"When you want to succeed as bad as you want to breathe,
then you'll be successful."
--- Eric Thomas

"I don't care if I was a ditch-digger at a dollar a day, I'd want to do my job better than the fellow next to me. I'd want to be the best at whatever I do."
-- Branch Rickey

*Jules, it would take me a book twice as big to fully express my gratitude and appreciation. From the bottom of my heart, thank you – for everything. My greatest accomplishment in life was to convince a girl like you to fall in love with a nerdy, baseball obsessed schlub like me.*

*The most impactful thing ever said to me was by mom: "You're the single most competitive person I've ever met. And I can't believe you're going to let this beat you." Where do you think I got that competitiveness from? Keep up the fight, mom.*

*Dad, I hope to be half the father you are one day.*

*And, of course, how could I forget my sister, Amanda, whose smile epitomizes all the good in life.*

*Cal, you're the best friend a guy could ever hope for. Thank you for all the reminders that it was time for a break during those long writing sessions. One of the greatest joys in my life is playing fetch and running through the house with you.*

**Author Bio:** Joseph Werner continues to provide further evidence that Jim Bouton was right when he wrote, "You spend your life gripping a baseball, and in the end it turns out that it was the other way around all the time."

As a lifelong Indians fan, Werner's lived and died multiple times over. First with the original revival of Cleveland baseball in the mid 90s, then languishing through the lean years before having his hopes dashed again in recent seasons.

All along the way, though, he's heard two of the greatest radio voices in the game: Herb Score and Tom Hamilton. Despite his youth at the time, he proudly — and somewhat embarrassingly — remembers falling asleep with his arms clutched around a portable radio as Score made his last radio call during Game 7 of 1997 World Series.

Werner continues to submerse himself in the game he passionately loves; be it on the playing field or writing about it.After serving as a video scout/analyst for *Baseball Info Solutions*, he began writing at his original site, ReleasePoints.com. He's since transitioned into his current niche, prospect analysis, at ProspectDigest.com.

Werner has been fortunate — and incredibly blessed — to have some of his work published and mentioned by several major media outlets, including: ESPN, Cleveland.com , The Baseball Research Journal, and Beyond the Box Score.

**A Note from the Author**: It's a labor of love, really. One in which I spend hundreds of hours poring through every statistic I can get my hands on. The challenging part for me is trying to entertain the reader from baseball's best prospect, Minnesota's Byron Buxton, all the way down to the guy who – ultimately – will never see the green grass of a Major League stadium – something I hope I have accomplished in the following pages.

Obvious hat tips go to Baseball-Reference, FanGraphs, TheBaseballCube, StatCorner, and the countless websites that provide the invaluable data that I glean. They make the baseball world a better place.

And a special thank you goes out to Blaise Terranova for the designing the cover for me again, as well as the emails I received asking about this year's book (those really helped me getting over the proverbial writing hump).

If you're so inclined I would love to hear your thoughts on the book – good, bad, or indifferent. You can reach me at JosephMWerner@yahoo.com. Any feedback is much appreciated.

Thank You,

JOE

# Table of Contents

# Another Introduction to CAL

# Another Introduction to CAL

*Author's Note:* This article appeared in last year's book, but I decided to include it again as a reference guide. The formulas/algorithms have been tweaked a bit for improvement, something that will likely happen as I seek to perfect the system.

Also, following the last page of this section is an email exchange between myself and Steve Moyer, former president of Baseball Info Solutions who is now with Inside Edge, another baseball analytics company. Mr. Moyer originally had some questions about CAL and as I answered them he suggested I include the email string in this year's book.

---

Let's play a game for a moment. You're a General Manager of a non-contending team and you're interested in dealing the club's most valuable trade chip, a perennial All-Star whose services no longer fit with the long term plans. Five teams are interested, each offering one of the following prospects as a potential centerpiece.

| Player | POS | Age | LVL | PA | 2B | 3B | HR | AVG | OBP | SLG | SB | CS | BB% | K% | wRC+ |
|--------|-----|-----|-----|-----|----|----|----|-------|-------|-------|----|----|-------|-------|------|
| Player A | SS | 21 | AA | 522 | 42 | 4 | 25 | 0.276 | 0.355 | 0.552 | 19 | 3 | 10.3% | 28.5% | 132 |
| | | 22 | AAA | 488 | 27 | 1 | 23 | 0.272 | 0.338 | 0.497 | 10 | 1 | 9.2% | 24.6% | 110 |
| | | 23 | AAA | 448 | 21 | 2 | 31 | 0.296 | 0.375 | 0.595 | 6 | 5 | 10.0% | 23.2% | 140 |

**Notes on Player A:** Standing a solid 6-foot-3 and 205 pounds, the former first rounder, 23rd overall, is one of the elite power bats in the minor leagues – a fact that becomes all that more impressive given his position (SS). Including his work in the Arizona Fall League, he once slugged 57 homeruns in a 163-game stretch. He was briefly called up during his age-23 season and struggled in 150 at bats (.200/.224/.327 with a 43/4 K/BB ratio). He's widely recognized as one of the top prospects in baseball – despite some swing-and-miss tendencies.

| Player | POS | Age | LVL | PA | 2B | 3B | HR | AVG | OBP | SLG | SB | CS | BB% | K% | wRC+ |
|--------|-----|-----|-----|-----|----|----|----|-------|-------|-------|----|----|-------|-------|------|
| Player B | 3B | 21 | AA | 298 | 25 | 0 | 21 | 0.347 | 0.413 | 0.687 | 0 | 1 | 8.7% | 14.1% | 194 |
| | | 21 | AAA | 236 | 16 | 0 | 15 | 0.293 | 0.314 | 0.564 | 2 | 0 | 3.4% | 10.6% | 114 |
| | | 22 | AAA | 250 | 15 | 1 | 10 | 0.287 | 0.347 | 0.498 | 1 | 1 | 7.6% | 17.6% | 105 |

**Notes on Player B:** Former second overall pick put a rough showing in High Class A behind him (.250/.397/.421), and put together one of the best showings in Class AA at the age of 21 in recent memory. 20-plus homerun potential with solid peripherals from the hot corner. He's widely recognized as one of the top prospects in baseball.

| Player | POS | Age | LVL | PA | 2B | 3B | HR | AVG | OBP | SLG | SB | CS | BB% | K% | wRC+ |
|--------|-----|-----|-----|-----|----|----|----|-------|-------|-------|----|----|-------|-------|------|
| Player C | C | 22 | A+ | 247 | 21 | 1 | 9 | 0.275 | 0.312 | 0.489 | 0 | 0 | 3.6% | 25.9% | 128 |
| | | 23 | AA | 309 | 18 | 1 | 13 | 0.250 | 0.317 | 0.464 | 0 | 0 | 8.1% | 24.3% | 111 |
| | | 24 | AAA | 334 | 29 | 1 | 13 | 0.328 | 0.380 | 0.557 | 4 | 0 | 7.5% | 21.6% | 140 |

**Notes on Player C:** Former 10th round pick transferred from the SEC to a small-time baseball college. Solid or better defensive backstop who's continually hit well with solid-average power, though that comes against mostly age appropriate levels of competition. He's a career .283/.344/.478 minor league hitter. Big league ready and a potential candidate to start for Team Brazil in the World Baseball Classic.

| Player | POS | Age | LVL | PA | 2B | 3B | HR | AVG | OBP | SLG | SB | CS | BB% | K% | wRC+ |
|--------|-----|-----|-----|-----|----|----|----|-------|-------|-------|----|----|------|------|------|
| Player D | CF | 20 | A+ | 350 | 14 | 5 | 10 | 0.304 | 0.393 | 0.486 | 25 | 6 | 12.3% | 23.7% | 145 |
| | | 21 | AA | 459 | 15 | 8 | 13 | 0.277 | 0.375 | 0.456 | 21 | 7 | 13.1% | 27.0% | 125 |
| | | 22 | AAA | 343 | 18 | 8 | 3 | 0.319 | 0.399 | 0.463 | 8 | 2 | 11.1% | 16.9% | 132 |

**Notes on Player D:** Former tenth overall pick is one of the premium defensive center fielders in the minors – a potential game changer on both sides of the ball. A potential 20/20 threat, he's s topped the league average production by at least 25% at each stop since his age-20 season in High Class A.

| Player | POS | Age | LVL | PA | 2B | 3B | HR | AVG | OBP | SLG | SB | CS | BB% | K% | wRC+ |
|--------|-----|-----|-----|-----|----|----|----|-------|-------|-------|----|----|------|------|------|
| Player E | 2B | 22 | AA | 350 | 21 | 4 | 2 | 0.260 | 0.386 | 0.381 | 8 | 2 | 15.7% | 11.7% | 118 |
| | | 22 | AAA | 237 | 12 | 4 | 5 | 0.274 | 0.338 | 0.439 | 2 | 1 | 8.4% | 16.0% | 96 |
| | | 23 | AAA | 331 | 17 | 3 | 9 | 0.303 | 0.421 | 0.487 | 7 | 3 | 16.6% | 11.5% | 130 |

**Notes on Player E:** Another former #2 overall pick, the lefty-swinging second baseman was considered the most polished, advanced bat in the entire class. Above-average patience with 15- to 17-homerun potential from a position up the middle. Big league ready.

The overall ranking would probably go something like:

1. **Player D** – he plays an up the middle position, has a history of performing well against much older competition and can provide value on both sides of the ball.
2. **Player A** – above-average power potential at a premium position is too hard to ignore. His 43-to-4 strikeout-to-walk ratio during his initial debut is alarming but, again, the power coming from shortstop is likely worth the risk.
3. **Player E** – a potential table-setter for the next decade.
4. **Player B** – Not quite a middle-of-the-order thumper, but a capable big league bat with plenty of potential.
5. **Player C** – just not enough of the "wow" factor/perceived upside.

Congratulations, you've just dealt the face of your franchise for a package (likely) centered on a complete disappointment. Player A is Brandon Wood. Player B is Mike Moustakas. Player C is Yan Gomes. Player D is Cameron Maybin. Player E is Dustin Ackley.

With the exception of Gomes, the remaining four have been well below-average offensive performers – if not flat out busts – for their respective big league careers – despite putting together some solid minor league production.

But CAL – the Comparison And Likeness prospect classification system I designed – would have suggested otherwise.

Based off of the idea of Bill James' Similarity Scores (which can be found on Baseball Reference), I re-worked the formula with different variables (age, position, level of competition, production, speed, power, plate discipline) each weighted accordingly to determine a prospect's top comparables based on a player's last three stops in the minors.

CAL attempts to answer the age old question - how have players with similar production between certain ages at specific levels fared in the future?

So what does CAL think of the aforementioned five? Let's take a look...

**Brandon Wood** (entering his age-24 season): Alex Liddi, Arismendy Alcantara, Luke Hughes, Sean Rodriguez, Matt Davidson. It's a collection of minor league flame outs/big league role players. And even Alcantara, the recent top prospect from the Cubs organization, looked completely overmatched during his respective debut (.205/.254/.367 70 wRC+ with massive contact issues a la Wood).

**Mike Moustakas** (after his final full season in the minors): Josh Vitters, Wilmer Flores, Andy LaRoche, Lonnie Chisenhall, Ryan Wheeler. With the exception of fringy big league regular Lonnie Chisenhall, it's a disappointing group. (Update: Moustakas is sporting a career 92 wRC+, Chisenhall has a career (98wRC+).

**Cameron Maybin** (after his final full season in the minors): Brett Jackson, John Tolisano, Trayvon Robinson, Michael Saunders, Robbie Grossman. Of the grouping, only Saunders and Grossman have seen a fair share of big league action.

- Maybin's career wRC+: 89 (2,623 PA)
- Saunders' career wRC+: 92 (1,955 PA)
- Grossman's career wRC+: 91 (764 PA)

**Dustin Ackley** (after his final full season in the minors): Nick Franklin, Blake DeWitt, Jose Pirela, Nate Spears, Adrian Cardenas. Not surprisingly, it's a ho-hum collection.

- Ackley's career wRC+: 92 (2,277 PA)
- DeWitt's career wRC+: 87 (1,247 PA)
- Franklin's career wRC+: 75 (611 PA)

And finally **Yan Gomes.** Following his acquisition from the Blue Jays Indians beat writer Paul Hoynes wrote, "[General Manager Chris] Antonetti said Gomes will go to Spring Training with a chance to make the team as a second or third catcher." Well, to everyone's surprise he's been one of the best backstops over the last two years. So what did CAL think?

Gomes' top comparables immediately following the trade (entering his age-25 season): Welington Castillo, Travis d'Arnaud, Lucas May, J.P. Arencibia, Cameron Rupp. While it lacks a lot of name recognition, there are a couple solid names.

- Gomes' career wRC+: 105 (1,340 PA)
- Castillo's career wRC+: 100 (1447 PA)
- d'Arnaud's career wRC+: 107 (801 PA)

And even Arencibia two semi-successful seasons before he cratered in 2013. Did CAL correctly assume that Gomes would be an All-Star caliber bat? No. But CAL did suggest that there was something close to league average offensive potential and subsequently starting caliber upside, something the Blue Jays – or Indians – probably wouldn't have initially guessed. After all, he was deal along with Mike Aviles for reliever re-tread Esmil Rogers.

In a nutshell, CAL uses a couple algorithms to search a database (FanGraphs' minor league stats which extends back to 2006) to find similar players.

## About CAL:

**Steve Moyer:** What I notice are that most of the comparison players — especially beyond a team's top few prospects - are dominated by guys I've never heard of. Seems weird to me, almost like saying almost none of these guys are ever going to make it, and a very minute number will become regulars or stars. Perhaps you can explain better than I interpret.

**Joseph Werner:** In terms of CAL, I think you hit it right on the head actually. I love Paul DePodesta (of Moneyball fame). He's remarkably smart and provides such insight. One of my favorite quotes by him is:

> *"Unfortunately, the attrition rate is gruesome. Out of the entire pool of drafted and signed players, only about 18% of them ever get even one day in the big leagues, and only about 7% of them actually accumulate three years in the Major Leagues. It's even scarier if you examine the rounds — fewer than 50% of 1st round picks get three years in the big leagues, and from rounds two through five that number drops to about 15%. After that it plummets to the low single digits. In short, it's very difficult to scout, draft, sign, and develop Major Leaguers, so having a plan to do so isn't enough."*

The fact is the overwhelming majority of prospects never pans out, let alone reach their projected ceilings. My goal with CAL was to provide some sort of context to properly view prospects through. More specifically, how have similar players (age, performance, level, position) in the past developed in the future.

For more examples of CAL's usefulness, check out my website: ProspectDigest.com

# Revisited: A Look Back at Past Bold Predictions

# Revisited: A Look Back at Past Bold Predictions

One of my favorite aspects about baseball analysis is that it often takes *years* to see if the projected outcomes actually come true. Sure, snap judgments are fun. But often times it takes three, four, maybe even five years to accurately measure a move in baseball.

Take, for example, one of the more widely panned moves in recent memory where the Diamondbacks – in an unprecedented deal – agreed to ship Dansby Swanson (the most recent #1 overall pick in the draft), right-hander Aaron Blair, and outfielder Ender Inciarte to the Braves for Shelby Miller and Gabe Speier.

Now on the onset of the deal it looks absolutely absurd.

In his best season to date Miller tallied a little over 3.0 wins above replacement (something that FanGraphs and Baseball-Reference both agree upon). But Inciarte, an overlooked prospect coming up in the Diamondbacks' system, totaled nearly the identical amount of WAR according to FanGraphs and bested that mark by 2.0 WAR according to BR.

And by going on that basis alone one could surmise that a Miller for Inciarte-and-Blair package would have been enough to satisfy both teams. But the Diamondbacks insisted on throwing in the supremely talented collegiate shortstop.

We now have the makings of a completely lopsided deal.

Or do we?

A lot of Inciarte's value comes from his defense; he's sporting a 21.3 UZR/150 over the course of his 250 career games. On offense, he's been 6% *below* the league average. Now let's say that our understanding of defensive value *greatly* improves in the coming years – which I happen to think that it will – and we later determine that (A) our previous numbers have been bloated or (B) the fact that he's bouncing between all three outfield spots somehow changes his numbers (meaning: is a good defensive center fielder far more valuable than a great corner outfielder?) or (C) that Arizona's staff finished the year just outside the Top 10 in groundballs somehow creates unwanted noise in the metrics.

The point is: we don't know what we don't know.

Maybe Inciarte never shags fly balls as efficiently. Or that Aaron Blair never becomes anything more than a #5 arm. Or that Swanson tops out as a league average shortstop (because of some shortcomings).

Baseball analysis is like trying to hit a moving target. We use all the data we have at our fingertips to project what we *think* will happen, but in the end it's important to remember that we're dealing with human behavior. Doubly important: we're humans dealing with the human element.

Anyway, I thought it would be interesting to look back at some articles I've written over the past several years and see how the hell I've done – both good and bad. And I think one constant portion of this section moving forward will be examining the previous year's predicted breakout prospects because, well, a one year snapshot for that is sufficient.

# Revisited: New Baltimore Regime Committing Same Old Mistakes

Throughout my writing career my personal site has evolved with each passing year. It morphed from an Indians blog to a general baseball blog to a prospect-central website.

The following article was originally posted – without future editing – on March 31st, 2012. I sincerely hope my writing style has improved since.

The original article is italicized and commentary will follow.

---

*New Baltimore Regime Committing Same Old Mistakes*

*First off, let me say this: I get it. And by that I mean I really get it. My future first born – who's still many, many years away – is more likely to make the big leagues before Baltimore is set to contend in the ultra-competitive American League East.*

*So it's not like the organization's most recent move – placing right-hander Alfredo Simon on waivers – is going to set its future back any more. But still. This, on so many levels, represents the type move a team like this should simply avoid. It's as if the old regime is picking up where the last one left off, and the one before that, and the one before that.*

*Either way, they've done it. They committed the cardinal sin in baseball: The Orioles failed to realize just, exactly, what they have – or had – in Simon.*

*Alfredo Simon's role during his four-year career with the Orioles was never defined. Was he a starter? Or was he a reliever? No one really knew which. Perhaps some of the blame could be laid at the feet of one of his previous franchises – I'm looking at you, San Francisco – but with an organization so deeply entrenched with losing they had very little to lose by defining his role – either one. Instead, during his four years in Baltimore he made 19 starts, 59 relief appearances, and actually served as quasi-closer in 2010.*

*Fine. Plenty of teams fail to properly utilize their players.*

*But let's look at Simon's production the past two seasons.*

*Truthfully, he was pretty bad in 2010. According to FanGraphs, he cost the team almost one full win, posted a horrendous walk rate for a reliever, 4.01 BB/9, and an equally pitiful ERA (4.93). But he was coming off of Tommy John surgery. Pitcher's never rebound – especially their command – completely during their first year back and Simon was no different. His 2010 walk rate was almost one full walk higher than his minor league numbers. And his SIERA (Skill Independent ERA), the most advanced ERA estimator, was also almost a full run better, at 4.11. His HR/9 that season, 1.82, was also unsustainably high too. So despite the poor showing there was reason to believe that 2011 would be a better year.*

*And it was.*

*Last season, Simon's numbers, unsurprisingly, began to improve. He tossed 115.2 innings, saw his walk rate improve to 3.11 BB/9 (close to his career track record), was worth more than one win above replacement, and posted a nearly identical SIERA.*

*In fact, among pitchers with at least 100 innings last season, his 4.19 SIERA was better than Francisco Liriano, Jeremy Guthrie, who they just traded away, Nick Blackburn, John Lannan, Jonathan Sanchez, Chad Billingsley, Mark Buehrle, Freddy Garcia, Jair Jurrjens, and Ivan Nova, just to name a few.*

*Whoops, Baltimore.*

*And this isn't a soft-tosser either. Simon's fastball averaged 94.2 MPH last season, the seventh hardest heater in baseball (among pitchers with 100+ innings). Given his 6-foot-6 inch frame, the ball looks much harder than that too.*

*Double whoops, Baltimore.*

*And the Orioles simply don't consider him good enough to roster this season. But they do have a place for the bespectacled Kevin Gregg, who happens to be the very definition of replacement level. Look it up. I bet you his name and/or picture is mentioned.*

*Yes, Gregg is making a lot of money – almost $6 million – but why keep an aging, replaceable reliever who's been worth 0.2 wins over the last three years instead of a higher upside player that the team could potentially flip for something semi-worthwhile during the season?*

*Just eat Gregg's salary and release him, not Simon.*

*Maybe the organization is hoping to squeak him through waivers because many teams are close to finalizing their Opening Day rosters? Don't bet on it. There will be 10 claims on him, easily. And he probably doesn't make it beyond the second or third one on the list.*

*Is this really a new regime or is it just an extension of the previous ones?*

*Either way, Dan Duquette has given no reason to believe that the Orioles are headed in the right direction. And this is just the latest example.*

---

OK. First thing, I completely whiffed on Baltimore's future chances at contending. They would quickly become the biggest surprise team that season and averaged more than 88 wins a year since.

I'm fine with that. Baltimore was coming off of a horrific stretch of five years where they failed to win more than 69 games in any season. And *nobody* saw them developing into a contender so quickly.

But the crux of the piece was about the fact that the front office soured on Simon when they should have stuck by his side.

Cincinnati eventually won the waiver claim and...voila...Simon morphed into a dominant force for the franchise over the following three seasons.

The big right-hander spent 2012 and 2013 working exclusively out of the Reds' bullpen, tallying an impressive 2.78 ERA with 115 strikeouts and 48 walks in 148.2 innings of work.

He (finally) made the move into the rotation in 2014, which eventually led to a trip to the All-Star game, 15 wins, and a 3.44 ERA (though his SIERA bloated up to 4.17).

Cincinnati would then ship Simon off to the Tigers last season in exchange for first rounder Jonathan Crawford and Eugenio Suarez, who batted .280/.315/.446 with the Reds in 2015.

As for Gregg, well, he tossed 125.1 innings with a 5.03 ERA over the same span and (fewer than 20 innings since 2014).

So, in the end, the Orioles foolishly gave Simon away for free, which didn't keep them from a complete turnaround. And the Reds, well, they played the game by the book – acquiring a promising hurler for nothing, extracting as much value from him, and then later shipped him off for two useful pieces.

# Revisited: Breakout Teams for 2015

One of my favorite analytical pieces I write centers on trying to forecast how teams will do several years down the line – though it's only because of the degree of difficulty in doing so. There are numerous variable to weigh: payroll, farm system, divisional foes, and, of course, what types of moves the front office will make over the course of time.

It's fun. But it's (enjoyably) difficult.

Here's an article I wrote on my site – prospectdigest.com – on August 22$^{nd}$, 2013. The original article is italicized with commentary following.

---

*After losing 93 games two years ago, the Baltimore Orioles shocked the baseball world by winning 93 last 2012 before eventually losing to the Yankees in the ALDS. The Oakland A's improved upon their record in 2012 by 20 games while winning the AL West last season too. Quick turnarounds are hardly an uncommon occurrence in Major League Baseball.*

*Here's a look at some of the club's that could see the biggest jumps within the next two years.*

### 1. Seattle Mariners

*After several years of rebuilding, a handful of the Mariners' top prospects have already started their exodus from the minors to the big league ball club. Along with rookies Brad Miller, Nick Franklin and Mike Zunino, Seattle has underrated third baseman Kyle Seager (.282/.352/.469 and 19 homeruns) and a resurgent Justin Smoak (.269/.363/.443) to give the organization one of the more promising young infields in the game.*

*On the pitching side, the Mariners have one of the best hurlers on the planet – Felix Hernandez, who's still only 27-years-old – as well as one of the game's top pitching prospects in Taijuan Walker, potentially giving the organization the best 1-2 punch in the game. Hisashi Iwakuma is under team control (potentially) through 2015.*

*Behind Walker, the club has lefty James Paxton, whose control has taken a noticeable step forward in Class AAA this season and could be ready to step into the big league rotation mid-2014. Right-hander Brandon Maurer has struggled during his rookie season, but is just 22 and has averaged more than a punch out per inning with solid-average control in the minor leagues.*

### 2. Chicago Cubs

*Team President Theo Epstein and GM Jed Hoyer have done wonders with the Cubs' farm system, be it by adding young talent through the draft, international free agents, or shrewd trades.*

*The club has lineup cornerstone Anthony Rizzo already in place and under team control for several years, as well as another in the enigmatic Starlin Castro. Right-hander Jeff Samardzija has developed into a solid #2/#3-type. Edwin Jackson is another good mid-rotation starter. And Travis Wood is a nice backend option.*

*Most of the club's top talent, however, is still a year or two away. Shortstop Javier Baez, 20, is hitting .280/.344/.565 with 31 homeruns between high Class A and AA. Recently acquired third baseman Mike Olt has struggled this season, but still profiles as a league average everyday player with on-base skills, good defense and above-average power. Behind that pair, Chicago has Daniel Vogelbach, Jorge Soler and Albert Almora all developing in the lower levels.*

*What makes Chicago so dangerous is that it has 60% of a good rotation in place and plenty of payroll room to add when the farm system starts burping up the big prospects mid-2014.*

### 3. *New York Mets*

*As I've previously highlighted [in a previous article],the Mets are a serious contender for a quick turnaround. The organization has Matt Harvey and Zack Wheeler already in place. Noah Syndergaard is quickly following suit. Rafael Montero could slide into the rotation today and become a solid backend option. Catcher Travis d'Arnaud recently made his big league debut, as did infielder Wilmer Flores. Throw in veterans David Wright, Daniel Murphy, Ike Davis (maybe?), and Lucas Duda and the Mets could be contenders before the end of 2015.*

### 4. *Miami Marlins*

*The oft-criticized franchise has potentially the best young outfield in the game, with Christian Yelich manning left field, Jake Marisnick in center, and Giancarlo Stanton in right. The rotation is sporting the best young pitcher in the game – Jose Fernandez – as well as Jacob Turner and Nathan Eovaldi. Add complementary players like Logan Morrison, Angel Hechavarria, and Justin Ruggiano and additional prospects like Marcell Ozuna, Andrew Heaney, and Adam Conley near big league ready.*

### 5. *Minnesota Twins*

*Minnesota arguably has the top two prospects in the entire game, Byron Buxton and Miguel Sano, as well as Oswaldo Arcia (.257/.313/.438) already with the big league club. After flopping for the majority of the big league year, it's still too early to give up on center fielder Aaron Hicks, and the same can be said for right-hander Kyle Gibson. Pitchers Alex Meyer and Trevor May are throwing well in Class AA. Plus, Justin Morneau's lofty contract comes off the books this offseason too.*

---

OK. So three-out-of-five isn't bad. And I do have to admit I was *ecstatic* when both the Mets and Cubs squared off in the National League Championship Series.

Mets: while I didn't get it perfectly right, the franchise made it to the World Series on the backs of the starting pitchers, something I alluded to in the original piece. New York saw an 11-win spike from their 2014 total.

Cubs: No one – and I do mean *no one* – could have foreseen Edwin Jackson's implosion or the fact that they'd deal Jeff Samardzija to Oakland for Addison Russell. But they finished the year with a 24-win improvement.

Twins: Surprisingly enough, Minnesota finished 2015 as the second-best club in the American League Central Division. Miguel Sano had a dynamic rookie season, slugging .269/.385/.530 with 18 dingers in just 80 games. Gibson finished the year as Minnesota's best starter with a 3.84 ERA and a solid 145-to-65 strikeout-to-walk ratio in 194.2 innings of work. Overall, the franchise saw a 13-game improvement from 2014.

Mariners: Definitely swung-and-missed on this one. Nick Franklin and Brandon Maurer were dealt away. Mike Zunino can't hit his weight. And the majority of the club's other top prospects from their once-great system haven't panned out.

Marlins: This one's simple. Never pick the Marlins – it's called the Jeffrey Loria factor. The foundation is still present – Giancarlo Stanton, Christian Yelich, Marcell Ozuna, whom Loria wants to deal because he doesn't like him, Conley, Jose Fernandez, and Dee Gordon – but, again, the Loria factor.

# Revisited: Breakout Prospects for 2015

So unlike the previous two *Revisited* articles, I'm going to handle this one a little differently – just for ease of reading (and writing). In the review of last year's predicted breakout prospects, I'm going to break them out into three separate categories: Hits, Misses, and Neutral.

The Hits, obviously, were correctly predicted breakouts. The Misses, likewise, were players that either (A) maintained status quo or (B) took a step back. And the Neutrals were somewhere in between; they had good, sometimes borderline great years, but I just didn't feel like they were breakout-y enough.

By my count there were 11 Hits, 7 Misses (which were mostly the result of aggressive promotions or my stubbornness), and 7 Neutrals. All in all, it's not bad work for predicting human behaviors through numbers.

## Hits:

**Orlando Arcia, SS, Milwaukee Brewers**: I was incredibly high on the young shortstop last season, ranking him as the 51st overall prospect. And he delivered in a *huge* way, hitting .307/.347/.453 as a 20-year-old in the Southern League.

**Roberto Osuna, RHP, Toronto Blue Jays**: He vaulted up from High Class A straight into the Jays' pen as one of the key contributors for the club last season. He finished his rookie season with 75 punch outs, just 16 walks, and a 2.58 ERA in 69.2 innings pitched *at the big league level*.

**Max Kepler, 1B/OF, Minnesota Twins**: Easily one of the biggest – if not *the* biggest – breakout players in 2015. The German-born Kepler finished the year with a .322/.416/.531 triple-slash line as he topped the Southern League average production line by 67%. Yeah, that qualifies as a breakout season.

**Michael Fulmer, RHP, Detroit Tigers**: The former first rounder was coming off of a season in which he posted a mediocre 3.98 ERA in 19 Florida State League starts. But he made stops at three different levels in 2015 as he finished the year with a 2.24 ERA, 125 strikeouts, and 30 walk in 124.2 innings.

**Amir Garrett, LHP, Cincinnati Reds**: Garrett finished the year with a career best 2.44 ERA while fanning a smidgeon under a bat per inning in High Class A. He also appeared in the Futures Game. Not bad work for a former Division I basketball player.

**Edwin Diaz, RHP, Seattle Mariners**: The former third round pick posted a strong 154-to-46 strikeout-to-walk ratio in 141.2 innings, three-quarters of which were spent in Class AA. As a 21-year-old. Again, a rotation fronted by King Felix, Taijuan Walker, and Diaz is going to open up a lot of doors for the franchise in the coming years.

**Frankie Montas, RHP, Los Angeles Dodgers**: Montas was absolutely brilliant in an injury-plagued campaign two years ago, and he carried that momentum into 2015. In a career high 112.0 innings, the hard-throwing right-hander fanned 108 and walked 48 with Birmingham in Class AA.

**Jake Bauers, 1B, Tampa Bay Rays**: Bauers absolutely ripped through the High Class A pitching at the start of the season, bashing to the tune of .267/.357/.433 en route to topping the league average offensive production by 42%. And he looked sturdy in his promotion up to Class AA.

**Joe Jimenez, RHP, Detroit Tigers**: He was absolutely, positively dominant during his time with West Michigan: 43.0 IP, 61 K, 11 BB, and a 1.47 ERA. I've mentioned it a million times before, but I hope the Tigers push the big hurler into a rotation spot...like...in 2016.

**J.B. Wendelken, LHP, Chicago White Sox**: I was hoping his breakout campaign would have come as a member of the rotation, but Wendelken, nonetheless, shined in his first taste as a reliever: 59.0 IP, 69 K, 16 BB, and a 3.20 ERA.

**Jordan Guerrero, LHP, Chicago White Sox**: In his first year in the rotation the lanky lefty out of California finished the year with 148 strikeouts and just 31 walks in a career high 149.0 total innings.


## Misses:

**Tyrone Taylor, CF, Milwaukee Brewers**: This was a result of just ignoring the numbers and merely continuing to stick by the toolsy outfielder. But Taylor's overall production has been in slow decline since his 2013 season. The tools are there, but the power's never taken the step forward that I thought it would. Still, though, he's only entering his age-22 season and already has a season in Class AA under his belt.

**Andrew Morales, RHP, St. Louis Cardinals**: One of most underrated arms in the 2014 draft class. St. Louis was betting as high on Morales as I was last season. They pushed the slight-framed right-hander straight up to Class AA with only 12.1 innings of minor league ball on his resume. So, with that respect, it's not surprising he didn't have that breakout season. But the Cardinals sense something in Morales, and so do I.

**Franmil Reyes, RF, San Diego Padres**: Very similar to Tyrone Taylor, Reyes has a ton of potential, particularly power, but he took a modest step forward in his repeat of the Midwest League.

**Taylor Lindsey, 2B, San Diego Padres**: Again, I ignored the numbers and was looking for a feel good aspect after Lindsey's demise. He batted .274/.339/.441 in the Texas League as a 21-year-old, but the lefty-swinging second baseman has posted OPSs of .678 and .581 in the two following seasons.

**Mitch Brown, RHP, Cleveland Indians**: The former second round pick was coming off of his finest professional season to date, something I thought would carry over into the 2016 season. I was wrong. His control regressed back to his 2013 showing as he finished the year with a poor 5.15 ERA and a walk rate hovering around 5.0 BB/9.

**LeVon Washington, OF, Cleveland Indians**: You know how parents so desperately want their kids to come up with the big game-winning hit? It's kind of like how I feel about Washington. When he's healthy the twice-drafted outfielder is an absolute OBP monster with a strong hit tool. But in six professional seasons, he's topped 50 games just twice and never appeared in more than 79 in a season. I think it's time I move on.

**Justin Williams, LF/RF, Arizona Diamondbacks**: He just stopped…walking. After posting OBPs hovering around .400 in 2013 and 2014, Williams walked just 14 times in 122 games and finished the year with a .298 OBP. That's what you call the anti-breakout season

## Neutrals:

**Michael Lorenzen, RHP, Cincinnati Reds**: I wavered between putting him here or in the "miss" category. Lorenzen, a former two-way player for Cal State Fullerton, only moonlighted as the team's closer. Well, fast forward 160 or so innings and he's making 21 starts (with six relief appearances) in Cincinnati. The numbers with the Reds, though, weren't all that impressive. He did open the by posting a 3.25 ERA in his first 80.1 innings between his time with Cincinnati and Louisville. But, again, he basically spent one full season in the minors (after hardly pitching in college) before getting thrust into the big league club's rotation.

**Nick Burdi, RHP, Minnesota Twins**: Another player that got aggressively pushed up to a level he wasn't particularly ready for. But Burdi finished the year on an incredibly high note: 33.1 IP, 50 K, 13 walks, and a 1.89 ERA. That's the stuff that qualifies as a breakout season. He could be closing out games for the Twins by the end of the year.

**Dillon Overton, LHP, Oakland A's**: Finally back from arm injuries, Overton was very good, but not quite breakout-y enough for my liking. He finished the year with a 3.43 ERA with 106 strikeouts and just 27 walks in 126.0 IP. Again, he was very good.

**Bobby Wahl, RHP, Oakland A's**: Sort of the poor man's version of Nick Burdi. Wahl's overall numbers were wrecked by two poor back-to-back outings in the early part of the season. Ignoring those, here's his line: 2.37 ERA, 34 K, and 14 BB in 30.1 IP. Again, a very good season, but not quite breakout-y enough for my liking.

**Daniel Mengden, RHP, Oakland A's**: Another one of these very good, not breakout-y enough seasons. The former Texas A&M hurler finished the year with a spectacular 125-to-36 strikeout-to-walk ratio in 130.2 innings.

**Tyler Danish, RHP, Chicago White Sox**: So the overall numbers aren't that impressive: 90 strikeouts, 60 walks, and a 4.50 ERA. But it's important to note that he spent the entire season hurling for the Birmingham Barons in the Southern League – where he was the youngest qualified arm in the league, *by two years*.

**Yoel Mecias, LHP, Philadelphia Phillies**: It's hard to be a breakout prospect when you throw just 10.0 innings (thanks to injuries).

# The Next Great Untapped Talent Pool:

# Failed College Quarterbacks

# The Next Great Untapped Talent Pool: Failed College Quarterbacks

Back in the 1960s Ewing Kauffman, the owner of the new Kansas City franchise, had an ingenious idea. He wanted to teach athletic, talented young men to play baseball – regardless if the sport was a part of their childhood or not. The entrepreneur dumped roughly $1.5 million into the idea – about $9 million in today's economy – and with a wide-ranging net he collected all the intriguing talent he could.

And so, the Royals Baseball Academy was born.

The Academy debuted in the Gulf Coast the following year, in 1971, and they were an immediate success. Strung together with a hodgepodge of talented young men, the GCL Royals went on an absolute tear: they finished first in the league in wins, runs, triples, stolen bases, batting average, slugging percentage, OPS, total bases, ERA, walks per nine innings, and shutouts. The ballclub would also finish second in hits, homeruns, and strikeouts per nine innings.

Three years later, though, Kaufman and the Royals would shut down the Academy – a move the stadium's namesake later referenced as, "the biggest mistake I made in baseball was letting them talk me into closing [it]." (*Author's note: The quote was mentioned in a August 2, 2014 column by the great Sam Mellinger.*)

But the baseball university left an indelible mark. In those four short seasons the program graduated three players that would spend a combined 39 years in the big leagues, tallying more 45 wins above replacement along the way: Frank White, Ron Washington, and U.L. Washington.

Innovation.

It's what led the great Branch Rickey – my personal baseball hero – to create the minor leagues. Hell, one could make the argument that the Royals don't win the '85 World Series without Frank White. And innovation.

The ability to think *outside* the proverbial box...

More than a decade ago – I can't believe it's been that long – Kyle Boller, the eventual 19th overall pick in the 2003 NFL draft, displayed jaw-dropping arm strength at the combine. He coiled his torso and unleashed an ungodly 60+ yard throw through the uprights – *from a kneeling position*.

It was a display of arm strength in the truest sense. No boost from his lower half. Just. Arm. Strength.

There are a few things in athletics that can't be taught: speed, size, and arm strength.

Sure, those skills – along with a multitude of others – can be honed or even improved upon. But the ability to get down on one knee and loft a football over 60 yards certainly can't be learned. It's a God-given ability thrust upon the lucky.

So why haven't MLB organizations taken advantage of collegiate QBs that don't garner enough attention from NFL scouts but display uncanny arm strength?

It's a conversation I've had with a very good friend of mine, who's worked on the outer fringes of Major League Baseball. He's told me, numerous times, that it's too cost ineffective. The return on investment is long at best, too small to throw gobs of money at, and most importantly, too time consuming.

But I don't buy it.

College basketball players have been lacing up NFL football cleats for *decades.*

The Cowboy's signed Cornell Green, the brother of Pumpsie Green, the first African-American player in Red Sox history, after a successful career with Utah State's basketball program. Cornell would go out to make five Pro Bowls. Antonio Gates, Marcus Pollard, Ken Johnson are just a couple more of the bigger success stories.

But you're probably saying, well...playing baseball is much more difficult as it relies less on brute strength and pure athleticism.

OK.

But the goal isn't to teach players to hit like Ted Williams. Instead, it's teaching throwers to become pitchers.

How many times have failed position players turned in their Louisville Sluggers and toed the rubber?

Joe Nathan. Kenley Jansen. Sean Doolittle, who once slugged .286/.385/.495 as a 21-year-old between the California and Texas Leagues. Jason Motte. Mychael Givens, one of the best prospects in the Orioles system. Jake Stinnett, a recent second round choice of the Cubs. Chris Hatcher. Alexi Ogando. The list goes on and on.

And, yes, I know these guys were constantly throwing baseballs during their life. I get it. I really do.

But in a cut-throat, multi-billion business wouldn't it be worth throwing a couple million dollars at another potentially innovative – or at least an interesting – idea just to see if it could work?

I don't pretend to think that it's going to be easy, but it's worth a shot – just in *hopes* of developing a useful big league arm. And I implore anyone, everyone to give it a shot. Please.

In the end, though, it all falls back on the "Moneyball" approach: it's exploiting unrealized value.

And, hell, while we're at it let's sign some Cricket players and start a whole new baseball academy.

# Ranking the Top 250 Prospects

# Ranking the Top 250 Prospects (1-100)

| Rank | Name | Team | POS |
|------|------|------|-----|
| 1 | Byron Buxton | Minnesota Twins | CF |
| 2 | Julio Urias | Los Angeles Dodgers | LHP |
| 3 | Lucas Giolito | Washington Nationals | RHP |
| 4 | Yoan Moncada | Boston Red Sox | 2B |
| 5 | Tyler Glasnow | Pittsburgh Pirates | RHP |
| 6 | Corey Seager | Los Angeles Dodgers | SS |
| 7 | Alex Reyes | St. Louis Cardinals | RHP |
| 8 | J.P. Crawford | Philadelphia Phillies | SS |
| 9 | Jose Berrios | Minnesota Twins | LHP |
| 10 | Steven Matz | New York Mets | LHP |
| 11 | Blake Snell | Tampa Bay Rays | LHP |
| 12 | Nomar Mazara | Texas Rangers | LF/RF |
| 13 | Jose De Leon | Los Angeles Dodgers | |
| 14 | Austin Meadows | Pittsburgh Pirates | CF |
| 15 | Rafael Devers | Boston Red Sox | 3B |
| 16 | Jesse Winker | Cincinnati Reds | LF/RF |
| 17 | Ryan McMahon | Colorado Rockies | 3B |
| 18 | Orlando Arcia | Milwaukee Brewers | SS |
| 19 | A.J. Reed | Houston Astros | 1B |
| 20 | Lewis Brinson | Texas Rangers | CF |
| 21 | Clint Frazier | Cleveland Indians | OF |
| 22 | Francis Martes | Houston Astros | RHP |
| 23 | Brent Honeywell | Tampa Bay Rays | RHP |
| 24 | Albert Almora | Chicago Cubs | CF |
| 25 | Taylor Guerrieri | Tampa Bay Rays | RHP |
| 26 | Anderson Espinoza | Boston Red Sox | RHP |
| 27 | Dansby Swanson | Atlanta Braves | SS |
| 28 | Nick Williams | Philadelphia Phillies | LF/CF |
| 29 | Aaron Judge | New York Yankees | RF |
| 30 | Jon Gray | Colorado Rockies | RHP |
| 31 | Brendan Rodgers | Colorado Rockies | SS |
| 32 | Robert Stephenson | Cincinnati Reds | RHP |
| 33 | Andrew Benintendi | Boston Red Sox | CF |
| 34 | Phil Bickford | San Francisco Giants | RHP |
| 35 | Michael Fulmer | Detroit Tigers | RHP |
| 36 | Trea Turner | Washington Nationals | 2B/SS |
| 37 | Frankie Montas | Los Angeles Dodgers | RHP |
| 38 | Edwin Diaz | Seattle Mariners | RHP |
| 39 | Miguel Almonte | Kansas City Royals | RHP |
| 40 | Mark Appel | Philadelphia Phillies | RHP |
| 41 | Archie Bradley | Arizona Diamondbacks | RHP |
| 42 | Cornelius Randolph | Philadelphia Phillies | LF |
| 43 | Brett Phillips | Milwaukee Brewers | LF/CF |
| 44 | Josh Bell | Pittsburgh Pirates | 1B/RF |
| 45 | Alex Verdugo | Los Angeles Dodgers | CF |
| 46 | Joey Gallo | Texas Rangers | 3B/LF |
| 47 | Rookie Davis | Cincinnati Reds | RHP |
| 48 | Justus Sheffield | Cleveland Indians | LHP |
| 49 | Alex Bregman | Houston Astros | SS |
| 50 | Jamie Westbrook | Arizona Diamondbacks | 2B |

| Rank | Name | Team | POS |
|------|------|------|-----|
| 51 | Franklin Barreto | Oakland A's | SS |
| 52 | Sean Manaea | Oakland A's | LHP |
| 53 | Joe Musgrove | Houston Astros | RHP |
| 54 | Anthony Alford | Toronto Blue Jays | CF |
| 55 | Jack Flaherty | St. Louis Cardinals | RHP |
| 56 | Daniel Robertson | Tampa Bay Rays | SS |
| 57 | Kyle Tucker | Houston Astros | RF |
| 58 | Sean Reid-Foley | Toronto Blue Jays | RHP |
| 59 | Yadier Alvarez | Los Angeles Dodgers | RHP |
| 60 | Bradley Zimmer | Cleveland Indians | OF |
| 61 | Willy Adames | Tampa Bay Rays | SS |
| 62 | Jeff Hoffman | Colorado Rockies | RHP |
| 63 | Chance Sisco | Baltimore Orioles | C |
| 64 | Tyler Jay | Minnesota Twins | LHP |
| 65 | Jake Bauers | Tampa Bay Rays | 1B |
| 66 | Billy McKinney | Chicago Cubs | LF/RF |
| 67 | Hunter Renfroe | San Diego Padres | RF |
| 68 | Spencer Adams | Chicago White Sox | RHP |
| 69 | Michael Kopech | Boston Red Sox | RHP |
| 70 | Carson Fulmer | Chicago White Sox | RHP |
| 71 | Grant Holmes | Los Angeles Dodgers | RHP |
| 72 | Victor Robles | Washington Nationals | CF |
| 73 | Raul Mondesi | Kansas City Royals | SS |
| 74 | Sean Newcomb | Atlanta Braves | LHP |
| 75 | Alex Jackson | Seattle Mariners | LF/RF |
| 76 | Manuel Margot | San Diego Padres | CF |
| 77 | Dillon Tate | Texas Rangers | RHP |
| 78 | Kyle Zimmer | Kansas City Royals | RHP |
| 79 | Brady Aiken | Cleveland Indians | LHP |
| 80 | Rob Kaminsky | Cleveland Indians | LHP |
| 81 | Joe Jimenez | Detroit Tigers | RHP |
| 82 | Tim Anderson | Chicago White Sox | SS |
| 83 | Gavin Cecchini | New York Mets | SS |
| 84 | Matt Olson | Oakland A's | 1B |
| 85 | Jacob Faria | Tampa Bay Rays | RHP |
| 86 | Amir Garrett | Cincinnati Reds | LHP |
| 87 | Eric Jagielo | Cincinnati Reds | 3B |
| 88 | Jacob Nottingham | Oakland A's | C/1B |
| 89 | Gleyber Torres | Chicago Cubs | SS |
| 90 | Michael Feliz | Houston Astros | RHP |
| 91 | Luke Weaver | St. Louis Cardinals | RHP |
| 92 | Tyler Beede | San Francisco Giants | RHP |
| 93 | Ian Happ | Chicago Cubs | LF/RF |
| 94 | Reynaldo Lopez | Washington Nationals | RHP |
| 95 | Luis Ortiz | Texas Rangers | RHP |
| 96 | Garrett Whitley | Tampa Bay Rays | CF |
| 97 | Tyler Kolek | Miami Marlins | RHP |
| 98 | Kodi Medeiros | Milwaukee Brewers | LHP |
| 99 | Javier Guerra | San Diego Padres | SS |
| 100 | Alex Meyer | Minnesota Twins | RHP |

# Ranking the Top 250 Prospects (101-200)

| Rank | Name | Team | POS | Rank | Name | Team | POS |
|------|------|------|-----|------|------|------|-----|
| 101 | Josh Naylor | Miami Marlins | 1B | 151 | Cody Reed | Cincinnati Reds | LHP |
| 102 | Daz Cameron | Houston Astros | CF | 152 | Mallex Smith | Atlanta Braves | CF |
| 103 | Jorge Mateo | New York Yankees | SS | 153 | Trey Mancini | Baltimore Orioles | 1B |
| 104 | Ashe Russell | Kansas City Royals | RHP | 154 | Casey Gillaspie | Tampa Bay Rays | 1B |
| 105 | Trevor Clifton | Chicago Cubs | RHP | 155 | Harold Ramirez | Pittsburgh Pirates | LF/RF |
| 106 | Cody Bellinger | Los Angeles Dodgers | 1B | 156 | Kohl Stewart | Minnesota Twins | RHP |
| 107 | Max Pentecost | Toronto Blue Jays | C | 157 | Tyler Stephenson | Cincinnati Reds | C |
| 108 | Max Kepler | Minnesota Twins | 1B/OF | 158 | Pedro Fernandez | Kansas City Royals | RHP |
| 109 | Marco Gonzales | St. Louis Cardinals | LHP | 159 | Beau Burrows | Detroit Tigers | RHP |
| 110 | Braden Shipley | Arizona Diamondbacks | RHP | 160 | Ian Clarkin | New York Yankees | LHP |
| 111 | Jake Thompson | Philadelphia Phillies | RHP | 161 | Ruddy Giron | San Diego Padres | SS |
| 112 | Jorge Alfaro | Philadelphia Phillies | C | 162 | Miguel Castro | Colorado Rockies | RHP |
| 113 | David Dahl | Colorado Rockies | CF | 163 | K.J. Woods | Miami Marlins | 1B/LF |
| 114 | Forrest Wall | Colorado Rockies | 2B | 164 | Carl Edwards | Chicago Cubs | RHP |
| 115 | Jorge Lopez | Milwaukee Brewers | RHP | 165 | Eloy Jimenez | Chicago Cubs | LF/RF |
| 116 | Keury Mella | Cincinnati Reds | RHP | 166 | Colin Moran | Houston Astros | 3B |
| 117 | Jordan Guerrero | Chicago White Sox | LHP | 167 | Cody Reed | Arizona Diamondbacks | LHP |
| 118 | Connor Greene | Toronto Blue Jays | RHP | 168 | Daniel Mengden | Oakland A's | RHP |
| 119 | Jorge Polanco | Minnesota Twins | 2B/SS | 169 | Josh Hader | Milwaukee Brewers | LHP |
| 120 | Stephen Gonsalves | Minnesota Twins | LHP | 170 | Jeremy Rhoades | Los Angeles Angels | RHP |
| 121 | Rowdy Tellez | Toronto Blue Jays | 1B | 171 | Alex Young | Arizona Diamondbacks | LHP |
| 122 | Dylan Bundy | Baltimore Orioles | RHP | 172 | Ryan Castellani | Colorado Rockies | RHP |
| 123 | Hunter Harvey | Baltimore Orioles | RHP | 173 | Nick Burdi | Minnesota Twins | RHP |
| 124 | Luiz Gohara | Seattle Mariners | LHP | 174 | Touki Toussaint | Atlanta Braves | RHP |
| 125 | Vladimir Guerrero Jr. | Toronto Blue Jays | 3B/OF | 175 | Francisco Mejia | Cleveland Indians | C |
| 126 | Trent Clark | Milwaukee Brewers | CF | 176 | Triston McKenzie | Cleveland Indians | RHP |
| 127 | Kolby Allard | Atlanta Braves | LHP | 177 | Jacob Lindgren | New York Yankees | LHP |
| 128 | Erick Fedde | Washington Nationals | RHP | 178 | Lucas Sims | Atlanta Braves | RHP |
| 129 | Jameson Taillon | Pittsburgh Pirates | RHP | 179 | Clayton Blackburn | San Francisco Giants | RHP |
| 130 | Jomar Reyes | Baltimore Orioles | 3B | 180 | Austin Riley | Atlanta Braves | 3B |
| 131 | Richard Urena | Toronto Blue Jays | SS | 181 | Austin Barnes | Los Angeles Dodgers | C/2B |
| 132 | Duane Underwood | Chicago Cubs | RHP | 182 | Chris Shaw | San Francisco Giants | 1B |
| 133 | Marcos Molina | New York Mets | RHP | 183 | Edmundo Sosa | St. Louis Cardinals | SS |
| 134 | Gary Sanchez | New York Yankees | C | 184 | Daniel Vogelbach | Chicago Cubs | 1B |
| 135 | Mike Clevinger | Cleveland Indians | RHP | 185 | Magneuris Sierra | St. Louis Cardinals | CF |
| 136 | James Kaprielian | New York Yankees | RHP | 186 | Yoan Lopez | Arizona Diamondbacks | RHP |
| 137 | Mychal Givens | Baltimore Orioles | RHP | 187 | Silvino Bracho | Arizona Diamondbacks | RHP |
| 138 | Aaron Blair | Atlanta Braves | RHP | 188 | Nick Longhi | Boston Red Sox | 1B/LF/RF |
| 139 | Devin Williams | Milwaukee Brewers | RHP | 189 | Donnie Dewees | Chicago Cubs | LF/CF |
| 140 | Christian Arroyo | San Francisco Giants | SS | 190 | Nick Plummer | St. Louis Cardinals | CF |
| 141 | Mac Williamson | San Francisco Giants | LF/RF | 191 | Jake Stinnett | Chicago Cubs | RHP |
| 142 | Michael Reed | Milwaukee Brewers | OF | 192 | Zach Davies | Milwaukee Brewers | RHP |
| 143 | Mark Zagunis | Chicago Cubs | OF | 193 | Jordan Patterson | Colorado Rockies | 1B/LF/RF |
| 144 | Ariel Jurado | Texas Rangers | RHP | 194 | Carlos Tocci | Philadelphia Phillies | CF |
| 145 | Jon Harris | Toronto Blue Jays | RHP | 195 | Travis Jankowski | San Diego Padres | CF |
| 146 | Renato Nunez | Oakland A's | 1B/3B | 196 | Junior Fernandez | St. Louis Cardinals | RHP |
| 147 | Dillon Overton | Oakland A's | LHP | 197 | Lucius Fox | San Francisco Giants | SS |
| 148 | D.J. Stewart | Baltimore Orioles | LF | 198 | Jose Peraza | Cincinnati Reds | 2B/SS/CF |
| 149 | Nick Gordon | Minnesota Twins | SS | 199 | Max Fried | Atlanta Braves | LHP |
| 150 | Bobby Bradley | Cleveland Indians | 1B | 200 | Oscar De La Cruz | Chicago Cubs | RHP |

# Ranking the Top 250 Prospects (201-250)

| Rank | Name | Team | POS |
|------|------|------|-----|
| 201 | Stone Garrett | Miami Marlins | CF |
| 202 | Gilbert Lara | Milwaukee Brewers | SS |
| 203 | Jake Woodford | St. Louis Cardinals | RHP |
| 204 | D.J. Peterson | Seattle Mariners | 1B/3B |
| 205 | Walker Buehler | Los Angeles Dodgers | RHP |
| 206 | Socrates Brito | Arizona Diamondbacks | OF |
| 207 | Brandon Drury | Arizona Diamondbacks | 2B/3B |
| 208 | Brandon Nimmo | New York Mets | CF |
| 209 | Amed Rosario | New York Mets | SS |
| 210 | Kyle Freeland | Colorado Rockies | LHP |
| 211 | Alec Mills | Kansas City Royals | RHP |
| 212 | Tyler O'Neill | Seattle Mariners | LF/RF |
| 213 | Michael Cederoth | Minnesota Twins | RHP |
| 214 | Chris Flexen | New York Mets | RHP |
| 215 | Chase Johnson | San Francisco Giants | RHP |
| 216 | Wulimer Becerra | New York Mets | LF/RF |
| 217 | Sam Travis | Boston Red Sox | 1B |
| 218 | German Marquez | Colorado Rockies | RHP |
| 219 | Brian Johnson | Boston Red Sox | LHP |
| 220 | Jon Kemmer | Houston Astros | LF/RF |
| 221 | Derek Fisher | Houston Astros | LF/CF |
| 222 | Pierce Johnson | Chicago Cubs | RHP |
| 223 | Willson Contreras | Chicago Cubs | C |
| 224 | Andrew Morales | St. Louis Cardinals | RHP |
| 225 | Austin Kubitza | Detroit Tigers | RHP |
| 226 | Sam Tuivailala | St. Louis Cardinals | RHP |
| 227 | Mariano Llorens | St. Louis Cardinals | RHP |
| 228 | Rio Ruiz | Atlanta Braves | 3B |
| 229 | Chad Pinder | Oakland A's | SS |
| 230 | Willy Garcia | Pittsburgh Pirates | OF |
| 231 | Taylor Ward | Los Angeles Angels | C |
| 232 | Alex Blandino | Cincinnati Reds | 2B/SS |
| 233 | Nathan Kirby | Milwaukee Brewers | LHP |
| 234 | Casey Meisner | Oakland A's | RHP |
| 235 | Brad Keller | Arizona Diamondbacks | RHP |
| 236 | Nate Smith | Los Angeles Angels | LHP |
| 237 | Kevin Newman | Pittsburgh Pirates | SS |
| 238 | Alen Hanson | Pittsburgh Pirates | 2B/SS |
| 239 | Scott Blewett | Kansas City Royals | RHP |
| 240 | Jeimer Candelario | Chicago Cubs | 3B |
| 241 | Wei-Chieh Huang | Arizona Diamondbacks | RHP |
| 242 | Ramon Flores | Milwaukee Brewers | CF |
| 243 | Tyler Naquin | Cleveland Indians | OF |
| 244 | Ozhaino Albies | Atlanta Braves | SS |
| 245 | Michael Matuella | Texas Rangers | RHP |
| 246 | Joe Gunkel | Baltimore Orioles | RHP |
| 247 | John Lamb | Cincinnati Reds | LHP |
| 248 | Rymer Liriano | Milwaukee Brewers | OF |
| 249 | Reymond Fuentes | Kansas City Royals | LF/CF |
| 250 | Kyle Kubitza | Los Angeles Angels | IF/OF |

# Ranking the Farm Systems

# Ranking the 2016 Farm Systems

1. **Los Angeles Dodgers (Last Year's Rank: #11)** – It almost doesn't seem fair does it? The organization with seemingly limitless pockets is also sporting the deepest, most talented farm system in baseball. There's plenty of high end, blue chip caliber prospects – Julio Urias, Corey Seager, Jose De Leon – with a surplus of depth to deal. But here's the impressive part: there are as many as 12 future big league regulars in the system (though with varying degrees of risk): Urias, Seager, De Leon, Montas, Alex Verdugo, Yadier Alvarez, Grant Holmes, Cody Bellinger, Austin Barnes (perhaps the next Justin Turner), Walker Buehler, hot-hitting Willie Calhoun, and Starling Heredia. We could be on the verge of a Yankees-type dynasty here.

2. **Tampa Bay Rays (#4)** – Once again, I'm not afraid to put my analytical neck on the line for the Rays as having one of the top farm systems in baseball. But let's briefly breakdown the system. Blake Snell is in competition with Steven Matz and Jose Berrios for the title as the minors' second best southpaw (behind Julio Urias, of course). Brent Honeywell and Taylor Guerrieri rank as the sixth and seventh best right-handers. Daniel Robertson is as steady as they come and looks like he could be a decade-plus big league veteran. Jake Bauers, who is only entering his age-20 season thanks to his late birthday, batted .276/.329/.405 in his first taste of Class AA. And shortstop Willy Adames ranks as the 61$^{st}$ best overall prospect. Expect a big bounce back from second baseman Ryan Brett.

3. **Minnesota Twins (#2)** – Welcome to the Byron Buxton Show, folks, because without him the club drops down to the bottom half of the rankings – a testament to his jaw-dropping ability. Jose Berrios is a budding front-of-the-rotation caliber arm who's nearing big league readiness. And keep your fingers crossed that the front office pushes the first round pick Tyler Jay into the rotation in 2016. Gargantuan right-hander Alex Meyer has the ability to dominate at the big league level, but whether the organization is as patient with him as Seattle was with Randy Johnson is an entirely different story.

4. **Chicago Cubs (#1)** – Even after the losses of Kris Bryant, Kyle Schwarber, Addison Russell, and Jorge Soler, Chicago's farm system is still brimming with plenty of talented youths. Albert Almora is never going to be an above-average big league bat, but he can run 'em down with the best of them. Billy McKinney, who lost a good chunk of 2015, should be knocking on the club's big league door by June – or July, which would afford the club a valuable trade chip. Duane Underwood offers up glimpses of front-of-the-rotation caliber production, but he's yet to string it together for more than two months at a time. Last year's first round pick Ian Happ could be a clone of new Cubbie Ben Zobrist.

5. **Houston Astros (#3)** – A.J. Reed is blossoming into the type of hitter everyone thought Jonathan Singleton and Chris Carter were going to be. Half the front office should be locked up for grand theft when they got Miami to throw in hard-throwing right-hander Frances Martes as part of the Jarred Cosart deal two years ago. And just to add to their stockpile of promise, the Astros added three high-ceiling first rounders last

| Rank | Franchise |
|------|-----------|
| 1 | Los Angeles Dodgers |
| 2 | Tampa Bay Rays |
| 3 | Minnesota Twins |
| 4 | Chicago Cubs |
| 5 | Houston Astros |
| 6 | Milwaukee Brewers |
| 7 | Colorado Rockies |
| 8 | Cincinnati Reds |
| 9 | Boston Red Sox |
| 10 | Philadelphia Phillies |
| 11 | St. Louis Cardinals |
| 12 | Pittsburgh Pirates |
| 13 | Atlanta Braves |
| 14 | Cleveland Indians |
| 15 | Oakland A's |
| 16 | Texas Rangers |
| 17 | Arizona Diamondbacks |
| 18 | New York Yankees |
| 19 | Kansas City Royals |
| 20 | San Francisco Giants |
| 21 | Washington Nationals |
| 22 | Baltimore Orioles |
| 23 | San Diego Padres |
| 24 | Toronto Blue Jays |
| 25 | Seattle Mariners |
| 26 | New York Mets |
| 27 | Detroit Tigers |
| 28 | Miami Marlins |
| 29 | Chicago White Sox |
| 30 | Los Angeles Angels |

June: Alex Bregman, Kyle Tucker, and Daz Cameron. Let's see if Jon Kemmer can keep bashing his way through the high minors.

6. **Milwaukee Brewers (#28)** – Made the single biggest jump among all the teams in a year's time. Milwaukee acquired toolsy outfielder Brett Phillips, along with enigmatic big leaguer Domingo Santana, as part of the Carlos Gomez deal with Houston. Shortstop Orlando Arica came through in a huge way as he caught fire in the opening couple months in Class AA. And lanky southpaw Kodi Medeiros fanned more than a bat per inning as a 19-year-old in the Midwest League. Speed demon first rounder Trent Clark looked at ease during his debut. There's not a whole lot of star quality to the system, but there's plenty of middle tier prospects – which quickly adds up. Michael Reed could be one of those saber darlings in the coming years.

7. **Colorado Rockies (#19)** – After promoting stud third baseman Nolan Arenado three years ago, Colorado has another promising hot corner making his way through the minors: Ryan McMahon. Former Oklahoma ace Jon Gray outpitched his big league ERA by nearly two full runs (5.53 ERA vs. 3.63 FIP). And shortstop Brendan Rodgers, the third pick last June, is the long term heir apparent to the recently vacated shortstop position. The organization also did well in adding right-hander Jeff Hoffman from Toronto.

8. **Cincinnati Reds (#10)** – Walt Jocketty did better than expected with everything swirling around Aroldis Chapman's head as he acquired one of the most underrated prospects in the game, right-hander Rookie Davis, and former Notre Dame third baseman Eric Jagielo. Corner outfielder Jesse Winker is one of the most talent prospects, as is fire-balling Robert Stephenson. Both of them could be the face of the franchise's next turnaround. Beyond that Cincinnati has some promising pitching depth with Amir Garrett, Cody Reed, Keury Mella, and John Lamb. Don't buy into the Jose Peraza hype, please.

9. **Boston Red Sox (#6)** – Yoan Moncada is proving to be quite the $60 million bargain. And teenage third baseman Rafael Devers has the makings of an above-average big leaguer. Right-hander Anderson Espinoza is going to be the biggest breakout prospect of 2016. He has everything you'd want in a young arm. Keep your fingers crossed that he doesn't fall victim to the injury nexus. Last year's first round pick, Andrew Benintendi, could be a fast mover to Boston, all aboard the train.

10. **Philadelphia Phillies (#14)** – Former General Manager Ruben Amaro Jr. did exceedingly well in the Cole Hamels deal with Texas last season, acquiring their eventual second, fifth, sixth, and eighteenth best prospects. It wouldn't be surprising to see J.P. Crawford eventually edge out Corey Seager in terms of wins above replacement thanks to his well-rounded game. And outfielder Nick Williams has All-Star potential as well. The front office gambled on former Stanford ace Mark Appel in the Ken Giles deal. It's not time to give up on the big right-hander, but it is quickly approaching. You're looking at the 2018 Surprise Team of the Year.

11. **St. Louis Cardinals (#21)** – The Cardinals have the innate ability to churn out impact arm after impact arm: Michael Wacha, Trevor Rosenthal, Carlos Martinez, Lance Lynn, Jaime Garcia, Shelby Miller, Jason Motte, etc... And right-hander Alex Reyes could eventually exceed them all. The club's first round pick two years ago, Jack Flaherty, looked ridiculously strong as a teenager in the Sally. Underrated Florida State hurler Luke Weaver, a 2014 pick, could be pitching in St. Louis by the end of the year. Very pitching heavy with most of the bats still cutting their minor league teeth.

12. **Pittsburgh Pirates (#9)** – Led off by a three-headed monster, the Pirates' competitive window is likely extended by several years as ace-in-waiting Tyler Glasnow, Austin Meadows, and Josh Bell graduate to the big leagues within the next year-plus. Former top prospect Jameson Taillon, who tantalized quite a bit during his early years, missed his second consecutive season. Outfielders Harold Ramirez and Willy Garcia have some big league upside. Don't buy into the Alen Hanson hype.

13. **Atlanta Braves (#15)** – Veteran General Manager John Hart fleeced the Diamondbacks out a decade-plus middle-of-the-order bat (at a premium position) in Dansby Swanson, a safe solid mid-rotation arm in Aaron Blair, and one of the more underrated outfielders at the big league level (Ender Inciarte) in one of the steals of this century. The system is chock full of flame-throwers with varying degrees of red flags. Touki Toussaint, another former member the Diamondbacks shipped off for pennies on the dollar, Sean Newcomb, Lucas Sims, Zachary Bird, and Chris Ellis all fall into that category. Mallex Smith could be a better version of Billy Hamilton.

14. **Cleveland Indians (#16)** – Very, very sneaky farm system. Justus Sheffield could easily vault up into the game's Top 20 prospects this time next year. Clint Frazier took some important strides last season as well, cutting his strikeout rate down to a career low 21.3%. Bradley Zimmer's second half collapse in Class AA is worrisome. The front office took the ultimate high risk, high reward by taking injured southpaw Brady Aiken with their first pick last June. And the Tribe swindled the always savvy St. Louis front office out of Rob Kaminsky as well. Right-hander Mike Clevinger, who was acquired from the Angels for Vinnie Pestano two years ago, might be a poor man's version of Corey Kluber.

15. **Oakland A's (#24)** – A typical Oakland-type system (go figure). There's not a whole lot of youth when compared to other systems, but there are plenty of intriguing names sprinkled throughout. Sean Manaea, if he can turn in a full season, is one of the minors' most promising southpaws. And the trio of Franklin Barreto, Matt Olson, and Jacob Nottingham give the organization a solid offensive foundation.

16. **Texas Rangers (#8)** – Took quite a stumble – and rightfully so – after dealing away three of the franchise's better prospects (Nick Williams, Jake Thompson, and Jorge Alfaro) for ace lefty Cole Hamels. Still, though, there's still plenty of firepower packed into the club's top 10 prospects. Nomar Mazara is one of the most talented outfielders in the minors, Lewis Brinson looked like a budding five-tool All-Star, and Joey Gallo can hit 'em as far as anyone on earth (when he connects). The club did well in adding collegiate arms Dillon Tate and Michael Matuella last June as well.

17. **Arizona Diamondbacks (#12)** – Easily a top 10 farm system – maybe even a top five – before GM Dave Stewart and Co. stared gutting the minors for what amounted to bargain shopping for other teams. Right-hander Archie Bradley has a chance to be special. Second baseman Jamie Westbrook is one of the most underrated players in the game. And we're all waiting for former collegiate-hitter-turned-first-round pick Braden Shipley to take the next step forward. Maybe it comes in 2016?

18. **New York Yankees (#17)** – Another one of these teams that could have found themselves in the Top 10 if not for some offseason wheeling-and-dealing, though it's hard to not justify acquiring the most dominant arm in the game (Aroldis Chapman). Aaron Judge looks like a Danny Tartabull-type player, offering up some intriguing power and speed. Speedy Jorge Mateo is likely going to fall victim to the "we finally found the replacement to Derek Jeter's throne." And after multiple sessions in Class AA backstop Gary Sanchez finally made his way to Scranton/Wilkes-Barre.

19. **Kansas City Royals (#22)** – Dayton Moore dealt away some promising future pieces for an eventual World Series title, so there's not too much left down on the farm. Miguel Almonte could be a mid-rotation arm. Raul Mondesi is still being talked about as the next best thing, but he hasn't hit since his debut in the Pioneer League four years ago. I'm still holding out hope – with my fingers *and* toes crossed – that Kyle Zimmer can make it through a season without succumbing to some type of injury.

20. **San Francisco Giants (#5)** – The Giants dropped 15 spots over the course of the year. A lot of that has to do with the continued downward spiral of right-hander Kyle Crick, as well as promotions (Andrew Susac, Matt Duffy), and some big league swapping. The system was also hurt by a lack of depth.

21. **Washington Nationals (#20)** – A quintet of blue chip prospects – Lucas Giolito, Trea Turner, Reynaldo Lopez, Victor Robles, and Erick Fedde – helped buoy the system's overall rankings. And once you get past A.J. Cole at #6, there's a very good chance that no one else sees considerable time in Washington. Still, though, Lucas Giolito...nothing else needs to be said.

22. **Baltimore Orioles (#27)** – Chance Sisco's become the best catching prospect in baseball. And, yet, no one is really talking about that. The injured duo of Dylan Bundy and Hunter Harvey are as talented as any hurlers in the minors, so hopefully they can bounce back fully. Mychal Givens, who I listed in last year's Top 20 list, looks the part of a dominant backend reliever. Hell, he *was one* during his debut last season. Let's see if sweet-swinging masher Trey Mancini can continue to hit in 2016.

23. **San Diego Padres (#23)** – GM A.J. Preller did well in restocking the farm as last offseason's purge as he acquired a pair of high ceiling youngsters – Manuel Margot and Javier Guerra – from Boston for veteran relief ace Craig Kimbrel. Hunter Renfroe figured out Class AA after a couple hundred plate appearances and he's likely to spend some significant time in San Diego in 2016. Hopefully, Alex Dickerson finally gets an extended look at the next level as well.

24. **Toronto Blue Jays (#13)** – Dealt away a significant part of the minor league depth as the club geared up with a surprising second half surge. Former Division I football player Anthony Alford arrived as one of the more exciting prospects in 2015. Hyphenated assassin Sean Reid-Foley has a limitless ceiling as long as he can get over some control yips. And one of the club's more recent first round selections, collegiate backstop Max Pentecost, missed the entire 2015 season and could be looking at a position change in the near future.

25. **Seattle Mariners (#18)** – A rotation featuring the likes of Felix Hernandez, Taijuan Walker, and Edwin Diaz could be special. But after the club's second and third top prospects, corner outfielder Alex Jackson and big southpaw Luiz Gohara, there is very little to note. D.J. Peterson stopped slugging. And masher Tyler O'Neill couldn't find first base if you strapped a homing beacon on his head.

26. **New York Mets (#7)** – And here, ladies and gentlemen, is the biggest faller of the group as the Mets dropped 19 positions over the previous 12 months. Of course, promotions to Noah Syndergaard, Dilson Herrera, Michael Conforto, Rafael Montero, and Kevin Plawecki have a lot to do with it. As do the trades of Michael Fulmer and Casey Meisner. Shortstop Gavin Cecchini finally had his coming out party and could be the organization's answer to their long running shortstop question. Brandon Nimmo has some David DeJesus-type value in his bat – *if he can solve southpaws.*

27. **<u>Detroit Tigers (#30)</u>** – No longer the worst system in baseball, thanks in large part to former GM Dave Dombrowski's deals at the deadline last June. Detroit has an incredible surplus of older pitching prospects headlined by Kevin Ziomek and Austin Kubitza. I'm hoping the organization finally pushes Joe Jimenez into a rotation spot. If that does happen, watch out.

28. **<u>Miami Marlins (#29)</u>** – Behind Tyler Kolek, the power-armed right-hander who hasn't missed many sticks, Miami is sporting a trio of interesting low level bats: Josh Naylor, K.J. Woods, and Stone Garrett. If they continue to progress – Kolek included – it wouldn't be surprising to see Miami jump eight to 10 spots next year as some of the associated risk drops.

29. **<u>Chicago White Sox (#25)</u>** – There's some solid talent upfront with Spencer Adams, Carson Fulmer, Tim Anderson, and Jordan Guerrero, but it becomes a who's who of nobodies quickly after. It wouldn't be overly surprising to see Fulmer pitching out of the Sox's bullpen by late September either a la Chris Sale from a couple seasons ago.

30. **<u>Los Angeles Angels of Anaheim (#26)</u>** – The lack of talent is absolutely laughable at this point. There's one potential big league player capable of becoming a regular: right-hander Jeremy Rhoades. After that it's a lot of fringy type prospects. I'll be shocked to see if Taylor Ward continues to hit like he did in his professional debut.

# The Top 25 Breakout Prospects for 2016

# The Top 25 Breakout Prospects for 2016

1. **Anderson Espinoza, RHP, Boston Red Sox** – The actual numbers by themselves are mindboggling: 58.1 IP, 65 K, 14, and a tidy 1.23 ERA. It's obviously a small sample size, by the soon-to-be 18-year-old in the lowest MiLB levels who is just scratching the surface of his seemingly limitless potential. Remember. This. Name.

2. **David Perez, RHP, Texas Rangers** – Limited to just over 10.0 innings between 2013 and 2014, the big right-hander made up for lost time in 2015. The Rangers eased Perez back into the rotation last season, but he should be ready to take on a much larger role in 2016. And here's why you should stop and take notice of Perez: his first two starts in the rotation he tossed 10 total innings with 20 punch outs and zero walks. That type of production – at any level – won't happen very often. He's a candidate for biggest breakout in 2016.

3. **Alex Verdugo, OF, Los Angeles Dodgers** – The former second round pick sparkled in his debut in the rookie leagues two years ago, hitting .353/.421/.511 in 216 plate appearances. And while his numbers from last season are more than solid, .311/.340/.441, take a look at how he performed over the final four months of the season: .356/.380/.520. He'll be on every Top 100-list come this time next year.

4. **Junior Fernandez, RHP, St. Louis Cardinals** – The next great flame-throwing St. Louis Cardinals prospect, Fernandez got a brief two-game taste of the Florida State League last season. At the age of 18. His career numbers, 85.0 IP, 76K, 29 BB, and a 4.31, are very misleading. He's like a ticking time bomb. Tick, tick, tick…

5. **Phil Bickford, RHP, San Francisco Giants** – Another prospect that's going to be thrust into the upper half of most other prospect lists, Bickford possesses the rare quality of superlative control and above-average to plus-strikeout ability. It wouldn't be surprising to see the big right-hander finish the year out in High Class A, maybe even Class AA.

6. **Justin Steele, LHP, Chicago Cubs** – A fourth round pick of the Cubbies two years ago, Steele proved his worth against the Arizona Summer and Northwest Leagues since then. He's going to miss a ton of bats with solid-average control.

7. **Grant Holmes, RHP, Los Angeles Dodgers** – Maybe it's due to the fact that he's buried in the deepest, most talented farm system on the planet, but no one is really talking the young right-hander – *yet*. Tremendous, tremendous ability to miss bats with some wavering control. Once he gets that fixed, watch out! He's another one that's likely going to make a lot of Top 100 lists next year.

8. **Johan Mieses, OF, Los Angeles Dodgers** – Another one of the baby-faced Dodgers that has been overlooked up to this point. Mieses batted .260/.309/.439 between the Midwest and California Leagues, numbers that don't warrant a whole lot of notice until you factor in his age (19).

9. **Reynaldo Lopez, RHP, Washington Nationals** – The wiry right-hander out of the Dominican Republic has been nothing short of dominant over the past two seasons. The problem, though? He's thrown less than 100.0 innings in each of those seasons. Washington is likely going to push Lopez up to Class AA for 2016. Expect his numbers to *pop*.

10. **Oscar De La Cruz, RHP, Chicago Cubs** – A former shortstop that converted to pitching in the last couple years, De La Cruz made the leap to short-season ball after two stints in the Dominican Summer League. And despite the aggressive promotion the 6-foot-4 right-hander saw a big uptick in his strikeout rate.

11. **Hunter Wood, RHP, Tampa Bay Rays** – After splitting last season between the Midwest and Florida State Leagues, it wouldn't be a surprise to see the former 29th round pick make his way up to Class AAA at some point in 2016. Impressive ability to miss bats with an equally strong feel for the strike zone. And, yet, no one's really talking about him. For now.

12. **Enyel De Los Santos, RHP, San Diego Padres** – Acquired along with Nelson Ward from the Mariners in exchange for veteran reliever Joaquin Benoit. De Los Santos, a 6-foot-3, 170-pound hurler out of San Pedro de Macoris, looked absolutely brilliant during his debut last season, averaging 10.3 K/9 and 2.6 BB/9 between the Arizona Summer and Northwest Leagues. He could be one of the major "pop-up guys" in 2016.

13. **Luiz Gohara, LHP, Seattle Mariners** – The talent and potential are in place to develop into a front line starting pitcher. The lone thing holding him back (other than his youth): some questionable control/command. This is a risky pick for a breakout prospect – only because he's set to spend the year with Clinton in the Midwest League at 19-years-old – but remember the name.

14. **Chris Kohler, LHP, Oakland A's** – After missing all of the 2014 season, the 6-foot-3 southpaw made his way back from Tommy John surgery last year. Oakland governed the lefty's innings pretty strictly, but he cobbled together an impressive 37-to-10 strikeout-to-walk ratio in 38.2 innings with Vermont in the NYPL.

15. **Matthew Strahm, LHP, Kansas City Royals** – A late, late round pick in 2012 out of Neosho County Community College, Strahm missed the entire 2013 season and much of 2014 recovering from Tommy John surgery. Finally healthy, the big southpaw fanned 121 in just 94 innings. Can't wait to see him over the course of a full season.

16. **David Paulino, RHP, Houston Astros** – Acquired from the Tigers as part of the Jose Veras trade a couple years ago, Paulino missed much of the 2013 season and all of the following year with – now everyone say it with me – Tommy John surgery. But the 6-foot-7 right-hander came back strong as he made stops in three different levels. Expect big, *big* things from him in 2016.

17. **Luis Castillo, RHP, Miami Marlins** – The not-so-typically-savvy Marlins acquired the 6-foot-2 righty from the Giants – along with Kendry Flores – for retread Casey McGehee. Miami started transitioning Castillo into a fulltime starting pitcher last year, and the results were quite favorable: 41.2 IP, 3.02 ERA, 28 K, and 12 BB.

18. <u>**Jean Cosme, RHP, San Diego Padres**</u> – A 17<sup>th</sup> round pick by the Orioles two years ago, and later flipped to the Padres, Cosme's exceeded the modest expectations placed before him as he's fanned 70 and walked just 26 in his first 72.1 innings of work. He's ticketed for Low Class A in 2016.

19. <u>**Ryan Castellani, RHP, Colorado Rockies**</u> – Not particularly overpowering in the traditional sense, Castellani, nonetheless, made it through the bandbox known as Asheville with a solid 3.27 FIP. He generates a ton of groundballs and he's headed for a more neutral field.

20. <u>**Brent Honeywell, RHP, Tampa Bay Rays**</u> – Like a simmering pot of water, Honeywell is edging towards a boiling point. He's entering his age-21 season and likely will spend a good chunk of it in Class AA. One of my favorite arms in the entire minors.

21. <u>**Francis Martes, RHP, Houston Astros**</u> – Technically, it's hard to declare a pitcher coming off a season in which he posted a 2.04 ERA as a breakout candidate. But in Martes case there's so much more in the tank. After making three starts in Class AA at the end of the year, the 6-foot-1 righty is likely headed back to Corpus Christi in 2016. There's a distinct chance he finishes the year with at least a small cup of coffee in Houston.

22. <u>**Jacob Nottingham, C/1B, Oakland A's**</u> – A typical Oakland A's type prospect with blossoming power. Nottingham handled himself well after two disappointing seasons in the rookie leagues. He could be an All-Star if he sticks behind the plate.

23. <u>**Pedro Fernandez, RHP, Kansas City Royals**</u> – A lively armed right-hander out of the Dominican Republic, Fernandez has been absolutely dominating at various points of his career. He could be one of those late-blooming hurlers that it takes a while to finally click.

24. <u>**Justin Williams, LF/RF, Tampa Bay Rays**</u> – I've picked Williams as a breakout prospect the past two years, so how can I just *not* pick him again for 2016? There's every reason to believe his walk rate will bounce back and perhaps his power potential finally starts to show up in games…

25. <u>**Jacob Faria, RHP, Tampa Bay Rays**</u> – This is so much predicated on the fact that he's going to improve upon his 2015 season – because how does one post a better ERA than 1.92 as he progresses up the minor league ladder? – but you'll end up hearing his naming talked about quite a bit by this time next season. People will eventually start to take notice.


**Bonus Player:**

<u>**Thomas Pannone, LHP, Cleveland Indians**</u> – Former two-way player looked impressive as he jumped from the Arizona Summer League to Low Class A. The Indians have typically done well in developing late-round arms for some reason.

# The Most Overrated Prospects

# The Most Overrated Prospects

So this is the section that will inevitably upset people. I've come to terms with that. I think. But here's a list of players that are more highly touted than they should be.

1.  **Jose Peraza, 2B/SS, Cincinnati Reds** – I make it a point to avoid as much prospect chatter as I can in fear of it swaying my opinion one way or the other. Keeping that in mind, just bear with me here. First, though, I ranked him as the Braves' seventh best prospect and the **228<sup>th</sup> overall prospect in the game**. Here's what I what I wrote about the speedy infielder in last year's book:

    > *"The biggest development for Peraza was his (slight) improvement in the power department last season, which is only amplified by the fact that he moved up two levels. The speed and bat are standout tools, but he rarely walks and the power is still lacking. With Andrelton Simmons fully entrenched at shortstop, Peraza was pushed to the keystone. CAL's not overly optimistic, linking him to a bunch of utility-type guys. He definitely needs to keep hitting for .300+ batting averages if he hopes to develop into an everyday guy."*

    And while it's not overly damning, per se, it certainly smacks with a strong undertone of caution – particularly when Peraza was widely viewed as a Top 100 prospect, many had him in their Top 50 lists. So, after a relatively disappointing 2015 – it's true he batted a healthy .293 as a 21-year-old in Class AAA, but it was an *empty* .293 – former General Manager Jim Bowden tweeted out the following after the trade:

    > *Executives and scouts from both the Braves and Dodgers have told me they Peraza as a utility player at best.*

    Peraza's not going to be a star – unless he can pick it like the Wizard Oz. He has a very, very limited offensive toolkit which is highly dependent upon his speed. Sounds like...Billy Hamilton doesn't it? Peraza's a useful guy, but the power and lack of plate discipline are going to be too damning.

2.  **Brandon Nimmo, CF, New York Mets** – Since I started writing the book two years ago no player analysis has enraged people as much as the former first round pick. And I do mean *ENRAGED*. The sheer amount of hate mail – and vitriol – is unlike anything I've never seen before, even for the internet. But let's just pose the question: what makes Brandon Nimmo so noteworthy? And let's ignore his lofty draft status as we ponder...

    Nimmo's entering his age-23 season as a career .268/.381/.391 hitter, slugging just 119 extra-base hits and swiping 30 bags (while getting caught 22 times) in 420 games. He's also batted just .259/.347/.381 in 133 games in Class AA.

    He's only been dominant just once in his career – a 62-game stint in the Florida State League – but it was buoyed by his ungodly .401 BABIP.

    He's never slugged more than 10 homeruns *or* 21 doubles in a season and *he still can't hit fellow southpaws!* He posted a .613 OPS against them last season, a .664 mark in 2014, a .635 showing the year before, and he scratched out a .594 total in 2012.

    He was two saving graces: (1) his nose for first base via the free pass and (2) he came from an incredibly small town in Wyoming, which obviously isn't a hotbed for talent (so there's the eternal hope for a breakout because of his limited past). But let's be honest: how long will he be able to sniff out a walk as often as he does when pitchers start challenging him more?

I don't hate Brandon Nimmo. He's a nice prospect. But he's flawed. He's in the same boat as Peraza – guys who could tally a two wins with a 90 wRC+ and above-average defense, but they aren't the cream of the crop.

3. **Raimel Tapia, CF, Colorado Rockies** – Yes, the numbers – without proper context – have been phenomenal during his four-year professional career. And 21-year-old outfielders that can bat .305/.333/.467 with double-digit homerun power and speed in High Class A are certainly noteworthy. But, according to *Weighted Runs Created Plus*, Tapia's (artificially bloated) production topped the league average mark by just 12%.

Just to put that into perspective, here's a short list of 21-year-old players that have topped the California League average production by about 12% over the years: Gabriel Guerrero (112 wRC+), Alex Yarbrough (108 wRC+), Theodis Bowe (110 wRC+), Beamer Weems (113 wRC+), Johnny Whittleman (108 wRC+), Travis Denker (117 wRC+), Jonathan Herrera (114 wRC+).

Throw in some pitiful walk rates and Tapia's top prospect status comes sliding back down. Now, again, this isn't to say he won't be a useful big leaguer; I just don't think he's top prospect worthy.

4. **Dominic Smith, 1B, New York Mets** – We're human. We do…human things. I'm guilty of it. You're guilty of it. Everyone's guilty of it. One of those human things is falling for the "Player X had a breakout season" hype train. And even worse, we hope for a prospect to do well, it's as if we're willing a family member to make it to the big leagues. Enter Dominic Smith, the 11th overall pick in the 2013 draft.

Smith had "the best season of his career last year" as he topped the High Class A league average mark by 33% - a tremendous showing for a 20-year-old in High Class A. Yay! All aboard the hype train! He also slugged a career high in homeruns, a total that more than doubled his previous best! Double yay!!

Except that he slugged six homeruns with a .112 ISO. As. A. First. Baseman.

Would you look at the time? I think my stop is this one; I'll be getting off the train now…

He has a promising hit tool, and if he were a middle infielder he might rank in the top 100 prospects. But he's a first baseman that's going to provide very little value on defense. Throw in a career ISO below.100 and just 10 homeruns to his name and it's easy to see the writing on the wall.

5. **Ozhaino Albies, SS, Atlanta** – At this point I feel – and you may agree – that I'm just kind of picking on the Mets and Braves. But, it is what it is. Albies is sort of the "next Jose Peraza," which is a nice thing to say – unless you're the team that dealt away two years of cost controlled All-Star caliber production from the third base position (I'm looking at you, Reds).

Anyway, the Braves, more than any other organization, have a knack for unearthing pocket-sized middle infielders that light the world on fire in the low levels before getting the bat knocked out of their hand when they progress up the ladder: Jose Peraza, Johan Camargo, Daniel Castro (who once hit

.286/.312/.398 as a 21-year-old between High Class A and Class AA), and Elmer Reyes (.285/.321/.406 as a 22-year-old in the Carolina League).

And while Albies is the best of the bunch – sort of a backhanded compliment – he's another very limited player. He's incredibly young, but hasn't shown much in terms of power and his slight 5-foot-nothing frame doesn't offer up a whole lot of hope down the line either.

Again, he's going to be one of those guys that could carve out of a super-sub role unless his defense proves to be otherworldly.

6. **Hector Olivera, 3B, Atlanta Braves** – Here's the thing about big dollar contracts, they often can be misleading as they suggest superstar status. Say, for example, Ryan Howard or Vernon Wells or Barry Zito or Kei Igawa...or Braves' 31-year-old prospect, Cuban-import Hector Olivera, who signed a rich $62.5 million with the Dodgers last year.

And a couple months later Los Angeles, one of the savviest teams in baseball, flips him to Atlanta. Curious move, wouldn't you say?

Let's consider Olivera's last season in Cuba. As a 28-year-old he batted .316/.412/.474 with 11 doubles, a pair of triples, and seven homeruns in 73 games. Fantastic production – until you consider the league had eight guys bat higher than .340 or that 23 other guys topped his .412 OBP.

Caution small sample coming: but Olivera, the Braves' supposed cornerstone to the rebuild as he's been referred to on the internet following his acquisition, batted a lowly .272/.326/.376 in 135 plate appearances in the minors and a mediocre .253/.310/.405 with Atlanta in 87 trips to the plate.

7. **Domingo Leyba, 2B/SS, Arizona Diamondbacks** – Part of that weird three-team deal with the Yankees and Tigers last offseason, Leyba first appeared on prospect charts when he slugged .348/.446/.577 as a 17-year-old in the Dominican Summer League in 2013. One year later he was freakin' ripping the cover off the ball as an 18-year-old in the Midwest League, mashing to the tune of .397/.431/.483 in 124 plate appearances. Damn.

But let's take a trip down to a little place called *Regression is a Bitch*.

Before he looked like the second coming of Cobb two years ago, Leyba spent the first part of 2014 hovering around the league average mark in short-season ball. So how'd he morph into a .397/.431/.483 hitter? Simple: .441 BABIP.

It was destined to come crashing down to earth this year. But the Diamondbacks, for whatever reason, decided that the 30-game sample was convincing enough to push him up to High Class A. And voila!

He batted .237/.277/.309.

Many will point out he was 19-years-old in High Class A. To that I'd like to say: he was 19-years-old and should have been in Low Class A.

8. **Alen Hanson, 2B/SS, Pittsburgh Pirates** – I spent the majority of my childhood either (A) with my nose buried in a baseball book, even at school because a last name of Werner affords a lot of nonsensical stuff in the back of a classroom, (B) memorizing baseball statistics on the back of cards, and (C) playing baseball.

One of my favorite quotes – or at least one that's always stuck with me – is by Frankie Frisch who said, "Baseball is like this. Have one good year and you can fool them for five more, because for five more years they expect you to have another good one."

Well, meet Alen Hanson.

The soon-to-be 23-year-old infielder looked like a budding superstar with the West Virginia Power in the South Atlantic League at the age of 19, hitting .309/.381/.528. But since then he's posted wRC+ totals of 121 (A+), 111 (AA), and 101 (AAA).

See a trend?

Don't be fooled by that aforementioned saying.

# 2016 MLB Projections

# 2016 MLB Projections

I decided to take CAL, the Comparison And Likeness program I've developed, to the next stage: projections. Below you'll find the results for the CAL Projection System 1.0. Also, as part of my summer work I will be focusing on projecting how minor league players will perform in the big leagues. Look for that – hopefully – in next year's book! For now, though, these are just for players that have spent some time in the big leagues.

# 2016 MLB Projections - Hitters

| Player | Age | PA | AB | AVG | OBP | SLG | OPS | ISO | 1B | 2B | 3B | HR | BB% | K% | SB | CS | HBP | wOBA |
|---|---|---|---|---|---|---|---|---|---|---|---|---|---|---|---|---|---|---|
| Jose Abreu | 29 | 617 | 564 | 0.292 | 0.342 | 0.513 | 0.855 | 0.221 | 98 | 38 | 1 | 28 | 5.61% | 21.18% | 1 | 0 | 12 | 0.372 |
| Abraham Almonte | 27 | 268 | 245 | 0.267 | 0.319 | 0.419 | 0.738 | 0.152 | 43 | 13 | 2 | 6 | 7.35% | 16.72% | 5 | 1 | 1 | 0.325 |
| Yonder Alonso | 29 | 520 | 473 | 0.263 | 0.319 | 0.416 | 0.735 | 0.153 | 81 | 28 | 1 | 14 | 7.25% | 10.55% | 7 | 3 | 4 | 0.325 |
| Jose Altuve | 26 | 680 | 626 | 0.338 | 0.382 | 0.468 | 0.850 | 0.129 | 157 | 40 | 4 | 11 | 6.11% | 9.70% | 61 | 16 | 6 | 0.374 |
| Elvis Andrus | 27 | 651 | 608 | 0.253 | 0.299 | 0.351 | 0.650 | 0.098 | 109 | 36 | 3 | 6 | 6.09% | 12.04% | 26 | 13 | 2 | 0.290 |
| Nolan Arenado | 25 | 665 | 611 | 0.275 | 0.324 | 0.514 | 0.838 | 0.239 | 90 | 42 | 3 | 32 | 6.45% | 16.33% | 2 | 1 | 4 | 0.364 |
| Erick Aybar | 32 | 578 | 539 | 0.279 | 0.319 | 0.374 | 0.693 | 0.095 | 114 | 28 | 3 | 6 | 4.92% | 10.60% | 13 | 5 | 5 | 0.308 |
| Jose Bautista | 35 | 641 | 529 | 0.251 | 0.373 | 0.508 | 0.880 | 0.256 | 71 | 25 | 2 | 36 | 15.69% | 17.17% | 5 | 2 | 5 | 0.386 |
| Brandon Belt | 28 | 582 | 524 | 0.274 | 0.339 | 0.492 | 0.830 | 0.218 | 83 | 32 | 4 | 25 | 8.21% | 27.39% | 7 | 2 | 6 | 0.363 |
| Carlos Beltran | 39 | 489 | 449 | 0.234 | 0.285 | 0.397 | 0.682 | 0.163 | 65 | 24 | 1 | 16 | 6.24% | 17.37% | 1 | 0 | 3 | 0.301 |
| Adrian Beltre | 37 | 615 | 561 | 0.296 | 0.346 | 0.455 | 0.801 | 0.159 | 111 | 37 | 1 | 16 | 7.03% | 10.10% | 1 | 0 | 4 | 0.352 |
| Mookie Betts | 23 | 655 | 590 | 0.306 | 0.367 | 0.486 | 0.853 | 0.180 | 109 | 51 | 7 | 13 | 8.61% | 13.30% | 21 | 8 | 3 | 0.373 |
| Greg Bird | 23 | 281 | 247 | 0.243 | 0.329 | 0.472 | 0.801 | 0.228 | 32 | 13 | 0 | 14 | 10.97% | 29.34% | 0 | 0 | 2 | 0.352 |
| Charlie Blackmon | 29 | 660 | 609 | 0.281 | 0.329 | 0.428 | 0.757 | 0.147 | 119 | 30 | 7 | 15 | 5.53% | 14.92% | 23 | 7 | 10 | 0.334 |
| Xander Bogaerts | 23 | 665 | 613 | 0.296 | 0.342 | 0.421 | 0.763 | 0.125 | 133 | 32 | 4 | 12 | 6.16% | 17.26% | 6 | 1 | 5 | 0.338 |
| Jackie Bradley | 26 | 552 | 487 | 0.296 | 0.346 | 0.464 | 0.810 | 0.199 | 76 | 29 | 5 | 19 | 9.87% | 23.20% | 11 | 0 | 7 | 0.357 |
| Michael Brantley | 29 | 412 | 365 | 0.304 | 0.374 | 0.498 | 0.872 | 0.194 | 65 | 33 | 0 | 12 | 9.60% | 9.53% | 8 | 0 | 4 | 0.382 |
| Ryan Braun | 32 | 601 | 545 | 0.273 | 0.335 | 0.481 | 0.816 | 0.208 | 93 | 25 | 5 | 26 | 7.87% | 20.01% | 23 | 5 | 5 | 0.358 |
| Jay Bruce | 29 | 631 | 571 | 0.222 | 0.285 | 0.416 | 0.701 | 0.194 | 68 | 32 | 2 | 25 | 8.22% | 25.34% | 11 | 4 | 1 | 0.308 |
| Kris Bryant | 24 | 667 | 576 | 0.269 | 0.362 | 0.483 | 0.845 | 0.213 | 91 | 32 | 6 | 26 | 11.50% | 30.03% | 12 | 3 | 10 | 0.371 |
| Billy Burns | 26 | 621 | 583 | 0.299 | 0.339 | 0.406 | 0.746 | 0.107 | 137 | 19 | 12 | 6 | 4.82% | 15.53% | 27 | 9 | 6 | 0.330 |
| Billy Butler | 30 | 602 | 551 | 0.258 | 0.312 | 0.380 | 0.692 | 0.123 | 99 | 31 | 0 | 12 | 7.17% | 18.03% | 0 | 0 | 2 | 0.308 |
| Asdrubal Cabrera | 30 | 527 | 478 | 0.241 | 0.300 | 0.385 | 0.685 | 0.144 | 73 | 26 | 6 | 11 | 7.28% | 23.07% | 6 | 2 | 4 | 0.303 |
| Miguel Cabrera | 33 | 649 | 537 | 0.334 | 0.440 | 0.549 | 0.988 | 0.214 | 111 | 45 | 1 | 23 | 15.33% | 15.45% | 1 | 1 | 6 | 0.431 |
| Melky Cabrera | 31 | 599 | 556 | 0.263 | 0.309 | 0.386 | 0.695 | 0.123 | 102 | 32 | 1 | 11 | 6.34% | 12.22% | 2 | 1 | 1 | 0.308 |
| Lorenzo Cain | 30 | 579 | 533 | 0.274 | 0.325 | 0.405 | 0.730 | 0.130 | 102 | 28 | 6 | 10 | 4.96% | 18.48% | 22 | 6 | 13 | 0.324 |
| Kole Calhoun | 28 | 634 | 574 | 0.265 | 0.329 | 0.444 | 0.773 | 0.179 | 100 | 26 | 3 | 24 | 8.28% | 25.13% | 2 | 1 | 4 | 0.341 |
| Robinson Cano | 33 | 669 | 611 | 0.295 | 0.351 | 0.430 | 0.781 | 0.135 | 127 | 39 | 1 | 14 | 7.37% | 11.30% | 2 | 3 | 5 | 0.346 |
| Matt Carpenter | 30 | 701 | 598 | 0.276 | 0.372 | 0.478 | 0.850 | 0.202 | 93 | 46 | 4 | 22 | 13.01% | 22.38% | 3 | 3 | 5 | 0.374 |
| Chris Carter | 29 | 567 | 495 | 0.220 | 0.310 | 0.456 | 0.766 | 0.236 | 58 | 18 | 0 | 33 | 10.99% | 32.26% | 2 | 2 | 5 | 0.338 |
| Nick Castellanos | 24 | 609 | 564 | 0.276 | 0.318 | 0.435 | 0.753 | 0.159 | 97 | 40 | 6 | 12 | 6.01% | 22.46% | 0 | 2 | 1 | 0.330 |
| Jason Castro | 29 | 412 | 367 | 0.212 | 0.291 | 0.370 | 0.661 | 0.158 | 42 | 24 | 0 | 11 | 9.03% | 29.04% | 0 | 0 | 5 | 0.296 |
| Starlin Castro | 26 | 637 | 595 | 0.266 | 0.309 | 0.378 | 0.688 | 0.113 | 119 | 24 | 1 | 14 | 5.52% | 19.50% | 8 | 3 | 4 | 0.306 |
| Lonnie Chisenhall | 27 | 512 | 469 | 0.264 | 0.322 | 0.426 | 0.748 | 0.161 | 77 | 32 | 1 | 14 | 7.26% | 20.60% | 5 | 1 | 4 | 0.331 |
| Shin-Soo Choo | 33 | 637 | 547 | 0.242 | 0.342 | 0.368 | 0.710 | 0.126 | 89 | 28 | 4 | 11 | 10.50% | 23.90% | 5 | 4 | 19 | 0.322 |
| Michael Conforto | 23 | 567 | 509 | 0.266 | 0.328 | 0.452 | 0.780 | 0.186 | 76 | 42 | 0 | 18 | 8.53% | 19.07% | 0 | 0 | 2 | 0.342 |
| Carlos Correa | 21 | 641 | 575 | 0.270 | 0.335 | 0.497 | 0.832 | 0.227 | 91 | 30 | 2 | 32 | 9.07% | 17.31% | 20 | 6 | 1 | 0.363 |
| Carl Crawford | 34 | 309 | 289 | 0.275 | 0.314 | 0.412 | 0.726 | 0.137 | 56 | 14 | 3 | 6 | 5.23% | 19.33% | 16 | 4 | 1 | 0.320 |
| Brandon Crawford | 29 | 567 | 512 | 0.257 | 0.318 | 0.439 | 0.757 | 0.181 | 85 | 21 | 6 | 20 | 7.78% | 23.26% | 5 | 4 | 5 | 0.333 |
| Coco Crisp | 36 | 531 | 476 | 0.220 | 0.289 | 0.326 | 0.615 | 0.106 | 70 | 26 | 2 | 7 | 9.15% | 14.04% | 12 | 3 | 0 | 0.277 |
| C.J. Cron | 26 | 537 | 505 | 0.259 | 0.295 | 0.454 | 0.749 | 0.195 | 82 | 23 | 1 | 25 | 4.20% | 20.31% | 5 | 1 | 5 | 0.328 |
| Nelson Cruz | 35 | 646 | 570 | 0.285 | 0.364 | 0.528 | 0.892 | 0.243 | 101 | 23 | 1 | 38 | 10.51% | 23.14% | 2 | 2 | 5 | 0.390 |
| Travis d'Arnaud | 27 | 531 | 484 | 0.255 | 0.316 | 0.452 | 0.768 | 0.196 | 72 | 29 | 1 | 22 | 7.53% | 17.61% | 0 | 0 | 4 | 0.338 |
| Khris Davis | 28 | 531 | 478 | 0.227 | 0.297 | 0.482 | 0.779 | 0.255 | 55 | 18 | 2 | 33 | 8.32% | 22.87% | 5 | 1 | 5 | 0.340 |
| Rajai Davis | 35 | 429 | 399 | 0.274 | 0.318 | 0.413 | 0.731 | 0.139 | 75 | 21 | 5 | 8 | 5.33% | 15.37% | 29 | 7 | 5 | 0.323 |
| Chris Davis | 30 | 633 | 547 | 0.253 | 0.344 | 0.532 | 0.876 | 0.279 | 70 | 26 | 0 | 42 | 10.68% | 31.89% | 1 | 0 | 12 | 0.381 |
| Delino DeShields Jr. | 23 | 520 | 468 | 0.258 | 0.326 | 0.368 | 0.694 | 0.111 | 84 | 23 | 11 | 2 | 8.73% | 21.22% | 22 | 8 | 4 | 0.310 |
| Josh Donaldson | 30 | 616 | 537 | 0.255 | 0.339 | 0.465 | 0.804 | 0.210 | 75 | 35 | 2 | 25 | 11.19% | 18.49% | 4 | 0 | 3 | 0.353 |
| Brian Dozier | 29 | 700 | 614 | 0.244 | 0.326 | 0.450 | 0.776 | 0.207 | 84 | 33 | 2 | 30 | 10.20% | 20.87% | 13 | 4 | 7 | 0.342 |
| Lucas Duda | 30 | 577 | 488 | 0.232 | 0.345 | 0.439 | 0.784 | 0.207 | 62 | 26 | 0 | 25 | 12.67% | 28.95% | 0 | 0 | 13 | 0.350 |
| Matt Duffy | 25 | 602 | 570 | 0.294 | 0.329 | 0.418 | 0.747 | 0.123 | 124 | 28 | 6 | 10 | 4.60% | 15.96% | 10 | 2 | 3 | 0.330 |
| Adam Eaton | 27 | 649 | 580 | 0.274 | 0.347 | 0.394 | 0.741 | 0.120 | 117 | 22 | 12 | 8 | 8.44% | 17.15% | 14 | 6 | 12 | 0.331 |
| Jacoby Ellsbury | 32 | 636 | 571 | 0.270 | 0.338 | 0.376 | 0.715 | 0.106 | 114 | 27 | 4 | 9 | 6.13% | 17.50% | 36 | 8 | 22 | 0.322 |
| Edwin Encarnacion | 33 | 619 | 528 | 0.273 | 0.370 | 0.574 | 0.944 | 0.301 | 72 | 28 | 0 | 44 | 12.32% | 15.24% | 3 | 3 | 8 | 0.408 |
| Yunel Escobar | 33 | 598 | 542 | 0.274 | 0.336 | 0.387 | 0.722 | 0.112 | 109 | 29 | 1 | 10 | 7.78% | 17.56% | 2 | 5 | 5 | 0.323 |
| Alcides Escobar | 29 | 633 | 593 | 0.271 | 0.312 | 0.350 | 0.662 | 0.079 | 126 | 26 | 5 | 3 | 4.49% | 12.00% | 19 | 4 | 9 | 0.296 |
| Andre Ethier | 34 | 374 | 329 | 0.270 | 0.351 | 0.402 | 0.753 | 0.133 | 64 | 13 | 5 | 7 | 10.00% | 21.02% | 1 | 3 | 5 | 0.336 |
| Prince Fielder | 32 | 700 | 614 | 0.269 | 0.353 | 0.427 | 0.780 | 0.158 | 112 | 31 | 0 | 22 | 10.15% | 13.00% | 0 | 0 | 11 | 0.348 |
| Logan Forsythe | 29 | 498 | 454 | 0.220 | 0.281 | 0.366 | 0.647 | 0.146 | 64 | 19 | 2 | 14 | 6.53% | 18.12% | 4 | 1 | 8 | 0.289 |

# 2016 MLB Projections - Hitters

| Player | Age | PA | AB | AVG | OBP | SLG | OPS | ISO | 1B | 2B | 3B | HR | BB% | K% | SB | CS | HBP | wOBA |
|---|---|---|---|---|---|---|---|---|---|---|---|---|---|---|---|---|---|---|
| Maikel Franco | 23 | 600 | 544 | 0.272 | 0.330 | 0.468 | 0.799 | 0.196 | 88 | 37 | 2 | 22 | 7.33% | 16.07% | 2 | 0 | 6 | 0.350 |
| Todd Frazier | 30 | 641 | 578 | 0.247 | 0.311 | 0.401 | 0.712 | 0.153 | 88 | 37 | 2 | 16 | 6.27% | 21.07% | 18 | 6 | 16 | 0.317 |
| Freddie Freeman | 26 | 664 | 560 | 0.301 | 0.404 | 0.531 | 0.935 | 0.230 | 99 | 39 | 3 | 28 | 13.63% | 19.69% | 5 | 2 | 9 | 0.409 |
| Avisail Garcia | 25 | 537 | 488 | 0.263 | 0.323 | 0.371 | 0.694 | 0.108 | 98 | 19 | 2 | 10 | 7.42% | 21.53% | 5 | 4 | 5 | 0.311 |
| Brett Gardner | 32 | 620 | 553 | 0.276 | 0.348 | 0.417 | 0.765 | 0.141 | 106 | 29 | 5 | 13 | 9.33% | 20.60% | 25 | 6 | 5 | 0.340 |
| Evan Gattis | 29 | 537 | 498 | 0.242 | 0.287 | 0.416 | 0.703 | 0.174 | 78 | 19 | 2 | 21 | 4.85% | 24.09% | 0 | 0 | 8 | 0.310 |
| Johnny Giavotella | 28 | 542 | 505 | 0.241 | 0.284 | 0.315 | 0.598 | 0.074 | 97 | 17 | 4 | 5 | 5.58% | 15.27% | 9 | 3 | 2 | 0.268 |
| Paul Goldschmidt | 28 | 700 | 556 | 0.318 | 0.448 | 0.566 | 1.014 | 0.247 | 93 | 57 | 2 | 26 | 19.16% | 20.40% | 25 | 6 | 3 | 0.440 |
| Yan Gomes | 28 | 463 | 424 | 0.242 | 0.294 | 0.415 | 0.709 | 0.172 | 60 | 27 | 1 | 15 | 5.19% | 24.24% | 0 | 0 | 9 | 0.312 |
| Carlos Gomez | 30 | 566 | 515 | 0.266 | 0.324 | 0.437 | 0.761 | 0.171 | 91 | 24 | 3 | 19 | 6.40% | 21.34% | 22 | 12 | 10 | 0.336 |
| Adrian Gonzalez | 34 | 659 | 591 | 0.299 | 0.360 | 0.487 | 0.846 | 0.188 | 119 | 31 | 0 | 27 | 8.66% | 16.18% | 1 | 1 | 3 | 0.371 |
| Carlos Gonzalez | 30 | 523 | 480 | 0.256 | 0.308 | 0.506 | 0.814 | 0.250 | 66 | 23 | 3 | 30 | 6.85% | 25.89% | 4 | 0 | 2 | 0.354 |
| Dee Gordon | 28 | 661 | 627 | 0.316 | 0.347 | 0.407 | 0.754 | 0.092 | 159 | 23 | 12 | 3 | 4.44% | 13.04% | 49 | 21 | 2 | 0.333 |
| Alex Gordon | 32 | 668 | 567 | 0.272 | 0.372 | 0.414 | 0.785 | 0.142 | 109 | 28 | 1 | 17 | 10.86% | 19.14% | 10 | 8 | 21 | 0.353 |
| Yasmani Grandal | 27 | 435 | 372 | 0.219 | 0.328 | 0.380 | 0.708 | 0.161 | 49 | 19 | 0 | 14 | 13.47% | 24.14% | 3 | 3 | 3 | 0.320 |
| Curtis Granderson | 35 | 627 | 549 | 0.229 | 0.320 | 0.355 | 0.674 | 0.126 | 84 | 28 | 1 | 13 | 11.19% | 23.98% | 10 | 1 | 4 | 0.306 |
| Didi Gregorius | 26 | 599 | 539 | 0.238 | 0.309 | 0.366 | 0.676 | 0.128 | 90 | 21 | 4 | 13 | 6.58% | 15.21% | 8 | 2 | 18 | 0.304 |
| Randal Grichuk | 24 | 530 | 491 | 0.269 | 0.319 | 0.500 | 0.819 | 0.231 | 69 | 33 | 11 | 20 | 6.16% | 30.97% | 6 | 2 | 4 | 0.356 |
| Josh Hamilton | 35 | 359 | 330 | 0.249 | 0.298 | 0.405 | 0.703 | 0.156 | 52 | 19 | 1 | 10 | 6.03% | 26.35% | 1 | 1 | 3 | 0.310 |
| Billy Hamilton | 25 | 578 | 545 | 0.239 | 0.281 | 0.338 | 0.619 | 0.100 | 96 | 19 | 9 | 6 | 5.05% | 15.05% | 63 | 13 | 3 | 0.276 |
| J.J. Hardy | 33 | 579 | 545 | 0.239 | 0.276 | 0.344 | 0.620 | 0.105 | 94 | 26 | 0 | 10 | 4.86% | 19.03% | 0 | 0 | 2 | 0.276 |
| Bryce Harper | 23 | 669 | 542 | 0.312 | 0.436 | 0.610 | 1.046 | 0.298 | 93 | 33 | 3 | 41 | 17.57% | 20.63% | 8 | 4 | 5 | 0.451 |
| Josh Harrison | 28 | 550 | 515 | 0.308 | 0.348 | 0.446 | 0.794 | 0.138 | 108 | 39 | 4 | 8 | 4.67% | 11.09% | 22 | 5 | 7 | 0.350 |
| Chase Headley | 32 | 575 | 514 | 0.242 | 0.319 | 0.363 | 0.682 | 0.121 | 88 | 24 | 1 | 12 | 8.46% | 23.14% | 4 | 1 | 10 | 0.308 |
| Adeiny Hechavarria | 27 | 577 | 544 | 0.244 | 0.280 | 0.335 | 0.615 | 0.091 | 101 | 18 | 10 | 4 | 4.76% | 17.55% | 7 | 2 | 1 | 0.273 |
| Odubel Herrera | 24 | 630 | 587 | 0.287 | 0.332 | 0.392 | 0.724 | 0.105 | 123 | 35 | 4 | 6 | 5.54% | 23.58% | 14 | 9 | 6 | 0.322 |
| Jason Heyward | 26 | 629 | 561 | 0.294 | 0.365 | 0.443 | 0.808 | 0.149 | 114 | 33 | 3 | 15 | 9.40% | 15.33% | 12 | 3 | 5 | 0.359 |
| Matt Holliday | 36 | 642 | 532 | 0.281 | 0.397 | 0.439 | 0.837 | 0.159 | 98 | 34 | 2 | 16 | 14.00% | 16.90% | 5 | 3 | 16 | 0.375 |
| Eric Hosmer | 26 | 670 | 609 | 0.300 | 0.354 | 0.448 | 0.802 | 0.147 | 123 | 42 | 4 | 13 | 7.72% | 15.64% | 8 | 2 | 3 | 0.353 |
| Ryan Howard | 36 | 367 | 331 | 0.236 | 0.299 | 0.435 | 0.734 | 0.199 | 40 | 24 | 0 | 14 | 7.68% | 27.60% | 0 | 0 | 3 | 0.323 |
| Chris Iannetta | 33 | 323 | 273 | 0.211 | 0.327 | 0.367 | 0.693 | 0.156 | 33 | 15 | 0 | 9 | 14.32% | 24.69% | 1 | 1 | 2 | 0.315 |
| Jose Iglesias | 26 | 557 | 513 | 0.279 | 0.334 | 0.362 | 0.696 | 0.083 | 114 | 21 | 3 | 5 | 5.34% | 13.43% | 10 | 7 | 13 | 0.313 |
| Ender Inciarte | 25 | 591 | 546 | 0.280 | 0.331 | 0.404 | 0.735 | 0.124 | 110 | 27 | 7 | 9 | 6.67% | 13.07% | 20 | 7 | 3 | 0.326 |
| John Jaso | 32 | 424 | 366 | 0.258 | 0.352 | 0.429 | 0.780 | 0.171 | 58 | 23 | 1 | 13 | 11.96% | 19.14% | 0 | 0 | 4 | 0.348 |
| Jon Jay | 31 | 601 | 540 | 0.257 | 0.327 | 0.333 | 0.660 | 0.077 | 109 | 22 | 3 | 4 | 7.61% | 16.95% | 4 | 5 | 12 | 0.300 |
| Desmond Jennings | 29 | 550 | 497 | 0.263 | 0.329 | 0.398 | 0.726 | 0.135 | 91 | 20 | 12 | 8 | 8.03% | 17.54% | 17 | 11 | 6 | 0.323 |
| Adam Jones | 30 | 682 | 645 | 0.261 | 0.295 | 0.458 | 0.753 | 0.197 | 104 | 31 | 2 | 30 | 3.60% | 18.89% | 8 | 2 | 8 | 0.330 |
| Jung-Ho Kang | 29 | 550 | 494 | 0.275 | 0.342 | 0.441 | 0.782 | 0.165 | 91 | 26 | 2 | 17 | 5.78% | 21.39% | 6 | 3 | 20 | 0.347 |
| Matt Kemp | 31 | 587 | 538 | 0.263 | 0.312 | 0.454 | 0.766 | 0.192 | 84 | 33 | 2 | 22 | 6.75% | 23.63% | 8 | 3 | 2 | 0.335 |
| Kevin Kiermaier | 26 | 558 | 517 | 0.254 | 0.302 | 0.416 | 0.718 | 0.161 | 81 | 27 | 15 | 9 | 6.20% | 19.36% | 16 | 6 | 2 | 0.314 |
| Ian Kinsler | 34 | 637 | 594 | 0.289 | 0.329 | 0.428 | 0.757 | 0.139 | 122 | 31 | 5 | 14 | 5.10% | 9.92% | 10 | 4 | 5 | 0.333 |
| Jason Kipnis | 29 | 627 | 559 | 0.263 | 0.334 | 0.399 | 0.733 | 0.136 | 97 | 35 | 4 | 11 | 8.98% | 18.10% | 15 | 5 | 6 | 0.326 |
| Jake Lamb | 25 | 511 | 458 | 0.266 | 0.332 | 0.393 | 0.724 | 0.127 | 87 | 20 | 7 | 8 | 9.15% | 20.59% | 4 | 3 | 1 | 0.322 |
| Adam LaRoche | 36 | 461 | 402 | 0.199 | 0.292 | 0.323 | 0.615 | 0.125 | 54 | 14 | 0 | 12 | 11.38% | 24.57% | 1 | 0 | 2 | 0.281 |
| Brett Lawrie | 26 | 555 | 512 | 0.242 | 0.294 | 0.380 | 0.674 | 0.138 | 83 | 23 | 3 | 14 | 6.30% | 17.16% | 6 | 3 | 4 | 0.299 |
| Adam Lind | 32 | 561 | 503 | 0.281 | 0.350 | 0.448 | 0.798 | 0.168 | 90 | 34 | 1 | 16 | 9.63% | 17.52% | 0 | 0 | 1 | 0.353 |
| Francisco Lindor | 22 | 555 | 515 | 0.310 | 0.351 | 0.468 | 0.820 | 0.158 | 114 | 26 | 5 | 15 | 6.15% | 15.53% | 15 | 3 | 1 | 0.359 |
| James Loney | 32 | 599 | 551 | 0.265 | 0.319 | 0.368 | 0.687 | 0.103 | 108 | 28 | 0 | 10 | 7.28% | 13.55% | 3 | 0 | 2 | 0.308 |
| Evan Longoria | 30 | 682 | 614 | 0.259 | 0.323 | 0.385 | 0.707 | 0.126 | 109 | 35 | 1 | 13 | 7.92% | 20.02% | 4 | 1 | 7 | 0.315 |
| Jed Lowrie | 32 | 541 | 478 | 0.232 | 0.310 | 0.376 | 0.686 | 0.145 | 70 | 26 | 1 | 14 | 9.26% | 15.87% | 1 | 0 | 7 | 0.307 |
| Jonathan Lucroy | 30 | 591 | 532 | 0.258 | 0.321 | 0.388 | 0.709 | 0.130 | 95 | 27 | 4 | 11 | 8.54% | 16.47% | 17 | 1 | 2 | 0.316 |
| Manny Machado | 23 | 641 | 585 | 0.294 | 0.350 | 0.505 | 0.855 | 0.211 | 109 | 31 | 2 | 29 | 7.32% | 18.28% | 13 | 5 | 5 | 0.374 |
| Nick Markakis | 32 | 700 | 627 | 0.289 | 0.355 | 0.373 | 0.728 | 0.084 | 145 | 28 | 2 | 7 | 9.09% | 14.26% | 2 | 1 | 3 | 0.327 |
| Starling Marte | 27 | 633 | 584 | 0.279 | 0.329 | 0.428 | 0.757 | 0.149 | 112 | 29 | 5 | 16 | 5.03% | 20.59% | 34 | 8 | 14 | 0.335 |
| Russell Martin | 33 | 489 | 422 | 0.251 | 0.346 | 0.469 | 0.815 | 0.219 | 62 | 20 | 1 | 24 | 10.43% | 22.16% | 8 | 3 | 12 | 0.360 |
| Leonys Martin | 28 | 557 | 510 | 0.240 | 0.297 | 0.368 | 0.665 | 0.128 | 86 | 20 | 3 | 13 | 7.26% | 19.35% | 26 | 12 | 3 | 0.297 |
| Victor Martinez | 37 | 539 | 494 | 0.267 | 0.316 | 0.409 | 0.725 | 0.142 | 92 | 26 | 0 | 15 | 6.08% | 10.57% | 0 | 0 | 6 | 0.320 |
| J.D. Martinez | 28 | 592 | 545 | 0.294 | 0.341 | 0.502 | 0.843 | 0.208 | 100 | 32 | 3 | 25 | 6.41% | 24.68% | 7 | 1 | 4 | 0.368 |
| Joe Mauer | 33 | 599 | 522 | 0.274 | 0.357 | 0.377 | 0.734 | 0.103 | 104 | 30 | 2 | 7 | 11.62% | 14.99% | 1 | 0 | 1 | 0.330 |
| Cameron Maybin | 29 | 547 | 494 | 0.248 | 0.317 | 0.373 | 0.691 | 0.126 | 81 | 27 | 6 | 7 | 8.93% | 21.33% | 15 | 6 | 2 | 0.309 |

# 2016 MLB Projections - Hitters

| Player | Age | PA | AB | AVG | OBP | SLG | OPS | ISO | 1B | 2B | 3B | HR | BB% | K% | SB | CS | HBP | wOBA |
|---|---|---|---|---|---|---|---|---|---|---|---|---|---|---|---|---|---|---|
| Brian McCann | 32 | 497 | 446 | 0.220 | 0.291 | 0.423 | 0.715 | 0.204 | 59 | 14 | 0 | 25 | 7.78% | 19.59% | 0 | 0 | 8 | 0.316 |
| Andrew McCutchen | 29 | 670 | 574 | 0.293 | 0.384 | 0.485 | 0.869 | 0.192 | 107 | 34 | 3 | 23 | 12.25% | 19.17% | 15 | 5 | 7 | 0.383 |
| Jordy Mercer | 29 | 547 | 508 | 0.274 | 0.320 | 0.409 | 0.729 | 0.135 | 97 | 28 | 2 | 12 | 6.17% | 16.43% | 4 | 0 | 2 | 0.323 |
| Devin Mesoraco | 25 | 581 | 534 | 0.237 | 0.288 | 0.346 | 0.633 | 0.109 | 90 | 20 | 10 | 6 | 6.20% | 11.73% | 73 | 14 | 5 | 0.282 |
| Yadier Molina | 33 | 523 | 483 | 0.270 | 0.315 | 0.365 | 0.679 | 0.095 | 99 | 23 | 1 | 7 | 6.11% | 10.95% | 3 | 2 | 2 | 0.303 |
| Miguel Montero | 32 | 427 | 375 | 0.218 | 0.302 | 0.342 | 0.643 | 0.124 | 59 | 10 | 0 | 12 | 9.83% | 25.19% | 0 | 1 | 5 | 0.292 |
| Kendry Morales | 33 | 550 | 491 | 0.290 | 0.360 | 0.475 | 0.835 | 0.185 | 91 | 31 | 1 | 19 | 8.82% | 14.61% | 0 | 0 | 7 | 0.368 |
| Mitch Moreland | 30 | 519 | 472 | 0.263 | 0.318 | 0.439 | 0.756 | 0.176 | 77 | 29 | 2 | 17 | 6.80% | 23.76% | 0 | 0 | 6 | 0.333 |
| Logan Morrison | 28 | 540 | 482 | 0.244 | 0.320 | 0.362 | 0.681 | 0.118 | 86 | 18 | 2 | 12 | 9.65% | 13.70% | 7 | 4 | 3 | 0.307 |
| Brandon Moss | 32 | 476 | 413 | 0.224 | 0.319 | 0.429 | 0.748 | 0.205 | 50 | 21 | 0 | 21 | 10.46% | 28.25% | 0 | 1 | 10 | 0.332 |
| Mike Moustakas | 27 | 559 | 505 | 0.257 | 0.320 | 0.440 | 0.759 | 0.183 | 79 | 29 | 0 | 21 | 6.38% | 14.09% | 1 | 1 | 13 | 0.335 |
| Daniel Murphy | 31 | 624 | 579 | 0.273 | 0.316 | 0.419 | 0.735 | 0.146 | 106 | 33 | 3 | 15 | 5.80% | 11.25% | 5 | 2 | 3 | 0.324 |
| Wil Myers | 25 | 557 | 493 | 0.235 | 0.315 | 0.331 | 0.645 | 0.096 | 85 | 21 | 1 | 8 | 10.52% | 21.07% | 8 | 2 | 1 | 0.293 |
| Mike Napoli | 34 | 434 | 362 | 0.212 | 0.337 | 0.378 | 0.715 | 0.166 | 46 | 15 | 0 | 15 | 14.84% | 23.92% | 3 | 1 | 5 | 0.325 |
| Derek Norris | 27 | 517 | 453 | 0.245 | 0.336 | 0.416 | 0.751 | 0.170 | 70 | 23 | 1 | 18 | 11.12% | 19.82% | 0 | 0 | 5 | 0.336 |
| Rougned Odor | 22 | 579 | 530 | 0.250 | 0.306 | 0.449 | 0.755 | 0.200 | 79 | 22 | 11 | 20 | 5.17% | 15.99% | 8 | 2 | 15 | 0.331 |
| David Ortiz | 40 | 601 | 523 | 0.274 | 0.358 | 0.494 | 0.852 | 0.220 | 86 | 28 | 0 | 29 | 11.71% | 15.62% | 0 | 0 | 1 | 0.373 |
| Marcell Ozuna | 25 | 632 | 580 | 0.263 | 0.317 | 0.431 | 0.748 | 0.168 | 98 | 32 | 3 | 20 | 7.20% | 24.00% | 6 | 4 | 2 | 0.330 |
| Angel Pagan | 34 | 478 | 446 | 0.277 | 0.320 | 0.369 | 0.689 | 0.091 | 96 | 21 | 2 | 5 | 5.86% | 13.42% | 13 | 4 | 1 | 0.307 |
| Joe Panik | 25 | 570 | 517 | 0.313 | 0.372 | 0.412 | 0.784 | 0.099 | 127 | 25 | 3 | 7 | 8.37% | 9.98% | 3 | 1 | 2 | 0.350 |
| Gerardo Parra | 29 | 601 | 559 | 0.281 | 0.325 | 0.434 | 0.759 | 0.152 | 105 | 33 | 6 | 14 | 5.43% | 17.33% | 9 | 7 | 6 | 0.334 |
| Joc Pederson | 24 | 599 | 492 | 0.221 | 0.356 | 0.430 | 0.786 | 0.209 | 61 | 20 | 1 | 27 | 15.93% | 26.62% | 4 | 7 | 9 | 0.353 |
| Dustin Pedroia | 32 | 593 | 526 | 0.309 | 0.379 | 0.397 | 0.776 | 0.088 | 132 | 22 | 1 | 7 | 10.03% | 9.53% | 10 | 4 | 2 | 0.348 |
| Hunter Pence | 33 | 668 | 613 | 0.265 | 0.321 | 0.484 | 0.805 | 0.219 | 93 | 34 | 7 | 29 | 7.63% | 22.09% | 13 | 4 | 1 | 0.352 |
| Jhonny Peralta | 34 | 631 | 582 | 0.272 | 0.322 | 0.385 | 0.707 | 0.113 | 122 | 22 | 0 | 15 | 6.82% | 20.03% | 3 | 6 | 2 | 0.315 |
| Roberto Perez | 27 | 189 | 159 | 0.227 | 0.341 | 0.389 | 0.730 | 0.162 | 22 | 8 | 1 | 5 | 14.26% | 26.21% | 0 | 0 | 1 | 0.329 |
| Sal Perez | 26 | 557 | 534 | 0.257 | 0.282 | 0.395 | 0.677 | 0.138 | 95 | 26 | 1 | 15 | 3.07% | 15.65% | 1 | 0 | 3 | 0.298 |
| Brandon Phillips | 35 | 581 | 545 | 0.278 | 0.315 | 0.373 | 0.688 | 0.095 | 122 | 19 | 1 | 10 | 4.41% | 11.67% | 10 | 3 | 6 | 0.306 |
| Stephen Piscotty | 25 | 550 | 495 | 0.299 | 0.359 | 0.502 | 0.861 | 0.203 | 91 | 31 | 9 | 18 | 8.47% | 21.25% | 6 | 2 | 3 | 0.375 |
| Trevor Plouffe | 30 | 614 | 553 | 0.232 | 0.300 | 0.359 | 0.659 | 0.127 | 76 | 42 | 3 | 7 | 8.53% | 17.52% | 3 | 1 | 3 | 0.295 |
| Gregory Polanco | 24 | 660 | 597 | 0.243 | 0.311 | 0.381 | 0.691 | 0.138 | 99 | 26 | 5 | 15 | 8.98% | 17.56% | 35 | 8 | 1 | 0.309 |
| A.J. Pollock | 28 | 639 | 580 | 0.296 | 0.352 | 0.489 | 0.841 | 0.193 | 104 | 41 | 10 | 17 | 7.80% | 15.50% | 37 | 7 | 3 | 0.367 |
| Buster Posey | 29 | 617 | 554 | 0.295 | 0.354 | 0.445 | 0.799 | 0.150 | 118 | 26 | 1 | 19 | 8.28% | 10.81% | 0 | 0 | 4 | 0.353 |
| Martin Prado | 32 | 589 | 542 | 0.279 | 0.326 | 0.385 | 0.711 | 0.106 | 116 | 23 | 2 | 10 | 5.78% | 12.51% | 1 | 1 | 7 | 0.316 |
| Yasiel Puig | 25 | 649 | 579 | 0.274 | 0.345 | 0.468 | 0.813 | 0.194 | 100 | 28 | 8 | 23 | 9.23% | 22.14% | 8 | 5 | 5 | 0.357 |
| Albert Pujols | 36 | 602 | 548 | 0.262 | 0.319 | 0.435 | 0.753 | 0.173 | 94 | 26 | 0 | 23 | 7.22% | 10.96% | 3 | 1 | 5 | 0.332 |
| Alexei Ramirez | 34 | 599 | 565 | 0.261 | 0.295 | 0.368 | 0.663 | 0.107 | 108 | 29 | 1 | 10 | 4.11% | 10.96% | 12 | 6 | 4 | 0.294 |
| Hanley Ramirez | 32 | 589 | 533 | 0.268 | 0.331 | 0.464 | 0.795 | 0.196 | 88 | 29 | 2 | 24 | 8.08% | 20.65% | 9 | 3 | 5 | 0.350 |
| Colby Rasmus | 29 | 431 | 385 | 0.240 | 0.316 | 0.502 | 0.818 | 0.262 | 47 | 18 | 1 | 27 | 9.78% | 28.77% | 1 | 0 | 2 | 0.358 |
| Josh Reddick | 29 | 566 | 521 | 0.251 | 0.301 | 0.388 | 0.689 | 0.137 | 92 | 20 | 5 | 14 | 6.88% | 16.14% | 6 | 2 | 1 | 0.305 |
| Anthony Rendon | 26 | 654 | 580 | 0.260 | 0.332 | 0.399 | 0.731 | 0.139 | 100 | 36 | 2 | 14 | 9.53% | 19.25% | 2 | 2 | 4 | 0.325 |
| Ben Revere | 28 | 633 | 604 | 0.306 | 0.337 | 0.384 | 0.721 | 0.078 | 151 | 24 | 8 | 2 | 3.81% | 9.16% | 37 | 8 | 4 | 0.320 |
| Jose Reyes | 33 | 489 | 453 | 0.264 | 0.312 | 0.375 | 0.687 | 0.111 | 87 | 23 | 3 | 7 | 6.68% | 12.52% | 16 | 5 | 0 | 0.306 |
| Anthony Rizzo | 26 | 646 | 548 | 0.288 | 0.388 | 0.537 | 0.925 | 0.249 | 86 | 37 | 4 | 31 | 12.14% | 16.92% | 14 | 4 | 14 | 0.403 |
| Alex Rodriguez | 40 | 547 | 469 | 0.263 | 0.360 | 0.491 | 0.852 | 0.228 | 74 | 20 | 0 | 29 | 12.23% | 26.94% | 8 | 2 | 7 | 0.375 |
| Addison Russell | 22 | 572 | 521 | 0.256 | 0.315 | 0.413 | 0.728 | 0.157 | 82 | 35 | 1 | 15 | 7.74% | 25.53% | 5 | 3 | 3 | 0.322 |
| Pablo Sandoval | 29 | 574 | 529 | 0.243 | 0.292 | 0.391 | 0.683 | 0.147 | 83 | 28 | 2 | 15 | 5.81% | 13.94% | 0 | 0 | 5 | 0.302 |
| Miguel Sano | 23 | 599 | 501 | 0.268 | 0.376 | 0.526 | 0.902 | 0.259 | 73 | 26 | 2 | 33 | 14.85% | 35.05% | 1 | 1 | 2 | 0.393 |
| Domingo Santana | 23 | 389 | 339 | 0.241 | 0.331 | 0.407 | 0.738 | 0.166 | 53 | 15 | 0 | 14 | 10.13% | 31.82% | 9 | 2 | 8 | 0.330 |
| Carlos Santana | 30 | 651 | 523 | 0.232 | 0.377 | 0.391 | 0.768 | 0.159 | 76 | 26 | 1 | 19 | 18.18% | 17.56% | 13 | 1 | 6 | 0.350 |
| Kyle Schwarber | 23 | 543 | 459 | 0.255 | 0.361 | 0.496 | 0.857 | 0.241 | 72 | 11 | 2 | 32 | 12.76% | 28.20% | 5 | 7 | 9 | 0.377 |
| Kyle Seager | 28 | 641 | 568 | 0.254 | 0.333 | 0.425 | 0.758 | 0.172 | 93 | 27 | 1 | 23 | 9.52% | 19.04% | 4 | 4 | 8 | 0.337 |
| Jean Segura | 26 | 585 | 559 | 0.262 | 0.292 | 0.353 | 0.645 | 0.091 | 115 | 18 | 8 | 6 | 3.55% | 13.36% | 19 | 7 | 4 | 0.286 |
| Marcus Semien | 25 | 431 | 400 | 0.251 | 0.300 | 0.418 | 0.719 | 0.168 | 64 | 16 | 11 | 10 | 6.26% | 20.02% | 8 | 2 | 2 | 0.316 |
| Andrelton Simmons | 26 | 647 | 601 | 0.262 | 0.309 | 0.380 | 0.689 | 0.118 | 116 | 25 | 2 | 14 | 5.86% | 8.52% | 8 | 4 | 4 | 0.306 |
| Jorge Soler | 24 | 502 | 452 | 0.268 | 0.332 | 0.421 | 0.753 | 0.154 | 83 | 22 | 2 | 15 | 8.08% | 29.94% | 3 | 1 | 5 | 0.334 |
| Giovanny Soto | 33 | 329 | 295 | 0.233 | 0.309 | 0.393 | 0.702 | 0.160 | 41 | 19 | 0 | 10 | 9.76% | 29.57% | 0 | 0 | 1 | 0.313 |
| Steven Souza | 27 | 519 | 454 | 0.229 | 0.314 | 0.382 | 0.696 | 0.152 | 70 | 16 | 1 | 17 | 10.28% | 31.35% | 12 | 4 | 6 | 0.312 |
| Denard Span | 32 | 446 | 401 | 0.293 | 0.360 | 0.425 | 0.784 | 0.132 | 81 | 27 | 3 | 6 | 8.93% | 11.12% | 12 | 2 | 3 | 0.349 |
| George Springer | 26 | 597 | 500 | 0.239 | 0.355 | 0.441 | 0.797 | 0.202 | 69 | 23 | 3 | 24 | 12.45% | 28.57% | 14 | 4 | 18 | 0.355 |
| Giancarlo Stanton | 26 | 559 | 478 | 0.253 | 0.358 | 0.559 | 0.916 | 0.306 | 57 | 22 | 0 | 41 | 13.60% | 31.56% | 7 | 2 | 3 | 0.398 |

# 2016 MLB Projections - Hitters

| Player | Age | PA | AB | AVG | OBP | SLG | OPS | ISO | 1B | 2B | 3B | HR | BB% | K% | SB | CS | HBP | wOBA |
|---|---|---|---|---|---|---|---|---|---|---|---|---|---|---|---|---|---|---|
| Kurt Suzuki | 32 | 461 | 418 | 0.252 | 0.315 | 0.323 | 0.638 | 0.070 | 84 | 17 | 0 | 4 | 7.18% | 15.70% | 0 | 0 | 7 | 0.290 |
| Mark Teixeira | 36 | 484 | 415 | 0.230 | 0.326 | 0.439 | 0.765 | 0.209 | 59 | 11 | 0 | 25 | 12.00% | 21.26% | 1 | 0 | 4 | 0.339 |
| Yasmany Tomas | 25 | 560 | 531 | 0.278 | 0.312 | 0.416 | 0.727 | 0.138 | 104 | 27 | 4 | 13 | 4.24% | 25.00% | 5 | 2 | 3 | 0.321 |
| Mike Trout | 24 | 701 | 587 | 0.317 | 0.417 | 0.648 | 1.064 | 0.330 | 94 | 38 | 6 | 48 | 14.06% | 24.47% | 14 | 4 | 7 | 0.454 |
| Mark Trumbo | 30 | 551 | 508 | 0.246 | 0.303 | 0.409 | 0.712 | 0.162 | 84 | 20 | 1 | 20 | 7.45% | 26.23% | 2 | 3 | 1 | 0.316 |
| Troy Tulowitzki | 31 | 489 | 439 | 0.290 | 0.355 | 0.451 | 0.806 | 0.160 | 90 | 21 | 0 | 16 | 8.11% | 20.71% | 4 | 1 | 7 | 0.357 |
| Justin Turner | 31 | 555 | 500 | 0.311 | 0.368 | 0.490 | 0.858 | 0.180 | 98 | 40 | 2 | 15 | 6.98% | 16.87% | 7 | 3 | 10 | 0.376 |
| Melvin Upton | 31 | 257 | 231 | 0.225 | 0.300 | 0.374 | 0.674 | 0.150 | 32 | 11 | 3 | 6 | 9.74% | 28.97% | 9 | 3 | 0 | 0.301 |
| Justin Upton | 28 | 621 | 546 | 0.262 | 0.341 | 0.506 | 0.846 | 0.244 | 77 | 31 | 2 | 33 | 9.96% | 22.70% | 13 | 4 | 7 | 0.369 |
| Giovanny Urshela | 24 | 367 | 339 | 0.227 | 0.281 | 0.335 | 0.617 | 0.109 | 57 | 11 | 1 | 8 | 6.69% | 20.84% | 0 | 1 | 2 | 0.277 |
| Chase Utley | 37 | 321 | 286 | 0.226 | 0.301 | 0.352 | 0.653 | 0.126 | 42 | 15 | 0 | 7 | 8.80% | 16.37% | 3 | 2 | 4 | 0.294 |
| Stephen Vogt | 31 | 523 | 458 | 0.229 | 0.311 | 0.375 | 0.686 | 0.147 | 68 | 21 | 2 | 14 | 10.72% | 19.46% | 0 | 0 | 2 | 0.307 |
| Joey Votto | 32 | 701 | 539 | 0.306 | 0.457 | 0.509 | 0.966 | 0.203 | 102 | 38 | 2 | 22 | 21.89% | 22.58% | 8 | 1 | 2 | 0.426 |
| Neil Walker | 30 | 592 | 532 | 0.259 | 0.329 | 0.415 | 0.744 | 0.156 | 89 | 29 | 4 | 15 | 7.27% | 20.95% | 4 | 1 | 14 | 0.331 |
| Jayson Werth | 37 | 509 | 449 | 0.244 | 0.324 | 0.377 | 0.701 | 0.133 | 73 | 25 | 0 | 11 | 9.80% | 19.38% | 4 | 1 | 5 | 0.315 |
| Matt Wieters | 30 | 551 | 499 | 0.303 | 0.353 | 0.469 | 0.822 | 0.165 | 109 | 22 | 1 | 19 | 7.88% | 19.95% | 1 | 1 | 0 | 0.360 |
| Kolten Wong | 25 | 621 | 567 | 0.262 | 0.320 | 0.438 | 0.758 | 0.176 | 94 | 27 | 11 | 17 | 5.68% | 13.09% | 14 | 13 | 14 | 0.334 |
| David Wright | 33 | 507 | 441 | 0.285 | 0.372 | 0.442 | 0.814 | 0.158 | 84 | 27 | 1 | 13 | 11.94% | 16.91% | 6 | 4 | 3 | 0.362 |
| Christian Yelich | 24 | 632 | 558 | 0.281 | 0.362 | 0.403 | 0.765 | 0.123 | 109 | 35 | 5 | 8 | 10.88% | 23.19% | 31 | 5 | 3 | 0.343 |
| Ryan Zimmerman | 31 | 501 | 447 | 0.279 | 0.343 | 0.486 | 0.829 | 0.207 | 72 | 33 | 0 | 20 | 9.25% | 19.64% | 1 | 0 | 1 | 0.362 |
| Ben Zobrist | 35 | 569 | 497 | 0.267 | 0.350 | 0.399 | 0.749 | 0.132 | 91 | 26 | 7 | 9 | 11.31% | 11.57% | 7 | 3 | 2 | 0.335 |

# 2016 MLB Projections – Pitchers

| Name | Age | IP | FIP | H | K | K/9 | BB | BB/9 | HR | HR/9 | HBP |
|------|-----|-----|------|-----|-----|------|-----|------|-----|------|-----|
| Cody Allen | 27 | 66.2 | 3.15 | 44 | 77 | 10.46 | 34 | 4.60 | 6 | 0.77 | 1 |
| Chase Anderson | 28 | 171.1 | 3.73 | 170 | 127 | 6.65 | 55 | 2.90 | 18 | 0.94 | 4 |
| Brett Anderson | 28 | 162.1 | 3.41 | 179 | 124 | 6.91 | 58 | 3.21 | 13 | 0.74 | 0 |
| Chris Archer | 27 | 203.1 | 3.39 | 198 | 223 | 9.88 | 93 | 4.11 | 21 | 0.91 | 7 |
| Jake Arrieta | 30 | 222.2 | 2.84 | 153 | 214 | 8.68 | 63 | 2.54 | 18 | 0.71 | 7 |
| Homer Bailey | 30 | 156.2 | 3.40 | 157 | 133 | 7.65 | 40 | 2.29 | 17 | 0.97 | 7 |
| Trevor Bauer | 25 | 180.2 | 3.78 | 165 | 164 | 8.20 | 69 | 3.44 | 22 | 1.08 | 6 |
| Dellin Betances | 28 | 78.0 | 2.02 | 62 | 128 | 14.76 | 35 | 4.06 | 6 | 0.72 | 3 |
| Brad Boxberger | 28 | 62.1 | 3.41 | 51 | 78 | 11.25 | 29 | 4.21 | 7 | 1.07 | 3 |
| Zach Britton | 28 | 75.1 | 2.80 | 65 | 72 | 8.66 | 24 | 2.87 | 5 | 0.64 | 1 |
| Clay Buchholz | 31 | 159.1 | 3.20 | 167 | 118 | 6.68 | 35 | 1.99 | 14 | 0.77 | 6 |
| Madison Bumgarner | 26 | 219.0 | 2.86 | 189 | 232 | 9.55 | 46 | 1.88 | 25 | 1.02 | 6 |
| Matt Cain | 31 | 163.1 | 4.96 | 186 | 130 | 7.17 | 70 | 3.86 | 29 | 1.62 | 7 |
| Carlos Carrasco | 29 | 209.0 | 3.10 | 168 | 182 | 7.84 | 51 | 2.19 | 20 | 0.84 | 6 |
| Andrew Cashner | 29 | 154.1 | 3.21 | 170 | 144 | 8.43 | 48 | 2.83 | 15 | 0.88 | 4 |
| Santiago Casilla | 35 | 61.0 | 3.34 | 52 | 61 | 9.02 | 22 | 3.27 | 6 | 0.89 | 4 |
| Aroldis Chapman | 28 | 70.0 | 2.80 | 50 | 106 | 13.61 | 46 | 5.86 | 4 | 0.57 | 6 |
| Steve Cishek | 30 | 65.0 | 3.16 | 63 | 66 | 9.08 | 29 | 3.98 | 5 | 0.70 | 1 |
| Alex Cobb | 28 | 160.2 | 3.84 | 132 | 112 | 6.27 | 55 | 3.11 | 14 | 0.81 | 12 |
| Gerrit Cole | 25 | 198.1 | 2.26 | 180 | 205 | 9.31 | 45 | 2.07 | 11 | 0.49 | 9 |
| Bartolo Colon | 43 | 186.1 | 4.89 | 257 | 132 | 6.41 | 37 | 1.77 | 41 | 2.01 | 2 |
| Adam Conley | 26 | 177.1 | 3.52 | 172 | 153 | 7.77 | 56 | 2.83 | 19 | 0.96 | 7 |
| Patrick Corbin | 26 | 170.0 | 3.20 | 180 | 147 | 7.76 | 40 | 2.11 | 17 | 0.91 | 6 |
| Jarred Cosart | 26 | 164.1 | 4.06 | 147 | 106 | 5.82 | 62 | 3.41 | 18 | 0.97 | 1 |
| Johnny Cueto | 30 | 209.1 | 3.59 | 178 | 179 | 7.70 | 52 | 2.23 | 26 | 1.11 | 11 |
| John Danks | 31 | 182.2 | 4.51 | 215 | 130 | 6.42 | 56 | 2.78 | 30 | 1.48 | 5 |
| Yu Darvish | 29 | 181.1 | 3.17 | 160 | 190 | 9.44 | 73 | 3.62 | 16 | 0.81 | 6 |
| Wade Davis | 30 | 74.1 | 1.98 | 46 | 88 | 10.73 | 27 | 3.31 | 2 | 0.27 | 2 |
| Jorge De La Rosa | 35 | 173.2 | 3.60 | 168 | 166 | 8.64 | 81 | 4.22 | 16 | 0.82 | 8 |
| Jacob deGrom | 28 | 201.2 | 2.37 | 154 | 222 | 9.94 | 42 | 1.89 | 17 | 0.78 | 2 |
| Anthony DeSclafani | 26 | 201.2 | 3.47 | 217 | 169 | 7.58 | 64 | 2.85 | 21 | 0.92 | 5 |
| R.A. Dickey | 41 | 188.1 | 4.68 | 205 | 130 | 6.24 | 66 | 3.17 | 28 | 1.36 | 15 |
| Sean Doolittle | 29 | 63.2 | 2.63 | 52 | 79 | 11.23 | 21 | 3.04 | 6 | 0.90 | 0 |
| Danny Duffy | 27 | 167.2 | 3.56 | 146 | 142 | 7.65 | 66 | 3.58 | 14 | 0.78 | 8 |
| Nathan Eovaldi | 26 | 187.1 | 3.13 | 198 | 148 | 7.14 | 52 | 2.48 | 15 | 0.71 | 4 |
| Marco Estrada | 32 | 202.0 | 4.66 | 173 | 155 | 6.90 | 65 | 2.91 | 36 | 1.61 | 6 |
| Jeurys Familia | 26 | 73.1 | 3.74 | 58 | 65 | 8.00 | 27 | 3.26 | 9 | 1.10 | 1 |
| Jose Fernandez | 23 | 187.1 | 2.38 | 171 | 198 | 9.53 | 47 | 2.25 | 12 | 0.59 | 6 |
| Brandon Finnegan | 23 | 167.1 | 4.07 | 130 | 157 | 8.47 | 71 | 3.81 | 24 | 1.27 | 3 |
| Doug Fister | 32 | 154.2 | 3.95 | 162 | 122 | 7.10 | 44 | 2.56 | 20 | 1.16 | 10 |
| Mike Foltynewicz | 24 | 166.0 | 4.24 | 210 | 150 | 8.12 | 56 | 3.04 | 27 | 1.46 | 7 |
| Jaime Garcia | 29 | 157.2 | 3.47 | 173 | 113 | 6.50 | 38 | 2.15 | 15 | 0.87 | 8 |
| Matt Garza | 32 | 169.0 | 4.32 | 176 | 146 | 7.76 | 65 | 3.46 | 27 | 1.42 | 3 |
| Kevin Gausman | 25 | 198.1 | 3.66 | 209 | 175 | 7.96 | 58 | 2.64 | 26 | 1.18 | 3 |
| Kyle Gibson | 28 | 199.0 | 4.10 | 228 | 144 | 6.49 | 79 | 3.57 | 23 | 1.02 | 5 |
| Ken Giles | 25 | 75.2 | 1.33 | 53 | 104 | 12.40 | 24 | 2.84 | 2 | 0.22 | 0 |
| Gio Gonzalez | 30 | 179.1 | 3.03 | 183 | 164 | 8.24 | 72 | 3.62 | 11 | 0.55 | 4 |
| Miguel Gonzalez | 32 | 167.2 | 3.79 | 148 | 125 | 6.74 | 48 | 2.58 | 19 | 1.04 | 7 |
| Kendall Graveman | 25 | 164.1 | 4.31 | 175 | 113 | 6.20 | 52 | 2.86 | 23 | 1.24 | 8 |
| Sonny Gray | 26 | 218.1 | 3.06 | 189 | 186 | 7.68 | 67 | 2.78 | 16 | 0.66 | 6 |

# 2016 MLB Projections – Pitchers

| Name | Age | IP | FIP | H | K | K/9 | BB | BB/9 | HR | HR/9 | HBP |
|------|-----|----|----|---|---|-----|----|----|----|----|-----|
| Jonathan Gray | 24 | 191.1 | 3.37 | 231 | 184 | 8.66 | 67 | 3.14 | 19 | 0.92 | 8 |
| Zack Greinke | 32 | 227.1 | 3.16 | 187 | 191 | 7.59 | 51 | 2.04 | 23 | 0.90 | 5 |
| Jesse Hahn | 26 | 168.1 | 3.16 | 145 | 137 | 7.33 | 57 | 3.06 | 10 | 0.53 | 12 |
| Cole Hamels | 32 | 216.0 | 3.31 | 205 | 205 | 8.54 | 59 | 2.46 | 24 | 1.00 | 11 |
| Jason Hammel | 33 | 164.0 | 4.12 | 168 | 132 | 7.26 | 46 | 2.54 | 25 | 1.36 | 7 |
| J.A. Happ | 33 | 191.0 | 3.73 | 185 | 157 | 7.40 | 63 | 2.96 | 23 | 1.09 | 1 |
| Matt Harvey | 27 | 210.0 | 2.39 | 163 | 223 | 9.54 | 44 | 1.89 | 16 | 0.67 | 7 |
| Andrew Heaney | 25 | 186.2 | 3.45 | 182 | 146 | 7.04 | 49 | 2.37 | 18 | 0.85 | 12 |
| Jeremy Hellickson | 29 | 168.2 | 3.97 | 199 | 150 | 8.05 | 50 | 2.69 | 25 | 1.35 | 6 |
| Kyle Hendricks | 26 | 191.0 | 3.26 | 203 | 127 | 5.99 | 50 | 2.34 | 13 | 0.63 | 6 |
| Felix Hernandez | 30 | 217.0 | 3.08 | 209 | 209 | 8.67 | 68 | 2.84 | 19 | 0.81 | 7 |
| Kelvin Herrera | 26 | 69.2 | 3.13 | 50 | 55 | 7.16 | 25 | 3.26 | 4 | 0.55 | 1 |
| Derek Holland | 29 | 141.0 | 4.12 | 150 | 98 | 6.23 | 42 | 2.69 | 17 | 1.11 | 10 |
| Phil Hughes | 30 | 169.0 | 3.68 | 195 | 112 | 5.99 | 21 | 1.10 | 23 | 1.24 | 3 |
| Raisel Iglesias | 26 | 157.1 | 3.27 | 131 | 167 | 9.55 | 48 | 2.77 | 17 | 0.98 | 13 |
| Hisashi Iwakuma | 35 | 171.2 | 3.35 | 166 | 162 | 8.54 | 24 | 1.26 | 26 | 1.39 | 1 |
| Kenley Jansen | 28 | 77.0 | 1.51 | 52 | 126 | 14.76 | 21 | 2.42 | 6 | 0.75 | 2 |
| Ubaldo Jimenez | 32 | 184.2 | 4.66 | 173 | 168 | 8.22 | 90 | 4.38 | 30 | 1.47 | 6 |
| Taylor Jungmann | 26 | 159.0 | 3.62 | 143 | 144 | 8.13 | 61 | 3.48 | 15 | 0.88 | 11 |
| Nate Karns | 28 | 164.2 | 3.78 | 152 | 152 | 8.31 | 62 | 3.41 | 20 | 1.10 | 5 |
| Scott Kazmir | 32 | 182.1 | 4.28 | 185 | 145 | 7.14 | 70 | 3.44 | 25 | 1.24 | 8 |
| Joe Kelly | 28 | 158.2 | 3.73 | 167 | 130 | 7.42 | 67 | 3.80 | 14 | 0.80 | 8 |
| Ian Kennedy | 31 | 190.0 | 4.04 | 213 | 206 | 9.75 | 73 | 3.45 | 31 | 1.48 | 7 |
| Clayton Kershaw | 28 | 237.0 | 1.95 | 167 | 277 | 10.52 | 46 | 1.74 | 15 | 0.59 | 5 |
| Dallas Keuchel | 28 | 224.1 | 2.97 | 210 | 205 | 8.23 | 51 | 2.06 | 22 | 0.86 | 5 |
| Craig Kimbrel | 28 | 66.2 | 2.55 | 40 | 90 | 12.24 | 29 | 3.90 | 5 | 0.73 | 2 |
| Corey Kluber | 30 | 217.0 | 2.79 | 171 | 229 | 9.48 | 57 | 2.37 | 19 | 0.81 | 10 |
| Tom Koehler | 30 | 203.1 | 4.42 | 209 | 155 | 6.86 | 86 | 3.80 | 27 | 1.21 | 9 |
| John Lackey | 37 | 207.0 | 3.88 | 232 | 141 | 6.13 | 51 | 2.22 | 26 | 1.14 | 4 |
| John Lamb | 25 | 163.1 | 2.99 | 191 | 175 | 9.63 | 64 | 3.54 | 13 | 0.72 | 6 |
| Mike Leake | 28 | 206.1 | 4.16 | 230 | 139 | 6.08 | 61 | 2.66 | 27 | 1.19 | 7 |
| Jon Lester | 32 | 207.1 | 3.30 | 196 | 183 | 7.94 | 57 | 2.48 | 22 | 0.94 | 5 |
| Colby Lewis | 36 | 182.0 | 3.98 | 196 | 147 | 7.29 | 40 | 1.96 | 27 | 1.34 | 13 |
| Francisco Liriano | 32 | 169.1 | 3.65 | 152 | 168 | 8.92 | 78 | 4.14 | 18 | 0.95 | 4 |
| Jeff Locke | 28 | 159.1 | 3.76 | 165 | 108 | 6.13 | 53 | 3.00 | 15 | 0.88 | 3 |
| Carlos Martinez | 24 | 200.0 | 3.19 | 202 | 196 | 8.81 | 77 | 3.48 | 16 | 0.73 | 9 |
| Steven Matz | 25 | 165.2 | 3.50 | 158 | 150 | 8.18 | 47 | 2.57 | 20 | 1.08 | 5 |
| Lance McCullers | 22 | 181.0 | 3.19 | 158 | 183 | 9.08 | 63 | 3.15 | 17 | 0.85 | 8 |
| Jake McGee | 29 | 69.0 | 2.93 | 51 | 76 | 9.94 | 20 | 2.59 | 8 | 0.99 | 1 |
| Collin McHugh | 29 | 197.1 | 3.36 | 196 | 203 | 9.27 | 56 | 2.55 | 22 | 0.99 | 22 |
| Mark Melancon | 31 | 71.0 | 2.54 | 54 | 57 | 7.23 | 14 | 1.79 | 4 | 0.47 | 2 |
| Wade Miley | 29 | 200.0 | 3.71 | 199 | 166 | 7.49 | 62 | 2.81 | 25 | 1.10 | 3 |
| Shelby Miller | 25 | 215.0 | 3.50 | 202 | 173 | 7.23 | 80 | 3.36 | 19 | 0.78 | 5 |
| Andrew Miller | 31 | 63.1 | 1.45 | 42 | 105 | 15.00 | 18 | 2.60 | 4 | 0.61 | 5 |
| Matt Moore | 27 | 166.2 | 4.23 | 192 | 128 | 6.92 | 55 | 2.98 | 23 | 1.23 | 11 |
| Charlie Morton | 32 | 147.1 | 3.75 | 131 | 117 | 7.13 | 54 | 3.23 | 13 | 0.81 | 13 |
| Jason Motte | 34 | 65.2 | 3.44 | 68 | 42 | 5.74 | 17 | 2.38 | 5 | 0.74 | 1 |
| Jimmy Nelson | 27 | 200.0 | 3.36 | 196 | 200 | 9.00 | 60 | 2.69 | 21 | 0.93 | 21 |
| Jon Niese | 29 | 190.0 | 3.98 | 226 | 141 | 6.69 | 55 | 2.59 | 25 | 1.20 | 5 |
| Aaron Nola | 23 | 182.1 | 3.65 | 172 | 156 | 7.71 | 48 | 2.36 | 24 | 1.18 | 4 |

# 2016 MLB Projections – Pitchers

| Name | Age | IP | FIP | H | K | K/9 | BB | BB/9 | HR | HR/9 | HBP |
|------|-----|------|------|-----|-----|-------|-----|------|-----|------|-----|
| Bud Norris | 31 | 162.0 | 4.80 | 194 | 135 | 7.49 | 66 | 3.67 | 28 | 1.57 | 9 |
| Daniel Norris | 23 | 170.0 | 4.16 | 142 | 128 | 6.78 | 53 | 2.83 | 25 | 1.30 | 3 |
| Ivan Nova | 29 | 171.1 | 4.61 | 211 | 128 | 6.73 | 52 | 2.76 | 28 | 1.46 | 16 |
| Jake Odorizzi | 26 | 189.1 | 3.27 | 179 | 163 | 7.74 | 54 | 2.58 | 18 | 0.87 | 5 |
| Roberto Osuna | 21 | 88.0 | 2.80 | 59 | 95 | 9.71 | 21 | 2.12 | 9 | 0.97 | 2 |
| Jonathan Papelbon | 35 | 64.0 | 3.19 | 59 | 59 | 8.24 | 14 | 1.93 | 6 | 0.87 | 7 |
| Jake Peavy | 35 | 159.1 | 4.03 | 157 | 117 | 6.60 | 45 | 2.53 | 22 | 1.23 | 4 |
| Mike Pelfrey | 32 | 169.1 | 5.71 | 223 | 83 | 4.42 | 75 | 4.00 | 31 | 1.64 | 10 |
| Wily Peralta | 27 | 180.2 | 3.85 | 199 | 121 | 6.05 | 45 | 2.25 | 22 | 1.08 | 5 |
| Martin Perez | 25 | 156.1 | 3.38 | 150 | 111 | 6.39 | 61 | 3.52 | 9 | 0.52 | 4 |
| Glen Perkins | 33 | 59.0 | 3.18 | 55 | 60 | 9.23 | 14 | 2.11 | 8 | 1.16 | 1 |
| Michael Pineda | 27 | 182.1 | 2.76 | 164 | 175 | 8.64 | 24 | 1.18 | 21 | 1.01 | 1 |
| Rick Porcello | 27 | 183.1 | 3.23 | 179 | 142 | 7.00 | 45 | 2.21 | 16 | 0.80 | 6 |
| David Price | 30 | 233.2 | 2.56 | 236 | 233 | 8.98 | 53 | 2.05 | 19 | 0.72 | 3 |
| Jose Quintana | 27 | 201.0 | 2.59 | 213 | 187 | 8.39 | 45 | 2.01 | 14 | 0.61 | 7 |
| A.J. Ramos | 29 | 73.1 | 3.32 | 48 | 71 | 8.75 | 37 | 4.54 | 5 | 0.59 | 3 |
| Robbie Ray | 24 | 171.2 | 3.20 | 158 | 167 | 8.77 | 67 | 3.51 | 13 | 0.69 | 11 |
| Garrett Richards | 28 | 200.2 | 3.27 | 171 | 181 | 8.14 | 79 | 3.54 | 15 | 0.67 | 9 |
| Tanner Roark | 29 | 199.2 | 4.47 | 244 | 122 | 5.53 | 53 | 2.41 | 30 | 1.34 | 11 |
| David Robertson | 31 | 65.0 | 2.43 | 52 | 86 | 11.96 | 17 | 2.30 | 7 | 1.03 | 1 |
| Carlos Rodon | 23 | 209.0 | 3.61 | 193 | 188 | 8.10 | 103 | 4.45 | 16 | 0.70 | 8 |
| Eduardo Rodriguez | 23 | 177.2 | 3.64 | 182 | 143 | 7.27 | 54 | 2.76 | 19 | 0.97 | 7 |
| Francisco Rodriguez | 34 | 66.0 | 3.79 | 58 | 67 | 9.10 | 20 | 2.79 | 10 | 1.43 | 0 |
| Hector Rondon | 28 | 69.2 | 2.58 | 59 | 71 | 9.20 | 18 | 2.39 | 5 | 0.68 | 1 |
| Trevor Rosenthal | 26 | 72.0 | 2.36 | 64 | 87 | 10.86 | 34 | 4.22 | 3 | 0.33 | 2 |
| Joe Ross | 23 | 154.1 | 2.91 | 123 | 127 | 7.42 | 45 | 2.66 | 10 | 0.56 | 4 |
| Tyson Ross | 29 | 197.1 | 2.98 | 202 | 189 | 8.65 | 82 | 3.73 | 11 | 0.50 | 9 |
| Hyun-Jin Ryu | 29 | 77.0 | 2.83 | 77 | 67 | 7.83 | 19 | 2.25 | 6 | 0.66 | 2 |
| CC Sabathia | 35 | 178.1 | 3.68 | 236 | 208 | 10.53 | 47 | 2.39 | 32 | 1.64 | 3 |
| Danny Salazar | 26 | 180.0 | 3.23 | 162 | 183 | 9.15 | 45 | 2.26 | 22 | 1.11 | 7 |
| Chris Sale | 27 | 215.1 | 2.77 | 188 | 265 | 11.07 | 47 | 1.97 | 26 | 1.08 | 15 |
| Jeff Samardzija | 31 | 203.1 | 3.62 | 206 | 169 | 7.50 | 57 | 2.53 | 23 | 1.01 | 13 |
| Anibal Sanchez | 32 | 177.1 | 3.54 | 150 | 185 | 9.38 | 63 | 3.22 | 23 | 1.18 | 3 |
| Ervin Santana | 33 | 189.0 | 3.80 | 180 | 165 | 7.86 | 67 | 3.19 | 23 | 1.11 | 5 |
| Max Scherzer | 31 | 222.2 | 2.79 | 180 | 237 | 9.59 | 45 | 1.80 | 25 | 1.01 | 4 |
| Luis Severino | 22 | 177.0 | 3.96 | 139 | 152 | 7.75 | 61 | 3.12 | 24 | 1.20 | 6 |
| James Shields | 34 | 208.1 | 4.20 | 214 | 157 | 6.77 | 80 | 3.48 | 26 | 1.14 | 7 |
| Matt Shoemaker | 29 | 149.1 | 3.28 | 133 | 126 | 7.62 | 36 | 2.16 | 16 | 0.96 | 3 |
| Will Smith | 26 | 64.0 | 2.38 | 54 | 87 | 12.20 | 24 | 3.35 | 5 | 0.77 | 1 |
| Drew Smyly | 27 | 168.1 | 3.30 | 142 | 177 | 9.48 | 51 | 2.71 | 22 | 1.16 | 2 |
| Drew Storen | 28 | 61.0 | 3.01 | 52 | 60 | 8.80 | 15 | 2.18 | 6 | 0.95 | 1 |
| Stephen Strasburg | 27 | 203.1 | 3.24 | 188 | 212 | 9.40 | 50 | 2.22 | 26 | 1.17 | 7 |
| Huston Street | 32 | 60.0 | 2.67 | 55 | 63 | 9.38 | 21 | 3.09 | 4 | 0.64 | 0 |
| Marcus Stroman | 25 | 182.1 | 2.67 | 186 | 151 | 7.44 | 40 | 2.00 | 11 | 0.54 | 4 |
| Noah Syndergaard | 23 | 180.1 | 2.96 | 153 | 183 | 9.14 | 34 | 1.70 | 22 | 1.08 | 3 |
| Masahiro Tanaka | 27 | 180.0 | 3.35 | 143 | 181 | 9.04 | 29 | 1.47 | 28 | 1.40 | 3 |
| Julio Teheran | 25 | 217.1 | 4.12 | 206 | 165 | 6.84 | 61 | 2.51 | 31 | 1.30 | 9 |
| Chris Tillman | 28 | 201.0 | 3.98 | 201 | 150 | 6.70 | 84 | 3.76 | 21 | 0.94 | 3 |
| Shawn Tolleson | 28 | 69.1 | 3.07 | 69 | 68 | 8.81 | 18 | 2.35 | 7 | 0.97 | 1 |
| Josh Tomlin | 31 | 157.1 | 4.19 | 140 | 121 | 6.93 | 19 | 1.10 | 30 | 1.72 | 4 |

# 2016 MLB Projections – Pitchers

| Name | Age | IP | FIP | H | K | K/9 | BB | BB/9 | HR | HR/9 | HBP |
|------|-----|------|------|-----|-----|------|-----|------|-----|------|-----|
| Yordano Ventura | 25 | 193.0 | 3.24 | 189 | 183 | 8.52 | 65 | 3.01 | 18 | 0.84 | 8 |
| Justin Verlander | 33 | 196.1 | 3.75 | 194 | 157 | 7.20 | 54 | 2.46 | 25 | 1.15 | 5 |
| Edinson Volquez | 32 | 210.2 | 3.75 | 206 | 167 | 7.16 | 80 | 3.42 | 20 | 0.88 | 10 |
| Michael Wacha | 25 | 203.0 | 3.21 | 174 | 186 | 8.27 | 58 | 2.59 | 21 | 0.92 | 4 |
| Adam Wainwright | 34 | 172.1 | 2.41 | 156 | 126 | 6.58 | 33 | 1.73 | 6 | 0.31 | 3 |
| Taijuan Walker | 23 | 189.2 | 3.72 | 185 | 173 | 8.21 | 43 | 2.05 | 28 | 1.32 | 10 |
| Jered Weaver | 33 | 174.2 | 3.81 | 171 | 135 | 6.98 | 46 | 2.40 | 22 | 1.15 | 6 |
| C.J. Wilson | 35 | 165.2 | 4.85 | 168 | 134 | 7.29 | 76 | 4.12 | 27 | 1.45 | 11 |
| Matthew Wisler | 23 | 156.0 | 4.13 | 168 | 104 | 6.01 | 54 | 3.11 | 18 | 1.06 | 5 |
| Brad Ziegler | 36 | 69.1 | 3.19 | 50 | 37 | 4.77 | 15 | 1.92 | 4 | 0.49 | 2 |
| Jordan Zimmermann | 30 | 207.1 | 3.20 | 221 | 179 | 7.79 | 38 | 1.65 | 23 | 1.01 | 8 |

# **Organizational Analysis**

**State of the Farm System:** Under the guidance of brand spankin' new General Manager Dave Stewart, the Diamondbacks have made some...questionable moves, to put it delicately. Let's recap some of the more interesting ones, shall we?

- November 14, 2014: Diamondbacks trade Justin Williams and Andrew Velazquez to the Rays for Jeremy Hellickson, who would be dealt exactly one year to the day later to Philadelphia for Sam McWilliams – a definite trade down.
- December 5, 2014: Arizona shipped Didi Gregorius, an underappreciated shortstop who finished third at the position in fWAR last season, for the overrated Domingo Leyba and Robbie Ray as part of the three-team trade involving the Yankees and Tigers. To be fair, it's not a horrible trade, but it doesn't make a whole lot of sense to acquire a young pitcher (which typically comes with an injury risk) for a solid offensive shortstop in an offensive-depleted era – especially for a team that gets the fortune of pitching to a hurler a couple times a game.
- June 20, 2015: Swapped 2014 first round pick, lively armed right-hander Touki Toussaint, and Bronson Arroyo for cash and minor leaguer Philip Gosselin. To be honest with you, it was a shit trade – even if Toussaint never pans out, it's the wrong type of gamble an organization should take.
- December 9, 2015: Easily one of the single worst trades over the past decade, the organization flipped #1 overall pick Dansby Swanson and supremely underrated outfielder Ender Inciarte, and future mid-rotation starter Aaron Blair for Shelby Miller and Gabe Speier.

These are the types of trades that can – and often – haunt an organization.

What's left for the Diamondbacks? Quite a bit, actually, including Archie Bradley (if he can stay healthy), Jamie Westbrook, who could be the single most underrated player in the minors, Braden Shipley, and Cody Reed. Maybe Alex Young.

| Rank | Name | POS |
|------|------|-----|
| 1 | Archie Bradley | RHP |
| 2 | Jamie Westbrook | 2B |
| 3 | Braden Shipley | RHP |
| 4 | Cody Reed | LHP |
| 5 | Alex Young | LHP |
| 6 | Yoan Lopez | RHP |
| 7 | Silvino Bracho | RHP |
| 8 | Socrates Brito | OF |
| 9 | Brad Keller | RHP |
| 10 | Wei-Chieh Huang | RHP |
| 11 | Brandon Drury | 2B/3B |
| 12 | Anthony Banda | LHP |
| 13 | Peter O'Brien | LF/RF |
| 14 | Zac Curtis | LHP |
| 15 | Isan Diaz | 2B/SS |
| 16 | Jake Barrett | RHP |
| 17 | Gabriel Guerrero | OF |
| 18 | Jimmie Sherfy | RHP |
| 19 | Joey Krehbiel | RHP |
| 20 | Ryan Burr | RHP |
| 21 | Dawel Lugo | SS |
| 22 | Domingo Leyba | 2B/SS |
| 23 | Mitchell Haniger | OF |
| 24 | Sergio Alcantara | SS |
| 25 | Taylor Clarke | RHP |

**Review of the 2015 Draft:** Well, they *had* a long term shortstop in place by selecting Dansby Swanson. But Stewart, in a shit move, dealt away the former Vanderbilt stud. The kicker: Arizona already picked up Swanson's hefty bonus. They followed that pick up by selecting 10 more collegiate players including TCU ace Alex Young, College of Charleston pin-point artist Taylor Clarke, who was ridiculously good during his debut in the Northwest League, and potential late-inning reliever Ryan Burr.

Frankly, it was a solid draft for the first year GM – had he kept Swanson in the organization.

## 1. Archie Bradley, RHP

| Born: 08/10/92 | Age: 23 | Bats: R | Top CALs: Franklin Morales, Jarred Cosart, |
| Height: 6-4 | Weight: 230 | Throws: R | Zach Davies, Dan Cortes, Sean Gallagher |

| YEAR | Age | Level | IP | W | L | ERA | FIP | K/9 | BB/9 | K% | BB% | HR/9 | LOB% |
|------|-----|-------|-----|---|---|-----|-----|-----|------|-----|-----|------|------|
| 2013 | 20 | A+ | 28.7 | 2 | 0 | 1.26 | 2.48 | 13.50 | 3.14 | 37.4% | 8.7% | 0.31 | 89.0% |
| 2013 | 20 | AA | 123.3 | 12 | 5 | 1.97 | 3.04 | 8.68 | 4.31 | 23.5% | 11.7% | 0.36 | 81.2% |
| 2014 | 21 | R | 4.0 | 0 | 0 | 4.50 | 1.78 | 13.50 | 2.25 | 31.6% | 5.3% | 0.00 | 66.7% |
| 2014 | 21 | AA | 54.7 | 2 | 3 | 4.12 | 4.23 | 7.57 | 5.93 | 19.2% | 15.0% | 0.33 | 70.9% |
| 2014 | 21 | AAA | 24.3 | 1 | 4 | 5.18 | 3.78 | 8.51 | 4.44 | 20.4% | 10.6% | 0.00 | 66.7% |
| 2015 | 22 | R | 4.0 | 0 | 0 | 0.00 | 3.82 | 13.50 | 6.75 | 33.3% | 16.7% | 0.00 | 100.0% |
| 2015 | 22 | A+ | 4.0 | 0 | 0 | 4.50 | 8.78 | 13.50 | 4.50 | 35.3% | 11.8% | 4.50 | 45.5% |
| 2015 | 22 | AAA | 21.3 | 1 | 0 | 2.95 | 4.26 | 8.44 | 2.11 | 21.7% | 5.4% | 1.27 | 89.6% |

**Background:** At one point in the not-so-distant past the only question swirling about Bradley's future was when – *not* if – he develops into a legitimate front-of-the-rotation caliber big league arm. But after two seasons of injury and misalignment the question that's jumped to the forefront of most minds is: Can Archie Bradley stay healthy enough to realize his potential? After missing much of his 2014 season due to injury – an elbow issue that limited him to just 83.0 innings, which includes his rehab work in the Arizona Summer League – Bradley broke camp with Arizona and made eight starts, though they weren't easy by any stretch of the means. The former seventh overall pick in the 2011 draft – taken between Anthony Rendon and Francisco Lindor, by the way – took a line drive to face off the bat of Rockies All-Star outfielder Carlos Gonzalez. Fortunately enough, Bradley would miss just a couple of week before returning to the Diamondbacks' rotation – briefly. Following another four starts, Bradley was shut down with shoulder inflammation. He would make one more late-June start with Reno in the PCL before being shut down until late August.

**Projection:** The talent's clearly there, even through another tumultuous injury-ravaged campaign. Bradley had his power arsenal on full display during his eight-game stint – a low- to mid-90s fastball, a snapdragon Uncle Charlie, and a mid-80s changeup. But just as he has throughout the duration of his professional career, the 6-foot-4, 230-pound right-hander battled some control issues when he was up in The Show; he posted a disappointing 23-to-22 strikeout-to-walk ratio in 35.2 innings.

One final note: CAL's not overly impressed by the hard-throwing hurler, tying him to a pair of disappointing top prospects in Franklin Morales and Jarred Cosart, and a career big league reliever in Sean Gallagher.

**Ceiling:** 3.5- to 4.0-win player
**Risk:** Moderate to High
**MLB ETA:** Debuted in 2015

## 2. Jamie Westbrook, 2B

| Born: 06/18/95 | Age: 21 | Bats: R | Top CALs: Jorge Polanco, Jose Altuve, |
| Height: 5-9 | Weight: 170 | Throws: R | Jonathan Schoop, Rougned Odor, Corban Joseph |

| Season | Age | LVL | PA | 2B | 3B | HR | AVG | OBP | SLG | BB% | K% | wRC+ | ISO |
|--------|-----|-----|-----|----|----|----|-----|-----|-----|-----|----|------|-----|
| 2013 | 18 | R | 177 | 8 | 8 | 1 | 0.292 | 0.373 | 0.468 | 9.6% | 11.9% | 133 | 0.175 |
| 2014 | 19 | A | 561 | 27 | 4 | 8 | 0.259 | 0.314 | 0.375 | 6.8% | 17.5% | 98 | 0.116 |
| 2015 | 20 | A+ | 524 | 33 | 4 | 17 | 0.319 | 0.357 | 0.510 | 4.6% | 13.2% | 132 | 0.192 |

**Background:** Just to put things into perspective a bit, consider this: among all stateside minor league second basemen Westbrook's 132 *Weighted Runs Created Plus* total tied for the second best showing. And that total's been topped by only five other second basemen with 400+ plate appearances in a season before the age of 21: Dilson Herrera, Rougned Odor, Mookie Betts, Eddie Rosario, and Joe Panik . The former fifth round pick out of Basha High School in 2013, Westbrook had a strong debut as he spent time in the Arizona Summer and Pioneer Leagues, hitting .281/.356/.430 with 11 doubles, eight triples, a pair of homeruns, and four stolen bases. He followed that up with a bit of downturn in production as the club aggressively pushed him up to full-season ball, hitting .259/.314/.375 with a bunch of extra-base firepower (27 doubles, four triples, eight homeruns). But Westbrook showed important progress in the second half of the year as he batted .285/.344/.425 from July through the end of the year.

And that momentum carried over into 2016 – in a *big* way.

As one of the youngest everyday players in the California League, Westbrook slugged a robust .319/.357/.510 with 33 doubles, four triples, 17 homeruns and 14 stolen bases in 18 attempts. And just a little more perspective: he ranked seventh in the league in doubles, 10th in homeruns, and eighth in *Weighted Runs Created Plus*.

**Projection:** Now here's the thing, the one, single solitary thing keeping Westbrook from leaping up the overwhelming majority of prospect lists: he stands just 5-foot-9 and 170 pounds. I don't give a damn. Hell, I don't give a shit either. And how's this for bold: Jamie Westbrook is one of the top second base prospects in all the minors. And how's this for bold part II: I would take Westbrook over any other prospect in the Diamondbacks system not named Archie Bradley.

So let's break him down, shall we? First off, he has surprising, above-average pop for the position – regardless of his short frame. A little bit of speed, but more of the sneaky variety and some defensive chops at the keystone. His lone issue is his subpar patience at the plate. But with an offensive premium at the position, he'll be just fine.

As for his CALs, well, I'll just list them here (again): Jorge Polanco, Jose Altuve, Jonathan Schoop, Rougned Odor, and Corban Joseph. That's one MVP candidate (Altuve), one perennial All-Star candidate (Rougned Odor), another top prospect (Jorge Polanco), and a guy who debuted in the big leagues at the age of 21.

**Ceiling:** 3.0- to 3.5-win player
**Risk:** Moderate
**MLB ETA:** 2017

## 3. Braden Shipley, RHP

**MiLB Rank: #110**
**Position Rank: N/A**

| Born: 02/02/92 | Age: 24 | Bats: R | **Top CALs:** Andrew Gagnon, Williams Perez, Raymar Diaz, Ronnie Martinez, Mark Peterson |
| Height: 6-2 | Weight: 185 | Throws: R | |

| YEAR | Age | Level | IP | W | L | ERA | FIP | K/9 | BB/9 | K% | BB% | HR/9 | LOB% |
|------|-----|-------|-----|---|---|------|------|-------|------|------|------|------|------|
| 2013 | 21 | A- | 19.0 | 0 | 2 | 7.58 | 2.58 | 11.37 | 2.84 | 25.8% | 6.5% | 0.47 | 53.4% |
| 2013 | 21 | A | 20.7 | 0 | 1 | 2.61 | 4.35 | 6.97 | 3.48 | 19.5% | 9.8% | 0.87 | 84.2% |
| 2014 | 22 | A | 45.7 | 4 | 2 | 3.74 | 2.83 | 8.08 | 2.17 | 21.7% | 5.8% | 0.20 | 64.2% |
| 2014 | 22 | A+ | 60.3 | 2 | 4 | 4.03 | 4.39 | 10.14 | 3.13 | 27.0% | 8.3% | 1.04 | 70.5% |
| 2014 | 22 | AA | 20.0 | 1 | 2 | 3.60 | 4.84 | 8.10 | 4.50 | 22.0% | 12.2% | 1.35 | 80.8% |
| 2015 | 23 | AA | 156.7 | 9 | 11 | 3.50 | 3.55 | 6.78 | 3.22 | 17.8% | 8.5% | 0.40 | 70.6% |

**Background:** One of my favorite collegiate prospects in the 2013 college-heavy draft class. So much so, in fact, I ranked the hard-throwing former position player as fourth best college prospect, trailing only the mighty triumvirate of Kris Bryant, Mark Appel, and Jon Gray. And for the first two seasons in professional ball Shipley looked every bit the budding #2/#3-type arm. He hung a 40-to-14 strikeout-to-walk ratio in 39.2 innings between the Northwest and Midwest Leagues during his debut. He followed that up by making stops at three different levels two years ago, throwing 126.0 innings with 127 strikeouts and 42 free passes with South Bend, Visalia, and Mobile. Last season, though, Shipley's strikeout rate tumbled to a career low 6.8% as he spent the entirety of the year pitching for Mobile.

**Projection**: Here's what I wrote prior to the 2013 draft:

> "[A]s a former infielder Shipley is likely more athletic than most hurlers and the wear-and-tear on his right arm isn't as great either. He looks like a decent bet to develop into a mid rotation-type guy with a peak as a good #2. He could have a higher ceiling than any college pitcher not named Jonathan Gray and Mark Appel ."

As noted his strikeout rate dropped to a career low last season, but Shipley showed progress over the course of the season – particularly in the second half as he posted a 63-to-18 strikeout-to-walk ratio with a 2.49 ERA over his final 79.2 innings of work. And while he may never average more than 7.5 punch outs per nine innings, he does show a strong feel for the zone and generates a lot of action on the ground.

**Ceiling:** 2.5-win player
**Risk:** Moderate
**MLB ETA:** 2016

## 4. Cody Reed, LHP

**MiLB Rank: #167**
**Position Rank: N/A**

| Born: 06/07/96 | Age: 20 | Bats: R | **Top CALs:** Enyel De Los Santos, Felix Jorge, Jonathan Coreea, Joshua Blanco, Keury Mella |
| Height: 6-3 | Weight: 245 | Throws: L | |

| YEAR | Age | Level | IP | W | L | ERA | FIP | K/9 | BB/9 | K% | BB% | HR/9 | LOB% |
|------|-----|-------|------|---|---|------|------|-------|------|-------|------|------|------|
| 2014 | 18 | R | 12.0 | 0 | 1 | 2.25 | 4.53 | 10.50 | 5.25 | 31.8% | 15.9% | 0.75 | 81.4% |
| 2014 | 18 | R | 20.7 | 0 | 1 | 2.18 | 2.68 | 11.32 | 2.18 | 30.2% | 5.8% | 0.00 | 72.0% |
| 2015 | 19 | A- | 63.3 | 5 | 4 | 3.27 | 3.40 | 10.23 | 2.98 | 27.8% | 8.1% | 0.71 | 66.7% |

**Background:** As tall as he is wide, the former 2014 second round pick looked at home in the Northwest League last season – he tossed 63.1 innings with 72 punch outs, 21 walks, and a solid 3.40 FIP. For his year-plus career, Reed has averaged 10.5 K and just 3.1 BB per nine innings.

**Projection**: Standing a solid 6-foot-3 and a potyly 245 pounds, Reed finished the year with the third most strikeouts in the Northwest League last season, trailing only the Cubs' Oscar De La Cruz and then-21-year-old rotation-mate Carlos Hernandez – despite throwing far less innings. And for a stretch beginning in late June, the big southpaw looked like one of the finest amateur hurlers on the planet – he posted a 42-to-6 strikeout-to-walk ratio in 35.1 innings in five starts. The main concern, obviously, is his love for food. If he doesn't eat himself out of the league, a la Calvin Pickering, Reed looks like a potential mid-rotation arm.

**Ceiling:** 2.0-win player
**Risk:** Moderate
**MLB ETA:** 2018

## 5. Alex Young, LHP

**MiLB Rank: #171**
**Position Rank: N/A**

| Born: 09/09/93 | Age: 22 | Bats: L | Top CALs: Michael Kirkman, Earl Oakes, |
| Height: 6-2 | Weight: 205 | Throws: L | Nicholas Pasquale, Austin Chambliss, Will Savage |

| YEAR | Age | Level | IP | W | L | ERA | FIP | K/9 | BB/9 | K% | BB% | HR/9 | LOB% |
|---|---|---|---|---|---|---|---|---|---|---|---|---|---|
| 2015 | 21 | R | 1.0 | 0 | 0 | 0.00 | 1.82 | 9.00 | 0.00 | 33.3% | 0.0% | 0.00 | 100.0% |
| 2015 | 21 | A- | 6.0 | 0 | 0 | 1.50 | 2.44 | 7.50 | 1.50 | 22.7% | 4.6% | 0.00 | 83.3% |

**Background:** After back-to-back years of dominance working out of the Horned Frogs' bullpen – he tallied a 77-to-26 strikeout-to-walk ratio in 83.2 innings of work – Young made a successful move into the rotation, eventually becoming the school's top arm. The 6-foot-2, 180-pound southpaw struck out 103, walked 22, and posted a 2.22 ERA in 97.1 innings last season. The lone – glaring – red flag on an otherwise impressive junior campaign: he coughed up 10 gopher balls. Following his selection as the first pick in the second round last June, 43rd overall, Arizona allowed Young just to dip his toes in the professional waters as he tossed another seven innings, six of them coming in the Northwest League. He finished with six strikeouts and one walk.

**Projection**: Here's what I wrote prior to the draft last June:

*"A solid mid- to back-of-the-rotation caliber starting pitcher with less risk [because of] his lack of wear-and-tear on his left arm courtesy of spending a couple years in the bullpen. Young will miss some bats and do a solid job limiting free passes. He's been a bit homer-prone this season, so that'll bear watching. For comps, think Marco Gonzales or Chi Chi Gonzalez."*

**Ceiling:** 2.0- to 2.5-win player
**Risk:** Moderate
**MLB ETA:** 2017/2018

## 6. Yoan Lopez, RHP

**MiLB Rank: #186**
**Position Rank: N/A**

| Born: 01/02/93 | Age: 23 | Bats: R | Top CALs: Fabio Castillo, Chris Mobley, |
| Height: 6-3 | Weight: 185 | Throws: R | Ben Hornbeck, Trevor Miller, Clario Perez |

| YEAR | Age | Level | IP | W | L | ERA | FIP | K/9 | BB/9 | K% | BB% | HR/9 | LOB% |
|---|---|---|---|---|---|---|---|---|---|---|---|---|---|
| 2015 | 22 | R | 6.0 | 1 | 0 | 0.00 | 1.82 | 9.00 | 0.00 | 31.6% | 0.0% | 0.00 | 100.0% |
| 2015 | 22 | AA | 48.0 | 1 | 6 | 4.69 | 4.55 | 6.00 | 4.50 | 15.6% | 11.7% | 0.75 | 66.8% |

**Background:** At that time of the signing in mid-January last year Lopez's $8.27 million bonus was a record for the largest given to an international amateur. After spending parts of three seasons in the Cuban National Series pitching for the Isla de la Juventud, Lopez made the leap straight into the Southern League last season – and looked a bit underprepared. He posted a 32-to-24 strikeout-to-walk in 48.0 innings of work.

**Projection**: We still don't have a whole lot of stateside information on the hard-throwing right-hander out of Cuba. But what we do have correlates well enough with his work as a teenager in the Cuban National Series, namely his inability to harness his power arsenal. He walked 11.7% of the batters he faced before defecting and followed that up by walking 11.7% of the batters he faced with Mobile in Class AA last season. He's still a massive wild card, but it's important to note that last season would have just been his senior year in a stateside college.

**Ceiling:** 2.0- to 2.5-win player
**Risk:** Moderate to High
**MLB ETA:** 2017

## 7. Silvino Bracho, RHP

**MiLB Rank: #187**
**Position Rank: N/A**

| Born: 07/17/92 | Age: 23 | Bats: R | Top CALs: Dan Barnes, Jonathan Ortiz, |
| Height: 5-10 | Weight: 190 | Throws: R | Tucker Healy, Mat Latos, Christian Friedrich |

| YEAR | Age | Level | IP | W | L | ERA | FIP | K/9 | BB/9 | K% | BB% | HR/9 | LOB% |
|------|-----|-------|------|---|---|------|-------|-------|------|------|-----|------|-------|
| 2013 | 20 | R | 26.3 | 0 | 2 | 1.71 | 2.53 | 12.99 | 1.03 | 36.2% | 2.9% | 0.68 | 86.2% |
| 2014 | 21 | A | 43.3 | 3 | 2 | 2.08 | 1.85 | 14.54 | 1.66 | 42.9% | 4.9% | 0.62 | 81.2% |
| 2015 | 22 | A+ | 6.0 | 0 | 0 | 0.00 | -0.39 | 21.00 | 1.50 | 70.0% | 5.0% | 0.00 | 100.0% |
| 2015 | 22 | AA | 44.7 | 2 | 1 | 1.81 | 2.21 | 11.89 | 1.81 | 33.3% | 5.1% | 0.60 | 85.4% |

**Background:** The Venezuelan-born right-hander opened the season with just 43.1 innings above rookie ball and finished it with 12.1 – dominant – innings in Arizona. In between, Bracho, a 5-foot-10, 190-pound right-hander, torched the California League by fanning 14 in just six innings of work and blew through the Southern League by posting a 73-to-10 strikeout-to-walk ratio in just 44.2 innings. Bracho finished his minor league season – likely career – by fanning a remarkable 37% and walking a smidgeon over 5% of the total batters he faced. And make no mistake: this type of production isn't an aberration either. He's fanned 211 and walked just 26 of the 573 minor league bats he's faced in his career.

**Projection**: His fastball isn't what you'd expect, on either end of the spectrum. He's not particularly overpowering, but isn't a typical soft-tosser relying purely on spotting a mediocre heater. Instead, it rests in the low-90s and complements with a low-80s slider. He has the chance to spend the next decade-plus – barring injury – working in high, high-leverage situations.

**Ceiling:** 1.5 – to 2.0-win player
**Risk:** Low to Moderate
**MLB ETA:** Debuted in 2015

## 8. Socrates Brito, OF

**MiLB Rank: #206**
**Position Rank: N/A**

| Born: 09/06/92 | Age: 23 | Bats: L | Top CALs: Lee Haydel, Jake Cave, |
| Height: 6-1 | Weight: 200 | Throws: L | Juan Portes, Peter Bourjos, Rudy Guillen |

| Season | Age | LVL | PA | 2B | 3B | HR | AVG | OBP | SLG | ISO | BB% | K% | wRC+ |
|--------|-----|-----|-----|----|----|----|-------|-------|-------|-------|------|-------|------|
| 2013 | 20 | A | 566 | 24 | 9 | 2 | 0.264 | 0.313 | 0.356 | 0.092 | 6.5% | 21.9% | 89 |
| 2014 | 21 | A+ | 561 | 30 | 5 | 10 | 0.293 | 0.339 | 0.429 | 0.135 | 6.4% | 19.4% | 99 |
| 2015 | 22 | AA | 522 | 17 | 15 | 9 | 0.300 | 0.339 | 0.451 | 0.151 | 5.6% | 16.1% | 122 |
| 2015 | 22 | MLB | 34 | 3 | 1 | 0 | 0.303 | 0.324 | 0.455 | 0.152 | 2.9% | 20.6% | 106 |

**Background:** A quiet, unheralded prospect signed out of the Dominican Republic, Brito continued his ascension up through the low and mid levels of the minor leagues – and one that culminated in an 18-game stint in Arizona – with another solid offensive showing. After filling up the stat sheet without truly dominating High Class A – he batted .293/.339/.429 with 30 doubles, five triples, 10 homeruns, and 38 stolen bases – Brito easily had his finest professional season to date. He batted .300/.339/.451 with 17 doubles, a career best 15 triples, nine homeruns, and 20 stolen bases (in 26 attempts). His overall production, according to *Weighted Runs Created Plus*, topped the league average mark by 22%.

**Projection**: A member of the *Bird Doggin' It* section in last year's book, Brito had a massive coming out party in 2015 – one that likely convinced the front office to include Ender Inciarte in the trade debacle with the Braves. Brito offers up a surprisingly well-rounded offensive toolkit: power, speed, and hit tool. His walk rate will ultimately eat into some of his overall value. But if he plays decent defense he should have no issues developing into a starter on a non-contending team.

**Ceiling:** 1.5- to 2.0-win player
**Risk:** Moderate
**MLB ETA:** Debuted in 2015

## 9. Brandon Drury, 2B/3B

**MiLB Rank: #207**

**Position Rank: #8 (2B),**

| Born: 08/21/92 | Age: 23 | Bats: R |
|---|---|---|
| Height: 6-1 | Weight: 215 | Throws: R |

**Top CALs:** Colin Moran, Cheslor Cuthbert, Jefry Marte, Blake Dewitt, Adrian Cardenas

| Season | Age | LVL | PA | 2B | 3B | HR | AVG | OBP | SLG | ISO | BB% | K% | wRC+ |
|---|---|---|---|---|---|---|---|---|---|---|---|---|---|
| 2013 | 20 | A | 583 | 51 | 4 | 15 | 0.302 | 0.362 | 0.500 | 0.198 | 8.1% | 15.8% | 138 |
| 2014 | 21 | A+ | 478 | 35 | 1 | 19 | 0.300 | 0.366 | 0.519 | 0.219 | 8.6% | 15.9% | 128 |
| 2014 | 21 | AA | 116 | 7 | 0 | 4 | 0.295 | 0.345 | 0.476 | 0.181 | 6.0% | 16.4% | 128 |
| 2015 | 22 | AA | 291 | 14 | 1 | 3 | 0.278 | 0.306 | 0.370 | 0.092 | 3.8% | 14.1% | 89 |
| 2015 | 22 | AAA | 276 | 26 | 0 | 2 | 0.331 | 0.384 | 0.458 | 0.127 | 7.6% | 12.7% | 127 |
| 2015 | 22 | MLB | 59 | 3 | 0 | 2 | 0.214 | 0.254 | 0.375 | 0.161 | 3.4% | 13.6% | 66 |

**Background:** So it all comes down to Brandon Drury, the former 2010 13th round pick out of Grants Pass High School. The stocky 6-foot-1 third baseman is the club's sole remaining hope for an impact player received in the Justin Upton/Chris Johnson deal with Atlanta. The ironic part: Drury was viewed as a throw-in wild card of sorts at the time of the trade. Anyway, after finishing the 2014 season with a 29-game stint with Mobile, Drury found himself back in the Southern League to begin last season. And let's just say he got off to a disappointing start. He batted .250/.282/.338 in his first 85 trips to the plate, didn't slug his first homerun until the second of May, and his second dinger didn't come until a June 14th game against the Jackson Generals. Arizona would push Drury up to Reno a couple weeks later – he would bat .331/.384/.458 with the Aces – and then eventually promote him to the big league club for help down the stretch.

**Projection**: If you hear sirens in the distance sounding off that's the red flags popping up all over Drury's prospect status. After slowly developing power – his homerun output moved from 3 to 8 to 6 to 15 to 23 through his five previous seasons – it all but dried up last season. He posted the lowest slugging percentage, .412, and Isolated Power, .109, since his struggles in the Sally at the age of 19. I remarked in last year's book that (A) CAL remained down on the young third baseman as it compared him to only one viable big leaguer in Lonnie Chisenhall and (B) his only standout tool is his power, which, coincidentally, all but abandoned him. Well, CAL continues to be hard on Drury, this time linking him to Colin Moran, Cheslor Cuthbert, Jefry Marte, Blake DeWitt, and Adrian Cardenas. But (B), the power decline might be explained by his switching to second base. The 2016 season is as important as any for Drury – if the power comes back, so does his prospect status. If not, well...

**Ceiling:** 2.0-win player
**Risk:** Moderate to High
**MLB ETA:** N/A

## 10. Brad Keller, RHP

**MiLB Rank: #235**

**Position Rank: N/A**

| Born: 07/27/95 | Age: 20 | Bats: R |
|---|---|---|
| Height: 6-5 | Weight: 230 | Throws: R |

**Top CALs:** Andrew Potter, Felix Doubront, Dallas Newton, Victor Gonzalez, Matthew Tenuta

| YEAR | Age | Level | IP | W | L | ERA | FIP | K/9 | BB/9 | K% | BB% | HR/9 | LOB% |
|---|---|---|---|---|---|---|---|---|---|---|---|---|---|
| 2013 | 17 | R | 6.0 | 0 | 0 | 4.50 | 4.76 | 6.00 | 6.00 | 14.3% | 14.3% | 0.00 | 70.0% |
| 2013 | 17 | R | 56.7 | 7 | 3 | 2.22 | 3.80 | 9.69 | 4.13 | 25.0% | 10.7% | 0.32 | 75.5% |
| 2014 | 18 | R | 33.7 | 1 | 4 | 6.95 | 6.44 | 8.02 | 4.81 | 18.1% | 10.8% | 1.60 | 63.9% |
| 2014 | 18 | R | 31.3 | 4 | 0 | 2.30 | 4.73 | 5.74 | 2.59 | 15.8% | 7.1% | 0.57 | 86.7% |
| 2014 | 18 | A- | 6.0 | 1 | 0 | 0.00 | 1.65 | 12.00 | 1.50 | 40.0% | 5.0% | 0.00 | 100.0% |
| 2015 | 19 | A | 142.0 | 8 | 9 | 2.60 | 3.13 | 6.91 | 2.35 | 18.6% | 6.3% | 0.19 | 69.1% |

**Background:** One of the more overlooked prospects in the system, perhaps because of his slow movement through the minors' lowest levels, but consider the following: among all qualified pitchers in either Low Class A league, Keller's 3.13 FIP ranked 11th overall and second among all teenage arms, trailing only Cleveland's Justus Sheffield. Keller, an eighth round pick out of Flowery Branch High School in 2013, *doubled* his previous career innings high as he tossed 142.0 innings with Kane Country last season. He fanned 109, walked just 37, and posted a 2.60 ERA. For his three-year professional career Keller is averaging 7.6 punch outs and just 3.1 walks per nine innings.

**Projection**: With the build of an innings eater, Keller, who stands 6-foot-5 and 230 pounds, has been a quiet, consistent performer throughout his career. His control, which flashed below-average during his debut, has been trending in the right direction since as he's posted walk rates of 4.3 BB/9 to 3.5 BB/9 to a career best 2.3 BB/9 last season. He has the look of a solid #3/#4-type arm and could begin to move quickly within the next 12 months.

**Ceiling:** 1.5- to 2.0-win player
**Risk:** Moderate
**MLB ETA:** 2017/2018

## 11. Wei-Chieh Huang, RHP

**MiLB Rank: #241**
**Position Rank: N/A**

| Born: 09/26/93 | Age: 22 | Bats: R | Top CALs: Travis Banwart, Carlos Hernandez, |
| Height: 6-1 | Weight: 170 | Throws: R | Danny Vais, Donn Roach, Eduardo Baeza |

| YEAR | Age | Level | IP | W | L | ERA | FIP | K/9 | BB/9 | K% | BB% | HR/9 | LOB% |
|---|---|---|---|---|---|---|---|---|---|---|---|---|---|
| 2015 | 21 | A | 76.7 | 7 | 3 | 2.00 | 2.53 | 7.98 | 1.88 | 22.5% | 5.3% | 0.12 | 70.1% |

**Background:** Signed out of Taiwan in early July two years ago for $450,000 after pitching for the National Taiwan University of Physical Education and Sport, Huang didn't make his stateside debut until last season when he spent the entire year with Kane County in the Midwest League. In 15 games, 12 of which were starts, the slight-framed 6-foot-1, 170-pounder right-hander posted an immaculate 68-to-16 strikeout-to-walk ratio.

**Projection**: Basically the equivalent of an incoming collegiate arm, but with far less data to analyze. Huang looked brilliant as he easily handled the Midwest League hitters. Huang was particularly dominant during his first five starts of the year: he tossed 31.2 innings with 32 punch outs, five walks, and a laughably low 0.85 ERA as he held opponents to a .502 OPS. He's not overpowering but is poised beyond his years. Above-average or better control, Huang could be a nice #4/#5-type arm down the line.

**Ceiling:** 1.5- to 2.0-win player
**Risk:** Moderate
**MLB ETA:** 2017/2018

## 12. Anthony Banda, LHP

**MiLB Rank: #N/A**
**Position Rank: N/A**

| Born: 08/10/93 | Age: 22 | Bats: L | Top CALs: Brooks Pounders, Jose Ramirez, |
| Height: 6-2 | Weight: 190 | Throws: L | Gregory Billo, Ivan Pineyro, Carlos Hernandez |

| YEAR | Age | Level | IP | W | L | ERA | FIP | K/9 | BB/9 | K% | BB% | HR/9 | LOB% |
|---|---|---|---|---|---|---|---|---|---|---|---|---|---|
| 2013 | 19 | R | 60.7 | 3 | 4 | 4.45 | 5.39 | 6.68 | 3.71 | 17.1% | 9.5% | 1.04 | 62.3% |
| 2014 | 20 | A | 118.7 | 9 | 6 | 3.03 | 3.36 | 8.87 | 3.41 | 23.2% | 8.9% | 0.46 | 75.0% |
| 2015 | 21 | A+ | 151.7 | 8 | 8 | 3.32 | 3.31 | 9.02 | 2.31 | 24.3% | 6.2% | 0.47 | 69.3% |

**Background:** A 10th round pick out of San Jacinto College, North Campus in 2012, the 6-foot-2 southpaw found his way to the Arizona system via the Gerardo Parra trade. And after a strong showing in the Midwest League two years ago – he tossed 118.2 innings while averaging 8.9 punch outs and 3.4 walks per nine innings – Banda put together his finest professional season to date. In a career best 151.2 innings of work with Visalia, Banda fanned 152, walked just 39, and posted nearly matching ERA and FIP (3.32 and 3.31, respectively). For his four-year professional career, he's fanned 357 and walked 133 in 372.2 innings.

**Projection**: Another highly underrated prospect in the system. Banda does a whole lot of things surprisingly well – he's always missed a strong number of bats; his control has taken a step forward into above-average territory, something that has happened since entering the organization, and he's generated a good amount of action on the ground. The 2016 season will go a long way in determining the likelihood of him developing into a #3/#4-type arm – thanks to the challenge of Class AA – but he's one to watch.

**Ceiling:** 1.5- to 2.0-win player
**Risk:** Moderate to High
**MLB ETA:** 2017/2018

## 13. Peter O'Brien, LF/RF

**MiLB Rank: #N/A**
**Position Rank: N/A**

| Born: 07/15/90 | Age: 25 | Bats: R | Top CALs: Bryce Brentz, Brandon Wood, |
| Height: 6-4 | Weight: 235 | Throws: R | Jerry Sands, Kyle Reynolds, Brandon Burgess |

| Season | Age | LVL | PA | 2B | 3B | HR | AVG | OBP | SLG | ISO | BB% | K% | wRC+ |
|---|---|---|---|---|---|---|---|---|---|---|---|---|---|
| 2013 | 22 | A | 226 | 22 | 1 | 11 | 0.325 | 0.394 | 0.619 | 0.294 | 9.7% | 25.7% | 181 |
| 2013 | 22 | A+ | 280 | 17 | 3 | 11 | 0.265 | 0.314 | 0.486 | 0.221 | 6.8% | 27.1% | 122 |
| 2014 | 23 | A+ | 119 | 9 | 1 | 10 | 0.321 | 0.353 | 0.688 | 0.366 | 3.4% | 24.4% | 189 |
| 2014 | 23 | AA | 294 | 14 | 1 | 23 | 0.245 | 0.296 | 0.555 | 0.310 | 5.4% | 26.2% | 131 |
| 2015 | 24 | AAA | 534 | 35 | 9 | 26 | 0.284 | 0.332 | 0.551 | 0.267 | 5.8% | 23.2% | 129 |
| 2015 | 24 | MLB | 12 | 1 | 0 | 1 | 0.400 | 0.500 | 0.800 | 0.400 | 16.7% | 41.7% | 247 |

**Background**: A collegiate backstop out of the University of Miami that, well, couldn't really catch – at least passably. O'Brien, who was acquired from the Yankees in exchange for Martin Prado at the trade deadline two years ago, continued to bounce between a couple positions as he spent the majority of year mashing for the Reno Aces in the Pacific Coast League in 2015. The former second round pick hit .284/.332/.551 with 35 doubles, nine triples, and 26 homeruns en route to topping the PCL league average production line by 29%. For his career, O'Brien's sporting a sturdy .273/.323/.539 triple-slash line with 107 doubles, 15 triples, and 92 homeruns in 408 games. He also managed to go 4-for-8 with the big league club.

**Projection**: O'Brien can do two things with authority: he can slug the long ball with the best of them and he can go down trying with the best of them. And while he's managed to post some solid batting averages throughout his minor league tenure, don't expect that trend to continue when he gets extended looks at the big league level. The power – even with the low averages and low equally depressing OBPs – will continue to get him enough looks and playing time.

**Ceiling:** 1.5-win player
**Risk:** Moderate
**MLB ETA:** Debuted in 2015

## 14. Zac Curtis, LHP

MiLB Rank: #N/A
Position Rank: N/A

| Born: 07/04/92 | Age: 23 | Bats: L | Top CALs: Will Harris, Justin Wright, |
| Height: 5-9 | Weight: 179 | Throws: L | Jonathan Ortiz, Chad Smith, Adam Parks |

| YEAR | Age | Level | IP | W | L | ERA | FIP | K/9 | BB/9 | K% | BB% | HR/9 | LOB% |
|------|-----|-------|------|---|---|------|------|-------|------|-------|------|------|------|
| 2014 | 21 | A- | 27.0 | 2 | 1 | 1.00 | 2.04 | 14.00 | 4.00 | 38.5% | 11.0% | 0.00 | 83.3% |
| 2015 | 22 | A | 54.0 | 4 | 4 | 1.33 | 1.82 | 12.50 | 2.00 | 36.4% | 5.8% | 0.33 | 85.7% |

**Background:** Among the Division I league leaders in strikeouts during his final season at Middle Tennessee State University, Curtis' small stature – he stands just 5-foot-9 and 179 pounds – likely cost him a shot as an early round pick. Arizona grabbed the diminutive southpaw in the sixth round, 180th overall, and immediately – and perhaps, wrongly – converted him into a fulltime reliever. And Curtis has been absolutely lights out over the past two seasons. He barely got touched in the Northwest League during his debut, posting a miniscule 1.00 ERA and 2.04 FIP with a staggering 42 punch outs and 12 walks in 27.0 innings. The little lefty got pushed up to the Midwest League last season – and he continued to dominate: in 54.0 innings with Kane County, Curtis tallied a 1.33 ERA and 1.82 FIP positing an impressive 75-to-12 strikeout-to-walk ratio while saving 33 games.

**Projection**: Here's what I wrote about the former Middle Tennessee State stud prior to the 2014 draft:

> *"There's going to be a lot of temptation – and rightly so – to push the small southpaw immediately into the bullpen because of concerns about his small frame and the ability to hold up over the course of a full season. Above-average or better ability to miss bats, good control, a lively arm.*
>
> *At the very least, Curtis looks like another Tim Collins-clone."*

There's really not too much else to add other than the fact that he should have been fast-tracked after his dominating debut. Like I said before, he's a budding Tim Collins.

**Ceiling:** 1.5-win player
**Risk:** Moderate
**MLB ETA:** 2018

## 15. Jake Barrett, RHP

MiLB Rank: #N/A
Position Rank: N/A

| Born: 07/22/91 | Age: 24 | Bats: R | Top CALs: Dan Cortes, Zach Phillips, |
| Height: 6-3 | Weight: 220 | Throws: R | Luis Cessa, John Gast, Robert Carson |

| YEAR | Age | Level | IP | W | L | ERA | FIP | K/9 | BB/9 | K% | BB% | HR/9 | LOB% |
|------|-----|-------|------|---|---|------|------|-------|------|-------|-------|------|------|
| 2013 | 21 | A+ | 27.3 | 2 | 1 | 1.98 | 3.33 | 12.18 | 2.96 | 31.4% | 7.6% | 0.66 | 86.1% |
| 2013 | 21 | AA | 24.7 | 1 | 1 | 0.36 | 2.55 | 8.03 | 1.09 | 22.9% | 3.1% | 0.73 | 93.4% |
| 2014 | 22 | AA | 26.3 | 1 | 2 | 2.39 | 2.73 | 8.20 | 4.10 | 21.8% | 10.9% | 0.00 | 81.1% |
| 2014 | 22 | AAA | 29.0 | 1 | 0 | 3.72 | 5.11 | 7.14 | 4.66 | 19.3% | 12.6% | 0.93 | 74.0% |
| 2015 | 23 | AA | 30.0 | 3 | 0 | 4.20 | 3.27 | 9.00 | 3.30 | 22.9% | 8.4% | 0.60 | 73.5% |
| 2015 | 23 | AAA | 23.0 | 1 | 3 | 5.09 | 3.90 | 8.22 | 4.70 | 20.2% | 11.5% | 0.39 | 63.8% |

**Background:** Fun fact: Barrett was originally taken by the Blue Jays in the third round coming out of high school in 2012; he was later drafted in the third round after a successful collegiate career at Arizona State University three years later. And since entering the Diamondbacks' farm system four years ago Barrett's been biding his time to take over as the club's latest hard-throwing closer. It was a move that seemed destined to happen – perhaps as soon as 2015 – if it weren't for a disappointing showing two years ago. Barrett blew through the Midwest, California, and Southern Leagues in abbreviated stops over his first two seasons, but control issues popped up in his return to the Southern League and didn't disappear for the remainder of the year, even after the club bumped him up to Reno. And guess what? They resurfaced (briefly) last season as well – something that precipitated his demotion back to the Southern League.

**Projection**: Here's what I wrote in last year's book:

> *"A lively, power-armed reliever with late-inning potential, Barrett has a long history – extending way back to his sophomore campaign with the Sun Devils – of better than average control, so last season's spike should prove to be nothing more than a blip on the screen. He's nearing big league readiness."*

Well, you know what? His control did bounce back at the start of last season. Over his first 19 games Barrett walked seven batters – or about 3.3 BB/9. But in a three-game span starting at the end of May, the hard-throwing right-hander coughed up five walks in four innings. And the front office had a major mental meltdown. They shipped him back to the Southern League where he would average 3.3 walks per nine innings.

A stupid, stupid move and a horrible kneejerk reaction to a minor blip on the screen.

Barrett's big league ready and could step in and control an eighth inning role today. Hell, he could've done it yesterday.

**Ceiling:** 1.0- to 1.5-win player
**Risk:** Low to Moderate
**MLB ETA:** 2016

## 16. Tyler Wagner, RHP

**MiLB Rank: #N/A**
**Position Rank: N/A**

| Born: 01/24/91 | Age: 25 | Bats: R | Top CALs: Sam Lecure, Robert Ray, |
|---|---|---|---|
| Height: 6-3 | Weight: 195 | Throws: R | Amaury Rivas, Graham Godfrey, Mark Leiter |

| YEAR | Age | Level | IP | W | L | ERA | FIP | K/9 | BB/9 | K% | BB% | HR/9 | LOB% |
|---|---|---|---|---|---|---|---|---|---|---|---|---|---|
| 2013 | 22 | A | 148.7 | 10 | 8 | 3.21 | 3.84 | 7.02 | 3.39 | 18.9% | 9.1% | 0.61 | 74.1% |
| 2014 | 23 | A+ | 150.0 | 13 | 6 | 1.86 | 3.66 | 7.08 | 2.88 | 19.8% | 8.1% | 0.60 | 82.4% |
| 2015 | 24 | AA | 152.3 | 11 | 5 | 2.25 | 3.27 | 7.09 | 2.66 | 19.7% | 7.4% | 0.41 | 79.1% |

**Background:** Armed with a fringy upper-80s fastball, Wagner spent the majority of the year twirling quality start after quality start for Biloxi in the Southern League: he would finish with a career high 152.1 innings while averaging 7.1 punch outs and just 2.7 walks per nine innings. The former University of Utah hurler also made three starts with Milwaukee last season.

**Projection**: Your typical soft-tossing right-hander that succeeds by doing the little things: limiting free passes, generating a crap-ton of action on the ground, and not surrendering a whole lot of long balls. Here's what I wrote in last year's book:

> *"A polished collegiate senior who hasn't been particularly dominating in the lower levels of the minors. Wagner has better than average control and generates a lot of action on the ground, sporting a groundball rate north of 55% in his career. Maybe a swing-man down the line."*

See, told you…

**Ceiling:** 1.0-win player
**Risk:** Low to Moderate
**MLB ETA:** Debuted in 2015

## 17. Gabriel Guerrero, OF

**MiLB Rank: #N/A**
**Position Rank: N/A**

| Born: 12/11/93 | Age: 22 | Bats: R | Top CALs: Tyler Henson, Avisail Garcia, |
|---|---|---|---|
| Height: 6-3 | Weight: 190 | Throws: R | Elier Hernandez, Leyson Septimo, Paulo Orlando |

| Season | Age | LVL | PA | 2B | 3B | HR | AVG | OBP | SLG | ISO | BB% | K% | wRC+ |
|---|---|---|---|---|---|---|---|---|---|---|---|---|---|
| 2013 | 19 | A | 499 | 23 | 3 | 4 | 0.271 | 0.303 | 0.358 | 0.087 | 4.2% | 22.6% | 85 |
| 2014 | 20 | A+ | 580 | 28 | 2 | 18 | 0.307 | 0.347 | 0.467 | 0.160 | 5.9% | 22.6% | 110 |
| 2015 | 21 | AA | 488 | 25 | 5 | 7 | 0.222 | 0.258 | 0.343 | 0.122 | 4.7% | 22.1% | 66 |

**Background:** Part of the four-man package Arizona received from Seattle in exchange for OBP-deficient outfielder Mark Trumbo and portly southpaw Vidal Nuno, Guerrero looked nothing like the player that batted .307/.347/.467 in High Class A two years ago as he struggled through the most difficult minor league test: Class AA. Splitting time between both organizations, though he didn't move out of the Southern League, the sinewy 6-foot-3, 190-pound Dominican-born outfielder hit a paltry .222/.258/.343 with 25 doubles, five triples, seven homeruns, and 11 stolen bases. His overall production, per *Weighted Runs Created Plus*, was more than 30% *below* the league average mark. For his career, Guerrero is sporting a .277/.316/.412 triple-slash line with 99 doubles, 14 triples, 45 homeruns, and 49 stolen bases in 507 games.

**Projection**: More of a stat sheet filler than prospect at any point during his five-year minor league career; Guerrero's never truly dominated outside of his 2012 stint in the Dominican Summer League, his *second* jaunt through the foreign rookie level. Otherwise, Guerrero's wRC+ totals have ranged from below-average (85) to slightly better than average (110). He flashes double-digit power and speed, but his inability to work the count will most assuredly limit his ceiling to that of a fourth outfielder capacity, maybe even less.

**Ceiling:** 1.5-win player
**Risk:** Moderate to High
**MLB ETA:** 2017

## 18. Jimmie Sherfy, RHP

**MiLB Rank: #N/A**
**Position Rank: N/A**

| | | | |
|---|---|---|---|
| **Born:** 12/27/91 | **Age:** 24 | **Bats:** R | **Top CALs:** Justin Wright, Ethan Martin, |
| **Height:** 6-0 | **Weight:** 175 | **Throws:** R | Dan Cortes, Jenrry Mejia, Daniel Haigwood |

| YEAR | Age | Level | IP | W | L | ERA | FIP | K/9 | BB/9 | K% | BB% | HR/9 | LOB% |
|------|-----|-------|------|---|---|------|------|-------|------|-------|-------|------|--------|
| 2013 | 21 | A- | 9.0 | 0 | 0 | 0.00 | 0.54 | 17.00 | 1.00 | 51.5% | 3.0% | 0.00 | 100.0% |
| 2013 | 21 | A | 8.3 | 1 | 1 | 2.16 | 1.54 | 12.96 | 3.24 | 30.8% | 7.7% | 0.00 | 84.6% |
| 2014 | 22 | A+ | 11.0 | 2 | 0 | 3.27 | 3.56 | 18.82 | 4.09 | 52.3% | 11.4% | 1.64 | 76.1% |
| 2014 | 22 | AA | 38.0 | 3 | 1 | 4.97 | 3.92 | 10.66 | 4.26 | 27.1% | 10.8% | 0.95 | 69.4% |
| 2015 | 23 | AA | 49.7 | 1 | 6 | 6.52 | 3.95 | 9.06 | 5.07 | 22.3% | 12.5% | 0.54 | 57.3% |

**Background:** A two-year dominant stay as Oregon's closer wasn't enough to convince a team to burn a pick on the hard-throwing right-hander until Arizona stopped his skid in the 10th round in 2013. Since then, however, the 6-foot, 175-pound reliever has looked every bit of a bargain. Sherfy posted an impeccable 29-to-4 strikeout-to-walk ratio in 17.1 innings during his pro debut. He followed that up by fanning 68 and walking 23 in 49.0 innings between Visalia and Mobile two years ago. But, unfortunately, he seemingly came down with a case of Jake Barrett-itis. Just like his counterpart, Sherfy lost sight of the strike zone during his full-season stint in the Southern League. He continued to miss bats (9.1 K/9), but coughed up 28 free passes in 49.2 innings.

**Projection**: Unlike Barrett, Sherfy doesn't have a lengthy track record of strong control/command. He walked about five guys every nine innings during his sophomore season with Oregon and averaged 4.2 BB/9 two years ago. So don't expect a huge bounce back in 2016. With that being said, he owns one of the best of arms in the system with the potential to develop into a dominant big league reliever.

**Ceiling:** 1.5-win player
**Risk:** Moderate to High
**MLB ETA:** 2016/2017

## 19. Joey Krehbiel, RHP

**MiLB Rank: #N/A**
**Position Rank: N/A**

| | | | |
|---|---|---|---|
| **Born:** 12/20/92 | **Age:** 23 | **Bats:** R | **Top CALs:** Thomas Palica, Vincent Velasquez, |
| **Height:** 6-2 | **Weight:** 185 | **Throws:** R | Adrian Rosario, Sean Newcomb, Alejandro Chacin |

| YEAR | Age | Level | IP | W | L | ERA | FIP | K/9 | BB/9 | K% | BB% | HR/9 | LOB% |
|------|-----|-------|------|---|---|------|------|-------|------|-------|-------|------|--------|
| 2013 | 20 | A | 65.7 | 6 | 5 | 2.74 | 3.22 | 9.59 | 3.84 | 25.6% | 10.2% | 0.41 | 76.5% |
| 2014 | 21 | A | 14.0 | 0 | 0 | 1.93 | 2.34 | 10.93 | 3.86 | 29.8% | 10.5% | 0.00 | 71.4% |
| 2014 | 21 | | 29.3 | 1 | 0 | 1.53 | 3.44 | 10.43 | 3.07 | 29.8% | 8.8% | 0.61 | 81.9% |
| 2015 | 22 | A+ | 68.0 | 0 | 6 | 3.71 | 3.43 | 12.71 | 3.71 | 33.5% | 9.8% | 0.79 | 72.8% |

**Background:** Another one of the system's promising minor league relief arms. Krehbiel, a 12th round pick out of the Angels out of Seminole High School in 2011, was acquired by Arizona – along with outfielder Zach Borenstein – as part of the Tony Campana swap in an early July trade two years ago. The 6-foot-2, 185-pound right-hander spent the year with Visalia, averaging nearly 13 K/9.

**Projection**: After aggressively pushing some players so quickly through the minors, one wonders why Krehbiel got the ticket back to the California League after a dominant 29.1-inning stint the previous season. He's shown a remarkable ability to miss bats, particularly since entering High Class A. The control is solid-average. And he should – *should* – be ready to jump up to Class AAA in the second half of 2016. Whether that happens, I don't know.

**Ceiling:** 1.0- to 1.5-win player
**Risk:** Moderate
**MLB ETA:** 2016/2017

## 20. Ryan Burr, RHP

MiLB Rank: #N/A
Position Rank: N/A

| Born: 05/28/94 | Age: 22 | Bats: R | Top CALs: Justin Wright Jose Mavare, |
| Height: 6-4 | Weight: 224 | Throws: R | Zac Curtis, Ben Hornbeck, Edgar Estanga |

| YEAR | Age | Level | IP | W | L | ERA | FIP | K/9 | BB/9 | K% | BB% | HR/9 | LOB% |
|------|-----|-------|-----|---|---|------|------|-------|------|-------|------|------|-------|
| 2015 | 21 | A- | 14.3 | 3 | 0 | 1.88 | 2.83 | 13.19 | 3.14 | 37.5% | 8.9% | 0.63 | 86.2% |
| 2015 | 21 | A | 19.7 | 1 | 0 | 0.46 | 1.46 | 12.81 | 2.75 | 36.8% | 7.9% | 0.00 | 94.4% |

**Background:** A dominant reliever out of the Arizona State University last season, Burr, who was taken in the 5th round, 136th overall, spent three seasons as the Sun Devils' closer. The 6-foot-4, 225-pound right-hander finished his collegiate career with a 190-to-86 strikeout-to-walk ratio in 135 innings.

**Projection**: It's not overly surprising that the hard-throwing Burr lasted until the mid-rounds of the draft given his propensity to avoid the strike zone. He averaged nearly six walks per nine innings during his collegiate career and would post walk rates above 4.60 BB/9 in each of his three seasons. With that being said, it's surprising to see him issue just 11 walks in 34.0 innings during his debut. He has the "future closer" label swirling about his head, but he needs to prove he can handle high leverage situations.

**Ceiling:** 1.5-win player
**Risk:** High
**MLB ETA:** 2018

## 21. Dawel Lugo, SS

MiLB Rank: #N/A
Position Rank: N/A

| Born: 12/31/94 | Age: 21 | Bats: R | Top CALs: Juan Rivera, Jonathan Mota, |
| Height: 6-0 | Weight: 190 | Throws: R | Juan Diaz, Abiatal Avelino, Luis Marte |

| Season | Age | LVL | PA | 2B | 3B | HR | AVG | OBP | SLG | ISO | BB% | K% | wRC+ |
|--------|-----|-----|-----|----|----|----|-------|-------|-------|-------|------|-------|------|
| 2013 | 18 | R | 202 | 11 | 2 | 6 | 0.297 | 0.317 | 0.469 | 0.172 | 2.5% | 13.9% | 122 |
| 2014 | 19 | A | 498 | 17 | 2 | 4 | 0.259 | 0.286 | 0.329 | 0.070 | 3.6% | 14.5% | 76 |
| 2015 | 20 | A | 218 | 7 | 2 | 2 | 0.335 | 0.358 | 0.419 | 0.084 | 4.1% | 17.0% | 124 |
| 2015 | 20 | A+ | 276 | 9 | 2 | 2 | 0.219 | 0.258 | 0.292 | 0.073 | 3.3% | 17.8% | 68 |

**Background:** If you ever wanted to know the going rate for a light-hitting, multi-million-dollar-a-year, defensive-minded backup infielder, here is your answer: Dawel Lugo. As the Blue Jays and Diamondbacks got together for a one-for-one swap in an early August deal last season, Lugo's mostly flown under the radar during his four-year professional career. He struggled in his debut in the Gulf Coast League as a 17-year-old (.224/.275/.329), but had a coming out party of sorts the following season as he slugged .297/.317/.469 with Bluefield in Appalachian League, though his overall production that season was marred by a poor showing in the Northwest League as a late-season promotion. Two years ago, Lugo spent the year mostly getting fooled by the Midwest League as he hit .259/.286/.329. And, perhaps, taking a page of the Arizona Book of Handling (under the chapter of Sergio Alcantara), Toronto pushed the soft-hitting shortstop up to High Class A to begin 2015. After an unsurprisingly poor showing, he got the boot back to the Low Class A where he batted .335/.358/.419 the rest of the way.

**Projection**: Let's pretend for a moment that Lugo was simply a 20-year-old shortstop prospect making his debut in the Midwest League. Had he hit .335/.358/.419 he'd likely be the talk of the town. But, unfortunately, his failings the previous season – as well as the ill-timed move of bumping him up to High Class A – dampen his shine a bit. And that's not including a BABIP hovering around .400. It's still a tremendous value for what amounted to a couple weeks of Cliff Pennington and cash. Lugo shows six- to eight-HR potential, no patience, very little speed, and strong contact skills.

**Ceiling:** 1.0- to 1.5-win player
**Risk:** Moderate to High
**MLB ETA:** 2018

## 22. Domingo Leyba, 2B/SS

| Born: 09/11/95 | Age: 21 | Bats: B | Top CALs: Derek Perlo, Carlos Triunfel, |
|---|---|---|---|
| Height: 5-11 | Weight: 160 | Throws: R | Wilfredo Tovar, Wilmer Flores, Jonathan Mota |

| Season | Age | LVL | PA | 2B | 3B | HR | AVG | OBP | SLG | ISO | BB% | K% | wRC+ |
|---|---|---|---|---|---|---|---|---|---|---|---|---|---|
| 2013 | 17 | R | 247 | 15 | 8 | 5 | 0.348 | 0.446 | 0.577 | 0.229 | 13.8% | 10.5% | 195 |
| 2013 | 17 | R | 247 | 15 | 8 | 5 | 0.348 | 0.446 | 0.577 | 0.229 | 13.8% | 10.5% | 195 |
| 2014 | 18 | A- | 154 | 11 | 1 | 1 | 0.264 | 0.303 | 0.375 | 0.111 | 5.2% | 11.0% | 99 |
| 2014 | 18 | A | 124 | 7 | 0 | 1 | 0.397 | 0.431 | 0.483 | 0.086 | 4.8% | 10.5% | 165 |
| 2014 | 18 | A | 124 | 7 | 0 | 1 | 0.397 | 0.431 | 0.483 | 0.086 | 4.8% | 10.5% | 165 |
| 2015 | 19 | A+ | 562 | 21 | 5 | 2 | 0.237 | 0.277 | 0.309 | 0.072 | 4.6% | 16.0% | 60 |

**Background:** Part of the package the Diamondbacks received along with Robbie Ray during that three-team swap which sent Didi Gregorius to New York and Shane Greene to Detroit. And despite the young middle infielder appearing in just 67 games above the Dominican Summer League – 37 with Connecticut in the NYPL and 30 with West Michigan in the Midwest League – Arizona threw caution to the wind and promoted the then-19-year-old up to the California League. And, unsurprisingly, he was incredibly overmatched. The 5-foot-11 switch-hitter out of Santo Domingo batted a lowly .237/.277/.309 with 21 doubles, five triples, a pair of long balls, and 10 stolen bases in 16 attempts. His overall production, according to *Weighted Runs Created Plus*, was 40% - 40 %$*&!@# percent – below the average.

**Projection**: And this is how you don't develop prospects. Leyba basically hovered around the league average mark during his stint in the New York-Penn League, posting a 94 wRC+. He gets bumped up to Low Class A – and thanks to a .441 BABIP – looks like the second coming of Cobb. And the Diamondbacks' front office bought it! As I noted in last year's book, Leyba is a budding utility guy, offering up no power, some speed, and low walk rates.

**Ceiling:** 1.0-win player
**Risk:** Moderate
**MLB ETA:** 2018/2019

## 23. Mitch Haniger, OF

| Born: 12/23/90 | Age: 25 | Bats: R | Top CALs: Tim Smith, Starlin Rodriguez, |
|---|---|---|---|
| Height: 6-2 | Weight: 215 | Throws: R | Drew Anderson, Sean Henry, Chris Swauger |

| Season | Age | LVL | PA | 2B | 3B | HR | AVG | OBP | SLG | ISO | BB% | K% | wRC+ |
|---|---|---|---|---|---|---|---|---|---|---|---|---|---|
| 2013 | 22 | A | 178 | 12 | 2 | 5 | 0.297 | 0.399 | 0.510 | 0.214 | 14.0% | 13.5% | 152 |
| 2013 | 22 | A+ | 365 | 24 | 3 | 6 | 0.250 | 0.323 | 0.396 | 0.146 | 8.8% | 18.6% | 107 |
| 2014 | 23 | AA | 301 | 10 | 1 | 10 | 0.262 | 0.328 | 0.419 | 0.157 | 7.3% | 15.0% | 109 |
| 2015 | 24 | A+ | 226 | 16 | 3 | 12 | 0.332 | 0.381 | 0.619 | 0.287 | 7.5% | 17.3% | 163 |
| 2015 | 24 | AA | 174 | 10 | 1 | 1 | 0.281 | 0.351 | 0.379 | 0.098 | 9.2% | 18.4% | 107 |

**Background:** Not to rub things in a bit, *but* following the two of the three picks following Haniger in the 2012 draft were Texas power-hitter Joey Gallo and already developed big league starter Lance McCullers. The former 38th overall pick's offensive development has stagnated over the past couple of years as he's bounced between the California and Southern Leagues. But even then it's hard to figure out how – or why – the Diamondbacks justified sending Haniger back down to High Class A in the second half of 2015 – particularly after he batted .281/.351/.379 with 10 doubles, one triple, and one homerun with a 107 wRC+ in 55 games. After the demotion Haniger torched the California League, hitting .332/.381/.619 with a 163 wRC+ in 49 games.

**Projection**: Another odd move by the new regime. If it was a numbers game, why not just bump the former first rounder up to Class AAA and see if he can hack it? What did the organization earn by demoting him? Nothing. Not a damn thing. Typical fourth/fifth outfielder type.

**Ceiling:** 1.0-win player
**Risk:** Moderate
**MLB ETA:** 2016/2017

## 24. Sergio Alcantara, SS

MiLB Rank: #N/A
Position Rank: N/A

| Born: 07/10/96 | Age: 19 | Bats: B | Top CALs: Jesus Lopez, Riley Unroe, |
|---|---|---|---|
| Height: 5-9 | Weight: 168 | Throws: R | Jeckson Flores, Franklin Torres, Luis Carpio |

| Season | Age | LVL | PA | 2B | 3B | HR | AVG | OBP | SLG | ISO | BB% | K% | wRC+ |
|---|---|---|---|---|---|---|---|---|---|---|---|---|---|
| 2013 | 16 | R | 218 | 5 | 4 | 0 | 0.243 | 0.398 | 0.320 | 0.077 | 20.2% | 16.5% | 116 |
| 2014 | 17 | R | 320 | 11 | 0 | 1 | 0.244 | 0.361 | 0.297 | 0.053 | 15.0% | 19.4% | 84 |
| 2015 | 18 | A- | 287 | 12 | 2 | 1 | 0.253 | 0.314 | 0.327 | 0.074 | 8.4% | 16.0% | 88 |
| 2015 | 18 | A- | 287 | 12 | 2 | 1 | 0.253 | 0.314 | 0.327 | 0.074 | 8.4% | 16.0% | 88 |
| 2015 | 18 | A | 79 | 1 | 0 | 0 | 0.113 | 0.169 | 0.127 | 0.014 | 5.1% | 21.5% | -12 |

**Background:** Chalk this up as another confounding move by the front office: after batting a lowly .244/.361/.297 two years ago in the Pioneer League – and a lowly .243/.398/.320 in the Arizona Summer League in 2013 – Arizona pushed the then-18-year-old shortstop up to the Midwest League. And he quickly – very quickly – proved that he couldn't handle the much older pitching. In 20 games with Kane County, the 5-foot-9, 168-pound switch-hitter batted a putrid .113/.169/.127 with just one extra-base hit in 79 plate appearances – a triple-slash line worth of a demotion to short-season ball. And here's the kicker: Alcantara strung together a .253/.314/.327 triple-slash line with Hillsboro, further cementing that he wasn't close to being ready for full-season action.

**Projection**: After remarking how Alcantara's patience was his sole savior during his first two professional seasons, the teenage shortstop's walk rate regressed back down to the league average as he faced better pitching. He hasn't shown any type of pop, not a whole lot of speed, and a (still) underwhelming hit tool. He is still only going to be 19 next season, but he doesn't look worth the $700,000 bonus he was signed to as a 16-year-old.

**Ceiling:** 1.0-win player
**Risk:** Moderate
**MLB ETA:** 2019

## 25. Taylor Clarke, RHP

MiLB Rank: #N/A
Position Rank: N/A

| Born: 07/10/96 | Age: 19 | Bats: B | Top CALs: N/A |
|---|---|---|---|
| Height: 5-9 | Weight: 168 | Throws: R | |

| YEAR | Age | Level | IP | W | L | ERA | FIP | K/9 | BB/9 | K% | BB% | HR/9 | LOB% |
|---|---|---|---|---|---|---|---|---|---|---|---|---|---|
| 2015 | 22 | A- | 21.0 | 0 | 0 | 0.00 | 1.74 | 11.57 | 1.71 | 36.0% | 5.3% | 0.00 | 100.0% |

**Background:** A third round pick out of the College of Charleston last season, Clarke was as dominant as *any incoming minor leaguer in the history of the game.* Period. Bar none. No argument. In 21.0 innings with Hillsboro, the 6-foot-4 right-hander posted a 27-to-4 strikeout-to-walk ratio without surrendering a run.

**Projection**: No matter what he turns out to be, it's literally going to be all downhill from here. Clarke, who was the highest player selected out of the College of Charleston, missed the majority of the 2013 season because of Tommy John surgery. He was incredibly dominant during his final year in college, posting 143-to-14 strikeout-to-walk ratio. Certainly a name to keep an eye on moving forward.

**Ceiling:** 1.0-win player
**Risk:** Moderate
**MLB ETA:** 2019

### *Barely Missed:*

- **J.R. Bradley, RHP** – Once problematic control seemed to clear up for the then-23-year-old right-hander working in High Class A. The former second round pick out Nitro High School – how badass is that name? – posted a 42-to-3 strikeout-to-walk ratio in 34.2 innings. He promptly walked five in eight innings after his promotion to Mobile.

- **Henry Castillo, 2B/SS** – Switch-hitting middle infielder out of Dominican Republic batted a respectable .315/.333/.429 with Kane County last season.  Not a whole lot of pop or speed, so the batting average will need to carry him every year.

- **Victor Reyes, OF** – Switch-hitting outfielder hit .311/.343/.389 with 17 doubles, five triples, two homeruns, and 13 stolen bases. Solid enough production, except that it was a repeat of Low Class A.

- **Jack Reinheimer, 2B/SS** – Pretty much a poor man's version of Matt Duffy, which, unfortunately, means he's going to be bench fodder/utility guy/minor league vagabond – something that CAL agrees with by comparing him to Cristhian Adames, Justin Sellers, Tyler Filliben, Reegie Corona, and Marcus Lemon. The problem for the former ECU infielder is his inability to drive the ball; he's sporting a career. 079 Isolated Power.

## *Bird Doggin' It – Additional Prospects to Keep an Eye in 2016*

| Player | Age | POS | Notes |
|--------|-----|-----|-------|
| Anfernee Benitez | 20 | RHP | Panamanian-born right-hander torched the Pioneer League across 14 starts last season, averaging more than 10.5 punch outs per nine innings. Solid-average control too. |
| Zach Borenstein | 25 | OF | Once-promising sabermetric prospect hasn't struggled in 257 plate appearances in two stints in Class AAA. |
| Colin Bray | 23 | OF | Switch-hitting outfielder batted .308/.370/.410 with hap gap power and plenty of speed in Low Class A. He's a candidate for regression in 2016. |
| Austin Byler | 23 | 1B | Hulking first baseman slugged a mind-boggling 42 extra-base hits in 66 Pioneer League games, including 15 dingers. Let's see how he handles full-season ball. |
| Kevin Cron | 23 | 1B | Younger brother of the Angels' C.J. Cron, Kevin's line looks impressive enough with Visalia – .272/.314/.494 – but he only topped the league average mark by 14%. |
| Todd Glaesmann | 25 | OF | Former 2009 third round pick rediscovered his stick with Reno last season, hitting .286/.327/.551. Don't buy into it. |
| Zach Godley | 26 | RHP | Low 90s fastball is probably better suited for relief work. Fringy big league starter. |
| Brent Jones | 23 | RHP | Former Ivy Leaguer with a big fastball hasn't missed enough bats as a starter in two years in the minors. He's a candidate to move quickly when he gets pushed into a relief role. |
| Jeferson Mejia | 21 | RHP | Posted a 17-to-31 strikeout-to-walk ratio in 34.1 innings with Kane County before getting demoted down to the Northwest League. Big arm. Let's see if he can harness it. |
| Blake Perry | 24 | RHP | 6-foot-5, 190-pound right-hander fanned 131 in 119.1 with Visalia. The problem: he walked 55 in that same span. |
| Stryker Trahan | 22 | C/RF | Former first round pick has as much power as anyone in the minors, but he's swinging Swiss Cheese at the plate. |
| Marcus Wilson | 19 | OF | A 2014 second round pick, Wilson looked overmatched during his debut in the Arizona Summer League as he batted .206/.297/.275. He fared much better in the Pioneer League last season, .258/.357/.338, but it's still not enough. By a long shot. |

**State of the Farm System:** Grab a pen, kids, because this is how you undergo a rebuild. And let's be honest too: it's eerily similar to the Astros' method of deal everything that isn't nailed down theory, which worked out pretty damn good. Here's the talent John Hart and John Coppolella added over the past couple of years: Arodys Vizcaino, Tyrell Jenkins, Shelby Miller, Max Fried, Dustin Peterson, Mallex Smith, Jace Peterson, Manny Banuelos, Nate Hyatt, Ricardo Sanchez, Rio Ruiz, Andrew Thurman, Mike Foltynewicz, Jordan Paroubeck, Cameron Maybin, Matt Wisler, Touki Toussaint, John Gant, Robert Whalen, Zachary Bird, Hector Olivera, Paco Rodriguez, Chris Ellis, Sean Newcomb, Erick Aybar, Aaron Blair, Dansby Swanson, Ender Inciarte, and Casey Kelly.

Now *that's* an incredible infusion of talent.

And, obviously, the coup d'état was the Jason Heyward for Shelby Miller and then immediately flipping the resurgent right-hander for an outfielder who was basically his equal in terms of WAR, a mid rotation arm in Blair and the most recent top pick in the draft. It's actually laughable how well Hart worked the trade wire.

Anyway, Atlanta's farm system is drastically improved, moving up from #26 in 2014 to #15 two years ago and finally settling in at #12 this season. But this is a system deep on depth, not so much on high caliber talent outside of Swanson and maybe Sean Newcomb (if he can improve his control/command) and Kolby Allard.

Otherwise, there are a lot of middle-tier prospects and wild cards.

**Review of the 2015 Draft:** One of the things that always haunted John Hart during his tenure in Cleveland was his inability to cobble together a strong pitching staff to complement his Hall of Fame-laden offense. So Atlanta's done a 180-degree turn and has been snapping up any young arm in the organization's ever-reaching net, including grabbing a couple prep starters in Allard and right-hander Mike Soroka with their first two picks in the opening round last June. Atlanta would also follow that up with two more high school players, Austin Riley, who slugged like the second coming of Babe Ruth in his debut, and backstop Lucas Herbert.

Riley mashed to the tune of .304/.389/.544 with a whopping 14 doubles and 12 homeruns in just 60 games.

Atlanta also did well by adding former Texas A&M hurler A.J. Minter in the second round as well.

The Braves are also equipped with three of the top 44 picks in the 2016, so it wouldn't be surprising to see them add some more high impact players.

| Rank | Name | Age |
|------|------|-----|
| 1 | Dansby Swanson | 21 |
| 2 | Sean Newcomb | 22 |
| 3 | Kolby Allard | 18 |
| 4 | Aaron Blair | 23 |
| 5 | Mallex Smith | 22 |
| 6 | Lucas Sims | 21 |
| 7 | Touki Toussaint | 19 |
| 8 | Austin Riley | 18 |
| 9 | Max Fried | 22 |
| 10 | Rio Ruiz | 21 |
| 11 | Ozhaino Albies | 18 |
| 12 | Mike Soroka | 18 |
| 13 | Chris Ellis | 23 |
| 14 | Zachary Bird | 20 |
| 15 | Hector Olivera | 30 |
| 16 | John Gant | 22 |
| 17 | Braxton Davidson | 19 |
| 18 | Ricardo Sanchez | 18 |
| 19 | Andrew Thurman | 23 |
| 20 | Dustin Peterson | 20 |
| 21 | Manny Banuelos | 24 |
| 22 | Jason Hursh | 23 |
| 23 | Lucas Herbert | 18 |
| 24 | Tyrell Jenkins | 22 |
| 25 | Mauricio Cabrera | 21 |

# 1. Dansby Swanson, SS

**MiLB Rank: #27**
**Position Rank: #4**

| Born: 02/11/94 | Age: 22 | Bats: R | **Top CALs:** Cole Figueroa, Alex Blandino, Dean Anna, Joaquin Rodriguez, Addison Maruszak |
|---|---|---|---|
| Height: 6-0 | Weight: 175 | Throws: R | |

| Season | Age | LVL | PA | 2B | 3B | HR | AVG | OBP | SLG | ISO | BB% | K% | wRC+ |
|---|---|---|---|---|---|---|---|---|---|---|---|---|---|
| 2015 | 21 | A- | 99 | 7 | 3 | 1 | 0.289 | 0.394 | 0.482 | 0.193 | 14.1% | 14.1% | 145 |

**Background:** It was assumed that one-sided deals involving multiple top prospects were a thing of the past – especially with the added emphasis placed on minor leaguers over the past handful of years. The days of Bartolo Colon and Tim Drew for Cliff Lee, Grady Sizemore, Brandon Phillips, and Lee Stevens had supposedly died away like bellbottom jeans. That is, of course, until Atlanta General Manager was able to finagle Swanson, the first pick in the draft last June, former Marshall ace right-hander Aaron Blair, and above-average big league outfielder Ender Inciarte from the Diamondbacks in exchange for a resurgent Shelby Miller and low level lefty reliever Gabe Speier. And just to sort of put this into some perspective – while beating the horse to death – Inciarte was worth about the same number of wins above replacement as Miller according to FanGraphs (3.3 vs. 3.4) and was far better according to Baseball Reference (5.3 vs. 3.6). As long as Inciarte can come close to matching his production from either 2014 *or* 2015 anything else the Braves get out of the deal is purely icing on the cake.

As for Swanson, well, he was simply one of the most dynamic, well-rounded collegiate bats in the entire draft class.

After being limited to barely a dozen at bats at Pitcher U., Swanson had a coming out party for the Commodores in two years. The 6-foot, 175-pound shortstop hit a robust .333/.411/.475 while leading the team in doubles (27), on base percentage (.411), and stolen bases (22). He would also finish tied fourth on the club in homeruns (3) and second in walks (37) and slugging percentage as well. Swanson, of course, followed that up with an even better showing during his junior campaign, hitting .335/.423/.623 with 24 doubles and career highs in triples (6), homeruns (15), and walks (43).

Following his selection as the top pick in the draft, his former organization pushed him down to Hillsboro in the Northwest League for his debut; he batted .289/.390/.482 with seven doubles, a trio of three-baggers, and one homerun.

**Projection**: Here's what I wrote about the quick-twitch middle infielder prior to the draft:

> "Arguably the top collegiate bat in the entire class, Swanson offers up a well-rounded offensive approach – solid plate discipline, hit tool, double-digit homerun power, and speed. He profiles as solid top-of-the-order-type hitter who could border on an All-Star caliber season if everything breaks just the right way, though he'll likely slide into a solid league-average status."

**Ceiling:** 3.5-win player
**Risk:** Moderate
**MLB ETA:** 2017

# 2. Sean Newcomb, LHP

**MiLB Rank: #74**
**Position Rank: N/A**

| Born: 06/12/93 | Age: 23 | Bats: L | **Top CALs:** Shawn Armstrong, Corey Young, Christian Meza, Charlis Burdie, Stephen Johnson |
|---|---|---|---|
| Height: 6-5 | Weight: 245 | Throws: L | |

| YEAR | Age | Level | IP | W | L | ERA | FIP | K/9 | BB/9 | K% | BB% | HR/9 | LOB% |
|---|---|---|---|---|---|---|---|---|---|---|---|---|---|
| 2014 | 21 | R | 3.0 | 0 | 0 | 3.00 | 7.36 | 9.00 | 3.00 | 25.0% | 8.3% | 3.00 | 100.0% |
| 2014 | 21 | A | 11.7 | 0 | 1 | 6.94 | 3.31 | 11.57 | 3.86 | 28.9% | 9.6% | 0.77 | 54.2% |
| 2015 | 22 | A | 34.3 | 1 | 0 | 1.83 | 2.90 | 11.80 | 4.98 | 31.3% | 13.2% | 0.26 | 82.6% |
| 2015 | 22 | A+ | 65.7 | 6 | 1 | 2.47 | 3.17 | 11.51 | 4.52 | 30.0% | 11.8% | 0.27 | 76.4% |
| 2015 | 22 | AA | 36.0 | 2 | 2 | 2.75 | 3.94 | 9.75 | 6.00 | 25.8% | 15.9% | 0.50 | 79.2% |

**Background:** Taking a page out of Jeff Luhnow's mantra of selling everything that isn't nailed down, the Braves dealt away shortstop incumbent Andrelton Simmons, as well as recently acquired Jose Briceno, to the Angels in exchange for Newcomb, the 15th overall pick in the 2014 draft, Erick Aybar, another *new* incumbent, right-hander Chris Ellis. Hailing from the University of Hartford, home to should-be-Hall-of-Famer Jeff Bagwell, Newcomb blew through three different levels last season, making stops with Burlington in the Midwest League, Inland Empire in High Class A, and the Arkansas Travelers in the Texas League. And at each stop Newcomb proved to be a dominant force to be reckoned with – even though he battled some extreme control issues at various times. In 27 combined starts, the 6-foot-5, 245-pound southpaw tallied 136.0 innings with a whopping 168 punch outs, 76 walks, and a barely-there 2.38 ERA.

**Projection**: Here's what I wrote about Newcomb prior to the draft two years ago:

> *"The good news: big bodied lefties with the rare ability to miss an above-average amount of bats are worth their weight in gold – literally. All of that by itself pushed Newcomb well up the draft charts but there are certainly more than a few red flags.*
>
> *First: The forearm injury in 2012. Was that really just an aberration or something more? And one of the key 'signs' – or terms – thrown around right before Tommy John surgery is a forearm injury. Obviously, it's not nearly that serious for Newcomb – he's thrown about 150 innings since – but it still has to be on teams' radars.*
>
> *Second: Level of competition. The Hartford player chosen highest in the draft prior to Newcomb's impending first round status: Jeff Bagwell, fourth round. How is he going to handle competing against vastly superior players than he was [the previous three years]?*
>
> *Third: Control. The control, even in his breakout season [last] year, is still below-average.*
>
> *Fourth: Decline in strikeout rate. After averaging 11.5 K/9 [in 2013], Newcomb averaged 10.26 in 2014.*
>
> *A bit of a first round wild card. The ceiling is certainly high, but so is the risk. A solid #2/#3-type arm, but, again, there's risk. Think of a left-handed version of Allen Webster.*

Most importantly, he's continued to distance himself from his previous forearm injury as he threw a solid amount of innings last season. And just like I mentioned previously, the control is going to be the ultimate determining factor between a mid- to upper-rotation caliber arm and a spot in the pen.

But, man, Newcomb was so dominant last season. Of his 27 starts, consider the following:

- He recorded eight games with at least eight punch outs and another ten games with at least six whiffs.
- He allowed more than two runs on just four occasions and more than three runs just twice.
- He surrendered four or fewer hits 17 times.

Finally, one final tidbit to chew on: Only one other southpaw, Tampa Bay's Blake Snell, fanned a higher percentage of hitters than Newcomb (31.3% vs. 29.2%) last season.

**Ceiling:** 3.0- to 3.5-win player
**Risk:** Moderate to High
**MLB ETA:** 2016/2017

## 3. Kolby Allard, RHP

**MiLB Rank: #127**
**Position Rank: N/A**

| Born: 08/13/97 | Age: 18 | Bats: L | Top CALs: N/A |
|---|---|---|---|
| Height: 6-1 | Weight: 175 | Throws: L | |

| YEAR | Age | Level | IP | W | L | ERA | FIP | K/9 | BB/9 | K% | BB% | HR/9 | LOB% |
|---|---|---|---|---|---|---|---|---|---|---|---|---|---|
| 2015 | 17 | R | 6.0 | 0 | 0 | 0.00 | -0.19 | 18.00 | 0.00 | 60.0% | 0.0% | 0.00 | 100.0% |

**Background:** For the first time since the organization grabbed Steve Avery with the third overall selection in 1988, Atlanta went with a prep southpaw among the draft's top 15 picks, taking Allard with the 14th overall pick. Allard, who underwent back surgery during the offseason, is expected to be ready for Spring Training. He tossed just six innings in rookie ball, fanning 12 without a walk.

**Projection:** There's nothing to go off of – literally. But here are the three games he tossed during his debut:

- 1.0 IP, 1 H, 3 K, 0BB
- 2.0 IP, 1H, 5 K, 0 BB
- 3.0 IP 1, H, 4 K, 0 BB

**Ceiling:** Too Soon to Tell
**Risk:** N/A
**MLB ETA:** N/A

## 4. Aaron Blair, RHP

**MiLB Rank: #138**

**Position Rank: N/A**

| Born: 05/26/92 | Age: 24 | Bats: R | Top CALs: Tanner Roark, Eduardo Morlan, |
|---|---|---|---|
| Height: 6-5 | Weight: 230 | Throws: R | John Gast, Brett Oberholtzer, Rob Rasmussen |

| YEAR | Age | Level | IP | W | L | ERA | FIP | K/9 | BB/9 | K% | BB% | HR/9 | LOB% |
|---|---|---|---|---|---|---|---|---|---|---|---|---|---|
| 2013 | 21 | A- | 31.0 | 1 | 1 | 2.90 | 3.80 | 8.13 | 3.77 | 22.1% | 10.2% | 0.58 | 80.7% |
| 2013 | 21 | A | 17.7 | 0 | 2 | 3.57 | 2.72 | 6.62 | 2.04 | 17.1% | 5.3% | 0.00 | 58.3% |
| 2014 | 22 | A | 35.7 | 1 | 2 | 4.04 | 3.01 | 11.10 | 3.53 | 29.3% | 9.3% | 0.50 | 56.5% |
| 2014 | 22 | A+ | 72.3 | 4 | 2 | 4.35 | 3.87 | 10.08 | 2.61 | 25.9% | 6.7% | 0.75 | 69.1% |
| 2014 | 22 | AA | 46.3 | 4 | 1 | 1.94 | 3.49 | 8.94 | 3.11 | 25.3% | 8.8% | 0.78 | 87.3% |
| 2015 | 23 | AA | 83.3 | 6 | 3 | 2.70 | 3.95 | 6.91 | 2.48 | 19.3% | 6.9% | 0.86 | 80.2% |
| 2015 | 23 | AAA | 77.0 | 7 | 2 | 3.16 | 4.08 | 6.55 | 3.16 | 17.7% | 8.5% | 0.58 | 72.7% |

**Background:** Also part of the franchise's bloated package it received in the Shelby Miller deal with Arizona. Blair, the 36th overall pick out of Marshall University in 2013, spent last season fine-tuning his approach on the mound, as well as biding his time until forcing his way onto a big league roster. Making 26 appearances, 25 of which were starts, the 6-foot-5, 230-pound hurler fanned 120, walked 50, and posted an aggregate 2.92 ERA. For his three-year professional career, Blair has struck out 22.2% and walked 7.9% of the batters he's faced throughout his career.

**Projection**: I've always been a particularly big fan since the right-hander's collegiate days. Here's what I wrote prior to the 2013 draft:

> "There is some concern that while Blair's ability to miss bats has improved during the past two seasons, his control has failed to do the same, basically remaining average-ish. He profiles as a decent option in a big league rotation with a ceiling as a #3 [starting pitcher] and a floor as a #5 [arm]."

After blowing away the Midwest, California, and Southern Leagues in his fast-tracked 2014 season, Blair's strikeout percentage dropped from a dominant 26.5% to a more average-ish 18.5% between Class AA and Class AAA in 2015. The decline is a bit worrisome, but not enough where he still doesn't profile as a solid backend arm. The control has continued to hover around the 3.0 BB/9-mark.

**Ceiling:** 2.0-win player
**Risk:** Moderate
**MLB ETA:** 2016

## 5. Mallex Smith, CF

**MiLB Rank: #152**

**Position Rank: N/A**

| Born: 05/06/93 | Age: 23 | Bats: L | Top CALs: L.J Hoes, Brett Gardner, |
|---|---|---|---|
| Height: 5-9 | Weight: 170 | Throws: R | John Andreoli, Jacoby Ellsbury, Dalton Pompey |

| Season | Age | LVL | PA | 2B | 3B | HR | AVG | OBP | SLG | ISO | BB% | K% | wRC+ |
|---|---|---|---|---|---|---|---|---|---|---|---|---|---|
| 2013 | 20 | A | 507 | 17 | 2 | 4 | 0.262 | 0.367 | 0.340 | 0.078 | 11.6% | 16.6% | 108 |
| 2014 | 21 | A | 303 | 13 | 6 | 0 | 0.295 | 0.393 | 0.394 | 0.098 | 12.5% | 18.2% | 131 |
| 2014 | 21 | A+ | 261 | 16 | 1 | 5 | 0.327 | 0.414 | 0.475 | 0.148 | 11.9% | 18.4% | 138 |
| 2015 | 22 | AA | 240 | 5 | 2 | 2 | 0.340 | 0.418 | 0.413 | 0.073 | 11.3% | 17.1% | 140 |
| 2015 | 22 | AAA | 307 | 12 | 6 | 0 | 0.281 | 0.339 | 0.367 | 0.086 | 7.8% | 14.3% | 106 |

**Background:** After speedster Billy Hamilton made it to the big leagues a couple seasons ago it was Smith, a fifth rounder out of Santa Fe Community College, who quickly ascended atop the list of fastest minor leaguers. Smith, a 5-foot-9, 170-pound center fielder, was acquired last offseason as part of the Justin Upton mega-deal with San Diego. The speedy outfielder strung together his best showing at level in his professional career in the first half of 2015, hitting .340/.418/.413 with five doubles, a pair of triples, two homeruns, and 23 stolen bases en route to topping the league average production line by 40%. His numbers took a bit of a dip once he got promoted up to the International League as he posted a league average-ish .281/.339/.367 with 12 doubles, six triples, and 34 stolen bases. Overall, he batted .306/.373/.386 with 17 doubles, eight triples, two homeruns, and 57 stolen bases (in 70 attempts).

**Projection:** Per the typical for a speedy center fielder, just like Billy Hamilton, Smith has nonexistent power; his career ISO is .092 and he's never slugged more than five homeruns in a single season. And it's no surprise that his walk rate tumbled from double-digit territory all the way down to 7.8% in Class AAA last season. CAL, however, seems to be a big fan, comparing him to Brett Gardner, Jacoby Ellsbury, and Dalton Pompey. If Smith's defense proves to be as valuable as it seems, he should have no trouble topping the two-win mark.

**Ceiling:** 2.5-win player
**Risk:** Moderate to High
**MLB ETA:** 2016

## 6. Touki Toussaint, RHP

**MiLB Rank: #174**

**Position Rank: N/A**

| Born: 06/20/96 | Age: 20 | Bats: R | **Top CALs:** Felix Sterling, Clevelan Santeliz, |
|---|---|---|---|
| Height: 6-3 | Weight: 185 | Throws: R | Alberto Cabrera, Tyler Vail, Luis Heredia |

| YEAR | Age | Level | IP | W | L | ERA | FIP | K/9 | BB/9 | K% | BB% | HR/9 | LOB% |
|---|---|---|---|---|---|---|---|---|---|---|---|---|---|
| 2014 | 18 | R | 13.7 | 1 | 3 | 12.51 | 8.35 | 9.88 | 3.95 | 20.6% | 8.2% | 3.29 | 40.0% |
| 2014 | 18 | R | 15.0 | 1 | 1 | 4.80 | 4.56 | 10.20 | 7.20 | 23.0% | 16.2% | 0.00 | 57.1% |
| 2015 | 19 | A | 48.7 | 3 | 5 | 5.73 | 5.74 | 7.03 | 6.10 | 17.7% | 15.4% | 1.11 | 63.6% |
| 2015 | 19 | A | 39.0 | 2 | 2 | 3.69 | 4.55 | 6.69 | 3.46 | 18.0% | 9.3% | 0.92 | 68.4% |

**Background**: Packaged along with aging – and injured – veteran Bronson Arroyo as part of salary dump that sent career minor league infielder Philip Gosselin to Arizona in late June. Diamondbacks General Manager Dave Stewart (in)famously said, according to an AZCentral report following the trade, that Toussaint "hasn't thrown 96 mph since he's been here." Esteemed reporter Ken Rosenthal followed that up a week later by writing that the 16th overall selection in 2014 touched 98 mph in a start for the Rome Braves. Oops. Between the organizations, as well as two different Low Class A leagues, the 6-foot-3, 185-pound right-hander posted a mediocre 67-to-48 strikeout-to-walk ratio in 87.2 innings of work.

**Projection**: Now to be completely fair to the former Oakland-A's-ace-turned-GM, Toussaint has hardly lived up to the expectations that follow a high first round selection. So far he's walked 12.6% of the total batters he's faced in his brief career, including issuing free passes to more than 15% of the guys he faced in the Atlanta organization. And perhaps as equally troublesome, the wiry right-hander's swing-and-miss total plummeted after a strong debut showing. He's still clearly young enough – he's only entering his age-20 season – to figure it out. Plus, there aren't too many hurlers his age that can nearly dial it up to triple digits. One final thought: he might be another Chris Archer dark horse type arm.

**Ceiling:** 2.0- to 2.5-win player
**Risk:** Moderate to High
**MLB ETA:** 2019

## 6. Lucas Sims, RHP

**MiLB Rank: #178**

**Position Rank: N/A**

| Born: 05/10/94 | Age: 22 | Bats: R | **Top CALs:** Ryan Searle, Dan Cortes, |
|---|---|---|---|
| Height: 6-2 | Weight: 225 | Throws: R | Phillippe Aumont, Mauricio Cabrera, Richard Castillo |

| YEAR | Age | Level | IP | W | L | ERA | FIP | K/9 | BB/9 | K% | BB% | HR/9 | LOB% |
|---|---|---|---|---|---|---|---|---|---|---|---|---|---|
| 2013 | 19 | A | 116.7 | 12 | 4 | 2.62 | 3.09 | 10.34 | 3.55 | 27.9% | 9.6% | 0.23 | 71.5% |
| 2014 | 20 | A+ | 156.7 | 8 | 11 | 4.19 | 4.56 | 6.15 | 3.27 | 15.8% | 8.4% | 0.69 | 68.4% |
| 2015 | 21 | R | 5.0 | 0 | 0 | 9.00 | 2.91 | 12.60 | 3.60 | 26.9% | 7.7% | 0.00 | 36.4% |
| 2015 | 21 | A+ | 40.0 | 3 | 4 | 5.18 | 4.01 | 8.33 | 5.18 | 20.7% | 12.9% | 0.45 | 61.1% |
| 2015 | 21 | AA | 47.7 | 4 | 2 | 3.21 | 3.30 | 10.57 | 5.48 | 28.1% | 14.6% | 0.19 | 72.6% |

**Background:** The former 21st overall pick in the 2012 draft continued his Jekyll-and-Hyde development curve last season. After a dominant debut between the Appalachian and Gulf Coast Leagues last season, he upped the ante during his follow-up campaign with Rome in 2013. As a 19-year-old Sims posted a 134-to-46 strikeout-to-walk ratio in 116.2 innings in the Sally. The organization continued to challenge the young hurler, promoting him up to Lynchburg in 2014, and Sims saw a noticeable decline in his punch out rate; it dropped from 10.3 K/9 to a worrisome 6.2 K/9. Then just like that…he started missing a ton of bats in 2015. Sims fanned 37 in 40.0 innings back in High Class A and another 56 in 47.2 innings of work with Mississippi in the second half. Of course, this time his control abandoned him as he walked a career worst 5.2 every nine innings.

**Projection**: In last year's book I highlighted how Sims' production suffered during his first 16 starts but rebounded nicely over his remaining 12 games two years ago, giving hope that 2015 would be much more successful. And it was – sort of. Sims' strikeout rate spiked back to above-average levels, but it was his control giving him all kinds of fits. But, again, he had glimpses of pure dominance at various points: He fanned 10 and walked a pair in six innings against Pensacola in late August or his mid-July contest against the Winston-Salem Dash where he fanned eight and walked one in six innings or his seven-inning game against Jacksonville where he posted a seven-to-one strikeout-to-walk ratio. Then on the other end of the spectrum he had seven games where he walked at least four.

And just like the previous season things seemed to click for Sims down the stretch; he walked 12 and fanned 33 over his final 30.2 innings.

Sims is still plenty young enough to put it all together. And if that ever happens, watch out.

**Ceiling:** 2.0- to 2.5-win player
**Risk:** Moderate to High
**MLB ETA:** 2017

## 8. Austin Riley, 3B

**MiLB Rank: #180**

**Position Rank: #9**

| Born: 04/02/97 | Age: 19 | Bats: R | Top CALs: Amaurys Minier, Oswaldo Morales, |
|---|---|---|---|
| Height: 6-2 | Weight: 230 | Throws: R | Miguel Sano, Jharmidy De Jesus, Zachary Green |

| Season | Age | LVL | PA | 2B | 3B | HR | AVG | OBP | SLG | ISO | BB% | K% | wRC+ |
|---|---|---|---|---|---|---|---|---|---|---|---|---|---|
| 2015 | 18 | R | 131 | 9 | 1 | 5 | 0.351 | 0.443 | 0.586 | 0.234 | 10.7% | 21.4% | 182 |
| 2015 | 18 | R | 121 | 5 | 0 | 7 | 0.255 | 0.331 | 0.500 | 0.245 | 9.9% | 30.6% | 146 |

**Background:** The third first round selection of the John Hart Era, Riley's professional career got off to a torrid start last season. He batted .255/.331/.500 in 30 games in the Gulf Coast League. Then he caught fire and torched the Appalachian league for another 30 contests. Overall, he hit an aggregate .304/.389/.544 with 14 doubles and a mind-boggling 12 long-balls in just 60 games.

**Projection:** Granted it's a rather limited sample size, just 60 games, but Riley was on pace to slug 32 homeruns over a 162-game season. The power, needless to say, looks like an above-average, perhaps even better, skill. He walked a solid amount of the time and his red flag-territory K-rate in the GCL declined all the way down to 21.4% in the Appalachian League. Let's see how he handles the Sally.

**Ceiling:** Too Soon to Tell
**Risk:** N/A
**MLB ETA:** N/A

## 9. Max Fried, LHP

**MiLB Rank: #199**

**Position Rank: N/A**

| Born: 01/18/94 | Age: 21 | Bats: L | Top CALs: N/A |
|---|---|---|---|
| Height: 6-4 | Weight: 170 | Throws: L | |

| YEAR | Age | Level | IP | W | L | ERA | FIP | K/9 | BB/9 | K% | BB% | HR/9 | LOB% |
|---|---|---|---|---|---|---|---|---|---|---|---|---|---|
| 2013 | 19 | A | 118.7 | 6 | 7 | 3.49 | 4.04 | 7.58 | 4.25 | 20.0% | 11.2% | 0.53 | 72.6% |
| 2014 | 20 | R | 5.0 | 0 | 0 | 5.40 | 2.63 | 14.40 | 5.40 | 30.8% | 11.5% | 0.00 | 72.7% |
| 2014 | 20 | A | 5.7 | 0 | 1 | 4.76 | 6.13 | 3.18 | 3.18 | 8.3% | 8.3% | 1.59 | 79.0% |

**Background:** Teaming with arguably the most dominant right-hander in the minor leagues, Lucas Giolito, during their tenure at Harvard-Westlake High School, Fried missed the entire 2015 recovering from Tommy John surgery, though that didn't stop John Hart from acquiring him from San Diego as part of the package for Justin Upton on December 19th, 2014.

**Projection:** First things first: After going down on July 21st, 2014, Fried should – barring any massive setbacks – be ready to resume his professional career in Spring Training. The last extended time we saw of the 6-foot-4, 170-pound southpaw he was handling himself well enough as a 19-year-old in the Midwest League. Hopefully, he comes back all the way.

**Ceiling:** Too Soon to Tell
**Risk:** N/A
**MLB ETA:** N/A

## 10. Rio Ruiz, 3B

**MiLB Rank: #228**

**Position Rank: N/A**

| Born: 05/22/94 | Age: 22 | Bats: L | Top CALs: Dante Bichette, Jefry Marte, |
|---|---|---|---|
| Height: 6-2 | Weight: 215 | Throws: R | Daniel Mateo, Matthew Cerda, Jonathan Meyer |

| Season | Age | LVL | PA | 2B | 3B | HR | AVG | OBP | SLG | ISO | BB% | K% | wRC+ |
|---|---|---|---|---|---|---|---|---|---|---|---|---|---|
| 2013 | 19 | A | 472 | 33 | 1 | 12 | 0.260 | 0.335 | 0.430 | 0.171 | 10.6% | 19.5% | 115 |
| 2014 | 20 | A+ | 602 | 37 | 2 | 11 | 0.293 | 0.387 | 0.436 | 0.143 | 13.6% | 15.1% | 119 |
| 2015 | 21 | AA | 489 | 21 | 1 | 5 | 0.233 | 0.333 | 0.324 | 0.090 | 12.9% | 19.2% | 91 |

**Background:** Keeping with the general theme of the franchise's write-up thus far, the Braves – you've guessed it – acquired the former fourth round Bonus Baby along with fire-balling right-hander Mike Foltynewicz, and Andrew Thurman in exchange for Evan Gattis and James Hoyt in a deal with Houston last January. The lefty-swinging third baseman, however, had a rough go of it as he moved in Class AA for the first – and not only – time in his professional career. Coming off of two back-to-back solid seasons against much older competition, Ruiz looked ill-equipped in the Southern League, hitting a paltry .233/.333/.324 with just 21 doubles, one triple, and five homeruns in 489 plate appearances. For his career, Ruiz is sporting a .263/.353/.399 triple-slash line.

**Projection**: A lot of Ruiz's basic skill set translated well into the minors' most challenging level: he walked in nearly 13% of his plate appearances; his K-rate was nearly identical to his 2013 season (19.2% vs. 19.5%), and his BABIP dipped a little bit but nothing to severe (.288). The main culprit appears to be his nosedive in the power department; after posted Isolated Power totals of .143 and .171 in High Class A and Low Class A the past two seasons, Ruiz cobbled together a slap-hitting .090 last season. He still looks like a capable #5/#6-type bat.

**Ceiling:** 1.5- to 2.0-win player
**Risk:** Moderate
**MLB ETA:** 2017

## 11. Ozhaino Albies, SS

**MiLB Rank: #244**
**Position Rank: N/A**

| Born: 01/07/97 | Age: 19 | Bats: B |
|---|---|---|
| Height: 5-9 | Weight: 150 | Throws: R |

**Top CALs:** Odubel Herrera, Kike Hernandez, Joseph Rosa, Abiatal Avelino, Manuel Guzman

| Season | Age | LVL | PA | 2B | 3B | HR | AVG | OBP | SLG | ISO | BB% | K% | wRC+ |
|---|---|---|---|---|---|---|---|---|---|---|---|---|---|
| 2014 | 17 | R | 161 | 4 | 3 | 1 | 0.356 | 0.429 | 0.452 | 0.096 | 10.6% | 10.6% | 156 |
| 2015 | 18 | A | 439 | 21 | 8 | 0 | 0.310 | 0.368 | 0.404 | 0.094 | 8.2% | 12.8% | 122 |

**Background:** Albies burst onto the scene two years ago by robustly hitting .364/.446/.444 as a 17-year-old between both rookie leagues. And he followed that up with another strong showing in the Sally last season, hitting .310/.368/.404. For those counting at home, Albies has cobbled together a .328/.395/.417 triple-slash line through his first 155 professional games – against much older competition.

**Projection**: Now that we have that out of the way. Here's what I really want to say: Welcome to one of the most overrated, overhyped prospects found anywhere, in any organization, on any planet. While it's true that his *Weighted Runs Created Plus* totals are astounding – he topped the league mark by about 60% two years ago and then followed that up with a 22% showing in 2015 – Albies is an extremely limited prospect. His power is nonexistent – he's slugged one homerun in his first 155 games – and his 5-foot-9, 150-pound frame doesn't offer up a whole lot of projection. His average-ish eye is also likely to decline as more advanced hitters challenge him as he moves up the ladder. He's going to end up sliding into a super-sub role unless his defense proves to be spectacular.

**Ceiling:** 1.5-win player
**Risk:** Moderate
**MLB ETA:** 2018

## 12. Mike Soroka, RHP

**MiLB Rank: #N/A**
**Position Rank: N/A**

| Born: 08/04/97 | Age: 18 | Bats: R |
|---|---|---|
| Height: 6-4 | Weight: 195 | Throws: R |

**Top CALs:** Genesis Cabrera, Jeremy Gabryszwski, Tyler Skaggs, Jesse Beal, Robert Whalen

| YEAR | Age | Level | IP | W | L | ERA | FIP | K/9 | BB/9 | K% | BB% | HR/9 | LOB% |
|---|---|---|---|---|---|---|---|---|---|---|---|---|---|
| 2015 | 17 | R | 24.0 | 0 | 2 | 3.75 | 2.10 | 9.75 | 1.50 | 24.8% | 3.8% | 0.00 | 64.7% |
| 2015 | 17 | R | 10.0 | 0 | 0 | 1.80 | 2.01 | 9.90 | 0.90 | 29.0% | 2.6% | 0.00 | 75.0% |

**Background:** Sandwiched between the club's other two first round selections, lefty Kolby Allard and third baseman Austin Riley, Soroka, like his two first round mates, had a surprisingly strong debut showing last season. Throwing 34.0 innings between the Gulf Coast and Appalachian Leagues, the 6-foot-4, 195-pound right-hander fanned 37 and walked just five.

**Projection**: He did everything you would want a high prep arm to do in his professional debut: Soroka made successful stops at multiple levels; he fanned more than a bat per inning; and he was like Scrooge when it came to issuing free passes. The best part: because of his late birthday he'll be entering his age-18, one in which he should spend as the one of the youngest players in any Low Class A in 2016.

**Ceiling:** 1.5- to 2.0-win player
**Risk:** Moderate to High
**MLB ETA:** 2017

## 13. Chris Ellis, RHP

**MiLB Rank: #N/A**
**Position Rank: N/A**

| Born: 09/22/92 | Age: 23 | Bats: R | **Top CALs:** Camilo Vasquez, John Gast, |
| Height: 6-4 | Weight: 220 | Throws: R | Robin Leyer, Tyson Ross, Jeremy Bleich |

| YEAR | Age | Level | IP | W | L | ERA | FIP | K/9 | BB/9 | K% | BB% | HR/9 | LOB% |
|------|-----|-------|------|---|---|------|------|-------|------|------|------|------|------|
| 2014 | 21 | R | 15.7 | 0 | 1 | 6.89 | 5.56 | 9.19 | 4.60 | 24.6% | 12.3% | 1.15 | 62.0% |
| 2015 | 22 | A+ | 62.7 | 4 | 5 | 3.88 | 3.79 | 10.05 | 2.87 | 27.0% | 7.7% | 0.86 | 71.7% |
| 2015 | 22 | AA | 78.0 | 7 | 4 | 3.92 | 4.98 | 7.15 | 4.96 | 17.9% | 12.4% | 1.04 | 73.4% |

**Background:** Acquired along with Sean Newcomb as part of the Andrelton Simmons deal with the Halos of Anaheim. Ellis was one of the bigger surprises of the first half last season, averaging a smidgeon over 10 punch outs and under 3.0 free passes per nine innings with Inland Empire in the California League. After the trade Atlanta sent Ellis to Class AA where his strikeout rate tumbled and control issues spiked.

**Projection**: Here's what I wrote about Ellis prior to the draft two years ago:

*"A lesser version of Ole' Miss' ace from [2013], Bobby Wahl, who was a fifth round pick by Oakland, Ellis hasn't missed a whole lot of bats since his freshman season. And while the control is a tangible, repeatable skill, it's not enough to compensate for his inability to miss bats. With that being said, there is some rotational upside."*

I continued,

*"Ellis has made just 16 starts with Ole Miss, 13 of which have come this season. And, again, he missed the majority of last year too. He's probably going to get two, maybe three seasons in the minors to prove he can stick in the rotation. If not, the arsenal definitely plays up in the pen."*

Well, he certainly proved that he could hack it in the High Class A rotation. But his control really abandoned him upon his promotion to Class AA. In a span of 42 innings he walked 31 hitters beginning in late June. Let's see how he handles the Texas League a second time through.

**Ceiling:** 1.5- to 2.0-win player
**Risk:** Moderate to High
**MLB ETA:** 2016/2017

## 14. Zachary Bird, RHP

**MiLB Rank: #N/A**
**Position Rank: N/A**

| Born: 07/14/94 | Age: 21 | Bats: R | **Top CALs:** Wilmer Font, Josh Hader, |
| Height: 6-4 | Weight: 205 | Throws: R | Zachary Fuesser, Nick Travieso, Chad James |

| YEAR | Age | Level | IP | W | L | ERA | FIP | K/9 | BB/9 | K% | BB% | HR/9 | LOB% |
|------|-----|-------|-------|---|----|------|------|------|------|-------|-------|------|-------|
| 2013 | 18 | R | 43.7 | 2 | 4 | 5.77 | 4.55 | 9.07 | 3.92 | 22.1% | 9.6% | 0.62 | 58.3% |
| 2013 | 18 | A | 60.0 | 2 | 5 | 5.10 | 5.11 | 7.50 | 6.75 | 18.0% | 16.2% | 0.75 | 67.7% |
| 2014 | 19 | A | 118.7 | 6 | 17 | 4.25 | 4.13 | 8.34 | 4.17 | 21.0% | 10.5% | 0.68 | 68.3% |
| 2015 | 20 | A+ | 89.0 | 5 | 7 | 4.75 | 4.24 | 9.61 | 4.85 | 24.7% | 12.5% | 0.61 | 62.6% |
| 2015 | 20 | AA | 12.7 | 1 | 1 | 4.26 | 4.88 | 5.68 | 8.53 | 14.6% | 21.8% | 0.00 | 70.0% |

**Background:** Just another young, promising arm acquired within the last year to help bolster a sagging system. The Braves, Marlins, and Dodgers got together for a mega 12-man (and one competitive balance pick) deal at the end of July. The abbreviated version: Atlanta shipped out Alex Wood, Jose Peraza, Bronson Arroyo, Luis Avilan, and Jim Johnson and received Bird, Hector Olivera, Paco Rodriguez, and a 2016 competitive balance round A pick. Once all the dust settled, Atlanta sent Bird, a lean 6-foot-4 right-hander out of Murrah High School, to the Southern League for three starts before shutting him down for the season. In totality, Bird tossed 101.2 innings while fanning 103 and walking 60.

**Projection**: Last year I ranked Bird as the Dodgers' #15 prospect, writing:

*"[He's] a wild card brewing in the lower levels for the Dodgers. Despite being in the organization for parts of the three seasons now, Bird's just entering his age-20 season, one in which would be spent in High Class A presumably. Left-handers feasted off of him last year (.288/.377/.441) and the control still has ways to go. Bird looks like fringy starter/potential late-inning reliever."*

Well, Bird seemingly solved left-handers, or at least more often than he has in the past, as he limited them to a .241/.340/.371 triple-slash line – a stark improvement over his previous two seasons. His control/command, on the other hand, continues to linger in the well below-average territory – just as it has for the previous three seasons. He's still only entering his age-21 season and already has a brief taste of Class AA experience. But he's going to need to showing he can hit the strike zone with some type of frequency.

**Ceiling:** 1.5-win player
**Risk:** Moderate
**MLB ETA:** 2017

## 15. Hector Olivera, 2B/3B

**MiLB Rank: #N/A**
**Position Rank: N/A**

| Born: 04/05/85 | Age: 31 | Bats: R | Top CALs: N/A |
|---|---|---|---|
| Height: 6-2 | Weight: 220 | Throws: R | |

| Season | Age | LVL | PA | 2B | 3B | HR | AVG | OBP | SLG | ISO | BB% | K% | wRC+ |
|---|---|---|---|---|---|---|---|---|---|---|---|---|---|
| 2015 | 30 | R | 18 | 1 | 0 | 0 | 0.313 | 0.389 | 0.375 | 0.063 | 11.1% | 5.6% | 129 |
| 2015 | 30 | AA | 25 | 0 | 0 | 1 | 0.318 | 0.400 | 0.455 | 0.136 | 12.0% | 20.0% | 144 |
| 2015 | 30 | AAA | 31 | 1 | 1 | 1 | 0.387 | 0.387 | 0.581 | 0.194 | 0.0% | 9.7% | 158 |
| 2015 | 30 | R | 5 | 0 | 0 | 0 | 0.000 | 0.000 | 0.000 | 0.000 | 0.0% | 20.0% | -100 |
| 2015 | 30 | A | 14 | 0 | 0 | 0 | 0.083 | 0.214 | 0.083 | 0.000 | 14.3% | 7.1% | 0 |
| 2015 | 30 | AAA | 42 | 3 | 0 | 0 | 0.231 | 0.286 | 0.308 | 0.077 | 4.8% | 9.5% | 72 |
| 2015 | 30 | MLB | 87 | 4 | 1 | 2 | 0.253 | 0.310 | 0.405 | 0.152 | 5.7% | 13.8% | 97 |

**Background:** The centerpiece of the club's three-team deal involving the Marlins and Dodgers, the Cuban-born infielder bounced around *a lot* during his initial taste of stateside leagues last season. For those keeping track at home he made appearances in: the Arizona Summer League, Gulf Coast League, Sally, Texas League, International League, PCL, and finally appearing in 24 games in Atlanta. Between all those minor league stops Olivera hit a mediocre .272/.326/.376. The soon-to-be 31-year-old is sporting a career .323/.407/.505 in 10 seasons in the Cuban National Series.

**Projection:** One year into his US-career and there's very little data to go on. He accrued just over 200 plate appearances between his time in the minors and Atlanta. And none of it is all that impressive either. The power looks average, the hit tool a bit underwhelming, and he didn't appear to be all that eager to take a free pass. Add in the fact that he's entering his age-21 season, and it's safe to say he doesn't look like more than a fringy big league regular.

**Ceiling:** 1.5-win player
**Risk:** Moderate
**MLB ETA:** Debuted in 2015

## 16. John Gant, RHP

**MiLB Rank: #N/A**
**Position Rank: N/A**

| Born: 08/06/92 | Age: 23 | Bats: R | Top CALs: Maikel Cleto, Aaron Blair, |
|---|---|---|---|
| Height: 6-5 | Weight: 205 | Throws: R | Johnny Barbato, Ronnie Martinez, Kevin Vance |

| YEAR | Age | Level | IP | W | L | ERA | FIP | K/9 | BB/9 | K% | BB% | HR/9 | LOB% |
|---|---|---|---|---|---|---|---|---|---|---|---|---|---|
| 2013 | 20 | A- | 71.7 | 6 | 4 | 2.89 | 2.40 | 10.17 | 3.52 | 27.7% | 9.6% | 0.13 | 66.2% |
| 2014 | 21 | A | 123.0 | 11 | 5 | 2.56 | 3.31 | 8.34 | 2.93 | 22.4% | 7.8% | 0.37 | 72.0% |
| 2015 | 22 | A+ | 40.3 | 2 | 0 | 1.79 | 2.89 | 10.71 | 2.23 | 29.6% | 6.2% | 0.89 | 89.5% |
| 2015 | 22 | AA | 59.3 | 4 | 5 | 4.70 | 3.62 | 6.52 | 3.94 | 16.2% | 9.8% | 0.30 | 61.4% |
| 2015 | 22 | AA | 40.7 | 4 | 0 | 1.99 | 2.54 | 9.52 | 3.10 | 27.4% | 8.9% | 0.22 | 76.4% |

**Background:** Yet another arm Hart Trading Co. have acquired in the last 12 or so months. Gant, who was dealt from the Mets along with Rob Whalen in exchange for Juan Uribe and Kelly Johnson, dominated the Florida State League for six starts though that was after he got demoted after struggling mightily in the Eastern League. After he got bounced back up he posted a 62-to-19 strikeout-to-walk ratio in 64.0 innings.

**Projection:** Underrated. The 6-foot-5, 205-pound right-hander has a huge supporter in CAL. The formulas compare him to new organization-mate Aaron Blair, hard-throwing Johnny Barbato, and the enigmatic but oh-so-talented Maikel Cleto. Gant has a long history of missing bats with solid-average control. The seven starts at the beginning of the season were nothing more than a blip on the radar. He has a chance to develop into a #4/#5-type arm.

**Ceiling:** 1.0- to 1.5-win player
**Risk:** Low to Moderate
**MLB ETA:** 2016/2017

## 17. Braxton Davidson, LF/RF

MiLB Rank: #N/A
Position Rank: N/A

| | | | | |
|---|---|---|---|---|
| Born: 06/18/96 | Age: 20 | Bats: L | **Top CALs:** Charles Jones, Richard Pena, Brandon Nimmo, Edison Sanchez, David Denson | |
| Height: 6-2 | Weight: 210 | Throws: L | | |

| Season | Age | LVL | PA | 2B | 3B | HR | AVG | OBP | SLG | ISO | BB% | K% | wRC+ |
|---|---|---|---|---|---|---|---|---|---|---|---|---|---|
| 2014 | 18 | R | 140 | 7 | 1 | 0 | 0.243 | 0.400 | 0.324 | 0.081 | 15.7% | 22.9% | 124 |
| 2015 | 19 | A | 494 | 23 | 0 | 10 | 0.242 | 0.381 | 0.374 | 0.132 | 17.0% | 27.3% | 122 |

**Background:** The last first round pick of the Frank Wren regime, Davidson rode an ungodly walk rate during his debut in the Gulf Coast League last season en route to topping the league average mark by 24%, despite batting an unimpressive .243/.400/.342.

The front office bumped him up to the more advanced rookie level, the Appalachian League, and the 32nd overall pick looked completely overmatched as he went 6-for-36. But despite a lowly triple-slash line during his debut, John Hart & Co. decided that Davidson was ready for the South Atlantic League – at the ripe age of 19. And for the most part he rewarded their faith. In 124 games with Rome last season, Davidson batted .242/.381/.374 as he posted another unearthly walk rate, 17.0%, en route to topping the league average production mark by 22%.

**Projection**: It's tough to get an accurate read on the 6-foot-2, 210-pound corner outfielder. On one hand, he's now put together back-to-back showings where he's topped the league average mark by more than 20% *and* his power took a nice step forward. But on the other hand, his overall toolkit leaves a lot to be desired, particularly his bat.

He did have a nice 54-game stretch from May through the end of June where he batted .281/.417/.411 so that offers up some home that his first month was an adjustment period and the final couple months of pathetic production could be due from the teenager simply tiring over the course of a long season. Right now, unless the power takes another step forward – his career ISO is just .117 – he looks like a fringy big league regular.

**Ceiling:** 1.5-win player
**Risk:** Moderate to High
**MLB ETA:** 2019

## 18. Ricardo Sanchez, LHP

MiLB Rank: #N/A
Position Rank: N/A

| | | | | |
|---|---|---|---|---|
| Born: 04/11/97 | Age: 19 | Bats: L | **Top CALs:** Jefferson Olacio, Jake Newberry, Adys Portillo, Anfernee Benitez, Luis Morel | |
| Height: 5-11 | Weight: 170 | Throws: L | | |

| YEAR | Age | Level | IP | W | L | ERA | FIP | K/9 | BB/9 | K% | BB% | HR/9 | LOB% |
|---|---|---|---|---|---|---|---|---|---|---|---|---|---|
| 2014 | 17 | R | 38.7 | 2 | 2 | 3.49 | 3.90 | 10.01 | 5.12 | 23.6% | 12.1% | 0.00 | 67.2% |
| 2015 | 18 | A | 39.7 | 1 | 6 | 5.45 | 4.95 | 7.03 | 4.76 | 17.2% | 11.7% | 0.68 | 60.2% |

**Background:** General Manager John Hart made some headlines for swapping limited mid-level bat Kyle Kubitza and Nate Hyatt for the promising, highly-touted left arm of Sanchez. Then, of course, injuries limited the 5-foot-11, 170-pound southpaw to just 39.2 innings in the Sally last season, averaged 7.0 K/9 and 4.8 BB/9.

**Projection**: Basically, Sanchez is the equivalent of a high round draft pick; he's tallied just 78.1 innings of professional ball before his 19th birthday. And even then that sample size was distributed across two different seasons. With that being said, Sanchez has offered up more than a couple promising glimpses in his young career. Sub-six-foot arms have to be good enough to convince teams not to push them into a bullpen role. It remains to be seen if that's in Sanchez's future.

**Ceiling:** 1.5-win player
**Risk:** Moderate to High
**MLB ETA:** 2019

## 19. Andrew Thurman, RHP

**MiLB Rank: #N/A**
**Position Rank: N/A**

| Born: 12/10/91 | Age: 24 | Bats: R | **Top CALs:** Danny Rosenbaum, Matthew Hobgood, |
|---|---|---|---|
| Height: 6-3 | Weight: 225 | Throws: R | Nathan Nery, Jeff Mandel, Justin Jones |

| YEAR | Age | Level | IP | W | L | ERA | FIP | K/9 | BB/9 | K% | BB% | HR/9 | LOB% |
|---|---|---|---|---|---|---|---|---|---|---|---|---|---|
| 2013 | 21 | A- | 39.7 | 4 | 2 | 3.86 | 3.63 | 9.76 | 2.50 | 25.2% | 6.4% | 1.13 | 80.0% |
| 2014 | 22 | A | 115.3 | 7 | 9 | 5.38 | 3.74 | 8.35 | 3.12 | 21.5% | 8.1% | 0.70 | 58.8% |
| 2015 | 23 | R | 8.0 | 1 | 0 | 3.38 | 3.06 | 10.13 | 1.13 | 30.0% | 3.3% | 1.13 | 71.4% |
| 2015 | 23 | A+ | 57.3 | 5 | 4 | 3.77 | 2.99 | 6.75 | 1.73 | 17.9% | 4.6% | 0.31 | 66.5% |
| 2015 | 23 | AA | 24.3 | 1 | 4 | 5.18 | 4.13 | 5.18 | 5.92 | 12.2% | 13.9% | 0.00 | 66.7% |

**Background:** The Braves acquired the former UC Irvine standout as part of the package for shipping Evan Gattis westward to Houston last offseason. Thurman, a second round pick in 2013, sandwiched 19 appearances between the Gulf Coast, Carolina, and Southern Leagues around a rather lengthy stint on the Disabled List courtesy of a serious team bus crash in early May – injuries, by the way, that forced him to miss nearly two full months of action. The 6-foot-3, 225-pound right-hander finished his season with 89.2 innings, 66 punch outs, 28 walks, and a decent 4.12 ERA. For his three-year professional career, Thurman has tallied 244.1 innings while averaging 8.0 strikeouts and just 2.9 walks per nine innings.

**Projection**: Here's what I wrote about him prior to the 2013 draft:

> *"Useful #4-type arm. He's always shown a strong ability to pound the zone, average-ish K-rates, and teams could certainly do worse in the latter part of the first or early second rounds."*

He got off to an impressive start in the Carolina League, posting a 23-to-7 strikeout-to-walk ratio while allowing nine earned runs in his first 32.1 innings (six of those runs, by the way, came in one start) and he continued that strong stretch with the Mudcats once he was healthy again. He got smacked around a bit in Class AA, which is to be expected, but he's looked strong in the Arizona Fall League. Thurman throws harder than one would think given his finesse-type stats, so if he doesn't work out as a #4/#5-type arm he could very easily slide into a late-inning relief role along the lines of Cleveland's Zach McAlister.

**Ceiling:** 1.0- to 1.5-win player
**Risk:** Moderate
**MLB ETA:** 2016/2017

## 20. Dustin Peterson, 3B/LF

**MiLB Rank: #N/A**
**Position Rank: N/A**

| Born: 09/10/94 | Age: 21 | Bats: R | **Top CALs:** Jefry Marte, Dorssys Paulino, |
|---|---|---|---|
| Height: 6-2 | Weight: 180 | Throws: R | Jonathan Meyer, Yefri Carvajal, Jonah Arenado |

| Season | Age | LVL | PA | 2B | 3B | HR | AVG | OBP | SLG | ISO | BB% | K% | wRC+ |
|---|---|---|---|---|---|---|---|---|---|---|---|---|---|
| 2013 | 18 | R | 172 | 8 | 0 | 0 | 0.293 | 0.337 | 0.344 | 0.051 | 5.2% | 19.2% | 95 |
| 2014 | 19 | A | 563 | 31 | 3 | 10 | 0.233 | 0.274 | 0.361 | 0.127 | 4.4% | 24.3% | 80 |
| 2015 | 20 | A+ | 498 | 15 | 2 | 8 | 0.251 | 0.317 | 0.348 | 0.096 | 8.8% | 18.3% | 96 |

**Background:** The younger brother of Mariners prospect D.J. Peterson, Dustin had a decent, though far from impressive, showing with the Carolina Mudcats last season. In 118 games, the former second round pick hit .251/.317/.348 with 15 doubles, a pair of triples, and eight homeruns en route to posting another below-average *Weighted Runs Created Plus* total.

**Projection**: The optimist would point out that Peterson's overall production jumped 16 percentage points relative to his level of competition as his wRC+ moved from 80 to 96 last year. And while his power took a noticeable step backward, he was able to shave off some percentage points off his K-rate and add some needed to his walk rate. It's progress – even if it's in small incremental steps.

**Ceiling:** 1.0- to 1.5-win player
**Risk:** Moderate to High
**MLB ETA:** 2017

## 21. Manny Banuelos, LHP

**MiLB Rank: #N/A**
**Position Rank: N/A**

| Born: 03/13/91 | Age: 25 | Bats: R | Top CALs: Eury De La Rosa, Nick Additon, |
|---|---|---|---|
| Height: 5-10 | Weight: 205 | Throws: L | J.C. Ramirez, Keyvius, Sampson, Matt Lollis |

| YEAR | Age | Level | IP | W | L | ERA | FIP | K/9 | BB/9 | K% | BB% | HR/9 | LOB% |
|---|---|---|---|---|---|---|---|---|---|---|---|---|---|
| 2014 | 23 | A+ | 12.7 | 0 | 0 | 2.84 | 1.89 | 9.95 | 1.42 | 28.0% | 4.0% | 0.00 | 69.2% |
| 2014 | 23 | AA | 49.0 | 1 | 3 | 4.59 | 5.03 | 8.08 | 3.49 | 21.4% | 9.2% | 1.47 | 66.9% |
| 2014 | 23 | AAA | 15.0 | 1 | 0 | 3.60 | 5.56 | 7.80 | 6.00 | 18.6% | 14.3% | 1.20 | 85.6% |
| 2015 | 24 | R | 2.0 | 0 | 0 | 0.00 | 4.81 | 13.50 | 9.00 | 23.1% | 15.4% | 0.00 | 40.0% |
| 2015 | 24 | AAA | 84.7 | 6 | 2 | 2.23 | 3.46 | 7.33 | 4.25 | 19.7% | 11.4% | 0.21 | 80.2% |

**Background:** Oh how the mighty have fallen. Once the Crown Jewel of the Yankees system – and recipient of mass amount of hype courtesy of New York media machine – Banuelos has hardly resembled the once-dominant, budding ace he was in his early 20s. The cause: Tommy John surgery. Just for comparison's sake: prior to the injury he posted a 125-to-71 strikeout-to-walk ratio in 129.2 innings between the Eastern and International Leagues; last season he posted a mediocre 72-to-42 strikeout-to-walk ratio in 86.2 innings in Class AAA. Banuelos also made seven appearances in Atlanta in 2015, six of which were starts, throwing 26.1 innings with 19 punch outs and 12 walks to go along with a 5.37 FIP.

**Projection**: Here's what I wrote about the former top prospect in last year's book:

> *"Prior to the injury, Banuelos looked like a budding #2-type arm, maybe even better. Now, though, the ceiling has to be tempered back towards the back of the rotation or maybe even a late-inning bullpen arm. A lot of that can change, but the list of 5-foot-10 starting pitchers who can toss 200+ innings at the big league level has been rather scant over the last decade-plus."*

After showing off a fringy upper 80s heater during his brief stint, Banuelos likely isn't long for a rotation spot – especially once his sub-average control/command is taken into account. One final thought: CAL isn't overly optimistic either, linking him to Eury De La Rosa, Nick Additon, J.C. Ramirez, Keyvius Sampson, and Matt Lollis.

**Ceiling:** 1.0-win player
**Risk:** Low to Moderate
**MLB ETA:** Debuted in 2015

## 22. Jason Hursh, RHP

**MiLB Rank: #N/A**
**Position Rank: N/A**

| Born: 10/02/91 | Age: 24 | Bats: R | Top CALs: Brian Broderick, Luis Mendoza, |
|---|---|---|---|
| Height: 6-3 | Weight: 200 | Throws: R | Richard Castillo, Kyle Waldrop, Zeke Spruill |

| YEAR | Age | Level | IP | W | L | ERA | FIP | K/9 | BB/9 | K% | BB% | HR/9 | LOB% |
|---|---|---|---|---|---|---|---|---|---|---|---|---|---|
| 2013 | 21 | A | 27.0 | 1 | 1 | 0.67 | 4.07 | 5.00 | 3.33 | 13.9% | 9.3% | 0.33 | 74.3% |
| 2014 | 22 | AA | 148.3 | 11 | 7 | 3.58 | 3.52 | 5.04 | 2.61 | 13.5% | 7.0% | 0.30 | 67.5% |
| 2015 | 23 | AA | 82.3 | 3 | 6 | 5.14 | 3.49 | 6.56 | 3.50 | 15.8% | 8.4% | 0.33 | 65.6% |
| 2015 | 23 | AAA | 15.0 | 1 | 0 | 5.40 | 5.42 | 3.00 | 3.00 | 7.8% | 7.8% | 1.20 | 67.7% |

**Background:** One of the more questionable moves under the Frank Wren regime, Hursh spent the majority of the year back in Class AA where his struggles fell somewhere on the Greek Tragedy scale. He completed five innings in one of his first six starts, throwing 21.2 innings and more walks (17) than strikeouts (14). He followed that up with a six-game stretch on the other side of the spectrum: 35.2 innings, 26 K, 10 BB, and a 3.03 ERA. Then he followed that up by allowing 11 runs in his next 13 innings – production that cost him his long-term spot in the rotation. The club bounced him to Mississippi's bullpen in last June where he would rattle off 12 strong innings before struggling with Gwinnett in the International League.

**Projection**: Well, I hate to say it but I called it. Here's what I wrote in last year's book:

> *"Including his 136 college innings, Hursh has averaged just 5.61 strikeouts per nine innings. He succeeds by limiting the free passes and generating a ton of action on the ground, more than 55% in his minor league career. There are not a whole lot of pitchers that can consistently win at the big league level with sub-6.0 strikeout rates – in fact there were only six pitchers at the big league level to strikeout fewer than 6.0 per nine innings and top two wins above replacement. He could very likely get pushed into the bullpen in the coming year or two."*

Obviously, when you burn a first round pick on a collegiate starter you assume that he's going to stay in that role longer than two seasons. It didn't happen with Hursh. But he has some upside as a solid seventh/eighth-inning guy.

**Ceiling:** 1.0win player
**Risk:** Low to Moderate
**MLB ETA:** 2016

## 23. Lucas Herbert, C

**MiLB Rank:** #N/A
**Position Rank:** N/A

| Born: 11/28/96 | Age: 19 | Bats: R | Top CALs: Sebastian Valle, Oscar Hernandez, |
|---|---|---|---|
| Height: 6-0 | Weight: 200 | Throws: R | Alex Murphy, Carlos Perez, Ryan Casteel |

| Season | Age | LVL | PA | 2B | 3B | HR | AVG | OBP | SLG | ISO | BB% | K% | wRC+ |
|---|---|---|---|---|---|---|---|---|---|---|---|---|---|
| 2015 | 18 | R | 5 | 0 | 0 | 1 | 0.500 | 0.600 | 1.250 | 0.750 | 0.0% | 20.0% | 411 |

**Background:** Taking a high school catcher in the opening two rounds for the first time since 2003 when Atlanta selected Jarrod Saltalamacchia, Herbert was limited to just five plate appearances during his professional debut.

**Projection:** Other than his lofty draft status there's virtually nothing to go off of. Zilch. Zippo. Nada.

**Ceiling:** Too Soon to Tell
**Risk:** N/A
**MLB ETA:** N/A

## 24. Tyrell Jenkins, RHP

**MiLB Rank:** #N/A
**Position Rank:** N/A

| Born: 07/20/92 | Age: 23 | Bats: R | Top CALs: Tim Alderson, Jhonathan Ramos, |
|---|---|---|---|
| Height: 6-4 | Weight: 180 | Throws: R | Ryan O'Sulivan, Richard Castillo, Tyler Herron |

| YEAR | Age | Level | IP | W | L | ERA | FIP | K/9 | BB/9 | K% | BB% | HR/9 | LOB% |
|---|---|---|---|---|---|---|---|---|---|---|---|---|---|
| 2013 | 20 | A | 49.3 | 4 | 4 | 4.74 | 4.53 | 6.20 | 4.38 | 15.6% | 11.0% | 0.73 | 68.2% |
| 2013 | 20 | A+ | 10.0 | 0 | 0 | 4.50 | 2.34 | 5.40 | 0.90 | 14.0% | 2.3% | 0.00 | 57.1% |
| 2014 | 21 | A+ | 74.0 | 6 | 5 | 3.28 | 4.31 | 4.99 | 2.80 | 13.3% | 7.4% | 0.73 | 73.7% |
| 2015 | 22 | AA | 93.0 | 5 | 5 | 3.00 | 3.84 | 5.71 | 3.97 | 14.9% | 10.4% | 0.29 | 70.0% |
| 2015 | 22 | AAA | 45.3 | 3 | 4 | 3.57 | 4.48 | 5.76 | 3.97 | 14.8% | 10.2% | 0.79 | 75.8% |

**Background:** Once considered the Crown Jewel in a flourishing St. Louis farm system, the Cardinals parted with the former 2010 first round pick – as well as Shelby Miller in the Jason Heyward/Jordan Walden two-for-two swap. And despite the 2015 season being the fire-balling right-hander's sixth professional season, Jenkins cracked the 100-inning mark for the first time. The oft-injured, perennially banged up enigma split last year between Mississippi and Gwinnett; he posted a mediocre 88-to-61 strikeout-to-walk ratio but somehow managed to finish 2015 with a nice-enough-looking 3.19 ERA. For his career, the 6-foot-4, 180-pound explosive hurler has averaged just 6.7 punch outs and just 3.5 walks per nine innings.

**Projection:** Here's the thing about the rocket-armed Jenkins: he hasn't posted a solid strikeout rate since 2012, when he was a 19-year-old making his way through an abbreviated season in the Sally. Otherwise, he's been mediocre, a victim of his own hype. Given his lengthy injury track record and subpar peripherals, it's probably time to start thinking about converting him into a relief role.

**Ceiling:** 1.0-win player
**Risk:** Moderate
**MLB ETA:** 2016

## 25. Mauricio Cabrera, RHP

**MiLB Rank:** #N/A
**Position Rank:** N/A

| Born: 11/22/93 | Age: 22 | Bats: R | Top CALs: Blake King, Jochi Ogando, |
|---|---|---|---|
| Height: 6-3 | Weight: 230 | Throws: R | Aaron Sanchez, Kevin Siegrist, Santo Frias |

| YEAR | Age | Level | IP | W | L | ERA | FIP | K/9 | BB/9 | K% | BB% | HR/9 | LOB% |
|---|---|---|---|---|---|---|---|---|---|---|---|---|---|
| 2013 | 19 | A | 131.3 | 3 | 8 | 4.18 | 3.91 | 7.33 | 4.87 | 18.7% | 12.4% | 0.21 | 63.4% |
| 2014 | 20 | R | 4.0 | 0 | 0 | 6.75 | 3.51 | 6.75 | 4.50 | 17.7% | 11.8% | 0.00 | 40.0% |
| 2014 | 20 | A+ | 29.0 | 1 | 1 | 5.59 | 4.41 | 8.69 | 5.90 | 21.5% | 14.6% | 0.31 | 54.8% |
| 2015 | 21 | A+ | 31.0 | 2 | 2 | 5.52 | 3.51 | 8.13 | 4.94 | 20.0% | 12.1% | 0.29 | 54.8% |
| 2015 | 21 | AA | 17.3 | 0 | 1 | 5.71 | 4.46 | 12.98 | 9.35 | 30.1% | 21.7% | 0.52 | 64.2% |

**Background:** Cabrera's stock has fallen rather fast since he established himself as a high-ceiling arm as a 19-year-old in the South Atlantic League in 2013. He posted a decent 107-to-71 strikeout-to-walk ratio in 131.1 innings. Since then the 6-foot-3, 230-pound right-hander battled a forearm injury, control issues, and a subsequent move to the pen.

**Projection:** Cabrera's always had the tenacity – and matching fastball – to miss a whole helluva lot of bats. Unfortunately, though, it required a move to the bullpen. But the hard-throwing Dominican-born hurler managed to fan 53 in 48.1 innings between the Carolina and Southern

Leagues last season. The problem: he walked 35 during that period as well. He could be a dominant, late-inning relief arm – *if* the control comes around.

**Ceiling:** 1.0 – to 1.5-win player
**Risk:** High
**MLB ETA:** 2017/2018

### *Barely Missed:*

- **Wes Parsons, RHP** – Parsons first popped up on my radar after dominating the Sally competition as a 20-year-old in 2013. He followed that up with a bit of a mediocre year as he battled some poor luck in the more advanced Class A. But it's hard to tell what he is moving forward. He'll be 24 with zero experience above the Carolina League and barely a dozen innings under his belt in 2015.

- **Casey Kelly, RHP** – The former top prospect famously made it look easy as he converted from a two-way player to a full-time starting pitcher in the low levels. His once-promising career got interrupted by injuries and he's struggled regaining his previous touch.

- **A.J. Minter, LHP** – Second round pick out of Texas A&M University last June, Minter was in the midst of a breakout season – one in which he moved from the bullpen to the rotation – before succumbing to Tommy John surgery. Through his four starts last season, the sub-six-foot lefty posted a 29-to-8 strikeout-to-walk ratio in 21.0 innings of work.

## *Bird Doggin' It – Additional Prospects to Keep an Eye in 2016*

| Player | Age | POS | Notes |
|---|---|---|---|
| Brandon Barker | 23 | RHP | A 14<sup>th</sup> round pick out of Mercer University two years ago, Barker made appearances at three different levels last season: Low Class A, High Class A, and a pair of Class AAA starts. He finished with a combined 109-to-41 strikeout-to-walk ratio. |
| Jose Briceno | 23 | C/1B | First time since his debut in the DSL in 2010 that Briceno failed to hit. The catcher/first baseman batted a putrid .183/.215/.267 with just 18 extra-base hits in 327 plate appearances. |
| Johan Camargo | 22 | SS | Once promising prospect stopped hitting once he jumped into full season ball a couple years ago. |
| Daniel Castro | 23 | IF | Prototypical middle infield backup fodder. Castro doesn't do a whole lot other than positional versatility and empty batting averages. |
| Kyle Kinman | 25 | LHP | Short southpaw fanned 65 in 51.2 innings between Rome, Carolina, and Mississippi last season. |
| Connor Lien | 22 | OF | A 12<sup>th</sup> round pick out of Olympia High School in 2012, Lien had a coming out party of sorts in High Class A: .285/.347/.415 with 22 doubles, five triples, nine homeruns, and 34 stolen bases. |
| Dilmer Mejia | 18 | LHP | 5-foot-11, 160-pound southpaw looked promising as a 17-year-old in the GCL last season: 21.2 IP, 19 K, and 4 BB. |
| Max Povse | 22 | RHP | Third round pick out of UNC two years ago, Povse breezed through the Sally but struggled adjusting to High Class A. |
| Evan Rutckyj | 24 | LHP | Rule 5 pick from the Yankees. Rutckyj split time between the Florida State and Eastern Leagues last season, averaging 12 punch outs and 3.1 walks per nine innings. He could be a serviceable middle relief arm in 2016. |
| Carlos Salazar | 21 | RHP | Strikeout artist's control issues reached a boiling point last season; he walked 50 in 56.2 innings. |
| Rob Whalen | 22 | RHP | Acquired along with John Gant from the Mets last season. Whalen, a 12<sup>th</sup> round pick in 2012, tossed 96.2 innings in High Class A last season, averaging 6.3 punch outs and 3.5 walks per nine innings. |
| Daniel Winkler | 26 | RHP | Soft-tossing control artist made it back from Tommy John. Think: poor man's Josh Tomlin. |
| Jorge Zavala | 22 | RHP | Posted a combined 2.28 ERA between Rome and Carolina last season, fanning 55 and walking 26 in 43.1 innings of work. |

**State of the Farm System:** Here's a crash course in how not to build a successful, long term farm system: do not, under any circumstance, put all your eggs – and subsequent hope – into a high upside, young, teenage arms. You know, sort of just like the Baltimore Orioles. The system has something that every other club yearns to have: a pair of high upside, often times dominant hard-throwing right-handers in Dylan Bundy and Hunter Harvey. Of course, though, they would succumb to nearly identical elbow injuries.

Important point #1: Once is an anomaly, but when your two young studs come down with identical elbow issues it can't be merely a coincidence, right? At least it deserves some type of exploration. And the ironic part is that the front office basically banned Bundy from throwing the cutter.

And make no mistake about it, the pair would easily rank as the club's top two prospects, but after weighting their age, severity of injury, and likelihood of bouncing back, they fall to #2 and #3 on this year's list as backstop Chance Sisco surpassed the duo.

Sisco, a second round pick out of Santiago High School three years ago, is the top backstop prospect in all of baseball. Owning a smooth left-hander swing, he's strung together back-to-back strong showings as he's passed through the South Atlantic and Carolina Leagues before earning a brief 20-trial in Class AA.

Third baseman Jomar Reyes is a big kid who's still learning to translate his raw power into in-game power at this point, but he looked solid in his first taste of full season action. Perhaps the single most intriguing prospect in the system, maybe even the minors, is infielder-bust-turned-budding-dominant-reliever Mychal Givens. Since converting to a fulltime moundsman three years ago, the 6-foot, 210-pound right-hander has posted a 170-to-74 strikeout-to-walk ratio in the minors and a video game-esque 38-to-6 mark in 30.0 innings with Baltimore last season. And Givens couldn't be in a better position to succeed because O's manager Buck Showalter is one of the game's best at deploying his relief corps.

| Rank | Name | POS |
|------|------|-----|
| 1 | Chance Sisco | C |
| 2 | Dylan Bundy | RHP |
| 3 | Hunter Harvey | RHP |
| 4 | Jomar Reyes | 3B |
| 5 | Mychal Givens | RHP |
| 6 | D.J. Stewart | LF |
| 7 | Trey Mancini | 1B |
| 8 | Joe Gunkel | RHP |
| 9 | Christian Walker | 1B |
| 10 | Ryan Mountcastle | SS |
| 11 | Mike Wright | RHP |
| 12 | Parker Bridwell | RHP |
| 13 | C.J. Riefenhauser | LHP |
| 14 | Tyler Wilson | RHP |
| 15 | Garrett Cleavinger | LHP |
| 16 | David Hess | RHP |
| 17 | Jon Keller | RHP |
| 18 | Travis Seabrooke | LHP |
| 19 | Branden Kline | RHP |
| 20 | Derrick Bleeker | RHP |
| 21 | Tanner Scott | LHP |
| 22 | Brian Gonzalez | LHP |
| 23 | Josh Hart | CF |
| 24 | Adrian Marin | SS |
| 25 | | |

Then there's Trey Mancini, the former Notre Dame masher who slugged .341/.375/.563 with a whopping 43 two-baggers, six triples, and 21 homeruns as one of the minors' most lethal bats last season.

**Review of the 2015 Draft:** For the first time since the club grabbed Nick Markakis in opening round in 2003, Baltimore grabbed a post-high school aged outfielder with their top pick in the draft when they selected Florida State University stud D.J. Stewart, who looked a bit underwhelming in his foray into the New York-Penn League last season. They followed that up with prep shortstop Ryan Mountcastle with their second first round pick.

They also did well in grabbing potential fast-moving Oregon lefty Garrett Cleavinger. Baltimore also failed to sign prep right-hander Jonathan Hughes, the 68th overall pick.

## 1. Chance Sisco, C

**MiLB Rank: #63**
**Position Rank: #1**

| Born: 02/24/95 | Age: 21 | Bats: L | Top CALs: Carlos Perez, JR Murphy, |
| Height: 6-2 | Weight: 193 | Throws: R | Jobduan Morales, Danny Arribas, Tucker Barnhart |

| Season | Age | LVL | PA | 2B | 3B | HR | AVG | OBP | SLG | ISO | BB% | K% | wRC+ |
|---|---|---|---|---|---|---|---|---|---|---|---|---|---|
| 2013 | 18 | R | 118 | 4 | 1 | 1 | 0.371 | 0.475 | 0.464 | 0.093 | 14.4% | 17.8% | 181 |
| 2014 | 19 | A | 478 | 27 | 2 | 5 | 0.340 | 0.406 | 0.448 | 0.108 | 8.8% | 16.5% | 141 |
| 2015 | 20 | A+ | 300 | 12 | 3 | 4 | 0.308 | 0.387 | 0.422 | 0.114 | 11.0% | 13.7% | 140 |
| 2015 | 20 | AA | 84 | 4 | 0 | 2 | 0.257 | 0.337 | 0.392 | 0.135 | 10.7% | 16.7% | 114 |

**Background:** And because the injury bug struck the club's top picks, why the hell should it avoid the system's top bat? Sisco, a lefty-swinging backstop taken in the second round three years ago, missed about a handful of games after fracturing his right ring finger on an opponent's bat during a stolen base attempt. And then he would miss about a month of action with another injury early in the season as well. But despite that, though, the big 6-foot-2, 193-pound backstop ripped through the Carolina League, hitting a robust .308/.387/.422 with 12 doubles, three triples, four homeruns, and eight stolen bases, before earning a 20-game promotion to Bowie, where he would bat a solid .257/.337/.392. Defensively last season, he threw out 25% of the attempted would-be base thieves.

**Projection**: Just to add a little bit of context to Sisco's dominant showing with Frederick last season, consider the following: no 20-year-old catcher with 300 or more plate appearances in the Carolina League topped Sisco's 140 wRC+ mark since 2006, the first year FanGraphs' minor league data is available. He has a very promising offensive foundation in place, particularly for a catcher: an above-average eye at the plate, 15- to 17-homer potential, and a hit tool that could threaten a .300 average annually. He's always shown some platoon splits so that'll bear watching. Defensively, he...remains a work in progress.

**Ceiling:** 3.0-win player
**Risk:** Moderate
**MLB ETA:** 2017

## 2. Dylan Bundy, RHP

**MiLB Rank: #122**
**Position Rank: N/A**

| Born: 11/15/92 | Age: 23 | Bats: B | Top CALs: N/A |
| Height: 6-1 | Weight: 200 | Throws: R | |

| YEAR | Age | Level | IP | W | L | ERA | FIP | K/9 | BB/9 | K% | BB% | HR/9 | LOB% |
|---|---|---|---|---|---|---|---|---|---|---|---|---|---|
| 2014 | 21 | A- | 15.0 | 0 | 1 | 0.60 | 1.11 | 13.20 | 1.80 | 39.3% | 5.4% | 0.00 | 92.3% |
| 2014 | 21 | A+ | 26.3 | 1 | 2 | 4.78 | 3.97 | 5.13 | 4.44 | 12.8% | 11.1% | 0.00 | 66.7% |
| 2015 | 22 | AA | 22.0 | 0 | 3 | 3.68 | 1.81 | 10.23 | 2.05 | 27.8% | 5.6% | 0.00 | 63.0% |

**Background:** Just a handful of years after capturing the imagination – and attention – of front office personnel and fans alike, Bundy barely registers a blip on the many prospect radars now – or at least that's what it seems. But then again, that's what happens when you make the big leagues at 19-years-old and then tally just 63.1 innings over the next three seasons. Bundy first missed the entire 2013 season and part of the following year with Tommy John surgery. And then he missed a good part of last year – and by good part, I mean more than three months – with an entirely new ailment: shoulder inflammation. Overall, he tossed 22.0 innings with Bowie, fanning 25 and walking five en route to totaling a 3.68 ERA. He would make two appearances with the Peoria Javelinas in the Arizona Summer League at the end the year.

**Projection**: So, what do you do at this point? Bundy clearly has – note the present tense used, not past – the potential to develop into a legitimate impact big league starter. But he has the durability of a cheap, wet paper towel. As a baseball fan in general you hope that Bundy can move beyond the shit luck and eventually realize his potential, because he'd be a lot of fun to watch. Keep your fingers crossed. Hell, even Rich Harden carved out three seasons with at least 140.0 innings.

**Ceiling:** 3.0- to 3.5-win player
**Risk:** High
**MLB ETA:** Debuted in 2012

## 3. Hunter Harvey, RHP

**MiLB Rank: #123**
**Position Rank: N/A**

| Born: 12/09/94 | Age: 21 | Bats: R | Top CALs: N/A |
| Height: 6-3 | Weight: 175 | Throws: R | |

| YEAR | Age | Level | IP | W | L | ERA | FIP | K/9 | BB/9 | K% | BB% | HR/9 | LOB% |
|------|-----|-------|------|---|---|------|------|-------|------|-------|------|------|-------|
| 2013 | 18 | R | 13.3 | 0 | 0 | 1.35 | 1.21 | 12.15 | 1.35 | 36.0% | 4.0% | 0.00 | 83.3% |
| 2013 | 18 | A- | 12.0 | 0 | 1 | 2.25 | 1.60 | 11.25 | 3.00 | 30.0% | 8.0% | 0.00 | 73.3% |
| 2014 | 19 | A | 87.7 | 7 | 5 | 3.18 | 3.42 | 10.88 | 3.39 | 29.0% | 9.0% | 0.51 | 68.9% |

**Background:** As if having one star-crossed, snake-bitten top pitching prospect wasn't enough, Baltimore is the proud owner of *two* star-crossed, snake-bitten top pitching prospects: Dylan Bundy, the original hurler right out of a William Shakespeare tragedy, and Harvey, the son of former All-Star closer Bryan Harvey. But here's where it gets…weird: the younger Harvey was originally diagnosed with a strained flexor mass in the middle of 2014, the exact same issue that first popped up with Bundy. But the Orioles opted to take the rest and rehab approach with the former first round pick. And Harvey came back last spring…until a comebacker slightly fractured his right fibula. Well, fast forward to the end the year, the first time Harvey toes the rubber against the Rays in the Instructional League he felt some elbow discomfort. I would assume that he's likely going to be facing the surgical scalpel at some point in the very near future – unfortunately.

**Projection**: I think the most important question facing the *identical* injuries to Bundy and Harvey is this: Is this merely a coincidence or does it have to do with an organizational philosophy, be it throwing, working out, etc…? Harvey, like his injured counterpart, also captured the quite a bit of press before succumbing to the injury. Here's hoping he can escape further issues/setbacks.

**Ceiling:** 3.0- to 3.5-win player
**Risk:** High
**MLB ETA:** 2019

## 4. Jomar Reyes, 3B

**MiLB Rank: #124**
**Position Rank: #6**

| Born: 02/20/97 | Age: 19 | Bats: R | Top CALs: Rafael Devers, Jorge Bonifacio, |
| Height: 6-3 | Weight: 220 | Throws: R | Victor Acosta, Zachary Green, Steven Fuentes |

| Season | Age | LVL | PA | 2B | 3B | HR | AVG | OBP | SLG | ISO | BB% | K% | wRC+ |
|--------|-----|-----|-----|----|----|----|-------|-------|-------|-------|-------|-------|------|
| 2014 | 17 | R | 207 | 10 | 2 | 4 | 0.285 | 0.333 | 0.425 | 0.140 | 7.2% | 18.4% | 112 |
| 2015 | 18 | R | 19 | 2 | 0 | 0 | 0.250 | 0.368 | 0.375 | 0.125 | 10.5% | 26.3% | 131 |
| 2015 | 18 | A | 335 | 27 | 4 | 5 | 0.278 | 0.334 | 0.440 | 0.162 | 5.4% | 21.8% | 119 |

**Background:** Signed out of the Dominican Republic for $350,000 in early February 2014, Reyes has quietly become one of the more interesting low level third baseman after two solid showings. The big, stocky Reyes batted a respectable .285/.333/.425 with 10 doubles, a pair of triples, four homeruns, and a stolen base in the Gulf Coast League in 2014. And he followed that up by slugging .278/.334/.440 with a whopping 27 doubles, four triples, five homeruns en route to topping the Sally offensive average mark by 19% in 84 games. For his career, he's sporting a solid .280/.335/.432 triple-slash line.

**Projection**: For those counting at home, here are Reyes' numbers pro-rated over a full 162-game season: 52 doubles, eight triples, 10 triples, and a pair of stolen bases. And just to add a little bit of perspective to that: the Dodgers prospect Kyle Farmer led all the minors with 47 two-baggers last season.

Here's what I wrote in last year's book:

> *"Outside of the sheer size, Reyes is a pretty promising prospect: he made a successful jump stateside, flashing above-average power potential, decent walk and strikeout rates, and a solid hit tool. He could be a fast riser next beginning next year."*

Well, how's that for a fast riser? He owns the best power potential in the entire system, something that will eventually come to fruition given all the doubles he's slugged. The lone knock on him at this point: a slightly below-average eye at the plate, though it's worth noting he was just 18 last season.

**Ceiling:** 2.5- to 3.0-win player
**Risk:** Moderate to High
**MLB ETA:** 2017/2018

## 5. Mychal Givens, RHP

**MiLB Rank: #137**

**Position Rank: N/A**

| **Born:** 05/13/90 | **Age:** 26 | **Bats:** R | **Top CALs:** Santos Rodriguez, Stephen Shackleford, |
|---|---|---|---|
| **Height:** 6-0 | **Weight:** 210 | **Throws:** R | Nathan Striz, Erik Davis, Barret Browning |

| YEAR | Age | Level | IP | W | L | ERA | FIP | K/9 | BB/9 | K% | BB% | HR/9 | LOB% |
|---|---|---|---|---|---|---|---|---|---|---|---|---|---|
| 2013 | 23 | A | 42.7 | 2 | 3 | 4.22 | 3.65 | 7.59 | 4.01 | 20.1% | 10.6% | 0.21 | 65.9% |
| 2014 | 24 | A+ | 33.3 | 1 | 2 | 3.24 | 4.30 | 7.29 | 4.32 | 19.2% | 11.4% | 0.54 | 52.5% |
| 2014 | 24 | AA | 25.3 | 0 | 0 | 3.91 | 4.58 | 9.95 | 8.17 | 23.0% | 18.9% | 0.00 | 75.0% |
| 2015 | 25 | AA | 57.3 | 4 | 2 | 1.73 | 1.73 | 12.40 | 2.51 | 34.8% | 7.1% | 0.16 | 77.3% |

**Background:** Finally, perhaps my single most favorite minor league prospect to date. Givens flamed out as a light-hitting, albeit rocket-armed shortstop in his first three seasons. He "batted" – a term used in the loosest of senses – a disappointing .247/.331/.311 with just 44 extra-base knocks in 1,043 plate appearances.

Add in the fact that he was a highly touted second round pick, and it was clear that he was encroaching upon bust territory. But then the heavens parted and Baltimore took advantage of his true God-given ability: to unleash a wicked power arsenal upon the opposition. Less than two years later he was up in the big leagues as arguably the Orioles' top relief arm. In 22 appearances in The Show last season, Givens fanned 32.5% and walked just 5.1% of the total batters he faced.

**Projection**: Here's the power arsenal: a mid-90s fastball, a snap-dragon of a slider, and a hard, mid-80s changeup. If the control is as good as advertised last season, the sky's the limit. He's a potential shut down, turn off the lights, empty the ballpark, game over caliber relief arm.

**Ceiling:** 2.0-win player
**Risk:** Low to Moderate
**MLB ETA:** Debuted in 2015

## 6. D.J. Stewart, LF

**MiLB Rank: #148**

**Position Rank: N/A**

| **Born:** 11/30/93 | **Age:** 22 | **Bats:** L | **Top CALs:** Michael Taylor, Carlos Moncrief, |
|---|---|---|---|
| **Height:** 6-0 | **Weight:** 230 | **Throws:** R | Ben Verlander, Tyler Marincov, Dan Gulbransen |

| Season | Age | LVL | PA | 2B | 3B | HR | AVG | OBP | SLG | ISO | BB% | K% | wRC+ |
|---|---|---|---|---|---|---|---|---|---|---|---|---|---|
| 2015 | 21 | A- | 268 | 8 | 2 | 6 | 0.218 | 0.288 | 0.345 | 0.126 | 8.6% | 19.4% | 89 |

**Background:** Built like Kirby Puckett, in the latter years, the sweet-swinging corner outfielder was a consistent – eerily consistent, to be exact – dominant force for three years at Florida State University. His yearly OPS totals: 1.029, 1.029, 1.093. He left the school as a .344/.481/.570 career hitter, slugging 54 doubles, four triples, 27 homeruns, 15 of which came during his final year with the Seminoles, and 24 stolen bases. Baltimore grabbed the 6-foot, 230-pound lefty-swinging outfielder in the first round last June, 25th overall, and pushed him to Aberdeen for his debut. In 62 games with Aberdeen, he batted a disappointing .218/.288/.345 with eight doubles, two triples, six homeruns, and four stolen bases (in five attempts).

**Projection**: Here's what I wrote prior to draft last season:

> "An OBP-machine. Through his first 165 games Stewart owns a .488 OBP. To put that into perspective a bit, look at some of the more notable careers of some past collegiate hitters: Kris Bryant (.486), Michael Conforto (.376), Colin Moran (.452), D.J. Peterson (.463), Mike Zunino (.393), Dustin Ackley (.489), Pedro Alvarez (.451).
>
> Stewart owns an elite eye at the plate – he's walked 18.4% of his career plate appearances and a staggering 25.8% this season – and enough pop to develop into an annual 15-HR threat. At 6-foot and 230 pounds, he's not overly quick, but his above-average hit tool helps compensate.
>
> He won't be your prototypical run-producing corner outfield bat, but has better-than-average production."

**Ceiling:** 2.0- to 2.5-win player
**Risk:** Moderate
**MLB ETA:** 2018

## 7. Trey Mancini, 1B

**MiLB Rank: #153**
**Position Rank: N/A**

| Born: 03/18/92 | Age: 24 | Bats: R | Top CALs: Henry Wrigley, Joe Mahoney, |
|---|---|---|---|
| Height: 6-4 | Weight: 215 | Throws: R | Curt Smith, Christian Marrero, Mitch Moreland |

| Season | Age | LVL | PA | 2B | 3B | HR | AVG | OBP | SLG | ISO | BB% | K% | wRC+ |
|---|---|---|---|---|---|---|---|---|---|---|---|---|---|
| 2013 | 21 | A- | 285 | 18 | 2 | 3 | 0.328 | 0.382 | 0.449 | 0.121 | 7.0% | 15.1% | 150 |
| 2014 | 22 | A | 291 | 13 | 3 | 3 | 0.317 | 0.357 | 0.422 | 0.104 | 4.8% | 17.9% | 118 |
| 2014 | 22 | A+ | 295 | 19 | 0 | 7 | 0.251 | 0.295 | 0.396 | 0.145 | 4.7% | 14.6% | 93 |
| 2015 | 23 | A+ | 217 | 14 | 3 | 8 | 0.314 | 0.341 | 0.527 | 0.213 | 4.1% | 16.1% | 150 |
| 2015 | 23 | AA | 354 | 29 | 3 | 13 | 0.359 | 0.395 | 0.586 | 0.227 | 6.2% | 16.4% | 180 |

**Background:** Alright, be honest, who in the hell saw this offensive surge coming? Really? Where the hell did this type of production come from? An eighth round pick out of Notre Dame three years ago, Mancini ripped the cover off the ball in 52 games with Frederick, slugging .314/.341/.527 with 14 doubles, three triples, and eight homeruns en route to topping the league average production by a whopping 50%. But it didn't stop there, either. In 84 games with Bowie, Mancini looked like the second-coming of Babe Ruth, mashing to the tune of .359/.395/.586 with 29 doubles, three triples, 13 homeruns, and a pair of stolen bases. Here's the best part: during his time with Bowie, the 6-foot-4, 215-pounder basher topped the league average production mark by 80 *freakin'* %. Overall, Mancini finished the year with a combined .341/.375/.563 triple-slash line with 43 doubles, six triples, and 21 homeruns – easily the greatest season of his career, amateur or professional.

**Projection:** Again, here's some perspective for you: Among *all stateside minor league hitters*, Mancini finished in the top five in doubles and tied for eighth in overall production (169 wRC). He was an **eighth round pick three years ago**. And as much as I want to say that this smacks of being a complete fluke, I'm not completely convinced he *can't* develop into a dominant big league bat. He still walked the same amount, the power took a noticeable uptick but (A) he slugged a lot of doubles two years ago and (B) he was an absolute force to be reckoned with during his time with Notre Dame, and even though his BABIPs were high, they aren't that far out of line with his 2013 and part of his 2014 showing. And here's something to keep in mind: Paul Goldschmidt, arguably the top hitter in the majors right now, absolutely annihilated the minor leagues but never garnered a whole lot of positive reviews. Could Trey Mancini be the next Paul Goldschmidt? Hell, even if he develops into 80% of that he'll be a league average player. CAL is a little optimistic, comparing him to Mitch Moreland, owner of a career 101 wRC+ in 2,259 big league plate appearances.

**Ceiling:** 2.5-win player
**Risk:** Moderate to High
**MLB ETA:** 2017

## 8. Joe Gunkel, RHP

**MiLB Rank: N/A**
**Position Rank: N/A**

| Born: 12/30/91 | Age: 24 | Bats: R | Top CALs: Jeff Manship, Andrew Gagnon, |
|---|---|---|---|
| Height: 6-5 | Weight: 225 | Throws: R | Corey Vanallen, Chris Schwinden Williams Perez |

| YEAR | Age | Level | IP | W | L | ERA | FIP | K/9 | BB/9 | K% | BB% | HR/9 | LOB% |
|---|---|---|---|---|---|---|---|---|---|---|---|---|---|
| 2013 | 21 | R | 1.0 | 0 | 0 | 0.00 | 1.46 | 9.00 | 0.00 | 33.3% | 0.0% | 0.00 | 100.0% |
| 2013 | 21 | A- | 20.0 | 3 | 0 | 1.35 | 0.50 | 14.40 | 1.35 | 43.2% | 4.1% | 0.00 | 66.7% |
| 2014 | 22 | A | 51.3 | 3 | 0 | 2.28 | 2.92 | 10.87 | 1.93 | 31.8% | 5.6% | 0.53 | 72.2% |
| 2014 | 22 | A+ | 52.3 | 3 | 5 | 4.64 | 3.63 | 6.71 | 2.24 | 16.9% | 5.6% | 0.52 | 61.8% |
| 2015 | 23 | A+ | 22.0 | 1 | 1 | 2.05 | 2.98 | 9.00 | 1.64 | 26.2% | 4.8% | 0.82 | 81.4% |
| 2015 | 23 | AA | 122.7 | 10 | 5 | 2.79 | 3.32 | 6.68 | 1.69 | 18.5% | 4.7% | 0.59 | 75.1% |

**Background:** Originally drafted by the Red Sox out of West Chester University of Pennsylvania in the 18th round three years ago, Boston flipped the underrated right-hander last June for the services of veteran outfielder Alejandro De Aza. As for Gunkel, well, he's been incredibly underrated – and highly successful – during his relatively short minor league career. Last season the 6-foot-5, 225-pound right-hander tossed a career high 144.2 innings while fanning 113 and walking just 27 en route to tallying a 2.68 ERA and a FIP hovering around 3.00. For his career, Gunkel has fanned 247 and walked just 54 in 269.1 innings of work.

**Projection:** Incredibly underrated. Most people won't give Gunkel a second look. But make no mistake about it – there is legitimate big league starting potential here. He's shown above-average control/command, a solid ability to miss bats, and the skill to churn out plenty of innings. He's a good bet to develop into a #4/#5 pitcher, one where you'll look up and ask: where the hell did this guy come from?

**Ceiling:** 1.5-win player
**Risk:** Moderate
**MLB ETA:** 2016

## 9. Christian Walker, 1B

**MiLB Rank: N/A**
**Position Rank: N/A**

| Born: 03/28/91 | Age: 25 | Bats: R | Top CALs: Matt Clark, Justin Huber, |
| Height: 6-0 | Weight: 220 | Throws: R | Brock Peterson, Danny Dorn, Mike Carp |

| Season | Age | LVL | PA | 2B | 3B | HR | AVG | OBP | SLG | ISO | BB% | K% | wRC+ |
|--------|-----|-----|-----|----|----|----|------|------|------|------|------|------|------|
| 2013 | 22 | A | 131 | 5 | 0 | 3 | 0.353 | 0.420 | 0.474 | 0.121 | 8.4% | 12.2% | 160 |
| 2013 | 22 | A+ | 239 | 17 | 0 | 8 | 0.288 | 0.343 | 0.479 | 0.191 | 7.1% | 17.2% | 126 |
| 2014 | 23 | AA | 411 | 15 | 2 | 20 | 0.301 | 0.367 | 0.516 | 0.216 | 9.2% | 20.2% | 144 |
| 2014 | 23 | AAA | 188 | 10 | 0 | 6 | 0.259 | 0.335 | 0.428 | 0.169 | 9.6% | 26.1% | 109 |
| 2015 | 24 | AAA | 592 | 33 | 1 | 18 | 0.257 | 0.324 | 0.423 | 0.167 | 8.3% | 23.0% | 116 |
| 2015 | 24 | MLB | 12 | 0 | 0 | 0 | 0.111 | 0.333 | 0.111 | 0.000 | 25.0% | 33.3% | 48 |

**Background:** A collegiate basher taken in the fourth round out of South Carolina University four years ago, things seemingly clicked for Walker in the Eastern League two years ago when he slugged .301/.367/.516 with 15 doubles, two triples, and 20 homeruns in just 95 games. But his production took a noticeable decline when the club bumped him up to the International League, hitting an average-ish .259/.335/.428 in 44 games. And that type of production followed him back to his return to Norfolk last season. In 138 games with the Tides, the 6-foot, 220-pound first baseman hit .257/.324/.423 with 33 doubles, one triples, and 18 homeruns en route to tallying a 116 wRC+.

**Projection**: Here's what I wrote in last year's book:

> "Walker answered some questions surrounding his power potential last season by doubling his career homerun total. Still, though, it's more of a line-drive type of bat with 15-homerun potential in the big leagues. CAL isn't overly optimistic, linking him to a bunch of minor league flame outs. And the overall skillset – decent patience, OK hit tool, and average power – is pretty underwhelming."

Well, CAL still isn't impressed, linking him to Matt Clark, Justin Huber, Brock Peterson, Danny Dorn, and Mike Carp. But, again, line-drive power, average eye, decent hit tool – it can be a promising combination for a middle infielder, just not a first baseman.

**Ceiling:** 1.0- to 1.5-win player
**Risk:** Low
**MLB ETA:** Debuted in 2014

## 10. Ryan Mountcastle, SS

**MiLB Rank: N/A**
**Position Rank: N/A**

| Born: 02/18/97 | Age: 19 | Bats: R | Top CALs: Richard Urena, Preston Mattingly |
| Height: 6-3 | Weight: 185 | Throws: R | Kenneth Peoples-Walls, Neftali Soto, Yeffry De Aza |

| Season | Age | LVL | PA | 2B | 3B | HR | AVG | OBP | SLG | ISO | BB% | K% | wRC+ |
|--------|-----|-----|-----|----|----|----|------|------|------|------|------|------|------|
| 2015 | 18 | R | 175 | 7 | 0 | 3 | 0.313 | 0.349 | 0.411 | 0.098 | 5.1% | 20.6% | 128 |
| 2015 | 18 | A- | 34 | 0 | 0 | 1 | 0.212 | 0.206 | 0.303 | 0.091 | 0.0% | 29.4% | 45 |

**Background:** Baltimore's had a pretty strong track record of draft prep shortstops in the first round over the past several decades, with names including Bobby Grich, Manny Machado, and Ricky Gutierrez. Note: Cal Ripken Jr. was taken in the second round – as a third baseman. Anyway, Mountcastle is the latest high school shortstop taken in the opening round by the franchise. He batted a combined .313/.349/.411 with seven doubles, four homeruns, and 10 stolen bases in 53 games between the Gulf Coast League and Aberdeen in the NYPL.

**Projection**: It was a relatively solid professional debut for the 36th overall pick; he squared up a couple pitches, took a couple walks, and swiped a handful of bags. Per the usual, we'll take a wait-and-see approach until we have a larger sample size to analyze.

**Ceiling:** 1.5-win player
**Risk:** Moderate
**MLB ETA:** 2019

## 11. Mike Wright, RHP

**MiLB Rank:** N/A
**Position Rank:** N/A

| Born: 01/03/90 | Age: 26 | Bats: R | Top CALs: Merrill Kelly, Randy Wells, |
|---|---|---|---|
| Height: 6-6 | Weight: 215 | Throws: R | Scott Diamond, Jeff Manship, Brooks Raley |

| YEAR | Age | Level | IP | W | L | ERA | FIP | K/9 | BB/9 | K% | BB% | HR/9 | LOB% |
|---|---|---|---|---|---|---|---|---|---|---|---|---|---|
| 2013 | 23 | AA | 143.7 | 11 | 3 | 3.26 | 3.27 | 8.52 | 2.44 | 21.8% | 6.2% | 0.56 | 72.2% |
| 2013 | 23 | AAA | 6.7 | 0 | 0 | 0.00 | 2.60 | 2.70 | 0.00 | 7.7% | 0.0% | 0.00 | 100.0% |
| 2014 | 24 | AAA | 142.7 | 5 | 11 | 4.61 | 3.79 | 6.50 | 2.59 | 16.6% | 6.6% | 0.63 | 61.8% |
| 2015 | 25 | AAA | 81.0 | 9 | 1 | 2.22 | 3.28 | 7.00 | 2.78 | 20.0% | 7.9% | 0.44 | 81.1% |

**Background:** Getting the Kevin Gausman treatment last season, Wright spent the entire year bouncing between the Norfolk Tides and Baltimore – all the while keeping his rookie eligibility because he tossed just 44.2 big league innings.

A third round pick out of East Carolina University in 2013, Wright showcased a 93 mph heater, a low-80s slider, a seldom used curveball, and an 80 mph changeup. The big right-hander got smacked around quite a bit during his big league tenure, posting a worrisome 26-to-18 strikeout-to-walk with a 6.13 FIP. He's never going to miss a whole lot of bats, but if the control regresses back his minor league track record he might be a serviceable #5. CAL's best case scenario: Randy Well and Scott Diamond.

**Ceiling:** 1.0- to 1.5-win player
**Risk:** Low to Moderate
**MLB ETA:** Debuted in 2015

## 12. Parker Bridwell, RHP

**MiLB Rank:** N/A
**Position Rank:** N/A

| Born: 02/02/91 | Age: 24 | Bats: R | Top CALs: James Houser, Bryan Mitchell, |
|---|---|---|---|
| Height: 6-4 | Weight: 190 | Throws: R | Rob Rasmussen, Alexander Smit, Dan Cortes |

| YEAR | Age | Level | IP | W | L | ERA | FIP | K/9 | BB/9 | K% | BB% | HR/9 | LOB% |
|---|---|---|---|---|---|---|---|---|---|---|---|---|---|
| 2013 | 21 | A | 142.7 | 8 | 9 | 4.73 | 3.71 | 9.08 | 3.72 | 22.8% | 9.4% | 0.57 | 62.6% |
| 2014 | 22 | A+ | 141.7 | 7 | 10 | 4.45 | 4.20 | 9.02 | 4.45 | 23.4% | 11.5% | 0.70 | 68.1% |
| 2015 | 23 | AA | 97.0 | 4 | 5 | 3.99 | 3.53 | 8.63 | 3.53 | 22.3% | 9.1% | 0.65 | 69.7% |

**Background:** A ninth round pick all the way back in 2010, which, by the way, was the same year the franchise selected cornerstone Manny Machado, Bridwell has been slowly – and, boy do I mean *slowly* – been making his through the *low* levels of the minor leagues. He spent his debut between the Gulf Coast and New York-Penn Leagues, followed that up with spending time back in short-season ball as well as a brief five-game stint in the Sally. He would then spend the next two seasons back with Delmarva, and he would eventually make it up to the Carolina League last season. At each stop, however, Bridwell has always missed a solid amount of wood. Baltimore finally bumped the big 6-foot-4, 190-pound right-hander up to Bowie last season. And in an injury-shortened campaign – he dealt with some elbow issues – Bridwell tossed 97.0 innings with 93 strikeouts, 38 walks, and a 3.53 FIP.

**Projection:** The control is really the only thing holding Bridwell back from becoming a viable big league starter – assuming the platelet-rich injection in his right elbow did the trick. He's *always* missed an impressive amount of bats – he's fanned 20.7% of the batters he's faced in his career – but his control, even during his finest seasons, is below-average. He could be a solid setup man in the near future, something Orioles manager Buck Showalter can capitalize on.

**Ceiling:** 1.0- to 1.5-win player
**Risk:** Moderate
**MLB ETA:** 2016

## 13. C.J. Riefenhauser, LHP

**MiLB Rank:** N/A
**Position Rank:** N/A

| Born: 01/30/90 | Age: 26 | Bats: L | Top CALs: Ryan Brasier, Vin Mazzaro, |
|---|---|---|---|
| Height: 6-0 | Weight: 195 | Throws: L | Alex Wilson, Michael Tonkin, Bryan Augenstein |

| YEAR | Age | Level | IP | W | L | ERA | FIP | K/9 | BB/9 | K% | BB% | HR/9 | LOB% |
|---|---|---|---|---|---|---|---|---|---|---|---|---|---|
| 2013 | 23 | AA | 53.0 | 4 | 0 | 0.51 | 2.52 | 8.15 | 1.87 | 24.4% | 5.6% | 0.51 | 83.8% |
| 2013 | 23 | AAA | 20.7 | 2 | 1 | 3.05 | 3.50 | 9.58 | 3.48 | 26.8% | 9.8% | 0.87 | 67.7% |
| 2014 | 24 | AAA | 57.7 | 3 | 3 | 1.40 | 3.60 | 8.27 | 3.90 | 22.1% | 10.4% | 0.47 | 86.2% |
| 2015 | 25 | A+ | 1.0 | 0 | 0 | 0.00 | 7.17 | 9.00 | 18.00 | 20.0% | 40.0% | 0.00 | 100.0% |
| 2015 | 25 | AAA | 34.7 | 4 | 2 | 2.86 | 2.44 | 8.83 | 1.82 | 24.5% | 5.0% | 0.26 | 68.5% |

**Background:** Passed around like an unwanted cold virus this offseason, Riefenhauser was originally traded by the Rays – along with Boog Powell and Nate Karns – to the Mariners as part of six-player deal that sent Brad Miller, Danny Farquhar, and Logan Morrison to sunny Florida. Less than one month later Seattle packaged the lefty reliever with OBP-deficient slugger Mark Trumbo in exchange for backstop Steve Clevenger. And here's the thing: Riefenhauser – no, it's not the kid from Rookie of the

Year – is going to be a very valuable lefty reliever – like, tomorrow. For his six-year minor league career, the former 20th round pick out of Chipola College has averaged 8.4 K/9 and just 2.7 BB/9 in nearly 450 innings of work.

**Projection**: A fringy upper 80s fastball with plenty of big league value is apparently unwanted. Riefenhauser has typically been death to fellow lefties, so at the very least he's going to be another Javier Lopez. Tremendous, tremendous pick up by the Orioles' front office. And how's this for a bold prediction: in terms of Wins Above Replacement, Riefenhauser is going post a higher total than his player he was traded with, multi-million slugger Mark Trumbo.

**Ceiling:** 1.0-win player
**Risk:** Low
**MLB ETA:** Debuted in 2014

## 14. Tyler Wilson, RHP

**MiLB Rank:** N/A
**Position Rank:** N/A

| Born: 09/25/89 | Age: 26 | Bats: R | Top CALs: Brett Oberholtzer, Reid Santos, |
|---|---|---|---|
| Height: 6-2 | Weight: 185 | Throws: R | Brad Lincoln, Travis Banwart, Travis Wood |

| YEAR | Age | Level | IP | W | L | ERA | FIP | K/9 | BB/9 | K% | BB% | HR/9 | LOB% |
|---|---|---|---|---|---|---|---|---|---|---|---|---|---|
| 2013 | 23 | A+ | 62.3 | 1 | 1 | 4.48 | 3.89 | 6.93 | 3.61 | 18.2% | 9.5% | 0.58 | 63.3% |
| 2013 | 23 | AA | 89.3 | 7 | 5 | 3.83 | 4.46 | 7.05 | 2.22 | 18.7% | 5.9% | 1.31 | 76.0% |
| 2014 | 24 | AA | 96.7 | 10 | 5 | 3.72 | 3.53 | 8.47 | 2.05 | 22.3% | 5.4% | 0.93 | 70.0% |
| 2014 | 24 | AAA | 70.0 | 4 | 3 | 3.60 | 3.90 | 8.49 | 2.70 | 23.2% | 7.4% | 1.03 | 73.8% |
| 2015 | 25 | AAA | 94.3 | 5 | 5 | 3.24 | 3.62 | 6.01 | 1.72 | 16.4% | 4.7% | 0.76 | 77.3% |

**Background:** One of the seemingly rare – at least nowadays – pitchers to make it through the system without a catastrophic injury. Wilson, like Kevin Gausman and Mike Wright, was placed on the franchise's odd development plan as he flip-flopped between the Tides and Orioles for pretty much the entire year. He tossed 94.1 innings with Norfolk last season, fanning 63 and walking just 18 en route to tallying a nice looking 3.24 ERA. And in his five trips to Baltimore, Wilson threw another 36.0 innings while posting a worrisome 13-to-11 strikeout-to-walk ratio. For his minor league career, the former University of Virginia hurler has averaged 7.8 strikeouts and 2.2 walks per nine innings.

**Projection**: During his multiple – and unnecessarily complicated – stints with the Orioles, Wilson showed an average to slightly below-average 90 mph fastball, a low-80s slider, curveball, and changeup, your typical standard four-pitch mix. Wilson's another one of these decent backend fillers who will either settle in as a #5-type or as a useful relief option. CAL offers up some hope by comparing him to Brett Oberholtzer and Travis, both comps seem quite reasonable.

**Ceiling:** 1.0- to 1.5-win player
**Risk:** Moderate
**MLB ETA:** Debuted in 2015

## 15. Garrett Cleavinger, LHP

**MiLB Rank:** N/A
**Position Rank:** N/A

| Born: 04/23/94 | Age: 22 | Bats: L | Top CALs: Hawtin Buchanan, Samuel Martinez, |
|---|---|---|---|
| Height: 6-1 | Weight: 220 | Throws: L | J.D. Osborne, Kyle Smith, Yeyfry Del Rosario |

| YEAR | Age | Level | IP | W | L | ERA | FIP | K/9 | BB/9 | K% | BB% | HR/9 | LOB% |
|---|---|---|---|---|---|---|---|---|---|---|---|---|---|
| 2015 | 21 | A- | 25.0 | 6 | 1 | 2.16 | 4.40 | 11.52 | 6.48 | 30.2% | 17.0% | 0.72 | 83.3% |

**Background:** A three-year workhorse out of the University of Oregon's bullpen, the hefty lefty averaged more than 13 punch outs across 116 collegiate innings. Of course, that came with some – *clears throat* – some questionable control. He averaged a 4.5 BB/9. Baltimore took the potentially fast-moving left-hander in the third round last June, 102nd overall, and sent him directly to the New York-Penn League. In 25.0 innings with Aberdeen, he fanned 32 and walked 18 en route to posting a 2.16 ERA.

**Projection**: Here's what I wrote prior to the draft last season:

> "As ridiculously dominant as he's been in his career – he's *averaged* 14.42 punch outs since he left high school – one has to wonder how he'd perform in the rotation. The Cincinnati Reds have transitioned several former collegiate hurlers – Tony Cingrani, Nick Howard, and Michael Lorenzen – so Cleavinger could be on the franchise's radar.
>
> Cleavinger owns a high floor – he's a potentially fast-moving backend reliever – with a potentially high ceiling as a starter."

I doubt the Orioles give the lefty a chance at starting, but he could move quickly if he posts even reasonable walk rates.

**Ceiling:** 1.0- to 1.5-win player
**Risk:** Moderate
**MLB ETA:** 2018

## 16. David Hess, RHP

MiLB Rank: N/A

Position Rank: N/A

| Born: 07/10/93 | Age: 22 | Bats: R | Top CALs: Sam Bragg, Adam Ottavino, |
|---|---|---|---|
| Height: 6-2 | Weight: 180 | Throws: R | Ryan Berry, Yeiper Castillo, Felix Carvallo |

| YEAR | Age | Level | IP | W | L | ERA | FIP | K/9 | BB/9 | K% | BB% | HR/9 | LOB% |
|---|---|---|---|---|---|---|---|---|---|---|---|---|---|
| 2014 | 20 | A- | 25.3 | 2 | 1 | 3.20 | 3.24 | 8.53 | 2.84 | 23.5% | 7.8% | 0.36 | 75.2% |
| 2014 | 20 | A | 8.0 | 0 | 0 | 3.38 | 0.59 | 13.50 | 0.00 | 40.0% | 0.0% | 0.00 | 57.1% |
| 2015 | 21 | A+ | 133.3 | 9 | 4 | 3.58 | 3.65 | 7.43 | 3.58 | 19.6% | 9.4% | 0.54 | 73.3% |
| 2015 | 21 | AA | 10.0 | 1 | 1 | 4.50 | 2.07 | 10.80 | 3.60 | 27.9% | 9.3% | 0.00 | 64.3% |

**Background:** The second highest pick in the June draft ever taken out of Tennessee Technological University, Hess was taken in the fifth round, 151st overall, two years ago. And since then, he's established himself as one of the better hurlers in the Orioles' system, albeit a very thin Orioles system. The 6-foot-2, 180-pound Tennessee-born right-hander looked dominant in 33.1 innings between Aberdeen and Delmarva during his debut, so the front office bumped him right up to Frederick in the Carolina League. And Hess didn't miss a beat. In 25 starts, 133.1 innings, the right-hander fanned 110, walked 53 and posted a 3.65 FIP. Baltimore bumped him up for a pair of starts in the Eastern League in early September, one of them rather dominant (6.2 IP, 4 H, 8 K, and 2 BB).

**Projection:** He's another of these fringy big league starter types. The control is merely OK and he hasn't missed enough bats to compensate for that. But he's handled his aggressive promotions with relative ease, so he might be able to carve out a career as a decent #5, though I wouldn't count on it. Look for him to make his mark in the bullpen in the coming years.

**Ceiling:** 1.0- to 1.5-win player
**Risk:** Moderate
**MLB ETA:** 2017

## 17. Jon Keller, RHP

MiLB Rank: N/A

Position Rank: N/A

| Born: 08/08/92 | Age: 23 | Bats: R | Top CALs: Tyler Chambliss, James Pugliese, |
|---|---|---|---|
| Height: 6-5 | Weight: 210 | Throws: R | Joel Bender, Devin Anderson, Doug Brandt |

| YEAR | Age | Level | IP | W | L | ERA | FIP | K/9 | BB/9 | K% | BB% | HR/9 | LOB% |
|---|---|---|---|---|---|---|---|---|---|---|---|---|---|
| 2013 | 20 | R | 15.3 | 1 | 2 | 4.11 | 1.70 | 10.57 | 1.17 | 27.7% | 3.1% | 0.00 | 55.0% |
| 2013 | 20 | A- | 3.0 | 1 | 0 | 3.00 | 2.76 | 6.00 | 3.00 | 18.2% | 9.1% | 0.00 | 50.0% |
| 2014 | 21 | A | 56.7 | 3 | 0 | 1.59 | 2.33 | 10.48 | 2.22 | 30.0% | 6.4% | 0.16 | 82.1% |
| 2014 | 21 | A+ | 4.3 | 0 | 0 | 8.31 | 6.06 | 10.38 | 14.54 | 18.5% | 25.9% | 0.00 | 66.7% |
| 2015 | 22 | A+ | 63.7 | 3 | 4 | 3.82 | 3.49 | 7.07 | 3.82 | 17.4% | 9.4% | 0.14 | 68.7% |
| 2015 | 22 | AA | 12.7 | 0 | 0 | 3.55 | 4.14 | 5.68 | 5.68 | 16.0% | 16.0% | 0.00 | 66.7% |

**Background:** After pegging the former 22nd round pick as one of the Top 25 Breakout Prospects in 2015, Keller regressed as he spent time with Frederick and Bowie last season; his strikeout rate dropped from a dominant 10.5 K/9 to a mediocre 6.8 K/9. And, of course, his walk rate ballooned to career high 4.1 BB/9.

**Projection:** Keller looked solid, though far from breakout-y, in his return to High Class A last season. But his control took a noticeable, tangible step backward. CAL isn't offering up much hope by linking him to Tyler Chambliss, James Pugliese, Joel Bender, Devin Anderson, and Dough Brandt. If he can bounce back he might be able to develop into a solid eighth inning guy, otherwise he's middle relief fodder.

**Ceiling:** 1.0-win player
**Risk:** Moderate
**MLB ETA:** 2017

## 18. Travis Seabrooke, LHP

**Born:** 09/16/95 | **Age:** 20 | **Bats:** R | **Top CALs:** Zach Britton, Luis Lugo,
**Height:** 6-6 | **Weight:** 205 | **Throws:** L | Casey Shane, Luis Diaz, Lucas Lanphere

| YEAR | Age | Level | IP | W | L | ERA | FIP | K/9 | BB/9 | K% | BB% | HR/9 | LOB% |
|------|-----|-------|------|---|---|------|------|------|------|-------|------|------|-------|
| 2013 | 17 | R | 8.0 | 0 | 0 | 1.13 | 5.96 | 7.88 | 5.63 | 20.6% | 14.7% | 1.13 | 94.3% |
| 2015 | 19 | A- | 63.7 | 3 | 7 | 4.95 | 3.31 | 6.08 | 2.12 | 15.6% | 5.4% | 0.14 | 63.7% |

**Background:** A projectable lefty taken fifth round out of a Canadian high school, Seabrooke missed the entire 2014 season due to injury. However, if a young hurler would miss an entire year due to injury you would want him to succumb to the type that Seabrooke suffered: a torn ACL in his right knee. Seabrooke, who signed for nearly $300,000, made it back – and healthy – last season, throwing 63.2 innings with the Aberdeen IronBirds, averaging 6.1 punch outs and just 2.1 walks per nine innings. Here's a fun little fact: Seabrooke's father, Glen, was the 21st overall pick in the 1985 NHL draft.

**Projection:** In terms of development, sure, the knee injury put him behind the curve. But (A) thanks to a late birthday he is only entering his age-20 season and (B) putting a positive spin on it, it's less wear-and-tear on his arm. He's basically the equivalent of a 2015 JuCo pick so the sample size is still quite limited.

**Ceiling:** Too Soon to Tell
**Risk:** N/A
**MLB ETA:** N/A

## 19. Branden Kline, RHP

**Born:** 09/29/91 | **Age:** 24 | **Bats:** R | **Top CALs:** Jake Brigham, Jhonatan Ramos,
**Height:** 6-3 | **Weight:** 210 | **Throws:** R | Hector Hernandez, Brian Rauh, Ulises Joaquin

| YEAR | Age | Level | IP | W | L | ERA | FIP | K/9 | BB/9 | K% | BB% | HR/9 | LOB% |
|------|-----|-------|-------|---|---|------|------|------|------|-------|-------|------|-------|
| 2013 | 21 | A | 35.3 | 1 | 2 | 5.86 | 4.50 | 8.15 | 3.57 | 19.9% | 8.7% | 1.02 | 62.3% |
| 2014 | 22 | A+ | 126.7 | 8 | 6 | 3.84 | 3.77 | 6.75 | 2.27 | 17.5% | 5.9% | 0.64 | 71.3% |
| 2014 | 22 | AA | 16.7 | 0 | 2 | 5.94 | 5.03 | 4.86 | 5.94 | 12.2% | 14.9% | 0.54 | 65.2% |
| 2015 | 23 | AA | 39.3 | 3 | 3 | 3.66 | 4.90 | 6.18 | 4.35 | 15.7% | 11.1% | 0.92 | 72.0% |

**Background:** And the arm injuries continue to mount for the organization's young hurlers, the latest elbow to crumble belonged to Kline, the club's 2012 second round pick out of the University of Virginia. Prior to the injury, Kline tallied just 39.1 innings with Bowie, averaging 6.2 K/9 and 4.3 BB/9. It also marked the second time in the last three seasons that the big righty failed to top 40 innings.

**Projection:** Once upon a time several years ago, Kline looked like a promising mid- to back-of-the-rotation caliber arm. But injuries – several of them – have been slowly adding up and now it's hopeful to just keep the 6-foot-3, 210-pound hurler on the mound for extended periods of time.

**Ceiling:** 1.0- to 1.5-win player
**Risk:** High
**MLB ETA:** 2017/2018

## 20. Derrick Bleeker, RHP

**Born:** 03/11/91 | **Age:** 25 | **Bats:** R | **Top CALs:** Jason Motte, Lee Ridenhour,
**Height:** 6-5 | **Weight:** 220 | **Throws:** R | Sheldon Mcdonald, Mike Adams, Jared Simon

| YEAR | Age | Level | IP | W | L | ERA | FIP | K/9 | BB/9 | K% | BB% | HR/9 | LOB% |
|------|-----|-------|------|---|---|------|------|-------|------|-------|------|------|--------|
| 2013 | 22 | R | 3.0 | 0 | 0 | 0.00 | 1.79 | 12.00 | 3.00 | 36.4% | 9.1% | 0.00 | 100.0% |
| 2014 | 23 | A- | 23.3 | 1 | 2 | 3.09 | 2.24 | 8.87 | 1.54 | 23.2% | 4.0% | 0.00 | 70.0% |
| 2014 | 23 | A | 12.3 | 0 | 0 | 2.19 | 2.37 | 10.22 | 0.00 | 29.8% | 0.0% | 0.73 | 60.6% |
| 2015 | 24 | A | 20.7 | 1 | 2 | 6.53 | 3.15 | 7.84 | 0.00 | 19.8% | 0.0% | 0.87 | 41.3% |

**Background:** Taking a page directly out of Mychal Givens' playbook, Bleeker began his pro career as a light-hitting, 37th round pick out of the University of Arkansas. And after batting .238/.304/.333 in his debut, Bleeker converted to the mound and has been...dominant in the lower levels. He's sporting a career 59-to-5 strikeout-to-walk ratio.

**Projection:** And, of course, Bleeker, who started out the season with a perfect 18-to-0 strikeout-to-walk ratio, succumbed to an arm injury – a sprained *freakin'* UCL, the ligament that's eventually replaced in Tommy John surgery. Luckily enough, he was able to avoid undergoing the knife. But, seriously, what the hell is going on with the Orioles' young arms? When he's healthy, he's dominant, though it's come against the lowest levels. He might be something down the road.

**Ceiling:** 1.0-win player
**Risk:** High
**MLB ETA:** 2017/2018

## 21. Tanner Scott, LHP

**MiLB Rank: N/A**
**Position Rank: N/A**

| Born: 07/22/94 | Age: 21 | Bats: R | Top CALs: Javier Avendano, Tyler Wilson, Drake Britton, Clayton Schrader, Jacob Dunnington |
|---|---|---|---|
| Height: 6-2 | Weight: 220 | Throws: L | |

| YEAR | Age | Level | IP | W | L | ERA | FIP | K/9 | BB/9 | K% | BB% | HR/9 | LOB% |
|---|---|---|---|---|---|---|---|---|---|---|---|---|---|
| 2014 | 19 | R | 23.0 | 1 | 5 | 6.26 | 4.51 | 9.00 | 7.83 | 20.4% | 17.7% | 0.00 | 50.0% |
| 2015 | 20 | A- | 21.3 | 4 | 0 | 3.38 | 2.72 | 13.08 | 5.06 | 33.3% | 12.9% | 0.00 | 71.0% |
| 2015 | 20 | A | 21.0 | 0 | 3 | 4.29 | 2.15 | 12.43 | 4.29 | 32.2% | 11.1% | 0.00 | 58.6% |

**Background:** The Warren, Ohio, native caught the eye of the organization after averaging more than 11 punch outs per nine innings during his year at Howard College. And after fanning more than 28% of the batters he's faced in his first two professional seasons, it's easy to see how the Orioles spent a sixth round pick on the 6-foot-2, 220-pound lefty.

**Projection**: Now here's the bad news, of course: after averaging 6.64 BB/9 during his year at Howard College, Scott has walked 42 of the 296 minor league hitters he's faced – or just over 14%. It's very likely that he'll never rein in his problematic control, but big, projectable, hard-throwing southpaws with impressive punch out rates will always get more than a couple head-turns – just ask the Mets' Jack Leathersich, who happens to be a reasonable comparison.

**Ceiling:** 1.0-win player
**Risk:** Moderate to High
**MLB ETA:** 2018

## 22. Brian Gonzalez LHP

**MiLB Rank: N/A**
**Position Rank: N/A**

| Born: 10/25/95 | Age: 20 | Bats: R | Top CALs: Tyler Kolek, Nick Bucci, Matt Kretzschmar, Daniel Mcgrath, Jamie Callahan |
|---|---|---|---|
| Height: 6-3 | Weight: 230 | Throws: L | |

| YEAR | Age | Level | IP | W | L | ERA | FIP | K/9 | BB/9 | K% | BB% | HR/9 | LOB% |
|---|---|---|---|---|---|---|---|---|---|---|---|---|---|
| 2014 | 18 | R | 24.7 | 0 | 0 | 0.00 | 2.70 | 9.12 | 2.92 | 26.9% | 8.6% | 0.00 | 95.2% |
| 2014 | 18 | A- | 9.0 | 0 | 1 | 5.00 | 1.66 | 11.00 | 2.00 | 29.7% | 5.4% | 0.00 | 58.3% |
| 2015 | 19 | A | 105.7 | 4 | 9 | 5.71 | 4.84 | 6.90 | 5.03 | 17.3% | 12.6% | 0.68 | 57.9% |

**Background:** The club's first pick in the 2014 draft, Gonzalez, who was taken in the third round, 90th overall, looked incredible during his debut between the GCL and NYPL, averaging 9.6 K/9 and just 2.7 BB/9. But his production took a dramatic downturn as he got pushed up

– prematurely? – to the Sally: 105.2 IP, 81 K, 59 BB.

**Projection**: The big lefty looked absolutely overmatched in the South Atlantic League last season – which, truthfully, happens all the time. But here's the issue: he showed no signs of progression as the season clicked by. He's still plenty young enough, but he'll need to show something else next season, one in which should be spent in a repeat of the Sally.

**Ceiling:** 1.0-win player
**Risk:** Moderate to High
**MLB ETA:** 2019

## 23. Josh Hart, CF

**MiLB Rank: N/A**
**Position Rank: N/A**

| Born: 10/02/94 | Age: 21 | Bats: L | Top CALs: Derrick Robinson, Eduardo Sosa, Avisail Garcia, Trayvon Robinson, John Matulia |
|---|---|---|---|
| Height: 6-1 | Weight: 180 | Throws: L | |

| Season | Age | LVL | PA | 2B | 3B | HR | AVG | OBP | SLG | ISO | BB% | K% | wRC+ |
|---|---|---|---|---|---|---|---|---|---|---|---|---|---|
| 2013 | 18 | R | 139 | 5 | 2 | 0 | 0.228 | 0.312 | 0.301 | 0.073 | 9.4% | 16.5% | 88 |
| 2014 | 19 | A | 352 | 5 | 1 | 1 | 0.255 | 0.301 | 0.285 | 0.031 | 6.0% | 24.4% | 67 |
| 2015 | 20 | A+ | 445 | 15 | 3 | 1 | 0.255 | 0.282 | 0.311 | 0.057 | 2.5% | 18.2% | 72 |

**Background:** Not to rub salt into an open wound, but here's a list of the players taken right before or immediately following his selection in the latter part of the first round three years ago: Aaron Judge, Sean Manaea, Aaron Blair, Michael Lorenzen, and Corey Knebel, the final two have already made their big league debut. As for Hart, well, he simply looked like a filled baby's diaper in the Sally two years ago, hitting a diarrhea-like .255/.301/.285, and continued his craptastic ways as the club – inexplicably – moved him up to High Class A (.255/.282/.311).

**Projection**: I'd like someone in the Orioles front office explain the decision to move the former supplemental first round pick up to High Class A after one of the worst offensive showings in 2014. I think the reasoning would be fascinating, perhaps telling as well. Anyway, he's nearly 1,000 plate appearances into his minor league career with a .586 OPS. He's a bust, but maybe his speed will get him a couple looks up the ladder.

**Ceiling:** 0.5- to 1.0-win player
**Risk:** Moderate to High
**MLB ETA:** 2019

## 24. Adrian Marin, SS

**MiLB Rank: N/A**
**Position Rank: N/A**

| Born: 03/08/94 | Age: 22 | Bats: R | Top CALs: Malquin Canelo, Abiatal Avelino, |
|---|---|---|---|
| Height: 6-0 | Weight: 180 | Throws: R | Oscar Tejeda, Juan Diaz, Leury Garcia |

| Season | Age | LVL | PA | 2B | 3B | HR | AVG | OBP | SLG | ISO | BB% | K% | wRC+ |
|---|---|---|---|---|---|---|---|---|---|---|---|---|---|
| 2013 | 19 | A | 422 | 19 | 2 | 4 | 0.265 | 0.311 | 0.356 | 0.090 | 5.5% | 21.3% | 93 |
| 2014 | 20 | A+ | 460 | 30 | 1 | 5 | 0.232 | 0.271 | 0.341 | 0.109 | 4.6% | 22.4% | 71 |

**Background:** A (disappointing) third round pick out of Gulliver Prep in Miami, Florida four years ago, Marin put together a couple solid seasons to open up his professional career, but his offense has *really* stagnated in High Class A over the past two seasons.

**Projection**: I think I'll just let CAL paint the picture for you: Malquin Canelo, Abiatal Avelino, Oscar Tejeda, Juan Diaz, and Leury Garcia. Pretty much nothing else needs to be written at this point, right?

**Ceiling:** 0.5- to 1.0-win player
**Risk:** Moderate to High
**MLB ETA:** 2018

## 25. Ryan McKenna, CF

**MiLB Rank: N/A**
**Position Rank: N/A**

| Born: 03/08/94 | Age: 22 | Bats: R | Top CALs: Malquin Canelo, Abiatal Avelino, |
|---|---|---|---|
| Height: 6-0 | Weight: 180 | Throws: R | Oscar Tejeda, Juan Diaz, Leury Garcia |

| Season | Age | LVL | PA | 2B | 3B | HR | AVG | OBP | SLG | ISO | BB% | K% | wRC+ |
|---|---|---|---|---|---|---|---|---|---|---|---|---|---|
| 2013 | 19 | A | 422 | 19 | 2 | 4 | 0.265 | 0.311 | 0.356 | 0.090 | 5.5% | 21.3% | 93 |
| 2014 | 20 | A+ | 460 | 30 | 1 | 5 | 0.232 | 0.271 | 0.341 | 0.109 | 4.6% | 22.4% | 71 |

**Background:** The club's most recent fourth round pick, McKenna, who hails from St. Thomas Aquinas High School in Dover, New Hampshire, batted .265/.366/.324 in a 10-game stint in the Gulf Coast League.

**Projection**: Only 41 trips to the plate. Per the usual, we'll wait and see.

**Ceiling:** Too Soon to Tell
**Risk:** N/A
**MLB ETA:** N/A

### *Barely Missed:*

- **Kevin Grendell, LHP** – Lefty was brilliant with Aberdeen last season, tallying a 36-to-12 strikeout-to-walk ratio in 38.1 innings of work. He might have a future as a middle relief arm down the line.

- **Mitch Horacek, LHP** – Big lefty out of Dartmouth College fanned nearly a bat per inning with solid control in High Class A last season. The problem: 22 gopher balls.

## *Bird Doggin' It – Additional Prospects to Keep an Eye in 2016*

| Player | Age | POS | Notes |
|---|---|---|---|
| Cristian Alvarado | 21 | RHP | Posted an impressive 1.83 between the Gulf Coast and New York-Penn Leagues on the back of a barely-there walk rate. |
| Jake Bray | 23 | RHP | Missed the entire 2014 season, but came back to post a 39-to-5 strikeout-to-walk ratio between the GCL and NYPL. |
| Drew Dosch | 24 | 3B | Lefty-swinging third baseman out of Youngstown State University, home of Jim Tressel, hit a combined .256/.316/.338 between the Carolina and Eastern Leagues last season. He might make it to the big leagues for a couple cups. |
| Donnie Hart | 25 | LHP | Small lefty out of Texas State University blew through three levels en route to averaging 7.6 K/9 and 2.7 BB/9. |
| Jason Heinrich | 20 | LF | Fifth round pick last year had a solid debut in the GCL, hitting .270/.360/.382. |
| Alex Murphy | 21 | C | Career .258/.327/.393 hitter, though he's spent just 36 games in the Sally at this point. |
| Nick Vespi | 20 | LHP | A late round prep pick last June, Vespi looked very promising during his debut in the GCL: 24.0 IP, 25 K, 3 BB. |
| Mike Yastrzemski | 25 | OF | Grandson of Boston great Carl Yastrzemski. Mike is in line to get a couple looks with Baltimore in the next two years. |

**State of the Farm System:** It didn't take long for new General Manager Dave Dombrowski to leave his thumbprint on the historic franchise. Just a little over a week after the Sox hired him, Dombrowski pulled off his first deal, swapping veteran replaceable outfielder Alejandro De Aza for low level lefty Luis Isla, who ranks as the club's 24th best prospect. A couple months later the Hall of Fame-bound GM build off a more sizeable deal, exchanging a quartet of prospects, three with relatively high upside, for Craig Kimbrel. When the dust settled Boston said goodbye to Manuel Margot, Javier Guerra, Logan Allen, and Carlos Asuaje.

Former GM Ben Cherington left the incoming regime with more than a handful of promising minor leaguers. The conversation begins with Cuban-import Yoan Moncada. After inking the 6-foot-2, 205-pound switch-hitter to a whopping $31.5 million bonus, though it topped $60 million once the 100% luxury tax was applied. And you know what? Knowing what we know now, Moncada could have signed for a nine-figure deal as he rebounded from a slow start to bat .310/.415/.500 over his final 56 games.

Falling behind the young Cuban is teenage third baseman Rafael Devers, who teamed with the club's top prospect to give the Greenville Drive an incredible one-two punch in the heart of the lineup. The lefty-swinging Devers slugged .288/.329/.443 with 38 doubles, one three-bagger, and 11 dingers in 508 trips to the plate.

And then there's Anderson Espinoza – ***the best pitching prospect you've likely never heard of.*** Yet.

Espinoza, a 6-foot, rail-thin right-hander out of Venezuela, burst onto the scene as a 17-year-old as he fanned 65 and walked just 14 as he tallied a miniscule 1.23 ERA between the Dominican Summer, Gulf Coast, and South Atlantic Leagues. ***Remember this kid's name.***

Rounding out their Top 5 are Andrew Benintendi, the club's most recent first round pick who will likely give Dansby Swanson a run for his money as the class' top collegiate bat, and right-hander Michael Kopech, who missed a ton of bats but forgot to pass on whatever banned substance that he got popped and subsequently banned for.

After that, though, the system gets awfully thin, awfully quick.

| Rank | Name | POS |
|------|------|-----|
| 1 | Yoan Moncada | 2B |
| 2 | Rafael Devers | 3B |
| 3 | Anderson Espinoza | RHP |
| 4 | Andrew Benintendi | CF |
| 5 | Michael Kopech | RHP |
| 6 | Nick Longhi | 1B/LF/RF |
| 7 | Sam Travis | 1B |
| 8 | Brian Johnson | LHP |
| 9 | Sean Coyle | 2B/3B/OF |
| 10 | Wendell Rijo | 2B |
| 11 | Michael Chavis | 3B |
| 12 | Jamie Callahan | RHP |
| 13 | Deven Marrero | IF |
| 14 | Marco Hernandez | SS |
| 15 | Williams Jerez | LHP |
| 16 | Pat Light | RHP |
| 17 | Josh Ockimey | 1B |
| 18 | Daniel Mcgrath | LHP |
| 19 | Trey Ball | LHP |
| 20 | Teddy Stankiewicz | RHP |
| 21 | Edwin Escobar | LHP |
| 22 | Ty Buttrey | RHP |
| 23 | Mauricio Dubon | IF |
| 24 | Luis Ysla | LHP |
| 25 | Luis Alejandro Basabe | 2B/SS |

**Review of the 2015 Draft:** Armed with the seventh overall pick for the second time in three years, Boston grabbed the supremely talented Arkansas outfielder Andrew Benintendi, who absolutely torched the competition by hitting a combined .313/.416/.556 with seven doubles, four triples, 11 homeruns, and 10 stolen bases during his debut between Lowell Spinners and Greenville Drive. The next pick, 81st overall, was used to grab University of Washington catcher Austin Rei in the third round.

One interesting player to note: fourth round outfielder Tate Matheny, son of Cardinals skipper Mike Matheny, though he looked overmatched during his pro debut.

## 1. Yoan Moncada, 2B

**MiLB Rank: #4**
**Position Rank: #1**

| Born: 05/27/95 | Age: 21 | Bats: B | **Top CALs:** Chris Bostick, Ryan Dent, |
| Height: 6-2 | Weight: 205 | Throws: R | Karexon Sanchez, Marc Wik, Forrest Wall |

| Season | Age | LVL | PA | 2B | 3B | HR | AVG | OBP | SLG | ISO | BB% | K% | wRC+ |
|---|---|---|---|---|---|---|---|---|---|---|---|---|---|
| 2015 | 20 | A | 363 | 19 | 3 | 8 | 0.278 | 0.380 | 0.438 | 0.160 | 11.6% | 22.9% | 135 |

**Background:** The club made a big splash in the international market season — and one that occurred after the publication of last year's book – by inking the Cuban-born infielder to a colossal $31.5 million deal. But that total more than doubled as the club paid the hefty 100% tax fee. Moncada, 6-foot-2, 205-pound switch-hitting infielder, started gaining notoriety when he first debuted in the Cuban National Series at the ripe age of 17. He would slug .283/.414/.348 for the Cienfuegos that year and would follow up with a better showing as an 18-year-old in 2013, hitting .273/.365/.406 with seven doubles, three triples, and three homeruns in 45 games. Once signed, the Red Sox pushed the highly-touted youngster straight in the Sally last season. And he fared well – especially once the calendar flipped to July.

After starting off a bit sluggish – he batted .200/.287/.289 over his first 25 games – Moncada looked every bit the budding star over his final 56 contests. In 262 trips to the plate, Moncada smoked the Sally pitching to the tune of .310/.415/.500 with 16 doubles, a pair of triples, seven homeruns, and a laughably absurd 45 stolen bases in just 48 attempts.

**Projection**: And just for fun here is his production over his final 56 games prorated to a full 162-game season: 46 doubles, six triples, 20 homeruns, and 130 (freaking) stolen bases. So now the $63 million price doesn't seem so outlandish, does it? Moncada is a bit large for second base. And just for some added context: there have been just 17 players since the turn of the 20th century to stand at least 6-foot-2 tall and appear in at least 162 games at second base in their career – Bobby Grich, Ben Zobrist, and Neil Walker being the best of the bunch. So it remains to be seen whether Moncada is the heir apparent to Dustin Pedroia's vaunted throne. He's a budding All-Star, potentially even a future MVP candidate.

**Ceiling:** 5.0- to 5.5-win player
**Risk:** Moderate
**MLB ETA:** 2017

## 2. Rafael Devers, 3B

**MiLB Rank: #15**
**Position Rank: #1**

| Born: 10/24/96 | Age: 19 | Bats: L | **Top CALs:** Jomar Reyes, Matt Dominguez |
| Height: 6-0 | Weight: 195 | Throws: R | Josh Vitters, Victor Acosta, Jarek Cunningham |

| Season | Age | LVL | PA | 2B | 3B | HR | AVG | OBP | SLG | ISO | BB% | K% | wRC+ |
|---|---|---|---|---|---|---|---|---|---|---|---|---|---|
| 2014 | 17 | R | 127 | 5 | 3 | 3 | 0.337 | 0.441 | 0.529 | 0.192 | 15.0% | 15.7% | 175 |
| 2014 | 17 | R | 174 | 11 | 2 | 4 | 0.312 | 0.374 | 0.484 | 0.172 | 8.0% | 17.2% | 146 |
| 2015 | 18 | A | 508 | 38 | 1 | 11 | 0.288 | 0.329 | 0.443 | 0.156 | 4.7% | 16.5% | 118 |

**Background:** Devers had his coming out party two years ago when he bashed his way through 28 Dominican Summer League games (.337/.445/.538) and torched the Gulf Coast League pitching to the tune of .312/.374/.484 with 11 doubles, a pair of triples, and four homeruns. So it seemed like a lock that the Dominican-born third baseman would head to the South Atlantic at the ripe age of 18 last year. And he did just that. In 115 contests with the Greenville Drive, the lefty-swinging Devers stroked a solid .288/.329/.443 with plenty of extra-base firepower; he nearly paced the circuit in doubles (trailing league leader Jose Marmolejos-Diaz of the Nationals 39 to 38) and tied for the 13th most dingers as well. Of course, I'd be remiss to mention that he was one of just two qualified 18-year-olds in the Sally last season (the other being the Braves' Ozhaino Albies).

**Projection**: Again, it's all about perspective. So let's add some. Since 2006, , the first season of FanGraphs' minor league numbers, no other 18-year-old prospect in the Sally has slugged as many two-baggers as Devers did last season; his closest competition was former top prospect Jurickson Profar, who knocked 37 doubles in 2011. So let's widen the parameters a bit, shall we? Since 2006 no 18-year-old *in any Low Class A league* has slugged more doubles than Devers.

Now onto the tangible skills: the lefty-swinging Devers showed a bit of a platoon effect last season, hitting .302/.343/.479 vs. RHP and .252/.297/.356 vs. LHP. But he wasn't completely helpless against southpaws either. The power has a chance to develop into an above-average or potentially even plus skill. And the hit tool is incredibly promising. He needs to continue to make strides against LHP, but there's an All-Star caliber ceiling here.

**Ceiling:** 4.0-win player
**Risk:** Moderate
**MLB ETA:** 2016

## 3. Anderson Espinoza, RHP

**MiLB Rank: #26**
**Position Rank: #12**

| Born: 03/09/98 | Age: 18 | Bats: R | **Top CALs:** Chris Luck, Jio Orozco, |
| Height: 6-0 | Weight: 160 | Throws: R | Fernando Romero, Junior Fernandez, Orlando Romero |

| YEAR | Age | Level | IP | W | L | ERA | FIP | K/9 | BB/9 | K% | BB% | HR/9 | LOB% |
|---|---|---|---|---|---|---|---|---|---|---|---|---|---|
| 2015 | 17 | R | 15.0 | 0 | 0 | 1.20 | 1.67 | 12.60 | 1.80 | 33.9% | 4.8% | 0.00 | 66.7% |
| 2015 | 17 | R | 40.0 | 0 | 1 | 0.68 | 2.28 | 9.00 | 2.03 | 26.0% | 5.8% | 0.00 | 86.5% |
| 2015 | 17 | A | 3.3 | 0 | 1 | 8.10 | 2.88 | 10.80 | 5.40 | 23.5% | 11.8% | 0.00 | 50.0% |

**Background:** The Pedro Martinez comparisons are going to come all too easy – and likely very soon. Gifted with an arm from the baseball gods – sort of like Nuke LaLoosh – the 6-foot-nothing right-hander out of Caracas, Venezuela, convinced Boston to hand a hefty $1.8 million deal – a deal, by the way, that essentially eliminates the franchise's ability to sign international amateur free agents to deals in surplus of $300,000 *through the 2016-2017 season*. And barring any horrific – or unfortunate – injury, Espinoza's going to prove that the club made the right deal, hands down. The 160-pound right-hander, who could stand to walk around with a couple Big Macs in his back pocket for snack time, was as dominant as *any* teenage prospect in baseball last season, small sample size be damned. Espinoza blew through the Dominican Summer League in four starts, put on his best Pedro impression in the Gulf Coast for another 10 games, and finished off his pro debut with one start in the Sally. The sinewy right-hander finished the year with an aggregate 1.23 ERA in 58.1 innings of work, fanning 65 and walking only 14.

**Projection**: New Sox General Manager Dave Dombrowski is going to have to write his predecessor Ben Cherington a rather lengthy thank you note for inking the supremely talented hurler. While the data is still rather limited – just under 60 innings of work – Espinoza's ceiling could be as high as any hurler in the minor leagues, including that of Julio Urias. Equipped with a bazooka for an arm and blessed with what appears to be pinpoint control, Espinoza is likely going to be a force to be reckoned with for the foreseeable future. Here's hoping the kid stays healthy.

**Ceiling:** 4.5- to 5.0-win player
**Risk:** High
**MLB ETA:** 2018

## 4. Andrew Benintendi, CF

**MiLB Rank: #33**
**Position Rank: N/A**

| Born: 07/06/94 | Age: 21 | Bats: L | **Top CALs:** Carlos Santana, Ian Happ, |
| Height: 5-10 | Weight: 170 | Throws: L | Brett Siddall, Reid Fronk, Garin Cecchini |

| Season | Age | LVL | PA | 2B | 3B | HR | AVG | OBP | SLG | ISO | BB% | K% | wRC+ |
|---|---|---|---|---|---|---|---|---|---|---|---|---|---|
| 2015 | 20 | A- | 153 | 2 | 4 | 7 | 0.290 | 0.408 | 0.540 | 0.250 | 16.3% | 9.8% | 175 |
| 2015 | 20 | A | 86 | 5 | 0 | 4 | 0.351 | 0.430 | 0.581 | 0.230 | 11.6% | 10.5% | 183 |

**Background:** Since 1968 the Red Sox have owned three top 10 draft selections and in each of those seasons – 1993, 2013, and 2015 – the organization's been armed with the seventh overall pick. The club selected former fan favorite outfielder Trot Nixon more than two decades ago, right-handed prepster Trey Ball in 2013, and, finally, grabbing Andrew Benintendi last June. The rare draft-eligible sophomore, Benintendi garnered a whole helluva lot of awards and recognitions during his final year with the Razorbacks, including:

- Golden Spikes Award
- Dick Howser Trophy
- SEC Male Athlete of the Year
- Baseball America National Player of the Year
- Collegiate Baseball National Player of the Year
- SEC Player of the Year (as chosen by the coaches)
- All-SEC First Team (as chosen by the coaches)
- Louisville Slugger All-America First Team
- ABCA/Rawlings All-America First Team
- D1 Baseball All-America First Team
- Baseball America All-America First Team
- Collegiate Baseball All-America First Team

The 5-foot-11 center fielder had a season for the records in 2015, hitting .376/.488/.717 with 13 doubles, two triples, an NCAA-leading 20 homeruns, and 24 stolen bases (in 28 attempts). Perhaps the most impressive statistic to note: Benintendi finished the year with a laughably absurd 32-to-50 strikeout-to-walk ratio. And as Arkansas' website states, Benintendi became just the third player in the SEC lengthy history to lead the conference in both batting average and homeruns. The other two occurrences were by Rafael Palmeiro in 1984 and Kurt Abbot ten years later. And Benintendi's impressive offensive run didn't end with his conversion to wood bats either.

The club had the seventh overall pick begin his professional career in the New York-Penn League, which lasted all of 35 games; of course, hitting .290/.408/.540 goes along way too. He got bounced up to Greenville for his final 19 games and still managed to swing a scorching stick, slugging .351/.430/.581. Overall, he finished his pro debut with an aggregate .313/.416/.556 with seven doubles, four triples, 11 homeruns ,and 10 stolen bases.

**Projection**: Here's what I wrote during his pre-draft evaluation:

> *"Not too much data to go off of, just about two seasons worth, but Benintendi is showcasing an incredible collection of offensive potential for Arkansas this season: power, speed, patience, and a solid hit tool. Making it more impressive is [the fact] that Arkansas' home ballpark tends to **deflate** offensive production.Benintendi has the potential to develop into a better-tha- average everyday MLB'er down the line, offering up 15/15 potential with solid on-base skills and perhaps the ability to hit in the upper third of team's lineup."*

That 15/15 projection looks a bit on the low side for now. I'd bump it up to 20/20, perhaps even going a touch higher to 25/25 now. If the defense grades out even as average, Benintendi has a chance to develop into a perennial All-Star.

**Ceiling:** 4.0-win player
**Risk:** Moderate
**MLB ETA:** 2017

## 5. Michael Kopech, RHP

**MiLB Rank: #69**
**Position Rank: N/A**

| Born: 04/30/96 | Age: 20 | Bats: R | Top CALs: John Lamb, Yoel Mecias, |
|---|---|---|---|
| Height: 6-3 | Weight: 205 | Throws: R | Frank Lopez, Jake Thompson, Robbie Ray |

| YEAR | Age | Level | IP | W | L | ERA | FIP | K/9 | BB/9 | K% | BB% | HR/9 | LOB% |
|---|---|---|---|---|---|---|---|---|---|---|---|---|---|
| 2014 | 18 | R | 13.7 | 0 | 1 | 4.61 | 3.14 | 10.54 | 5.93 | 26.7% | 15.0% | 0.00 | 65.0% |
| 2015 | 19 | A | 65.0 | 4 | 5 | 2.63 | 3.35 | 9.69 | 3.74 | 25.9% | 10.0% | 0.28 | 73.9% |

**Background:** The supremely talented Kopech was in the midst of a breakout season before he got slapped – and slapped *hard* – by the minor league drug testing system. The former supplemental first round pick got popped – and subsequently suspended for 50 games – for having the performance enhancer Oxilofrine in his system. The drug falls under the amphetamine umbrella. Before the punishment was doled out, Kopech was a force to be reckoned with in the South Atlantic League last season, fanning nearly 26% and walking 10.0% of the total hitters he faced. He was sporting a 2.35 ERA to go along with a 3.35 FIP before being shut down for the season.

**Projection**: Equipped with a power-pitcher's arsenal, the 6-foot-3, 195-pound right-hander can sling it with the best 'em. And unlike so many other teenagers blessed with an above-average- to plus-fastball, Kopech actually knew where it was going the majority of the time. Look for him to have a big, *big* year in 2016.

**Ceiling:** 3.0-win player
**Risk:** Moderate
**MLB ETA:** 2018

## 6. Nick Longhi, 1B/LF/RF

**MiLB Rank: #188**
**Position Rank: N/A**

| Born: 08/16/95 | Age: 20 | Bats: R | Top CALs: Austin Dean, Justin Williams, |
|---|---|---|---|
| Height: 6-2 | Weight: 205 | Throws: L | Reid Engel, Jose Martinez, Luis Domoromo |

| Season | Age | LVL | PA | 2B | 3B | HR | AVG | OBP | SLG | ISO | BB% | K% | wRC+ |
|---|---|---|---|---|---|---|---|---|---|---|---|---|---|
| 2014 | 18 | A- | 121 | 10 | 1 | 0 | 0.330 | 0.388 | 0.440 | 0.110 | 9.1% | 18.2% | 144 |
| 2015 | 19 | A | 488 | 27 | 3 | 7 | 0.281 | 0.338 | 0.403 | 0.122 | 7.0% | 18.0% | 112 |
| 2015 | 19 | A | 488 | 27 | 3 | 7 | 0.281 | 0.338 | 0.403 | 0.122 | 7.0% | 18.0% | 112 |

**Background:** Don't let the 30th round draft selection fool you. The franchise signed the former 2013 pick to a hefty $440,000 bonus – basically the equivalent to late third/early fourth round money that year. And the low risk/high reward signing has been paying off in big way over the past two seasons – something that is very likely to continue despite General Manager Ben Cherington earning his walking papers. Longhi, a lefty-swinging corner outfielder/first baseman, had a less-than-auspicious debut in the Gulf Coast in 2013, hitting .178/.245/.356 in 50 plate appearances, but he's handled the New York-Penn and South Atlantic Leagues with aplomb. As an 18-year-old in 2014, Longhi topped the NYPL average offensive production by 44% en route to hitting a robust .330/.388/.440 – despite failing to hit a single homerun. The club pushed him to the Sally last season, and he responded with a .281/.338/.403 showing, hitting 27 doubles, three triples, and seven dingers.

**Projection**: The power hasn't come through in the typical over-the-fence fashion, but it's slowly taking the appropriate steps forward – especially with the then-19-year-old bashing 37 extra-base hits last season. Decent plate discipline with the ability to develop an above-average hit tool, Longhi hasn't shown any favoritism towards facing lefties or righties – another positive sign. If everything breaks the right way for the former 30th round pick could develop into a quasi-Eric Hosmer type bat.

**Ceiling:** 2.0- to 2.5- to 3.0-win player
**Risk:** Moderate to High
**MLB ETA:** 2018

## 7. Sam Travis, 1B

**MiLB Rank: #217**
**Position Rank: N/A**

| Born: 08/27/93 | Age: 22 | Bats: R | Top CALs: Rangel Ravelo, Gregory Polanco, |
|---|---|---|---|
| Height: 6-0 | Weight: 195 | Throws: R | Aaron Cunningham, Josh Bell, Logan Morrison |

| Season | Age | LVL | PA | 2B | 3B | HR | AVG | OBP | SLG | ISO | BB% | K% | wRC+ |
|---|---|---|---|---|---|---|---|---|---|---|---|---|---|
| 2014 | 20 | A- | 174 | 5 | 1 | 4 | 0.333 | 0.364 | 0.448 | 0.115 | 2.3% | 10.3% | 140 |
| 2014 | 20 | A | 115 | 11 | 1 | 3 | 0.290 | 0.330 | 0.495 | 0.206 | 6.1% | 12.2% | 124 |
| 2015 | 21 | A+ | 278 | 15 | 4 | 5 | 0.313 | 0.378 | 0.467 | 0.154 | 9.4% | 15.5% | 146 |
| 2015 | 21 | AA | 281 | 17 | 2 | 4 | 0.300 | 0.384 | 0.436 | 0.136 | 11.7% | 12.1% | 140 |

**Background:** I *hate* the phrase "Professional Hitter." If you get paid to play baseball as an everyday guy – regardless if it's multi-millions of dollars or a small pittance handed out to Indy League players – you are, in fact, a Professional Hitter. Some are definitely better than others, but they all fall under the same umbrella. Now with that little rant behind me, I can't believe I'm going write/say this: when the phrase inevitably pops up it could easily be slapped on Sam Travis, the former University of Indiana slugger who teamed with – and was overshadowed by – Kyle Schwarber to form an NCAA version of the Bash Brothers. Travis, the second round pick of the Sox in 2014, bashed his way through the New York-Penn and Sally Leagues during his debut, hitting a combined .316/.351/.467 with 16 doubles, a pair of triples, and seven homeruns in 67. And he continued his upward-and-onward march towards Boston last season. He opened the year by slugging .313/.378/.467 in 66 games with Salem and closed it up by batting .300/.384/.436 in 65 Eastern League games.

**Projection**: For a jog down memory lane, here's what I wrote prior to the 2014 draft:

> "While his contact rates have improved – and ignoring some vagaries in BABIP – Travis has seemingly plateaued as a hitter. Solid-average power with the chance to top out in the 15- to 20-HR area, a pretty good hit tool, and a decent eye at the plate, which will likely become below-average in the professional ranks.
>
> Depending upon his defense, Travis could develop into a league-average everyday third baseman or a below-average first baseman (where the bat clearly doesn't play well), give or take a half-win either way.
>
> He could, however, just as easily flame out as a Quad-A guy too. There's some risk, but one that's worth taking in the late second/third rounds."

Well, there's an awful lot of right *and* wrong in that pre-draft evaluation. The right: solid-average power and a pretty good hit tool. The wrong: Travis didn't plateau as a hitter and his patience at the plate held firm. CAL remains rather impressed, linking him to Gregory Polanco, Josh Bell, and Logan Morrison. Think of a big league triple-slash line that hovers between 95 and 105 wRC+ when it's all said and done.

**Ceiling:** 1.5- to 2.0-win player
**Risk:** Moderate
**MLB ETA:** 2016

## 8. Brian Johnson, LHP

**MiLB Rank: #219**
**Position Rank: N/A**

| Born: 12/07/90 | Age: 25 | Bats: L | Top CALs: Nick Tropeano, Jeff Locke, |
|---|---|---|---|
| Height: 6-4 | Weight: 235 | Throws: L | Robert Ray, Alex Wilson, Boone Whiting |

| YEAR | Age | Level | IP | W | L | ERA | FIP | K/9 | BB/9 | K% | BB% | HR/9 | LOB% |
|---|---|---|---|---|---|---|---|---|---|---|---|---|---|
| 2013 | 22 | R | 5.0 | 0 | 0 | 0.00 | 1.86 | 12.60 | 3.60 | 41.2% | 11.8% | 0.00 | 100.0% |
| 2013 | 22 | A | 69.0 | 1 | 6 | 2.87 | 3.63 | 9.00 | 3.65 | 24.0% | 9.7% | 0.52 | 69.4% |
| 2013 | 22 | A+ | 11.0 | 1 | 0 | 1.64 | 3.26 | 6.55 | 4.09 | 17.8% | 11.1% | 0.00 | 85.7% |
| 2014 | 23 | A+ | 25.7 | 3 | 1 | 3.86 | 1.76 | 11.57 | 2.45 | 30.3% | 6.4% | 0.00 | 56.7% |
| 2014 | 23 | AA | 118.0 | 10 | 2 | 1.75 | 3.15 | 7.55 | 2.44 | 21.9% | 7.1% | 0.46 | 79.7% |
| 2015 | 24 | AAA | 96.0 | 9 | 6 | 2.53 | 3.22 | 8.44 | 3.00 | 23.1% | 8.2% | 0.56 | 74.8% |

**Background:** The lanky lefty out of the University of Florida battled a fairly serious injury for the second time in his professional career. The 31st overall selection in the 2012 draft, Johnson took a line-drive off the face, breaking several bones, and limiting his professional debut to just over five innings of work. Fast forward a couple years – and a couple hundred innings – and Johnson was shut down in early August with elbow tightness, an injury that precipitated a trip to the MRI machine which, thankfully, revealed no structural damage. The 6-foot-4, 235-pound southpaw made 18 starts with Pawtucket in the International League last season, throwing 96 innings with 90 punch outs, 32 walks, and a 3.22 FIP. The club bounced him up for a disastrous start in late July; he would face off against the Astros and allow four walks and four earned runs in 4.1 innings.

**Projection**: During his brief big league stint – and it should be noted he would be shut down for the season shortly after – Johnson's fastball averaged a smidgeon over 87 mph. And once again CAL links a bunch of backend starter types to the lefty: Nick Tropeano, Jeff Locke, Robbie Ray, etc… He's not going to miss nearly the amount of bats he has in his minor league career, but, again, as I stated in last year's book, every team needs a #5, right? Here's hoping that the elbow doesn't slow him down at any point in the future.

**Ceiling**: 1.5- to 2.0-win player
**Risk**: Moderate
**MLB ETA**: Debuted in 2015

## 9. Sean Coyle, 2B/3B/OF

**MiLB Rank: N/A**
**Position Rank: N/A**

| Born: 01/17/92 | Age: 24 | Bats: R | Top CALs: Bruce Caldwell, Josh Tolisano, |
| Height: 5-8 | Weight: 175 | Throws: R | Trevor Story, Brandon Woods, Javier Baez |

| Season | Age | LVL | PA | 2B | 3B | HR | AVG | OBP | SLG | ISO | BB% | K% | wRC+ |
|---|---|---|---|---|---|---|---|---|---|---|---|---|---|
| 2013 | 21 | A+ | 224 | 9 | 1 | 14 | 0.241 | 0.321 | 0.513 | 0.272 | 10.7% | 29.0% | 125 |
| 2014 | 22 | AA | 384 | 23 | 1 | 16 | 0.295 | 0.371 | 0.512 | 0.217 | 9.9% | 24.7% | 144 |
| 2015 | 23 | R | 42 | 4 | 0 | 1 | 0.289 | 0.357 | 0.474 | 0.184 | 7.1% | 45.2% | 149 |
| 2015 | 23 | A- | 13 | 1 | 0 | 0 | 0.250 | 0.308 | 0.333 | 0.083 | 7.7% | 23.1% | 92 |
| 2015 | 23 | AAA | 148 | 3 | 0 | 5 | 0.159 | 0.274 | 0.302 | 0.143 | 13.5% | 29.7% | 71 |

**Background**: Disappointing in nearly every sense of the word. Coyle's initial trip to the International League was hampered by injury, more specifically left elbow inflammation, and a subsequent lack of production. The once-budding sabermetric darling hit a paltry .159/.274/.305 with just eight extra-base knocks –

three doubles and five homeruns – en route to tallying a career low 71 wRC+. It's quite a fall from grace for the same player that batted .295/.371/.512 with plenty of extra-base firepower in Class AA the year before. For his career, Coyle is sporting a solid .251/.338/.445 triple-slash line, hitting 102 doubles, 11 triples, 61 homeruns, and 66 stolen bases in 434 total games.

**Projection**: A do-over is in definite order. When he is right Coyle offers up an average or better package of offensive skills: plate discipline, power, and speed. Here's what I wrote in last year's book:

> "Of course there's going to be bad news, right? For everything Coyle does well, his strikeout rates have always toed the line between high and red flag territory. Fringy every day guy who could – and likely will – succeed in a super-sub role."

**Ceiling**: 1.5-win player
**Risk**: Moderate
**MLB ETA**: 2016

## 10. Wendell Rijo, 2B

**MiLB Rank: N/A**
**Position Rank: N/A**

| Born: 09/04/95 | Age: 20 | Bats: R | Top CALs: John Tolisano, Yamaico Navarro, |
| Height: 5-11 | Weight: 170 | Throws: R | Luis Mateo, Chris Bostick, Delino Deshields |

| Season | Age | LVL | PA | 2B | 3B | HR | AVG | OBP | SLG | ISO | BB% | K% | wRC+ |
|---|---|---|---|---|---|---|---|---|---|---|---|---|---|
| 2013 | 17 | R | 203 | 15 | 0 | 0 | 0.271 | 0.368 | 0.359 | 0.088 | 10.8% | 14.3% | 121 |
| 2014 | 18 | A | 473 | 27 | 6 | 9 | 0.254 | 0.348 | 0.416 | 0.161 | 11.8% | 21.8% | 115 |
| 2015 | 19 | A+ | 455 | 27 | 2 | 6 | 0.260 | 0.324 | 0.381 | 0.121 | 7.5% | 20.7% | 107 |

**Background**: Originally signed out of the Dominican Republic in 2011 for a little over $600,000. Rijo's aggressive developmental plan continued without a hitch in 2015 – he was one of just five qualified teenage bats in any High Class A level last year. Rijo was the rare international free agent signing that would bypass the foreign leagues and head straight into the stateside rookie leagues, where he more than held his own (.271/.368/.359). Boston bounced him to Greenville two years ago and once again he handled the test with aplomb: .254/.348/.416. Last year Rijo batted .260/.324/.381 with plenty of gap power (27 doubles and a pair of triples) while slugging six dingers. He finished the year with a 107 wRC+ - the third best showing among those teenage bats in High Class A.

**Projection**: A fairly well-rounded middle infield prospect. Rijo packs more wallop than his 5-foot-11, 170-pound frame would lead you to believe. He can swipe 15 or so bags, take the occasional walk, and won't get burned chasing too many pitches outside the zone. He's a fringy big league regular, something CAL seems to agree with (Delino Deshields, Yamaico Navarro, and Chris Bostick).

**Ceiling:** 1.5-win player
**Risk:** Moderate
**MLB ETA:** 2017

## 11. Michael Chavis, 3B

<u>**MiLB Rank:**</u> N/A
<u>**Position Rank:**</u> N/A

| Born: 08/11/95 | Age: 20 | Bats: R | Top CALs: Levi Carolus, Miguel Tejada, |
|---|---|---|---|
| Height: 5-10 | Weight: 190 | Throws: R | Jomar Reyes, Alex Liddi, Javier Azcona |

| Season | Age | LVL | PA | 2B | 3B | HR | AVG | OBP | SLG | ISO | BB% | K% | wRC+ |
|---|---|---|---|---|---|---|---|---|---|---|---|---|---|
| 2014 | 18 | R | 150 | 12 | 3 | 1 | 0.269 | 0.347 | 0.425 | 0.157 | 10.0% | 25.3% | 124 |
| 2014 | 18 | R | 150 | 12 | 3 | 1 | 0.269 | 0.347 | 0.425 | 0.157 | 10.0% | 25.3% | 124 |
| 2015 | 19 | A | 471 | 29 | 1 | 16 | 0.223 | 0.277 | 0.405 | 0.182 | 6.2% | 30.6% | 91 |

**Background**: The club's first pick in the draft two years ago, Chavis got off to an abysmal start in 2015, his first taste of full season action. After a solid, though far from spectacular debut in the Gulf Coast in 2014, the club aggressively pushed the 5-foot-10, 190-pound third baseman to the Sally. And he promptly "batted," a term used in the loosest sense, .197/.263/.336 in his first 60 games of action. Chavis did manage to pick it up in early July; he hit a more respectable .250/.292/.476 with 16 doubles, one triple, and 10 homeruns over his final 49 contests. For his brief career, Chavis is sporting a .234/.277/.405 triple-slash line, hitting 41 doubles, four triples, and 17 dingers in 148 games.

**Projection**: Here's what we know about the short, well-built third baseman in roughly a year-plus worth of action: above-average power, now and in the foreseeable future; questionable contact rates and hit tool; a little bit of speed. But even during his "hot stretch" in the Sally last season Chavis punched out in over 27% of his plate appearances. An optimist would respond by saying (A) it's an improvement and (B) he was incredibly young for the level. I would respond by pointing out that he fanned in over a quarter of his plate appearances in the Gulf Coast two years ago, an age-appropriate level of competition.

**Ceiling:** 1.5-win player
**Risk:** Moderate to High
**MLB ETA:** 2018

## 12. Jamie Callahan, RHP

<u>**MiLB Rank:**</u> N/A
<u>**Position Rank:**</u> N/A

| Born: 08/24/94 | Age: 21 | Bats: R | Top CALs: Yeiper Castillo, Omar Poveda, |
|---|---|---|---|
| Height: 6-2 | Weight: 230 | Throws: R | Jose Alvarez, David Baker, Zachary Fuesser |

| YEAR | Age | Level | IP | W | L | ERA | FIP | K/9 | BB/9 | K% | BB% | HR/9 | LOB% |
|---|---|---|---|---|---|---|---|---|---|---|---|---|---|
| 2013 | 18 | A- | 59.7 | 5 | 1 | 3.92 | 3.11 | 8.15 | 2.56 | 22.6% | 7.1% | 0.60 | 65.2% |
| 2014 | 19 | A | 108.7 | 3 | 13 | 6.96 | 5.34 | 7.37 | 5.47 | 17.1% | 12.7% | 0.99 | 59.1% |
| 2015 | 20 | A | 89.3 | 7 | 6 | 4.53 | 3.17 | 9.47 | 3.32 | 23.7% | 8.3% | 0.40 | 62.7% |

**Background:** The club's second round pick all the way back in 2012 – and just to put that into perspective that's the same year Carlos Correa, Byron Buxton, and Addison Russell were picked – made another go-round in the Sally last season. Callahan, at the ripe age of 19-years-old, battled some rather serious control issues during his first stint with Greenville, issuing 66 base-on-balls in just 108.2 innings of work. Last season, though, Callahan faired far better: in 31 appearances with Greenville he tossed 89.1 innings while fanning 94 and walking just 33.

**Projection**: After a disastrous start to the year – Callahan coughed up 22 earned runs in his first 21.2 innings of work – the 6-foot-2 right-hander was demoted to a multi-inning reliever and the results were far better: 68 IP, 75 strikeouts, 23 walks, and a tidy 3.04 ERA. It's still far too early to give up on the promising right-hander's career aspirations as a starter, but at least there's always the possibility of a dominant backend reliever.

**Ceiling:** 1.5-win player
**Risk:** Moderate
**MLB ETA:** 2018

## 13. Deven Marrero, SS

MiLB Rank: N/A
Position Rank: N/A

| Born: 08/25/90 | Age: 25 | Bats: R | Top CALs: Omar Quintanilla, Tim Beckham, |
| Height: 6-1 | Weight: 195 | Throws: R | Trevor Plouffe, Brent Lillibridge, Ramiro Pena |

| Season | Age | LVL | PA | 2B | 3B | HR | AVG | OBP | SLG | ISO | BB% | K% | wRC+ |
|---|---|---|---|---|---|---|---|---|---|---|---|---|---|
| 2013 | 22 | A+ | 376 | 20 | 0 | 2 | 0.256 | 0.341 | 0.334 | 0.078 | 11.2% | 16.0% | 94 |
| 2014 | 23 | AA | 307 | 19 | 2 | 5 | 0.291 | 0.371 | 0.433 | 0.142 | 11.1% | 18.6% | 126 |
| 2014 | 23 | AAA | 202 | 11 | 0 | 1 | 0.210 | 0.260 | 0.285 | 0.075 | 5.9% | 18.3% | 48 |
| 2015 | 24 | AAA | 419 | 13 | 1 | 6 | 0.256 | 0.316 | 0.344 | 0.088 | 7.9% | 20.8% | 92 |
| 2015 | 24 | MLB | 56 | 0 | 0 | 1 | 0.226 | 0.268 | 0.283 | 0.057 | 5.4% | 33.9% | 46 |

**Background:** After three-plus years of being selected with the 24th overall pick in the draft – ahead of the likes of Lewis Brinson, Jose Berrios, Daniel Robertson, Stephen Piscotty, Joey Gallo, and Lance McCullers; just to name a few – the defensive artist known as Devin "The Disappointing" Marrero appeared from the murky waters of the International League to make his big league debut. To be completely fair, it's not his fault he went as high in the draft as he did. After all, his production had dropped severely over his final two seasons at Arizona State. But it is what it is. Marrero appeared in 102 games with Pawtucket in 2015, making 419 trips to the plate, hitting .256/.316/.344 with little power and speed – numbers that are eerily similar to his MiLB career marks (.258/.333/.350).

**Projection:** The defense is above-average, big league caliber. The question – and it's *always* been the question – is whether he was ever going to hit enough to get an extended opportunity at the game's pinnacle level. After 1,673 plate appearances in the minors the answer is a resounding *no*. His walk rate has tumbled over the past couple years as more advanced pitchers have continually – and successfully – challenged him. Cliff Pennington wannabe. Or according to CAL he's another Omar Quintanilla/Tim Beckham/Brent Lillibridge/Ramiro Pena..

**Ceiling:** 1.0-win player
**Risk:** Low
**MLB ETA:** Debuted in 2015

## 14. Marco Hernandez, SS

MiLB Rank: N/A
Position Rank: N/A

| Born: 09/06/92 | Age: 23 | Bats: L | Top CALs: Trevor Plouffe, Yadiel Rivera, |
| Height: 6-0 | Weight: 170 | Throws: R | Erik Gonzalez, Didi Gregorius, Heiker Menses |

| Season | Age | LVL | PA | 2B | 3B | HR | AVG | OBP | SLG | ISO | BB% | K% | wRC+ |
|---|---|---|---|---|---|---|---|---|---|---|---|---|---|
| 2013 | 20 | A | 443 | 17 | 3 | 4 | 0.254 | 0.287 | 0.338 | 0.084 | 3.6% | 16.3% | 75 |
| 2014 | 21 | A+ | 486 | 13 | 7 | 3 | 0.270 | 0.315 | 0.351 | 0.082 | 6.2% | 18.5% | 89 |
| 2015 | 22 | AA | 294 | 21 | 4 | 5 | 0.326 | 0.349 | 0.482 | 0.156 | 3.1% | 16.7% | 139 |
| 2015 | 22 | AAA | 190 | 9 | 2 | 4 | 0.271 | 0.300 | 0.409 | 0.138 | 4.2% | 20.5% | 100 |
| 2015 | 22 | AAA | 190 | 9 | 2 | 4 | 0.271 | 0.300 | 0.409 | 0.138 | 4.2% | 20.5% | 100 |

**Background:** The player to be named later in the Felix Doubront deal with the Cubs at the trade deadline two years ago, the lefty-swinging shortstop tore up the Class AA competition, hitting .326/.349/.482 with 21 doubles, four triples, five homeruns, and four stolen bases in 68 games, before hovering around the International League average for 46 games.

**Projection:** The power really came back in a big way last season for Hernandez as he posted an aggregate .149 ISO. And after looking lost against fellow left-handers the previous season, the Dominican-born shortstop batted .317/.336/.387 against them in 2015. The eye is below-average and he didn't run nearly as frequently as he did the previous couple of years. Fringy big league regular who is destined to be a backup.

**Ceiling:** 1.0- to 1.5-win player
**Risk:** Low to Moderate
**MLB ETA:** 2017

## 15. Williams Jerez, LHP

**MiLB Rank: N/A**
**Position Rank: N/A**

| Born: 05/16/92 | Age: 24 | Bats: L | **Top CALs:** Brad Mills, Dan Merklinger, |
|---|---|---|---|
| Height: 6-4 | Weight: 190 | Throws: L | Mark Peterson, Barret Browning, Kyle Gunderson |

| YEAR | Age | Level | IP | W | L | ERA | FIP | K/9 | BB/9 | K% | BB% | HR/9 | LOB% |
|---|---|---|---|---|---|---|---|---|---|---|---|---|---|
| 2014 | 22 | R | 24.3 | 3 | 1 | 2.22 | 2.15 | 9.99 | 1.85 | 27.0% | 5.0% | 0.00 | 70.4% |
| 2014 | 22 | A- | 10.0 | 1 | 1 | 4.50 | 3.24 | 11.70 | 5.40 | 26.0% | 12.0% | 0.00 | 71.4% |
| 2015 | 23 | A | 39.3 | 3 | 1 | 2.06 | 3.13 | 9.84 | 2.29 | 25.9% | 6.0% | 0.69 | 76.3% |
| 2015 | 23 | A+ | 12.3 | 1 | 0 | 0.73 | 2.53 | 8.76 | 2.92 | 23.1% | 7.7% | 0.00 | 87.5% |
| 2015 | 23 | AA | 37.0 | 1 | 2 | 3.65 | 3.67 | 7.54 | 4.14 | 19.5% | 10.7% | 0.49 | 74.7% |

**Background:** The club's second round pick in 2011, Jerez quickly proved that he couldn't handle professional, low level pitching; he hit .221/.254/.275 through his first 107 games. So the Sox did the only reasonable thing: they converted the rocket-armed center fielder into a pitcher and two years later he's knocking on the big league club's door. The 6-foot-4, 190-pound left-hander made stops at three different levels in 2015, tallying 88.2 innings between the South Atlantic, Carolina, and Eastern Leagues. He fanned 86, walked 31, and finished with an aggregate 2.54 ERA. For his [pitching] career, Jerez has averaged 9.2 punch outs and just 3.1 free passes per nine innings. Not bad work for a former second round bust.

**Projection**: Listed among the *Bird Doggin' It* section of last year's book; there's so much promised wrapped up in Jerez's left arm. He has very little wear-and-tear that would be associated with the typical 23-year-old arm; he's thrown just 123.0 innings since 2011. And he's been *healthy* during that time. Strong strikeouts, solid control.

**Ceiling:** 1.0-win player
**Risk:** Low to Moderate
**MLB ETA:** 2016

## 16. Pat Light, RHP

**MiLB Rank: N/A**
**Position Rank: N/A**

| Born: 03/29/91 | Age: 25 | Bats: R | **Top CALs:** Robert Hinton, Grant Johnson, |
|---|---|---|---|
| Height: 6-5 | Weight: 195 | Throws: R | Steven Hensley, Kyle Bloom, Chris Stratton |

| YEAR | Age | Level | IP | W | L | ERA | FIP | K/9 | BB/9 | K% | BB% | HR/9 | LOB% |
|---|---|---|---|---|---|---|---|---|---|---|---|---|---|
| 2013 | 22 | R | 6.0 | 0 | 0 | 0.00 | 3.46 | 4.50 | 3.00 | 13.0% | 8.7% | 0.00 | 100.0% |
| 2013 | 22 | A | 28.3 | 1 | 4 | 8.89 | 4.93 | 8.89 | 4.45 | 19.6% | 9.8% | 1.27 | 48.7% |
| 2014 | 23 | A | 17.3 | 2 | 0 | 4.15 | 2.84 | 9.87 | 2.08 | 27.1% | 5.7% | 0.52 | 56.8% |
| 2014 | 23 | A+ | 115.0 | 6 | 6 | 4.93 | 4.67 | 4.46 | 2.58 | 11.2% | 6.5% | 0.78 | 66.9% |
| 2015 | 24 | AA | 29.7 | 1 | 1 | 2.43 | 3.54 | 9.71 | 3.34 | 27.1% | 9.3% | 0.91 | 72.6% |
| 2015 | 24 | AAA | 33.0 | 2 | 4 | 5.18 | 4.28 | 9.55 | 7.09 | 22.7% | 16.9% | 0.55 | 70.7% |

**Background:** Another wildly disappointing year in the books for the 2012 first rounder. Light, who was grabbed with the 37th overall pick, split his season between Portland and Pawtucket, his first year working exclusively in relief, throwing 62.2 innings with 67 strikeouts and a whopping 37 free passes. For his career, the 6-foot-5, 195-pound hurler has averaged 7.1 K/9 and 3.3 BB/9 en route to tallying a 4.64 ERA.

**Projection**: So, according to a WEEI.com report in late November, the former Monmouth University hurler was tipping his pitches – which would be completely believable if not for the fact that his strikeout rate was more than a punch per inning and his homerun rate was basically in line with his career norms. The control will likely regress back to his previous showings, making him a prime candidate to see some seventh inning action in Boston in 2016.

**Ceiling:** 1.0-win player
**Risk:** Low to Moderate
**MLB ETA:** 2017

## 17. Josh Ockimey, 1B

**MiLB Rank: N/A**
**Position Rank: N/A**

| Born: 10/18/95 | Age: 20 | Bats: L | **Top CALs:** Oliver Ortiz, Drew Rundle, |
|---|---|---|---|
| Height: 6-1 | Weight: 215 | Throws: R | Manuel Sanchez, Matthew Spath, David Medina |

| Season | Age | LVL | PA | 2B | 3B | HR | AVG | OBP | SLG | ISO | BB% | K% | wRC+ |
|---|---|---|---|---|---|---|---|---|---|---|---|---|---|
| 2014 | 18 | R | 130 | 3 | 1 | 0 | 0.188 | 0.292 | 0.232 | 0.045 | 10.8% | 28.5% | 63 |
| 2015 | 19 | A- | 229 | 13 | 3 | 4 | 0.266 | 0.349 | 0.422 | 0.156 | 10.9% | 34.1% | 128 |

**Background:** A fifth round pick out of Sts. Neumann and Goretti High School in 2014, Ockimey spent last season battering anything he could get his hands on in the New York-Penn League. In 229 PA, the hulking first baseman slugged .266/.349/.422 with 13 doubles, three triples, and four dingers.

**Projection**: Lefties have chewed up and spit up Ockimey throughout his brief career. After batting .176/.326/.265 against LHP two years ago, Ockimey followed that up with another putrid showing in the NYPL (.196/.291/.304). Ockimey has promising power for a teenager – he posted a .156 ISO last season – but he needs to shave off more than a few percentage points from his abysmal K-rate. The player development system has their work cut out.

**Ceiling:** 1.5-win player
**Risk:** Moderate to High
**MLB ETA:** 2018

## 18. Daniel McGrath, LHP

**MiLB Rank: N/A**
**Position Rank: N/A**

| Born: 07/07/94 | Age: 21 | Bats: R | Top CALs: Wilmer Font, Zachary Fuesser, |
|---|---|---|---|
| Height: 6-3 | Weight: 205 | Throws: L | Efrain Nieves, Jason Garcia, Travis Ott |

| YEAR | Age | Level | IP | W | L | ERA | FIP | K/9 | BB/9 | K% | BB% | HR/9 | LOB% |
|---|---|---|---|---|---|---|---|---|---|---|---|---|---|
| 2013 | 18 | R | 20.0 | 0 | 1 | 1.35 | 2.66 | 13.50 | 2.70 | 43.5% | 8.7% | 0.90 | 98.2% |
| 2013 | 18 | A- | 33.3 | 3 | 3 | 4.86 | 3.04 | 9.45 | 3.51 | 25.6% | 9.5% | 0.54 | 54.7% |
| 2014 | 19 | A | 97.3 | 6 | 6 | 4.07 | 4.79 | 7.49 | 4.81 | 19.2% | 12.3% | 0.83 | 68.4% |
| 2015 | 20 | R | 6.0 | 0 | 0 | 0.00 | 0.97 | 10.50 | 0.00 | 33.3% | 0.0% | 0.00 | 100.0% |
| 2015 | 20 | A+ | 84.3 | 4 | 6 | 3.84 | 3.88 | 7.58 | 3.95 | 19.8% | 10.3% | 0.64 | 66.3% |

**Background:** The 6-foot-3 Aussie made the successful – albeit injury-shortened – jump in High Class A last season. Left elbow inflammation limited McGrath's campaign to just 84.1 innings, though he managed to fan 71 and walk 37 while finishing with a decent 3.88 FIP. For his career, McGrath has averaged 8.4 punch outs and 4.0 base-on-balls per nine innings.

**Projection**: I tabbed the Australian-born hurler as a *"fringy"* prospect in last year's book, and, to be truthful, McGrath was on pace to prove he was something more. Before being shut down for several weeks in mid-May, opponents were batting just .119/.258/.208 against him through his first six starts. And then the elbow issues popped up. Once he made his way back to Salem in mid-July McGrath hardly resembled the same pitcher: 54.1 IP, 4.97 ERA, 40 K, and 19 walks. One year later and he still looks like a fringy-type prospect, one with the ceiling of a backend starter.

**Ceiling:** 1.0- to 1.5-win player
**Risk:** Moderate to High
**MLB ETA:** 2018

## 19. Trey Ball, RHP

**MiLB Rank: N/A**
**Position Rank: N/A**

| Born: 06/27/94 | Age: 22 | Bats: L | Top CALs: Zach Jemiola, Arismendy Ozoria, |
|---|---|---|---|
| Height: 6-6 | Weight: 185 | Throws: L | Thomas Melgarejo, Michael Schiact, Jake Sisco |

| YEAR | Age | Level | IP | W | L | ERA | FIP | K/9 | BB/9 | K% | BB% | HR/9 | LOB% |
|---|---|---|---|---|---|---|---|---|---|---|---|---|---|
| 2013 | 19 | R | 7.0 | 0 | 1 | 6.43 | 6.46 | 6.43 | 7.71 | 13.9% | 16.7% | 1.29 | 61.6% |
| 2014 | 20 | A | 100.0 | 5 | 10 | 4.68 | 4.66 | 6.12 | 3.51 | 15.1% | 8.7% | 0.81 | 59.8% |
| 2015 | 21 | A+ | 129.3 | 9 | 13 | 4.73 | 5.13 | 5.36 | 4.18 | 13.7% | 10.6% | 1.11 | 67.2% |

**Background:** The 2013 draft will always be remembered for the first three players selected: Mark Appel, Kris Bryant, and Jon Gray. But let's take a look at whom the Red Sox bypassed in order to take left-hander Trey Ball with the seventh overall pick: Austin Meadows (9th), J.P. Crawford (16th), Tim Anderson (17th), Marco Gonzales (19th), Hunter Harvey (22nd), Chi-Chi Gonzalez (23rd), Eric Jagielo (26th), Rob Kaminsky (28th), Aaron Judge (32nd), Sean Manaea (34th), Aaron Blair (36th), Michael Lorenzen (38th), and Corey Knebel (39th). One would be hard-pressed now to make a logical argument as to picking Ball ahead of any of those other prospects. The 6-foot-6, 185-pound lefty spent last season barely missing bats and walking way too many Carolina League hitters, averaging just 5.4 punch outs and 4.2 free passes per nine innings. Those numbers were a slight decline from his production line in the Sally two years ago: 100.0 IP, 68 K, and 39 BB.

**Projection**: Here's what I wrote in last year's book:

> "Big and projectab e, Ball still has a puncher's chance to rebound from a slow start to his professional career. But – sticking with the boxing theme – the southpaw's stock has taken a Rocky Balboa-esque beating. Fingers crossed, kid. Yo! Adrian!"

Ball's prospect status continued to take an ass-beating last year. And he's quickly approaching the final round with the score card heavily in favor of anyone who's stepping in against him.

**Ceiling:** 1.0- to 1.5-win player

**Risk:** Moderate to High
**MLB ETA:** 2018

## 20. Teddy Stankiewicz, RHP

**MiLB Rank: N/A**
**Position Rank: N/A**

| Born: 11/25/93 | Age: 21 | Bats: R | Top CALs: Kyle Greenwalt, Kyle Ryan, |
| Height: 6-4 | Weight: 200 | Throws: R | Myles Jaye, Austin Reed, Mike Broadway |

| YEAR | Age | Level | IP | W | L | ERA | FIP | K/9 | BB/9 | K% | BB% | HR/9 | LOB% |
|------|-----|-------|------|----|----|------|------|------|------|-------|------|------|-------|
| 2013 | 19 | A- | 19.7 | 0 | 0 | 2.29 | 2.69 | 6.86 | 0.92 | 19.2% | 2.6% | 0.46 | 75.3% |
| 2014 | 20 | A | 140.3 | 11 | 8 | 3.72 | 3.63 | 6.54 | 1.86 | 17.5% | 5.0% | 0.58 | 67.8% |
| 2015 | 21 | A+ | 141.3 | 5 | 11 | 4.01 | 4.03 | 4.90 | 2.04 | 13.2% | 5.5% | 0.70 | 66.2% |

**Background:** The twice-drafted second rounder spent the year fine tuning his game – and shaving off some precious punch outs from his K-rate – with Salem in the Carolina League last season. A big, durable right-hander out of Seminole State College, Stankiewicz's strikeout rate has declined in each of his past two seasons, going from 6.9 K/9 during his pro debut to 6.5 K/9 in the Sally the following year and, finally, down to a career worst 4.9 K/9. Stankiewicz finished 2015 with nearly matching 4.01 ERA and 4.03 FIP. For his career he's sporting a 194-to-63 strikeout-to-walk ratio.

**Projection:** Here's the thing about Stankiewicz: he's never missed – or will miss – an extraordinary amount of bats; unless, of course, he develops a new pitch. Stankiewicz has always done a fantastic job keeping unwanted runners off base with exceptional control. If everything breaks the right way he could be a #5.

**Ceiling:** 1.0-win player
**Risk:** Moderate
**MLB ETA:** 2017

## 21. Edwin Escobar, LHP

**MiLB Rank: N/A**
**Position Rank: N/A**

| Born: 04/22/92 | Age: 24 | Bats: L | Top CALs: Pedro Hernandez, Jesus Rodriguez, |
| Height: 6-2 | Weight: 225 | Throws: L | Rafael Rodriguez, Simon Castro, Eddie Mckiernan |

| YEAR | Age | Level | IP | W | L | ERA | FIP | K/9 | BB/9 | K% | BB% | HR/9 | LOB% |
|------|-----|-------|-------|----|----|------|------|-------|------|-------|-------|------|--------|
| 2013 | 21 | A+ | 74.7 | 3 | 4 | 2.89 | 2.55 | 11.09 | 2.05 | 29.3% | 5.4% | 0.36 | 64.8% |
| 2013 | 21 | AA | 54.0 | 5 | 4 | 2.67 | 2.64 | 9.00 | 2.17 | 24.8% | 6.0% | 0.33 | 73.0% |
| 2014 | 22 | AAA | 111.0 | 3 | 8 | 5.11 | 5.01 | 7.78 | 3.00 | 19.2% | 7.4% | 1.30 | 68.6% |
| 2014 | 22 | AAA | 27.3 | 0 | 2 | 4.28 | 4.20 | 6.59 | 2.63 | 16.7% | 6.7% | 0.99 | 70.7% |
| 2015 | 23 | A | 1.0 | 0 | 0 | 0.00 | 3.48 | 0.00 | 0.00 | 0.0% | 0.0% | 0.00 | 100.0% |
| 2015 | 23 | AAA | 49.7 | 3 | 3 | 5.07 | 5.92 | 4.35 | 4.53 | 10.9% | 11.3% | 1.45 | 73.8% |

**Background:** The 6-foot-2, 225-pound left-hander has hardly resembled the pitcher Boston thought they were acquiring near the trade deadline two years ago. Or maybe San Francisco dealt Escobar away at the most opportune time. Anyway, the Venezuelan-born lefty missed the first couple of months dealing with some elbow issues, but managed to make it back to Pawtucket in early June. He would make just 19 appearances in the International League, six of which were starts, throwing 49.2 innings of work while posting an alarmingly poor 24-to-25 strikeout-to-walk ratio. For his career, Escobar is averaging 8.5 punch outs and just 3.1 walks per nine innings to go along with a blasé 4.20 ERA.

**Projection:** The elbow injury was serious enough that Boston brought Escobar slowly up to speed. Including his one-inning tune-up in the Sally, Escobar didn't throw more than three innings until his final five appearances. But even those brought about more than a few red flags: he posted a lackluster 10-to-13 strikeout-to-walk ratio in 27.0 innings of work. Unless he takes a large leap forward, expect Escobar to get pushed into a bullpen role.

**Ceiling:** 1.0-win player
**Risk:** Moderate
**MLB ETA:** Debuted in 2014

## 22. Ty Buttrey, RHP

**MiLB Rank: N/A**
**Position Rank: N/A**

| Born: 03/31/93 | Age: 23 | Bats: L | Top CALs: Brian Rauh, Kyle Fernandes, |
|---|---|---|---|
| Height: 6-6 | Weight: 235 | Throws: R | Myles Jaye, Austin Reed, Mike Broadway |

| YEAR | Age | Level | IP | W | L | ERA | FIP | K/9 | BB/9 | K% | BB% | HR/9 | LOB% |
|---|---|---|---|---|---|---|---|---|---|---|---|---|---|
| 2013 | 20 | A- | 61.0 | 4 | 3 | 2.21 | 3.23 | 5.16 | 3.10 | 13.8% | 8.3% | 0.00 | 73.8% |
| 2014 | 21 | R | 5.0 | 0 | 0 | 1.80 | 3.11 | 7.20 | 1.80 | 21.1% | 5.3% | 0.00 | 75.0% |
| 2014 | 21 | A- | 11.7 | 0 | 0 | 3.09 | 3.18 | 9.26 | 5.40 | 23.1% | 13.5% | 0.00 | 66.7% |
| 2014 | 21 | A | 46.0 | 0 | 5 | 6.85 | 4.89 | 7.83 | 4.70 | 18.1% | 10.9% | 0.98 | 55.8% |
| 2015 | 22 | A | 22.0 | 1 | 0 | 2.45 | 3.21 | 9.00 | 1.23 | 25.6% | 3.5% | 0.82 | 71.4% |
| 2015 | 22 | A+ | 115.7 | 8 | 10 | 4.20 | 3.71 | 6.30 | 3.50 | 16.4% | 9.1% | 0.39 | 65.6% |

**Background:** A 6-foot-6, 235-pound right-hander out of Providence High School, it's taken Buttrey longer than expected but he appears to be ready for the minors' biggest test: Class AA. Buttrey, an older prep arm taken in the fourth round, opened the year up in the Sally for four quick starts before getting promoted to Salem for his final 21 contests. Overall, he finished with a combined 103-to-48 strikeout-to-walk ratio in 137.2 innings of work. For his career, Buttrey has averaged 6.7 punch outs and 3.5 walks per nine innings to go along with a 3.92 ERA in 266.0 innings.

**Projection**: Back of the rotation/middle relief fodder. Buttrey has the size and frame to chew innings, but his swing-and-miss ability ebbs-and-flows from year-to-year, as does his control.

**Ceiling:** 1.0-win player
**Risk:** Moderate
**MLB ETA:** 201

## 23. Mauricio Dubon, IF

**MiLB Rank: N/A**
**Position Rank: N/A**

| Born: 07/19/94 | Age: 21 | Bats: R | Top CALs: Drew Cumberland, Christian Arroyo, |
|---|---|---|---|
| Height: 6-0 | Weight: 160 | Throws: R | Thairo Estrada, Jose Pirela, Ramon Torres |

| Season | Age | LVL | PA | 2B | 3B | HR | AVG | OBP | SLG | ISO | BB% | K% | wRC+ |
|---|---|---|---|---|---|---|---|---|---|---|---|---|---|
| 2014 | 19 | A- | 274 | 8 | 1 | 3 | 0.320 | 0.337 | 0.395 | 0.074 | 3.3% | 9.5% | 114 |
| 2015 | 20 | A | 261 | 12 | 3 | 4 | 0.301 | 0.354 | 0.428 | 0.127 | 6.9% | 13.0% | 123 |
| 2015 | 20 | A | 261 | 12 | 3 | 4 | 0.301 | 0.354 | 0.428 | 0.127 | 6.9% | 13.0% | 123 |

**Background:** Not too shabby for a former 26th round pick. Dubon, the 773rd player chosen in 2013, had a solid showing as a 19-year-old in the NYPL two years ago, hitting .320/.337/.395 with eight doubles, one triples, and three homeruns. Dubon was able to keep the momentum moving forward last season as he split time between Greenville and Salem, hitting a combined .288/.349/.376 with 29 extra-base hits and a career high 30 stolen bases (in 37 attempts). For his career, Dubon is batting .295/.342/.377 with 32 doubles, four triples, eight homeruns, and 43 swipes.

**Projection**: My word of warning in last year's book about Dubon's abhorrence to the free pass seemed to be unfounded last season; he walked in a career best 8.6% of his plate appearances. The power took a tremendous leap forward in the Sally, but basically disappeared upon his promotion to High Class A. There are bits-and-pieces of a solid big league backup here.

**Ceiling:** 1.0-win player
**Risk:** Moderate
**MLB ETA:** 2018

## 24. Luis Ysla, LHP

**MiLB Rank: N/A**
**Position Rank: N/A**

| Born: 04/27/92 | Age: 24 | Bats: L | Top CALs: Dan Griffin, Chase Johnson, |
|---|---|---|---|
| Height: 6-1 | Weight: 185 | Throws: L | Matthew Loosen, Jake Cowan, Dan Merklinger |

| YEAR | Age | Level | IP | W | L | ERA | FIP | K/9 | BB/9 | K% | BB% | HR/9 | LOB% |
|---|---|---|---|---|---|---|---|---|---|---|---|---|---|
| 2013 | 21 | R | 51.0 | 4 | 0 | 2.65 | 3.16 | 9.18 | 2.29 | 25.6% | 6.4% | 0.18 | 68.4% |
| 2014 | 22 | A | 121.3 | 6 | 7 | 2.45 | 3.93 | 8.53 | 3.34 | 22.4% | 8.8% | 0.59 | 79.3% |
| 2015 | 23 | A+ | 79.7 | 3 | 6 | 6.21 | 4.52 | 10.73 | 4.63 | 25.1% | 10.8% | 1.02 | 66.2% |
| 2015 | 23 | A+ | 5.0 | 0 | 0 | 0.00 | 2.06 | 10.80 | 3.60 | 35.3% | 11.8% | 0.00 | 100.0% |

**Background:** A late August deal with the Giants sent outfield extraordinaire Alejandro De Aza to San Francisco in exchange for Ysla, a 6-foot-1, 185-pound lefty out of Venezuela. Ysla made 33 appearances in the Giants' organization, nine of which were starts, throwing 79.2 innings with a whopping 95 punch outs and 41 walks. He tossed another five frames in the Boston organization after the late deal.

**Projection**: Massive strikeout potential with the caveat that his control/command has been trending in the wrong direction over the past couple of seasons. The idea of making him a full-time starter is likely a pipedream, but he could develop into a solid bullpen arm.

**Ceiling:** 1.0-win player
**Risk:** Moderate
**MLB ETA:** 2017

## 25. Luis Alejandro Basabe, 2B/SS

MiLB Rank: N/A
Position Rank: N/A

| Born: 04/27/92 | Age: 24 | Bats: L | **Top CALs:** Luis Liberato, Sandber Pimentel, |
|---|---|---|---|
| Height: 6-1 | Weight: 185 | Throws: L | Delbis Arcila, Alexy Palma, Adalfi Almonte |

| Season | Age | LVL | PA | 2B | 3B | HR | AVG | OBP | SLG | ISO | BB% | K% | wRC+ |
|---|---|---|---|---|---|---|---|---|---|---|---|---|---|
| 2013 | 16 | R | 198 | 5 | 4 | 1 | 0.192 | 0.332 | 0.295 | 0.103 | 16.7% | 24.2% | 97 |
| 2014 | 17 | R | 141 | 3 | 2 | 0 | 0.229 | 0.413 | 0.295 | 0.067 | 22.0% | 21.3% | 124 |
| 2015 | 18 | R | 124 | 5 | 0 | 0 | 0.260 | 0.387 | 0.310 | 0.050 | 16.9% | 26.6% | 121 |
| 2015 | 18 | R | 124 | 5 | 0 | 0 | 0.260 | 0.387 | 0.310 | 0.050 | 16.9% | 26.6% | 121 |
| 2013 | 16 | R | 268 | 13 | 2 | 1 | 0.225 | 0.385 | 0.321 | 0.096 | 18.3% | 21.6% | 123 |
| 2014 | 17 | R | 168 | 7 | 10 | 0 | 0.287 | 0.405 | 0.485 | 0.199 | 15.5% | 17.9% | 152 |
| 2014 | 17 | R | 123 | 5 | 0 | 1 | 0.248 | 0.328 | 0.324 | 0.076 | 10.6% | 18.7% | 93 |
| 2015 | 18 | A- | 256 | 8 | 3 | 7 | 0.243 | 0.340 | 0.401 | 0.158 | 12.5% | 26.2% | 122 |

**Background:** Basabe looked absolutely overwhelmed in two previous stints in the Dominican Summer League, hitting an aggregate .204/.360/.286, but Boston opted to push the switch-hitting middle infielder stateside last season and, lo and behold, his production spiked to .260/.387/.310.

**Projection**: An absolute OBP monster during his first three seasons in the minor leagues. Basabe is sporting an 18.1% career walk rate, including a 16.9% showing in the Gulf Coast League last season. He's yet to show any type of power – literally, my younger sister probably packs more of a wallop – but a player with such a tremendous eye at the plate is at least intriguing.

**Ceiling:** 0.5- to 1.0-win player
**Risk:** Moderate to High
**MLB ETA:** 2019

### Barely Missed:

- **Daniel Gonzalez, RHP** – 6-foot-5, 180-pound man-child has showcased impeccable control during his three-year professional career, averaging just 1.6 walks every nine innings. After posting a solid 51-to-16 strikeout-to-walk ratio in the New York-Penn League, Gonzalez looks ready for full-season ball.

- **Tzu-Wei Lin, SS** – Pint-sized shortstop had a coming out party with the bat in High Class A last season, hitting .281/.331/.367 – all career bests. And then he tanked when he was promoted to Class AA (.202/.268/.266).

## Bird Doggin' It – Additional Prospects to Keep an Eye in 2016

| Player | Age | POS | Notes |
|---|---|---|---|
| Victor Acosta | 20 | 3B | Batted .251/.307/.351 as a 19-year-old in the NYPL. He hasn't shown much power since coming stateside two years ago. |
| Jalen Beeks | 22 | LHP | Former Arkansas rotation stalwart struggled in his first taste of full season ball: 145.2 IP, 100 K, 28 BB, and a 4.32 ERA. His control could keep him relevant in the lower levels. |
| Jake Cosart | 22 | RHP | 2014 third round pick couldn't harness his lively arm in the New York-Penn League last season, walking 20 in 33.0 innings. Strong candidate for a bullpen role. |
| William Cuevas | 25 | RHP | Posted a 91-to-41 strikeout-to-walk ratio in 95.1 innings in Class AA and followed that up with a 37-to-14 showing in 41.0 innings in Class AAA. He could be a sufficient swing-man in 2016. |
| Keury De La Cruz | 24 | OF | Wiry outfielder hasn't looked the same since making the leap up to High Class A in 2013. |
| Enmanuel De Jesus | 19 | LHP | 6-foot-3, 190-pound lefty tallied a 1.66 ERA in 43.1 innings in the Gulf Coast League. Fantastic control, but he hasn't missed a whole lot of wood yet. |
| Nick Duron | 20 | RHP | A 31st round pick last June out of Clark College looked awfully solid in the Gulf Coast: 26.1 IP, 28 K, 5 BB. |
| Edwar Garcia | 22 | RHP | Fanned 26 in 23.0 innings with Lowell in the NYPL. Of course, well, he happened to walk 15 during the same time span. |
| Bryan Hudson | 21 | CF | A fourth/fifth outfielder type with a nose for first base and speed. |
| Dedgar Jimenez | 20 | LHP | Hefty lefty is a curmudgeon when it comes to issuing free passes but his strikeout rate has dropped from 8.2 K/9 in the DSL three years ago to 6.8 in the GCL to 4.7 in the Sally last year. |
| Pat Light | 25 | RHP | The 37th overall pick in 2012 had very little success as a member of the rotation, so the club moved him into a relief role. And...voila...instant success! |
| Kyle Martin | 25 | RHP | 6-foot-7 right-hander fanned 48 in 42 innings with Portland last season. He could be a middle relief option for the big league club at some point. |
| Kevin McAvoy | 22 | RHP | 2014 fourth round pick made the leap from the New York-Penn League into High Class A last season. He battled some control issues, but handled it better than expected. |
| Mike Meyers | 22 | OF | Posted a 126 wRC+ mark in the Sally last season, but struggled in a brief promotion to High Class A. Looked semi-toolsy. |
| Yankory Pimentel | 22 | RHP | Punched out 42 in just over 33 innings in the Gulf Coast. Of course, that came at the ripe ol' age 21. |
| Noe Ramirez | 26 | RHP | Uncorked an upper 80s heater during his stint in Boston. Solid middle reliever. |
| Henry Ramos | 24 | OF | Toolsy outfielder struggled in a shortened 2015, hitting .244/.317/.359 with Portland. |
| Roniel Raudes | 18 | RHP | Nicaraguan-born right-hander looked very promising in the DSL and nearly unhittable in the Gulf Coast. |
| Kevin Steen | 19 | RHP | A ninth round pick in 2014, Steen split his year between the Gulf Coast and New York-Penn, posting a 47-to-20 strikeout-to-walk ratio in 56.2 innings. |
| Aneury Tavarez | 24 | OF | Once promising prospect couldn't find first base if Marco Polo was standing on it. |

# Chicago Cubs

**State of the Farm System:** Even after the losing many of the system's previous blue chip prospects over the past couple years – including the likes of Kris Bryant, Kyle Schwarber, Jorge Soler, Anthony Rizzo, and Addison Russell – the Cubs' farm system *still* ranks among the best in baseball, a true testament of player development engine.

Center fielder Albert Almora, whose bat won't likely ever live up to the expectations thrust upon a player taken with the sixth overall pick, continues to hover around the league average mark offensively, but his defensive reputation precedes him – so much so, in fact, that the roving outfielder should have no issues cobbling together 3.0+ win seasons.

Falling in right behind Almora is another young outfielder: Billy McKinney. Acquired along with Addison Russell and right-hander Dan Straily as part of the deal that sent Jeff Samardzija and Jason Hammel to Oakland, McKinney got off to a scorching hot start in High Class A and continued to show offensive promise following a promotion to the Southern League before an injury prematurely ended his season.

Gleyber Torres is just the latest young shortstop the farm system is manufacturing. And just think about it: this comes on the heels of churning out Starlin Castro, Javier Baez, and Addison Russell. Anyway, Torres more than handled himself in his first taste of full-season action in the Midwest League, hitting .293/.353/.386 with 24 doubles, five triples, three homeruns, and 22 stolen bases en route to topping the league average offensive production by 16%. As an 18-year-old.

Rounding out the Top 5 is Ian Happ, one of the more polished collegiate bats available last June, and young right-hander Trevor Clifton, a prime candidate for a massive breakout season in 2016.

Chicago's system, per the usual, is sprinkled with plenty of high upside talent throughout, including former catcher-turned-Kyle-Schwarber-impressionist Mark Zagunis, potential mid-rotation caliber arm Duane Underwood, who offers up plenty of glimpses of dominance but has yet to string it together for an entire year, and the oft-injured Carl Edwards.

| Rank | Name | POS |
|---|---|---|
| 1 | Albert Almora | CF |
| 2 | Billy McKinney | LF/RF |
| 3 | Gleyber Torres | SS |
| 4 | Ian Happ | LF/RF |
| 5 | Trevor Clifton | RHP |
| 6 | Mark Zagunis | OF |
| 7 | Duane Underwood | RHP |
| 8 | Carl Edwards | RHP |
| 9 | Eloy Jimenez | LF/RF |
| 10 | Daniel Vogelbach | 1B |
| 11 | Donnie Dewees | LF/CF |
| 12 | Jake Stinnett | RHP |
| 13 | Oscar De La Cruz | RHP |
| 14 | Pierce Johnson | RHP |
| 15 | Willson Contreras | C |
| 16 | Jeimer Candelario | 3B |
| 17 | Jen-Ho Tseng | RHP |
| 18 | Justin Steele | LHP |
| 19 | Corey Black | RHP |
| 20 | Victor Caratini | C/1B/3B |
| 21 | Carson Sands | LHP |
| 22 | Paul Blackburn | RHP |
| 23 | Rob Zastryzny | LHP |
| 24 | Daury Torrez | RHP |
| 25 | Erick Leal | RHP |

**Review of the 2015 Draft:** In my first book I highlighted – and gushed about – Chicago's approach when it came to honing in on young power bats, not only a safer prospect type when compared to pitchers, but also because of the league-wide downward trend in offense. And guess what? That trend continued in last year's draft.

Chicago grabbed University of Cincinnati stud Ian Happ with the ninth overall pick last June. Happ, a defensive vagabond, slugged an impressive .338/.463/.552 during his tenure at the school including a .369/.492/.672 mark during his junior campaign. After that the front office – once again – dipped into the collegiate ranks and grabbed University of North Florida outfielder Donnie Dewees with the 47th overall pick. Dewees bounced back from an injury-marred sophomore season to slug .422/.483/.749 with 12 doubles, eight triples, 18 homeruns, and 23 stolen bases against some less than stellar competition.

They followed that up with big prep lefty Bryan Hudson in the third round and Canton, Ohio, high schooler Darryl Wilson in the fourth round.

Finally, my absolute favorite hands down collegiate prospect – perhaps ever – was taken by the club in the fifth round last June: submariner Dave Berg. In an article for *Beyond the Box Score* I opined that Berg would become the first member of the 2015 draft class to make the big leagues – and I'm still putting my money down on the relief arm.

## 1. Albert Almora, CF

**MiLB Rank: #24**
**Position Rank: #7**

| Born: 04/16/94 | Age: 22 | Bats: R | Top CALs: Jae-Hoon Ha, Teodoro Martinez, |
|---|---|---|---|
| Height: 6-2 | Weight: 180 | Throws: R | Tyrone Taylor, Shane Peterson, Jose Tabata |

| Season | Age | LVL | PA | 2B | 3B | HR | AVG | OBP | SLG | ISO | BB% | K% | wRC+ |
|---|---|---|---|---|---|---|---|---|---|---|---|---|---|
| 2013 | 19 | A | 272 | 17 | 4 | 3 | 0.329 | 0.376 | 0.466 | 0.137 | 6.3% | 11.0% | 137 |
| 2014 | 20 | A+ | 385 | 20 | 2 | 7 | 0.283 | 0.306 | 0.406 | 0.123 | 3.1% | 11.9% | 100 |
| 2014 | 20 | AA | 145 | 7 | 2 | 2 | 0.232 | 0.248 | 0.352 | 0.120 | 1.4% | 15.9% | 63 |
| 2015 | 21 | AA | 451 | 26 | 4 | 6 | 0.272 | 0.327 | 0.400 | 0.128 | 7.1% | 10.4% | 105 |

**Background:** I always like to play a bit of a mental game when I'm looking at early first round picks. OK, Almora was the sixth overall pick in the draft in 2016 – also the first selection in the Jed Hoyer/Theo Epstein era. Knowing what we know now how does Almora stack up against some of the more known members of that draft class? Well, let's take a look, shall we?

(Note: Obviously, Almora falls short when it comes to the class' first two pick, Carlos Correa and Byron Buxton.)

- Almora vs. Mike Zunino (#3 pick).
  - Winner: Almora. The bar's set fairly low with this one; Zunino's sporting a career .193/.252/.353 triple-slash line in over 1,050 big league plate appearances to go along with a rancid 71 wRC+.
- Almora vs. Kevin Gausman (#4):
  - Winner: Tie. For a while there it didn't seem like the Orioles knew how to handle the donut-devouring right-hander as they bounced him between the minor and major leagues. But Gausman's averaged over 3.2 fWAR per 220 innings in his career. But you could go either way on this one.
- Almora vs. Mark Appel (#8):
  - Winner: Tie. One could make the argument either way at this point as Appel's hype/power-arsenal hasn't been anything close to his dominance with Stanford.
- Almora vs. Addison Russell (#11)/Corey Seager (#18)/Michael Wacha (#19)/Marcus Stroman (#22):
  - Winner: Each player not named Albert Almora.
- Almora vs. Joey Gallo:
  - Winner: Gallo, whose power potential is Ruthian. And his ability to swing-and-miss is just as large. But Almora will add value on defense. It's closer than you would think.

Anyway, Almora got a second crack at Southern League pitching after closing out the 2014 season with a disappointing 36-game stint with Tennessee, and the results – unsurprisingly – were much improved, even in another shortened season. Playing in fewer than 110 games for the second time in the last three years, Almora batted .272/.327/.400 with 26 doubles, four triples, six homeruns, and eight stolen bases.

**Projection**: Almora's another one of these guys where I have one very distinct – and prominent – thought:

1. He's a victim of his own hype, sort of the Cubs' version of Brandon Nimmo. While Almora brings enough to the kitchen table, it's very possible that his defensive contributions will outweigh his offensive production. Not necessarily bad by any stretch of the means, but he's been hyped for so long, ad nauseam, that's he's going to have trouble living up to the lofty expectations.

With that being said, he can fill out the back of a baseball card well enough – plenty of doubles, a handful of triples, 10 homeruns, and double-digit stolen bases. As a potential big league hitter he'll hover around the league average, but it's his defense that will push him over 3.0-win a year.

**Ceiling:** 3.0- to 3.5-win player
**Risk:** Low to Moderate
**MLB ETA:** 2016

## 2. Billy McKinney, LF/RF

**MiLB Rank: #66**
**Position Rank: #18**

| Born: 08/23/94 | Age: 21 | Bats: L | **Top CALs:** Jorge Bonifacio, John Drennen, |
| Height: 6-1 | Weight: 205 | Throws: L | Austin Gallagher, Cheslor Cuthbert, Dustin Fowler |

| Season | Age | LVL | PA | 2B | 3B | HR | AVG | OBP | SLG | ISO | BB% | K% | wRC+ |
|---|---|---|---|---|---|---|---|---|---|---|---|---|---|
| 2013 | 18 | R | 206 | 7 | 2 | 2 | 0.320 | 0.383 | 0.414 | 0.094 | 8.3% | 14.1% | 126 |
| 2014 | 19 | A+ | 333 | 12 | 2 | 10 | 0.241 | 0.330 | 0.400 | 0.159 | 10.8% | 17.4% | 92 |
| 2014 | 19 | A+ | 210 | 12 | 4 | 1 | 0.301 | 0.390 | 0.432 | 0.131 | 11.9% | 20.0% | 136 |
| 2015 | 20 | A+ | 125 | 5 | 2 | 4 | 0.340 | 0.432 | 0.544 | 0.204 | 13.6% | 10.4% | 182 |
| 2015 | 20 | AA | 308 | 26 | 1 | 3 | 0.285 | 0.346 | 0.420 | 0.135 | 8.8% | 15.3% | 116 |

**Background:** For the first couple weeks last season there was no hotter – or better – hitter on the planet than Billy McKinney, the 24th overall pick in the 2013 draft. The 6-foot-1, 205-pound corner outfielder put on his best impression of Ted Williams for the season's first 29 games by hitting a scorching .340/.432/.544 with some absurd peripherals in High Class A: 13.6% walk rate, 10.4% strikeout rate, .204 Isolated Power, five doubles, two triples, four homeruns, and a 182 wRC+. The club promoted him up to Class AA in mid-May where he continued to hit well before a knee issue – and subsequent hairline fracture surgery – sidelined him after the second week of August. McKinney would finish the year with an aggregate .300/.371/.454 triple-slash line, setting a new career high with 31 two-baggers, three triples, and seven homeruns.

**Projection**: The knee injury was more of a freak accident type of thing, the result of him fouling off a pitch. Last year marked the first time in his career that the left-handed McKinney failed to produce against fellow southpaws (.212/.296/.247), so there's reason to believe that it shouldn't be more than just a brief speed bump. When he's healthy, McKinney showcases an above-average eye at the plate, the ability to consistently hit .300+, and no worse than solid-average power with some more in the tank. Eventually the doubles – and he's slugged a ton of them over his past two seasons – will turn into some significant power output. And just to put that into perspective, since 2014 McKinney's averaged nearly 39 doubles for a full 162-game season. Think of McKinney as a David DeJesus clone circa 2008, someone who can slug .300/.360/.450 at the big league level.

**Ceiling:** 3.0-win player
**Risk:** Moderate
**MLB ETA:** 2016

## 3. Gleyber Torres, SS

**MiLB Rank: #89**
**Position Rank: N/A**

| Born: 12/13/96 | Age: 19 | Bats: R | **Top CALs:** Cole Tucker, Cito Culver, |
| Height: 6-1 | Weight: 175 | Throws: R | Luis Reynoso, Alejandro Salazar, Osvaldo Abreu |

| Season | Age | LVL | PA | 2B | 3B | HR | AVG | OBP | SLG | ISO | BB% | K% | wRC+ |
|---|---|---|---|---|---|---|---|---|---|---|---|---|---|
| 2014 | 17 | R | 183 | 6 | 3 | 1 | 0.279 | 0.372 | 0.377 | 0.097 | 13.7% | 18.0% | 119 |
| 2015 | 18 | A | 514 | 24 | 5 | 3 | 0.293 | 0.353 | 0.386 | 0.093 | 8.4% | 21.0% | 116 |

**Background:** The latest Chicago prospect to offer up significant offensive upside at an offensive deficient position. Torres, a leggy 6-foot-1, 175-pound shortstop out of Caracas, Venezuela, signed a rather impressive deal at the ripe ol' age of 16 – an ice cold $1.7 million. Torres would wait another season until making his debut, a rather aggressive approach by the Cubs who pushed the then 17-year-old prospect straight into the Arizona Summer League. Torres responded well, hitting .279/.372/.377 with doubles power before catching fire during a seven-game promotion (.393/.469/.786). And once again the front office challenged Torres for the 2015 season: he spent all but seven games with South Bend in the Midwest League; and those other seven games were spent with Myrtle Beach in the Carolina League. Overall, Torres hit .293/.353/.386 with 24 doubles, five triples, three homeruns, and 22 stolen bases (in 35 attempts) in the Midwest League.

**Projection**: First, here's what I wrote in last year's book:

> *"Tremendous eye for such a young kid, solid contact s kills and enough pop to suggest it becomes an average-ish skill down the line. It's still incredibly early, but CAL's suggesting there's quite a bit of upside between 2014 first rounder Cole Tucker and Colorado's Trevor Story. Looks like a solid find on the international market."*

Well, he certainly looks like a potential steal – and I can't believe I'm about to write this – for $1.7 million. But it's true. Torres took some important steps forward with his defense last season, commanded the strike zone well for a teenager making his full-season debut, flashed doubles power that will likely develop into 12 or so homeruns down the line, and a potential above-average stick.

**Ceiling:** 2.5- to 3.0-win player
**Risk:** Moderate
**MLB ETA:** 2017/2018

# 4. Ian Happ, LF/RF

**MiLB Rank: #93**

**Position Rank: N/A**

| Born: 08/12/94 | Age: 21 | Bats: B | **Top CALs:** Jonathan Rodriguez, Grolmann |
| Height: 6-0 | Weight: 205 | Throws: R | Gonzalez, Dylan Cozens, Reid Fronk, Jaff Decker |

| Season | Age | LVL | PA | 2B | 3B | HR | AVG | OBP | SLG | ISO | BB% | K% | wRC+ |
|--------|-----|-----|-----|----|----|----|-------|-------|-------|-------|-------|-------|------|
| 2015 | 20 | A- | 130 | 8 | 1 | 4 | 0.283 | 0.408 | 0.491 | 0.208 | 17.7% | 21.5% | 156 |
| 2015 | 20 | A | 165 | 9 | 3 | 5 | 0.241 | 0.315 | 0.448 | 0.207 | 10.3% | 23.6% | 118 |

**Background:** Let's take a quick look back at General Manager Jed Hoyer's draft track record in the first round since taking over the Cubs:

2012.    Albert Almora, OF
2013.    Kris Bryant, 3B
2014.    Kyle Schwarber, C

So it only makes sense that Hoyer would once again hone in on another polished stick, taking the University of Cincinnati outfielder with the ninth overall selection last June. Happ, a 6-foot, 205-pound corner outfielder who bounced around UC's infield at various times as well, was a three-year mainstay in the heart of the Bearcat lineup. He opened up his collegiate career on a high note, hitting .322/.451/.483 while tying for the team lead in doubles (13) and triples (1), while finishing with the most dingers, six. The switch-hitting Happ followed that up with an eerily similar campaign his sophomore season: .322/.443/.497 with 13 doubles, one triple, and five homeruns. And then the pre-season awards started rolling in, like Garth Brooks' Thunder:

- College Sports Madness Preseason All-American Conference
- College Sports Madness Preseason American Athletic Conference Player of the Year
- Perfect Game Preseason All-American Athletic Conference
- Perfect Game Preseason American Athletic Conference
- National College Baseball Writers of America Preseason All-America Third Team
- Louisville Slugger Preseason All-American Third Team
- College Sports Madness Preseason All-America First Team
- Baseball America Preseason All-America First Team
- Golden Spikes Preseason Watch List

And he surpassed – by leaps and bounds – every single expectation. In 56 games with the Bearcats, Happ bashed to the tune of .369/.492/.672 with career bests in doubles (18) and homeruns (14) while posting a 49-to-49 strikeout-to-walk ratio. Then the awards and recognition really poured in:

- Capital One Academic All-America First Team and All-District First Team
- ABCA First Team All-America
- D1Baseball.com First Team All-America
- Collegiate Baseball Second Team All-America
- Louisville Slugger Second Team All-America
- National College Baseball Writers of America Second Team All-America
- Baseball America Second Team All-America
- College Sports Madness Second Team All-America
- College Sports Madness American Player of the Year
- College Sports Madness First Team All-America
- Golden Spikes Semifinalist

**Projection**: I would be remiss to mention Happ's back-to-back appearances in the premier Cape Cod League in 2013 and 2014 as well. So I will. Here's what I wrote for his pre-draft write-up last year:

> *"A bit of an odd prospect because he really doesn't have a set position once he transitions to the pro level. He could easily find himself at a corner outfield spot – where the bat doesn't play extraordinarily well – [or] third base, where it has a chance to be league average for the position, or second base, a potential reincarnation of the Indians' Jason Kipnis.*
>
> *Offensively speaking, Happ has a lengthy track record of success with his time in a Bearcats' uniform as well as – and more importantly – in the Cape Cod Summer League. He has an elite eye at the plate – he's walked in nearly 18% of his career plate appearances (as of May 6th) – and enough pop to slug 25 doubles and 10 homeruns in a pro season. Happ's decline in stolen base frequency **and** success are the only red flags to speak of during his final collegiate season.*

> *He's in the mold of a Jason Kipnis/Dustin Ackley-type player – solid league-average offensive performers. He's a typical Oakland A's-type prospect – college bat with some defensive versatility – but likely won't be around when the franchise goes on the clock with the 20th pick."*

And, really, how much of a difference is there between Oakland's front office and the Theo Epstein/Jed Hoyer regime? Not much.

**Ceiling:** 2.5- to 3.0-win player
**Risk:** Moderate
**MLB ETA:** 2017

## 5. Trevor Clifton, RHP

**MiLB Rank: #105**
**Position Rank: N/A**

| Born: 05/11/95 | Age: 21 | Bats: R | Top CALs: Yelper Castillo, Paul Demny, |
|---|---|---|---|
| Height: 6-4 | Weight: 170 | Throws: R | Zachary Fuesser, Jason Garcia, Wilmer Font |

| YEAR | Age | Level | IP | W | L | ERA | FIP | K/9 | BB/9 | K% | BB% | HR/9 | LOB% |
|---|---|---|---|---|---|---|---|---|---|---|---|---|---|
| 2013 | 18 | R | 10.3 | 0 | 0 | 6.97 | 3.43 | 13.06 | 6.97 | 29.4% | 15.7% | 0.00 | 61.9% |
| 2014 | 19 | A- | 61.0 | 4 | 2 | 3.69 | 4.31 | 7.97 | 4.43 | 20.2% | 11.2% | 0.44 | 70.6% |
| 2015 | 20 | A | 108.7 | 8 | 10 | 3.98 | 3.94 | 8.53 | 3.89 | 22.3% | 10.2% | 0.58 | 67.5% |

**Background:** A big, projectable 6-foot-4 right-hander taken out of Heritage High School in 2013, Clifton received the highest bonus for a 12th rounder that year, nearly $400,000, the equivalent of late fourth round money. And Clifton's paying off in a *large* way. The Tennessee native had a bit of a coming out party with Boise in the Northwest League two years ago, averaging nearly a punch out per inning as he battled some below-average control/command issues. But Clifton took a rather big – and important – developmental step forward with South Bend in 2015. In 108.2 innings of work, he fanned 103, walked 47, and posted nearly matching 3.98 ERA and 3.94 FIP.

**Projection**: Here's the thing about long shots, or in this case late round over-slot signings – sometimes they pay off. And less than 200 innings under his professional belt, Clifton's making an awful lot of noise as an up-and-comer in the Chicago system; so much so, in fact, that he could have as much potential as *any* hurler in the organization's farm system. His strikeout rate is creeping up while he's slowly improving his control/command. He's big and projectable – with plenty of gas left in the projection tank. And only two other qualified starters under the age of 21 in the Midwest League last season missed more bats (Justus Sheffield and Grant Holmes, a pair of high round draft picks). Clifton has a chance to be an impact arm at the big league level. Watch out.

**Ceiling:** 3.0-win player
**Risk:** Moderate to High
**MLB ETA:** 2018

## 6. Duane Underwood, RHP

**MiLB Rank: #132**
**Position Rank: N/A**

| Born: 07/20/94 | Age: 21 | Bats: R | Top CALs: Carlos Pimentel, Tyler Green, |
|---|---|---|---|
| Height: 6-2 | Weight: 215 | Throws: R | Travis Ott, Robert Hernandez, Luis Heredia |

| YEAR | Age | Level | IP | W | L | ERA | FIP | K/9 | BB/9 | K% | BB% | HR/9 | LOB% |
|---|---|---|---|---|---|---|---|---|---|---|---|---|---|
| 2013 | 18 | A- | 54.3 | 3 | 4 | 4.97 | 4.77 | 5.96 | 4.47 | 13.9% | 10.4% | 0.66 | 57.1% |
| 2014 | 19 | A | 100.7 | 6 | 4 | 2.50 | 4.42 | 7.51 | 3.22 | 20.3% | 8.7% | 0.89 | 80.0% |
| 2015 | 20 | R | 5.0 | 0 | 0 | 0.00 | 1.42 | 10.80 | 0.00 | 33.3% | 0.0% | 0.00 | 100.0% |
| 2015 | 20 | A+ | 73.3 | 6 | 3 | 2.58 | 4.16 | 5.89 | 2.95 | 16.7% | 8.3% | 0.74 | 75.4% |

**Background:** The 2012 second round pick gave the organization quite a scare in late June – Underwood, a 6-foot-2, 215-pound well-built right-hander, started experiencing some discomfort in his powerful right-elbow, an ailment that worried the club enough that he underwent an MRI in early July where no structural damage was revealed. He would make just a pair of tune-up starts in late August in the Arizona Summer League, throwing five innings of pure dominance. Before the injury, Underwood was in the midst of breakout campaign: through his first 11 starts, the burly hurler tossed 63.1 innings, punched out 41, walked 17, and tallied a barely-there 1.85 ERA. For his career, he's sporting a 3.12 ERA with a 181-to-93 strikeout-to-walk ratio.

**Projection**: Here's what I wrote in last year's book,

> *"Then something clicked for the former second rounder and over his final 11 games he fanned 55, walked 16, and posted a tidy 2.13 ERA in 55.0 innings of work."*

I continued:

> *"Finally the real Underwood showed up. Granted it's just an 11-game stretch, but the lively armed right-hander was simply too dominant to ignore. Opponents hit .199/.268/.346 off of him. If, and it's a big if, he can carry that momentum forward – and there's no reason to believe he can't – Underwood's going to start garnering a lot of attention outside of Chicago. At the very least he's a dominant bullpen arm."*

Well, he carried that momentum into 2015 season...and straight onto the DL. So now he has 22 starts of just ridiculous dominance. The only question is whether his arm will slow him down or not. Assuming it doesn't spontaneously explode, he has front-of-the-rotation potential and the strikeouts could come in bunches.

**Ceiling:** 3.0-win player
**Risk:** High
**MLB ETA:** 2018

## 7. Mark Zagunis, OF

**MiLB Rank: #143**
**Position Rank: N/A**

| Born: 02/05/93 | Age: 23 | Bats: R | Top CALs: Wesley Cunningham, Joey Rickard, |
|---|---|---|---|
| Height: 6-0 | Weight: 205 | Throws: R | Jose Constanza, Mark Payton, Lucas Duda |

| Season | Age | LVL | PA | 2B | 3B | HR | AVG | OBP | SLG | ISO | BB% | K% | wRC+ |
|---|---|---|---|---|---|---|---|---|---|---|---|---|---|
| 2014 | 21 | A- | 191 | 9 | 2 | 2 | 0.299 | 0.429 | 0.422 | 0.123 | 16.2% | 16.2% | 145 |
| 2014 | 21 | A- | 191 | 9 | 2 | 2 | 0.299 | 0.429 | 0.422 | 0.123 | 16.2% | 16.2% | 145 |
| 2015 | 22 | A+ | 512 | 24 | 5 | 8 | 0.271 | 0.406 | 0.412 | 0.140 | 15.6% | 16.8% | 146 |

**Background:** Can I get whatever the front office is feeding college bats? Because that superhuman potion the club fattened Kris Bryant and Kyle Schwarber with apparently made its way down the line to Mark Zagunis, an overlooked backstop out of Virginia Tech a couple years back. Zagunis, who would eventually be tabbed in the third round in 2014, was an absolute force in the middle of VT's lineup over the course of his three year career, hitting an aggregate .338/.430/.495 with 37 doubles, seven triples, 16 homeruns, and 52 stolen bases in 164 games. And much like Bryant and Schwarber, Zagunis tore through a few levels during his debut two years ago, slugging a combined .288/.420/.420 while making stops in the Arizona Summer, Northwest, and Midwest Leagues. Chicago bumped the backstop-turned-outfielder to High Class A for 2015, and he responded by hitting .271/.406/.412 with 24 doubles, five triples, eight homeruns, and a wRC+ of 146, the seventh best mark among *all* High Class A bats.

**Projection**: I've always been a fan of the budding sabermetric star; here's what I wrote during his pre-draft evaluation:

> *"English Field [Virginia Tech's home park] tends to inflate offensive numbers, but the tools are strong across the board. Solid-average power, above-average hit tool, good speed for a catcher, strong eye at the plate, and solid contact skills. The lone red flag – and it's pretty glaring at this point – is his inability to control the [running] game. He has nabbed just 20% of would-be base stealer [so far in 2014].*
>
> *His overall skillset is fairly similar to Zane Evans, the Georgia Tech backstop taken in the fourth round last year by the Royals, though Zagunis has a higher ceiling.*
>
> *Overall, the Hokie catcher looks like a solid bet to develop into a league average everyday player with a peak around .270/.340/.400 with double-digit homeruns and stolen bases."*

Well, the analysis still looks spot on. The plate discipline has proven to be an elite skill; he's walked in over 15% of his career plate appearances. The power is solid-average, as is the hit tool. And the club wisely moved him away from behind the plate. Simply put, Zagunis is one of the better prospects you've never heard about. I could easily see him carving out a 10-year career with average offensive production north of 100 wRC+.

**Ceiling:** 2.0- to 2.5-win player
**Risk:** Moderate
**MLB ETA:** 2017

## 8. Carl Edwards, RHP

**MiLB Rank: #164**

**Position Rank: N/A**

| Born: 09/03/91 | Age: 24 | Bats: R | **Top CALs:** Shawn Armstrong, Corey Knebel, |
| Height: 6-3 | Weight: 170 | Throws: R | Pedro Strop, Maikel Cieto, Sam Demel |

| YEAR | Age | Level | IP | W | L | ERA | FIP | K/9 | BB/9 | K% | BB% | HR/9 | LOB% |
|---|---|---|---|---|---|---|---|---|---|---|---|---|---|
| 2013 | 21 | A | 93.3 | 8 | 2 | 1.83 | 2.06 | 11.76 | 3.28 | 32.4% | 9.0% | 0.00 | 71.7% |
| 2013 | 21 | A+ | 23.0 | 0 | 0 | 1.96 | 1.85 | 12.91 | 2.74 | 36.3% | 7.7% | 0.39 | 81.6% |
| 2014 | 22 | R | 5.7 | 0 | 0 | 1.59 | 3.33 | 12.71 | 6.35 | 36.4% | 18.2% | 0.00 | 83.3% |
| 2014 | 22 | AA | 48.0 | 1 | 2 | 2.44 | 2.92 | 8.63 | 3.94 | 23.8% | 10.9% | 0.19 | 75.1% |
| 2015 | 23 | AA | 23.7 | 2 | 2 | 2.66 | 2.97 | 13.69 | 6.46 | 36.0% | 17.0% | 0.38 | 60.2% |
| 2015 | 23 | AAA | 31.7 | 3 | 1 | 2.84 | 3.50 | 11.08 | 6.82 | 29.6% | 18.2% | 0.00 | 72.5% |

**Background**: It's been a bit of a roller-coaster ride for the pitcher formerly known as C.J. Edwards. A late, late, *late* round pick by the Rangers in 2011, Edwards' career was on an impressive trajectory – especially for a 48th round pick – until shoulder issues derailed his speedy ascension last season. The rail-thin right-hander out of Mid-Carolina High School tore through the Arizona and Northwest Leagues during his pro debut, leaped through the Sally and FSL in his sophomore campaign, and opened up the 2014 season with four promising starts with the Tennessee Smokies. But Edwards, not to be confused with the NASCAR driver with the same name, would miss more than three months (with injury) before returning in late July. Chicago converted him to a full-time reliever in 2015 and Edwards made stops at three different levels: Class AA, Class AAA, and MLB. He would finish the minor league season with 55.1 innings, 75 punch outs, and a whopping 41 base on balls. He would also issue another three walks in 4.2 innings with Chicago down the stretch.

**Projection**: "We certainly, in no way, shape or form, have given up on him as a starter. But we also realize we [have] to manage his innings a little bit this year and start him off in that role allows us to do that, and then make an assessment which way we want to go with him." – Cubs GM Jed Hoyer, April 8, 2015 via the Chicago Tribune.

Well, do you think after the season that the club is any closer in determining Edwards' future? Likely not. The 6-foot-3, 170-pound right-hander has, *historically speaking*, always offered up solid-average control. But consider this: since coming back from the shoulder injury in late July 2014, Edwards has walked 68 in 105 innings of work, or nearly six free passes every nine innings.

The arsenal – an above-average fastball, hard upper 70s curveball, and an 88 mph changeup – plays very well in the rotation, obviously, but if he doesn't recapture his previous control there's no way he makes it back to the big leagues as a starting pitcher.

**Ceiling**: 2.5- to 3.0-win player
**Risk**: High
**MLB ETA**: Debuted in 2015

## 9. Eloy Jimenez, LF/RF

**MiLB Rank: #165**

**Position Rank: N/A**

| Born: 11/27/96 | Age: 19 | Bats: R | **Top CALs:** Zolio Almonte, Zacrey Law, |
| Height: 6-4 | Weight: 205 | Throws: R | Oscar Rojas, Wander Franco, Natanael Delgado |

| Season | Age | LVL | PA | 2B | 3B | HR | AVG | OBP | SLG | ISO | BB% | K% | wRC+ |
|---|---|---|---|---|---|---|---|---|---|---|---|---|---|
| 2014 | 17 | R | 164 | 8 | 2 | 3 | 0.227 | 0.268 | 0.367 | 0.140 | 6.1% | 19.5% | 80 |
| 2015 | 18 | A- | 250 | 10 | 0 | 7 | 0.284 | 0.328 | 0.418 | 0.134 | 6.0% | 17.2% | 113 |

**Background:** One of the club's biggest expenditures in the international market over the past several seasons, Jimenez, who signed a massive $2.8 million deal out of the Dominican Republic as a 16-year-old, struggled to adapt to a brand new culture and far more advanced pitching during his pro debut in the Arizona Summer League the following season. The 6-foot-4, 205-pound man-child batted .227/.268/.367 with just 13 extra-base hits in 42 games. But the organization, keeping with their original aggressive approach, pushed Jimenez up to the Northwest League where his production rebounded greatly; he hit .284/.328/.418 with 10 doubles and seven dingers in 57 games as an 18-year-old against hurlers that averaged three years his senior.

**Projection**: Again, here's some more context: only one other 18-year-old slugged more short-season dingers than Jimenez: Colorado's Kevin Padlo, with 10. Jimenez has massive, *massive* power potential – something that his 6-foot-4, 205-pound frame only hints at. Solid-eye with some room to grow as he familiarizes himself with more advanced pitching. He also has strong contact rates, another encouraging sign for a budding power-hitter.

**Ceiling**: 2.0-win player
**Risk**: Moderate to High
**MLB ETA**: 2018

## 10. Daniel Vogelbach, 1B

| Born: 12/17/92 | Age: 23 | Bats: L | Top CALs: Mike Carp, Max Muncy, |
|---|---|---|---|
| Height: 6-0 | Weight: 250 | Throws: R | Stefan Welch, Chris Parmalee, Austin Gallagher |

| Season | Age | LVL | PA | 2B | 3B | HR | AVG | OBP | SLG | ISO | BB% | K% | wRC+ |
|---|---|---|---|---|---|---|---|---|---|---|---|---|---|
| 2013 | 20 | A | 500 | 21 | 0 | 17 | 0.284 | 0.364 | 0.450 | 0.166 | 11.4% | 15.2% | 128 |
| 2014 | 21 | A+ | 560 | 28 | 1 | 16 | 0.268 | 0.357 | 0.429 | 0.162 | 11.8% | 16.3% | 126 |
| 2015 | 22 | R | 17 | 2 | 0 | 0 | 0.455 | 0.647 | 0.636 | 0.182 | 35.3% | 5.9% | 265 |
| 2015 | 22 | AA | 313 | 16 | 1 | 7 | 0.272 | 0.403 | 0.425 | 0.154 | 18.2% | 19.5% | 140 |

**Background:** One of the last holdovers from the pre-Theo Epstein/Jed Hoyer era that's still considered a top prospect. Vogelbach continued his slow, arduous trek through the minor leagues last season, spending the entire year with Tennessee – and partly on the Disabled List. Appearing in 76 games with the Smokies in the Southern League, the hefty lefty-swinging first baseman, who battled a semi-serious oblique injury, mashed to the tune of .272/.403/.425 with 16 doubles, one triple, and seven homeruns en route to posting a whopping 140 wRC+. And just for argument's sake, here are those counting stats pro-rated for a full 162-game season: 35 doubles, 2 triples, and 15 homeruns. For his career Vogelbach is sporting an impressive .284/.382/.473 triple-slash line, most of which was done against much older competition.

**Projection**: For everything that Vogelbach does well – an above-average or better eye at the plate, 15- to 20-homer power potential, squares up the baseball – he has yet to consistently solve left-handed pitching. Here are his OPS totals against southpaws since 2013: .1200, .660, .637, and .769. And those two successful seasons can be easily explained away: rookie ball and a small sample size buoyed by his walk rate. If he can solve LHP, he's a slam dunk solid-average or better MLB first baseman. If not, well, he'll make a lot of money as a bench bat/platoon option.

**Ceiling:** 2.0- to 2.5-win player
**Risk:** Moderate to High
**MLB ETA:** 2016

## 11. Donnie Dewees, OF

| Born: 09/29/93 | Age: 22 | Bats: L | Top CALs: Walker Gourley, Julian Ridings, |
|---|---|---|---|
| Height: 5-11 | Weight: 180 | Throws: L | Michael Rockett, Austin Cousino, Luis Veras |

| Season | Age | LVL | PA | 2B | 3B | HR | AVG | OBP | SLG | ISO | BB% | K% | wRC+ |
|---|---|---|---|---|---|---|---|---|---|---|---|---|---|
| 2015 | 21 | A- | 303 | 14 | 1 | 5 | 0.266 | 0.306 | 0.376 | 0.110 | 4.6% | 17.8% | 96 |

**Background:** The second highest draft pick in University of North Florida's less-than-illustrious history and just the second player taken before the sixth round. Dewees, nonetheless, garnered a whole helluva lot attention throughout his career for the Ospreys:

- Atlantic Sun Conference All-Freshman
- All-Atlantic Sun Conference
- Perfect Game All-Freshman
- 2014 Atlantic Sun Preseason All-Conference Team
- 2015 Atlantic Sun Preseason All-Conference Team
- Perfect Game Atlantic Sun Preseason Player of the Year
- Atlantic Sun First Team All-Conference
- Golden Spikes Award Semifinalist
- Dick Howser Trophy Semifinalist
- Atlantic Sun All-Tournament Team
- Louisville Slugger First Team All-American

Small school be damned; that's an awful lot of notoriety for any prospect, at any school. And that's not including what he might have earned had he not suffered a broken wrist during his sophomore campaign. Anyway, Dewees slugged a hearty .422/.483/.749 with 12 doubles, eight triples, and 18 homeruns while swiping 23 bags in 26 attempts – all career bests. The club pushed Dewees to Eugene in the Northwest League for his debut where he hit .266/.306/.376 with 14 doubles, one triple, five homeruns, and 19 stolen bags.

**Projection**: Here's what I wrote during his pre-draft evaluation:

*"Obviously North Florida's level of competition doesn't stack up to an elite team like LSU or UCLA, but Dewees' production in the Cape last summer helps alleviate some of those concerns. Solid plate discipline, surprising power, and speed. If Dewees can stick in center field – which isn't a certainty – he could become one of the better prospects in this year's draft class. Otherwise, he's a strong candidate to be a better-than-average regular."*

Well, he's *still* not certain to spend the duration of his professional life in center field; he spent about one-third of his debut in a corner outfield position. But everything else still holds, though.

**Ceiling:** 2.0- to 2.5-win player
**Risk:** Moderate to High
**MLB ETA:** 2018

## 12. Jake Stinnett, RHP

**MiLB Rank: #191**
**Position Rank: N/A**

| Born: 04/25/92 | Age: 24 | Bats: R | Top CALs: Esmerlin Jimenez, Andrew Hess, |
| Height: 6-4 | Weight: 202 | Throws: R | Luis Noel, Blake Holovach, Jason Fernandez |

| YEAR | Age | Level | IP | W | L | ERA | FIP | K/9 | BB/9 | K% | BB% | HR/9 | LOB% |
|---|---|---|---|---|---|---|---|---|---|---|---|---|---|
| 2014 | 22 | R | 4.7 | 0 | 1 | 7.71 | 2.75 | 5.79 | 0.00 | 13.6% | 0.0% | 0.00 | 55.6% |
| 2014 | 22 | A- | 6.3 | 0 | 0 | 2.84 | 4.61 | 9.95 | 2.84 | 28.0% | 8.0% | 1.42 | 83.3% |
| 2015 | 23 | A | 117.0 | 7 | 6 | 4.46 | 4.20 | 7.00 | 3.85 | 17.7% | 9.8% | 0.46 | 67.0% |

**Background:** Sure, it's funny to chuckle about the freak accidents that can send a player DL-bound – the time Marty Cordova cooked himself a tad too long in the tanning bed, or when knuckleballer Steve Sparks dislocated his shoulder ripping a phonebook in half, or when Greg W. Harris missed a handful of games with elbow inflammation after spending the day flicking sunflower seeds. But what happened to Stinnett is hardly a laughing matter. The former senior pop-up at Maryland nearly lost a testicle during pitcher fielding practices during the offseason last year. Uhhh...cringe. So maybe that's why the big right-hander got off to a bit of slow start in the Midwest League last season? I sure as hell know that would have a lingering effect on me.

Through his first nine games of the season Stinnett coughed up 26 earned runs to go along with a nearly 1-to-1 strikeout-to-walk in 38.1 innings of work. After that, however, he hardly resembled that pitcher: in 78.2 innings he allowed 32 earned runs while posting a 59-to-23 strikeout-to-walk ratio, as well as a much more slightly 3.66 ERA.

**Projection**: I was so, so incredibly high on Stinnett entering the 2014 draft, writing:

*"Fresh, developing arm with the potential to help fill out the fron thalf of a big league rotation. Above-average ability to miss bats with solid-average or better control. And, again, Stinnett still has room to grow as he continues honing his craft."*

While his numbers during his first full season are...ugh huh...not so hot, I'm still not ready to give up on Stinnett's promising right arm. And it's still important to remember that he's only been pitching on a consistent basis for just three seasons now. He's already entering his age-24 season, so if it doesn't click within the next year-plus he'll likely find himself as a late-inning option.

**Ceiling:** 2.0- to 2.5-win player
**Risk:** Moderate to High
**MLB ETA:** 2017

## 13. Oscar De La Cruz, RHP

**MiLB Rank: #200**
**Position Rank: N/A**

| Born: 03/04/95 | Age: 21 | Bats: R | Top CALs: Jose Rodriguez, Hector Silvestre, |
| Height: 6-4 | Weight: 200 | Throws: R | Reiwal Gonzalez, Matt Spann, Rafael Volquez |

| YEAR | Age | Level | IP | W | L | ERA | FIP | K/9 | BB/9 | K% | BB% | HR/9 | LOB% |
|---|---|---|---|---|---|---|---|---|---|---|---|---|---|
| 2013 | 18 | R | 11.0 | 1 | 0 | 6.55 | 5.73 | 9.82 | 4.09 | 22.2% | 9.3% | 1.64 | 76.6% |
| 2014 | 19 | R | 75.0 | 8 | 1 | 1.80 | 2.89 | 7.68 | 2.28 | 21.0% | 6.2% | 0.24 | 71.8% |
| 2015 | 20 | A- | 73.0 | 6 | 3 | 2.84 | 3.18 | 9.00 | 2.10 | 25.2% | 5.9% | 0.49 | 70.0% |

**Background:** Another one of these low level arms with a potentially high ceiling. De La Cruz, a 6-foot-4, 200-pound right-hander signed out of the Dominican Republic a couple years back, took as big of a step forward developmentally speaking as any young arm the Cubs have last season. After spending roughly a year-plus in the Dominican Summer League, De La Cruz made the jump straight into the Northwest League where he made 13 starts while fanning more than a quarter of the total hitters he faced. He finished the year with a 73-to-17 strikeout-to-walk ratio in 73.0 innings of work.

**Projection**: An absolute force to be reckoned with at various points last season. De La Cruz twirled a six-inning, nine punch out, zero walk performance against the Hillsboro Hops in early July and had an even better showing in late August; he tossed a season-high seven innings against the Spokane Indians, fanning 13, walking one, and giving up one single solitary base knock. Again, like Justin Steele and Carson Sands, the sample size is incredibly limited, but there's an awful lot to like here.

**Ceiling:** 2.5-win player
**Risk:** High
**MLB ETA:** 2018

## 14. Pierce Johnson, RHP

**MiLB Rank: #222**
**Position Rank: N/A**

| Born: 05/10/91 | Age: 25 | Bats: R | **Top CALs:** Michael O'Brien, Justin Thomas, |
| Height: 6-3 | Weight: 200 | Throws: R | Zach Stewart, Rob Rasmussen, Barret Browning |

| YEAR | Age | Level | IP | W | L | ERA | FIP | K/9 | BB/9 | K% | BB% | HR/9 | LOB% |
|---|---|---|---|---|---|---|---|---|---|---|---|---|---|
| 2014 | 19 | A | 105.0 | 6 | 1 | 2.40 | 3.28 | 7.29 | 1.29 | 21.3% | 3.8% | 0.60 | 77.5% |
| 2015 | 20 | A+ | 119.0 | 7 | 7 | 3.55 | 3.30 | 6.58 | 2.27 | 17.6% | 6.1% | 0.38 | 71.9% |

**Background:** Johnson's career trajectory isn't what the Cubs envisioned when they selected the Missouri State University with the 43rd overall pick in the 2012. But Johnson, a 6-foot-3, 200-pound right-hander, just completed his second stint in Class AA – albeit a wildly successful, injury-shortened campaign. A back issue limited him to just 16 starts last season, throwing 95.0 innings while averaging 6.8 punch outs and 32 free passes while posting a 2.08 ERA and 3.47 FIP. And despite this being Johnson's second tenure with the Smokies, he's tallied 34 total games (186.2 innings, 163 strikeouts, and 86 walks).

**Projection**: Here's what I wrote in last year's book:

> "Johnson showed far better command of the strike zone two years ago, so there's hope that last season was just a hiccup. If it does [prove to be a hiccup] he could develop into a good #4 arm. If not, well, there's always the backend of the Cubs' bullpen where his fantastic strikeout ability would spike even higher."

Johnson's problematic control in 2014 – he averaged 5.0 free passes per nine innings – proved to be a hiccup, but his punch out rate tumbled to a career low in 2015. Still, though, he looks like a good #4.

**Ceiling:** 1.5- to 2.0-win player
**Risk:** Moderate
**MLB ETA:** 2016

## 15. Willson Contreras, C

**MiLB Rank: #223**
**Position Rank: #9**

| Born: 05/13/92 | Age: 24 | Bats: R | **Top CALs:** Luis Exposito, Mark Thomas, |
| Height: 6-1 | Weight: 175 | Throws: R | John Ryan Murphy, J.T. Realmuto, Dane Phillips |

| Season | Age | LVL | PA | 2B | 3B | HR | AVG | OBP | SLG | ISO | BB% | K% | wRC+ |
|---|---|---|---|---|---|---|---|---|---|---|---|---|---|
| 2013 | 21 | A | 345 | 11 | 5 | 11 | 0.248 | 0.320 | 0.423 | 0.174 | 7.5% | 19.1% | 109 |
| 2014 | 22 | A+ | 317 | 14 | 2 | 5 | 0.242 | 0.320 | 0.359 | 0.117 | 8.8% | 20.8% | 97 |
| 2015 | 23 | AA | 521 | 34 | 4 | 8 | 0.333 | 0.413 | 0.478 | 0.145 | 10.9% | 11.9% | 156 |

**Background:** I feel like we've seen this one before. Oh, yeah, that's because we have. Once upon a time in the not-so-distant past, the Cubs had a stocky young minor league backstop with a career track record the equivalent of vanilla ice cream. And then – BAM! – something clicked for the 24-year-old catcher known as Geovany Soto, and he bashed his way through the PCL – and up the prospect charts. Soto slugged .354/.424/.652 with 31 doubles, three triples, and 26 homeruns. Fast forward a couple more years and we now have Wilson Contreras, a once-non-descript backstop in the Cubs' organization who is forcing everyone to take notice after a breakout campaign in 2015. Contreras, who batted .242/.320/.359 as a 22-year-old with Daytona in 2014, hit a robust .333/.413/.478 during his initial foray into Class AA, slugging 34 doubles, four triples, eight homeruns, and posting a 62-to-57 strikeout-to-walk ratio in 521 trips to the plate.

**Projection**: Just to put Contreras' massive breakout into proper perspective consider this: among all stateside backstops with at least 300+ plate appearances, no other catcher topped Contreras' production. But let's take it a step further: among *all* stateside minor league prospects with 400+ prospects, Contreras' wRC+ total, 155, was tied for 16th.

So here's what we know about the Venezuelan-born backstop – he's a new convert to catcher, moving to the position in 2012; his plate discipline spiked to the best mark of his career, 10.9%; he has solid-average power, but not necessarily a double-digit homerun threat; and he was seemingly very lucky in 2015 as his BABIP spiked to .370, easily the highest mark of his career.

Add it all up and Contreras hardly looks like a top level prospect. He's a nice fringy big league regular that's likely headed for a steep decline in 2016. Remember: you've heard it hear first.

**Ceiling:** 1.5- to 2.0-win player
**Risk:** Moderate
**MLB ETA:** 2016

## 16. Jeimer Candelario, 3B

**MiLB Rank: #240**
**Position Rank: N/A**

| Born: 11/24/93 | Age: 22 | Bats: B | Top CALs: Aderlin Rodriguez, Wilmer Flores, |
|---|---|---|---|
| Height: 6-1 | Weight: 210 | Throws: R | Blake Dewitt, Cheslor Cuthbert, Brandon Drury |

| Season | Age | LVL | PA | 2B | 3B | HR | AVG | OBP | SLG | ISO | BB% | K% | wRC+ |
|---|---|---|---|---|---|---|---|---|---|---|---|---|---|
| 2013 | 19 | A | 572 | 35 | 1 | 11 | 0.256 | 0.346 | 0.396 | 0.140 | 11.9% | 15.4% | 112 |
| 2014 | 20 | A | 263 | 19 | 3 | 6 | 0.250 | 0.300 | 0.426 | 0.176 | 6.8% | 17.1% | 105 |
| 2014 | 20 | A+ | 244 | 10 | 2 | 5 | 0.193 | 0.275 | 0.326 | 0.133 | 9.4% | 18.0% | 73 |
| 2015 | 21 | A+ | 343 | 25 | 3 | 5 | 0.270 | 0.318 | 0.415 | 0.145 | 5.8% | 18.1% | 113 |
| 2015 | 21 | AA | 182 | 10 | 1 | 5 | 0.291 | 0.379 | 0.462 | 0.171 | 12.1% | 11.5% | 140 |

**Background:** Just how badly did Candelario struggle in 2014? Well, Chicago promoted the then-20-year-old up to the Florida State League to begin the year – a move that was widely expected given his showing in Low Class A the previous season – and Candelario wasn't simply overmatched, he was underpowered and nearly left for dead. The 6-foot-1, 210-pound third baseman "batted" a paltry .193/.275/.326 with 17 extra-base hits in 62 games. The club bounced him back down to Low Class A in mid-June and Candelario responded by hitting .250/.300/.426 with 19 doubles, three triples, and a half dozen dingers – good, not fantastic production. So you'll have to excuse me if I was a bit pessimistic moving forward. But the New York-born Candelario responded beautifully in his return to High Class A in 2015, batting .270/.318/.415 – enough production to warrant a mid-season promotion to Tennessee. Overall, he finished the year with an aggregate .277/.339/.431 with 35 doubles, four triples, and 10 homeruns.

**Projection:** The skill that made Candelario so damn promising as a teenager in the Midwest League finally returned during his stint in Class AA last season: he started working the count more often, which in turn pushed his walk rate north of 10%. Candelario has solid-average power, strong contact rates, and granny-like speed. He's a fringy big league regular, though his odds are much better than they were this time last year.

**Ceiling:** 1.5- to 2.0-win player
**Risk:** Moderate
**MLB ETA:** 2016

## 17. Jen-Ho Tseng, RHP

**MiLB Rank: N/A**
**Position Rank: N/A**

| Born: 10/03/94 | Age: 21 | Bats: L | Top CALs: Arquimedes Nieto, Edgar Garcia, |
|---|---|---|---|
| Height: 6-1 | Weight: 195 | Throws: R | Zach Eflin, Jonathan Martinez, Shairon Martis |

| YEAR | Age | Level | IP | W | L | ERA | FIP | K/9 | BB/9 | K% | BB% | HR/9 | LOB% |
|---|---|---|---|---|---|---|---|---|---|---|---|---|---|
| 2014 | 18 | R | 18.7 | 0 | 0 | 2.89 | 2.80 | 12.05 | 3.86 | 31.7% | 10.1% | 0.00 | 75.0% |
| 2015 | 19 | A- | 40.7 | 3 | 1 | 2.66 | 2.84 | 8.41 | 3.32 | 21.7% | 8.6% | 0.00 | 54.7% |

**Background:** After establishing himself as one of just six 19-year-old starters to throw at least 100 innings in the Midwest League two seasons ago, Tseng once again stood out among a class of older competition. He was the only 20-year-old starter to hurl 100+ innings in the Carolina League and one of just five to accomplish the feat in *any* High Class A level (the others being Antonio Senzatela, Kohl Stewart, German Marquez, and Victor Arano). Tseng, who signed on the international market for a touch over $1.6 million, made 22 starts with the Myrtle Beach Pelicans, throwing a career high 119.0 innings while fanning 17.6% and walking 6.1% of the total batters he faced. He finished the year with a solid 3.30 FIP.

**Projection:** Tseng's one of those guys that could easily go one way or the other – he could continue to progress through the minor leagues and develop into a backend starting pitcher *or* just as easily become the latest finesse right-hander that failed to take the necessary steps to succeed. He doesn't miss a whole lot of bats – he's fanned 19.2% of the batters he's faced in his career – but compensates by limiting free passes. With that being said, he's heading to Class AA as a 21-year-old coming off of back-to-back seasons in which he's posted a 3.28 and 3.30 FIPs against much older competition.

**Ceiling:** 1.5- to 2.0-win player
**Risk:** Moderate to High
**MLB ETA:** 2017

## 18. Justin Steele, LHP

**MiLB Rank:** N/A
**Position Rank:** N/A

| Born: 07/11/95 | Age: 20 | Bats: L | **Top CALs:** Kenny Mathews, Wilfredo Diaz, |
| Height: 6-2 | Weight: 195 | Throws: L | Ryan Morris, Andrew Bellatti, Austin Malinowski |

| YEAR | Age | Level | IP | W | L | ERA | FIP | K/9 | BB/9 | K% | BB% | HR/9 | LOB% |
|------|-----|-------|-----|---|---|------|------|-------|------|-------|-------|------|-------|
| 2013 | 21 | A+ | 107.7 | 7 | 8 | 3.93 | 3.47 | 9.70 | 4.60 | 23.8% | 11.3% | 0.42 | 64.6% |
| 2014 | 22 | AA | 124.3 | 6 | 7 | 3.47 | 4.68 | 8.61 | 5.14 | 22.0% | 13.2% | 0.94 | 77.9% |
| 2015 | 23 | AA | 86.0 | 3 | 5 | 4.92 | 3.86 | 10.57 | 4.92 | 27.2% | 12.7% | 0.73 | 62.3% |

**Background:** File this one under one of the more bizarre stat lines of 2015. Steele, a big time over slot signee two years ago, had an impressive showing in the Northwest League as a 19-year-old, averaging nearly a punch out per inning with solid-average control. The interesting part: he allowed 12 earned runs, but 24 runs total. Steele would finish the year with a 2.84 FIP in 40.2 innings of work.

**Projection:** The club signed the former fifth round pick for an even $1 million bonus. Steele has been an exciting prospect during his 59-inning run in pro ball. He's posted a combined 63-to-18 strikeout-to-walk ratio to go along with a 2.75 ERA. He has a sturdy, innings-eater frame with promising peripherals. Let's see how he performs when the reins get eased a bit in full season ball.

**Ceiling:** 1.5- to 2.0-win player
**Risk:** Moderate to High
**MLB ETA:** 2018

## 19. David Berg, RHP

**MiLB Rank:** N/A
**Position Rank:** N/A

| Born: 03/17/95 | Age: 21 | Bats: R | **Top CALs:** N/A |
| Height: 6-3 | Weight: 180 | Throws: R | |

**Background:** How's this for an impressive, dominant career at a collegiate powerhouse: in 267.0 innings with the Bruins, Berg tallied an impressive 241-to-44 strikeout-to-walk ratio en route to saving 49 games with a barely-there 1.11 ERA. Just pure, filthy dominance.

**Projection:** Here's what I wrote prior to the 2014 draft when the Rangers grabbed the young right-hander in the 17th round:

> "Now the motion: The quick, easy and wrong comparison to throw out would be the submarining Chad Bradford. But Berg's motion isn't as exaggerated. Instead of a release point from way down under, his is more sidearm with a release point close to parallel to the ground.
>
> He's going to be a right-hander specialist in the professional ranks: left-handed hitters are going to see the ball way too long. But Berg should move quickly, perhaps being one of the first players from the 2014 draft class to make it to the big leagues, and should settle in nicely as a solid or better late-inning arm."

Berg eventually bypassed the Rangers' option and headed back to school. Here's what I wrote before the Cubs grabbed him:

> "Admittedly, I was absolutely shocked when Berg last until the 17th round last season. Granted, he's not going to impact a game the way a potential first or second round pick would, but he has as long of a track record of pure dominance as anyone in college baseball.
>
> And as I noted in a question posed by a reader following that draft last season, MLB teams are still afraid of the unknown. Meaning: his atypical throwing motion.
>
> Now, Berg likely isn't going to be able to handle left-handers, but he's a strong candidate to develop into a Joe Smith, Pat Neshek, Brad Ziegler caliber performer.
>
> As far as his draft grade goes, I think nabbing him in the third round, but I would guess a team wouldn't take him before the fourth, especially considering that's where the Indians grabbed – and quickly promoted – southpaw reliever Kyle Crockett.

*Please. Someone. Anyone. Give Berg a chance."*

I also projected the right-hander to be the first player from the 2015 draft class to make it to the big leagues. Let's see what happens.

**Ceiling:** 1.0- to 1.5-win player
**Risk:** Low to Moderate
**MLB ETA:** 2018

## 20. Corey Black, RHP

**MiLB Rank:** N/A
**Position Rank:** N/A

| Born: 08/04/91 | Age: 24 | Bats: R | Top CALs: Dan Cortes, Chris Withrow, |
|---|---|---|---|
| Height: 5-11 | Weight: 175 | Throws: R | Justin Wright, Alexander Smit, Mike Foltynewicz |

| YEAR | Age | Level | IP | W | L | ERA | FIP | K/9 | BB/9 | K% | BB% | HR/9 | LOB% |
|---|---|---|---|---|---|---|---|---|---|---|---|---|---|
| 2014 | 19 | R | 19.0 | 3 | 1 | 1.89 | 3.19 | 9.47 | 3.32 | 26.0% | 9.1% | 0.00 | 69.6% |
| 2015 | 20 | A- | 57.3 | 3 | 4 | 3.92 | 3.58 | 6.44 | 3.30 | 16.1% | 8.2% | 0.00 | 55.1% |

**Background:** The diminutive right-hander out of Falkner University took the expected step towards a full time relief role in 2015. After posting some impressive – and often times dominant – peripherals in the lower levels, Black's control abandoned him in 2013 and

he's struggled regain his previous form. Couple that with his 5-foot-11, 175-pound frame, and big-time fastball; and Black was seemingly destined for his new role. After nine appearances – albeit, nine surprisingly impressive appearances – the organization pushed the hard-throwing hurler into a late-inning role. He finished the year with 101 punch outs and 47 walks in 86 innings of work.

**Projection**: First, here's what I wrote in last year's book:

> *"CAL's a big fan of the little right-hander, comparing him to an above-average starting pitcher (Willy Peralta) and a top prospect (Mike Foltynewicz). He probably has one, maybe two seasons to figure out how to find the plate with some level of consistency before the brass pushes him into the bullpen. And given his small stature it could end up happening anyways. At worst he's a good backend guy."*

So, as I've mentioned before his size was ultimately going to push him into a short-inning role. But the timing of it was a bit peculiar given how successful Black was in his first nine starts. Anyway, he's going to be a potentially above-average or better setup man.

**Ceiling:** 1.0- to 1.5-win player
**Risk:** Low to Moderate
**MLB ETA:** 2016

## 21. Victor Caratini, C/1B

**MiLB Rank:** N/A
**Position Rank:** N/A

| Born: 08/17/93 | Age: 22 | Bats: B | Top CALs: John Ryan Murphy, Christian Vazquez, |
|---|---|---|---|
| Height: 6-1 | Weight: 215 | Throws: R | Tucker Barnhart, Jair Fernandez, Chance Sisco |

| Season | Age | LVL | PA | 2B | 3B | HR | AVG | OBP | SLG | ISO | BB% | K% | wRC+ |
|---|---|---|---|---|---|---|---|---|---|---|---|---|---|
| 2013 | 19 | R | 246 | 23 | 1 | 1 | 0.290 | 0.415 | 0.430 | 0.140 | 15.9% | 19.9% | 148 |
| 2014 | 20 | A | 365 | 18 | 4 | 5 | 0.279 | 0.352 | 0.406 | 0.127 | 9.3% | 16.2% | 112 |
| 2015 | 21 | A+ | 453 | 31 | 1 | 4 | 0.257 | 0.342 | 0.372 | 0.115 | 10.8% | 16.6% | 111 |

**Background:** A 2013 second round pick out of JuCo powerhouse Miami-Dade, Caratini was shipped to the north side of Chicago at the trade deadline two years ago in exchange for lefty James Russell and utility man extraordinaire Emilio Bonifacio. Caratini, a 6-foot-1,

215-pound switch-hitter, continued his song-and-dance across the infield last season, seeing time behind the plate – his natural position – and at first base as well. He's also seen action at the hot corner and a little bit at shortstop during his three-year pro career. Last year, his first in High Class A, Caratini batted a respectable .257/.342/.372 with 31 doubles, one triple, and four homeruns en route to tallying a 111 wRC+.

**Projection**: Caratini has hit well enough against older competition over the past two seasons without truly dominating. And for the most part the skills are average across the board – patience, hit tool, power, etc... Obviously, the bat plays much better behind the plate, but that would also require him to – you know – field the position, unfortunately.

**Ceiling:** 1.0- to 1.5-win player
**Risk:** Moderate
**MLB ETA:** 2017

## 22. Carson Sands, LHP

Position Rank: N/A

| Born: 03/28/95 | Age: 21 | Bats: L | Top CALs: Robert Whitenack, Tayler Scott, |
| Height: 6-3 | Weight: 205 | Throws: L | Zach Dials, Sandobal Septimo, Miquel Celestino |

| YEAR | Age | Level | IP | W | L | ERA | FIP | K/9 | BB/9 | K% | BB% | HR/9 | LOB% |
|---|---|---|---|---|---|---|---|---|---|---|---|---|---|
| 2013 | 19 | A- | 46.0 | 2 | 3 | 3.33 | 4.47 | 7.43 | 5.67 | 18.7% | 14.3% | 0.59 | 67.4% |
| 2014 | 20 | A | 117.0 | 9 | 4 | 3.23 | 3.84 | 5.77 | 2.38 | 15.5% | 6.4% | 0.46 | 71.2% |
| 2015 | 21 | A+ | 89.7 | 7 | 5 | 3.11 | 3.22 | 6.32 | 2.21 | 17.0% | 5.9% | 0.30 | 71.8% |

**Background:** Taken one round before Justin Steele and signed to a slightly bigger deal (at $1.1 million), Sands is another high profile over slot prep hurler from the 2014 draft class. But unlike Steele, Sands, a 6-foot-3, 205-pound southpaw, couldn't carry his debut momentum into the Northwest League last season; he tossed 57.1 innings while fanning 41 and walking 21 to go along with a 3.58 FIP.

**Projection:** Despite being taken a round earlier and paid $100,000 more than his rotation-mate Justin Steele, Sands has been the lesser of the prospects. He's big and lanky with projectability, but his swing-and-miss ability really took a step backward last season. He's still young enough with enough limited innings to go anyway from here, but I'm still giving the long-term nod to Steele.

**Ceiling:** 1.0- to 1.5-win player
**Risk:** Moderate to High
**MLB ETA:** 2016

## 23. Paul Blackburn, RHP

MiLB Rank: N/A

Position Rank: N/A

| Born: 12/04/93 | Age: 22 | Bats: R | Top CALs: Zeke Spruill, Myles Jaye, |
| Height: 6-1 | Weight: 195 | Throws: R | Colton Cain, Ryan Searle, Joely Rodriguez |

| YEAR | Age | Level | IP | W | L | ERA | FIP | K/9 | BB/9 | K% | BB% | HR/9 | LOB% |
|---|---|---|---|---|---|---|---|---|---|---|---|---|---|
| 2013 | 19 | A- | 46.0 | 2 | 3 | 3.33 | 4.47 | 7.43 | 5.67 | 18.7% | 14.3% | 0.59 | 67.4% |
| 2014 | 20 | A | 117.0 | 9 | 4 | 3.23 | 3.84 | 5.77 | 2.38 | 15.5% | 6.4% | 0.46 | 71.2% |
| 2015 | 21 | A+ | 89.7 | 7 | 5 | 3.11 | 3.22 | 6.32 | 2.21 | 17.0% | 5.9% | 0.30 | 71.8% |

**Background:** One of the first picks of the Theo Epstein/Jed Hoyer era, Blackburn has remained remarkably consistent – and slowly improving – throughout his four-year minor league career. After a decent debut in rookie ball in 2012, the former 56th overall pick battled control issues as he moved into the Northwest League, walking more than 5.5 batters per nine innings. The club bumped him up to the Midwest League the following year, 2014, and his control rebounded, but his K-rate plummeted to sub-6.0-territory. Last year with Myrtle Beach, Blackburn made 18 starts; throwing 89.2 innings with 63 punch outs and 22 free passes. He finished with the best ERA, 3.11, and FIP, 3.22, of his pro career.

**Projection:** An absolute groundball machine – he's averaged well over 50% since 2013 – Blackburn's slight improvements each season should be noted:

| Year | IP | ERA | FIP |
|---|---|---|---|
| 2012 | 20.2 | 3.48 | 5.39 |
| 2013 | 46.0 | 3.33 | 4.47 |
| 2014 | 117.0 | 3.23 | 3.84 |
| 2015 | 89.2 | 3.11 | 3.22 |

Blackburn, in a lot of ways, is similar to that of fellow rotation-mate Jen-Ho Tseng – both aren't overpowering and won't miss a whole lot of bats; each shows strong control and has had success against older competition. The nod, however, goes to the younger Tseng, but Blackburn could carve out a role as a fringy #5.

**Ceiling:** 1.0-win player
**Risk:** Moderate
**MLB ETA:** 2017

## 24. Rob Zastryzny, LHP

MiLB Rank: N/A
Position Rank: N/A

| Born: 03/26/92 | Age: 24 | Bats: R | Top CALs: Daniel Gibson, Jason Garcia, |
|---|---|---|---|
| Height: 6-3 | Weight: 205 | Throws: L | Dylan De Meyer, Cody Penny, Trevor Hurley |

| YEAR | Age | Level | IP | W | L | ERA | FIP | K/9 | BB/9 | K% | BB% | HR/9 | LOB% |
|---|---|---|---|---|---|---|---|---|---|---|---|---|---|
| 2013 | 21 | A- | 14.3 | 0 | 0 | 3.14 | 2.34 | 10.05 | 2.51 | 25.8% | 6.5% | 0.00 | 76.2% |
| 2013 | 21 | A | 9.7 | 1 | 0 | 0.93 | 3.34 | 5.59 | 3.72 | 15.4% | 10.3% | 0.00 | 92.3% |
| 2014 | 22 | A+ | 110.0 | 4 | 6 | 4.66 | 3.66 | 9.00 | 2.70 | 23.0% | 6.9% | 0.82 | 70.1% |
| 2015 | 23 | R | 4.0 | 0 | 0 | 2.25 | 3.32 | 9.00 | 4.50 | 23.5% | 11.8% | 0.00 | 80.0% |
| 2015 | 23 | AA | 60.7 | 2 | 5 | 6.23 | 5.03 | 7.12 | 4.15 | 17.0% | 9.9% | 1.34 | 62.8% |

**Background:** And this is what happens when a polished collegiate, early round pick who breezes through the lower levels only to have Class AA smack him back down to earth. Zastryzny posted a 110-to-33 strikeout-to-walk ratio in 110.0 innings with Daytona two years ago. But those numbers declined to a 48-to-28 strikeout-to-walk ratio in 60.2 innings during an injury-shortened campaign.

**Projection**: So, I should have *totally* taken my own advice – and followed what CAL was suggesting. Here's what I wrote in last year's book:

> "CAL's a bit tough on the former second round pick, comparing him to a career minor league reliever (Dan Meadows), a former top prospect turned bust (Deck McGuire), two potential backend starting pitchers (Matthew Bowman and Kendry Flores), and a decent MLB reliever (Jenson Lewis). He seemed to handle the FSL well, so it's at least intriguing that the front office didn't push him to Class AA. Backend starting pitcher and/or reliever."

Well, CAL seemed to hit this one squarely on its head. Zastryzny looked helpless and hapless against the minors' biggest test, Class AA. He's a bit of tweener, but he's fairly likely to slide into a bullpen role in the coming year.

**Ceiling:** 1.0-win player
**Risk:** Moderate
**MLB ETA:** 2016

## 25. Daury Torrez, RHP

MiLB Rank: N/A
Position Rank: N/A

| Born: 06/11/93 | Age: 23 | Bats: R | Top CALs: Keith Couch, Aaron Brooks, |
|---|---|---|---|
| Height: 6-3 | Weight: 210 | Throws: R | Luis Cessa, Brian Broderick, Ryan Merritt |

| YEAR | Age | Level | IP | W | L | ERA | FIP | K/9 | BB/9 | K% | BB% | HR/9 | LOB% |
|---|---|---|---|---|---|---|---|---|---|---|---|---|---|
| 2013 | 20 | R | 49.0 | 4 | 2 | 3.31 | 2.84 | 9.00 | 0.92 | 24.8% | 2.5% | 0.37 | 64.5% |
| 2013 | 20 | A | 5.0 | 0 | 1 | 5.40 | 5.74 | 3.60 | 1.80 | 10.5% | 5.3% | 1.80 | 65.2% |
| 2014 | 21 | A | 131.3 | 11 | 7 | 2.74 | 3.64 | 5.55 | 1.44 | 15.5% | 4.0% | 0.55 | 68.9% |
| 2015 | 22 | A+ | 134.3 | 10 | 6 | 3.75 | 3.62 | 5.76 | 1.41 | 15.6% | 3.8% | 0.74 | 69.8% |

**Background:** The Dominican-born right-hander continued to defy the skeptics (like me) on his march towards the big leagues. Torrez, a 6-foot-3, 210-pound right-hander, spent the year with Myrtle Beach in the Carolina League last season where his lack of punch outs (5.8) clearly didn't slow him down. He posted a 3.62 FIP as a 22-year-old hurler against slightly older competition.

**Projection**: The name of the game for the hard-throwing right-hander – for whatever reason – has *always* been ability limiting free passes. In fact, he's issued free passes just 3.3% of the hitters he's faced *in his entire career*. He could be a solid backend starting pitcher, but the odds are long – especially considering he hasn't missed more than six bats per nine innings since entering pro ball.

**Ceiling:** 1.0-win player
**Risk:** Moderate to High
**MLB ETA:** 2017

### Barely Missed:

- **Dylan Cease, RHP** – Another big time over-slot signing by the club. Cease, who would eventually undergo Tommy John surgery, signed a staggering $1.5 million as a sixth rounder in 2014 – the same draft that added fellow Bonus Babies Carson Sands and Justin Steele. Cease made it back last year – as well as his above-average or better heater – but he battled the expected control/command issues.

- **Erick Leal, RHP** – The lanky right-hander is more about pitchability than power. He's always done a solid job limiting free passes and generates a decent amount of action on the ground. But unless he starts ramping up the punch out totals, he's likely not going to be very successful.

- **Bryan Hudson, RHP** – A massive, massive prep lefty taken in the third round last June. Hudson, who stands 6-foot-8 and 220 pounds, tossed just 6.2 innings during his debut, fanning five and walking a pair.

- **Jeremy Null, RHP** – Another member of the club's astonishing 2014 draft class. Null, a 6-foot-7, 200-pound right-hander out of Western Carolina University, didn't miss a whole lot of sticks during his stints with South Bend and Myrtle Beach (6.3 K/9), but he was a curmudgeon with the free passes (11 in 117.1 innings).

- **Ryan Williams, RHP** – Another finesse right-hander with extremely low walk totals – the type the club seems to churn out with ease. Williams split the 2015 season between the Midwest and Southern Leagues last seasons, posting a combined 98-to-18 strikeout-to-walk ratio in 141.2 innings of work.

## *Bird Doggin' It – Additional Prospects to Keep an Eye in 2016*

| Player | Age | POS | Notes |
|---|---|---|---|
| Gioskar Amaya | 23 | C/2B | Made the conversion from second base to behind the plate last season, so it's no surprise he tossed out just 18% of would-be base thieves. Club demoted him down to Low Class A to work on the defensive intricacies. He could be in the Top 25 next season. |
| Pedro Araujo | 22 | RHP | Racked up a staggering 70 punch outs in just a shade over 50 innings in the Northwest League. Let's see how he handles full season ball. |
| Jeffrey Baez | 22 | OF | Very slow and steady, it's taken Baez five years to make it from the Dominican Summer League to a successful showing in the Midwest League. |
| Charcer Burks | 21 | OF | Stuffed the Midwest League stat sheet last season, slugging 22 doubles, four triples, and three homeruns while nabbing 28 bags. |
| Rashad Crawford | 22 | CF | Toolsy center fielder hasn't quite figured out how to tap into the power his 6-foot-3 frame would allow you to believe. |
| David Garner | 23 | RHP | The 6-foot-1 reliever posted a solid 67-to-20 strikeout-to-walk ratio in 55.2 innings split between Low Class A and High Class A. |
| Jae-Hoon Ha | 25 | RHP | Converted from a light-hitting outfielder to the mound last season, striking out 9.7 K/9 as he bounced all the way to the Northwest League. |
| Michael Jensen | 25 | RHP | Reliever with a history of missing bats with solid-average control. |
| Brad Markey | 24 | RHP | Sub-6-foot right-hander walked 10 in 84 combined innings with South Bend and Myrtle Beach. Of course, he only averaged 6.8 strikeouts per nine innings as well. |
| Jose Paulino | 21 | LHP | Skinny lefty fanned 57 in 55.0 innings with Eugene in the Northwest League. Solid control. He's ready for the Midwest League. |
| Bijan Rademacher | 25 | OF | Four-year minor league vet hit .261/.379/.370 as a 24-year-old making his Class AA debut. He's always had a knack for first base with plus-speed. |
| Carlos Rodriguez | 20 | LHP | Former DSL star continued to post impressive peripherals but has yet to make it past rookie ball in four seasons. Why? |
| Tyler Skulina | 24 | RHP | Former Kent State stud looked solid in his return to the Carolina League in another shortened campaign. He averaged 8.7 punch outs and just 3.7 walks per nine innings. |
| Matt Szczur | 26 | CF | Speedy fourth outfielder type that could be useful in short stints. He's had a couple big league looks but hasn't lived up to the once prescribed hype. |
| Christian Villanueva | 25 | 1B/3B | Former top prospect never turned the expected corner. Spent the 2015 season hitting .259/.313/.437 with 18 dingers in the PCL. |
| Darryl Wilson | 19 | CF | Last June's fourth round pick hit a respectable .266/.322/.354 in the Arizona Summer League. |
| Chesny Young | 22 | IF/OF | Torched the Carolina League last season, hitting .321/.394/.388 with 18 doubles, three triples, one dinger, and 12 stolen bases. Utility guy. |

**State of the Farm System:** Easily one of the weakest systems in all of baseball. And that's even *before* top prospect Frankie Montas, infielder Micah Johnson, and outfielder – and brother of Golden State Warriors star – Trayce Thompson were dealt to the Dodgers as part of the three-team deal that sent All-Star third baseman Todd Frazier to the Sox.

What's left?

That's a pretty damn good question, actually. The answer: Not a whole helluva lot.

Chicago has a trio of promising hurlers in Spencer Adams, 2015 first round pick Carson Fulmer, and southpaw Jordan Guerrero. Adams, a second round pick two years ago, posted a ridiculously dominant 59-to-4 strikeout-to-walk ratio during his debut and he was able to carry that momentum in the South Atlantic and Carolina Leagues last season as well. Fulmer, a 6-foot-1, 190-pound right-hander out of Pitcher University, has the makings of a frontline starting pitcher – if he can get his sometimes bloated walk rate under control. The former Vanderbilt star looked solid in his respective debut as he walked just nine in 23.0 innings of work, all but one of those coming with the Winston-Salem Dash. A late round pick in 2012, Guerrero was finally converted into a fulltime starting pitcher for the first time last season – a role he blossomed in.

The system is sporting one caliber big league everyday player in speedy shortstop Tim Anderson. But other than that it's a list of flawed, red flag-pocked prospects.

| Rank | Name | POS |
|------|------|-----|
| 1 | Spencer Adams | RHP |
| 2 | Carson Fulmer | RHP |
| 3 | Tim Anderson | SS |
| 4 | Jordan Guerrero | LHP |
| 5 | Jacob May | CF |
| 6 | Micker Adolfo | RF |
| 7 | Tyler Danish | RHP |
| 8 | Trey Michalczewski | 3B |
| 9 | Chris Beck | RHP |
| 10 | Courtney Hawkins | LF/CF |
| 11 | Jordan Stephens | RHP |
| 12 | Keon Barnum | 1B |
| 13 | Jake Peter | 2B |
| 14 | Brian Clark | LHP |
| 15 | Onelki Garcia | LHP |
| 16 | Jace Fry | LHP |
| 17 | Will Lamb | LHP |
| 18 | Matt Davidson | 3B |
| 19 | Robin Leyer | RHP |
| 20 | Omar Narvaez | C |
| 21 | Michael Ynoa | RHP |
| 22 | Johan Cruz | SS |
| 23 | Nolan Sanburn | RHP |
| 24 | Maiker Feliz | 3B |
| 25 | Peter Tago | RHP |

**Review of the 2015 Draft:** Sitting with the eighth pick in the draft last June, Fulmer was basically a no-doubter as he offers up as high of a ceiling as any collegiate arm in the draft class. But, again, his ability to move quickly and efficiently will largely be predicated on the team's ability to help him hone his spotty control. Chicago was left without a second and third round pick, so Clemson lefty Zack Erwin was their next selection, the 112th player chosen. A few months later the franchise would turn around and deal the young southpaw to the A's as part of the Brett Lawrie package. Fifth rounder Jordan Stephens, a graduate from Arm Shredder University, also known locally as Rice University, underwent Tommy John surgery in early 2014, but looked solid in his return.

Overall, because the loss of the second and third round picks, Chicago added very little to their already beleaguered farm system. Good news, though, they're on the cusp of contending with their big league club.

## 1. Spencer Adams, RHP

MiLB Rank: #68
Position Rank: N/A

| Born: 04/13/96 | Age: 20 | Bats: R | Top CALs: Jonathan Martinez, Jen-Ho Tseng, |
| Height: 6-3 | Weight: 171 | Throws: R | Zach Eflin, Arquimedes Nieto, Ryan Weber |

| YEAR | Age | Level | IP | W | L | ERA | FIP | K/9 | BB/9 | K% | BB% | HR/9 | LOB% |
|---|---|---|---|---|---|---|---|---|---|---|---|---|---|
| 2015 | 19 | A | 100.0 | 9 | 5 | 3.24 | 3.29 | 6.57 | 0.99 | 17.1% | 2.6% | 0.63 | 65.4% |
| 2015 | 19 | A+ | 29.3 | 3 | 0 | 2.15 | 2.95 | 7.06 | 2.15 | 18.4% | 5.6% | 0.31 | 79.8% |

**Background:** Fun fact: The first – and only – Spencer Adams to appear in the big leagues appeared in just 180 games between 1923 and 1927, but he managed to play alongside some pretty impressive talent: Babe Ruth, Lou Gehrig, Walter Johnson, George Sisler, Bob Meusel, Sam Rice, Tony Lazzeri, Goose Goslin, Max Carey, Pie Traynor, Rabbit Maranville, Stan Coveleski, Herb Pennock, and Waite Hoyt. Imagine the stories he could… Anyway, Chicago's Adams burst onto the scene as a second round pick two years ago when he posted a flawless 59-to-4 strikeout-to-walk ratio in 41.2 innings with the franchise's Arizona Summer League affiliate. Last season the front – correctly – decided to aggressively challenge the 6-foot-3, 171-pound right-hander. And he responded in kind. As one of the youngest arms in the Sally, Adams tossed 100.0 innings with Kannapolis, fanning 17.1% and walking just 2.6% of the total batters he faced. Adams would also make five starts in the High Class A with Winston-Salem with similar results: 29.1 IP, 18.4% K%, and 5.6% BB%. Overall, he finished the year with an aggregate 2.99 ERA with 96 strikeouts and just 18 walks over 120.1 innings.

**Projection:** Just to put his 2015 season into perspective, consider the following:

- Only two other teenage pitchers with more than 100 innings in 2015 appeared above Low Class A: Spencer Adams and Houston's Francis Martes.
- Only four other teenage arms with 100 or more innings posted a better strikeout-to-walk percentage than Adams: Justus Sheffield, Francis Martes, David Burkhalter, and Grant Holmes.
- And, of course, the pièce de résistance: Adams walk percentage was the 16th *lowest* among all hurlers with 100 or more innings *at any level.*

Here's what I wrote in last year's book:

> "Adams was as dominant as [any] high school pitcher entering rookie ball in a long, long time. There's some very intriguing swing-and-miss potential, and if the control/command proves to be an above-average skill then the 6-foot-3 right-hander could be the latest member of the farm to fly through the minors."

Well, the control/command proved to be a repeatable above-average skill [clearly] and it wouldn't be out of the question to see his strikeout rates starts to creep upward as he gets older. In terms of teenage arms, he's a solid bet to develop into a mid-rotation caliber arm, perhaps even peaking as a decent #2 for a couple years.

**Ceiling:** 3.0-win player
**Risk:** Moderate
**MLB ETA:** 2018

## 2. Carson Fulmer, RHP

MiLB Rank: #70
Position Rank: N/A

| Born: 12/13/93 | Age: 22 | Bats: R | Top CALs: Nick Bucci, Blake Wood, |
| Height: 6-1 | Weight: 190 | Throws: R | Robbie Ray, Benny Suarez, Vincent Velasquez |

| YEAR | Age | Level | IP | W | L | ERA | FIP | K/9 | BB/9 | K% | BB% | HR/9 | LOB% |
|---|---|---|---|---|---|---|---|---|---|---|---|---|---|
| 2015 | 21 | R | 1.0 | 0 | 0 | 0.00 | 1.82 | 9.00 | 0.00 | 33.3% | 0.0% | 0.00 | 100.0% |
| 2015 | 21 | A+ | 22.0 | 0 | 0 | 2.05 | 3.66 | 10.23 | 3.68 | 27.8% | 10.0% | 0.82 | 90.9% |

**Background:** For the second consecutive season the White Sox took a high profile, high ceiling collegiate hurler with their first pick in the draft. After snapping up ace-to-be Carlos Rodon with the third overall pick, Chicago happily grabbed the Vanderbilt product with the eighth pick last June. Fulmer, a two-year mainstay in Pitcher U.'s rotation, opened up his collegiate career in the school's bullpen where he would post a 51-to-25 strikeout-to-walk ratio in 52.2 innings of work, some of which was spent as the club's closer. Head Coach Tim Corbin promoted the hard-throwing right-hander to the rotation the following year and the rest, as they say, is history. Fulmer would fan 262 and walk 91 with a 1.89 ERA over his final two seasons. After the draft Chicago pushed the 6-foot-1, 190-pound hurler to the Arizona Summer League for an inning before aggressively – and unsurprisingly – bumping him up to the Carolina League. And, of course, he would dominate.

**Projection**: Prior to the draft here's what I wrote:

> *"Vanderbilt University has certainly churned out plenty of high-caliber big league pitching prospects throughout over the last decade-plus: David Price, Sonny Gray, Mike Minor, Tyler Beede, Jeremy Sowers, Jensen Lewis, Kevin Ziomek, Drew VerHagen, Casey Weathers, and Grayson Garvin.*
>
> *And the club's current ace has the potential to slide right up next to Sonny Gray as a potential top-of-the-rotation caliber arm – if he continues to take positive strides with his control/command.*
>
> *While Fulmer's walk rates have been trending in the right direction – it's improved from 4.27 BB/9 to 4.05 BB/9 to a career best 3.59 BB/9 in 2015 – it's still no better than slightly below average. And another leap forward certainly wouldn't be unheard of either. Gray averaged 3.79 BB/9 over his final 234.2 collegiate innings. Over his last 168.2 innings, Fulmer's averaged 3.84 BB/9.*
>
> *In terms of ceiling, Fulmer looks like a potential 3.0- to 3.5-win starting pitcher, though that comes with the risk of not being able to corral his power arsenal. If not, he's a dominant, shutdown backend reliever with the ability to move quickly."*

**Ceiling:** 3.0- to 3.5-win player
**Risk:** Moderate to High
**MLB ETA:** 2017/2018

## 3. Tim Anderson, SS

**MiLB Rank: #82**
**Position Rank: N/A**

| Born: 06/23/93 | Age: 23 | Bats: R | **Top CALs:** Junior Lake, Jeff Bianchi, |
|---|---|---|---|
| Height: 6-1 | Weight: 185 | Throws: R | Leury Garcia, Heiker Menses, Chris Owings |

| Season | Age | LVL | PA | 2B | 3B | HR | AVG | OBP | SLG | ISO | BB% | K% | wRC+ |
|---|---|---|---|---|---|---|---|---|---|---|---|---|---|
| 2013 | 20 | A | 301 | 10 | 5 | 1 | 0.277 | 0.348 | 0.363 | 0.086 | 7.6% | 25.9% | 109 |
| 2014 | 21 | A+ | 300 | 18 | 7 | 6 | 0.297 | 0.323 | 0.472 | 0.175 | 2.3% | 22.7% | 120 |
| 2015 | 22 | AA | 550 | 21 | 12 | 5 | 0.312 | 0.350 | 0.429 | 0.117 | 4.4% | 20.7% | 121 |

**Background:** In the franchise's illustrious history the White Sox have taken six shortstops in the first round – Rich McKinney, Lee Richard, Steve Buechele, Jason Dellaero, and Tim Anderson. Five of those shortstops made it to the big leagues and the sixth, Anderson, is well on his way to making it a perfect six-for-six. Drafted out of East Central Community College in the first round three years ago, 17th overall, Anderson has handled the aggressive development path placed ahead of him: Anderson batted a respectable .277/.348/.363 as the club aggressively pushed him right into the South Atlantic League for his debut; he followed that up by slugging .297/.323/.472 in 68 games in High Class A before catching fire – briefly – in the Southern League; and last season, he continued to prove that he was one of the better shortstops in the minors. In a career best 125 games with Birmingham, Anderson hit .312/.350/.429 with 21 doubles, 12 triples, five homeruns, and 49 stolen bases (in 62 attempts). His overall production, according to *Weighted Runs Created Plus*, topped the league average mark by 21%. And for his career, Anderson is sporting a .301/.343/.429 triple-slash line.

**Projection**: Here's what I wrote in last year's book:

> *"Talk about jumping all over the place – Anderson was pretty much a polar opposite player during his first and second years in the pros. Initially, he was a speed-first, no pop, average walk rate guy. And then he followed that up as a power-minded shortstop that stopped running and walking. The reality is probably somewhere in between: enough walks to help buoy a sagging OBP, 15-HR power, and 15- to 20-stolen base potential. The defense has been absolutely atrocious at this point – 53 errors in his first 145 games. Anderson's a potential solid league average regular, maybe a tick better if he can improve his defense."*

First off, Anderson's defense is still a work in progress. He committed another 25 errors in 110 games at the position last season, though that was a positive step in the right direction. Offensively speaking, his skill set fell pretty much in between his first two pro stops: he walked in 4.4% of his plate appearances, showed solid pop as a shortstop, and plenty of above-average speed. He's like a poor man's version of future Hall of Famer Jimmy Rollins – which, to be fair, is basically saying he has a shot to be an above-average regular.

**Ceiling:** 2.5- to 3.0-win player
**Risk:** Moderate
**MLB ETA:** 2016

## 4. Jordan Guerrero, LHP

MiLB Rank: #117

Position Rank: N/A

| Born: 05/31/94 | Age: 22 | Bats: L | Top CALs: Johnny Cueto, Joe Wieland, |
| Height: 6-3 | Weight: 190 | Throws: L | Edwin Diaz, Michael Torrealba, Nick Tropeano |

| YEAR | Age | Level | IP | W | L | ERA | FIP | K/9 | BB/9 | K% | BB% | HR/9 | LOB% |
|---|---|---|---|---|---|---|---|---|---|---|---|---|---|
| 2013 | 19 | R | 25.3 | 0 | 3 | 4.26 | 4.89 | 5.33 | 1.78 | 14.0% | 4.7% | 1.42 | 69.1% |
| 2014 | 20 | A | 78.0 | 6 | 2 | 3.46 | 3.52 | 9.23 | 3.12 | 23.8% | 8.0% | 0.58 | 75.0% |
| 2015 | 21 | A | 55.3 | 6 | 1 | 2.28 | 2.20 | 9.76 | 1.63 | 28.2% | 4.7% | 0.16 | 74.1% |
| 2015 | 21 | A+ | 93.7 | 7 | 3 | 3.56 | 3.04 | 8.46 | 2.02 | 23.4% | 5.6% | 0.58 | 67.3% |

**Background:** Another of the youngsters I listed on the Top 25 Breakout Prospects for 2015 in last year's book. The organization unearthed the budding big leaguer in the 15th round out of Moorpark High School four years ago. And after slowly bringing the 6-foot-3, 190-pound southpaw up to speed, Guerrero responded with the best season of his minor league career in 2015 – a definite breakout campaign for the first time starting pitcher. In a career high 149.0 innings between his time with Kannapolis and Winston-Salem, the big lefty fanned more than a quarter of the guys he faced while posting a 5.3% walk percentage. For his career, Guerrero, who made just eight starts prior to the year, is sporting a 29-to-67 strikeout-to-walk ratio in just 261.1 innings of work.

**Projection:** Ignoring the impeccable 148-to-31 strikeout-to-walk ratio for a moment, perhaps the most encouraging aspect of Guerrero's season was his ability to hold up – *and improve* – over the course of year. Over his final 49.2 innings, all of which came with Winston-Salem in the Carolina League, Guerrero surrendered just 10 earned runs while tallying a laughable 49-to-8 strikeout-to-walk ratio.

And now the impressive part: among all stateside minor league hurlers with at least 140 innings under their belt last season, Guerrero's strikeout-to-walk percentage, 19.9%, was the second highest, trailing only Minnesota's budding ace Jose Berrios. Kind of adds quite a bit of perspective, doesn't it? Guerrero isn't as dominating as Berrios, but Chicago's young hurler could carve out a role as #3/#4-type arm in the coming years. Don't sleep on him.

**Ceiling:** 2.5-win player
**Risk:** Moderate
**MLB ETA:** 2017/2018

## 5. Jacob May, CF

MiLB Rank: N/A

Position Rank: N/A

| Born: 01/23/92 | Age: 24 | Bats: B | Top CALs: Sean Henry, Juan Portes, |
| Height: 5-10 | Weight: 180 | Throws: R | Tyler Massey Whit Merrifield, Shannon Wilkerson |

| Season | Age | LVL | PA | 2B | 3B | HR | AVG | OBP | SLG | ISO | BB% | K% | wRC+ |
|---|---|---|---|---|---|---|---|---|---|---|---|---|---|
| 2013 | 21 | A | 230 | 6 | 3 | 8 | 0.286 | 0.346 | 0.461 | 0.175 | 7.0% | 18.7% | 131 |
| 2014 | 22 | A+ | 472 | 31 | 10 | 2 | 0.258 | 0.326 | 0.395 | 0.137 | 8.9% | 15.0% | 103 |
| 2015 | 23 | AA | 432 | 15 | 1 | 2 | 0.275 | 0.329 | 0.334 | 0.059 | 6.7% | 16.9% | 90 |

**Background:** Originally drafted by the Reds in the 39th round in 2010, May bypassed the opportunity to turn pro and headed to Coastal Carolina University. Three years later he turned himself into a third round pick. May had one of the more impressive debuts following his selection as the 91st overall pick, hitting a combined .303/.372/.458 between Great Falls and Kannapolis. Chicago bounced the switch-hitting center fielder up to Winston-Salem the next season where his overall production took a noticeable downturn (.258/.326/.395). Last season he spent the year with the Birmingham Barons in the Southern League, hitting a decent .275/.329/.334 with 15 doubles, one triple, two homeruns, and 37 stolen bases (in 54 attempts).

**Projection:** The extra-base firepower May flashed during his debut is all but a pipedream at this point as his ISOs have been in steady decline since then, going from .155 to .137 to .059. But here's where it gets interesting: May actually got off to a tremendous start with Birmingham last season, hitting .311/.359/.359 over his first 52 games. But a midseason collision with Tim Anderson, which resulted in a lengthy stint on the DL with a concussion, wrecked his production as he hit .235/.295/.306 after July 24th.

May is a fringy big league regular depending upon his value on defense. He'll take the occasional walk, flash plus-speed, and leg out a couple two baggers. Expect him to have a major bounce back year in 2016, one that will likely end up at some point in Chicago.

**Ceiling:** 1.5-win player
**Risk:** Moderate
**MLB ETA:** 2016

## 6. Micker Adolfo, RF

**MiLB Rank: N/A**
**Position Rank: N/A**

| Born: 09/11/96 | Age: 19 | Bats: R | **Top CALs:** Rashad Brown, Alan Garcia, |
| Height: 6-3 | Weight: 200 | Throws: R | Charcer Burks, Aldemar Burgos, Cory Scammell |

| Season | Age | LVL | PA | 2B | 3B | HR | AVG | OBP | SLG | ISO | BB% | K% | wRC+ |
|---|---|---|---|---|---|---|---|---|---|---|---|---|---|
| 2015 | 18 | R | 93 | 3 | 1 | 0 | 0.253 | 0.323 | 0.313 | 0.060 | 6.5% | 26.9% | 92 |

**Background:** The recipient of the largest international bonus handed out to an amateur two years ago, Adolfo looked ill-prepared for his debut in the Arizona Summer League, hitting a lowly .218/.279/.380. Chicago opted to keep the 6-foot-3, 200-pound right fielder back in the rookie league last season and he responded with a .253/.323/.313 triple-slash line with three doubles, one triple, and three stolen bases.

**Projection:** Adolfo was limited to just 22 games as a fractured left fibula – with ankle ligament damage for added fun – forced a premature end to his season. He's still only accrued just 55 games, so we'll take a wait-and-see approach heading into 2016. He did manage to shave nearly 20-percentage points of his strikeout rate, though it was still 26.9% last season.

**Ceiling:** Too Soon to Tell
**Risk:** N/A
**MLB ETA:** N/A

## 7. Tyler Danish, RHP

**MiLB Rank: N/A**
**Position Rank: N/A**

| Born: 09/12/94 | Age: 21 | Bats: R | **Top CALs:** Chris Volstad, Arquimedes Nieto, |
| Height: 6-4 | Weight: 205 | Throws: R | Jacob Turner, Ryan Searle, Ronald Herrera |

| YEAR | Age | Level | IP | W | L | ERA | FIP | K/9 | BB/9 | K% | BB% | HR/9 | LOB% |
|---|---|---|---|---|---|---|---|---|---|---|---|---|---|
| 2013 | 18 | R | 26.0 | 1 | 0 | 1.38 | 2.82 | 7.62 | 1.73 | 22.7% | 5.2% | 0.35 | 75.3% |
| 2013 | 18 | A | 4.0 | 0 | 0 | 0.00 | 0.48 | 13.50 | 0.00 | 42.9% | 0.0% | 0.00 | 100.0% |
| 2014 | 19 | A | 38.0 | 3 | 0 | 0.71 | 3.06 | 5.92 | 2.37 | 17.1% | 6.9% | 0.00 | 79.0% |
| 2014 | 19 | A+ | 91.7 | 5 | 3 | 2.65 | 3.69 | 7.66 | 2.26 | 20.6% | 6.1% | 0.69 | 75.8% |
| 2015 | 20 | AA | 142.0 | 8 | 12 | 4.50 | 4.60 | 5.70 | 3.80 | 14.2% | 9.5% | 0.82 | 71.2% |

**Background:** Another member of the club's minor league system that I placed on last year's Top Breakout Prospects. Danish, a former second round pick three years ago, was an absolute dominant force over his first two professional seasons: he tallied an impressive 28-to-5 strikeout-to-walk ratio in 30 innings between the Appalachian and South Atlantic Leagues during his debut, and he followed that up with an immaculate showing with Kannapolis and Winston-Salem in 2014 (129.2 innings, 103 strikeouts, 33 walks, and an aggregate 2.08 ERA). Last season, Danish got his first – bitter – taste of Class AA, though it didn't start off terribly. Over his first 12 starts with the Barons, Danish fanned 56 and walked 25 in 65.2 innings. But over his final 14 appearances he posted a 34-to-35 strikeout-to-walk ratio in 76.1 innings.

**Projection:** Here's what I wrote in last year's book:

> "One of those sleeper-type prospects that pops up in the major leagues without any really noticing. Danish isn't overpowering; in fact, he's sort of the opposite – pitchability over power. The Zach McAllister and Jacob Turner comparisons suggested by CAL push him into back-of-the-rotation territory. In my writings for ESPN Network site *Its Pronounced Lajaway*, I've trumpeted McAllister for a long time, so here's hoping Danish reaches his potential (I'm still waiting on the Tribe's starter, by the way)."

Well, given his previous two seasons, his second half collapse is likely going to be a speed bump. CAL still compares him to some backend starters in Chris Volstad and Turner as well.

**Ceiling:** 1.5-win player
**Risk:** Moderate to High
**MLB ETA:** 2017

## 8. Trey Michalczewski, 3B

**MiLB Rank:** N/A
**Position Rank:** N/A

| Born: 02/27/95 | Age: 21 | Bats: B | **Top CALs:** Tyler Goeddel, Matt West, |
| Height: 6-3 | Weight: 210 | Throws: R | Karexon Sanchez, Drew Ward, Bobby Borchering |

| Season | Age | LVL | PA | 2B | 3B | HR | AVG | OBP | SLG | ISO | BB% | K% | wRC+ |
|--------|-----|-----|-----|----|----|----|-------|-------|-------|-------|------|------|------|
| 2013 | 18 | R | 222 | 5 | 2 | 3 | 0.236 | 0.324 | 0.328 | 0.092 | 10.4% | 25.2% | 94 |
| 2014 | 19 | A | 495 | 25 | 7 | 10 | 0.273 | 0.348 | 0.433 | 0.160 | 9.1% | 28.3% | 117 |
| 2015 | 20 | A+ | 532 | 35 | 4 | 7 | 0.259 | 0.335 | 0.395 | 0.135 | 9.4% | 21.4% | 113 |

**Background:** A seventh round pick out of Jenks High School three years ago, Michalczewski turned in another quietly solid year in High Class A last season. In 127 games with Winston-Salem, the switch-hitting third baseman batted .259/.335/.395 with a career best 35 doubles, four triples and seven homeruns en route to topping the league average mark by 13%.

**Projection**: Just like he did the previous year, Michalczewski's first half of the year was far more impressive than the second half. He slugged .267/.348/.426 through his first 68 games, but hit a lowly .251/.320/.359 over his final 59 contests. The power could turn into 15- to 20-homeruns down the line, but the rest of his skill sets is merely average. And CAL remains unimpressed, linking him to Tyler Goeddel, Matt West, Karexon Sanchez, Drew Ward, and Bobby Borchering.

**Ceiling:** 1.0- to 1.5-win player
**Risk:** Moderate
**MLB ETA:** 2017/2018

## 9. Chris Beck, RHP

**MiLB Rank:** N/A
**Position Rank:** N/A

| Born: 09/04/90 | Age: 25 | Bats: R | **Top CALs:** Merrill Kelly, Scott Diamond, |
| Height: 6-3 | Weight: 225 | Throws: R | Jeremy Sowers, Daniel Barone, Lucas Harrell |

| YEAR | Age | Level | IP | W | L | ERA | FIP | K/9 | BB/9 | K% | BB% | HR/9 | LOB% |
|------|-----|-------|-------|----|----|------|------|------|------|-------|------|------|------|
| 2013 | 22 | A+ | 118.7 | 11 | 8 | 3.11 | 4.76 | 4.32 | 3.19 | 11.4% | 8.4% | 0.83 | 75.9% |
| 2013 | 22 | AA | 28.0 | 2 | 2 | 2.89 | 1.88 | 7.07 | 0.96 | 20.0% | 2.7% | 0.00 | 67.7% |
| 2014 | 23 | AA | 116.7 | 5 | 8 | 3.39 | 3.92 | 4.40 | 2.39 | 11.6% | 6.3% | 0.54 | 71.7% |
| 2014 | 23 | AAA | 33.3 | 1 | 3 | 4.05 | 3.42 | 7.56 | 3.51 | 18.4% | 8.6% | 0.27 | 70.6% |
| 2015 | 24 | AAA | 54.3 | 3 | 2 | 3.15 | 3.29 | 6.63 | 2.32 | 17.7% | 6.2% | 0.50 | 74.4% |

**Background:** Georgia Southern University is home to some pretty big leaguers over the past several decades including Scott Fletcher, Joey Hamilton, John Tudor, and Jim Morrison. Unfortunately for Beck, his name won't be listed among the school's top performers. A second round pick in 2012, 76th overall, red flags started swirling about the big right-hander's head as soon as he jumped into full season ball a year later. In 146.2 innings between Winston-Salem and Birmingham, Beck averaged a disappointingly low 4.8 punch outs per nine innings. That number edged up a bit as he spent the next season between Class AA and Class AAA, though it was still well below-average. And that's completing disregarding his lofty draft status. Last season Beck made eight starts with Charlotte before getting the call up to Chicago. And then shit luck struck: during his May 29th start against the Orioles, Beck slipped and ended up injuring his Ulnar Nerve. He sat out a month, made two starts in Class AAA, and called it a wrap. Beck would eventually undergo the knife for Ulnar Nerve Transposition surgery, a procedure, according to reports, where the nerve is repositioned.

**Projection**: Prior to the injury Beck's strikeout numbers were slowly – and I do mean *slowly* – edging upwards. Of course, when you start up missing as many bats as your sick grandmother toeing the rubber it can only go up from there. Anyway, Beck showed a low-90s heater, a mid-80s changeup, curveball, and slider. CAL ties him to a trio of fringy big league starters: Scott Diamonds, Jeremy Sowers, and Lucas Harrell. Yeah, that seems about right.

**Ceiling:** 1.0-win player
**Risk:** Low to Moderate
**MLB ETA:** Debuted in 2015

## 10. Courtney Hawkins, LF/CF

**MiLB Rank:** N/A
**Position Rank:** N/A

| Born: 11/12/93 | Age: 22 | Bats: R | **Top CALs:** Willy Garcia, Denny Almonte, |
|---|---|---|---|
| Height: 6-3 | Weight: 230 | Throws: R | Trayce Thompson, Bobby Borchering, Jason Pace |

| Season | Age | LVL | PA | 2B | 3B | HR | AVG | OBP | SLG | ISO | BB% | K% | wRC+ |
|---|---|---|---|---|---|---|---|---|---|---|---|---|---|
| 2013 | 19 | A+ | 425 | 16 | 3 | 19 | 0.178 | 0.249 | 0.384 | 0.206 | 6.8% | 37.6% | 72 |
| 2014 | 20 | A+ | 515 | 25 | 4 | 19 | 0.249 | 0.331 | 0.450 | 0.200 | 10.3% | 27.8% | 117 |
| 2015 | 21 | AA | 330 | 19 | 2 | 9 | 0.243 | 0.300 | 0.410 | 0.167 | 6.1% | 30.3% | 99 |

**Background:** Taken just a handful of picks before Lucas Giolito, Corey Seager, Michael Wacha, and Marcus Stroman, Hawkins – unfortunately – has quite lived up to his lofty draft status as the 13th overall pick. Of course, a lot of that could be – and should be – attributed to the Sox's handling of the young outfielder. After a strong, albeit not overly impressive 38-game stint in the Appalachian League, Hawkins got pushed up to Kannapolis for 16 red-hot games before capping off his successful pro debut with five games in the Carolina League. So what does the front office do? Well, they decided to push him right back into High Class A – at the ripe age of 19 and with just under 250 plate appearances above the high school level. And he failed, miserably (.178/.249/.384). For. The. Entire. Year. Chicago opted to keep Hawkins back with Winston-Salem in 2014 with much improved production (.249/.331/.450). Last season he got the call-up to Birmingham and he basically was a league-average bat, hitting .243/.300/.410 with 19 doubles, two triples, and nine homeruns in 78 games.

**Projection**: It's not difficult to see why Hawkins became a first round pick: he offers up gobs of power, can swipe a dozen or so bags, and he can handle an outfield position well enough. And it's not difficult to see why Hawkins is heading down the path of former Chicago first rounder Jared Mitchell: he has a canyon the size of Montana in his swing. Hawkins has fanned in over 30% of his career plate appearances. He might be able to carve out a couple seasons as a backup outfielder, but I wouldn't count on it.

**Ceiling:** 1.5-win player
**Risk:** High
**MLB ETA:** 2017

## 11. Jordan Stephens, RHP

**MiLB Rank:** N/A
**Position Rank:** N/A

| Born: 09/12/92 | Age: 23 | Bats: R | **Top CALs:** N/A |
|---|---|---|---|
| Height: 6-0 | Weight: 180 | Throws: R | |

| YEAR | Age | Level | IP | W | L | ERA | FIP | K/9 | BB/9 | K% | BB% | HR/9 | LOB% |
|---|---|---|---|---|---|---|---|---|---|---|---|---|---|
| 2015 | 22 | R | 3.0 | 0 | 0 | 0.00 | 3.15 | 9.00 | 3.00 | 25.0% | 8.3% | 0.00 | 100.0% |
| 2015 | 22 | R | 14.7 | 0 | 0 | 0.61 | 1.98 | 11.05 | 1.23 | 32.7% | 3.6% | 0.00 | 90.0% |

**Background:** In the running as a potential first round pick entering his junior year at Arm Shredder U. – the little pet name I've bestowed on Rice University for their propensity of overworking pitchers, Stephenson, unsurprisingly, underwent the knife during his junior season. The result: Tommy John surgery. The 6-foot, 180-pound right-hander made it back for his senior season, tossing 59.2 innings with an impressive 75-to-17 strikeout-to-walk ratio. He finished his career with 231 innings, 230 strikeouts, 78 walks, and a 2.96 ERA. Chicago grabbed Stephens in the fifth round last June, 142nd overall, and sent him to the Arizona Summer League before eventually promoting him up to the advanced rookie level.

**Projection**: Here's what I wrote prior to the draft last June:

> "Obviously, there's some additional risk – admitted or not – with hurlers coming out of Rice University. And Stephens is no different. The 6hurler looked like a potential first round pick heading into his junior season – something that looked to be coming to fruition through his first three starts [in 2014].
>
> His overall production in 2015 measures up with the best of them: his strikeout rate [at the time of the original writing] ranks 17th among all DI hurlers. He's shown a strong ability to miss bats and limit free passes, something that would suggest at least middle-of-the-rotation potential. But, again, the injury coupled with Rice's history doesn't bode well.
>
> Stephens would be an excellent gamble for a team in the second round, one that could easily exceed expectations – if he doesn't self-implode."

Needless to say, after the Sox unearthed him in the fifth round, Stephens could be a big time value pick moving forward.

**Ceiling:** 1.5-win player
**Risk:** High
**MLB ETA:** 2018

## 12. Keon Barnum, 1B

**MiLB Rank:** N/A
**Position Rank:** N/A

| Born: 01/16/93 | Age: 23 | Bats: L | Top CALs: Jonathan Talley, Calvin Anderson, |
|---|---|---|---|
| Height: 6-5 | Weight: 225 | Throws: L | Bobby Borchering, Tyler Henson, Brian Ragira |

| Season | Age | LVL | PA | 2B | 3B | HR | AVG | OBP | SLG | ISO | BB% | K% | wRC+ |
|---|---|---|---|---|---|---|---|---|---|---|---|---|---|
| 2013 | 20 | A | 223 | 13 | 1 | 5 | 0.254 | 0.315 | 0.403 | 0.149 | 8.5% | 29.1% | 106 |
| 2014 | 21 | A+ | 533 | 29 | 1 | 8 | 0.253 | 0.306 | 0.365 | 0.112 | 6.9% | 30.6% | 90 |
| 2015 | 22 | A+ | 428 | 24 | 0 | 9 | 0.257 | 0.322 | 0.390 | 0.134 | 8.2% | 26.2% | 108 |

**Background:** Big, hulking, and in steady decline as he moves up the minor league ladder. Barnum, the 48th overall pick in 2012, one pick before Cincinnati grabbed Jesse Winker, took two passes at High Class A with mediocre – and only slightly improved – results. After batting .253/.306/.365 with Winston-Salem two years ago, the 6-foot-5, 225-pound first baseman batted .257/.322/.390 with 24 doubles and nine homeruns. His overall production, per *Weighted Runs Created Plus*, topped the league average mark by just 8%. For his career, Barnum is sporting a lowly .255/.315/.386 triple-slash line with 67 doubles, a pair of triples, 25 homeruns, and three stolen bases in 306 games.

**Projection:** One would assume that a player that could swing Paul Bunyan's axe would run into more than the rare extra-base hit, but that's not the case for Barnum, who owns a career .131 Isolated Power. On the positive side, last season was the first time Barnum didn't look absolutely helpless against fellow southpaws. He actually hit a promising .291/.350/.418 against them in 124 trips to the plate. He's eventually going to slide into a vagabond type role in the minor leagues.

**Ceiling:** 1. 0-win player
**Risk:** Moderate
**MLB ETA:** 2018

## 13. Jake Peter, 2B

**MiLB Rank:** N/A
**Position Rank:** N/A

| Born: 04/05/93 | Age: 23 | Bats: L | Top CALs: Mike Bell, Isaias Velasquez, |
|---|---|---|---|
| Height: 6-1 | Weight: 185 | Throws: R | Hunter Cole, Jordany Valdespin, Ryne Malone |

| Season | Age | LVL | PA | 2B | 3B | HR | AVG | OBP | SLG | ISO | BB% | K% | wRC+ |
|---|---|---|---|---|---|---|---|---|---|---|---|---|---|
| 2014 | 21 | R | 171 | 11 | 6 | 2 | 0.388 | 0.444 | 0.579 | 0.191 | 7.6% | 7.6% | 162 |
| 2015 | 22 | A+ | 562 | 25 | 5 | 3 | 0.260 | 0.330 | 0.348 | 0.089 | 9.4% | 15.8% | 100 |

**Background:** A three-year regular for Creighton University, the Sox grabbed the budding utility player in the 7th round, 198th overall, two years ago. And after a strong debut (mostly spent in the Pioneer League) Peter handled himself well as the club pushed him directly into the Carolina League last season, hitting .260/.330/.348 with 25 doubles, five triples, three homeruns, and 23 stolen bases (in 26 attempts). His overall production, according to *Weighted Runs Created Plus*, was exactly the league average mark (100 wRC+).

**Projection:** Your prototypical future utility infielder – if he could prove his ability to handle more than second base. Peter shows a solid-average, maybe slightly better, eye at the plate with subpar power. Last season marked the first time since before his days at Creighton that he ran as frequently – and as successfully – as he did in 2015. According to CAL, Peter's offensive ceiling – as it stands now – is Jordany Valdespin, who's more famous for taking one off the family jewels instead of his offensive prowess.

**Ceiling:** 1.0-win player
**Risk:** Moderate
**MLB ETA:** 2018

## 14. Brian Clark, LHP

**MiLB Rank:** N/A
**Position Rank:** N/A

| Born: 04/27/93 | Age: 23 | Bats: R | Top CALs: Trevor Bell, Jason Garcia, |
|---|---|---|---|
| Height: 6-3 | Weight: 225 | Throws: L | Eduardo Baeza, Michael O'Brien, Ivan Pineyro |

| YEAR | Age | Level | IP | W | L | ERA | FIP | K/9 | BB/9 | K% | BB% | HR/9 | LOB% |
|---|---|---|---|---|---|---|---|---|---|---|---|---|---|
| 2014 | 21 | R | 48.3 | 3 | 4 | 3.35 | 3.20 | 9.68 | 2.61 | 25.2% | 6.8% | 0.19 | 59.1% |
| 2015 | 22 | A+ | 89.0 | 10 | 4 | 2.33 | 2.66 | 8.60 | 3.84 | 22.8% | 10.2% | 0.00 | 75.2% |

**Background:** Kent State's been one of the more underrated programs in the country over the past decade plus. Just take a look at their notable alums: Andrew Chafin, Travis Shaw, Emmanuel Burriss, Andy Sonnanstine, and Dirk Hayhurst. Granted, it's not a who's who list of future Hall of Famers, but for a small-ish DI school out of Northeastern Ohio it's pretty impressive. And Clark could be the latest Golden Flash to make it to the big leagues. The 6-foot-3, 225-pound lefty spent his first two collegiate seasons working out of the pen, posting a combined 61-to-29 strikeout-to-walk ratio in 63 innings of work. Given the opportunity to start for the first time in his career as junior – he had yet to make a single start up to the point – Clark shined: 88.1 IP, 70 K, 35 BB, and a 3.77 ERA. After a successful stint in the Pioneer League during his debut, Chicago pushed Clark up to High Class A last season. And in 29 games, five of which were starts, he averaged 8.6 strikeouts and 3.8 walks per nine innings while tallying a 2.66 FIP.

**Projection:** The club's handling of the southpaw is a bit…perplexing – especially down the stretch. After having him work out of the pen for the first couple of months, Chicago began extending Clark's outings down the stretch. The weird part, though: he would throw at least five innings in his final seven games; only one of those games was a start. In other words, he entered the game until at least the second inning. I do wonder what the thought process on this was… Anyway, he has missed more bats than I would have guessed at this point in his career. He's sort of like a Brian Tallett-type. Meaning: he might be able to carve out role as a big league swing-man.

**Ceiling:** 1.0-win player
**Risk:** Moderate
**MLB ETA:** 2017/2018

## 15. Onelki Garcia, LHP

**MiLB Rank:** N/A
**Position Rank:** N/A

| Born: 08/02/89 | Age: 26 | Bats: L | Top CALs: Michael Bowden, Darin Downs, |
|---|---|---|---|
| Height: 6-3 | Weight: 225 | Throws: L | Jose Rosario, Jose Veras, Javy Guerra |

| YEAR | Age | Level | IP | W | L | ERA | FIP | K/9 | BB/9 | K% | BB% | HR/9 | LOB% |
|---|---|---|---|---|---|---|---|---|---|---|---|---|---|
| 2013 | 23 | AA | 52.3 | 2 | 3 | 2.75 | 3.58 | 9.11 | 5.50 | 23.4% | 14.1% | 0.52 | 79.1% |
| 2013 | 23 | AAA | 9.7 | 0 | 1 | 3.72 | 1.91 | 13.03 | 2.79 | 36.8% | 7.9% | 0.00 | 60.0% |
| 2014 | 24 | A+ | 0.7 | 0 | 1 | 27.00 | 8.24 | 0.00 | 13.50 | 0.0% | 20.0% | 0.00 | 33.3% |
| 2015 | 25 | AA | 17.7 | 1 | 0 | 5.09 | 1.95 | 12.23 | 3.57 | 29.6% | 8.6% | 0.00 | 51.9% |
| 2015 | 25 | AAA | 38.3 | 0 | 1 | 4.70 | 3.47 | 11.27 | 5.17 | 26.4% | 12.1% | 0.70 | 70.5% |

**Background:** Just another example that power-armed southpaws with a tendency to miss large amounts of wood will always get another opportunity – no matter how many free passes they issue. Chicago, and their increasingly savvy front office, plucked the hard-throwing Cuban-defector off of waivers from the Dodgers two years ago. Garcia spent last season – *clears throat* – fine-tuning his control with Birmingham and later in Charlotte, though the course in commanding the strike zone did little good. The 6-foot-3, 225-pound southpaw continued to miss a tremendous amount of bats – he fanned 72 in 56.0 innings of work – but he surrendered nearly five free passes per nine innings. For his career, Garcia is averaging 10.7 punch outs and 4.8 walks every nine innings.

**Projection:** A couple years ago Garcia made a brief – and I do mean brief – one-plus inning stint with the Dodgers, during which he flashed a mid-90s heater and a hard curveball. At this point he's entering his age-26 season so he's pretty much going to be what he is right now. He might be able to carve out a career as a middle relief arm, unless the control ticks up a couple notches.

**Ceiling:** 1.0-win player
**Risk:** Moderate
**MLB ETA:** Debuted in 2013

## 16. Jace Fry, LHP

**MiLB Rank:** N/A
**Position Rank:** N/A

| Born: 07/09/93 | Age: 22 | Bats: L | Top CALs: Adam Blackley, Cory Rauschenberger, |
|---|---|---|---|
| Height: 6-1 | Weight: 190 | Throws: L | Jeff Locke, John Stilson, B.J. Hermsen |

| YEAR | Age | Level | IP | W | L | ERA | FIP | K/9 | BB/9 | K% | BB% | HR/9 | LOB% |
|---|---|---|---|---|---|---|---|---|---|---|---|---|---|
| 2014 | 20 | R | 9.7 | 1 | 0 | 2.79 | 2.89 | 9.31 | 2.79 | 26.3% | 7.9% | 0.00 | 70.0% |
| 2015 | 21 | A+ | 52.0 | 1 | 8 | 3.63 | 2.99 | 6.75 | 2.94 | 16.9% | 7.4% | 0.17 | 67.5% |

**Background:** Taking the road less traveled is always the best approach. The 6-foot-1, 190-pound southpaw out of Oregon State University joined a relatively small group of unfortunate hurlers to succumb to multiple Tommy John surgeries – the first coming way back in 2012 near the end of his freshman season. He lasted just 52.0 innings last season before shutting it down.

**Projection:** Here's what I wrote prior to the 2014 draft (note the ominous tone):

> "Absolutely amazing [production] given that fact that he's on the comeback trail from Tommy John surgery, **which raises a red flag about the number of innings he's already thrown this season.** A higher ceiling than that of rotation-mate [Ben] Wetzler, though only slightly, Fry profiles as a better-than-average #5/fringe #4-type arm.

It'll be interesting to see if his K-rate spikes a little more than the average collegiate hurler in the minors as he moves further away from the surgery/rehab." I tagged him with a third/fourth round grade."

Prior to the injury Fry looked solid, though far from spectacular in his aggressive promotion up to the Carolina League last season. He finished the year with 39-to-1 strikeout-to-walk ratio. He still looked like a budding backend starter. Here's hoping for a full recovery...

**Ceiling:** 1.0- to 1.5-win player
**Risk:** High
**MLB ETA:** 2018

## 17. Will Lamb, LHP

MiLB Rank: N/A
Position Rank: N/A

| Born: 09/09/90 | Age: 25 | Bats: L | Top CALs: N/A |
| Height: 6-6 | Weight: 180 | Throws: L | |

| YEAR | Age | Level | IP | W | L | ERA | FIP | K/9 | BB/9 | K% | BB% | HR/9 | LOB% |
|---|---|---|---|---|---|---|---|---|---|---|---|---|---|
| 2013 | 22 | A+ | 69.7 | 5 | 3 | 5.17 | 5.04 | 8.01 | 5.04 | 20.2% | 12.7% | 1.03 | 67.5% |
| 2014 | 23 | A+ | 18.7 | 1 | 1 | 2.41 | 2.29 | 12.05 | 4.34 | 30.9% | 11.1% | 0.00 | 80.8% |
| 2014 | 23 | AA | 33.0 | 4 | 2 | 1.09 | 3.91 | 9.27 | 7.09 | 24.6% | 18.8% | 0.27 | 91.7% |
| 2015 | 24 | AA | 26.0 | 1 | 1 | 3.12 | 3.07 | 8.31 | 3.81 | 20.2% | 9.2% | 0.00 | 73.2% |
| 2015 | 24 | AAA | 31.0 | 2 | 3 | 5.52 | 4.76 | 7.84 | 4.35 | 19.3% | 10.7% | 0.87 | 64.7% |

**Background:** Chicago picked up the former second round pick near the Rule 5 draft in exchange for Myles Jaye in a straight-up one-for-one challenge trade. Lamb split last season between Class AA and Class AAA, averaging 8.1 strikeouts and 4.1 walks per nine innings.

**Projection:** Texas gave up on Lamb as a starting pitcher – or a *potential* starting pitcher – many years ago. But his problematic control issues have always been a limiting factor. Still, though, much like Onelki Garcia, hard-throwing southpaws with the ability to miss bats will always be worth a gamble.

**Ceiling:** 1.0-win player
**Risk:** Moderate to High
**MLB ETA:** 2018

## 18. Matt Davidson, 3B

MiLB Rank: N/A
Position Rank: N/A

| Born: 03/26/91 | Age: 25 | Bats: R | Top CALs: Alex Liddi, Mike Costanzo |
| Height: 6-3 | Weight: 230 | Throws: R | Pedro Alvarez, Ian Stewart, Oswaldo Arcia |

| Season | Age | LVL | PA | 2B | 3B | HR | AVG | OBP | SLG | ISO | BB% | K% | wRC+ |
|---|---|---|---|---|---|---|---|---|---|---|---|---|---|
| 2013 | 22 | AAA | 500 | 32 | 3 | 17 | 0.280 | 0.350 | 0.481 | 0.201 | 9.2% | 26.8% | 117 |
| 2014 | 23 | AAA | 539 | 18 | 0 | 20 | 0.199 | 0.283 | 0.362 | 0.163 | 9.1% | 30.4% | 77 |
| 2015 | 24 | AAA | 602 | 22 | 0 | 23 | 0.203 | 0.293 | 0.375 | 0.172 | 10.3% | 31.7% | 94 |

**Background:** It was a deal that marked a change in organizational philosophy: the Sox shipped off a luxury item for a rebuilding, non-contending team, closer Addison Russell, for one of the better minor league third baseman in Davidson. And then – just like that – the former first rounder forgot how to hit. Or more importantly: he forgot how to make consistent contact. Over the past two seasons Davidson has hit .199/.283/.362 and .203/.293/.375, respectively. Prior to that he consistently – like clockwork – topped an .800 OPS annually. Last season, his second stint with Charlotte, Davidson hit a lonely .203/.293/.375 with 22 doubles and a career best 23 homeruns en route to posting a 94 wRC+ mark.

**Projection:** Very briefly at the start of last season Davidson looked like he found his previous mojo by hitting .260/.325/.534 with five homeruns over his first 19 games. After that he batted a lowly .193/.288/.349 the rest of the way. What makes Davidson so intriguing is that he passed the minors' toughest challenge, Class AA, with flying colors as he batted .261/.367/.469. And he followed that up with an even better showing in the PCL three years ago. But since then, though, he just can't seem to solve the International League – oddly enough.

**Ceiling:** 1.0-win player
**Risk:** High
**MLB ETA:** Debuted in 2013

## 19. Robin Leyer, RHP

**MiLB Rank: N/A**
**Position Rank: N/A**

**Born:** 03/13/93 | **Age:** 23 | **Bats:** R | **Top CALs:** Tim Alderson, Jhonatan Garcia,
**Height:** 6-2 | **Weight:** 175 | **Throws:** R | Silfredo Garcia, Blake Hassebrock, Rick Zagone

| YEAR | Age | Level | IP | W | L | ERA | FIP | K/9 | BB/9 | K% | BB% | HR/9 | LOB% |
|------|-----|-------|------|---|---|------|------|------|------|------|------|------|------|
| 2013 | 20 | R | 56.7 | 2 | 7 | 6.35 | 5.20 | 6.04 | 4.76 | 14.1% | 11.2% | 0.79 | 63.5% |
| 2014 | 21 | A | 134.7 | 5 | 9 | 3.81 | 4.25 | 5.75 | 2.87 | 15.1% | 7.5% | 0.60 | 66.3% |
| 2015 | 22 | A+ | 83.7 | 3 | 6 | 4.30 | 3.82 | 6.88 | 2.80 | 17.7% | 7.2% | 0.75 | 61.7% |
| 2015 | 22 | AA | 38.3 | 3 | 1 | 4.93 | 4.16 | 7.04 | 3.99 | 17.7% | 10.0% | 0.70 | 60.9% |

**Background:** Signed out of the Dominican Republic in November of 2011, Leyer turned in an OK showing between Winston-Salem and Birmingham last season, posting a 94-to-43 strikeout-to-walk ratio in 122.0 innings of work. For his career, he's averaging 6.1 strikeouts and just 3.3 walks per nine innings.

**Projection:** There's been plenty of hype surrounding Leyer as one of the system's hardest throwers. But it's always concerning when a player with a highly touted heater fails to miss many bats *at any point in his professional career*. And last season was no different – even after they decided to push him into a relief role down the stretch. In 12.0 innings between mid-August to early-September Leyer allowed three runs on seven hits while fanning nine and walking four. It's not particularly dominant, but it *is* the path that he's probably better suited for. He was also kept in the bullpen during his stint in the Arizona Fall League as well. His control isn't terrible, so why isn't he missing more bats? It's basically the equivalent of the "How many licks does it take to get to the center of Tootsie Pop?"

**Ceiling:** 0.5- to 1.0-win player
**Risk:** Moderate
**MLB ETA:** 2017

## 20. Omar Narvaez, C

**MiLB Rank: N/A**
**Position Rank: N/A**

**Born:** 02/10/92 | **Age:** 24 | **Bats:** L | **Top CALs:** Raywilly Gomez, Bruce Maxwell,
**Height:** 5-10 | **Weight:** 175 | **Throws:** R | Rossmel Perez, Craig Manuel, Charlie Cutler

| Season | Age | LVL | PA | 2B | 3B | HR | AVG | OBP | SLG | ISO | BB% | K% | wRC+ |
|--------|-----|-----|-----|----|----|----|------|------|------|------|------|------|------|
| 2013 | 21 | A- | 162 | 6 | 2 | 0 | 0.267 | 0.311 | 0.333 | 0.067 | 4.9% | 13.0% | 96 |
| 2014 | 22 | A | 142 | 3 | 0 | 0 | 0.291 | 0.331 | 0.315 | 0.024 | 6.3% | 7.7% | 83 |
| 2014 | 22 | A+ | 174 | 8 | 0 | 2 | 0.279 | 0.393 | 0.379 | 0.100 | 15.5% | 12.1% | 124 |
| 2015 | 23 | A+ | 385 | 10 | 0 | 1 | 0.274 | 0.352 | 0.313 | 0.038 | 10.4% | 8.1% | 100 |

**Background:** Far from an overly exciting prospect, Narvaez, nonetheless, turned in a solid season in High Class A last season, hitting a perfectly league average .274/.352/.313 with 10 doubles and one dinger. For his career the Venezuelan-born backstop is sporting another perfectly average .282/.361/.339.

**Projection:** He's a future backup – nothing more, nothing less. Narvaez hasn't shown type of power in parts of seven minor league seasons as he's swatted five homeruns in 1,559 plate appearances. For those keeping track at home that's about a homer every 311+ plate appearances. Still, though, he has a nose for first base and can control a running game fairly well.

**Ceiling:** 0.5- to 1.0-win player
**Risk:** Moderate
**MLB ETA:** 2018

## 21. Michael Ynoa, RHP

**MiLB Rank: N/A**
**Position Rank: N/A**

**Born:** 09/24/91 | **Age:** 24 | **Bats:** R | **Top CALs:** Ryan Searle, Carlos Contreras,
**Height:** 6-7 | **Weight:** 210 | **Throws:** R | Lee Tabor, Jake Brigham, Stephen Harrold

| YEAR | Age | Level | IP | W | L | ERA | FIP | K/9 | BB/9 | K% | BB% | HR/9 | LOB% |
|------|-----|-------|------|---|---|------|------|------|------|------|------|------|------|
| 2013 | 21 | A | 54.7 | 2 | 1 | 2.14 | 3.67 | 7.90 | 2.96 | 21.0% | 7.9% | 0.49 | 77.5% |
| 2013 | 21 | A+ | 21.0 | 1 | 2 | 7.71 | 5.82 | 8.57 | 7.29 | 19.2% | 16.4% | 0.86 | 56.1% |
| 2014 | 22 | A+ | 45.7 | 4 | 2 | 5.52 | 4.07 | 12.61 | 4.14 | 31.8% | 10.5% | 0.99 | 65.6% |
| 2015 | 23 | A+ | 38.0 | 0 | 2 | 2.61 | 3.65 | 9.47 | 3.79 | 23.7% | 9.5% | 0.47 | 80.4% |

**Background:** In typical Moneyball fashion the cash-strapped Oakland A's shocked the baseball world by handing out a then-record $4.25 million to the one-ace-in-waiting all the way back in early July 2008, a then-record handed out to an international amateur. Raymond Abreu, Oakland's director of Latin America operations at the time, was quoted in an ESPN article saying, "In my opinion, he's the most impressive Latin America player since Felix Hernandez." Talk about heaping praise on a 16-year-old (fragile) arm. By now, though, the fanfare surrounding the big right-hander has subsided – injuries, a lengthy track record of bumps, bruises, strains, and surgical incisions, have all but derailed his once promising career.

Chicago grabbed Ynoa as a wild card throw-in as part of the Jeff Samardzija deal. For the third consecutive season, the frail right-hander appeared in High Class A, this time with the Winston-Salem Dash, throwing 38.0 innings with 40 punch outs and just 16 walks en route to tallying a 2.61 ERA and 3.65 FIP.

**Projection**: Throughout the injuries one thing has remained an absolute: Ynoa can still miss bats with relative ease, thanks in part to his sizzling fastball. He's fanned more than 23% of the batters he's faced in his career. Ynoa's control has been trending upward over the past couple seasons as well. Of course, though, it needs to be stated that he missed more than a month last season too. Some day old timers – or maybe just me – will speak about the what-might-have-been when it comes to the next best thing since Felix Hernandez. With that being said, if I were in the Chicago front office I'd bump Ynoa up to Class AAA and see if he can hack. Hell, they might even get a season or two of big league value out of his arm before it finally falls off.

**Ceiling**: 1.0-win player
**Risk**: Moderate
**MLB ETA**: 2016

## 22. Johan Cruz, 3B/SS

**MiLB Rank: N/A**
**Position Rank: N/A**

| Born: 08/08/95 | Age: 20 | Bats: R | Top CALs: Randy Cesar, Ramon Hernandez, |
|---|---|---|---|
| Height: 6-2 | Weight: 170 | Throws: R | Jesus Soto, Chris Rivera, Adam Coe |

| Season | Age | LVL | PA | 2B | 3B | HR | AVG | OBP | SLG | ISO | BB% | K% | wRC+ |
|---|---|---|---|---|---|---|---|---|---|---|---|---|---|
| 2013 | 17 | R | 277 | 7 | 1 | 0 | 0.123 | 0.216 | 0.160 | 0.037 | 9.0% | 20.6% | 26 |
| 2014 | 18 | R | 103 | 7 | 1 | 1 | 0.329 | 0.424 | 0.471 | 0.141 | 11.7% | 17.5% | 159 |
| 2015 | 19 | R | 285 | 17 | 0 | 6 | 0.312 | 0.338 | 0.442 | 0.130 | 4.2% | 21.4% | 98 |

**Background**: Signed out of Guananico, Puerto Plato, Dominican Republic, for $450,000 four years ago, it took Cruz a couple stints to in the foreign rookie league before getting his first taste of stateside action late in 2014. And let's just say it didn't go all that swimmingly either. But Cruz, a 6-foot-2, 170-pound shortstop/third baseman, seemed to make up for lost time as the club pushed him up to the Pioneer League last season, hitting .312/.338/.442 with 17 doubles and six homeruns, but his overall production – thanks to a piss-poor walk rate – actually fell 2% *below* the league average, an impressive feat considering that he finished tied with the 11th most doubles.

**Projection**: Cruz displayed some previously unknown free-swinging ways last season, leading to a lowly 4.2% walk rate. He has solid-average power with 15 or so in the tank, but it profiles far better at shortstop. Of course, the White Sox began transitioning Cruz to the hot corner. If the walk rate rebounds, Cruz might be a solid second or third tier prospect down the line.

**Ceiling**: 1.0-win player
**Risk**: High
**MLB ETA**: 2019

## 23. Nolan Sanburn, RHP

**MiLB Rank: N/A**
**Position Rank: N/A**

| Born: 07/21/91 | Age: 24 | Bats: R | Top CALs: Mark Peterson, Cody Hebner, |
|---|---|---|---|
| Height: 6-1 | Weight: 205 | Throws: R | Paul Clemens, Chi-Chi Gonzalez, Joan Gregorio |

| YEAR | Age | Level | IP | W | L | ERA | FIP | K/9 | BB/9 | K% | BB% | HR/9 | LOB% |
|---|---|---|---|---|---|---|---|---|---|---|---|---|---|
| 2013 | 21 | R | 4.0 | 0 | 0 | 2.25 | 2.51 | 13.50 | 2.25 | 35.3% | 5.9% | 0.00 | 80.0% |
| 2013 | 21 | A | 26.0 | 1 | 3 | 1.38 | 3.34 | 6.92 | 3.12 | 19.8% | 8.9% | 0.35 | 89.4% |
| 2014 | 22 | A+ | 71.3 | 3 | 1 | 3.28 | 3.93 | 9.21 | 3.15 | 23.8% | 8.1% | 0.76 | 78.7% |
| 2015 | 23 | AA | 30.0 | 0 | 2 | 6.60 | 4.14 | 9.00 | 6.90 | 21.1% | 16.2% | 0.30 | 53.5% |

**Background**: It was another Nolan Sanburn-like year for the former University of Arkansas stud. He missed a promising amount of bats *and* a lot of time in the process. The hard-throwing right-hander, who was acquired from Oakland in the Adam Dunn trade, tallied just 30.0 innings with Birmingham, fanning 30 and walking 23.

**Projection**: Here's what I wrote in my first back three years ago:

> *"[He has a] promising ability to miss bats and average-ish control/command. Sanburn came out as a draft-eligible sophomore, so the lost year basically puts him on the same developmental path as the most recent draft picks. He's very raw for a starting pitcher, but has an intriguingly high ceiling, maybe a decent #2."*

Needless to say, injuries have taken quite a toll on Sanburn's prospect status, almost completely decimating it at this point. The bloated walk rate from last season is just another added level of complexity. Still, though, in a system as thin as Chicago's, Sanburn finds his way on the Top 25 list.

**Ceiling:** 0.5- to 1.0-win player
**Risk:** High
**MLB ETA:** 2019

## 24. Maiker Feliz, 3B

**MiLB Rank: N/A**
**Position Rank: N/A**

| Born: 08/17/97 | Age: 18 | Bats: R | **Top CALs:** Wander Guillen, Victor Estevez, |
|---|---|---|---|
| Height: 6-0 | Weight: 195 | Throws: R | Brett Anderson, Carlos Baez, Ryan Dale |

| Season | Age | LVL | PA | 2B | 3B | HR | AVG | OBP | SLG | ISO | BB% | K% | wRC+ |
|---|---|---|---|---|---|---|---|---|---|---|---|---|---|
| 2014 | 16 | R | 251 | 5 | 1 | 0 | 0.198 | 0.315 | 0.231 | 0.033 | 12.7% | 21.1% | 73 |
| 2015 | 17 | R | 211 | 4 | 5 | 1 | 0.349 | 0.455 | 0.446 | 0.097 | 14.7% | 19.0% | 161 |
| 2015 | 17 | R | 35 | 0 | 0 | 0 | 0.161 | 0.229 | 0.161 | 0.000 | 8.6% | 28.6% | 24 |

**Background:** Signed on the dotted line for a little less than $500,000 two years ago, Felix looked absolutely putrid in his debut in the Dominican Summer League, hitting .198/.315/.231. Last season, though, he torched the DSL to the tune of .349/.455/.446 before earning a call-up to the Arizona Summer League.

**Projection**: Not a whole lot to go on. And what is available is basically unreliable because it's from the Dominican Summer League, a place where free-swingers post bloated walk rates and slap-hitters slug long balls. Just a name to watch in the coming years.

**Ceiling:** Too Soon to Tell
**Risk:** N/A
**MLB ETA:** N/A

## 25. Peter Tago, RHP

**MiLB Rank: N/A**
**Position Rank: N/A**

| Born: 07/05/92 | Age: 23 | Bats: R | **Top CALs:** Eric Smith, Trey Haley, Leroy Hunt, |
|---|---|---|---|
| Height: 6-3 | Weight: 190 | Throws: R | Fabian Williamson, Ryan O'Sullivan |

| YEAR | Age | Level | IP | W | L | ERA | FIP | K/9 | BB/9 | K% | BB% | HR/9 | LOB% |
|---|---|---|---|---|---|---|---|---|---|---|---|---|---|
| 2013 | 20 | R | 58.0 | 3 | 5 | 7.14 | 6.11 | 5.90 | 5.74 | 13.2% | 12.8% | 0.62 | 55.7% |
| 2013 | 20 | A- | 9.0 | 0 | 2 | 9.00 | 5.98 | 6.00 | 10.00 | 13.6% | 22.7% | 0.00 | 35.3% |
| 2014 | 21 | A+ | 60.0 | 0 | 6 | 6.00 | 5.71 | 7.20 | 7.05 | 16.8% | 16.4% | 0.60 | 59.6% |
| 2015 | 22 | A | 12.0 | 0 | 1 | 3.75 | 3.90 | 7.50 | 1.50 | 21.3% | 4.3% | 0.75 | 71.4% |
| 2015 | 22 | A+ | 35.3 | 2 | 0 | 2.80 | 2.66 | 11.97 | 4.58 | 30.3% | 11.6% | 0.25 | 81.4% |
| 2015 | 22 | AA | 19.0 | 1 | 0 | 1.89 | 3.36 | 7.58 | 4.26 | 22.2% | 12.5% | 0.00 | 70.6% |

**Background:** A first round pick by the Rockies all the way back in 2010, believe it or not. And for the majority of his professional career – at least prior to entering the White Sox's organization – Tago looked like a complete bust. But Chicago may have unearthed a little gem in the 6-foot-3, 190-pound right-hander as they've seemingly solved his once-problematic control. Or they at least got him to shave off a large part of his walk rate. Last season he split time between Winston-Salem and Birmingham, fanning a combined 73, walking 29, and tallying an aggregate 2.71 ERA. Tago also earned a trip to the Arizona Fall League.

**Projection**: I'm not overly convinced Tago's once well-below-average walk rates are going to come back in 2016. But the franchise has a history of polishing turd pitching prospects into gems. Tago could be the latest.

**Ceiling:** 0.5-win player
**Risk:** High
**MLB ETA:** 2017

### Barely Missed:

- **Jason Coats, OF** – A late round pick out of TCU in 2012, Coats spent the majority of the year bashing in the International League, hitting .270/.313/.438 with 29 doubles, one triple, and 17 homeruns. He won't walk much, but he might be able to carve out a role as a useful piece on the big league club's bench.

## *Bird Doggin' It – Additional Prospects to Keep an Eye in 2016*

| Player | Age | POS | Notes |
|---|---|---|---|
| Yency Almonte | 22 | RHP | Tallied a 110-to-38 strikeout-to-walk ratio in 137.1 innings of work between Kannapolis and Winston-Salem. |
| Miguel Chalas | 24 | RHP | Short, slight-framed right-hander won't miss many bats, but he limits walks well enough. He might pop up in Chicago for a couple brief stints. |
| Matt Cooper | 24 | RHP | Ridiculously dominant in the South Atlantic and Carolina Leagues last season, but his strikeout rate declined from 14.5 K/9 to 8.5 K/9 as he moved up to the advanced A-ball. |
| Nick Delmonico | 23 | 1B/3B | Former sabermetric darling hasn't looked the same since his showing in High Class A three years. Delmonico also can't seem to stay healthy. |
| Adam Engel | 24 | CF | Speed demon swiped a career best 65 bags with Winston-Salem last season. Batting a lowly .251/.335/.369 doesn't help his big league chances. |
| Thad Lowry | 21 | RHP | Lowry, a 2013 fifth round pick, hasn't missed many bats, but he's sporting a career 2.9 BB/9 walk rate. |
| Andre Wheeler | 24 | LHP | Former Texas Tech southpaw bounced between Winston-Salem's bullpen and rotation last season, averaging 8.7 K/9 and 4.0 BB/9. |

# Cincinnati Reds

**State of the Farm System:** The Reds' competitive core of Joey Votto, Brandon Phillips, Jay Bruce, Mike Leake, Devin Mesoraco, Johnny Cueto, Edinson Volquez, Homer Bailey, Aroldis Chapman, Bronson Arroyo, Mat Latos, and Alfredo Simon couldn't get the club over the proverbial hump – which, of course, means getting past the League Division Series – so long time General Manager Walt Jocketty did what had to be done: he started shipping off the aging, increasingly expensive veterans – a decision that actually started in early December 2014.

And in just over a little more than a year's time Cincinnati has pulled off seven – *seven!* – big deals:

- December 11, 2014: The club shipped former ace right-hander Mat Latos to the Marlins for Anthony DeSclafani, one my favorite minor league arms, and overrated backstop Chad Wallach.
- December 11, 2014: Cincinnati dealt All-Star starter Alfredo Simon to Detroit for former first round pick Jonathon Crawford and utility man Eugenio Suarez.
- July 26th, 2015: The Reds received a trio of young arms – Brandon Finnegan, John Lamb, and Cody Reed – for one of the best arms in franchise history (Johnny Cueto).
- July 20th, 2015: Dealt Mike Leake to San Francisco for Keury Mella and Adam Duvall.
- August 20th, 2015: Flipped Marlon Byrd to the Giants in exchange for Stephen Johnson.
- December 16th, 2015: Acquired overrated Jose Peraza, Scott Schebler, and Brandon Dixon as part of a three-team deal that shipped All-Star third baseman Todd Frazier to the White Sox.
- December 28th, 2015: Flipped Aroldis Chapman to the Yankees for Rookie Davis, Eric Jagielo, Tony Renda, and Caleb Cotham.

When the dust had (finally) settled, Jocketty & Co. acquired one solid underrated for the next six or so years (DeSclafani), another mid- to upper-rotation big league-ready arm (Finnegan), and seven prospects (Davis, Reed, Peraza, Mella, Lamb, Schebler, and Crawford) that all fall into the club's Top 25 list.

That, of course, ignores three of the club's top four prospects: outfielder – and sabermetric darling – Jesse Winker, potential ace right-hander Robert Stephenson, and big lefty Amir Garrett, whom I named as one of the Top 25 Breakout Prospects in last year's book.

It's a vastly improved farm system, one that ranks within the ten best in baseball, with deep, potentially impactful talent sprinkled throughout. Whether or not they can gear up for another run before Votto's declining years is a completely different discussion.

**Review of the 2015 Draft:** Armed with the club's earliest selection since they grabbed Mike Leake with the eighth overall pick in 2009, Cincinnati grabbed prep backstop Tyler Stephenson at the #11 spot last June. The big 6-foot-4, 225-pound catcher had a solid debut in the Pioneer League, hitting .268/.352/.361 with 15 doubles and one dinger in 54 games with Billings.

After that the club grabbed hurlers with five of the next seven selections, taking high school right-hander Antonio Santillan, Tanner Rainey, Ian Kahaloa, Jimmy Herget, and Jordan Ramsey. The two sticks taken in between were underrated Louisiana at Lafayette shortstop Blake Trahan and center fielder Miles Gordon.

| Rank | Name | POS |
|------|------|-----|
| 1 | Jesse Winker | LF/RF |
| 2 | Robert Stephenson | RHP |
| 3 | Rookie Davis | RHP |
| 4 | Amir Garrett | LHP |
| 5 | Eric Jagielo | 3B |
| 6 | Keury Mella | RHP |
| 7 | Cody Reed | LHP |
| 8 | Tyler Stephenson | C |
| 9 | Jose Peraza | 2B/SS/CF |
| 10 | Alex Blandino | 2B/SS |
| 11 | John Lamb | LHP |
| 12 | Phillip Ervin | OF |
| 13 | Tanner Rainey | RHP |
| 14 | Scott Schebler | OF |
| 15 | Tyler Mahle | RHP |
| 16 | Nick Travieso | RHP |
| 17 | Jon Moscot | RHP |
| 18 | Sal Romano | RHP |
| 19 | Blake Trahan | SS |
| 20 | Antonio Santillan | RHP |
| 21 | Kyle Waldrop | 1B/LF/RF |
| 22 | Jonathon Crawford | RHP |
| 23 | Taylor Sparks | 3B |
| 24 | Nick Howard | RHP |
| 25 | Jackson Stephens | RHP |

## 1. Jesse Winker, LF/RF

**MiLB Rank: #16**

**Position Rank: #4**

| Born: 08/17/93 | Age: 22 | Bats: L | **Top CALs:** Caleb Gindl, Nick Weglarz, |
|---|---|---|---|
| Height: 6-3 | Weight: 210 | Throws: L | Brett Phillips, Josh Bell, Aaron Cunningham |

| Season | Age | LVL | PA | 2B | 3B | HR | AVG | OBP | SLG | ISO | BB% | K% | wRC+ |
|---|---|---|---|---|---|---|---|---|---|---|---|---|---|
| 2013 | 19 | A | 486 | 18 | 5 | 16 | 0.281 | 0.379 | 0.463 | 0.182 | 13.0% | 15.4% | 138 |
| 2014 | 20 | A+ | 249 | 15 | 0 | 13 | 0.317 | 0.426 | 0.580 | 0.263 | 16.1% | 18.5% | 160 |
| 2015 | 21 | AA | 526 | 24 | 2 | 13 | 0.282 | 0.390 | 0.433 | 0.151 | 14.1% | 15.8% | 137 |

**Background:** It took the former supplemental first rounder to get his Class AA feet under him – especially after reaching the level briefly two years ago. But Winker, who appeared in 21 games with the Blue Wahoos in 2014 before a semi-serious career accident forced him to miss the remainder of the year, caught fire in the second half of last season and never looked back. After starting out with a disappointing .229/.343/.314 showing through his first 42 games, the young corner outfielder ripped through the Southern League in the second half, hitting a robust .310/.414/.497 with 19 doubles, one triple, 11 homeruns, and a quartet of stolen bases. Overall, Winker slugged a combined .282/.390/.433 with a career best 24 doubles, two triples, 13 homeruns, and eight stolen bases (in 12 attempts). His production, according to *Weighted Runs Created Plus*, topped the league average mark by 37%.

But the best part – which bodes oh-so-well for his future – was his always impeccable strikeout-to-walk ratio last season: he posted an 83-to-74 KK/B, the eighth best showing in the league last season.

Best Part II: Among the 14 prospect under the age of 22 to get at least 350 plate appearances in Class AA last season, Winker's strikeout-to-walk ratio was the second highest, trailing only Philadelphia's J.P. Crawford.

**Projection**: I've long been on the outfielder's bandwagon. Here's what I wrote two years ago:

> *"A budding analytic superstar, Winker not only showed a well-rounded offensive approach, but one that's mature beyond his years. Incredible plate discipline, developing power, and, perhaps the best news, the lefty-swinging Winker has handled southpaws well throughout his professional career, hitting .293/.393/.420 off of them. It wouldn't be surprising to see him develop into .300/.400/.500 hitter down the line, capable of 25+ homerun pop."*

I followed that up by writing the following in last year's book:

> *"The brief, unsuccessful stint he suffered through in Class AA should prove to be nothing more than an anomaly, a minor speed bump. He's still showing plus-power potential, an above-average eye at the plate, solid contact skills, and an amazing ability to handle southpaws. CAL links him to Justin Upton, which would be his ultimate offensive ceiling."*

Fast forward another year and there's nothing that's changed. He's still: walking at an elite rate, making consistent contact, and flashing 20- to 25-homer pop. The only problem: his struggles with southpaws last season (.211/.328/.326), though it should prove to be nothing more than a blip on the screen given his lengthy track record against them.

Simply put, Winker's a budding perennial All-Star. And he should slide in nicely alongside Joey Votto, Jay Bruce, and Devin Mesoraco to give the Reds a potentially potent lineup – though one that's going to be a bit too lefty-heavy.

**Ceiling:** 3.5-win player
**Risk:** Low to Moderate
**MLB ETA:** 2016

## 2. Robert Stephenson, RHP

MiLB Rank: #32
Position Rank: #14

| Born: 02/24/93 | Age: 23 | Bats: R | Top CALs: Dan Cortes, Mike Foltynewicz, |
| Height: 6-2 | Weight: 200 | Throws: R | Chris Withrow, Corey Black, Andy Oliver |

| YEAR | Age | Level | IP | W | L | ERA | FIP | K/9 | BB/9 | K% | BB% | HR/9 | LOB% |
|------|-----|-------|-----|---|---|-----|-----|-----|------|-----|-----|------|------|
| 2013 | 20 | A | 77.0 | 5 | 3 | 2.57 | 2.59 | 11.22 | 2.34 | 31.3% | 6.5% | 0.58 | 68.1% |
| 2013 | 20 | A+ | 20.7 | 2 | 2 | 3.05 | 3.82 | 9.58 | 0.87 | 26.5% | 2.4% | 1.31 | 71.4% |
| 2013 | 20 | AA | 16.7 | 0 | 2 | 4.86 | 4.65 | 9.72 | 7.02 | 24.0% | 17.3% | 1.08 | 73.5% |
| 2014 | 21 | AA | 136.7 | 7 | 10 | 4.74 | 4.58 | 9.22 | 4.87 | 23.3% | 12.3% | 1.19 | 66.8% |
| 2015 | 22 | AA | 78.3 | 4 | 7 | 3.68 | 4.16 | 10.23 | 4.94 | 27.4% | 13.2% | 0.92 | 72.1% |
| 2015 | 22 | AAA | 55.7 | 4 | 4 | 4.04 | 3.35 | 8.25 | 4.37 | 21.1% | 11.2% | 0.32 | 71.2% |

**Background**: Easily the top arm in the Cincinnati system – as well as one of the most potentially dominant young hurlers in all of the minor leagues – Stephenson found himself back in the Southern League for the third consecutive season. He first made it up to the minors' most challenging test as a 20-year-old three years ago, throwing 16.2 innings during his wildly successful breakout campaign. The front office opted to keep the 6-foot-2, 200-pound hurler with the Blue Wahoos for the entirety of the 2014 season. And while he would finish the year with 140 punch outs in just 134.0 innings of work, Stephenson's once strong control regressed towards below-average status as he issues 70 walks.

So back in Class AA – again – Stephenson missed a ton of bats in 78.1 innings (89), but continued to deal with those pesky control/command issues as he posted an identical walk rate (4.9 BB/9). The club bumped him up to the International League for another 11 starts. He would finish the year with a 140-to-70 strikeout-to-walk ratio in 134.0 innings of work.

**Projection**: Here's what I wrote in last year's book:

*"A big time arm that's coming along at the most opportune team as Cincinnati begins shuffling towards rebuilding/retooling the big league club. As I noted in [2014's] book, Stephenson has true ace potential. And while his control/command regressed last season, there's no reason to believe that it won't bounce back to his previous career norms next season."*

Well, the control didn't really bounce back as I originally suspected. But – and it's a big but – over his final 49.2 innings with Pensacola Stephenson walked just 20 batters – or about 3.6 BB/9. And his control in Class AAA was a bit clouded by three games in which he walked four batters each. Otherwise, he averaged 3.09 BB/9.

He's a legitimate shutdown ace – if he can learn to keep his walk rates around the league average. In terms of ceiling think a right-hander version of Gio Gonzalez.

**Ceiling:** 3.5-win player
**Risk:** Moderate
**MLB ETA:** Debuted in 2015

## 3. Rookie Davis, RHP

MiLB Rank: #47
Position Rank: N/A

| Born: 04/29/93 | Age: 23 | Bats: R | Top CALs: Bryan Flynn, Andrew Gagnon, |
| Height: 6-5 | Weight: 245 | Throws: R | Chi-Chi Gonzalez, Jesse Beal, Luis Diaz |

| YEAR | Age | Level | IP | W | L | ERA | FIP | K/9 | BB/9 | K% | BB% | HR/9 | LOB% |
|------|-----|-------|-----|---|---|-----|-----|-----|------|-----|-----|------|------|
| 2013 | 20 | A- | 42.0 | 2 | 4 | 2.36 | 2.62 | 8.36 | 2.79 | 20.6% | 6.9% | 0.21 | 70.5% |
| 2013 | 20 | A | 10.0 | 0 | 0 | 0.00 | 2.48 | 7.20 | 0.00 | 20.0% | 0.0% | 0.00 | 100.0% |
| 2014 | 21 | A | 126.0 | 7 | 8 | 4.93 | 3.79 | 7.57 | 3.00 | 19.1% | 7.6% | 0.50 | 63.5% |
| 2015 | 22 | A+ | 97.3 | 6 | 6 | 3.70 | 2.22 | 9.71 | 1.66 | 25.9% | 4.4% | 0.37 | 61.6% |
| 2015 | 22 | AA | 33.3 | 2 | 1 | 4.32 | 3.21 | 6.48 | 2.16 | 16.7% | 5.6% | 0.27 | 63.0% |

**Background:** Plucked out of Dixon High School in the 14th round in 2011, William "Rookie" Davis parlayed an above-average heater into a second round bonus. The well-built right-hander finally began to repay the club back with a breakout stint with Tampa in the Florida State League last season. In 19 starts with the Baby Yanks, Davis strung together an impeccable 105-to-18 strikeout-to-walk ratio to go along with a 2.22 FIP, the second best showing among hurlers with 90+ innings in any of the High Class A leagues last season. And the big North Carolina-born hurler particularly shined during a nine-game run beginning in late May: he tossed 52.1 innings, fanned 59, walked seven, and posted a 2.58 ERA. New York bounced Davis up to the Eastern League for another six games, five of which were starts; he fanned 24 and walked eight in 33.1 innings.

**Projection**: Just to shine some more light on Davis' 2015 season, considering the following: the 6-foot-5 right-hander posted an 18.7% strikeout-to-walk percentage, the sixth best showing among all MiLB'ers with 130+ innings *at any level*. That puts him squarely with the likes of some of the game's most promising arms – Blake Snell, Jose Berrios, and Brent Honeywell, among others. Davis has always showed a tremendous ability to miss bats and limit free passes; he's fanned 21.3% and walked just 6.0% of the total hitters he's faced over his four professional seasons. He isn't quite on Luis Severino's level, but he sure as hell isn't far off either.

**Ceiling:** 3.0- to 3.5-win player
**Risk:** Moderate
**MLB ETA:** 2017

## 4. Amir Garrett, LHP

**MiLB Rank: #86**
**Position Rank: N/A**

| Born: 05/03/92 | Age: 21 | Bats: L | Top CALs: Jake Brigham, Josh Wall, |
|---|---|---|---|
| Height: 6-5 | Weight: 210 | Throws: L | Douglas Arguello, Ryan Searle, Dan Griffin |

| YEAR | Age | Level | IP | W | L | ERA | FIP | K/9 | BB/9 | K% | BB% | HR/9 | LOB% |
|---|---|---|---|---|---|---|---|---|---|---|---|---|---|
| 2013 | 21 | R | 23.7 | 1 | 1 | 2.66 | 4.05 | 6.46 | 3.80 | 16.8% | 9.9% | 0.00 | 63.6% |
| 2013 | 21 | A | 34.0 | 1 | 3 | 6.88 | 5.57 | 3.97 | 4.24 | 9.7% | 10.3% | 1.06 | 61.1% |
| 2014 | 22 | A | 133.3 | 7 | 8 | 3.65 | 3.87 | 8.57 | 3.44 | 22.6% | 9.1% | 0.74 | 67.7% |
| 2015 | 23 | A+ | 140.3 | 9 | 7 | 2.44 | 2.90 | 8.53 | 3.53 | 23.1% | 9.6% | 0.26 | 73.9% |

**Background:** A successful – wildly successful, if I may toot my own horn – inclusion on last season's Top 25 Breakout Prospects for 2015, here's what I wrote in that portion of the book: *'The big lefty, who moonlighted as a basketball player at St. John's during the offseason, walked away from his two-sport dream to concentrate fully on baseball. He posted a 127-to-51 strikeout-to-walk ratio in the Midwest League last season."* Well, Garrett went from a late-round two-sport player into a member – and winning pitcher – of last season's Future's Game. So here's the breakout season: the 6-foot-5, 210-pound southpaw posted an impressive 133-to-55 strikeout-to-walk ratio to go along with a 2.44 ERA and 2.90 FIP in 140.1 innings of work. Here are some more impressive tidbits about qualified Florida State League arms:

- His strikeout percentage, 23.1%, ranked first.
- His strikeout-to-walk percentage, 13.7%, ranked fourth best.
- His 2.90 FIP ranked third.

And here's where those numbers rank among all qualified High Class A arms last season: sixth in K%, 14th in K/BB%, sixth in FIP.

**Projection:** Here's what I wrote in his projection section last season:

> *"A wild card in the truest sense, Garrett has the one thing you can't teach – size. Six-foot-5 southpaws will always garner a second look. He hasn't been challenged yet in terms of competition, so his 2015 season – one where he's likely to move to High Class A – could be very telling. And because he's been splitting his time between baseball and basketball, his experience is incredibly limited."*

Needless to say, the former hoopster passed the High Class A test with flying colors. The big lefty is still working through some average-ish control; in his 26 starts, he walked four or more five times. Garrett looks like a backend starter, perhaps peaking as a #4-type arm.

**Ceiling:** 2.5- to 3.0-win player
**Risk:** Moderate
**MLB ETA:** 2017

## 5. Eric Jagielo, 3B

**MiLB Rank: #87**
**Position Rank: #4**

| Born: 05/17/92 | Age: 24 | Bats: L | Top CALs: Marvin Lowrance, Pedro Alvarez, |
|---|---|---|---|
| Height: 6-2 | Weight: 215 | Throws: R | J.D. Davis, Josh Bell, Danny Valencia |

| Season | Age | LVL | PA | 2B | 3B | HR | AVG | OBP | SLG | ISO | BB% | K% | wRC+ |
|---|---|---|---|---|---|---|---|---|---|---|---|---|---|
| 2013 | 21 | A- | 218 | 14 | 1 | 6 | 0.266 | 0.376 | 0.451 | 0.185 | 11.9% | 24.8% | 152 |
| 2014 | 22 | A+ | 359 | 14 | 0 | 16 | 0.259 | 0.354 | 0.460 | 0.201 | 10.6% | 25.9% | 132 |
| 2015 | 23 | AA | 248 | 16 | 2 | 9 | 0.284 | 0.347 | 0.495 | 0.212 | 7.3% | 23.4% | 141 |

**Background:** Acquired along with the supremely underrated Rookie Davis as part of a four-for-one deal that shipped All-Star closer Aroldis Chapman to The Big Apple. Jagielo just can't seem to shake the injury bug. After taking an upper-80s heater to the face during the Instructional League last offseason and before that missing two months with an oblique injury, the lefty-swinging third baseman's 2015 season was interrupted – and ultimately ended – by midseason knee injury. Jagielo tore up his left knee in a mid-June slide into home and an MRI later revealed that he had some loose bodies floating around. Prior to going down, Jagielo was handling himself nicely with Trenton in the Eastern League, hitting .284/.347/.495 with 16 doubles, a pair of triples, and nine homeruns.

**Projection**: Here's what I wrote about the former third baseman for the Fighting Irish three years ago prior to the draft:

> "Jagielo has two red flags to be wary of: Notre Dame's home field tends to inflate numbers and his strikeout rate, 13.7%, while not high, is a bit of concern given his average power. He won't be a star, but he could be a solid-average everyday player, peaking with 15 or so homeruns and a .260/.330/.420 line. And, of course, a lot of that will hinge on his ability to his southpaws."

Jagielo has elevated the ball – and subsequently hit far more dingers - with a higher frequency since entering professional baseball. He's shown a solid-average eye at the plate and has handled lefties without too much of an issue either. Just as I wrote three years ago, his offensive ceiling resides somewhere close to a .260/.330/.420 line – assuming, of course, that his injuries won't hold him back.

**Ceiling**: 2.5- to 3.0-win player
**Risk**: Moderate
**MLB ETA**: 2016/2017

# 6. Keury Mella, RHP

**MiLB Rank: #116**
**Position Rank: N/A**

| | | | |
|---|---|---|---|
| **Born**: 08/02/93 | **Age**: 22 | **Bats**: R | **Top CALs**: Allen Harrington, Jon Kibler, |
| **Height**: 6-2 | **Weight**: 200 | **Throws**: R | Jhoulys Chacin, Danny Miranda, Dustin Antolin |

| YEAR | Age | Level | IP | W | L | ERA | FIP | K/9 | BB/9 | K% | BB% | HR/9 | LOB% |
|---|---|---|---|---|---|---|---|---|---|---|---|---|---|
| 2013 | 19 | R | 36.0 | 3 | 2 | 2.25 | 2.73 | 10.25 | 2.75 | 27.7% | 7.4% | 0.00 | 73.9% |
| 2014 | 20 | A- | 19.7 | 1 | 1 | 1.83 | 3.01 | 9.15 | 2.75 | 24.7% | 7.4% | 0.00 | 79.2% |
| 2014 | 20 | A | 66.3 | 3 | 3 | 3.93 | 2.79 | 8.55 | 1.76 | 22.0% | 4.6% | 0.14 | 60.5% |
| 2015 | 21 | A+ | 81.7 | 5 | 3 | 3.31 | 3.79 | 9.15 | 2.87 | 24.0% | 7.5% | 0.55 | 66.7% |
| 2015 | 21 | A+ | 21.3 | 3 | 1 | 2.95 | 4.62 | 9.70 | 6.33 | 25.3% | 16.5% | 0.84 | 83.3% |

**Background**: Cincinnati acquired the 6-foot-2, 200-pound right-hander as part of straight-up one-for-one swap with San Francisco that sent free-agent-to-be Mike Leake to the Bay Area. And after another solid season in which Mella missed a whole lot of bats with above-average control, the deal looks like a win-win for both organizations. Mella spent the entire season hurling gems in High Class A where he would make 16 starts in the California League and another four starts in the Florida State League following his trade. The Dominican-born hurler finished the year by fanning 24.3% and walking 9.4% of the total batters he faced en route to totaling a 3.23 ERA. For his career, Mella is averaging 9.3 punch outs and 3.0 walks per nine innings.

**Projection**: Mella's one of those intriguing, sneaky good arms that nobody's really talking about – yet. And some of that may be from the fact that he's totaled just 293.2 career innings, spanning parts of four seasons. But they're some pretty impressive innings nonetheless. His four-game stint in the Cincinnati organization muddied the waters a bit in terms of his overall production, especially his walk numbers. But make no mistake about it – Mella owns above-average control. He's likely headed to Class AA in 2016 and has a chance of finishing it in the International League. Sneaky good #4-type arm.

**Ceiling**: 1.5- to 2.0-win player
**Risk**: Moderate
**MLB ETA**: 2017

# 7. Cody Reed, LHP

**MiLB Rank: #151**
**Position Rank: N/A**

| | | | |
|---|---|---|---|
| **Born**: 04/15/93 | **Age**: 23 | **Bats**: L | **Top CALs**: Aaron Blair, Gil De La Vara, |
| **Height**: 6-5 | **Weight**: 220 | **Throws**: L | Justin De Fratus, Brad Meyers, Jhonny Nunez |

| YEAR | Age | Level | IP | W | L | ERA | FIP | K/9 | BB/9 | K% | BB% | HR/9 | LOB% |
|---|---|---|---|---|---|---|---|---|---|---|---|---|---|
| 2013 | 20 | R | 29.7 | 0 | 1 | 6.07 | 5.13 | 7.58 | 6.98 | 17.2% | 15.9% | 0.00 | 58.6% |
| 2014 | 21 | A | 84.0 | 3 | 9 | 5.46 | 4.37 | 6.21 | 3.86 | 15.0% | 9.3% | 0.54 | 56.9% |
| 2015 | 22 | A+ | 67.3 | 5 | 5 | 2.14 | 2.75 | 8.69 | 2.41 | 23.4% | 6.5% | 0.40 | 80.7% |
| 2015 | 22 | AA | 28.7 | 2 | 2 | 3.45 | 4.27 | 5.97 | 2.51 | 15.8% | 6.7% | 0.94 | 61.7% |
| 2015 | 22 | AA | 49.7 | 6 | 2 | 2.17 | 2.24 | 10.87 | 2.90 | 29.9% | 8.0% | 0.18 | 77.3% |

**Background**: The first signs of rebuild – that dreaded word – occurred when the Reds' front office, led by the underappreciated Walt Jocketty, shipped off veteran ace and free-agent-to-be Johnny Cueto to the eventual World Champs for former TCU ace Brandon Finnegan, John Lamb, and Reed, a massive 6-foot-5, 220-pound lefty out of Northwest Mississippi Community College. Reed, a 2013 second round pick, had a massive coming out party in 2015. After posting some lackluster – or worse – peripherals across his first two stints in professional ball, Reed blew away the Carolina League competition for 13 games; he posted a 65-to-18 strikeout-to-walk ratio to go along with a 2.14 ERA with Wilmington. Kansas City would bump the big southpaw up to Northwest Arkansas in the Texas League for five starts before the midseason deal. Cincinnati would keep Reed in Class AA for another eight starts – eight very, very dominant starts. Overall, he finished the year with 144 punch outs, 42 walks, and an aggregate 2.41 ERA.

**Projection**: Reed looked like the second coming of Koufax in his brief tenure in the Reds' system late last year. Of his eight starts, he fanned 10 or more twice and at least eight batters three other times. And he coughed up 10 of his 12 earned runs in two disastrous outings. His control has been trending in the right direction since his horrible debut and it now grades out as above-average. He has an innings eater body, generates a solid amount of groundballs, and a potential above-average *big league* ability to miss bats. Reed could develop into a #3/#4 type arm.

**Ceiling:** 2.5-win player
**Risk:** Moderate to High
**MLB ETA:** 2016

## 8. Tyler Stephenson, C

**MiLB Rank: #116**
**Position Rank: #6**

| Born: 08/16/96 | Age: 19 | Bats: R | Top CALs: Jobduan Morales, Tomas Nido, |
|---|---|---|---|
| Height: 6-4 | Weight: 225 | Throws: R | Oberto Munoz, Pedro Gonzalez, Jose Garcia |

| Season | Age | LVL | PA | 2B | 3B | HR | AVG | OBP | SLG | ISO | BB% | K% | wRC+ |
|---|---|---|---|---|---|---|---|---|---|---|---|---|---|
| 2015 | 18 | R | 219 | 15 | 0 | 1 | 0.268 | 0.352 | 0.361 | 0.093 | 10.0% | 19.2% | 90 |

**Background:** The Reds have drafted just three prep catchers in the first round of the draft since 1965: Danny Lamar (1979), Devin Mesoraco (2007), and Stephenson. The first backstop taken last June, Stephenson had a solid debut as he transitioned to the professional game, hitting .268/.352/.361 in 54 games with Billings.

**Projection**: The offensive output hardly screamed opening top draft pick, but an incoming young backstop is taking on far more responsibilities. And most importantly, he didn't look overmatched. It wouldn't be surprising to see the Reds challenge the former 11th overall pick by pushing him up to full season action next season.

**Ceiling:** Too Soon to Tell
**Risk:** N/A
**MLB ETA:** N/A

## 9. Jose Peraza, 2B/SS/CF

**MiLB Rank: #198**
**Position Rank: #7 (2B),**

| Born: 04/30/94 | Age: 22 | Bats: R | Top CALs: Alexi Casilla, Ronald Torreyes, |
|---|---|---|---|
| Height: 6-0 | Weight: 180 | Throws: R | Hanser Alberto, Ketel Marte, DJ Lemahieu |

| Season | Age | LVL | PA | 2B | 3B | HR | AVG | OBP | SLG | ISO | BB% | K% | wRC+ |
|---|---|---|---|---|---|---|---|---|---|---|---|---|---|
| 2013 | 19 | A | 504 | 18 | 8 | 1 | 0.288 | 0.341 | 0.371 | 0.083 | 6.7% | 12.7% | 106 |
| 2014 | 20 | A+ | 304 | 13 | 8 | 1 | 0.342 | 0.365 | 0.454 | 0.113 | 3.3% | 10.5% | 129 |
| 2014 | 20 | AA | 195 | 7 | 3 | 1 | 0.335 | 0.363 | 0.422 | 0.086 | 3.6% | 7.7% | 121 |
| 2015 | 21 | AAA | 94 | 3 | 1 | 1 | 0.289 | 0.304 | 0.378 | 0.089 | 2.1% | 10.6% | 79 |
| 2015 | 21 | AAA | 427 | 10 | 7 | 3 | 0.294 | 0.318 | 0.379 | 0.084 | 3.5% | 8.2% | 97 |
| 2015 | 21 | MLB | 25 | 1 | 1 | 0 | 0.182 | 0.250 | 0.318 | 0.136 | 8.0% | 8.0% | 44 |

**Background:** Funny how a change in regime can dramatically shift an organization's view of a player. Take for example, say, Jose Peraza – the once near crown jewel of the Atlanta system but dealt away by (savvy) veteran General Manager John Hart. Acquired as part of the three-team mega-deal involving Miami and Atlanta, Peraza was coming off of his best professional season to date, hitting a combined .339/.364/.441 as a 20-year-old splitting his time between the Carolina and Southern Leagues. But the speedy second baseman/center fielder fell back to earth in Class AAA last season, as his BABIP dropped to his typical career norms. He would bat .294/.318/.379 with the Braves and .289/.304/.378 in 22 games in the Dodgers system.

But the story didn't end there!

Cincinnati acquired Peraza as the centerpiece (oops!) in the three-team deal that shipped Todd Frazier to the White Sox. The Reds also acquired outfielder Scott Schebler and infielder Brandon Dixon.

**Projection**: Here's what I wrote in the book last year:

> "The biggest development for Peraza was his (slight) improvement in the power department [in 2014], which is only amplified by the fact that he moved up two levels. The speed and bat are standout tools, but he rarely walks and the power is still lacking. With Andrelton Simmons fully entrenched at shortstop, Peraza was pushed to the keystone. CAL's not overly optimistic, linking him to a bunch of utility-type guys. He definitely needs to keep hitting for .300-plus batting averages if he hopes to develop into an everyday guy."

Well, he walked just 17 times in his 521 plate appearances in Class AAA. And, of course, the power is still a well below-average skill set. So it's not surprising to see CAL link him to a bunch of utility-type guys (again). If he can handle multiple positions like a utility guy, hits like a utility guy, and looks like a utility guy – well, he must be a utility guy.

**Ceiling:** 1.5-win player
**Risk:** Low
**MLB ETA:** Debuted in 2015

## 10. Alex Blandino, 2B/SS

**MiLB Rank: #232**
**Position Rank: #9 (2B),**

| Born: 11/06/92 | Age: 23 | Bats: R | Top CALs: Brad Miller, Jason Donald, |
| Height: 6-0 | Weight: 190 | Throws: R | Chase D'Arnaud, Justin Bohn, Eugenio Suarez |

| Season | Age | LVL | PA | 2B | 3B | HR | AVG | OBP | SLG | ISO | BB% | K% | wRC+ |
|---|---|---|---|---|---|---|---|---|---|---|---|---|---|
| 2014 | 21 | R | 131 | 10 | 1 | 4 | 0.309 | 0.412 | 0.527 | 0.218 | 12.2% | 13.7% | 141 |
| 2014 | 21 | A | 152 | 10 | 1 | 4 | 0.261 | 0.329 | 0.440 | 0.179 | 8.6% | 27.6% | 118 |
| 2015 | 22 | A+ | 342 | 18 | 2 | 7 | 0.294 | 0.370 | 0.438 | 0.144 | 9.1% | 16.4% | 148 |
| 2015 | 22 | AA | 138 | 7 | 0 | 3 | 0.235 | 0.350 | 0.374 | 0.139 | 13.0% | 15.2% | 111 |

**Background:** When Cincinnati selected Blandino in the opening round two years ago it marked the fourth consecutive season in which Stanford had a first round pick – though to be fair Mark Appel was two of those selections as he returned back to school. That first round streak ended last season, for what it's worth.

Anyway, the club continued to aggressively push the former Cardinal through the minors last season. After splitting his debut between Billings and Dayton, Blandino jumped up to the Florida State League at the start of last season. In 80 games with Dayton, the 6-foot, 190-pound middle infielder batted a solid .294/.370/.438 with 18 doubles, two triples, seven homeruns, and seven stolen bases. His overall production, per *Weighted Runs Created Plus*, topped the league average mark by 48%, the third best mark in the FSL among hitters with at least 300 plate appearances. Blandino would eventually get promoted to the Eastern League in early August; he would bat .235/.350/.374 the rest of the way – though he still managed to top the average production line by 11%.

**Projection:** Here's what I wrote prior to the 2014 draft:

> *"The dreaded 'Stanford Swing' aside, Blandino looks like a potential above-average everyday player in the making. He has a pretty good idea at the plate – strong contact skills with a decent eye – to go along with some sneaky power. The problem, however, is that there's no true standout tool. Solid across the board, yes, but nothing that screams can't miss."*

Blandino certainly shined in his aggressive promotion to High Class A last season, flashing solid-average or better tools across the board. And he was able to rebound after a slow start in Class AA, hitting .268/.391/.394 over his final 88 plate appearances.

Again, Blandino doesn't have a true standout tool, but he does show enough offensive promise to develop into a solid big league middle infielder.

**Ceiling:** 1.5- to 2.0-win player
**Risk:** Moderate
**MLB ETA:** 2017

## 11. John Lamb, LHP

**MiLB Rank: #247**
**Position Rank: N/A**

| Born: 07/10/90 | Age: 25 | Bats: L | Top CALs: Nick Additon, Nick Tropeano, |
| Height: 6-4 | Weight: 205 | Throws: L | Travis Chick, Wade Leblanc, John Gast |

| YEAR | Age | Level | IP | W | L | ERA | FIP | K/9 | BB/9 | K% | BB% | HR/9 | LOB% |
|---|---|---|---|---|---|---|---|---|---|---|---|---|---|
| 2013 | 22 | A+ | 92.7 | 4 | 12 | 5.63 | 4.28 | 7.38 | 1.85 | 19.1% | 4.8% | 1.26 | 62.4% |
| 2013 | 22 | AAA | 16.0 | 1 | 2 | 6.75 | 4.82 | 5.63 | 3.94 | 13.9% | 9.7% | 0.56 | 53.1% |
| 2014 | 23 | AAA | 138.3 | 8 | 10 | 3.97 | 5.26 | 8.52 | 4.42 | 21.3% | 11.0% | 1.24 | 72.6% |
| 2015 | 24 | AAA | 94.3 | 9 | 1 | 2.67 | 3.58 | 9.16 | 2.77 | 25.1% | 7.6% | 0.67 | 75.6% |
| 2015 | 24 | AAA | 17.0 | 1 | 1 | 2.65 | 2.10 | 11.12 | 3.71 | 29.2% | 9.7% | 0.00 | 77.3% |

**Background:** Back from whatever scrapheap he was cast upon, the once Crown Jewel of the Royals' brimming farm system – which, by the way, was talked about as one of the greatest *ever* – was acquired as part of the midseason swap that sent Johnny Cueto a World Series ring. It's been a hard, *hard* battle for Lamb since his breakout 2010 season. He underwent Tommy John surgery in 2011, missed the majority of 2012 and got smacked around like nobody's business in 2013. But Lamb, a 6-foot-4, 205-pound lefty out of Laguna Hills High School, started showing signs of life in Class AAA two years ago when he averaged nearly a punch out per inning, though his control had a *long* ways to go. Last season, it went.

In 17 starts with the Royals Class AAA affiliate, the Omaha Storm Chasers, Lamb posted an impressive 96-to-29 strikeout-to-walk ratio in 94.1 innings of work. He was back. Finally. After the trade he made three starts in the International League and another 10 with the Reds.

**Projection**: Lamb was pumping his heater in the low-90s during his big league debut, complementing it with a hard cutter, a loopy curveball, and an upper-70s changeup. He was still missing plenty of bats during his big league stint – he averaged 10.51 K/9 – and his control remained average, workable even (3.44 BB/9). Simply put, John Lamb came back from the baseball graveyard and returned as a #4-type arm.

**Ceiling:** 1.5-win player
**Risk:** Low to Moderate
**MLB ETA:** Debuted in 2015

## 12. Phil Ervin, OF

**MiLB Rank:** N/A
**Position Rank:** N/A

| Born: 07/15/92 | Age: 23 | Bats: R | Top CALs: Casey Craig, Max Kepler, |
|---|---|---|---|
| Height: 5-10 | Weight: 205 | Throws: R | Christian Marrero, Juan Portes, Jabari Henry |

| Season | Age | LVL | PA | 2B | 3B | HR | AVG | OBP | SLG | ISO | BB% | K% | wRC+ |
|---|---|---|---|---|---|---|---|---|---|---|---|---|---|
| 2013 | 20 | R | 149 | 9 | 1 | 8 | 0.326 | 0.416 | 0.597 | 0.271 | 11.4% | 16.1% | 155 |
| 2014 | 21 | A | 561 | 34 | 7 | 7 | 0.237 | 0.305 | 0.376 | 0.139 | 8.2% | 19.6% | 94 |
| 2015 | 22 | A+ | 475 | 18 | 0 | 12 | 0.242 | 0.338 | 0.375 | 0.133 | 11.2% | 17.5% | 120 |
| 2015 | 22 | AA | 66 | 3 | 0 | 2 | 0.235 | 0.409 | 0.412 | 0.176 | 19.7% | 22.7% | 143 |

**Background:** A consistent force during his three-year career at Samford University, Ervin left the school as a .344/.433/.541 tool-laden hitter. Cincinnati would use – or burn, depending upon your thoughts – the 27th overall pick in the 2013 draft on the enigmatic outfielder. And after a surprisingly strong .331/.425/.564 showing during his debut, Ervin fell flat on his face in the Midwest League two years ago. In 132 games with the Dayton Dragons, Ervin did little more than stuff the stat sheet: he finished the year with 34 doubles, seven triples, seven homeruns, and 30 stolen bases. But his triple-slash line, .237/.305/.376, and overall production, 94 wRC+, painted a much different picture. The front office bumped Ervin up to the Florida State League where his numbers ticked up quite a bit: he topped the league average production line by 20% last season en route to hitting .242/.338/.375 with 18 doubles, 12 dingers, and 30 stolen bases. He would finish the year with a 17-game stint in the Southern League.

**Projection**: The highest drafted player in Samford University's history – by a wide margin. The next highest drafted player in the school's history was Brandon Miller, the 144th overall pick in the 2012 draft. Anyway, Ervin has a very promising offensive toolkit in place – 15-HR pop, above-average speed, strong contact rates – but it's ultimately undone by a well below-average hit tool. His ability to man all three outfield positions also adds value. He looks like a poor man's version of Mike Cameron.

**Ceiling:** 1.5-win player
**Risk:** Moderate
**MLB ETA:** 2016/2017

## 13. Tanner Rainey, RHP

**MiLB Rank:** N/A
**Position Rank:** N/A

| Born: 12/25/92 | Age: 21 | Bats: R | Top CALs: Paul Coleman, Andrew Virgili, |
|---|---|---|---|
| Height: 6-2 | Weight: 235 | Throws: R | Ben Norton, Benjamin Cornwell, Brent Bonvillain |

| YEAR | Age | Level | IP | W | L | ERA | FIP | K/9 | BB/9 | K% | BB% | HR/9 | LOB% |
|---|---|---|---|---|---|---|---|---|---|---|---|---|---|
| 2015 | 22 | R | 59.0 | 2 | 2 | 4.27 | 4.33 | 8.69 | 4.27 | 21.8% | 10.7% | 0.31 | 61.2% |

**Background:** The club's second round pick out of the University of West Alabama, Rainey was, according to the school's website, All Region and All-Gulf Conference as both first baseman and pitcher. He slugged .386/.491/.842 with 37 extra-base hits and posted an impressive 50-to-14 strikeout-to-walk ratio in just 28.1 innings of work during his final amateur year.

**Projection**: I love the way the Reds are willing to take calculated risks and convert collegiate relievers into starting pitchers – whether it's success or not doesn't matter. They think outside the box. And Rainey is simply following in the footsteps of Tony Cingrani, Michael Lorenzen, and Nick Howard. He was 15 starts in the Pioneer League during his debut, posting a 57-to-28 strikeout-to-walk ratio. Very, very intriguing. He's probably headed to the Midwest League.

**Ceiling:** 2.0-win player
**Risk:** High
**MLB ETA:** 2018

## 14. Scott Schebler, OF

MiLB Rank: N/A
Position Rank: N/A

| Born: 10/06/90 | Age: 25 | Bats: L | Top CALs: Jerry Sands, Steve Murphy, |
| Height: 6-0 | Weight: 225 | Throws: R | Cody Puckett, Erik Lis, Trayce Thompson |

| Season | Age | LVL | PA | 2B | 3B | HR | AVG | OBP | SLG | ISO | BB% | K% | wRC+ |
|---|---|---|---|---|---|---|---|---|---|---|---|---|---|
| 2013 | 22 | A+ | 534 | 29 | 13 | 27 | 0.296 | 0.360 | 0.581 | 0.285 | 6.6% | 26.2% | 140 |
| 2014 | 23 | AA | 560 | 23 | 14 | 28 | 0.280 | 0.365 | 0.556 | 0.276 | 8.0% | 19.6% | 154 |
| 2015 | 24 | AAA | 485 | 16 | 9 | 13 | 0.241 | 0.322 | 0.410 | 0.169 | 8.2% | 19.2% | 91 |
| 2015 | 24 | MLB | 40 | 0 | 0 | 3 | 0.250 | 0.325 | 0.500 | 0.250 | 7.5% | 32.5% | 124 |

**Background:** Well, it finally happened. For the first time since 2012 — and just the second time since entering pro ball as a late, late round pick in 2010 — Schebler failed to top the league average production mark. The former 26th round pick out of Des Moines Area Community College easily transitioned to rookie ball, took a modest step back in the Midwest League, and then took off like an old Meatloaf song for the next two years, hitting .296/.360/.581 in High Class A and topping that mark by slugging .280/.365/.556 in Class AA. And then the inevitable step back in the PCL happened last season: he posted a 91 wRC+, the worst mark of his career, en route to hitting .241/.322/.410. Schebler also made two trips to LA, the first for a one game stint in June and the second during the month of September. He finished his initial MLB debut by hitting .250/.325/.500.

Schebler, along with Jose Peraza and Brandon Dixon, was part of the package the organization received from the Dodgers in the poorly-constructed Todd Frazier trade with the White Sox and Dodgers.

**Projection**: Here's what I wrote in last year's book:

> "A poor man's version of Joc Pederson, Schebler has continued to defy the odds at each stop along the way. The hit tool is below average, the plate discipline is so-so, and he doesn't run nearly enough to suggest that his 27 triples the last two seasons aren't some sort of mirage, but the power potential is definitely intriguing. The best case scenario, according to CAL, would be a Tyler Colvin-esque player. Fringy regular/solid role bat on a championship squad."

Fast forward a year and the analysis rings as true as it did then. Well, except the part about the triples; he's now bagged 36 in the last three years. CAL remains even more pessimistic, linking him to Jerry Sands, Steve Murphy, Cody Puckett, Erik Lis, and Trayce Thompson.

**Ceiling:** 1.0- to 1.5-win player
**Risk:** Low to Moderate
**MLB ETA:** Debuted in 2015

## 15. Tyler Mahle, RHP

MiLB Rank: N/A
Position Rank: N/A

| Born: 09/29/94 | Age: 21 | Bats: R | Top CALs: Felix Jorge, Ian McKinney, |
| Height: 6-4 | Weight: 200 | Throws: R | Brent Oberholtzer, Adrian Salcedo, Mitchell Clarke |

| YEAR | Age | Level | IP | W | L | ERA | FIP | K/9 | BB/9 | K% | BB% | HR/9 | LOB% |
|---|---|---|---|---|---|---|---|---|---|---|---|---|---|
| 2013 | 18 | R | 34.3 | 1 | 3 | 2.36 | 2.96 | 7.86 | 2.10 | 20.8% | 5.6% | 0.00 | 55.0% |
| 2014 | 19 | R | 76.7 | 5 | 4 | 3.87 | 3.69 | 8.33 | 1.76 | 21.9% | 4.6% | 0.59 | 60.0% |
| 2015 | 20 | A | 152.0 | 13 | 8 | 2.43 | 2.93 | 7.99 | 1.48 | 21.8% | 4.0% | 0.41 | 74.2% |

**Background:** Well, *HELLO* there, Mr. Breakout Season. Mahle, a 6-foot-4, 200-pound right-hander out of Westminster High School in 2013, quietly had one of the best seasons you haven't heard about — yet. The then-20-year-old hurler finished the year with the following:

- The sixth best strikeout percentage, 21.8%, among all qualified Midwest League arms. Four of the five pitchers that posted higher marks were older than Mahle.
- The fifth lowest walk percentage, 4.0%.
- The third highest strikeout-to-walk percentage, 17.7%.
- Tied with the lowest ERA (2.43).
- The second lowest FIP (2.93).

**Projection**: All of that glorious production and he *still* can't hardly get a mention in the national media. For his part, the big right-hander has always — *always* — shown a strong propensity to limit free passes while missing a solid amount of bats in his three-year career. He's averaged 8.1 K/9 and just 1.6 BB/9 in 263.0 innings of work. Throw in a groundball rate right around 50% and you have the makings of a big league starter.

**Ceiling:** 1.0- to 1.5-win player
**Risk:** Moderate
**MLB ETA:** 2018/2019

## 16. Nick Travieso, RHP

**MiLB Rank:** N/A
**Position Rank:** N/A

| | | |
|---|---|---|
| **Born:** 01/31/94 | **Age:** 22 | **Bats:** R |
| **Height:** 6-2 | **Weight:** 225 | **Throws:** R |

**Top CALs:** Myles Jaye, Ryan Searle, Jeanmar Gomez, Jason Adam, Jacob Rasner

| YEAR | Age | Level | IP | W | L | ERA | FIP | K/9 | BB/9 | K% | BB% | HR/9 | LOB% |
|------|-----|-------|-----|----|---|------|------|------|------|-------|------|------|-------|
| 2013 | 19 | A | 81.7 | 7 | 4 | 4.63 | 4.10 | 6.72 | 2.98 | 17.5% | 7.8% | 0.77 | 64.3% |
| 2014 | 20 | A | 142.7 | 14 | 5 | 3.03 | 3.93 | 7.19 | 2.78 | 19.2% | 7.4% | 0.63 | 70.6% |
| 2015 | 21 | A+ | 93.3 | 6 | 6 | 2.70 | 3.32 | 7.33 | 2.89 | 19.2% | 7.6% | 0.39 | 69.9% |

**Background:** Solidly built at 6-foot-2 and 225 pounds, the Reds grabbed the big right-hander with the 14th overall selection in the 2012 draft – only picks ahead of Lucas Giolito, Corey Seager, Michael Wacha, and Marcus Stroman. And unlike his fast-moving counterparts, Travieso continued to hone his craft in the low- to mid-levels last season as he spent the year in the Florida State League.

**Projection**: Again, he falls into the Jon Moscot, Sal Romano, and Jackson Stephens group of hurlers that have posted solid walk rates with mediocre strikeout numbers. He'd generated a groundball rate just north of 42%. Again, he's sort of backend starting pitcher/long reliever/swing man waiting in the wings.

**Ceiling:** 1.0 to 1.5-win player
**Risk:** Moderate
**MLB ETA:** 2018

## 17. Jon Moscot, RHP

**MiLB Rank:** N/A
**Position Rank:** N/A

| | | |
|---|---|---|
| **Born:** 08/15/91 | **Age:** 24 | **Bats:** R |
| **Height:** 6-4 | **Weight:** 210 | **Throws:** R |

**Top CALs:** Gaby Hernandez, Tim Alderson, John Simms, John Gast, Aaron Thompson

| YEAR | Age | Level | IP | W | L | ERA | FIP | K/9 | BB/9 | K% | BB% | HR/9 | LOB% |
|------|-----|-------|-------|---|----|------|------|------|------|-------|------|------|-------|
| 2013 | 21 | A+ | 115.7 | 2 | 14 | 4.59 | 4.83 | 8.71 | 2.80 | 22.8% | 7.3% | 1.32 | 66.8% |
| 2013 | 21 | AA | 31.0 | 2 | 1 | 3.19 | 3.82 | 8.13 | 3.48 | 20.3% | 8.7% | 0.87 | 82.6% |
| 2014 | 22 | AA | 149.3 | 7 | 10 | 3.13 | 3.68 | 6.69 | 2.59 | 17.5% | 6.8% | 0.66 | 75.3% |
| 2014 | 22 | AAA | 17.3 | 1 | 1 | 5.71 | 7.28 | 4.67 | 3.63 | 12.2% | 9.5% | 2.60 | 73.3% |
| 2015 | 23 | AAA | 54.3 | 7 | 1 | 3.15 | 4.15 | 5.63 | 3.15 | 15.1% | 8.4% | 0.83 | 79.0% |

**Background:** A slow, steady riser through Cincinnati's system over the past four seasons, Moscot climbed his way up from a former fourth round pick all the way to his debut in The Show last season. He was limited to just over 60 combined innings as a dislocated shoulder from a dive attempt – and a follow up surgery – ended his season in mid-June.

**Projection**: Here's what I wrote in last year's book:

> "[He's] a fringy big league starter. Moscot hasn't missed a whole lot of bats since entering Class AA at the end of the 2013 season. The control's a solid skill and while he's been aggressively pushed through the system, none of his stops have been particularly impressive.

Moscot has a low-90s fastball, a low-80s slider, curveball, and changeup – your typical four-pitch mix. His strikeout rates have been trending in the wrong direction since his strong showing in the Pioneer League during his debut four years ago. At this point, Moscot will get some starts, but he's eventually going to be pushed into a relief role.

**Ceiling:** 1.0-win player
**Risk:** Low
**MLB ETA:** Debuted in 2015

## 18. Sal Romano, RHP

**MiLB Rank: N/A**
**Position Rank: N/A**

| Born: 10/12/93 | Age: 22 | Bats: L | Top CALs: Nick Travieso, Myles Jaye, |
| Height: 6-4 | Weight: 250 | Throws: R | Brody Colvin, Jeanmar Gomez, Tim Berry |

| YEAR | Age | Level | IP | W | L | ERA | FIP | K/9 | BB/9 | K% | BB% | HR/9 | LOB% |
|------|-----|-------|------|----|----|-------|------|------|------|------|------|------|------|
| 2013 | 19 | A | 120.3 | 7 | 11 | 4.86 | 4.61 | 6.66 | 4.26 | 16.6% | 10.6% | 0.75 | 64.2% |
| 2014 | 20 | A | 148.7 | 8 | 11 | 4.12 | 3.56 | 7.75 | 2.54 | 19.9% | 6.5% | 0.54 | 64.0% |
| 2015 | 21 | A+ | 104.0 | 6 | 5 | 3.46 | 2.91 | 6.84 | 2.86 | 18.2% | 7.6% | 0.17 | 66.6% |
| 2015 | 21 | AA | 23.0 | 0 | 4 | 10.96 | 6.35 | 3.52 | 4.70 | 7.9% | 10.5% | 1.57 | 45.9% |

**Background:** A late, late round pick out of a Connecticut High School all the way back in 2011, Romano's slowly, slowly making his way through the low levels of the minor leagues. After not making an appearance in 2011, the big right-hander spent the following season in the Pioneer League where he posted a solid 52-to-23 strikeout-to-walk ratio in 64.1 innings as an 18-year-old. He struggled as the club bumped him up to the Midwest League the following year, averaging just 6.7 punch outs and 4.3 walks per nine innings. Cincinnati kept him in the Low Class A league for another go-round in 2014 as his production crept back up: 148.1 IP, 128 K, 42 BB. Last year he tossed 104.0 innings with Daytona in the Florida State League, averaging 6.8 K/9 and 2.9 BB/9. The club decided to challenge him a bit and pushed him up to the Southern League for another seven (disastrous) starts.

**Projection**: Romano falls into the same category as Jon Moscot, Jackson Stephens, and Nick Travieso as polished low- or mid-level arms with limited ceilings. He's never going to miss a whole lot of bats and the control could stand to improve another tick, but he might be able to carve out a role as fifth starter/long man out of the pen.

**Ceiling:** 1.0- to 1.5-win player
**Risk:** Moderate
**MLB ETA:** 2016/2017

## 19. Blake Trahan, SS

**MiLB Rank: N/A**
**Position Rank: N/A**

| Born: 09/05/93 | Age: 22 | Bats: R | Top CALs: Mike Brownstein, Elio Castillo, |
| Height: 5-9 | Weight: 180 | Throws: R | Jecksson Flores, Yancarlos Ortiz, Yoel Campusano |

| Season | Age | LVL | PA | 2B | 3B | HR | AVG | OBP | SLG | ISO | BB% | K% | wRC+ |
|--------|-----|-----|-----|----|----|----|-------|-------|-------|-------|-------|-------|------|
| 2015 | 21 | R | 216 | 8 | 3 | 1 | 0.312 | 0.400 | 0.403 | 0.091 | 11.6% | 8.8% | 115 |
| 2015 | 21 | A+ | 36 | 0 | 0 | 0 | 0.114 | 0.139 | 0.114 | 0.000 | 0.0% | 13.9% | -26 |

**Background:** A diminutive shortstop taken in the third round last June out of the University of Louisiana at Lafayette, Trahan had a stellar career with the Ragin' Cajuns. He left the school a .331/.431/.432 hitter, adding 37 doubles, three triples, 10 homeruns, and 45 stolen bases. He spent the majority of his debut in the Pioneer League, hitting .312/.402/.403.

**Projection**: Here's what I wrote prior to the draft last June:

*"Trahan's production more or less stacks up with the best of them [Alex Bregman, Dansby Swanson, and Trea Turner]. Granted, he doesn't hit for nearly the same power, but his ability to sniff out first base via the free pass helps compensate a bit. Better-than-average plate discipline, strong hit tool, speedy. Trahan looks like a solid league average regular, though he'll likely be forced to move to the other side of second base."*

After ending the year in High Class A, it wouldn't be shocking to see him back there to start 2016.

**Ceiling:** 1.0- to 1.5-win player
**Risk:** Moderate
**MLB ETA:** 2017/2018

## 20. Antonio Santillan, RHP

**MiLB Rank: N/A**
**Position Rank: N/A**

| Born: 04/15/97 | Age: 19 | Bats: R | Top CALs: Young-Il Jung, Luis Morel, |
| Height: 6-3 | Weight: 240 | Throws: R | Aneurys Zabala, Onassis Sirrett, Angel German |

| YEAR | Age | Level | IP | W | L | ERA | FIP | K/9 | BB/9 | K% | BB% | HR/9 | LOB% |
|------|-----|-------|------|----|----|------|------|------|------|-------|-------|------|------|
| 2015 | 18 | R | 19.7 | 0 | 2 | 5.03 | 4.68 | 8.69 | 5.03 | 22.4% | 12.9% | 0.46 | 61.6% |

**Background:** The club's most recent second round pick out of Seguin High School had an OK debut in the Arizona Summer League last season, posting a 19-to-11 strikeout-to-walk ratio in 19.2 innings.

**Projection:** Nothing to see here, folks. Come back after 2016.

**Ceiling:** Too Soon to Tell
**Risk:** N/A
**MLB ETA:** N/A

## 21. Kyle Waldrop, 1B/LF/RF

**MiLB Rank: N/A**
**Position Rank: N/A**

| Born: 11/26/91 | Age: 24 | Bats: L | Top CALs: Fernando Martinez, Donald Lutz, |
|---|---|---|---|
| Height: 6-2 | Weight: 215 | Throws: L | Raul Reyes, Alex Liddi, Mark Shorey |

| Season | Age | LVL | PA | 2B | 3B | HR | AVG | OBP | SLG | ISO | BB% | K% | wRC+ |
|---|---|---|---|---|---|---|---|---|---|---|---|---|---|
| 2013 | 21 | A+ | 540 | 32 | 4 | 21 | 0.258 | 0.304 | 0.462 | 0.204 | 5.9% | 22.4% | 96 |
| 2014 | 22 | A+ | 288 | 20 | 1 | 6 | 0.359 | 0.409 | 0.516 | 0.156 | 7.6% | 19.4% | 142 |
| 2014 | 22 | AA | 252 | 17 | 3 | 8 | 0.315 | 0.359 | 0.517 | 0.203 | 6.7% | 17.5% | 143 |
| 2015 | 23 | AA | 259 | 13 | 3 | 6 | 0.277 | 0.313 | 0.430 | 0.153 | 4.6% | 23.6% | 107 |
| 2015 | 23 | AAA | 213 | 6 | 0 | 1 | 0.185 | 0.211 | 0.229 | 0.044 | 3.3% | 25.4% | 19 |

**Background:** The former 12th round pick out of Riverdale High School was one of the bigger surprises in the system after a breakout 2014 season. The corner outfielder/part-time first baseman dominated the California League to the tune of .359/.409/.516 for 65 games and continued to perform well when he got the call-up to Class AA. In 66 games with Pensacola, Waldrop posted a 143 wRC+ en route to slugging .315/.359/.517. Cincinnati did the prudent thing – perhaps because they weren't entirely convinced by his unprecedented success – and had him repeat the Southern League in the first half of 2015. Lo and behold, Waldrop's production line regressed back his career norms – or at least very close to it. He hit .277/.313/.430 with a league average-ish 107 wRC+. Just as they did the year before, the organization pushed him up a level in the second half – this time, though, he looked overmatched.

**Projection:** Here's what I wrote in last year's book:

> "Now that constitutes a breakout year. And now the bad news: not only doesn't CAL think too highly of Waldrop by linking him to Christian Marrero, Jeremy Baltz, Brandon Jones, Luis Domoromo, and Mikie Mahtook, but he hasn't solved fellow left-handers yet. Waldrop hit .258/.306/.337 against LHs in 2014 and owns a career .262/.305/.389 triple-slash line against them. He's a fringy everyday guy, who would likely get exposed in longer stints in the lineup. "

Southpaws continued to confound the budding platoon bat as posted a lowly .198/.253/.337 mark against them last season. His lone calling card has been his power. Other than that, he doesn't walk, or hit LHP, or run any more.

**Ceiling:** 1.0- to 1.5-win player
**Risk:** Moderate to High
**MLB ETA:** Debuted in 2015

## 22. Jonathon Crawford, RHP

**MiLB Rank: N/A**
**Position Rank: N/A**

| Born: 11/01/91 | Age: 24 | Bats: R | Top CALs: Matt Taylor, Harrison Cooney, |
|---|---|---|---|
| Height: 6-2 | Weight: 205 | Throws: R | Matthew Hobgood, Tyler Skulina, Drew Tyson |

| YEAR | Age | Level | IP | W | L | ERA | FIP | K/9 | BB/9 | K% | BB% | HR/9 | LOB% |
|---|---|---|---|---|---|---|---|---|---|---|---|---|---|
| 2013 | 21 | A- | 19.0 | 0 | 2 | 1.89 | 2.46 | 9.95 | 4.26 | 25.3% | 10.8% | 0.00 | 80.0% |
| 2014 | 22 | A | 123.0 | 8 | 3 | 2.85 | 3.88 | 6.22 | 3.66 | 17.2% | 10.1% | 0.22 | 75.3% |
| 2015 | 23 | R | 8.3 | 0 | 0 | 4.32 | 3.34 | 8.64 | 1.08 | 22.2% | 2.8% | 0.00 | 58.3% |
| 2015 | 23 | A+ | 5.3 | 0 | 1 | 8.44 | 2.60 | 10.13 | 5.06 | 25.0% | 12.5% | 0.00 | 37.5% |

**Background:** It was a completely wasted season for the former first rounder out of the University of Florida. Shoulder tendonitis limited the former Collegiate Team USA ace to just 13.2 innings in 2015, though he did manage to post a 14-to-4 strikeout-to-walk ratio.

**Projection:** Here's what I wrote prior to the 2013 draft:

> "There's some upside here given his track record, including his dominant sophomore season as well as his work during the summer. But he's taken a large step back, developmentally speaking, and one wonders if it's from a long 2012 season. Unless he can rediscover some of his peripheral-magic, Crawford looks like backend filler, potentially peaking as a #4/#5-type guy."

At this point the 6-foot-2, 205-pound right-hander is a complete and utter Wild Card. The lackluster showing in the Midwest League two years ago combined with a lengthy stint on the DL due to wonky shoulder will likely push him into a late-inning relief role – assuming, of course, that the shoulder bounces back to full strength.

# Cincinnati Reds

**Ceiling:** 1.0- to 1.5-win player
**Risk:** Moderate to High
**MLB ETA:** 2018

## 23. Taylor Sparks, 3B

**MiLB Rank: N/A**
**Position Rank: N/A**

| Born: 04/03/93 | Age: 23 | Bats: R | **Top CALs:** Tyler Johnson, David Christensen, |
|---|---|---|---|
| Height: 6-4 | Weight: 200 | Throws: R | Scott Krieger, Jeramy Laster, Bruce Caldwell |

| Season | Age | LVL | PA | 2B | 3B | HR | AVG | OBP | SLG | ISO | BB% | K% | wRC+ |
|---|---|---|---|---|---|---|---|---|---|---|---|---|---|
| 2014 | 21 | R | 240 | 7 | 7 | 10 | 0.232 | 0.350 | 0.490 | 0.258 | 12.9% | 35.0% | 111 |
| 2015 | 22 | A+ | 493 | 22 | 4 | 13 | 0.247 | 0.302 | 0.401 | 0.155 | 6.1% | 32.9% | 114 |

**Background:** Sparks' production line at UC Irvine went from disappointing when he batted .202/.277/.363 as a true freshman to outstanding the following year (.360/.388/.581) to some place in between during his final season (.308/.389/.506).

Cincinnati drafted the Long Beach, California, native in the second round two years, 58th overall. And despite a bit of a disappointing showing in the Pioneer League two years ago – he batted .232/.350/.490 with seven doubles, seven triples, and 10 homeruns en route to posting a 111 wRC+ – the front office pushed the young third baseman up to High Class A in 2015, completely bypassing the Midwest League. And Sparks looked solid, all things considered. He batted .247/.302/.401 with 22 doubles, four triples, 13 homeruns, and 14 stolen bases while topping the league average production mark by 14%.

**Projection**: Here's what I wrote prior to the 2014 draft:

> "He's going to swing-and-miss a whole lot during his professional career, likely regularly topping 120 strikeouts in a year, and he isn't going to walk a whole lot either. The power, though, is solid average to a tick better, with the potential to reach 25-HRs if everything breaks right."

He's certainly punching out at an epic rate: he fanned 35% of the time during his debut and only trimmed a smidge off of that last season as well. He's also not walking very much either. The power remains his sole saving skill. He's nothing more than a fringy backup.

**Ceiling:** 1.0-win player
**Risk:** Moderate
**MLB ETA:** 2018

## 24. Nick Howard, RHP

**MiLB Rank: N/A**
**Position Rank: N/A**

| Born: 04/06/93 | Age: 23 | Bats: R | **Top CALs:** Mark Diapoules, Fabian Williamson, |
|---|---|---|---|
| Height: 6-4 | Weight: 215 | Throws: R | Benjamin Wells, Chris Armstrong, Austin Urban |

| YEAR | Age | Level | IP | W | L | ERA | FIP | K/9 | BB/9 | K% | BB% | HR/9 | LOB% |
|---|---|---|---|---|---|---|---|---|---|---|---|---|---|
| 2014 | 21 | A | 33.7 | 2 | 1 | 3.74 | 4.73 | 6.15 | 2.94 | 16.9% | 8.1% | 1.07 | 72.7% |
| 2015 | 22 | A+ | 38.0 | 3 | 2 | 6.63 | 5.80 | 7.34 | 11.84 | 16.4% | 26.5% | 0.00 | 63.6% |

**Background:** Well *that* didn't go as expected. Howard was one of the more dominant arms for the University of Virginia, one of college's premier powerhouses, as he bounced between strong reliever to an ever better starting pitcher and then back to the pen where he became the club's shutdown ninth-inning option. During my pre-draft evaluation I implored whichever team that would eventually grab the hard-throwing right-hander to give him an opportunity to develop into a potential mid-rotation caliber arm. And just like they had done with Tony Cingrani and Michael Lorenzen, the Reds afforded the big right-hander that very specific opportunity. Howard looked up to the challenge during his debut as the club pushed him up to the Midwest League; he tossed 33.2 innings with 23 punch outs and 11 walks. The club, unsurprisingly, opted to push Howard up to the Florida State League for 2015. Then all hell broke out – in a craptastic way.

Howard opened the year with five horrendous starts: 18.2 IP, 17 K, 23 BB, and 10 ER. After that Cincinnati quickly pushed him into a relief role and he would post a 14-to-27 strikeout-to-walk ratio in 19.1 innings. Ouch.

**Projection**: I was so, so high on Howard entering the 2014. And since I mentioned on my hits – or near hits – it's only fair to list my big swings-and-misses as well:

> "[He's] poised to move quickly if he remains in the pen, but his 2013 success in the rotation offers a glimpse of some interesting upside as a starting pitcher. Plus, he was rather competitive pitching out of the rotation in the Cape last summer [2013] too, striking out 25 and walking just four in 24.2 innings."

Frankly, Howard's collapse last season was absolutely, 100% completely unsuspected. But…he just lost it. There are no ifs, ands, or buts about it. He simply…lost it. It's unclear whether he'll ever find it again. Hopefully, he does.

**Ceiling:** 1.0- to 1.5-win player
**Risk:** High
**MLB ETA:** 2018

## 25. Jackson Stephens, RHP

| | | |
|---|---|---|
| **Born:** 05/11/94 | **Age:** 22 | **Bats:** R |
| **Height:** 6-3 | **Weight:** 205 | **Throws:** R |

**Top CALs:** Nick Travieso, Chase Dejong, Zach Jemiola, Brian Rauh, Ryan Crowley

| YEAR | Age | Level | IP | W | L | ERA | FIP | K/9 | BB/9 | K% | BB% | HR/9 | LOB% |
|------|-----|-------|-----|---|---|------|------|------|------|------|------|------|-------|
| 2013 | 19 | A | 64.7 | 3 | 7 | 4.59 | 3.86 | 7.65 | 2.51 | 19.4% | 6.3% | 0.84 | 67.0% |
| 2014 | 20 | A | 67.3 | 2 | 7 | 4.81 | 4.72 | 7.22 | 2.94 | 18.4% | 7.5% | 1.07 | 67.2% |
| 2015 | 21 | A+ | 145.3 | 12 | 7 | 2.97 | 3.62 | 6.01 | 1.86 | 15.8% | 4.9% | 0.68 | 77.5% |

**Background:** Prior to the year, Stephens' minor league career could be easily summed up: slow, arduous, frustrating. But the 6-foot-3, 205-pound right-hander out of Oxford, Alabama, took all those frustrations and unused energy out as he made his way up to High Class A last season – in doing so he nearly equaled his entire career innings limit which spanned three seasons. Needless to say, Stephens set numerous career bests: starts (26), innings (145.1), ERA (2.97), and FIP (3.62). Stephens finished his breakout campaign with 90 strikeouts and 30 walks. For his career, Stephens has averaged 6.9 punch outs and 2.2 free passes per nine innings.

**Projection:** Stephens' wonky elbow, which limited him to just 67.0 innings last season, appears well at this point. He's a potential #5-type arm in a big league rotation, though he still has some room for growth given his limited experience.

**Ceiling:** 1.0- to 1.5-win player
**Risk:** High
**MLB ETA:** 2018

### *Barely Missed:*

- **Mark Armstrong, RHP** – A 2013 third round pick out of Clarence High School, Armstrong held his own as a 20-year-old in the Midwest League last season: 64.2 IP, 44 K, and 14 BB. He finished the year with a 3.20 ERA.

- **Jose Lopez, RHP** – Former Seton Hall University hurler made his pro debut last season after getting selected in the fifth round two years ago. The hard-throwing right-hander fanned 67 and walked 19 in 57.0 innings in the Pioneer League.

- **Yorman Rodriguez, OF** – The then-22-year-old outfielder batted a league average-ish 112 wRC+ to go along with a .269/.308/.429 triple slash line in Class AAA. Classic Quad-A type player.

- **Jake Turnbull, C** – The Aussie batted a respectable .291/.395/.373 as a 17-year-old in the Arizona Summer League. Don't overlook the fact that he was also moving stateside for the first time as well.

- **Seth Varner, LHP** – A late round pick out of Miami University of Ohio, Varner's promising strikeout rates haven't stopped as he's continued to march up the minor league ladder. He finished the year with 134 punch outs and just 11 – ELEVEN – walks in 138.2 innings of work.

## *Bird Doggin' It – Additional Prospects to Keep an Eye in 2016*

| Player | Age | POS | Notes |
|---|---|---|---|
| Mark Astin | 24 | RHP | Former Arkansas right-hander spilt his season between High Class A and Class A last season, averaging 7.3 punch outs and 3.4 walks per nine innings. |
| Ty Broyles | 20 | LHP | 6-foot-3, but weighs an impressive – or troubling? – 270 pounds, Boyles may be something but he'll need to get in better shape. |
| Jake Cave | 23 | OF | Picked up from the Yankees in the Rule 5 draft this past offseason, Cave is sporting a solid .285/.346/.391 triple-slash line in four professional seasons. He could be a useful bench option. |
| Alejandro Chacin | 23 | RHP | Smallish right-hander fanned a remarkable 56 in just 36.2 innings with Daytona. |
| Juan Duran | 24 | OF | 6-foot-7 power-hitter lacks any type of OBP value. |
| Ian Kahaloa | 18 | RHP | Fifth round pick out of a Hawaiian High School posted a 31-to-6 strikeout-to-walk ratio in 24.0 innings. |
| Shedric Long | 20 | 2B | Former backstop hit .283/.363/.474 in limited action Low Class A. He could be something or not. He's appeared in just 95 games in three pro seasons. |
| Steve Selsky | 26 | 1B/OF | Hit .315/.386/.428 across 51 games with Louisville in the International League last season. |
| Wyatt Strahan | 23 | RHP | Former USC stud posted a 132-to-53 strikeout-to-walk ratio in 164.1 innings. He's probably not long for the rotation, but could develop into a decent middle relief arm. |
| Zack Weiss | 24 | RHP | Averaged 11.8 K/9 and just 2.4 BB/9 in 52.0 innings as Pensacola's closer. |

# Cleveland Indians

**State of the Farm System:** With the official hiring of Chris Antonetti as the club's General Manager following the 2010, the franchise has undergone a radical philosophical change in terms of drafting – a weakness under Mark Shapiro's tenure. Instead of focusing on low ceiling, safe collegiate prospects, the front office honed in on drafting upside – and admittedly more risky – high school players. Five of the club's last eight first round picks – including supplemental selections – have been prep prospects. With Shapiro at the helm the Tribe grabbed just two high school-aged prospects – outfielder Johnny Drennen and former budding ace turned injury plagued wonder Adam Miller – out of 11 first round picks between 2003 and 2010.

And, as they say, the proof is in the pudding (or in the famous Bertman Stadium Mustard if you happen call Cleveland home).

The farm system just graduated shortstop wunderkind Francisco Lindor, who was the first selection under the Antonetti regime, to the big leagues. Outside of that, Cleveland's top two prospects – toolsy outfielder Clint Frazier and Justus Sheffield, one of the most underrated prospects in baseball – are both former high schoolers sitting atop their system. The front office brain trust also shocked the baseball world when the risk-mitigating organization took a flier on injured southpaw (and former 2014 #1 overall pick) Brady Aiken with the 17th overall pick last June. They would follow that up with another high-upside young arm in Triston McKenzie.

Helping round out their Top 5 are former University of San Francisco slugger Bradley Zimmer, who ripped through the Carolina League before getting doused with cold water in Class AA, and young lefty Rob Kaminsky, who was acquired in the Brandon Moss deal with St. Louis midseason – both of whom figure prominently into the club's long term big league plans.

Beyond that the system is sporting several intriguing names including hard-throwing right-hander Mike Clevinger, who could easily become a poor man's version of former Cy Young award winner Corey Kluber, and power-hitting, swing-at-everything first baseman Bobby Bradley, another one of the high reward high school kids selected early in the 2014 draft.

| Rank | Name | POS |
|---|---|---|
| 1 | Clint Frazier | OF |
| 2 | Justus Sheffield | P |
| 3 | Bradley Zimmer | OF |
| 4 | Brady Aiken | P |
| 5 | Rob Kaminsky | P |
| 6 | Mike Clevinger | P |
| 7 | Bobby Bradley | 1B |
| 8 | Francisco Mejia | C |
| 9 | Triston McKenzie | P |
| 10 | Tyler Naquin | OF |
| 11 | Nelson Rodriguez | 1B |
| 12 | Luis Lugo | P |
| 13 | Adam Plutko | P |
| 14 | Juan Hillman | P |
| 15 | James Ramsey | OF |
| 16 | Jesus Aguilar | 1B |
| 17 | Shawn Morimando | P |
| 18 | Thomas Pannone | P |
| 19 | Erik Gonzalez | SS |
| 20 | Mike Papi | OF |
| 21 | Luigi Rodriguez | OF |
| 22 | Mitch Brown | P |
| 23 | Yoiber Marquina | P |
| 24 | Sean Brady | P |
| 25 | Eric Haase | C |

**Review of the 2015 Draft:** After grabbing Aiken and McKenzie with their first two selections last June, the club triple-downed on prep-aged arms by grabbing southpaw Juan Hillman in the second round, 59th overall. Hillman, a lanky 6-foot-2 and 183 pounds, had a promising debut in the Arizona Summer League, posting a respectable 20-to-5 strikeout-to-walk in 24.0 innings of work.

The organization did well in landing a pair of collegiate infielders, Mark Mathias and Tyler Krieger, as buy-low options in the third and fourth rounds as well.

Two mid- to late-round names to remember: former Cal State Fullerton right-hander Justin Garza and high school shortstop – and son of former big league manager Don Wakamatsu – Luke Wakamatsu.

Here's what I wrote about Garza prior to the draft last June: "Solid, sturdy, and steady. Garza falls into the same category as so many polished collegiate hurlers in the past couple of years: Andrew Thurman, Marco Gonzales, and Chi Chi Gonzalez. Meaning: Garza profiles as a back-of-the-rotation caliber arm, who, potentially, could move quickly through the minors."

# Cleveland Indians

## 1. Clint Frazier, CF/RF

MiLB Rank: #21
Position Rank: #6

| Born: 09/06/94 | Age: 21 | Bats: R | |
|---|---|---|---|
| Height: 6-1 | Weight: 190 | Throws: R | |

**Top CALs:** Domingo Santana, Cameron Maybin, Angel Morales, Johermyn Chavez, Trayce Thompson

| Season | Age | LVL | PA | 2B | 3B | HR | AVG | OBP | SLG | ISO | BB% | K% | wRC+ |
|---|---|---|---|---|---|---|---|---|---|---|---|---|---|
| 2013 | 18 | R | 196 | 11 | 5 | 5 | 0.297 | 0.362 | 0.506 | 0.209 | 8.7% | 31.1% | 137 |
| 2014 | 19 | A | 542 | 18 | 6 | 13 | 0.266 | 0.349 | 0.411 | 0.146 | 10.3% | 29.7% | 120 |
| 2015 | 20 | A+ | 588 | 36 | 3 | 16 | 0.285 | 0.377 | 0.465 | 0.180 | 11.6% | 21.3% | 147 |

**Background:** One could make the argument – with a high percentage of success – that Frazier took the biggest developmental steps (not step) forward last season – not only in the system, but perhaps the entire minor leagues as well. After posting enough whiffs to knock a hair loose on Donald Trump's head, the former fifth overall pick cut nearly eight percentage points off his strikeout rate – it dropped from 30.1% in 2013-2014 to 21.3% in 2015 – while seeing a surge in the power department. The flaming-haired outfielder put a sluggish April behind him (.247/.317/.301) and batted an impressive .292/.387/.493 over his final 114 games. And his overall production, per *Weighted Runs Created Plus*, was 47% better than the league average last season, tied for the second best mark. And, oh yeah, he was one of just seven qualified hitters under the age of 21 in the Carolina League.

**Projection:** Just to put this into perspective a bit more consider this: among those seven qualified hitters under the age of 21, the White Sox's Trey Michalczewski's 113 wRC+ total was closet to Frazier's 147 mark. A difference *in percentage points* of 34, for those counting at home. Frazier's a supremely gifted athlete who offers up plus-power potential, above-average walk rates, and 20-stolen base speed; all the while adding value on the defensive side of the ball. It's a bit uncertain as to whether he, or Bradley Zimmer, or Tyler Naquin (probably not) will get pushed from center field to right field. But Frazier has a chance to be one of the better homegrown Tribe bats in a long, long time.

**Ceiling:** 4.0- to 4.5-win player
**Risk:** Moderate to High
**MLB ETA:** 2017

## 2. Justus Sheffield, LHP

MiLB Rank: #48
Position Rank: N/A

| Born: 05/13/96 | Age: 20 | Bats: L | |
|---|---|---|---|
| Height: 5-10 | Weight: 196 | Throws: L | |

**Top CALs:** Angel Reyes, Jake Thompson, Mitchell Taylor, Lucas Giolito, Felix Jorge

| YEAR | Age | Level | IP | W | L | ERA | FIP | K/9 | BB/9 | K% | BB% | HR/9 | LOB% |
|---|---|---|---|---|---|---|---|---|---|---|---|---|---|
| 2014 | 18 | R | 20.7 | 3 | 1 | 4.79 | 2.68 | 12.63 | 3.92 | 30.9% | 9.6% | 0.00 | 52.9% |
| 2015 | 19 | A | 127.7 | 9 | 4 | 3.31 | 2.99 | 9.73 | 2.68 | 24.9% | 6.9% | 0.56 | 70.2% |

**Background:** The Indians' second first round pick in 2014, 31st overall, Sheffield continued to shine in the lower levels of the minor leagues last season. After posting a 29-to-9 strikeout-to-walk ratio in the Arizona Summer League during his debut, the smallish lefty maintained an impressive ratio as he moved up to full-season ball for the first time, finishing the year with 138 punch outs – the second best mark in the Midwest League – and just 34 free passes in 127+ innings of work. That strikeout total is the highest mark for a 19-year-old in any Class A league since 2012, when Archie Bradley (156) and Clayton Blackburn (143) accomplished the feat. Sheffield also became the first left-hander in Class A to rack up that many swing-and-misses since Madison Bumgarner did so in 2008.

**Projection:** In last year's book I wrote how small starting pitchers just don't total a whole lot of innings at the big league level; between 2000 and 2014 there have been just six starters 5-foot-10 or less to throw 100 or more innings at the highest level (Chad Guadin, Jesus Sanchez, Kris Medlen, Mike Hampton, Mike Leake, and Wandy Rodriguez). And it was accomplished just once in 2015 (Mike Leake, again). So Sheffield is going to always have that hanging over his head. However, southpaws that limit free passes, punch out hitters like Mike Tyson in his prime, and succeed against much older competition will *always* garner more than a few shots to stay in the rotation. You don't have to squint too hard to see a mid-rotation caliber arm with some added upside. Whether his body can withstand grabbing the ball every fifth day for multiple seasons is a whole other question.

**Ceiling:** 3.5-win player
**Risk:** Moderate
**MLB ETA:** 2017

## 3. Bradley Zimmer, CF/RF

**MiLB Rank: #60**
**Position Rank: #17**

| Born: 11/27/92 | Age: 23 | Bats: L | Top CALs: Mike Daniel, Aaron Cunningham, |
| Height: 6-4 | Weight: 185 | Throws: R | Zoilo Almonte, Brett Jackson, Brandon Jones |

| Season | Age | LVL | PA | 2B | 3B | HR | AVG | OBP | SLG | ISO | BB% | K% | wRC+ |
|---|---|---|---|---|---|---|---|---|---|---|---|---|---|
| 2014 | 21 | A- | 197 | 11 | 2 | 4 | 0.304 | 0.401 | 0.464 | 0.161 | 9.6% | 15.2% | 157 |
| 2015 | 22 | A+ | 335 | 17 | 3 | 10 | 0.308 | 0.403 | 0.493 | 0.185 | 11.0% | 23.0% | 164 |
| 2015 | 22 | AA | 214 | 9 | 1 | 6 | 0.219 | 0.313 | 0.374 | 0.155 | 8.4% | 25.2% | 102 |

**Background:** For quite a while it was Zimmer, not Frazier, who was the toast of the baby-faced Tribe. The former University of San Francisco byproduct – and younger brother of KC's Kyle Zimmer – battered the Carolina League pitching like one of those back-handed chest chops akin to professional wrestling. Then Zimmer got promoted and the Eastern League pitchers started hitting back. Hard. The 23rd overall pick in 2014 went from slugging .308/.403/.493 in the age-appropriate High Class A to batting – a term used loosely – a paltry .219/.313/.374. Overall, Zimmer would finish his first full professional season with a combined .273/.368/.446 triple-slash line, with 26 doubles, four triples, 16 homeruns, and a surprising 44 stolen bases, the 18th best mark among all minor leaguers.

**Projection:** Prior to the 2014 draft I likened the toolsy 6-foot-4, 185-pound outfielder to a healthy Corey Hart, the former two-time Milwaukee All-Star whose career was ravaged by injuries over the past couple seasons. So let's take a look at how each player's age-22 seasons stack up against each other:

| Player | Age | Level | AVG | OBP | SLG | 2B | 3B | HR | SB |
|---|---|---|---|---|---|---|---|---|---|
| Zimmer | 22 | A+/AA | 0.273 | 0.368 | 0.446 | 26 | 4 | 16 | 44 |
| Hart | 22 | AAA | 0.281 | 0.342 | 0.485 | 29 | 8 | 15 | 17 |

Now to be completely fair, Hart spent the year at the highest MiLB level and Zimmer was just making his way through the middle rungs. But Zimmer did, however, jump straight from short-season ball all the way up to the Carolina League. Needless to say, I think the comparison still stands in the grand scheme of things. Don't expect the sneaky-quick outifleder to be a regular member of the 40+ stolen base club – it's very likely last season was one of those fluky year's like Garin Cecchini had in 2012 when he swiped 51 bags, but has only totaled a 43 since – but he could approach 20/20 territory in his prime. Solid-average or better power, speed, a strong idea at the plate with some defensive value – add it all up and Zimmer has a chance to develop into a quasi-All-Star caliber player for the Indians down the line.

**Ceiling:** 3.0-win player
**Risk:** Moderate
**MLB ETA:** 2017

## 4. Brady Aiken, LHP

**MiLB Rank: #79**
**Position Rank: N/A**

| Born: 08/16/96 | Age: 19 | Bats: L | Top CALs: N/A |
| Height: 6-4 | Weight: 205 | Throws: L | |

**Background:** At this point Aiken's draft story – or stories – is as well documented as it's going to get. The Astros took the 6-foot-4 southpaw with the first overall pick in 2014, offered him a cool $6.5 million to sign, later withdrew that offer based on post-draft medical concerns, tried to low-ball him with a $5 million offer, and eventually failed to sign the promising youngster. Fast forward a handful of months and it appears that the Astros' concerns about a "smaller than average" UCL ligament proved to be correct; Aiken succumbed to injury – and eventually Tommy John surgery – during his first game with IMG. The Indians, sitting with the 17th overall pick last June, swooped in, and signed him to a slightly above-average slot bonus of $2,513,280.

**Projection:** It can likely be taken with a grain of salt until Aiken actually toes a professional rubber against live competition, but after Houston grabbed him with the first pick Jeff Luhnow, the club's GM, quipped: "It's the most advanced high school pitcher I've ever seen in my entire career. He has command like I've never seen before of his stuff." The internet's littered with GMs for every sport gushing about their most recent picks – especially first rounders – so who knows if this is actually the case. But this is exactly the type of gamble the Indians (A) should have made sitting in the middle of the first round and (B) would have never made at any point under the guidance of former GM-turned-president Mark Shapiro, who often took low ceiling, low risk college prospects that quite never panned out. I'm looking at you Jeremy Sowers…Is Aiken going to be able to shake off having an abnormal UCL? Who knows? But the draft is a crapshoot anyways, so why not gamble on a player that likely would have been the #1 overall pick for the second year in a row if not for some injury concerns?

**Ceiling:** Too Soon to Tell
**Risk:** N/A
**MLB ETA:** N/A

## 5. Rob Kaminsky, LHP

**MiLB Rank: #80**
**Position Rank: N/A**

| Born: 09/02/94 | Age: 21 | Bats: R | Top CALs: Jairo Heredia, Randall Delgado, |
|---|---|---|---|
| Height: 5-11 | Weight: 190 | Throws: L | Spencer Adams, Clayton Tanner, Ian McKinney |

| YEAR | Age | Level | IP | W | L | ERA | FIP | K/9 | BB/9 | K% | BB% | HR/9 | LOB% |
|---|---|---|---|---|---|---|---|---|---|---|---|---|---|
| 2013 | 18 | R | 22.0 | 0 | 3 | 3.68 | 2.87 | 11.45 | 3.68 | 28.6% | 9.2% | 0.41 | 60.1% |
| 2014 | 19 | A | 100.7 | 8 | 2 | 1.88 | 3.28 | 7.06 | 2.77 | 19.4% | 7.6% | 0.18 | 77.0% |
| 2015 | 20 | A+ | 9.7 | 0 | 1 | 3.72 | 3.98 | 3.72 | 4.66 | 9.3% | 11.6% | 0.00 | 66.7% |
| 2015 | 20 | A+ | 94.7 | 6 | 5 | 2.09 | 2.51 | 7.51 | 2.66 | 20.1% | 7.1% | 0.00 | 74.6% |

**Background:** The 20-year-old southpaw out of Englewood Cliffs, New Jersey, got off to a typical Kaminsky-like season in the Florida State League last year: he limited free passes, missed a handful of bats, posted a tidy 2.51 FIP, and *failed to surrender a homerun through his first 17 starts*. And then the Cardinals sent the promising youngster packing for ~~a potent middle-of-the-order bat~~ Brandon Moss, who hit roughly the league average during his tenure in St. Louis. On the outset it looks like the Chris Antonetti-led Indians fleeced the Cardinals by sending a useful, albeit declining, power bat for the system's second or third best pitching prospect.

But here's the thing when it comes to the Red Birds: When's the last time the Cardinals genuinely got swindled when dealing away their homegrown talent? Just think about that for a moment. Here's the best I could come up since the 2000 season:

- On July 29, 2000, the Cardinals acquired lefty reliever Jason Christiansen for a light-hitting minor league defensive wizard at shortstop. Four years later that shortstop, Jack Wilson, slugged .308/.335/.459 en route to earning his first and only All Star game.

There have been deals that haven't worked out as well as the front office would have liked – shipping Dan Haren and Co. to Oakland for what amounted to one healthy season of Mark Mulder – but St. Louis rarely (*if ever*) commits *the* cardinal sin in baseball (no pun intended): they never fail to properly evaluate their own talent. Remember this is an organization that turned Brett Wallace/Shane Peterson/Clayton Mortensen into Matt Holliday, or Allen Craig and Joe Kelly into John Lackey. And let's not forget when they were criticized for dealing James Ramsey (see below) for a struggling Justin Masterson. So what, exactly, gives with dealing Kaminsky?

**Projection:** Here's what we do know about Kaminsky: he's incredibly young for his levels of competition; has never failed for any duration during his three-year professional career; is an absolute curmudgeon when it comes to allowing the long ball; and pitches well beyond his years. He's not overpowering by any stretch of the means, but his fastball certainly won't bounce off a pane of glass either. I pegged him as a mid-rotation caliber arm in last year's book, and he's done nothing to dissuade me from that opinion now either. Unless, of course, there's something the Cardinals' brain trust knows that we don't yet... Either way, though, this was a fantastic deal for the Tribe; they essentially turned Joey Wendle, a nondescript minor league second baseman shipped to Oakland last offseason, into Rob Kaminsky.

**Ceiling:** 2.5-win player
**Risk:** Low to Moderate
**MLB ETA:** 2017

## 6. Mike Clevinger, RHP

**MiLB Rank: #135**
**Position Rank: N/A**

| Born: 12/21/90 | Age: 25 | Bats: R | Top CALs: Chris Stratton, Tim Layden, |
|---|---|---|---|
| Height: 6-4 | Weight: 220 | Throws: R | Atahualpa Severino, Hipolito Guerrero, Rob Rasmussen |

| YEAR | Age | Level | IP | W | L | ERA | FIP | K/9 | BB/9 | K% | BB% | HR/9 | LOB% |
|---|---|---|---|---|---|---|---|---|---|---|---|---|---|
| 2013 | 22 | R | 2.7 | 0 | 1 | 16.88 | 5.96 | 6.75 | 6.75 | 11.8% | 11.8% | 0.00 | 33.3% |
| 2013 | 22 | R | 3.0 | 0 | 0 | 3.00 | 4.01 | 9.00 | 6.00 | 23.1% | 15.4% | 0.00 | 75.0% |
| 2014 | 23 | A | 24.0 | 3 | 0 | 1.88 | 2.94 | 10.13 | 1.88 | 29.4% | 5.4% | 0.75 | 87.9% |
| 2014 | 23 | A+ | 55.3 | 1 | 3 | 5.37 | 5.21 | 9.43 | 4.39 | 23.4% | 10.9% | 1.30 | 61.7% |
| 2014 | 23 | A+ | 20.7 | 0 | 1 | 4.79 | 4.73 | 6.53 | 4.79 | 17.1% | 12.5% | 0.44 | 67.5% |
| 2015 | 24 | AA | 158.0 | 9 | 8 | 2.73 | 3.02 | 8.26 | 2.28 | 22.7% | 6.3% | 0.46 | 74.6% |

**Background:** Acquired for the baseball corpse of once-dominant eighth-inning setup man Vinnie Pestano in 2014, Clevinger spent the season teaming Adam Plutko, Shawn Morimando, Ryan Merritt, and Cody Anderson (for a bit, at least) to help form one of the more formidable rotations in the minor leagues. For his part, Clevinger, the Angels' fourth round pick in 2011, had his finest professional season to date, setting a career low in walk percentage (6.3%) while somehow managing to uncork a career best 11 wild pitches – go figure. The big right-hander finished the year with a steady 145-to-40 strikeout-to-walk ratio en route to posting a 3.02 FIP, another career best.

**Projection:** Sort of the anti-Adam Plutko in the sense that Clevinger typically survives by missing nearly a bat per inning, not limiting an extreme amount of free passes (though his control took a tremendous step forward last season). He's typically played in age-appropriate levels of competition, but has always handled himself adequately. Truthfully, he's one of those guys that you could look up in a couple years and think, "It doesn't surprise he's developed into a decent, underrated mid-rotation arm." Then again, one could easily be saying, "Yeah, he's turned himself into one helluva late-inning reliever."

**Ceiling:** 2.0- to 2.5-win player
**Risk:** Moderate
**MLB ETA:** 2016

## 7. Bobby Bradley, 1B

**MiLB Rank: #150**
**Position Rank: N/A**

| Born: 05/29/96 | Age: 20 | Bats: L | Top CALs: Amarys Minier, Oswaldo Morales, Giancarlo Stanton, Ravel Santana, Roberto Ramos |
|---|---|---|---|
| Height: 6-1 | Weight: 225 | Throws: R | |

| Season | Age | LVL | PA | 2B | 3B | HR | AVG | OBP | SLG | ISO | BB% | K% | wRC+ |
|---|---|---|---|---|---|---|---|---|---|---|---|---|---|
| 2014 | 18 | R | 176 | 13 | 4 | 8 | 0.361 | 0.426 | 0.652 | 0.290 | 9.1% | 20.5% | 192 |
| 2015 | 19 | A | 465 | 15 | 4 | 27 | 0.269 | 0.361 | 0.529 | 0.259 | 12.0% | 31.8% | 153 |
| 2015 | 19 | A+ | 9 | 0 | 0 | 0 | 0.000 | 0.111 | 0.000 | 0.000 | 11.1% | 22.2% | -60 |

**Background:** Fun fact: prior to the 2015 season, the last time a 19-year-old led the Midwest League in homeruns was Minnesota's Miguel Sano, who slugged .258/.373/.521 with 28 dingers in 2012. Fast forward three seasons and Bradley, the Tribe's 2014 third round pick out of a Mississippi high school, batted a Sano-esque .269/.361/.529 with 27 long balls. Sano, by the way, appeared in 19 more games. For Bradley, though, it marked a successful conversion to full-season ball in 2015, proving that his monster debut in the Arizona Summer League (.361/.426/.652) was no accident.

**Projection:** And now for the bad news: Bradley's swing-and-miss tendencies are a bit alarming at this point in his career. After whiffing in just about 20% of his plate appearances as a rookie, the lefty-swinging first baseman punched out in nearly 32% of his trips to the dish last season, the second highest mark in the Midwest League. Bradley offers up the system's best power potential – grading out well above-average to plus – and looks like the typical Three True Outcomes hitter. Think of a not-so-quite-poor-man's version of Ryan Howard, if everything breaks the right way.

**Ceiling:** 2.5-win player
**Risk:** Moderate to High
**MLB ETA:** 2019

## 8. Francisco Mejia, C

**MiLB Rank: #175**
**Position Rank: #7**

| Born: 10/27/95 | Age: 20 | Bats: B | Top CALs: Sebastian Valle, Oscar Hernandez, Alex Murphy, Carlos Perez, Ryan Casteel |
|---|---|---|---|
| Height: 5-10 | Weight: 175 | Throws: R | |

| Season | Age | LVL | PA | 2B | 3B | HR | AVG | OBP | SLG | ISO | BB% | K% | wRC+ |
|---|---|---|---|---|---|---|---|---|---|---|---|---|---|
| 2013 | 17 | R | 113 | 9 | 1 | 4 | 0.305 | 0.348 | 0.524 | 0.219 | 4.4% | 15.9% | 139 |
| 2014 | 18 | A- | 274 | 17 | 4 | 2 | 0.282 | 0.339 | 0.407 | 0.125 | 6.6% | 17.2% | 119 |
| 2015 | 19 | A | 446 | 13 | 0 | 9 | 0.243 | 0.324 | 0.345 | 0.102 | 8.5% | 17.5% | 99 |

**Background:** The Dominican-born backstop became *the* pop-up guy in the Cleveland system a couple years ago, bashing his way through the Arizona Summer League with a .305/.348/.524 triple-slash line in 30 games. The switch-hitting Mejia has followed that up with some good, not great, production in short-season ball in 2014 (.282/.339/.407) and in his first full-season action in the Midwest League last year. Playing for the Lake County Captains, the then-19-year-old batted a league average-ish .243/.324/.345 with handful of doubles (13) and nine long balls while posting a 78-to-38 strikeout-to-walk ratio in 446 trips to the plate. For his career, Mejia is sporting a .265/.333/.391 mark, coming mostly against older competition.

**Projection:** Important context. Here's a list of the teenaged backstop in any Class A league with at least 300 plate appearances and a wRC+ total above 95 and an Isolated Power of at least .100 since 2006: Francisco Mejia, Chase Vallot, Chance Sisco, Carson Kelly, Jorge Alfaro, Austin Hedges, Gary Sanchez, Sebastian Valle, JR Murphy, Austin Romine, Jesus Montero, Wilson Ramos, Hank Conger, and Bryan Anderson. Of that group of 14, only two backstops – Mejia and Conger – were switch-hitters. Obviously, it's a fairly strong amalgamation of backstop prospects. So Mejia's place as a budding top prospect seems fitting. He's shown no true holes in his skill set at this point: average or better power, strong contact skills, decent eye at the plate. On the defensive side of the plate, Mejia will never be confused with Ivan Rodriguez, but he won't let the opposing running game get out of hand either.

**Ceiling:** 2.0- to 2.5-win player
**Risk:** Moderate to High
**MLB ETA:** 2019

## 9. Triston McKenzie, RHP

**MiLB Rank: #176**
**Position Rank: N/A**

| Born: 08/02/97 | Age: 18 | Bats: R | Top CALs: N/A |
|---|---|---|---|
| Height: 6-5 | Weight: 160 | Throws: R | |

| YEAR | Age | Level | IP | W | L | ERA | FIP | K/9 | BB/9 | K% | BB% | HR/9 | LOB% |
|---|---|---|---|---|---|---|---|---|---|---|---|---|---|
| 2015 | 17 | R | 12.0 | 1 | 1 | 0.75 | 1.73 | 12.75 | 2.25 | 39.5% | 7.0% | 0.00 | 85.7% |

**Background:** After bemoaning about the Tribe's inability to successfully develop high school-aged hurlers at length in last year's book, the front office decided to open the 2015 draft with three teenaged arms: Aiken, right-hander Triston McKenzie, and lefty Juan Hillman. Hailing from Royal Palm Beach High School (FL), home to Jarrod Saltalamacchia and former big leaguer Kason Gabbard, McKenzie was the eighth and final prep arm taken in the first round last June. Standing a lanky 6-foot-5 and 160 pounds soaking wet, McKenzie briefly dominated the Arizona Summer League competition last year as a 17-year-old, posting an eye-catching 17-to-3 strikeout-to-walk ratio in 12 innings of work during his debut.

**Projection:** Very little information to go off of, but McKenzie does has the size and lack of weight where his fastball could tick up another notch or two as he begins to fill out – or as us people on the wrong side of 30 say, pack on the pounds. Justus Sheffield had a similar debut in the AZL two years ago, so it wouldn't be shocking to see the Tribe push McKenzie up to the Midwest League where he'll undoubtedly be one of – if not *the* – youngest player.

**Ceiling:** Too Soon to Tell
**Risk:** N/A
**MLB ETA:** N/A

## 10. Tyler Naquin, CF

**MiLB Rank: #243**
**Position Rank: N/A**

| Born: 04/24/91 | Age: 25 | Bats: L | Top CALs: Mel Rojas Jr., Roger Bernadina, |
|---|---|---|---|
| Height: 6-2 | Weight: 190 | Throws: R | Ryan Rua, Brandon Jones, Tim Smith |

| Season | Age | LVL | PA | 2B | 3B | HR | AVG | OBP | SLG | ISO | BB% | K% | wRC+ |
|---|---|---|---|---|---|---|---|---|---|---|---|---|---|
| 2013 | 22 | A+ | 498 | 27 | 6 | 9 | 0.277 | 0.345 | 0.424 | 0.147 | 8.2% | 22.5% | 115 |
| 2014 | 23 | AA | 341 | 12 | 5 | 4 | 0.313 | 0.371 | 0.424 | 0.112 | 8.5% | 20.8% | 122 |
| 2015 | 24 | AA | 160 | 12 | 1 | 1 | 0.348 | 0.419 | 0.468 | 0.121 | 9.4% | 15.0% | 158 |
| 2015 | 24 | AAA | 218 | 13 | 0 | 6 | 0.263 | 0.353 | 0.430 | 0.167 | 11.5% | 22.5% | 127 |

**Background:** The last member of the system's triumvirate of center fielders/right fielders with a legitimate shot of seeing regular big league action. Naquin, the club's first round pick out of Texas A&M in 2012, 15th overall, smoked the Eastern League to the tune of .348/.419/.468 before getting promoted up to Columbus last season. It should be noted, however, that it was his third stint with at least 85 plate appearances in Akron. He handled himself in perfect Tyler Naquin-form after the jump up to the International League, hitting .263/.353/.430. The former Aggie finished the year with a combined .300/.381/.446 triple-slash line with 25 doubles, one triple, seven homeruns, and 13 stolen bases (16 attempts).

**Projection:** In last year's book I wrote:

> *"An everyday player for a non-contending team and a part-timer everywhere else. Naquin's overall skill set is largely underwhelming. Coming out of college his hit tool was touted as a potential above-average to plus skill. But now that he's entering his age-24 season with a .283 career average and more than 1,000 plate appearances under his belt, it looks like a solid-average skill, nothing more. Oh, and let's not forget about his struggles against southpaws in his minor league career: .238/.334/.309."*

OK. Let's update those numbers a bit. His career mark in nearly 1,500 plate appearances stands at .289/.361/.413. And he did manage to (slightly) improve against those pesky southpaws as well: he batted .262/.312/.369 in 95 trips to the plate against them. Naquin doesn't run very often, hit for a whole lot of power (his career ISO is just .124), and he's now entering his age-25 season with just a little over 200 plate appearances above Class AA. If he plays defense at an above-average clip he might able to break the two-win mark. I just don't see it happening on a consistent enough basis, though. He's a very good fourth outfielder/fringey everyday guy.

**Ceiling:** 1.5-win player
**Risk:** Low to Moderate
**MLB ETA:** 2016

## 11. Nellie Rodriguez, 1B

**Position Rank: N/A**

| Born: 06/12/94 | Age: 22 | Bats: R | **Top CALs:** Anthony Rizzo, Jonathan Rodriguez, |
| Height: 6-2 | Weight: 250 | Throws: R | Chris Carter, Matt Clark, Jeff Malm |

| Season | Age | LVL | PA | 2B | 3B | HR | AVG | OBP | SLG | ISO | BB% | K% | wRC+ |
|--------|-----|-----|-----|----|----|----|-------|-------|-------|-------|-------|-------|------|
| 2013 | 19 | A- | 295 | 16 | 0 | 9 | 0.287 | 0.366 | 0.452 | 0.165 | 9.8% | 20.7% | 148 |
| 2013 | 19 | A | 188 | 7 | 0 | 1 | 0.194 | 0.305 | 0.256 | 0.063 | 13.8% | 28.2% | 67 |
| 2014 | 20 | A | 550 | 32 | 3 | 22 | 0.268 | 0.349 | 0.482 | 0.214 | 10.9% | 25.8% | 137 |
| 2015 | 21 | A+ | 460 | 32 | 2 | 17 | 0.275 | 0.357 | 0.495 | 0.220 | 11.1% | 26.5% | 147 |
| 2015 | 21 | AA | 105 | 2 | 0 | 4 | 0.118 | 0.200 | 0.269 | 0.151 | 8.6% | 35.2% | 34 |

**Background:** Let's play a game for a minute: Among qualified hitters at any High Class A level, name the two most productive bats under the age of 22. The answer: Clint Frazier (age 20, 147 wRC+) and his teammate Nellie Rodriguez (age 21, also a 147 wRC+). Rodriguez, a 15th round pick in 2012, quietly put together a strong year in the Midwest League two years ago, batting .268/.349/.482 while tying for the league lead in homeruns with 22. Well, if two years ago was a quietly strong year, then last season's work in the Carolina League declarative statement by the slugging first baseman. Rodriguez mashed to the tune of .275/.357/.495 with 32 doubles, a pair of triples, and 17 homeruns in 108 games before getting promoted to Akron for his final 105 plate appearances. And just for good measure, Rodriguez swiped his first – and only – professional bag with Lynchburg as well. He struggled at an epic proportion during his tenure in the Eastern League, so his overall numbers looks less than impressive: .245/.328/.452.

**Projection**: Rodriguez has struggled twice in his brief four-year career: when he was initially promoted to full season ball in 2013 and last year's disappointing showing in Class AA. He walks and hits for gobs of power (even if it hasn't translated into true-homerun pop quite yet). The hit tool is a bit sketchy, as is his ability to make consistent contact, but 21-year-olds that top High Class A league average production by 47% will garner some looks. He has a chance to be what Cleveland fans were hoping with Jesus Aguilar: a decent #5/#6-type bat with 20-HR potential and a ceiling nearing league average.

**Ceiling:** 1.5- to 2.0-win player
**Risk:** Moderate to High
**MLB ETA:** 2017

## 12. Luis Lugo, LHP

**MiLB Rank: N/A**

**Position Rank: N/A**

| Born: 03/05/94 | Age: 21 | Bats: L | **Top CALs:** Nick Travieso, Jeffry Antigua, |
| Height: 6-5 | Weight: 200 | Throws: L | David Baker, Chase DeJong, Ryan Searle |

| YEAR | Age | Level | IP | W | L | ERA | FIP | K/9 | BB/9 | K% | BB% | HR/9 | LOB% |
|------|-----|-------|-------|----|----|------|------|-------|------|-------|------|------|-------|
| 2013 | 19 | A- | 50.3 | 1 | 4 | 1.97 | 3.12 | 5.36 | 1.97 | 15.5% | 5.7% | 0.18 | 74.6% |
| 2013 | 19 | A | 14.3 | 0 | 1 | 3.77 | 3.34 | 8.79 | 3.14 | 23.0% | 8.2% | 0.63 | 68.2% |
| 2014 | 20 | A | 126.3 | 10 | 9 | 4.92 | 3.86 | 10.40 | 2.85 | 27.1% | 7.4% | 1.14 | 61.1% |
| 2015 | 21 | A+ | 125.7 | 8 | 10 | 4.15 | 3.81 | 8.52 | 3.72 | 21.7% | 9.5% | 0.79 | 59.9% |

**Background:** Lugo has continued his quiet march through the bottom rungs of the minor league ladder. After a slight coming out party in short-season ball in 2013, the 6-foot-5 Venezuelan-born southpaw brightly shone in the Midwest League two years ago as he posted a ridiculous 146-to-40 strikeout-to-walk ratio as a 20-year-old. The front office brass bumped him up to Lynchburg in the Carolina League last season, and the results remained positive for the most part. Lugo tossed a smidgeon over 125 innings, struck out 119 and walked 52 en route to posting a 3.81 FIP. According to StatCorner, he also finished the year with the second lowest line-drive rate of his career as well (16.2%).

**Projection**: Despite the massive 6-foot-5, 200-pound frame, Lugo falls into the same category as Rob Kaminsky: sort of the not-quite-finesse-but-far-from-dominant southpaw. Lugo's control took a slight step backward last season, but remains average-ish. He'll get burned by the occasional homerun at times as well.

More than five years ago the Tribe shipped Jhonny Peralta off to Detroit for Giovanni Soto, another lanky left-hander with solid peripherals. Soto got banished to the pen, but think of Lugo as a slightly better version of that; a back-end starter with the downside of a solid middle reliever.

**Ceiling:** 1.5-win player
**Risk:** Moderate
**MLB ETA:** 2017

## 13. Adam Plutko, RHP

MiLB Rank: N/A
Position Rank: N/A

| Born: 10/03/91 | Age: 24 | Bats: R | Top CALs: Mark Leiter, Joe Gunkel, |
|---|---|---|---|
| Height: 6-3 | Weight: 195 | Throws: R | Anthony Desclafani, Todd Redman, Brandon Workman |

| YEAR | Age | Level | IP | W | L | ERA | FIP | K/9 | BB/9 | K% | BB% | HR/9 | LOB% |
|---|---|---|---|---|---|---|---|---|---|---|---|---|---|
| 2014 | 22 | A | 52.7 | 3 | 1 | 3.93 | 1.97 | 11.28 | 2.05 | 30.3% | 5.5% | 0.17 | 59.4% |
| 2014 | 22 | A+ | 97.0 | 4 | 9 | 4.08 | 4.00 | 7.24 | 1.67 | 19.7% | 4.5% | 1.02 | 69.5% |
| 2015 | 23 | A+ | 49.7 | 4 | 2 | 1.27 | 2.51 | 8.52 | 0.91 | 25.8% | 2.8% | 0.54 | 91.2% |
| 2015 | 23 | AA | 116.3 | 9 | 5 | 2.86 | 3.37 | 6.96 | 1.78 | 19.4% | 5.0% | 0.70 | 75.7% |

**Background:** One of the guys that just missed last year's Top 20 rankings for the franchise, the former UCLA ace was brilliantly effective in both his quick refresher in High Class A and in his 19-start performance with Akron in the Eastern League. Plutko, a 6-foot-3, 195-pound right-hander, opened the season by posting a mind-boggling 47-to-5 strikeout-to-walk ratio with Lynchburg while tallying a barely-there 1.27 ERA. Just a quick side note: he allowed just 12 *combined* runs (not just earned runs) *and* walks in nearly 50 innings of work. He was then bumped up to Akron, a more age-appropriate level of competition, and barely missed a beat: he tossed another 116.1 innings while fanning 90 and issuing just 23 free passes. The savvy right-hander finished the year with a combined 2.39 ERA while averaging 7.4 strikeouts and just 1.5 walks per nine innings.

**Projection**: Prior to the 2013 draft I wrote:

> "Plutko has a pretty decent pedigree: drafted in the sixth round out of high school, three solid years at UCLA, and a member for the USA Collegiate National Team. He's another one of these arms that has a high floor/low ceiling. [He's going to be] back rotation-type fodder."

I also slapped a second/third round draft grade on the promising hurler and ranked him as the 45th best collegiate prospect. Well, fast forward a handful of weeks and Plutko, who finished his collegiate career with a sparkling 2.26 ERA against some of the nation's toughest competition, inexplicably lasted until the 11th round.

Well, he certainly doesn't look like an 11th round talent now. Plutko won't blow the doors off of the competition – if we're sticking with the car theme think Toyota Camry, not a Ferrari – but there is definite big league value here, potentially peaking as a good #4-type arm. Very Josh Tomlin-esque. Plutko will chew innings, post an upper 3.0s/lower 4.0s ERA and keep his team in the game. Still sticking by what I wrote more than two years ago – he's a 1.0- to 1.5-win player.

**Ceiling:** 1.0- to 1.5-win player
**Risk:** Low to Moderate
**MLB ETA:** 2016

## 14. Juan Hillman, LHP

MiLB Rank: N/A
Position Rank: N/A

| Born: 05/15/97 | Age: 19 | Bats: L | Top CALs: N/A |
|---|---|---|---|
| Height: 6-2 | Weight: 183 | Throws: L | |

| YEAR | Age | Level | IP | W | L | ERA | FIP | K/9 | BB/9 | K% | BB% | HR/9 | LOB% |
|---|---|---|---|---|---|---|---|---|---|---|---|---|---|
| 2015 | 18 | R | 24.0 | 0 | 2 | 4.13 | 3.15 | 7.50 | 1.88 | 19.4% | 4.9% | 0.00 | 61.8% |

**Background:** Fun Fact #1: Prior to the 2015 draft, the last time the Indians grabbed pitchers with their first three selections was in 2004 when the club tabbed Jeremy Sowers, Justin Hoyman, and Scott Lewis in rounds one, two, and three. Fun Fact #2: the last time the franchise grabbed three consecutive teenage arms to open a draft is the 2001 debacle when they selected Dan Denham (pitched 163.2 innings in Class AAA before sputtering out), Alan Horne (who didn't sign with the club and would later peter out in Class AA), and J.D. Martin (totaled 125.0 IP in the big leagues, zero of which occurred donning a Cleveland uniform). Hillman, the club's second round pick out of Olympia High School (Orlando, FL), was the second prep southpaw taken in last June's draft, despite being pegged as the 59th overall selection. The 6-foot-2 lefty tossed 24.0 solid innings in the Arizona Summer League, getting his professional feet wet by punching out 20 and walking five.

**Projection**: Olympia High School has churned out some impressive talent in the past couple years: Nick Gordon, the fifth overall pick two years ago, and Jesse Winker, one of the minors' top young bats in 2012, and San Diego massive right-hander Walker Weickel, another supplemental first round pick. Hillman, similar to McKenzie, has likely punched his ticket to full season ball after a solid debut.

**Ceiling:** Too Soon to Tell
**Risk:** N/A
**MLB ETA:** N/A

## 15. James Ramsey, OF

MiLB Rank: N/A
Position Rank: N/A

| Born: 12/19/89 | Age: 26 | Bats: L | Top CALs: Kyeong Kang, Blake Smith, |
| Height: 6-0 | Weight: 200 | Throws: R | Marvin Lowrance, Matt Clark, Jai Miller |

| Season | Age | LVL | PA | 2B | 3B | HR | AVG | OBP | SLG | ISO | BB% | K% | wRC+ |
|---|---|---|---|---|---|---|---|---|---|---|---|---|---|
| 2013 | 23 | AA | 416 | 11 | 2 | 15 | 0.251 | 0.356 | 0.424 | 0.173 | 12.7% | 26.0% | 123 |
| 2014 | 24 | AA | 281 | 14 | 1 | 13 | 0.300 | 0.389 | 0.527 | 0.226 | 11.0% | 23.5% | 161 |
| 2014 | 24 | AAA | 127 | 9 | 1 | 3 | 0.284 | 0.365 | 0.468 | 0.183 | 10.2% | 26.8% | 130 |
| 2015 | 25 | AAA | 503 | 21 | 2 | 12 | 0.243 | 0.327 | 0.382 | 0.139 | 10.5% | 25.4% | 107 |

**Background:** Remember under the Rob Kaminsky evaluation I had stated how well the Cardinals do when assessing their own homegrown talent? Well, here's another example. Let's take a brief trip back in time, back to the day before the trade deadline in 2014. The Indians were under .500, and Justin Masterson was chucking high 80 heaters with little to no luck. Masterson, an impending free agent, was shipped off to St. Louis for a resurgent James Ramsey in what looked like a bit of steal for the Tribe. A former first round pick, 23rd overall in 2012, Ramsey was in the midst of a career year in his second stint in Class AA, hitting a robust .300/.389/.527 with 13 homeruns in less than 300 trips to the plate. After the deal the Tribe promoted Ramsey to Columbus and he continued to perform admirably, hitting .284/.365/.468. Well, this year rolled around and the lefty-swinging outfielder found himself back in Class AAA – where he batted a league average-ish .243/.327/.382.

**Projection:** So, what exactly happened? Well, the Cardinals appeared to have found a taker at the most opportune time for Ramsey – his potential peak in value. Ignoring his 18-game stint in High Class A in 2013, let's look at his extended action throughout his professional career:

- He batted a disappointing .229/.333/.314 as the Cards bumped him all the way to High Class A for his debut, posting an 89 wRC+ and a .309 BABIP.
- Ramsey would then spend the majority of the next year, 2013, in Class AA, where he managed to get his feet under him a bit more while hitting .251/.356/.424 while posting a 123 wRC+ with a .316 BABIP.
- Then Ramsey goes off in 2014, hitting .300/.389/.527 in Class AA and follows that up by hitting .284/.365/.468 in Class AAA. His BABIPs? Glad you asked: .364 and .378, respectively.
- Finally, Ramsey declines down to a .243/.327/.382 showing in Class AAA. Good enough for a 107 wRC+ while posting a .315 BABIP.

See the outliers?

His BABIPs, for whatever reason (luck?), spiked in 2014. Otherwise, he's been a nice, decent outfield prospect. The perfect risk a team like the Indians should have gambled on, but one that could – and eventually would – decline in 2015. He's your typical fourth/fifth outfielder on a championship squad, sort of a similar version of Tyler Naquin (just a bit older).

**Ceiling:** 1.0- to 1.5-win player
**Risk:** Moderate
**MLB ETA:** 2016

## 16. Jesus Aguilar, 1B

MiLB Rank: N/A
Position Rank: N/A

| Born: 06/30/90 | Age: 26 | Bats: R | Top CALs: Mark Canha, Matt Clark, |
| Height: 6-3 | Weight: 250 | Throws: R | Joey Votto, Allen Craig, Justin Bour |

| Season | Age | LVL | PA | 2B | 3B | HR | AVG | OBP | SLG | ISO | BB% | K% | wRC+ |
|---|---|---|---|---|---|---|---|---|---|---|---|---|---|
| 2013 | 23 | AA | 567 | 28 | 0 | 16 | 0.275 | 0.349 | 0.427 | 0.152 | 9.9% | 18.9% | 116 |
| 2014 | 24 | AAA | 499 | 31 | 0 | 19 | 0.304 | 0.395 | 0.511 | 0.206 | 12.8% | 19.2% | 149 |
| 2015 | 25 | AAA | 570 | 29 | 1 | 19 | 0.267 | 0.332 | 0.439 | 0.173 | 8.2% | 20.2% | 121 |
| 2015 | 25 | MLB | 20 | 1 | 0 | 0 | 0.316 | 0.350 | 0.368 | 0.053 | 0.0% | 35.0% | 102 |
| 2015 | 25 | MLB | 20 | 1 | 0 | 0 | 0.316 | 0.350 | 0.368 | 0.053 | 0.0% | 35.0% | 102 |

**Background:** The hulking first baseman spent his second consecutive season fine-tuning his offensive approach in Columbus. After batting a respectable .304/.395/.511 with the Clippers in 2014, Aguilar's production took a noticeable dip in his follow-up campaign: he slugged .267/.332/.439 while he saw downturns in nearly every meaningful statistic category. His Isolated Power dropped from .206 to .173; his BABIP (unsurprisingly) normalized, moving from the second highest of his career (.350) all the way down to .305; and his peripherals at the plate (strikeout and walk rates) both moved a touch in the wrong direction. For his career, Aguilar is sporting a .275/.353/.451 triple-slash line, slugging 110 homeruns in 816 games.

**Projection:** The book's pretty much well-written on Aguilar at this point: he's a nice, serviceable minor league first baseman. His power, which never really took another expected step forward, is merely average for a run-producing position. His patience will hover around the league average mark. He's definitely not a starter on a championship-contending team.

**Ceiling:** 1.0-win player
**Risk:** Low to Moderate
**MLB ETA:** Debuted in 2014

## 17. Shawn Morimando, LHP

**MiLB Rank: N/A**
**Position Rank: N/A**

| Born: 11/20/92 | Age: 23 | Bats: L | Top CALs: Richard Castillo, Tyler Herron, |
|---|---|---|---|
| Height: 5-11 | Weight: 195 | Throws: L | Alberto Cabrera, Chi-Chi Gonzalez, Joely Rodriguez |

| YEAR | Age | Level | IP | W | L | ERA | FIP | K/9 | BB/9 | K% | BB% | HR/9 | LOB% |
|---|---|---|---|---|---|---|---|---|---|---|---|---|---|
| 2013 | 20 | A+ | 135.0 | 8 | 13 | 3.73 | 4.36 | 6.80 | 5.07 | 17.5% | 13.0% | 0.53 | 68.9% |
| 2014 | 21 | A+ | 96.3 | 8 | 3 | 2.99 | 4.19 | 6.54 | 3.27 | 17.7% | 8.8% | 0.65 | 67.9% |
| 2014 | 21 | AA | 56.3 | 2 | 6 | 3.83 | 3.37 | 6.07 | 2.72 | 15.5% | 6.9% | 0.32 | 63.5% |
| 2015 | 22 | AA | 158.7 | 10 | 12 | 3.18 | 3.64 | 7.26 | 3.69 | 19.5% | 9.9% | 0.51 | 74.3% |

**Background:** One of the members of the RubberDucks' vaunted Class AA rotation, Morimando proved that his 10-game stint as a 21-year-old in the Eastern League two years ago was no fluke. The 5-foot-11 southpaw tossed 158.2 innings, punched out 128, and walked 65 en route to finishing the year with the second best FIP of his young professional career (3.64).

**Projection:** Fast-tracked since entering professional ball as a 19th round pick in 2011, Morimando, who tossed just six innings of rookie ball before jumping in the Midwest League, continued his rapid ascension up the minor league chain. Combined with his work in 2014, the southpaw has now tallied 215.0 innings of decent Class AA production before his 23rd birthday: 6.9 K/9, 3.4 BB/9, and a 3.35 ERA. So, needless to say there's some definite big league value here.

Morimando basically falls into the T.J. House/T.J. McFarland/Scott Lewis category as a successful minor league lefty without any truly standout underlying numbers. His control has merely been average; his strikeout rates slightly below. One of the major factors working for him is his age. If the command takes another step forward he could be a useful backend starter. If not, well, left arms tend to find homes regardless – especially ones that hold left-handed hitters to a miniscule .163/.242/.199 line as he did this season.

**Ceiling:** 1.0-win player
**Risk:** Low to Moderate
**MLB ETA:** 2016

## 18. Thomas Pannone, LHP

**MiLB Rank: N/A**
**Position Rank: N/A**

| Born: 04/28/94 | Age: 22 | Bats: L | Top CALs: Edgar Tejada, Ryne Slack,, |
|---|---|---|---|
| Height: 6-0 | Weight: 195 | Throws: L | Richard Ortiz, Torey Deshazier, Rony Bautista |

| YEAR | Age | Level | IP | W | L | ERA | FIP | K/9 | BB/9 | K% | BB% | HR/9 | LOB% |
|---|---|---|---|---|---|---|---|---|---|---|---|---|---|
| 2013 | 19 | R | 16.0 | 1 | 0 | 9.00 | 3.76 | 11.25 | 5.63 | 24.4% | 12.2% | 0.00 | 45.7% |
| 2014 | 20 | R | 45.0 | 5 | 0 | 3.20 | 3.36 | 12.40 | 4.80 | 31.2% | 12.1% | 0.20 | 60.8% |
| 2015 | 21 | A | 116.3 | 7 | 6 | 4.02 | 3.76 | 9.28 | 2.86 | 25.4% | 7.8% | 0.93 | 66.6% |

**Background:** Likely one of the two more underrated arms that you've never heard of developing in the lower levels of the Tribe's system (See #23 for the other), the front office unearthed this budding little gem in the ninth round out of the College of Southern Nevada in 2013. Originally drafted by the Cubs as a prep outfield bat in 2012, the Indians have slowly been developing the promising southpaw, having him debut in the Arizona Summer League, bouncing him back down to the rookie league in 2014, and finally promoting him to full season ball last year. In 27 appearances with Lake County (20 starts), the 6-foot lefty averaged more than a punch out per inning while issuing a free pass to less than 8% of the hitters he faced.

**Projection:** Not counting his foray into pitching as a prepster, Pannone's totaled just 231 innings since entering college – or an average of 77 each year. The front office finally started to ease the reins a bit last season, having him nearly triple his previous innings total, and the results were downright impressive: his strikeout percentage, 25.4%, and strikeout-to-walk percentage, 17.6%, ranked third and fourth among all qualified Midwest League hurlers.

Pannone's taken steps forward in each of his three seasons in the Indians organization, improving his control from below-average to slightly above-average. He still has quite a ways to go, but if everything breaks right he could niche out a nice little career as a backend starter with the big league club. Plus, he hasn't been a fulltime pitcher for a long time, so he could be one of the breakout players in 2016.

**Ceiling:** 1.0- to 1.5-win player
**Risk:** Moderate to High
**MLB ETA:** 2018

## 19. Erik Gonzalez, SS

**MiLB Rank: N/A**
**Position Rank: N/A**

| Born: 08/31/91 | Age: 24 | Bats: R | **Top CALs:** Yadiel Rivera, Estarlin De Los Santos, |
|---|---|---|---|
| Height: 6-3 | Weight: 195 | Throws: R | Trevor Plouffe, Juan Perez, Matt Reynolds |

| Season | Age | LVL | PA | 2B | 3B | HR | AVG | OBP | SLG | ISO | BB% | K% | wRC+ |
|---|---|---|---|---|---|---|---|---|---|---|---|---|---|
| 2013 | 21 | A | 383 | 23 | 7 | 9 | 0.259 | 0.307 | 0.439 | 0.180 | 6.3% | 18.5% | 108 |
| 2013 | 21 | A+ | 163 | 9 | 5 | 0 | 0.242 | 0.259 | 0.366 | 0.124 | 3.1% | 23.3% | 66 |
| 2014 | 22 | A+ | 336 | 14 | 7 | 3 | 0.289 | 0.336 | 0.409 | 0.120 | 6.8% | 19.3% | 109 |
| 2014 | 22 | AA | 136 | 6 | 3 | 1 | 0.357 | 0.390 | 0.473 | 0.116 | 5.1% | 16.9% | 141 |
| 2015 | 23 | AA | 327 | 18 | 4 | 6 | 0.280 | 0.304 | 0.421 | 0.141 | 3.4% | 17.1% | 106 |
| 2015 | 23 | AAA | 261 | 6 | 3 | 3 | 0.223 | 0.277 | 0.311 | 0.088 | 5.7% | 18.0% | 70 |

**Background:** *The* helium guy in the club's farm system following his breakout 2014 campaign, Gonzalez batted a steady .289/.336/.409 in the Carolina League but went nuclear upon a promotion to Class AA, slugging like he was the second coming of Alex Rodriguez. In 31 games with Akron, the lanky shortstop batted a scorching .357/.390/.473 with six doubles, three triples, one homerun, and six stolen bases. And, of course, everyone went (mildly) wild. For his encore, however, Gonzalez followed up that red hot 30-game stint with a more Gonzalez-like showing in 2015: he batted .280/.304/.421 in 72 games with Akron and looked absolutely overmatched in 65 contests with Columbus, hitting .223/.277/.311. He would finish the year with a combined .255/.292/.373 triple-slash line.

**Projection:** I was completely underwhelmed by Gonzalez's production two years ago, so much so, in fact, that I didn't even bother listing him among the club's top 20 prospects. Under the *Bird Doggin' Section* I wrote:

> *"One of the system's biggest breakout prospects in 2014. Gonzalez batted a combined .308/.352/.428 between the Carolina and Eastern Leagues, which has vaulted him most prospect lists. Don't buy it. His work in 336 PA in High Class A: 109 wRC+. His work in the [Eastern League] in 136 PA: 141 wRC+."*

Once Gonzalez's BABIP normalized this season his overall production drooped back down towards the league average in Class AA. Gonzalez is a nice prospect, but there's no true standout tool. He doesn't walk, won't hit for a ton of pop, has OK speed, and won't ever be mistaken for the next Ozzie Smith. It all sums up to a nice, but replaceable, backup infielder at the big league level. He'll help at times, a little here, some more there, but he'll end up getting exposed in long stints.

**Ceiling:** 1.0-win player
**Risk:** Moderate
**MLB ETA:** 2016

## 20. Mike Papi, 1B/LF/RF

**MiLB Rank: N/A**
**Position Rank: N/A**

| Born: 09/19/92 | Age: 23 | Bats: L | **Top CALs:** Evan Chambers, Ryan Bottger, |
|---|---|---|---|
| Height: 6-2 | Weight: 190 | Throws: R | Gilbert Gomez, Juan Silva, Derrick Loveless |

| Season | Age | LVL | PA | 2B | 3B | HR | AVG | OBP | SLG | ISO | BB% | K% | wRC+ |
|---|---|---|---|---|---|---|---|---|---|---|---|---|---|
| 2014 | 21 | A | 165 | 4 | 0 | 3 | 0.178 | 0.305 | 0.274 | 0.096 | 15.8% | 19.4% | 73 |
| 2015 | 22 | A+ | 505 | 34 | 2 | 4 | 0.236 | 0.362 | 0.356 | 0.120 | 16.0% | 23.4% | 117 |

**Background:** My absolute favorite bat entering the 2014 draft, I predicted some pretty hefty things in the future for Big Papi. And...that's quickly gone to hell. The former University of Virginia stud looked like a budding sabermetric superstar prior to being grabbed in the supplemental first round two years ago, offering up solid-average power, the ability to play first base or a corner outfield position, and one of the finest damn eyes this side of whatever river you can think of. I even likened him to the Tribe's – or ex-Tribe member – Nick Swisher. Then Mike Papi entered pro ball with a wet noodle. The Indians, agreeing (more or less) with my assessment that Papi was a potential quick-moving college stick, almost immediately bounced him up to Lake County, where he promptly hit – a term used loosely here – .178/.305/.274. Despite the lack of offensive firepower, the club bounced him up a level to begin the 2015 and...he still didn't hit. Sort of.

Over the season's first two months Papi batted – again, a term used in the most liberal sense – .175/.326/.234 with just nine extra-base hits, all doubles, in 190 trips to the plate. But something seemed to click for Papi in June, and the former apple of my sabermetric eye mashed – literally. He hit .343/.477/.486 with seven doubles and one homerun in his next 90 plate appearances. He tailed off for a bit, hitting .250/.333/.402 in July and completely petered out in August (.218/.340/.346) before picking up a little bit of steam in the first week of September. Overall, he finished the year with .236/.362/.356 triple-slash line, slugging 34 doubles, a pair of triples, and four homeruns in 500+ plate appearances.

**Projection:** Now here's where it gets a bit...interesting. Despite the clearly disappointing offensive punch he showed last season, Papi's overall production, per *Weighted Runs Created Plus*, was 17% better than average, the 11th best mark in the Carolina League. A lot – like the overwhelming majority – of that can be attributed to his still elite eye at the plate; he walked in 16.0% of his plate appearances last season. Another positive note: he finished third in the league with 34 doubles.

I still haven't given up hope for a massive turnaround for Papi yet – at least in terms of what I originally forecasted – but it's getting very close to the time where I jump off the bandwagon. The 2016 season will likely be a make-it-or-break-it type of year.

**Ceiling:** 1.0- to 1.5-win player
**Risk:** High
**MLB ETA:** 2017

# 21. Luigi Rodriguez, OF

**MiLB Rank: N/A**
**Position Rank: N/A**

| Born: 11/13/92 | Age: 23 | Bats: L | **Top CALs:** Edgardo Baez, Zoilo Almonte, |
|---|---|---|---|
| Height: 5-11 | Weight: 160 | Throws: R | Justin Justice, Angel Morales, Rafael Fernandez |

| Season | Age | LVL | PA | 2B | 3B | HR | AVG | OBP | SLG | ISO | BB% | K% | wRC+ |
|---|---|---|---|---|---|---|---|---|---|---|---|---|---|
| 2013 | 20 | A+ | 134 | 11 | 1 | 0 | 0.283 | 0.383 | 0.398 | 0.115 | 13.4% | 26.9% | 123 |
| 2014 | 21 | A+ | 393 | 13 | 4 | 6 | 0.250 | 0.347 | 0.366 | 0.116 | 12.7% | 22.4% | 106 |
| 2015 | 22 | A+ | 399 | 22 | 8 | 12 | 0.293 | 0.335 | 0.492 | 0.199 | 6.0% | 20.6% | 139 |

**Background:** The scrappy Dominican-born Rodriguez can do everything – he began his career as second baseman but later plied his trade as a center/left fielder; he can swipe some bags, take a walk, and hit a long ball or two. Unfortunately, Rodriguez can also take PEDs. The switch-hitting minor leaguer got popped with an 80-game suspension after testing positive for the drug Stanozolol, an anabolic steroid. Rodriguez did manage to get into 99 games before the mid-August suspension, hitting .293/.335/.492 with 12 homeruns and 24 stolen bases in the Carolina League. His overall production, per *Weighted Runs Created Plus*, topped the league average mark by 39%.

**Projection:** Look, as much as I'd like to downplay the PED suspension the truth is I don't know how this will impact his production – and eventual prospect status – moving forward. There's a lot of things we, as an industry, don't fully understand when it comes to improved performance. But to give Rodriguez the benefit of the doubt, he *has* performed like this in previous years. When he's at his best, he shows an above-average eye at the plate, double-digit homerun pop, and speed.

**Ceiling:** 1.0- to 1.5-win player
**Risk:** High
**MLB ETA:** 2017

# 22. Mitch Brown, RHP

**MiLB Rank: N/A**
**Position Rank: N/A**

| Born: 04/13/94 | Age: 22 | Bats: R | **Top CALs:** Evan Rutckyj, Shawn Morimando, |
|---|---|---|---|
| Height: 6-1 | Weight: 195 | Throws: R | Jose Ramirez, Tyler Green, Paul Demny |

| YEAR | Age | Level | IP | W | L | ERA | FIP | K/9 | BB/9 | K% | BB% | HR/9 | LOB% |
|---|---|---|---|---|---|---|---|---|---|---|---|---|---|
| 2013 | 19 | R | 52.0 | 2 | 4 | 5.37 | 4.80 | 8.31 | 5.02 | 20.0% | 12.1% | 0.35 | 68.0% |
| 2013 | 19 | A | 15.7 | 1 | 1 | 11.49 | 7.23 | 10.34 | 6.32 | 22.5% | 13.8% | 2.30 | 49.3% |
| 2014 | 20 | A | 138.7 | 8 | 8 | 3.31 | 3.64 | 8.24 | 3.57 | 22.2% | 9.6% | 0.39 | 69.8% |
| 2015 | 21 | A+ | 141.7 | 9 | 12 | 5.15 | 4.89 | 6.92 | 4.89 | 17.4% | 12.3% | 0.95 | 65.4% |

**Background:** If the enigmatic right-hander's career could be likened to a roller coaster at Sandusky's Cedar Point, then we're staring at a car stuck at the bottom of the coaster's biggest hill. Brown, the club's second round pick in 2012, looked like he finally turned the corner last season after a troublesome 2013 campaign, one in which he was demoted back down to rookie ball as struggling mightily with Lake County. That, however, proved to be a bit unfounded. The then-21-year-old Minnesota-born hurler finished last season the same way he started it – on a sour note. He threw 141.2 innings; posted a sickly 4.89 FIP, punched out 109, and walked a staggering 77. And when he did find the plate – which, let's be honest, wasn't all that often – he was averaging nearly a dinger every nine innings.

**Projection:** With that being said, I am still quite fond of the once-promising right-hander. When he's right, Brown will average about a strikeout per inning with average-ish control – everything you'd expect out of early 20s hurler. But when he's wrong, man, there's not a whole lot to like. At some point in the coming years he might take the road most traveled and wind up in the bullpen. But let's wait-and-see what happens after a repeat in the Carolina League.

**Ceiling:** 1.0-win player
**Risk:** Moderate to High
**MLB ETA:** 2018

## 23. Yoiber Marquina, RHP

**MiLB Rank:** N/A
**Position Rank:** N/A

| Born: 02/03/96 | Age: 20 | Bats: R | **Top CALs:** Fabian Cota, Will White, |
|---|---|---|---|
| Height: 5-10 | Weight: 190 | Throws: R | Eddie Ahorrio, Connor Bennett, Geuris Grullon |

| YEAR | Age | Level | IP | W | L | ERA | FIP | K/9 | BB/9 | K% | BB% | HR/9 | LOB% |
|---|---|---|---|---|---|---|---|---|---|---|---|---|---|
| 2014 | 18 | R | 21.0 | 3 | 1 | 2.57 | 3.13 | 12.43 | 5.14 | 29.9% | 12.4% | 0.00 | 59.4% |
| 2015 | 19 | A- | 23.7 | 2 | 2 | 2.28 | 4.32 | 8.75 | 4.56 | 21.9% | 11.4% | 0.76 | 67.4% |

**Background:** Back in the summer of 2012 the Indians inked a couple high-profile international catchers – one being Francisco Mejia, the club's seventh best prospect, and the other Marquina, who no longer dons the tools of ignorance. Known more for his defensive ability – particularly his cannon behind the plate – than his offensive firepower, it didn't take long for the Venezuelan-born Marquina to convince the organization that his future was on the mound. After batting a putrid .133/.278/.133 in 54 plate appearances in the Dominican Summer League in 2013 – Yes, that's right, he didn't hit a single extra-base knock – Marquina made the conversion to the mound and the results have been fairly promising, especially for a non-pitcher. The 5-foot-10, 190-pound right-hander fanned 29 in 21.0 innings in the Arizona Summer League in 2014 and followed that up by whiffing 23 in 23.2 innings in the New York-Penn League last season. The control is… Well, have I mentioned he owns one of the system's best fastballs?

**Projection**: Pure power arsenal with late-inning, backend dominant potential. If he can start honing his control a bit. Marquina's walked more than 11.5% of the batters he's faced in his career. He has the ability to throw the damn ball through the side of a barn, but he's going to have to find it first.

**Ceiling:** 1.0- to 1.5-win player
**Risk:** High to Extremely High
**MLB ETA:** 2018/2019

## 24. Eric Haase, C

**MiLB Rank:** N/A
**Position Rank:** N/A

| Born: 12/18/92 | Age: 23 | Bats: R | **Top CALs:** Kellin Deglan, William Swanner, |
|---|---|---|---|
| Height: 5-10 | Weight: 180 | Throws: R | Jorge Alfaro, Daniel Rams, Gary Sanchez |

| Season | Age | LVL | PA | 2B | 3B | HR | AVG | OBP | SLG | ISO | BB% | K% | wRC+ |
|---|---|---|---|---|---|---|---|---|---|---|---|---|---|
| 2013 | 20 | A | 420 | 23 | 3 | 14 | 0.250 | 0.322 | 0.439 | 0.189 | 9.5% | 27.9% | 113 |
| 2014 | 21 | A | 328 | 16 | 4 | 16 | 0.270 | 0.338 | 0.514 | 0.243 | 8.5% | 25.6% | 140 |
| 2015 | 22 | A+ | 370 | 26 | 7 | 9 | 0.247 | 0.341 | 0.456 | 0.209 | 9.7% | 30.8% | 133 |

**Background:** The Robin to Sabermetric's Batman; Haase, a seventh round pick all the way back in 2011, has continued his slow, methodical trek through the belly of the minor leagues. After hitting a sturdy .250/.322/.439 as a 20-year-old in the Midwest League – good enough for a 113 wRC+ – Haase found himself back in Low Class A for the majority of the 2014 season, improving his triple-slash line to an impressive .270/.338/.514 – enough to convince the front office that he was ready for the next step: the Carolina League.

He wasn't.

The 5-foot-10 backstop flailed away at the more advanced pitching, hitting a paltry .185/.243/.292 in 70 plate appearances. Last season, however, Haase found himself back with Lynchburg and the results were much improved: he slugged .247/.341/.456 and led fellow catchers in homeruns and finished second among the position with 26 doubles.

**Projection**: Haase draws some fairly impressive comparables as CAL links him to the Phillies' prized backstop, Jorge Alfaro, and the Yankees' forever backstop of the future Gary Sanchez. Haase packs a wallop, especially for a position as offensive deficient as catcher and he'll walk a bit as well, but the hit tool and contact rates are questionable at best. He could easily be one of these late blooming power-backstops that blossoms five years down the round. Or he could just as easily flame out in the next two or three years. The power, though, will garner him more than a few looks.

**Ceiling:** 1.0-win player
**Risk:** High
**MLB ETA:** 2018

## 25. Sean Brady, LHP

MiLB Rank: N/A
Position Rank: N/A

| Born: 06/09/94 | Age: 22 | Bats: L | Top CALs: Charles Haslup, Bryan Salsbury, |
|---|---|---|---|
| Height: 6-0 | Weight: 175 | Throws: L | Nick Gardewine, Patrick Arnold, Yeiper Castillo |

| YEAR | Age | Level | IP | W | L | ERA | FIP | K/9 | BB/9 | K% | BB% | HR/9 | LOB% |
|---|---|---|---|---|---|---|---|---|---|---|---|---|---|
| 2013 | 19 | R | 32.0 | 0 | 1 | 1.97 | 3.69 | 8.44 | 1.69 | 23.6% | 4.7% | 0.56 | 71.9% |
| 2014 | 20 | A- | 71.0 | 2 | 4 | 2.79 | 3.79 | 5.58 | 3.42 | 14.5% | 8.9% | 0.25 | 73.3% |
| 2014 | 20 | A | 2.7 | 0 | 1 | 13.50 | 13.99 | 6.75 | 6.75 | 12.5% | 12.5% | 6.75 | 38.5% |
| 2015 | 21 | A | 146.3 | 7 | 12 | 3.81 | 3.75 | 7.26 | 1.78 | 19.4% | 4.8% | 0.92 | 65.8% |

**Background:** After slowly breaking in the fifth round prep arm the previous two seasons, the Indians finally pushed Brady up to Class A for a full season in 2015. And the young left-hander more or less responded as expected: he missed a handful of bats, did a phenomenal job limiting free passes, and surrendered a few dingers.

**Projection**: If Morimando falls into the House/McFarland/Lewis category, then Brady's like one of the hurlers' less talented brethren. He won't blow his fastball past a whole lot of guys, but he has a pretty decent idea on how to attack the zone. The homerun rate last season was a bit wonky, so expect that to creep back toward the 0.70 HR/9 mark next season. Fringe big league starter with some LOOGY upside.

**Ceiling:** 0.5- to 1.0-win player
**Risk:** Moderate
**MLB ETA:** 2018

### Barely Missed:

- **Shawn Armstrong, RHP** – Missed bats with the best of them in the International League last season, Armstrong, who averaged 14.5 punch outs per nine innings with Columbus, earned a brief call-up down the stretch. The former 18th round pick flashed a mid-90s fastball, a hard upper 80s cutter, and a curveball. Armstrong's never really had any semblance of control – he's averaged 4.5 BB/9 throughout his minor league career – so that's likely going to be the difference between a shutdown setup man and a serviceable, though sometimes dominant, middle reliever.

- **J.P. Feyereisen, RHP** – A personal favorite of my future father-in-law's, Feyereisen is just the latest example of the Tribe's uncanny ability to unearth late-round power-armed relief prospects a la Vinnie Pestano, Cody Allen, and Shawn Armstrong, to name a few. Feyereisen, a 16th round pick two years ago, dominated short-season ball during his debut (17.0 IP, 24 K, and 1 BB), breezed through the Midwest League at the start of last year (16.2 IP, 25 K, and 6 BB), and continued to handle the Carolina League competition with ease (31.0 IP, 31 K, 10 BB). Because of the unpredictability of major league bullpens Feyereisen has positioned himself nicely to be among the first wave of reinforcements when things go awry.

## *Bird Doggin' It – Additional Prospects to Keep an Eye in 2016*

| Player | Age | POS | Notes |
|---|---|---|---|
| Greg Allen | 23 | OF | Prior to the draft two years ago I wrote, "Allen has one true standout tool, his speed, and a couple average-ish skills (bat and plate discipline), but the complete lack of power will push into a backup role in the professional levels. He's only 21-years-old, but in terms of a baseball ceiling, Allen's already near his peak." He spent last year hitting .273/.386/.382 in Class A. He's a fourth/fifth outfielder at best. |
| Claudio Bautista | 22 | 2B | Batted .300/.349/.466 as a 21-year-old in the Midwest League. The problem? He made his first appearance with the Captains as a 19-year-old. And he promptly tanked in High Class A (.197/.260/.287). |
| Justin Brantley | 25 | RHP | The cousin of Tribe All-Star left fielder Michael Brantley, Justin is coming off of two solid back-to-back seasons where he's averaged 9.1 punch outs and 2.8 walks per nine innings between the Midwest and Carolina Leagues. |
| Ivan Castillo | 21 | SS | Switch-hitting shortstop posted a respectable 90 wRC+ as a 20-year-old in High Class A. He'll offer up 20+ stolen base potential, but his absolute lack of power limits his ceiling to a borderline backup infielder. |
| Willi Castro | 19 | 2B/SS | Another switch-hitting middle infielder with speed and a decent hit tool. But similar to Ivan Castillo, Castro's lack of pop severely limits his overall ceiling. |
| Yu-Cheng Chang | 20 | SS | One of the most likely players that missed this year's top 25 to make a significant impact next season. Chang slugged 29 extra-base hits in 105 games as a 19-year-old in the Midwest League. Maybe another Ronny Rodriguez... Not sure if that's good or bad. Proab |
| Yandy Diaz | 24 | 3B | Cuban-born third baseman owns a quasi-impressive career minor league triple-slash line: .301/.401/.389. Plus patience, above-average hit tool, and little pop. |
| Luke Eubank | 22 | RHP | Fifteenth round pick out of Oxnard College in 2014. Eubank finished off 26 games for the Captains last season, averaging 9.4 strikeouts and just 2.0 free passes per nine innings. |
| Trey Haley | 26 | RHP | The late Yogi Berra would likely describe the former second round pick as 50% talented, 60% enigmatic. |
| Caleb Hamrick | 22 | RHP | Made the conversion to full-time reliever last season and, unsurprisingly, saw a huge spike in strikeouts, jumping from 5.7 K/9 to 9.7 K/9. |
| Cameron Hill | 22 | RHP | Ridiculously dominant with the Captains last season. Hill posted a 70-to-20 strikeout-to-walk ratio in 59.0 innings. |
| Ben Heller | 23 | RHP | In last year's *Bird Doggin' It* section I wrote, "[Heller] could follow in the footsteps of Vinnie Pestano and Cody, two late-round picks who developed into dominant relievers." Well, after blowing away the Carolina League and succeeding in a brief call-up to Akron, Heller is one step closer to fulfilling that promise. |
| Sam Hentges | 19 | RHP | Fourth round pick two years ago manhandled the Arizona Summer League before flopping in two starts with Mahoning Valley. |
| Jeffrey Johnson | 26 | RHP | Back after missing all of 2014 courtesy of Tommy John surgery, Johnson posted a 1.05 ERA and 2.20 FIP while averaging 9.82 K/9 and 3.33 BB/9. Future big league middle relief arm. Maybe. |
| Dace Kime | 24 | RHP | Likely nearing the end of the Dace-Kime-is-a-starter-experiment. Former third round pick out of Louisville could be a quick moving relief arm. |
| Tyler Krieger | 22 | SS | Fourth round pick out of Clemson tore up the ACC for three seasons, hitting a combined .312/.404/.394. Krieger's always displayed a strong eye, but a torn labrum cost his draft stock to tumble. Could be a very nice buy low gamble. |
| Nick Maronde | 25 | RHP | Low 90s fastball with the upside as a decent swing-man out of the big league bullpen. |
| Josh Martin | 26 | RHP | Big 6-foot-5 right-hander posted an 80-to-19 strikeout-to-walk ratio with Akron last season. |
| Mark Mathias | 21 | 2B | Taken a round earlier than Krieger, Mathias is another high round low risk/moderate reward gamble the Indians made in the 2015 draft. Despite shoulder woes, he bounced back to hit .356/.424/.436 for Cal Poly. Mathias hit .282/.389/.408 in the New York-Penn League. |
| Gabriel Mejia | 20 | CF | Switch-hitting center fielder mashed through the Arizona Summer League (.357/.438/.417) before getting a call-up to Mahoning Valley, where his success died down a bit (.304/.316/.321). Plus speed. |

## *Bird Doggin' It – Additional Prospects to Keep an Eye in 2016*

| Player | Age | POS | Notes |
|---|---|---|---|
| Ryan Merritt | 24 | LHP | Finesse lefty walked just a smidge over 3% of the batters he faced between Akron and Columbus last season. The downside: he fanned just 15%. |
| Dorssys Paulino | 21 | LF | Set the prospect world ablaze in 2012 when he slugged .333/.380/.558 as a 17-year-old in the Arizona Summer League. Since then he's moved to left field and struggled to hit in three trips through the Midwest League. He did look very promising in 43 games with Lynchburg when he batted .305/.371/.526. |
| Michael Peoples | 24 | RHP | Repeated the Carolina League with far less success than two years ago. He could be headed for a bullpen role by the end of the 2016. |
| Anderson Polanco | 23 | LHP | A bit old for the Midwest League with some control issues. Left arms will travel, though. |
| Anthony Santander | 21 | LF/RF | Posted the second highest wRC+ mark of his career last season (129). Of course, that comes with a rather large caveat: it was his third stop in the Midwest League. |
| Casey Shane | 20 | RHP | Posted some decent FIPs with Mahoning Valley (3.43) and Lake County (3.78). Doesn't miss enough bats, though the control could be something. |
| David Speer | 23 | LHP | Ivy League lefty passed the full-season test with ease (1.73 ERA, 8.5 K/9, and 2.0 BB/9). He might be a useful arm in a couple years. |
| Giovanni Soto | 25 | LHP | The booty brought from Detroit in exchange for Jhonny Peralta a few years back. Soto once looked like a promising starter, but has settled in nicely as a relief option. Bread-and-butter pitch: the cutter. |
| Ronny Rodriguez | 24 | 1B/2B | Rodriguez had his finest season to date in 2015, posting a career high 129 wRC+ in Akron. Again, it was his third stop through. |
| Emmanuel Tapia | 20 | 1B/RF | Hulking youngster batted .286/.350/.413 with 10 doubles and a pair of homeruns in 33 games in the NYPL last season. He's ready for full season ball. Tapia could be the next Jesus Aguilar. |
| Gregori Vasquez | 18 | RHP | Dominated the DSL as a 17-year-old, averaging nearly 11 punch outs while walking fewer than two batters per nine innings. |
| Luke Wakamatsu | 19 | SS | Son of big league coach Don Wakamatsu, Luke signed for top round money and looked solid in the Arizona Summer League (.267/.339/.400). |
| LeVon Washington | 24 | LF/RF | Oh, how the mighty have fallen. I've officially jumped off Washington's bandwagon after another season in which he failed to top 80 games. Ugh… |
| Tony Wolters | 24 | C | Scrappy infielder-turned-backstop looked like a potential big leaguer after he batted .260/.320/.404 as a 20-year-old in High Class A. He's never really recovered his stroke since moving behind the plate. He could be a late bloomer – hopefully. |

# Colorado Rockies

**State of the Farm System:** In their never ending quest to determine the formula for pitching success in Coor's Field, Colorado continues to cast a wide net for any – and every type – of young arm available , a move that's reminiscent of people hoarding food and water for an impending natural disaster.

After failing with every other arm – sans, of course, a brief run of success by Ubaldo Jimenez – the front office is ready to turn loose – with fingers crossed, prayers spoken – a brand new collection of young hurlers led by former #3 overall pick Jon Gray who made a brief – and successful – 40.2-inning stint in the big leagues. The former Oklahoma stud suffered through some bad luck but finished his big league debut with an impressive 40-to-14 strikeout-to-walk ratio en route to tallying a 3.63 FIP.

Outside of Gray, the system is sporting a pair of hard-throwing right-handers Jeff Hoffman, a recent Tommy John survivor, and Miguel Castro, both of whom were acquired as the centerpieces of the Troy Tulowitzki mega-deal with Toronto near the trade deadline last season. Hoffman hardly missed a beat as he was aggressively pushed through High Class A and Class AA in an effort to make up for lost time. And he handled it with relative ease, posting an aggregate 3.03 ERA in 104.0 innings. Castro, who possesses a mid- to upper-90s heater, made the move to fulltime relief for the first time last season and subsequently jumped from High Class A into Class AAA before eventually earning a big league call-up.

Former second round pick Ryan Castellani is a nice middle tier hurler who outpitched his mediocre ERA by more than a full run as a 19-year-old surviving the Asheville bandbox. And Kyle Freeland, the club's first round pick two years ago, lasted only a couple dozen innings before succumbing to another injury.

And just with life, death, and taxes, the Rockies sure as hell have more than a couple promising bats developing down on the farm as well. Brendan Rodgers, last year's #3 overall pick, is the long-term heir apparent to Troy Tulowitzki's old position. The teenage shortstop slugged a solid .273/.340/.420 with Grand Junction in the advanced rookie league. Second baseman Forrest Wall, the rare high school second baseman, offers another long-term solution to a key infield spot.

A couple words of warning: don't buy into the hype surrounding Raimel Tapia.

**Review of the 2015 Draft:** Following the club's selection of Rodgers with the third overall pick, Colorado grabbed a pair of high-ceiling prepsters with their other two first round picks: hard-throwing right-hander Mike Nikorak, who couldn't find the strike zone during his debut, and Tyler Nevin, son of former big leaguer Phil Nevin.

Their second and third round picks, right-handers Peter Lambert and Javier Medina, completed the perfect five-for-five on the high school front. Former Texas Longhorn hurler Parker French should breeze through the lower levels before stalling in the mid levels.

| Rank | Name | POS |
|---|---|---|
| 1 | Ryan McMahon | 3B |
| 2 | Jon Gray | RHP |
| 3 | Brendan Rodgers | SS |
| 4 | Jeff Hoffman | RHP |
| 5 | David Dahl | CF |
| 6 | Forrest Wall | 2B |
| 7 | Miguel Castro | RHP |
| 8 | Ryan Castellani | RHP |
| 9 | Jordan Patterson | 1B/LF/RF |
| 10 | Kyle Freeland | LHP |
| 11 | Kevin Padlo | 3B |
| 12 | Raimel Tapia | OF |
| 13 | Antonio Senzatela | RHP |
| 14 | Trevor Story | IF |
| 15 | Tyler Nevin | 3B |
| 16 | Jairo Diaz | RHP |
| 17 | Cristhian Adames | IF |
| 18 | Dom Nunez | C |
| 19 | Mike Nikorak | RHP |
| 20 | Carlos Estevez | RHP |
| 21 | Tommy Murphy | C |
| 22 | Sam Moll | LHP |
| 23 | Peter Lambert | RHP |
| 24 | Alex Balog | RHP |
| 25 | Rosell Herrera | 3B/SS/OF |

## 1. Ryan McMahon, 3B

**MiLB Rank: #17**
**Position Rank: #2**

| Born: 12/14/94 | Age: 21 | Bats: L | **Top CALs:** Josh Bell, Domingo Santana, |
|---|---|---|---|
| Height: 6-2 | Weight: 185 | Throws: R | Johermyn Chavez, Matt Davidson, Clint Frazier |

| Season | Age | LVL | PA | 2B | 3B | HR | AVG | OBP | SLG | ISO | BB% | K% | wRC+ |
|---|---|---|---|---|---|---|---|---|---|---|---|---|---|
| 2013 | 18 | R | 251 | 18 | 3 | 11 | 0.321 | 0.402 | 0.583 | 0.261 | 11.2% | 23.5% | 147 |
| 2014 | 19 | A | 552 | 46 | 3 | 18 | 0.282 | 0.358 | 0.502 | 0.220 | 9.8% | 25.9% | 137 |
| 2015 | 20 | A+ | 556 | 43 | 6 | 18 | 0.300 | 0.372 | 0.520 | 0.220 | 8.8% | 27.5% | 141 |

**Background:** Hailing from Mater Dei High School in Santa Ana, California – home to, among others, Sergio Santos, Matt Treanor, and recently retired minor league homerun leader Mike Hessman – McMahon did something that Trevor Story, Rosell Herrera, and other Colorado top prospects have failed to do over the past years: the lefty-swinging third baseman didn't fall prey to Asheville's bandbox and actually improved as he moved up to Modesto last season. After robustly slugging .282/.358/.502 – including a .256/.349/.496 triple-slash line on the road – with the Tourists, McMahon batted .300/.372/.572 with a whopping 43 doubles and six triples while tying a career-high with 18 dingers. His overall production, according to *Weighted Runs Created Plus*, topped the league average mark by 41% last season, the fourth best showing in the California League in 2015.

**Projection**: Now for some bad news of sorts – his K-rate two years ago, 25.9%, was already bordering on red flag territory, but it ticked up a bit as he faced the more advanced pitchers (27.5%). The power is an above-average skill as it stands now, but it has a chance to move into plus-territory given his infield position – especially considering all those doubles he's bit over the past two seasons. McMahon handles lefties and righties equally well and should be in Colorado by the end of 2017. With Nolan Arenado fully entrenched at the hot corner it will be interesting to see where McMahon winds up. Second base? Corner outfield? First base?

**Ceiling: 3**.5- to 4.0-win player
**Risk:** Moderate
**MLB ETA:** 2017

## 2. Jon Gray, RHP

**MiLB Rank: #30**
**Position Rank: #13**

| Born: 11/05/91 | Age: 24 | Bats: R | **Top CALs:** Andre Rienzo, Garrett Olson, |
|---|---|---|---|
| Height: 6-4 | Weight: 235 | Throws: R | Jeff Manship, David Rollins, Nick Tropeano |

| YEAR | Age | Level | IP | W | L | ERA | FIP | K/9 | BB/9 | K% | BB% | HR/9 | LOB% |
|---|---|---|---|---|---|---|---|---|---|---|---|---|---|
| 2013 | 21 | R | 13.3 | 0 | 0 | 4.05 | 2.51 | 10.13 | 1.35 | 25.9% | 3.5% | 0.00 | 55.6% |
| 2013 | 21 | A+ | 24.0 | 4 | 0 | 0.75 | 1.52 | 13.50 | 2.25 | 41.9% | 7.0% | 0.00 | 81.3% |
| 2014 | 22 | AA | 124.3 | 10 | 5 | 3.91 | 3.43 | 8.18 | 2.97 | 22.2% | 8.1% | 0.72 | 68.1% |
| 2015 | 23 | AAA | 114.3 | 6 | 6 | 4.33 | 3.88 | 8.66 | 3.23 | 21.7% | 8.1% | 0.71 | 70.0% |

**Background:** Part of one of the more memorable three-headed draft giants in recent memory, the former Oklahoma ace teamed with former Stanford hurler Mark Appel and University of San Diego basher Kris Bryant to create a perceived – and important word here – triumvirate of can't-miss blue chip prospects. Bryant's already established himself as one of the most lethal big league bats. And Gray, a 6-foot-4, 235-pound right-hander, has proven that he's ready to attempt to take on the hitter-friendly confines of Coors Field. After successfully spending the first couple months fine-tuning his game with Albuquerque in the Pacific Coast League – he tossed 114.1 innings while fanning 21.7% and walking just 8.1% of the hitters he faced – Gray got the call-up to Colorado where he would make another nine starts for the Rockies. And the results were…mixed. At best.

The hard-throwing right-hander certainly looked impressive in his second career start against the eventual NL Champs, hurling six innings with five strikeouts, two walks, and one hit. He followed that up with another solid start against the hapless Padres: 5.0 IP, 5 K, and 0 BB. He would also dominate San Diego in early September again as well: 5.0 IP, 6 K, 2 BB.

And now the bad: his second time facing off against the Mets lasted 1.2 innings; he coughed up seven earned runs on eight hits. Arizona and Pittsburgh would also smack him around a bit as well. His finished his big league debut with a 40-to-14 strikeout-to-walk ratio in 40.2 innings of work.

**Projection**: During his underrated debut in Colorado Gray came as advertised: he unleashed a mid-90s heater, a hard-biting slider, and a mid-80s change-up. He also continued to average about a punch out per inning with solid-average control/command. And, unsurprisingly, his homerun rate spiked to a career high 0.89 HR/9 with the Rockies. He has the right pitching makeup to succeed in Colorado: a blistering fastball, limits free passes, and generates an above-average amount of action on the ground. Let's see if he can do what virtually no other pitcher has done on a consistent basis.

**Ceiling:** 3.0- to 3.5-win player
**Risk:** Low to Moderate
**MLB ETA:** N/A

## 3. Brendan Rodgers, SS

MiLB Rank: #31
**Position Rank: #5**

| Born: 08/09/96 | Age: 19 | Bats: R | Top CALs: Edwin Diaz, Rosell Herrera, |
|---|---|---|---|
| Height: 6-0 | Weight: 180 | Throws: R | Luis Reynoso, Leonardo Gil |

| Season | Age | LVL | PA | 2B | 3B | HR | AVG | OBP | SLG | ISO | BB% | K% | wRC+ |
|---|---|---|---|---|---|---|---|---|---|---|---|---|---|
| 2015 | 18 | R | 159 | 8 | 2 | 3 | 0.273 | 0.340 | 0.420 | 0.147 | 9.4% | 23.3% | 95 |

**Background:** Just how historic was Rodgers' selection as the third overall pick in the 2015 draft? Only one other time in history had shortstops gone with the first two picks in the draft: 1982 when the Cubs grabbed Shawon Dunston and the Blue Jays picked Augie Schmidt. But after the Diamondbacks and Astros picked Dansby Swanson and Alex Bregman, the Rockies' choice of Rodgers made the 2015 draft the only time since the first year of the modern draft, 1965, that shortstops went one-two-three. Rodgers, who stands an even 6-foot and 180 pounds, had a solid debut with Grand Junction in the Pioneer League last season, hitting .273/.340/.420 with eight doubles, a pair of triples, and three homeruns with four stolen bases (in seven attempts). His overall production, per *Weighted Runs Created Plus*, was 5% *below* the league average mark.

**Projection**: The sample size is a bit limited, just under 160 plate appearances, but Rodgers showed off an impressive offensive foundation during his debut in the advanced rookie league: solid-average power, a strong eye at the plate, and a little bit of speed. He's ready for full-season ball next season, but a word of warning: Asheville is going inflate his offensive production so dig deeper into the actual numbers.

**Ceiling:** Too Soon to Tell
**Risk:** N/A
**MLB ETA:** N/A

## 4. Jeff Hoffman, RHP

**MiLB Rank: #31**
**Position Rank: N/A**

| Born: 01/08/93 | Age: 23 | Bats: R | Top CALs: Robin Leyer, Kevin Siegrist, |
|---|---|---|---|
| Height: 6-4 | Weight: 185 | Throws: R | Duke Von Schamann, Jeremy Bleich, Aaron Thompson |

| YEAR | Age | Level | IP | W | L | ERA | FIP | K/9 | BB/9 | K% | BB% | HR/9 | LOB% |
|---|---|---|---|---|---|---|---|---|---|---|---|---|---|
| 2015 | 22 | A+ | 56.0 | 3 | 3 | 3.21 | 3.70 | 6.11 | 2.41 | 16.7% | 6.6% | 0.64 | 79.8% |
| 2015 | 22 | AA | 48.0 | 2 | 2 | 2.81 | 3.41 | 6.94 | 2.25 | 19.7% | 6.4% | 0.56 | 74.2% |

**Background:** There's going to be a whole lot of pressure riding on Hoffman's surgically repaired right elbow as the centerpiece of the deal that sent longtime Colorado icon Troy Tulowitzki out of town. Hoffman, who was acquired along with veteran infielder Jose Reyes and a pair of intriguing minor league arms in Miguel Castro and Jesus Tinoco, finally made his way back from Tommy John surgery after missing some of his final season at East Carolina University. Despite not making his big league debut until late May, the Blue Jays seemed determined to make up for lost time: his former organization pushed him straight in the Florida State League. And the 6-foot-4, 185-pound fire-balling right-hander took to it with relative ease, especially if you ignore his first two starts of the year. After the Tampa Yankees and Jupiter Hammerheads smacked him around a bit, Hoffman posted a 31-to-14 strikeout-to-walk ratio in 46.2 innings of work.

Toronto promoted him up to the Eastern League in mid-July, which lasted two starts, before dealing the right-hander away. Colorado pushed Hoffman to their Class AA affiliate, the New Britain Rock Cats, for another nine starts. He would finish his time in Class AA with a 2.81 ERA to go along with 37 strikeouts and 12 walks in 48.0 innings of work. Not bad work for pitcher that missed a tremendous amount of time and virtually leapt into the mid-levels of the minors.

**Projection:** First things first, here's what I wrote prior to the 2013 draft:

> *"He isn't ace-type potential, at least not in the same way as [Carlos] Rodon or TCU's Brandon Finnegan. Instead, Hoffman's more of a good #2-type option that can offer glimpses of the ability to take games over. Think like a lite version of Gerrit Cole – a live-armed starting pitcher capable of chewing innings and averaging 7.8 K/9 with solid average control."*

Hoffman still doesn't profile as a legitimate ace arm – namely because his lack of punch outs will stop him from ascending into that role. But Hoffman, like his future rotation mate Jon Gray, has a skill set that should be suited for surviving – perhaps even succeeding in –Colorado: an above-average fastball, solid control command, especially once he continues to put distance between himself and the surgery, and an enormous amount of groundballs. I was probably a bit overzealous in ranking him as a #2-type arm; I would downgrade that to a #3-type ceiling now with some additional upside.

**Ceiling:** 3.0-win player
**Risk:** Moderate
**MLB ETA:** 2016/2017

## 5. David Dahl, CF

**MiLB Rank: #62**
**Position Rank: N/A**

| Born: 04/01/94 | Age: 22 | Bats: L | Top CALs: Avisail Garcia, Juan Silverio, |
|---|---|---|---|
| Height: 6-2 | Weight: 195 | Throws: R | Dustin Fowler, Tyler Colvin, Yorman Rodriguez |

| Season | Age | LVL | PA | 2B | 3B | HR | AVG | OBP | SLG | ISO | BB% | K% | wRC+ |
|---|---|---|---|---|---|---|---|---|---|---|---|---|---|
| 2014 | 20 | A | 422 | 33 | 6 | 10 | 0.309 | 0.347 | 0.500 | 0.191 | 5.5% | 15.4% | 133 |
| 2014 | 20 | A+ | 125 | 8 | 2 | 4 | 0.267 | 0.296 | 0.467 | 0.200 | 4.0% | 21.6% | 93 |
| 2015 | 21 | A- | 24 | 1 | 0 | 0 | 0.125 | 0.125 | 0.167 | 0.042 | 0.0% | 37.5% | -21 |
| 2015 | 21 | AA | 302 | 16 | 3 | 6 | 0.278 | 0.304 | 0.417 | 0.139 | 3.6% | 23.8% | 106 |

**Background:** The Colorado front office hasn't been shy about aggressively challenging the 2012 first round pick. And last season's push into the Eastern League with just 125 plate appearances in High Class A under his belt is no different. Dahl, a 6-foot-2, 195-pound lefty-swinging center fielder, took some initial lumps – he batted .212/.256/.294 with just four extra-base hits in his first 20 games – but made the right adjustments and slugged .320/.333/.454 over his next 24 games. Unfortunately for Dahl, though, he would once again miss some significant time as he ruptured his spleen in a scary collision with second baseman Juan Ciriaco. Dahl, according to A Yahoo! Sports report, opted to have the spleen removed – a decision that didn't come lightly. According to the report at the time, Dahl will have to take additional precautions in the form of medicine to avoid getting sick. Incredibly, he would make it back onto the field in mid-July and basically pick up where he left off: he batted .292/.318/.481 over the remainder of the season.

**Projection**: Dahl's had some serious hype bubbling about since his explosion in rookie ball during his pro debut – he slugged .379/.423/.625 – and he's continued to handle the club's aggressive promotion well since then. But one thing to highlight is the fact that his offensive toolkit hasn't been able to catch up to his quick-push through the minors. Take for example his power: two years ago Dahl was showcasing above-average power (though some of that was inflated by Asheville) but it was slightly below-average for his duration in Class AA. Meaning: expect it to bounce back in large way in 2016.

Dahl doesn't spend a whole lot of energy working the count as his subpar walk rates would indicate, so that'll eventually limit his ceiling. But center fielders with 20+ homerun pop and the ability to hit .290 who can play the hell out of the position on defense are valuable. In terms of offensive ceiling think Avisail Garcia's 2013 showing: .283/.309/.422.

**Ceiling:** 2.5-win player
**Risk:** Moderate
**MLB ETA:** 2016

## 6. Forrest Wall, 2B

**MiLB Rank: #113**
**Position Rank: #4**

| Born: 11/20/95 | Age: 20 | Bats: L | Top CALs: Erick Mejia, Abraham Almonte, |
|---|---|---|---|
| Height: 6-0 | Weight: 176 | Throws: R | Rayner Contreras, Claudio Bautista, Carlos Aquino |

| Season | Age | LVL | PA | 2B | 3B | HR | AVG | OBP | SLG | ISO | BB% | K% | wRC+ |
|---|---|---|---|---|---|---|---|---|---|---|---|---|---|
| 2014 | 18 | R | 188 | 6 | 6 | 3 | 0.318 | 0.416 | 0.490 | 0.172 | 14.4% | 17.0% | 136 |
| 2015 | 19 | A- | 17 | 0 | 0 | 0 | 0.500 | 0.647 | 0.500 | 0.000 | 35.3% | 11.8% | 234 |
| 2015 | 19 | A | 416 | 16 | 10 | 7 | 0.280 | 0.355 | 0.438 | 0.158 | 9.9% | 17.3% | 125 |

**Background**: The lone second baseman chosen in the opening round two years ago. Wall, who hails from the same high school as Yankees prospect Dante Bichette Jr. (Orangewood Christian High School), had one of the better professional debuts among all incoming prep players that season, hitting .318/.416/.490 with six doubles, six triples, three homeruns, 18 stolen bases, and a promising 136 wRC+ -- enough production to convince the front office that he was ready for the South Atlantic League. And – boy – was he. In a bit of an injury-shortened season, the lefty-swinging second baseman hit a solid .280/.355/.438 with 16 doubles, 10 triples, seven homeruns, and 23 stolen bases in 32 attempts. His overall production, per *Weighted Runs Created Plus*, topped the league average mark by 25% - the second best showing among all teenage prospects in the Sally last season.

**Projection**: One of the key statistics to look at for prospects that spend a lot of time feasting off of Asheville's hitter-friendly confines is the home/road splits. Just look at the splits for a couple other Colorado prospects that blew up with the Tourists:

| Player | Home OPS | Road OPS |
|---|---|---|
| Trevor Story | 0.961 | 0.775 |
| Rosell Herrera | 1.090 | 0.797 |

But Wall, on the other hand, basically replicated his home production while he was on the road last season: 0.823 vs. 0.785. Meaning: his overall skill set is far more reliable, analytically speaking. He has a slightly-better-than-average eye at the plate with matching pop and above-average- to plus-speed. Look for him to post another high wRC+ mark in High Class A in 2016. And it wouldn't be out of the norm to see him finish the year in Class AA.

**Ceiling:** 2.5-win player
**Risk:** Moderate
**MLB ETA:** 2019

## 7. Miguel Castro, RHP

**MiLB Rank: #114**
**Position Rank: N/A**

**Background:** Also included as part of the Troy Tulowitzki-to-Toronto package, Castro, a hard-throwing hurler out of the Dominican Republic, made the big leap from High Class A straight to the big leagues with former teammate Roberto Osuna – except Castro's stint didn't last nearly as long as his former counterpart's. Working exclusively out of Toronto's bullpen at the start of the year, the 6-foot-5, 190-

| Born: 12/24/94 | Age: 21 | Bats: R | Top CALs: Manny Banuelos, Randall Delgado, |
| Height: 6-5 | Weight: 190 | Throws: R | Aaron Sanchez, Phillippe Aumont, Brad Hand |

| YEAR | Age | Level | IP | W | L | ERA | FIP | K/9 | BB/9 | K% | BB% | HR/9 | LOB% |
|------|-----|-------|------|---|---|------|------|-------|------|-------|-------|------|--------|
| 2013 | 18 | R | 53.0 | 5 | 2 | 1.36 | 1.37 | 12.06 | 2.04 | 33.8% | 5.7% | 0.00 | 75.4% |
| 2013 | 18 | R | 2.0 | 0 | 0 | 0.00 | 0.43 | 13.50 | 0.00 | 33.3% | 0.0% | 0.00 | -100.0% |
| 2013 | 18 | R | 15.0 | 1 | 0 | 2.40 | 1.99 | 8.40 | 1.20 | 25.0% | 3.6% | 0.00 | 69.2% |
| 2014 | 19 | A- | 50.3 | 6 | 2 | 2.15 | 3.48 | 9.48 | 3.58 | 26.4% | 10.0% | 0.36 | 81.2% |
| 2014 | 19 | A | 21.7 | 1 | 1 | 3.74 | 3.95 | 8.31 | 2.91 | 24.1% | 8.4% | 0.83 | 59.2% |
| 2014 | 19 | A+ | 8.7 | 1 | 0 | 3.12 | 6.28 | 5.19 | 3.12 | 16.1% | 9.7% | 2.08 | 95.2% |
| 2015 | 20 | A+ | 5.0 | 0 | 0 | 0.00 | 0.97 | 12.60 | 1.80 | 43.8% | 6.3% | 0.00 | 100.0% |
| 2015 | 20 | AAA | 19.7 | 1 | 3 | 4.58 | 5.80 | 9.61 | 5.49 | 21.2% | 12.1% | 1.83 | 72.7% |
| 2015 | 20 | AAA | 13.7 | 2 | 0 | 1.32 | 3.89 | 6.59 | 4.61 | 18.2% | 12.7% | 0.00 | 78.6% |

pound man-child looked like he belonged at the big league level: he posted a 12-to-6 strikeout-to-walk ratio in 12.1 innings. The front office brass, however, sent him to the International League in an effort to stretch him out as a starting pitcher. He looked solid for four outings but struggled in his fifth start with the Bison, so Toronto, in a kneejerk reaction, demoted him all the way down to Dunedin for a couple appearances before shipping him to the Rocky Mountain State. After the trade Colorado wisely pushed him back up to Class AAA and then onto the big leagues as a September call-up.

**Projection:** Adding to the plethora of power arms the organization is suddenly collecting. Castro can uncork a fastball in the mid- to upper-90s with relative ease. He complements that with a low 80s slider and a hard changeup. He struggled with his control somewhat, but his minor league track record – he's averaged just 3.2 walks per nine innings in his career – suggests that it's going to rebound in the coming years. It's still too early to give up on him as a starting pitcher; hopefully the brass comes to the same conclusion.

**Ceiling:** 2.5- to 3.0-win player
**Risk:** High
**MLB ETA:** Debuted in 2015

## 8. Ryan Castellani, RHP

**MiLB Rank: #172**
**Position Rank: N/A**

**Background:** The club's second round selection out of Brophy College Preparatory two years ago, Colorado made the unusual move and pushed the 6-foot-3, 193-pound right-hander up to the Northwest League for his debut and he looked at home – he posted a

| Born: 04/01/96 | Age: 20 | Bats: R | Top CALs: Lino Martinez, Edgar Garcia, |
| Height: 6-3 | Weight: 193 | Throws: R | Brett Devall, Luis Reyes, Zack Littell |

| YEAR | Age | Level | IP | W | L | ERA | FIP | K/9 | BB/9 | K% | BB% | HR/9 | LOB% |
|------|-----|-------|-------|---|---|------|------|------|------|-------|------|------|-------|
| 2014 | 18 | A- | 37.0 | 1 | 2 | 3.65 | 4.23 | 6.08 | 2.19 | 15.9% | 5.7% | 0.49 | 62.0% |
| 2015 | 19 | A | 113.3 | 2 | 7 | 4.45 | 3.27 | 7.46 | 2.30 | 18.7% | 5.8% | 0.40 | 60.0% |

25-to-9 strikeout-to-walk ratio in 37.0 innings of work. The front office continued to challenge the young hurler by pushing him up to the South Atlantic League last season where he was just one of two qualified teenage arms last season (the other being Boston's Dedgar Jimenez). In 113.1 innings with the Tourists, Castellani fanned 18.7% and walked just 5.8% of the batters he faced last season. For his year-plus professional career Castellani has fanned 119 and walked 38 in 150.1 innings.

**Projection:** Impressive Part I: his strikeout-to-walk percentage, 12.9%, tied for the tenth best mark in the Sally last season. Impressive Part II: no qualified hurler under the age of 20 posted a better total in the league last season. Impressive Part III: only one other teenager, Justus Sheffield, posted a better strikeout-to-walk percentage in either Low Class A level. Impressive Part IV: Castellani has the foundation to succeed in Colorado, assuming, of course, he can make his way through the dreaded injury nexus. The big right-hander shows poise beyond his years with an improving strikeout rate; between the beginning of June through the end of August he posted a 73-to-19 strikeout-to-walk ratio in 73 innings. He's a candidate for 2016 Breakout Prospect of the Year.

**Ceiling:** 2.0-win player
**Risk:** Moderate
**MLB ETA:** 2018

## 9. Jordan Patterson, 1B/LF/RF

**MiLB Rank: #193**
**Position Rank: N/A**

| Born: 02/12/92 | Age: 24 | Bats: L | Top CALs: Brandon Barnes, Zoilo, |
|---|---|---|---|
| Height: 6-4 | Weight: 215 | Throws: L | Nick Evans, Sean Ratliff, Michael Hernandez |

| Season | Age | LVL | PA | 2B | 3B | HR | AVG | OBP | SLG | ISO | BB% | K% | wRC+ |
|---|---|---|---|---|---|---|---|---|---|---|---|---|---|
| 2013 | 21 | R | 249 | 12 | 0 | 10 | 0.291 | 0.389 | 0.495 | 0.204 | 7.6% | 14.9% | 128 |
| 2014 | 22 | A | 532 | 27 | 0 | 14 | 0.278 | 0.359 | 0.430 | 0.152 | 8.6% | 22.2% | 121 |
| 2015 | 23 | A+ | 339 | 26 | 12 | 10 | 0.304 | 0.378 | 0.568 | 0.264 | 5.6% | 26.0% | 153 |
| 2015 | 23 | AA | 202 | 19 | 0 | 7 | 0.286 | 0.342 | 0.503 | 0.216 | 5.4% | 20.8% | 143 |
| 2015 | 23 | AA | 202 | 19 | 0 | 7 | 0.286 | 0.342 | 0.503 | 0.216 | 5.4% | 20.8% | 143 |

**Background:** Following in the footsteps – and ready take up the torch – of former Clemson QB turned slugging minor league bat Kyle Parker, Patterson proved that his strong showing with Asheville two years ago was just a harbinger of the things to come, not an aberration. Patterson, a 2013 fourth round pick out of the University of South Alabama, hit .278/.359/.430 with the Tourists in his sophomore campaign. He followed that up with a dominant 77-game run with Modesto last season – he batted .304/.378/.568 with 26 doubles, 12 triples, 10 homeruns, and nine stolen bases – and he continued that torrid pace once he got the phone call to move up to New Britain. In 48 games with the Rock Cats, Patterson slugged .286/.342/.503. He finished the year with an aggregate .297/.364/.543 triple-slash line with a whopping 45 doubles, 12 triples, 17 dingers, and 18 stolen bases.

**Projection:** Incredibly toolsy for a 6-foot-4, 215-pound first baseman/corner outfielder. He consistently squares the ball up as uses his long arms to create solid lift leading to all those extra-base hits. While he benefited from playing half his season in the California League, Patterson's numbers in Class AA help solidify his status as a prospect – particularly after his BABIP dropped from .400 to .336.

**Ceiling:** 2.0- to 2.5-win player
**Risk:** Moderate to High
**MLB ETA:** 2016/2017

## 10. Kyle Freeland, LHP

**MiLB Rank: #209**
**Position Rank: N/A**

| Born: 05/14/93 | Age: 21 | Bats: L | Top CALs: Waner Mateo, Matt Mcswain, |
|---|---|---|---|
| Height: 6-3 | Weight: 170 | Throws: L | Trevor Harden, Kevin Johnson, Chris Lugo |

| YEAR | Age | Level | IP | W | L | ERA | FIP | K/9 | BB/9 | K% | BB% | HR/9 | LOB% |
|---|---|---|---|---|---|---|---|---|---|---|---|---|---|
| 2014 | 21 | R | 17.3 | 1 | 0 | 1.56 | 2.82 | 7.79 | 1.04 | 22.7% | 3.0% | 0.00 | 79.0% |
| 2014 | 21 | A | 21.7 | 2 | 0 | 0.83 | 3.08 | 7.48 | 1.66 | 22.0% | 4.9% | 0.42 | 84.3% |
| 2015 | 22 | R | 7.0 | 0 | 0 | 0.00 | 3.29 | 11.57 | 2.57 | 33.3% | 7.4% | 0.00 | 100.0% |
| 2015 | 22 | A+ | 39.7 | 3 | 2 | 4.76 | 5.06 | 4.31 | 1.82 | 11.2% | 4.7% | 1.13 | 69.4% |

**Background:** As if questions surrounding his – and every other hurlers' – ability to survive pitching in Coors Field weren't enough, Freeland, the eighth overall selection in the 2014 draft, basically lost his sophomore season as he suffered through some serious shoulder fatigue and underwent the knife for a minor procedure to remove bone chips in his left elbow. Not including his seven-inning rehab stint in the Pioneer League, the 6-foot-3, 170-pound southpaw tallied a disappointing 19-to-8 strikeout-to-walk ratio in 39.2 innings of work. And the steep decline in his punch out rate all carried over to the Arizona Fall League as well: through his first six starts he fanned just 13 of the 104 batters he faced, or just over 12%.

**Projection:** Freeland really took advantage of squaring off against the University of Evansville's lackluster competition throughout his three-year run with the school; he fanned 282 hitters in his 284 career innings. But that swing-and-miss ability –one which looked so promising – hasn't carried over into the professional ranks at all, even during his quick jaunt through the Pioneer and South Atlantic Leagues two years ago. Still, though, the control is an above average ability. I originally opined in last year's book that he could be a good #3-type arm, but I'd push him down a bit now.

**Ceiling:** 2.0-win player
**Risk:** Moderate to High
**MLB ETA:** 2018

## 11. German Marquez, RHP

**MiLB Rank: #218**
**Position Rank: N/A**

| Born: 02/22/95 | Age: 21 | Bats: R | Top CALs: Arquimedes Nieto, Zeke Spruill, |
|---|---|---|---|
| Height: 6-1 | Weight: 184 | Throws: R | Ryan Castellani, Clayton Cook, Spencer Adams |

| YEAR | Age | Level | IP | W | L | ERA | FIP | K/9 | BB/9 | K% | BB% | HR/9 | LOB% |
|---|---|---|---|---|---|---|---|---|---|---|---|---|---|
| 2013 | 18 | R | 53.3 | 2 | 5 | 4.05 | 3.73 | 6.41 | 3.38 | 16.9% | 8.9% | 0.34 | 62.9% |
| 2014 | 19 | A | 98.0 | 5 | 7 | 3.21 | 3.22 | 8.72 | 2.66 | 23.9% | 7.3% | 0.46 | 67.0% |
| 2015 | 20 | A+ | 139.0 | 7 | 13 | 3.56 | 3.14 | 6.73 | 1.88 | 17.5% | 4.9% | 0.39 | 67.0% |

**Background:** I ranked the Venezuelan-born right-hander as Tampa's 20th best prospect heading into last season when he was coming off of a solid 98-inning campaign as a 19-year-old in the Midwest League. And after another solid campaign against older competition Marquez found himself even high on his new team's list. The 6-foot-1 hurler spent the entirety of the year twirling gems in the Florida State League as one of just three 20-year-old qualified arms. Across 26 games, 23 starts, Marquez tossed 139.0 innings, punched out 104, walked 29, and coughed up just six dingers. His 3.14 FIP ranked eighth among all FSL qualified hurlers. For his career, Marquez is averaging 7.4 punch outs and just 2.7 walk per nine innings.

**Projection:** There's really not a whole lot to not like about Marquez at this point in his development: he misses a decent amount of sticks, has improved his walk rate in each of his four professional seasons, and has had success against much older competition. He's primed and ready for Class AA. He's a potential mid-rotation arm with tremendous upside as a backend reliever.

**Ceiling:** 1.5- to 2.0-win player
**Risk:** Moderate
**MLB ETA:** 2016

## 12. Raimel Tapia, OF

**MiLB Rank: N/A**
**Position Rank: N/A**

| Born: 02/04/94 | Age: 22 | Bats: L | Top CALs: Rafael Ortega, Francisco Peguero, |
|---|---|---|---|
| Height: 6-2 | Weight: 160 | Throws: L | Austin Dean, Gerardo Parra, Harold Ramirez |

| Season | Age | LVL | PA | 2B | 3B | HR | AVG | OBP | SLG | ISO | BB% | K% | wRC+ |
|---|---|---|---|---|---|---|---|---|---|---|---|---|---|
| 2013 | 19 | R | 286 | 20 | 6 | 7 | 0.357 | 0.399 | 0.562 | 0.205 | 5.2% | 10.8% | 141 |
| 2014 | 20 | A | 539 | 32 | 1 | 9 | 0.326 | 0.382 | 0.453 | 0.127 | 6.5% | 16.7% | 134 |
| 2015 | 21 | A+ | 593 | 34 | 9 | 12 | 0.305 | 0.333 | 0.467 | 0.162 | 4.0% | 17.7% | 112 |

**Background:** A wiry 6-foot-2, 160-pound outfielder out of the Dominican Republic, Tapia passed the important test in proving his Asheville-inflated production line two years ago wasn't a mirage as he moved up to Modesto last season. In 131 games with the Nuts, Tapia batted a solid .305/.333/.467 triple-slash line with career highs in doubles (34), triples (nine), and homeruns (12). He also swiped 26 bags.

**Projection:** But here's the single most important statistic that needs to be noted: despite the appearance of some gaudy numbers – and let's be honest, they *appear* quite garish – Tapia's overall production topped the California League average production mark by just 12%. That's certainly not the mark of a top-notch prospect – a nice one, sure, but not a top blue chipper. Tapia has solid pop, but it's not likely going to develop any further. The speed is an above-average tool. But his walk rates have been *terrible*. CAL's best comparison is Gerardo Parra, a below-average big league bat.

**Ceiling:** 1.5-win player
**Risk:** Moderate
**MLB ETA:** 2017

## 13. Antonio Senzatela, RHP

**MiLB Rank: N/A**
**Position Rank: N/A**

| Born: 01/21/95 | Age: 21 | Bats: R | Top CALs: Tyler Viza, Wilfredo Boscan, |
|---|---|---|---|
| Height: 6-1 | Weight: 180 | Throws: R | Zeke Spruill, Parker Frazier, Arquimedes Nieto |

| YEAR | Age | Level | IP | W | L | ERA | FIP | K/9 | BB/9 | K% | BB% | HR/9 | LOB% |
|---|---|---|---|---|---|---|---|---|---|---|---|---|---|
| 2013 | 18 | R | 51.0 | 6 | 1 | 1.76 | 2.13 | 8.12 | 0.53 | 24.2% | 1.6% | 0.18 | 69.0% |
| 2013 | 18 | A- | 42.3 | 2 | 4 | 3.83 | 3.81 | 4.25 | 2.76 | 10.6% | 6.9% | 0.21 | 65.5% |
| 2014 | 19 | A | 144.7 | 15 | 2 | 3.11 | 4.19 | 5.54 | 2.24 | 14.8% | 6.0% | 0.68 | 71.4% |
| 2015 | 20 | A+ | 154.0 | 9 | 9 | 2.51 | 3.56 | 8.36 | 1.93 | 23.0% | 5.3% | 0.58 | 75.3% |

**Background:** A 6-foot-1, 180-pound right-hander signed out of Venezuela, Senzatela had a coming out party with the Modesto Nuts in the California League last season. After treading water with some sub-optimal strikeout rates since entering professional baseball in 2012, Senzatela fanned a career high 8.4 punch outs per nine innings. And the best part: his above-average control/command maintained status quo as he averaged just 1.9 free passes per nine innings. For his four-year professional career, Senzatela has posted an impressive 333-to-99 strikeout-to-walk ratio in 454.1 innings of work. He's also sporting a solid 2.50 ERA – if you're into that sort of thing.

**Projection**: Very intriguing low level arm. Senzatela has always shown a tremendous feel for the strike zone, but if he can replicate his ability to miss a solid amount of bats as he moves up he might just force his way into the ballclub's future plans for the rotation. He's generated a solid amount of groundballs throughout his career and has success against much older competition. Add it all up, he's an underrated prospect.

**Ceiling:** 1.5- to 2.0-win player
**Risk:** Moderate to High
**MLB ETA:** 2017/2018

## 14. Trevor Story, 2B/3B/SS

**MiLB Rank: N/A**
**Position Rank: N/A**

**Born:** 11/15/92 **Age:** 23 **Bats:** R
**Height:** 6-1 **Weight:** 180 **Throws:** R

**Top CALs:** Javier Baez, Brandon Wood, JaCoby Jones, Jonathan Villar, Arismendy Alcantara

| Season | Age | LVL | PA | 2B | 3B | HR | AVG | OBP | SLG | ISO | BB% | K% | wRC+ |
|---|---|---|---|---|---|---|---|---|---|---|---|---|---|
| 2013 | 20 | A+ | 554 | 34 | 5 | 12 | 0.233 | 0.305 | 0.394 | 0.161 | 8.1% | 33.0% | 83 |
| 2014 | 21 | A+ | 218 | 17 | 7 | 5 | 0.332 | 0.436 | 0.582 | 0.250 | 14.2% | 27.1% | 164 |
| 2014 | 21 | AA | 237 | 8 | 1 | 9 | 0.200 | 0.302 | 0.380 | 0.180 | 11.8% | 34.6% | 98 |
| 2015 | 22 | AA | 300 | 20 | 6 | 10 | 0.281 | 0.373 | 0.523 | 0.242 | 11.7% | 24.3% | 155 |
| 2015 | 22 | AAA | 275 | 20 | 4 | 10 | 0.277 | 0.324 | 0.504 | 0.227 | 5.8% | 24.7% | 115 |

**Background:** Also a member of one of the most memorable first rounds in recent memory, 2011, Story's pendulum-like minor league career was on the upswing last season. After dominating the South Atlantic League as a 19-year-old in 2012, Story looked overmatched as he moved up to Modesto the following season, hitting a paltry .233/.305/.394 while his overall production fell to 17% *below* the league average mark. Colorado had the young infielder repeat the California League for the first half of 2014, and he looked like the second coming of Alex Rodriguez, hitting a whopping .332/.436/.582 to go along with a 164 wRC+. But, once again, he struggled as the club bumped him up to Class AA later in the year (.200/.302/.380). Last season Story repeated – again – the previous level with much better results: he slugged .281/.373/.523. Unlike previous years, however, Story looked comfortable as he got pushed up to the PCL, hitting .277/.324/.504.

**Projection**: Despite some impressive production at numerous points throughout his career, CAL remains incredibly down on the former 45th overall pick. His top five comparisons: Javier Baez, whom I wrote about in an article on Beyond the Box Score highlighting the long odds he's facing after such a dismal start to his career, Brandon Wood, JaCoby Jones, Jonathan Villar, and Arismendy Alcantara.

Story has a tremendous eye at the plate with above-average power, but his swing-and-miss tendencies have been – and will continue to be – an issue. Jose Reyes is fully entrenched at shortstop and Brendan Rodgers is the long-term heir apparent, Story might have a shot to beat out D.J. LeMahieu for the second base spot.

**Ceiling:** 1.5-win player
**Risk:** Moderate to High
**MLB ETA:** 2016

## 15. Tyler Nevin, 3B

**MiLB Rank: N/A**
**Position Rank: N/A**

**Born:** 05/29/97 **Age:** 19 **Bats:** R
**Height:** 6-4 **Weight:** 200 **Throws:** R

**Top CALs:** Jason Taylor, Rafael Medina, Trevor Story, Gerald Bautista, Randy Cesar

| Season | Age | LVL | PA | 2B | 3B | HR | AVG | OBP | SLG | ISO | BB% | K% | wRC+ |
|---|---|---|---|---|---|---|---|---|---|---|---|---|---|
| 2015 | 18 | R | 223 | 15 | 1 | 2 | 0.265 | 0.368 | 0.386 | 0.122 | 13.0% | 18.8% | 100 |

**Background:** Taken with the 38th overall selection last June, the young third baseman, who is also the son of former big league All-Star and winner of college baseball's Golden Spikes Award Phil Nevin, had a solid, league-average debut as he transitioned to wood bats last June, hitting .265/.368/.386 with 15 doubles, one triple, and two homeruns en route to posting a 100 wRC+.

**Projection**: It was a solid, though far from impressive, debut. He showed a tremendous eye and solid contact skills, and the average pop is likely going to continue to grow as his 6-foot-4 frame begins to fill out. He's probably headed for the Sally in 2016.

**Ceiling:** 1.5- to 2.0-win player
**Risk:** Moderate to High
**MLB ETA:** 2016/2017

## 16. Jairo Diaz, RHP

**MiLB Rank:** N/A
**Position Rank:** N/A

| Born: 05/27/91 | Age: 25 | Bats: R | Top CALs: Jeff Stevens, Brad Mills, |
| Height: 6-0 | Weight: 200 | Throws: R | Ryan Rodebaugh, Andrew Heaney, Sam Demel |

| YEAR | Age | Level | IP | W | L | ERA | FIP | K/9 | BB/9 | K% | BB% | HR/9 | LOB% |
|---|---|---|---|---|---|---|---|---|---|---|---|---|---|
| 2013 | 22 | A | 34.0 | 0 | 3 | 3.97 | 4.16 | 7.41 | 2.91 | 19.9% | 7.8% | 0.79 | 68.8% |
| 2013 | 22 | A+ | 22.3 | 0 | 2 | 8.87 | 5.52 | 8.46 | 5.64 | 17.8% | 11.9% | 1.21 | 52.3% |
| 2014 | 23 | A+ | 32.0 | 2 | 3 | 4.78 | 3.27 | 10.41 | 2.81 | 26.4% | 7.1% | 0.56 | 61.2% |
| 2014 | 23 | AA | 32.7 | 2 | 1 | 2.20 | 1.99 | 13.22 | 2.76 | 35.8% | 7.5% | 0.55 | 86.4% |
| 2015 | 24 | AAA | 55.0 | 3 | 5 | 4.58 | 5.44 | 8.18 | 6.05 | 19.9% | 14.7% | 0.98 | 73.0% |

**Background:** Acquired from the Halos of Anaheim last offseason in exchange for utility man-extraordinaire Josh Rutledge, Diaz spent last season uncorking his plus-upper-90s heater between Albuquerque and Colorado. In 55.0 innings with the Isotopes, the Venezuelan-born gunslinger fanned 19.9% of the total hitters he faced. The problem: he walked nearly 15% of the guys that dared to dig in. Colorado called Diaz up in late August and *miraculously* he stopped issuing free passes like a little league hurler. His walk percentage dropped to a more manageable 7.7% *and* still missed about a bat per inning. For his minor league career, Diaz is averaging 7.9 strikeouts and 3.3 free passes per nine innings. And for his brief big league career he's sporting an impressive 26-to-9 strikeout-to-walk ratio in 24.2 innings of work.

**Projection:** Diaz can sling it up there with the best of them as his fastball has averaged a smidgeon more than 97 mph in both of stints in the big leagues. He's had various points in his seven-year career where his control has all but abandoned him, but when he's on he's as dominant as any setup man in professional baseball.

**Ceiling:** 1.5-win player
**Risk:** Moderate to High
**MLB ETA:** Debuted in 2014

## 17. Cristhian Adames, IF

**MiLB Rank:** N/A
**Position Rank:** N/A

| Born: 07/26/91 | Age: 24 | Bats: B | Top CALs: Pedro Lopez, Diory Hernandez, |
| Height: 6-0 | Weight: 185 | Throws: R | Darwin Barney, Jorge Flores, Martin Prado |

| Season | Age | LVL | PA | 2B | 3B | HR | AVG | OBP | SLG | ISO | BB% | K% | wRC+ |
|---|---|---|---|---|---|---|---|---|---|---|---|---|---|
| 2013 | 21 | AA | 446 | 19 | 2 | 3 | 0.267 | 0.331 | 0.350 | 0.082 | 7.6% | 17.5% | 95 |
| 2014 | 22 | AA | 380 | 9 | 4 | 2 | 0.267 | 0.324 | 0.336 | 0.070 | 7.6% | 15.3% | 90 |
| 2014 | 22 | AAA | 163 | 12 | 0 | 1 | 0.338 | 0.392 | 0.441 | 0.103 | 8.0% | 15.3% | 122 |
| 2014 | 22 | AAA | 163 | 12 | 0 | 1 | 0.338 | 0.392 | 0.441 | 0.103 | 8.0% | 15.3% | 122 |
| 2015 | 23 | AAA | 511 | 20 | 3 | 11 | 0.311 | 0.362 | 0.438 | 0.127 | 7.0% | 11.0% | 114 |
| 2015 | 23 | MLB | 58 | 1 | 1 | 0 | 0.245 | 0.298 | 0.302 | 0.057 | 5.2% | 19.0% | 44 |

**Background:** The quintessential utility infielder, Adames turned in another solid minor league offensive showing in 2015 as he spent the majority of the year fine-tuning his approach with the Isotopes in the Pacific Coast League. Adames, a switch-hitter out of the Dominican Republic, hit .311/.362/.438 with 20 doubles, three triples, and a career best – by a large margin – 11 homeruns, and 11 stolen bases to go along with a 114 wRC+ mark. And just like the previous season, Adames earned a trip up to the Rocky Mountain State where he would post a .245/.298/.302 triple-slash line in limited action. For his minor league career Adames is sporting a solid .281/.348/.375 mark.

**Projection:** It's always going to come down to Adames' ability – or inability – to hit for any type of power. If he does, like he did with the Isotopes, Adames has a chance to spend a couple seasons manning a fulltime infield position before quietly bowing out. If he doesn't, like he's shown at numerous points in his minor league career, then he'll take the path of a perennial as the 25th-man on any roster.

**Ceiling:** 1.0-win player
**Risk:** Low
**MLB ETA:** Debuted in 2014

## 18. Mike Nikorak, RHP

MiLB Rank: N/A
Position Rank: N/A

| Born: 09/16/96 | Age: 19 | Bats: R | Top CALs: Michael Richez, Victor Perez, |
| Height: 6-5 | Weight: 220 | Throws: R | Zach Russell, Dennis, Moya, Brandon Koch |

| YEAR | Age | Level | IP | W | L | ERA | FIP | K/9 | BB/9 | K% | BB% | HR/9 | LOB% |
|------|-----|-------|-----|---|---|------|-----|------|------|------|------|------|------|
| 2015 | 18 | R | 17.7 | 0 | 4 | 11.72 | 9.07 | 7.13 | 16.30 | 12.8% | 29.4% | 0.51 | 54.6% |

**Background:** The second of the club's four consecutive prep players taken last June. Nikorak *really* struggled with his control/command during his time with Grand Junction, walking a mind-boggling 32 hitters in just 17.2 innings.

**Projection:** Granted it's an incredibly limited sample size, but *DAMN* did he walk a helluva lot of guys.

**Ceiling:** Too Soon to Tell
**Risk:** N/A
**MLB ETA:** N/A

## 19. Carlos Estevez, RHP

MiLB Rank: N/A
Position Rank: N/A

| Born: 12/28/92 | Age: 23 | Bats: R | Top CALs: Justin De Fratus, Dan Jennings, |
| Height: 6-4 | Weight: 210 | Throws: R | Matt Garza, Jeffrey Johnson, Sean Nolin |

| YEAR | Age | Level | IP | W | L | ERA | FIP | K/9 | BB/9 | K% | BB% | HR/9 | LOB% |
|------|-----|-------|------|---|---|------|------|-------|------|-------|------|------|--------|
| 2013 | 20 | R | 35.7 | 5 | 1 | 3.79 | 4.71 | 7.82 | 3.53 | 21.0% | 9.5% | 0.76 | 67.0% |
| 2013 | 20 | A- | 3.7 | 1 | 0 | 2.45 | 4.95 | 12.27 | 2.45 | 33.3% | 6.7% | 2.45 | 100.0% |
| 2014 | 21 | A | 53.3 | 1 | 3 | 4.73 | 3.36 | 8.44 | 1.86 | 22.1% | 4.9% | 0.68 | 58.5% |
| 2015 | 22 | A+ | 19.7 | 5 | 0 | 1.37 | 2.00 | 11.44 | 2.29 | 34.7% | 6.9% | 0.00 | 82.4% |
| 2015 | 22 | AA | 36.0 | 0 | 3 | 4.50 | 2.44 | 10.75 | 2.25 | 27.4% | 5.7% | 0.50 | 64.9% |

**Background:** Apparently the organization is literally going out in their backyard and plucking hard-throwing, potentially dominant arms. And Estevez, a 6-foot-4, 210-pound right-hander out of the Dominican Republic, is just another example. After trying to hone the craft – and his fastball – in two stints in the Dominican Summer League in 2011 and 2012, the organization pushed the young fire-baller into a fulltime relief role. And after two seasons of relief work with solid strikeout totals, Estevez's punch out *exploded* as he split his time between Modesto and New Britain last season: he fanned 68 of the 229 total batters he faced, or just about 30%. He finished the year with 55.2 combined innings, fanning 68 and walking just 14 to go along with 18 saves and a 3.40 ERA.

**Projection:** A potentially dominant backend relief arm. Estevez's control, which has always been solid-average, took another step forward last season. CAL's tied him to an at-times dominant big league starter (Matt Garza) and another solid starting prospect (Sean Nolin). Just remember the name: Carlos Estevez.

**Ceiling:** 1.0- to 1.5-win player
**Risk:** Moderate
**MLB ETA:** 2016/2017

## 20. Tommy Murphy, C

MiLB Rank: N/A
Position Rank: N/A

| Born: 04/03/91 | Age: 25 | Bats: R | Top CALs: Dusty Ryan, Yan Gomes, |
| Height: 6-1 | Weight: 220 | Throws: R | Chris Wallace, Welington Castillo, Colt Morton |

| Season | Age | LVL | PA | 2B | 3B | HR | AVG | OBP | SLG | ISO | BB% | K% | wRC+ |
|--------|-----|-----|-----|----|----|----|-------|-------|-------|-------|-------|-------|------|
| 2013 | 22 | A | 341 | 26 | 2 | 19 | 0.288 | 0.385 | 0.590 | 0.302 | 10.9% | 25.5% | 174 |
| 2014 | 23 | AA | 109 | 4 | 0 | 5 | 0.213 | 0.321 | 0.415 | 0.202 | 12.8% | 24.8% | 113 |
| 2015 | 24 | AA | 294 | 17 | 1 | 13 | 0.249 | 0.320 | 0.468 | 0.219 | 7.8% | 27.2% | 126 |
| 2015 | 24 | AAA | 136 | 9 | 2 | 7 | 0.271 | 0.301 | 0.535 | 0.264 | 3.7% | 31.6% | 113 |
| 2015 | 24 | MLB | 39 | 1 | 0 | 3 | 0.257 | 0.333 | 0.543 | 0.286 | 10.3% | 25.6% | 116 |

**Background:** The highest draft pick hailing from the University of Buffalo since Cincinnati's selection of Pete Grimm with the 56th overall pick in the 1983 draft, Murphy, who was taken with the 105th pick in 2012, rebounded after a disastrous 2014 showing to help establish his prospect status a potential solid big league backup backstop. After hitting a career worst .213/.321/.415 in an injury-shortened season, Murphy batted .249/.320/.468 with 17 doubles, one triple, and 13 homeruns in 72 games with the New Britain Rock Cats. Colorado bumped the 6-foot-1, 220-pound backstop up to the PCL in last July where he hit .271/.301/.535 the rest of the way. Overall, he finished his minor league season with a combined .256/.314/.490 triple-slash line with 26 doubles, three triples, and 20 homeruns. He also spent 11 games with the Rockies, going 9-for-35 with a double and three homeruns.

**Projection**: Here's what I wrote following his injury-laden 2014 campaign:

> *"A potential Three Tree Outcomes hitter behind the plate, Murphy has a history of good, not great walk rates, above-average power, and a concerning K-rate. CAL links him to a bunch of backup-type bats in Andrew Knapp, Luis Exposito, and Kellin Deglan. Throw in some massive question marks about controlling the running game – he's thrown out 20% in his career – and Murphy definitely has some hurdles to jump over to make a big league career possible."*

And one year later much of the same thing could still be said (or written). Murphy – once again – displayed some Three True Outcomes potential as he posted an ISO above .230 and a punch out rate north of 28.5%. His walk rate stumbled a bit effectively costing him the triumvirate. A reasonable big league comparison: J.P. Arencibia.

**Ceiling**: 1.0-win player
**Risk**: Low
**MLB ETA**: Debuted in 2015

# 21. Dom Nunez, C

**MiLB Rank**: N/A
**Position Rank**: N/A

| Born: 01/17/95 | Age: 21 | Bats: L | Top CALs: Carlos Perez, Oscar Hernandez, |
| Height: 6-0 | Weight: 175 | Throws: R | Jesus Araiza, Travis D'Arnaud, Alex Murphy |

| Season | Age | LVL | PA | 2B | 3B | HR | AVG | OBP | SLG | ISO | BB% | K% | wRC+ |
|---|---|---|---|---|---|---|---|---|---|---|---|---|---|
| 2013 | 18 | R | 217 | 13 | 1 | 3 | 0.200 | 0.269 | 0.323 | 0.123 | 8.3% | 15.7% | 54 |
| 2013 | 18 | R | 217 | 13 | 1 | 3 | 0.200 | 0.269 | 0.323 | 0.123 | 8.3% | 15.7% | 54 |
| 2014 | 19 | R | 198 | 12 | 0 | 8 | 0.313 | 0.384 | 0.517 | 0.205 | 10.6% | 14.1% | 129 |
| 2015 | 20 | A | 441 | 23 | 0 | 13 | 0.282 | 0.373 | 0.448 | 0.166 | 12.0% | 12.5% | 135 |

**Background**: A 2013 sixth round pick out of Elk Grove High School, Nunez continued to show some chops as a catcher after converting to the position two years ago. Nunez, a lefty-swinging former middle infielder, also handled himself surprisingly well as he moved up to full season ball last season. The 6-foot, 175-pound backstop hit a solid .282/.373/.448 with 23 doubles and 13 homeruns en route to posting a career best 135 wRC+ total. The 2015 season also marked the second consecutive year in which his overall production remained on an upward trend: he posted a lowly 54 wRC+ mark during his debut season in the Pioneer League three years ago and fared much better in his second go-round in the rookie league the following year, posting a 129 wRC+. Defensively, he's thrown out 26% of would-be base stealers in his 136 career games behind the dish.

**Projection**: So now we need to dig deeper into the offensive surge last season because he spent so much time mashing pitching in Asheville's home park. His home vs. road splits: .304/.398/.470 vs. .260/.351/.428. While it's not as dramatic as other players plying their trades with the Tourists, there's a definite – and rather steep – decline as he moved away from home. But that's not the most damning split he's shown; his work out against southpaws last season, .223/.304/.693, could prove to be too much to overcome as well. He looks like a better version of Tommy Murphy.

**Ceiling**: 1.0- to 1.5-win player
**Risk**: Moderate
**MLB ETA**: 2018

# 22. Sam Moll, LHP

**MiLB Rank**: N/A
**Position Rank**: N/A

| Born: 01/03/92 | Age: 24 | Bats: L | Top CALs: Brayan Villarreal, Jose Arredondo, |
| Height: 5-10 | Weight: 185 | Throws: L | Marco Estrada, Gabe Medina, Tyler Carpenter |

| YEAR | Age | Level | IP | W | L | ERA | FIP | K/9 | BB/9 | K% | BB% | HR/9 | LOB% |
|---|---|---|---|---|---|---|---|---|---|---|---|---|---|
| 2013 | 21 | A- | 30.0 | 3 | 1 | 1.80 | 2.38 | 8.70 | 3.00 | 24.2% | 8.3% | 0.00 | 70.0% |
| 2014 | 22 | A- | 13.0 | 0 | 1 | 4.15 | 4.90 | 4.85 | 2.77 | 11.9% | 6.8% | 0.69 | 77.7% |
| 2015 | 23 | A+ | 53.7 | 0 | 1 | 3.02 | 4.13 | 9.56 | 2.01 | 27.1% | 5.7% | 1.17 | 76.9% |
| 2015 | 23 | AA | 14.7 | 0 | 0 | 1.23 | 1.77 | 10.43 | 2.45 | 31.5% | 7.4% | 0.00 | 81.8% |

**Background**: Colorado plucked the small 5-foot-10, 185-pound left-hander out of the University of Memphis in 2013. And despite a dominant showing in the rotation during his junior campaign with the Tigers – he posted a 106-to-32 strikeout-to-walk ratio with a 2.30 ERA in 94.0 innings of work – the Rockies' front office brass pushed the diminutive hurler into a full time reliever, a combination of his small stature and the fact that he was limited to just 13.0 innings two years ago courtesy of an elbow injury. Moll split his 2015 season between Modesto and New Britain, fanned 74 and walking 16 in 68.1 combined innings to go along with a solid 2.63 ERA.

**Projection**: Here's what I wrote prior to the 2013 draft:

*"Moll is always going to have to answer questions about his stature, and he's almost assuredly smaller than the listed height as schools tend to exaggerate players' sizes. With that being said, there's really no reason that he shouldn't be given a shot to develop as a starter, maybe [peaking as a] #3/#4-type guy down the line. And at the very worst, the little lefty could easily become this year's version of Paco Rodriguez and Rob Rasmussen."*

Well, he's settled in nicely as a power-armed southpaw hurling an inning at a time. The strikeout numbers have been impressive, especially with the combination of above-average control. He has a chance to spend the next decade-plus as a lights-out seventh/eighth-inning arm.

**Ceiling:** 1.0 – to 1.5-win player
**Risk:** Moderate
**MLB ETA:** 2016/2017

## 23. Peter Lambert, RHP

**MiLB Rank: N/A**
**Position Rank: N/A**

| Born: 04/18/97 | Age: 19 | Bats: R | **Top CALs:** James Needy, Anfernee Benitez, |
|---|---|---|---|
| Height: 6-2 | Weight: 185 | Throws: R | Andress Sanchez, Geordy Parra, Tyler Vail |

| YEAR | Age | Level | IP | W | L | ERA | FIP | K/9 | BB/9 | K% | BB% | HR/9 | LOB% |
|---|---|---|---|---|---|---|---|---|---|---|---|---|---|
| 2015 | 18 | R | 31.3 | 0 | 4 | 3.45 | 5.17 | 7.47 | 3.16 | 18.2% | 7.7% | 0.86 | 65.3% |

**Background:** The club's most recent second round pick, Lambert, a 6-foot-1, 185-pound right-hander, posted a decent 26-to-11 strikeout-to-walk ratio in 31.1 innings of work in the Pioneer League during his debut.

**Projection**: The highest selected player out of San Dims High School, Lambert's overall production was mired by two three-plus-inning stints when he walked six total batters. Otherwise, his strikeout-to-walk ratio improves to 19-to-5 in 23.2 innings of work. Per the usual, we'll take a wait-and-see approach until he accrues more experience.

**Ceiling:** Too Soon to Tell
**Risk:** N/A
**MLB ETA:** N/A

## 24. Alex Balog, RHP

**MiLB Rank: N/A**
**Position Rank: N/A**

| Born: 07/16/92 | Age: 23 | Bats: R | **Top CALs:** Kyle Mcpherson, Pedro Encarnacion, |
|---|---|---|---|
| Height: 6-5 | Weight: 210 | Throws: R | Scott Allen, Jesus Rodriguez, Anvioris Ramirez |

| YEAR | Age | Level | IP | W | L | ERA | FIP | K/9 | BB/9 | K% | BB% | HR/9 | LOB% |
|---|---|---|---|---|---|---|---|---|---|---|---|---|---|
| 2013 | 20 | R | 30.0 | 1 | 4 | 9.30 | 6.99 | 5.10 | 2.40 | 11.7% | 5.5% | 2.10 | 44.9% |
| 2014 | 21 | A | 150.3 | 8 | 5 | 3.95 | 4.01 | 6.82 | 2.45 | 18.0% | 6.5% | 0.72 | 65.5% |
| 2015 | 22 | A+ | 97.0 | 3 | 8 | 3.71 | 3.74 | 6.68 | 1.76 | 18.1% | 4.8% | 0.46 | 66.7% |

**Background:** One of the fast-rising collegiate prospects in the latter part of the 2013 collegiate season, Balog was always going to be ill-fitted as a early round draft pick as the hype – and there was certainly enough of it swirling about – would never, *ever* match the actual production, even extending back to his collegiate days. The 6-foot-5, 210-pound right-hander, whom the club burned the 60th overall pick on, has made just 16 starts in the California League last season, posting another subpar punch out rate – he fanned just 18.1% of the total hitters he faced – with promising control. He finished the year with 72 strikeouts, 19 walks, and staggering 16 wild pitches in 97.0 innings of work. For his professional career, he's averaged 6.6 punch outs and just 2.2 free passes per nine innings.

**Projection**: Prior to the 2013 draft I wrote the following:

*"Balog has the size scouts crave but the production has failed to impress. And statistically speaking, there's really no reason to believe he will be anything more than organization depth right now."*

Three years later he hasn't done anything else to convince me otherwise. The control is an above-average skill and he's sporting a groundball rate north of 45%, but the lack of strikeouts will ultimately push him into a relief role.

**Ceiling:** 1.0-win player
**Risk:** Moderate
**MLB ETA:** 2016

## 25. Rosell Herrera, 3B/SS/OF

**MiLB Rank:** N/A
**Position Rank:** N/A

| | | | |
|---|---|---|---|
| **Born:** 10/16/92 | **Age:** 23 | **Bats:** B | **Top CALs:** Justin Sellers, Tyler Filliben, |
| **Height:** 6-3 | **Weight:** 195 | **Throws:** R | Chris Mcconnell, Juan Perez, Frank Martinez |

| Season | Age | LVL | PA | 2B | 3B | HR | AVG | OBP | SLG | ISO | BB% | K% | wRC+ |
|--------|-----|-----|-----|----|----|----|-------|-------|-------|-------|------|------|------|
| 2013 | 20 | A | 546 | 33 | 0 | 16 | 0.343 | 0.419 | 0.515 | 0.172 | 11.2% | 17.6% | 168 |
| 2014 | 21 | A+ | 302 | 11 | 1 | 4 | 0.244 | 0.302 | 0.335 | 0.091 | 7.9% | 17.2% | 68 |
| 2014 | 21 | A+ | 302 | 11 | 1 | 4 | 0.244 | 0.302 | 0.335 | 0.091 | 7.9% | 17.2% | 68 |
| 2015 | 22 | A+ | 512 | 20 | 6 | 4 | 0.260 | 0.314 | 0.354 | 0.094 | 7.2% | 18.9% | 84 |

**Background:** Herrera's spectacular showing – he slugged .343/.419/.515 with 33 doubles, 16 homeruns, and 21 stolen bases – with Asheville three years ago is all but distant memory at this point. Since then he's batted a lowly .244/.302/.335 in 72 games with Modesto two years ago and only moderately improved upon that in a redo of the High Class A level last season; in 123 games with the Modesto Nuts, Herrera batted .260/.314/.354 with 20 doubles, a career high six triples, four homeruns, and nine stolen bases in 17 attempts en route to posting a disastrous 84 wRC+ total.

**Projection**: Here's what I wrote about the former top prospect in last year's book:

> "Rule #1: when a below-average hitter – no matter how young he is – starts smacking the ball around like the second coming of Cobb in an extreme hitter's park, DON'T BUY INTO IT! Because that's exactly what Herrera did two years ago. While making his way through the rookie leagues and short season ball, the 6-foot-3 switch-hitter posted a wRC+ total above 100 just once. And then – BOOM! – he goes off like the ghost of Cobb in 2013 for Asheville, hitting .343/.419/.515 with 33 doubles and 16 homeruns en route to topping the league average by 68%. Fast forward to last season, and, wouldn't ya know it, Herrera fell completely on his face in Modesto: .244/.302/.335."

I continued,

> "So now we have five full seasons of data – or at least five sample sizes greater than 250 plate appearances – and Herrera's stood out for one season. Otherwise, his production has ranged from blah to abysmal. Pure utility guy. And that's if everything breaks just right."

After another dismal showing everything still holds.

**Ceiling:** 1.0-win player
**Risk:** Moderate to High
**MLB ETA:** 2018

### Barely Missed:

- **Ryan Casteel, 1B** – Former backstop-turned-first-baseman made the unconventional move back behind the plate last season. Though he was limited to just 34 games in the Pacific Coast League, he hit .292/.301/.415. He might be able to carve out a couple seasons as a spot-starter/bench guy.

- **Carlos Herrera, SS** – Hit a respectable .267/.316/.339 with plenty of speed as an 18-year-old in the Northwest League last season. He hasn't shown much power at any point during his three-year professional career.

- **Harrison Musgrave, LHP** – Portly lefty out of WVU two years ago breezed through the California League after 16 starts and made it look easy with New Britain. He's not going to be a big league starter, but he could serve as a valuable relief arm.

- **Will Swanner, C/1B** – He's bounced between backstop and first base throughout his six-year professional career. Swanner made it up to Class AA last season, hitting a solid .260/.343/.455. He's strictly a Quad-A type bat.

- **Jesus Tinoco, RHP** – A near lock to appear on next season's Top 25 list, Tinoco, who was acquired from Toronto in the Troy Tulowitzki deal, tallied a 105-to-30 strikeout-to-walk ratio in 121.1 innings in Low Class A. He finished with a combined 2.97 ERA.

## *Bird Doggin' It – Additional Prospects to Keep an Eye in 2016*

| Player | Age | POS | Notes |
|---|---|---|---|
| Mike Benjamin | 24 | IF | Former ASU standout continued his power surge with Modesto last season, posting a .450 slugging percentage. Below-average hit tool and patience will doom him into a life of a minor league vagabond. |
| Shane Broyles | 24 | RHP | Converted from starter to reliever a couple years ago, Broyles posted a 76-to-31 strikeout-to-walk ratio in 64.1 innings between Modesto, New Britain, and Albuquerque. |
| Matt Carasiti | 24 | RHP | 6-foot-3, 205-pound hurler saved 22 games for Modesto in 2015 while averaging more than a punch out per inning. |
| Omar Carrizales | 21 | OF | Venezuelan-born outfielder hit .286/.333/.410 with speed and gap power with Asheville. Let's see if he can carry it into High Class A. |
| Yonathan Daza | 22 | OF | Hasn't stopped hitting since leaping into the Pioneer League a couple years ago, though it's mostly been in limited action. |
| Sam Howard | 23 | LHP | Third rounder out of Georgia Southern in 2014, Howard posted a 122-to-32 strikeout-to-walk ratio in 134.0 innings with Asheville. |
| Javier Medina | 19 | RHP | Sahuaro High School alum taken in the third round last season, Medina averaged 7.9 punch outs and just 2.6 walks per nine innings during his debut. |
| Roberto Ramos | 21 | 1B | The latest beneficiary of Asheville's favorable park, Ramos slugged .341/.413/.610 with 10 dingers in 46 games. He's going to crash back to earth in 2016. |

**State of the Franchise:** Former Tigers General Manager Dave Dombrowski is one *helluva* guy – seriously. With the proverbial writing clearly

written on the wall – especially when he told cranky owner Mike Ilitch that the club didn't have the minor league resources to acquire a top notch starter for the stretch run – Dombrowski picked himself up by the bootstraps and pulled off three impressive Tiger-friendly deals before being fired.

The future Hall of Famer swapped David Price for a trio of young arms – Daniel Norris, who's ready to step into a mid-rotation role tomorrow, big southpaw Jairo Labourt, and Matt Boyd. Both Norris and Labourt figure into the club's long term plans. The same day he pulled off the mega-deal with Toronto, Dombrowski turned to Pittsburgh and got infielder – and recently suspended – JaCoby Jones for Joakim Soria. And then the next day he acquired the club's eventual top prospect right-hander Michael Fulmer and useful hurler Luis Cessa from the Mets for Yoenis Cespedes.

The rest of the farm system, just like their recently acquired talent, is incredibly heavy on pitching. Right-hander Joe Jimenez has front-of-the-rotation caliber potential, but the front office has kept him mired away in a late-inning relief role. Hopefully, though, that changes in the coming season or two.

Former collegiate studs Austin Kubitza and Kevin Ziomek are nearing big league readiness and could fill out some backend starts by mid-season, particularly if injuries strike the aging club. And last year's first round pick, right-hander Beau Burrows, looked awfully dominant during his 28.0-inning debut in the Gulf Coast League.

In terms of offensive talent, the farm's...lacking firepower.

Power-hitting outfielder Steven Moya abhors the free pass, but can slug 'em a mile long...when he makes contact. Former University of Tennessee standout – and another of the club's first round selections last June – looked strong during his respective debut, hitting a combined .285/.372/.508 between three different levels.

Overall, it's a poor system. One that's incredibly weak on top tier talent outside of its first two, maybe three prospects.

**Review of the 2015 Draft:** Straying from Dombrowski's mantra of grabbing collegiate arms early and often, Detroit picked up Burrows with the 22nd overall pick and Stewart just 12 selections later.

After that It's the useful smattering of low end, safe collegiate picks: Tyler Alexander, Drew Smith, Kade Scivicque, Cam Gibson (Kirk's kid), and Matt Hall, likely going to be the best of the aforementioned bunch.

| Rank | Name | POS |
|------|------|-----|
| 1 | Michael Fulmer | RHP |
| 2 | Joe Jimenez | RHP |
| 3 | Beau Burrows | RHP |
| 4 | Austin Kubitza | RHP |
| 5 | Jairo Labourt | LHP |
| 6 | Kevin Ziomek | LHP |
| 7 | Steven Moya | RF |
| 8 | Christin Stewart | LF |
| 9 | Zach Shepherd | 3B |
| 10 | Derek Hill | CF |
| 11 | Dixon Machado | SS |
| 12 | Matt Hall | LHP |
| 13 | Spencer Turnbull | RHP |
| 14 | JaCoby Jones | SS |
| 15 | Artie Lewicki | RHP |
| 16 | Wynton Benard | OF |
| 17 | Tyler Alexander | LHP |
| 18 | Jefry Marte | 1B/3B |
| 19 | Jose Valdez | RHP |
| 20 | Melvin Mercedes | RHP |
| 21 | Michael Gerber | RF |
| 22 | Drew Smith | RHP |
| 23 | Jeff Thompson | RHP |
| 24 | Steven Fuentes | 3B/SS |
| 25 | Drew Verhagen | RHP |

## 1. Michael Fulmer, RHP

MiLB Rank: #35
Position Rank: #16

| Born: 03/15/93 | Age: 23 | Bats: R | Top CALs: Richard Castillo, Randall Delgado, |
|---|---|---|---|
| Height: 6-3 | Weight: 200 | Throws: R | Eduardo Rodriguez, Johnny Barbato, Ryan Searle |

| YEAR | Age | Level | IP | W | L | ERA | FIP | K/9 | BB/9 | K% | BB% | HR/9 | LOB% |
|---|---|---|---|---|---|---|---|---|---|---|---|---|---|
| 2013 | 20 | R | 12.0 | 1 | 1 | 3.00 | 1.79 | 9.75 | 0.75 | 27.7% | 2.1% | 0.00 | 63.6% |
| 2013 | 20 | A+ | 34.0 | 2 | 2 | 3.44 | 3.86 | 7.68 | 4.76 | 19.9% | 12.3% | 0.26 | 74.0% |
| 2014 | 21 | A+ | 95.3 | 6 | 10 | 3.97 | 3.77 | 8.12 | 2.93 | 19.8% | 7.1% | 0.66 | 70.1% |
| 2014 | 21 | AA | 3.3 | 0 | 1 | 16.20 | 9.35 | 2.70 | 8.10 | 5.3% | 15.8% | 2.70 | 39.5% |
| 2015 | 22 | A+ | 7.0 | 0 | 0 | 3.86 | 2.45 | 11.57 | 0.00 | 36.0% | 0.0% | 1.29 | 38.5% |
| 2015 | 22 | AA | 117.7 | 10 | 3 | 2.14 | 2.86 | 8.87 | 2.29 | 24.5% | 6.3% | 0.54 | 79.2% |

**Background**: Here's a little snippet from *The Detroit News'* Lynn Henning in the days immediately following the Tigers' dismissal of Dave Dombrowski:

*"Tigers owner Mike Ilitch was disgusted over his 2015 Tigers team and its fraying as a playoff club. He was no happier when Dombrowski, following heavy meetings with his staff in Florida, said that lacked the trade pieces to add a starting pitcher that might salvage 2015's playoff chase."* (Author's Note: The article, submitted on August 8, 2015, was titled *Henning: Failure in 2015 was too much for Ilitch*.) So, clearly, the writing was on the wall for Dombrowski – despite piloting the organization to its most successful run since the start of the 19th century. But Dombrowski, the obvious consummate professional, pulled off a string of impressive deals to better the serve the organization – and his predecessor Al Avila – in the coming years. And no trade better exemplifies that than the Yoenis Cespedes-for-Michael-Fulmer (and Luis Cessa) swap with the Mets at the trade deadline.

I listed Fulmer among the Top 25 Breakout Prospects in 2015 in last year's book, writing the following:

> *"Overlooked because of New York's impressive collection of minor league arms, Fulmer, a former first round pick, missed most of the 2013 season because of [a] torn meniscus in his knee. [He shows a] a promising swing-and-miss ability with solid-average control."*

Well, Fulmer put together his finest season to date in 2015. In a career high 22 starts, 21 of which coming in the Eastern League, the 6-foot-3, 200-pound right-hander tossed 124.1 with 125 punch outs, just 30 walks, an impeccable 2.24 ERA, and a sub-2.90 FIP. Yeah, that qualifies as a breakout campaign.

**Projection**: In his projection section in last year's book I wrote the following:

> *"Fulmer's been quietly flying under the radar now for quite some time, even more so now thanks to missing so much time two years ago. But he's continued to handle the club's aggressive promotion schedule without showing any major hiccups along the way. He's a very, very underrated young arm that could be poised to shoot up quite a bit in 2015. Fulmer's another back-of-the-rotation caliber ceiling that could be capable of a lot more if everything breaks the right way."*

Well, he certainly falls under the "a lot more" category after his dominant showing last year. But just how dominant was he you ask? Consider the following:

- Between the Eastern, Southern, and Texas Leagues last season, Fulmer was one of just 11 qualified arms under the age of 23.
- His 2.86 FIP ranked second among all qualified Class AA arms.
- His strikeout-to-walk percentage, 18.2%, also ranked second among all qualified Class AA arms.
- His strikeout percentage, 24.5%, ranked third and his walk rate, 6.3%, tied for 20th lowest among all qualified Class AA arms.
- And, finally, among stateside hurlers with 120+ innings under their belt last season, Fulmer's strikeout-to-walk ratio ranked seventh.

Basically, Fulmer's developed into one of the most complete arms in the entire minor leagues. And while he doesn't profile as an elite-level, front-of-the-rotation caliber big league arm, the young right-hander looks like a very, very good #3-type hurler.

Overall, it was a fantastic – *fantastic* – deal for Detroit and its former shot-caller.

**Ceiling:** 3.0-win player
**Risk:** Low to Moderate
**MLB ETA:** 2016

# 2. Joe Jimenez, RHP

**MiLB Rank: #81**

**Position Rank: N/A**

| Born: 01/17/95 | Age: 21 | Bats: R | Top CALs: Dan Barnes, Justin Wright, |
| Height: 6-3 | Weight: 220 | Throws: R | Stephen Gonsalves, Chance Adams, Christian Friedrich |

| YEAR | Age | Level | IP | W | L | ERA | FIP | K/9 | BB/9 | K% | BB% | HR/9 | LOB% |
|---|---|---|---|---|---|---|---|---|---|---|---|---|---|
| 2013 | 18 | R | 18.0 | 3 | 0 | 0.50 | 1.79 | 12.00 | 3.00 | 35.3% | 8.8% | 0.00 | 93.3% |
| 2014 | 19 | A- | 26.7 | 3 | 2 | 2.70 | 1.75 | 13.84 | 2.03 | 37.3% | 5.5% | 0.34 | 69.9% |
| 2015 | 20 | A | 43.0 | 5 | 1 | 1.47 | 1.93 | 12.77 | 2.30 | 37.7% | 6.8% | 0.42 | 83.3% |

**Background:** Just another one of the incredibly savvy moves under the Dave Dombrowski regime – I hope you're taking note, Mr. Ilitch – the club signed the hard-throwing Puerto Rican-born hurler for the relative paltry sum of $100,000 as an undrafted free agent. Since then the 6-foot-3, 220-pound right-hander has been damn near unhittable spanning parts of three minor leagues seasons. Jimenez burst onto the scene as an 18-year-old in the Gulf Coast League, fanning 24 and walking just six in 18.0 innings of work. He got bumped up to the New York-Penn League the following season and continued to dominate: 26.2 IP, a ridiculous 41 strikeouts, and an equally ridiculous six walks. And that dominance continued into his action with the Gigantes de Carolina in the Puerto Rican Winter League as well. Making 12 appearances with the foreign club, Jimenez failed to surrender a run while posting another impeccable strikeout-to-walk ratio (15-to-1).

Heading into last season I named the then-20-year-old pitcher as one of the Top 25 Breakout Prospects for 2015. And he certainly didn't disappoint.

Spending the entire year with the West Michigan Whitecaps, Jimenez tossed a career best 43.0 innings while *averaging* 12.8 punch outs and just 2.3 walks per nine innings – production that earned him the nod as the Tigers' Minor League Pitcher of the Year.

One final note: Jimenez has fanned 37.1% of the total batters he's faced.

**Projection**: Here's what I wrote in last year's book:

> "Granted, it's two small sample sizes, but he's been utterly dominant. And as far as initial returns on an investment, Jimenez has rewarded the club with more than enough hope. You'd have to assume that given the dominance and ease, the Tigers would think about moving him into the rotation down the line."

Unfurling an upper-90s heater in the MLB Futures Game, Jimenez has the potential to develop into a top-notch starting pitcher – if the organization eases the reins a bit on the dominant hurler. Please, *please* push him into the rotation. I'm literally begging. He's thrown just 87.2 innings in his career; it's time to find out what he's capable of.

One thing to watch in the coming years: he lived – without dying – by the fly ball last season, so homeruns may become an issue at some point in the near future, maybe.

**Ceiling:** 2.5- to 3.0-win player
**Risk:** Moderate
**MLB ETA:** 2018

# 3. Beau Burrows, RHP

**MiLB Rank: #159**

**Position Rank: N/A**

| Born: 09/18/96 | Age: 19 | Bats: R | Top CALs: Brian Gonzalez, Michael Blazek, |
| Height: 6-2 | Weight: 200 | Throws: R | Miguel Gonzalez, Sean Reid-Foley, Jacob Partridge |

| YEAR | Age | Level | IP | W | L | ERA | FIP | K/9 | BB/9 | K% | BB% | HR/9 | LOB% |
|---|---|---|---|---|---|---|---|---|---|---|---|---|---|
| 2015 | 18 | R | 28.0 | 1 | 0 | 1.61 | 2.34 | 10.61 | 3.54 | 29.7% | 9.9% | 0.00 | 77.4% |

**Background:** For the first time since taking Jacob Turner in 2009, the Tigers drafted a prep arm in the opening round of the June draft. Burrows, who signed for the full slot-value of $2.154 million, tossed 28.0 innings in the Gulf Coast during his debut, posting an impressive 1.61 ERA with a 33-to-11 strikeout-to-walk ratio.

**Projection**: Under the Dave Dombrowski regime the Tigers were a perfect two-for-two in drafting prep arms in the first round of the draft, first taking Rick Porcello and then grabbing Turner two years later. And Burrows looks like he could be the next to develop into a viable big league arm. He's likely headed to the Midwest League in 2016.

**Ceiling:** Too Soon to Tell
**Risk:** N/A
**MLB ETA:** N/A

## 4. Austin Kubitza, RHP

**MiLB Rank: #225**
**Position Rank: N/A**

| Born: 11/16/91 | Age: 24 | Bats: R | **Top CALs:** Scott Diamond, James Needy, |
|---|---|---|---|
| Height: 6-5 | Weight: 225 | Throws: R | Carlos Hernandez, Josh Collmenter, Esmerling Vasquez |

| YEAR | Age | Level | IP | W | L | ERA | FIP | K/9 | BB/9 | K% | BB% | HR/9 | LOB% |
|---|---|---|---|---|---|---|---|---|---|---|---|---|---|
| 2013 | 21 | R | 8.3 | 0 | 0 | 2.16 | 2.98 | 5.40 | 1.08 | 16.7% | 3.3% | 0.00 | 57.1% |
| 2013 | 21 | A+ | 17.0 | 0 | 1 | 5.82 | 4.24 | 7.41 | 5.29 | 18.0% | 12.8% | 0.00 | 61.3% |
| 2014 | 22 | A | 131.0 | 10 | 2 | 2.34 | 2.99 | 9.62 | 2.95 | 26.0% | 8.0% | 0.34 | 72.3% |
| 2015 | 23 | AA | 133.7 | 9 | 13 | 5.79 | 3.65 | 6.46 | 3.23 | 15.1% | 7.6% | 0.40 | 58.1% |

**Background:** Arguably my favorite collegiate arm in the entire 2014 draft – which should be noted as being different than the collegiate arm available. Kubitza was an absolute stud during his time at Arm Shredder U. – also known, by me at least, Rice University. After his impressive three-year run, he left the school with a dominant 309-to-110 strikeout-to-walk ratio in a quasi-mind-boggling 290 innings. Detroit would take the wiry right-hander in the fourth round, 126th overall, as part of their effort to take every collegiate arm available. Since then he's dominated the Midwest League (131.0 IP, 140 K, 43 BB, 2.34 ERA, and a 2.99 FIP) and looked passable in the Eastern League as he bypassed High Class A last season (133.2 IP, 96 K, and 48 BB).

**Projection**: Here's what I wrote about the 6-foot-5, 225-pound right-hander prior to the draft:

> "There's some concern with Kubitza's ability to throw strikes and his walk rate has worsened in each of his three seasons, going from 2.16 BB/9 to 4.26 BB/9 to 4.32 BB/9. He's clearly got front of the rotation potential, but there's a decent amount of risk because of his control problems. Still, though, he's allowed just 11 extra-base hits and the ability to miss bats looks like a premium."

So let's fast forward two years, shall we? Kubitza passed the most important minor league challenge – Class AA – even if he was sporting an unsightly 5.79 ERA. His true measure of performance, according to his 3.65 FIP, was much more in line with his particular skill set as he battled through a lot of crap luck (.387 BABIP, 58.1% strand-rate). He did seem to tire in the second half of the season. In his first 13 starts with the SeaWolves he posted an impressive 56-to-25 strikeout-to-walk ratio, but that declined to a mediocre 40-to-23 over his final 14 starts.

On the positive side, he continues to generate a crap-ton of groundballs, averaging 59.2% last season and a freakin' ridiculous 70.4% two years ago.

Kubitza no longer profiles as a top-of-the-rotation arm, but he could develop into a steady #4.

**Ceiling:** 1.5- to 2.0-win player
**Risk:** Moderate
**MLB ETA:** 2016

## 5. Jairo Labourt, LHP

**MiLB Rank: N/A**
**Position Rank: N/A**

| Born: 03/07/94 | Age: 22 | Bats: L | **Top CALs:** Yeiper Castillo, Jose Ramirez, |
|---|---|---|---|
| Height: 6-4 | Weight: 205 | Throws: L | Tyler Vail, David Baker, Arquimedes Nieto |

| YEAR | Age | Level | IP | W | L | ERA | FIP | K/9 | BB/9 | K% | BB% | HR/9 | LOB% |
|---|---|---|---|---|---|---|---|---|---|---|---|---|---|
| 2013 | 19 | R | 51.7 | 2 | 2 | 1.92 | 3.43 | 7.84 | 2.44 | 21.3% | 6.6% | 0.52 | 77.2% |
| 2014 | 20 | A- | 71.3 | 5 | 3 | 1.77 | 3.41 | 10.35 | 4.67 | 27.5% | 12.4% | 0.00 | 81.5% |
| 2014 | 20 | A | 14.0 | 0 | 0 | 6.43 | 7.77 | 7.07 | 12.86 | 14.9% | 27.0% | 0.64 | 68.3% |
| 2015 | 21 | A+ | 116.0 | 3 | 12 | 5.12 | 4.01 | 8.07 | 4.58 | 19.5% | 11.1% | 0.70 | 61.7% |

**Background:** In one of his final moves as a member of the Detroit Tigers, Dave Dombrowski shipped David Price to the Toronto Blue Jays for a package of three players: former top prospect Daniel Norris, who narrowly exhausted his rookie status, Matt Boyd, and Labourt, a sinewy 6-foot-4, 205-pounder out of the Dominican Republic. And despite changing organizations at the season's midpoint, Labourt spent the entire year in the Florida State League where he would throw a career high 116.0 innings while averaging 8.1 strikeouts and 4.6 walks per nine innings. His 4.01 FIP was quite a bit lower than his combined 5.12 ERA. It was an aggressive promotion for the young lefty as he bypassed Low Class A after just 14.0 innings in 2014. For his career, Labourt has fanned 310 and walked 167 in 327.0 innings of work.

**Projection**: The Tigers did well enough by acquiring Norris, a solid bet to develop into a #2 or #3-type arm in the coming years. But Labourt is a nice gamble by the former regime-head. Last year, the then-21-year-old southpaw encountered his real struggles in professional baseball after more or less breezing through the Dominican Summer Leagues all the way up through short-season ball. And Labourt seemed to handle the aggressive promotion to High Class A last season. Given his relative youth and solid peripherals, Labourt has a chance to develop into a #4-type arm.

# Detroit Tigers

**Ceiling:** 1.5- to 2.0-win player
**Risk:** Moderate to High
**MLB ETA:** 2017/2018

## 6. Kevin Ziomek, LHP

**MiLB Rank:** N/A
**Position Rank:** N/A

| Born: 03/21/92 | Age: 24 | Bats: R | Top CALs: Aaron Blair, Juan Nicasio, |
| Height: 6-3 | Weight: 200 | Throws: L | Brad Mills, Steven Matz, Garrett Richards |

| YEAR | Age | Level | IP | W | L | ERA | FIP | K/9 | BB/9 | K% | BB% | HR/9 | LOB% |
|---|---|---|---|---|---|---|---|---|---|---|---|---|---|
| 2013 | 21 | A- | 8.0 | 0 | 1 | 4.50 | 4.97 | 3.38 | 5.63 | 8.8% | 14.7% | 0.00 | 58.3% |
| 2014 | 22 | A | 123.0 | 10 | 6 | 2.27 | 2.98 | 11.12 | 3.88 | 29.8% | 10.4% | 0.37 | 73.1% |
| 2015 | 23 | A+ | 154.7 | 9 | 11 | 3.43 | 2.38 | 8.32 | 1.98 | 22.6% | 5.4% | 0.17 | 64.0% |

**Background:** Picked behind a couple arms that are no longer in the organization thanks to some trades, Ziomek was part of Detroit's incredible collegiate-pitcher-heavy 2013 draft. The organization took an astounding 24 pitchers from four-year colleges and two from JUCOs out of their 41 overall picks. Hailing from Pitcher U. – also known as Vanderbilt University – Ziomek's been on the slow and steady development plan in his first three years in the organization, or the Anti-Buck Farmer path as it's known. After tossing a career-high 119.0 innings for the Commodores during his junior season, Detroit limited the 6-foot-3, 200-pound southpaw to just eight innings with Connecticut in the NYPL during his debut. Ziomek would spend the next year, 2014, with West Michigan, throwing a 123.0 innings while posting an impressive 152-to-53 strikeout-to-walk ratio. The club bumped him up another level last year, to the Florida State League, where he would throw a career best 154.2 innings while averaging 8.3 K/9. But more importantly he finished the year with his lowest walk rate, 1.98 BB/9, of his career – extending all the way back to his days before college. Ziomek was named the Tigers' Pitching Prospect of the Year as well.

**Projection**: First things first, here's what I wrote prior to the 2013 draft:

*"Along with the impressive K-rate (8.89 K/9) is the fact that it's come against a difficult schedule, something not every lefty can boast. Once adjusted for park and schedule – thanks to CollegeSplits.com – Ziomek's peripherals are even more impressive 9.29 K/9 and 2.88 BB/9. He's not an elite prospect, but he's right up there with Gonzaga's Marco Gonzalez."*

Well, despite the impressive peripherals and subsequent award recognition, Ziomek still isn't an elite prospect – namely because he's spent the past couple of years twirling gems against less-polished hitters in an age-appropriate level of competition. His once dominant punch out rate in the Midwest League plummeted to above-average status last season and it's going to take another step down as he moves up to the Eastern League in 2016, finishing around 7.2 K/9. With that being said, he has the makeup, build, and production to develop into a capable backend starter at the big league level.

One final thought: it wouldn't be surprising to see Detroit ship off the big lefty as part of mid-season trade to bolster the big league club.

**Ceiling:** 1.5-win player
**Risk:** Moderate
**MLB ETA:** 2016/2017

## 7. Steven Moya, RF

**MiLB Rank:** N/A
**Position Rank:** N/A

| Born: 08/09/91 | Age: 24 | Bats: L | Top CALs: Willy Garcia, Quincy Latimore, |
| Height: 6-7 | Weight: 260 | Throws: R | Denny Almonte, Greg Golson, Wilkin Ramirez |

| Season | Age | LVL | PA | 2B | 3B | HR | AVG | OBP | SLG | ISO | BB% | K% | wRC+ |
|---|---|---|---|---|---|---|---|---|---|---|---|---|---|
| 2013 | 21 | A+ | 388 | 19 | 5 | 12 | 0.255 | 0.296 | 0.433 | 0.178 | 4.6% | 27.3% | 106 |
| 2014 | 22 | AA | 549 | 33 | 3 | 35 | 0.276 | 0.306 | 0.555 | 0.280 | 4.2% | 29.3% | 131 |
| 2015 | 23 | A+ | 42 | 3 | 0 | 3 | 0.275 | 0.286 | 0.575 | 0.300 | 2.4% | 31.0% | 152 |
| 2015 | 23 | AAA | 535 | 30 | 0 | 20 | 0.240 | 0.283 | 0.420 | 0.180 | 5.0% | 30.3% | 101 |
| 2015 | 23 | MLB | 25 | 0 | 1 | 0 | 0.182 | 0.280 | 0.273 | 0.091 | 12.0% | 40.0% | 54 |

**Background:** With enough power to be named in the same conversation as Joey Gallo, the Rangers' bopping hulkster, Moya seemingly bashed every pitch during his breakout 2014 season (one in which was predicted in the book two years ago), slugging an impressive 33 doubles, three triples, and 35 homeruns en route to posting a solid .276/.306/.555 triple-slash line. Last season, however, the massive 6-foot-7, 260-pound right fielder looked a bit underwhelming in his first – and not last – go-round with the Toledo Mud Hens. After a quick nine-game tune-up with the Flying Tigers in High Class A, Moya batted a league average-ish .240/.283/.420 with 30 doubles and 20 homeruns in 535 trips to the plate in the International League. For his career, Moya is sporting a .249/.292/.441 mark with 122 doubles, 14 triples, and 100 dingers in 606 games.

**Projection:** I remained quite leery of Moya's ability to maintain his massive breakout, writing the following in last year's book:

> *"Moya finally tapped in his massive raw power and he continued his abhorrence to the free pass as well as battling contact issues; he walked just 4.2% and whiffed in 29.3% of his plate appearances last season. The lefty-swinging Moya has – surprisingly – handled fellow southpaws relatively well in his career. But, again, the K-rate has been trending in the wrong direction for years and he's made zero improvement in his low walk rates. There's certainly big league value here, but there's a ton of risk. Luckily, he's only entering his age-23 season."*

So the walk-abhorrence continued well into the 2015 season as he found first base via the free pass just 27 times out of his 535 plate appearances with Toledo. And, of course, his swing-and-miss tendencies ticked back up over the 30% mark as well. And just for added he fun: he struggled against southpaws last season as well, hitting a lowly .209/.231/.379 against them.

The big league club has Anthony Gose, Cameron Maybin, and J.D. Martinez penciled in at the outfield positions and veteran switch-hitting Victor Martinez at designated hitter, so Moya isn't likely going to find a whole lot of ABs until an injury – or a rash of injuries – strikes. With that being said, the current run environment in the big leagues is so putrid and power deprived that Moya could become something along the lines of a lesser version of Mark Trumbo with some defensive contributions.

**Ceiling:** 1.5-win player
**Risk:** Moderate
**MLB ETA:** Debuted in 2014

## 8. Christin Stewart, LF

**MiLB Rank: N/A**
**Position Rank: N/A**

| Born: 12/10/93 | Age: 22 | Bats: L | Top CALs: Harrison Bader, Derek Fisher, Michael Gerber, Jacob Scavuzzo, Zoilo Almonte |
|---|---|---|---|
| Height: 6-0 | Weight: 205 | Throws: R | |

| Season | Age | LVL | PA | 2B | 3B | HR | AVG | OBP | SLG | ISO | BB% | K% | wRC+ |
|---|---|---|---|---|---|---|---|---|---|---|---|---|---|
| 2015 | 21 | R | 26 | 2 | 1 | 1 | 0.364 | 0.462 | 0.682 | 0.318 | 11.5% | 19.2% | 233 |
| 2015 | 21 | A- | 59 | 2 | 2 | 2 | 0.245 | 0.322 | 0.490 | 0.245 | 8.5% | 30.5% | 130 |
| 2015 | 21 | A | 216 | 9 | 4 | 7 | 0.286 | 0.375 | 0.492 | 0.205 | 8.3% | 20.8% | 151 |

**Background:** Here's an interesting little tidbit for you: Prior to Stewart's selection as the 34th overall player in the 2015 draft, the last collegiate player taken in the first round was Southern University and A&M College second baseman Michael Woods – the year *before* Dave Dombrowski pulled up a chair at the front of the organization's table. So let's meet the man that broke Dombrowski's mantra of taking high-ceiling prepsters and polished collegiate arms in the first round. Stewart was a three-year mainstay for the University of Tennessee. After failing to turn enough pro heads coming out of high school, the solidly-built corner outfielder looked at ease as a true freshman in the SEC, hitting .310/.414/.455. He would follow that up with an even better showing during his sophomore season: .330/.386/.541 with a mind-boggling 19 doubles, six triples, five dingers, and seven stolen bases. And then he upped the ante even further during his final run with the school. In 221 plate appearances for the Volunteers, Stewart slugged a robust .311/.443/.633 with eight doubles, a pair of triples, and 15 homeruns, nearly double his career total at that point.

Detroit bounced the young outfielder through three levels during his debut, though most of his offensive damage was done with West Michigan in the Midwest League. He would bat .286/.375/.492 with plenty of extra-base firepower (nine doubles, four triples, and seven homeruns) in 216 PAs.

**Projection:** Here's what I wrote about Stewart prior to the draft last year:

> *"Solid overall offensive toolkit without a true standout tool that would play well in the professional ranks. Stewart has an average approach at the plate, decent hit tool, and 15- to 17-homerun power. While his career ISO stands a couple ticks above .220, it's important to remember that Tennessee's home ballpark, Lindsey Nelson Stadium, slightly enhances offensive production as well.*
>
> *In terms of professional ceiling, Stewart looks like a backup outfielder."*

**Ceiling:** 1.5-win player
**Risk:** Moderate
**MLB ETA:** 2018

## 9. Zach Shepherd, 3B

**MiLB Rank: N/A**
**Position Rank: N/A**

| Born: 09/14/95 | Age: 20 | Bats: R | Top CALs: Alex Liddi, Kevin Ahrens, |
|---|---|---|---|
| Height: 6-3 | Weight: 185 | Throws: R | Trey Michalczewski, Drew Ward, Jake Hanson |

| Season | Age | LVL | PA | 2B | 3B | HR | AVG | OBP | SLG | ISO | BB% | K% | wRC+ |
|---|---|---|---|---|---|---|---|---|---|---|---|---|---|
| 2014 | 18 | R | 201 | 12 | 5 | 4 | 0.301 | 0.373 | 0.497 | 0.197 | 10.4% | 21.9% | 146 |
| 2015 | 19 | A | 443 | 17 | 2 | 5 | 0.245 | 0.327 | 0.339 | 0.094 | 10.6% | 26.4% | 97 |

**Background:** Signed from the Land Down Under for $325,000 as a 16-year-old in 2012. Detroit waited a year before moving the 6-foot-3, 185-pound third baseman stateside, pushing him right into the Gulf Coast League two years ago. Shepherd responded by hitting an impressive .301/.373/.497 in 201 trips to the plate. The front office bumped the hot corner up to the Midwest League with far less impressive results.

**Projection**: One of the key components in evaluating teenage prospects in full-season ball is to look at how the prospect fared after the initial shock wears off *and* before they wear down. So let's do that, shall we? Ignoring Shepherd's hideous first month and his equally poor August, he hit a more-than-respectable .274/.366/.361 between May 1st and July 31st, a span of 74 games and 287 plate appearances. While it's not exactly a run of dominance, it's more than respectable for a 19-year-old getting his first taste of the Sally. If he can flash the above-average pop he showed two years ago he might have a shot to develop into a big league starter.

**Ceiling:** 1.5-win player
**Risk:** Moderate
**MLB ETA:** 2019

## 10. Derek Hill, CF

**MiLB Rank: N/A**
**Position Rank: N/A**

| Born: 12/30/95 | Age: 20 | Bats: R | Top CALs: Gregory Polanco, Cord Sandberg, |
|---|---|---|---|
| Height: 6-2 | Weight: 195 | Throws: R | Troy Stokes, Michael Swinson, Josh Roberts |

| Season | Age | LVL | PA | 2B | 3B | HR | AVG | OBP | SLG | ISO | BB% | K% | wRC+ |
|---|---|---|---|---|---|---|---|---|---|---|---|---|---|
| 2014 | 18 | R | 119 | 2 | 2 | 2 | 0.212 | 0.331 | 0.333 | 0.121 | 13.4% | 16.0% | 99 |
| 2015 | 19 | A | 235 | 6 | 5 | 0 | 0.238 | 0.305 | 0.314 | 0.076 | 8.5% | 18.7% | 82 |

**Background:** Fun fact: Derek Hill was selected as the 23rd overall pick in the 2014 draft; his father Orsino Hill, a baseball-lifer, was chosen with the 24th overall pick in the 1982 draft out of University of Nebraska. But, unfortunately, the parallels between father-and-son don't end there either. Orsino struggled through his first taste of the Midwest Leagues, hitting a lowly .229/.318/.384 with Cedar Rapids in 1983. And Derek, the toolsy center fielder with a couple million bucks in his pocket already, hit an unimpressive .238/.305/.314 in his first taste in an injury-shortened campaign in the Midwest League. For his career, Hill is sporting a lowly .225/.301/.305 triple-slash line with just nine doubles, eight triples, and two homeruns in 100 games.

**Projection:** The positives: Hill has a fairly solid approach at the plate, at least in terms of peripherals. He's walked in 8.8% and punched out in 20.6% of his career plate appearances. And he's offering up plenty of speed; he's swiped 36 bags in 45 attempts; or about 58 bags in a typical 162-game season.

Now the negatives: an underwhelming hit tool and basically no power.

Hill's still plenty young enough to start driving the ball with more authority – especially given his 6-foot-2, 195-pound frame – but it has to start happening like…tomorrow.

**Ceiling:** 2.0-win player
**Risk:** High
**MLB ETA:** 2019

## 11. Dixon Machado, SS

**MiLB Rank:** N/A
**Position Rank:** N/A

| Born: 02/22/92 | Age: 24 | Bats: R | Top CALs: Justin Sellers, Tyler Saladino, |
|---|---|---|---|
| Height: 6-1 | Weight: 170 | Throws: R | Cristhian Adames, Trevor Plouffe, Daniel Mayora |

| Season | Age | LVL | PA | 2B | 3B | HR | AVG | OBP | SLG | ISO | BB% | K% | wRC+ |
|---|---|---|---|---|---|---|---|---|---|---|---|---|---|
| 2013 | 21 | A+ | 163 | 5 | 2 | 1 | 0.215 | 0.264 | 0.295 | 0.081 | 6.1% | 11.7% | 57 |
| 2014 | 22 | A+ | 187 | 8 | 1 | 1 | 0.252 | 0.348 | 0.333 | 0.082 | 12.3% | 18.2% | 101 |
| 2014 | 22 | AA | 342 | 23 | 1 | 5 | 0.305 | 0.391 | 0.442 | 0.137 | 11.7% | 10.5% | 135 |
| 2015 | 23 | AAA | 567 | 22 | 1 | 4 | 0.261 | 0.313 | 0.332 | 0.071 | 6.3% | 15.0% | 88 |
| 2015 | 23 | MLB | 78 | 3 | 0 | 0 | 0.235 | 0.307 | 0.279 | 0.044 | 9.0% | 17.9% | 64 |

**Background:** The Venezuelan-born shortstop's production came crashing back to earth after his breakout 2014 when he slugged .305/.391/.442 in 90 games in the Eastern League, a stark rise from his 41-game stint in High Class A (.252/.348/.333). Machado batted a lowly .261/.313/.332 in the International League and failed to set the world ablaze in his 24-game stint in Detroit.

**Projection**: Here's how I closed out Machado's projection part in last year's book:

*"CAL thinks he has a chance to develop into a decent hitter, something along the lines of a 90 wRC+, which could in turn push him close to league average status with good defense."*

For the record, he finished last season with an 88 wRC+. Anyway, the cause for Machado's rapid decline was his complete lack of power in Class AAA last season – his ISO dropped from .137 in Class AA to a lowly .071 with Toledo last season – and he stopped walking an above-average clip. He still looks like a decent utility guy, nothing more. As for CAL, well, it seems to agree: Justin Sellers, Tyler Saladino, Cristhian Adames, Trevor Plouffe (the lone exception), and Daniel Mayora.

**Ceiling:** 1.0- to 1.5-win player
**Risk:** Low to Moderate
**MLB ETA:** Debuted in 2015

## 12. Matt Hall, LHP

**MiLB Rank:** N/A
**Position Rank:** N/A

| Born: 07/23/93 | Age: 22 | Bats: L | Top CALs: Jose Macias, Elih Villanueva, |
|---|---|---|---|
| Height: 6-0 | Weight: 200 | Throws: L | James Shepherd, Yoervis, Tony Rizzotti |

| YEAR | Age | Level | IP | W | L | ERA | FIP | K/9 | BB/9 | K% | BB% | HR/9 | LOB% |
|---|---|---|---|---|---|---|---|---|---|---|---|---|---|
| 2015 | 21 | R | 3.0 | 0 | 0 | 3.00 | 1.64 | 12.00 | 3.00 | 28.6% | 7.1% | 0.00 | 80.0% |
| 2015 | 21 | A- | 31.0 | 0 | 1 | 2.90 | 3.52 | 8.71 | 2.03 | 24.0% | 5.6% | 0.87 | 78.6% |

**Background:** The 6-foot, 200-pound lefty was an absolute dominant force to be reckoned with during his junior season with Missouri State: in a career best 125.0 innings he tallied a 2.02 ERA with 45 walks and 171 strikeouts, the most among any Division I hurler. Detroit eventually grabbed Hall in the sixth round last June and sent him to the Gulf Coast briefly before promoting him up to Connecticut in the NYPL.

**Projection**: Here's what I wrote prior to last year's draft:

*"Not overpowering in the traditional sense, Hall relies more on pitchability and guile. His control has never been great, but it grades out as an average skillset. He'll miss a handful of bats in the professional ranks – something around 7.2 K/9 – and should easily dominate the lower levels. Nice mid- to back-of-the-rotation caliber arm, maybe peaking around a decent #4. Think something along the lines of Mike Leake."*

Needless to say, I think the Tigers got a tremendous find in the sixth round last June.

**Ceiling:** 1.0-win player
**Risk:** Low to Moderate
**MLB ETA:** 2016

## 13. Spencer Turnbull, RHP

**MiLB Rank: N/A**
**Position Rank: N/A**

| Born: 09/18/92 | Age: 23 | Bats: R | **Top CALs:** Frank Garces, Jayson Ruhlman, Kyle Parker, Edward Rodriguez, AJ Schugel |
| Height: 6-3 | Weight: 215 | Throws: R | |

| YEAR | Age | Level | IP | W | L | ERA | FIP | K/9 | BB/9 | K% | BB% | HR/9 | LOB% |
|---|---|---|---|---|---|---|---|---|---|---|---|---|---|
| 2014 | 21 | R | 3.0 | 0 | 0 | 3.00 | 6.17 | 12.00 | 3.00 | 36.4% | 9.1% | 3.00 | 100.0% |
| 2014 | 21 | A- | 28.3 | 0 | 2 | 4.45 | 4.15 | 6.04 | 4.45 | 14.5% | 10.7% | 0.32 | 67.3% |
| 2015 | 22 | A | 116.7 | 11 | 3 | 3.01 | 3.10 | 8.18 | 4.01 | 21.1% | 10.3% | 0.00 | 72.7% |

**Background:** The club's second round pick two years ago, Turnbull was taken with the 63rd overall selection out of the University of Alabama after a largely mediocre career in the school's rotation. He averaged just 5.99 K/9 and 4.23 BB/9. The 6-foot-3, 215-pound right-hander spent all of last season working out of West Michigan's rotation, posting a 106-to-52 strikeout-to-walk ratio in 116.2 innings of work.

**Projection**: Turnbull saw a dramatic uptick in his strikeout rate since entering pro ball, but, unfortunately for him, his control has followed suit. He did have a nine-game stretch to close out the season where he tallied an impeccable 50-to-14 strikeout-to-walk ratio in 49.2 innings of work. Turnbull will head to the Florida State League in 2016. And if he can't carry that momentum into the league, expect him to get pushed into a relief role.

**Ceiling:** 1.0- to 1.5-win player
**Risk:** Moderate
**MLB ETA:** 2018

## 14. JaCoby Jones, SS

**MiLB Rank: N/A**
**Position Rank: N/A**

| Born: 05/10/92 | Age: 24 | Bats: R | **Top CALs:** Jason Martinson, Bruce Caldwell, Cody Puckett, Danny Espinosa, Brandon Wood |
| Height: 6-2 | Weight: 205 | Throws: R | |

| Season | Age | LVL | PA | 2B | 3B | HR | AVG | OBP | SLG | ISO | BB% | K% | wRC+ |
|---|---|---|---|---|---|---|---|---|---|---|---|---|---|
| 2014 | 22 | A | 501 | 21 | 3 | 23 | 0.288 | 0.347 | 0.503 | 0.216 | 6.6% | 26.3% | 134 |
| 2015 | 23 | A+ | 423 | 18 | 3 | 10 | 0.253 | 0.313 | 0.396 | 0.142 | 7.3% | 26.7% | 116 |
| 2015 | 23 | AA | 171 | 7 | 2 | 6 | 0.267 | 0.345 | 0.466 | 0.199 | 10.5% | 30.4% | 131 |

**Background:** Acquired at the trade deadline last season from the Pirates in a straight-up one-for-one deal that sent veteran right-hander Joakim Soria to the NL Central. Jones initially burst onto the scenes as a hot-shot freshman dominating for one of the top collegiate programs in the world, hitting a robust .338/.395/.467 with doubles power and speed for the LSU Tigers. His production would crater the following year (.253/.308/.363), as well as at the start of his junior campaign before a late-season surge buoyed his overall production (.294/.390/.448). Pittsburgh would eventually grab Jones in the third round, 87th overall, three years ago. Since then he's: dominated the South Atlantic League, looked decent in High Class A, remained solid in a relatively brief trip to the Eastern League, and got popped – twice – for a drug of abuse, the most recent time in early November. Jones was subsequently suspended for 50 games – a move that essentially cost him the first half of arguably the most important season to date.

**Projection**: First, here's what I wrote prior to the 2013 draft:

> He has some useful skills: solid speed, a pretty decent eye at the plate, and a little bit of pop. But Jones strikes out an awful lot (19%) and his total production is hardly noteworthy (.283/.382/.417) Still, though, with the current state of the game, it wouldn't be surprising to find him being taken as soon as the third round. Jones probably won't be an everyday player and may not even be serviceable bench option, but he provides some depth with a little bit of upside. If a team's lucky, maybe, just maybe, they might be able to unlock the key to his successful freshman year."

Fast forward a couple seasons and Jones as squarely fallen into the "depth option" in terms of his ceiling. And basically the same things could be said now as I wrote three years ago: decent eye, solid-average power, and problematic strikeout tendencies. He's fanned in 26.8% of his career plate appearances. Still, though, power from the middle infield position is valuable, but that's what they said about Brandon Wood, one of Jones' top CALs, too.

**Ceiling:** 1.0- to 1.5-win player
**Risk:** Moderate
**MLB ETA:** 2017

## 15. Artie Lewicki, RHP

**MiLB Rank: N/A**
**Position Rank: N/A**

| Born: 04/08/92 | Age: 24 | Bats: R | Top CALs: Manolin De Leon, Philip Wetherell, |
|---|---|---|---|
| Height: 6-3 | Weight: 195 | Throws: R | Josh Taylor, Dan Merklinger, Jared Lakind |

| YEAR | Age | Level | IP | W | L | ERA | FIP | K/9 | BB/9 | K% | BB% | HR/9 | LOB% |
|---|---|---|---|---|---|---|---|---|---|---|---|---|---|
| 2014 | 22 | R | 2.0 | 0 | 0 | 0.00 | 1.01 | 18.00 | 4.50 | 40.0% | 10.0% | 0.00 | 100.0% |
| 2014 | 22 | A | 25.7 | 2 | 2 | 2.45 | 3.84 | 7.71 | 3.16 | 22.0% | 9.0% | 0.70 | 79.4% |
| 2015 | 23 | A | 79.3 | 3 | 4 | 3.52 | 3.13 | 8.74 | 2.84 | 22.4% | 7.3% | 0.45 | 71.0% |

**Background:** Despite spending four years in college the 6-foot-3, 195-pound right-hander tallied just 158.0 career innings while at the University of Virginia – of course, losing a year-plus to Tommy John surgery will do that for you. Detroit would eventually grab the surgically repaired right arm in the eighth round two years ago, 250th overall, and he – once again – battled through injuries last season. After making his first start of the year on April 10th, a four-plus-inning clunker against the Dayton Dragons, Lewicki hit the DL for two months with a strained right pectoral. He eventually made it back for another 14 starts beginning on June 11th. And he would finish the year with 79.1 innings, a solid 3.52 ERA, 77 punch outs, and just 25 walks.

**Projection:** Lewicki falls into the same category as pretty much every other hurler making an appearance in Detroit's Top Prospect List this season: an older, polished collegiate arm that's simply too good for his particular level of competition. Lewicki didn't miss a beat going from pitching against some of the best collegiate competition to the lowest level of full season ball in the minors. He never missed a whole lot of bats during his amateur career, so his 8.7% K-rate will likely prove to be a mirage. He's another one of these backend/relief types.

**Ceiling:** 1.0- to 1.5-win player
**Risk:** Moderate
**MLB ETA:** 2018

## 16. Wynton Bernard, OF

**MiLB Rank: N/A**
**Position Rank: N/A**

| Born: 09/24/90 | Age: 25 | Bats: R | Top CALs: Tom Belza, Brett Nommensen, |
|---|---|---|---|
| Height: 6-2 | Weight: 195 | Throws: R | Whit Merrifield, Ryan Lollis, Tim Smith |

| Season | Age | LVL | PA | 2B | 3B | HR | AVG | OBP | SLG | ISO | BB% | K% | wRC+ |
|---|---|---|---|---|---|---|---|---|---|---|---|---|---|
| 2013 | 22 | A- | 161 | 5 | 1 | 1 | 0.250 | 0.333 | 0.324 | 0.074 | 11.2% | 20.5% | 96 |
| 2014 | 23 | A | 583 | 30 | 6 | 6 | 0.323 | 0.394 | 0.442 | 0.118 | 9.6% | 14.8% | 142 |
| 2015 | 24 | AA | 587 | 29 | 8 | 4 | 0.301 | 0.352 | 0.408 | 0.107 | 6.5% | 12.4% | 121 |

**Background:** A late, late round pick of the Padres out of Niagara University back in 2012, Bernard found his way into the Detroit organization as a minor league free agent two years ago. And since then the former 35th round pick has been an offensive revelation. After failing to top a .656 OPS in the lowest levels of the minors in his two seasons with San Diego, things seemed to click for Bernard over the past two seasons as he's slugged .323/.394/.442 with 30 doubles, six triples, six homeruns, and 45 stolen bases (in 64 attempts) in the Midwest League and he handled the aggressive push up to Class AA last season, hitting .301/.352/.408 with 29 doubles, eight triples, four homeruns, and 43 stolen bases (in 59 attempts). His overall production since entering the Tigers' development engine has been at least 21% better than the league average.

**Projection:** All the credit in the world goes to both the Tigers' scouting/analytical department for quickly signing the former minor league free agent *and* to Bernard for making the necessary adjustments to develop into a surprisingly strong minor league hitter. Obviously, the speed is an above-average skill, but he'll flash gap-to-gap power and take the occasional walk. He's not going to be a full-time regular, but there's no reason to suggest that he can't carve out a lengthy big league career as a backup. Tremendous, tremendous, tremendous find by the Tigers. I can't reiterate that enough.

**Ceiling:** 1.0- to 1.5-win player
**Risk:** Moderate
**MLB ETA:** 2016

## 17. Tyler Alexander, LHP

**MiLB Rank:** N/A
**Position Rank:** N/A

| Born: 07/14/94 | Age: 21 | Bats: R | Top CALs: Cody Poteet, Mitchell Lambson, |
| Height: 6-3 | Weight: 200 | Throws: L | Lorenzo Mendoza, Daniel Oliver, Adam Veres |

| YEAR | Age | Level | IP | W | L | ERA | FIP | K/9 | BB/9 | K% | BB% | HR/9 | LOB% |
|------|-----|-------|-----|---|---|------|------|------|------|-------|------|------|-------|
| 2015 | 20 | A- | 37.0 | 0 | 2 | 0.97 | 3.27 | 8.03 | 1.22 | 24.4% | 3.7% | 0.73 | 85.1% |

**Background:** A finesse lefty in the traditional sense, Alexander spent two seasons in TCU's rotation. He left the school with a career 131-to-21 strikeout-to-walk ratio and a 2.70 ERA in 193.0 innings. Detroit sent him to the New York-Penn League for his debut where he would throw another 37.0 innings of nearly unhittable ball: 0.97 ERA, 33 K, 5 BB.

**Projection:** So it's probably goes without saying that Alexander isn't going to miss many bats in the future. Hell, his strikeout rate last season, 8.03 K/9, is probably the only time he cracks the 7.5 K/9-mark in the coming years. But, damn, he sure as hell can pitch his ass off. Plus, he generates a ton of action on the ground (64.6% GB-rate during his debut). He might have an outside shot to develop into a traditional #5.

**Ceiling:** 1.0- to 1.5-win player
**Risk:** Moderate to High
**MLB ETA:** 2018

## 18. Jefry Marte, 1B/3B

**MiLB Rank:** N/A
**Position Rank:** N/A

| Born: 06/21/91 | Age: 25 | Bats: R | Top CALs: Conor Gillaspie, Tyler Kuhn, |
| Height: 6-1 | Weight: 220 | Throws: R | Zelous Wheeler, Pete Ciofrone, Zack Cox |

| Season | Age | LVL | PA | 2B | 3B | HR | AVG | OBP | SLG | ISO | BB% | K% | wRC+ |
|--------|-----|-----|-----|----|----|----|-------|-------|-------|-------|------|-------|------|
| 2013 | 22 | AA | 278 | 17 | 1 | 2 | 0.278 | 0.349 | 0.380 | 0.102 | 9.0% | 17.6% | 107 |
| 2014 | 23 | AA | 460 | 17 | 0 | 10 | 0.259 | 0.333 | 0.375 | 0.116 | 9.8% | 15.0% | 105 |
| 2015 | 24 | AAA | 399 | 25 | 3 | 15 | 0.275 | 0.341 | 0.487 | 0.213 | 7.8% | 16.0% | 139 |
| 2015 | 24 | MLB | 90 | 4 | 0 | 4 | 0.213 | 0.284 | 0.413 | 0.200 | 8.9% | 24.4% | 89 |

**Background:** He's bounced around quite a bit during his eight-year minor league career, going from the Mets and Oakland before landing with the Detroit organization last season. Marte had his finest professional season to date, though, hitting .275/.341/.487 with 25 doubles, three triples, and 15 homeruns en route to posting a 139 wRC+.

**Projection:** I've always been a bit of fan of Marte's over the past couple of seasons. He's always shown a decent eye at the plate with a reasonable ability to make contact. And he's flashed solid pop at various points in his career as well. But last season's surge – he posted a .213 ISO – was completely unexpected. Think of him as a poor man's version of J.D. Martinez, another Detroit reclamation project.

**Ceiling:** 1.0-win player
**Risk:** Moderate
**MLB ETA:** Debuted in 2015

## 19. Jose Valdez, RHP

**MiLB Rank:** N/A
**Position Rank:** N/A

| Born: 03/01/90 | Age: 21 | Bats: R | Top CALs: Joe Bisenius, Jay Buente, |
| Height: 6-1 | Weight: 200 | Throws: R | Santos Rodriguez, Edgar Ibarra, Joe Testa |

| YEAR | Age | Level | IP | W | L | ERA | FIP | K/9 | BB/9 | K% | BB% | HR/9 | LOB% |
|------|-----|-------|------|---|---|------|------|-------|------|-------|-------|------|-------|
| 2013 | 23 | A | 26.3 | 1 | 1 | 2.73 | 2.96 | 11.96 | 6.84 | 31.8% | 18.2% | 0.00 | 75.0% |
| 2013 | 23 | A+ | 23.0 | 1 | 1 | 2.74 | 2.98 | 12.52 | 5.48 | 33.0% | 14.4% | 0.39 | 81.1% |
| 2014 | 24 | AA | 57.0 | 2 | 3 | 4.11 | 3.83 | 10.42 | 4.11 | 26.8% | 10.6% | 0.95 | 75.1% |
| 2015 | 25 | AAA | 57.0 | 4 | 5 | 3.32 | 4.33 | 6.79 | 6.00 | 17.4% | 15.4% | 0.47 | 77.3% |

**Background:** Just another one of the system's hard-throwing gunslingers, Valdez had such an incredibly odd season with Toledo in 2015. The good: he tallied a 3.32 ERA across 57.0 innings in his first stint in Class AAA. The weird: after averaging more than 10 strikeouts per nine innings in each of the previous four seasons, Valdez managed to fan just 43 batters, or 5.8 K/9. The weirder: he posted a near one-to-one strikeout-to-walk ratio. Valdez also tossed another nine innings with the Tigers in two different stints in the second half of year, fanning four and walking four. For his minor league career, the 6-foot-1, 200-pound right-hander has fanned 282 and walked 154 in 256.2 innings.

**Projection:** An even harder thrower than his teammate Melvin Mercedes, Valdez routinely ran his fastball into the mid- to upper-90s during his brief stint in the big leagues. He complemented that plus-pitch with a mid-80s slider and a hard 87 mph changeup. Valdez's control took a dramatic leap forward two years ago – though it remained firmly in the below average territory – but it regressed back to it's terrible ways in 2015. There might be some relief value extracted from his powerful right arm, but it's not going to be easy.

**Ceiling:** 1.0-win player
**Risk:** Moderate to High
**MLB ETA:** Debuted in 2015

## 20. Melvin Mercedes, RHP

MiLB Rank: N/A
Position Rank: N/A

| Born: 11/02/90 | Age: 25 | Bats: R | Top CALs: Chris Mason, Jeffry Antigua, |
|---|---|---|---|
| Height: 6-3 | Weight: 250 | Throws: R | David Buchanan, Bobby Doran, Daniel Strange |

| YEAR | Age | Level | IP | W | L | ERA | FIP | K/9 | BB/9 | K% | BB% | HR/9 | LOB% |
|---|---|---|---|---|---|---|---|---|---|---|---|---|---|
| 2013 | 22 | A+ | 28.0 | 3 | 1 | 0.96 | 3.13 | 5.46 | 1.61 | 15.5% | 4.6% | 0.32 | 79.7% |
| 2013 | 22 | AA | 25.0 | 2 | 1 | 1.44 | 4.68 | 6.84 | 3.24 | 17.1% | 8.1% | 1.08 | 80.5% |
| 2014 | 23 | AAA | 60.3 | 0 | 3 | 4.92 | 4.85 | 4.62 | 2.39 | 11.8% | 6.1% | 1.19 | 67.8% |
| 2015 | 24 | AA | 26.3 | 1 | 1 | 2.73 | 3.00 | 6.84 | 3.08 | 17.5% | 7.9% | 0.00 | 76.9% |
| 2015 | 24 | AAA | 33.7 | 0 | 1 | 6.68 | 3.75 | 8.55 | 3.74 | 19.5% | 8.5% | 0.80 | 58.8% |

**Background:** The American League version of Jumbo Diaz, Mercedes stands an imposing 6-foot-3 and 250 pounds and can dial it up to the mid-90s with relative ease. A career reliever during his eight professional seasons – all of which were spent hurling peas in the Detroit organization with mixed results. Last season the hefty right-hander split the year between Erie and Toledo, averaging 7.8 K/9 and 3.4 BB/9.

**Projection:** Mercedes made up to the big league level – briefly – two years ago, showing a mid-90s heater, a low-80s slider, and a changeup. But despite the prototypical power arsenal, Mercedes has never really missed a whole lot of bats at any point in his lengthy minor league career. In fact, his best overall punch rate was 8.1 K/9 during his stint as a 17-year-old in the Dominican Summer League. His showing last season, 7.8 K/9, was the only other time he's posted a punch out rate higher than 7.0 K/9. The control has come around over the past couple of years, so he might have a future role as a seventh-inning guy.

**Ceiling:** 0.5- to 1.0-win player
**Risk:** Moderate
**MLB ETA:** Debuted in 2014

## 21. Mike Gerber, RF

MiLB Rank: N/A
Position Rank: N/A

| Born: 07/08/92 | Age: 23 | Bats: L | Top CALs: Jeremy Synan, Miguel Velazquez, |
|---|---|---|---|
| Height: 6-2 | Weight: 175 | Throws: R | Steffan Wilson, Chris Swauger, Kyle Jensen |

| Season | Age | LVL | PA | 2B | 3B | HR | AVG | OBP | SLG | ISO | BB% | K% | wRC+ |
|---|---|---|---|---|---|---|---|---|---|---|---|---|---|
| 2014 | 21 | A- | 243 | 16 | 4 | 7 | 0.286 | 0.354 | 0.493 | 0.207 | 7.0% | 19.8% | 147 |
| 2015 | 22 | A | 583 | 31 | 10 | 13 | 0.292 | 0.355 | 0.468 | 0.175 | 8.4% | 16.6% | 135 |

**Background:** A late round senior pick out of Creighton University, Gerber earned the (meaningless) distinction as the club's Top Hitting Prospect after his showing in the Midwest League in 2015. In 135 games with West Michigan, the former 15th round pick slugged a robust .292/.355/.468 with 31 doubles, 10 triples, 13 homeruns, and 16 stolen bases (in 20 attempts). He topped the league average production by 35%.

**Projection:** While the title of Tigers' Top Hitting Prospect certainly sounds nice, it's more of the backhanded compliment kind – because someone *has* to earn the award. Right? Gerber doesn't have a true standout tool – unsurprisingly average eye, decent hit tool, eight- to 10-homer pop, a little speed. Plus he was a touch old for the Midwest League. He might get a couple sniffs at the big league level as a fourth/fifth outfielder but nothing more.

**Ceiling:** 0.5- to 1.0-win player
**Risk:** Moderate
**MLB ETA:** 2018

## 22. Drew Smith, RHP

**MiLB Rank:** N/A
**Position Rank:** N/A

| Born: 09/24/93 | Age: 22 | Bats: R | **Top CALs:** Tyler James Kaprielian, Justin Kamplain, |
|---|---|---|---|
| Height: 6-2 | Weight: 190 | Throws: R | Zech Zinicola, Jordan Flasher, Daniel Mengden |

| YEAR | Age | Level | IP | W | L | ERA | FIP | K/9 | BB/9 | K% | BB% | HR/9 | LOB% |
|---|---|---|---|---|---|---|---|---|---|---|---|---|---|
| 2015 | 21 | R | 1.7 | 0 | 0 | 0.00 | 1.51 | 16.20 | 0.00 | 42.9% | 0.0% | 0.00 | 100.0% |
| 2015 | 21 | A- | 27.7 | 2 | 0 | 0.33 | 1.67 | 10.73 | 1.30 | 32.4% | 3.9% | 0.00 | 95.0% |
| 2015 | 21 | A | 1.7 | 1 | 0 | 0.00 | 2.79 | 10.80 | 5.40 | 28.6% | 14.3% | 0.00 | 50.0% |

**Background:** The former Dallas Baptist University hurler bounced back from a control-plagued sophomore campaign to have a solid, yet uninspiring junior season: he tossed 45.1 innings with a 38-to-17 strikeout-to-walk ratio. Detroit grabbed the career reliever in the third round last June and bounced him from the Gulf Coast to the NYPL to the Midwest League during his debut.

**Projection**: Impressive, impressive debut – he tossed 31.0 innings with an impeccable 38-to-5 strikeout-to-walk ratio while surrendering one earned run – until you consider the fact that (A) he's never thrown that well in college and (B) most of the damage was done in the New York-Penn League. He profiles as a middle relief arm, but he's certainly needs to show his improvement in control is the real deal.

**Ceiling:** 0.5- to 1.0-win player
**Risk:** Moderate
**MLB ETA:** 2018

## 23. Jeff Thompson, RHP

**MiLB Rank:** N/A
**Position Rank:** N/A

| Born: 09/23/91 | Age: 24 | Bats: R | **Top CALs:** Matt Marksbury, Matthew Shepherd, |
|---|---|---|---|
| Height: 6-6 | Weight: 245 | Throws: R | Brian Leach, Yeiper Castillo, Justin Amlung |

| YEAR | Age | Level | IP | W | L | ERA | FIP | K/9 | BB/9 | K% | BB% | HR/9 | LOB% |
|---|---|---|---|---|---|---|---|---|---|---|---|---|---|
| 2013 | 21 | A | 45.0 | 2 | 2 | 3.80 | 3.74 | 8.40 | 3.80 | 21.7% | 9.8% | 0.60 | 70.9% |
| 2014 | 22 | A | 8.0 | 0 | 0 | 6.75 | 5.98 | 11.25 | 10.13 | 24.4% | 22.0% | 1.13 | 68.2% |
| 2015 | 23 | A | 118.7 | 7 | 11 | 3.79 | 3.90 | 7.96 | 3.56 | 20.6% | 9.2% | 0.68 | 69.3% |

**Background:** The ace of Louisville's *loaded* pitching 2013 staff – which included Chad Green, Dace Kime, Nick Burdi, and Kyle "Bringin' the Funk" Funkhouser – Thompson sparkled like the shimmering moonlight off of a glass bay during his junior season. Throwing a career best 107.0 innings, the 6-foot-6, 245-pound right-hander tallied a 2.19 ERA with a fantastic 113-to-34 strikeout-to-walk ratio. Detroit eventually grabbed the behemoth hurler in the third round three years ago, though we just got our first extended look of him last season. Thompson, who missed all but eight innings two years ago, tossed 118.0 innings with West Michigan in the Midwest League last season, averaging 8.0 strikeouts and 3.6 walks per nine innings.

**Projection**: So here's the thing: Thompson tied for the second oldest qualified hurler in the Midwest League last season at the ripe *old* age of 23. In fact the list of 23-year-old arms in the league reads like a list of who's who among minor league nobodies (except Cubs' Jake Stinnett). And here's the other thing: Thompson didn't exactly set the world ablaze either, posting nice enough peripherals with a mediocre 3.90 FIP. It wouldn't be surprising to see the big righty get pushed all the way up to Class AA to start 2016.

**Ceiling:** 1.0-win player
**Risk:** High
**MLB ETA:** 2018

## 24. Steven Fuentes, 3B/SS

**MiLB Rank:** N/A
**Position Rank:** N/A

| Born: 10/21/94 | Age: 21 | Bats: B | **Top CALs:** Hector Veloz, Jose Rivero, |
|---|---|---|---|
| Height: 5-11 | Weight: 180 | Throws: R | David Bote, Burt Reynolds, Victor Acosta |

| Season | Age | LVL | PA | 2B | 3B | HR | AVG | OBP | SLG | ISO | BB% | K% | wRC+ |
|---|---|---|---|---|---|---|---|---|---|---|---|---|---|
| 2013 | 18 | R | 174 | 10 | 2 | 2 | 0.272 | 0.353 | 0.404 | 0.132 | 6.9% | 23.6% | 126 |
| 2014 | 19 | A- | 222 | 13 | 7 | 3 | 0.295 | 0.356 | 0.475 | 0.180 | 7.2% | 23.0% | 143 |
| 2015 | 20 | A- | 137 | 2 | 4 | 1 | 0.150 | 0.243 | 0.258 | 0.108 | 9.5% | 32.1% | 50 |
| 2015 | 20 | A | 56 | 2 | 0 | 0 | 0.163 | 0.236 | 0.204 | 0.041 | 8.9% | 32.1% | 32 |

**Background:** Fuentes was one of the system's pleasant surprises two years ago when he slugged .295/.356/.475 with an impressive 143 wRC+ as a 19-year-old in the New York-Penn League. But everything that went right two years ago went oh-so-wrong in 2015: he got off to a late start and never rebounded as he hit .163/.236/.204 with West Michigan and didn't fare better upon a demotion to the NYPL.

**Projection**: Here's what I wrote in last year's book following his breakout 2014 campaign:

"Along with the uptick in his overall production, Fuentes' power has been on the steady rise – his ISOs over the last three years are .097, .132, and .180. He's not built like your typical third baseman and I'm not convinced that the bat's going to play there either. He's also struggled against southpaws in his career (.213/.299/.354). Looks like a utility guy with a little bit of upside."

He's still only entering his age-21 season so I'm certainly willing to give the 5-foot-11, 180-pound switch-hitter a do-over. And, again, in a system in dire need for any type of minor league bat, Fuentes still qualifies as an interesting low level wild card.

**Ceiling:** 1.0-win player
**Risk:** High
**MLB ETA:** 2019

## 25. Drew VerHagen, RHP

MiLB Rank: N/A
Position Rank: N/A

**Background:** A fourth round pick out of Vanderbilt University in 2012, VerHagen made stops at three different levels last season, bouncing an awful lot between Erie, Toledo, and Detroit. He would finish his minor league season with 34.1 innings, 26 strikeouts, and 13 walks. As for his time in Detroit, well, it wasn't all that spectacular: 26.1 IP, 13 K, and

| Born: 10/22/90 | Age: 25 | Bats: R | Top CALs: Scott Diamond, Jeremy Sowers, |
| Height: 6-6 | Weight: 230 | Throws: R | Merrill Kelly, Chris Beck, Dallas Keuchel |

| YEAR | Age | Level | IP | W | L | ERA | FIP | K/9 | BB/9 | K% | BB% | HR/9 | LOB% |
|---|---|---|---|---|---|---|---|---|---|---|---|---|---|
| 2013 | 22 | A+ | 67.3 | 5 | 3 | 2.81 | 3.82 | 4.68 | 3.61 | 12.7% | 9.8% | 0.13 | 67.8% |
| 2013 | 22 | AA | 60.0 | 2 | 5 | 3.00 | 3.69 | 6.00 | 2.55 | 16.1% | 6.9% | 0.45 | 71.6% |
| 2014 | 23 | AAA | 110.3 | 6 | 7 | 3.67 | 3.70 | 5.14 | 2.04 | 13.6% | 5.4% | 0.41 | 72.0% |
| 2015 | 24 | AA | 6.7 | 2 | 0 | 2.70 | 4.62 | 6.75 | 2.70 | 20.0% | 8.0% | 1.35 | 90.9% |
| 2015 | 24 | AAA | 27.7 | 1 | 3 | 3.58 | 2.94 | 6.83 | 3.58 | 18.0% | 9.4% | 0.00 | 65.8% |

14 walks.

**Projection**: VerHagen and his well-documented disdain for the punch out continued on in 2015. He showed an average 90 mph heater, a mid-70s curveball, and a mid-80s slider during his tenure in Motown last year. He's the vanilla, replaceable arm that every team eventually needs at some point. And there's value in that.

**Ceiling:** 0.5-win player
**Risk:** Low
**MLB ETA:** Debuted in 2014

### Barely Missed:

- **Harold Castro, IF** – The Tigers continued to aggressively push the young infielder through the system despite some underwhelming offensive production. After hitting .311/.343/.420 as an 18-year-old in the Gulf Coast League, Castro batted .245/.266/.318 between the Midwest and Florida State Leagues a year later. He followed that up with a combined .286/.327/.322 in 2014 and then batted .256/.283/.313 with Erie last season. He might be a utility infielder.

- **Grayson Greiner, C** – For one 12-game stretch in June last season, Greiner looked the part of an offensive-minded backstop, something the organization envisioned when they selected him with the 99th overall pick two years ago. But other than that not a helluva lot went Greiner's way as he batted a shockingly dreadful .183/.254/.250 in 343 plate appearances for Lakeland last season.

- **Joshua Turley, LHP** – Former late round pick out of Baylor University continued to post a strikeout rate in the 6.0s and a walk rate in the low 2.0s. He's dominated southpaws at various points so he might be able to carve out a role as a LOOGY.

- **Paul Voelker, RHP** – A 2014 tenth round pick out of Dallas Baptist University, the small right-hander made stops at three different levels last season, totaling 63 strikeouts and just 20 walks in 55.1 innings between the Midwest, Florida State, and Eastern Leagues.

# Detroit Tigers

## *Bird Doggin' It – Additional Prospects to Keep an Eye in 2016*

| | | | |
|---|---|---|---|
| Jeff Ferrell | 25 | RHP | Offered up a low-90s fastball during his 11.1-inning debut in Detroit. After a couple seasons of mediocre results, the club pushed him into a relief role in 2015 and…voila…instant success. |
| Dominic Ficociello | 24 | 1B | Former University of Arkansas alumnus hit a respectable .293/.349/.415, though his lack of over-the-fence pop will ultimately push him into Quad-A status. |
| Francisco German | 19 | RHP | The teenage right-hander posted an impressive 26-to-6 strikeout-to-walk ratio in 21.0 innings in the GCL. He could be something. Or he could be nothing. |
| Joe Mantiply | 25 | LHP | Big league ready after posting a career 2.35 ERA while averaging 84 K/9 and 2.2 BB/9. Middle relief fodder. |
| Gabe Speier | 21 | RHP | Small-ish southpaw has posted some solid peripherals in a relief role. He might be a candidate to move into the rotation in the next year or two. |
| Adenson Verastegui | 23 | RHP | Posted a 40-to-17 strikeout-to-walk ratio in 41.2 innings with Lakeland last year. |

**State of the Farm System:** Just to put some perspective into how plentiful the talent has been in the Houston system, considering the following:

- Here's a list of prospects that have been promoted – and subsequently lost their rookie eligibility – *or* dealt away since 2014:
  - Carlos Correa, George Springer, Jonathan Singleton, Lance McCullers, Mike Foltnewicz, Rio Ruiz, Delino DeShields Jr., Nick Tropeano, Vincent Velasquez, Preston Tucker, Andrew Thurman, David Rollins, Brett Phillips, Daniel Mengden, Jacob Nottingham, Josh Hader, Domingo Santana, Mark Appel, Harold Arauz, and Thomas Eshelman.

That right there is a list of prospects that would easily rank among the Top Five farm systems in baseball, perhaps even *the* top system in the game. But even after the mass departure – either through promotions or trades – Houston's system *still* ranks as the fifth best in all of baseball. Think about that for a moment. Which other organization in baseball – *at any other time* – could have withstood such a tremendous amount of talent leaving the minor leagues and still rank among the game's best?

Quite frankly, Houston isn't just going to be a perennial playoff contender; they're edging up to dynasty type levels.

Leading the way for the baby 'Stros is hulking first baseman – and former two-way star at the University of Kentucky – A.J. Reed. The former second round pick bashed to the tune of .340/.432/.612 with a whopping 30 doubles, five triples, and 34 homeruns in just 135 games.

Third baseman Colin Moran easily had his finest professional season to date as he slugged .306/.381/.459 with Corpus Christi in the Texas League, hitting a career best nine dingers. And

Jon Kemmer, a former 21st round pick in 2013, was among the game's biggest surprises as he batted .327/.414/.574 with 28 doubles, four triples, and 18 long balls in Class AA.

In terms of impact arms, former Blue Jay Joe Musgrove took a huge leap forward. Hard-throwing right-hander Michael Feliz is poised to be a big contributor in 2016. And one can't forget about budding ace – and one of the candidates for biggest breakout prospect in 2016 – Francis Martes.

And just like some late night infomercial salesman – *there's more*.

Houston added a tremendous amount of talent in the first two rounds last June as well: outfielders Kyle Tucker and Daz Cameron, and LSU shortstop Alex Bregman.

It's deep. It's filled with to the brim with potential big league regulars. And it's showing no signs of slowing down.

**Review of the 2015 Draft:** Easily one of the top – if not *the* top – draft class last June. Houston had two top five selections, thanks in part due to their failure to sign Brady Aiken two years ago. Alex Bregman is poised to move quickly and looks like an above-average infielder. Kyle Tucker, younger brother to current outfielder Preston, was the second prep player taken last year.

Second rounder Daz Cameron, son of the supremely underrated Mike Cameron, had Top 5 pick hype potential heading into the draft.

The club dealt away second rounder Thomas Eshelman as part of the Ken Giles deal. And third rounder Riley Ferrell has late-inning, high-leverage potential.

| Rank | Name | POS |
|---|---|---|
| 1 | A.J. Reed | 1B |
| 2 | Francis Martes | RHP |
| 3 | Alex Bregman | SS |
| 4 | Joe Musgrove | RHP |
| 5 | Kyle Tucker | RF |
| 6 | Michael Feliz | RHP |
| 7 | Daz Cameron | CF |
| 8 | Colin Moran | 3B |
| 9 | Jon Kemmer | LF/RF |
| 10 | Derek Fisher | LF/CF |
| 11 | David Paulino | RHP |
| 12 | Akeem Bostick | RHP |
| 13 | Teoscar Hernandez | CF |
| 14 | Riley Ferrell | RHP |
| 15 | Nolan Fontana | 2B/3B/SS |
| 16 | Tyler White | 1B/3B |
| 17 | J.D. Davis | 3B |
| 18 | Kyle Smith | RHP |
| 19 | Cy Sneed | RHP |
| 20 | Tony Kemp | 2B/OF |
| 21 | Jason Martin | LF/CF |
| 22 | Jandel Gustave | RHP |
| 23 | Danry Vasquez | LF/RF |
| 24 | Elieser Hernandez | RHP |
| 25 | Brendan Mccurry | RHP |

## 1. A.J. Reed, 1B

**MiLB Rank: #19**
**Position Rank: #1**

| Born: 05/10/93 | Age: 23 | Bats: L | Top CALs: Jerry Sands, Ji-Man Choi, |
| Height: 6-4 | Weight: 240 | Throws: L | Rhys Hoskins, Nick Evans, Kala Ka'Aihue |

| Season | Age | LVL | PA | 2B | 3B | HR | AVG | OBP | SLG | ISO | BB% | K% | wRC+ |
|--------|-----|-----|-----|-----|-----|-----|-------|-------|-------|-------|-------|-------|------|
| 2014 | 21 | A- | 150 | 11 | 0 | 5 | 0.306 | 0.420 | 0.516 | 0.210 | 14.7% | 14.7% | 174 |
| 2014 | 21 | A | 135 | 9 | 1 | 7 | 0.272 | 0.326 | 0.528 | 0.256 | 5.9% | 23.7% | 141 |
| 2015 | 22 | A+ | 385 | 16 | 4 | 23 | 0.346 | 0.449 | 0.638 | 0.292 | 15.3% | 19.0% | 190 |
| 2015 | 22 | AA | 237 | 14 | 1 | 11 | 0.332 | 0.405 | 0.571 | 0.239 | 11.4% | 20.7% | 168 |

**Background:** Arguably the top offensive performer in the minor leagues – and the likely winner of said argument – Reed's breakout 2015 has to be leaving a lot of front office personnel shaking their heads, wondering how the hell the hulking first baseman lasted until the 42nd pick in the draft two years ago. A two-way player at the University of Kentucky, Reed capped off his three-year collegiate career on a high note: as a southpaw toeing the rubber he posted a career best 2.09 ERA in 112 innings, striking out 71 and walking 29, and as the team's top bat he slugged .336/.476/.735 with an NCAA leading 23 dingers. Fearing that Reed would be a one dimensional slugger, he dropped completely out of the first round and squarely into the waiting lap of the Astros.

Reed had a dominant professional debut – easing a lot of fears about his hit tool – by slugging a combined .289/.375/.522 with 33 extra-base hits in just 68 games between Tri-City and Quad Cities. But *nobody* could have expected him to string together a season like he did last year, making quick work of the California League and later torching Class AA pitching. In total, he mashed to the tune of .340/.432/.612 with 30 doubles, five triples, and a MiLB-leading 34 bombs. His 177 wRC+ total also ranked first among all prospect to not appear in rookie ball.

**Projection:** Just for comparison's sake let's take a quick look at two of the top bats from some recent drafts:

| Player | Age | Levels | AVG | OBP | SLG | HR | BB% | K% |
|--------|-----|--------|-------|-------|-------|-----|--------|--------|
| A.J. Reed | 22 | A+/AA | 0.340 | 0.432 | 0.612 | 34 | 13.83% | 19.61% |
| Kris Bryant | 22 | AA/AAA | 0.325 | 0.438 | 0.661 | 43 | 14.48% | 27.27% |

Obviously, there are couple factors in play here: (1.) Bryant split his age-22 season between AA/AAA and Reed split his season between A+/AA and (2.) Lancaster's home field is an absolute bandbox. But it's still an interesting comparison nonetheless.

Prior to the draft I wrote:

> "As a pitcher, Reed's game is based purely on [pitchability].And while his control/command is a tangible skill his complete lack of strikeouts would almost assuredly push him into an eventual bullpen [role] in the minor leagues where he would – at best – be a middle reliever.
>
> His bat, however, could be something special, potential pushing him up towards the latter half of the first round.
>
> Reed's plate discipline has been trending in the right direction and it wouldn't be surprising to see him post walk rates hovering near 9.5% to 10.0% in the minor leagues. Obviously, the power is an above-average to potentially plus skill. He's a nice…#5/#6 hitter. He'll probably never hit for average."

While he did hit for a (very) high average last season, I'd like to point out that his walk rate was 13.8% – so the trend definitely continued. CAL's a big fan, linking him to Brandon Belt and Ike Davis (and let's not forget Davis had some pretty solid seasons). I'm still not convinced he's going to be a perennial .280-hitter, but the power/patience combo is #4-hitter worthy. One more thing: he hit .271/.362/.512 against southpaws – very, very good news.

**Ceiling:** 3.5- to 4.0-win player
**Risk:** Moderate
**MLB ETA:** 2016

## 2. Francis Martes, RHP

**MiLB Rank: #22**
**Position Rank: #9**

| Born: 11/24/95 | Age: 20 | Bats: R | Top CALs: Drew Hutchison, David Holmberg , |
| Height: 6-1 | Weight: 225 | Throws: R | Francellis Montas, Julio Teheran, Ian Mckinney |

| YEAR | Age | Level | IP | W | L | ERA | FIP | K/9 | BB/9 | K% | BB% | HR/9 | LOB% |
|------|-----|-------|------|---|---|------|------|------|------|------|------|------|------|
| 2013 | 17 | R | 50.3 | 3 | 3 | 3.04 | 3.23 | 5.90 | 2.50 | 15.2% | 6.5% | 0.18 | 71.8% |
| 2014 | 18 | R | 44.0 | 3 | 3 | 4.09 | 3.17 | 9.20 | 4.70 | 23.7% | 12.1% | 0.00 | 59.3% |
| 2015 | 19 | A | 52.0 | 3 | 2 | 1.04 | 2.78 | 7.79 | 2.25 | 22.4% | 6.5% | 0.17 | 79.4% |
| 2015 | 19 | A+ | 35.0 | 4 | 1 | 2.31 | 2.81 | 9.51 | 2.06 | 25.7% | 5.6% | 0.26 | 77.7% |
| 2015 | 19 | AA | 14.7 | 1 | 0 | 4.91 | 4.32 | 9.82 | 4.30 | 23.2% | 10.1% | 1.23 | 77.6% |

**Background:** Martes, who was originally recognized as a throw-in type of prospect as part the mega-deal involving Jared Cosart, Jake Marisnick, and Colin Moran with Miami at the deadline two years ago, took a *huge* developmental step forward in 2015 as he spent the year breezing through three levels of minors'. As a 19-year-old. The sturdy, well-built right-hander began the year on a ridiculous note in the Midwest League: he made 10 appearances with Quad Cities, throwing 52 innings with a 1.04 ERA while averaging 7.8 punch outs and 2.2 walks per nine innings. Martes would make another six impressive appearances in Lancaster, where he didn't succumb to pressure of the bandbox, by averaging 9.5 K/9 and 2.1 BB/9. The club would bump him up again to Class AA for his final three starts. Overall, he finished the year with 90 strikeouts, 28 walks, and a 2.04 ERA in 101.2 innings of work.

**Projection**: Without a doubt the single biggest riser in Houston's system and in the conversation for all of the minor leagues, Martes went from relative obscurity to becoming one of the best teenage arms around. Big, *BIG* time arm with the uncanny ability to find the strike zone on more than a consistent basis, you'll be hard pressed to find a more talented teenage arm outside of the Dodgers' Julio Urias or Boston's Anderson Espinoza.. Simply put, the 6-foot-1, 235-pound Martes is the best prospect you've likely never heard of. Yet. Legit front-of-the-rotation caliber upside as long as he can avoid the injury nexus. Given his relative youth he's likely headed for an innings limit around130.0 next season.

**Ceiling:** 4.0- to 4.5-win player
**Risk:** Moderate to High
**MLB ETA:** 2017

## 3. Alex Bregman, SS

**MiLB Rank: #49**
**Position Rank: #7**

| Born: 03/30/94 | Age: 22 | Bats: R | Top CALs: Greg Garcia, Sergio Miranda, |
| Height: 6-0 | Weight: 180 | Throws: R | Brandon Wikoff, David Fletcher, Jorge Flores |

| Season | Age | LVL | PA | 2B | 3B | HR | AVG | OBP | SLG | ISO | BB% | K% | wRC+ |
|--------|-----|-----|-----|----|----|----|-------|-------|-------|-------|------|------|------|
| 2015 | 21 | A | 133 | 5 | 0 | 1 | 0.259 | 0.368 | 0.330 | 0.071 | 12.8% | 9.8% | 108 |
| 2015 | 21 | A+ | 178 | 8 | 4 | 3 | 0.319 | 0.364 | 0.475 | 0.156 | 6.7% | 9.6% | 126 |

**Background:** For the first time in modern draft history three consecutive shortstops – Dansby Swanson, Bregman, and Brendan Rodgers – were taken with the opening three selections. Bregman, who was shoehorned between the Vanderbilt star and the prep middle infielder, was a consistent, dominant force in the middle of LSU's lineup for the duration of collegiate career. The 6-foot, 180-pound Bregman was named 2013 National Freshman of the Year by *Baseball America*, hitting .369/.417/.546 with 18 doubles, seven triples, six homeruns, and 16 stolen bases (in 17 attempts). His production took a modest downturn the following season (.316/.397/.455), but rebounded nicely during his final campaign (.323/.412/.535). Bregman, a career .337/.409/.514 hitter at LSU, earned numerous other awards throughout his storied career, including: twice-recognized as an All-American (2013, 2015), First-Team All-SEC (2013, 2015), National Shortstop of the Year (2013), SEC All-Defensive Team (2015), ABCA Gold Glove Award Team, Golden Spike Award Finalist.

After Houston grabbed him with the second overall pick, the compensatory pick for failing to sign Brady Aiken as the first pick two years ago, the club sent him straight into full-season ball where he initially struggled – he batted .237/.308/.322 during his first 14 game – but managed to turn it around for the rest of his debut (.310/.381/.441).

**Projection**: Here's what I wrote prior to the draft:

> *"Bregman, who's likely to move across the bag to second base in the pros, [has] one of the best collegiate hit tools in the class. Above-average speed with 15-stolen base potential, 10- to 12-homeruns, and slightly below-average walk rates. He's a potential top-of-the-order hitter, not quite a leadoff bat but a solid #2 who could easily carve out a 12- to 15-year professional career. In terms of ceiling, think something like Adam Kennedy circa 2009 when he batted .289/.348/.410."*

Bregman had a solid, sometimes spectacular debut, but he clearly benefited from spending a portion of his year slugging at Lancaster – a place that would make Mario Mendoza – of Mendoza Line fame – look like a big league hitter. According to StatCorner, High Class A line from .317/.362/.472 to .303/.347/.431 once adjusted for the park.

**Ceiling:** 3.0- to 3.5-win player
**Risk:** Moderate
**MLB ETA:** 2017

## 4. Joe Musgrove, RHP

**MiLB Rank: #53**
**Position Rank: N/A**

| Born: 12/04/92 | Age: 23 | Bats: R | **Top CALs:** Marco Gonzalez, Hector Noesi, |
| Height: 6-5 | Weight: 255 | Throws: R | P.J. Walters, Kender Villegas, Seth Maness |

| YEAR | Age | Level | IP | W | L | ERA | FIP | K/9 | BB/9 | K% | BB% | HR/9 | LOB% |
|------|-----|-------|------|---|---|------|------|-------|------|-------|------|------|-------|
| 2013 | 20 | R | 32.7 | 1 | 3 | 4.41 | 2.57 | 8.27 | 1.10 | 20.1% | 2.7% | 0.28 | 56.7% |
| 2014 | 21 | A- | 77.0 | 7 | 1 | 2.81 | 2.84 | 7.83 | 1.17 | 22.3% | 3.3% | 0.47 | 72.4% |
| 2015 | 22 | A | 25.7 | 4 | 1 | 0.70 | 1.84 | 8.06 | 0.35 | 23.0% | 1.0% | 0.00 | 83.3% |
| 2015 | 22 | A+ | 30.0 | 4 | 0 | 2.40 | 2.08 | 12.90 | 0.30 | 36.4% | 0.9% | 0.60 | 78.0% |
| 2015 | 22 | AA | 45.0 | 4 | 0 | 2.20 | 4.25 | 6.60 | 1.20 | 19.0% | 3.5% | 1.40 | 89.7% |

**Background:** A part of the 10-player megadeal involving Brandon Lyon, J.A. Happ, and David Carpenter heading to Toronto and Musgrove, Francisco Cordero, Asher Wojciechowski, David Rollins, Carlos Perez, Kevin Comer, and Ben Francisco coming back to Houston. Musgrove, a former first round pick, 46th overall, in 2011, took a huge, unsuspected leap forward last season, going from a solid prospect to something much more promising. The big right-hander's always shown an above-average or better feel for the strike zone – he's averaged no worse than 2.1 walks per nine innings in any professional season – but his strikeout rate exploded to above-average territory last season. The 6-foot-5, 255-pound hurler was seemingly shot out of cannon last season, making five ridiculously dominant appearances in the Midwest League, another six near-perfect games with Lancaster, and eight promising contests with Corpus Christi. Musgrove finished the year by tallying a 1.82 ERA to go along with a laughably videogame-esque 99-to-8 strikeout-to-walk ratio.

**Projection:** Not quite front-of-the-rotational caliber arm, but something along the lines as a very good #2/#3-type ceiling. Think John Lackey. Musgrove has an elite ability to limit base on balls, above-average groundball rates, and the ability to chew up plenty of innings thanks to his size.

**Ceiling:** 3.0- to 3.5-win player
**Risk:** Moderate
**MLB ETA:** 2016

## 5. Kyle Tucker, RF

**MiLB Rank: #57**
**Position Rank: #16**

| Born: 01/17/97 | Age: 19 | Bats: L | **Top CALs:** Jean Carlos Valdez, Zacrey Law, |
| Height: 6-4 | Weight: 190 | Throws: R | Zoilo Almonte, Kurt Fleming, Wander Franco |

| Season | Age | LVL | PA | 2B | 3B | HR | AVG | OBP | SLG | ISO | BB% | K% | wRC+ |
|--------|-----|-----|-----|----|----|----|-------|-------|-------|-------|------|-------|------|
| 2015 | 18 | R | 121 | 9 | 0 | 1 | 0.286 | 0.322 | 0.393 | 0.107 | 5.8% | 12.4% | 93 |
| 2015 | 18 | R | 133 | 3 | 2 | 2 | 0.208 | 0.267 | 0.317 | 0.108 | 6.8% | 10.5% | 78 |

**Background:** Beginning the 2015 family draft theme, Houston grabbed Kyle, the younger brother of Preston Tucker, who happened to patrol the outfield for Houston as a rookie last season. The younger Tucker, the club's second top five pick last season, hails from H.B. Plant HS, home to several top draft picks and former big leaguers including Wade Boggs, John Hudek, Jake Woodford, and Mychal Givens. The 6-foot-4, 190-pound outfielder, like fellow 2015 first round pick Daz Cameron, got off to a bit of a slow start, hitting .208/.267/.317 but rebounded nicely in the Appalachian League (.286/.322/.393). Overall, he batted .246/.294/.353 with 12 doubles, a pair of triples, and three homeruns.

**Projection:** Granted the sample size is rather limited – just 254 plate appearances – but Tucker showed an interesting talent package: decent-ish eye, a bit of power potential, solid hit tool, and speed.

**Ceiling:** Too Soon to Tell
**Risk:** N/A
**MLB ETA:** N/A

## 6. Michael Feliz, RHP

MiLB Rank: #90

Position Rank: N/A

| Born: 06/28/93 | Age: 23 | Bats: R | Top CALs: Aaron Blair, Chad Thall, |
| Height: 6-4 | Weight: 225 | Throws: R | Andres Santiago, Nick Martinez, Jose Guzman |

| YEAR | Age | Level | IP | W | L | ERA | FIP | K/9 | BB/9 | K% | BB% | HR/9 | LOB% |
|------|-----|-------|------|---|---|------|------|-------|------|-------|------|------|-------|
| 2013 | 19 | A- | 69.0 | 4 | 2 | 1.96 | 1.91 | 10.17 | 1.70 | 28.6% | 4.8% | 0.26 | 75.5% |
| 2014 | 20 | A | 102.7 | 8 | 6 | 4.03 | 3.31 | 9.73 | 3.24 | 25.2% | 8.4% | 0.53 | 67.6% |
| 2015 | 22 | A+ | 32.7 | 1 | 1 | 4.41 | 3.84 | 9.09 | 3.31 | 22.9% | 8.3% | 0.55 | 60.7% |
| 2015 | 22 | AA | 78.7 | 6 | 3 | 2.17 | 3.11 | 8.01 | 2.29 | 23.3% | 6.6% | 0.57 | 81.5% |

**Background:** Just another one of the seemingly endless supply of power-armed right-handers developing in the Houston system. Feliz, a 6-foot-4, 225-pound right-hander, continued his dramatic rise in 2015, making two minor league stops – High Class A and Class AA – as well as a brief eight-inning stint with the big league club. Feliz's journey looks more like a road trip across the western part of the state as he bounced from Lancaster, California, to Houston, Texas, to Corpus Christi, Texas, and finally back to Houston to close out a widely successful season. His combined minor league numbers from 2015: 111.1 innings, 103 punch outs, just 32 walks, and a 2.83 ERA. And while his big league numbers are a bit deceiving – seven earned runs in eight innings – his big mid 90s heater offers up plenty of optimism.

**Projection**: In last year's book I wrote:

> "Feliz is nothing more than a wild card right now. He's consistently missed a solid amount of bats while flashing decent control/command, but that all comes with the caveat that it's been in the lowest levels of the minor leagues and against players more or less the same age."

Well, just like Rocky Balboa taught us – sometimes wild cards pay off. The organization has capped his innings rather judiciously throughout his career, never allowing him to top more than 120 frames in a season, so he could be due for another bump up in the coming year. Very promising package: power arsenal, strong K-rates, above-average control, sturdy build, and dominating performances vs. older competition.

**Ceiling:** 2.5- to 3.0-win player
**Risk:** Low to Moderate
**MLB ETA:** 2016

## 7. Daz Cameron, CF

MiLB Rank: #102

Position Rank: N/A

| Born: 01/15/97 | Age: 19 | Bats: R | Top CALs: Marquise Cooper, Connor Lien, |
| Height: 6-2 | Weight: 185 | Throws: R | Ty Morrison, Max Kepler, Cristian Toribio |

| Season | Age | LVL | PA | 2B | 3B | HR | AVG | OBP | SLG | ISO | BB% | K% | wRC+ |
|--------|-----|-----|-----|----|----|----|-------|-------|-------|-------|-------|-------|------|
| 2015 | 18 | R | 124 | 2 | 3 | 0 | 0.272 | 0.372 | 0.350 | 0.078 | 12.9% | 25.0% | 106 |
| 2015 | 18 | R | 87 | 2 | 0 | 0 | 0.222 | 0.326 | 0.250 | 0.028 | 10.3% | 20.7% | 81 |

**Background:** The son of former All-Star center fielder Mike Cameron, Daz was widely rumored to be a potential Top 10, maybe even a Top 5 pick in last June's draft, but tumbled all the way down to Houston with the 37th overall selection. The younger Cameron, who hails from Eagle's Landing HS, home to former big league outfielder Matt Murton, initially got off to a slow start but batted .271/.378/.340 over his final 43 games between the Gulf Coast and Appalachian Leagues. And just on a side note: the elder Cameron totaled 46.5 wins above replacement (Baseball Reference's version) throughout his career; let's put that into perspective.

- Sandy Koufax, 49.0 bWAR
- Earl Averill, 48.0 bWAR
- Jim Rice, 47.4 bWAR
- Mike Cameron, 46.5 bWAR
- Jimmy Rollins, 46.0 bWAR
- Lou Brock, 45.2 bWAR
- Rocky Colavito, 44.8 bWAR

**Projection**: Not quite as filled out as his All-Star – and borderline Hall of Fame – father, Daz showed above-average or better speed and a decent eye at the plate. There's some concern about whether he'll hit for much of an average. But as his body begins to mature he should be able to drive the ball with more consistency.

**Ceiling:** Too Soon to Tell
**Risk:** N/A
**MLB ETA:** N/A

## 8. Colin Moran, 3B

**MiLB Rank: #166**
**Position Rank: #8**

| Born: 10/01/92 | Age: 23 | Bats: L | **Top CALs:** Cheslor Cuthbert, Nick Tanielu, |
| Height: 6-4 | Weight: 215 | Throws: R | Adrian Cardenas, Brandon Drury, Taylor Green |

| Season | Age | LVL | PA | 2B | 3B | HR | AVG | OBP | SLG | ISO | BB% | K% | wRC+ |
|---|---|---|---|---|---|---|---|---|---|---|---|---|---|
| 2013 | 20 | A | 175 | 8 | 1 | 4 | 0.299 | 0.354 | 0.442 | 0.143 | 8.6% | 14.3% | 127 |
| 2014 | 21 | A+ | 392 | 21 | 0 | 5 | 0.294 | 0.342 | 0.393 | 0.100 | 7.1% | 13.5% | 110 |
| 2014 | 21 | AA | 123 | 6 | 0 | 2 | 0.304 | 0.350 | 0.411 | 0.107 | 7.3% | 18.7% | 114 |
| 2015 | 22 | AA | 417 | 25 | 2 | 9 | 0.306 | 0.381 | 0.459 | 0.153 | 10.3% | 18.9% | 136 |

**Background:** Moran's name was famously floated as a potential under-slot target Houston was mulling about as the 2013 draft approached. And while the franchise opted to go with Mark Appel, Houston finally got its guy in a mid-season deal with the Marlins a year later. The former UNC star third baseman turned in another quietly strong performance in 2015, hitting .306/.381/.459 with 25 doubles, a pair of triples, and nine homeruns in Class AA – his second stop at the level. The lefty-swinging third baseman topped the league average production mark by 36%, his best professional showing. For his career, Moran is sporting a lifetime .300/.360/.427 triple-slash line, including a .305/.374/.448 mark in 124 games in the Texas League.

**Projection**: Here's what I wrote prior to the draft in 2013:

*"Moran will find his way into the top of the first round and profiles as a solid-average big league bat, capable of hitting .280/.380/.460-type hitter with 20+ homerun potential, though I'd be interested in how he handles fellow southpaws."*

And here's what I wrote in last year's book:

*"Solid, yet uninspiring numbers thus far for the then-22-year-old. The power has yet to develop for Moran, who's slugged just 11 homeruns in his first 690 plate appearances. The hit tool and his glove are his best offerings; otherwise, he's simply been average."*

OK, so obviously the power just hasn't taken the step forward I expected. It happens. But the bat, patience, and glove should carry him all the way to becoming a league average big leaguer. Take this for what you will, but he came close to developing into the type of hitter I thought he would eventually become: I wrote in 2013 that he'd be a .280/.380/.460 hitter and last season he slugged .301/.381/.459. Not too shabby (even if I was wrong on the power).

**Ceiling:** 2.0-win player
**Risk:** Moderate
**MLB ETA:** 2016

## 9. Jon Kemmer, 1B

**MiLB Rank: #220**
**Position Rank: N/A**

| Born: 11/17/90 | Age: 25 | Bats: L | **Top CALs:** Jordan Patterson, Steven Souza Jr., |
| Height: 6-2 | Weight: 220 | Throws: L | Scott Van Slyke, Patrick Kivlehan, Eric Thames |

| Season | Age | LVL | PA | 2B | 3B | HR | AVG | OBP | SLG | ISO | BB% | K% | wRC+ |
|---|---|---|---|---|---|---|---|---|---|---|---|---|---|
| 2013 | 22 | A- | 225 | 7 | 1 | 4 | 0.221 | 0.304 | 0.327 | 0.106 | 7.6% | 18.2% | 95 |
| 2014 | 23 | A | 204 | 15 | 1 | 4 | 0.289 | 0.369 | 0.450 | 0.161 | 9.8% | 19.1% | 136 |
| 2014 | 23 | A | 204 | 15 | 1 | 4 | 0.289 | 0.369 | 0.450 | 0.161 | 9.8% | 19.1% | 136 |
| 2014 | 23 | A+ | 159 | 10 | 1 | 12 | 0.294 | 0.314 | 0.608 | 0.314 | 2.5% | 20.8% | 130 |
| 2015 | 24 | AA | 425 | 28 | 4 | 18 | 0.327 | 0.414 | 0.574 | 0.247 | 10.6% | 20.9% | 174 |

**Background:** Trivia Time: Name the top *two* minor league bats according to *Weighted Runs Created Plus* with 425 or more plate appearances. The answer: Houston's dynamic left-handed duo of A.J. Reed and Jon Kemmer, one a former Golden Spikes Award Winner and the latter a 21st round pick out of tiny Brewton-Parker College, home to just one MLB draft pick taken before the 12th round (Johnnie Wiggins). Kemmer looked every bit the part of late round, small college pick during his professional debut, hitting a paltry .221/.304/.327 in 65 games with the franchise's short-season club. Since then, however, he's done nothing but mash. A 6-foot-2, 220-pound corner outfielder/first baseman, Kemmer had a bit of coming out party in 2014, hitting a combined .291/.345/.523 with plenty of extra-base pop (25 doubles, two triples, and 16 homeruns) between Quad Cities and Lancaster. But, again, he was an older prospect at the time, 23, with some level of college. Last season, though, Kremmer took the expectations to entirely new level: spending the year in an age appropriate environment, Class AA, he *slugged* .327/.474/.547 with career highs in doubles (28), triples (4), homeruns (18), stolen bases (9), and walk rate (10.6%). Not too shabby...

**Projection**: On one hand you can't entirely look past the fact that he was a late, late round pickup and he's never really had a chance to face off against older competition. But on the other hand he's been so damn productive. Above-average power but more of the gap-to-gap doubles kind, not over-the-fence taters. Solid-average plate discipline; the ability to handle both left- and right-handers; and reasonable contact rates. Add it all and it looks like a potential big league contributor, perhaps even as a league average regular. CAL offers up some hope as well, tying him to Steven Souza, Scott Van Slyke, and Eric Thames – all of whom have been league average offensive performers.

**Ceiling:** 1.5- to 2.0-wins above replacement
**Risk:** Moderate
**MLB ETA:** 2016

## 10. Derek Fisher, LF/CF

**MiLB Rank: #221**
**Position Rank: N/A**

| Born: 08/21/93 | Age: 22 | Bats: L | Top CALs: Marc Wik, Zoilo Almonte, |
| Height: 6-1 | Weight: 207 | Throws: R | Dan Brewer, Dalton Pompey, Aaron Cunningham |

| Season | Age | LVL | PA | 2B | 3B | HR | AVG | OBP | SLG | ISO | BB% | K% | wRC+ |
|---|---|---|---|---|---|---|---|---|---|---|---|---|---|
| 2014 | 20 | A- | 172 | 4 | 3 | 2 | 0.303 | 0.378 | 0.408 | 0.105 | 9.3% | 20.3% | 133 |
| 2015 | 21 | A | 171 | 11 | 1 | 6 | 0.305 | 0.386 | 0.510 | 0.205 | 11.1% | 21.6% | 159 |
| 2015 | 21 | A+ | 398 | 10 | 7 | 16 | 0.262 | 0.354 | 0.471 | 0.209 | 11.8% | 23.9% | 124 |

**Background:** The Lebanon, Pennsylvania, native looked like a potential breakout star heading into his junior season at Virginia. He was coming off of a year in which he showed plenty of power with an upward trend in plate discipline. And then the injury – a broken hamate – happened, one that typically saps a hitter's power for quite some time. Fisher would eventual make it back for the university's stretch run, but his overall numbers – .260/.316/.362 – took a massive hit. Nonetheless, the Astros grabbed the lefty-swinging outfielder with the 37th overall pick and pushed him into short-season ball. Last season, with the injury fully out of the way, Fisher's power rebounded as he hit a combined .275/.364/.483 with 21 doubles, eight triples, 22 homeruns, and 31 stolen bases between Quad Cities and Lancaster.

**Projection:** I've always been a relatively big fan of Fisher's, writing at the time of the draft:

> "[He's] never going to hit for average, probably peaking around .265 or .270 in the big leagues, but there's 25-HR pop I his bat with at least a solid-average eye at the plate. Again, though, he's not likely to show any significant pop until at least the end of 2014and more likely at some early point in 2015 [because of the hamate injury]."

The power came storming back last year – though playing a large part of his games in the Lancaster Bandbox thoroughly helps. Fisher ran more than at any other point in his career, likely the result of picking on less experience batteries. He's not going to be a star by any stretch of the imagination, but there's some starter potential here. He's sort of like what Indians MiLB outfielder James Ramsey was supposed to be.

**Ceiling:** 1.5- to 2.0-win player
**Risk:** Moderate
**MLB ETA:** 2017

## 11. David Paulino, RHP

**MiLB Rank: N/A**
**Position Rank: N/A**

| Born: 02/06/94 | Age: 22 | Bats: R | Top CALs: Sean Mclaughlin, Johan Belisario, |
| Height: 6-7 | Weight: 215 | Throws: R | Michael Vinson, Keury Mella, Michael Boyle |

| YEAR | Age | Level | IP | W | L | ERA | FIP | K/9 | BB/9 | K% | BB% | HR/9 | LOB% |
|---|---|---|---|---|---|---|---|---|---|---|---|---|---|
| 2013 | 19 | R | 20.0 | 2 | 1 | 2.70 | 2.21 | 9.90 | 0.90 | 29.7% | 2.7% | 0.45 | 72.3% |
| 2015 | 21 | A- | 9.3 | 1 | 0 | 0.00 | 2.02 | 9.64 | 1.93 | 29.4% | 5.9% | 0.00 | 100.0% |
| 2015 | 21 | A | 28.7 | 3 | 2 | 1.57 | 2.00 | 10.05 | 2.20 | 28.6% | 6.3% | 0.00 | 79.3% |
| 2015 | 21 | A+ | 29.3 | 1 | 1 | 4.91 | 3.40 | 9.20 | 3.07 | 24.8% | 8.3% | 0.31 | 54.9% |

**Background:** Another smart, calculated gamble GM Jeff Luhnow has taken. Paulino, a massive hard-throwing right-hander out of the Dominican, was acquired as a PTBNL as part of the Jose Veras deal with the Tigers a couple years back. The catch: he was on the DL recovering from Tommy John surgery and last hurled a meaningful pitch on July 13, 2013. Finally healthy, the 6-foot-7, 215-pound Paulino made stops at three different levels last season, making two abbreviated tune-ups in the New York-Penn League, another five dominant starts with Quad Cities, and closing out his year with six deceptively strong games in the California League. When it was all said and done Paulino posted an impressive 72-to-19 strikeout-to-walk ratio in 67.1 innings of work.

**Projection:** Primed for a breakout in 2016, Paulino's control bounced back without missing a beat as he returned from surgery. There's a whole lot to like about the lanky right-hander: size, projection, power arsenal, dominating strikeout totals, and surprising control – especially for a 6-foot-7 pitcher. Paulino's innings will likely be capped around 100 or so, but he should spend some significant time in Class AA. In terms of potential ceiling, he's still a bit of wild card, but I like his odds to develop into a mid-rotation arm.

**Ceiling:** 1.0- to 1.5-win player
**Risk:** High
**MLB ETA:** 2017

## 12. Akeem Bostick, RHP

**MiLB Rank: N/A**
**Position Rank: N/A**

| Born: 05/04/95 | Age: 21 | Bats: R | Top CALs: Luc Rennie, Nick Travieso, |
|---|---|---|---|
| Height: 6-6 | Weight: 215 | Throws: R | Jackson Stephens, Nickolas Sarianides, Garrett Gould |

| YEAR | Age | Level | IP | W | L | ERA | FIP | K/9 | BB/9 | K% | BB% | HR/9 | LOB% |
|---|---|---|---|---|---|---|---|---|---|---|---|---|---|
| 2013 | 18 | R | 41.3 | 4 | 1 | 2.83 | 3.35 | 7.19 | 2.61 | 19.0% | 6.9% | 0.00 | 70.9% |
| 2014 | 19 | A | 92.3 | 5 | 6 | 5.17 | 4.65 | 6.24 | 2.73 | 16.0% | 7.0% | 0.97 | 61.2% |
| 2015 | 20 | A | 42.0 | 3 | 1 | 1.50 | 3.11 | 7.07 | 0.64 | 21.2% | 1.9% | 0.64 | 80.5% |
| 2015 | 20 | A+ | 64.3 | 6 | 4 | 5.88 | 4.63 | 6.72 | 2.52 | 16.6% | 6.2% | 0.98 | 53.9% |

**Background:** Acquired from the Texas Rangers for what amounted to 121 plate appearances of well below-average offensive production from backstop Carlos Corporan. Bostick, a 2013 second round pick out of West Florence High School, opened the year back up in Low Class A where he was brilliant for 42 innings (33 strikeouts, three walks, 1.50 ERA, and 3.11 FIP. Houston then promoted the lanky 6-foot-6 right-hander to Lancaster where still posted solid peripherals (6.72 K/9 and 2.52 BB/9) but saw a noticeable downturn in overall effectiveness as his ERA, FIP, and homerun rate all spiked. For his career, Bostick, who is sporting a 4.32 ERA, has fanned 17.5% and walked just 6.0% of the total batters he's faced.

**Projection:** Bostick has missed a surprisingly scant amount of bats considering his promising, budding power arsenal. The control/command is incredibly strong given his size and youth, so he has a chance to move once he begins to click. Bostick has the upside as a back-of-the-rotation caliber arm with the floor of a potential late-inning relief arm.

**Ceiling:** 1.5- to 2.0-win player
**Risk:** Moderate to High
**MLB ETA:** 2017

## 13. Teoscar Hernandez, CF

**MiLB Rank: N/A**
**Position Rank: N/A**

| Born: 10/15/92 | Age: 23 | Bats: R | Top CALs: Michael A Taylor, Bubba Starling, |
|---|---|---|---|
| Height: 6-2 | Weight: 180 | Throws: R | Trayvon Robinson, Tyler Henson, Quincy Latimore |

| Season | Age | LVL | PA | 2B | 3B | HR | AVG | OBP | SLG | ISO | BB% | K% | wRC+ |
|---|---|---|---|---|---|---|---|---|---|---|---|---|---|
| 2013 | 20 | A | 565 | 25 | 9 | 13 | 0.271 | 0.328 | 0.435 | 0.164 | 7.3% | 23.9% | 114 |
| 2014 | 21 | A+ | 455 | 33 | 8 | 17 | 0.294 | 0.376 | 0.550 | 0.256 | 10.8% | 25.7% | 137 |
| 2015 | 22 | AA | 514 | 12 | 2 | 17 | 0.219 | 0.275 | 0.362 | 0.143 | 6.4% | 24.5% | 75 |

**Background:** This time last year Houston fans were dreaming on the Brett Philips/Teoscar Hernandez duel to the finish with the winner taking a firm hold of the starting center fielder's job for the better part of the next decade. Well, neither is likely going to happen: Phillips got shipped off to Milwaukee in the Carlos Gomez deal and Hernandez – poor, poor Hernandez – looked lost, overmatched, and out of place with Corpus Christi in the Texas League. The wiry 6-foot-2, 180-pound center fielder, who slugged .292/.362/.535 in 2014, cobbled together a lowly .219/.275/.362 triple-slash line with 12 doubles, two triples, 17 homeruns, and 33 stolen bases (in 40 attempts). His overall production, per *Weighted Runs Created Plus*, was 25% below the league average mark.

**Projection:** In last year's book I warned about the hype surrounding Hernandez, writing:

> *"[He] is a nice little prospect – he'll flash above-average pop at times, swipe a surprisingly [amount] of bags, and will occasionally flirt with some impressive walk rates. But the overall package is far less impressive than the individual pieces, something CAL tends to agree with. The Dominican-born outfielder will get more than a few looks from big league clubs as a potential everyday guy, but in the end he's going to find himself as a part-timer. Watch out for some swing-and-miss totals."*

Hernandez once again filled up the stat sheet while showing off a promising combination of power and speed. But all the holes in his bat were exposed in Class AA. I'm still sticking by the analysis from last year: he's a toolsy, enigmatic part-timer.

**Ceiling:** 1.5-win player
**Risk:** Moderate
**MLB ETA:** 2017

## 14. Riley Ferrell, RHP

**MiLB Rank:** N/A
**Position Rank:** N/A

| Born: 10/18/93 | Age: 22 | Bats: R | Top CALs: N/A |
| Height: 6-1 | Weight: 230 | Throws: R | |

| YEAR | Age | Level | IP | W | L | ERA | FIP | K/9 | BB/9 | K% | BB% | HR/9 | LOB% |
|------|-----|-------|-----|---|---|------|------|------|------|-------|-------|------|-------|
| 2015 | 21 | A | 16.7 | 0 | 0 | 1.08 | 3.70 | 9.18 | 7.02 | 23.9% | 18.3% | 0.00 | 87.0% |

**Background:** It wasn't too long ago that a potential fast-moving dominant backend relief arm would be snapped up in the opening round of the draft a la Huston Street or Chad Cordero. But Ferrell, a hard-throwing right-hander out of TCU, racked up a tremendous amount of punch outs during his three-year run as the Horned Frogs' closer. Ferrell fanned an impressive 162 batters in 110 career innings, or a touch over 13 per nine innings. Houston hastily grabbed the promising reliever in the third round and immediately sent him straight into full season where he showed a tremendous amount of promise – he fanned 17 in 16.2 innings while posting a 1.08 ERA – but also struggled with his control as well (13 walks).

**Projection**: Here's what I wrote prior to the draft:

> "Shutdown dominant closer in waiting. And the minor control hiccup this season [should prove to be of no concern because] Ferrell has historically shown better-than-average control. Throw in one of the better fastballs in the draft and he's primed to move quickly through the minors. In terms of comparable think Nick Burdi, Minnesota's second round pick last season."

Well, that minor hiccup continued to haunt Ferrell during his pro debut as he averaged more than seven free passes per nine innings. But, again, he averaged about three walks every nine innings during his first two college seasons, so there's no reason to worry. Yet.

**Ceiling:** 1.5-win player
**Risk:** Moderate
**MLB ETA:** 2017

## 15. Nolan Fontana, 2B/3B/SS

**MiLB Rank:** N/A
**Position Rank:** N/A

| Born: 06/06/91 | Age: 21 | Bats: L | Top CALs: Jake Lemmerman, Chris Gutierrez, |
| Height: 5-11 | Weight: 205 | Throws: R | Darwin Perez, Steve Tolleson, Greg Garcia |

| Season | Age | LVL | PA | 2B | 3B | HR | AVG | OBP | SLG | ISO | BB% | K% | wRC+ |
|--------|-----|-----|-----|----|----|----|-------|-------|-------|-------|-------|-------|------|
| 2013 | 22 | A+ | 499 | 18 | 6 | 8 | 0.259 | 0.415 | 0.399 | 0.140 | 20.4% | 20.0% | 125 |
| 2014 | 23 | AA | 305 | 21 | 1 | 1 | 0.262 | 0.418 | 0.376 | 0.114 | 20.0% | 24.9% | 138 |
| 2014 | 23 | AA | 305 | 21 | 1 | 1 | 0.262 | 0.418 | 0.376 | 0.114 | 20.0% | 24.9% | 138 |
| 2015 | 24 | AAA | 456 | 21 | 6 | 3 | 0.241 | 0.369 | 0.357 | 0.116 | 16.2% | 21.7% | 102 |
| 2015 | 24 | AAA | 456 | 21 | 6 | 3 | 0.241 | 0.369 | 0.357 | 0.116 | 16.2% | 21.7% | 102 |

**Background:** The single most fascinating prospect in the minor leagues – and the likely winner of that category over the last decade (at least to me), Fontana is *the* Sabermetric Superstar we've all been dreaming about. An absolute on-base machine, the University of Florida product who owns a career .409 OBP, sports a ridiculous 20.4% walk rate – *in nearly 1,500 plate appearances*. He's literally walking one out of every five trips to the plate. It's comical. It's incredible. It's…Nolan Fontana. The shortstop-turned-jack-of-all-trades spent the year refining his approach with Fresno in the PCL, hitting a less than impressive .241/.369/.357 but still managed to top the league average production mark by 2%. And for what it's worth, his walk rate last season, 16.2%, was the first time he failed to crack the 20%-mark.

**Projection**: I want him to succeed as if he's my own kid. I really do. Because it's such an interesting test case: the hit tool and power are below-average, the speed is nothing to write home about, but the patience is like finding the pot of gold at the end of the rainbow. Fontana is going to have to bounce between various infield positions to get some big league bats with Houston, but it's one of the few organizations that will put him in the perfect place to succeed.

**Ceiling:** 1.0- to 1.5-win player
**Risk:** Low to Moderate
**MLB ETA:** 2016

## 16. Tyler White, 1B/3B

MiLB Rank: N/A
Position Rank: N/A

| Born: 10/29/90 | Age: 25 | Bats: R | Top CALs: Jason Rogers, Yonder Alonso, |
| Height: 5-11 | Weight: 225 | Throws: R | Brad Emaus, Ole Sheldon, Dan Paolini |

| Season | Age | LVL | PA | 2B | 3B | HR | AVG | OBP | SLG | ISO | BB% | K% | wRC+ |
|---|---|---|---|---|---|---|---|---|---|---|---|---|---|
| 2013 | 22 | A- | 127 | 2 | 0 | 3 | 0.286 | 0.362 | 0.384 | 0.098 | 10.2% | 7.1% | 130 |
| 2014 | 23 | A | 290 | 20 | 1 | 7 | 0.305 | 0.414 | 0.485 | 0.180 | 12.1% | 13.8% | 159 |
| 2014 | 23 | A+ | 186 | 13 | 1 | 8 | 0.267 | 0.403 | 0.527 | 0.260 | 15.1% | 14.5% | 142 |
| 2015 | 24 | AA | 236 | 6 | 0 | 7 | 0.284 | 0.415 | 0.426 | 0.142 | 17.8% | 14.8% | 142 |
| 2015 | 24 | AAA | 259 | 19 | 1 | 7 | 0.362 | 0.467 | 0.559 | 0.197 | 16.2% | 14.7% | 178 |

**Background:** Another late, late round afterthought that, despite the seemingly insurmountable odds, has surpassed and exceeded expectations at every single stop along the way. White, a 33rd round pick out of Western Carolina University in 2013, has gone from having no realistic shot at the big leagues to someone that's likely to receive multiple looks at the game's pinnacle level. The stout 5-foot-11, 225-pound corner infielder burst onto the scene during his debut (.322/.406/.456), followed that up by hitting .290/.410/.501 between the Midwest and California Leagues, and upped the ante even more by slugging .325/.442/.496 with Corpus Christi and Fresno. For his career, White is sporting an impressive .311/.422/.489 triple-slash line, hitting 72 doubles, three triples, and 35 homeruns.

**Projection**: Another production vs. projection argument. White's background and draft selection all suggest he's going to barely leave a thumbnail scratch at the big league level. But he has not stopped hitting since his junior season with West Carolina University. One of the best walk rates in the minors, better-than-average power, a surprising hit tool, and strong contact rates. He's a player, for sure. And while CAL links him to only one big league, Yonder Alonso, it's a solid comp for peak performance.

**Ceiling:** 1.0- to 1.5-win player
**Risk:** Low to Moderate
**MLB ETA:** 2015

## 17. J.D. Davis, 3B

MiLB Rank: N/A
Position Rank: N/A

| Born: 04/27/93 | Age: 23 | Bats: R | Top CALs: Zoilo Almonte, David Vidal, |
| Height: 6-3 | Weight: 215 | Throws: R | Eric Jagielo, D.J. Peterson, Chris Dennis |

| Season | Age | LVL | PA | 2B | 3B | HR | AVG | OBP | SLG | ISO | BB% | K% | wRC+ |
|---|---|---|---|---|---|---|---|---|---|---|---|---|---|
| 2014 | 21 | A- | 131 | 7 | 1 | 5 | 0.279 | 0.382 | 0.495 | 0.216 | 11.5% | 19.1% | 158 |
| 2014 | 21 | A | 171 | 9 | 0 | 8 | 0.303 | 0.363 | 0.516 | 0.213 | 7.6% | 24.0% | 150 |
| 2015 | 22 | A+ | 552 | 28 | 3 | 26 | 0.289 | 0.370 | 0.520 | 0.231 | 9.8% | 28.4% | 140 |

**Background:** A three-year regular at Cal State Fullerton, Davis broke out as a two-way sensation during his sophomore season when he slugged .318/.407/.436 with 11 doubles, one triple, and four homeruns and moonlighted as a late-inning relief arm (23 IP, 17 strikeouts, seven walks, 2.74 ERA, and four saves). Davis' production improved during his final year as he mashed .338/.419/.528 with 27 extra-base hits and posted a 22-to-4 strikeout-to-walk ratio in 20.1 innings of work. Houston grabbed the right-hander/third base in the third round, converted him to a full-time stick, and set him off on his path of offensive destruction. He made quick work of the New York-Penn League (.279/.382/.495) and tore up Low Class A (.303/.363/.516) during his debut. The front office pushed him straight into High Class A last season and his numbers remained impressively positive: .289/.370/.520 with 28 doubles, three triples, and 26 homeruns.

**Projection**: Prior to the 2014 draft I pegged the former Titan as a third/fourth round and wrote:

> "Another prospect that could potentially shift to the mound if he fails to hit in the minor leagues, Davis' offensive toolkit grades out as merely average across the board – he isn't likely to hit for enough power for [third base], the plate discipline is good, not great, and he isn't likely to hit for a high average. Add in the fact that Cal State's home field is definitely hitter-friendly, and all of a sudden his draft prospects aren't so hot. At the very best Davis becomes a James Loney-type hitter. But that's if everything breaks the right way."

I raised the bar a little bit after his impressive debut, writing this in last year's book:

> "I'm not entirely sold on the homerun power just yet, but last year's output [in the minors] was at least a little eye-catching. And despite totaling just 171 plate appearances in Low Class A, he's punched his train ticket to Lancaster – where we still won't have a solid read on his power [because of Lancaster's bandbox effect]."

That one was a bit more on par. But there was a clear and distinct difference in production between his home and road splits last season: he batted .352/.434/683 at Lancaster and .231/.310/.373 everywhere else while slugging just seven of his 26 homeruns on the road. So maybe the initial pre-draft evaluation wasn't all that wrong in the first place.

Again, Davis' production remains quite cloudy – first because of Cal State's home ballpark and now because of Lancaster. He could be an interesting bat bench if the creep up in power remains steady. One more red flag: he's swinging-and-missing at some fairly prodigious rates.

**Ceiling:** 1.5-win player
**Risk:** Moderate to High
**MLB ETA:** 2017

## 18. Kyle Smith, RHP

**MiLB Rank: N/A**
**Position Rank: N/A**

| Born: 09/10/92 | Age: 23 | Bats: R | Top CALs: N/A |
| Height: 6-0 | Weight: 170 | Throws: R | |

| YEAR | Age | Level | IP | W | L | ERA | FIP | K/9 | BB/9 | K% | BB% | HR/9 | LOB% |
|---|---|---|---|---|---|---|---|---|---|---|---|---|---|
| 2013 | 20 | A+ | 104.3 | 5 | 4 | 2.85 | 3.61 | 8.28 | 2.50 | 22.2% | 6.7% | 0.78 | 77.8% |
| 2013 | 20 | A+ | 23.3 | 1 | 1 | 7.33 | 5.74 | 8.10 | 3.47 | 20.2% | 8.7% | 1.54 | 58.6% |
| 2014 | 21 | A+ | 27.7 | 4 | 0 | 2.60 | 4.21 | 10.08 | 3.90 | 27.2% | 10.5% | 0.98 | 77.5% |
| 2014 | 21 | AA | 95.3 | 5 | 5 | 4.34 | 3.86 | 9.06 | 2.36 | 24.2% | 6.3% | 1.32 | 72.4% |

**Background:** Always a favorite of mine, Smith succumbed to what so many young – and old – arms have fallen to: Tommy John surgery. The former 6th round pick underwent the operation in early April.

**Projection:** Since Smith failed to throw a pitch in 2015, here's what I wrote in last year's book:

> *"Arguably the most underrated prospect in the system, which is pretty tough to do considering the sheer depth of the farm, Smith has an extended history of success against much, much older competition. He's the kind of guy who shows up in a club's big league rotation and leaves six or seven years later for a contract that pays $8- to $10-million dollars a year."*

As much as we like to think as Tommy John surgery as a 100% solution, it's not. So I'm going to temper the expectations a bit on Smith, whose fastball was far from dominant, until after he starts chewing up innings again. He should be ready to go at some early point in 2016.

**Ceiling:** 1.5-win player
**Risk:** Moderate to High
**MLB ETA:** 2018/2019

## 19. Cy Sneed, RHP

**MiLB Rank: N/A**
**Position Rank: N/A**

| Born: 10/01/92 | Age: 23 | Bats: R | Top CALs: Cory Vanallen, Ivan Pineyro, |
| Height: 6-4 | Weight: 185 | Throws: R | Ramon Garcia, Justin Edwards, Francisco Jimenez |

| YEAR | Age | Level | IP | W | L | ERA | FIP | K/9 | BB/9 | K% | BB% | HR/9 | LOB% |
|---|---|---|---|---|---|---|---|---|---|---|---|---|---|
| 2014 | 21 | R | 38.0 | 0 | 2 | 5.92 | 5.11 | 7.34 | 3.32 | 16.9% | 7.7% | 0.95 | 58.6% |
| 2015 | 22 | A | 77.3 | 3 | 7 | 2.68 | 2.74 | 7.80 | 1.98 | 21.1% | 5.4% | 0.23 | 65.0% |
| 2015 | 22 | A+ | 62.0 | 3 | 4 | 2.47 | 2.44 | 7.98 | 1.60 | 22.1% | 4.4% | 0.29 | 70.8% |

**Background:** The third highest draft selection out of Dallas Baptist University – right-handers Vic Black and Jake Johansen being the top two – Sneed was taken in the third round in 2014, 85th overall. A three-year stalwart in the Patriots rotation, Sneed averaged just 6.82 K/9 and 3.13 BB/9 during his amateur career. Last season he split time between the Midwest and Florida State Leagues.

**Projection:** Sneed's seen a dramatic improvement since entering pro ball two years ago – he's already averaged more punch outs with fewer walks in roughly one full season's of data than at any point in college. And last season he sparkled as he finished the year with a 122-to-28 strikeout-to-walk ratio. He's likely headed to Class AA in 2016. And he profiles as a #5-type arm, though he could very easily head down the path to middle relief-dom.

**Ceiling:** 1.0 to 1.5-win player
**Risk:** Moderate
**MLB ETA:** 2018

## 20. Tony Kemp, 2B/OF

**MiLB Rank:** N/A
**Position Rank:** N/A

| Born: 10/31/91 | Age: 24 | Bats: L | Top CALs: Angel Franco, DJ Lemahieu, |
|---|---|---|---|
| Height: 5-6 | Weight: 165 | Throws: R | Adrian Cardenas, Jake Elmore, Kevin Russo |

| Season | Age | LVL | PA | 2B | 3B | HR | AVG | OBP | SLG | ISO | BB% | K% | wRC+ |
|---|---|---|---|---|---|---|---|---|---|---|---|---|---|
| 2013 | 21 | A- | 204 | 7 | 2 | 1 | 0.282 | 0.355 | 0.362 | 0.079 | 10.3% | 14.2% | 119 |
| 2013 | 21 | A | 120 | 1 | 1 | 1 | 0.255 | 0.387 | 0.316 | 0.061 | 15.8% | 15.0% | 112 |
| 2014 | 22 | A+ | 356 | 19 | 4 | 4 | 0.336 | 0.433 | 0.468 | 0.132 | 12.6% | 9.8% | 141 |
| 2014 | 22 | AA | 275 | 11 | 4 | 4 | 0.292 | 0.381 | 0.425 | 0.133 | 10.2% | 11.6% | 135 |
| 2015 | 23 | AA | 230 | 10 | 1 | 0 | 0.358 | 0.457 | 0.420 | 0.062 | 15.2% | 12.2% | 155 |
| 2015 | 23 | AAA | 311 | 9 | 3 | 3 | 0.273 | 0.334 | 0.362 | 0.089 | 6.8% | 11.9% | 88 |
| 2015 | 23 | AAA | 311 | 9 | 3 | 3 | 0.273 | 0.334 | 0.362 | 0.089 | 6.8% | 11.9% | 88 |

**Background:** Cornering the market on pocket-sized second baseman – or more likely smart enough to look beyond what a player is, rather than isn't – Houston grabbed the 5-foot-6, 165-pound lefty-swinging second baseman out of Vanderbilt in the fifth round three years ago. And he hasn't stopped hitting since. A career .329/.434/.431 hitter with the Commodores, Kemp batted .273/.366/.345 between the New York-Penn and Midwest Leagues during his debut, followed that up with a .316/.411/.449 mark between High Class A and Class AA two years ago, and posted a .308/.388/.386 line between Corpus Christi and Fresno last season.

**Projection:** One of the major helium guys during the first half of last season (.358/.457/.420), Kemp cooled off dramatically once he was promoted to the PCL. But more importantly: his power took a *huge* developmental step backward last season as well, falling from slightly below-average to well below-average. Kemp's a nice utility guy with a solid hit tool, numerous defensive positions, and speed. CAL isn't a particular fan either, linking him to Angel Franco, D.J. Lemahieu, Adrian Cardenas, Jake Elmore, and Kevin Russo.

**Ceiling:** 1.0-win player
**Risk:** Low to Moderate
**MLB ETA:** 2016

## 21. Jason Martin, CF/LF

**MiLB Rank:** N/A
**Position Rank:** N/A

| Born: 09/05/95 | Age: 20 | Bats: L | Top CALs: Fafael Valera, Abraham Almonte, |
|---|---|---|---|
| Height: 5-11 | Weight: 190 | Throws: R | Manuel Margot, Roderick Bernadina, Jose Gonzalez |

| Season | Age | LVL | PA | 2B | 3B | HR | AVG | OBP | SLG | ISO | BB% | K% | wRC+ |
|---|---|---|---|---|---|---|---|---|---|---|---|---|---|
| 2013 | 17 | R | 214 | 8 | 4 | 0 | 0.251 | 0.357 | 0.341 | 0.089 | 13.6% | 14.5% | 113 |
| 2014 | 18 | R | 192 | 11 | 6 | 0 | 0.274 | 0.363 | 0.415 | 0.140 | 12.5% | 15.6% | 125 |
| 2015 | 19 | A | 460 | 12 | 7 | 8 | 0.270 | 0.346 | 0.396 | 0.126 | 10.2% | 16.1% | 116 |

**Background:** A nice under-the-radar find out of Orange Lutheran High School, home to Gerrit Cole and Brandon Maurer, in the eighth round three years ago. The lacking tool that Martin has yet to display during his tenure in professional baseball, power, finally took a huge development step forward last season. Owner of one career homerun in his first 113 games, Martin stepped up to the plate and slugged eight dingers last season, as well as 12 doubles and seven triples en route to posting a more than respectable .270/.346/.396 triple-slash line with a 116 wRC+ as a 19-year-old. Martin also swiped 14 bags, but that came with a rather unfortunate caveat: he was nabbed 15 times.

**Projection:** There are some interesting parallels that can be drawn between Martin and his former org-mate – and current Brewers prospect – Brett Phillips. For instance, let's take a gander at their work in the Gulf Coast, Appalachian, and New York-Penn Leagues during their first two pro seasons:

| Player | Age | Level | PA | AVG | OBP | SLG | SB | BB% | K% |
|---|---|---|---|---|---|---|---|---|---|
| Jason Martin | 17-18 | R/A- | 496 | 0.255 | 0.346 | 0.366 | 24 | 12.10% | 14.92% |
| Brett Phillips | 18-19 | R/A- | 376 | 0.247 | 0.355 | 0.348 | 12 | 12.77% | 21.01% |

Obviously, the duo's production is closely mirrored. The big change, however, came when Phillips decimated the Midwest League (.302/.362/.521) and Martin merely performed well (.270/.346/.396), though the latter was a year younger in baseball terms. Martin has a firm offensive foundation in place: solid hit tool, developing power, and sneaky speed. But there's a massive, canyon-sized hole he's going to need to jump over to achieve his potential: his inability – and that's a complete understatement – to handle fellow left-handers. Martin's yearly OPSs against southpaws since 2013: .628, .511, and .590. If he can solve that issue – which I don't think he ever will – Martin has a shot to develop into a league average player. If not, he's merely a fourth- or fifth-outfielder.

**Ceiling:** 1.0- to 1.5-win player
**Risk:** Moderate to High
**MLB ETA:** 2018

## 22. Jandel Gustave, RHP

MiLB Rank: N/A

Position Rank: N/A

| Born: 10/12/92 | Age: 23 | Bats: R | Top CALs: Carlos Hernandez, Kevin Comer, |
| Height: 6-2 | Weight: 160 | Throws: R | Jose Ramirez, Jasner Severino, Waldis Joaquin |

| YEAR | Age | Level | IP | W | L | ERA | FIP | K/9 | BB/9 | K% | BB% | HR/9 | LOB% |
|---|---|---|---|---|---|---|---|---|---|---|---|---|---|
| 2013 | 20 | R | 43.7 | 2 | 3 | 2.68 | 3.64 | 10.10 | 4.74 | 25.4% | 11.9% | 0.41 | 67.5% |
| 2014 | 21 | A | 79.0 | 5 | 5 | 5.01 | 3.50 | 9.34 | 3.30 | 22.1% | 7.8% | 0.34 | 59.9% |
| 2015 | 22 | AA | 58.7 | 5 | 2 | 2.15 | 3.45 | 7.52 | 3.84 | 19.8% | 10.1% | 0.31 | 79.8% |

**Background:** Passed around like yesterday's leftovers last offseason, Gustave would eventually find his way back to the Houston for his sixth professional season. The hard-throwing right-hander converted to a full-time reliever in 2015 and completed a rather rare feat: his strikeout rate actually declined, dropping all the way down to 7.5 K/9.

**Projection**: Armed with not only one of the organization's best arms, but also one of the minors' finest as well. After posting walk rates north of eight free passes per nine innings during his first three professional seasons, Gustave's control has been trending in the right direction ever since. His walk rates have declined from 15.8 BB/9 to 8.7 BB/9 to 4.7 BB/9 to 3.3 BB/9 before ticking back up to 3.8 BB/9. Dominant late-inning reliever with some risk.

**Ceiling:** 1.0- to 1.5-win player
**Risk:** High
**MLB ETA:** 2016

## 23. Danry Vasquez, LF/RF

MiLB Rank: N/A

Position Rank: N/A

| Born: 01/08/94 | Age: 22 | Bats: L | Top CALs: Bridger Hunt, Gerardo Parra, |
| Height: 6-3 | Weight: 190 | Throws: R | Teodoro Martinez, L.J. Hayes, Willie Cabrera |

| Season | Age | LVL | PA | 2B | 3B | HR | AVG | OBP | SLG | ISO | BB% | K% | wRC+ |
|---|---|---|---|---|---|---|---|---|---|---|---|---|---|
| 2013 | 19 | A | 549 | 18 | 6 | 9 | 0.284 | 0.331 | 0.400 | 0.116 | 6.7% | 12.9% | 104 |
| 2014 | 20 | A+ | 475 | 30 | 2 | 5 | 0.291 | 0.353 | 0.407 | 0.116 | 8.4% | 14.3% | 101 |
| 2015 | 21 | A+ | 182 | 13 | 2 | 3 | 0.315 | 0.365 | 0.470 | 0.155 | 7.1% | 13.2% | 128 |
| 2015 | 21 | AA | 296 | 13 | 1 | 0 | 0.245 | 0.294 | 0.300 | 0.054 | 5.4% | 14.2% | 67 |

**Background:** A savvy pickup from Detroit for what amounted to 19+ innings of average relief work from Jose Veras at the 2013 trade deadline. Vasquez has always been one of these fill-up-the-stat-sheet guys, but never truly dominated at any point during his five-year pro career. Three years ago, at the ripe old age of 19, the lefty-swinging corner outfielder slugged 16 doubles, five triples, six homeruns, and swiped 11 bags while hitting a combined .284/.331/.400 between both organizations. Fantastic production at first glance, but according to *Weighted Runs Created Plus*, he basically hovered around the league average mark. He did the same thing the following year with Lancaster, stuffing the stat sheet but posting another average-ish 101 wRC+. Last season, everything seemed to click for the lanky corner outfielder as he started off on a bang back in Lancaster, hitting a robust .315/.365/.470 while posting a career high 125 wRC+. And then it all came crashing down once he got promoted to Class AA; he batted .245/.294/.300 with a career low 67 wRC+.

**Projection**: Chewed up, spit out, and left for dead by any left-hander in the minor leagues over the past two seasons. Vasquez's production over the past two seasons have been so poor that if you **added** OPS totals against LHP stands at a .945. Yes, that's right. He tallied a .433 OPS against them in 2014 and fared only slightly better last season (.512). Vasquez has always been a quasi-interesting prospect – he's shown, at times, an average eye at the plate, developing power, a little bit of speed, and a decent hit tool – but his complete inability to handle southpaws will ultimately doom him into minor league purgatory.

**Ceiling:** 1.0-win player
**Risk:** Moderate to High
**MLB ETA:** 2018

## 24. Elieser Hernandez, RHP

**MiLB Rank: N/A**
**Position Rank: N/A**

| Born: 05/03/95 | Age: 21 | Bats: R | **Top CALs:** Connor Greene, Jhonathan Ramos, |
|---|---|---|---|
| Height: 6-0 | Weight: 210 | Throws: R | Aaron Fuhrman, Luis Severino, Jose Gusman |

| YEAR | Age | Level | IP | W | L | ERA | FIP | K/9 | BB/9 | K% | BB% | HR/9 | LOB% |
|---|---|---|---|---|---|---|---|---|---|---|---|---|---|
| 2013 | 18 | R | 57.3 | 5 | 1 | 1.26 | 2.92 | 7.22 | 3.30 | 20.6% | 9.4% | 0.16 | 83.3% |
| 2014 | 19 | R | 10.0 | 1 | 0 | 0.00 | 3.77 | 7.20 | 4.50 | 19.1% | 11.9% | 0.00 | 100.0% |
| 2014 | 19 | R | 35.7 | 4 | 1 | 2.78 | 3.26 | 8.58 | 2.02 | 24.6% | 5.8% | 0.50 | 73.1% |
| 2015 | 20 | A- | 20.7 | 0 | 1 | 1.31 | 1.19 | 13.06 | 0.87 | 38.0% | 2.5% | 0.00 | 70.6% |
| 2015 | 20 | A | 45.7 | 3 | 3 | 3.94 | 3.29 | 9.07 | 2.17 | 23.1% | 5.5% | 0.59 | 66.9% |

**Background:** Tipping the scales at an already portly 210 pounds for an average-sized pitcher, the Venezuelan-born Hernandez, who stands 6-foot tall, got his first taste of full-season action in 2015 – and he loved it so much he's going back for seconds. After taking several years to mull his way through the lowest levels, Hernandez made quick work of the New York-Penn League last season, posting a 30-to-2 strikeout-to-walk ratio in 20.2 innings, and he continued his run of strong performances in the Midwest League (45.2 innings, 46 strikeouts, and 11 walks). Overall he finished the year with a combined 3.12 ERA while averaging 10.3 punch outs and just 1.8 walks per nine innings.

**Projection**: Hernandez's strikeout-to-walk ratios have been steadily trending in the right direction over the past couple years, and last season's mark is by far-and-away the best of his young career. And despite the fact that he's tallied just 45.2 innings above short-season ball, Hernandez could be headed to Lancaster to open the 2016 season. Very intriguing pitcher with some upside as a backend starter. But let's hold off a bit until he gets some more innings under his belt.

**Ceiling:** 1.0-win player
**Risk:** Moderate to High
**MLB ETA:** 2018

## 25. Brendan McCurry, RHP

**MiLB Rank: N/A**
**Position Rank: N/A**

| Born: 11/14/93 | Age: 21 | Bats: B | **Top CALs:** Oneli Perez, Matt Frevent, |
|---|---|---|---|
| Height: 5-11 | Weight: 175 | Throws: R | T.J. House, Mat Batts, Doug Brandt |

| YEAR | Age | Level | IP | W | L | ERA | FIP | K/9 | BB/9 | K% | BB% | HR/9 | LOB% |
|---|---|---|---|---|---|---|---|---|---|---|---|---|---|
| 2014 | 22 | R | 1.3 | 0 | 0 | 0.00 | 1.03 | 13.50 | 0.00 | 33.3% | 0.0% | 0.00 | 100.0% |
| 2014 | 22 | A | 26.3 | 2 | 0 | 0.34 | 1.97 | 11.62 | 1.03 | 37.0% | 3.3% | 0.34 | 100.0% |
| 2014 | 22 | A+ | 1.0 | 0 | 0 | 0.00 | 1.74 | 9.00 | 0.00 | 33.3% | 0.0% | 0.00 | 100.0% |
| 2015 | 23 | A+ | 46.3 | 1 | 2 | 1.94 | 3.17 | 10.88 | 2.14 | 30.9% | 6.1% | 0.58 | 78.4% |
| 2015 | 23 | AA | 16.7 | 0 | 1 | 1.62 | 2.04 | 14.04 | 3.24 | 40.0% | 9.2% | 0.54 | 88.2% |

**Background:** A fantastic scouting – or analytical – find in the 22nd round out of Oklahoma State University. I'm not sure what's more impressive, either his dominant 2015 season or career numbers? Let's talk about both. McCurry spent the season making quick work of both the California and Texas Leagues. In 63.0 combined innings, he surrendered 13 earned runs, punched out 82, and walked just 17. He also finished with an aggregate 1.86 ERA and saved 27 games. And now the career numbers: in 91.2 innings, he's sporting a 1.37 ERA while averaging 11.7 K/9 and just 2.0 BB/9.

**Projection**: Not overly big. Hell, he's actually rather small; he's listed at 5-foot-10 and 165 pounds. And he's not your typical flame-throwing right-handed closer either. But McCurry gets results, which gets the attention of the Oakland front office and eventually the Houston brass. He could be a solid, better-than-average middle relief arm, something every team needs.

**Ceiling:** 0.5- to 1.0-win player
**Risk:** Low to Moderate
**MLB ETA:** 2016

### Barely Missed:

- **Andrew Aplin, OF** – A solid fourth outfielder type out of Arizona State University. Aplin made waves as an early season breakout in 2015, hitting a robust .343/.458/.448 in 31 games with Corpus Christi, but his production fell back to his usual norms once promoted to Fresno (.275/.392/.348).

- **Chris Devenski, RHP** – Former late round pick out of Cal State Fullerton in 2011, Devenski spent the season back in Class AA last season. He tossed 119.2 innings, fanned 104, and walked 33. Basically, he's a younger version of Asher Wojciechowski (see below).

- **Reymin Guduan, LHP** – A power-armed southpaw out of the Dominican Republic, Guduan can rack up strikeout totals with the best of them. The lone issue: he literally has no idea where the hell it's going. He averaging more than seven free passes per nine innings *for his entire career* – a career that spans nearly 200 innings. Last season he made stops at three different levels – Midwest, California, and Texas Leagues – and averaged 11.6 K/9 and "just" 6.5 BB/9. Progress, I guess.

- **Brady Rodgers, RHP** – Rodgers, a third round pick out of Arizona State University in 2012, is yet another older-ish right-hander with a limited skill set knocking on the Big League door. For his career he's averaged 7.2 K/9 and just 1.7 BB/9. Among the trio of Rodgers, Devenski, and Wojciechowski, Rodgers has the best chance to succeed with Houston.

- **Asher Wojciechowski, RHP** – Big league ready with a limited ceiling. The former first round pick out of The Citadel flashed a low 90s fastball, low 80s slider, cutter, and changeup during his brief debut in Houston. Fringy backend start whose finest quality – the ability to chew innings – will get him a couple looks.

## *Bird Doggin' It – Additional Prospects to Keep an Eye in 2016*

| Player | Age | POS | Notes |
|---|---|---|---|
| Harold Arauz | 21 | RHP | Got smacked around a bit in the NYPL last season, but his nearly 6.00 ERA resulted from a .400+ BABIP the opposition was sporting. Strong peripherals and a decent sub-4.00 FIP. |
| Rogelio Armenteros | 22 | RHP | Cuban defector simply overmatched the New York-Penn and Midwest Leagues last season, posting a 61-to-24 strikeout-to-walk ratio in 61.0 innings. His brief stint with Quad Cities was as nothing short of breathtaking: 17.0 IP, 21 K, 7 BB. |
| Bobby Boyd | OF | 23 | Small 5-foot-9 outfielder out of West Virginia University. Boyd batted .283/.347/.363 with 19 doubles, seven triples, one homerun, and 40 stolen bases (in 52 attempts). Speed is the only tool, but not enough to make him a legit prospect. |
| Kevin Comer | RHP | 23 | Acquired along with Joe Musgrove, the former first round pick was mediocre with his stints in Quad Cities and Lancaster. |
| Brock Dykxhoorn | RHP | 21 | Massive, massive 6-foot-8 right-hander could find himself among the system's top 25 prospects after next year. Shows a strong feel for the strikeout, despite his frame size, but didn't miss a whole lot of bats with Quad Cities. |
| Alfredo Gonzalez | C | 23 | Had a breakout season as he hit .321/.409/.378 between three levels. Gonzalez has thrown out 37% of would-be base stealers in his career, so he might be able to carve out a backup role. |
| Conrad Gregor | 1B | 24 | Former fourth round pick out of Vanderbilt continued to struggle in Class AA in 2015, nearly replicating his production for the previous season. |
| Tyler Heineman | C | 25 | A better version of Alfredo Gonzalez with a longer track record. He batted .285/.334/.379 between the minors' top two levels. |
| Brian Holmes | LHP | 25 | Big time strikeout rates with solid-average control. He could be a serviceable middle-relief/LOOGY option down the line. |
| Mott Hyde | 2B/SS | 24 | A late round pick out of Georgia Tech two years ago, Hyde hit a combined .304/.384/.433 between Quad Cities and Lancaster. Let's see how he handles an age-appropriate level of competition. |
| Ramon Laureano | OF | 21 | Short, stocky outfielder with speed, average power, and posted a 114 wRC+ as a 20-year-old in the Midwest League. |
| Chase McDonald | 1B | 24 | Mashed 61 extra-base hits in 105 games, though that comes with two caveats: his age and the fact that he played in Lancaster. |
| Bryan Radziewski | LHP | 24 | Wrote this prior to the 2014 draft: "Not particularly overpowering, Radziewski lands firmly in the Jeremy Sowers camp – left-handers with decent stuff and an idea how to use it." He's ready for Class AA. |
| Juan Robles | RHP | 18 | Incredibly fascinating prospect. Robles made three stops – including a two-game stint in the Midwest League – at the ripe age of 17. Finished the year with a 56-to-21 strikeout-to-walk ratio in 54.2 innings. |
| Troy Scribner | RHP | 24 | The good news: he punched out 111 in 100.0 innings. The bad news: he walked 57. |
| Miguelangel Sierra | SS | 18 | International Bonus Baby chewed up the DSL (.302/.406/.479), but got spit out once he moved stateside (.160/.267/.213). He could find himself in the Top 20 next year. |
| Max Stassi | C | 25 | Hasn't looked – or performed – the same since the late 2013 concussion. |
| Kristian Trompiz | IF | 20 | Looked OK, far from great, as a 19-year-old in the Midwest League; he posted a .251/.285/.367 with an 87 wRC+. |

**State of the Farm System:** Kansas City's system has taken quite a hit over the past couple years – of course, back-to-back World Series

appearances and one big ring is more than worth it. Needless to say, the farm system that was once touted as "Greatest in Baseball History" easily lived up to those lofty expectations – which is a good thing nowadays as there aren't nearly the numbers of high ceiling, high impact big league hopefuls making their way through the minors. It's the result of churning out so many big leaguers in so little time and then dealing away top prospects to plug holes in the championship aspirations.

But that doesn't mean the cupboard is completely barren.

Hard-throwing Dominican-born right-hander Miguel Almonte made stops at three different levels last season, going from Northwest Arkansas to Omaha before settling in with the big league club down the stretch. He displayed a mid- to upper-90s heater in limited action, complementing the above-average to plus-pitch with a hard 80 mph curveball and a wickedly fast 90 mph changeup. The Royals' rotation is filled at the moment – Edinson Volquez, Yordano Ventura, newly inked Ian Kennedy, Kris Medlen, Danny Duffy, Chris Young, and eventually Jason Vargas, who's on the comeback trail from Tommy John surgery – so Almonte will likely have to bide his time back with the Storm Chasers in the Pacific Coast League.

Equally hard-throwing right-hander Kyle Zimmer – a personal favorite of mine – finally seemed to shake the injury bug last season as he lasted 64.0 innings, his most since 2013. The front office also grabbed another potentially dominant young arm in the first round last June as well, taking right-hander Ashe Russell with the 21st overall pick and signing him to a deal which was about $600,000 more than the allotted bonus.

| Rank | Name | POS |
|---|---|---|
| 1 | Miguel Almonte | RHP |
| 2 | Raul Mondesi | SS |
| 3 | Kyle Zimmer | RHP |
| 4 | Ashe Russell | RHP |
| 5 | Pedro Fernandez | RHP |
| 6 | Scott Blewett | RHP |
| 7 | Alec Mills | RHP |
| 8 | Reymond Fuentes | LF/CF |
| 9 | Foster Griffin | LHP |
| 10 | Matthew Strahm | LHP |
| 11 | Balbino Fuenmayor | 1B/3B |
| 12 | Bubba Starling | CF |
| 13 | Eric Skoglund | LHP |
| 14 | Glenn Sparkman | RHP |
| 15 | Nolan Watson | RHP |
| 16 | Elier Hernandez | CF/RF |
| 17 | Alfredo Escalera-Maldonado | OF |
| 18 | Jorge Bonifacio | LF/RF |
| 19 | Cheslor Cuthbert | 1B/3B |
| 20 | Josh Staumont | RHP |
| 21 | Christian Binford | RHP |
| 22 | Hunter Dozier | 3B |
| 23 | Jake Junis | RHP |
| 24 | Ryan O'Hearn | 1B/RF |
| 25 | Chase Vallot | C |

Raul Mondesi made history by becoming the first player to make his big league debut in the World Series. The then-19-year-old shortstop was coming off of a decent – though far from impressive – showing in the Texas League where he batted .243/.2779/.372.

Beyond that, though, there are a lot of young arms in the lower levels: Pedro Fernandez, Alec Mills, Foster Griffin, Matthew Strahm, and Eric Skoglund, who could turn into a cheap backend option in a couple years.

As far as hitters go, Reymond Fuentes is ready to take over a backup outfield spot with the big league club; former first round pick Bubba Starling made tremendous strides to help shed some of the bust label hanging over his head; and former prospect-turned-Indy-star Balbino Fuenmayor looked like the second coming of the Bambino in his second chance at the minor leagues.

**Review of the 2015 Draft:** Kansas City opened up the draft by taking three highly touted right-handers: Russell, the 21st overall pick, Nolan Watson, who was chosen 11 picks later, and DII flame-thrower Josh Staumont. The problem, though, is each looked a bit underwhelming during their admittedly brief professional debuts. Russell and Watson didn't miss a whole lot of bats and Staumont found the strike zone with as much regularity as a blind-folded drunk guy peeing in a urinal.

Former Western Kentucky University outfielder Anderson Miller, who was taken in the third round, looked decent during his 43-game stint with Lexington in the South Atlantic League, hitting .260/.319/.355.

## 1. Miguel Almonte, RHP

| Born: 04/04/93 | Age: 23 | Bats: R | Top CALs: Richard Castillo, Tyler Herron, |
|---|---|---|---|
| Height: 6-2 | Weight: 180 | Throws: R | Ryan Searle, Allen Webster, James Parr |

| YEAR | Age | Level | IP | W | L | ERA | FIP | K/9 | BB/9 | K% | BB% | HR/9 | LOB% |
|---|---|---|---|---|---|---|---|---|---|---|---|---|---|
| 2013 | 20 | A | 130.7 | 6 | 9 | 3.10 | 3.04 | 9.09 | 2.48 | 24.7% | 6.7% | 0.41 | 70.2% |
| 2014 | 21 | A+ | 110.3 | 6 | 8 | 4.49 | 3.92 | 8.24 | 2.61 | 21.8% | 6.9% | 0.73 | 65.5% |
| 2015 | 22 | AA | 67.0 | 4 | 4 | 4.03 | 4.00 | 7.39 | 3.63 | 18.8% | 9.2% | 0.54 | 73.1% |
| 2015 | 22 | AAA | 36.7 | 2 | 2 | 5.40 | 3.90 | 10.06 | 3.68 | 26.5% | 9.7% | 0.74 | 57.7% |

**Background:** Following in the footsteps of another hard-throwing Dominican-born hurler (Yordano Ventura) Almonte's rapid ascension over the past three-plus seasons culminated with a September call-up to help reinforce the eventual World Champion's bullpen. Almonte, a lean 6-foot-2, 180-pound right-hander, has been making waves since his age-19 season when he combined to throw 77.0 inning between the Dominican and Arizona Summer Leagues, fanning 74 and walking just 13. Since then, he's torched the South Atlantic League (130.2 IP, 132 K, 36 BB), breezed through High Class A (110.0 IP, 101 K, 32 BB), and looked at ease between his stint with Northwest Arkansas and Omaha last season. Almonte began the year as one of the youngest hurlers in the Texas League in 2015, though you wouldn't know it by his level of production. In 17 starts and 67.0 innings with the Naturals, he fanned 55, walked 27, and posted a decent 4.00 FIP. Kansas City pushed the young hurler up to the PCL in early July, and after seven mostly favorable starts – he posted a 38-to-11 strikeout-to-walk ratio in 32.2 innings of work – Almonte got pushed into a late-inning relief role to prep him for the big league club's stretch run. He would finish his minor league season with 103.2 combined innings, with 96 punch outs and 42 walks. As for his time in Kansas City, well, let's just say the long ball proved to be too much to overcome; he surrendered four dingers in 8.2 innings.

**Projection**: Almonte has shown the not-too-common combination of swing-and-miss ability with low walk totals. For his career, he's averaged 8.6 strikeouts and just 2.7 walks per nine innings. He showed a dominant mid- to upper-90s fastball during his brief – and admittedly disappointing – stint in Kansas City. He complemented with a curveball and hard, low-90s changeup. The Royals are chock full of pitching at the big league level, with the rotation currently featuring Edinson Volquez, Yordano Ventura, Kris Medlen, Danny Duffy, and Chris Young, and the bullpen is ridiculously deep with power arms; so Almonte probably won't see a whole lot of action unless a rash of injuries break out. I'm a big, big fan of the burgeoning right-hander – a power arsenal with the ability to maximize his potential as a mid- to upper-half of the rotation starter.

**Ceiling:** 3.0-win player
**Risk:** Low to Moderate
**MLB ETA:** Debuted in 2015

## 2. Kyle Zimmer, RHP

| Born: 09/13/91 | Age: 24 | Bats: R | Top CALs: Sean Nolin, Aaron Blair, |
|---|---|---|---|
| Height: 6-3 | Weight: 215 | Throws: R | Johnny Cueto, Jharel Cotton, Justin Garcia |

| YEAR | Age | Level | IP | W | L | ERA | FIP | K/9 | BB/9 | K% | BB% | HR/9 | LOB% |
|---|---|---|---|---|---|---|---|---|---|---|---|---|---|
| 2013 | 21 | A+ | 89.7 | 4 | 8 | 4.82 | 3.27 | 11.34 | 3.11 | 29.8% | 8.2% | 0.90 | 59.2% |
| 2013 | 21 | AA | 18.7 | 2 | 1 | 1.93 | 2.68 | 13.02 | 2.41 | 36.0% | 6.7% | 0.96 | 92.1% |
| 2014 | 22 | R | 4.7 | 0 | 0 | 1.93 | 4.46 | 9.64 | 7.71 | 21.7% | 17.4% | 0.00 | 88.9% |
| 2015 | 23 | A | 16.0 | 1 | 0 | 1.13 | 2.80 | 11.81 | 3.38 | 32.8% | 9.4% | 0.56 | 89.7% |
| 2015 | 23 | AA | 48.0 | 2 | 5 | 2.81 | 3.13 | 9.56 | 2.63 | 25.9% | 7.1% | 0.75 | 71.4% |

**Background:** And this is why there are no such things as pitching prospects. A couple years ago – prior to his string of rather serious injuries – I would have taken the former San Francisco stud ahead of nearly any arm in the minor leagues. Then the former fifth overall pick got smacked upside the head with the injury stick. He's suffered through numerous setbacks on nearly every major part of a pitcher's body – elbow tendonitis, shoulder surgery to repair damaged tissue in his labrum and rotator cuff, bicep issues, and a latssimusi dorsi strain that forced him to miss the majority of 2014. Quite frankly, it's a surprise he hasn't spontaneously combusted at this time. But after throwing just 4.2 innings with Idaho Falls and another 9.2 in the Arizona Fall League two years ago, Zimmer looked healthy – and dominant – for the first time in long while last season.

After a quick nine-game tune-up with Lexington in the Sally, Zimmer got pushed back up to the Texas League for his 15 games. He would throw 48.0 innings with the Naturals, fanning 51 and walking only 14 to go along with a 2.81 ERA and 3.13 FIP. And just to put this whole thing into some perspective consider this: despite being limited to 152.2 innings between 2012 and 2014, Zimmer's strikeout-to-walk percentage in Class AA last season ranked 11th among all Texas League hurlers with 40+ innings.

**Projection**: Here's what I wrote about Zimmer in my first book two years ago:

*"The very definition of outpitching one's ERA. Zimmer, who posted an unsustainably low strand rate in High Class A, showed tremendous swing-and-miss ability and strong control en route to posting a combined 2.56 Skill Independent ERA. True ace potential and one of the top pitching prospects in the minors, Zimmer also has a relatively fresh arm, lacking the typical wear-and-tear of the normal collegiate hurler."*

Well, he *did* lack the typical wear-and-tear of many early 20s hurlers. But now his body and arm have the equivalent age of your Aunt Ida. But here's what we know (minus the lengthy injury history): Zimmer still has an incredibly high, albeit risky, ceiling; he showcases an above-average- to plus-fastball and a matching ability to miss sticks. If he can stay healthy – and that's an iceberg-sized *if* – Zimmer still looks like a potential ace. Keep your fingers crossed.

One final thought: CAL still remains rather optimistic, tying him to Aaron Blair and Johnny Cueto.

**Ceiling:** 3.5- to 4.0-win player
**Risk:** High
**MLB ETA:** 2017

# 3. Raul Mondesi, SS

**MiLB Rank: #78**
**Position Rank: N/A**

| Born: 07/27/95 | Age: 20 | Bats: B | Top CALs: Junior Lake, Elvis Andrus, |
| Height: 6-1 | Weight: 185 | Throws: R | Danny Santana, Jonathan Villar, Chris Owings |

| Season | Age | LVL | PA | 2B | 3B | HR | AVG | OBP | SLG | ISO | BB% | K% | wRC+ |
|---|---|---|---|---|---|---|---|---|---|---|---|---|---|
| 2013 | 17 | A | 536 | 13 | 7 | 7 | 0.261 | 0.311 | 0.361 | 0.100 | 6.3% | 22.0% | 94 |
| 2014 | 18 | A+ | 472 | 14 | 12 | 8 | 0.211 | 0.256 | 0.354 | 0.143 | 5.1% | 25.8% | 68 |
| 2015 | 19 | AA | 338 | 11 | 5 | 6 | 0.243 | 0.279 | 0.372 | 0.128 | 5.0% | 26.0% | 77 |

**Background:** I've previously mentioned this on numerous occasions, but I find it so fascinating I think it's worth repeating: Mondesi's old man, who also goes by the same name, spent 13 seasons in the big leagues, hitting .273/.331/.485 with 319 doubles, 49 triples, 271 homeruns, and 229 stolen bases; he was also named the 1994 strike-shortened Rookie of the Year, beating out such dignitaries as Ryan Klesko, Javy Lopez, and Cliff Floyd; the elder Mondesi was also named to an All-Star squad, slugged 30 homeruns in a season three times, mashed 20 or more another six times, and played on teams with Gary Sheffield , Mike Piazza, Eric Karros, Charles Johnson, a young Adrian Beltre, and Eric Young among others during his peak seasons. But he never topped 100 RBI in a season, at any point in his career. You know who's accomplished that feat? Guys like Jeff King, John Jaha, and Jay Bell.

Anyway, the younger Mondesi also made some headlines this year, though in a much more positive light: the then-19-year-old shortstop became the first player in modern history, which dates back to 1903 by the way, to make his big league debut in the World Series.

Prior to his historic showing, Mondesi had spent the entire year – albeit injury-shortened – 2015 season with the Northwest Arkansas Naturals. Unsurprisingly, he was the only teenage prospect to receive at least 10 plate appearances in the Texas League and one of just two teenagers to match that feat in any Class AA level.

Mondesi batted a disappointing .243/.279/.372 with 11 doubles, five triples, six homeruns, and 19 stolen bases in 81 games. His overall production, per *Weighted Runs Created Plus*, was 23% *below* the Texas League average. For his career, he's sporting a .246/.293/.365 triple-slash line, though that's exclusively come against significantly older competition.

**Projection**: Despite the paltry triple-slash line, Mondesi did offer up flashes of promising offensive production during the year. Mondesi, who missed five or six weeks after injuring his back in his first game, slugged .270/.289/.426 in his first 31 games and posted a .309/.330/.457 line in the month of August. The problem: his production in July, .178/.238/.274, wrecked his yearly stats. The switch-hitting shortstop, who profiles as an above-average defender, has turned in two back-to-back showings of surprising power which could develop into 15-homer territory down the line. Above-average or better speed, his lone downfall – at least what's going to limit his ultimate ceiling – is his in ability to take a free pass.

**Ceiling:** 3.0- to 3.5-win player
**Risk:** Moderate to High
**MLB ETA:** Debuted in 2015

## 4. Ashe Russell, RHP

**MiLB Rank: #104**

**Position Rank: N/A**

| Born: 08/28/96 | Age: 19 | Bats: R | Top CALs: Ryan Warner, Joel Pierce, |
|---|---|---|---|
| Height: 6-4 | Weight: 201 | Throws: R | Kazuya Takano, John Gant, Jose Calero |

| YEAR | Age | Level | IP | W | L | ERA | FIP | K/9 | BB/9 | K% | BB% | HR/9 | LOB% |
|---|---|---|---|---|---|---|---|---|---|---|---|---|---|
| 2015 | 18 | R | 36.3 | 0 | 3 | 4.21 | 6.22 | 5.94 | 3.22 | 16.0% | 8.7% | 1.98 | 80.5% |

**Background:** Dipping back into the prep ranks for another high ceiling youngster, the Royals selected the 6-foot-4, 201-pound right-hander with the 21st overall pick last June. Russell, hailing from Cathedral High School in Indianapolis, IN, tossed 36.1 innings with Burlington during his debut, fanned 24 and walking 13.

**Projection:** Per the usual, the sample size is incredibly limited, but one thing that should be noted was his propensity for giving up the long ball; Russell surrendered eight dingers in 36.1 innings – or just about two per nine innings. And his low K-rate picked up as he got his professional feet underneath him. He fanned 21 over his final 26.1 innings of work.

**Ceiling:** Too Soon to Tell
**Risk:** N/A
**MLB ETA:** N/A

## 5. Pedro Fernandez, RHP

**MiLB Rank: #158**

**Position Rank: N/A**

| Born: 05/25/94 | Age: 22 | Bats: R | Top CALs: Victor Capellan, David Baker, |
|---|---|---|---|
| Height: 6-0 | Weight: 175 | Throws: R | Ivan Pineyro, Myles Jaye, Shane Dawson |

| YEAR | Age | Level | IP | W | L | ERA | FIP | K/9 | BB/9 | K% | BB% | HR/9 | LOB% |
|---|---|---|---|---|---|---|---|---|---|---|---|---|---|
| 2013 | 19 | R | 12.0 | 0 | 0 | 0.75 | 1.34 | 11.25 | 2.25 | 34.9% | 7.0% | 0.00 | 87.5% |
| 2013 | 19 | R | 34.7 | 0 | 1 | 1.82 | 3.63 | 9.87 | 2.08 | 27.3% | 5.8% | 0.78 | 81.8% |
| 2014 | 20 | A | 61.3 | 1 | 8 | 4.99 | 4.71 | 8.80 | 4.84 | 22.6% | 12.5% | 0.88 | 64.9% |
| 2015 | 21 | A | 78.0 | 6 | 2 | 3.12 | 2.65 | 10.27 | 3.12 | 28.8% | 8.7% | 0.23 | 64.4% |
| 2015 | 21 | A+ | 32.7 | 0 | 6 | 8.82 | 3.35 | 6.89 | 2.20 | 15.4% | 4.9% | 0.55 | 49.8% |

**Background:** Kansas City has been, uncharacteristically so, slowly developing the hard-throwing Dominican-born right-hander since signing him in 2011. Fernandez spent his debut season in the Dominican Summer League. He then followed that up by splitting his time between the DSL and Arizona Summer League the next year. Finally taking the training wheels off a bit, Fernandez got pushed up to Lexington in the South Atlantic League two years ago, and he responded by averaging nearly a punch out per inning with some wavering control. The front office had the 6-foot, 175-pound right-hander repeat Low Class A for the first part of 2015; he averaged a remarkable 10.3 strikeouts per nine innings with much improved control. Fernandez got bumped up to Wilmington in early August, making another seven – largely disappointing – starts. Overall, he finished the year with 114 strikeouts and 35 walks in 110.2 innings of work.

**Projection:** One of the more underrated and overlooked arms in the entire system, Fernandez is a ticking time bomb of potential – you just have to ignore some unsightly ERAs to realize that though. Among hurlers with 70 or more innings thrown at any Low Class A level last season, Fernandez's strikeout percentage, 28.8%, ranks first and his strikeout-to-walk percentage, 20.1%, ranks sixth. Granted, he was repeating the level after making 16 appearances there two years ago, but that's an impressive amount of punch outs either way.

Fernandez has always shown the propensity to miss bats – he's fanned nearly a quarter of the hitters he's faced in his career – with incredible control. He's likely headed back to High Class A in 2016, but he should be up to Northwest Arkansas by the middle of the season. In terms of ultimate ceiling, Fernandez has a mid-rotation-caliber ceiling with the floor of a dominant relief arm. Assuming, of course, that he stays healthy.

**Ceiling:** 2.5-win player
**Risk:** Moderate to High
**MLB ETA:** 2017

## 6. Alec Mills, RHP

**MiLB Rank: #210**
**Position Rank: N/A**

| Born: 11/30/91 | Age: 24 | Bats: R | Top CALs: Terance Marin, Austin Voth, |
|---|---|---|---|
| Height: 6-4 | Weight: 185 | Throws: R | Tyson Corley, Ben Pfinsgraff, Nathaniel Kilcrease |

| YEAR | Age | Level | IP | W | L | ERA | FIP | K/9 | BB/9 | K% | BB% | HR/9 | LOB% |
|---|---|---|---|---|---|---|---|---|---|---|---|---|---|
| 2013 | 21 | A | 45.3 | 2 | 3 | 1.59 | 2.42 | 9.33 | 1.79 | 26.9% | 5.1% | 0.20 | 74.5% |
| 2014 | 22 | R | 19.3 | 2 | 2 | 4.66 | 3.51 | 6.52 | 1.86 | 17.3% | 4.9% | 0.00 | 53.9% |
| 2014 | 22 | A | 38.0 | 2 | 1 | 1.18 | 2.72 | 7.82 | 2.37 | 23.6% | 7.1% | 0.00 | 83.3% |
| 2015 | 23 | A+ | 113.3 | 7 | 7 | 3.02 | 2.09 | 8.81 | 1.11 | 23.5% | 3.0% | 0.24 | 72.0% |

**Background:** A recipient of the all-too-common Tommy John surgery, Mills missed most of the 2013 *and* 2014 seasons. The injury, unfortunately for the 6-foot-4 hurler, interrupted his breakout, coming-of-age 2013 campaign; in 45.2 innings he fanned 47, walked only nine, and posted a video game-esque 1.59 ERA. Mills spent the majority of the 2014 season getting back up to speed, but he looked as strong as ever with Wilmington in the Carolina League last season. With the reins eased, Mills throw a career best 113.1 innings while fanning 111 and walking only 14 to go along with another video game-esque 2.09 FIP. For his career, the big right-hander has issued just 54 free passes, fanned 255, and owns a 2.94 ERA.

**Projection**: Just to add some perspective to Mills' resurgence, consider the following:

- The former late round pick out of University of Tennessee at Martin finished the year with a 2.09 FIP. His closest competitor in the Carolina League, the soon to be 27-year-old Seth Webster, tallied a 2.51 mark.
- Among all Carolina League hurlers with 100+ innings, Mills' strikeout-to-walk percentage, 20.6%, also ranked first. His closest competitor, again, was Seth Webster, who finished the year with a 16.9% K/BB percentage.
- Among all High Class A hurlers with 100+ innings, Mills' 2.09 FIP ranked first and his strikeout-to-walk percentage was topped by only one other hurler, Martin Agosta.
- Finally, here's where his FIP and K/BB percentage stacks up against any hurler with at least 100+ innings at *any* level: first and tenth

Needless to say, Mills is ready for the minors' biggest test: Class AA. He has a solid to above-average ability to miss bats, some of the system's finest control, and he generates a tremendous amount of action on the ground as well. Last season he finished with a groundball rate just north of 49%; the year before that it was 56.8%; and before that it was 60.9%. Mills has the potential to be a mid-rotation arm, but he needs to prove that he can handle Class AA first.

**Ceiling:** 2.0-win player
**Risk:** Moderate to High
**MLB ETA:** 2017

## 7. Scott Blewett, RHP

**MiLB Rank: #239**
**Position Rank: N/A**

| Born: 04/10/96 | Age: 20 | Bats: R | Top CALs: Doug Salinas, Brandon Barrow, |
|---|---|---|---|
| Height: 6-6 | Weight: 210 | Throws: R | Justin Edwards, Rigoberto Garcia, Juan Perez |

| YEAR | Age | Level | IP | W | L | ERA | FIP | K/9 | BB/9 | K% | BB% | HR/9 | LOB% |
|---|---|---|---|---|---|---|---|---|---|---|---|---|---|
| 2014 | 18 | R | 28.0 | 1 | 2 | 4.82 | 4.82 | 9.32 | 4.82 | 23.0% | 11.9% | 0.96 | 71.1% |
| 2015 | 19 | A | 81.3 | 3 | 5 | 5.20 | 3.96 | 6.64 | 2.66 | 17.0% | 6.8% | 0.66 | 60.0% |

**Background:** The club's second round pick in 2014, Blewett spent the year as one of just eight 19-year-old hurlers to throw at least 80 innings in the South Atlantic League last season. And among those baby faced hurlers, Blewett's strikeout percentage, 17.0%, ranked fifth. He finished the year with a 3.96 FIP and a 60-to-24 strikeout-to-walk ratio in 81.1 innings of work.

**Projection**: Despite spending parts of two seasons in the minors the data is still rather limited for Blewett; he's thrown just 109.1 innings of work. And while he didn't dominate the Sally, the massive 6-foot-6, 210-pound right-hander didn't look overwhelmed at any point either. He also flashed some glimpses of dominance as well: he fanned eight in four innings against Greenville in his first start and fanned seven in five innings a couple weeks later against Greensboro. It's still too early to accurately gauge his ceiling, but he's certainly promising.

**Ceiling:** Too Soon to Tell
**Risk:** N/A
**MLB ETA:** N/A

## 8. Reymond Fuentes, LF/CF

**MiLB Rank: #249**
**Position Rank: N/A**

| Born: 02/12/91 | Age: 25 | Bats: L | **Top CALs:** Kevin Kiermaier, Anthony Webster, |
|---|---|---|---|
| Height: 6-0 | Weight: 160 | Throws: L | Eury Perez, Lorenzo Cain, Julio Borbon |

| Season | Age | LVL | PA | 2B | 3B | HR | AVG | OBP | SLG | ISO | BB% | K% | wRC+ |
|---|---|---|---|---|---|---|---|---|---|---|---|---|---|
| 2013 | 22 | AA | 403 | 21 | 2 | 6 | 0.316 | 0.396 | 0.441 | 0.125 | 10.2% | 17.6% | 139 |
| 2014 | 23 | AA | 194 | 6 | 2 | 4 | 0.324 | 0.386 | 0.453 | 0.129 | 8.2% | 19.1% | 142 |
| 2014 | 23 | AAA | 178 | 9 | 3 | 1 | 0.261 | 0.337 | 0.376 | 0.115 | 9.6% | 15.2% | 88 |
| 2015 | 24 | AAA | 445 | 10 | 4 | 9 | 0.308 | 0.360 | 0.422 | 0.114 | 6.7% | 16.2% | 110 |

**Background**: Passed around a bit throughout his career, Fuentes, who was sent by Boston as part of the Adrian Gonzalez deal in 2010 and then shipped by the Padres to the Royals for Kyle Bartsch, has seemingly found a home on the Royals' 40-man roster. The former first round pick in 2009 – 28th overall – spent last season with the Storm Chasers, his third stop in Class AAA, hitting a solid .308/.360/.422.

**Projection**: Here's what I wrote in my first book two years ago:

*"He might have a shot to carve out a couple seasons of fringy league average production, maybe better depending upon his defense. Above-average walk rates and speed. Doubles power. [He] struggles against southpaws a bit."*

I further commented in last year's book by writing:

*"The platoon splits are still an issue – he's batted .278/.354/.390 vs. RHs and .264/.338/.326 against LHs in his career. But CAL remains pretty optimistic, linking him to two underrated MLB'ers: Jon Jay and Kevin Kiermaier. Fuentes is more of a quality fourth outfielder now. Very, very savvy move by the defending AL Champs."*

Well, his production against southpaws came roaring back in a big way last season; he batted .342/.373/.400 in 131 plate appearances against them. CAL remains equally optimistic as well, linking him to Kevin Kiermaier (again) and Lorenzo Cain. He could be one of those late-blooming guys that flashes a solid year or two before retreating back into a backup role.

**Ceiling:** 1.5-win player
**Risk:** Low to Moderate
**MLB ETA:** Debuted in 2013

## 9. Foster Griffin, LHP

**MiLB Rank: N/A**
**Position Rank: N/A**

| Born: 07/27/95 | Age: 20 | Bats: R | **Top CALs:** Jose Molina, Jose Torres, |
|---|---|---|---|
| Height: 6-3 | Weight: 200 | Throws: L | Raul Batis, Tyree Hayes, Victor Gonzalez |

| YEAR | Age | Level | IP | W | L | ERA | FIP | K/9 | BB/9 | K% | BB% | HR/9 | LOB% |
|---|---|---|---|---|---|---|---|---|---|---|---|---|---|
| 2014 | 18 | R | 28.0 | 0 | 2 | 3.21 | 4.53 | 6.11 | 3.86 | 16.5% | 10.4% | 0.64 | 75.3% |
| 2015 | 19 | A | 102.7 | 4 | 6 | 5.44 | 4.22 | 6.22 | 3.07 | 15.5% | 7.6% | 0.70 | 58.7% |

**Background**: Griffin teamed with fellow 2014 draft pick Scott Blewett to give Lexington a pair of potentially high-ceiling teenaged arms in their rotation. Griffin, like his draft-mate, took some lumps in his first exposure in the Sally as he posted a 5.44 ERA with a 71-to-35 strikeout-to-walk ratio.

**Projection**: Griffin got past some early season struggles to finish strong. After posting an ERA north of 7.00 through his first 14 starts, the 6-foot-3, 200-pound southpaw out of The First Academy posted a 27-to-11 strikeout-to-walk ratio with a 3.22 ERA over his final eight games (spanning 44.2 innings). Griffin hasn't missed a whole lot of bats at any point in his young career, including his 28.0-inning stint in the Appalachian League two years ago, so that's a bit worrisome. He could be a decent backend starter as it stands now.

**Ceiling:** 1.5- to 2.0-win player
**Risk:** Moderate to High
**MLB ETA:** 2018

## 10. Matthew Strahm, LHP

MiLB Rank: N/A
Position Rank: N/A

| Born: 11/12/91 | | Age: 24 | | Bats: R | | Top CALs: Brennan Garr, Bryce Bandilla, |
| Height: 6-4 | | Weight: 180 | | Throws: L | | Evan Rutckyj, Christopher Perry, Richie Lentz |

| YEAR | Age | Level | IP | W | L | ERA | FIP | K/9 | BB/9 | K% | BB% | HR/9 | LOB% |
|------|-----|-------|-----|---|---|------|------|-------|------|-------|-------|------|-------|
| 2014 | 22 | R | 19.7 | 1 | 0 | 2.29 | 3.62 | 12.36 | 4.58 | 34.2% | 12.7% | 0.46 | 76.5% |
| 2015 | 23 | A | 26.0 | 2 | 1 | 2.08 | 2.68 | 13.15 | 4.15 | 38.0% | 12.0% | 0.35 | 77.2% |
| 2015 | 23 | A+ | 68.0 | 1 | 6 | 2.78 | 3.21 | 10.99 | 2.51 | 30.2% | 6.9% | 0.93 | 75.6% |

**Background:** Hailing from little Neosho County Community College in Chanute, Kansas, Strahm became just the fifteenth player taken since 1974 in the school's history. And only of the previous 14, southpaw Paul Lindblad, made it to the big leagues, though he did manage to spend 14 years there. Anyway, Strahm was a late, late round gem unearthed in the 21st round in 2012. After a solid debut in the Pioneer League that season – he fanned 42 in 30.1 innings with control issues – the 6-foot-4, 180-pound lefty missed all of the 2013 and the majority of 2014 recovering from Tommy John surgery. But Strahm certainly made up for all the lost time last season. As the club began to stretch out the budding hurler in Lexington last season, Strahm fanned a remarkable 38 batters in just 26.0 innings of work. And he continued to dominate with Wilmington upon his promotion to High Class A as well: 68.0 IP, 83 K, 19 BB. Overall, he finished the year with 121 strikeouts, 31 walks, and a combined 2.59 ERA in 94.0 innings of work.

**Projection**: The lanky lefty is a definite candidate for Breakout Prospect of the Year in 2016. Despite missing so much time due to the injury and subsequent rehab work, Strahm looked like a potential mid- to back-of-the-rotation caliber arm. He missed a *ton* of bats, showed much improved control – especially when the club moved him back into the rotation – and he was able to grab the ball every fifth day without any signs of slowing down.

And here's just a glimpse of his 2015 dominance: In his first five appearances with the Blue Rocks, Strahm fanned 36 in just 21.1 innings, or just about 15.2 K/9. At the very least he looks like a taller version of Tim Collins. But Strahm's ultimate ceiling is quite higher.

**Ceiling:** 1.5- to 2.0-win player
**Risk:** Moderate to High
**MLB ETA:** 2017

## 11. Balbino Fuenmayor, 1B/3B

MiLB Rank: N/A
Position Rank: N/A

| Born: 11/26/89 | | Age: 26 | | Bats: R | | Top CALs: Mike Eylward, Gabe Jacobo, |
| Height: 6-3 | | Weight: 230 | | Throws: R | | Jairo Perez, Mike Marjama, John Whitaker |

| Season | Age | LVL | PA | 2B | 3B | HR | AVG | OBP | SLG | ISO | BB% | K% | wRC+ |
|--------|-----|-----|-----|----|----|----|-------|-------|-------|-------|------|-------|------|
| 2013 | 23 | A | 108 | 4 | 1 | 4 | 0.208 | 0.287 | 0.396 | 0.188 | 7.4% | 29.6% | 91 |
| 2015 | 25 | AA | 308 | 22 | 1 | 15 | 0.354 | 0.386 | 0.591 | 0.237 | 3.9% | 14.9% | 169 |
| 2015 | 25 | AAA | 70 | 6 | 1 | 2 | 0.377 | 0.371 | 0.580 | 0.203 | 0.0% | 18.6% | 150 |

**Background:** Like the mythical phoenix rising from the ashes of his burned out professional career, Fuenmayor resurrected his big league hopes as he bounced back from life in the Independent Leagues to become one of the most lethal bats in the minors last season. Before the crescendo of the Great Balbino, let's take a look back at what led to this. Balbino made his professional debut as a 17-year-old in the Gulf Coast League in 2007, though he looked overmatched and unprepared as he batted .174/.244/.242 in the Toronto organization. The Blue Jays brass had him repeat the level the following year – with much better results – before bouncing him up to the Midwest League in 2010. He would then bounce between Vancouver, Lansing, and a variety of Indy Leagues before signing with Kansas City last offseason, a move that was precipitated by his dominant showing with Les Capitales de Quebec when he slugged .347/.383/.610.

Now onto the present – or at least the relatively close past: upon his signing with the Royals, Fuenmayor slugged a robust .354/.386/.591 with 22 doubles, one triple, and 15 homeruns en route to topping the league average production by 69%. Kansas City bounced the husky first baseman up to the PCL in early July and he continued to mash before suffering a knee injury that required surgery and a subsequent four- to six-month recovering time.

**Projection**: One of the most intriguing prospects I couldn't wait to write about in this year's book. Fuenmayor's story itself is fascinating, but he's also revamped his overall offensive toolkit. His power has taken an unexpected step forward into above-average territory; he's making hard contact more often; and he's stopped walking – literally. In 70 plate appearances with the Storm Chasers he didn't walk one, single, solitary time. He also made mincemeat of lefties last season, batting .427/.434/.867 with eight homeruns in 76 plate appearances; so at the very least he could be a potentially dominant platoon stick. In terms of offensive ceiling, Fuenmayor could be an average or better big league stick, something along the lines of a .280/.315/.460-type slugger. Think Mark Trumbo with a better bat.

**Ceiling:** 1.5- to 2.0-win player
**Risk:** Moderate to High
**MLB ETA:** 2016

## 12. Bubba Starling, CF

**MiLB Rank: N/A**
**Position Rank: N/A**

| Born: 08/03/92 | Age: 23 | Bats: R | Top CALs: Michael A Taylor, Tyler Henson, |
|---|---|---|---|
| Height: 6-4 | Weight: 210 | Throws: R | Brian Pointer, Michael Burgess, Brandon Jacobs |

| Season | Age | LVL | PA | 2B | 3B | HR | AVG | OBP | SLG | ISO | BB% | K% | wRC+ |
|---|---|---|---|---|---|---|---|---|---|---|---|---|---|
| 2013 | 20 | A | 498 | 21 | 4 | 13 | 0.241 | 0.329 | 0.398 | 0.156 | 10.6% | 25.7% | 111 |
| 2014 | 21 | A+ | 549 | 23 | 4 | 9 | 0.218 | 0.304 | 0.338 | 0.120 | 8.9% | 27.3% | 84 |
| 2015 | 22 | A+ | 51 | 4 | 0 | 2 | 0.386 | 0.471 | 0.614 | 0.227 | 13.7% | 33.3% | 214 |
| 2015 | 22 | AA | 366 | 19 | 4 | 10 | 0.254 | 0.318 | 0.426 | 0.172 | 8.2% | 24.9% | 105 |

**Background:** Finally tapping into the potential that allowed him to be picked as the fifth overall pick in one of the most top-heavy/loaded drafts in recent memory. On a side note: the 2011 first round included the likes of Gerrit Cole, Trevor Bauer, Dylan Bundy, Anthony Rendon, Archie Bradley, Francisco Lindor, Javier Baez, George Springer, Brandon Nimmo, Jose Fernandez, Sonny Gray, Kolten Wong, Alex Meyer, Blake Swihart, Roberto Stephenson, Joe Panik, Jackie Bradley Jr., and Blake Snell among others. Sorry, I digress. Starling began last season back in the Carolina League, though that lasted just 12 games because he batted .386/.471/.614 with a 214 wRC+ before getting the call up to the minors' toughest test, Class AA. And with the Northwest Arkansas Naturals the toolsy outfielder looked solid, batting a league-average-ish .254/.318/.426 with 19 doubles, four triples, 10 homeruns, and four stolen bases in 91 games. For his career – and one that will inevitably be measured in what ifs – Starling sporting a .245/.329/.403 tripe-slash line in 413 games.

**Projection**: I pretty much wrote off the former NCAA QB recruit in last year's book, writing:

> "A better athlete than ballplayer, CAL links Starling to, no surprise, a bunch of minor league flameouts. And it's easy to spot out why. The righty-swinging center field has struggled against RHs, hitting a pathetic .224/.316/.369 against them (compared to the .281/.360/.450 line against southpaws), and he struggles putting the ball in play. Starling's fanned in 27% of his career plate appearances. Minor league depth. Great story about what was supposed to be."

And while CAL still remains quite pessimistic about his ultimate future by comparing him to Michael A. Taylor, Tyler Henson, Brian Pointer, Michael Burgess, and Brandon Jacobs ; Starling did makes some important developmental strides last season. He proved that his two previous showings against RHP pitchers weren't a harbinger of things to come as he posted the highest OPS vs. RHP since his debut in 2012. Above-average power and speed with the potential to be a 20/20 threat, Starling's ultimate undoing will come down to a subpar hit tool. With that being said, his big league outlook looks much more promising now than it did a year ago. He could be a fringy starter on a non-contending team.

**Ceiling:** 1.5-win player
**Risk:** Moderate
**MLB ETA:** 2016

## 13. Eric Skoglund, LHP

**MiLB Rank: N/A**
**Position Rank: N/A**

| Born: 10/26/92 | Age: 23 | Bats: L | Top CALs: Kyle Hendricks, Justin Freeman, |
|---|---|---|---|
| Height: 6-7 | Weight: 200 | Throws: L | Chadwick Bell, Dillon Gee, Anthony Fernandez |

| YEAR | Age | Level | IP | W | L | ERA | FIP | K/9 | BB/9 | K% | BB% | HR/9 | LOB% |
|---|---|---|---|---|---|---|---|---|---|---|---|---|---|
| 2014 | 21 | R | 23.0 | 0 | 2 | 5.09 | 4.29 | 9.78 | 3.52 | 23.6% | 8.5% | 0.78 | 61.8% |
| 2015 | 22 | A+ | 84.3 | 6 | 3 | 3.52 | 2.53 | 7.04 | 1.17 | 19.4% | 3.2% | 0.21 | 65.1% |

**Background:** After bypassing the opportunity to jump into the big leagues as a member of the Pirates organization as a 16th round pick coming out of high school, Skoglund packed his bags and headed off to college to attend the University of Central Florida. The lanky 6-foot-7, 200-pound lefty would spend the majority of the next three seasons working out of the Knights' rotation, totaling 214.0 collegiate innings with 165 punch outs, 75 walks, and a 3.36 ERA. Kansas City took him in the third round two years ago and sent him to Idaho Falls for a quick crash course in minor league baseball. The front office aggressively pushed him up to Wilmington in 2015, and Skoglund responded by tallying a 2.53 FIP, the third best mark in the Carolina League, before an undisclosed elbow injury forced him to prematurely end his breakout season.

**Projection**: Here's what I wrote about Skoglund prior to the 2014 draft:

> *"Skoglund has the one thing that can't be taught – size. Standing 6-foot-7 and barely an apple slice over 200 pounds, he still has plenty of room to fill out. Decent strikeout numbers, though they'll decline in the middle levels of the minor leagues. He's a nice back-of-the-rotation option down the line, someone in the mold of Brian Tallet early in his career or Brian Flynn, who is currently working his way through the minors."*

Assuming the elbow injury won't slow him down in the future, Skoglund could easily carve out a career as the backend starter I was projecting a couple years ago. His control really took a massive step forward last season, particularly so if you ignore his final two appearances of the year; he posted a 58-to-9 strikeout-to-walk ratio in his first 75.2 innings. Let's hope that (A) he can stay healthy and (B) the uptick in control is a repeatable skill.

**Ceiling:** 1.5-win player
**Risk:** Moderate
**MLB ETA:** 2017

## 14. Glenn Sparkman, RHP

MiLB Rank: N/A
Position Rank: N/A

| Born: 05/11/92 | Age: 24 | Bats: B | Top CALs: Andre Rienzo, Jeffrey Johnson, Daniel Hudson, Charles Brewer, Dan Jennings |
|---|---|---|---|
| Height: 6-2 | Weight: 210 | Throws: R | |

| YEAR | Age | Level | IP | W | L | ERA | FIP | K/9 | BB/9 | K% | BB% | HR/9 | LOB% |
|---|---|---|---|---|---|---|---|---|---|---|---|---|---|
| 2013 | 21 | R | 36.7 | 1 | 0 | 1.72 | 2.78 | 11.54 | 2.45 | 32.6% | 6.9% | 0.25 | 80.9% |
| 2014 | 22 | A+ | 121.0 | 8 | 3 | 1.56 | 2.42 | 8.70 | 1.86 | 24.8% | 5.3% | 0.15 | 78.3% |
| 2015 | 23 | AA | 20.0 | 2 | 2 | 3.60 | 3.35 | 9.45 | 4.05 | 24.7% | 10.6% | 0.45 | 70.3% |

**Background:** The fast-rising former 20th round pick continued to generate some buzz through his first four starts of 2015 – he posted a 21-to-9 strikeout-to-walk ratio in 20.0 innings – but a wonky elbow, and subsequent Tommy John surgery, knocked him out in late April. Sparkman has quickly risen through the ranks, going from a late round pick to Class AA starter in fewer than 160 innings.

**Projection:** A member of the Bird Doggin' It section in last year's book, Sparkman could have been knocking on the club's big league door by the end of last season if not for the injury. He's shown a tremendous feel for missing bats and limiting free passes during his brief career, fanning 26.4% and walking 6.3% of the total hitters he's faced. If the injury and related rehab don't prove to be too big to overcome, Sparkman has a very real shot of developing into a backend big league starting pitcher – something that wasn't planned just three years ago.

**Ceiling:** 1.5-win player
**Risk:** Moderate to High
**MLB ETA:** 2017

## 15. Nolan Watson, RHP

MiLB Rank: N/A
Position Rank: N/A

| Born: 01/25/97 | Age: 19 | Bats: R | Top CALs: RJ Peace, Ugueth Urbina, Nick Wells, Colin Rodgers, Jose Oliveros |
|---|---|---|---|
| Height: 6-2 | Weight: 195 | Throws: R | |

| YEAR | Age | Level | IP | W | L | ERA | FIP | K/9 | BB/9 | K% | BB% | HR/9 | LOB% |
|---|---|---|---|---|---|---|---|---|---|---|---|---|---|
| 2015 | 18 | R | 29.3 | 0 | 3 | 4.91 | 4.75 | 4.91 | 3.38 | 11.7% | 8.0% | 0.61 | 57.8% |

**Background:** Never afraid to double-up on risky draft selections, Kansas City dipped back into the prep ranks and grabbed a second consecutive high school arm in the opening round last June, taking Nolan Watson with the 33rd overall selection, just 12 picks after taking Ashe Russell. Watson posted a 16-to-11 strikeout-to-walk ratio in 29.1 innings with Burlington during his debut.

**Projection:** Again, per the typical for incoming prep players, the data's incredibly limited at this point – just a smidge over 29.0 innings. And it was a bit underwhelming to be honest. Watson posted a near one-to-one strikeout-to-walk ratio and got hit pretty hard overall.

**Ceiling:** Too Soon to Tell
**Risk:** N/A
**MLB ETA:** N/A

## 16. Elier Hernandez, CF/RF

**MiLB Rank:** N/A
**Position Rank:** N/A

| Born: 11/21/94 | Age: 21 | Bats: R | Top CALs: Reid Engel, Yorman Rodriguez, |
|---|---|---|---|
| Height: 6-3 | Weight: 197 | Throws: R | Yefri Carvajal, Eduardo Sosa, Isaac Galloway |

| Season | Age | LVL | PA | 2B | 3B | HR | AVG | OBP | SLG | ISO | BB% | K% | wRC+ |
|---|---|---|---|---|---|---|---|---|---|---|---|---|---|
| 2013 | 18 | R | 319 | 15 | 8 | 3 | 0.301 | 0.350 | 0.439 | 0.138 | 5.6% | 19.4% | 103 |
| 2014 | 19 | A | 446 | 19 | 4 | 9 | 0.264 | 0.296 | 0.393 | 0.129 | 3.6% | 22.2% | 90 |
| 2015 | 20 | A | 314 | 19 | 2 | 5 | 0.290 | 0.331 | 0.421 | 0.131 | 4.5% | 23.2% | 113 |
| 2015 | 20 | A+ | 196 | 7 | 2 | 1 | 0.232 | 0.281 | 0.311 | 0.079 | 5.1% | 24.0% | 72 |

**Background:** Signed to the third largest international bonus given out a couple years ago, Hernandez has hardly looked the part of a $3 million Bonus Baby through his first four professional seasons. Kansas City aggressively – and wrongly – promoted the then-17-year-old up to the Pioneer League for his debut, and he responded by stringing together a rancid .208/.256/.280 triple-slash line. Hernandez did fare much better in a redo of the rookie league the next season, hitting .301/.350/.439 with 15 doubles, eight triples, and three homeruns, but he stumbled in his move to the Sally in 2014. Hernandez batted .264/.296/.393 with a 90 wRC+ mark as one of the league's youngest bats. Last season he spent the first part of the year back in the Sally where he hit .290/.331/.421 but stumbled once again on his promotion to High Class A (.232/.281/.311).

**Projection:** Despite tallying more than 1,500 professional plate appearances across parts of four seasons, Hernandez is still only entering his age-21 season. And in a lot of ways he's similar to that of Alfredo Escalera-Maldonado – both loathe the free pass, show solid-average power, some speed, and some borderline questionable punch out rates. Hernandez is never likely going to live up to his lofty signing bonus expectations, but he might be able to squeak out a couple decent big league seasons.

**Ceiling:** 1.5- to 2.0-win player
**Risk:** Moderate to High
**MLB ETA:** 2018

## 17. Alfredo Escalera-Maldonado, OF

**MiLB Rank:** N/A
**Position Rank:** N/A

| Born: 02/17/95 | Age: 21 | Bats: R | Top CALs: Elier Hernandez, Isaac Galloway, |
|---|---|---|---|
| Height: 6-1 | Weight: 186 | Throws: R | Yorman Rodriguez, Eduardo Sosa, Daniel Carroll |

| Season | Age | LVL | PA | 2B | 3B | HR | AVG | OBP | SLG | ISO | BB% | K% | wRC+ |
|---|---|---|---|---|---|---|---|---|---|---|---|---|---|
| 2013 | 18 | R | 204 | 14 | 1 | 1 | 0.277 | 0.333 | 0.380 | 0.103 | 6.9% | 20.6% | 108 |
| 2014 | 19 | A | 475 | 17 | 4 | 9 | 0.221 | 0.267 | 0.340 | 0.119 | 3.8% | 23.4% | 69 |
| 2015 | 20 | A | 285 | 13 | 3 | 8 | 0.313 | 0.356 | 0.477 | 0.164 | 3.5% | 20.4% | 135 |
| 2015 | 20 | A+ | 222 | 7 | 2 | 2 | 0.206 | 0.285 | 0.291 | 0.085 | 7.7% | 27.5% | 71 |

**Background:** In the running – and the likely winner – for longest name in professional baseball, the hyphenated outfielder was originally taken in the eighth round out of The Pendleton School, home to JR Murphy and Tyler Pastornicky, in 2012. Escalera-Maldonado had a solid showing in the Arizona Summer League during his debut that year, hitting .303/.344/.361, though he lacked pop and plate discipline. The front office bumped the then-18-year-old Puerto Rican-born outfielder up to the Appalachian League the following season, and he handled himself well enough (.277/.333/.380). But things hit the skids for Escalera-Maldonado when the club promoted him to Low Class A; he batted a lowly .221/.267/.340 with a laughably poor 111-to-18 strikeout-to-walk ratio. Kansas City kept Escalera-Maldonado in the Sally for the first part of last season and after his best showing in professional ball to date – he slugged .313/.356/.477 – he got the call up to High Class A (where he would look overmatched). Overall, he finished the year with a .267/.325/.397 triple-slash line with 20 doubles, five triples, 10 homeruns, and 19 stolen bases.

**Projection:** Regardless of everything else Escalera-Maldonado has to offer, the focal point is always going to be his inability to work the count. Through his first 303 professional games, spanning 1,314 plate appearances, the 6-foot-1, 186-pound outfielder has walked just 64 times – or just about 4.9% of the time. Escalera-Maldonado has – at various times – showed some semblance of plate discipline, but those have been few and far between.

Outside of a swing-at-everything mantra, he does offer up solid-average power and speed, potentially peaking as a 20/20 threat down the line. And the high punch out rate he exhibited with Wilmington should regress back down in his repeat of the level in 2016. He looks like, at best, a starter on a non-contending team – sort of the anti-Saber guy. And CAL isn't offering up a whole lot of long term big league potential either, comparing him to Elier Hernandez, Isaac Galloway, Yorman Rodriguez, Eduardo Sosa, and Daniel Carroll.

**Ceiling:** 1.5-win player
**Risk:** Moderate to High
**MLB ETA:** 2018

## 18. Jorge Bonifacio, LF/RF

**MiLB Rank: N/A**
**Position Rank: N/A**

| Born: 06/04/93 | Age: 23 | Bats: R | **Top CALs:** Shane Peterson, Andrew Lambo, |
|---|---|---|---|
| Height: 6-1 | Weight: 195 | Throws: R | Jake Cave, John Drennen, Juan Portes |

| Season | Age | LVL | PA | 2B | 3B | HR | AVG | OBP | SLG | ISO | BB% | K% | wRC+ |
|---|---|---|---|---|---|---|---|---|---|---|---|---|---|
| 2013 | 20 | A+ | 234 | 11 | 3 | 2 | 0.296 | 0.368 | 0.408 | 0.112 | 9.8% | 17.1% | 118 |
| 2013 | 20 | AA | 105 | 7 | 0 | 2 | 0.301 | 0.371 | 0.441 | 0.140 | 10.5% | 21.9% | 129 |
| 2014 | 21 | AA | 566 | 20 | 4 | 4 | 0.230 | 0.302 | 0.309 | 0.079 | 8.8% | 22.4% | 77 |

**Background:** It's been nearly three years since Bonifacio has had a productive, above-average minor league season. That time frame, by the way, also coincides with the Dominican-born corner outfielder missing some significant time due to a broken hamate bone, an injury, as I've previously warned, that typically takes much longer for a full recovery. But Bonifacio, who once hit .282/.336/.432 with a 116 wRC+ as a 19-year-old in Low Class A, has really struggled to right the proverbial ship since. After batting a solid .301/.371/.441 in his initial 25-game debut in Class AA – and return from the injury – Bonifacio followed that up with a paltry .230/.302/.309 showing with Northwest Arkansas two years ago and a .240/.305/.416 production line during his third trip with the club last season as well. Perhaps the most troubling aspect of his stagnated development: much of Bonifacio's production was generated during his 22-game run in the month of July when he batted .289/.348/.566; otherwise, he dialed to post an OPS above .740 in any other month.

**Projection**: CAL's pretty much already sentenced the soon-to-be 23-year-old to a life a fourth/fifth outfielder-dom. Last year the system compared him to John Drennen, Leyson Septimo, Jake Cave, Henry Ramos, and Mitch Dening. And after another disappointing season CAL remains equally unimpressed: Shane Peterson, Andrew Lambo, Jake Cave, John Drennen, and Juan Portes.

When he's at his best, Bonifacio shows off solid-average or better power with the ability to smack to 15- to 20-homeruns in a big league season. His plate discipline remains passable, though far from impressive, and he has a little bit of speed. The problem, however, has been the fact that his hit tool hasn't progressed any over his past couple of seasons.

**Ceiling:** 1.0- to 1.5-win player
**Risk:** Moderate
**MLB ETA:** 2017

## 19. Cheslor Cuthbert, 1B/3B

**MiLB Rank: N/A**
**Position Rank: N/A**

| Born: 11/16/92 | Age: 23 | Bats: R | **Top CALs:** Jefry Marte, Lonnie Chisenhall, |
|---|---|---|---|
| Height: 6-1 | Weight: 190 | Throws: R | Matt Dominguez, Andrew Lambo, Juan Portes |

| Season | Age | LVL | PA | 2B | 3B | HR | AVG | OBP | SLG | ISO | BB% | K% | wRC+ |
|---|---|---|---|---|---|---|---|---|---|---|---|---|---|
| 2013 | 20 | A+ | 254 | 21 | 2 | 2 | 0.280 | 0.354 | 0.418 | 0.138 | 10.6% | 14.6% | 116 |
| 2013 | 20 | AA | 264 | 16 | 0 | 6 | 0.215 | 0.279 | 0.359 | 0.143 | 7.6% | 19.3% | 77 |
| 2014 | 21 | AA | 395 | 19 | 1 | 10 | 0.276 | 0.342 | 0.420 | 0.144 | 9.1% | 17.0% | 118 |
| 2014 | 21 | AAA | 100 | 5 | 0 | 2 | 0.264 | 0.330 | 0.385 | 0.121 | 9.0% | 12.0% | 87 |
| 2015 | 22 | AAA | 438 | 22 | 1 | 11 | 0.277 | 0.339 | 0.421 | 0.144 | 8.4% | 13.7% | 103 |
| 2015 | 22 | MLB | 50 | 2 | 1 | 1 | 0.217 | 0.280 | 0.370 | 0.152 | 8.0% | 18.0% | 76 |

**Background:** A perennial member of the franchise's better prospect lists – despite never truly standing out – Cuthbert finally made his way up to the big leagues after six long, arduous minor league seasons. In between his couple cups of coffee in Kansas City, Cuthbert spent the majority of the year with the Omaha Storm Chasers, his second stint in the Pacific Coast League. Cuthbert had a very Cuthbert-like showing in 2015, hitting a league average-ish .277/.339/.421 with some pop – he slugged 22 doubles, one triple, and 11 homeruns – and decent peripherals at the plate. He looked lost and overmatched in his 50 plate appearances in The Show, hitting a paltry .217/.280/.370. For his minor league career, Cuthbert is sporting .259/.324/.388 triple-slash line.

**Projection**: Despite toiling away in the minors for six complete seasons now, Cuthbert is still quite young; he's entering his age-23 season. But he's not really a top prospect now either. He's never posted a *Weighted Runs Created Plus* total north of 118. His power is below-average, particularly for a corner infield position. He doesn't walk all that often, but makes a lot of contact. So, yeah... Every organization has guys like this, the ones that can be plugged into a role in a pinch but ultimately get exposed in longer stints.

**Ceiling:** 1.0-win player
**Risk:** Low to Moderate
**MLB ETA:** Debuted in 2015

## 20. Josh Staumont, RHP

**MiLB Rank:** N/A

**Position Rank:** N/A

| Born: 12/21/93 | Age: 22 | Bats: R | Top CALs: Scott Griggs, Zachary Jones, |
|---|---|---|---|
| Height: 6-2 | Weight: 190 | Throws: R | Santos Rodriguez, Reid Scoggins, Jarrett Miller |

| YEAR | Age | Level | IP | W | L | ERA | FIP | K/9 | BB/9 | K% | BB% | HR/9 | LOB% |
|---|---|---|---|---|---|---|---|---|---|---|---|---|---|
| 2015 | 21 | R | 31.3 | 3 | 1 | 3.16 | 3.38 | 14.65 | 6.89 | 38.1% | 17.9% | 0.00 | 75.0% |
| 2015 | 21 | R | 8.7 | 0 | 0 | 0.00 | 5.32 | 7.27 | 8.31 | 18.4% | 21.1% | 0.00 | 100.0% |

**Background:** Equipped with arguably the top fastball in the entire 2015 draft class, Staumont fell to the second round as – legitimate – concerns about his control surrounded him. Staumont, who bounced between Biola University and Azusa Pacific during his collegiate run, walked 32 in 40.0 innings of work during his debut between the Arizona Summer and Pioneer Leagues.

**Projection**: It doesn't really matter if you can throw it through a brick wall if you can't hit it. Staumont has a premium fastball and matching swing-and-miss ability, but his control is really going to inhibit his potential of making it to the big leagues. For instance, Staumont fanned a remarkable 109 batters in just 68.2 innings with Azusa Pacific last season, but he also walked 54. He has the potential to be a top relief arm – if he can figure out the strike zone.

**Ceiling:** 1.5- to 2.0-win player
**Risk:** High to Extremely High
**MLB ETA:** 2019

## 21. Christian Binford, RHP

**MiLB Rank:** N/A

**Position Rank:** N/A

| Born: 12/20/92 | Age: 23 | Bats: R | Top CALs: Ross Seaton, Tim Alderson, |
|---|---|---|---|
| Height: 6-6 | Weight: 220 | Throws: R | Tyler Herron, Gabriel Ynoa, Matthew Heidenreich |

| YEAR | Age | Level | IP | W | L | ERA | FIP | K/9 | BB/9 | K% | BB% | HR/9 | LOB% |
|---|---|---|---|---|---|---|---|---|---|---|---|---|---|
| 2015 | 22 | AA | 91.3 | 4 | 7 | 5.03 | 3.66 | 5.91 | 2.27 | 14.9% | 5.7% | 0.59 | 63.2% |
| 2015 | 22 | AAA | 27.7 | 1 | 4 | 5.86 | 6.45 | 2.93 | 4.88 | 7.1% | 11.9% | 1.30 | 66.8% |

**Background:** A 30th round pick in 2011, Binford, the 906th overall pick, has exceeded expectations all along the way – even if you do consider his sizeable six-figure bonus. Binford split his 2015 campaign between Northwest Arkansas and Omaha, though he took the unfavorable path of moving from the PCL down to Class AA. The 6-foot-6, 220-pounder got smacked around in each of his six starts with the Storm Chasers; he coughed up 18 earned runs in 27.3 innings while walking more than he fanned (15 and nine). Following his demotion Binford seemed to recapture his previous gumption – he tossed seven innings with five punch outs and zero walks against the Arkansas Travelers – but that proved to be short lived; he got lit up in his next four starts. Overall, Binford finished the year with an aggregate 5.22 ERA while averaging 5.2 punch outs and 2.9 free passes per nine innings.

**Projection**: Binford's successful eight-game stint with Northwest Arkansas two years ago proved to be a mirage of sorts as the club's tried to aggressively push him back up to the PCL as a starter in 2015. He showcases some of the best control/command in the entire system, but his lack of strikeouts last season is highly alarming. He's still only entering his age-23 season, so there's some hope that he'll bounce back, though I wouldn't necessarily count on it.

**Ceiling:** 1.0-win player
**Risk:** Moderate
**MLB ETA:** 2016

## 22. Hunter Dozier, 3B

**MiLB Rank:** N/A

**Position Rank:** N/A

| Born: 08/22/91 | Age: 24 | Bats: R | Top CALs: Niko Vasquez, Deibinson Romero, |
|---|---|---|---|
| Height: 6-4 | Weight: 220 | Throws: R | Edward Salcedo, Patrick Wisdom, B.A. Vollmuth |

| Season | Age | LVL | PA | 2B | 3B | HR | AVG | OBP | SLG | ISO | BB% | K% | wRC+ |
|---|---|---|---|---|---|---|---|---|---|---|---|---|---|
| 2013 | 21 | R | 258 | 24 | 0 | 7 | 0.303 | 0.403 | 0.509 | 0.206 | 13.6% | 12.4% | 135 |
| 2014 | 22 | A+ | 267 | 18 | 0 | 4 | 0.295 | 0.397 | 0.429 | 0.134 | 13.1% | 21.0% | 136 |
| 2014 | 22 | AA | 267 | 12 | 0 | 4 | 0.209 | 0.303 | 0.312 | 0.103 | 11.6% | 26.2% | 81 |
| 2015 | 23 | AA | 523 | 27 | 1 | 12 | 0.213 | 0.281 | 0.349 | 0.137 | 8.6% | 28.9% | 75 |

**Background:** Dozier was never going to live up to the lofty expectations that come with being the eighth overall pick in the draft, but the Royals grabbed the former Stephen F. Austin State University stud with full knowledge that he'd be a well below-slot signing, allowing the money saved to eventually ink the recently traded Sean Manaea to a big deal. But Dozier's offensive stagnation in Class AA over the past two seasons was quite unsuspected. After handling himself well enough in High Class A two years ago, the front office bumped the third baseman up to the Texas League for the second half of the season. And Dozier stumbled. Badly. He "hit" .209/.303/.312 in 267 plate appearances with the Naturals. He also followed that up with another putrid – albeit full-season – showing with Northwest Arkansas; he batted .312/.281/.349 with 27 doubles, one triple, and 12 homeruns in 523 trips to the plate.

**Projection**: At this point in time – which includes a .212/.289/.337 triple-slash line in 790 total plate appearances in the Texas League – Dozier's prospect status can all but be left for dead. Average eye at the plate with matching power, the 6-foot-4, 220-pound third baseman's shitty hit tool will all but doom him as a minor league vagabond.

**Ceiling:** 1.0-win player
**Risk:** Moderate to High
**MLB ETA:** 2017

## 23. Jake Junis, RHP

**MiLB Rank: N/A**
**Position Rank: N/A**

| Born: 09/16/92 | Age: 23 | Bats: R | Top CALs: Ryan Crowley, Ryan Kelly, |
|---|---|---|---|
| Height: 6-2 | Weight: 225 | Throws: R | Ian Dickson, Chase DeJong, Jose Ramirez |

| YEAR | Age | Level | IP | W | L | ERA | FIP | K/9 | BB/9 | K% | BB% | HR/9 | LOB% |
|---|---|---|---|---|---|---|---|---|---|---|---|---|---|
| 2013 | 20 | R | 59.7 | 2 | 6 | 7.39 | 6.18 | 8.30 | 2.56 | 19.3% | 6.0% | 1.96 | 54.1% |
| 2014 | 21 | A | 136.0 | 9 | 8 | 4.30 | 4.57 | 7.21 | 2.51 | 19.0% | 6.6% | 1.06 | 68.1% |
| 2015 | 22 | A+ | 155.7 | 5 | 11 | 3.64 | 3.27 | 7.11 | 1.68 | 19.7% | 4.6% | 0.64 | 66.2% |
| 2015 | 22 | AA | 4.0 | 0 | 1 | 9.00 | 3.30 | 6.75 | 2.25 | 14.3% | 4.8% | 0.00 | 44.4% |

**Background:** A 29th round pick out of Rock Falls High School in 2011, Junis teamed Alec Mills, Eric Skoglund, Matthew Strahm, Cody Reed, before his trade, and Pedro Fernandez to form one of the better – and consistently deep – rotation in the minors. For his part, Junis, a 6-foot-2, 225-pound right-hander, made 26 starts with the Blue Rocks, throwing a career best 155.2 innings with 123 strikeouts and 29 walks en route to posting a 3.64 ERA and an even better 3.27 FIP. Junis also made a brief, and unsuccessful, start with the Northwest Arkansas Naturals. He lasted four innings but managed to surrender four earned runs on seven hits. For his career, Junis has fanned 312 and walked 90 in 390.0 innings of work.

**Projection**: Not particularly fascinating as a potential starting pitcher, Junis may have some upside as a middle relief/swing man down the line. He hasn't missed a lot of bats at any point during his four year career, but compensates with above-average or better control. He's also been homer-prone at various points in his career as well.

**Ceiling:** 0.5 to 1. 0-win player
**Risk:** Moderate
**MLB ETA:** 2017

## 24. Chase Vallot, C

**MiLB Rank: N/A**
**Position Rank: N/A**

| Born: 08/21/96 | Age: 19 | Bats: R | Top CALs: Tyler Weeden, Daniel Rams, |
|---|---|---|---|
| Height: 6-0 | Weight: 215 | Throws: R | Brett Whiteside, Lucas Bailey, Gary Sanchez |

| Season | Age | LVL | PA | 2B | 3B | HR | AVG | OBP | SLG | ISO | BB% | K% | wRC+ |
|---|---|---|---|---|---|---|---|---|---|---|---|---|---|
| 2014 | 17 | R | 222 | 14 | 0 | 7 | 0.215 | 0.329 | 0.403 | 0.188 | 11.7% | 36.5% | 112 |
| 2015 | 18 | A | 333 | 13 | 3 | 13 | 0.219 | 0.331 | 0.427 | 0.208 | 12.3% | 31.5% | 116 |

**Background:** The good: Vallot, the second prep catcher taken two years ago, finished his first stint – albeit a shortened one – with 13 long balls, tied for 12th among all Sally League hitters and tied fourth for the backstops in the leagues. The bad: Vallot batted a putrid .219 last season, which, of course, comes on the heels of his .215 showing during his pro debut. The ugly: he fanned 105 of his 333 plate appearances with Lexington, or 31.5% of the time, the fourth highest mark in the Sally. For his young career, the 6-foot, 215-pound backstop out of St. Thomas Moore High School is sporting a .217/.330/.417 triple-slash line with 27 doubles, three triples, and 20 homeruns in 133 games. He's also managed to throw out only 19% of the would-be base stealers in his career as well.

**Projection**: There are a couple certainties in play here: Vallot has as much power as any bat in the Royals' system, flashing above-average pop with potential to slug 25 long balls in a season; the actual hit tool is a poor as one could imagine; he's going to swing-and-miss *a lot* during his minor league tenure. And while Vallot is still just 133 games into his professional career, there's not a whole lot of hope at this juncture that he develops into anything of tangible big league value. The bat and propensity to whiff are just too great to overcome. Not to add fuel to the fire, but a position switch is probably in the near future as well.

**Ceiling:** 1.0 -win player
**Risk:** High
**MLB ETA:** 2019

## 25. Ryan O'Hearn, 1B/RF

**MiLB Rank:** N/A
**Position Rank:** N/A

| | | |
|---|---|---|
| **Born:** 07/26/93 | **Age:** 22 | **Bats:** L |
| **Height:** 56-3 | **Weight:** 200 | **Throws:** L |

**Top CALs:** Xavier Scruggs, Matt Clark, Nelson Rodriguez, Chris Dennis, Gerardo Rodriguez

| Season | Age | LVL | PA | 2B | 3B | HR | AVG | OBP | SLG | ISO | BB% | K% | wRC+ |
|---|---|---|---|---|---|---|---|---|---|---|---|---|---|
| 2014 | 20 | R | 293 | 16 | 1 | 13 | 0.361 | 0.444 | 0.590 | 0.229 | 13.3% | 20.1% | 162 |
| 2015 | 21 | A | 356 | 11 | 0 | 19 | 0.277 | 0.351 | 0.494 | 0.217 | 10.1% | 24.4% | 136 |
| 2015 | 21 | A+ | 181 | 10 | 0 | 8 | 0.236 | 0.315 | 0.447 | 0.211 | 10.5% | 29.8% | 120 |

**Background:** An eighth round pick out of Sam Houston State University two years ago, O'Hearn carried over his debut momentum – he batted .361/.444/.590 in the Pioneer League – into the 2015 season. Spending time between Lexington and Wilmington last year, O'Hearn hit a combined .263/.339/.478 with 21 doubles, 27 homeruns, and seven stolen bases.

**Projection**: The typical collegiate bat that tends to dominate in the low levels of the minor leagues. O'Hearn's production dropped from .277/.351/.494 in Low Class A to a more reasonable – and expected – 236/.315/.447. His strikeout rate spiked and his BABIP took a 21-point nosedive when he made the jump as well. The power is an above-average skill, clearly. And the eye at the plate looks like a nice skill in his tool belt as well. Final note: CAL, unsurprisingly, compares O'Hearn to a bunch of Quad-A bats: Xavier Scruggs, Matt Clark, Nelson Rodriguez, Chris Dennis, and Gerardo Rodriguez.

**Ceiling:** 0.5- to 1.0-win player
**Risk:** Moderate
**MLB ETA:** 2018

### Barely Missed:

- **Wander Franco, 3B** – The then-20-year-old hot corner hit a league average .268/.310/.403 with Lexington last season, adding 30 doubles, a pair of triples, and 10 homeruns. Franco has always a brief history of solid performances, posting wRC+ marks of 151, 104, 124 in the Dominican Summer, Arizona Summer, and Pioneer Leagues prior to 2015.

- **Marten Gasparini, SS** – Italian-born switch-hitting speedster batted .259/.341/.411 with four doubles, a mind-boggling 10 triples, a pair of homeruns, and 26 stolen bases in 54 games in the Pioneer League last season. He's a near lock to be listed among the club's Top 25 next season.

- **Luis Rico, LHP** – 6-foot-1, 175-pound lefty out of Venezuela missed some bats – he averaged 8.7 punch outs per nine innings – but struggled with control during his stint with Wilmington last season.

## *Bird Doggin' It – Additional Prospects to Keep an Eye in 2016*

| Player | Age | POS | Notes |
|---|---|---|---|
| Jacob Bodner | 23 | RHP | A smallish right-hander plucked in the 27th round out of Xavier last June, Bodner, who battled control issues during his collegiate career, started pounding the zone unlike anything he had ever shown before: he posted a 26-to-3 strikeout-to-walk ratio in 23.1 innings with Burlington. Then he promptly walked five in 2.2 innings with Idaho Falls. |
| Brandon Downes | 23 | RF | Former University of Virginia slugger showed off his trademark power with Lexington last season, mashing 29 doubles, three triples, and 14 homeruns, but struggled to find first base. |
| Samir Duenez | 20 | 1B | The then-19-year-old first baseman hit .266/.314/.332 in the Sally last season. He's yet to show any type of reasonable power though. |
| Jonathan Dziedzic | 25 | RHP | The former 13th round pick in 2013 made it all the way up to Class AAA last season, even if it was for one unsuccessful start. He finished the year with a 97-to-37 strikeout-to-walk ratio in 141.2 innings. |
| Zane Evans | 24 | C | Georgia Tech's old backstop struggled a bit adjusting to the minors' toughest challenge, hitting .252/.278/.387 in a shortened campaign in the Texas League. |
| Xavier Fernandez | 20 | C | It's taken a while – three years to be exact – but Fernandez looks like he's ready for full season ball. He batted .329/.396/.500 in the Appalachian League last season, his second stint with Burlington. |
| Amalani Fukofuka | 20 | CF | After disappointing for the better part of two years, the former fifth rounder had a coming out party in the Pioneer League in 2015, hitting .339/.401/.500. |
| Ashton Goudeau | 23 | RHP | Massive 6-foot-6, 205-pound right-hander out of Maple Woods Community College posted a 61-to-10 strikeout-to-walk ratio in 69.0 innings with Wilmington last season. |
| Chad Johnson | 22 | C | Lefty-swinging backstop had his finest showing to date in 77 games with Lexington last season, hitting .284/.401/.402. I'm not ready to anoint him a serious prospect until he can replicate that mark moving forward – especially when he's sporting a .398 BABIP. |
| Rudy Martin | 20 | OF | Pint-sized outfielder taken in the 25th round two years ago finally made his debut in 2015, hitting .338/.477/.541 in the Arizona Summer League. |
| Anderson Miller | 22 | CF | Third round pick last June out of Western Kentucky, Miller torched the Appalachian League for 10 games before settling in with Lexington in the Sally (.260/.319/.355). |
| Jake Newberry | 21 | RHP | Posted a 55-to-18 strikeout-to-walk ratio in 60.2 relief innings with Lexington last season. He might be a candidate to get stretched out in the rotation. |
| Sam Selman | 25 | LHP | Big, lanky lefty out of Vanderbilt maintained status quo: he missed a lot of bats and walked a ton of guys in Class AA last season. |
| Daniel Stumpf | 25 | LHP | Older lefty reliever with some big league upside, Stumpf has transitioned nicely into a multi-inning arm. He could see some action in KC in 2016. |
| Ramon Torres | 23 | IF | Hit a combined .264/.308/.354 between Wilmington and Northwest Arkansas last season. |

**State of the Farm System:** Well, this one can be summed up in one word: *terrible*. Years of missing out on first and second round picks due to big league signings followed by poor overall drafts and dealing away whatever tangible minor leaguers they've had on hand left the stockroom empty.

Former Illinois State right-hander Jeremy Rhoades put together an impressive run as the club – correctly – moved him into the rotation fulltime for the first time since his high school days. The 6-foot-4, 225-pound hurler finished the year with 135 strikeouts and just 37 walks in 137.2 innings across the Midwest and California Leagues. His overall ERA, 4.77, was a bit bloated as his homerun rate spiked to 2.5 dingers per nine innings during his time with Inland Empire. Expect that number to come crashing back down in 2016.

Lefty Nate Smith, a 2013 eighth round pick out of Furman University, followed up a strong 2014 campaign by splitting time with Arkansas and Salt Lake last season. He might be able to carve out a role as a backend starter, particularly when injuries strike the big league club.

Last year's first round pick, Fresno State catcher Taylor Ward, was widely panned as a big reach with the 26th overall pick, but he rewarded the club's faith by slugging .348/.457/.438 between the Pioneer and Midwest League during his debut.

And then it gets thin. Fast.

Infielder/outfielder Kyle Kubitza could help the club in 2016 as a solid bench option. And former top prospect-turned-complete-bust Kaleb Cowart seemed to figure things out last season. But after barely hitting his weight for so long, let's see how he responds to 2016 before we re-anoint him.

I've always liked big southpaw Tyler DeLoach, who might be able to carve out a relief role in the next season or two.

Overall, it's the worst system in baseball. Bar none. And the organization is now caught in the dangerous game of spending big money to get the club an extra win or two in a season.

| Rank | Name | POS |
|------|------|-----|
| 1 | Jeremy Rhoades | RHP |
| 2 | Nate Smith | LHP |
| 3 | Taylor Ward | C |
| 4 | Kyle Kubitza | IF/OF |
| 5 | Victor Alcantara | RHP |
| 6 | Alex Yarbrough | 2B |
| 7 | Kaleb Cowart | 3B |
| 8 | Joe Gatto | RHP |
| 9 | Tyler Deloach | LHP |
| 10 | Eduardo Paredes | RHP |
| 11 | Natanael Delgado | LF/RF |
| 12 | Jahmai Jones | CF |
| 13 | Kyle McGowin | RHP |
| 14 | Jett Bandy | C |
| 15 | Grayson Long | RHP |
| 16 | Roberto Baldoquin | 2B/SS |
| 17 | Greg Mahle | LHP |
| 18 | Caleb Adams | OF |
| 19 | Hunter Green | LHP |
| 20 | Jake Jewell | RHP |
| 21 | Kody Eaves | 2B |
| 22 | Austin Robichaux | RHP |
| 23 | Julio Garcia | SS |
| 24 | Jonah Wesely | LHP |
| 25 | Keynan Middleton | RHP |

**Review of the 2015 Draft:** Again, Ward's selection near the end of the first round was widely panned – particularly for a player that batted a solid, though far from dominant .304/.413/.486 during his final collegiate year. And as I wrote in the following pages he sort of a fringy everyday guy.

The club's second round pick, outfielder Jahmai Jones, batted a lowly .244/.330/.344 in the Arizona Summer League. And their third round pick, big right-hander Grayson Long out of Texas A&M, missed some bats in the advanced rookie leagues.

Overall, it's a very, very underwhelming draft class.

## 1. Jeremy Rhoades, RHP

**MiLB Rank: #170**
**Position Rank: N/A**

| Born: 02/12/93 | Age: 23 | Bats: R | Top CALs: Jasner Severino, Brandon Barker, |
| Height: 6-4 | Weight: 225 | Throws: R | Kevin Comer, Dan Griffin, Billy Muldowney |

| YEAR | Age | Level | IP | W | L | ERA | FIP | K/9 | BB/9 | K% | BB% | HR/9 | LOB% |
|------|-----|-------|-----|---|---|------|------|-------|------|-------|------|------|-------|
| 2014 | 21 | R | 38.7 | 2 | 1 | 4.42 | 4.29 | 9.31 | 3.49 | 23.1% | 8.7% | 0.70 | 62.7% |
| 2015 | 22 | A | 87.0 | 5 | 5 | 2.69 | 3.03 | 8.07 | 1.97 | 22.2% | 5.4% | 0.41 | 77.1% |
| 2015 | 22 | A+ | 50.7 | 4 | 5 | 8.35 | 6.54 | 10.13 | 3.20 | 24.1% | 7.6% | 2.49 | 57.6% |

**Background:** One of my favorite arms, especially as a sleeper type, in the entire 2014 draft class. And needless to say I thought the Los Angeles front office found one helluva deal in grabbing Rhoades in the fourth round two years ago, the 119th overall player selected. Rhoades, another wiry right-hander, spent the majority of his first two seasons working out of Illinois State's bullpen where he made 43 total appearances, six of which were starts, all coming during his freshman season. But Rhoades had a major coming out party during his sophomore campaign when he posted a 1.37 ERA while fanning 37 and walking 10 in 41.0 innings of work. I'd like to think that my perpetual finger-crossing helped convince the university's head coach, Mark Kingston, to push the promising reliever into the rotation, though it might not be the case. Anyway, Rhoades became a revelation during his final season with the school: 76.2 IP, 92 punch outs, 25 walks, and a 2.35 ERA.

Rhoades had a promising debut in rookie ball after his selection in the amateur draft: he posted a 40-to-15 strikeout-to-walk ratio in 38.2 innings. Last season the front office bumped the 6-foot-4, 225-pound right-hander up to the Midwest League and he was as a strong as I would have guessed: he fanned 78, walked 19, and posted a 3.03 FIP in 87.0 innings. Rhoades got the bump up to the California League in mid-July and his numbers took a left turn at wacky. He still missed a whole lot of bats (10.13 K/9), limited walks well enough (3.20), but finished with an 8.35 ERA and a 6.54 FIP.

**Projection**: First off, here's what I wrote two years ago during his pre-draft evaluation:

> "Sneaky upside here. A team will likely be tempted to push Rhoades back into the bullpen and fast-track him to the big leagues, but, again, the real value comes from his spot in the rotation. Strong, strong control. The ability to miss bats jumped to a premium this season, despite having worked the majority of his innings out of the rotation. And similar numbers in the Cape last season: 21.1 IP, 19 K's, and 8 BB's. You don't have to squint to hard too hard to see a potential fringe #3-type arm here."

Secondly, some updated analysis: I still remain high on the former Illinois State University hurler. He's continued to miss a whole lot of bats in the professional level and the control has remained a constant as well. His one singular downfall so far has been his propensity to surrender the long ball – *quite often*, particularly when he got the call up to High Class A. But here's some encouragement: Rhoades' homerun rate is going to regress – and push his ceiling higher – thanks to an above-average groundball rate. He's a quality #3/#4-type arm.

**Ceiling:** 2.0-win player
**Risk:** Moderate
**MLB ETA:** 2017

## 2. Nate Smith, LHP

**MiLB Rank: #231**
**Position Rank: N/A**

| Born: 08/28/91 | Age: 24 | Bats: L | Top CALs: Michael O'Brien, Tanner Roark, |
| Height: 6-3 | Weight: 205 | Throws: L | Paul Clemens, Brett Oberholtzer, Ryan Searle |

| YEAR | Age | Level | IP | W | L | ERA | FIP | K/9 | BB/9 | K% | BB% | HR/9 | LOB% |
|------|-----|-------|-------|---|---|------|------|------|------|-------|-------|------|-------|
| 2013 | 21 | R | 35.0 | 2 | 2 | 3.86 | 4.75 | 7.97 | 1.80 | 21.8% | 4.9% | 1.03 | 66.0% |
| 2014 | 22 | A+ | 55.7 | 6 | 3 | 3.07 | 3.37 | 8.25 | 2.26 | 23.2% | 6.4% | 0.49 | 65.0% |
| 2014 | 22 | AA | 62.3 | 5 | 3 | 2.89 | 3.04 | 9.67 | 4.33 | 26.3% | 11.8% | 0.43 | 77.2% |
| 2015 | 23 | AA | 101.7 | 8 | 4 | 2.48 | 3.90 | 7.17 | 2.48 | 19.6% | 6.8% | 0.89 | 82.8% |
| 2015 | 23 | AAA | 36.0 | 2 | 4 | 7.75 | 6.10 | 5.75 | 3.75 | 13.3% | 8.7% | 1.75 | 50.8% |

**Background:** Hailing from Furman University as an eighth round pick in 2013, Smith, a 6-foot-3, 205-pound southpaw, had a chance to be one of the school's most successful big league alum. Of course, it should be noted that since the mid-1920s only nine players from the college have appeared in the big leagues with Jimmie Coker, Jerry Martin, Tom Mastny, and Rick Wilkins as the only alums to appear in more than six games. Anyway, Smith has been a fast-riser, not only in the Angels' system but also through the minors as well. After throwing 35.0 innings in the Pioneer League during his debut, the organization aggressively promoted the lefty up to High Class A to begin the next season. And Smith responded in kind: He made 10 starts for Inland Empire, throwing 55.2 innings while posting 51-to-14 strikeout-to-walk ratio – enough production to convince the front office he was ready for the Texas League. And once again, he handled the promotion with ease: 62.1 innings, 67 K, and 30 BB. But the torrid stretch didn't end there either. Smith tossed another 22.0 innings in the Arizona Fall League two years ago as well, where he continued to miss bats (8.6 K/9) with solid-average control (3.3

BB/9). The Angels had the then-23-year-old hurler repeat Class AA last season, and in 17 starts he fanned 104 and walked just 28 before getting a brief – and disastrous – seven-game look in the Pacific Coast League.

**Projection**: A nice little find out of small school in the mid-rounds two years ago. Smith has a chance to develop into a backend big league starter. His work in Class AAA should prove to be nothing more than a speed bump: his strand rate was barely over 50% and his homerun rate spiked to an unreasonable 1.75 HR/9. Smith is far from dominant, but is no worse than a solid middle relief/setup man out of the pen. CAL links him to a couple backend arms like Paul Clemons and Brett Oberholtzer with a surprise comparison to Tanner Roark. Don't sleep on Smith.

**Ceiling**: 1.5-win player
**Risk**: Moderate
**MLB ETA**: 2016

## 3. Taylor Ward, C

**MiLB Rank: #236**
**Position Rank: #10**

| Born: 12/14/93 | Age: 22 | Bats: R | **Top CALs:** Juan Fuentes, Charlie Cutler, |
| Height: 6-1 | Weight: 180 | Throws: R | Beau Taylor, Jamie Ritchie, Camden Maron |

| Season | Age | LVL | PA | 2B | 3B | HR | AVG | OBP | SLG | ISO | BB% | K% | wRC+ |
|--------|-----|-----|-----|----|----|----|-------|-------|-------|-------|------|------|------|
| 2015 | 21 | R | 141 | 4 | 1 | 2 | 0.349 | 0.489 | 0.459 | 0.110 | 20.6% | 5.7% | 156 |
| 2015 | 21 | A | 103 | 3 | 0 | 1 | 0.348 | 0.412 | 0.413 | 0.065 | 9.7% | 14.6% | 145 |

**Background:** Widely panned as a one of the biggest reaches, if not *the* biggest reach, in the opening round last June. Needless to say, the Angels surprised more than a few scouts and pundits by taking the Fresno State University backstop with the 26th overall pick. But it was the Angels who initially got the last laugh. After torching the Mountain West Conference during his final two seasons with the Bulldogs, Taylor, who was originally drafted in the 31st round by the Rays back in 2012 as a prep player, made quick work of the Pioneer League during his debut, hitting a robust .349/.489/.459 with four doubles, one triple, and a pair of homeruns while swiping five bags in seven attempts. The club would eventually bump the 6-foot-1, 180-pound backstop up to full-season ball and he didn't miss a beat – or anything else. In 24 games with Burlington, Ward mashed .348/.412/.413 with three more doubles and one homerun. Overall, he finished the year with an aggregate .348/.457/.438 triple-slash line.

**Projection**: A promising receiver that displayed a tremendous feel for the strike zone over his final two seasons with Fresno State – he sported a 63-to-63 strikeout-to-walk ratio in 116 games – and that continued into the low levels of the minors; he actually finished with 16 more walks than strikeouts in pro ball. Ward isn't going to offer up a whole lot of power in the minors, specifically when he gets past High Class A, but a catcher with gap power, a strong eye at the plate, and some defensive value will certainly make some waves as a potential every day big leaguer.

**Ceiling**: 1.5- to 2.0-win player
**Risk**: Moderate
**MLB ETA**: 2018

## 4. Kyle Kubitza, 2B/3B/LF

**MiLB Rank: #250**
**Position Rank: N/A**

| Born: 07/15/90 | Age: 25 | Bats: L | **Top CALs:** Mike Costanzo, Mike Walker, |
| Height: 6-3 | Weight: 210 | Throws: R | Cole Gillespie, Logan Forsythe, Jai Miller |

| Season | Age | LVL | PA | 2B | 3B | HR | AVG | OBP | SLG | ISO | BB% | K% | wRC+ |
|--------|-----|-----|-----|----|----|----|-------|-------|-------|-------|------|------|------|
| 2013 | 22 | A+ | 527 | 28 | 6 | 12 | 0.260 | 0.380 | 0.434 | 0.175 | 15.2% | 25.0% | 130 |
| 2014 | 23 | AA | 529 | 31 | 11 | 8 | 0.295 | 0.405 | 0.470 | 0.175 | 14.6% | 25.1% | 145 |
| 2015 | 24 | AAA | 526 | 43 | 5 | 7 | 0.271 | 0.357 | 0.433 | 0.162 | 11.4% | 23.8% | 112 |
| 2015 | 24 | MLB | 39 | 0 | 0 | 0 | 0.194 | 0.256 | 0.194 | 0.000 | 7.7% | 38.5% | 32 |

**Background:** Acquired from the Braves last January for Nate Hyatt and Ricardo Sanchez, Kubitza continued to show some offensive promise with the bat during his first year with his new organization. Making his Class AAA debut, the lefty-swinging third baseman batted a solid .271/.357/.433 with a career best 43 doubles, five triples, and seven homeruns while going 7-for-8 in the stolen base department. It marked the sixth consecutive time that the former third round pick out Texas State University not only posted a *Weighted Runs Created Plus* total above 100, but also finished the year with a walk rate north of 10%, an Isolated Power above .150, and a BABIP topping .333. For his career, Kubitza is sporting a .271/.376/.436 triple-slash line with 142 doubles, 34 triples, 37 homeruns, and 63 stolen bases.

**Projection**: Here's what I wrote in last year's book:

*"Wade Boggs made a career out of being the non-typical third baseman, as did Bill Mueller and a variety of others. But [Kubitza's] not Boggs – or Mueller for that matter. Kubitza's a solid depth guy who should probably add some positional versatility to help his big league chances."*

Kubitza did just that: add positional versatility to his resume within the last year. He made a couple appearances at first base with Licey in the Dominican Winter League and, according to RotoWire, worked out at second base. Kubitza handles southpaws and right-handers equally well, will take a walk, and flash some serious gap power. His strikeout rate has always tended to toe the line between moderation and problematic, so it'll be interesting to see how he responds with extended big league looks. Again, fringy everyday guy.

**Ceiling:** 1.5-win player
**Risk:** Low to Moderate
**MLB ETA:** Debuted in 2015

## 5. Victor Alcantara, RHP

**MiLB Rank: N/A**
**Position Rank: N/A**

| Born: 04/03/93 | Age: 23 | Bats: R | Top CALs: Josh Ravin, Anthony Ortega, |
|---|---|---|---|
| Height: 6-2 | Weight: 190 | Throws: R | Jose Ramirez, Myles Jaye, Josh Wall |

| YEAR | Age | Level | IP | W | L | ERA | FIP | K/9 | BB/9 | K% | BB% | HR/9 | LOB% |
|---|---|---|---|---|---|---|---|---|---|---|---|---|---|
| 2015 | 22 | A+ | 136.0 | 7 | 12 | 5.63 | 4.37 | 8.27 | 3.84 | 20.4% | 9.5% | 0.66 | 59.0% |

**Background:** Sinewy, explosive, and incredibly raw, just four years removed from making his professional debut in the Dominican Summer League – at the age of 19 no less - the 6-foot-2, 190-pound right-hander now sits close to the top of the Angels' farm system – albeit an incredibly *weak* Angels farm system. After battling some semi-serious control/command issues in his first couple seasons – including walking 40 in 72.0 DSL innings and another 35 in 59 innings in the Pioneer League – Alcantara's ability to locate the strike zone with regularity took another important step forward last season. In 27 starts with Inland Empire in the California League, Alcantara walked 9.5% of the total batters he faced – the first time in his young career that he walked fewer than 11.5% of the hitters he faced in any one season. The Dominican-born hurler also managed to punch out 20.4% of the hitters he faced as well, the eighth best mark among all qualified hurlers in the California League last season. For his career, Alcantara has fanned 367, walked 193, and posted a rather unsightly 4.68 ERA.

**Projection**: So...I was incredibly harsh on the fire-balling hurler in last year's book, writing:

*"Not to disparage his big step forward in the Midwest League that fact is Alcantara was basically pitching against an age-appropriate level of competition. On the whole, he was neither dominant nor overly impressive. He looks like a fringy starter whose strikeout rate could tick up in the pen."*

But, look, let's call it as it is: (A) the Angels have a farm system as devoid of impact caliber talent, on either side of the ball, as any in Major League Baseball and (B) Alcantara's production during his four-year career has never been anything noteworthy.

Here's what the numbers have told us to this point:

- He can miss a good amount of bats as evidenced by his career strikeout percentage is 21.4%.
- In terms of production as measured by FIP, well, Alcantara's been an average pitcher since coming stateside, sometimes better, sometimes worse.
- Despite his solid strikeout ability, one which would be associated with a power arm, Alcantara has been hit fairly hard in two of the past three years as he's surrendered BABIPs of .345 and .341.

Add it all up – and not to mention some unfavorable CALs – and Alcantara doesn't look like a top-of-the-line caliber arm. In fact, as I wrote in the book two years ago, I wouldn't be surprised if he ended up as a power-armed, high-leverage, late-inning relief arm in the near future.

**Ceiling:** 1.5- to 2.0-win player
**Risk:** Moderate to High
**MLB ETA:** 2018

## 6. Alex Yarbrough, 2B

**MiLB Rank: N/A**
**Position Rank: N/A**

| Born: 08/03/91 | Age: 24 | Bats: B | **Top CALs:** Charlie Culberson, Daniel Mayora |
|---|---|---|---|
| Height: 6-0 | Weight: 200 | Throws: R | Kurt Mertins, Marcus Lemon, Scooter Gennett |

| Season | Age | LVL | PA | 2B | 3B | HR | AVG | OBP | SLG | ISO | BB% | K% | wRC+ |
|---|---|---|---|---|---|---|---|---|---|---|---|---|---|
| 2013 | 21 | A+ | 615 | 32 | 10 | 11 | 0.313 | 0.341 | 0.459 | 0.146 | 4.4% | 17.2% | 108 |
| 2014 | 22 | AA | 592 | 38 | 4 | 5 | 0.285 | 0.321 | 0.397 | 0.112 | 5.6% | 20.9% | 103 |
| 2015 | 23 | AAA | 545 | 29 | 3 | 3 | 0.236 | 0.274 | 0.324 | 0.088 | 4.8% | 25.0% | 56 |

**Background:** Prior to the year the switch-hitting second baseman was a bit of a dark horse candidate to leapfrog up to the top spot in the system following 2015. And then he shat the bed. Yarbrough, who was drafted in the fourth round out of the University of Mississippi, made waves during his first three seasons in pro ball. He handled the Midwest League with ease during his debut, batting .287/.320/.410 with 12 doubles and nine triples in 58 games, and followed that up with another favorable showing in the California League by hitting .313/.341/.459 with plenty of extra-base fire-power (32 doubles, 10 triples, 11 homeruns) and a smattering of speed (14-for-18 in stolen bases). He then continued to hover around the league average production line when he batted .285/.321/.397 with a 103 wRC+ total last season in Class AA as well. And, of course, the wheels fell the hell off last season. In 128 games with Salt Lake in the Pacific Coast League, the 6-foot, 200-pound infielder batted .236/.274/.324 with a career worst 56 wRC+.

**Projection**: Steadily consistent until 2015, Yarbrough hit the proverbial brick wall – and it damn near killed him last season. His power has been in decline since his career best showing in 2013 as it's dropped from .146 to .112 to .088. But the most troubling statistic from last season: despite a solid-average .313 BABIP, Yarbrough's production line still cratered. But just like two years ago, CAL is linking the once-promising second baseman to Scooter Gennett, which, again, would be his ultimate ceiling. Yarbrough could be a late-bloomer, just like CAL is suggesting. Final thought: he could be a nice little buy-low candidate for a potential trade partner.

**Ceiling:** 1.5-win player
**Risk:** Moderate
**MLB ETA:** Debuted in 2015

## 7. Kaleb Cowart, 3B

**MiLB Rank: N/A**
**Position Rank: N/A**

| Born: 06/02/92 | Age: 24 | Bats: B | **Top CALs:** Niko Goodrum, Edward Salcedo, |
|---|---|---|---|
| Height: 6-3 | Weight: 225 | Throws: R | Deibinson Romero, Seth Mejias-Brean, Jared Hoying |

| Season | Age | LVL | PA | 2B | 3B | HR | AVG | OBP | SLG | ISO | BB% | K% | wRC+ |
|---|---|---|---|---|---|---|---|---|---|---|---|---|---|
| 2013 | 21 | AA | 546 | 20 | 1 | 6 | 0.221 | 0.279 | 0.301 | 0.080 | 7.0% | 22.7% | 65 |
| 2014 | 22 | AA | 487 | 18 | 4 | 6 | 0.223 | 0.295 | 0.324 | 0.101 | 8.8% | 20.3% | 77 |
| 2015 | 23 | A+ | 221 | 14 | 4 | 2 | 0.242 | 0.326 | 0.387 | 0.144 | 10.0% | 19.5% | 96 |
| 2015 | 23 | AAA | 253 | 13 | 3 | 6 | 0.323 | 0.395 | 0.491 | 0.168 | 11.5% | 25.3% | 136 |
| 2015 | 23 | MLB | 52 | 2 | 0 | 1 | 0.174 | 0.255 | 0.283 | 0.109 | 9.6% | 36.5% | 54 |

**Background:** Like Lazarus brought back to life, the switch-hitting third baseman has arisen from his deep slumber, one that clouded his once-promising sheen. Taken in the middle of first round in 2010, just picks ahead of Mike Foltynewicz, Christian Yelich, and fellow organization-mate Cam Bedrosian, Cowart had a solid showing in the Pioneer League at the age 19 in 2011, hitting .283/.345/.420 with solid pop. He followed that up with a dominant burst in the Midwest the next year – he batted .293/348/.479 with 16 doubles, three triples, and nine homeruns – but cooled a bit when the organization pushed him up to Inland Empire during the second half (.259/.366/.426). And then it went dark, like the Northeast Blackout of 2003 that affected 45 million people in eight states and another 10 million in Ontario, Canada. The blackout, on a side note, began just minutes away from my childhood home when a tree came in contact with a 345kV transmission line in Walton Hills, Ohio.

Anyway, sorry, now back to Cowart.

The former 18th overall pick looked lost in Class AA in 2013; he batted a putrid .221/.279/.301. And he promptly followed that up with another rancid Class AA line: .223/.295/.324. He also struggled mightily during his trip the Arizona Fall League that year, hitting .185/.224/.259. But something seemed to click for Cowart in 2015, though not initially.

The Angels bounced him all the way back down to High Class A to begin the year, where he promptly batted .163/.217/.276 in his first 25 games. And just like that he figured it out – again. Over his next 26 games with Inland Empire he slugged .323/.426/.500 and then continued to mash when the club promoted him all the way to the PCL (.323/.395/.491). Cowart eventually earned a 34-game stint with the big league club too.

**Projection**: Where to begin, honestly? Cowart once looked like a solid #6-type stick when he was originally an up-and-comer. Then his bat took a *long* hiatus where he was as effective as I would be battling against Class AA arms. Finally, he rebounds and looks even better than he previously showed during his early seasons.

Obviously, there's a ton of risk involved here, and his work in Anaheim only adds to that. Even during his down times he showed a solid eye at the plate, with reasonable contact skills. The power, while it's in the double-digit homerun area, doesn't play very well at the hot corner. Add it up and he looks like a fringy every day guy, one that's probably better suited for a Quad-A role.

**Ceiling**: 1.5-win player
**Risk**: Moderate to High
**MLB ETA**: Debuted in 2015

## 8. Joe Gatto, RHP

**MiLB Rank:** N/A
**Position Rank:** N/A

| Born: 06/14/95 | Age: 21 | Bats: R | Top CALs: Andres Santiago, Carter Hope, |
|---|---|---|---|
| Height: 6-3 | Weight: 204 | Throws: R | Luis Pina, Reinaldo Lopez, Igol Feliz |

| YEAR | Age | Level | IP | W | L | ERA | FIP | K/9 | BB/9 | K% | BB% | HR/9 | LOB% |
|---|---|---|---|---|---|---|---|---|---|---|---|---|---|
| 2014 | 19 | R | 2.0 | 0 | 0 | 4.50 | 9.53 | 4.50 | 0.00 | 12.5% | 0.0% | 4.50 | 100.0% |
| 2014 | 19 | R | 25.0 | 2 | 1 | 5.40 | 4.55 | 5.40 | 3.24 | 13.0% | 7.8% | 0.36 | 62.5% |
| 2015 | 20 | R | 54.3 | 2 | 3 | 4.31 | 4.64 | 6.29 | 2.82 | 16.2% | 7.3% | 0.66 | 69.9% |

**Background:** Gatto, who was one of just two prep players taken by the franchise in the first 33 rounds two years ago, is also the sole holdover remaining of the club's first three selections – thanks to the trades of Sean Newcomb and Chris Ellis in the Andrelton Simmons deal with Atlanta. A 6-foot-3 right-hander, Gatto spent the year with Orem, posting a 38-to-17 strikeout-to-walk ratio in 54.1 innings.

**Projection**: There's really nothing to go off of here, just 81.1 innings. And even then it's not all that promising. Personally, I find it downright concerning when a high round prep arm fails to miss a whole lot of bats in the lowest levels of the minors. He's fanned just 15.2% of the total batters he faced so far. Still, though, it's a very limited sample size. We'll see what 2016 brings.

**Ceiling**: Too Soon to Tell
**Risk**: N/A
**MLB ETA**: N/A

## 9. Tyler DeLoach, LHP

**MiLB Rank:** N/A
**Position Rank:** N/A

| Born: 04/12/91 | Age: 25 | Bats: R | Top CALs: Robert Hinton, Ronald Uviedo, |
|---|---|---|---|
| Height: 6-6 | Weight: 240 | Throws: L | Steve Johnson, William Cuevas, Dellin Betances |

| YEAR | Age | Level | IP | W | L | ERA | FIP | K/9 | BB/9 | K% | BB% | HR/9 | LOB% |
|---|---|---|---|---|---|---|---|---|---|---|---|---|---|
| 2013 | 22 | A | 70.0 | 5 | 5 | 3.34 | 3.21 | 10.16 | 2.83 | 27.9% | 7.8% | 0.64 | 70.4% |
| 2014 | 23 | A+ | 112.0 | 10 | 4 | 3.21 | 4.00 | 9.80 | 3.94 | 25.5% | 10.2% | 0.48 | 73.8% |
| 2014 | 23 | AA | 35.3 | 4 | 0 | 2.29 | 3.97 | 9.93 | 4.33 | 27.5% | 12.0% | 0.76 | 86.6% |
| 2015 | 24 | AA | 45.0 | 3 | 2 | 2.40 | 3.30 | 8.40 | 2.00 | 23.5% | 5.6% | 0.60 | 79.5% |
| 2015 | 24 | AAA | 94.3 | 2 | 6 | 6.20 | 4.87 | 8.68 | 4.48 | 21.7% | 11.2% | 1.05 | 63.9% |

**Background:** A massive 6-foot-6, 240-pound southpaw taken in the 26th round in 2012 out of the University of North Carolina at Wilmington, DeLoach has perpetually been on my radar as a sleeper pick. Back in 2013, his sophomore campaign, DeLoach made 13 starts with Burlington in the Midwest League while averaging 10.2 punch outs and just 2.8 walks per nine innings. He followed that up by splitting the season between Inland Empire and Arkansas, throwing 147.1, more than double his previous career high, with 161 strikeouts, 66 walks, and an aggregate 3.36 ERA. Last year the promising lefty was bounced between the Texas and Pacific Coast Leagues, averaging 8.6 punch outs and 3.7 walks per nine innings. For his career, DeLoach has fanned 24.7% and walked 10.3% of the total hitters he's faced thus far.

**Projection**: In my first book three years ago I ranked the big southpaw as the club's ninth best prospect, writing at that time:

> "Very, very interesting. Big, big frame. Huge K-rate. Solid control. Definitely a breakout candidate for next season."

Then in last year's book I bumped him down a couple slots, more indicative of some of the higher-ceiling arms the team drafted, and wrote:

> "DeLoach took to Class AA like a fish in water. In his second and third starts, both coming against Corpus Christi, he posted a 19-to-3 strikeout-to-walk ratio. The big lefty out of the University of North Carolina at Wilmington still largely flies under the radar largely because of his age and level of competition. But if he can even come close

to duplicating his 2014 success, he might find himself on the outer fringes of the game's top 100. Right now, DeLoach looks like a backend arm or dominant late-inning reliever."

Well, DeLoach did come close to replicating his 2014 production last year – sort of. He missed nearly a bat per inning with slightly subpar control. But some of his underlying numbers in the PCL were a bit wacky: he walked 11.2% of the hitters he faced, the second highest mark of his career; his BABIP was .366; he surrendered 1.05 homeruns per nine innings; and he finished with the highest FIP, 4.87, of his four-year pro career.

DeLoach, who's entering his age-25 season, might not get too many more looks as a potential starting candidate – especially once big league injuries strike. But tall lefties with decent control and the ability to miss bats always get a few chances to realize their potential.

**Ceiling:** 1.0- to 1.5-win player
**Risk:** Moderate
**MLB ETA:** 2016

## 10. Eduardo Paredes, RHP

**MiLB Rank:** N/A
**Position Rank:** N/A

| Born: 03/06/95 | Age: 21 | Bats: R | Top CALs: Francisco Jimenez, Abel De Los Santos, |
|---|---|---|---|
| Height: 6-1 | Weight: 170 | Throws: R | Jose Fernandez, Cortland Cox, Joe Jimenez |

| YEAR | Age | Level | IP | W | L | ERA | FIP | K/9 | BB/9 | K% | BB% | HR/9 | LOB% |
|---|---|---|---|---|---|---|---|---|---|---|---|---|---|
| 2013 | 18 | R | 22.3 | 2 | 1 | 2.82 | 3.23 | 5.64 | 1.61 | 14.4% | 4.1% | 0.40 | 72.8% |
| 2014 | 19 | R | 20.3 | 2 | 1 | 1.33 | 2.60 | 13.72 | 3.54 | 37.8% | 9.8% | 0.00 | 79.0% |
| 2015 | 20 | A | 42.0 | 0 | 2 | 1.71 | 1.99 | 12.64 | 1.71 | 35.8% | 4.9% | 0.43 | 81.6% |
| 2015 | 20 | A+ | 13.3 | 0 | 0 | 4.73 | 2.28 | 8.78 | 1.35 | 23.6% | 3.6% | 0.00 | 53.3% |

**Background:** A less-than-imposing lefty with a penchant for big punch out totals. Paredes made it up to full-season ball in 2015 after spending parts of the three previous seasons making his way from the Dominican Summer League (twice) and a quick jaunt through with Orem in the Pioneer League. And the 6-oot-1, 170-pound right-hander looked at ease in the Midwest and California Leagues last year. In 37 games with Burlington, Paredes tossed 42.0 innings and racked up an incredible 59 strikeouts and issued just eight walks. He followed that up with another 13 punch outs – as well as seven free passes – in 13.1 innings. For his career, the dominant young reliever has fanned over 30% of the total batters to dig in against him.

**Projection**: A fast-moving righty that could conceivably be called up by June 2017. Paredes has been a dominant force during his four-year professional career, offering up huge strikeout totals and barely-there walk totals. And just to add some context to this: among all hurlers with at least 50+ innings last season, *at any level* (minus the Mexican League), Paredes finished 10th in strikeout-to-walk percentage with 28.2%. He's going to be a force.

**Ceiling:** 1.0- to 1.5-win player
**Risk:** Moderate
**MLB ETA:** 2017

## 11. Natanael Delgado, LF/RF

**MiLB Rank: N/A**
**Position Rank: N/A**

| Born: 10/23/95 | Age: 20 | Bats: L | Top CALs: Elier Hernandez, Jem Argenal, |
|---|---|---|---|
| Height: 6-1 | Weight: 170 | Throws: L | Elvis Escobar, Brian Mathews, Juan Ortiz |

| Season | Age | LVL | PA | 2B | 3B | HR | AVG | OBP | SLG | ISO | BB% | K% | wRC+ |
|---|---|---|---|---|---|---|---|---|---|---|---|---|---|
| 2013 | 17 | R | 209 | 16 | 2 | 3 | 0.271 | 0.311 | 0.422 | 0.151 | 5.3% | 20.6% | 101 |
| 2014 | 18 | R | 162 | 8 | 4 | 3 | 0.301 | 0.333 | 0.464 | 0.163 | 3.1% | 21.0% | 102 |
| 2015 | 19 | A | 438 | 19 | 5 | 6 | 0.241 | 0.276 | 0.355 | 0.114 | 4.3% | 23.7% | 81 |

**Background:** Keeping with the theme of underwhelming performances and general disappointment from the club's better prospects; Delgado's offensive showing in the Midwest League left an awful lot to be desired, even if he was just 19-years-old at the time. A 6-foot-1, 170-pound corner outfielder out of the Dominican Republic, Delgado was coming off of two solid back-to-back showings in the rookie leagues. He batted .271/.311/.422 with 16 doubles, a pair of triples, and three homeruns with four stolen bases en route to posting a league average-ish 101 wRC+ in the Arizona Summer League. Delgado followed that up with another league average performance in the advanced rookie league: .301/.333/.464 with eight doubles, four triples, and three homeruns. Last season, though, Delgado struggled in his transition to full season ball, batting .241/.276/.355 in 108 games with Burlington in the Midwest League.

**Projection**: The optimist in me would like to point out that Delgado slugged .310/.349/.454 during a torrid 49-game stretch between late April and the end of June. The pessimist would point out that (A) he hit .178/.209/.270 over his final 46 games and (B) that lefties were absolutely death on the left-handed outfielder (.192/.221/.274). And, of course, the pessimist would also point out that he finished the year with a 104-to-19 strikeout-to-walk ratio. Delgado looks like a fringy big leaguer: there's some offensive promise here, but he's going to have to overcome an awful lot moving forward.

**Ceiling:** 1.0- to 1.5-win player
**Risk:** Moderate
**MLB ETA:** 2019

## 12. Jahmai Jones, CF

**MiLB Rank: N/A**
**Position Rank: N/A**

| Born: 08/04/97 | Age: 18 | Bats: R | **Top CALs:** Aaron Siliga, Antonio Arias, |
| Height: 5-11 | Weight: 210 | Throws: R | Zacrey Law, Oliver Zapata, Ricardo Marcano |

| Season | Age | LVL | PA | 2B | 3B | HR | AVG | OBP | SLG | ISO | BB% | K% | wRC+ |
|--------|-----|-----|-----|----|----|----|-------|-------|-------|-------|------|-------|------|
| 2015 | 17 | R | 183 | 6 | 2 | 2 | 0.244 | 0.330 | 0.344 | 0.100 | 9.3% | 18.0% | 101 |

**Background:** The club's second round pick last June. Jones, a stocky center fielder from a prep school in Georgia, had a decent debut in the Arizona Summer League, hitting .244/.330/.344 with six doubles, two triples, two homeruns, and 16 stolen bases (in 23 attempts). His overall production, according to *Weighted Runs Created Plus*, topped the league average mark by a whopping 1%.

**Projection:** Toolsy, but the actual bat left a bit to be desired during his 40-game stint in the Arizona Summer League. Jones' production has been OK, nothing great, but far from terrible as well. Per the usual, it's too soon to get a solid analytical read on the 5-foot-11, 210-pound center fielder.

**Ceiling:** Too Soon to Tell
**Risk:** N/A
**MLB ETA:** N/A

## 13. Kyle McGowin, RHP

**MiLB Rank: N/A**
**Position Rank: N/A**

| Born: 11/27/91 | Age: 24 | Bats: R | **Top CALs:** William Cuevas, Nick Tepesch, |
| Height: 6-3 | Weight: 200 | Throws: R | Jeff Manship, Jesse Beal, Mitchell Boggs |

| YEAR | Age | Level | IP | W | L | ERA | FIP | K/9 | BB/9 | K% | BB% | HR/9 | LOB% |
|------|-----|-------|-------|---|---|------|------|------|------|-------|-------|------|-------|
| 2013 | 21 | R | 14.3 | 1 | 1 | 6.28 | 5.48 | 7.53 | 3.14 | 19.7% | 8.2% | 1.26 | 46.1% |
| 2014 | 22 | R+ | 2.0 | 0 | 0 | 0.00 | 3.53 | 9.00 | 4.50 | 22.2% | 11.1% | 0.00 | 100.0% |
| 2014 | 22 | A+ | 58.3 | 1 | 5 | 2.93 | 3.86 | 7.41 | 2.47 | 20.1% | 6.7% | 0.62 | 70.5% |
| 2014 | 22 | AA | 5.0 | 0 | 1 | 5.40 | 4.52 | 5.40 | 0.00 | 14.3% | 0.0% | 1.80 | 65.2% |
| 2015 | 23 | AA | 154.0 | 9 | 9 | 4.38 | 4.13 | 7.31 | 2.92 | 19.4% | 7.7% | 0.94 | 68.5% |

**Background:** A fifth rounder out of little Savannah State University in 2013, McGowin looked like a nice mid-round find by the organization shortly after he made his full season debut two years ago. McGowin, who made a quick jaunt through the Pioneer League in 2013, but got aggressively pushed up to the California League at the start of the 2014 season. The 6-foot-3, 200-pound right-hander made 10 starts for Inland Empire that year, throwing 58.1 innings with 48 punch outs, 16 walks, and a 3.86 FIP. After that he would make one more start, a five-inning performance with the Arkansas Travelers in the Texas League, before a wonky elbow would force a premature end to his season. McGowin spent last season back with the Travelers where he would make 27 starts, toss a career best 154.0 innings, fan 125, and walk 50 en route to tallying a decent 4.13 FIP.

**Projection:** Well, it looks like the elbow is fully healed, thankfully. And as a fifth round pick out of a small school he's already exceeded many – or most – expectations that were previously laid out. McGowin's control remained steady as he transitioned from school to the low levels on up through the minors' biggest test. He'll also miss a handful of bats, but his inability to keep the ball in the park is going to doom him. He's coughed up 23 gopher balls in 233.2 innings. He looks like a fringy #5 with the high probability as a middle relief arm thanks to a solid fastball.

**Ceiling:** 1.0-win player
**Risk:** Low to Moderate
**MLB ETA:** 2016

## 14. Jett Bandy, C

| Born: 03/26/90 | Age: 26 | Bats: R | Top CALs: Bobby Wilson, Sean Ochinko, |
|---|---|---|---|
| Height: 6-4 | Weight: 235 | Throws: R | David Freitas, Cole Armstrong, Wyatt Toregas |

| Season | Age | LVL | PA | 2B | 3B | HR | AVG | OBP | SLG | ISO | BB% | K% | wRC+ |
|---|---|---|---|---|---|---|---|---|---|---|---|---|---|
| 2013 | 23 | AA | 272 | 17 | 2 | 4 | 0.241 | 0.303 | 0.376 | 0.135 | 5.1% | 14.3% | 91 |
| 2014 | 24 | AA | 363 | 12 | 0 | 13 | 0.250 | 0.348 | 0.413 | 0.163 | 9.1% | 17.4% | 121 |
| 2015 | 25 | AAA | 344 | 21 | 0 | 11 | 0.291 | 0.347 | 0.466 | 0.175 | 4.7% | 18.3% | 116 |
| 2015 | 25 | MLB | 2 | 0 | 0 | 1 | 0.500 | 0.500 | 2.000 | 1.500 | 0.0% | 0.0% | 599 |

**Background:** When parents bestow a name like Jett to their new-born son it's almost a guarantee that he grows up as either: (A) a star – and local badass – of a childhood movie like The Sandlot, which starred Benny "The Jet" Rodriguez or (B) a slap-hitting speedster in the mold of Kerry Robinson, the former Cardinals outfielder that carved out a niche as chop-at-the-ball-and-run role player about a decade ago. But Bandy, a former late, late round pick in 2011 has broken through his deceiving name to develop into a slow moving – some would say methodically developing – backstop that was a chance to carve out his own role with Angels moving forward. Bandy, a 6-foot-4, 235-pound former 31st round pick out of the University of Arizona, put his second consecutive solid season together as he made his debut in Class AAA last season. After batting .250/.348/.413 with 12 doubles and 13 homeruns in the Texas League two years ago, Bandy posted another respectable line in 2015: .291/.347/.466 with 21 doubles and 11 homeruns. He's also thrown out 33% of would-be base stealers in his career.

**Projection**: It's not surprising to see CAL throw a couple backup comparisons Bandy's way, tying him to Bobby Wilson, another Angels second-string backstop, and Wyatt Toregas. Bandy won't kill a team with his defensive abilities while offering up double-digit homerun power, a below-average eye, and some batting averages in the .230s or .240s. On an interesting note: Bandy's sporting a career 599 wRC+ in the big leagues; of course, going 1-for-2 with a dinger does that for you.

**Ceiling:** 1.0-win player
**Risk:** Low to Moderate
**MLB ETA:** Debuted in 2015

## 15. Grayson Long, RHP

| Born: 05/27/94 | Age: 22 | Bats: R | Top CALs: Scott Harkin, Drayton Riekenberg, |
|---|---|---|---|
| Height: 6-5 | Weight: 200 | Throws: R | Bryan Ball, Chase Boruff, Luis Garcia |

| YEAR | Age | Level | IP | W | L | ERA | FIP | K/9 | BB/9 | K% | BB% | HR/9 | LOB% |
|---|---|---|---|---|---|---|---|---|---|---|---|---|---|
| 2015 | 21 | R | 19.7 | 0 | 0 | 5.03 | 4.10 | 10.07 | 4.58 | 25.9% | 11.8% | 0.46 | 61.6% |

**Background:** Continuing the long-standing tradition of Aggies arms going in the draft, the Angels of Anaheim grabbed the 6-foot-5, 200-pound right-hander in the third round last June, the 104th overall pick. Long, a three-year mainstay in Texas A&M's rotation, was a rare starter in the rotation as a true freshman, throwing 46.0 innings with a 38-to-25 strikeout-to-walk ratio. He followed that up with a bit of a downturn in production as his innings total nearly doubled – his strikeout rate dropped from 7.43 K/9 to 5.54 K/9 – but he came back strong during his junior campaign. In 17 starts, he averaged a career best 9.97 punch outs and 3.67 free passes per nine innings. Following his selection in the draft, Long tossed another 19.2 innings in the Pioneer League, fanning 22 and walking 10.

**Projection**: Not particularly overpowering, the big right-hander offers up a ceiling somewhere between two of the system's more advanced arms, Nate Smith and Kyle McGowin. Long isn't going to miss a whole lot of bats in the professional ranks, maybe averaging around 7.3 or so punch outs per nine innings. But if he can show the type of control that was on display during his sophomore year season, he has a shot at developing into a backend starter.

**Ceiling:** 1.0- to 1.5-win player
**Risk:** Moderate to High
**MLB ETA:** 2018

## 16. Roberto Baldoquin, 2B/SS

**MiLB Rank:** N/A
**Position Rank:** N/A

| Born: 05/14/94 | Age: 22 | Bats: R | Top CALs: Ogui Diaz, Pedro Ciriaco, |
| Height: 5-11 | Weight: 185 | Throws: R | Alexis Aguilar, Angel Gonzalez, Angel Ortega |

| Season | Age | LVL | PA | 2B | 3B | HR | AVG | OBP | SLG | ISO | BB% | K% | wRC+ |
|---|---|---|---|---|---|---|---|---|---|---|---|---|---|
| 2015 | 21 | A+ | 309 | 12 | 1 | 1 | 0.235 | 0.266 | 0.294 | 0.059 | 2.9% | 22.7% | 52 |

**Background:** Proving that not every big dollar import from Cuba immediately makes a stateside impact, Baldoquin made waves by signing an $8 million deal with the Angels last January but the club had to pay double that amount as they exceeded their international bonus pool which required them to pay 100% luxury tax on the contract. And what the franchise got in return was...well...an injury-shortened lackluster offensive performance with some tinges of disappointment from Inland Empire's manager – and former big leaguer – Denny Hocking. After a lengthy stint on the DL early in the season with a lat injury, Hocking, according to a May 28th article by *The Orange Country Register*, quipped: "For him to be out this long, I think there's more in there (in his lat area) that we're not finding. That's what I think. I'm not around it, but I hope there's something more because he needs to be on the field to develop his skills."

Doesn't sound like a ringing endorsement now, does it? At the time of the lat issue Baldoquin was batting a paltry .154/.233/.205, though that's through 11 games. The 5-foot-11, 185-pound middle infielder missed six or so weeks and returned to bat .248/.271/.308 with just 12 extra-base hits and one homerun.

**Projection**: Granted it's a relatively small sample size, just 309 plate appearances across 77 games, but the overall production was disappointing no matter how you dice it. He didn't walk or hit for power or run with any type of frequency or hit...anything. He did seem to hit his stride over his final 39 contests, but even then it didn't offer up a whole lot of hope (.287/.301/.333). Baldoquin, while still plenty young, looks like a backup at the game pinnacle level, nothing more, perhaps something less.

**Ceiling:** 1.0-win player
**Risk:** Moderate
**MLB ETA:** 2019

## 17. Greg Mahle, LHP

**MiLB Rank:** N/A
**Position Rank:** N/A

| Born: 04/17/93 | Age: 23 | Bats: L | Top CALs: Jeffrey Johnson, Dan Jennings, |
| Height: 6-2 | Weight: 225 | Throws: L | Justin De Fratus, Joey Krehbiel, Austin Voth |

| YEAR | Age | Level | IP | W | L | ERA | FIP | K/9 | BB/9 | K% | BB% | HR/9 | LOB% |
|---|---|---|---|---|---|---|---|---|---|---|---|---|---|
| 2014 | 21 | R | 8.0 | 1 | 1 | 0.00 | 2.78 | 12.38 | 3.38 | 32.4% | 8.8% | 0.00 | 44.4% |
| 2014 | 21 | A | 29.3 | 0 | 1 | 3.38 | 2.77 | 11.66 | 3.68 | 31.4% | 9.9% | 0.31 | 67.5% |
| 2015 | 22 | A+ | 22.7 | 0 | 1 | 3.57 | 2.28 | 12.31 | 1.19 | 33.3% | 3.2% | 0.40 | 71.0% |
| 2015 | 22 | AA | 35.3 | 3 | 3 | 3.06 | 2.56 | 9.17 | 2.80 | 24.5% | 7.5% | 0.25 | 66.5% |

**Background:** A three-year relief arm during his tenure with UC Santa Barbara, Mahle, who tossed 177 innings during his collegiate career, posted some solid, uninspiring peripherals including averaging just 6.81 punch outs and 3.00 walks per nine innings. He finished with a lackluster 3.56 ERA as well. The Angels took the 6-foot-2, 225-pound southpaw in the 15th round and apparently sprinkled magic strikeout dust over his left arm because, well, he's missing far more bats in the minors than he did at any point during his time with UC Santa Barbara. He split his debut between the Pioneer and the Midwest Leagues two years ago, fanning 49 and walking 15 in 37.1 innings. The club bumped him up to Inland Empire and eventually to Arkansas during last season; he tallied a 67-to-14 strikeout-to-walk ratio. And through his first 95.1 innings, Mahle has averaged 11 strikeouts per nine innings.

**Projection**: Stocky with a newfound ability to miss an enormous amount of bats, Mahle's already ascended up to – and breezed through – the minors' hardest test, Class AA. And just a couple seasons after entering pro ball as late round pick, the big lefty is already knocking on the club's big league door. Don't expect those punch out numbers to continue at the game's highest level, but Mahle could be a serviceable lefty out of the pen.

**Ceiling:** 1.0-win player
**Risk:** Moderate
**MLB ETA:** 2016

## 18. Caleb Adams, OF

**MiLB Rank:** N/A
**Position Rank:** N/A

| | | | | | |
|---|---|---|---|---|---|
| **Born:** 01/26/93 | **Age:** 23 | **Bats:** R | **Top CALs:** Mike Daniel, David Medina, | |
| **Height:** 5-10 | **Weight:** 185 | **Throws:** R | Jarred Bogany, Brian Rike, Rafael Fernandez | |

| Season | Age | LVL | PA | 2B | 3B | HR | AVG | OBP | SLG | ISO | BB% | K% | wRC+ |
|---|---|---|---|---|---|---|---|---|---|---|---|---|---|
| 2014 | 21 | R | 235 | 9 | 2 | 7 | 0.252 | 0.325 | 0.414 | 0.162 | 8.9% | 29.8% | 90 |
| 2015 | 22 | A | 277 | 10 | 5 | 3 | 0.302 | 0.398 | 0.426 | 0.123 | 11.6% | 27.8% | 144 |
| 2015 | 22 | A+ | 208 | 11 | 3 | 4 | 0.293 | 0.380 | 0.453 | 0.160 | 10.6% | 28.8% | 129 |

**Background:** Over the past two drafts there have been eight players drafted out of the University of Louisiana at Lafayette; two of those players – Caleb Adams and right-hander Austin Robichaux – have been taken by the Angels of Anaheim, both in 2014. Adams, a 10th round pick, had a decent debut in the Pioneer league, hitting .252/.325/.414 with nine doubles, a pair of triples, and seven homeruns while swiping seven bags in eight attempts. The front office bumped the 5-foot-10, 185-pound outfielder up to the Midwest League to begin last season, and the results were…well…promising; he slugged .302/.398/.426 in 65 games. Adams got the call up to Inland Empire in late June, and he, once again, handled himself well, slugging .293/.380/.453. Overall, Adams hit .298/.390/.438 with 21 doubles, eight triples, seven homeruns, and 10 stolen bases.

**Projection**: An interesting, intriguing low level prospect in a system bereft of a lot of impact talent. Adams is sporting a career .283/.369/.430 triple-slash line through his first 177 minor league games. He's been on the end of some favorable BABIPs – he posted a .343 during his debut and followed that up with a .436 showing in Low Class A and a .415 mark with the 66ers – and his strikeout rates are bordering on red flag territory. He could develop into a similar player as Tigers outfielder Tyler Collins, a quasi-serviceable bench bat with some fourth outfielder upside.

**Ceiling:** 1.0-win player
**Risk:** Moderate
**MLB ETA:** 2018

## 19. Hunter Green, LHP

**MiLB Rank:** N/A
**Position Rank:** N/A

| | | | | | |
|---|---|---|---|---|---|
| **Born:** 07/12/95 | **Age:** 20 | **Bats:** L | **Top CALs:** Shane Hill, Nash Walters, | |
| **Height:** 6-4 | **Weight:** 175 | **Throws:** L | Luis Guerrero, Andres Santiago, Curtis Petersen | |

| YEAR | Age | Level | IP | W | L | ERA | FIP | K/9 | BB/9 | K% | BB% | HR/9 | LOB% |
|---|---|---|---|---|---|---|---|---|---|---|---|---|---|
| 2013 | 17 | R | 16.7 | 0 | 1 | 4.32 | 5.75 | 5.94 | 8.64 | 13.6% | 19.8% | 0.00 | 57.6% |

**Background:** As if the franchise didn't have enough trouble drafting, developing, and/or not dealing away their young talent for aging veterans, Green, the club's second round pick in 2013, has not thrown a meaningful pitch since August 20th, 2013. Since then he's missed the entire 2014 season with a back injury and failed to appear in a game last year as he dealt with a stress fracture in his left elbow.

**Projection**: So heading into year three of his development and the big 6-foot-4, 175-pound southpaw out of Warren East High School has thrown just 16.2 innings. In the Arizona Summer League. At this point, one has to think that the Angels' brass just want to see Green on the mound regardless of his performance. And I hope it happens in 2016.

**Ceiling:** 1.0- to 1.5-win player
**Risk:** Moderate to High
**MLB ETA:** 2018

## 20. Jake Jewell, RHP

**MiLB Rank:** N/A
**Position Rank:** N/A

| | | | | | |
|---|---|---|---|---|---|
| **Born:** 05/16/93 | **Age:** 23 | **Bats:** R | **Top CALs:** Luid Perdomo, Erick Abreu, | |
| **Height:** 6-3 | **Weight:** 200 | **Throws:** R | Polin Trinidad, Brad Furnish, Harold Mozingo | |

| YEAR | Age | Level | IP | W | L | ERA | FIP | K/9 | BB/9 | K% | BB% | HR/9 | LOB% |
|---|---|---|---|---|---|---|---|---|---|---|---|---|---|
| 2014 | 21 | R | 12.3 | 0 | 2 | 8.76 | 5.09 | 6.57 | 2.92 | 14.3% | 6.4% | 0.73 | 60.2% |
| 2014 | 21 | R | 30.3 | 1 | 0 | 1.48 | 3.60 | 7.71 | 3.56 | 21.3% | 9.8% | 0.00 | 83.3% |
| 2015 | 22 | A | 111.3 | 6 | 8 | 4.77 | 3.51 | 8.89 | 2.51 | 23.1% | 6.5% | 0.65 | 60.7% |

**Background:** A fifth round pick two years ago. And I don't mean the University of Miami or even Miami University. Nope, Miami, Oklahoma – home to Northeast Oklahoma A&M College. Who the hell knew there was a Miami in Oklahoma? Anyway, Jewell had a nice showing with Burlington last season, posting a 110-to-31 K-to-BB ratio in 111.1 IP.

**Projection**: Similar to Kyle McGowin, minus the fast-tracked development schedule. Jewell isn't going to be long for the rotation, despite some borderline dominant peripherals last season. But once you factor in age – he was 22-years-old – and the fact that he has some collegiate experience, the overall picture doesn't look as rosy. He could be a middle relief/potential late-inning arm if all else fails.

**Ceiling:** 1.0- to 1.5-win player
**Risk:** Low to Moderate
**MLB ETA:** 2016

## 21. Kody Eaves, 2B

**MiLB Rank: N/A**
**Position        Rank:**

**N/A**

| Born: 07/08/93 | Age: 22 | Bats: L | Top CALs: Luis Mateo, Frank Martinez, |
|---|---|---|---|
| Height: 6-0 | Weight: 175 | Throws: R | Karexon Sanchez, Christopher Mcfarland, Chris Bostick |

| Season | Age | LVL | PA | 2B | 3B | HR | AVG | OBP | SLG | ISO | BB% | K% | wRC+ |
|---|---|---|---|---|---|---|---|---|---|---|---|---|---|
| 2013 | 19 | R | 292 | 14 | 6 | 1 | 0.277 | 0.326 | 0.386 | 0.110 | 6.8% | 13.7% | 85 |
| 2014 | 20 | A | 587 | 37 | 7 | 10 | 0.268 | 0.308 | 0.415 | 0.148 | 4.9% | 24.2% | 104 |
| 2015 | 21 | A+ | 575 | 17 | 11 | 11 | 0.248 | 0.308 | 0.387 | 0.138 | 7.8% | 26.1% | 88 |

**Background:** A bit of an over-slot bonus as a prep bat in the 16th round, Eaves, who signed a six-figure bonus as the 507th overall pick in 2012, has been methodically moving through the low levels of the minor leagues: He spent his debut in the ASL, followed that up with a year in the Pioneer League, then a quick stop in Low Class A before last year's stop with Inland Empire.

**Projection**: A speedy second baseman with a decent overall toolkit, Eaves has been a below-average offensive performer throughout his four-year professional career, only topping a 100 wRC+ two years ago with Burlington. He sports a slightly below-average eye at the plate, decent power, and the ability to swipe 30 bags in a 162-game season. Unfortunately for him, however, is that it doesn't add up to anything more than a minor league lifer.

**Ceiling:** 1.0-win player
**Risk:** Moderate to High
**MLB ETA:** 2018

## 22. Austin Robichaux, RHP

**MiLB Rank: N/A**
**Position Rank: N/A**

| Born: 11/23/92 | Age: 23 | Bats: R | Top CALs: Mario Santiago, Alex McRae, |
|---|---|---|---|
| Height: 6-5 | Weight: 170 | Throws: R | Jimmy Ballinger, Starlin Gerson, Matthew Borens |

| YEAR | Age | Level | IP | W | L | ERA | FIP | K/9 | BB/9 | K% | BB% | HR/9 | LOB% |
|---|---|---|---|---|---|---|---|---|---|---|---|---|---|
| 2014 | 21 | R | 40.3 | 2 | 3 | 4.91 | 5.05 | 6.02 | 1.79 | 16.4% | 4.9% | 1.12 | 61.7% |
| 2015 | 22 | A | 142.0 | 9 | 8 | 3.74 | 4.40 | 5.83 | 3.17 | 15.4% | 8.4% | 0.76 | 70.9% |

**Background:** A three-year starter at the University of Louisiana at Lafayette under his father – and head coach – Tony Robichaux, the Angels grabbed Austin in the 18th round two years ago after a solid three-year run in the Ragin Cajuns' rotation. Robichaux, a 6-foot-5 170-pound right-hander, hurled 40.1 innings in the Pioneer League during his debut, punching out 27, walking just eight, and posting an unsightly 5.05 FIP. Robichaux got promoted to the Midwest League last season and he had an OK, not good, not great showing with Burlington. He averaged 5.8 strikeouts and 3.2 walks per nine innings.

**Projection**: The long ball has been a problem for Robichaux since entering pro ball a couple years ago. He surrendered nearly as many dingers (five) as walks issued (eight) during his debut, and he promptly followed that up with 12 more homeruns with his time in the Low Class A last season. His strikeout rates have been disappointing and his control took a noticeably large step backwards as well. He could be a serviceable middle relief arm, probably nothing more.

**Ceiling:** 0.5- to 1.0-win player
**Risk:** Moderate
**MLB ETA:** 2018

## 23. Julio Garcia, SS

**MiLB Rank: N/A**

**Position Rank: N/A**

| Born: 07/31/97 | Age: 18 | Bats: R | Top CALs: Cristian Santana, Andury Acevado, |
| Height: 6-0 | Weight: 175 | Throws: R | Ronaldo Lopez, Jose Rodriguez, Angel Rojas |

| Season | Age | LVL | PA | 2B | 3B | HR | AVG | OBP | SLG | ISO | BB% | K% | wRC+ |
|--------|-----|-----|-----|----|----|----|-------|-------|-------|-------|------|-------|------|
| 2015 | 17 | R | 127 | 1 | 2 | 0 | 0.214 | 0.242 | 0.256 | 0.043 | 3.1% | 22.0% | 45 |
| 2015 | 17 | R | 61 | 2 | 0 | 0 | 0.224 | 0.250 | 0.259 | 0.034 | 3.3% | 26.2% | 52 |

**Background**: Signed out of the Dominican Republic for $565,000 two years ago, Garcia has done very little to live up to the lofty expectations that comes with a big signing bonus. The 6-foot, 175-pound shortstop owns a career .202/.241/.235 triple-slash line through his first 64 games spanning parts of two seasons in the Dominican Summer League and the Arizona Summer League.

**Projection**: Typically, I'd throw a younger prospect with a bigger bonus and craptastic production as part of the *Bird Doggin' It* section, but...it's the Angels. And their system is disappointing, at best. Garcia hasn't walked, hit, or hit for power during his two-years in the minors. And even though he's just entering his age-18 season, it's hard to imagine him resurrecting his career back towards his pre-signing bonus hype.

**Ceiling:** 1.0-win player
**Risk:** High
**MLB ETA:** 2018

## 24. Jonah Wesely, LHP

**MiLB Rank: N/A**

**Position Rank: N/A**

| Born: 12/08/94 | Age: 21 | Bats: L | Top CALs: Jonathan Escudero, Michael Torrealba |
| Height: 6-1 | Weight: 215 | Throws: L | Blake King, Alejandro Chacin, Thomas Pannone |

| YEAR | Age | Level | IP | W | L | ERA | FIP | K/9 | BB/9 | K% | BB% | HR/9 | LOB% |
|------|-----|-------|------|---|---|------|------|-------|------|-------|-------|------|-------|
| 2013 | 18 | R | 1.0 | 0 | 0 | 0.00 | 7.01 | 0.00 | 9.00 | 0.0% | 20.0% | 0.00 | 100.0% |
| 2014 | 19 | R | 35.3 | 0 | 0 | 4.08 | 4.77 | 9.68 | 4.58 | 24.7% | 11.7% | 0.76 | 67.7% |
| 2015 | 20 | A | 30.3 | 4 | 2 | 2.97 | 2.57 | 12.76 | 3.86 | 33.1% | 10.0% | 0.30 | 61.2% |

**Background:** Hailing from Tracy High School where he became just the third prospect selected in the school's history, Wesely was in the midst of a breakout season in 2015, averaging nearly 13 punch outs and a sub-4.0 walk rate before succumbing to Tommy John surgery. The stocky lefty owns a career 81-to-32 strikeout-to-walk ratio throughout his career.

**Projection**: A slightly lesser – and currently a less healthy – version of another lefty in the system, Eduardo Paredes, Wesely might have earned a late-season promotion to the California League if not for the surgery. Assuming he bounces back fully, he could be a solid middle relief arm.

**Ceiling:** 0.5- to 1. 0-win player
**Risk:** Moderate to High
**MLB ETA:** 2018

## 25. Keynan Middleton, RHP

**MiLB Rank: N/A**

**Position Rank: N/A**

| Born: 09/12/93 | Age: 22 | Bats: R | Top CALs: Miguel Socolovich, Hudson Boyd, |
| Height: 6-2 | Weight: 185 | Throws: R | Pedro Lambertus, Starlyn Suriel, Dovydas Neverauskas |

| YEAR | Age | Level | IP | W | L | ERA | FIP | K/9 | BB/9 | K% | BB% | HR/9 | LOB% |
|------|-----|-------|-------|---|----|------|------|------|------|-------|-------|------|-------|
| 2013 | 19 | R | 23.3 | 1 | 3 | 8.10 | 7.22 | 5.79 | 5.79 | 13.8% | 13.8% | 1.54 | 54.5% |
| 2013 | 19 | R | 5.7 | 0 | 0 | 6.35 | 3.83 | 7.94 | 4.76 | 20.8% | 12.5% | 0.00 | 33.3% |
| 2014 | 20 | R | 67.0 | 5 | 4 | 6.45 | 5.81 | 7.12 | 4.03 | 17.6% | 9.9% | 1.21 | 50.9% |
| 2015 | 21 | A | 125.7 | 6 | 11 | 5.30 | 4.74 | 6.30 | 3.37 | 16.0% | 8.6% | 1.07 | 67.8% |

**Background:** A third round pick out of Lane Community College in 2013, Middleton struggled in his full-season debut last year, averaging just 6.3 strikeouts and 3.4 walks per nine innings to go along with an unsightly 4.74 FIP.

**Projection**: There's really not too much to add here. As a third round community college pick, Middleton's been a disappointment over the past three seasons, though his control has been trending in the right direction. He's probably headed to a relief role. And quick.

**Ceiling:** 0.5-win player
**Risk:** Moderate
**MLB ETA:** 2018

### *Barely Missed:*

- **Jose Briceno, C/1B** –Acquired from the Braves as part of the Andrelton Simmons deal, Briceno had a massively disappointing season in High Class A last year, his first and only showing in Atlanta's system. Coming off of a .283/.336/.476 campaign in Low Class A two years ago, Briceno batted just .183/.215/.267. There's some power potential in his bat.

- **Andrew Daniel, 2B/3B** – An 11th round pick out of the University of San Diego, Daniel hit a combined .264/.329/.422 with a whopping 34 doubles, six triples, nine homeruns, and 11 stolen bases (in 18 attempts). But his work with Inland Empire, .265/.333/.408, was basically league average production.

- **Brendon Sanger, OF** – Plucked out of Florida Atlantic University in the fourth round last June, Sanger torched the Pioneer League during his debut, hitting .300/.420/.456 with 20 doubles, one triple, and four homeruns.

## *Bird Doggin' It – Additional Prospects to Keep an Eye in 2016*

| Player | Age | POS | Notes |
|---|---|---|---|
| Alex Abbott | 21 | LF/RF | Showed some promising power potential in the Pioneer League last season, slugging 14 doubles, a pair of triples, and eight homeruns. Below-average hit tool. |
| Austin Adams | 25 | RHP | Fanned an impressive 71 in just 55.0 innings between High Class A, Class AA, and Class AAA. Of course, he happened to walk 47 too. |
| Justin Anderson | 23 | RHP | Former 14th round pick two years ago, Anderson posted a 3.41 ERA and a 112-to-51 strikeout-to-walk ratio. |
| Geoff Broussard | 25 | RHP | Averaged more than 14 punch outs per nine innings last season in High Class A. Too old for the level, but that's a *ton* of strikeouts. |
| David Fletcher | 22 | SS | A sixth round pick out of Loyola Marymount University last June, Fletcher tore through the Pioneer League (.331/.391/.456) and held his own in a 32-game stint with Burlington (.283/.358/.358). |
| Chad Hinshaw | 25 | OF | Batted a respectable .289/.391/.356 with 17 doubles and one homerun in 71 games in Class AA. |
| Edward Santos | 26 | RHP | Averaged 12.03 strikeouts per nine innings in Class AA last season, though the then-25-year-old's control took a noticeable step backward. |
| Jose Suarez | 18 | LHP | Small-ish left-hander spent time between the Dominican and Arizona Summer Leagues last season, posting a 46-to-12 strikeout-to-walk ratio in 72.2 innings. |
| Kyle Survance | 22 | CF | Eighth rounder out of the University of Houston last June, Survance mashed the Pioneer League pitching to the tune of .363/.434/.484. Let's see how he handles full season ball. |

**State of the Farm System:** The rich keep getting…better? As if sporting the highest payroll entering the 2016 season wasn't enough, the Dodgers also own the top farm system in the game with elite level, blue-chip caliber talent sprinkled throughout.

Southpaw wunderkind Julio Urias has more upside as any minor league hurler in baseball, offering up dominating performance after dominating performance against much older competition.

Shortstop Corey Seager is being handed the club's everyday gig after blowing through the minor leagues since his selection in the 2012 first round.

And Jose De Leon was simply an out-of-nowhere revelation in 2015 as he posted an impeccable 163-to-37 strikeout-to-walk ratio in just 114.1 innings between Rancho Cucamonga and Tulsa – not bad work for a former 24th round pick.

But what makes the franchise so strong is their ability to turn a couple fringy everyday big leaguers – Jose Peraza and Scott Schebler – and turn them into another high ceiling, hard-throwing right-hander in Frankie Montas, a speedy second baseman who is better suited as a bench option (Micah Johnson), and a wild card in toolsy outfielder Trayce Thompson.

The farm system is so deep that the club's fifth, sixth, seventh, and maybe even their eighth best prospects – Alex Verdugo, Yadier Alvarez, Grant Holmes, and Cody Bellinger – would easily rank among many teams' top two or three.

If the Kansas City Royals were talked about as having the Game's Best Farm System a couple years back, then this one isn't that far behind. It's absolutely ridiculous to think that there could be as many as 11 different players in their minor league clubs that could develop into at least league average regulars. It's absurd abundance of riches.

| Rank | Name | POS |
|------|------|-----|
| 1 | Julio Urias | LHP |
| 2 | Corey Seager | SS |
| 3 | Jose De Leon | RHP |
| 4 | Frankie Montas | RHP |
| 5 | Alex Verdugo | CF |
| 6 | Yadier Alvarez | RHP |
| 7 | Grant Holmes | RHP |
| 8 | Cody Bellinger | 1B |
| 9 | Austin Barnes | C/2B |
| 10 | Walker Buehler | RHP |
| 11 | Willie Calhoun | 2B |
| 12 | Starling Heredia | OF |
| 13 | Micah Johnson | 2B |
| 14 | Zach Lee | RHP |
| 15 | Johan Mieses | OF |
| 16 | Chris Anderson | RHP |
| 17 | Chase Dejong | RHP |
| 18 | Jacob Rhame | RHP |
| 19 | Trayce Thompson | CF/RF |
| 20 | Ross Stripling | RHP |
| 21 | Jharel Cotton | RHP |
| 22 | Mitch Hansen | OF |
| 23 | Jordan Paroubeck | LF/RF |
| 24 | Josh Sborz | RHP |
| 25 | Scott Barlow | RHP |

**Review of the 2015 Draft:** The Dodgers' top pick, former Vanderbilt stud Walker Buehler immediately underwent elbow surgery and they failed to sign their other first round selection, Kyle Funkhouser. Fine. It happens all the time, on both accounts. But they absolutely struck gold in the fourth round by drafting JuCo stud second baseman Willie Calhoun.

The 5-foot-9, 177-pound lefty-swinging Calhoun ripped through three levels en route to tallying a .316/.390/.519 triple-slash line during his debut. He could very easily be the best pick in the Dodgers' entire draft class.

Second rounder Mitch Hansen looked underwhelming as he struggled to hit his weight (and much of anything else). Former Virginia hurler Josh Sborz could move quickly as a solid relief option, but will likely be given some time to develop as a starter.

# 1. Julio Urias, LHP

| Born: 08/12/96 | Age: 19 | Bats: L | Top CALs: Tyler Skaggs, Julio Teheran, |
| Height: 6-2 | Weight: 205 | Throws: L | Noah Syndergaard, Lucas Giolito, Arodys Vizcaino |

| YEAR | Age | Level | IP | W | L | ERA | FIP | K/9 | BB/9 | K% | BB% | HR/9 | LOB% |
|---|---|---|---|---|---|---|---|---|---|---|---|---|---|
| 2013 | 16 | A | 54.3 | 2 | 0 | 2.48 | 3.01 | 11.10 | 2.65 | 31.8% | 7.6% | 0.83 | 85.2% |
| 2014 | 17 | A+ | 87.7 | 2 | 2 | 2.36 | 3.36 | 11.19 | 3.80 | 30.6% | 10.4% | 0.41 | 80.3% |
| 2015 | 18 | R | 3.0 | 0 | 0 | 0.00 | 1.48 | 15.00 | 3.00 | 45.5% | 9.1% | 0.00 | 100.0% |
| 2015 | 18 | A+ | 4.7 | 0 | 0 | 7.71 | 4.85 | 7.71 | 0.00 | 19.1% | 0.0% | 1.93 | 53.6% |
| 2015 | 18 | AA | 68.3 | 3 | 4 | 2.77 | 2.59 | 9.75 | 1.98 | 27.6% | 5.6% | 0.53 | 71.0% |
| 2015 | 18 | AAA | 4.3 | 0 | 1 | 18.69 | 5.45 | 10.38 | 12.46 | 16.7% | 20.0% | 0.00 | 47.1% |

**Background:** Question: Is Julio Urias the greatest pitching prospect in baseball since the institution of the draft in 1965? Move beyond the initial absurdity of it for a moment and just think about it for a few minutes. Is Julio Urias, the teenage wunderkind twirling gems in the Dodgers' system, the greatest pitching prospect in baseball since the institution of the draft in 1965? It was worth repeating, I think. For this purpose, as sort of a quick and easy study, let's take a brief snapshot of top pitching prospects since 1965 and their age-18 seasons:

| Player | Age | Level(s) | IP | K | BB | K/9 | BB/9 | K/BB |
|---|---|---|---|---|---|---|---|---|
| Julio Urias | 18 | A+/AA/AAA | 80.1 | 88 | 22 | 9.9 | 2.5 | 4.0 |
| Felix Hernandez | 18 | A+/AA | 149.1 | 172 | 47 | 10.4 | 2.8 | 3.7 |
| Vida Blue | 18 | A | 152.0 | 231 | 80 | 13.7 | 4.7 | 2.9 |
| Jose Rijo | 18 | A/AA | 200.2 | 184 | 65 | 8.3 | 2.9 | 2.9 |
| Dwight Gooden | 18 | A | 191.0 | 300 | 112 | 14.1 | 5.3 | 2.7 |

A few things to note here: Obviously, limiting the study to age-18 seasons eliminates any collegiate players (Stephen Strasburg, Mark Prior, etc...) and because the sample size is usually under 30 innings, a lot of prep arms too. But there also serves a point in highlighting just how rare a prospect like Urias comes along.

OK, now onto the study. First, how absolutely ridiculous was it to have teenage arms, barely beyond high school, hurl upwards of 200 innings? Secondly, Urias' numbers – while admittedly in a much small sample, thanks to increased injury awareness – compare decently with each of the four listed prospects. He may not have the pure power that Blue or Gooden had (judging by K-rate), but he's exhibited superior control/command as evidenced by his walk rate and strikeout-to-walk ratio. Does that make the young Dodgers lefty the greatest? No, not by itself. But it does certainly show he at least belongs in the conversation.

Los Angeles wisely capped the Mexican-born hurler's innings last year, allowing Urias to toss a smidgeon over 80 frames – most of which were spent in the Texas League, an environment where the average hitter *was six years his senior*. Urias would finish his Class AA campaign with a 2.59 FIP while fanning 27.6% of the batters he faced.

**Projection:** The best pitching prospect in baseball. Bar none. Urias has an uncanny ability to control the zone like few other teenage pitchers in the history of the game. He mixes an above-average ability to miss bats while limiting free passes. And like I noted in last year's book, Urias is next in line to the throne of southpaw Dodger greats, following in the footsteps of Sandy Koufax, Fernando Valenzuela, and Clayton Kershaw.

**Ceiling:** 6.5-win player
**Risk:** Moderate
**MLB ETA:** 2016

## 2. Corey Seager, SS

MiLB Rank: #6
Position Rank: #1

| Born: 04/27/94 | Age: 22 | Bats: L | Top CALs: Reid Brignac, Dilson Herrera, Xander Bogaerts, Nick Franklin, Arismendy Alcantara |
| Height: 6-4 | Weight: 215 | Throws: R | |

| Season | Age | LVL | PA | 2B | 3B | HR | AVG | OBP | SLG | ISO | BB% | K% | wRC+ |
|---|---|---|---|---|---|---|---|---|---|---|---|---|---|
| 2013 | 19 | A | 312 | 18 | 3 | 12 | 0.309 | 0.389 | 0.529 | 0.221 | 10.9% | 18.6% | 155 |
| 2013 | 19 | A+ | 114 | 2 | 1 | 4 | 0.160 | 0.246 | 0.320 | 0.160 | 10.5% | 27.2% | 46 |
| 2014 | 20 | A+ | 365 | 34 | 2 | 18 | 0.352 | 0.411 | 0.633 | 0.281 | 8.2% | 20.8% | 167 |
| 2014 | 20 | AA | 161 | 16 | 3 | 2 | 0.345 | 0.381 | 0.534 | 0.189 | 6.2% | 24.2% | 154 |
| 2015 | 21 | AA | 86 | 7 | 1 | 5 | 0.375 | 0.407 | 0.675 | 0.300 | 5.8% | 12.8% | 196 |
| 2015 | 21 | AAA | 464 | 30 | 2 | 13 | 0.278 | 0.332 | 0.451 | 0.173 | 6.9% | 14.0% | 106 |
| 2015 | 21 | MLB | 113 | 8 | 1 | 4 | 0.337 | 0.425 | 0.561 | 0.224 | 12.4% | 16.8% | 175 |

**Background:** The 2012 first round has the potential to go down in history as baseball's version of the 1983 NFL draft, which was famous for having seven quarterbacks taken in the first round, including Hall of Famers John Elway, Jim Kelly, and Dan Marino as well as solid starter Ken O'Brien. The 2012 MLB draft churned out three perennial All-Star caliber shortstops within the first 18 picks: Carlos Correa (1st overall), Addison Russell (11th overall), and Corey Seager (18th overall), each of whom, coincidentally enough, all made their big league debuts last season. Seager began the year by torching the Texas League arms to the tune of .375/.407/.675 with 13 extra-base hits in 20 games. The front office promoted the lefty-swinging infielder up to the PCL on the first of May and the results were solid: he batted .278/.332/.451 with a not-quite-impressive 106 wRC+. He would eventually get the call up to LA in early September, where his hot hitting (.337/.425/.561) allowed him to wrestle the starter's role from future Hall of Famer Jimmy Rollins.

**Projection:** In last year's book I wrote:

*"Seager is the complete offensive package – he hits for average and power, has a strong approach at the plate which leads to solid walk and contact rates, runs well, shows no discernible platoon split. Defensively speaking, well, did I mention how promising the bat is? He has a chance to be a star, whether it's at shortstop or third base."*

Ditto; though his defense did take a bit of a step forward last season. He's going to be a superior player than his older brother Kyle, who garnered a nine-figure deal from the Mariners. On the flip, though, CAL isn't overly convinced, linking him to just one above-average regular, Xander Bogaerts.

**Ceiling:** 4.0-win player
**Risk:** Low to Moderate
**MLB ETA:** Debuted in 2015

## 3. Jose De Leon, RHP

MiLB Rank: #13
Position Rank: #8

| Born: 08/07/92 | Age: 23 | Bats: R | Top CALs: Jonathan Ortiz, Addison Reed, Clay Buchholz, Casey Mulligan, Will Harris |
| Height: 6-2 | Weight: 185 | Throws: R | |

| YEAR | Age | Level | IP | W | L | ERA | FIP | K/9 | BB/9 | K% | BB% | HR/9 | LOB% |
|---|---|---|---|---|---|---|---|---|---|---|---|---|---|
| 2013 | 20 | R | 19.3 | 1 | 2 | 12.10 | 6.83 | 8.38 | 1.40 | 17.8% | 3.0% | 2.33 | 36.1% |
| 2013 | 20 | R | 33.7 | 2 | 3 | 4.01 | 4.27 | 9.36 | 4.81 | 23.5% | 12.1% | 0.27 | 68.4% |
| 2014 | 21 | R | 54.3 | 5 | 0 | 2.65 | 2.95 | 12.75 | 3.15 | 33.8% | 8.3% | 0.33 | 65.4% |
| 2014 | 21 | A | 22.7 | 2 | 0 | 1.19 | 0.62 | 16.68 | 0.79 | 48.8% | 2.3% | 0.40 | 82.2% |
| 2015 | 22 | A+ | 37.7 | 4 | 1 | 1.67 | 2.00 | 13.86 | 1.91 | 39.2% | 5.4% | 0.24 | 79.2% |
| 2015 | 22 | AA | 76.7 | 2 | 6 | 3.64 | 3.64 | 12.33 | 3.40 | 33.1% | 9.2% | 1.29 | 74.4% |

**Background:** As if unearthing Julio Urias on the sandlots of Mexico weren't fortunate enough, the Dodgers polished this former 24th round draft pick into a legitimate prospect gem – within two years. The 724th player taken in the 2013 draft, De Leon, who was grabbed out of Southern University and A&M College, had a rather inauspicious debut as a 20-year-old splitting his time between the Pioneer and Appalachian Leagues, posting a nearly 7.00 ERA courtesy of some poor luck (.341 BABIP, 2.33 HR/9). But the 6-foot-2 right-hander did finish the year with a stellar 53-to-21 strikeout-to-walk rate. De Leon found himself back in the Pioneer League to begin the following season, 2014, but dispatched the younger competition with relative ease: he fanned 77 and walked 19 in 54.1 innings. It was enough to convince the organization that he was finally ready for full season ball. He would make four successful starts in the Midwest League to cap off his year.

Those four starts, believe it or not, were enough to earn a shot at High Class A coming straight out of Spring Training in 2015. And De Leon didn't look back. He was as dominant as any pitcher in baseball for seven starts with Rancho Cucamonga (37.2 IP, 58 K, and 8 BB) and continued to buzz-saw the Texas League competition (76.2 IP, 105 K, 29 BB).

**Projection:** I listed the Puerto Rican-born hurler in the Bird Doggin' Section last season, writing: "I'll start believing once he spends more than 22.2 innings above the rookie leagues." Well, consider me converted. De Leon has transformed from a late-round gamble into a legitimate front-of-the-rotation caliber arm, who, laughably, would be the system's top hurler if it weren't for Urias. Strikeouts come in gobs. The walks barely materialize.

**Ceiling:** 4.0-win player
**Risk:** Moderate
**MLB ETA:** 2016

## 4. Frankie Montas, RHP

**MiLB Rank: #37**
**Position Rank: #17**

| Born: 03/21/93 | Age: 23 | Bats: R | Top CALs: Randall Delgado, Luke Jackson, |
|---|---|---|---|
| Height: 6-2 | Weight: 185 | Throws: R | Michael Feliz, Jose Ortegano, Eduardo Rodriguez |

| YEAR | Age | Level | IP | W | L | ERA | FIP | K/9 | BB/9 | K% | BB% | HR/9 | LOB% |
|---|---|---|---|---|---|---|---|---|---|---|---|---|---|
| 2013 | 20 | A | 111.0 | 5 | 11 | 5.43 | 3.91 | 10.30 | 4.05 | 25.7% | 10.1% | 0.89 | 60.7% |
| 2014 | 21 | A+ | 62.0 | 4 | 0 | 1.60 | 2.90 | 8.13 | 2.03 | 23.1% | 5.8% | 0.29 | 77.3% |
| 2014 | 21 | AA | 5.0 | 0 | 0 | 0.00 | 3.39 | 1.80 | 1.80 | 5.9% | 5.9% | 0.00 | 50.0% |
| 2015 | 22 | AA | 112.0 | 5 | 5 | 2.97 | 3.04 | 8.68 | 3.86 | 23.2% | 10.3% | 0.24 | 66.5% |

**Background:** When it comes to the Dodgers' portion of the Todd Frazier deal involving the White Sox and Reds, it's a clear win for the analytically thinking front office. Los Angeles shipped out a couple fringy big league regulars in Jose Peraza and Scott Schebler and a career minor leaguer, Brandon Dixon, for Montas, easily the best prospect in the entire seven-player deal, Micah Johnson, and Trayce Thompson. For his part, Montas, a 6-foot-2, 195-pound right-hander out of the Dominican Republic, took his plus-fastball to Class AA last season, easily the minors' toughest challenge, and he passed with flying colors. In a career high 112.0 innings with the Birmingham Barons Montas tallied 108 punch outs, 48 walks, a 2.97 ERA, and a sparkling 3.04 FIP. For his career, he has fanned 24.0% and walked 10.0% of the total hitters he's faced en route to totaling a 3.86 ERA.

**Projection:** Another of the prospects I've hitched my analytical wagon to for the past couple of years, I ranked Montas as Chicago's #2 and #5 prospects the last two seasons. Here's what I wrote in my first book in 2014:

> "As with any young arm there's going to be a lot of injury risk associated with Montas, but the peripherals are too good to ignore. His control was far better during his 85+ innings with Boston (3.38 BB/9) than the 25+ innings with Chicago (6.31 BB/9). There's quite a bit of upside here."

And I followed that up with this in last year's book:

> "The knee injuries added some level of complexity to the analysis, but the gifted right-hander has now fanned over 24% of the batters he's faced in his young career. He's not on the level of some of the game's top pitching prospect, but Montas still looks like a good bet to develop into a #3-type arm."

A couple interesting tidbits:

- During his 15.0-inning stint with Chicago last season Montas' fastball averaged a shade over 96 mph. He complemented with a mid-80s slider, and a ridiculously hard, upper-80s changeup.
- Last season his strikeout percentage, 23.2%, ranked fourth among all qualified arms in the Southern League.
- His strikeout-to-walk percentage, 12.9%, finished as the fifth best mark in the league.
- Among all qualified arms in any Class AA level, his strikeout percentage was the sixth best; his strikeout-to-walk percentage ranked 15th.

Needless to say, he's an incredibly promising arm – and the Dodgers picked him up for what amounts to a song-and-dance. At the very worst, he's a late-inning relief arm. Here's hoping the Dodgers don't decide to relegate him to that role too soon.

**Ceiling:** 3.0-win player
**Risk:** Moderate
**MLB ETA:** Debuted in 2015

## 5. Alex Verdugo, CF

**MiLB Rank: #45**
**Position Rank: #13**

| Born: 05/15/96 | Age: 20 | Bats: L | Top CALs: Gerardo Parra, Jose Osuna, |
|---|---|---|---|
| Height: 6-0 | Weight: 205 | Throws: L | Gorkys Hernandez, Danry Vasquez, Teodoro Martinez |

| Season | Age | LVL | PA | 2B | 3B | HR | AVG | OBP | SLG | ISO | BB% | K% | wRC+ |
|---|---|---|---|---|---|---|---|---|---|---|---|---|---|
| 2014 | 18 | R | 196 | 14 | 3 | 3 | 0.347 | 0.423 | 0.518 | 0.171 | 10.2% | 7.1% | 165 |
| 2015 | 19 | A | 444 | 23 | 2 | 5 | 0.295 | 0.325 | 0.394 | 0.100 | 3.8% | 11.9% | 108 |
| 2015 | 19 | A+ | 96 | 9 | 2 | 4 | 0.385 | 0.406 | 0.659 | 0.275 | 4.2% | 12.5% | 183 |

**Background:** A second round pick two years ago, Verdugo had one of – if not *the* – top debuts of the 2014 draft class. Spending all but five of his 54 games in the Arizona Summer League, the young center fielder slugged .353/.421/.511 with 15 doubles, a trio of triples, and three homeruns while going a perfect 11-for-11 in stolen bases. His overall production topped the league average mark by more than 60%. So, needless to say, expectations were riding quite high entering his sophomore campaign. And after a bit of a lengthy adaption period, Verdugo – once again – caught fire. He opened the season hitting .213/.254/.274 across his first 40 games, but slugged .346/.370/.471 over his final 61 contests in the Midwest League. And he didn't slow down after getting a promotion to Rancho Cucamonga (.385/.406/.659).

**Projection**: For those counting at home, after the rough start Verdugo looked like a baby-faced Ted Williams at the plate, hitting .356/.380/.520 over his final 84 games. The power grades out merely average now, but has the potential to develop into 15-HR territory at the game's top level. Above-average hit tool, but his patience at the plate took a noticeable downturn, dropping nearly six percentage points from his first season. Gerardo Parra, his top CAL, seems like a reasonable comparison, but there's room to grow here.

**Ceiling:** 3.0-win player
**Risk:** Moderate
**MLB ETA:** 2017

## 6. Yadier Alvarez, RHP

**MiLB Rank: #59**
**Position Rank: N/A**

| Born: 11/14/93 | Age: 21 | Bats: B | Top CALs: N/A |
|---|---|---|---|
| Height: 5-11 | Weight: 175 | Throws: R | |

**Background:** The latest Cuban import to ink a big dollar deal. Alvarez, a 6-foot-2, 170-pound fire-balling right-hander, signed a contract with a reported bonus just north of $16 million – the second highest bonus ever given out to an international amateur free agent. The Dodgers eventually outbid the Phillies and Diamondbacks for the services of the promising young hurler.

**Projection**: Absolutely nothing to go off in terms of statistical data. But his signing created quite the buzz. We'll know more once he moves stateside.

**Ceiling:** Too Soon to Tell
**Risk:** N/A
**MLB ETA:** N/A

## 7. Grant Holmes, RHP

**MiLB Rank: #71**
**Position Rank: N/A**

| Born: 03/22/96 | Age: 21 | Bats: L | Top CALs: Michael Main, Lucas Giolito, |
|---|---|---|---|
| Height: 6-1 | Weight: 215 | Throws: R | Angel Reyes, Casey Mulligan, Will Harris |

| YEAR | Age | Level | IP | W | L | ERA | FIP | K/9 | BB/9 | K% | BB% | HR/9 | LOB% |
|---|---|---|---|---|---|---|---|---|---|---|---|---|---|
| 2014 | 18 | R | 18.3 | 1 | 1 | 4.91 | 3.16 | 12.27 | 2.95 | 32.1% | 7.7% | 0.49 | 65.0% |
| 2014 | 18 | R | 30.0 | 1 | 2 | 3.00 | 3.60 | 9.90 | 2.10 | 28.0% | 5.9% | 0.60 | 68.7% |
| 2015 | 19 | A | 103.3 | 6 | 4 | 3.14 | 3.48 | 10.19 | 4.70 | 26.6% | 12.3% | 0.52 | 71.6% |

**Background:** Received a pretty hefty over-slot bonus as the 22nd overall pick two years ago, Holmes, who inked a deal with the Dodgers for over $2.2 million, started paying dividends for the franchise almost immediately. The 6-foot-1 fire-balling right-hander breezed through both levels of rookie ball during his debut, totaling an impressive 58-to-13 strikeout-to-walk ratio in just over 48 innings of work. The front office pushed Holmes into the Midwest League last season where he...dominated. Pitching no more than six innings in any of his 24 starts, Holmes fanned at least five batters in 12 contests and allowed 1 or fewer runs in 13 times. He finished the year with 103.1 innings, 117 strikeouts, 54 walks, and a solid 3.48 FIP. Among all Low Class A starters with at least 100 innings last season Holmes' strikeout percentage, 26.6%, ranks second.

**Projection**: Control still has a ways to go – he walked over 12% of the batters he faced last season – but it should at least develop into a solid-average skill. For instance, he walked nine of his total 54 batters in two games – or just under 17% of his total. The strikeout rate is plenty promising and he's likely going to find his way into at least #3-type role in a big league starting rotation – barring injury, of course.

**Ceiling:** 3.0- to 3.5-win player
**Risk:** Moderate to High
**MLB ETA:** 2018

## 8. Cody Bellinger, 1B

**MiLB Rank: #106**
**Position Rank: #7**

| Born: 07/13/95 | Age: 20 | Bats: L | Top CALs: Kyle Blanks, Dylan Cozens, |
|---|---|---|---|
| Height: 6-4 | Weight: 180 | Throws: L | Joe Benson, Jason Smit, Juan Ortiz |

| Season | Age | LVL | PA | 2B | 3B | HR | AVG | OBP | SLG | ISO | BB% | K% | wRC+ |
|---|---|---|---|---|---|---|---|---|---|---|---|---|---|
| 2013 | 17 | R | 195 | 9 | 6 | 1 | 0.210 | 0.340 | 0.358 | 0.148 | 15.9% | 23.6% | 102 |
| 2014 | 18 | R | 212 | 13 | 6 | 3 | 0.328 | 0.368 | 0.503 | 0.174 | 6.6% | 16.5% | 120 |
| 2015 | 19 | A+ | 544 | 33 | 4 | 30 | 0.264 | 0.336 | 0.538 | 0.274 | 9.6% | 27.6% | 130 |

**Background:** Bellinger looked awfully raw – and overmatched – during his debut in the Arizona Summer League three years ago, cobbling together a paltry triple slash line (.210/.340/.358). But the incoming fourth round pick did have a fairly strong foundation to build upon: a solid eye at the plate (that was undoubtedly aided by the level of pitching), decent power, and he didn't swing-and-miss too often. Well, the disappointing debut eventually led to only a slight promotion: spending another year developing at the rookie level, this time the Pioneer League. Bellinger's numbers ticked up noticeably during his sophomore campaign: he slugged .328/.368/.503 with 13 doubles, six triples, and three homeruns. The production was good enough to earn him a trip to full season ball – except I would've never guessed that he would bypass the Midwest League and head straight to the California League. And then *dominate*. As a 19-year-old.

The left-handed thumper mashed at an impressive clip – .264/.336/.538 – while finishing tied for second in the league with 30 dingers. His overall production, per *Weighted Runs Created Plus*, topped the league average mark by 30%. And just for comparison's sake here's a brief list of 19-year-old qualified prospects to post a 130 wRC+ in the Cal League since 2006: Addison Russell and Domingo Santana. That's it, just two other players.

**Projection**: During my initial pre-pre-rank I fully expected to opine about how the 6-foot-4 first baseman was likely overhyped. But the more research I did, the more in-depth I delved into the numbers I came to a vastly different conclusion. Take for example the list of 19-year-olds at any High Class A league that have posted a walk rate above 9% and an ISO north of .200 since 2006: Domingo Santana, Xander Bogaerts, Addison Russell, and Bellinger, of course.

Granted, the California League tends to inflate offensive numbers, but Bellinger didn't just top a .200 ISO, he surpassed it by a whopping 74 points. The power is going to play in any league, at any level. The patience at the plate is more than serviceable. It will likely come down to Bellinger's ability to make consistent enough contact. But any 19-year-old that can slug 30 bombs in High Class A is a legitimate prospect. He could be a middle-of-the-lineup force, but there's risk here.

**Ceiling:** 3.0-win player
**Risk:** Moderate to High
**MLB ETA:** 2017

## 9. Austin Barnes, 2B/C

**MiLB Rank: #181**
**Position Rank: #8 (C), #6 (2B)**

| Born: 12/28/89 | Age: 26 | Bats: R | Top CALs: Charlie Cutler, John Jaso, |
|---|---|---|---|
| Height: 5-10 | Weight: 185 | Throws: R | Josmil Pinto, Robinosn Chirinos, Kris Watts |

| Season | Age | LVL | PA | 2B | 3B | HR | AVG | OBP | SLG | ISO | BB% | K% | wRC+ |
|---|---|---|---|---|---|---|---|---|---|---|---|---|---|
| 2013 | 23 | A+ | 417 | 15 | 1 | 4 | 0.260 | 0.367 | 0.343 | 0.083 | 12.5% | 14.1% | 110 |
| 2014 | 24 | A+ | 200 | 11 | 2 | 1 | 0.317 | 0.385 | 0.417 | 0.100 | 9.5% | 12.5% | 132 |
| 2014 | 24 | AA | 348 | 20 | 2 | 12 | 0.296 | 0.406 | 0.507 | 0.211 | 14.4% | 10.3% | 157 |
| 2015 | 25 | AAA | 335 | 17 | 2 | 9 | 0.315 | 0.389 | 0.479 | 0.164 | 10.4% | 10.7% | 133 |
| 2015 | 25 | MLB | 37 | 2 | 0 | 0 | 0.207 | 0.361 | 0.276 | 0.069 | 16.2% | 16.2% | 93 |

**Background:** Sort of a poor man's Craig Biggio, Barnes continued his best impression of the Hall of Famer in 2015 – though not to the extent he showcased two years ago. Last season marked the fifth consecutive time that the former ninth round pick appeared in at least one game behind the plate and another game at the keystone.

Keeping with the theme of consistency, 2015 also marked the third time out of his last four seasons that he posted an OPS of at least .869. Barnes, a career .300/.390/.439 minor league hitter, appeared in 80 games with Oklahoma City last season, slugging .315/.389/.479 with 17 doubles, two triples, nine homeruns, and 12 stolen bases (in just 14 attempts). He also bounced up to LA a couple times as well, where his overall numbers – .207/.361/.276 – look far less impressive, but he still managed to finish his MLB debut with a solid 93 wRC+ courtesy of a walk rate just north of 16%.

**Projection**:  An incredibly savvy pickup as part of the Dee Gordon deal with the Marlins last offseason. In last year's book I wrote:

> *"A potential interesting bench option for the Dodgers. Barnes could act as both a backup infielder and catcher for the club, which in turn would allow them to carry an additional late-inning [bullpen] option. He's a career .298/.390/.431 hitter, htough he's never appeared in a game above Class AA. Solid power with a tremendous nose for first base."*

Let's just compare Barnes' MiLB production to Yan Gomes, whom I always find incredibly intriguing because he was *so* overlooked:

| Player | PA | AVG | OBP | SLG | ISO | BB% | K% |
|---|---|---|---|---|---|---|---|
| Austin Barnes | 2,190 | 0.300 | 0.390 | 0.439 | 0.139 | 11.51% | 11.37% |
| Yan Gomes | 1,390 | 0.288 | 0.347 | 0.483 | 0.195 | 7.55% | 21.85% |

Gomes, likely the greatest pickup in Cleveland GM Chris Antonetti's career, has the noticeable edge in power. But in every other offensive category the nod goes to Barnes. On the defensive side, both backstops tossed out 30% of potential thieves during their respective MiLB runs. CAL is also a rather large fan of Barnes as well, linking him to John Jaso (career 120 wRC+), Josmil Pinto (120 wRC+), and Robinson Chirinos (92 wRC+). Is Barnes the top catcher in the minors? Absolutely, unequivocally no. But can he hold down a starting position on a championship caliber squad. If I were a small market GM, I'd bet on it. Too bad he's in LA.

**Ceiling:** 1.5- to 2.0-win player
**Risk:** Low to Moderate
**MLB ETA:** Debuted in 2015

# 10. Walker Buehler, RHP

**MiLB Rank: #205**
**Position Rank: N/A**

| Born: 11/14/93 | Age: 21 | Bats: B | Top CALs: N/A |
|---|---|---|---|
| Height: 5-11 | Weight: 175 | Throws: R | |

**Background:** The club's first pick last June, 24th overall, provided quite the surprise following his selection from Pitcher U. (aka Vanderbilt): the Commodores' ace hurler immediately underwent the knife upon signing his $1.78 million deal. According to Dodgers GM Farhan Zaidi via the Los Angeles Times, Buehler exhibited some elbow discomfort prior to the draft, but the team felt comfortable spending their first pick on the injured right-hander. And, according to Zaidi, "[A] week before we drafted him, he pitched in the College World Series and hit 97 miles per hour." Despite dealing with the discomfort Buehler turned arguably his finest collegiate season: he tossed 88.1 IP, fanned 92, walked 30, and posted a 2.95 ERA as he helped propel the Commodores to the final round.

**Projection**: Prior to the draft I wrote:

> *"Physically speaking, he's a bit thin and could stand to add to his 6-foot-2 frame. Production-wise, though, Buehler's been incredibly consistent throughout his career, always showing a strong ability to limit free passes – he's averaged just 2.72 walk per nine innings over his last two seasons – with an equally impressive talent to miss bats in one of college baseball's better conferences."*

I continued:

> *And his early season elbow issues seem to be firmly in the past: he fanned a career best 13 hitters against Ole' Miss in early April and followed that up with nine more punch outs against South Carolina. There are always going to be questions about his durability, and those notwithstanding, Buehler looks like a potential fast-moving, back-of-the-rotation caliber arm."*

Well, apparently the elbow issues weren't firmly in the past. One does wonder how well he would have performed with a healthy wing. I previously slapped a Mid- to Late-First Round tag on him, as well as a 2.0-win ceiling. I'll stick with that until proven otherwise – injury or not.

**Ceiling:** 2.0-win player
**Risk:** Moderate to High
**MLB ETA:** 2018

## 11. Willie Calhoun, 2B

MiLB Rank: N/A
Position Rank: N/A

| Born: 11/04/94 | Age: 21 | Bats: L | Top CALs: Jose Altuve, Brett Wiley, |
| Height: 5-9 | Weight: 177 | Throws: R | Avery Romero, Jake Smolinski, Corban Joseph |

| Season | Age | LVL | PA | 2B | 3B | HR | AVG | OBP | SLG | ISO | BB% | K% | wRC+ |
|--------|-----|-----|-----|----|----|----|-------|-------|-------|-------|-------|-------|------|
| 2015 | 20 | R | 175 | 13 | 1 | 7 | 0.278 | 0.371 | 0.517 | 0.238 | 13.1% | 10.3% | 124 |
| 2015 | 20 | A | 66 | 3 | 0 | 1 | 0.393 | 0.439 | 0.492 | 0.098 | 7.6% | 10.6% | 174 |
| 2015 | 20 | A+ | 82 | 7 | 0 | 3 | 0.329 | 0.390 | 0.548 | 0.219 | 8.5% | 15.9% | 152 |

**Background:** Not So Big Willie Calhoun packs a big wallop. But first: a jog down memory lane. Hailing from Benicia HS, home to just four other previous draft picks, the Rays originally grabbed the tiny left-handed swinging second baseman in the 17th round. Calhoun would eventually decline and pack his bags for the University of Arizona. And despite a decent showing as a true freshman – he hit .247/.345/.301 – Calhoun once again packed his bags and transferred to tiny Yavapai College – where he would morph into some sort of Barry Bonds/Babe Ruth hybrid. In 63 games for the RoughRiders, Calhoun slugged a ridiculous .432/.520/.952with 23 doubles, one triple, and a laughably high 31 homeruns. OK. Fine. Beau Mills once put up massive numbers at small college too. But Calhoun didn't stop hitting after the organization grabbed him in the fourth round last season. Hell, he didn't stop in the Pioneer League (.278/.371/.517) or the Midwest League (.393/.439/.492) or even with Rancho Cucamonga (.329/.390/.548) in the California League.

**Projection**: Obviously, CALs already a big fan by comparing him to another pocket-sized power-packed second baseman: Jose Altuve. While the data on Calhoun is limited, it's also otherworldly as well. He finished the year with a combined .316/.390/.519 with a staggering 35 extra-base hits. Just to put that into perspective, Calhoun slugged one extra-base hit every other game.

Now is he this good. Nope. His BABIPs spiked once he moved out of the rookie league, so he's going to seemingly take a step back in 2016. But the patience is average, the power is going to be in the 15- to 20-HR territory if everything breaks the right way, and the hit tool could continue to push him up the ladder. He could be a solid big leaguer, but there's some risk until we see his BABIP normalize.

**Ceiling:** 2.0- to 2.5-win player
**Risk:** High
**MLB ETA:** 2017

## 12. Starling Heredia, OF

MiLB Rank: N/A
Position Rank: N/A

| Born: N/A | Age: N/A | Bats: N/A | Top CALs: N/A |
| Height: N/A | Weight: N/A | Throws: N/A | |

**Background:** When I was 16 years old I spent my free time doing a couple things: playing baseball, thinking about baseball, and working at the local Drug Mart. I hated that job, stocking shelves, pushing a broom, picking up the slack of fellow lazy teenagers – all for something like $6.75 an hour. All Heredia did was sign Heredia to a deal worth a cool $2.5 million.

**Projection:** The pudgy baby-faced outfielder didn't make his professional debut after signing, so there's no statistical data to go off of other than his massive bonus. But to put that bonus in some comparative terms, Brady Aiken, the former #1 overall pick in the 2014 draft, signed for nearly an identical amount as the 17th overall pick last June.

**Ceiling:** Too Soon to Tell
**Risk:** N/A
**MLB ETA:** N/A

## 13. Micah Johnson, 2B

**MiLB Rank: N/A**
**Position Rank: N/A**

| | | | |
|---|---|---|---|
| **Born:** 12/18/90 | **Age:** 25 | **Bats:** L | **Top CALs:** Kevin Russo, Cord Phelps, |
| **Height:** 6-0 | **Weight:** 210 | **Throws:** R | Chris Taylor, Chris Nelson, Jason Kipnis |

| Season | Age | LVL | PA | 2B | 3B | HR | AVG | OBP | SLG | ISO | BB% | K% | wRC+ |
|---|---|---|---|---|---|---|---|---|---|---|---|---|---|
| 2013 | 22 | A | 351 | 17 | 11 | 6 | 0.342 | 0.422 | 0.530 | 0.188 | 11.4% | 19.1% | 172 |
| 2013 | 22 | A+ | 228 | 7 | 4 | 1 | 0.275 | 0.309 | 0.360 | 0.085 | 4.4% | 11.8% | 86 |
| 2014 | 23 | AA | 170 | 9 | 1 | 3 | 0.329 | 0.414 | 0.466 | 0.137 | 12.4% | 15.9% | 151 |
| 2014 | 23 | AAA | 302 | 10 | 5 | 2 | 0.275 | 0.314 | 0.370 | 0.095 | 5.3% | 13.9% | 87 |
| 2015 | 24 | AAA | 351 | 17 | 3 | 8 | 0.315 | 0.375 | 0.466 | 0.151 | 9.1% | 17.9% | 145 |
| 2015 | 24 | MLB | 114 | 4 | 0 | 0 | 0.230 | 0.306 | 0.270 | 0.040 | 7.9% | 26.3% | 62 |

**Background:** Also part of the big seven-player, three-team mega-deal involving Cincinnati and the White Sox, Johnson had a bit of an up-and-down season last year. He opened 2015 as the Sox's everyday second baseman, though that lasted just 27 games before he got sent back down to Charlotte for more seasoning. The former ninth round pick out of Indiana University then caught fire for 66 games with the Knights, slugging .328/.383/.487 with 15 doubles, three triples, seven homeruns, and 26 stolen bases before missing a month of action. The lefty-swinging second baseman made it back with the Knights for a dozen more games before getting called back up to Chicago for a handful of games down the stretch.

**Projection**: When he's at his best he'll flash gap power, an above-average eye at the plate, and plus-speed. He's not really big league regular material, thanks in large part to his inability to consistently drive the ball with authority, but he'll bring some value to the Dodgers in 2015.

**Ceiling:** 1.0- to 1.5-win player
**Risk:** Low to Moderate
**MLB ETA:** Debuted in 2015

## 14. Zach Lee, RHP

**MiLB Rank: N/A**
**Position Rank: N/A**

| | | | |
|---|---|---|---|
| **Born:** 09/13/91 | **Age:** 24 | **Bats:** R | **Top CALs:** Jeanmar Gomez, Sean O'Sullivan, |
| **Height:** 6-4 | **Weight:** 210 | **Throws:** R | Adrian Sampson, Casey Coleman, Simon Castro |

| YEAR | Age | Level | IP | W | L | ERA | FIP | K/9 | BB/9 | K% | BB% | HR/9 | LOB% |
|---|---|---|---|---|---|---|---|---|---|---|---|---|---|
| 2013 | 21 | AA | 142.7 | 10 | 10 | 3.22 | 3.08 | 8.26 | 2.21 | 22.5% | 6.0% | 0.82 | 74.6% |
| 2014 | 22 | AAA | 150.7 | 7 | 13 | 5.38 | 5.16 | 5.79 | 3.23 | 14.5% | 8.1% | 1.08 | 62.3% |
| 2015 | 23 | AAA | 113.3 | 11 | 6 | 2.70 | 3.35 | 6.43 | 1.51 | 18.0% | 4.2% | 0.40 | 73.2% |

**Background:** The onetime Bonus Baby, who famously signed a lucrative $5.25 million deal as a late first rounder in 2010, rebounded from his worst statistical season to date. Coming on the heels of several career worsts (walk rate, strikeout rate, ERA, and FIP, to name a few) Lee – unsurprisingly – landed back in the PCL for the 2015 season, and all his numbers fell back in line with his expected/career norms – though some poor circulation issues led to a minor stint on the DL mid-season. Once destined for a potential front-of-rotation gig, Lee's numbers were solid, yet uninspiring last season: he tossed 123.1 innings between a couple rehab appearances and 19 Class AAA starts, striking out 85, walking 20, and posting a combined 2.63 ERA, the lowest mark of his five-year career. The Dodgers called Lee up for one (horrific) spot on July 25th, but he lasted just 4.2 innings while allowing seven earned runs.

**Projection**:  Lee sported an upper 80s/low 90s fastball, a cutter-like slider, curveball, and changeup during his brief debut. Never one to miss a whole lot of bats, Lee, who's averaged just 7.1 K/9 during his career, has been more about pitchability, not power. The hype he garnered as a prep signee has long passed and his ultimate development will likely be looked at as a bit of a disappointment, but there's certainly backend starting potential here.

**Ceiling:** 1.0- to 1.5-win player
**Risk:** Low to Moderate
**MLB ETA:** Debuted in 2015

## 15. Johan Mieses, OF

MiLB Rank: N/A
Position Rank: N/A

| Born: 07/13/95 | Age: 20 | Bats: R | Top CALs: Anthony Santander, Dustin Fowler, |
| Height: 6-2 | Weight: 185 | Throws: R | Jonathan Garcia, Randal Grichuk, Kyeong Kang |

| Season | Age | LVL | PA | 2B | 3B | HR | AVG | OBP | SLG | ISO | BB% | K% | wRC+ |
|--------|-----|-----|-----|-----|-----|-----|-------|-------|-------|-------|------|-------|------|
| 2014 | 18 | R | 230 | 11 | 8 | 5 | 0.298 | 0.370 | 0.502 | 0.205 | 9.1% | 17.4% | 146 |
| 2015 | 19 | A | 181 | 10 | 1 | 5 | 0.277 | 0.320 | 0.440 | 0.163 | 6.1% | 17.1% | 118 |
| 2015 | 19 | A+ | 214 | 18 | 1 | 6 | 0.245 | 0.299 | 0.439 | 0.194 | 6.1% | 26.6% | 98 |

**Background:** Already a bit of a man-child, the Dominican-born outfielder stands an impressive 6-foot-2 and a solid 185 pounds. Mieses began his pro career looking overmatched against the Dominican Summer League competition three years ago, hitting a paltry .222/.323/.259 in his brief 16-game stint. He would follow that up with a far better showing as an 18-year-old the next year, slugging .299/.371/.505 – enough production to not only earn him a trip to the stateside league but also allowing him to bypass the remaining rookie leagues. Mieses quickly passed that test – he hit .277/.320/.440 while topping the league average production by 18% - before earning another promotion; this time to High Class A. And after a slight adjustment period to the more advanced league, Mieses, who batted .210/.255/.340 in his first 25 games with Rancho Cucamonga, caught fire and slugged .281/.343/.542 over his remaining 26 contests.

**Projection**: A newcomer to the book this season, Mieses is an interesting prospect. He was too old to be taken seriously in the DSL two years ago, but handled the aggressive promotion schedule with relative ease last season. The hit tool is a bit underdeveloped at this point, but there's intriguing potential as a power/speed outfielder with 20/20 ability. His strikeout rate spiked as he moved into the Cal League, but he should shave a couple percentage points off that total this season, moving him closer to his previous career norms.

**Ceiling:** 1.5- to 2.0-win player
**Risk:** Moderate to High
**MLB ETA:** 2018

## 16. Chris Anderson, RHP

MiLB Rank: N/A
Position Rank: N/A

| Born: 07/29/92 | Age: 23 | Bats: R | Top CALs: Alexander Smit, Jake Thompson, |
| Height: 6-3 | Weight: 235 | Throws: R | Nick Barnese, T.J. House, Jordan Walden |

| YEAR | Age | Level | IP | W | L | ERA | FIP | K/9 | BB/9 | K% | BB% | HR/9 | LOB% |
|------|-----|-------|-------|---|---|-------|-------|------|-------|-------|-------|------|-------|
| 2013 | 20 | A | 46.0 | 3 | 0 | 1.96 | 2.79 | 9.78 | 4.70 | 26.9% | 12.9% | 0.00 | 73.7% |
| 2014 | 21 | A+ | 134.3 | 7 | 7 | 4.62 | 4.26 | 9.78 | 4.22 | 24.3% | 10.5% | 0.74 | 69.9% |
| 2015 | 22 | AA | 126.7 | 9 | 7 | 4.05 | 4.57 | 6.96 | 4.19 | 17.8% | 10.7% | 0.85 | 71.6% |
| 2015 | 22 | AAA | 6.3 | 0 | 3 | 18.47 | 11.34 | 2.84 | 12.79 | 4.9% | 22.0% | 2.84 | 39.6% |

**Background:** The 18th overall pick in the 2013 draft, Anderson, who became Jacksonville University's highest selected player in school history, put together his worst professional season to date. After a solid and sometimes dominating debut in the Midwest League – he posted a 50-to-24 strikeout-to-walk ratio in 46.0 innings – Anderson saw a modest improvement in his below-average control the following year in High Class A to suggest he might be able to carve out a role as a backend starter. But last year's work with Tulsa in the Texas League makes me believe otherwise: while he topped 130 innings for the second consecutive time, the 6-foot-3 right-hander walked a staggering 68 batters in 2015 – or just under 11.5% of the totals guys he faced. Only adding to his now cloudy future as a starter is the fact that his K-rate tumbled all the way down to sub-average 7.0 K/9.

**Projection**: "Something to wary of: this is largely the first time in his career that he's shown this particular combination of strikeouts and solid control/command," I stated in his pre-draft evaluation. Anderson was coming off of a season in which he averaged 2.32 BB/9, by far his best total since entering college.

Anderson was a bit young for the draft – he's only entering his age-23 season – so he'll likely get one, maybe two more seasons to figure it out in the rotation. The Dodgers' depth, both in terms of talent and money, will likely mean that he's headed for a rotation spot or a place on the team's trading block.

**Ceiling:** 1.5-win player
**Risk:** Moderate to High
**MLB ETA:** 2016

## 17. Chase De Jong, RHP

**MiLB Rank: N/A**
**Position Rank: N/A**

| Born: 12/29/93 | Age: 22 | Bats: L | Top CALs: Ryan Crowley, Jeffry Antigua, |
|---|---|---|---|
| Height: 6-4 | Weight: 205 | Throws: R | Zach Jemiola, Jack Spradlin, Jeanmar Gomez |

| YEAR | Age | Level | IP | W | L | ERA | FIP | K/9 | BB/9 | K% | BB% | HR/9 | LOB% |
|---|---|---|---|---|---|---|---|---|---|---|---|---|---|
| 2013 | 19 | R | 56.0 | 2 | 3 | 3.05 | 2.13 | 10.61 | 1.61 | 28.1% | 4.3% | 0.32 | 72.5% |
| 2014 | 20 | A | 97.0 | 1 | 6 | 4.82 | 4.48 | 6.77 | 2.04 | 17.2% | 5.2% | 1.11 | 66.3% |
| 2015 | 21 | A | 86.3 | 7 | 4 | 3.13 | 3.70 | 8.03 | 1.88 | 21.9% | 5.1% | 0.94 | 71.9% |
| 2015 | 21 | A+ | 50.0 | 4 | 3 | 3.96 | 4.22 | 9.36 | 2.70 | 24.6% | 7.1% | 1.08 | 64.0% |

**Background:** I always joke with people about the cost of my education and ask them if they know what $90,000 looks like? The answer, of course, is always a weird look followed by some version of no. I then point to my diploma from The Ohio State University. Damn, I wish I was funny. Anyway, ever wonder what $1,071,300 looks like in terms of discarded minor league talent? Well, that's essentially what the Blue Jays sold De Jong, a 2012 second round pick, and middle infielder Tim Locastro for in bonus money. And the 2016 season will go long way in proving if the Blue Jays were penny wise or pound foolish. Prior to the 2015 season De Jong looked like a nice prospect, but nothing spectacular. He'd always shown a strong feel for the strike zone, but failed to miss a whole lot of bats during his debut in the full season ball the season before. And then all of sudden he started missing bats – a lot of bats. He fanned 77 and walked just 18 in a repeat with Lansing before the trade to LA. The Dodgers promoted him to High Class A immediately after acquiring him and De Jong continued to miss sticks (9.4 K/9 and 2.7 BB/9).

**Projection**: He's not going to be a top- or mid-rotation big leaguer, but a good #4 if definitely worth a million dollars in the baseball world. Fantastic control and the ability to miss bats should be no worse than an average skill. One word of caution: In last year's book I wrote about some trepidation about his propensity for the long ball, which could be a harbinger of things to come. Well, it continued last season as he served up a dinger on average for every nine innings.

**Ceiling:** 1.0- to 1.5-win player
**Risk:** Moderate
**MLB ETA:** 2017

## 18. Jacob Rhame, RHP

**MiLB Rank: N/A**
**Position Rank: N/A**

| Born: 03/16/93 | Age: 23 | Bats: R | Top CALs: James McDonald, Yordano Ventura, |
|---|---|---|---|
| Height: 6-1 | Weight: 190 | Throws: R | Brian Matusz, Kurt Yacko, Thomas Palica |

| YEAR | Age | Level | IP | W | L | ERA | FIP | K/9 | BB/9 | K% | BB% | HR/9 | LOB% |
|---|---|---|---|---|---|---|---|---|---|---|---|---|---|
| 2013 | 20 | R | 19.7 | 1 | 2 | 4.58 | 4.80 | 9.61 | 4.12 | 24.7% | 10.6% | 0.92 | 61.1% |
| 2014 | 21 | A | 67.3 | 5 | 4 | 2.00 | 2.01 | 12.03 | 1.87 | 34.4% | 5.3% | 0.40 | 79.6% |
| 2015 | 22 | A+ | 7.0 | 0 | 0 | 0.00 | 0.49 | 16.71 | 1.29 | 56.5% | 4.4% | 0.00 | 100.0% |
| 2015 | 22 | AA | 50.0 | 3 | 3 | 3.06 | 3.52 | 10.26 | 3.42 | 28.4% | 9.5% | 0.90 | 78.7% |

**Background:** One of my favorite background stories of any prospect in the book. Because, really, who doesn't love a good redemption story? Rhame entered his freshman season at Oklahoma weighing just 190 pounds, a nice, solid number for 6-foot hurler. Jump a head a few months and the once-promising hurler was tipping the scales at an NFL linebacker-like 260 pounds. Oklahoma would eventually part ways with Rhame, who would move onto Grayson County Community College. The right-hander lost the weight, got back in shape, and has been an absolute force to be reckoned with since. Spending the majority of his season with Tulsa in the Texas League, Rhame fanned 70, walked just 20, and finished with a FIP hovering around 3.50. For his professional career, he's average 11.3 strikeouts and 2.7 walks per nine innings.

**Projection**: In last year's book I wrote:

> *"Big time power arm with pinpoint control, Rhame could be poised to fly through the minor leagues – if given the chance. Another late-inning arm."*

He did jump quite a bit in terms of placement in the minor league food chain, essentially going the Midwest League to the Tulsa with just seven innings in between. The control/command took a little bit of back-step, but it's still a solid, repeatable skill. He could be a dominant setup man as soon as mid-2016.

**Ceiling:** 1.5-win player
**Risk:** Moderate
**MLB ETA:** 2016

## 19. Trayce Thompson, CF/RF

| Born: 03/15/91 | Age: 25 | Bats: R | Top CALs: John Selby, Matt Spencer, |
|---|---|---|---|
| Height: 6-3 | Weight: 210 | Throws: R | Jai Miller, Quincy Latimore, Todd Frazier |

| Season | Age | LVL | PA | 2B | 3B | HR | AVG | OBP | SLG | ISO | BB% | K% | wRC+ |
|---|---|---|---|---|---|---|---|---|---|---|---|---|---|
| 2013 | 22 | AA | 590 | 23 | 5 | 15 | 0.229 | 0.321 | 0.383 | 0.154 | 10.2% | 23.6% | 107 |
| 2014 | 23 | AA | 595 | 34 | 6 | 16 | 0.237 | 0.324 | 0.419 | 0.181 | 10.9% | 25.4% | 108 |
| 2015 | 24 | AAA | 417 | 23 | 4 | 13 | 0.260 | 0.304 | 0.441 | 0.180 | 5.5% | 18.9% | 114 |
| 2015 | 24 | MLB | 135 | 8 | 3 | 5 | 0.295 | 0.363 | 0.533 | 0.238 | 9.6% | 19.3% | 144 |

**Background:** The third and final piece Los Angeles received from Chicago this offseason, Thompson, a former second round pick, continued to showcase a promising – albeit flawed – offensive toolkit with Charlotte last season, hitting .260/.304/.441 with 23 doubles, four triples, 13 homeruns, and 11 stolen bases. He also played his ass off in 44 games with the Sox as well, hitting .295/.363/.533.

Projection: The brother of Golden State Warriors' Klay Thompson, the center fielder/right fielder has the always sought after power-speed combo with an impressive eye at the plate. But his hit tool is lacking. And as he enters his age-25 season there's no reason to expect that it'll suddenly tick upward. He typically murders right-hander pitching so he might be useful as a platoon option with Andre Ethier and/or Carl Crawford.

Ceiling: 1.0- to 1.5-win player
Risk: Moderate to High
MLB ETA: Debuted in 2015

## 20. Ross Stripling, RHP

| Born: 11/23/89 | Age: 26 | Bats: R | Top CALs: Leo Rosales, Andres Avila, |
|---|---|---|---|
| Height: 6-3 | Weight: 190 | Throws: R | Clint Goocher, Jesse Carlson, Michael Recchia |

| YEAR | Age | Level | IP | W | L | ERA | FIP | K/9 | BB/9 | K% | BB% | HR/9 | LOB% |
|---|---|---|---|---|---|---|---|---|---|---|---|---|---|
| 2013 | 23 | A+ | 33.7 | 2 | 0 | 2.94 | 3.12 | 9.09 | 2.94 | 25.4% | 8.2% | 0.27 | 71.4% |
| 2013 | 23 | AA | 94.0 | 6 | 4 | 2.78 | 2.31 | 7.95 | 1.82 | 21.5% | 4.9% | 0.38 | 73.8% |
| 2015 | 25 | AA | 67.3 | 3 | 6 | 3.88 | 3.86 | 7.35 | 2.54 | 20.2% | 7.0% | 0.94 | 72.7% |

**Background:** Former fifth rounder out of Texas A&M in 2012. Stripling was on the fast-track to Los Angeles early in his career, reaching Class AA with only 100 career innings under his belt, but Tommy John surgery sidelined him for more than a season. Last season marked the first time Stripling tossed a meaningful pitch since August 29, 2013 – a seven-inning gem against the Tennessee Smokies. Finally healthy, the 6-foot-3 right-hander picked up right where he left off in Class AA: 67.1 IP, 55 K, 21 BB, and a 3.86 FIP. For his career, Stripling is sporting a 2.83 ERA while averaging 8.1 strikeouts and 2.2 base on balls per nine innings.

Projection: Assuming the injury is completely in the past, Stripling looks like a nice little backend starter. He's always pounded the strike zone, missed enough bats to be successful, and has never really stumbled in the professional ranks.

Ceiling: 1.0- to 1.5-win player
Risk: Moderate
MLB ETA: 2016

## 21. Jharel Cotton, RHP

| Born: 01/19/92 | Age: 24 | Bats: R | Top CALs: Aaron Blair, Adalberto Flores, |
|---|---|---|---|
| Height: 5-11 | Weight: 195 | Throws: R | Nelvin Fuentes, Tyler Thornburg, Nick Tropeano |

| YEAR | Age | Level | IP | W | L | ERA | FIP | K/9 | BB/9 | K% | BB% | HR/9 | LOB% |
|---|---|---|---|---|---|---|---|---|---|---|---|---|---|
| 2013 | 21 | A | 58.3 | 2 | 5 | 3.55 | 3.17 | 8.95 | 2.62 | 25.2% | 7.4% | 0.62 | 68.0% |
| 2013 | 21 | A+ | 5.7 | 0 | 0 | 1.59 | 4.30 | 4.76 | 4.76 | 12.5% | 12.5% | 0.00 | 85.7% |
| 2013 | 21 | AA | 10.0 | 0 | 2 | 8.10 | 1.61 | 9.90 | 2.70 | 22.9% | 6.3% | 0.00 | 33.3% |
| 2014 | 22 | A+ | 126.7 | 6 | 10 | 4.05 | 4.24 | 9.81 | 2.42 | 26.6% | 6.6% | 1.28 | 63.5% |
| 2015 | 23 | A+ | 22.3 | 1 | 0 | 1.61 | 2.79 | 11.28 | 2.82 | 32.9% | 8.2% | 0.40 | 86.7% |
| 2015 | 23 | AA | 62.7 | 5 | 2 | 2.30 | 2.87 | 10.20 | 3.02 | 28.6% | 8.5% | 0.57 | 80.8% |
| 2015 | 23 | AAA | 7.3 | 0 | 0 | 4.91 | 1.96 | 11.05 | 2.45 | 28.1% | 6.3% | 0.00 | 63.6% |

**Background:** Always one of the minors' top performing prospects since entering pro ball as a 20th round pick out of East Carolina University in 2012, Cotton turned in a typical Cotton-like season last year as he made stops at four different levels: the diminutive 5-foot-11 right-hander punched out 114 and walked just 31 in 95.2 innings of work. It was just the latest example of Cotton's ability to miss a ton of sticks while limiting free passes. His strikeout-to-walk ratios since 2012: 20-to-3, 72-to-23, 138-to-34, and 114-to-31. For his career, Cotton's fanned over 27% and walked just 7.4% of the batters he's faced in his career.

**Projection**: In last year's book I wrote:

> *"There aren't too many sub-6-foot starting pitchers in the big leagues, and given the club's…ahem…limitless pockets, Cotton's probably going to get pushed into a late-inning relief role. Sneaky good."*

The transition to the bullpen is apparently underway: after making 16 starts between the Midwest, California, and Texas Leagues last season, Cotton pitched exclusively out of the pen over the season's final six weeks. And the move wasn't likely precipitated by an innings cap either; he tossed 126.2 innings two years ago and finished last season with 95.2 frames. His work as a reliever: 12.0 IP, 18 strikeouts, and four walks. He could bounce between a very good middle relief arm and solid setup man.

**Ceiling:** 1.0-win player
**Risk:** Low to Moderate
**MLB ETA:** 2016

---

## 22. Mitch Hansen, OF

**MiLB Rank:** N/A
**Position Rank:** N/A

| | | |
|---|---|---|
| **Born:** 05/01/96 | **Age:** 20 | **Bats:** L |
| **Height:** 6-4 | **Weight:** 195 | **Throws:** L |

**Top CALs:** Juan Polonia, Ranyelmy Mendoza, Riley King, Rashad Crawford, Hilton Richardson

| Season | Age | LVL | PA | 2B | 3B | HR | AVG | OBP | SLG | ISO | BB% | K% | wRC+ |
|---|---|---|---|---|---|---|---|---|---|---|---|---|---|
| 2015 | 19 | R | 167 | 6 | 3 | 0 | 0.201 | 0.281 | 0.282 | 0.081 | 9.0% | 30.5% | 71 |

**Background:** A touch old for a prospect coming out of high school, Hansen, who is already entering his age-20 season, looked like anything *but* a second round pick during his dreadful debut, hitting .201/.281/.282 across 44 Arizona Summer League games.

**Projection**: The 6-foot-4, 195-pound outfielder did show some signs of life once he got his proverbial minor league feet wet: he batted .279/.353/.410 with six extra-base hits over his final 18 games. The problem: even during the "hot streak" Hansen fanned 20 times in 68 plate appearances. It's still way too early to get an accurate read on his potential, but any time a prospect whiffs in 30% of the plate appearances *and* fails to post an ISO above .081 usually spells trouble.

**Ceiling:** Too Soon to Tell
**Risk:** N/A
**MLB ETA:** N/A

---

## 23. Jordan Paroubeck, LF/RF

**MiLB Rank:** N/A
**Position Rank:** N/A

| | | |
|---|---|---|
| **Born:** 11/02/94 | **Age:** 21 | **Bats:** B |
| **Height:** 6-2 | **Weight:** 190 | **Throws:** R |

**Top CALs:** Jon Del Campo, Juan Ortiz, Pedro Urena, Andy Diaz, Nicholas Francis

| Season | Age | LVL | PA | 2B | 3B | HR | AVG | OBP | SLG | ISO | BB% | K% | wRC+ |
|---|---|---|---|---|---|---|---|---|---|---|---|---|---|
| 2014 | 19 | R | 157 | 8 | 2 | 4 | 0.286 | 0.346 | 0.457 | 0.171 | 8.3% | 26.8% | 127 |
| 2015 | 20 | R | 99 | 7 | 1 | 4 | 0.379 | 0.455 | 0.621 | 0.241 | 12.1% | 27.3% | 173 |
| 2015 | 20 | R | 55 | 4 | 1 | 1 | 0.245 | 0.327 | 0.429 | 0.184 | 10.9% | 23.6% | 120 |

**Background:** The two most famous things about Paroubeck have nothing to do with his actual on-field production: #1 hailing from the same alma mater as Barry Bonds, the all-time homerun king worked out Paroubeck before the 2013 draft and #2 the young corner outfielder has been passed around as if he were baseball's greatest pariah over the past dozen-plus months. The Padres would ship Paroubeck to the Braves as part of the Craig Kimbrel mega-deal. Roughly three months later Atlanta would package Paroubeck and Caleb Dirks for the #87 international bonus slot. All that movement for a prospect that's tallied just 311 minor league plate appearances, none of which have come above the rookie leagues.

**Projection**: When he's healthy and on the field Paroubeck's performances have ranged from solid to above-average. But it's come against younger, less polished competition. The switch-hitting outfielder has shown a decent eye at the plate, solid-average or better pop, and a little bit of speed. He looks like a fourth outfielder-type right now, but he has a chance to move up if he performs in full season ball.

**Ceiling:** 1.0-win player
**Risk:** Moderate
**MLB ETA:** 2018

## 24. Josh Sborz, RHP

**MiLB Rank:** N/A
**Position Rank:** N/A

| Born: 12/17/93 | | Age: 22 | | Bats: R | | Top CALs: N/A | |
|---|---|---|---|---|---|---|---|
| Height: 6-2 | | Weight: 209 | | Throws: R | | | |

| YEAR | Age | Level | IP | W | L | ERA | FIP | K/9 | BB/9 | K% | BB% | HR/9 | LOB% |
|---|---|---|---|---|---|---|---|---|---|---|---|---|---|
| 2015 | 21 | R | 4.0 | 0 | 1 | 4.50 | 5.15 | 9.00 | 9.00 | 23.5% | 23.5% | 0.00 | 66.7% |
| 2015 | 21 | A | 6.3 | 0 | 1 | 2.84 | 5.61 | 12.79 | 2.84 | 31.0% | 6.9% | 2.84 | 71.4% |
| 2015 | 21 | A+ | 12.0 | 0 | 0 | 1.50 | 3.86 | 9.00 | 2.25 | 23.5% | 5.9% | 0.75 | 95.9% |

**Background:** A mainstay at one of college baseball's top programs, the University of Virginia. The 6-foot-3, 225-pound Sborz spent his three-year tenure bouncing between the Cavaliers' bullpen and rotation, making 21 starts and another 62 appearances as a reliever. Despite being one of Virginia's better starters as sophomore in 2014 (he posted a 2.92 ERA to go along with a 72-to-44 strikeout-to-walk ratio in 77.0 innings), Sborz entered a completely different role during his final amateur campaign: full-time closer. The well-built right-hander would save 15 games for the eventual champions – and made one start, a complete game shutout – while finishing the year with 62 punch outs and just 25 walks in 73 innings of work.

**Projection:** In a post-draft recap for each team I wrote that, "Sborz could be a sleeper as a #4-type arm if he can demonstrate the type of control/command [he's exhibited] closing out game." The issue with that is his control really took a noticeable step backwards during his lone season as a full-time starter. Not overpowering even when working as a late-inning option, Sborz will likely be given a couple chances to start before being pushed into some sort of middle relief/set up role.

**Ceiling:** 1.0-win player
**Risk:** Moderate
**MLB ETA:** 2018

## 25. Scott Barlow, RHP

**MiLB Rank:** N/A
**Position Rank:** N/A

| Born: 12/18/92 | | Age: 23 | | Bats: R | | Top CALs: Jose Ramirez, Sugar Ray Marimon, Josh Ravin, Tyree Hayes, Brian Rauh | |
|---|---|---|---|---|---|---|---|
| Height: 6-3 | | Weight: 170 | | Throws: R | | | |

| YEAR | Age | Level | IP | W | L | ERA | FIP | K/9 | BB/9 | K% | BB% | HR/9 | LOB% |
|---|---|---|---|---|---|---|---|---|---|---|---|---|---|
| 2013 | 20 | R | 69.7 | 4 | 3 | 6.20 | 6.60 | 6.59 | 4.13 | 15.8% | 9.9% | 1.68 | 64.1% |
| 2014 | 21 | A | 106.0 | 6 | 7 | 4.50 | 4.09 | 8.83 | 2.97 | 22.3% | 7.5% | 0.93 | 65.4% |
| 2015 | 22 | A | 4.7 | 0 | 1 | 5.79 | 9.18 | 1.93 | 1.93 | 4.2% | 4.2% | 3.86 | 16.1% |
| 2015 | 22 | A+ | 71.3 | 8 | 3 | 2.52 | 4.23 | 8.07 | 4.04 | 21.3% | 10.7% | 0.50 | 73.3% |
| 2015 | 22 | AAA | 3.7 | 0 | 1 | 14.73 | 4.42 | 7.36 | 7.36 | 15.8% | 15.8% | 0.00 | 40.0% |

**Background:** It's take a while – something along the lines of five or so years – but the 2011 sixth round pick out of Golden Valley High School is finally starting to live up to his potential. And this should be further proof that not all Tommy John cases result in immediate bounce-back-type scenarios. Barlow made two appearances following his professional debut in the Arizona Summer League before succumbing to TJ. But it took another full year before he regained the type of peripherals/skills to make him a legitimate prospect. He posted a 104-to-35 strikeout-to-walk ratio in the Midwest League two years ago and followed that up with another solid showing (79-to-40 K-to-BB) spread across 88-plus innings over four different levels.

**Projection:** He's still battling some control/command issues. Couple that with the fact that he's never topped 106 innings in a season, and it's pretty easy to see a clear path to the bullpen. Solid middle relief arm.

**Ceiling:** 0.5- to 1.0-win player
**Risk:** Moderate
**MLB ETA:** 2016

- **Victor Gonzalez, LHP** - This marks the second consecutive season in which the southpaw has been plagued by a huge, unsustainable (I think) batting average on balls in play; he finished 2014 with a .381 mark and faired only slightly better than that last season (.371). There might be some upside as a #5-type arm, but he'll more than likely get pushed into a relief role down the line. And despite the terrible ERA, he's probably ready for High Class A.

- **Julian Leon, C** – The rotund backstop failed to his for the first time since entering pro ball in 2013. Leon had a respectable debut as a 17-year-old in the Arizona Summer League (.247/.319/.420) and exploded the following year in the Pioneer League (.332/.420/.565). Plenty of power potential and a likely member of next year's top 25.

## Bird Doggin' It – Additional Prospects to Keep an Eye in 2016

| Player | Age | POS | Notes |
|---|---|---|---|
| Devan Ahart | 23 | OF | 16th round pick out of the University of Akron two years ago tore through the Pioneer and Midwest Leagues during his debut (.344/.376/.463) and performed surpisingly well when he was aggressively pushed to Rancho Cucamonga. Sneaky good tools. |
| Joe Broussard | 25 | RHP | Too old to be taken seriously as a prospect. Broussard, nonetheless, is averaging 9.8 K/9 and 2.0 BB/9 during his two-year career as a low level reliever. |
| Ralston Cash | 24 | RHP | Former second round pick all the way back in 2010 converted to a full time relief role two years and the results have been promising. Still battling spotty control. |
| Justin Chigbogu | 21 | 1B | Gobs of power and a career .226 batting average while whiffing on nearly 36% of his plate appearances. Enough said. |
| Joey Curletta | 22 | RF | With a name straight out of the Sopranos, "Brass Knuckles" Curletta has some tools – speed, pop – but a massive hole in his swing. |
| Brendon Davis | 18 | SS | Huge for a shortstop – 6-foot-4 – but rail thin (163 pounds). Last year's fifth round pick had a decent debut, hitting .278/.309/.322 in the Arizona Summer League. |
| O'Koyea Dickson | 26 | 1B/LF | Classic Quad-A slugger: power, but not enough for a run producing position, questionable hit tool. |
| Kyle Farmer | 25 | C/3B | Career numbers, .300/.349/.435, seem far less impressive when age and level of competition factored in. |
| Kyle Garlick | 24 | RF | Odiferous 2015 late round pick already cracked High Class A. Hit a combined .349/.397/.591 during debut spanning four teams. |
| Juan Jaime | 28 | RHP | Big time mid 90s fastball, monstrous strikeout rates, and horrifically poor walk rates. |
| Tim Locastro | 23 | 2B/SS | Purchased along with Chase De Jong from the Blue Jays. Locastro ripped through the Midwest League (.310/.409/.421), but really struggled to adjust in High Class A (.224/.328/.327). |
| Jairo Pacheco | 19 | LHP | Saw a massive drop off in K-rate as he moved from Arizona Summer League to the Pioneer League, going from 10.1 K/9 to 7.3 K/9. |
| Philip Pfeifer | 23 | LHP | Third round pick from Vanderbilt. Pfeifer's strikeout rate nearly doubled during his junior campaign. Of course, spending two-thirds of the year working out of the pen helps that. |
| Jacob Scavuzzo | 22 | OF | Promising power potential (career .179) but the hit tool is a little questionable. Scavuzzo hit a combined .286/.337/.500 with 32 doubles, four triples, and 18 homeruns. |
| Brock Stewart | 24 | LHP | Posted a 103-to-24 strikeout-to-walk ratio in 101.0 innings between Great Lakes and Rancho Cucamonga. |

**State of the Farm System:** Following along the company's tagline, Miami is sporting a paper-thin, top-end heavy farm system loaded with high risk, high reward youngsters.

Texas-born right-hander Tyler Kolek, the organization's first pick two years ago, spent the year getting battered with the Greensboro Grasshoppers in the South Atlantic League. Armed with a reported triple-digit heater, Kolek managed to fan just 81 of the 501 hitters he faced last season – or just about 16%. Throw in some subpar, questionable control/command and it's easy to see how he falls into the high risk/high reward category.

The farm does have a trio of intriguing low level bats in Josh Naylor, their most recent first round pick, K.J. Woods, and Stone Garrett.

Naylor, the 12th overall pick last June, slugged a solid .327/.352/.418 with four doubles, one triple, and one dinger in 25 games with the organization Gulf Coast League affiliate.

Woods had a massive breakout season, though some of it was due to statistical noise, as he batted .277/.364/.496 with 28 doubles, one triple, and 18 long balls as a 19-year-old in the Sally.

And Garrett, an eighth round pick two years ago, slugged a solid .297/.352/.581 with 35 extra-base hits in just 58 games in the New York-Penn League.

After that it gets...thin. Quick.

There's a handful of arms – Kendry Flores, Brett Lilek, Austin Brice, Nick Wittgren, Brian Ellington, Luis Castillo, and the often on the move Ivan Pineyro – who could eventually see some time with the big league club in some backend starter/relief capacity. Right-hander Colby Suggs has some late-inning relief potential if he can bounce back from TJ surgery.

| Rank | Name | POS |
|------|------|-----|
| 1 | Tyler Kolek | RHP |
| 2 | Josh Naylor | 1B |
| 3 | K.J. Woods | 1B/LF |
| 4 | Stone Garrett | CF |
| 5 | Kendry Flores | RHP |
| 6 | Brett Lilek | LHP |
| 7 | Austin Brice | RHP |
| 8 | Nick Wittgren | RHP |
| 9 | Brian Ellington | RHP |
| 10 | Luis Castillo | RHP |
| 11 | Avery Romero | 2B |
| 12 | Ivan Pineyro | RHP |
| 13 | Colby Suggs | RHP |
| 14 | Jarlin Garcia | LHP |
| 15 | Austin Dean | LF |
| 16 | Victor Araujo | RHP |
| 17 | Jeff Brigham | RHP |
| 18 | Brian Schales | 3B |
| 19 | Brian Anderson | 2B/3B |
| 20 | Isaiah White | CF |
| 21 | Justin Twine | SS |
| 22 | Justin Cohen | C |
| 23 | Blake Anderson | C |
| 24 | Chris Reed | LHP |
| 25 | Anfernee Seymour | SS |

**Review of the 2015 Draft:** The Marlins went against tradition thinking and took a prep first baseman in the opening round – largely because these type of prospects are tied solely to their ability to hit, and hit with power – but Naylor has a chance to be special, particularly when he begins to tap into his above-average power potential.

Their second round pick, big lefty Brett Lilek out of Arizona State, has a chance to move quickly through the system. Outfielder Isaiah White hit a respectable .294/.321/.381 – of course, though, he posted a putrid 44-to-3 strikeout-to-walk ratio in just 132 trips to the plate. Cody Poteet and Justin Jacome were nice finds in the fourth and fifth rounds.

Overall, it was a solid draft, though it'll largely be tied to Naylor's ability to hit the long ball.

## 1. Tyler Kolek, RHP

**MiLB Rank: #97**

**Position Rank: N/A**

| | | |
|---|---|---|
| Born: 12/15/95 | Age: 20 | Bats: R |
| Height: 6-5 | Weight: 260 | Throws: R |

**Top CALs:** Brian Gonzalez, Matt Kretzschmar, Juan Minaya, Fabian Jimenez-Angulo, Shawn Morimando

| YEAR | Age | Level | IP | W | L | ERA | FIP | K/9 | BB/9 | K% | BB% | HR/9 | LOB% |
|---|---|---|---|---|---|---|---|---|---|---|---|---|---|
| 2014 | 18 | R | 22.0 | 0 | 3 | 4.50 | 3.92 | 7.36 | 5.32 | 18.2% | 13.1% | 0.00 | 54.1% |
| 2015 | 19 | A | 108.7 | 4 | 10 | 4.56 | 4.87 | 6.71 | 5.05 | 16.2% | 12.2% | 0.58 | 65.0% |

**Background**: Possessing one of the biggest right arms in the minors didn't exactly add up to a dominant 2015 performance for the former second overall pick. Kolek, who's sometimes triple-digit fastball caused scout and front office personnel to flock in droves to little Shepherd High School in Texas two years ago, jumped up to the South Atlantic League last season where he posted a mediocre 81-to-61 strikeout-to-walk ratio in 108.2 innings of work. In other words, he fanned just 16.2% and walked 12.2% of the total batters he faced last season. And those numbers aren't that much different than those during his debut in the Gulf Coast League two years ago either (18.2% K% and 13.1% BB%).

**Projection**: Personally, I always find it troublesome – though it's not always proven – when incoming high prep picks fail to perform at an above-average level in lowest rookie leagues, something that could be said about Kolek's debut in the GCL two years ago. And after another so-so year in 2015, Kolek's still no closer to capitalizing on his God-given talent.

But here's something incredibly bothersome: Kolek and his 100 mph fastball made 25 starts in 2015; of those games, the big Texas-born right-hander averaged more than one punch out per inning seven times. That's it, seven times. Or in other words, that's 28% of his starts. Yes, he still has the *potential* to peak as a front-end starting pitcher, but he needs to start taking some dramatic leaps forward in the next year or two.

**Ceiling:** 3.5-win player
**Risk:** High
**MLB ETA:** 2018

## 2. Josh Naylor, 1B

**MiLB Rank: #101**

**Position Rank: #6**

| | | |
|---|---|---|
| Born: 06/22/97 | Age: 19 | Bats: L |
| Height: 6-1 | Weight: 225 | Throws: L |

**Top CALs:** Luis Bandes, Telmito Agustin, Wilson Ramos, Yonathan Mejia, Brandon Drury

| Season | Age | LVL | PA | 2B | 3B | HR | AVG | OBP | SLG | ISO | BB% | K% | wRC+ |
|---|---|---|---|---|---|---|---|---|---|---|---|---|---|
| 2015 | 18 | R | 105 | 4 | 1 | 1 | 0.327 | 0.352 | 0.418 | 0.092 | 3.8% | 10.5% | 130 |

**Background:** Never one to shy away from taking high-ceiling prep players at any point in the amateur draft, Miami grabbed the hulking first baseman out of St. Joan of Arc Catholic SS with the 12th overall selection last June. The front office, per the usual, sent Naylor down to the Gulf Coast League for his debut – a largely successful debut. He slugged .327/.352/.418 with four doubles, one triple, and one homerun with a 130 wRC+.

**Projection**: One of the Golden Rules when it comes to prep players is to avoid taking first basemen in the opening rounds, largely because they're viewed as un-athletic and will provide no value on the defensive side of the ball. So it's not surprising that Naylor was the first prep first baseman taken in the opening round since Dominic Smith in 2013. Anyway, he wasn't particularly patient at the plate last season, nor did he flash a whole lot of power at any point. But, most importantly, he didn't look overwhelmed with the transition to wood bats either.

**Ceiling:** Too Soon to Tell
**Risk:** N/A
**MLB ETA:** N/A

## 3. K.J. Woods, 1B/LF

**MiLB Rank: #163**

**Position Rank: N/A**

| | | |
|---|---|---|
| Born: 07/09/95 | Age: 20 | Bats: L |
| Height: 6-3 | Weight: 230 | Throws: R |

**Top CALs:** Bobby Bradley, Michael Burgess, Telvin Nash, Nelson Rodriguez, Tyler O'Neill

| Season | Age | LVL | PA | 2B | 3B | HR | AVG | OBP | SLG | ISO | BB% | K% | wRC+ |
|---|---|---|---|---|---|---|---|---|---|---|---|---|---|
| 2013 | 17 | R | 168 | 4 | 6 | 1 | 0.201 | 0.310 | 0.250 | 0.049 | 10.1% | 31.5% | 78 |
| 2014 | 18 | A- | 117 | 6 | 1 | 1 | 0.219 | 0.282 | 0.324 | 0.105 | 6.8% | 28.2% | 77 |
| 2015 | 19 | A | 439 | 28 | 1 | 18 | 0.277 | 0.364 | 0.496 | 0.219 | 10.3% | 30.3% | 143 |

**Background:** The Marlins unearthed their latest gem in the fourth round in 2013, signing him to a deal worth in excess of $500,000. And after struggling *mightily* during his first two professional seasons – he "slugged" .201/.310/.250 during his debut in the Gulf Coast and followed that up with a .226/.287/.323 showing between the rookie league and Batavia two years ago – Woods had a massive breakout party in 2015, his first –

and only – stint in the South Atlantic League. In 104 games with Greensboro, Woods mashed to the tune of .277/.364/.496 with 28 doubles, one three-bagger, and 18 homeruns. His overall production, according *Weighted Runs Created Plus*, topped the league average production by a whopping 43% last season – the second best total among all qualified hitters in the Sally.

**Projection**: First, some context as to just how dominant Woods' 2015 season was:

- The next highest *Weighted Runs Created Plus* total by a 19-year-old in the Sally last season was Colorado's Forrest Wall, who tallied a 125 wRC+.
- The last time a 19-year-old bat posted a wRC+ above Woods' 143 was three years ago when Texas' Joey Gallo and Nick Williams exceed the total (163 and 148, respectively).
- Woods' 18 homeruns finished second in the league, trailing only teammate Arturo Rodriguez who appeared in 21 games.

Second, Woods' overall production was actually far better through his first 77 games: he batted .293/.375/.541 with 23 doubles, one triple, and 15 homeruns through August 3rd. He would string together a lowly .230/.336/.370 over his final 27 games. So more context (of course): it's common for a teenage player to struggle down the stretch in their first exposure in full-season ball. Take for example Jake Bauers: two years ago he slugged .354/.429/.523 in his first 55 contests, but batted .242/.325/.313 over his final 57 games. Bauers would follow that up with one of the biggest breakouts in 2015.

Third, the Greensboro Grasshoppers' home field, NewBridge Bank Park (yes, NewBridge is one word), is an incredibly favorable ballpark for hitters. According to StatCorner, Woods' park adjusted triple-slash line drops from .277/.364/.496 to a .266/.361/.455 – which, by itself, is a strong showing for a 19-year-old in the Sally. More evidence of the ballparks offense-inducing environment: Woods' home/road splits were .289/.366/.510 vs. .261/.363/.455.

Taking each of the three into account, Woods is a fine prospect, one that should be getting more notoriety. But there is some added risk though, especially since he hasn't performed like this in years past. Finally, it wouldn't be surprising to see Woods handle High Class A with relative ease – even if his production takes a small step backwards.

**Ceiling:** 2.5- to 3.0-win player
**Risk:** High
**MLB ETA:** 2018

# 4. Stone Garrett, CF

**MiLB Rank: #201**
**Position Rank: N/A**

| Born: 11/22/95 | Age: 20 | Bats: R | Top CALs: Joseph Monge, Elvis Escobar, |
| Height: 6-2 | Weight: 195 | Throws: R | Keury De La Cruz, Bralin Jackson, Dylan Cozens |

| Season | Age | LVL | PA | 2B | 3B | HR | AVG | OBP | SLG | ISO | BB% | K% | wRC+ |
|--------|-----|-----|-----|----|----|----|-------|-------|-------|-------|------|-------|------|
| 2014 | 18 | R | 156 | 3 | 1 | 0 | 0.236 | 0.269 | 0.270 | 0.034 | 4.5% | 19.9% | 58 |
| 2015 | 19 | A- | 247 | 18 | 6 | 11 | 0.297 | 0.352 | 0.581 | 0.284 | 7.7% | 24.3% | 167 |

**Background:** Hailing from George Ranch High School in Richmond, Texas, two years ago, Garrett, a former eighth round pick, rebounded from a poor showing in the Gulf Coast League by slugging an impressive .297/.352/.581 with 18 doubles, six triples, and 11 homeruns in 58 games with Batavia. His overall production, per *Weighted Runs Created Plus*, topped the league average mark by 67%.

**Projection**: Granted it was just short-season ball, but here are Garrett's numbers pro-rated over a 162-game season: 50 doubles, 17 triples, and 31 bombs. Yeah, that'll play. The power is absolute premium, particularly coming from the center field position, but Garrett's strikeout rate crept up to red flag territory last season as he posted a 24.3% total. Average eye, a little bit of speed, but the power could encroach the 25-HR mark in the coming years.

**Ceiling:** 2.5-win player
**Risk:** Moderate to High
**MLB ETA:** 2019

## 5. Kendry Flores, RHP

MiLB Rank: N/A
Position Rank: N/A

| Born: 11/24/91 | Age: 24 | Bats: R | Top CALs: Robert Ray, Robert Rohrbaugh, |
|---|---|---|---|
| Height: 6-2 | Weight: 175 | Throws: R | Ronnie Martinez, Jeff Manship, Chad Rogers |

| YEAR | Age | Level | IP | W | L | ERA | FIP | K/9 | BB/9 | K% | BB% | HR/9 | LOB% |
|---|---|---|---|---|---|---|---|---|---|---|---|---|---|
| 2013 | 21 | A | 141.7 | 10 | 6 | 2.73 | 3.00 | 8.70 | 1.08 | 24.9% | 3.1% | 0.70 | 73.4% |
| 2014 | 22 | A+ | 105.7 | 4 | 6 | 4.09 | 4.40 | 9.54 | 2.73 | 25.1% | 7.2% | 1.19 | 68.4% |
| 2015 | 23 | A+ | 2.7 | 0 | 0 | 0.00 | 2.42 | 3.38 | 0.00 | 11.1% | 0.0% | 0.00 | 100.0% |
| 2015 | 23 | AA | 56.7 | 3 | 3 | 2.06 | 3.41 | 6.67 | 2.38 | 19.9% | 7.1% | 0.48 | 78.6% |
| 2015 | 23 | AAA | 58.7 | 3 | 2 | 2.61 | 3.60 | 6.44 | 2.15 | 18.0% | 6.0% | 0.46 | 75.3% |

**Background:** Kudos to Miami and their front office for extracting a year of league average production from Casey McGehee and then flipping the big league veteran – and his BABIP inflated triple-slash line – last offseason to San Francisco in exchange for anything of value, let alone acquiring Kendry Flores and Luis Castillo. Flores, a wiry 6-foot-2, 175-pound right-hander out of the Dominican Republic, made stops at four different levels in 2015 – though they weren't in the typical ascending order. Flores opened the year up with nine starts in the Southern League before getting promoted up to Miami for a pair of relief stints. He then got sent down to the Pacific Coast League for 10 starts before getting recalled back up to The Show for another five games. And then he got sent all the way back down to Jupiter after missing a couple weeks. Overall, Flores finished his minor league campaign with 118.0 innings while averaging 6.5 punch outs and just 2.2 walks per nine innings. And in both his stints with the Marlins he would tally 12.2 innings with a 9-to-4 strikeout-to-walk ratio.

**Projection**: Sporting a fringy 90 mph fastball – as well as a slider, cutter, curveball, and changeup – Flores' success is predicated on doing the small things: limiting free passes, surrendering the occasional (not frequent) homerun, and getting a little bit of action on the ground. He's another one of these backend starters.

**Ceiling:** 1.5-win player
**Risk:** Low to Moderate
**MLB ETA:** Debuted in 2015

## 6. Brett Lilek, LHP

MiLB Rank: N/A
Position Rank: N/A

| Born: 08/10/93 | Age: 22 | Bats: L | Top CALs: Ralph Garza, Brandon Leibrandt, |
|---|---|---|---|
| Height: 6-4 | Weight: 194 | Throws: L | Jordan Zimmermann, Austin Wright, Jess Todd |

| YEAR | Age | Level | IP | W | L | ERA | FIP | K/9 | BB/9 | K% | BB% | HR/9 | LOB% |
|---|---|---|---|---|---|---|---|---|---|---|---|---|---|
| 2015 | 21 | A- | 35.0 | 1 | 2 | 3.34 | 2.20 | 11.06 | 1.80 | 30.7% | 5.0% | 0.26 | 66.5% |

**Background:** A two-year member of Arizona State's rotation, the 6-foot-4, 195-pound southpaw battled control issues during tenure with the Sun Devils. He averaged 4.18 walks per nine innings as a sophomore and 4.69 free passes per nine innings as a junior. Miami grabbed Lilek with the 50th overall pick last June. Lo and behold, his control issues all but disappeared once he entered professional baseball. In 35.0 innings with Batavia in the New York-Penn League, Lilek posted a dominant 43-to-7 strikeout-to-walk ratio en route to tallying a 3.34 ERA and 2.20 FIP.

**Projection**: It wasn't just an uptick in control, Lilek looked like a completely different hurler during his debut – granted, he only turned over the line a handful of times during his debut. He's not particularly overpowering – especially if you focus on his work in college – but he might be able to carve out a role as a #5-type arm in a couple years.

**Ceiling:** 1.5-win player
**Risk:** Moderate
**MLB ETA:** 2018

## 7. Austin Brice, RHP

MiLB Rank: N/A
Position Rank: N/A

| Born: 06/19/92 | Age: 24 | Bats: R | Top CALs: Jake Brigham, Ryan Chaffee, |
|---|---|---|---|
| Height: 6-4 | Weight: 205 | Throws: R | Alexander Smit, Rob Rasmussen, Adam Ottavino |

| YEAR | Age | Level | IP | W | L | ERA | FIP | K/9 | BB/9 | K% | BB% | HR/9 | LOB% |
|---|---|---|---|---|---|---|---|---|---|---|---|---|---|
| 2013 | 21 | A | 113.0 | 8 | 11 | 5.73 | 5.33 | 8.84 | 6.53 | 20.5% | 15.2% | 0.88 | 65.5% |
| 2014 | 22 | A+ | 127.3 | 8 | 9 | 3.60 | 3.79 | 7.70 | 3.89 | 19.8% | 10.0% | 0.35 | 66.3% |
| 2015 | 23 | AA | 125.3 | 6 | 9 | 4.67 | 4.36 | 9.12 | 4.95 | 22.8% | 12.4% | 0.79 | 67.4% |

**Background:** An enigmatic hard-throwing right-hander taken in the ninth round out of Northwood High School in 2010, Brice continued to offer up glimpses as a mid-rotation caliber arm – when all things were clicking. Otherwise, he looked like a potential late-inning wild card. Brice, a 6-

foot-4, 205-pound hurler, has long been on the system's list of most intriguing arms since his 2011 season with the Gulf Coast; he would average 10.2 strikeouts and just 6.1 walks per nine innings. Brice would follow that up with a plethora of punch outs and a high walk rate in each of the following two seasons. But he seemed to take a noticeable step forward two years ago with Jupiter when he walked a career best 10.0% of the total batters he faced. Brice's control would regress back to his previous lows as the club bounced him up Class AA.

**Projection:** Here's what I wrote in last year's book:

> "Brice could be a backend starting pitcher, though his best shot at being a serviceable big league arm would be best taking the bullpen path. He's going to need another season in which he posts a sub-4.0 walk rate before I start to believe, but there's a little bit of upside here."

After averaging 5.0 free passes per nine innings last season, it's clear Brice's future is now as a potential late-inning relief arm. But it'd be prudent to wait one more season in hopes that Brice can figure it out during his age-24 season. Again there's plenty of potential here – he fanned 13 and walked 1 in an eight-inning, one-hitter against Biloxi last June – and it's not like the Marlins plan on contending any time soon.

**Ceiling:** 2.0-win player
**Risk:** High
**MLB ETA:** 2017

# 8. Nick Wittgren, RHP

**MiLB Rank:** N/A
**Position Rank:** N/A

**Born:** 05/29/91 **Age:** 25 **Bats:** R
**Height:** 6-3 **Weight:** 210 **Throws:** R

**Top CALs:** Bryan Woodall, Fernando Abad, Brandon Workman, Anthony Desclafani, Hector Noesi

| YEAR | Age | Level | IP | W | L | ERA | FIP | K/9 | BB/9 | K% | BB% | HR/9 | LOB% |
|------|-----|-------|------|---|---|------|-------|-------|------|-------|------|------|-------|
| 2013 | 22 | A+ | 54.3 | 2 | 1 | 0.83 | 1.97 | 9.77 | 1.66 | 27.6% | 4.7% | 0.17 | 89.4% |
| 2013 | 22 | AA | 4.0 | 0 | 0 | 0.00 | 0.91 | 9.00 | 0.00 | 30.8% | 0.0% | 0.00 | 100.0% |
| 2014 | 23 | AA | 66.0 | 5 | 5 | 3.55 | 3.40 | 7.64 | 1.91 | 20.0% | 5.0% | 0.82 | 72.0% |
| 2015 | 24 | AA | 1.7 | 0 | 0 | 0.00 | -0.30 | 16.20 | 0.00 | 60.0% | 0.0% | 0.00 | 100.0% |
| 2015 | 24 | AAA | 62.3 | 1 | 6 | 3.03 | 3.23 | 9.24 | 1.16 | 25.5% | 3.2% | 0.87 | 76.8% |

**Background:** A ninth round pick out of Purdue University in 2012, Wittgren continued his rapid – and highly successful – rise through the minor leagues last season. The former Boilermaker blew through two levels during his debut, the New York-Penn and South Atlantic Leagues, posting an impeccable 47-to-5 strikeout-to-walk ratio in just 30.2 innings of work. The 6-foot-3, 210-pound right-hander followed that up with another two stops in 2013 – albeit the second stop, the Southern League, was just a late-season promotion. But he continued to show little regression during sophomore campaign: 58.1 IP, 63 K, and just 10 walks. Miami would keep the relief stalwart with Jupiter the entire 2014 season as he saw a noticeable downturn in his strikeout rate; he fanned just 20.0% of the total batters he faced, by far the worst mark of his career. Wittgren would open 2015 back in Class AA, though it lasted just two games, before earning a trip to New Orleans in the Pacific Coast League.

**Projection:** Here's what I wrote in my first book two years ago:

> "Nice strikeout ability, solid groundball rates and pinpoint control. Not sure if Wittgren will ever ascend to closer status in the big leagues, but he should be a solid setup man for quite a while."

I followed that up by writing the following in last year's book:

> "Not particularly overpowering in the typical sense. Wittgren combines a solid ability to miss bats and a premium ability to limit free passes. The Marlins have spent part of the last couple of months reworking the pen, so Wittgren will likely have to bide his time until injuries strike."

Well, that time never came – obviously. But Wittgren is big league ready, and he could ascend to a seventh/eighth-inning role like…yesterday. He still limits walks, misses quite a few bats, and his groundball rate has been hovering around 45% to 50% over the past couple years. I like him…a lot. And with a big league bullpen with as little name-power as the Marlins – it's literally like opening a phonebook and throwing your finger down – Wittgren will – hopefully – get his big league opportunity.

**Ceiling:** 1.0- to 1.5-win player
**Risk:** Low to Moderate
**MLB ETA:** Debuted in 2015

## 9. Brian Ellington, RHP

**MiLB Rank:** N/A
**Position Rank:** N/A

| Born: 08/04/90 | Age: 25 | Bats: R | Top CALs: Brad Meyers, Chris Leroux, |
|---|---|---|---|
| Height: 6-4 | Weight: 195 | Throws: R | Jose Guzman, Luis Perdomo, Jose Flores |

| YEAR | Age | Level | IP | W | L | ERA | FIP | K/9 | BB/9 | K% | BB% | HR/9 | LOB% |
|---|---|---|---|---|---|---|---|---|---|---|---|---|---|
| 2013 | 22 | R | 3.0 | 0 | 0 | 0.00 | 3.79 | 12.00 | 9.00 | 30.8% | 23.1% | 0.00 | 100.0% |
| 2013 | 22 | A- | 19.3 | 1 | 2 | 3.72 | 2.79 | 9.78 | 4.19 | 24.4% | 10.5% | 0.00 | 50.0% |
| 2013 | 22 | A | 42.7 | 3 | 2 | 4.64 | 5.38 | 5.70 | 4.85 | 13.9% | 11.9% | 0.63 | 67.9% |
| 2014 | 23 | A+ | 47.3 | 2 | 2 | 4.75 | 3.29 | 10.65 | 4.56 | 25.8% | 11.1% | 0.38 | 66.5% |
| 2015 | 24 | AA | 43.0 | 4 | 1 | 2.51 | 2.09 | 9.84 | 2.72 | 27.8% | 7.7% | 0.00 | 69.1% |
| 2015 | 24 | AAA | 1.3 | 0 | 0 | 0.00 | 2.10 | 6.75 | 0.00 | 25.0% | 0.0% | 0.00 | 100.0% |

**Background:** Interesting fact about the University of West Florida: Since the school's first MLB draft pick in 1982, 24th rounder Thomas Cruz, only three players have been selected within the top 500 picks (LeDarious Clark, Jordan DeLorenzo, and Brian Ellington). And it took Ellington, the 497th overall pick in 2012, parts of just four seasons to make his way up to the big leagues. The 6-foot-4, 195-pound right-hander split his 2015 season between Jacksonville – where he would post a 47-to-13 strikeout-to-walk ratio – and Miami. During his time with the Marlins, Ellington would throw another 25.0 innings, fanning 17.1% and walking 12.4% of the total hitters he faced. For his minor league career, the big hurler has averaged 9.1 punch outs and 4.7 walks per nine innings to go along with a 3.62 ERA.

**Projection:** And here's how a former 16th round pick hailing from a small school with a minor league walk rate approaching 5.0 BB/9 gets an extended look in the big leagues: his fastball averaged nearly 97 mph. He complemented that with a low-80s curveball and a hard, seldom-used changeup. Ellington's control took a dramatic leap forward with Jacksonville (2.7 BB/9), but he really struggled with Miami. He has ability to develop into an above-average setup man, maybe even ascending to the club's closer role, but he needs to limit the walks.

**Ceiling:** 1.5-win player
**Risk:** Moderate to High
**MLB ETA:** Debuted in 2015

## 10. Luis Castillo, RHP

**MiLB Rank:** N/A
**Position Rank:** N/A

| Born: 12/12/92 | Age: 23 | Bats: R | Top CALs: Kevin Comer, Dan Griffin, |
|---|---|---|---|
| Height: 6-2 | Weight: 170 | Throws: R | Braden Shipley, Carlos Contreras, Brandon Barker |

| YEAR | Age | Level | IP | W | L | ERA | FIP | K/9 | BB/9 | K% | BB% | HR/9 | LOB% |
|---|---|---|---|---|---|---|---|---|---|---|---|---|---|
| 2013 | 20 | R | 28.3 | 0 | 1 | 0.64 | 1.12 | 10.80 | 0.95 | 32.1% | 2.8% | 0.00 | 73.7% |
| 2014 | 21 | A | 58.7 | 2 | 2 | 3.07 | 4.00 | 10.13 | 3.84 | 25.8% | 9.8% | 0.92 | 80.2% |
| 2015 | 22 | A | 63.3 | 4 | 3 | 2.98 | 2.74 | 8.95 | 2.70 | 23.9% | 7.2% | 0.14 | 70.4% |
| 2015 | 22 | A+ | 43.7 | 2 | 3 | 3.50 | 3.67 | 6.39 | 2.89 | 17.0% | 7.7% | 0.62 | 76.6% |

**Background:** Also acquired from the Giants in Miami's savvy dump of Casey McGehee last offseason. Castillo continued his methodical move through the low levels of the minors, splitting last season between Greensboro and Jupiter. In a career best 107.0 innings, the 6-foot-2, 170-pound right-hander fanned 94, walked 33, and posted an aggregate 3.20 ERA.

**Projection:** The deal to swap out Casey McGehee for Kendry Flores and Luis Castillo was enough. But Miami took it to a whole other level when they started transitioning the full-time reliever into a first time starting pitcher. And the results were...intriguing. Over his 16 starts, six coming in the Sally and the rest occurring in the Florida State League, Castillo tossed 76.1 innings while posting a 2.48 ERA and a 60-to-20 strikeout-to-walk ratio. There's some sneaky upside as a backend starter – albeit there's some obvious risk as well.

**Ceiling:** 1.5-win player
**Risk:** Moderate to High
**MLB ETA:** 2018

## 11. Avery Romero, 2B

**MiLB Rank: N/A**
**Position Rank: N/A**

| Born: 05/11/93 | Age: 23 | Bats: R | **Top CALs:** Matt Wessinger, Isaias Velasquez, |
| Height: 5-11 | Weight: 195 | Throws: R | Ramon Torres, Casey Mcelroy, Frank Martinez |

| Season | Age | LVL | PA | 2B | 3B | HR | AVG | OBP | SLG | ISO | BB% | K% | wRC+ |
|--------|-----|-----|-----|----|----|----|-------|-------|-------|-------|------|------|------|
| 2013 | 20 | A- | 235 | 18 | 0 | 2 | 0.297 | 0.357 | 0.411 | 0.115 | 6.4% | 14.5% | 133 |
| 2014 | 21 | A | 399 | 23 | 1 | 5 | 0.320 | 0.366 | 0.429 | 0.109 | 6.3% | 11.8% | 124 |
| 2014 | 21 | A+ | 108 | 8 | 0 | 0 | 0.320 | 0.370 | 0.400 | 0.080 | 6.5% | 12.0% | 123 |
| 2015 | 22 | A+ | 505 | 14 | 1 | 3 | 0.259 | 0.315 | 0.314 | 0.055 | 7.5% | 14.1% | 94 |

**Background:** Romero had trouble following up his breakout 2014 campaign when he batted .320/.367/.423 with 31 doubles, one triple, five homeruns, and 10 stolen bases between Greensboro and Jupiter. Miami had the offensive-minded second baseman spend the entire year back with Jupiter, though the results were far less impressive: .259/.315/.314 with 14 doubles, one triple, and a trio of homers.

**Projection**: After topping the league average production mark by about 24% two years ago, Romero's *Weighted Runs Created Plus* total dropped to six-percent *below* the league average mark as his .360-ish BABIP crated to .297 last season. Below-average pop with a decent eye at the plate, Romero's destined to become a minor league vagabond as his defensive value is limited to just second base.

**Ceiling:** 1.0- to 1.5-win player
**Risk:** Moderate
**MLB ETA:** 2018

## 12. Ivan Pineyro, RHP

**MiLB Rank: N/A**
**Position Rank: N/A**

| Born: 09/29/91 | Age: 24 | Bats: R | **Top CALs:** Marco Carrillo, Robert Carson, John Gast, Stolmy Pimentel, Aaron Thompson |
| Height: 6-1 | Weight: 200 | Throws: R | |

| YEAR | Age | Level | IP | W | L | ERA | FIP | K/9 | BB/9 | K% | BB% | HR/9 | LOB% |
|------|-----|-------|-------|---|---|------|------|------|------|-------|-------|------|-------|
| 2013 | 21 | A | 66.0 | 5 | 3 | 3.14 | 3.21 | 8.86 | 2.32 | 24.6% | 6.4% | 0.55 | 71.4% |
| 2013 | 21 | A+ | 14.7 | 1 | 0 | 3.68 | 4.17 | 4.91 | 3.07 | 13.1% | 8.2% | 0.61 | 73.9% |
| 2013 | 21 | A+ | 45.0 | 3 | 1 | 3.40 | 2.93 | 7.60 | 1.80 | 20.5% | 4.9% | 0.40 | 73.3% |
| 2014 | 22 | R | 11.3 | 0 | 2 | 5.56 | 4.12 | 7.15 | 1.59 | 18.0% | 4.0% | 0.79 | 51.3% |
| 2014 | 22 | AA | 48.7 | 0 | 4 | 5.55 | 4.85 | 7.58 | 4.25 | 17.9% | 10.0% | 1.29 | 65.1% |
| 2015 | 23 | AA | 109.3 | 7 | 6 | 3.87 | 3.32 | 7.57 | 2.72 | 20.0% | 7.2% | 0.49 | 69.8% |
| 2015 | 23 | AAA | 36.7 | 2 | 2 | 2.70 | 3.71 | 6.38 | 1.96 | 17.9% | 5.5% | 0.49 | 78.5% |

**Background:** The well-traveled right-hander has now been a member of three different organizations during his five-year professional career, bouncing from Washington to the Cubs and finally landing with Marlins of Miami last season as part of the Dan Haren swap at the trade deadline last season. Pineyro, for his part, has continued to showcase a big league worthy line of production at each of his numerous stops. And last season was no different. In 26 starts between both organizations, 20 of which coming in Class AA, Pineyro tossed a career best 146.0 innings while fanning 118 and walking 41 en route to posting a serviceable 3.58 ERA. For his career, the 6-foot-1, 200-pound right-hander has averaged 7.9 strikeouts and 2.6 walks per nine innings.

**Projection**: He's such an interesting prospect because everyone wants him – and then they don't. But Pineyro's always looked like a backend big league starter: he misses bats, shows above-average control, and generates decent groundball rates. And the forearm strain that limited him to 60.0 innings two years ago proved to be non-surgery worthy. He could serve as a decent #5 arm.

**Ceiling:** 1.0-win player
**Risk:** Low to Moderate
**MLB ETA:** 2016

## 13. Colby Suggs, RHP

**MiLB Rank: N/A**
**Position Rank: N/A**

| Born: 10/25/91 | Age: 24 | Bats: R | Top CALs: Kevin Siegrist, Lucas Luetge, |
| Height: 5-11 | Weight: 235 | Throws: R | Arquimedes Nieto, Rafael Dolis, Edgar Olmos |

| YEAR | Age | Level | IP | W | L | ERA | FIP | K/9 | BB/9 | K% | BB% | HR/9 | LOB% |
|------|-----|-------|-----|---|---|------|------|-------|------|-------|-------|------|-------|
| 2013 | 21 | R | 1.0 | 0 | 0 | 9.00 | 10.46 | 9.00 | 18.00 | 14.3% | 28.6% | 0.00 | 75.0% |
| 2013 | 21 | A- | 8.0 | 1 | 0 | 1.13 | 1.47 | 12.38 | 2.25 | 39.3% | 7.1% | 0.00 | 75.0% |
| 2013 | 21 | A+ | 18.3 | 1 | 3 | 3.93 | 2.70 | 12.76 | 6.87 | 32.9% | 17.7% | 0.00 | 65.2% |
| 2014 | 22 | A+ | 58.3 | 1 | 6 | 5.09 | 4.09 | 7.25 | 3.86 | 18.3% | 9.7% | 0.46 | 63.4% |
| 2015 | 23 | A | 5.3 | 0 | 0 | 0.00 | 1.80 | 10.13 | 1.69 | 28.6% | 4.8% | 0.00 | 100.0% |

**Background:** Tabbed in the second round out of the University of Arkansas three years ago, Suggs may have had a shot at going in the opening round if not for his...*clears throat*...inability to accurately locate his above-average fastball. He walked 17 in 20.0 innings during his freshman season, another 19 in 39.0 innings the next year, and 17 more in 20.2 innings during his junior campaign. So it's no surprise that the 5-foot-11, 235-pound right-hander has battled those same control issues during his pro career. He posted an 18-to-10 strikeout-to-walk ratio in 27.1 innings between the Gulf Coast, New York-Penn, and Florida State Leagues. But things seemed to click for Suggs as he spent the entire 2014 season back in Jupiter; he would average just 3.9 walks per nine innings. He would toss just 5.1 innings before undergoing the knife for Tommy John surgery last season.

**Projection**: Here's what I wrote prior to the 2013 draft:

> *"Forget command, control doesn't even exist for the hard-throwing right-hander yet. He certainly has the talent to make into the top 50 or so picks, but it likely won't happen come June. He's eventually going to develop into a shutdown backend reliever, but it could take a few seasons."*

Suggs certainly looked like he was taking the necessary steps towards the big leagues before elbow surgery shut him down. Here's hoping for a full and speedy recovery...

**Ceiling:** 1.0- to 1.5-win player
**Risk:** Moderate to High
**MLB ETA:** 2017/2018

## 14. Jarlin Garcia, LHP

**MiLB Rank: N/A**
**Position Rank: N/A**

| Born: 01/18/93 | Age: 23 | Bats: L | Top CALs: Jon Moscot, Ryan Crowley, |
| Height: 6-2 | Weight: 170 | Throws: L | Robin Leyer, Mike Tarsi, Kevin Comer |

| YEAR | Age | Level | IP | W | L | ERA | FIP | K/9 | BB/9 | K% | BB% | HR/9 | LOB% |
|------|-----|-------|-------|----|---|------|------|------|------|-------|-------|------|-------|
| 2013 | 20 | A- | 69.7 | 2 | 3 | 3.10 | 3.14 | 9.56 | 2.33 | 26.1% | 6.3% | 0.90 | 68.9% |
| 2014 | 21 | A | 133.7 | 10 | 5 | 4.38 | 3.77 | 7.47 | 1.41 | 19.5% | 3.7% | 0.88 | 62.6% |
| 2015 | 22 | A+ | 97.0 | 3 | 5 | 3.06 | 3.05 | 6.40 | 2.13 | 17.2% | 5.7% | 0.37 | 70.2% |
| 2015 | 22 | AA | 36.7 | 1 | 3 | 4.91 | 4.20 | 8.59 | 4.17 | 21.7% | 10.6% | 0.98 | 62.8% |

**Background:** Signed out of Santo Domingo at the age of 17 in 2010, Garcia's taken the level-by-level approach in each of the succeeding seasons prior to 2015. Garcia spent the entire 2011 campaign twirling games in the Dominican Summer League. He followed that up with a year in the Gulf Coast, then another year with Batavia, then another year with Greensboro. Last season, however, marked the first time in his five-year career that Garcia appeared at two different levels. The 6-foot-2, 170-pound southpaw opened the year with 18 starts in Jupiter, fanning 17.2% and walking 5.7% of the batters he faced in 97.0 innings of work. Miami bumped him up to Jacksonville in late July for another seven starts. Overall, Garcia tallied a 104-to-40 strikeout-to-walk ratio in 133.2 innings to go along with a 3.57 ERA.

**Projection**: Garcia looks better in a weak system like Miami. He's continued to plod along the lower levels without truly differentiating himself among his peers – sans his strong showing with Batavia in 2013. Otherwise, he's never fanned more than 21.7% of the batters he's faced in a season. He might develop into a backed starting pitcher, but he could just as easily (A) flame out in the upper minors or get pushed into a relief role in the next two or three years.

**Ceiling:** 1.0-win player
**Risk:** Moderate
**MLB ETA:** 2018

## 15. Austin Dean, LF

**MiLB Rank:** N/A
**Position Rank:** N/A

| Born: 10/14/93 | Age: 22 | Bats: R | Top CALs: Danry Vasquez, Drew Vettleson, |
| Height: 6-1 | Weight: 190 | Throws: R | Juan Portes, Ka'Ai Tom, Casey Craig |

| Season | Age | LVL | PA | 2B | 3B | HR | AVG | OBP | SLG | ISO | BB% | K% | wRC+ |
|--------|-----|-----|-----|----|----|----|-------|-------|-------|-------|------|------|------|
| 2013 | 19 | A- | 231 | 12 | 7 | 2 | 0.268 | 0.325 | 0.418 | 0.150 | 7.4% | 20.3% | 125 |
| 2014 | 20 | A | 449 | 20 | 4 | 9 | 0.308 | 0.371 | 0.444 | 0.136 | 8.5% | 16.0% | 128 |
| 2015 | 21 | A+ | 578 | 32 | 2 | 5 | 0.268 | 0.318 | 0.366 | 0.098 | 6.7% | 13.1% | 107 |

**Background:** One of the better surprises in the system two years ago, Dean's production took a noticeable downturn as the club pushed him up to Jupiter for the first time in 2015. Coming off of a .308/.371/.444 showing with Greensboro, Dean hit a league average-ish .268/.318/.366 – though he managed to slug a career best 32 doubles as well as a pair of triples, five homeruns, and 18 stolen bases.

 **Projection**: I really had high hopes for the semi-toolsy outfielder, but his recent stumble clouds his future as a potential big league outfielder. The former fourth rounder's power took a dramatic step backward en route to posting the second lowest slugging percentage of his career. It's no surprise that CAL links him to a pair of similarly toolsy outfielders with cloudy big league futures in Danry Vasquez and Drew Vettleson.

**Ceiling:** 1.0-win player
**Risk:** Moderate
**MLB ETA:** 2018

## 16. Victor Araujo, RHP

**MiLB Rank:** N/A
**Position Rank:** N/A

| Born: 11/09/92 | Age: 23 | Bats: R | Top CALs: Michael Marby, T.J. Large, |
| Height: 5-11 | Weight: 170 | Throws: R | Brandon Kloess, Pedro Vidal, Cole Johnson |

| YEAR | Age | Level | IP | W | L | ERA | FIP | K/9 | BB/9 | K% | BB% | HR/9 | LOB% |
|------|-----|-------|------|---|---|------|------|-------|------|-------|------|------|-------|
| 2013 | 23 | R | 76.3 | 5 | 3 | 6.48 | 4.30 | 8.84 | 2.36 | 22.2% | 5.9% | 0.83 | 54.2% |
| 2014 | 24 | A | 68.0 | 5 | 2 | 1.32 | 2.57 | 9.79 | 1.99 | 28.7% | 5.8% | 0.26 | 81.9% |
| 2014 | 24 | A+ | 5.0 | 0 | 1 | 7.20 | 5.94 | 7.20 | 3.60 | 18.2% | 9.1% | 1.80 | 53.6% |
| 2015 | 25 | A+ | 50.0 | 3 | 3 | 5.40 | 4.16 | 9.90 | 2.52 | 25.4% | 6.5% | 1.08 | 52.9% |
| 2015 | 25 | A+ | 20.3 | 0 | 0 | 0.89 | 1.94 | 10.18 | 2.21 | 27.7% | 6.0% | 0.00 | 91.3% |

**Background:** Acquired along with Jeff Brigham as part of the Marlins' deal that shipped Mat Latos westward, Araujo had a very Araujo-like year in High Class A last season: he posted an impeccable – damn near impressive – 78-to-19 strikeout-to-walk ratio in 70.1 innings of work between both organizations. It comes on the heels of his breakout 2014 season, which was also the first one working as a fulltime reliever, when he posted a nearly identical 75-to-20 strikeout-to-walk ratio in 73.0 innings between the Midwest and California Leagues. For his career, the 5-foot-11, 170-pound Dominican-born right-hander is averaging a spectacular 9.2 punch outs and just 2.4 walks per nine innings across six different seasons.

**Projection**: Overall, it was nice little haul for the rapidly aging Mat Latos. Both Jeff Brigham and Araujo could develop into serviceable middle relief types. Araujo has proven – time and time again – that he's ready to be pushed quickly through the minors. Hopefully, the Marlins realize that in 2016

**Ceiling:** 1.0-win player
**Risk:** Moderate
**MLB ETA:** 2016/2017

## 17. Jeff Brigham, RHP

**MiLB Rank:** N/A
**Position Rank:** N/A

| Born: 02/16/92 | Age: 24 | Bats: R | Top CALs: Pedro Figueroa, Dennis O'Grady, |
| Height: 6-0 | Weight: 200 | Throws: R | Jeff Kaplan, Robert Nixon, Luis De Paula |

| YEAR | Age | Level | IP | W | L | ERA | FIP | K/9 | BB/9 | K% | BB% | HR/9 | LOB% |
|------|-----|-------|------|---|---|------|------|-------|------|-------|-------|------|-------|
| 2014 | 22 | R | 32.7 | 0 | 3 | 3.58 | 4.37 | 9.09 | 4.41 | 23.6% | 11.4% | 0.55 | 75.8% |
| 2015 | 23 | A | 7.0 | 2 | 0 | 1.29 | 1.11 | 14.14 | 2.57 | 42.3% | 7.7% | 0.00 | 80.0% |
| 2015 | 23 | A+ | 68.0 | 4 | 5 | 5.96 | 5.28 | 8.47 | 4.76 | 20.0% | 11.3% | 1.06 | 63.4% |
| 2015 | 23 | A+ | 33.7 | 2 | 2 | 1.87 | 2.75 | 5.88 | 2.41 | 16.1% | 6.6% | 0.00 | 77.3% |

**Background:** Part of the July 20th three-team mega-deal that sent declining veteran Mat Latos to the Dodgers – briefly – Brigham, a 6-foot, 200-pound hard-throwing righty out of Washington, tossed 108.2 innings, all but seven coming in High Class A, while averaging 8.0 strikeouts and 3.9 walks per nine innings. For his career,

he's posted a 130-to-63 K/BB ratio in 141.1 IP.

**Projection**: Brigham isn't long for the rotation, but he does have some upside as a hard-throwing reliever if – or when – the organization decides to push him into a relief role. One thing that's incredibly intriguing: the 2014 fourth round pick averaged just 4.42 strikeouts per nine innings in his entire collegiate career, but since entering pro ball he's averaged 8.3 punch outs per nine innings.

**Ceiling:** 1.0-win player
**Risk:** Moderate
**MLB ETA:** 2018

## 18. Brian Schales, 3B

**MiLB Rank:** N/A
**Position Rank:** N/A

| Born: 02/13/96 | Age: 20 | Bats: R | Top CALs: Juremi Profar, Miguel Andujar, |
| Height: 6-1 | Weight: 170 | Throws: R | Janluis Castro, Sergio Alcantara, Trace Loehr |

| Season | Age | LVL | PA | 2B | 3B | HR | AVG | OBP | SLG | ISO | BB% | K% | wRC+ |
|---|---|---|---|---|---|---|---|---|---|---|---|---|---|
| 2014 | 18 | R | 200 | 8 | 0 | 1 | 0.243 | 0.318 | 0.306 | 0.064 | 8.0% | 14.0% | 86 |
| 2015 | 19 | A | 497 | 21 | 3 | 4 | 0.260 | 0.330 | 0.348 | 0.088 | 7.6% | 15.3% | 97 |

**Background:** Plucked out of Edison High School in the fourth round two years ago, Schales didn't look all that promising during his debut in the Gulf Coast League, hitting .243/.318/.306 with eight doubles and one homerun en route to tallying an 86 wRC+. But the club aggressively pushed him up the Sally last season, and Schales saw a significant rise in production: .260/.330/.348 with a 97 wRC+.

**Projection**: As noted in other parts of the book, Greensboro's home park massively inflates offensive production. But the best part of Schales' development is the fact that he fared much better away from the Grasshoppers ballpark, hitting .257/.316/.324 at home vs. .262/.344/.371 on the road. Obviously, it's still far from top prospect status, but it's something to build upon. He still hasn't shown much power either.

**Ceiling:** 1.0-win player
**Risk:** Moderate
**MLB ETA:** 2019

## 19. Brian Anderson, 2B/3B

**MiLB Rank:** N/A
**Position Rank:** N/A

| Born: 05/19/93 | Age: 23 | Bats: R | Top CALs: Kevin Ahrens, juan Avila, |
| Height: 6-3 | Weight: 185 | Throws: R | Joe Leonard, Danny Valencia, David Vidal |

| Season | Age | LVL | PA | 2B | 3B | HR | AVG | OBP | SLG | ISO | BB% | K% | wRC+ |
|---|---|---|---|---|---|---|---|---|---|---|---|---|---|
| 2014 | 21 | A | 172 | 7 | 0 | 8 | 0.314 | 0.378 | 0.516 | 0.203 | 7.6% | 16.3% | 148 |
| 2015 | 22 | A+ | 530 | 22 | 2 | 8 | 0.235 | 0.304 | 0.340 | 0.105 | 7.5% | 20.6% | 99 |

**Background:** A consistent, polished collegiate bat taken in the third round two years ago out of the University of Arkansas, Anderson left the school as a career .318/.418/.467 player, hitting 30 doubles, eight triples, and 13 homeruns while swiping 17 bags in 171 total games. The Marlins aggressively pushed the second/third baseman through the lower levels during his debut. And Anderson responded well, hitting .300/.363/.496 between his brief stops with Batavia and Greensboro. Keeping with the rapid development plan, Miami sent Anderson up to Jupiter for the 2015. And let's just say that he wasn't nearly as ready as they thought he would be. In 132 games with the Hammerheads, the 6-foot-3, 185-pound infielder batted a lowly .235/.304/.340 with 22 doubles, two triples, eight homeruns, and a pair of stolen bases. Also, at the time of the writing Anderson was sporting an equally troubling .115/.111/.115 line in the Arizona Fall League.

**Projection**: Here's what I wrote prior to the 2014 draft:

*"The bat plays well in the middle infield, but his size may eventually push him to an outfield role. Anderson's sort of like a poor man's Jason Kipnis – the tools aren't as impressive across the board but manage to grade out as solid average. Decent plate discipline, though his willingness to take one off the elbow helps the OBP, double-digit power potential, handful of stolen bases, and a .260- to .270-ish average."*

*"If Anderson can stay at second, which, again, isn't a certainty, he has an outside shot of being a league average regular down the line – if everything breaks the right way. More likely, though, his ceiling will fall somewhere between Quad-A status and solid big league bench bat."*

After that ugly showing in High Class A last season, it's pretty safe to assume that he's heading down the Quad-A status road. And not to pile on, but here's the most damning aspect: he never made any adjustments throughout the long season as his OPS totals ranged from .580 through .667 from May through September.

**Ceiling:** 1.0-win player
**Risk:** Moderate
**MLB ETA:** 2017

## 20. Isaiah White, CF

**MiLB Rank:** N/A
**Position Rank:** N/A

| Born: 01/07/97 | Age: 19 | Bats: R | Top CALs: Raphael Ramirez, Lance Jeffries, |
|---|---|---|---|
| Height: 6-0 | Weight: 170 | Throws: R | Jeffrey Diehl, Yair Lopez, Trayvon Robinson |

| Season | Age | LVL | PA | 2B | 3B | HR | AVG | OBP | SLG | ISO | BB% | K% | wRC+ |
|---|---|---|---|---|---|---|---|---|---|---|---|---|---|
| 2015 | 18 | R | 132 | 7 | 2 | 0 | 0.294 | 0.321 | 0.381 | 0.087 | 2.3% | 33.3% | 111 |

**Background:** The club's most recent third round pick, White, who was plucked out of Greenfield School in Wilson, North Carolina, hit a solid .294/.321/.381 with seven doubles, two triples, and 13 stolen bases (in 13 attempts) en route to posting a 111 wRC+.

**Projection:** Again, not too much data to go off of, just 132 total trips to the plate, but it's encouraging nonetheless. Or it's at least more encouraging than most of the club's past top draft picks. White didn't show a whole lot of power or patience, which is troubling, but the base-thievery is very intriguing.

**Ceiling:** Too Soon to Tell
**Risk:** N/A
**MLB ETA:** N/A

## 21. Justin Twine, SS

**MiLB Rank:** N/A
**Position Rank:** N/A

| Born: 10/07/95 | Age: 20 | Bats: R | Top CALs: Junior Lake, Jeudy Valdez, |
|---|---|---|---|
| Height: 5-11 | Weight: 205 | Throws: R | Gari Pena, Felix Gonzalez, Garabez Rosa |

| Season | Age | LVL | PA | 2B | 3B | HR | AVG | OBP | SLG | ISO | BB% | K% | wRC+ |
|---|---|---|---|---|---|---|---|---|---|---|---|---|---|
| 2014 | 18 | R | 179 | 8 | 5 | 1 | 0.229 | 0.285 | 0.355 | 0.127 | 3.4% | 29.1% | 86 |
| 2015 | 19 | A | 473 | 20 | 3 | 7 | 0.206 | 0.235 | 0.310 | 0.104 | 1.3% | 22.8% | 53 |

**Background:** A second round pick out of Fall City High School in 2014, Twine looked craptastic during his professional debut in the Gulf Coast League, hitting a lowly .229/.285/.355 in 179 trips to the plate. And the organization, not known for making the most prudent of decisions (two words: Marcell Ozuna) opted to push the unproven shortstop up to the Sally. He, of course, struggled – *mightily*.

**Projection:** At one point when it's become as clear as death-and-taxes does the organization just say, "Hey, you know what? The kid we've invested a lot of money in is clearly overmatched in the Sally, just like he was in his debut two years ago, let's bounce him down a level, OK?" Then again...this is the Marlins we're talking about.

I guess if you wanted to point at a silver lining – or at least a quasi-silver lining – you could look at his month of August when he batted .255/.267/.431. Defensively, he committed 29 errors in 117 games...

**Ceiling:** 1.0-win player
**Risk:** Moderate to High
**MLB ETA:** 2018

## 22. Justin Cohen, C

**MiLB Rank:** N/A
**Position Rank:** N/A

| Born: 09/26/96 | Age: 19 | Bats: R | Top CALs: Jonathan Talley, Mike Meyers, |
|---|---|---|---|
| Height: 6-0 | Weight: 190 | Throws: R | Jon Egan, Jorge Alfaro, Daniel Diaz |

| Season | Age | LVL | PA | 2B | 3B | HR | AVG | OBP | SLG | ISO | BB% | K% | wRC+ |
|---|---|---|---|---|---|---|---|---|---|---|---|---|---|
| 2015 | 18 | R | 63 | 4 | 0 | 2 | 0.321 | 0.371 | 0.500 | 0.179 | 7.9% | 38.1% | 158 |

**Background:** I typically avoid writing about any new incoming picks – especially prep players – taken beyond the third, maybe fourth rounds. But Cohen's .321/.371/.500 triple-slash line, even if it was just in 18 games, offers up hope in a system as bereft of impact talent as Miami's. The club's latest sixth rounder hit .321/.371/.600 with six extra-base hits in 63 plate appearances.

# Miami Marlins

**Projection**: He could be something. Or nothing. But he signed a deal in excess of $500,000, the largest deal given to a sixth round pick.

**Ceiling:** Too Soon to Tell
**Risk:** N/A
**MLB ETA:** N/A

## 23. Blake Anderson, C

**MiLB Rank: N/A**
**Position Rank: N/A**

| Born: 01/05/96 | Age: 20 | Bats: R | Top CALs: Brandon Snyder, Tyler Weeden, |
| Height: 6-3 | Weight: 180 | Throws: R | Alixon Suarez, Charles Moorman, Steven Baron |

| Season | Age | LVL | PA | 2B | 3B | HR | AVG | OBP | SLG | ISO | BB% | K% | wRC+ |
|---|---|---|---|---|---|---|---|---|---|---|---|---|---|
| 2015 | 19 | A- | 128 | 6 | 0 | 2 | 0.220 | 0.273 | 0.322 | 0.102 | 2.3% | 32.8% | 78 |

**Background:** Widely regarded as a significant reach as the 36th overall pick two years ago, Anderson's first two professional seasons have done nothing to dispel that notion. After batting a Freddy Krueger-esque .108/.287/.135 (because it was downright scary), Anderson batted a lowly .220/.273/.322 (six doubles and two dingers) with just eight extra-base hits in 31 games with Batavia.

**Projection**: On the positive side, Anderson's overall production improved by more than 60%. Of course, jumping from a truly putrid 48 wRC+ to a less-putrid 78 wRC+ isn't worth celebrating. And let's not mention that Anderson walked just three times in 128 plate appearances last season as well. Then there's the punch out rate: 32.8%. He looks solid behind the plate, so there's that...

**Ceiling:** 1.0-win player
**Risk:** High
**MLB ETA:** 2020

## 24. Chris Reed, LHP

**MiLB Rank: N/A**
**Position Rank: N/A**

| Born: 05/20/90 | Age: 26 | Bats: L | Top CALs: Eduardo Sierra, Alex Sogard, |
| Height: 6-3 | Weight: 225 | Throws: L | Steven Hensley, David Kopp, Heath Rollins |

| YEAR | Age | Level | IP | W | L | ERA | FIP | K/9 | BB/9 | K% | BB% | HR/9 | LOB% |
|---|---|---|---|---|---|---|---|---|---|---|---|---|---|
| 2013 | 23 | AA | 137.7 | 4 | 11 | 3.86 | 3.73 | 6.93 | 4.12 | 18.1% | 10.7% | 0.59 | 72.1% |
| 2014 | 24 | AA | 137.0 | 4 | 8 | 3.22 | 3.80 | 7.62 | 3.61 | 20.1% | 9.5% | 0.66 | 65.4% |
| 2014 | 24 | AAA | 21.3 | 0 | 3 | 10.97 | 6.89 | 7.59 | 4.64 | 15.9% | 9.7% | 2.11 | 51.2% |
| 2015 | 25 | AA | 23.7 | 2 | 2 | 7.23 | 5.32 | 6.08 | 6.85 | 14.7% | 16.5% | 0.76 | 51.1% |
| 2015 | 25 | AAA | 31.7 | 1 | 0 | 3.69 | 4.77 | 7.96 | 4.83 | 20.7% | 12.6% | 0.85 | 79.4% |

**Background:** Miami acquired the lefty in a straight-up one-for-one challenge trade with the Dodgers mid-July last season, sending another big lefty, Grant Dayton, to Dodgers. Reed was the 16th overall pick in the famous – at least what I keep telling people, or anyone that will listen – 2011 draft. Los Angeles grabbed the former Stanford Cardinal just picks ahead of Sonny Gray, Kolten Wong, Alex Meyer, Robert Stephenson, Joe Panik, etc... Anyway, after his failed conversion into the rotation, LA pushed the 6-foot-3, 225-pound southpaw back into the bullpen for the first time since entering pro ball. And the results were...actually much worse. Reed's always struggled with his control/command, but his walk rates were slowly trending in the right way, averaging 4.1 BB/9 in 2013 and 3.8 BB/9 two years ago. Last season, though, he walked 35 in 55.1 innings of work. He also made a brief, two-game appearance with the Marlins following the trade.

**Projection**: The fastball isn't nearly as dominant as his lofty draft status would lead you to believe; it averaged just a smidge over 91 mph during his four-inning big league stint. He might be able to carve out a role as a middle relief arm, but the roads to The Show are littered with plenty of former first round arms that couldn't quite hack it. And, unfortunately, Reed may be the next to fall in line.

**Ceiling:** 1.0-win player
**Risk:** Moderate to High
**MLB ETA:** Debuted in 2015

## 25. Anfernee Seymour, SS

**MiLB Rank: N/A**
**Position Rank: N/A**

| Born: 06/24/95 | Age: 21 | Bats: B | **Top CALs:** Matt Bouchard, Estarlin De Los Santos, Deiner Lopez, Aaron Blanton, Jorge Flores |
|---|---|---|---|
| Height: 5-11 | Weight: 165 | Throws: R | |

| Season | Age | LVL | PA | 2B | 3B | HR | AVG | OBP | SLG | ISO | BB% | K% | wRC+ |
|---|---|---|---|---|---|---|---|---|---|---|---|---|---|
| 2014 | 19 | R | 112 | 0 | 1 | 0 | 0.245 | 0.333 | 0.265 | 0.020 | 10.7% | 24.1% | 84 |
| 2014 | 19 | R | 112 | 0 | 1 | 0 | 0.245 | 0.333 | 0.265 | 0.020 | 10.7% | 24.1% | 84 |
| 2015 | 20 | A- | 266 | 10 | 4 | 0 | 0.273 | 0.338 | 0.349 | 0.076 | 7.5% | 19.5% | 107 |

**Background:** A Bahamian-born shortstop taken in the seventh round out of Florida High School two years ago, Seymour had a solid sophomore season in the New York-Penn League in 2015. In 266 plate appearances with Batavia, the 5-foot-11 switch-hitter batted a league average-ish .273/.338/.349 – though he slugged just 10 doubles and a quartet of triples.

**Projection**: Again, why the club opted to keep Justin Twine up in the Sally when he clearly wasn't ready and forced Seymour to stay in short-season ball is beyond me. Is Seymour the heir-apparent to the big league job? Nope. But he was better suited for the South Atlantic League. He has speed, but brings a sieve to the field. Maybe Seymour develops into a big league backup.

**Ceiling:** 0.5- to 1.0-win player
**Risk:** Moderate to High
**MLB ETA:** 2019

## Barely Missed:

- **Tim Berry, LHP** – Claimed off of waivers from the Orioles this offseason, the former 50th round pick got strung with a millstone around his neck in the form of a 7.32 ERA in Class AA last season, though his 4.53 FIP is far less damning. Once upon a time he looked like a backend starter, but his career has stagnated the past two years. He might be able to carve out a role as a LOOGY.

- **Justin Bohn, IF** – The former seventh round pick's production cratered in Class AA which prompted a demotion back to the Florida State League. Here's what I wrote in last year's book: "A future utility guy without a true above-average tool. He'll take the occasional walk, flash doubles pop, and can swipe a bag or two. He also looks solid with the glove."

- **Gabriel Castellanos, LHP** – The then-21-year-old hasn't made a whole lot of progress since passing the GCL test in 2012. He offers up some swing-and-miss potential – particularly if he gets pushed into a relief role – but his problematic control leave an awful lot to be desired.

- **J.T. Riddle, IF** – League average minor league bat hit a combined .283/.323/.368 mainly between Jupiter and Jacksonville last season. He might be able to get a couple cups of coffee as a bench option.

## *Bird Doggin' It – Additional Prospects to Keep an Eye in 2016*

| Player | Age | POS | Notes |
|---|---|---|---|
| Samuel Castro | 18 | 2B/SS | Hit a respectable .265/.332/.325 as a 17-year-old in the Gulf Coast League. Just another name to watch in 2016. |
| Miguel Del Pozo | 23 | LHP | Posted an impressive 43-to-15 strikeout-to-walk ratio in 37.0 innings as a reliever last season. Miami pushed him into the rotation for a handful starts at the end of the season. |
| Ben Holmes | 24 | LHP | Former Oregon State University stud made 24 starts – and three relief appearances – between Greensboro and Jupiter, averaging 7.0 K/9 and 3.3 BB/9. |
| Justin Jacome | 22 | LHP | Club's most recent fifth round pick out of UC Santa Barbara, Jacome posted a solid 96-to-26 strikeout-to-walk in 116.2 innings during his final collegiate season. He profiles as a middle relief arm. |
| Blake Logan | 24 | RHP | Hefty right-hander out of East Oklahoma State College averaged 9.1 K/9 and 3.2 BB/9 between Jacksonville and New Orleans. |
| Michael Mader | 22 | LHP | A third round pick two years ago, Mader tossed 140.2 innings with just 86 punch outs and 57 walks. He's headed for relief-dom. |
| Nefi Ogando | 27 | RHP | Re-claimed from Philly on waivers, Ogando's heater has averaged 95+ mph during his big league stint last season, but he's never missed a whole lot of bats at any point. |
| Chris Paddack | 20 | RHP | Typical big Texas-born prep arm taken in the eighth round last June. Paddack, who stands 6-foot-4 and 195 pounds, posted an impressive 39-to-7 strikeout-to-walk ratio in 45.1 innings in the Gulf. |
| Cody Poteet | 21 | RHP | Three-year starter at UCLA, Marlins grabbed the 6-foot-2 right-hander in the fourth round last June. After a brief stint in the NYPL he's headed to the Sally in 2016. |
| Tomas Telis | 25 | C | A solid backup option at the big league level, Telis hit a combined .297/.336/.394 in Class AAA between the Rangers and Marlins organization. |

# Milwaukee Brewers

**State of the Farm System:** Brewers' new General Manager David Stearns, the youngest GM in baseball right now, has been busy since taking office in late September:

- November 18th, 2015: Flipped veteran reliever Francisco Rodriguez to Detroit for minor league infielder Javier Betancourt and the (in)famous player to be named later.
- November 19th, 2015: Dealt right-hander Cy Sneed to Houston for infielder Jonathan Villar
- November 20th, 2015: Shipped infielder Luis Sardinas to Seattle for highly, highly underrated outfielder Ramon Flores.
- December 9th, 2015: Acquired a trio of low level arms – Daniel Missaki, Carlos Herrera, and Freddy Peralta – from the Mariners for Adam Lind.
- December 17th, 2015: Traded Jason Rogers to Pittsburgh for Trey Supak and Keon Broxton.

Only three of the players the franchise acquired – Missaki, Betancourt, and Supak – made their Top 25. But Stearns is walking into a pretty favorable position.

The farm has decade-plus big future league shortstop in Orlando Arcia, whom I named as one of the minors' Top 25 Breakout Prospects heading into last season, tools-laden outfielder Brett Phillips, 2014 first round lefty Kodi Medeiros, big league ready right-hander Jorge Lopez, and Trent Clark, the club's dynamic first round pick last June. Arcia, Phillips, and Lopez all figure to see plenty of time with the Brew Crew in 2016.

Outside of that, Milwaukee's farm has several complementary-type prospects who all have a chance to develop into solid big leaguers down the line, including: Devin Williams, sabermetric darling Michael Reed, Josh Hader, Zach Davies, and Ramon Flores.

Clint Coulter, one of the system's breakout prospects two years ago, took a tremendous step backward in 2015.

| Rank | Name | POS |
|---|---|---|
| 1 | Orlando Arcia | SS |
| 2 | Brett Phillips | LF/CF |
| 3 | Kodi Medeiros | LHP |
| 4 | Jorge Lopez | RHP |
| 5 | Trent Clark | CF |
| 6 | Devin Williams | RHP |
| 7 | Michael Reed | OF |
| 8 | Josh Hader | LHP |
| 9 | Zach Davies | RHP |
| 10 | Gilbert Lara | SS |
| 11 | Nathan Kirby | LHP |
| 12 | Ramon Flores | CF |
| 13 | Rymer Liriano | OF |
| 14 | Clint Coulter | RF |
| 15 | Daniel Missaki | RHP |
| 16 | Adrian Houser | RHP |
| 17 | Isan Diaz | 2B/SS |
| 18 | Tyrone Taylor | OF |
| 19 | David Burkhalter | RHP |
| 20 | Monte Harrison | CF/RF |
| 21 | Cody Ponce | RHP |
| 22 | Tyler Wagner | RHP |
| 23 | Jacob Gatewood | SS |
| 24 | Marcos Diplan | RHP |
| 25 | Trey Supak | RHP |

**Review of the 2015 Draft:** Former General Manager Doug Melvin, who stepped down from the position in mid-August, had a strong final draft class for the organization. Toolsy center fielder Trent Clark, the 15th overall pick, had a tremendously positive debut as he split time between the Arizona Summer and Pioneer Leagues, hitting .309/.424/.430 with seven doubles, six triples, two homeruns, and 25 stolen bases.

Former Virginia lefty Nathan Kirby has a chance to move quickly and land into #4/#5-type role with the big league club in a couple seasons. And second round pick, Cody Ponce, could be a gem unearthed out of Division II powerhouse California Polytechnic State University. Fourth round pick Demi Orimoloye slugged .292/.319/.518 with nine doubles, a pair of triples, six dingers, and 19 stolen bases in 33 games in rookie ball.

## 1. Orlando Arcia, SS

**MiLB Rank: #18**
**Position Rank: #3**

| Born: 08/04/94 | Age: 21 | Bats: R | Top CALs: Jorge Polanco, Jose Pirela, |
|---|---|---|---|
| Height: 6-0 | Weight: 165 | Throws: R | Francisco Lindor, Odubel Herrera, Reegie Corona |

| Season | Age | LVL | PA | 2B | 3B | HR | AVG | OBP | SLG | ISO | BB% | K% | wRC+ |
|---|---|---|---|---|---|---|---|---|---|---|---|---|---|
| 2013 | 18 | A | 486 | 14 | 5 | 4 | 0.251 | 0.314 | 0.333 | 0.081 | 7.2% | 8.2% | 84 |
| 2014 | 19 | A+ | 546 | 29 | 5 | 4 | 0.289 | 0.346 | 0.392 | 0.102 | 7.7% | 11.9% | 113 |
| 2014 | 19 | A+ | 546 | 29 | 5 | 4 | 0.289 | 0.346 | 0.392 | 0.102 | 7.7% | 11.9% | 113 |
| 2015 | 20 | AA | 552 | 37 | 7 | 8 | 0.307 | 0.347 | 0.453 | 0.146 | 5.4% | 13.2% | 126 |

**Background:** "Arcia's one of the biggest sleeper prospects in all of baseball." That's how I concluded the write-up on the 6-foot, 165-pound shortstop out of Venezuela. In last year's book I ranked Arcia as Milwaukee's #1 prospect – ahead of a surging Clint Coulter, in front of the club's most recent first round pick, 12th overall, Kodi Medeiros, and besting toolsy center fielder – and another personal favorite – Tyrone Taylor. Well, Arcia isn't a sleeper prospect anymore – not after his dominant showing in the Southern League. After making his debut in the Dominican Summer League at the age of 16, Arcia would eventually miss his entire sophomore campaign as he recovered from a broken ankle. And this is where the front office made one of the boldest moves imaginable when it comes to player development: when Arcia returned to full health for the start of 2013, Milwaukee pushed the then-18-year-old up to the Midwest League – despite (A) being one of the youngest players in the level, (B) completely bypassing all the stateside rookie and short-season leagues, and (C) having missed a full season of action.

Arcia responded by hitting .251/.314/.333, a showing that appears far less impressive without the proper context.

He would earn another aggressive promotion up to High Class A the following season, hitting .289/.346/.392 en route to topping the league average production mark by 13%. And then he set the baseball world ablaze...

Arcia took off like a bat-out-of-hell to open the 2015 season: he slugged .409/.468/.545 in the season's opening month and was sporting an impressive .341/.393/.495 by the time the end of May rolled around. He cooled off a bit in June (.247/.267/.361), but rebounded to hit .305/.341/.459 over his final 59 games. He finished the year with a .307/.347/.453 triple-slash line with career bests in doubles (37), triples (seven), homeruns (eight) while swiping 25 bags and topping the league average mark by 26%.

**Projection:** Here's what I wrote in last year's book:

> Consider this little comparison between 19-year-old middle infielders in the FSL:
>
> - Player A: .302/.340/.391 with a 112 wRC+
> - Arcia: .289/.346/.392 with a 113 wRC+
>
> Player A is none other than one of the most dynamic young shortstops in baseball right now – Starlin Castro. You get the sense that Arcia's offensive game is just going to explode once his body begins to catch up with his level of competition. Above-average speed, improving power that could top out in the 15-HR range and a ton of youth; add it all up and Arcia's one of the biggest sleeper prospects in all of baseball.

Just to add some additional context to his 2015 numbers, consider the following:

- Among all hitters with 400+ plate appearances, Arcia's overall production, 126 wRC+, was the best showing among all 20-year-olds in the Southern League. It also bested a couple offensively-minded 20-year-old top prospects as well (Nomar Mazara and J.P. Crawford).

So here's where we stand with Arcia after his wildly successful 2015 season: he's still showing above-average speed with a below-average walk rate, but the power has blossomed – and is still blossoming – into double-digit homer territory. Add in defensive value, and Arcia has a chance to peak as an All-Star caliber shortstop – perhaps as soon as 2017.

**Ceiling:** 3.5- to 4.0-win player
**Risk:** Moderate
**MLB ETA:** 2016/2017

## 2. Brett Phillips, LF/CF

**MiLB Rank: #43**
**Position Rank: #11**

| Born: 05/30/94 | Age: 22 | Bats: L | Top CALs: Aaron Cunningham, Jake Marisnick, |
|---|---|---|---|
| Height: 6-0 | Weight: 180 | Throws: R | Gregory Polanco, Josh Reddick, Dalton Pompey |

| Season | Age | LVL | PA | 2B | 3B | HR | AVG | OBP | SLG | ISO | BB% | K% | wRC+ |
|---|---|---|---|---|---|---|---|---|---|---|---|---|---|
| 2013 | 19 | R | 113 | 7 | 1 | 0 | 0.247 | 0.371 | 0.353 | 0.106 | 15.0% | 18.6% | 114 |
| 2014 | 20 | A | 443 | 21 | 12 | 13 | 0.302 | 0.362 | 0.521 | 0.219 | 8.1% | 17.2% | 148 |
| 2014 | 20 | A+ | 128 | 8 | 2 | 4 | 0.339 | 0.421 | 0.560 | 0.220 | 10.9% | 15.6% | 156 |
| 2015 | 21 | A+ | 322 | 19 | 7 | 15 | 0.320 | 0.379 | 0.588 | 0.268 | 6.8% | 19.9% | 159 |
| 2015 | 21 | AA | 145 | 8 | 4 | 1 | 0.321 | 0.372 | 0.463 | 0.142 | 5.5% | 17.9% | 134 |
| 2015 | 21 | AA | 98 | 7 | 3 | 0 | 0.250 | 0.361 | 0.413 | 0.163 | 14.3% | 30.6% | 120 |

**Background**: One of the top prospects in a heavily loaded Houston farm system, Milwaukee acquired Philips – along with polished lefty Josh Hader, enigmatic outfielder Domingo Santana, and right-hander Adrian Houser – from the Astros prior to the trade deadline in exchange for All-Star outfielder Carlos Gomez and underrated veteran Mike Fiers. Phillips, a former sixth round pick out of Seminole High School in 2012, had a massive coming out party two years ago when he robustly slugged .310/.375/.529 with 29 doubles, 14 triples, 17 homeruns, and 23 stolen bases as he spent time between Quad Cities and Lancaster. The toolsy outfielder responded by mashing to the tune of .320/.379/.588 for 66 games – though those numbers drop to .297/.356/.528 once adjusted for the park, according to StatCorner – before earning a promotion up to the minors' most daunting Challenge: Class AA.

And Phillips hardly missed a beat.

In his final 31 games in the Astros' development engine, Phillips batted .321/.372/.463 en route to topping the Texas League offensive average by 34%. Milwaukee would send their shiny new prospect to their respective Class AA affiliate, the Biloxi Shuckers in the Southern League, for another 23 games.

Phillips would finish the year with an aggregate .309/.374/.527 – an eerily similar showing from the previous year.

**Projection**: Outside of once-in-a-generational talents like Bryce Harper or Mike Trout, if one would build an outfielder from the ground up it might resemble something similar to Phillips. He shows a tremendous eye at the plate, ranging from above-average to plus at time. He's equipped with the rare combination of power and speed with a 20/20 big league season on the horizon. He handles lefties and righties well, makes consistent contact, and has handled older competition with aplomb.

And CAL seems to be a fan as well, comparing him to a quartet of potentially above-average big league outfielders in Jake Marisnick, Gregory Polanco, Josh Reddick, and Dalton Pompey.

**Ceiling:** 3.0- to 3.5-win player
**Risk:** Moderate
**MLB ETA:** 2016/2017

## 3. Kodi Medeiros, LHP

**MiLB Rank: #98**
**Position Rank: N/A**

| Born: 05/25/96 | Age: 20 | Bats: L | Top CALs: Robbie Ray, Frank Lopez, |
|---|---|---|---|
| Height: 6-2 | Weight: 180 | Throws: L | Eduardo Sanchez, Jack Flaherty, David Holmberg |

| YEAR | Age | Level | IP | W | L | ERA | FIP | K/9 | BB/9 | K% | BB% | HR/9 | LOB% |
|---|---|---|---|---|---|---|---|---|---|---|---|---|---|
| 2014 | 18 | R | 17.7 | 0 | 2 | 7.13 | 4.94 | 13.25 | 6.62 | 28.0% | 14.0% | 1.02 | 48.3% |
| 2015 | 19 | A | 93.3 | 4 | 5 | 4.44 | 2.96 | 9.06 | 3.86 | 23.5% | 10.0% | 0.00 | 60.9% |

**Background:** Hailing from paradise – quite literally – Milwaukee grabbed the fireball-slinging southpaw out of a Hawaiian high school with the 12th overall pick in the 2014. The 6-foot-2, 180-pound southpaw was the seventh hurler taken that year, though he was just the second prep lefty. Medeiros had a fairly positive debut in the Arizona Summer League two years ago, sans a horrific start against the Dodgers' farm team. He would finish the year with 26 strikeouts in 17.1 innings. Milwaukee opted – unsurprisingly given their precedent with past top prospects – to push Medeiros up to the Midwest League for the start of 2015. And as one of just seven teenage arms to throw 90+ innings in the league, Medeiros would finish his first taste of full season action by fanning 23.5% and walking 10.0% of the total batters he faced en route to finishing with an impressive 2.96 FIP.

**Projection**: Here's how the wiry southpaw stacks up against all other hurlers to throw at least 90 innings in either Low Class A league:

- His strikeout percentage, 23.5%, ranked 12th.
- His 2.93 FIP ranked the 7th lowest.
- His strikeout rate, 9.06 K/9, ranked as the 9th highest.

And perhaps the single best statistic: his generated a **61.5% groundball rate** last season.

Again, that's for hurlers with at least 90 innings in either the Midwest or South Atlantic Leagues. One of the knocks on the promising lefty coming out of the draft was his low arm slot, perhaps creating an advantage for right-handed bats that will inevitably see the ball longer. But so far righties haven't had too much success against Medeiros: they batted a lowly .241/.339/.285 against him last season. His control still has a bit to go, but Medeiros looks like a potential mid-rotation-caliber arm.

**Ceiling:** 2.5- to 3.0-win player
**Risk:** Moderate to High
**MLB ETA:** 2018

## 4. Jorge Lopez, RHP

**MiLB Rank:** #115
**Position Rank:** N/A

| Born: 02/10/93 | Age: 23 | Bats: R | Top CALs: Jeanmar Gomez, Jason Adam, |
|---|---|---|---|
| Height: 6-3 | Weight: 190 | Throws: R | Jon Moscot, James Houser, Kyle Lobstein |

| YEAR | Age | Level | IP | W | L | ERA | FIP | K/9 | BB/9 | K% | BB% | HR/9 | LOB% |
|---|---|---|---|---|---|---|---|---|---|---|---|---|---|
| 2013 | 20 | A | 117.0 | 7 | 8 | 5.23 | 4.67 | 7.08 | 3.69 | 17.9% | 9.4% | 1.00 | 62.3% |
| 2014 | 21 | A+ | 137.7 | 10 | 10 | 4.58 | 3.88 | 7.78 | 3.01 | 20.4% | 7.9% | 0.78 | 64.3% |
| 2015 | 22 | AA | 143.3 | 12 | 5 | 2.26 | 3.36 | 8.60 | 3.27 | 24.0% | 9.1% | 0.57 | 83.5% |

**Background:** The system's pitching equivalent of Orlando Arcia, Lopez had his own breakout season in Class AA in 2015. A second round pick out of Caguas Military Academy in Puerto Rico in 2011, Lopez looked a bit underwhelming during his first two professional seasons: he tossed only 12 innings during his debut in the Arizona Summer League and followed that up with some up-and-down moments as he split his 2012 season between the Dominican and Arizona Summer Leagues. But the front office began to challenge the 6-foot-3, 190-pound right-hander a year later as they pushed him up to Wisconsin in the Midwest League; he finished with an unsightly – or downright ugly – 5.23, the second consecutive season in which he posted an ERA in the 5.00s. Undeterred, however, Milwaukee continued to challenge Lopez as they bumped him up to Brevard County in 2014, and his number started to tick upward: 137.1 IP, 119 K, 46 BB, and a 3.88 FIP.

And that trend continued all the way through last season with The Shuckers.

In 24 starts in the Southern League, Lopez set career bests in innings (143.1), ERA (2.26), FIP (3.36), strikeout percentage (21.7%), and strikeout-to-walk percentage (14.9%). He would also toss another 10 innings in Milwaukee in two late-season starts as well.

**Projection:** Lopez has quietly built a strong case to be included in the team's depleted Opening Day rotation, one that currently includes Wily Peralta, Jimmy Nelson, Taylor Jungmann, Zach Davies, and Matt Garza. When he's at his best, Lopez pumps his sinking fastball in the low- to mid-90s – which has generated groundball rates hovering around 50% in the minors – to go along with a low-80s curveball, and hard changeup. He has the look of a potential #3/#4-type arm.

**Ceiling:** 2.5-win player
**Risk:** Moderate
**MLB ETA:** Debuted in 2015

## 5. Trent Clark, CF

**MiLB Rank:** #126
**Position Rank:** N/A

| Born: 11/01/96 | Age: 19 | Bats: L | Top CALs: Aaron Hicks, Cornelius Randolph, |
|---|---|---|---|
| Height: 6-0 | Weight: 205 | Throws: L | Jesse Winker, Royce Consigli, Brandon Diaz |

| Season | Age | LVL | PA | 2B | 3B | HR | AVG | OBP | SLG | ISO | BB% | K% | wRC+ |
|---|---|---|---|---|---|---|---|---|---|---|---|---|---|
| 2015 | 18 | R | 52 | 0 | 0 | 1 | 0.310 | 0.431 | 0.381 | 0.071 | 17.3% | 15.4% | 119 |
| 2015 | 18 | R | 200 | 7 | 6 | 1 | 0.309 | 0.422 | 0.442 | 0.133 | 15.0% | 18.0% | 154 |

**Background:** For the third consecutive time the Brewers grabbed a promising high school prospect in the opening round – though it should be noted that this doesn't include 2013 when the club didn't own a first round pick. Clark got off to an impressive start in his burgeoning professional career, hitting a combined .309/.424/.430 between his stops in the Arizona Summer and Pioneer Leagues.

**Projection:** Obviously, the sample size is still quite limited, just over 250 plate appearances, but Clark showcased an impressive offensive toolkit during his debut: a tremendous eye at the plate to help utilize his above-average to plus-speed, gap-to-gap power (he slugged seven doubles, six triples, and one homerun), and a strong hit tool. He's likely to spend his 2016 season in the Midwest League where we'll have a better feel for his status as a (potential) top prospect.

**Ceiling:** Too Soon to Tell
**Risk:** N/A
**MLB ETA:** N/A

## 6. Devin Williams, RHP

**MiLB Rank: #139**
**Position Rank: N/A**

| Born: 09/21/94 | Age: 21 | Bats: R | Top CALs: Torey Deshazier, Jake Newberry, |
|---|---|---|---|
| Height: 6-3 | Weight: 165 | Throws: R | Eduar Lopez, Tyler Cravy, Alexander Santana |

| YEAR | Age | Level | IP | W | L | ERA | FIP | K/9 | BB/9 | K% | BB% | HR/9 | LOB% |
|---|---|---|---|---|---|---|---|---|---|---|---|---|---|
| 2013 | 18 | R | 34.7 | 1 | 3 | 3.38 | 4.01 | 10.13 | 5.71 | 24.7% | 13.9% | 0.00 | 68.5% |
| 2014 | 19 | R | 66.3 | 4 | 7 | 4.48 | 4.02 | 8.95 | 2.71 | 23.2% | 7.0% | 0.68 | 64.0% |
| 2015 | 20 | A | 89.0 | 3 | 9 | 3.44 | 3.28 | 9.00 | 3.64 | 23.5% | 9.5% | 0.30 | 69.4% |

**Background:** Combined with Kodi Medeiros, David Burkhalter, Angel Ventura, and Cy Sneed, Williams helped the Timber Rattlers form one of the better – and deeper – rotations in the lower levels of the minors last season. A 2013 second round pick out of Hazelwood High School, home to former big leaguer Kyle McClellan, Williams hasn't been thrust through the system as quickly as some of his counterparts. He opened his career up in the Arizona Summer League three years ago, posting a solid 39-to-22 strikeout-to-walk ratio in 34.2 innings. But the club opted to push him only up to the Pioneer League the next season instead of sending him straight into Low Class A – a decision that was more likely than not precipitated by his control issues. And it proved to the right decision: he walked 20 in 66.0 innings of work with Helena while averaging a punch out per inning.

He finally made it up to the Midwest League last season. And he shined.

Like Medeiros and Burkhalter, Williams offered up a promising 89-to-36 strikeout-to-walk ratio in 89.0 innings. He finished the year with a 3.44 ERA and a slightly better 3.28 FIP.

**Projection**: Continually offering up an above-average ability to miss bats, Williams has proven on back-to-back occasions that his control issues three years ago were just a tiny blip on the map. Since walking 5.7 BB/9 in 2013, he's averaged a solid 3.25 BB/9. Williams is another mid-rotation caliber arm, sliding between Medeiros and Burkhalter.

**Ceiling:** 2.0- to 2.5-win player
**Risk:** Moderate
**MLB ETA:** 2018

## 7. Michael Reed, OF

**MiLB Rank: #142**
**Position Rank: N/A**

| Born: 11/18/92 | Age: 23 | Bats: R | Top CALs: Brandon Nimmo, Robbie Grossman, |
|---|---|---|---|
| Height: 6-0 | Weight: 190 | Throws: R | Shane Peterson, Aaron Hicks, Daryl Jones |

| Season | Age | LVL | PA | 2B | 3B | HR | AVG | OBP | SLG | ISO | BB% | K% | wRC+ |
|---|---|---|---|---|---|---|---|---|---|---|---|---|---|
| 2013 | 20 | A | 539 | 23 | 13 | 1 | 0.286 | 0.385 | 0.400 | 0.114 | 13.2% | 20.0% | 125 |
| 2014 | 21 | A+ | 457 | 20 | 5 | 5 | 0.255 | 0.396 | 0.378 | 0.123 | 17.1% | 17.3% | 130 |
| 2015 | 22 | AA | 377 | 20 | 5 | 5 | 0.278 | 0.379 | 0.422 | 0.144 | 14.1% | 21.2% | 129 |
| 2015 | 22 | AAA | 148 | 13 | 2 | 0 | 0.246 | 0.351 | 0.381 | 0.135 | 13.5% | 20.9% | 100 |
| 2015 | 22 | MLB | 6 | 1 | 0 | 0 | 0.333 | 0.333 | 0.500 | 0.167 | 0.0% | 50.0% | 123 |

**Background:** An on-base percentage dynamo, the speedy Texas-born outfielder continued to ride his wave of high walk rates into another solid, some would say underrated, season. After looking lost and overmatched during his first two professional seasons, Reed established himself as a solid prospect during his 2013 stint in the Midwest League when he batted .286/.385/.400. He followed that up with an even better showing in High Class A the following season – at least in terms of overall production as measured by *Weighted Runs Created Plus* – when he hit .255/.396/.378 with a 130 wRC+. Reed spent the majority of last year in Biloxi, but made brief stints in the PCL and an even shorter tenure as a late season call-up in Milwaukee.

**Projection**: Speed, incredibly strong walk rates, and enough power to keep most pitchers honest. It's really a dangerous combination for opponents. Reed is sporting an incredible 14.1% walk rate for his *career*. The hit tool isn't particularly strong, but the power's been slowly coming along. His yearly ISOs since 2013: .114, .123, and .141. Add it all up and you're talking about a potential better than average big league regular.

**Ceiling:** 2.0- to 2.5-win player
**Risk:** Moderate
**MLB ETA:** 2016/2017

## 8. Josh Hader, LHP

**MiLB Rank: #169**

**Position Rank: N/A**

| Born: 04/07/94 | Age: 22 | Bats: L | Top CALs: Randall Delgado, Luke Jackson, |
|---|---|---|---|
| Height: 6-3 | Weight: 160 | Throws: L | Jordan Walden, Edwin Diaz, Johnny Barbato |

| YEAR | Age | Level | IP | W | L | ERA | FIP | K/9 | BB/9 | K% | BB% | HR/9 | LOB% |
|---|---|---|---|---|---|---|---|---|---|---|---|---|---|
| 2013 | 19 | A | 85.0 | 3 | 6 | 2.65 | 3.93 | 8.36 | 4.45 | 21.4% | 11.4% | 0.42 | 67.6% |
| 2013 | 19 | A | 22.3 | 2 | 0 | 3.22 | 4.05 | 6.45 | 4.84 | 17.2% | 12.9% | 0.00 | 73.3% |
| 2014 | 20 | A+ | 103.3 | 9 | 2 | 2.70 | 4.10 | 9.75 | 3.31 | 26.6% | 9.0% | 0.78 | 74.5% |
| 2014 | 20 | AA | 20.0 | 1 | 1 | 6.30 | 4.87 | 10.80 | 7.20 | 25.5% | 17.0% | 0.90 | 65.2% |
| 2015 | 21 | AA | 65.3 | 3 | 3 | 3.17 | 3.47 | 9.51 | 3.31 | 24.2% | 8.4% | 0.69 | 70.4% |
| 2015 | 21 | AA | 38.7 | 1 | 4 | 2.79 | 2.81 | 11.64 | 2.56 | 32.9% | 7.2% | 0.70 | 76.1% |

**Background:** Proving yet again that minor league awards and organizational recognitions are meaningless, Hader was named the California League Pitcher of the Year *and* Houston's Minor League Pitcher of the Year after his successful 2014 season. And then he was traded by the Astros a handful of months later as part of the package for All-Star outfielder Carlos Gomez. Hader spent all of last season hurling games in Class AA, despite changing organizations. In a combined 104.0 innings, Hader posted a 119-to-35 strikeout-to-walk ratio to go along with a 3.03 ERA. For his career the 6-foot-3, 160-pound southpaw out of Old Mill High School has averaged 9.9 punch outs and 3.8 walks every nine innings spanning his four-year career.

**Projection**: At 6-foot-3 and barely a dried plantain slice above 160 pounds, Hader's consistently missed a whole lot of bats – no more important that the 10.3 K/9 he fanned last season in Class AA, the minors' most important level. The control is subpar, but it's not too far off from being average. He looks like a solid bet to develop into a #4-type arm. And there's a chance he takes another step into a legitimate #3. He could be an Erik Bedard if everything breaks the right way.

One final note: CAL is incredibly impressed by Hader by comparing him to Randall Delgado, Luke Jackson, Jordan Walden, Edwin Diaz, and Johnny Barbato.

**Ceiling:** 2.0-win player
**Risk:** Moderate
**MLB ETA:** 2016

## 9. Zach Davies, RHP

**MiLB Rank: #192**

**Position Rank: N/A**

| Born: 02/07/93 | Age: 23 | Bats: R | Top CALs: Jonathon Niese, Eduardo Rodriguez, |
|---|---|---|---|
| Height: 6-0 | Weight: 160 | Throws: R | James Parr, Randall Delgado, Jameson Taillon |

| YEAR | Age | Level | IP | W | L | ERA | FIP | K/9 | BB/9 | K% | BB% | HR/9 | LOB% |
|---|---|---|---|---|---|---|---|---|---|---|---|---|---|
| 2013 | 20 | A+ | 148.7 | 7 | 9 | 3.69 | 3.28 | 7.99 | 2.30 | 21.3% | 6.1% | 0.61 | 66.3% |
| 2014 | 21 | AA | 110.0 | 10 | 7 | 3.35 | 3.30 | 8.92 | 2.62 | 23.4% | 6.9% | 0.65 | 70.3% |
| 2015 | 22 | AAA | 101.3 | 5 | 6 | 2.84 | 3.08 | 7.19 | 2.93 | 19.3% | 7.9% | 0.36 | 77.1% |
| 2015 | 22 | AAA | 27.0 | 1 | 2 | 5.00 | 4.45 | 7.00 | 4.00 | 16.4% | 9.4% | 0.67 | 70.5% |

**Background:** On July 31st, 2014, the Brewers flipped underrated southpaw Anthony Banda and first round bust Mitch Haniger to the Diamondbacks for Gerardo Parra. One year later, to the day, Milwaukee flipped the quintessential league average outfielder to the Orioles for right-armed stick-figure known as Zach Davies. Originally taken in the late, late rounds of the 2011 draft, Davies, who stands an average 6-foot but weighs in at an Olive Oyl-esque 160 pounds, has quickly – and quietly – moved up the minor league ladder. The rail-thin starter made his pro debut in the Midwest League a year after being selected in the 26th round; he would average 7.2 punch outs and 3.6 walks per nine innings. He would follow that up with an even better showing in the Carolina League in 2013: 148.2 IP, 132 K, 38 BB, and a 3.28 FIP. He would eventually make stops in the Eastern, International, and Pacific Coast Leagues over the next two seasons before making a six-start debut in Milwaukee.

**Projection**: Fringy upper-80s fastball highlighted by his strong pitchability and a trio of secondary offerings (cutter, changeup, and curveball), Davies hasn't really shown anything but success in professional baseball, including his six-game stint with the Brewers. He obviously won't throw it by anyone, but he does everything else well enough. CAL is obviously a big fan, comparing him to Jonathan Niese, Eduardo Rodriguez, Randall Delgado, and Jameson Taillon.

**Ceiling:** 1.5- to 2.0-win player
**Risk:** Low to Moderate
**MLB ETA:** Debuted in 2015

## 10. Gilbert Lara, SS

**MiLB Rank: #202**
**Position Rank: N/A**

| Born: 10/30/97 | Age: 18 | Bats: R | Top CALs: Amed Rosario, Yeyson Yrizarri, |
|---|---|---|---|
| Height: 6-2 | Weight: 190 | Throws: R | Willi Castro, Luis Joseph, Byron Capellan |

| Season | Age | LVL | PA | 2B | 3B | HR | AVG | OBP | SLG | ISO | BB% | K% | wRC+ |
|---|---|---|---|---|---|---|---|---|---|---|---|---|---|
| 2015 | 17 | R | 49 | 3 | 0 | 0 | 0.205 | 0.286 | 0.273 | 0.068 | 10.2% | 24.5% | 50 |
| 2015 | 17 | R | 214 | 4 | 5 | 1 | 0.248 | 0.285 | 0.332 | 0.084 | 4.2% | 19.2% | 81 |

**Background:** Given a massive $3.2 million bonus on the international market in 2014, the Brewers waited until last season to debut their shiny new young shortstop. The organization pushed him straight into the Arizona Summer League and later the advanced rookie level as Lara hit a combined .240/.285/.321 with seven doubles, five triples, one homerun, and three stolen bases.

**Projection**: Basically the equivalent of an incoming high first round pick, it can't be overlooked that the Dominican-born shortstop was also tasked with leaving home and moving to another country. He didn't show too much offensively, but it's only 200 or so plate appearances.

**Ceiling:** Too Soon to Tell
**Risk:** N/A
**MLB ETA:** N/A

## 11. Nathan Kirby, LHP

**MiLB Rank: #233**
**Position Rank: N/A**

| Born: 11/23/93 | Age: 22 | Bats: L | Top CALs: N/A |
|---|---|---|---|
| Height: 6-2 | Weight: 185 | Throws: L | |

| YEAR | Age | Level | IP | W | L | ERA | FIP | K/9 | BB/9 | K% | BB% | HR/9 | LOB% |
|---|---|---|---|---|---|---|---|---|---|---|---|---|---|
| 2015 | 21 | A | 12.7 | 0 | 1 | 5.68 | 4.18 | 4.97 | 4.97 | 12.3% | 12.3% | 0.00 | 60.9% |

**Background:** Here are some interesting tidbits about draft success stories and the University of Virginia:

- The collegiate powerhouse had seven players taken in the 2015 draft and eight players taken the year before.
- The school has had a total of 39 players selected since 2010 – an average of more than six per year.
- Over the past two years the Cavaliers have had an astounding four first round picks: Kirby (2015), Nick Howard (2014), Derek Fisher (2014), and Mike Papi (2014).

Kirby's just the last in a long line of successful collegiate players recruited and churned out by Virginia. Taken with the 40th pick last year, Kirby was in the midst of another strong campaign – 64.0 IP, 81 K, 32 BB, and a 2.53 FIP – before a lat injury prematurely ended the year. He tossed another 12.2 inning in the Midwest League during his debut, posting a 7-to-7 strikeout-to-walk ratio.

**Projection**: Here's what I wrote about the eventual first rounder prior to the draft:

> The best southpaw prospect to come out of the University of Virginia since Danny Hultzen in 2011 and arguably the second best in the school's illustrious history, Kirby doesn't own the arm strength of many of the class' top hurlers (Carson Fulmer, Kyle Funkhouser, Mike Matuella, Phil Bickford, etc…). But he's generally around the plate, despite the noticeable backwards step in control this season. And one wonders if a strained lat, which will likely force him to miss the season's final weeks, may have been an issue before he was eventually shut down.
>
> In terms of ceiling, Kirby is very similar to that of St. Louis' Marco Gonzales, another polished southpaw who posted solid peripherals through his three-year collegiate run.
>
> Kirby's a solid #4-type arm – safe, low ceiling/high floor guy who should move rather quickly.

**Ceiling:** 1.5- to 2.0-win player
**Risk:** Moderate
**MLB ETA:** 2017/2018

## 12. Ramon Flores, OF

**MiLB Rank: #242**
**Position Rank: N/A**

| Born: 03/26/92 | Age: 24 | Bats: L | Top CALs: Logan Morrison, L.J. Hoes, |
|---|---|---|---|
| Height: 5-10 | Weight: 190 | Throws: L | Jake Smolinski, Andrew McCutchen, Ryan Sweeney |

| Season | Age | LVL | PA | 2B | 3B | HR | AVG | OBP | SLG | ISO | BB% | K% | wRC+ |
|---|---|---|---|---|---|---|---|---|---|---|---|---|---|
| 2013 | 21 | AA | 620 | 25 | 6 | 6 | 0.260 | 0.353 | 0.363 | 0.103 | 12.4% | 15.8% | 104 |
| 2014 | 22 | AAA | 271 | 17 | 4 | 7 | 0.247 | 0.339 | 0.443 | 0.196 | 12.2% | 16.6% | 116 |
| 2015 | 23 | AAA | 63 | 6 | 0 | 2 | 0.423 | 0.524 | 0.654 | 0.231 | 17.5% | 9.5% | 217 |
| 2015 | 23 | AAA | 321 | 11 | 2 | 7 | 0.286 | 0.377 | 0.417 | 0.130 | 12.1% | 13.4% | 133 |
| 2015 | 23 | MLB | 33 | 1 | 0 | 0 | 0.219 | 0.219 | 0.250 | 0.031 | 0.0% | 12.1% | 21 |

**Background:** A fantastic little pick up from the Yankees for infielder Luis Sardinas, Flores turned in another highly underrated campaign last season, hitting .308/.401/.454 between Scranton/Wilkes-Barre and Tacoma, with 17 doubles, two triples, nine homeruns, and three stolen bases in 87 games.

**Projection**: There's really nothing to not like about Flores: he's a career .275/.363/.405 hitter with surprising power, a tremendous eye at the plate, sneaky speed, and a decent hit tool. The real question is how come he's never received an extended stint in the big leagues at this point, even after hitting a combined .282/.376/.449 in 150 Class AAA games in his career? You'll look up one day and Flores will be putting together a Gerardo Parra-like career.

**Ceiling:** 1.5-win player
**Risk:** Low to Moderate
**MLB ETA:** Debuted in 2014

## 13. Rymer Liriano, OF

**MiLB Rank: 248**
**Position Rank: N/A**

| Born: 08/11/91 | Age: 25 | Bats: R | Top CALs: Jeremy Hazelbaker, Justin Huber, |
|---|---|---|---|
| Height: 6-0 | Weight: 230 | Throws: R | Dustin Martin, Todd Frazier, Johan Limonta |

| Season | Age | LVL | PA | 2B | 3B | HR | AVG | OBP | SLG | ISO | BB% | K% | wRC+ |
|---|---|---|---|---|---|---|---|---|---|---|---|---|---|
| 2014 | 23 | AA | 415 | 20 | 2 | 14 | 0.264 | 0.335 | 0.442 | 0.178 | 8.4% | 24.6% | 122 |
| 2014 | 23 | MLB | 121 | 2 | 0 | 1 | 0.220 | 0.289 | 0.266 | 0.046 | 7.4% | 32.2% | 62 |
| 2015 | 24 | AAA | 549 | 31 | 3 | 14 | 0.292 | 0.383 | 0.460 | 0.167 | 11.7% | 24.0% | 128 |

**Background:** It's been a rough couple of years for the Dominican-born outfielder: he lost the entire 2013 season recovering from Tommy John surgery, then came back and looked OK – in his return to the upper levels of minors, but looked overmatched in a 38-game cup of coffee in San Diego (.220/.289/.266). The front office bounced the once-promising bat back to the Pacific Coast League for the entirety of 2015 where he would bat a solid .292/.383/.460 with 31 doubles, three triples, 14 homeruns, and 18 stolen bases while topping the league average mark by 28%. For his seven-year minor league career, Liriano is sporting a .277/.350/.435 triple-slash line, slugging 172 doubles, 28 triples, and 68 homeruns while swiping 190 bags in 738 games.

**Projection**: Liriano was always a bit overrated as a prospect, something that I mentioned in my first book two years ago. It's not that he's a terrible minor leaguer – because he's not – but his overall skill set, as promising as it looks on paper, hasn't led to any type of extended dominance since his breakout season in 2011. But he could find a home on a non-contending team like San Diego where he'll carve out some league-average offensive production and defensive value.

**Ceiling:** 2.0-win player
**Risk:** Moderate
**MLB ETA:** Debuted in 2014

## 14. Clint Coulter, RF

**MiLB Rank: N/A**
**Position Rank: N/A**

| Born: 07/30/93 | Age: 22 | Bats: R | Top CALs: Mike Moustakas, Gary Sanchez, |
|---|---|---|---|
| Height: 6-3 | Weight: 222 | Throws: R | Christian Vazquez, Tyler Marlette, Ronny Rodriguez |

| Season | Age | LVL | PA | 2B | 3B | HR | AVG | OBP | SLG | ISO | BB% | K% | wRC+ |
|---|---|---|---|---|---|---|---|---|---|---|---|---|---|
| 2013 | 19 | A | 135 | 5 | 1 | 3 | 0.207 | 0.299 | 0.345 | 0.138 | 8.1% | 23.0% | 84 |
| 2014 | 20 | A | 529 | 28 | 3 | 22 | 0.287 | 0.410 | 0.520 | 0.233 | 13.8% | 19.5% | 165 |
| 2015 | 21 | A+ | 569 | 30 | 3 | 13 | 0.246 | 0.329 | 0.397 | 0.150 | 8.1% | 16.2% | 123 |

**Background:** Likely in an effort to help speed up his development path to the big leagues Milwaukee moved Coulter from behind the plate and into right field for the first time in his four-year career last year. And for the first month of the season that path looked like it would happen far

sooner than not for the former the first rounder pick. Coulter battered the Florida State League pitching to the tune of .325/.429/.649 with three doubles, a pair of triples, and six homeruns in his first 20 games with Brevard County. But the FSL started to hit back – in a major way. Coulter posted a .196/.281/.330 triple-slash line over his next 29 games and he wouldn't post an OPS above .712 in any of the remaining months. Overall, Coulter finished the year with a .246/.329/.397 triple-slash line with a career best 30 doubles, three triples, 13 homeruns, and half-a-dozen stolen bases.

**Projection**: Despite the noticeable downturn in his triple-slash line Coulter still managed to top the FSL average production by 23% last season – tied for the 12th best showing in the league. The hit tool is a bit underwhelming at this point, but he compensates with a decent eye and above-average in-game power. The soon-to-be-22-year-old needs to prove that his breakout 2014 season was just that...a breakout, and not an aberration.

**Ceiling:** 2.0- to 2.5-win player
**Risk:** High
**MLB ETA:** 2017/2018

## 15. Daniel Missaki, RHP

**MiLB Rank: N/A**
**Position Rank: N/A**

| Born: 04/09/96 | Age: 20 | Bats: R | Top CALs: Luis Ortiz, Frankie Montas, |
| Height: 6-0 | Weight: 170 | Throws: R | Felix Jorge, Jose Campos, Allen Webster |

| YEAR | Age | Level | IP | W | L | ERA | FIP | K/9 | BB/9 | K% | BB% | HR/9 | LOB% |
|------|-----|-------|------|---|---|------|------|-------|------|-------|------|------|-------|
| 2013 | 17 | R | 13.0 | 0 | 1 | 6.23 | 4.08 | 10.38 | 3.46 | 25.0% | 8.3% | 0.69 | 64.8% |
| 2014 | 18 | R | 58.7 | 6 | 3 | 2.76 | 3.14 | 9.51 | 2.45 | 26.2% | 6.8% | 0.46 | 74.4% |
| 2015 | 19 | A | 34.3 | 1 | 2 | 3.41 | 1.85 | 8.91 | 1.31 | 25.6% | 3.8% | 0.00 | 61.1% |

**Background:** Signed out of Brazil at 16-years-old around the same time the club inked Luiz Gohara, Missaki had a strong showing in the Appalachian League two years ago, posting a 2.76 ERA and 3.14 FIP while averaging 9.51 K/9 and just 2.45 BB/9 in 58.2 innings of work. The 6-foot, 170-pound hurler got off to an impressive start in 2015 – he was sporting an impressive 34-to-5 strikeout-to-walk ratio through his first six starts – before succumbing to injury woes – the dreaded Tommy John surgery. For his brief, brief career, Missaki has thrown 106.0 innings with 111 strikeouts, 26 walks, and a tidy 3.40 ERA.

**Projection**: There's very little data to go off of, obviously, but Missaki's been far more impressive than his Brazilian counterpart Luiz Gohara, who also has a far superior power repertoire. Missaki isn't particularly overpowering, but he shows poise beyond his years with the rare ability to miss bats *and* limit walks before the age of 20. Hopefully, he makes a full recovery from TJ because he was showing some backend big league starting potential.

**Ceiling:** 1.5- to 2.0-win player
**Risk:** Moderate to High
**MLB ETA:** 2019

## 16. Adrian Houser, RHP

**MiLB Rank: N/A**
**Position Rank: N/A**

| Born: 02/02/93 | Age: 23 | Bats: R | Top CALs: Kevin Comer, Brian Flynn, |
| Height: 6-4 | Weight: 230 | Throws: R | Richard Castillo, Dan Griffin, Brandon Barker |

| YEAR | Age | Level | IP | W | L | ERA | FIP | K/9 | BB/9 | K% | BB% | HR/9 | LOB% |
|------|-----|-------|-------|---|---|------|------|------|------|-------|------|------|-------|
| 2013 | 20 | A- | 50.0 | 0 | 4 | 3.42 | 2.70 | 7.02 | 1.80 | 18.1% | 4.6% | 0.18 | 66.6% |
| 2014 | 21 | A | 108.7 | 5 | 6 | 4.14 | 3.70 | 7.70 | 3.06 | 20.3% | 8.1% | 0.41 | 65.7% |
| 2015 | 22 | A+ | 49.7 | 2 | 2 | 4.35 | 4.04 | 9.97 | 3.62 | 25.1% | 9.1% | 0.54 | 64.1% |
| 2015 | 22 | AA | 33.3 | 1 | 2 | 6.21 | 5.70 | 6.21 | 4.05 | 15.1% | 9.9% | 1.62 | 62.2% |
| 2015 | 22 | AA | 37.0 | 4 | 1 | 2.92 | 3.55 | 7.78 | 1.46 | 21.1% | 4.0% | 0.97 | 69.8% |

**Background:** Also part of the four-for-two swap that sent Carlos Gomez and Mike Fiers packing to Houston, Houser, who was acquired along with Domingo Santana, Josh Hader, and Brett Phillips, made stops at four different leagues last season: he opened the year with 12 appearances (eight starts) in the California League, made another seven starts in the Texas League, then he started seven more games with Biloxi following the trade, and he made two more appearances in Milwaukee to cap off a wild 2015 campaign. Overall, the former 2011 second round pick finished his minor league season with a career high 120.0 innings while fanning 110 and walking 41 en route to posting an unsightly – and unlucky – 4.42 ERA.

**Projection**: The 6-foot-4 right-hander featured a hard mid-90s heater during his debut, complementing it with a low-80s curveball, and a changeup to finish off the typical three-pitch mix. Houser suffered through a bit of bad luck during his rapid rise to The Show last season – particularly his wonky homerun rate in Class AA. Houser surrendered 10 homeruns in 70.1 innings – or about 1.28 HR/9, a number incredibly high given his above-average groundball rates.

He's big, sturdy, and equipped with an above-average fastball and slightly below-average control. Teams could do far worse than run Houser out as their #5. He's likely headed to Class AAA to start the year, but he'll be among the first wave of arms called up.

**Ceiling:** 1.5-win player
**Risk:** Moderate
**MLB ETA:** Debuted in 2015

## 17. Isan Diaz, 2B/SS

**MiLB Rank: N/A**
**Position Rank: N/A**

| Born: 05/27/96 | Age: 20 | Bats: L | **Top CALs:** Moises Grance, David Bote, |
| Height: 5-10 | Weight: 185 | Throws: R | Jensi Peralta, Jorge Vega-Rosado, Danienger Perez |

| Season | Age | LVL | PA | 2B | 3B | HR | AVG | OBP | SLG | ISO | BB% | K% | wRC+ |
|---|---|---|---|---|---|---|---|---|---|---|---|---|---|
| 2014 | 18 | R | 212 | 7 | 5 | 3 | 0.187 | 0.289 | 0.330 | 0.143 | 11.8% | 26.4% | 83 |
| 2015 | 19 | R | 312 | 25 | 6 | 13 | 0.360 | 0.436 | 0.640 | 0.279 | 10.9% | 20.8% | 169 |

**Background:** After looking overmatched – and ill-suited – for professional baseball, even at its lowest levels, Diaz completely resurrected his status as a 2014 second round pick with a dominant showing in the Pioneer League last season. The lefty-swinging middle infielder batted .360/.436/.640 with a whopping 25 doubles, six triples, and 13 homeruns in just 68 games. Milwaukee acquired Diaz as part of a five-player trade this offseason.

**Projection:** Granted it's just 68 games in the Pioneer League, but here are those numbers prorated over the course of a 162-game season: 60 doubles, 14 triples, and 31 homeruns. That's impressive production at *any* level. And it goes without saying that Diaz likely paved the way straight to the Midwest League.

Here's the best part of Diaz's dominance last season: a lot of his underlying skill set should be easily maintained as he moves forward. Here are his peripherals between his disastrous showing in 2014 and his monstrous campaign last year:

| Year | League | BB% | K% | ISO | BABIP |
|---|---|---|---|---|---|
| 2014 | ARIZ | 11.80% | 26.40% | 0.143 | 0.248 |
| 2015 | PION | 10.90% | 20.80% | 0.279 | 0.434 |

He's still fairly combustible given that he was 19-years-old and dominating the Pioneer League, but above-average walk rates with no worse than solid-average power at a middle infielder position are very promising. But even as his BABIP normalizes in 2016 he should still be a force to be reckoned with.

**Ceiling:** 2.0-win player
**Risk:** High
**MLB ETA:** 2018

## 18. Tyrone Taylor, OF

**MiLB Rank: N/A**
**Position Rank: N/A**

| Born: 01/22/94 | Age: 22 | Bats: R | **Top CALs:** Teodoro Martinez, Albert Almora, |
| Height: 6-0 | Weight: 185 | Throws: R | Danry Vasquez, Jae-Hoon Ha, Cedric Hunter |

| Season | Age | LVL | PA | 2B | 3B | HR | AVG | OBP | SLG | ISO | BB% | K% | wRC+ |
|---|---|---|---|---|---|---|---|---|---|---|---|---|---|
| 2013 | 19 | A | 549 | 33 | 2 | 8 | 0.274 | 0.338 | 0.400 | 0.126 | 6.4% | 11.5% | 109 |
| 2014 | 20 | A+ | 559 | 36 | 3 | 6 | 0.278 | 0.331 | 0.396 | 0.118 | 7.0% | 10.4% | 107 |
| 2015 | 21 | AA | 504 | 20 | 3 | 3 | 0.260 | 0.312 | 0.337 | 0.077 | 6.2% | 10.9% | 84 |

**Background:** I've literally tried to will the former second round pick into a breakout season since I began writing about prospects. And it seemed, I'm sure, that I was practically pleading for him to realize his potential as a lesser version – albeit still quite valuable – of Mike Cameron. But, alas, the toolsy outfielder just hasn't cooperated as I had hoped. Taylor, the 92nd overall pick in the 2012 draft and just one selection before Phillies top prospect Nick Williams, looked lost during his first taste of the Southern League last season, hitting a disappointingly low .260/.312/.337 with full-season career lows in doubles (20), homeruns (3), and stolen bases (10). His overall production, per *Weighted Runs Created Plus*, 16% *below* the league average mark – another career low.

**Projection:** Taylor just hasn't been able to keep up with the club's slightly aggressive development plan at this point. He looked promising as a 19-year-old in the Midwest League three years ago, but his production has been in slow decline ever since. And it's now reached a point where he's going to need to rediscover so much of his once-promising offensive foundation. He's stopped running and hitting for power. He looks like a backup outfielder at this point, unfortunately.

**Ceiling:** 1.5-win player
**Risk:** Moderate to High
**MLB ETA:** 2017

## 19. David Burkhalter, RHP

**MiLB Rank:** N/A
**Position Rank:** N/A

| Born: 07/25/95 | Age: 20 | Bats: R | **Top CALs:** Steve Garrison, Will Smith, |
| Height: 6-3 | Weight: 190 | Throws: R | Victor Arano, Jeffry Antigua, Jackson Stephens |

| YEAR | Age | Level | IP | W | L | ERA | FIP | K/9 | BB/9 | K% | BB% | HR/9 | LOB% |
|------|-----|-------|-----|---|---|------|------|------|------|-------|------|------|-------|
| 2014 | 18 | R | 22.7 | 0 | 5 | 7.15 | 3.99 | 7.54 | 2.78 | 16.8% | 6.2% | 0.40 | 51.7% |
| 2015 | 19 | A | 101.0 | 5 | 9 | 4.99 | 3.51 | 8.29 | 1.96 | 21.7% | 5.1% | 0.80 | 57.1% |

**Background:** A sixth round pick out of Ruston High School two years ago, Burkhalter – ironically enough – bypassed an opportunity to work with former Brewers ace and four-time All-Star Ben Sheets, who is the pitching coach at the University of Louisiana-Monroe, and opted to sign with Milwaukee instead. The 6-foot-3, 190-pound right-hander had a decent showing in the Arizona Summer League during his debut as he posted a 19-to-7 strikeout-to-walk ratio in 22.2 innings of work – enough production to convince the organization's powers-that-be that he was ready for the Midwest League.

And he was.

Burkhalter tossed 101.0 innings with the Wisconsin Timber Rattlers last season, fanning nearly 22% and walking just 5.1% of the total batters he faced. His overall production was mired by an unlucky strand rate, 57.1%, as his 3.51 FIP clearly outshone his 4.99 ERA.

**Projection:** A sneaky good low level arm in the Brewers' system, Burkhalter's overall production is fairly similar to that of his more highly touted draft/teammate Kodi Medeiros. Consider the following:

| Player | Age | IP | K% | BB% | K/BB% | FIP |
|--------|-----|------|--------|--------|--------|------|
| David Burkhalter | 19 | 101.0 | 21.70% | 5.10% | 16.60% | 3.51 |
| Kodi Medeiros | 19 | 93.1 | 23.50% | 10.00% | 13.50% | 2.96 |

Burkhalter doesn't possess the power-based arsenal of Medeiros, but he does show better pitchability in terms of limiting walks. He could be a nice #4/#5 arm down the line.

**Ceiling:** 1.5-win player
**Risk:** Moderate to High
**MLB ETA:** 2018

## 20. Taylor Williams, RHP

**MiLB Rank:** N/A
**Position Rank:** N/A

| Born: 07/21/91 | Age: 24 | Bats: B | **Top CALs:** Edgmer Escalona, James Shepherd, |
| Height: 5-11 | Weight: 195 | Throws: R | Matthew Loosen, Cole Mccurry, Rohn Pierce |

| YEAR | Age | Level | IP | W | L | ERA | FIP | K/9 | BB/9 | K% | BB% | HR/9 | LOB% |
|------|-----|-------|-------|---|---|------|------|------|------|-------|------|------|-------|
| 2013 | 21 | R | 42.3 | 3 | 1 | 4.25 | 4.99 | 8.93 | 3.61 | 23.0% | 9.3% | 1.06 | 72.2% |
| 2014 | 22 | A | 107.0 | 8 | 1 | 2.36 | 2.69 | 9.42 | 1.93 | 26.4% | 5.4% | 0.34 | 72.0% |
| 2014 | 22 | A+ | 25.3 | 1 | 2 | 4.26 | 4.18 | 8.88 | 1.78 | 23.2% | 4.6% | 1.42 | 71.4% |

**Background:** Perhaps the single most impressive statistic I've stumbled across as I've written/researched the book this season: According to a report by Adam McCalvy on MLB.com, when Taylor Williams underwent the knife in early August last season he was the first player in the Milwaukee organization to undergo Tommy John surgery. And it bears repeating: in an age when it's more commonplace than not, the Milwaukee organization lost their first arm to Tommy John surgery in early August. Williams actually failed to appear in a game last year as he tried the rest-and-rehab approach. It didn't work – clearly. For his career, Williams has fanned 179 and walked just 45 in 174.2 innings between stints in the Pioneer, Midwest, and Florida State Leagues.

**Projection:** Since there's no new data on the hurler, here's what I wrote prior to the organization selecting in the fourth round in 2013:

> "The data's exceptionally limited – good, but limited. And there are not too many DI hurlers that can match his ability to miss bats and pound the zone. But the problem will come down to size, where teams shy away from sub-6-foot right-handers, particularly starters. He's probably headed for the third round or so, but he's going to be a steal – if the drafting team keeps him in the rotation."

Here's hoping that he makes a full recovery...

**Ceiling:** 1.5-win player
**Risk:** High
**MLB ETA:** 2018/2019

## 21. Monte Harrison, CF/RF

**MiLB Rank:** N/A
**Position Rank:** N/A

| Born: 08/10/95 | Age: 20 | Bats: R | Top CALs: Hilton Richardson, James Harris, |
|---|---|---|---|
| Height: 6-3 | Weight: 220 | Throws: R | Eduardo Sosa, Kenny Wilson, Jordon Austin |

| Season | Age | LVL | PA | 2B | 3B | HR | AVG | OBP | SLG | ISO | BB% | K% | wRC+ |
|---|---|---|---|---|---|---|---|---|---|---|---|---|---|
| 2014 | 18 | R | 224 | 7 | 2 | 1 | 0.261 | 0.402 | 0.339 | 0.078 | 13.8% | 21.4% | 126 |
| 2015 | 19 | R | 119 | 4 | 2 | 3 | 0.299 | 0.410 | 0.474 | 0.175 | 11.8% | 19.3% | 131 |
| 2015 | 19 | A | 184 | 6 | 2 | 2 | 0.148 | 0.246 | 0.247 | 0.099 | 7.6% | 41.8% | 49 |

**Background:** It took 46 games and a putrid .148/.246/.247 showing to convince the front office that he should be demoted down to the Pioneer League. Harrison, the club's second round pick two years ago hit .299/.410/.474 in 28 rookie league games before a gruesome broken ankle knocked him out of the remainder of the year following a late-July game.

**Projection:** The ankle injury, according to an MLB.com report, was so bad that his foot was pointing sideways after slipping on wet grass after rounding third base. And, obviously, injuries are always an unfortunate accident. But Harrison was in the midst of establishing his bat in the advanced rookie league. He batted .345/.456/.548 over his final 26 games. It's a bit surprising that Harrison was left up in the Midwest League for so long – especially considering his punch out rate was north of **41%**. Here's hoping for a full recovery.

**Ceiling:** 1.5-win player
**Risk:** Moderate to High
**MLB ETA:** 2019

## 22. Cody Ponce, RHP

**MiLB Rank:** N/A
**Position Rank:** N/A

| Born: 04/25/94 | Age: 22 | Bats: R | Top CALs: Justin Erasmus, Chris Rhoads, |
|---|---|---|---|
| Height: 6-6 | Weight: 240 | Throws: R | Scott Diamond, Jade Todd, Daniel Turpen |

| YEAR | Age | Level | IP | W | L | ERA | FIP | K/9 | BB/9 | K% | BB% | HR/9 | LOB% |
|---|---|---|---|---|---|---|---|---|---|---|---|---|---|
| 2015 | 21 | R | 5.0 | 0 | 0 | 3.60 | 2.55 | 7.20 | 0.00 | 21.1% | 0.0% | 0.00 | 50.0% |
| 2015 | 21 | A | 46.0 | 2 | 1 | 2.15 | 2.76 | 7.04 | 1.76 | 19.3% | 4.8% | 0.20 | 73.6% |

**Background:** Milwaukee dipped in the Division II ranks and selected the big right-hander in the second round of the draft last June. Ponce finished his amateur career with 159 punch outs and 49 walks in 183 innings. He tossed another 51.0 innings in pro ball during his debut, all but five of them coming in the Midwest League. He posted a 36-to-9 strikeout-to-walk ratio to go along with a 2.15 ERA and a 2.76 FIP.

**Projection:** Here's what I wrote prior to the draft last year:

> *"So this is where it gets tricky – sort of. Ponce has enough talent to compete – and succeed – against some of the best collegiate talent in nation as evidenced by his work in the Cape Cod, where he also earned a nod as one of the league's All-Stars. The problem, however, is that in three years at a suboptimal level – Division II – Ponce has never really stood out above the rest in terms of production.*
>
> *His control is solid-average but has wavered at times. When he's at his best he'll miss about one bat per inning. But, again, he's not facing the likes of Stanford, LSU, Oregon, Arizona, Vanderbilt, etc...*
>
> *Ignoring the shoulder issues he dealt with early this season, there's definitely some risk with Ponce.*
>
> *He could very easily – and likely – slide into the bullpen in the coming seasons."*

He's off to a promising start, and it wouldn't be surprising to see him start 2016 in High Class A.

**Ceiling:** 1.5-win player
**Risk:** Moderate to High
**MLB ETA:** 2018

## 23. Jacob Gatewood, SS

MiLB Rank: N/A
Position Rank: N/A

| Born: 09/25/95 | Age: 20 | Bats: R | Top CALs: Wilfredo, Sosa, Anthony Chavez, |
| Height: 6-5 | Weight: 190 | Throws: R | Jeudy Valdez, Luis Aviles, Francisco Sanchez |

| Season | Age | LVL | PA | 2B | 3B | HR | AVG | OBP | SLG | ISO | BB% | K% | wRC+ |
|---|---|---|---|---|---|---|---|---|---|---|---|---|---|
| 2014 | 18 | R | 222 | 6 | 0 | 3 | 0.206 | 0.249 | 0.279 | 0.074 | 5.9% | 32.0% | 56 |
| 2015 | 19 | R | 238 | 23 | 1 | 6 | 0.274 | 0.331 | 0.476 | 0.203 | 7.6% | 28.6% | 102 |
| 2015 | 19 | A | 193 | 5 | 1 | 4 | 0.209 | 0.275 | 0.316 | 0.107 | 7.3% | 33.7% | 74 |

**Background:** Easily the biggest boom-or-bust prospect in the entire 2014 draft class. Milwaukee opted to take the status quo approach with high ceiling prospect and aggressively challenge the former first round pick by pushing him directly up to the Midwest League to start last season – *despite looking completely out of whack during his debut in the Arizona Summer League*. The power-hitting shortstop batted a nightmarish .206/.249/.279 in 50 games as he fanned in nearly one-third of his plate appearances. And, lo and behold, he did the same damn thing when he was – wrongly! – pushed up to the Timber Rattlers: he "batted" .209/.275/.316 with another strikeout rate well on the wrong side of 30%. Those struggles continued when he was demoted back to Helena as well; he hit .238/.283/.393 over his first 21 games. But things seemed to click for him in the middle of July when he went on tear, batting .292/.361/.523. Milwaukee would – once again – bump him back up to the Midwest League at the end of the year and he promptly went 8-for-47.

**Projection**: Here's what I wrote in last year's book:

*"The book on Gatewood was quite simple: the power's a potential premium skill, but will he make enough contact in order to capitalize on it? Right now, the answer's a resounding no. Not only did he finish with the fifth worst production in the Arizona Summer League, but he whiffed in nearly one-third of his plate appearances. Power's at an absolute premium in professional ball, so it was a gamble worth taking. It just doesn't look like one that's going to pay off."*

Well, ditto... Although I should add that I'm shocked he's lasted this long at shortstop.

**Ceiling:** 1.5-win player
**Risk:** High
**MLB ETA:** 2016/2017

## 24. Marcos Diplan, RHP

MiLB Rank: N/A
Position Rank: N/A

| Born: 11/18/96 | Age: 19 | Bats: R | Top CALs: Zachary Bird, Hector Garcia, |
| Height: 6-0 | Weight: 160 | Throws: R | Joshua Blanco, Fabian Williamson, Leondy Perez |

| YEAR | Age | Level | IP | W | L | ERA | FIP | K/9 | BB/9 | K% | BB% | HR/9 | LOB% |
|---|---|---|---|---|---|---|---|---|---|---|---|---|---|
| 2014 | 17 | R | 64.3 | 7 | 2 | 1.54 | 4.05 | 7.97 | 5.04 | 22.4% | 14.1% | 0.28 | 79.2% |
| 2015 | 18 | R | 50.3 | 2 | 2 | 3.75 | 4.40 | 9.66 | 3.75 | 25.7% | 10.0% | 0.72 | 76.1% |

**Background:** As I noted in last year's book, Diplan, who was originally signed by the Texas Rangers for $1.3 million, was flipped to Milwaukee as part of the Yovani Gallardo package. Diplan moved up from the Dominican Summer League and straight into the Pioneer League last season. In 50.1 innings with Helena, the 6-foot, 160-pound right-hander posted an impressive 54-to-21 strikeout-to-walk ratio with a 4.40 FIP.

**Projection**: Diplan was a bit hittable when he wasn't unhittable last season. Meaning: he averaged nearly a base-knock per inning but helped compensate with a strong strikeout rate. He fanned more than a quarter of the batters he faced last season. At 6-foot and just 160-pounds, he doesn't offer up a whole lot projection. Let's see how he handles the Midwest League next year.

**Ceiling:** Too Soon to Tell
**Risk:** N/A
**MLB ETA:** N/A

# Milwaukee Brewers

## 25. Trey Supak, RHP

MiLB Rank: N/A
Position Rank: N/A

| Born: 05/31/96 | Age: 20 | Bats: R | Top CALs: Christopher Santamaria, Patrick Arnold, |
| Height: 6-5 | Weight: 210 | Throws: R | Julio Mateo, Orlando Munoz, Ronnie Williams |

| YEAR | Age | Level | IP | W | L | ERA | FIP | K/9 | BB/9 | K% | BB% | HR/9 | LOB% |
|------|-----|-------|------|---|---|------|------|------|------|-------|------|------|-------|
| 2014 | 18 | R | 24.0 | 1 | 3 | 4.88 | 5.67 | 7.88 | 4.13 | 19.1% | 10.0% | 1.50 | 79.1% |
| 2015 | 19 | R | 28.3 | 1 | 2 | 6.67 | 3.55 | 7.31 | 1.59 | 18.6% | 4.0% | 0.64 | 51.0% |

**Background:** Just like fellow 2014 second rounder Mitch Keller, Supak was limited to just over two-dozen innings with Bristol in the Appalachian League last summer, though Supak's numbers – 28.1 IP, 23 K, 5 BB – were far more impressive.

**Projection**: Just as I wrote for Mitch Keller down below, there's basically zero information to go on in terms of projecting this former second rounder's future. He tossed 24.0 innings in the Gulf Coast League during his debut and only topped that by 4.1 innings last year. The control, for what it's worth, was far better in 2015. But, again, super small sample size.

**Ceiling:** Too Soon to Tell
**Risk:** N/A
**MLB ETA:** N/A

## _Barely Missed:_

- **Javier Betancourt, 2B** – Milwaukee acquired the then-20-year-old second baseman in the Francisco Rodriguez swap with Detroit. Betancourt spent the year in High Class A hovering around the league average mark en route to hitting .263/.304/.336. He hasn't hit well since entering full-season ball last season.

- **Garin Cecchini, 1B/3B** – Just straight up purchased the former top prospect from the Red Sox. Cecchini's production has regressed mightily since hitting .322/.443/.471 between the Carolina and Eastern Leagues last in 2013. He followed that up with a .263/.341/.371 with Pawtucket in 2014 and looked absolutely putrid last season (.213/.286/.296).

- **Christopher McFarland, 2B** – A poor man's version of Scooter Gennett, McFarland batted .274/.317/.335 in High Class A last season. No power will ultimately push him on a path of minor league vagabond.

- **Tucker Neuhaus, 2B/3B/SS** – A second round pick in 2013, Neuhaus looked a bit overmatched as he moved into full season ball last season, hitting .249/.307/.355 with 19 doubles, four triples, and four homeruns.

- **Victor Roache, LF/RF** – A former first round pick out of out of Georgia Southern university in 2012, Roache is up there with Jacob Gatewood as having the most power in the entire Milwaukee system. And similiarly to Gatewood, Roache is sporting some problematic punch out rates. The slugging left fielder hit a solid .237/.326/.448 in the Florida State League, topping the average production line by 37%. Of course, swinging and missing in more than 35% of his plate appearances tends to put a damper on that success. Roache got bumped up to Class AA in the second half of the season, and while his overall numbers took a bit of a dive – .247/.321/.430 – he did manage to shave about 10 percentage points off of his K-rate. Above-average power with a subpar bat. Roache hasn't shown a propensity to bash lefties, ultimately ruling him out as a potential platoon bat. At this point, he is what he is.

- **Angel Ventura, RHP:** It was just that – an age-appropriate level of competition. The success would look differently had he been two years younger. Now, though, he's a 22-year-old dominating the lowest full season league in the minors. Let's see how he handles moving into the Florida State League next season. One final question: why didn't Milwaukee, a normally aggressive organization, bump Ventura up any time last season?

The 2016 Prospect Digest Handbook

Page 310

## *Bird Doggin' It – Additional Prospects to Keep an Eye in 2016*

| Player | Age | POS | Notes |
|---|---|---|---|
| Tyler Cravy | 26 | RHP | Former late round pick tossed 42.2 innings in Milwaukee last season. Average arsenal and matching peripherals add up to nothing special. |
| Demi Orimoloye | 19 | LF/RF | Last year's fourth round pick looked awfully promising during his run in the Arizona Summer League, hitting .292/.319/.518. He slugged 17 extra-base hits in 33 games. |
| Gian Rizzo | 22 | RHP | I've long been intrigued by the right-hander as evidenced by my previous two books. He finally got his first taste of action in the Midwest League last season – albeit one that was spent pitching on the bullpen. He posted a 38-to-7 strikeout-to-walk ratio in 55.1 innings. |
| Nash Walters | 19 | RHP | Big right-hander taken in the third round last June walked 20 in 21.2 innings in the Arizona Summer League. |
| Brandon Woodruff | 23 | RHP | Former Mississippi State University stud didn't miss nearly enough bats in High Class A last season. He did average only 2.7 walks per nine innings though… |
| Kyle Wren | 25 | CF | Son of baseball executive Frank Wren, Kyle hit .272/.330/.322 between Biloxi and Colorado Springs. He's quick, not a whole lot else. |

# Minnesota Twins

**State of the Farm System:** Beginning with my first book three years ago, here's how I've ranked the Twins' farm heading into each season (beginning with 2014): #4, #2, and #3. And once again Minnesota's system is brimming with plenty of top tier talent. Of course, the conversation begins – and ends – with the injury-plagued Byron Buxton.

Buxton, the #2 overall pick in 2012, made stops at three different levels last season, beginning the year in Class AA before yo-yoing the remaining months between Class AAA, the big leagues, and the Disabled List. Overall, the supremely talented center fielder batted .305/.367/.500 with 10 doubles, 13 triples, seven homeruns, and 22 stolen bases in 72 minor league contests, but cobbled together a lowly .209/.250/.326 in 46 games in Minnesota.

Behind Buxton is budding ace Jose Berrios, who was also taken in the first round of the 2012 draft. The 6-foot, 185-pound southpaw absolutely dominated the Southern and International Leagues as he posted an impeccable 175-to-38 strikeout-to-walk ratio.

Last year's first round pick, Tyler Jay, also has front-of-the-rotation caliber potential, as does towering right-hander Alex Meyer, if he can get his control under...control.

First baseman/outfielder Max Kepler was one of the biggest breakout prospects last season, something that was predicted in last year's book. The German-born Kepler slugged .322/.416/.531 with Chattanooga in Class AA.

Expect the system to tumble quite a bit – potentially to the bottom 15 – as it loses the majority of this year's top prospects (Buxton, Berrios, Meyer, Kepler, and Jorge Polanco).

Whether or not some of the system's other minor leaguers – I'm looking at you, Nick Gordon – can help pick up the slack is an entirely different question.

| Rank | Name | POS |
|------|------|-----|
| 1 | Byron Buxton | CF |
| 2 | Jose Berrios | |
| 3 | Tyler Jay | LHP |
| 4 | Alex Meyer | |
| 5 | Max Kepler | 1B/OF |
| 6 | Jorge Polanco | 2B/SS |
| 7 | Stephen Gonsalves | LHP |
| 8 | Nick Gordon | SS |
| 9 | Kohl Stewart | RHP |
| 10 | Nick Burdi | RHP |
| 11 | Michael Cederoth | RHP |
| 12 | Lewis Thorpe | LHP |
| 13 | Zachary Jones | RHP |
| 14 | JT Chargois | RHP |
| 15 | Adam Walker | RF |
| 16 | Daniel Palka | 1B |
| 17 | Travis Harrison | RF |
| 18 | Ryan Eades | RHP |
| 19 | Jake Reed | RHP |
| 20 | Lachlan Wells | RHP |
| 21 | Aaron Slegers | RHP |
| 22 | Taylor Rogers | LHP |
| 23 | Stuart Turner | C |
| 24 | Fernando Romero | RHP |
| 25 | Levi Michael | 2B |

**Review of the 2015 Draft:** Fun fact: beginning in 2012 the Twins have had the second, third, fourth, and sixth picks in the draft; the last time the organization had a stretch like that was between 1994 and 2001 when they had the eighth, second, ninth, sixth, fifth, second, and first choices. Anyway, the Twins went with high upside collegiate reliever Tyler Jay with the intention – *hopefully* – of converting him into a fulltime starting pitcher. The wiry southpaw finished his collegiate career with a 143-to-30 strikeout-to-walk ratio in 129.0 innings of work. All but two of his 71 career games came in relief.

Minnesota failed to sign big University of Kentucky right-hander Kyle Cody, their second round pick.

The club's third and fourth round picks, Travis Blankenhorn and Trey Cabbage, both looked quite underwhelming during their respective debuts in the rookie leagues.

## 1. Byron Buxton, CF

| Born: 12/18/93 | Age: 22 | Bats: R | Top CALs: Christian Yelich, Brett Phillips, |
| Height: 6-2 | Weight: 190 | Throws: R | Aaron Cunningham, Brett Jackson, Justin Upton |

| Season | Age | LVL | PA | 2B | 3B | HR | AVG | OBP | SLG | ISO | BB% | K% | wRC+ |
|---|---|---|---|---|---|---|---|---|---|---|---|---|---|
| 2013 | 19 | A | 321 | 15 | 10 | 8 | 0.341 | 0.431 | 0.559 | 0.219 | 13.7% | 17.4% | 176 |
| 2013 | 19 | A+ | 253 | 4 | 8 | 4 | 0.326 | 0.415 | 0.472 | 0.147 | 12.6% | 19.4% | 155 |
| 2014 | 20 | A+ | 134 | 4 | 2 | 4 | 0.240 | 0.313 | 0.405 | 0.165 | 7.5% | 24.6% | 106 |
| 2015 | 21 | AA | 268 | 7 | 12 | 6 | 0.283 | 0.351 | 0.489 | 0.207 | 9.7% | 19.0% | 135 |
| 2015 | 21 | AAA | 59 | 3 | 1 | 1 | 0.400 | 0.441 | 0.545 | 0.145 | 6.8% | 20.3% | 190 |
| 2015 | 21 | MLB | 138 | 7 | 1 | 2 | 0.209 | 0.250 | 0.326 | 0.116 | 4.3% | 31.9% | 54 |

**Background:** Let's run down the litany of baseball bruises – and so much worse – that Buxton's succumbed to over the past couple of seasons:

• The former #2 overall pick injured his shoulder after a dominant, breakout showing in 2013. The cause, according to the club's press release, was swinging a bat.

• Buxton would injure his wrist in Spring Training the following season, an injury that would hamper the top prospect for the next several months.

• In mid-August, Buxton, finally shaking off the effects of the wrist injury, collided with a diving Mike Kvasnicka, a impact so forceful that the club's promising center fielder was rendered unconscious for approximately 10 minutes and eventually left the park via an ambulance. Buxton would be diagnosed with a concussion and would miss nearly two months before making it back to the Arizona Fall League.

• Eleven games into his big league debut Buxton injured his thumb and would eventually miss about six weeks of action before returning back to the International League for a quick refresher.

Now onto the stats from last season: Back in Class AA after his brief – *very brief* – one-game stint the previous season, Buxton batted a solid .283/.351/.489 with seven doubles, 12 triples, six homeruns and 20 stolen bases (in 22 attempts) in 58 games before his big league call up. And then after the injury he slugged .400/.441/.545 in 13 games in Class AAA. But his work in Minnesota leaves a lot to be desired: .209/.250/.326.

**Projection:** Fun fact: his 12 triples with Chattanooga tied for the third most in the Southern League last season – despite playing in fewer than 60 games. Easily the most explosive two-way prospect since Mike Trout tore through the minors. Buxton offers up an array of above-average to plus tools across the board. So much so, in fact, here's what I wrote in last year's book:

*"Earlier in [2014] I described Buxton's offensive ceiling as Barry Bonds-esque circa the Pittsburgh Pirates, particularly his 1992 season in which he hit .311/.456/.624 with 36 doubles, five triples, 34 homeruns, and 38 stolen bases."*

His work with Chattanooga is the true talent level, so why change the why praise now? Finally, one bold prediction: In 2017 Buxton's going to top a 145 wRC+ total at the big league level.

**Ceiling:** 7.5-win player
**Risk:** Moderate
**MLB ETA:** Debuted in 2015

## 2. Jose Berrios, LHP

| Born: 05/27/94 | Age: 22 | Bats: R | Top CALs: Johnny Cueto, Eduardo Sanchez, |
| Height: 6-0 | Weight: 185 | Throws: R | Eduardo Rodriuez, Josh Hader, Sean Gallagher |

| YEAR | Age | Level | IP | W | L | ERA | FIP | K/9 | BB/9 | K% | BB% | HR/9 | LOB% |
|---|---|---|---|---|---|---|---|---|---|---|---|---|---|
| 2013 | 19 | A | 103.7 | 7 | 7 | 3.99 | 3.58 | 8.68 | 3.47 | 22.0% | 8.8% | 0.52 | 65.9% |
| 2014 | 20 | A+ | 96.3 | 9 | 3 | 1.96 | 2.51 | 10.18 | 2.15 | 28.0% | 5.9% | 0.37 | 76.5% |
| 2014 | 20 | AA | 40.7 | 3 | 4 | 3.54 | 3.65 | 6.20 | 2.66 | 17.2% | 7.4% | 0.44 | 67.9% |
| 2014 | 20 | AAA | 3.0 | 0 | 1 | 18.00 | 4.36 | 9.00 | 9.00 | 15.8% | 15.8% | 0.00 | 40.0% |
| 2015 | 21 | AA | 90.7 | 8 | 3 | 3.08 | 3.09 | 9.13 | 2.38 | 25.1% | 6.5% | 0.60 | 75.8% |
| 2015 | 21 | AAA | 75.7 | 6 | 2 | 2.62 | 2.79 | 9.87 | 1.67 | 27.7% | 4.7% | 0.71 | 77.9% |

**Background:** While he didn't make his big league debut last season, the promising came awfully damn close. A breakout prospect two years ago, Berrios, who made stops at three different levels in 2014, began the year back in Class AA and quickly proved that he was ready for the next stop. In 15 starts with Chattanooga, the 6-foot _____ punched out 92 and walked just 24 in 90.2 innings of work. The organization bumped him up to Rochester for the remainder of the season – a final 12 starts – where he fanned nearly 28% and walked just 4.7% of the batters he faced. His overall 2015 stat line: 166.1 innings, 175 punch outs, just 38 walks, and a neat-and-tidy 2.87 ERA. For his career, Berrios has fanned 25.7% and walked 6.6% of the total batters he's faced.

**Projection**: Berrios would easily be the most talked about _____ in the minor leagues – if it weren't for the Dodgers' Julio Urias. Proof is in the pudding: among all minor league hurlers with at least 150+ innings in 2015, his strikeout percentage, 26.2%, and strikeout-to-walk percentage, 20.5%, both ranked first. Berrios possesses an above-average to plus-heater, something he displayed during his second Futures Game appearance last season. Above-average control, ~~success~~ dominance against older competition, and a healthy track record; name it and he possesses it. He'll hover around front-of-the-rotation status, even if he never ascends to Johnny Cueto (his top CAL) levels.

**Ceiling:** 4.0- to 4.5-win player
**Risk:** Moderate
**MLB ETA:** 2016

## 3. Tyler Jay, LHP

**MiLB Rank: #64**
**Position Rank: N/A**

| | | |
|---|---|---|
| **Born:** 04/19/94 | **Age:** 22 | **Bats:** L |
| **Height:** 6-1 | **Weight:** 180 | **Throws:** L |

**Top CALs:** Jose Ortega, Abel De Los Santos, Joey Krehbiel, Casey Mulligan, Daniel Stange

| YEAR | Age | Level | IP | W | L | ERA | FIP | K/9 | BB/9 | K% | BB% | HR/9 | LOB% |
|------|-----|-------|------|---|---|------|------|-------|------|-------|------|------|-------|
| 2015 | 21 | A+ | 18.3 | 0 | 1 | 3.93 | 2.07 | 10.80 | 3.93 | 27.2% | 9.9% | 0.00 | 61.5% |

**Background:** Apparently the Alex Wimmers selection had a bit of a lasting effect on the organization, because Jay, a hard-throwing southpaw out of the University of Illinois, was the first time the club took a collegiate arm with their first pick since 2010. The lanky lefty spent the overwhelming majority of his collegiate career working out of the Illini's bullpen. To be exact, all but two of his 71 career appearances were of the relief variety. Jay was nearly unhittable of his last two seasons: he tallied 123 punch outs and coughed out 20 free passes over his final 108.1 innings. For his amateur career, Jay averaged 9.98 K/9 and 2.09 BB/9. He also spent the summer of 2014 working out of the pen for Team USA, where he posted a 21-to-6 strikeout-to-walk ratio in 16.2 innings.

**Projection**: Prior to the draft I wrote the following:

> *"Despite [Coach] Hartlieb's erroneous decision to leave the dominant southpaw in the pen during his final season, Jay will likely become the school's highest drafted player in history. Former right-hander John Ericks is the university's only [other] first rounder (22nd overall).*
>
> *For his part, Jay offers up an incredible package of strong control, better-than-average swing-and-miss ability, and a tremendous [talent] to keep the ball in the park; he's allowed just two homeruns over his last 93.0 innings of work.*
>
> *There's some obvious risk that comes along, namely, will Jay be able to handle the rigors of not only taking the ball every fifth day, but also hurling more than a couple innings in each outing? [He's] mid-rotation caliber ceiling with the floor as a better version of Kyle Crockett, the former fourth round pick by the Indians who vaulted through the minor leagues."*

**Ceiling:** 3.0-win player
**Risk:** Moderate
**MLB ETA:** 2017

## 4. Alex Meyer,

**MiLB Rank: #100**
**Position Rank: N/A**

| | | |
|---|---|---|
| **Born:** 01/03/90 | **Age:** 26 | **Bats:** R |
| **Height:** 6-9 | **Weight:** 225 | **Throws:** R |

**Top CALs:** Randy Wells, C.J. Riefenhauser, Alex Wilson, heath Hembree, Garrett Olson

| YEAR | Age | Level | IP | W | L | ERA | FIP | K/9 | BB/9 | K% | BB% | HR/9 | LOB% |
|------|-----|-------|-------|---|---|------|------|-------|------|-------|-------|------|-------|
| 2013 | 23 | R | 8.3 | 0 | 0 | 1.08 | 0.70 | 17.28 | 3.24 | 47.1% | 8.8% | 0.00 | 90.0% |
| 2013 | 23 | AA | 70.0 | 4 | 3 | 3.21 | 2.85 | 10.80 | 3.73 | 28.1% | 9.7% | 0.39 | 71.8% |
| 2014 | 24 | AAA | 130.3 | 7 | 7 | 3.52 | 3.66 | 10.57 | 4.42 | 27.1% | 11.3% | 0.69 | 74.7% |
| 2015 | 25 | AAA | 92.0 | 4 | 5 | 4.79 | 3.28 | 9.78 | 4.70 | 23.9% | 11.5% | 0.39 | 67.4% |

**Background:** It took a couple years of consistently grabbing the ball every week in college, but Meyer – and his massive 6-foot-9 frame – turned himself into a viable starting pitcher, or at least one that wouldn't walk half-a-dozen batters every nine innings. The problem, of course, is that Meyer's control never really took another step forward as it's remained firmly in the below-average or worse category. And his work with Rochester in the International League was just the latest example. Acquired in the one-for-one swap with Washington a couple years back for Denard Span, Meyer's 2015 campaign got off on a rocky start as he coughed up 31 earned runs across his first eight starts while posting a hideous 41-to-24 strikeout-to-walk ratio. The organization pushed him into a full time relief role for the remainder of the season and, lo and behold, his production spiked: across his next nine games Meyer allowed one earned run to go along with his spectacular 20-to-6 strikeout-to-walk ratio, a stretch that would earn him a (brief) trip to Minneapolis for two games. Overall, Meyer would finish his year with by whiffing 23.9% and walking 11.5% of the Class AAA batters he faced.

**Projection**: Officially among the largest human beings to ever don a Major League uniform, Meyer has a whole helluva lot of moving parts to control; thus explaining his problematic control. But I would like to point one thing out: Randy Johnson didn't become *Randy Johnson* until his age-29 season. Just take a look:

| Player | Ages | IP | BB/9 | K/9 |
|---|---|---|---|---|
| Randy Johnson | 24-28 | 818.0 | 5.7 | 9.0 |
| Randy Johnson | 29+ | 3317.1 | 2.7 | 11.0 |

And that includes leading baseball in free passes for three consecutive seasons. Now, is Meyer the next Randy Johnson? Certainly not. But just ask yourself this question: If Randy Johnson was coming up through the minors in today's age of deep, specialized bullpens, would he have been given more than 800 innings at the big league level – with a walk rate approach 6.0 BB/9 – to figure it out? Certainly not. With that being said, I'm still a big, big fan – no pun intended – of Meyer. He unleashed a mid- to upper-90s fastball during his debut, which only plays up due to his massive wing span, and he has the build to chew up plenty of meaningful innings. Sure, he's entering his age-26 season but let's see if the kid can figure it out. He *is* in the right organization for that. At the very least, he's a dominant, shutdown closer.

**Ceiling:** 3.0-win player
**Risk:** Moderate to High
**MLB ETA:** Debuted in 2015

# 5. Max Kepler, 1B/OF

**MiLB Rank: #108**
**Position Rank: #8 (1B)**

| Born: 02/10/93 | Age: 23 | Bats: L | **Top CALs:** Sean Henry, Gregory Polanco, |
|---|---|---|---|
| Height: 6-4 | Weight: 205 | Throws: L | Casey Craig, Dwight Smith, Aaron Cunningham |

| Season | Age | LVL | PA | 2B | 3B | HR | AVG | OBP | SLG | ISO | BB% | K% | wRC+ |
|---|---|---|---|---|---|---|---|---|---|---|---|---|---|
| 2013 | 20 | A | 263 | 11 | 3 | 9 | 0.237 | 0.312 | 0.424 | 0.186 | 9.1% | 16.3% | 105 |
| 2014 | 21 | A+ | 407 | 20 | 6 | 5 | 0.264 | 0.333 | 0.393 | 0.129 | 8.4% | 15.2% | 109 |
| 2015 | 22 | A+ | 26 | 2 | 0 | 0 | 0.250 | 0.308 | 0.333 | 0.083 | 7.7% | 19.2% | 97 |
| 2015 | 22 | AA | 482 | 32 | 13 | 9 | 0.322 | 0.416 | 0.531 | 0.209 | 13.9% | 13.1% | 167 |
| 2015 | 22 | MLB | 7 | 0 | 0 | 0 | 0.143 | 0.143 | 0.143 | 0.000 | 0.0% | 42.9% | -33 |

**Background:** Another one of the club's baby-faced youngsters to debut last season, I listed the German-born first baseman/outfielder among my Top 25 Breakout Prospects for 2015. And he did just that. In. A. Huge. Way. In 482 trips to the plate for Chattanooga, Kepler torched the opposition to the tune of .322/.416/.531 with 32 doubles (4th best mark in the Southern League), 13 triples (2nd best), nine homeruns, and a league-leading 167 wRC+. Kepler saw just three games in Minnesota, making seven plate appearances, and going 1-for-7. For his minor league career Kepler is sporting a steady .281/.362/.445 triple-slash line, slugging 98 doubles, 31 triples, and 34 homeruns in 427 total games.

**Projection**: In last year's book I wrote:

> *"CAL offers more hope than one would suspect based on his numbers. Of his top five comparisons, three – Jake Marisnick, Josh Reddick, and Gregory Polanco – have a shot or have already developed into league average or better players. And a fourth, Aaron Cunningham, carved out a nice enough career as a fourth/fifth outfielder. Kepler's power has stagnated after his 2012 season grading out as slightly better than average. He'll walk a little bit and swipe a couple bags. The hit tool is questionable now. Again, [he's a] league average starter – maybe a tick better."*

Let's take a look at that analysis, piece by piece. CAL still remains a rather big fan, tying him to Gregory Polanco and Desmond Jennings, who ranked as his sixth comparable. Kepler's power still isn't the over-the-fence-type; instead, he relies on gap-to-gap pop resulting in tons of doubles and triples. He did set a career high in walk rate (13.9%) and his hit tool jumped up to better-than-average. I'm still sticking with last year's conclusion: league average to slightly better regular.

**Ceiling:** 2.5-win player
**Risk:** Moderate
**MLB ETA:** Debuted in 2015

## 6. Jorge Polanco, 2B/SS

**MiLB Rank: #119**
**Position Rank: #5 (2B)**

| Born: 07/05/93 | Age: 22 | Bats: B | Top CALs: Orlando Arcia, Daniel Robertson, |
|---|---|---|---|
| Height: 5-11 | Weight: 200 | Throws: R | Jose Pirela, Tyler Pastornicky, Francisco Lindor |

| Season | Age | LVL | PA | 2B | 3B | HR | AVG | OBP | SLG | ISO | BB% | K% | wRC+ |
|---|---|---|---|---|---|---|---|---|---|---|---|---|---|
| 2013 | 19 | A | 523 | 32 | 10 | 5 | 0.308 | 0.362 | 0.452 | 0.144 | 8.0% | 11.3% | 127 |
| 2014 | 20 | A+ | 432 | 17 | 6 | 6 | 0.291 | 0.364 | 0.415 | 0.124 | 10.6% | 13.9% | 124 |
| 2014 | 20 | AA | 157 | 6 | 0 | 1 | 0.281 | 0.323 | 0.342 | 0.062 | 5.7% | 17.8% | 86 |
| 2015 | 21 | AA | 431 | 17 | 3 | 6 | 0.289 | 0.346 | 0.393 | 0.104 | 8.1% | 14.6% | 111 |
| 2015 | 21 | AAA | 94 | 6 | 0 | 0 | 0.284 | 0.309 | 0.352 | 0.068 | 4.3% | 10.6% | 88 |
| 2015 | 21 | MLB | 12 | 0 | 0 | 0 | 0.300 | 0.417 | 0.300 | 0.000 | 16.7% | 8.3% | 111 |

**Background:** A short, stocky switch-hitting middle infielder out of the Dominican Republic, Polanco fared much better in his return Class AA after his 37-game stint the previous season. He hit .289/.346/.393 with 17 doubles, three triples, and half a dozen dingers in his 95 games with Chattanooga. Minnesota bumped him up to Rochester for another 22 games (.284/.309/.352).

**Projection**: Well, CAL's certainly a huge fan, comparing the young shortstop/second baseman to one budding All-Star (Francisco Lindor) and another pair of promising prospects (Orlando Arcia and Daniel Robertson). Polanco's power has stagnated over the past couple of years as he's been aggressively pushed up the minor league chain, but the skill should develop into at least an average offering at the big league level once he's finished filling out. He has solid-average or better tools across the board, as well as the potential to develop into a similar big league player.

**Ceiling:** 2.5-win player
**Risk:** Moderate
**MLB ETA:** Debuted in 2014

## 7. Stephen Gonsalves, LHP

**MiLB Rank: #120**
**Position Rank: N/A**

| Born: 07/08/94 | Age: 21 | Bats: L | Top CALs: Drew Hutchison, Lucas Giolito, |
|---|---|---|---|
| Height: 6-5 | Weight: 190 | Throws: L | David Holmberg, Joey Krehbiel, Luis Severino |

| YEAR | Age | Level | IP | W | L | ERA | FIP | K/9 | BB/9 | K% | BB% | HR/9 | LOB% |
|---|---|---|---|---|---|---|---|---|---|---|---|---|---|
| 2013 | 18 | R | 14.0 | 1 | 1 | 1.29 | 1.29 | 13.50 | 2.57 | 38.2% | 7.3% | 0.00 | 85.7% |
| 2013 | 18 | R | 14.3 | 1 | 0 | 0.63 | 2.41 | 11.30 | 4.40 | 32.1% | 12.5% | 0.00 | 93.3% |
| 2014 | 19 | R | 29.0 | 2 | 0 | 2.79 | 3.36 | 8.07 | 3.10 | 22.8% | 8.8% | 0.31 | 67.5% |
| 2014 | 19 | A | 36.7 | 2 | 3 | 3.19 | 2.50 | 10.80 | 2.70 | 29.3% | 7.3% | 0.25 | 63.4% |
| 2015 | 20 | A | 55.0 | 6 | 1 | 1.15 | 2.10 | 12.60 | 2.45 | 36.8% | 7.2% | 0.33 | 88.5% |
| 2015 | 20 | A+ | 79.3 | 7 | 2 | 2.61 | 3.58 | 6.24 | 4.31 | 16.5% | 11.4% | 0.23 | 77.3% |

**Background:** Hailing from the same high school as former #1 pick – and later #17th overall – Brady Aiken, Gonsalves continues to make scouts, analysts, and prognosticators take notice. The big southpaw made it look easy in 28.1 innings across both rookie ball levels during his debut (0.95 ERA, 39 strikeouts, and 11 walks), breezed through a second round of the Appalachian League and a brief stop with Cedar Rapids a year later, and made quick work of the Midwest and Florida State Leagues last season. In totality, Gonsalves made 24 starts in 2015, throwing 134.1 innings while fanning 132 and walking 53. He finished the year with an aggregate 2.01 ERA. For his career, he's tallied a 2.17 ERA with a 241-to-85 strikeout-to-walk ratio in 228.1 innings of work.

**Projection**: CAL stands impressed, comparing him to established big leaguer Drew Hutchison and a pair of high-ceiling youngsters (Luis Severino and Lucas Giolito). And the trio of comparables is quite reasonable: Gonsalves has done nothing but succeede – often against older competition – since signing on the dotted line; his peripherals are above-average; and he does a fine job limiting the long ball (especially considering his groundball rates have been blasé). He's a solid mid-rotation caliber arm who could jump up a bit as his lanky frame begins to fill out. Needless to say, Gonsalves has proven to be an incredible mid-round find for the organization.

**Ceiling:** 2.5-win player
**Risk:** Moderate
**MLB ETA:** 2017

## 8. Nick Gordon, SS

MiLB Rank: #149
Position Rank: N/A

| Born: 10/24/95 | Age: 20 | Bats: L | Top CALs: Adrian Marin, Hak-Ju Lee, |
| Height: 6-0 | Weight: 160 | Throws: R | Amed Rosario, Jose Pirela, Humberto Arteaga |

| Season | Age | LVL | PA | 2B | 3B | HR | AVG | OBP | SLG | ISO | BB% | K% | wRC+ |
|---|---|---|---|---|---|---|---|---|---|---|---|---|---|
| 2014 | 18 | R | 255 | 6 | 4 | 1 | 0.294 | 0.333 | 0.366 | 0.072 | 4.3% | 17.6% | 101 |
| 2015 | 19 | A | 533 | 23 | 7 | 1 | 0.277 | 0.336 | 0.360 | 0.083 | 7.3% | 16.5% | 104 |

**Background:** The son of former hard-throwing, sometimes dominant right-hander Tom "Flash" Gordon, the young Minnesota prospect not only has his famous father's footsteps to walk in, but his older brother, Dee, is also setting the bar high by winning the batting title last year as well. The youngest Gordon, the fifth overall pick in 2014, cobbled together another solid, though far from spectacular stat line in 2015. In fact, I think we've seen this one before. Here are his 2014 statistics prorated for 120 games, the number of contests he appeared in with Cedar Rapids last season:

| Year | G | AVG | OBP | SLG | 2B | 3B | HR | SB | CS | wRC+ |
|---|---|---|---|---|---|---|---|---|---|---|
| 2014 | 120 | 0.294 | 0.333 | 0.366 | 13 | 8 | 2 | 23 | 15 | 101 |
| 2015 | 120 | 0.277 | 0.336 | 0.360 | 23 | 7 | 1 | 25 | 8 | 104 |

**Projection**: After struggling for the first 45 games in his full season debut, Gordon, who batted .320/.305/.281 through the first two months of the season, hit a more-than-respectable .304/.355/.406 over his final 75 contests. The speed's already an above-average tool, but he's nowhere close to becoming the base thief that his older brother is. Nick doesn't offer up a whole lot of power – even during his final 75 games his ISO barely cracked the .100-mark – so the hit tool will need to carry him the rest of the way. And CAL isn't overly optimistic either, ranking him with several highly touted former top prospects that never figured it out.

**Ceiling:** 2.5-win player
**Risk:** Moderate to High
**MLB ETA:**

## 9. Kohl Stewart, RHP

MiLB Rank: #156
Position Rank: N/A

| Born: 10/07/94 | Age: 21 | Bats: R | Top CALs: Marwin Vega, Vin Mazzaro, |
| Height: 6-3 | Weight: 195 | Throws: R | Brett Duvall, Clayton Cook, T.J. Mcfarland |

| YEAR | Age | Level | IP | W | L | ERA | FIP | K/9 | BB/9 | K% | BB% | HR/9 | LOB% |
|---|---|---|---|---|---|---|---|---|---|---|---|---|---|
| 2013 | 18 | R | 4.0 | 0 | 0 | 0.00 | 0.93 | 18.00 | 2.25 | 53.3% | 6.7% | 0.00 | 100.0% |
| 2013 | 18 | R | 16.0 | 0 | 0 | 1.69 | 2.21 | 9.00 | 1.69 | 23.2% | 4.4% | 0.00 | 56.3% |
| 2014 | 19 | A | 87.0 | 3 | 5 | 2.59 | 3.73 | 6.41 | 2.48 | 17.2% | 6.7% | 0.41 | 69.7% |
| 2015 | 20 | A+ | 129.3 | 7 | 8 | 3.20 | 3.45 | 4.94 | 3.13 | 12.8% | 8.1% | 0.14 | 67.0% |

**Background:** For the second consecutive season the highly touted hurler out of St. Pius X High School (Houston, TX) succeeded against older competition despite some underwhelming, subpar peripherals. Stewart – the fourth overall pick in 2013 and the long time apple of the Twins' eye – had a solid showing as a teenage arm with Cedar Rapids in the Midwest League two years ago; in an injury-shortened campaign the 6-foot-3 right-hander fanned 62, walked 24, and a 2.59 ERA in 87.0 innings of work. Stewart would follow that up with another odd showing in 2015. In 22 starts (129.1 IP), the hard-throwing right-hander fanned just 12.8% and walked 8.1% of the total batters he faced, but surprisingly enough he posted a sturdy 3.45 FIP.

**Projection**: Just to put this into a bit of perspective consider the following: only one other pitcher, New York Mets right-hander Kevin McGowan, finished with a worse strikeout-to-walk percentage among all qualified Florida State League hurlers. What makes Stewart so interesting – at least from an analytical perspective – is that he possesses an above-average fastball with a solid offering of secondary pitches, but still hasn't missed a whole lot bats. He compensates for the lack of swings-and-misses by generating a ton of action on the ground (55% for his career). Statistically speaking, he looks like a backend arm. But his draft pedigree and overall athleticism suggest otherwise.

**Ceiling:** 2.5-win player
**Risk:** Moderate to High
**MLB ETA:** 2017

## 10. Nick Burdi, RHP

**MiLB Rank: #173**
**Position Rank: N/A**

| Born: 01/19/93 | Age: 23 | Bats: R | Top CALs: Ethan Martin, Dan Cortes, |
|---|---|---|---|
| Height: 6-5 | Weight: 215 | Throws: R | Paul Voelker, Cody Satterwhite, Ben Lively |

| YEAR | Age | Level | IP | W | L | ERA | FIP | K/9 | BB/9 | K% | BB% | HR/9 | LOB% |
|---|---|---|---|---|---|---|---|---|---|---|---|---|---|
| 2014 | 21 | A | 13.0 | 0 | 0 | 4.15 | 1.33 | 18.00 | 5.54 | 48.2% | 14.8% | 0.00 | 62.5% |
| 2014 | 21 | A+ | 7.3 | 2 | 0 | 0.00 | 1.35 | 14.73 | 2.45 | 42.9% | 7.1% | 0.00 | 100.0% |
| 2015 | 22 | A+ | 20.0 | 2 | 2 | 2.25 | 1.37 | 13.05 | 1.35 | 39.7% | 4.1% | 0.45 | 58.8% |
| 2015 | 22 | AA | 43.7 | 3 | 4 | 4.53 | 3.99 | 11.13 | 6.60 | 26.3% | 15.6% | 0.62 | 69.8% |

**Background:** It was such an up-and-down season for the 2014 second round pick – literally in every sense of the word. Another one of my picks for the Top 25 Breakout Prospects, Burdi opened the year on a sour note: his first game of the season he lasted less than one inning, but the hard-throwing former Louisville closer managed to cough up four earned runs and four base-on-balls. And that's pretty much how it went for the next 12 or so weeks, a span covering 30+ innings and a horribly grotesque 5.93 ERA. The front office bounced him down to High Class A for a bit of a breather – or to stop the bleeding – and Burdi looked like the hurler I envisioned: 20.0 innings of work, a tidy, barely-there 1.37 FIP, 29 punch outs, and just three walks. The dominance convinced the club to push him back up to Class AA for the season's last couple of weeks. And, lo and behold, he continued to dominate: 13.1 IP, 1.35 ERA, 21 strikeouts, and 10 walks.

**Projection**: Here's what I wrote prior to his selection in the 2014 draft:

*"Craig Kimbrel of the collegiate ranks – a pitcher that simply overpowers the competition with an elite ability to miss bats with a strong enough feel for the strike zone. His control has been steadily improving in each of his last seasons, going from 3.97 BB/9 in 2011 to 3.28 as a sophomore and finally 3.12 BB/9 this season (as of 4/16/14).*

*Perhaps the most impressive stat, however, is the number one. The big right-hander's surrendered just one homerun in his first 75.2 career innings. Near big league-ready, he should be among this class' first waves to [The Show]. Big, big strikeout ability with the potential to average nearly a punch and a half per inning. He's a very safe selection in terms of big league potential, though his career value will ultimately fall short in comparison with players like Carlos Rodon and Casey Gilaaspie."*

Burdi's production from July 2nd through the end of the year – 33.1, 1.89 ERA, 50 K, and 13 BB – is the true talent level, definitely not the hurler that battled control issues in the first half. As I wrote two years ago, the burly 6-foot-5 Burdi is going to be a force to be reckoned with at the big league level. And soon.

**Ceiling:** 1.5- to 2.0-win player
**Risk:** Low to Moderate
**MLB ETA:** 2016

## 11. Michael Cederoth, RHP

**MiLB Rank: #213**
**Position Rank: N/A**

| Born: 11/25/92 | Age: 23 | Bats: R | Top CALs: Yensi Lopez, A.J. Wideman, |
|---|---|---|---|
| Height: 6-6 | Weight: 195 | Throws: R | HakReed Garrett, Colton Murray, John Baird |

| YEAR | Age | Level | IP | W | L | ERA | FIP | K/9 | BB/9 | K% | BB% | HR/9 | LOB% |
|---|---|---|---|---|---|---|---|---|---|---|---|---|---|
| 2014 | 21 | R | 45.7 | 4 | 2 | 3.55 | 3.65 | 8.28 | 3.55 | 20.1% | 8.6% | 0.20 | 61.9% |
| 2015 | 22 | A | 35.3 | 1 | 4 | 4.08 | 3.73 | 9.42 | 4.58 | 22.7% | 11.0% | 0.51 | 59.8% |

**Background:** One of my favorite arms in the 2014 draft class, the big fire-balling right-hander out of San Diego State University made just 11 appearances (six starts) totaling just 35.1 innings – 10 frames fewer than he compiled during his pro debut – and failed to appear in a meaningful game after the fourth of June. Cederoth landed on the organization's DL with an "undisclosed illness," an ailment that was severe enough to not only knock him out for the remainder of the season but also limit him from most physical activity for nearly nine weeks. The 6-foot-6 hurler would finish the year with a 37-to-18 strikeout-to-walk ratio en route to posting a 3.73 FIP in the Midwest League. Through his first 81.0 career innings, Cederoth has punched out 79 and walked 36.

**Projection**: Here's what I wrote prior to the 2014 draft:

*"In terms of big league upside, Cederoth is right up there with some of the bigger names in the draft – [Tyler] Beede, [Jeff] Hoffman, [Sean] Newcomb, etc...*

*The problem, which could actually be a plus in the long run, is that Cederoth has spent two seasons in the bullpen, thus limiting his experience to polish his secondary offerings but also keeping his arm relatively free from wear-and-tear.*

*Assuming whichever team that grabs him in the opening round converts him back into a starting pitcher – please let that happen – Cederoth could develop into an upper-rotation-type arm, maybe peaking as a fringe #2 for a couple seasons, though the likelihood of this happening is a bit lower. He should have the **floor** along the lines of a Bud Norris-type."*

And here's what I wrote months later in last year's book:

*"Armed with one of the two or three best fastball in college last season, Cederoth inexplicably dropped to the third round last June. Thankfully, so far the Twins look content on keeping him in the rotation. And the results during his debut – 45.2 IP, 42 K, 18 BB – were better than solid. [I] love this pick."*

Clearly, I've been wearing my fan-boy badge for quite some time. And I'm certainly not going to back down after a non-baseball injury/illness limited him to a handful of games last season.

And just for argument's sake, consider the following age-22 seasons by Cederoth and Norris, whom I compared the former San Diego University to a couple years ago:

| Player | Year | LVL | IP | K/9 | BB/9 | FIP |
|---|---|---|---|---|---|---|
| Michael Cederoth | 2015 | A | 35.1 | 9.4 | 4.6 | 3.75 |
| Bud Norris | 2007 | A | 96.2 | 10.9 | 3.8 | 3.65 |

Given that Cederoth missed so much of his year, that's actually a pretty spot on comparison. Again, think Bud Norris as a floor. And despite a rather limited appearance in the Midwest League in 2015, it wouldn't be shocking to see the club challenge a healthy Cederoth by pushing him up to High Class A for 2016.

**Ceiling:** 2.0-win player
**Risk:** Moderate to High
**MLB ETA:**

## 12. Lewis Thorpe, LHP

**MiLB Rank: N/A**
**Position Rank: N/A**

| Born: 11/23/95 | Age: 20 | Bats: R | Top CALs: Adonys Cardona, Arodys Vicaino, |
|---|---|---|---|
| Height: 6-1 | Weight: 160 | Throws: L | Clayton Cook, Lucas Giolito, Michael Main |

| YEAR | Age | Level | IP | W | L | ERA | FIP | K/9 | BB/9 | K% | BB% | HR/9 | LOB% |
|---|---|---|---|---|---|---|---|---|---|---|---|---|---|
| 2013 | 17 | R | 44.0 | 4 | 1 | 2.05 | 1.69 | 13.09 | 1.23 | 38.1% | 3.6% | 0.41 | 72.6% |
| 2014 | 18 | A | 71.7 | 3 | 2 | 3.52 | 4.24 | 10.05 | 4.52 | 25.6% | 11.5% | 0.88 | 70.8% |

**Background:** The left-hander from down under, who was coming off of an impressive showing in the Midwest League as an 18-year-old, succumbed to the always present danger of Tommy John surgery in early March, an injury that forced him to miss the entire 2015 season.

**Projection**: For starters here's what I wrote in last year's book,

*"Assuming the elbow injury isn't too serious Thorpe should see some action very early on in the Florida State League. Young lefties with solid strikeout numbers and matching control are usually worth their weight in gold. Thorpe should could be a solid #3/#4-type arm."*

Oops. Double oops. The elbow injury was, ahem, pretty serious. So I'm not going to jinx him and write something like, "If there aren't any setbacks…" Here's hoping for a full recovery, kid.

**Ceiling:** 2.0- to 2.5-win player
**Risk:** High
**MLB ETA:** 2018

## 13. Zach Jones, RHP

**MiLB Rank:** N/A
**Position Rank:** N/A

| Born: 12/04/90 | Age: 25 | Bats: R | **Top CALs:** Jaye Chapman, Kevin Whelan, |
|---|---|---|---|
| Height: 6-1 | Weight: 185 | Throws: R | Omar Duran, Luis Lebron, Christopher Perry |

| YEAR | Age | Level | IP | W | L | ERA | FIP | K/9 | BB/9 | K% | BB% | HR/9 | LOB% |
|---|---|---|---|---|---|---|---|---|---|---|---|---|---|
| 2013 | 22 | A+ | 48.7 | 4 | 3 | 1.85 | 2.75 | 12.95 | 5.18 | 35.7% | 14.3% | 0.37 | 85.1% |
| 2014 | 23 | R | 5.3 | 0 | 0 | 3.38 | 2.38 | 15.19 | 6.75 | 39.1% | 17.4% | 0.00 | 71.4% |
| 2014 | 23 | A+ | 5.0 | 0 | 0 | 0.00 | 2.59 | 9.00 | 3.60 | 25.0% | 10.0% | 0.00 | 100.0% |
| 2015 | 24 | A+ | 24.7 | 2 | 2 | 2.19 | 1.67 | 13.86 | 3.65 | 37.3% | 9.8% | 0.00 | 70.4% |
| 2015 | 24 | AA | 27.0 | 3 | 2 | 6.00 | 4.64 | 10.00 | 6.00 | 24.6% | 14.8% | 1.00 | 64.4% |

**Background:** Armed with a big, big time fastball and a potentially dominant ability to miss bats – when he isn't missing the strike zone – Jones has quickly moved through the minor leagues since entering the professional ranks as a fourth round pick in 2012. A 6-foot-1, 185-pound right-hander out of San Jose State University, Jones opened the year up in the Southern League on a rather significant tear: from his first appearance on April 10th to his 21st appearance more than two months later, the hard-throwing right-hander allowed just five earned runs in 22.0 innings of work while punching out 26 and walking just seven – dominance that would earn his a trip to the Southern League All Star Game. And then the wheels fell off. Over his next six appearances with Chattanooga, Jones coughed up 13 earned runs in five innings while posting a 4-to-11 strikeout-to-walk ratio. Minnesota promptly – in a potential knee-jerk reaction – demoted him down to High Class A where he quickly regained his previous dominant form.

**Projection**: Jones can run his fastball up with the best of them – both in the minors *and* majors. The problem, though, is that often times he literally has no idea where it's going, sort of an early version of Nuke LaLoosh. Quick! Someone know Susan Sarandon? On the positive side, not including the hideous little stint to end his tenure with Chattanooga, Jones seemingly turned the corner – so the potential for at least solid-average control is there. If he can repeat that game-in and game-out, Jones could be a dominant late-inning reliever. He's likely headed back to the Southern League, but could very well end up in Class AAA or even Minnesota if everything goes well.

**Ceiling:** 1.5-win player
**Risk:** Moderate
**MLB ETA:** 2016

## 14. J.T. Chargois, RHP

**MiLB Rank:** N/A
**Position Rank:** N/A

| Born: 12/03/90 | Age: 25 | Bats: B | **Top CALs:** Drew Hayes, Kam Mickolio, |
|---|---|---|---|
| Height: 6-3 | Weight: 200 | Throws: R | Tyler Clark, Chad Reineke, Atahualpa Severino |

| YEAR | Age | Level | IP | W | L | ERA | FIP | K/9 | BB/9 | K% | BB% | HR/9 | LOB% |
|---|---|---|---|---|---|---|---|---|---|---|---|---|---|
| 2015 | 24 | A+ | 15.0 | 1 | 0 | 2.40 | 1.63 | 11.40 | 3.00 | 28.8% | 7.6% | 0.00 | 52.9% |
| 2015 | 24 | AA | 33.0 | 1 | 1 | 2.73 | 3.64 | 9.27 | 5.45 | 24.1% | 14.2% | 0.27 | 77.3% |

**Background:** A late-blooming dominant relief arm for Rice University several years back, Chargois, who posted a career best 38-to-12 strikeout-to-walk ratio in 37.2 innings with the collegiate baseball powerhouse, managed to make just 12 professional appearances in 2012 before his elbow promptly exploded like Humpy Dumpy when he fell off that damn wall. Well, guess what? It took all the king's horses and all the king's men *and nearly all of the king's time*, to piece Chargois' elbow back together again. Nine-hundred and 59 days, to be exact. Because that's the how long the hard-throwing right-hander went in between minor league games. Finally healthy, the club pushed Chargois up to High Class A to being the year where he looked like he never missed a beat: 15 IP, 19 K, and 5 BB. He got promoted up to Class AA where he continued to miss a ton of bats (9.3 K/9) as he battled some control issues (5.5 BB/9).

One final thought: I don't call it Arm Shredder U. for nothing...

**Projection**: It's pretty easy to dismiss the mid- to late-season control issues with Chattanooga. After all, he missed more than two full years of regular season action. The fastball – and subsequent strikeout rates – bounced back with authority. And while he's always going to have to answer to the past injury issues, Chargois looks like a dominant backend reliever – a better option of Zach Jones, though his risk pushes him down the list.

**Ceiling:** 1.5-win player
**Risk:** Moderate to High
**MLB ETA:** 2016

## 15. Adam Walker, RF

**MiLB Rank:** N/A
**Position Rank:** N/A

| Born: 10/18/91 | Age: 24 | Bats: R | **Top CALs:** Carlos Peguero, Victor Roache, |
|---|---|---|---|
| Height: 6-4 | Weight: 225 | Throws: R | Brock Kjeldgaard, Trayce Thompson, Brandon Burgess |

| Season | Age | LVL | PA | 2B | 3B | HR | AVG | OBP | SLG | ISO | BB% | K% | wRC+ |
|---|---|---|---|---|---|---|---|---|---|---|---|---|---|
| 2013 | 21 | A | 552 | 31 | 7 | 27 | 0.278 | 0.319 | 0.526 | 0.248 | 5.6% | 20.8% | 130 |
| 2014 | 22 | A+ | 554 | 19 | 1 | 25 | 0.246 | 0.307 | 0.436 | 0.190 | 7.9% | 28.2% | 111 |
| 2015 | 23 | AA | 560 | 31 | 3 | 31 | 0.239 | 0.309 | 0.498 | 0.259 | 9.1% | 34.8% | 125 |

**Background:** Just close your eyes for a moment and ignore what you know about Walker for the time being. What organization would you likely find a player with the following production line: 560 plate appearances, average or slightly better walk rate, *massive* swing-and-miss tendencies, a pitiful batting average, above-average or better in-game power, and an overall production line that top the league average mark by 25%? Kind of sounds like a Billy Beane-type of bat doesn't it? The type of offensive package that's fairly narrow, but has proven to be successful at every stop of the way. Anyway, that's Adam Walker, a former third round pick out of Jacksonville University in 2012. Walker spent the year whipping up hurricane-like winds and battering fastballs with Chattanooga in the Southern League, hitting .239/.309/.498 with 31 doubles, a pair of triples, 31 homeruns, and 13 stolen bases (in 17 attempts).

**Projection:** CAL's certainly not impressed with Walker's prodigious power, linking him to a bunch of toolsy, talented, flawed minor league sticks like Carlos Peguero, Victor Roache, and Trayce Thompson. And at this point in his career the book on Walker is already written: massive power and a crater the size of Texas in his right-handed swing. He hasn't shown a propensity to bash left-handed arms, so he's likely going to fall into the fourth-outfielder/part-time bench bat role in Minnesota.

**Ceiling:** 1.0- to 1.5-win player
**Risk:** Moderate
**MLB ETA:** 2016

## 16. Travis Harrison, RF

**MiLB Rank:** N/A
**Position Rank:** N/A

| Born: 10/17/92 | Age: 23 | Bats: R | **Top CALs:** Michael Burgess, Juan Portes, |
|---|---|---|---|
| Height: 6-1 | Weight: 215 | Throws: R | Robbie Grossman, Lance Ray, Jeremy Barfield |

| Season | Age | LVL | PA | 2B | 3B | HR | AVG | OBP | SLG | ISO | BB% | K% | wRC+ |
|---|---|---|---|---|---|---|---|---|---|---|---|---|---|
| 2013 | 20 | A | 537 | 28 | 0 | 15 | 0.253 | 0.366 | 0.416 | 0.162 | 12.7% | 23.3% | 124 |
| 2014 | 21 | A+ | 537 | 33 | 1 | 3 | 0.269 | 0.361 | 0.365 | 0.096 | 11.9% | 16.0% | 112 |
| 2015 | 22 | AA | 479 | 23 | 4 | 5 | 0.240 | 0.363 | 0.356 | 0.116 | 13.6% | 21.3% | 111 |

**Background:** Fun Fact: there have been two players chosen in the first round from Tustin High School (Tustin, CA) – Harrison, a supplemental first rounder in 2011 and All-Star outfielder Shawn Green. Obvious Fact: Travis Harrison is no Shawn Green. After taking to third base in the pros like a fish to land, Harrison made the conversion to left field two years ago and then to right field last season. His bat, however, has continued to disappoint at each level. Spending the year with Chattanooga, Harrison hit a decent .241/.363/.356 with 23 doubles, four triples, five homeruns and three stolen bases (in a laughable 12 attempts). His overall production, according to *Weighted Runs Created Plus*, topped the league average mark by 11% -- a surprisingly strong total by a 22-year-old in Class AA.

**Projection:** Harrison has one single, solitary saving tool – an above-average eye at the plate. Otherwise, his skill set leaves a lot to be desired: below-average hit tool, questionable power, and decent speed with horrendously poor base running instincts. He's a fringy big league bench option, nothing more.

**Ceiling:** 1.0-win player
**Risk:** Moderate
**MLB ETA:** 2017

## 17. Ryan Eades, RHP

MiLB Rank: N/A
Position Rank: N/A

| Born: 12/15/91 | Age: 24 | Bats: R | Top CALs: Jesse Darrah, Trey Watten, |
|---|---|---|---|
| Height: 6-2 | Weight: 200 | Throws: R | Yorfrank Lopez, Cody Dickson, Dennis Tepera |

| YEAR | Age | Level | IP | W | L | ERA | FIP | K/9 | BB/9 | K% | BB% | HR/9 | LOB% |
|---|---|---|---|---|---|---|---|---|---|---|---|---|---|
| 2013 | 21 | R | 15.7 | 0 | 0 | 4.60 | 4.46 | 7.47 | 6.89 | 18.8% | 17.4% | 0.00 | 66.7% |
| 2014 | 22 | A | 133.0 | 10 | 11 | 5.14 | 4.44 | 6.63 | 3.38 | 16.6% | 8.5% | 0.74 | 63.7% |
| 2015 | 23 | A+ | 118.7 | 6 | 3 | 3.11 | 3.48 | 6.07 | 2.88 | 16.4% | 7.8% | 0.38 | 75.3% |

**Background:** If there was ever a pitcher to better personify the organization's past philosophy it's Ryan Eades, a second rounder out of Louisiana State University in 2013. The former Bayou stalwart was a three-year mainstay for university's staff, tallying 237.0 career innings with a 172-to-78 strikeout-to-walk ratio and a solid 3.57 ERA. And after getting battered during his stints in the Appalachian and Midwest Leagues, the 6-foot-2 right-hander found his groove in the Florida State League last season: he made 20 starts, throwing 118.2 innings while posting a 3.11 ERA and averaging 6.1 punch outs and 2.9 walks per nine innings.

**Projection:** Eades is one of the guys that won't wow a whole lot of folks in the scouting/statistical community, but he could sneak up on some people as a #5 caliber arm. He doesn't miss a whole lot of bats or generate a ton of action on the ground, but he maximizes his abilities fairly well. He's head for Class AA in 2016 and then the big leagues soon after.

**Ceiling:** 1.0-win player
**Risk:** Moderate
**MLB ETA:** 2017

## 18. Jake Reed, RHP

MiLB Rank: N/A
Position Rank: N/A

| Born: 09/29/92 | Age: 23 | Bats: R | Top CALs: Mark Appel, Taylor Guerrieri, |
|---|---|---|---|
| Height: 6-2 | Weight: 190 | Throws: R | David Roberts, Paul Phillips, Zach Stewart |

| YEAR | Age | Level | IP | W | L | ERA | FIP | K/9 | BB/9 | K% | BB% | HR/9 | LOB% |
|---|---|---|---|---|---|---|---|---|---|---|---|---|---|
| 2014 | 21 | R | 6.0 | 0 | 0 | 0.00 | 0.90 | 12.00 | 0.00 | 42.1% | 0.0% | 0.00 | 100.0% |
| 2014 | 21 | A | 25.0 | 3 | 0 | 0.36 | 1.48 | 11.16 | 1.08 | 34.4% | 3.3% | 0.00 | 85.7% |
| 2015 | 22 | A+ | 12.3 | 1 | 0 | 0.00 | 2.27 | 5.11 | 0.73 | 16.3% | 2.3% | 0.00 | 77.8% |
| 2015 | 22 | AA | 47.0 | 4 | 4 | 6.32 | 4.20 | 7.47 | 4.02 | 17.6% | 9.5% | 0.57 | 50.1% |

**Background:** After doubling down on hard-throwing collegiate right-handers with their second and third round picks in 2014, the Twins just flat-out cornered the market by grabbing the supremely underrated right-hander out of the University of Oregon. A two-year member of the Ducks' rotation, Reed was pushed to the closer's role during his junior campaign and, unsurprisingly, he flourished. In 37 innings that year, Reed punched out 34, walked 15, and saved 13 games. He followed that up with an impressive 31.0-inning run in the lower levels of the minor leagues, posting an incredible 39-to-3 strikeout-to-walk ratio. And just like fellow 2014 draftee Nick Burdi, Reed struggled mightily as the club aggressively pushed him up to Class AA to start the season before an eventual demotion down to High Class A.

**Projection:** Here's what I wrote two years ago:

> "Hopefully, whichever team drafts Reed will push him back into the rotation to see if he has the chops to hang, though he still profiles as a backend guy. At the very least, he can be pushed back into the bullpen where he should slide into a seventh/eighth-inning role."

I also successfully predicted his draft status as a fourth/fifth rounder. And despite the hiccup in Class AA last season, Reed still profiles as a nice little setup arm. His strikeout rate plummeted as he battled control problems, but let's remember he's barely a year removed from pitching against collegiate metal bats (and those cool ping-y sounds).

**Ceiling:** 1.0-win player
**Risk:** Moderate
**MLB ETA:** 2016

## 19. Lachlan Wells, RHP

**MiLB Rank: N/A**
**Position Rank: N/A**

| Born: 02/27/97 | Age: 19 | Bats: R | Top CALs: Felix Sterling, Jose Espada, |
|---|---|---|---|
| Height: 5-8 | Weight: 163 | Throws: R | Gilmael Troya, Shane Dawson, Manuel Barreda |

| YEAR | Age | Level | IP | W | L | ERA | FIP | K/9 | BB/9 | K% | BB% | HR/9 | LOB% |
|---|---|---|---|---|---|---|---|---|---|---|---|---|---|
| 2015 | 18 | R | 47.3 | 5 | 2 | 2.09 | 3.22 | 9.32 | 2.09 | 26.5% | 6.0% | 0.76 | 85.3% |

**Background:** Very few teams are as aggressive – or successful – as the Twinkies when it comes to signing prospects from the Land Down Under. And Wells is just the latest example. A pint-sized right-hander, Wells, who stands a less-than-imposing 5-foot-8 and 160+ pounds, spent the 2013 and 2014 seasons pitching in the Australian Baseball League, but finely made the move stateside last year. In 47.1 innings in the Gulf Coast League, Wells posted an impressive 49-to-11 strikeout-to-walk ratio with a 2.09 ERA and a 3.22 FIP.

**Projection:** He's basically going to be treated as an incoming prep pick due to his lack of track record. But the season was wildly successful, especially for a young prospect making such a large move to an entirely new continent. His frame size will likely limit his potential to somewhere between a middle relief/late-inning role.

**Ceiling:** Too Soon to Tell
**Risk:** N/A
**MLB ETA:** N/A

## 20. Aaron Slegers, RHP

**MiLB Rank: N/A**
**Position Rank: N/A**

| Born: 09/04/92 | Age: 23 | Bats: R | Top CALs: Mike Mcclendon, Joely Rodriguez, |
|---|---|---|---|
| Height: 6-10 | Weight: 245 | Throws: R | Brian Flynn, Egan Smith, Will Roberts |

| YEAR | Age | Level | IP | W | L | ERA | FIP | K/9 | BB/9 | K% | BB% | HR/9 | LOB% |
|---|---|---|---|---|---|---|---|---|---|---|---|---|---|
| 2013 | 20 | R | 19.0 | 0 | 0 | 0.47 | 2.01 | 8.53 | 0.95 | 26.5% | 2.9% | 0.00 | 89.5% |
| 2014 | 21 | A | 113.3 | 7 | 7 | 4.53 | 3.41 | 7.15 | 1.59 | 19.0% | 4.2% | 0.56 | 58.4% |
| 2014 | 21 | A+ | 19.0 | 2 | 1 | 3.32 | 4.44 | 5.68 | 1.89 | 16.0% | 5.3% | 0.95 | 75.6% |
| 2015 | 22 | A+ | 119.3 | 8 | 6 | 2.87 | 2.96 | 6.03 | 1.58 | 16.6% | 4.4% | 0.30 | 66.2% |
| 2015 | 22 | AA | 36.7 | 1 | 4 | 4.91 | 4.20 | 5.89 | 2.95 | 14.8% | 7.4% | 0.74 | 64.3% |

**Background:** We can say one thing with some relative accuracy: the Twins could field the best front court basketball team among all MLB organizations. Slegers out-towers fellow Oak Tree right-hander Alex Meyer, 6-foot-10 to 6-foot-9. A former fifth round pick out of Indiana University, Slegers split the year between Fort Myers and Chattanooga, totaling 156.0 innings of work with a steady, yet unimpressive, 104-to-33 strikeout-to-walk ratio. For his career, he's averaging 6.6 strikeouts and 1.7 free passes per nine innings.

**Projection:** Bucking the typical trend that massive hurlers struggle repeating their delivery – and subsequently trouble with the strike zone – Slegers can pound the zone with the best of them – big or small. He doesn't have an overpowering fastball, though it definitely plays up due to his frame, but he knows how to pitch. He could be a fringy backend start/serviceable relief arm.

**Ceiling:** 1.0-win player
**Risk:** Moderate
**MLB ETA:** 2017

## 21. Taylor Rogers, LHP

**MiLB Rank: N/A**
**Position Rank: N/A**

| Born: 12/17/90 | Age: 25 | Bats: L | Top CALs: Danny Rosenbaum, Robert Ray, |
|---|---|---|---|
| Height: 6-3 | Weight: 180 | Throws: L | Mario Santiago, Scott Diamond, Jeff Manship |

| YEAR | Age | Level | IP | W | L | ERA | FIP | K/9 | BB/9 | K% | BB% | HR/9 | LOB% |
|---|---|---|---|---|---|---|---|---|---|---|---|---|---|
| 2013 | 22 | A | 10.0 | 0 | 1 | 7.20 | 3.84 | 9.00 | 3.60 | 20.0% | 8.0% | 0.90 | 36.1% |
| 2013 | 22 | A+ | 130.7 | 11 | 6 | 2.55 | 3.41 | 5.72 | 2.20 | 15.7% | 6.1% | 0.34 | 74.5% |
| 2014 | 23 | AA | 145.0 | 11 | 6 | 3.29 | 3.04 | 7.01 | 2.30 | 18.7% | 6.1% | 0.25 | 69.4% |
| 2015 | 24 | AAA | 174.0 | 11 | 12 | 3.98 | 3.21 | 6.52 | 2.28 | 17.2% | 6.0% | 0.47 | 68.8% |

**Background:** One of those lefties that every system keeps around. Rogers is actually on the cusp of forcing the organization's hand a bit. The then-24-year-old southpaw spent the entire year navigating the waters of the International League, tallying a career high 174.0 innings while averaging 6.5 punch outs and 2.3 walks per nine innings to go along with a bloated 3.98 ERA.

**Projection**: He's a LOOGY in the making – the club just hasn't realized it…yet. Here's how fellow left-handers have fared against Rogers since 2013:

- 2013: .214/.264/.260
- 2014: .217/.268/.287
- 2015: .177/.209/.193

And here's how right-handers have performed during the same time span:

- 2013: .266/.326/.363
- 2014: .285/.336/.367
- 2015: .326/.374/.457

I'm assuming you probably don't need any further convincing. Now someone tell the Twins…

**Ceiling:** 0.5- to 1.0-win player
**Risk:** Low
**MLB ETA:** 2016

---

## 22. Stuart Turner, C

**MiLB Rank:** N/A
**Position Rank:** N/A

| Born: 12/27/91 | Age: 24 | Bats: R | Top CALs: Michael Blanke, Parker Berberet, |
|---|---|---|---|
| Height: 6-2 | Weight: 230 | Throws: R | Jair Fernandez, John Ryan Murphy, Luis Sierra |

| Season | Age | LVL | PA | 2B | 3B | HR | AVG | OBP | SLG | ISO | BB% | K% | wRC+ |
|---|---|---|---|---|---|---|---|---|---|---|---|---|---|
| 2013 | 21 | R | 142 | 5 | 0 | 3 | 0.264 | 0.340 | 0.380 | 0.116 | 8.5% | 15.5% | 110 |
| 2014 | 22 | A+ | 364 | 16 | 2 | 7 | 0.249 | 0.322 | 0.375 | 0.126 | 8.5% | 16.8% | 101 |
| 2015 | 23 | AA | 379 | 13 | 1 | 4 | 0.223 | 0.322 | 0.306 | 0.083 | 11.9% | 18.2% | 83 |

**Background:** The former Ole Miss backstop had a massive coming out part during his junior season with the Rebs. Turner, a transfer from LSU-Eunice following a dominant sophomore season, hit a robust .374/.444/.518 with 15 doubles, one triple, and five homeruns in 266 trips to the plate in 2013 – production that earned him a hefty $600,000 signing bonus as a third round pick in 2013. Turner's solid, better-than-average showing in the Appalachian League during his debut (.264/.340/.380) gave way to a decent production line as the club bumped him all the way up to High Class A the following season (.249/.322/.375), but his production crated in his first taste of the Southern League last season. In nearly 400 trips to the plate with Chattanooga, Turner posted the lowest wRC+ total of his professional career, 83, en route to cobbling together a .223/.322/.306 showing.

**Projection**: Here's what I wrote prior to the 2015 draft:

> "Turner's a few rungs behind Georgia Tech's Zane Evans and Cal's Andrew Knapp, but he does have the ability to develop into a capable backup. But he's likely not going to become a starter. His power is below-average and he doesn't own a true standout tool."

Well, fast forward a couple years and Turner still doesn't possess a true standout tool. He does have a nose for first base via the free pass and handles himself well behind the plate, so that should earn him several looks as the organization's backup backstop.

**Ceiling:** 0.5- to 1.0-win player
**Risk:** Low to Moderate
**MLB ETA:** 2016

---

## 23. Fernando Romero, RHP

**MiLB Rank:** N/A
**Position Rank:** N/A

| Born: 12/24/94 | Age: 21 | Bats: R | Top CALs: N/A |
|---|---|---|---|
| Height: 6-0 | Weight: 215 | Throws: R | |

| YEAR | Age | Level | IP | W | L | ERA | FIP | K/9 | BB/9 | K% | BB% | HR/9 | LOB% |
|---|---|---|---|---|---|---|---|---|---|---|---|---|---|
| 2013 | 18 | R | 45.0 | 2 | 0 | 1.60 | 2.44 | 9.40 | 2.60 | 26.0% | 7.2% | 0.00 | 75.0% |
| 2014 | 19 | A | 12.0 | 0 | 0 | 3.00 | 4.32 | 6.75 | 3.75 | 18.0% | 10.0% | 0.75 | 84.3% |

**Background:** A fast-rising prospect a couple years ago, Romero fell victim to Tommy John surgery in mid-October 2014 – an injury that forced the promising right-hander to miss the remainder of the 2014 as well as the entire 2015 campaign as well.

**Projection**: The sample size is incredibly limited – he's thrown just 88.0 innings in his three-year career and just 12 innings above rookie ball – and he's coming off of major arm surgery. So basically, he could be anything at this point. But he sports a massive fastball and showed some promising control during his 45-inning run in the Gulf Coast in 2013.

**Ceiling**: Too Soon to Tell
**Risk**: N/A
**MLB ETA**: N/A

## 24. Levi Michael, 2B

**MiLB Rank: N/A**
**Position Rank: N/A**

| Born: 02/09/91 | Age: 25 | Bats: B | Top CALs: Estarlin De Los Santos, Raul Barron, |
|---|---|---|---|
| Height: 5-10 | Weight: 180 | Throws: R | Coly Sedbrook, Mott Hyde, Steve Tolleson |

| Season | Age | LVL | PA | 2B | 3B | HR | AVG | OBP | SLG | ISO | BB% | K% | wRC+ |
|---|---|---|---|---|---|---|---|---|---|---|---|---|---|
| 2013 | 22 | A+ | 375 | 15 | 4 | 4 | 0.229 | 0.331 | 0.340 | 0.111 | 13.1% | 17.9% | 95 |
| 2014 | 23 | A+ | 201 | 9 | 2 | 1 | 0.305 | 0.375 | 0.395 | 0.090 | 9.5% | 12.4% | 124 |
| 2015 | 24 | AA | 264 | 12 | 5 | 5 | 0.267 | 0.369 | 0.434 | 0.167 | 11.7% | 20.1% | 131 |

**Background**: If you ever needed further evidence as to how much of a crapshoot the draft – even in the latter part of the first round – is, just take a gander at picks #30 through #48 in the 2011 draft: Levi Michael, Mikie Mahtook, Jake Hager, Kevin Matthews, Brian Goodwin, Jacob Anderson, Henry Owens, Zach Cone, Brandon Martin, Larry Greene, Jackie Bradley, Tyler Goeddel, Jeff Ames, Andrew Chafin, Michael Fulmer, Trevor Story, Joseph Musgrove, Keenyn Walker, Michael Kelly, Kyle Crick, and Travis Harrison. Michael missed some significant time due to a thumb injury, but managed to sandwich in 63 games with Chattanooga, hitting a respectable .267/.369/.434 with 12 doubles, five triples, five homeruns, and 18 stolen bases. For his career, Michael is sporting a blasé .259/.352/.356 triple-slash line in 339 games.

**Projection**: The closest Michael is going to come to big league dominance is the fact that he shared a University of North Carolina bus with the Dark Knight himself, Matt Harvey. Michael's never topped 117 games in a season or performed well enough to justify his high round selection or shown enough power. And the only time the hit tool looked playable was in his third trip through High Class A. Maybe he develops into a useful bench option. Maybe not.

**Ceiling**: 0.5- to 1.0-win player
**Risk**: Moderate
**MLB ETA**: 2016

## 25. Mason Melotakis, LHP

**MiLB Rank: N/A**
**Position Rank: N/A**

| Born: 06/28/91 | Age: 25 | Bats: R | Top CALs: Mario Alvarez, Mike Mcquire, |
|---|---|---|---|
| Height: 6-2 | Weight: 206 | Throws: L | Parker Markel, Paul Clemens, Jose Jimenez |

| YEAR | Age | Level | IP | W | L | ERA | FIP | K/9 | BB/9 | K% | BB% | HR/9 | LOB% |
|---|---|---|---|---|---|---|---|---|---|---|---|---|---|
| 2013 | 22 | A | 111.0 | 11 | 4 | 3.16 | 3.72 | 6.81 | 3.16 | 17.7% | 8.2% | 0.49 | 70.6% |
| 2014 | 23 | A+ | 47.0 | 3 | 1 | 3.45 | 4.03 | 8.62 | 4.60 | 21.0% | 11.2% | 0.57 | 78.3% |
| 2014 | 23 | AA | 16.0 | 1 | 0 | 2.25 | 1.98 | 9.56 | 1.69 | 25.4% | 4.5% | 0.00 | 76.2% |

**Background**: The 2012 second round pick succumbed to Tommy John surgery in October 2014 and failed to make it back to throw a meaningful pitch in 2015. For his career – and prior to the injury – Melotakis has fanned 180 and walked 72 in 198.0 IP.

**Projection**: Again, before the injury, Melotakis flashed a whole lot of upside as a potential dominant lefty out of the pen; he averaged nearly a punch out per inning with solid-average control. But it's a least somewhat concerning that the former Northwestern State University of Louisiana hurler didn't make it back to register a meaningful pitch in 2015. We'll have to wait-and-see what the 2016 season holds.

**Ceiling**: 1.0-win player
**Risk**: High
**MLB ETA**: 2017

Minnesota Twins

## Barely Missed:

- **Yorman Landa, RHP** – It took the Venezuelan-born right-hander a while, but he finally started coming into his own in 2014, his fourth professional season, before a minor shoulder issue raised some red flags. The 6-foot, 170-pound hurler made 15 appearances last season, throwing 27 innings while averaging 10.3 punch outs and 4.7 walks per nine innings. He'll likely be found in next year's Top 25 list.

- **Aderlin Mejia, IF** – Eerily similar to a million other prospects in a million other locales, Mejia's a solid minor league middle infielder when he's right, but lacks any type of wallop with the wood. He's a career .268/.342/.314. Defensive versatility with speed. Yada, yada, yada...

- **Engelb Vielma, SS** – A small switch-hitting middle infielder, he batted .270/.321/.306 with just 12 extra-base knocks in 120 games. Easy math: that's one every 10 games. Vielma has a decent stick with above-average speed, but his complete and utter lack of power will ultimately cap his value as a backend bench option.

## *Bird Doggin' It – Additional Prospects to Keep an Eye in 2016*

| Player | Age | POS | Notes |
|---|---|---|---|
| Luis Arraez | 19 | IF/OF | Jack-of-all-trades while in the field, Arraez made the successful move to the Gulf Coast League last season, hitting .309/.377/.391. Again no power. He's failed to bash a four-bagger in his first 88 games. |
| Luke Bard | 25 | RHP | Finally healthy after missing the majority of 2013 and all of 2014, Bard dominated the Midwest League. Not bad work for a former first round pick against much younger competition. |
| Mat Batts | 24 | LHP | A freakin' awesome name for player carrying a big stick. Unfortunately, Batts is a pitcher – albeit one that's experienced some lower level success. He posted a 2.61 ERA between Low Class A and High Class A. |
| Travis Blankenhorn | 19 | IF/OF | Last year's third round pick batted .244/.321/.347 with seven doubles, a pair of triples, and three homeruns in 53 games between the Appalachian and Gulf Coast Leagues. |
| Cameron Booser | 24 | LHP | Fanned 64 in 46.0 innings with Cedar Rapids. The problem(s): he was 23 and walked 40. Sometimes it clicks late for these guys though. |
| Jean Carlos Arias | 18 | CF | Destroyed the DSL as a 17-year-old (.311/.378/.537). Let's see how he handles the stateside leagues. |
| Sam Clay | 23 | LHP | Former Georgia Tech southpaw lost his way with Cedar Rapids. He's now entering his age-23 season with just 33.1 innings above rookie ball. |
| John Curtiss | 24 | RHP | Bounced between the Midwest and Gulf Coast Leagues last season. Curtiss was incredibly homer-friendly, like your kid sister could have belted one. |
| Tanner English | 23 | CF | Speedy little center fielder out of the University of South Carolina, English bated .265/.359/.406 with 22 doubles, eight triples, five homeruns, and 37 stolen bases. |
| Sam Gibbons | 22 | RHP | Another one of the club's Aussie finds, Gibbons spent the year with Cedar Rapids: 90.1 innings, 68 punch outs, and 23 walks. There could be some more projection left in his 6-foot-4 frame. |
| Trevor Hildenberger | 25 | RHP | Older, late round pick in 2014, Hildenberger absolutely destroyed the Midwest League competition (45.0 IP, 59 K, 5 BB, and 4 ER) before continuing to miss a whole lot of bats and limit free passes with Fort Myers. |
| C.K. Irby | 24 | RHP | After averaging just 6.6 K/9 during his debut, Irby has fanned 115 over the next 83 innings. Granted it's against the lowest levels, but intriguing none the less. |
| Felix Jorge | 22 | RHP | Dominican-born hurler posted a solid 114-to-32 strikeout-to-walk ratio in 142 with Cedar Rapids. Maybe he turns into a backend starter. |
| Andriu Marin | 17 | RHP | 6-foot-1, 183-pound right-hander fanned 39 in 37.2 innings in the DSL as a 16-year-old. He's likely to spend another year before moving stateside. |
| Brandon Peterson | 24 | RHP | A 2013 13th round pick out of Wichita State, Peterson fanned 77 in 61.0 innings between Fort Myers and Chattanooga. He has a legitimate chance to see a bundle of big league innings. |
| Brandon Poulson | 26 | RHP | Big time fastball with massive control issues; he's walked 32 in his first 27.3 innings. But the story of truck-driver-turned-minor-league-flame-thrower is quite fascinating. Here's hoping the positive narrative continues. |
| Rafael Valera | 21 | IF/OF | 20-year-old utility guy batted .283/.378/.338 with a 115 wRC+ in the Midwest League. |
| Trey Vavra | 24 | 1B/LF | 33rd round pick out of Florida Southern College two years ago, Vavra slugged .346/.406/.538 against the younger Midwest League. |

**State of the Farm System:** One of the surprise teams of 2015 – see the *Revisited* section – the Mets leapt up from the bowels of the NL East to finish the year with 90 wins, the most since the club's National League Championship Series appearance in 2006. And the driving force for the Mets' resurgence – other than Yoenis Cespedes' ungodly 57-game run with the club – was the ballclub's pitching staff, namely their rotation.

Behind hefty right-hander Bartolo Colon's pinpoint control with his running two-seamer was a collection of homegrown talent: Matt Harvey, Jacob deGrom, Noah Syndergaard, Jon Niese, and Steven Matz. And despite the promotions of so many top prospects over the past couple of years, the Mets' system is still home to some intriguing prospects.

Former 2012 first round pick Gavin Cecchini broke out in a big way – finally – with Binghamton last season, hitting .317/.377/.442 as a 21-year-old in the minors' toughest level of competition. It marked the first time in his career that he posted an OPS north of .707 at any point.

Outfielder Brandon Nimmo, who was plucked out of East High School in Cheyenne, Wyoming, as the 13th overall pick five years ago, continued to hover around the league average production line as he split time between the Eastern and Pacific Coast Leagues – though he continued to struggle against fellow southpaws.

The system's next four bats on the Top 25 list – Amed Rosario, Wuilmer Becerra, Matt Reynolds, and Dominic Smith – all had varying degrees of success in 2015.

Rosario looked OK as the front office continued to aggressively challenge him; he batted .257/.307/.335 as a 19-year-old in High Class A. Becerra, an often forgotten piece of the R.A. Rickey deal with Toronto, continued to slowly develop in the low levels of the minors and owns some of the system's top power. Reynolds' production took a noticeable step backward as his BABIP regressed, but he has the look of a solid backup infielder – sort of a poor man's version of San Francisco's Matt Duffy. And Smith, the powerless first baseman, batted a career best .305/.354/.4187 with six dingers.

In terms of arms, well, let's just say the system isn't sporting the impressive depth it has in the past (obviously). But big righty Marcos Molina has a high ceiling assuming he can move beyond Tommy John surgery unscathed. Former 12th round pick Chris Flexen finally made his way up to the Sally. And Robert Gsellman could eventually fill out a rotation in the next year or two.

**Review of the 2015 Draft:** Without a first round pick last June, New York grabbed a couple prep prospects in the second and third rounds. Toolsy outfielder Desmond Lindsay ripped through the Gulf Coast for 21 games before earning a promotion to Brooklyn in the New York-Penn League. Max Wotell, a lanky lefty out of North Carolina, was limited to just 10.2 innings during his debut. Their fourth round pick was used on Miami slugging third baseman David Thompson – the power's there, whether or not he'll hit enough is an entirely different question.

| Rank | Name | POS |
|------|------|-----|
| 1 | Steven Matz | LHP |
| 2 | Gavin Cecchini | SS |
| 3 | Marcos Molina | RHP |
| 4 | Brandon Nimmo | CF |
| 5 | Amed Rosario | SS |
| 6 | Chris Flexen | RHP |
| 7 | Wuilmer Becerra | LF/RF |
| 8 | Dominic Smith | 1B |
| 9 | Matt Reynolds | SS |
| 10 | Robert Gsellman | RHP |
| 11 | Gabriel Ynoa | RHP |
| 12 | Jhoan Urena | 3B |
| 13 | Desmond Lindsay | CF |
| 14 | Akeel Morris | RHP |
| 15 | Seth Lugo | RHP |
| 16 | Jack Leathersich | LHP |
| 17 | Corey Oswalt | RHP |
| 18 | David Thompson | 3B |
| 19 | Michael Gibbons | RHP |
| 20 | Eudor Garcia-Pacheco | 3B |
| 21 | Luis Carpio | 2B/SS |
| 22 | Dario Alvarez | LHP |
| 23 | Max Wotell | LHP |
| 24 | Milton Ramos | 2B/SS |
| 25 | Dash Winningham | 1B |

## 1. Steven Matz, LHP

**MiLB Rank: #10**

**Position Rank: #6**

| Born: 05/29/91 | Age: 25 | Bats: R | **Top CALs:** Kea Komentani, Andrew Heaney, |
| Height: 6-2 | Weight: 200 | Throws: L | Brad Mills, Manny Parra, Cory Mazzoni |

| YEAR | Age | Level | IP | W | L | ERA | FIP | K/9 | BB/9 | K% | BB% | HR/9 | LOB% |
|------|-----|-------|-----|---|---|------|------|-------|------|-------|------|------|-------|
| 2013 | 22 | A | 106.3 | 5 | 6 | 2.62 | 2.91 | 10.24 | 3.22 | 28.3% | 8.9% | 0.34 | 75.4% |
| 2014 | 23 | A+ | 69.3 | 4 | 4 | 2.21 | 2.73 | 8.05 | 2.73 | 21.5% | 7.3% | 0.00 | 77.2% |
| 2014 | 23 | AA | 71.3 | 6 | 5 | 2.27 | 2.64 | 8.71 | 1.77 | 24.0% | 4.9% | 0.38 | 75.8% |
| 2015 | 24 | A+ | 3.7 | 0 | 0 | 4.91 | 2.35 | 7.36 | 2.45 | 16.7% | 5.6% | 0.00 | 75.0% |
| 2015 | 24 | AA | 11.3 | 1 | 0 | 0.00 | 2.03 | 7.94 | 1.59 | 27.0% | 5.4% | 0.00 | 100.0% |
| 2015 | 24 | AAA | 90.3 | 7 | 4 | 2.19 | 3.44 | 9.37 | 3.09 | 26.2% | 8.6% | 0.60 | 82.1% |

**Background:** Matz, a promising, often dominant lefty that would uncork mid-90s heat who captured the imagination of the hometown crowd for six starts last season, was taken with the Mets' first pick all the way back in 2009. But Matz, the 72nd player chosen that year, sandwiched between David Holmberg and Max Walla in the second round, wouldn't make his professional debut for nearly *three full seasons*. Here's a story about perseverance: early in Spring Training in 2010 Matz underwent the knife – Tommy John surgery – but had numerous setbacks for the next two seasons. At one point the famed Dr. James Andrews told the young lefty, according to the New York Post in article published by Howie Kussoy July 27, 2015, "that there was chance [he] would need a second Tommy John surgery." But here's the catch: as told by Matz to Kussoy, the only way that would be determined is after he started throwing again; either it would rip again or the scar tissue would break up. Luckily for Matz, the scar tissue broke up.

Just pause and think about that for a moment. You're barely out of high school with your dream job in front of you – and every single aspiration lined up – but you may not ever get the chance to see if you're good enough to hack it. It's quite the sobering feeling, isn't it?

Anyway, Matz would appear in six games for Kingsport in the Appalachian League in 2012. He would top 100 innings in the Sally the following year. Then in 2014, with the lengthy injury history firmly in his past, Matz started leaping through the minor leagues. He made two stops that year, splitting the season between St. Lucie and Binghamton. And then blew the doors of the PCL competition before making his brief six-game debut with Mets last year.

Long odds be damned; perseverance – and some luck – pays off.

**Projection**: I've always had a special place in my analytical heart for the 6-foot-2, 200-pound lefty. In my first book in I listed Matz among the Top 25 Breakout Prospects for 2014, writing:

> "[He] finished fourth in the Sally with 10.04 K/9. Matz also showed surprising control for a pitcher that had thrown fewer than 30 innings prior to the year. He also was able to maintain his K-rate towards the end of the season, another positive sign. Still, though, that injury past is troublesome. He could be a mid-rotation guy, peaking as a #3, or more likely a dominant reliever. For now, though, I'll go with the former."

Even back then I thought Matz had a potentially special left arm. He also proved that he was one of the bigger breakout prospects for 2014. And here's what I wrote in last year's book:

> "Well, now Matz looks like a sleeping giant in terms of ceiling. Fantastic numbers, though they have mostly come against an age-appropriate level of competition, but dominance in the mid-levels of the minors is a plus."

That dominance continued into the PCL and through the six starts with the Mets before a lat tear shut him down. When he's right – and healthy – the budding ace sports a mid-90s heater, hard upper-80s slider, curve, and change. Above-average punch out potential with matching control; the only thing limiting his ceiling would be the injury bug.

**Ceiling:** 4.0- to 4.5-win player
**Risk:** Moderate
**MLB ETA:** Debuted in 2015

## 2. Gavin Cecchini, SS

**MiLB Rank: #83**
**Position Rank: N/A**

| Born: 12/22/93 | Age: 22 | Bats: R | Top CALs: Tyler Pastornicky, Jonathan Mota, |
|---|---|---|---|
| Height: 6-2 | Weight: 200 | Throws: R | J.P . Crawford, Daniel Robertson, Jorge Polanco |

| Season | Age | LVL | PA | 2B | 3B | HR | AVG | OBP | SLG | ISO | BB% | K% | wRC+ |
|---|---|---|---|---|---|---|---|---|---|---|---|---|---|
| 2013 | 19 | A- | 212 | 8 | 0 | 0 | 0.273 | 0.319 | 0.314 | 0.041 | 6.6% | 14.2% | 94 |
| 2014 | 20 | A | 259 | 17 | 4 | 3 | 0.259 | 0.333 | 0.408 | 0.149 | 9.7% | 15.8% | 106 |
| 2014 | 20 | A+ | 271 | 10 | 1 | 5 | 0.236 | 0.325 | 0.352 | 0.116 | 11.8% | 14.8% | 96 |
| 2015 | 21 | AA | 485 | 26 | 4 | 7 | 0.317 | 0.377 | 0.442 | 0.125 | 8.7% | 11.3% | 139 |

**Background:** As his older brother Garin's stock continues to plummet, Gavin, the Mets' first pick in 2012, is moving skyward after a breakout season in Class AA at the age of 21. Taken with the 12th overall pick, one selection behind future All-Star Addison Russell, Cecchini struggled to make any type of offensive impact during his first three professional seasons: he had a lackluster debut with Kingsport in the Appalachian League (.246/.311/.330), fared slightly better in the New York-Penn League during his sophomore campaign (.273/.319/.314), continued his slight uptick in performance in the Sally (.259/.333/.408) and held his own after a midseason promotion to St. Lucie (.236/.325/.352). But the 6-foot-2, 200-pound shortstp finally separated himself from the minor league pack last season: he slugged a career best .317/.377/.442 with 26 doubles, four triples, seven homeruns, and a trio of stolen bases. His overall production, according to *Weighted Runs Created Plus*, was 39% better than the Eastern League average, the fifth best showing.

**Projection**: On one hand Cecchini's offensive spike was a bit predictable: he was constantly facing off against more advanced pitching and his underlying numbers were slowly creeping upwards. On the other hand, however, there's no one on this planet that would have surmised the young shortstop outperforming J.P. Crawford, widely recognized as one of the top MiLB shortstops, in the Eastern League. But Cecchini did just that, 139 wRC+ vs. 121 wRC+. With that being said, Cecchini doesn't own a true standout tool. The power is merely average, perhaps even slightly below. He doesn't offer up a whole lot of foot speed. The plate discipline is merely average. And the hit tool, well, this is the first time he's topped a .273 average; coincidentally (or not), Cecchini's also sporting the highest BABIP of his career (.348). Cecchini, as CAL would agree, looks like a solid big league regular, perhaps a few ticks better.

**Ceiling:** 2.5- to 3.0-win player
**Risk:** Moderate
**MLB ETA:** 2017

## 3. Marcos Molina, RHP

**MiLB Rank: #133**
**Position Rank: N/A**

| Born: 03/08/95 | Age: 21 | Bats: R | Top CALs: Ian Mckinney, Carlos Vasquez, |
|---|---|---|---|
| Height: 6-3 | Weight: 188 | Throws: R | Jose Guzman, Casey Meisner, Sam Gibbons |

| YEAR | Age | Level | IP | W | L | ERA | FIP | K/9 | BB/9 | K% | BB% | HR/9 | LOB% |
|---|---|---|---|---|---|---|---|---|---|---|---|---|---|
| 2013 | 18 | R | 53.3 | 4 | 3 | 4.39 | 3.76 | 7.26 | 2.36 | 18.6% | 6.1% | 0.51 | 63.2% |
| 2014 | 19 | A- | 76.3 | 7 | 3 | 1.77 | 2.34 | 10.73 | 2.12 | 30.7% | 6.1% | 0.24 | 77.4% |
| 2015 | 20 | A+ | 41.3 | 1 | 5 | 4.57 | 2.68 | 7.84 | 2.40 | 19.7% | 6.0% | 0.22 | 59.4% |

**Background:** In a year that started off with so much promise – Molina, who made the jump from the Gulf Coast League straight into High Class A – it ended with nothing but doubt and disappointment. The lanky 6-foot-3, 188-pound right-hander was coming off of an absolutely dominating campaign, something that's seemingly commonplace in this organization; in 12 starts with Brooklyn in 2014 Molina posted a barely there 1.73 ERA, a slightly higher FIP (2.34), and finished with an impeccable 91-to-18 strikeout-to-walk ratio. And, of course, like so many young, promising arms before him, Molina succumbed to Tommy John surgery in 2015, essentially limiting him to 41.1 innings – albeit 41.1 *really good* innings. Removing the poor statistical luck, he posted a 2.68 FIP while averaging 7.84 K/9 and 2.40 BB/9.

**Projection**: I couldn't have been higher on the big right-hander coming into the season, writing this in last year's book:

> "Simply put, Molina's the best pitching prospect you've never heard of – YET. Molina, who stands a solid 6-foot-3 and nearly 190 pounds, has improved his strikeout rate for the second consecutive season, going from a lackluster 6.5 K/9 in the DSL to 7.3 K/9 in his stateside jump in 2013 to a career high 10.89 K/9 in the NYPL last season. What makes It even more impressive: his walk rate has essentially remained the same. It wouldn't be surprising to see him ascend to the club's top pitching prospect – or overall prospect, for that matter – as soon as next season (assuming Noah Syndergaard is promoted). You've been warned."

And through his first five starts of 2015 Molina looked up to the challenge; he tallied a 28-to-7 strikeout-to-walk ratio in 27.0 innings. And remember: he closed out the previous season in the New York-Penn League. Assuming there aren't any Steven Matz – or worse – setbacks,

Molina still offers up plenty of upside in his powerful right arm. Last year I pegged him as a three-win player with a high risk, and he's done nothing to change that – unfortunately.

**Ceiling:** 3.0-win player
**Risk:** Moderate
**MLB ETA:** 2018

## 4. Brandon Nimmo, CF

**MiLB Rank: #208**
**Position Rank: N/A**

| Born: 03/27/93 | Age: 23 | Bats: L | Top CALs: Andrew Lambo, Shane Peterson, |
|---|---|---|---|
| Height: 6-3 | Weight: 205 | Throws: R | Daryl Jones, Tyler Austin, Michael Reed |

| Season | Age | LVL | PA | 2B | 3B | HR | AVG | OBP | SLG | ISO | BB% | K% | wRC+ |
|---|---|---|---|---|---|---|---|---|---|---|---|---|---|
| 2013 | 20 | A | 480 | 16 | 6 | 2 | 0.273 | 0.397 | 0.359 | 0.086 | 14.8% | 27.3% | 127 |
| 2014 | 21 | A+ | 279 | 9 | 5 | 4 | 0.322 | 0.448 | 0.458 | 0.137 | 17.9% | 18.3% | 165 |
| 2014 | 21 | AA | 279 | 12 | 4 | 6 | 0.238 | 0.339 | 0.396 | 0.158 | 12.9% | 19.4% | 107 |
| 2015 | 22 | A+ | 20 | 1 | 0 | 0 | 0.125 | 0.300 | 0.188 | 0.063 | 20.0% | 15.0% | 65 |
| 2015 | 22 | AA | 302 | 12 | 3 | 2 | 0.279 | 0.354 | 0.368 | 0.089 | 8.6% | 18.2% | 111 |
| 2015 | 22 | AAA | 112 | 3 | 1 | 3 | 0.264 | 0.393 | 0.418 | 0.154 | 16.1% | 17.9% | 121 |

**Background:** I can, with as much certainty as *anything else in this entire book,* say no other prospect can stir up the type of emotional swell amongst the hometown faithful than the 6-foot-3, 205-pound lefty-swinging center fielder out of a little Wyoming town. And for Brandon Nimmo the 2015 season was another very Brandon Nimmo-like showing.

The 13<sup>th</sup> overall selection in the 2011 draft – and one pick ahead of ace right-hander Jose Fernandez – Nimmo spent the majority of last season battling a couple serious injuries as he split time between Binghamton and Las Vegas. The young center fielder sprained his ACL trying to leg out an infield single in mid-May, an injury that forced him to miss about four weeks of action. And then a couple months later he would miss a handful of games as he recovered from a fractured nose, the result of a BP incident. In total, Nimmo would hit an aggregate .269/.362/.372 between the Eastern and Pacific Coast Leagues last season (including a four-game rehab stint with St. Lucie).

As for his production, it more or less falls in line with his yearly marks since entering the New York-Penn League as a 19-year-old in 2012. Consider the following:

| YEAR | LEVEL(S) | AVG | OBP | SLG | OPS |
|---|---|---|---|---|---|
| 2012 | A- | 0.248 | 0.372 | 0.406 | 0.778 |
| 2013 | A- | 0.273 | 0.397 | 0.359 | 0.756 |
| 2014 | A+/AA | 0.278 | 0.394 | 0.426 | 0.820 |
| 2015 | AA/AAA | 0.269 | 0.362 | 0.372 | 0.734 |

**Projection:** Let's take a trip into the WayBack Machine and re-visit what I wrote in my first book two years ago:

*"Sorry, Mets' fans. Nimmo is going to be another Sam Bowie. Or Steve Chilcott, the high school catcher the club picked instead of Reggie Jackson; [whichever] analogy you prefer, of course. Nimmo has one above-average tool: his ability to walk. He hasn't run at all, or hit for power, or hit left-handers. And, not to pile on, but his K-rate, 27.3%, is encroaching red flag territory. Maybe he develops into a useful fourth/fifth outfielder."*

And here's what I wrote in last year's book:

*"Alright, maybe I was a bit too harsh on the guy the Mets chose instead of Jose Fernandez, but let's delve into the numbers a little bit deeper, ok? Nimmo started off the year as hot as Pete Rose walking through Hell wearing a gasoline suit – he hit .384/.508/.515 over his first 26 games – but he cooled dramatically afterwards, hitting .250/.361/.402 over his final 101 games – numbers more or less in line with his career norms by the way. (And that's not including his chilly .202/.306/.238 performance in the Arizona Summer League, either.)*

*And, yes, he still walked at a tremendous rate. But the power was simply average for the majority of the year; he still ran rather infrequently (at least not enough to boost his value) and – here's the doozy – he still can't hit southpaws (.232/.347/.317 against them [in 2014] and .220/.331/.298 in his career).*

*So, I'm not backing off of my evaluation from last year. And CAL is suggesting that I could be right by listing Aaron Hicks, Robbie Grossman, Dan Brewer, and LeVon Washington as four of his top five comps. [He's a] fourth/fifth outfielder guy."*

OK, so where do I begin?

Well, Nimmo is sporting a tremendous strong eye at the plate; he walked in 11.1% of his plate appearances last season and has found first base via the free pass in about 14% of the time in his career. It's safe to say it's an above-average, repeatable skill with the floor of something around 8.5% to 9% at the big league level.

Going down the list from two years ago, Nimmo still isn't running very frequently or successfully at this point in his career. Last season he swiped five bags in 11 tries, and he's gone 30-for-52 in his five-year professional career. He also isn't hitting for a whole lot of power either. Even prior to the knee injury he posted a .123 Isolated Power. And then, of course, is his complete inability to hit fellow southpaws; he "batted" .242/.349/.264 against them in 2015, numbers that more or less far in line with his career mark. Finally, CAL remains utterly unimpressed as well, linking him to Andrew Lambo, Shane Peterson, Daryl Jones, Tyler Austin, and Michael Reed.

In the end, I think, people associate Nimmo's lofty draft status as a harbinger of things to come, but in reality he's never likely going to live up to those expectations. Instead, the former first rounder looks like a platoon specialist given his inability to hit LHP. There's definite value in that, especially if he proves to be an adequate defender, but there's no way he can overcome it.

**Ceiling:** 1.5- to 2.0-win player
**Risk:** Moderate
**MLB ETA:** 2016

## 5. Amed Rosario, SS

**MiLB Rank:** #209
**Position Rank:** N/A

| Born: 11/20/95 | Age: 20 | Bats: R | Top CALs: Oscar Tejeda, Milton Ramos, |
|---|---|---|---|
| Height: 6-2 | Weight: 170 | Throws: R | Malquin Canelo, Arismendy Alcantara, Cleuluis Rondon |

| Season | Age | LVL | PA | 2B | 3B | HR | AVG | OBP | SLG | ISO | BB% | K% | wRC+ |
|---|---|---|---|---|---|---|---|---|---|---|---|---|---|
| 2013 | 17 | R | 226 | 8 | 4 | 3 | 0.241 | 0.279 | 0.358 | 0.118 | 4.9% | 19.0% | 82 |
| 2014 | 18 | A- | 290 | 11 | 5 | 1 | 0.289 | 0.337 | 0.380 | 0.090 | 5.9% | 16.2% | 111 |
| 2015 | 19 | A+ | 417 | 20 | 5 | 0 | 0.257 | 0.307 | 0.335 | 0.078 | 5.5% | 17.5% | 97 |
| 2015 | 19 | AA | 10 | 0 | 0 | 0 | 0.100 | 0.100 | 0.100 | 0.000 | 0.0% | 50.0% | -54 |

**Background:** The organization didn't just quickly move Rosario through the lower levels they damn near shoved him through kicking-and-screaming. Rosario, a lean 6-foot-2, 170-pound shortstop out of the Dominican Republic, bypassed all the foreign rookie leagues and jumped straight into the Appalachian League for his debut, hitting a decent-ish .241/.279/.358 en route to posting an 82 wRC+. He began the following season, 2014, in short-season ball and finished it with a seven-game stint in the Sally. But despite the fact that he hit a combined .274/.320/.372 two years ago, the front office pushed Rosario straight into the Florida State League where he would be one of just two qualified everyday teenage regulars (the other being Tampa Bay's Willy Adames). And for the most part Rosario handled the aggressive development curve: he essentially performed at the FSL league average mark.

**Projection:** A wrist injury – and subsequent trip to the DL – limited Rosario's High Class A stint to 105 games. Rosario continued to show a below-average eye at the plate, something to be expected given his youth and level of competition. The hit tool is slowly trending upward. But the power hasn't started to surface just yet either. CAL's not overly impressed, but a 19-year-old that can post a 97 wRC+ in High Class A has some upside. He might turn into a Didi Gregorius down the line, offensively speaking, of course.

**Ceiling:** 2.0-win player
**Risk:** Moderate to High
**MLB ETA:** 2017

## 6. Chris Flexen, RHP

**MiLB Rank:** #214
**Position Rank:** N/A

| Born: 07/01/94 | Age: 21 | Bats: R | Top CALs: Yelper Castillo, David Baker, |
|---|---|---|---|
| Height: 6-3 | Weight: 215 | Throws: R | Aaron Fuhrman, Chris Lugo, Jayson Aquino |

| YEAR | Age | Level | IP | W | L | ERA | FIP | K/9 | BB/9 | K% | BB% | HR/9 | LOB% |
|---|---|---|---|---|---|---|---|---|---|---|---|---|---|
| 2013 | 19 | R | 69.0 | 8 | 1 | 2.09 | 3.55 | 8.09 | 1.57 | 22.9% | 4.4% | 0.78 | 84.7% |
| 2014 | 20 | A | 69.0 | 3 | 5 | 4.83 | 4.98 | 6.00 | 4.83 | 14.5% | 11.6% | 0.65 | 68.8% |
| 2015 | 20 | R | 6.0 | 0 | 0 | 0.00 | 2.14 | 7.50 | 1.50 | 23.8% | 4.8% | 0.00 | 100.0% |
| 2015 | 20 | A- | 12.3 | 0 | 2 | 5.11 | 3.60 | 9.49 | 5.84 | 21.7% | 13.3% | 0.00 | 66.7% |
| 2015 | 20 | A | 33.7 | 4 | 0 | 1.87 | 2.15 | 8.82 | 1.87 | 24.8% | 5.3% | 0.00 | 74.3% |

**Background:** A younger prep prospect taken in the 14th round out of Memorial High in 2012, New York inked the big right-hander for a $400,000 over-slot bonus as the 440th player selected that year. Flexen made seven appearances with Kingsport during his debut and spent the following season back in the Appalachian League where he would dominate the competition to the tune of 62 punch outs, 12 walks, and a 2.09 ERA in 69.0 innings of work. The front office bumped the then-19-year-old hurler up to Savannah in 2014, but that lasted just 13 starts before Tommy John surgery interrupted his development. Finally healthy, Flexen made three tune-up starts in the Gulf Coast, another three with the Brooklyn Cyclones, and six mostly dominant starts with the Sand Gnats to wrap up a successful return.

**Projection:** Flexen really seemed to turn the corner once the club eased the reins on him a bit in the Sally. Through his first five starts with Savannah the young right-hander posted a 31-to-5 strikeout-to-walk ratio in 31.0 innings, including a ridiculous eight-inning, 10-strikeout, and zero-walk performance against the Kannapolis Intimidators in late August. Flexen could be the latest young Mets prospect to move quickly through the minors.

**Ceiling:** 2.0-win player
**Risk:** Moderate to High
**MLB ETA:** 2017

## 7. Wuilmer Becerra, LF/RF

**MiLB Rank: #216**
**Position Rank: N/A**

| Born: 10/01/94 | Age: 21 | Bats: R | Top CALs: Jose Rivero, Elier Hernandez, |
| Height: 6-4 | Weight: 190 | Throws: R | Edwin Gomez, Manuel Hernandez, David Bote |

| Season | Age | LVL | PA | 2B | 3B | HR | AVG | OBP | SLG | ISO | BB% | K% | wRC+ |
|---|---|---|---|---|---|---|---|---|---|---|---|---|---|
| 2013 | 18 | R | 206 | 6 | 0 | 1 | 0.243 | 0.351 | 0.295 | 0.052 | 9.7% | 29.1% | 102 |
| 2014 | 19 | R | 228 | 9 | 2 | 7 | 0.300 | 0.351 | 0.464 | 0.164 | 6.1% | 24.1% | 132 |
| 2015 | 20 | A | 487 | 27 | 3 | 9 | 0.290 | 0.342 | 0.423 | 0.134 | 6.8% | 19.7% | 118 |

**Background:** The lesser known piece of the R.A. Dickey swindling from Toronto a handful of years ago. At the time of the deal Becerra was a 17-year-old international Bonus Baby with just 39 professional plate appearances on his resume – all of which came in the Gulf Coast League. Since then, however, Becerra has *slowly* progressed from a toolsy outfielder that had trouble driving the baseball into a South Atlantic League middle-of-the-lineup thumper. In 118 games with Savannah last season, the 6-foot-4, 190-pound corner outfielder slugged a solid .290/.342/.423 with 27 doubles, three triples, nine homeruns, and 16 stolen bases en route to posting a 118 wRC+. For his career Becerra is sporting a .281/.347/.407 triple-slash line.

**Projection:** Becerra has now strung together back-to-back seasons of noteworthy production. After a slow April, he batted an impressive .298/.350/.419. The power is solid-average, but there's 20-homer pop in the barrel of his bat. The eye has taken a step backward since posting a 9.7% walk rate in 2013, but it should be no less than an average skill when it's all said and done.

**Ceiling:** 2.0-win player
**Risk:** Moderate to High
**MLB ETA:** 2018

## 8. Dominic Smith, 1B

**MiLB Rank: N/A**
**Position Rank: N/A**

| Born: 06/15/95 | Age: 21 | Bats: L | Top CALs: Nick Longhi, Austin Gallagher, |
| Height: 6-0 | Weight: 185 | Throws: L | Jake Bauers, Jose Osuna, Kristopher Hobson |

| Season | Age | LVL | PA | 2B | 3B | HR | AVG | OBP | SLG | ISO | BB% | K% | wRC+ |
|---|---|---|---|---|---|---|---|---|---|---|---|---|---|
| 2013 | 18 | R | 198 | 9 | 1 | 3 | 0.287 | 0.384 | 0.407 | 0.120 | 12.1% | 18.7% | 131 |
| 2014 | 19 | A | 518 | 26 | 1 | 1 | 0.271 | 0.344 | 0.338 | 0.067 | 9.8% | 14.9% | 95 |
| 2015 | 20 | A+ | 497 | 33 | 0 | 6 | 0.305 | 0.354 | 0.417 | 0.112 | 7.0% | 15.1% | 133 |

**Background:** And just like everything else the Mets touched last year, the once-punch-less first baseman had a career year in 2015. The 11th overall pick in the 2013 draft, Smith hasn't driven the ball as expected, both in terms of his lofty draft status or his run-producing position. The 6-foot, 185-pound first baseman batted .301/.398/.439 during his debut between the Gulf Coast and Appalachian Leagues in 2013, though he posted just a .138 Isolated Power. He followed that up with a disappointing campaign in the South Atlantic League two years ago, hitting a paltry .271/.344/.338 with just one single, solitary dinger. But Smith continued to defy the critics – like myself – by slugging .305/.354/.417 as a 20-year-old in the Florida State League, setting a career high with 33 doubles and six homeruns.

**Projection:** But everything that went well last season, Smith still only managed to finish the year with a **.112 Isolated Power**. And just to put that into perspective a bit, when follow Mets prospect Gavin Cecchini was making his way through the FSL two years ago he tallied a slightly higher ISO (.116). Another red flag to be wary of: all six of Smith's dingers last season came against right-handers. If everything breaks the right way he could develop into a James Loney-type bat. Maybe.

**Ceiling:** 1.5-win player
**Risk:** Moderate
**MLB ETA:** 2017

## 9. Matt Reynolds, SS

**MiLB Rank:** N/A
**Position Rank:** N/A

| Born: 12/03/90 | Age: 25 | Bats: R | **Top CALs:** Chris Taylor, Omar Quintanilla, |
| Height: 6-1 | Weight: 205 | Throws: R | Ivan Ochoa, Daniel Mayora, Brian Bixler |

| Season | Age | LVL | PA | 2B | 3B | HR | AVG | OBP | SLG | ISO | BB% | K% | wRC+ |
|--------|-----|-----|-----|-----|----|----|-------|-------|-------|-------|-------|-------|------|
| 2013 | 22 | A+ | 488 | 21 | 6 | 5 | 0.226 | 0.302 | 0.337 | 0.111 | 7.4% | 16.4% | 83 |
| 2014 | 23 | AA | 242 | 5 | 3 | 1 | 0.355 | 0.430 | 0.422 | 0.066 | 12.0% | 16.9% | 144 |
| 2014 | 23 | AAA | 301 | 16 | 4 | 5 | 0.333 | 0.385 | 0.479 | 0.146 | 7.0% | 19.9% | 124 |
| 2015 | 24 | AAA | 490 | 32 | 5 | 6 | 0.267 | 0.319 | 0.402 | 0.135 | 6.5% | 18.8% | 90 |

**Background:** And this, kids, is what happens when your fantastic luck turns to, well, normal everyday luck. After two seasons of sub-optimal offensive performances – he batted .259/.335/.367 during his pro debut in the Sally and followed that up with .226/.302/.337 mark with St. Lucie the next season –

Reynolds had a *massive* breakout campaign two years ago, torching the Eastern League to the tune of .355/.430/.422 and wreaking havoc on the PCL with a .333/.385/.479 triple-slash line. The former second round pick out of Arkansas hit an aggregate .343/.405/.454 with 21 doubles, seven triples, six homeruns, and 20 stolen bases. An impressive showing, sure, until you factor in his ungodly BABIPs. He posted a .433 BABIP in Class AA and an only slightly worse .404 in Class AAA. So once those numbers normalized, Reynolds' overall production slipped closer to his actual expected results in 2015: he batted .267/.319/.402 with 32 doubles, five triples, six homeruns, and 13 swipes as his production fell to 10% *below* the league average mark.

**Projection**: And here's what I wrote in last year's book:

> "The overall numbers are as impressive as it gets for a middle infielder. But the outcome far outweighs the individual skill set. Reynolds has never really hit for a whole lot of pop at [any] point in his career, even extending back to college. At best, it'll peak as slightly below-average. The eye, which bordered on plus in college, has been average sans his 58-game stint in Class AA [two years ago]. Solid, better than average speed. And the hit tool was inflated this season by a pair of .400+ BABIPs. Good defense and enough of an offensive profile to not kill a team, Reynolds looks like a solid utility guy."

He's as good as it's going to get right now. And CAL links him to a handful of disappointing prospects/big leaguers: Chris Taylor, Omar Quintanilla, Ivan Ochoa, Daniel Mayora, and Brian Bixler. He's a fringy everyday regular who will get exposed in everyday situations.

**Ceiling:** 1.5-win player
**Risk:** Moderate
**MLB ETA:** 2016

## 10. Robert Gsellman, RHP

**MiLB Rank:** N/A
**Position Rank:** N/A

| Born: 07/18/93 | Age: 22 | Bats: R | **Top CALs:** Arquimedes Nieto, Eduardo Rodriguez, |
| Height: 6-4 | Weight: 200 | Throws: R | Jake Thompson, Sebastian Vader, Nick Barnese |

| YEAR | Age | Level | IP | W | L | ERA | FIP | K/9 | BB/9 | K% | BB% | HR/9 | LOB% |
|------|-----|-------|-------|----|----|------|------|------|------|-------|-------|------|-------|
| 2013 | 19 | A- | 70.0 | 3 | 3 | 2.06 | 2.41 | 8.23 | 1.54 | 22.2% | 4.2% | 0.26 | 72.8% |
| 2013 | 19 | A | 29.0 | 2 | 3 | 3.72 | 4.14 | 4.34 | 1.86 | 11.5% | 4.9% | 0.62 | 63.8% |
| 2013 | 19 | A+ | 9.0 | 1 | 0 | 3.00 | 5.24 | 5.00 | 5.00 | 13.2% | 13.2% | 1.00 | 81.4% |
| 2014 | 20 | A | 116.3 | 10 | 6 | 2.55 | 3.34 | 7.12 | 2.63 | 18.4% | 6.8% | 0.15 | 75.8% |
| 2015 | 21 | A+ | 51.0 | 6 | 0 | 1.76 | 2.79 | 6.53 | 1.94 | 18.9% | 5.6% | 0.18 | 82.7% |
| 2015 | 21 | AA | 92.3 | 7 | 7 | 3.51 | 3.65 | 4.78 | 2.53 | 12.7% | 6.7% | 0.39 | 62.5% |

**Background**: It's easy to get overlooked in a system that's churned out, among others, Matt Harvey, Zack Wheeler, Noah Syndergaard, Steven Martz, and Jacob deGrom over the past couple of seasons. And that's exactly what's happened to Robert "the Gazelle" Gsellman. A late round pick in 2011, the 6-foot-4, 200-pound right-hander has continued to make rapid progress through

the low – and now mid – levels of the minor leagues. The former 13th round pick opened the season up with a bang in the Florida State League, hurling 51 innings of impressive ball including his four final games at the level when he posted a 1.50 ERA in 30 innings. Sandy Alderson and Co. bumped the hurler up to the Eastern League for the remainder of the year last May. And after a bit of a rude welcoming – he allowed six earned in four innings with against the Altoona Curve – Gsellman rattled off 14 strong starts before getting smacked around by the Curve (again) in his final start. Overall, Gsellman finished the year with an aggregate 2.89 ERA to go along with an 86-to-37 strikeout-to-walk ratio in a career best 143.1 innings of work.

**Projection**: An intriguing young arm that's never really missed a whole lot of sticks at any point in his career, sans a 12 game stint with Brooklyn in the New York-Penn League several years ago. But Gsellman offers up poise well beyond his years. He compensates for a lack of punch outs by generating a ton of action on the ground; he's totaled at least a 51% groundball rate at any level since 2013. He could be a solid backend starter, whether he gets the chance in New York's loaded rotation is a whole other question. Look for him to be eased in at the big league level, perhaps making a mid-season call up to bolster the club's pen.

**Ceiling:** 1.5-win player
**Risk:** Moderate
**MLB ETA:** 2016

## 11. Gabriel Ynoa, RHP

**MiLB Rank:** N/A
**Position Rank:** N/A

| Born: 05/26/93 | Age: 23 | Bats: R | Top CALs: Tim Alderson, Aaron Siegers, |
| Height: 6-2 | Weight: 160 | Throws: R | Ross Seaton, Blake Johnson, Will Roberts |

| YEAR | Age | Level | IP | W | L | ERA | FIP | K/9 | BB/9 | K% | BB% | HR/9 | LOB% |
|---|---|---|---|---|---|---|---|---|---|---|---|---|---|
| 2013 | 20 | A | 135.7 | 15 | 4 | 2.72 | 3.16 | 7.03 | 1.06 | 19.6% | 3.0% | 0.60 | 74.6% |
| 2014 | 21 | A+ | 82.0 | 8 | 2 | 3.95 | 3.45 | 7.02 | 1.43 | 18.2% | 3.7% | 0.77 | 69.6% |
| 2014 | 21 | AA | 66.3 | 3 | 2 | 4.21 | 4.53 | 5.70 | 1.63 | 15.0% | 4.3% | 1.22 | 74.6% |
| 2015 | 22 | AA | 152.3 | 9 | 9 | 3.90 | 4.12 | 4.84 | 1.83 | 12.9% | 4.9% | 0.83 | 71.1% |

**Background:** The younger brother of the once highly touted prospect Michael Ynoa, Gabriel, nonetheless, has developed – or is developing – into a far superior minor league pitcher. After a bit of sluggish start to his professional career – he made his pro debut in 2010 but didn't appear in a full season contest until 2013 – Ynoa has been making up for lost time lately. The Dominican-born right-hander split his 2014 campaign between St. Lucie and Binghamton, and then spent the entire 2015 season back in the Eastern League. In 25 games with the Class AA Mets Ynoa tallied a career high 152.1 innings with his prototypical sub-2.0 walk rate with some questionable strikeout numbers. For his career Ynoa has punched out just 16% and walked an impressive 3.6% of the total batters he faced.

**Projection:** Just to put this into a bit of perspective – something I strive to do with every prospect in the book – consider the following: in 641 career innings Ynoa has issued just 94 base-on-balls; on the other hand, San Francisco fire-balling right-hander – and one of the club's top prospects – Kyle Crick has walked 241 in just 340 innings. Ynoa's never missed a whole helluva lot of bats at any stop during his six-year minor league career; his best showing was 7.5 punch outs per nine innings. But the control is among the finest in the minor leagues. He doesn't generate a whole lot of action on the ground either. Unlike a lot of other control-style starters Ynoa actually possesses a strong fastball, so maybe there's hope he can carve out a role in the backend of the Mets' rotation if needed in a pinch.

**Ceiling:** 1.0- to 1.5-win player
**Risk:** Low to Moderate
**MLB ETA:** 2016

## 12. Jhoan Urena, 3B

**MiLB Rank:** N/A
**Position Rank:** N/A

| Born: 09/01/94 | Age: 21 | Bats: B | Top CALs: Victor Acosta, Deiner Lopez, |
| Height: 6-1 | Weight: 200 | Throws: R | Mario Martinez, Tim Kennelly, Jean Carlos Valdez |

| Season | Age | LVL | PA | 2B | 3B | HR | AVG | OBP | SLG | ISO | BB% | K% | wRC+ |
|---|---|---|---|---|---|---|---|---|---|---|---|---|---|
| 2013 | 18 | R | 171 | 6 | 3 | 0 | 0.299 | 0.351 | 0.376 | 0.076 | 7.6% | 19.9% | 115 |
| 2014 | 19 | A- | 315 | 20 | 1 | 5 | 0.300 | 0.356 | 0.431 | 0.131 | 8.6% | 18.4% | 128 |
| 2015 | 20 | A+ | 222 | 5 | 3 | 0 | 0.214 | 0.257 | 0.267 | 0.052 | 5.0% | 18.0% | 60 |

**Background:** A decidedly risky move that flamed out in a spectacular manner for the club's development system. New York decided to shove the then-20-year-old third baseman into High Class A straight from the New York-Penn League to start the year, making him one of just a handful of prospects under the age of 21 in the Florida State League. And after a promising initial debut – he went 3-for-5 with a triple and two RBIs against the Bradenton Marauders in his first game – Urena posted a rancid .215/.254/.259 triple-slash line over his next 37 games before a wrist injury – a broken hamate bone – shut him down for about six weeks. After a quick trip through the GCL for a tune-up, Urena came back to St. Lucie in mid-July and batted an even worse .186/.240/.229 the rest of the season.

**Projection:** A very, very tough read – analytically speaking, of course. Urena was simply overmatched by the more advanced High Class A pitching, and then he suffered the broken hamate, an injury that saps a player's power for 12 or so months. Two years ago in the NYPL Urena showcased solid-average or better power and a decent eye at the plate. I'm willing to overlook the misstep last year, but he's going need to show something more in 2016.

**Ceiling:** 1.5- to 2.0-win player
**Risk:** High
**MLB ETA:** 2017/2018

## 13. Desmond Lindsay, CF

| Born: 01/15/97 | Age: 19 | Bats: R | Top CALs: N/A |
| Height: 6-0 | Weight: 200 | Throws: R | |

| Season | Age | LVL | PA | 2B | 3B | HR | AVG | OBP | SLG | ISO | BB% | K% | wRC+ |
|---|---|---|---|---|---|---|---|---|---|---|---|---|---|
| 2015 | 18 | R | 81 | 4 | 2 | 1 | 0.304 | 0.400 | 0.464 | 0.159 | 13.6% | 25.9% | 157 |
| 2015 | 18 | A- | 53 | 3 | 0 | 0 | 0.200 | 0.308 | 0.267 | 0.067 | 13.2% | 35.8% | 79 |

**Background:** Without a true first round pick for the first time since 2009 courtesy of signing the rapidly declining Michael Cuddyer, the front office selected prep outfielder Desmond Lindsay with the 53rd overall selection last June. Lindsay was able to hold own in the Gulf Coast League (.304/.400/.464) before falling back to earth in the New York-Penn League (.200/.308/.267).

**Projection**: Lindsay looked incredibly toolsy during his 21-game tour of the GCL last season, showing an above-average eye at the plate, solid or better power, a little bit of speed, and decent hit tool (though that was buoyed by a .426 BABIP). I'm willing to overlook the 35.8% K-rate in the New York-Penn League given his age, and one wonders if he'll be placed on an aggressive development path and head to full season ball next season.

**Ceiling:** Too Soon to Tell
**Risk:** N/A
**MLB ETA:** N/A

## 14. Akeel Morris, RHP

| Born: 11/14/92 | Age: 23 | Bats: R | Top CALs: Adrian Rosario, Clayton Schrader, |
| Height: 6-1 | Weight: 195 | Throws: R | Joey Krehbiel, Casey Mulligan, Paul Voelker |

| YEAR | Age | Level | IP | W | L | ERA | FIP | K/9 | BB/9 | K% | BB% | HR/9 | LOB% |
|---|---|---|---|---|---|---|---|---|---|---|---|---|---|
| 2013 | 20 | A- | 45.0 | 4 | 1 | 1.00 | 2.32 | 12.00 | 4.60 | 32.8% | 12.6% | 0.20 | 89.2% |
| 2014 | 21 | A | 57.0 | 4 | 1 | 0.63 | 1.90 | 14.05 | 3.47 | 42.2% | 10.4% | 0.16 | 91.1% |
| 2015 | 22 | A+ | 32.0 | 0 | 1 | 1.69 | 2.01 | 12.94 | 3.94 | 38.3% | 11.7% | 0.28 | 80.5% |
| 2015 | 22 | AA | 29.3 | 0 | 1 | 2.45 | 2.86 | 10.74 | 4.60 | 29.9% | 12.8% | 0.31 | 78.4% |

**Background:** After moving at a slow-and-steady pace for the first five seasons of his professional career, Morris, who only made one stop each year, threw it into high gear in 2015. The former late round pick, another theme of the organization, blew away the Florida State League competition, made a brief – and unsuccessful – appearance in New York, and then settled in nicely with the Binghamton Mets in the Eastern League. The 6-foot-1, 195-pound right-hander finished his sixth minor league campaign with a total of 61.1 innings, fanning a whopping 81 and walking 29. For his career he's averaging 12 punch outs and 4.9 free passes per nine innings to go along with a 2.76 ERA.

**Projection**: A budding late-inning star if Morris can ever reel in his problematic control, though he continued to take another step in the right direction last year by issuing the second fewest walks in his career. Morris churned out a low- to mid-90s fastball, an upper 80s slider, and a mid-70s change.

**Ceiling:** 1.0- to 1.5-win player
**Risk:** Moderate
**MLB ETA:** Debuted in 2015

## 15. Jacob Lugo, RHP

| Born: 11/17/89 | Age: 26 | Bats: R | Top CALs: Reid Santos, Ronald Uviedo, |
| Height: 6-4 | Weight: 185 | Throws: R | Dave Johnson, Robert Hinton, Ryan Mckeller |

| YEAR | Age | Level | IP | W | L | ERA | FIP | K/9 | BB/9 | K% | BB% | HR/9 | LOB% |
|---|---|---|---|---|---|---|---|---|---|---|---|---|---|
| 2013 | 23 | A- | 34.3 | 2 | 4 | 4.19 | 3.88 | 7.08 | 3.41 | 18.5% | 8.9% | 0.79 | 73.1% |
| 2013 | 23 | A | 32.0 | 2 | 2 | 2.53 | 2.51 | 10.97 | 1.69 | 32.2% | 5.0% | 0.56 | 76.3% |
| 2014 | 24 | A+ | 105.0 | 8 | 3 | 4.11 | 3.91 | 9.77 | 3.26 | 25.1% | 8.4% | 1.03 | 69.5% |
| 2015 | 25 | AA | 109.0 | 6 | 5 | 3.80 | 3.41 | 8.01 | 2.48 | 20.8% | 6.4% | 0.66 | 67.5% |
| 2015 | 25 | AAA | 27.0 | 2 | 2 | 4.00 | 3.60 | 10.00 | 1.67 | 26.3% | 4.4% | 1.00 | 70.5% |

**Background:** I once had a pitching coach – who happened to spend some time in the low levels of the minors in the Texas organization – tell me that no matter where you play, if you're good enough scouts will find you. Well, that's certainly the case for Lugo. Plucked out Division III Centenary College of Louisiana in the 34th round in 2011, the 6-foot-4 right-hander not only beat the odds by coming from a small school with a lackluster track record – Lugo tallied a 3-and-7 record to go along with a 5.57 ERA during his final collegiate campaign – but he overcame a near-career-ending injury. During offseason workouts following his big league debut Lugo injured his back so badly that doctors told him he may never play ball again. The diagnosis: Spondylolisthesis, a displacement of a vertebra in the spine. Well, he missed the entire 2012 season, but came back in a big way in 2013; he made stops in the New York-Penn League and the Sally. He spent the next year in Florida State, and then blew through the Eastern and Pacific Coast Leagues last year.

**Projection**: Lugo's already exceeded every possible expectation thrown his way and dealt with every perceived limitation as well. He has a long history of above-average peripherals – he's fanned nearly a punch out per inning with a sub-3.0 walk rate – but he's always been a bit old for his levels of competition. New York's rotation is chock full of high level arms and a big waistband with the likes of Matt Harvey, Noah Syndergaard, Jacob deGrom, Steven Matz, Zack Wheeler, and Bartolo Colon so it's safe to assume that Lugo's likely to be bounced into a bullpen role in the next 12 months.

**Ceiling:** 1.0-win player
**Risk:** Moderate
**MLB ETA:** 2016

## 16. Jack Leathersich, LHP

MiLB Rank: N/A
Position Rank: N/A

| Born: 07/14/90 | Age: 25 | Bats: R |
|---|---|---|
| Height: 5-11 | Weight: 200 | Throws: L |

**Top CALs:** J.J. Hoover, Corey Knebel, Lisalverto Bonilla, Shae Simmons, David Robertson

| YEAR | Age | Level | IP | W | L | ERA | FIP | K/9 | BB/9 | K% | BB% | HR/9 | LOB% |
|---|---|---|---|---|---|---|---|---|---|---|---|---|---|
| 2013 | 22 | AA | 29.3 | 2 | 0 | 1.53 | 1.76 | 16.88 | 4.91 | 44.4% | 12.9% | 0.31 | 89.6% |
| 2013 | 22 | AAA | 29.0 | 2 | 0 | 7.76 | 4.54 | 14.59 | 9.00 | 31.8% | 19.6% | 0.62 | 50.7% |
| 2014 | 23 | AA | 46.0 | 3 | 3 | 2.93 | 1.83 | 15.46 | 4.11 | 39.7% | 10.6% | 0.20 | 74.7% |
| 2014 | 23 | AAA | 8.3 | 0 | 0 | 5.40 | 6.34 | 15.12 | 7.56 | 33.3% | 16.7% | 2.16 | 75.8% |
| 2015 | 24 | AAA | 13.3 | 0 | 0 | 5.40 | 5.02 | 14.85 | 4.73 | 38.6% | 12.3% | 2.03 | 72.5% |

**Background:** The book on Leathersich is – and had been – written ad nauseam: a dominant left-handed reliever with an incredible ability to miss a ton of bats *and* the strike zone at a high frequency. So it's no surprise that last season, his fifth in professional baseball, was no different. Leathersich did the tango between the Pacific Coast League and New York before succumbing to the all-too-common Tommy John surgery. Prior to the injury, Leathersich punched out 22 and walked seven in 13.1 innings with Las Vegas and fanned another 14 and issued another seven walks in 11.2 innings with the Mets. For his career, the former 2011 fifth round pick out of the University of Massachusetts Lowell has averaged a mind-boggling 15.2 strikeouts per nine innings.

**Projection**: Here's what I opined in last year's book:

> "Leathersich belongs in the merry bunch that helped Dorothy find the Wizard of Oz. The Lion lacked courage; the Tin Man, a heart; the Scarecrow needs a brain; and the Mets' lefty desperately wishes for some control. Quick! Someone tell him he was born with it already! The potential to be an absolutely devastating reliever is right there for the taking – if he could cut about a walk-and-a-half off his career walk rate. Guys like this, though, often find it later in their careers. Fingers firmly crossed."

Leathersich didn't showcase the typical mid- to upper-90s fastball one would contribute to such absurd strikeout numbers; instead it rested in the low-90s, averaging 91.2 mph during his run with the big league club. Assuming the Tommy John surgery and rehab continues without a hitch, Leathersich could still develop into a dominant reliever. I just don't think, however, that it'll be with the Mets. Most pitchers battle control issues when they successfully return from the injury, but how longer do you think the front office will stick by Leathersich?

**Ceiling:** 1.0- to 1.5-win player
**Risk:** Moderate to High
**MLB ETA:** Debuted in 2015

## 17. Corey Oswalt, RHP

MiLB Rank: N/A
Position Rank: N/A

| Born: 09/03/93 | Age: 22 | Bats: R |
|---|---|---|
| Height: 6-4 | Weight: 200 | Throws: R |

**Top CALs:** Justin De Fratus, Jesus Tinoco, Ryan Weber, Nick Hernandez, Domingo German

| YEAR | Age | Level | IP | W | L | ERA | FIP | K/9 | BB/9 | K% | BB% | HR/9 | LOB% |
|---|---|---|---|---|---|---|---|---|---|---|---|---|---|
| 2013 | 19 | R | 13.0 | 0 | 1 | 3.46 | 1.97 | 7.62 | 0.69 | 20.0% | 1.8% | 0.00 | 60.0% |
| 2014 | 20 | A- | 67.7 | 6 | 2 | 2.26 | 2.69 | 7.85 | 2.00 | 21.5% | 5.5% | 0.13 | 74.0% |
| 2015 | 21 | A | 128.7 | 11 | 5 | 3.36 | 3.06 | 6.92 | 1.47 | 18.3% | 3.9% | 0.42 | 69.6% |

**Background:** The 230th player taken in the 2012 draft, Oswalt, nonetheless, signed for a hefty half-million dollar bonus – not bad work for a seventh round pick. Standing 6-foot-4 and an even 200 pounds, Oswalt has climbed through the low levels of the minor leagues and finally made it into full season ball for the first time in his four-year career. In 23 starts with the Savannah Sand Gnats, the right-hander out of Madison High School whiffed 99, walked 21, and posted a promising 3.06 FIP in a career best 128.2 innings of work. For his career, Oswalt has struck out 189 and walked 44 of the 1,033 total hitters he's faced – or 18.3% and 4.3%, respectively.

**Projection**: The front office's mid- to late-round over-slot bonus babies continue to payoff. And despite posting a solid 3.36 ERA and an equally strong 3.06 FIP, Oswalt suffered through some pretty poor luck; opponent's posted a .355 BABIP against the then-21-year-old hurler. He also improved over the course of the season as well: over his final 75 innings Oswalt allowed 20 earned runs (2.40 ERA), fanned 52, and walked 13. He's a nice low level hurler who has a chance to develop into a useful #5 or a solid bullpen contributor.

**Ceiling**: 1.0-win player
**Risk**: Moderate
**MLB ETA**: 2018

## 18. David Thompson, 3B

MiLB Rank: N/A
Position Rank: N/A

| Born: 08/28/93 | Age: 22 | Bats: R | Top CALs: Jhonny Medrano, Tyler Bream, |
|---|---|---|---|
| Height: 6-2 | Weight: 220 | Throws: R | Garrett Buechele, Wade Gaynor, Ben Verlander |

| Season | Age | LVL | PA | 2B | 3B | HR | AVG | OBP | SLG | ISO | BB% | K% | wRC+ |
|---|---|---|---|---|---|---|---|---|---|---|---|---|---|
| 2015 | 21 | A- | 228 | 10 | 1 | 3 | 0.218 | 0.268 | 0.320 | 0.102 | 4.8% | 19.3% | 72 |

**Background**: A big college bopper out of the University of Miami, Thompson seemingly came out of nowhere during his junior campaign to finish with the second most homeruns, 19, among all Division I players. In his final season with the Hurricanes Thompson slugged a robust .328/.434/.640 with 18 doubles and a pair of triples to go along with massive power supply. New York grabbed the 6-foot-1, 180-pound third baseman in the fourth round last June, 119th overall, and pushed him into the New York-Penn League where he struggled to make the proper adjustments at the professional level; he batted a paltry .218/.274/.320 with a horrific 44-to-11 strikeout-to-walk ratio. His overall production, according to *Weighted Runs Created Plus*, was a whopping 28% *below* the league average mark.

**Projection**: Here's what I wrote in his pre-draft evaluation:

> *"The most impressive part of his breakout season: he's sporting an impeccable 24-to-41 strikeout-to-walk ratio. Thompson [shows] an above-average to plus-power, something in the range of 25-homeruns in a full professional season, with a surprisingly solid hit tool and a decent eye at the plate.*
>
> *Defensively, he needs a lot of work. He's already committed 12 errors this year.*
>
> *Overall, though, Thompson's best showing – his power potential – comes at a time when it's in dire need at the professional level. And, quite frankly, it's a bit surprising he's not more talked about. He's one of those guys that could very easily slide out of the first round and become an instant steal."*

Well, it looks like I clearly overvalued Thompson's power potential as he not only slid out of the first round – *well* out of the first round – but Thompson looked awful during his debut.

**Ceiling**: 1. 0- to 1.5-win player
**Risk**: High
**MLB ETA**: 2018

## 19. Michael Gibbons, RHP

MiLB Rank: N/A
Position Rank: N/A

| Born: 04/24/93 | Age: 23 | Bats: R | Top CALs: Garrett Cortright, Chase Lirette, |
|---|---|---|---|
| Height: 6-4 | Weight: 205 | Throws: R | Zach Isler, Ethan Katz, Alex Powers |

| YEAR | Age | Level | IP | W | L | ERA | FIP | K/9 | BB/9 | K% | BB% | HR/9 | LOB% |
|---|---|---|---|---|---|---|---|---|---|---|---|---|---|
| 2015 | 22 | A- | 10.7 | 2 | 0 | 5.91 | 3.98 | 8.44 | 2.53 | 21.7% | 6.5% | 0.84 | 58.8% |
| 2015 | 22 | A | 34.3 | 2 | 3 | 2.88 | 4.33 | 6.03 | 2.88 | 15.3% | 7.3% | 0.79 | 74.8% |
| 2015 | 22 | A+ | 18.0 | 0 | 1 | 3.50 | 2.78 | 5.50 | 1.50 | 14.9% | 4.1% | 0.00 | 63.6% |
| 2015 | 22 | AA | 6.3 | 0 | 1 | 4.26 | 4.85 | 4.26 | 1.42 | 12.0% | 4.0% | 1.42 | 55.6% |

**Background**: In a page taken out of St. Louis hurler Zack Petrick's book, the undrafted free agent out of little Wheaton College is making a quick – and lasting – impression with every slugger that digs in against him. Gibbons, a 6-foot-4, 205-pound right-hander, signed in late-August 2014, but made his professional debut last year.

And it was one helluva debut. Gibbons made stops at four different levels last season, and for those keeping track at home it went something like this:

- One start in the Florida State League
- Two starts in the New York-Penn League
- One start in the Eastern League

- Six starts in the Sally
- Two starts in the Florida State League

In one of the more – or most – bizarre seasons in recent memory, Gibbons would finish the season with a 47-to-18 strikeout-to-walk ratio in 69.1 innings, as well as a 3.63 ERA.

**Projection**: Who the hell knows the exact reason Gibbons bounced around like a rubber pancake, but he showed obvious flashes – especially considering that only months before he was struggling to latch onto a team. He's one to watch in 2016.

**Ceiling:** Too Soon to Tell
**Risk:** N/A
**MLB ETA:** N/A

## 20. Eudor Garcia, 3B

**MiLB Rank:** N/A
**Position Rank:** N/A

| Born: 05/17/94 | Age: 22 | Bats: L | Top CALs: Matt Weaver, Ron Garth, |
| Height: 6-0 | Weight: 225 | Throws: R | David Bote, Jovan Rosa, Zachary Green |

| Season | Age | LVL | PA | 2B | 3B | HR | AVG | OBP | SLG | ISO | BB% | K% | wRC+ |
|---|---|---|---|---|---|---|---|---|---|---|---|---|---|
| 2014 | 20 | R | 226 | 9 | 1 | 2 | 0.262 | 0.327 | 0.347 | 0.084 | 7.1% | 14.2% | 98 |
| 2015 | 21 | A | 429 | 23 | 4 | 9 | 0.296 | 0.340 | 0.442 | 0.146 | 5.1% | 22.1% | 121 |

**Background:** A fourth round pick out of El Paso Community College in 2014, Garcia had a bit of a disappointing professional debut two years ago, hitting a lackadaisical .262 /.327/.347 with Kingsport in the Appalachian League. The organization bumped him up to Savannah last season and he responded in kind: in 105 games for the Sand Gnats Garcia batted .296/.340/.442 with a 121 wRC+.

**Projection**: The power took a nice developmental step forward for Savannah last season; he posted a solid-average .146 ISO in a slightly favorable pitcher's ballpark. The patience at the plate is sub-par and the defensive numbers aren't too thrilling either. He's a nice organizational soldier.

**Ceiling:** 1.0-win player
**Risk:** Moderate to High
**MLB ETA:** 2018

## 21. Luis Carpio, SS

**MiLB Rank:** N/A
**Position Rank:** N/A

| Born: 07/11/97 | Age: 18 | Bats: R | Top CALs: Rehiner Cordova, Oscar Tejeda, |
| Height: 6-0 | Weight: 165 | Throws: R | Griffin Garabito, Juniel Querecuto, Leobaldo Pina |

| Season | Age | LVL | PA | 2B | 3B | HR | AVG | OBP | SLG | ISO | BB% | K% | wRC+ |
|---|---|---|---|---|---|---|---|---|---|---|---|---|---|
| 2014 | 16 | R | 250 | 9 | 1 | 1 | 0.234 | 0.347 | 0.301 | 0.067 | 13.2% | 13.2% | 98 |
| 2015 | 17 | R | 207 | 10 | 0 | 0 | 0.304 | 0.372 | 0.359 | 0.055 | 8.2% | 16.4% | 109 |

**Background:** Signed his name on the dotted line on his sixteenth birthday for $300,000 on July 11, 2013, Caprio, 6-foot, 165-pound shortstop, looked underwhelming during his debut in the Dominican Summer League, hitting .234/.347/.301. But the organization took a calculated risk and pushed the then-17-year-old straight up to Kingsport in the Appalachian League last season. And Carpio looked like a completely different player. He slugged .304/.372/.359 with 10 doubles and nine stolen bases. His overall production, according to *Weighted Runs Created Plus*, topped the league average mark by 9%.

**Projection**: Solid eye with a promising hit tool and a smattering of speed, Carpio could go one of two ways: either he develops into a solid big league regular or a sparsely used backup infielder. The deciding factor, of course, is if he'll development enough power – which may not happen because it looks like he's swinging one of those foam Nerf bats now.

**Ceiling:** 1.0-win player
**Risk:** Moderate to High
**MLB ETA:** 2019

## 22. Dario Alvarez, LHP

MiLB Rank: N/A
Position Rank: N/A

| Born: 01/17/89 | Age: 27 | Bats: L | Top CALs: Pete Ruiz, Brian Akin, |
| Height: 6-1 | Weight: 170 | Throws: L | Seth Simmons, Beck Wheeler, Matt Langwell |

| YEAR | Age | Level | IP | W | L | ERA | FIP | K/9 | BB/9 | K% | BB% | HR/9 | LOB% |
|------|-----|-------|-----|---|---|-----|-----|-----|------|-----|-----|------|------|
| 2013 | 24 | A- | 58.0 | 2 | 4 | 3.10 | 3.06 | 8.84 | 4.03 | 22.4% | 10.2% | 0.16 | 67.8% |
| 2014 | 25 | A | 61.3 | 7 | 1 | 1.32 | 1.70 | 13.94 | 2.05 | 39.1% | 5.8% | 0.29 | 83.6% |
| 2014 | 25 | A+ | 6.3 | 2 | 0 | 0.00 | 1.65 | 14.21 | 4.26 | 50.0% | 15.0% | 0.00 | 100.0% |
| 2014 | 25 | AA | 5.7 | 1 | 0 | 0.00 | 0.71 | 14.29 | 0.00 | 42.9% | 0.0% | 0.00 | 100.0% |
| 2015 | 26 | AA | 31.0 | 1 | 1 | 3.19 | 3.17 | 12.48 | 4.65 | 32.1% | 11.9% | 0.58 | 69.9% |
| 2015 | 26 | AAA | 11.0 | 2 | 1 | 2.45 | 2.33 | 15.55 | 4.09 | 43.2% | 11.4% | 0.00 | 78.6% |

**Background:** A lefty with a lengthy track record of high punch out totals and some wavering control. Alvarez split his season between Class AA and Class AAA last season, totaling 42 innings with 62 strikeouts and 21 free passes to go along with a 3.00 ERA. For his career, Alvarez has fanned 28.6% and walked 9.5% of the total hitters he's faced in MiLB.

**Projection**: In his two brief stints in New York over the past couple of seasons Alvarez has unleashed an upper 80s to lower 90s fastball and a slurvy-type slider. He's been death on minor league lefties since 2011, holding them to a lowly .177/.284/.238 triple-slash line. At worst, he's the prototypical LOOGY.

**Ceiling:** 0.5- to 1.0-win player
**Risk:** Low to Moderate
**MLB ETA:** Debuted in 2014

## 23. Max Wotell, LHP

MiLB Rank: N/A
Position Rank: N/A

| Born: 09/13/96 | Age: 19 | Bats: R | Top CALs: Trevor Cahill, Jose Morel, |
| Height: 6-3 | Weight: 180 | Throws: L | Wander Marte, Cody Reed, Andrea Lucati |

| YEAR | Age | Level | IP | W | L | ERA | FIP | K/9 | BB/9 | K% | BB% | HR/9 | LOB% |
|------|-----|-------|-----|---|---|-----|-----|-----|------|-----|-----|------|------|
| 2015 | 18 | R | 10.7 | 0 | 1 | 2.53 | 3.12 | 13.50 | 7.59 | 35.6% | 20.0% | 0.00 | 58.3% |

**Background:** The club's third round pick out of Marvin Ridge High School last June. Wotell, a 6-foot-3, 180-pound lefty, made nine appearances in the Gulf Coast League during his debut, throwing 10.2 innings while fanning 16 and walking a staggeringly high nine hitters.

**Projection**: Nothing much to go on other than the lofty draft status and 10+ innings of work. Wotell started off his professional debut well enough, striking out 10 and walking three in 5.2 innings of work. But he coughed up six free passes in his final five innings.

**Ceiling:** Too Soon to Tell
**Risk:** N/A
**MLB ETA:** N/A

## 24. Milton Ramos, 2B/SS

MiLB Rank: N/A
Position Rank: N/A

| Born: 10/26/95 | Age: 20 | Bats: R | Top CALs: Angelo More, Randoll Santana, |
| Height: 5-11 | Weight: 158 | Throws: R | Jeudy Valdez, Cleuluis Rondon, Jose Garcia |

| Season | Age | LVL | PA | 2B | 3B | HR | AVG | OBP | SLG | ISO | BB% | K% | wRC+ |
|--------|-----|-----|-----|----|----|----|-----|-----|-----|-----|-----|-----|------|
| 2014 | 18 | R | 185 | 9 | 5 | 0 | 0.241 | 0.299 | 0.355 | 0.114 | 7.6% | 18.4% | 87 |
| 2015 | 19 | R | 179 | 11 | 1 | 1 | 0.317 | 0.341 | 0.415 | 0.098 | 3.9% | 16.8% | 108 |
| 2015 | 19 | R | 39 | 1 | 0 | 0 | 0.194 | 0.256 | 0.222 | 0.028 | 2.6% | 23.1% | 52 |

**Background:** Hailing from American Heritage High School, home to such dignitaries as Eric Hosmer, Deven Marrero, Darnell Sweeney, and Adrian Nieto, the Mets plucked the 5-foot-11, 165-pound middle infielder in the third round two years ago. Ramos looked overmatched during his professional debut in the Gulf Coast League, hitting a mediocre .241/.299/.355. Ramos spent the majority of last season bouncing between the Appalachian League and GCL, hitting a combined .295/.326/.380.

**Projection**: Ramos is now entering his age-20 season without much experience above the Appalachian. The hit tool is questionable, the walk rates were subpar last year, and he showed very little power – even for a middle infielder. He looks like organization depth right.

**Ceiling:** 1.0-win player
**Risk:** Moderate to High
**MLB ETA:** 2019

## 25. Dash Winningham, 1B

**MiLB Rank:** N/A
**Position Rank:** N/A

| Born: 10/11/95 | Age: 20 | Bats: L | Top CALs: Juan Ortiz, Elio De La Rosa, |
|---|---|---|---|
| Height: 6-2 | Weight: 230 | Throws: L | Jonas Lantigua, Jose Pena, Pedro Perez |

| Season | Age | LVL | PA | 2B | 3B | HR | AVG | OBP | SLG | ISO | BB% | K% | wRC+ |
|---|---|---|---|---|---|---|---|---|---|---|---|---|---|
| 2014 | 18 | R | 199 | 10 | 1 | 5 | 0.231 | 0.322 | 0.391 | 0.160 | 8.5% | 19.6% | 107 |
| 2015 | 19 | R | 290 | 19 | 1 | 12 | 0.266 | 0.310 | 0.479 | 0.213 | 5.2% | 21.7% | 113 |

**Background:** A big hulky first baseman out of Trinity Catholic High School, the 6-foot-2, 230-pound Winningham slugged an Appalachian-league best 12 dingers during his sophomore campaign. The former 8th round pick batted .266/.310/.479 with 19 doubles and one triple to go along with all the homeruns. His overall production, per *Weighted Runs Created Plus*, topped the league average mark by 13%.

**Projection:** Decent eye with reasonably strong contact rates against the advanced rookie league pitching. But the power can be a potential above-average skill moving forward. Of course, there's a rather large red flag: Winningham batted a paltry .139/.195/.250 against fellow left-handers. He's not really an MLB-caliber prospect yet, but there's some hope he can develop into a big league platoon option.

**Ceiling:** 1.0-win player
**Risk:** Moderate to High
**MLB ETA:** 2017

## Barely Missed:

- **Anderson Baldonado, LHP** – A wiry 6-foot-2 left-hander out of the Dominican Republic, Baldonado posted an absurd 74-to-24 strikeout-to-walk ratio to go along with a barely-there 1.91 ERA. At 22-years-old, he's a bit too old for the Sally, but he's poised to move after stagnating the past couple of seasons.

- **Luis Carpio, 2B/SS** – Hit a respectable .304/.372/.359 as a 17-year-old in the Appalachian League. Carpio has only slugged one career homerun in his first 105 professional games. He's likely to be included in next year's top 25. It wouldn't be surprising to see the club push the teenager to at least the NYPL and maybe even the Sally in 2016.

- **Luis Guillorme, SS** – Topped the South Atlantic League offensive production by 20% last year as a 20-year-old. This, of course, is only complicated by the fact that he's yet to slug a homerun in 217 professional games.

- **Jeff McNeil, 2B/3B/SS** – Another late round pick by the organization, McNeil continued to hold his own in the lower levels of the minors. The former 12th round pick hit a respectable .312/.373/.382 with St. Lucie in the Florida State League. He owns a career .305/.375/.389. Potential utility guy.

## *Bird Doggin' It – Additional Prospects to Keep an Eye in 2016*

| Player | Age | POS | Notes |
|---|---|---|---|
| Jace Boyd | 25 | 1B/LF | Typical Quad-A caliber bat. Boyd owns a respectable .295/.373/.416 triple-slash line, but has only slugged 23 homeruns in his four-year professional career. |
| Kevin Canelon | 22 | LHP | Advanced lefty chewed up the younger New York-Penn League competition, averaging 8.2 punch outs and 1.8 free passes per nine innings. |
| Darrell Ceciliani | 25 | OF | A seven-year minor league vet, Ceciliani had a massive breakout in the PCL last season, hitting a robust .345/.398/.581 |
| Nabil Crismatt | 21 | RHP | Columbian-born right-hander has posted a sub-2.91 ERA in each of his previous three seasons including last year's work in the Appalachian. Likely headed to the NYPL. |
| Yeffrey De Aza | 19 | IF | Career .305/.337/.384 hitter through two years between the Dominican Summer and Gulf Coast Leagues. |
| Jimmy Duff | 22 | RHP | Massive 6-foot-6 right-hander out of the 20th round in 2014. Duff split his season between the Sally and FSL last year, averaging 8.6 punch outs and just 1.4 walks per nine innings. |
| Jake Kuebler | 25 | RHP | Former minor league stick a career .222/.301/.326 line, Kuebler made the move to the mound in 2013. Within that time he's already moved up to Class AA. He's long shot, but a good story nonetheless. |
| Matt Oberste | 24 | 1B | Hit a solid .301/.359/.430, but the first baseman has slugged just 12 dingers in 270 career games. A lesser Jace Boyd. |
| David Roseboom | 24 | LHP | Dominated the Sally with a 35-to-8 strikeout-to-walk ratio in 31.1 innings and continued to impress with a 29-to-8 showing in the FSL. Solid middle relief option. |
| Blake Taylor | 20 | LHP | Former second round pick of the Pirates was acquired as part of the Ike Davis deal. Taylor made it back from Tommy John surgery, throwing 23 innings between the GCL and NYPL. |
| Ivan Wilson | 21 | CF | Former third round pick in 2013. Wilson's stick hasn't lived up to the lofty draft expectations: he's batting .214/.306/.357 through his first three pro seasons. |

**State of the Farm System:** Prior to dealing away two of the club's better prospects – supremely underrated right-hander Rookie Davis and former Notre Dame third baseman Eric Jagielo – the Yankees, believe it or not, had a Top 10 farm system. Since the Aroldis Chapman deal with Cincinnati, the Yanks' system tumbled down to the 18th best in baseball.

Right fielder Aaron Judge has proven to be one of the system's better first round picks in the last decade. The former Fresno State behemoth batted a combined .255/.330/.448 with 26 doubles, three triples, 20 homeruns, and seven stolen bases between his time with Trenton and Scranton/Wilkes-Barre.

Young shortstop Jorge Mateo – who is already being hailed as Derek Jeter's long term replacement; never mind the fact Didi Gregorius is more than capable – offers up plenty of speed with gap power and a decent hit tool. The Dominican-born infielder batted .278/.345/.392 with 23 doubles, 11 triples, a pair of homeruns, and a whopping 82 stolen bases.

And catcher Gary Sanchez finally made it past Class AA after three different stints, though he's still blocked long term by Brian McCann.

The club's fourth, fifth, and sixth best prospects – James Kaprielian, Ian Clarkin, and Jacob Lindgren – all have solid big league futures. Kaprielian, the Yankees' most recent first round pick out of UCLA, is poised to move quickly, particularly through the low levels. Clarkin, a supplemental first round pick in 2013, missed the entire year with elbow issues. And Lindgren has the ability to be one of the top lefty relievers in baseball, like tomorrow.

| Rank | Name | POS |
|------|------|-----|
| 1 | Aaron Judge | RF |
| 2 | Jorge Mateo | SS |
| 3 | Gary Sanchez | C |
| 4 | James Kaprielian | RHP |
| 5 | Ian Clarkin | LHP |
| 6 | Jacob Lindgren | LHP |
| 7 | Rob Refsnyder | 2B |
| 8 | Jeff Degano | LHP |
| 9 | Kyle Holder | SS |
| 10 | Miguel Andujar | 3B |
| 11 | Dustin Fowler | CF |
| 12 | Chad Green | RHP |
| 13 | Luis Cessa | RHP |
| 14 | Benjamin Gamel | OF |
| 15 | Tyler Wade | SS |
| 16 | Johnny Barbato | RHP |
| 17 | Jonathan Holder | RHP |
| 18 | Mason Williams | CF |
| 19 | Mark Montgomery | RHP |
| 20 | Bryan Mitchell | RHP |
| 21 | James Pazos | LHP |
| 22 | Domingo Acevedo | RHP |
| 23 | Jordan Montgomery | LHP |
| 24 | Brady Lail | RHP |
| 25 | Jordan Foley | RHP |

**Review of the 2015 Draft:** It's been more than 20 years since the Yankees held a selection as early in the draft as last year's #16 pick. And the club grabbed highly touted UCLA stud James Kaprielian, who also became the Yankees' first collegiate right-hander taken in the opening round since Andrew Brackman in 2007. The big right-hander finished his collegiate career with 275 punch outs and 75 walks in 253 innings with the Bruins.

New York grabbed University of San Diego shortstop Kyle Holder with their second first round pick and dipped into the collegiate ranks for a third consecutive time and grabbed Indiana State University southpaw Jeff Degano, who could be one of the draft's biggest steals.

The club's third round pick, right-hander Drew Finley, missed plenty of bats (41 in 32.0 IP), but walked more than his fair share of hitters as well (5.3 BB/9).

## 1. Aaron Judge, RF

**MiLB Rank: #29**

**Position Rank: #9**

| Born: 04/26/92 | Age: 24 | Bats: R | **Top CALs:** Matt Joyce, Marvin Lowrance, |
|---|---|---|---|
| Height: 6-7 | Weight: 275 | Throws: R | Jai Miller, James Ramsey, Victor Roache |

| Season | Age | LVL | PA | 2B | 3B | HR | AVG | OBP | SLG | ISO | BB% | K% | wRC+ |
|---|---|---|---|---|---|---|---|---|---|---|---|---|---|
| 2014 | 22 | A | 278 | 15 | 2 | 9 | 0.333 | 0.428 | 0.530 | 0.197 | 14.0% | 21.2% | 167 |
| 2014 | 22 | A+ | 285 | 9 | 2 | 8 | 0.283 | 0.411 | 0.442 | 0.159 | 17.5% | 25.3% | 149 |
| 2015 | 23 | AA | 280 | 16 | 3 | 12 | 0.284 | 0.350 | 0.516 | 0.232 | 8.6% | 25.0% | 147 |
| 2015 | 23 | AAA | 260 | 10 | 0 | 8 | 0.224 | 0.308 | 0.373 | 0.149 | 11.2% | 28.5% | 98 |

**Background:** Here are a couple interesting tidbits about the Yankees and drafting outfielders:

- The last time the ball club had an outfielder picked in the first round make the big leagues was former top prospect turned bust Slade Heathcott.

- Prior to Judge's selection as the 32nd overall pick in the draft three years ago, the last time the franchise picked a collegiate outfielder in the opening round was way back in 2001 when they selected former Florida State slugger John-Ford Griffin

- In the storied – and lengthy – history of Yankees, Carl Everett was the most successful first round outfielder in the team record books. And every last win-above-replacement Everett tallied in his career was done outside the organization.

So, needless to say, the former Fresno State herculean right-fielder has a fairly decent shot to go down in the Yankees' record books. Judge, who stands a monstrous 6-foot-7 and 275-pounds, was a three-year mainstay in the heart of the Bulldogs' lineup. He burst onto the scene as a true freshman, hitting a robust .358/.437/.465 while filling the stat-sheet with 12 doubles, one triple, a pair of homeruns, and 11 stolen bases.

Judge followed that up with another giant season during his sophomore campaign, slugging .308/.453/.458 with another 14 doubles, two triples, four homeruns, and 13 stolen bases. But the Paul Bunyan-esque right-fielder had a season for the ages for Fresno State during his final year: in 56 games, 246 plate appearances, Judge posted a .369/.461/.655 triple-slash line, adding career bests in doubles (15), triples (four), and homeruns (12) while adding 12 stolen bases.

And he's continued that torrid approach at the plate since entering pro ball two years ago.

Judge tore through the South Atlantic League (.333/.428/.530); the Florida State League pitching hardly fazed him (.283/.411/.442); he took to the minors' toughest level, Class AA, with aplomb (.284/.350/.516), though he finally showed signs of slowing down in the International League late season (.224/.308/.373).

**Projection**: Here's what I wrote in his pre-draft evaluation three years ago:

> "Judge, a hulking 6-foot-7, will always have to contend with an abnormally large strike zone and the subsequent questions surrounding it. But he's incredibly athletic, has a history of solid plate discipline, and could be another 20/20 candidate down the line. A reasonable comp might be Milwaukee 's Corey Hart, another gangly, athletic outfielder with a similar skill set."

Since then, Judge has proven to be a dynamic middle-of-the-order thumper. Through his first 1,100+ professional plate appearances he's walked nearly 13% of the time, shown 25- to 30-homerun potential, and hit for a decent average. In terms of offensive ceiling think something along the lines of Matt Joyce's 2011 season with the Rays: .277/.347/.478. And if he doesn't make the club come Opening Day, which is a possibility given his struggles in Class AAA, he won't – or shouldn't – be kept down for long

**Ceiling:** 3.5-win player
**Risk:** Moderate
**MLB ETA:** 2016

## 2. Jorge Mateo, SS

**MiLB Rank: #103**

**Position Rank: N/A**

| Born: 06/23/95 | Age: 21 | Bats: R | **Top CALs:** Roman Quinn, Yamaico Navarro, |
|---|---|---|---|
| Height: 6-0 | Weight: 188 | Throws: R | Argenis Diaz, Nick Franklin, Danny Santana |

| Season | Age | LVL | PA | 2B | 3B | HR | AVG | OBP | SLG | ISO | BB% | K% | wRC+ |
|---|---|---|---|---|---|---|---|---|---|---|---|---|---|
| 2015 | 20 | A | 409 | 18 | 8 | 2 | 0.268 | 0.338 | 0.378 | 0.110 | 8.8% | 19.6% | 106 |
| 2015 | 20 | A+ | 91 | 5 | 3 | 0 | 0.321 | 0.374 | 0.452 | 0.131 | 7.7% | 19.8% | 152 |

**Background:** Like a poorly produced reality show featuring a bunch of Hollywood rejects and C-list types, the franchise has been on the search for Derek Jeter's heir apparent seemingly for the past decade-plus, anointing – among others – C.J. Henry, Eduardo Nunez, Ferdin Tejeda, and D'Angelo Jimenez at various points. So, needless to say, a lot of hope is riding on the slender shoulders of the Dominican-born middle infielder. Mateo, who stands 6-foot and 188 pounds, originally signed in January 2012 for a fairly scant sum – at least to 99.999% of the world – of $250,000. And for much of his first three professional seasons the young shortstop had a hard time appearing in a whole lot of games; he tallied just 93 games between 2012 and 2014. But Mateo had a bit of coming out party with Charleston in the South Atlantic League last season, his first year in full-season ball, hitting a respectable .268/.338/.378 with 18 doubles, eight triples, and a pair of homeruns. The most impressive part of his 96-game stint in Low Class A: he swiped 71 bags in 86 attempts. New York bumped the then-20-year-old shortstop up to the Florida State League in early August and he batted .321/.374/.452 in 21 games.

**Projection**: It probably goes without saying, but I'll write it anyway: the speed is a plus-plus skill and a game-changer in every respect. But Mateo refuses to be pigeonholed into the typical slap-hitting speedster; he flashes solid-average power with the ability – down the line – to slug 12 to 15 dingers in a season. And after a bit of slow start in the Sally last season he batted .280/.344/.400 over his remaining 106 contests. Mix in some solid defensive abilities and Mateo has a strong foundation to develop into an above-average – perhaps even an All-Star caliber – big leaguer.

**Ceiling:** 3.0-win player
**Risk:** Moderate to High
**MLB ETA:** 2018

## 3. Gary Sanchez, C

**MiLB Rank: #134**
**Position Rank: #5**

| Born: 12/02/92 | Age: 23 | Bats: R | Top CALs: Travis D'Arnaud, John Ryan Murphy, |
|---|---|---|---|
| Height: 6-2 | Weight: 230 | Throws: R | Ryan Lavarnway, Wilin Rosario, Nick Hundley |

| Season | Age | LVL | PA | 2B | 3B | HR | AVG | OBP | SLG | ISO | BB% | K% | wRC+ |
|---|---|---|---|---|---|---|---|---|---|---|---|---|---|
| 2013 | 20 | A+ | 399 | 21 | 0 | 13 | 0.254 | 0.313 | 0.420 | 0.166 | 7.0% | 17.8% | 108 |
| 2013 | 20 | AA | 110 | 6 | 0 | 2 | 0.250 | 0.364 | 0.380 | 0.130 | 11.8% | 14.5% | 113 |
| 2014 | 21 | AA | 477 | 19 | 0 | 13 | 0.270 | 0.338 | 0.406 | 0.135 | 9.0% | 19.1% | 108 |
| 2015 | 22 | AA | 254 | 14 | 0 | 12 | 0.262 | 0.319 | 0.476 | 0.215 | 7.1% | 19.7% | 127 |
| 2015 | 22 | AAA | 146 | 9 | 0 | 6 | 0.295 | 0.349 | 0.500 | 0.205 | 7.5% | 19.2% | 145 |

**Background:** The highly-touted Dominican-born backstop finally passed the Class AA test – it just took 191 games spread across parts of three seasons. Since bursting onto the scene – and by scene I mean the Gulf Coast League and the NYPL – as a 17-year-old, Sanchez has historically been an offensive force at an offensive deficient position.

But his bat seemingly plateaued in Trenton beginning back in 2013. The 6-foot-2, 230-pound backstop hit a league-average-ish .250/.364/.380 in a 23-game stint at the level three years ago, followed that up with a full season triple-slash line of .270/.338/.406, and finally upped the ante to .262/.319/.476 last season. Sanchez finally got the call-up to the International League in mid-July and batted .295/.349/.500 with Scranton/Wilkes Barre the remainder of the way. He also got a quick two-game trip up to Baseball's Cathedral in early October and promptly went 0-for-2.

**Projection**: Double-digit homerun potential with the caveat of poor batting averages, Sanchez isn't nearly the prospect he was once a couple years ago when he ranked among the game's best. He'll take a walk once in a while, flash solid contact skills, and above-average power for the position. CAL is reasonably optimistic about Sanchez's future, linking him to Travis d'Arnaud, John Ryan Murphy, Wilin Rosario, and Nick Hundley. Think of a backstop that will add some value on defense and post a wRC+ mark between 90 and 110.

**Ceiling:** 2.0- to 2.5-win player
**Risk:** Moderate
**MLB ETA:** Debuted in 2015

## 4. James Kaprielian, RHP

**MiLB Rank: #136**
**Position Rank: N/A**

| Born: 03/02/94 | Age: 22 | Bats: R | Top CALs: N/A |
|---|---|---|---|
| Height: 6-4 | Weight: 200 | Throws: R | |

| YEAR | Age | Level | IP | W | L | ERA | FIP | K/9 | BB/9 | K% | BB% | HR/9 | LOB% |
|---|---|---|---|---|---|---|---|---|---|---|---|---|---|
| 2015 | 21 | R | 2.3 | 0 | 0 | 11.57 | 4.16 | 7.71 | 7.71 | 18.2% | 18.2% | 0.00 | 0.0% |
| 2015 | 21 | A- | 9.0 | 0 | 1 | 2.00 | 1.52 | 12.00 | 2.00 | 32.4% | 5.4% | 0.00 | 80.0% |

**Background:** Armed with a top 16 selection for the first time since the club picked some guy named Derek Jeter with the sixth overall selection in 1992, New York grabbed Kaprielian out of UCLA in the middle of the opening round last June. A three-year member of the Bruins – and a two-year member of the rotation – Kaprielian showed a certain tenacity for the punch out during his collegiate run: he fanned 53 in 40.2 relief innings as a true freshman; he then punched out 108 in 106 innings during his first year as a starting pitcher, and upped the ante slightly by fanning 114 in 106.2 innings as a junior. For his collegiate career, Kaprielian fanned 275 and walked 92 in 253 innings of work. The club selected the 6-foot-4, 200-pound right-hander with the 16th overall pick last June and sent him – briefly – to the Gulf Coast before bumping him up to the New York-Penn League. He would throw just 11.1 innings during his debut, fanning 14 and walking four.

**Projection**: Here's what I wrote prior to his selection in the draft last June:

*"Very, very little to dislike about Kaprielian: he's not overpowering, per se, but his advanced approach allows him to miss plenty of bats; he does a solid job of limiting free passes; he's performed well at the highest amateur levels of competition, against premium opponents; he's sturdy, but hasn't been overworked.*

*Kaprielian is, quite frankly, everything one would look for in a polished collegiate arm – one that is very likely to move quickly through the minor leagues.*

*The lone knock on the big right-hander has been his inability to avoid the long ball over the past two seasons with UCLA; he's allowed nine dingers in his last 198.2 innings of work, or about 0.41 HR per nine innings."*

**Ceiling:** 2.0- to 2.5-win player
**Risk:** Moderate
**MLB ETA:** 2017/2018

## 5. Ian Clarkin, LHP

**MiLB Rank: #160**
**Position Rank: N/A**

| Born: 02/14/95 | Age: 21 | Bats: L | |
|---|---|---|---|
| Height: 6-2 | Weight: 190 | Throws: L | Top CALs: Greg Harris, Michael Main, Randall Delgado, Jameson Taillon, Jake Thompson |

| YEAR | Age | Level | IP | W | L | ERA | FIP | K/9 | BB/9 | K% | BB% | HR/9 | LOB% |
|---|---|---|---|---|---|---|---|---|---|---|---|---|---|
| 2013 | 18 | R | 5.0 | 0 | 2 | 10.80 | 10.06 | 7.20 | 7.20 | 16.0% | 16.0% | 3.60 | 55.6% |
| 2014 | 19 | A | 70.0 | 3 | 3 | 3.21 | 3.74 | 9.13 | 2.83 | 25.0% | 7.8% | 0.77 | 75.7% |
| 2014 | 19 | A+ | 5.0 | 1 | 0 | 1.80 | 2.39 | 7.20 | 1.80 | 20.0% | 5.0% | 0.00 | 87.5% |

**Background:** After whetting the appetites of fans and front office personnel alike while briefly shining in the South Atlantic and Florida State Leagues in 2014, Clarkin missed the entire 2015 campaign as a result of lingering – and pesky – elbow inflammation.

**Projection**: Just as I noted in last year's book, CAL remains quite impressed by Clarkin's limited action, linking him to Greg Harris, Michael Main, Randall Delgado, Jameson Taillon, and Jake Thompson. The 6-foot-2, 190-pound former Bonus Baby did make it back finally as he was named as a participant of the Arizona Summer League. And through his first six starts, the big lefty has – unsurprisingly – struggled a bit against some of the top lower level prospects: he tossed 24.2 IP with 17punch outs and 14 walks.

**Ceiling:** 2.5-win player
**Risk:** High
**MLB ETA:** 2018

## 6. Jacob Lindgren, LHP

**MiLB Rank: #177**
**Position Rank: N/A**

| Born: 03/12/93 | Age: 23 | Bats: L | |
|---|---|---|---|
| Height: 5-11 | Weight: 205 | Throws: L | Top CALs: Mike Minor, Bruce Rondon, Carlos Rodon, Gregory Infante, David Robertson |

| YEAR | Age | Level | IP | W | L | ERA | FIP | K/9 | BB/9 | K% | BB% | HR/9 | LOB% |
|---|---|---|---|---|---|---|---|---|---|---|---|---|---|
| 2014 | 21 | R | 1.0 | 0 | 0 | 0.00 | -0.49 | 18.00 | 0.00 | 40.0% | 0.0% | 0.00 | 100.0% |
| 2014 | 21 | A | 5.0 | 1 | 0 | 1.80 | -0.21 | 19.80 | 0.00 | 57.9% | 0.0% | 0.00 | 50.0% |
| 2014 | 21 | A+ | 7.3 | 0 | 0 | 0.00 | 0.39 | 20.86 | 4.91 | 54.8% | 12.9% | 0.00 | 85.7% |
| 2014 | 21 | AA | 11.7 | 1 | 1 | 3.86 | 2.58 | 13.89 | 6.94 | 36.7% | 18.4% | 0.00 | 60.0% |
| 2015 | 22 | AAA | 22.0 | 1 | 1 | 1.23 | 1.88 | 11.86 | 4.09 | 31.5% | 10.9% | 0.00 | 73.1% |

**Background:** The 5-foot-11, 205-pound southpaw was a consistent dominant force working out of Mississippi State University's bullpen and rotation, though the latter was a brief – albeit highly – successful experiment. During his three-year run with the Bulldogs, Lindgren posted a ridiculous 189-to-50 strikeout-to-walk ratio in just 140.0 innings. For those keeping track at home that's 12.2 punch out and just 3.2 walks per nine innings. The Yankees plucked the lefty in the second round two years ago, 55th overall, and he's been light's out ever since. Lindgren's basically leapfrogged up to Class AAA last season and was in New York soon after. So far he's tallied 46.2 minor league innings, fanning a laughable 77 and walking 23. During his seven-game stint in New York he fanned eight and walked four. Not bad production for a hurler with barely any minor league experience.

**Projection**: Here's what I wrote prior to the draft in 2014:

*"If left in the bullpen Lindgren could very easily be pitching in the big leagues by the end of the year a la Chris Sale in 2010. And make no mistake about it; the Mississippi product has all the tools to become a dominant backend reliever – namely above-average control and an elite ability to miss bats."*

Well, I wasn't too far off. It only took 46.2 innings for the lefty to ascend to the game's highest level. Despite his high strikeout ability Lindgren isn't overpowering in the traditional sense as his fastball averaged just a tick over 89 mph during his big league debut. But he complements that with a dominant low-80s slider, giving him a solid one-two punch. He should bring back memories of Mike Stanton as early as Opening Day 2016.

**Ceiling:** 1.5- to 2.0-win player
**Risk:** Low to Moderate
**MLB ETA:** Debuted in 2015

## 7. Rob Refsnyder, 2B

<u>MiLB Rank: N/A</u>
<u>Position Rank: N/A</u>

| Born: 03/26/91 | Age: 25 | Bats: R | Top CALs: Cord Phelps, Jason Kipnis, |
|---|---|---|---|
| Height: 6-1 | Weight: 205 | Throws: R | Chris Nelson, Scott Sizemore, Chris Taylor |

| Season | Age | LVL | PA | 2B | 3B | HR | AVG | OBP | SLG | ISO | BB% | K% | wRC+ |
|---|---|---|---|---|---|---|---|---|---|---|---|---|---|
| 2013 | 22 | A+ | 507 | 28 | 2 | 6 | 0.283 | 0.408 | 0.404 | 0.121 | 15.4% | 13.8% | 140 |
| 2014 | 23 | AA | 244 | 19 | 5 | 6 | 0.342 | 0.385 | 0.548 | 0.206 | 5.7% | 15.6% | 159 |
| 2014 | 23 | AAA | 333 | 19 | 1 | 8 | 0.300 | 0.389 | 0.456 | 0.157 | 12.3% | 20.1% | 137 |
| 2015 | 24 | AAA | 522 | 28 | 2 | 9 | 0.271 | 0.359 | 0.402 | 0.131 | 10.7% | 14.0% | 123 |
| 2015 | 24 | MLB | 47 | 3 | 0 | 2 | 0.302 | 0.348 | 0.512 | 0.209 | 6.4% | 14.9% | 130 |

**Background:** Refsnyder's string of strong offensive performances pre-dates his time in the Yankees' organization. A three-year starter with the University of Arizona, the solidly built second baseman burst onto the scene as a true freshman in 2010, slugging an impressive .344/.397/.440 with nine doubles, three triples, and a pair of homeruns in a lineup laden with future minor league talent such as Jett Bandy, Seth Mejias-Brean, and Joey Rickard (among others). Refsnyder followed that up with another dominant performance during his sophomore season, flashing significantly more power en route to hitting .320/.371/.498. But despite an otherworldly junior campaign with the Wildcats – he batted .364/.453/.562 – New York didn't call his name until the fifth round in 2012.

Since then, however, all Refsnyder has done is cobble together a minor league triple-slash line of .290/.380/.432 with 106 doubles, 11 triples, 33 homeruns, and 55 stolen bases in 430 total games. The 6-foot-1, 205-pound Korean-born second baseman spent the majority of last season in Class AAA, his second extended stint in the International League, and batted a quality .271/.359/.402. He also spent 16 games in Baseball's Palace, hitting .302/.348/.512 in 47 plate appearances.

**Projection**: In last year's book I ranked the offensive-minded second baseman as the club's eighth overall pick, writing:

> "CAL's a big fan of the former Wildcat, comparing his production over the last three stops to an All-Star (Jason Kipnis) and another former top prospect (Nick Franklin). Prior to the year the power was below-average, but it flashed 15-HR potential last season. Strong walk rates, solid contact skills, and sneaky speed all add up to [a] solid, below-the-radar prospect. As far as his ceiling is concerned: think a slightly better than average offensive performer with decent, not great defensive ability."

Well, let's update that a bit – shall we? CAL still remains quite optimistic in terms of his offensive ceiling, linking him to Jason Kipnis and Scott Sizemore. But the power, which peaked two years ago, regressed some in his repeat of Class AAA; it now remains squarely in the below-average to average territory. Solid plate discipline and hit tool, Refsnyder remains an under-the-radar prospect – one that is only further clouded by the recent acquisition of Starlin Castro. In terms of offensive output, think somewhere along the lines of him posting a 100 wRC+.

**Ceiling:** 1.5-win player
**Risk:** Low to Moderate
**MLB ETA:** Debuted in 2015

## 8. Jeff Degano, LHP

<u>MiLB Rank: N/A</u>
<u>Position Rank: N/A</u>

| Born: 10/30/92 | Age: 23 | Bats: R | Top CALs: N/A |
|---|---|---|---|
| Height: 6-4 | Weight: 215 | Throws: L | |

| YEAR | Age | Level | IP | W | L | ERA | FIP | K/9 | BB/9 | K% | BB% | HR/9 | LOB% |
|---|---|---|---|---|---|---|---|---|---|---|---|---|---|
| 2015 | 22 | R | 10.7 | 0 | 4 | 5.06 | 4.43 | 6.75 | 3.38 | 16.0% | 8.0% | 0.84 | 62.5% |
| 2015 | 22 | A- | 10.7 | 0 | 0 | 2.53 | 2.86 | 11.81 | 4.22 | 29.2% | 10.4% | 0.00 | 82.4% |

**Background:** The immediate comparisons between this tall lefty out of Indiana State University and another former tall lefty hailing from the college, Sean Manaea, are going to be all too easy to make – especially once you consider each hurlers injury history. But unlike Manaea, Degano missed a lengthy amount of time – more than 12 months – recovering from Tommy John surgery, which limited his collegiate tenure to just 108.0 innings, all but eight of those spent during his final season with the Sycamores. But, damn, Degano was as dominant as any collegiate hurler last season. In 15 starts, the 6-foot-4, 215-pound southpaw punched out 126 and walked just 28 to go along with a 2.36 ERA in 99.0 innings of work. New York grabbed him with the 57th overall pick and signed him to one of the lowest second round bonuses last season. Degano tossed another 21.1 innings between the Gulf Coast and New York-Penn Leagues during his debut, fanning 22 and walking just nine.

**Projection**: Very, very little statistical data to go off of, but it was as dominant as one would expect for an early round pick – so much so, in fact, that one wonders how (A) he lasted until the middle of the second round and (B) how the Yankees were able to finagle the sleeping giant to a well below-slot bonus. Because of the injury he's already entering his age-23 season, but he's one to pay attention to in the coming years, though he may be forced – undeservedly so – into a bullpen role within the next year or two to accelerate his path to the big leagues.

**Ceiling:** 2.0- to 2.5-win player
**Risk:** High
**MLB ETA:** 2017/2018

## 9. Kyle Holder, SS

**MiLB Rank: N/A**
**Position Rank: N/A**

| Born: 05/25/94 | Age: 22 | Bats: L | Top CALs: Alec Sole, Ismael Tijerina, |
|---|---|---|---|
| Height: 6-1 | Weight: 185 | Throws: R | Emmanuel Marrero, Ryan Jackson, James Roberts |

| Season | Age | LVL | PA | 2B | 3B | HR | AVG | OBP | SLG | ISO | BB% | K% | wRC+ |
|---|---|---|---|---|---|---|---|---|---|---|---|---|---|
| 2015 | 21 | A- | 250 | 7 | 1 | 0 | 0.213 | 0.273 | 0.253 | 0.040 | 6.8% | 13.6% | 57 |

**Background:** The franchise's second first round pick last June, Holder was taken with the 30th overall selection out of the University of San Diego. A two-year member of the Toreros by way of Grossmont College, the lefty-swinging shortstop emerged as one of college baseball's top middle infielders after a breakout 2015 campaign. In 55 games with the school, Holder batted .348/.418/.482 with career highs in doubles (14) and homeruns (four) while tying a career best with two triples. He also swiped five bags, though it took 11 attempts, and posted a 19-to-19 strikeout-to-walk ratio in 260 trips to the plate. Perhaps the most impressive part: in 645 career plate appearances at the college level Holder fanned just 34 times, or just about 5.2%. New York pushed him to short-season ball for his debut and, well, let's just summarize that by saying things didn't go swimmingly (.213/.273/.253).

**Projection**: Here's what I wrote prior to the 2015 draft:

> "Defensive-minded middle infielder who won't hurt his team too much at the plate. Holder isn't going to walk a whole lot – his career walk rate [at the time of the original writing] with San Diego is 7.3% - but he's not going to swing-and-miss in bunches either. Not overly quick on the base paths and power's a below-average skill, Holder looks like a fringy big league regular. If his defense is as good as advertised he might be able to carve out a couple Zack Cozart, Adeiny Hechavarria, Brandon Crawford-type seasons."

**Ceiling:** 1.5-win player
**Risk:** Moderate
**MLB ETA:** 2017

## 10. Dustin Fowler, CF

**MiLB Rank: N/A**
**Position Rank: N/A**

| Born: 12/29/94 | Age: 21 | Bats: L | Top CALs: Dorssys Paulino, Jorge Bonifacio, |
|---|---|---|---|
| Height: 6-0 | Weight: 185 | Throws: L | D'Arby Myers, Max Kepler, Delta Cleary |

| Season | Age | LVL | PA | 2B | 3B | HR | AVG | OBP | SLG | ISO | BB% | K% | wRC+ |
|---|---|---|---|---|---|---|---|---|---|---|---|---|---|
| 2013 | 18 | R | 117 | 8 | 4 | 0 | 0.241 | 0.274 | 0.384 | 0.143 | 3.4% | 19.7% | 89 |
| 2014 | 19 | A | 272 | 13 | 6 | 9 | 0.257 | 0.292 | 0.459 | 0.202 | 4.8% | 19.5% | 104 |
| 2015 | 20 | A | 256 | 9 | 3 | 4 | 0.307 | 0.340 | 0.419 | 0.112 | 4.3% | 18.4% | 114 |
| 2015 | 20 | A+ | 262 | 11 | 3 | 1 | 0.289 | 0.328 | 0.370 | 0.081 | 5.7% | 16.4% | 111 |

**Background:** Tell me if you've heard this one before: the franchise unearthed the 6-foot, 185-pound center fielder in the late, late rounds of the draft. Fowler, an 18th round pick out of West Laurens High School in 2013, split the season between Low Class A and High Class A last year, hitting a combined .298/.334/.394 with 20 doubles, six triples, and five HRs while swiping 30 bags in 43 attempts.

**Projection**: Similar ilk to that of Ben Gamel. Fowler's power took a tremendous step backward after his surge in the Sally two years ago. After slugging nine dingers in 66 games, Fowler followed that up with five long balls in 123 games in 2015. He hasn't handled fellow southpaws that well in his career, so unless the power rebounds he looks like a backup outfielder.

**Ceiling:** 2.0-win player
**Risk:** High
**MLB ETA:** 2018

## 11. Miguel Andujar, 3B

MiLB Rank: N/A

Position Rank: N/A

| Born: 03/02/95 | Age: 21 | Bats: R | Top CALs: Daniel Mateo, Edward Salcedo, |
| Height: 6-0 | Weight: 175 | Throws: R | Zachary Green, Mike Moustakas, Jefry Marte |

| Season | Age | LVL | PA | 2B | 3B | HR | AVG | OBP | SLG | ISO | BB% | K% | wRC+ |
|---|---|---|---|---|---|---|---|---|---|---|---|---|---|
| 2013 | 18 | R | 144 | 11 | 0 | 4 | 0.323 | 0.368 | 0.496 | 0.173 | 4.9% | 14.6% | 152 |
| 2014 | 19 | A | 527 | 25 | 4 | 10 | 0.267 | 0.318 | 0.397 | 0.130 | 6.6% | 15.7% | 99 |
| 2015 | 20 | A+ | 520 | 24 | 5 | 8 | 0.243 | 0.288 | 0.363 | 0.120 | 5.6% | 17.3% | 98 |

**Background:** An up-and-coming power-hitting third baseman out of San Cristobal, Dominican Republic, the Yankees continued to aggressively push Andujar through the low levels of the minor leagues. After debuting – albeit unsuccessfully – in the Gulf Coast League at the age of 17, Andujar repeated the rookie level with much improved results the following season: he batted .323/.368/.496 with 11 doubles, four triples, and a staggeringly high 152 wRC+ in 34 games. New York bumped the then-19-year-old hot corner up to the Sally in 2014 and he responded with a solid .267/.318/.397 showing. Last season, keeping with their current development scheme, Andujar spent the year in High Class A, hitting .243/.288/.363 with 24 doubles, five triples, and eight homeruns. For his career he's sporting a .259/.308/.381 triple-slash line.

**Projection:** The overall production – sans his 34-game redo in the Gulf Coast League a couple years back – have been clouded by the fact that Andujar has been squaring off against older pitching. With that being said, his numbers have merely been league average the past two seasons. And not to pile on, but Andujar hasn't really shown the ability to take more than the rare free pass either; he's walked in just 6.1% of his career plate appearances as well. The power, though, has a chance to develop into 20-homer territory.

**Ceiling:** 1.5-win player
**Risk:** Moderate
**MLB ETA:** Debuted in 2015

## 12. Chad Green, RHP

MiLB Rank: N/A

Position Rank: N/A

| Born: 05/24/91 | Age: 24 | Bats: L | Top CALs: David Rollins, Matt Shoemaker, |
| Height: 6-3 | Weight: 210 | Throws: R | Mark Leiter, Jason Berken, Alex Wilson |

| YEAR | Age | Level | IP | W | L | ERA | FIP | K/9 | BB/9 | K% | BB% | HR/9 | LOB% |
|---|---|---|---|---|---|---|---|---|---|---|---|---|---|
| 2013 | 22 | R | 3.0 | 1 | 0 | 3.00 | 3.79 | 18.00 | 0.00 | 50.0% | 0.0% | 3.00 | 100.0% |
| 2013 | 22 | A+ | 17.3 | 3 | 0 | 3.63 | 3.13 | 5.19 | 3.12 | 13.9% | 8.3% | 0.00 | 68.2% |
| 2014 | 23 | A | 130.3 | 6 | 4 | 3.11 | 3.08 | 8.63 | 1.93 | 23.9% | 5.4% | 0.55 | 71.7% |
| 2015 | 24 | AA | 148.7 | 5 | 14 | 3.93 | 3.22 | 8.29 | 2.60 | 20.9% | 6.6% | 0.54 | 65.6% |

**Background:** After spending the majority of his first two seasons pitching out of Louisville's bullpen, the 6-foot-3, 210-pound right-hander made a wildly successful conversion into the collegiate powerhouse's rotation. He would make 18 starts for the Cardinals in 2013, throwing 104.1 innings while posting a solid 74-to-27 strikeout-to-walk ratio to go along with a solid 2.42 ERA. Detroit took the hurler in the 11th round, 336th overall, as part of…wait for it…their collegiate pitching grab in 2013. Green would spend the majority of his debut pitching for Lakeland in the Florida State League, but got bumped down a level for the entire 2014. Last year Green took the same path as his West Michigan teammate Austin Kubitza and jumped all the way up to the Eastern League. In 27 starts with the SeaWolves he would throw a career best 148.2 innings with 137 punch outs and just 43 walks. The Yankees acquired Green – along with Luis Cessa – from the Tigers in exchange for Justin Wilson.

**Projection:** One of the more underrated arms in the entire minor leagues, something that extended back to his collegiate days as well, Green's knocking on the big league club's door ready-and-willing to step right into the back of its rotation. Now for the analysis: Green finished the year with the fifth best strikeout-to-walk ratio in the Easter League last season; he also generates a metric-ton of groundballs as well. He's not overpowering, but does all the small things well enough to succeed at the game's pinnacle level. He's a solid #5.

**Ceiling:** 1.0 to 1.5-win player
**Risk:** Low to Moderate
**MLB ETA:** 2016

## 13. Luis Cessa, RHP

**MiLB Rank: N/A**
**Position Rank: N/A**

| Born: 04/25/92 | Age: 24 | Bats: R | Top CALs: Randy Wells, Bryan Augenstein, |
|---|---|---|---|
| Height: 6-3 | Weight: 190 | Throws: R | Jeff Locke, Josh Lindblom, Scott Diamond |

| YEAR | Age | Level | IP | W | L | ERA | FIP | K/9 | BB/9 | K% | BB% | HR/9 | LOB% |
|---|---|---|---|---|---|---|---|---|---|---|---|---|---|
| 2013 | 21 | A | 130.0 | 8 | 4 | 3.12 | 3.11 | 8.58 | 1.32 | 23.1% | 3.5% | 0.76 | 73.1% |
| 2014 | 22 | A+ | 114.7 | 7 | 8 | 4.00 | 3.52 | 6.51 | 2.12 | 17.6% | 5.7% | 0.55 | 66.1% |
| 2014 | 22 | AA | 3.7 | 0 | 1 | 12.27 | 11.26 | 7.36 | 4.91 | 14.3% | 9.5% | 4.91 | 69.4% |
| 2015 | 23 | AA | 77.3 | 7 | 4 | 2.56 | 2.69 | 7.10 | 1.98 | 19.2% | 5.4% | 0.23 | 75.7% |
| 2015 | 23 | AAA | 24.3 | 0 | 3 | 8.51 | 3.85 | 8.88 | 1.48 | 20.2% | 3.4% | 1.11 | 49.0% |
| 2015 | 23 | AAA | 37.7 | 1 | 3 | 5.97 | 3.40 | 8.12 | 3.58 | 20.0% | 8.8% | 0.48 | 59.8% |

**Background:** Acquired with Chad Green from the Tigers for lefty reliever Justin Wilson. Cessa split last season between Class AA and Class AAA as he was shuffled from the Mets to the Tigers as part of the Yoenis Cespedes deal at the deadline. Overall, the 6-foot-3, 190-pound right-hander tossed 139.1 innings with 119 strikeouts and just 36 walk en route to tallying a 4.52 ERA.

**Projection**: An underrated starter who will likely get lost in the New York money machine. Cessa has always shown a tremendous feel for the strike zone with decent swing-and-miss ability. Throw in some above-average groundball numbers and you have the making of a decent big leaguer – be it as a reliever or as a #4/#5 starter. He's sort of a Carlos Villanueva knockoff.

**Ceiling:** 1.0- to 1.5-win player
**Risk:** Low to Moderate
**MLB ETA:** 2016

## 14. Ben Gamel, OF

**MiLB Rank: N/A**
**Position Rank: N/A**

| Born: 05/17/92 | Age: 24 | Bats: L | Top CALs: Sean Henry, Caleb Gindl, |
|---|---|---|---|
| Height: 5-11 | Weight: 185 | Throws: L | Xavier Paul, Mikie Mahtook, Juan Portes |

| Season | Age | LVL | PA | 2B | 3B | HR | AVG | OBP | SLG | ISO | BB% | K% | wRC+ |
|---|---|---|---|---|---|---|---|---|---|---|---|---|---|
| 2013 | 21 | A+ | 423 | 28 | 4 | 3 | 0.272 | 0.352 | 0.396 | 0.124 | 11.3% | 18.2% | 114 |
| 2014 | 22 | AA | 586 | 31 | 3 | 2 | 0.261 | 0.308 | 0.340 | 0.079 | 6.1% | 15.0% | 80 |
| 2015 | 23 | AAA | 551 | 28 | 14 | 10 | 0.300 | 0.358 | 0.472 | 0.172 | 8.3% | 19.6% | 138 |

**Background:** The younger brother of former Brewers top prospect – who eventually became a failed top prospect – Mat Gamel, Ben has pushed his name up among the system's better minor leaguers – despite getting plucked out of the tenth round as a prep player in 2010. The speedy center fielder out of Bishop Kennedy High School rebounded after a dismal showing in the Eastern League two years ago to have his finest season to date in Class AAA last season: he batted .300/.358/.472 with 28 doubles and career bests in triples (14) and homeruns (10) en route to tallying a 138 wRC+ mark. For his career, the 5-foot-11, 185-pound outfielder owns a career .284/.340/.400 triple-slash line in parts of six minor league seasons.

**Projection**: I'm not quite sure – or in other words entirely convinced – that Gamel's power surge with Scranton/Wilkes-Barre is a repeatable skill; his career Isolated Power mark is .100 vs. his .172 showing last season. And, unsurprisingly, his HR/FB ratio nearly doubled his previous career high as well. Gamel has typically handled LHP and RHP equally well, showcases double-digit stolen base potential, and a fringy-decent eye at the plate. Combine that with his CALs – Sean Henry, Caleb Gindl, Xavier Paul, Mikie Mahtook, and Juan Portes – and it's easy to see how he's likely to slide into a backup outfield role in the near future.

**Ceiling:** 1.0- to 1.5-win player
**Risk:** Low to Moderate
**MLB ETA:** 2016

## 15. Tyler Wade, 2B/SS

**MiLB Rank:** N/A
**Position Rank:** N/A

| Born: 11/23/94 | Age: 21 | Bats: L | **Top CALs:** Hak-Ju Lee, Darwin Perez, |
|---|---|---|---|
| Height: 6-1 | Weight: 180 | Throws: R | Jose Pirela, Francisco Lindor, Reegie Corona |

| Season | Age | LVL | PA | 2B | 3B | HR | AVG | OBP | SLG | ISO | BB% | K% | wRC+ |
|---|---|---|---|---|---|---|---|---|---|---|---|---|---|
| 2013 | 18 | R | 198 | 10 | 0 | 0 | 0.309 | 0.429 | 0.370 | 0.062 | 16.2% | 21.2% | 146 |
| 2014 | 19 | A | 576 | 23 | 6 | 1 | 0.272 | 0.350 | 0.347 | 0.075 | 9.9% | 20.5% | 100 |
| 2015 | 20 | A+ | 418 | 11 | 5 | 2 | 0.280 | 0.349 | 0.353 | 0.073 | 9.3% | 15.6% | 117 |
| 2015 | 20 | AA | 117 | 4 | 0 | 1 | 0.204 | 0.224 | 0.265 | 0.062 | 1.7% | 20.5% | 37 |

**Background:** The Yankees grabbed the lefty-swinging prep shortstop in the fourth round out of Murrieta High School in 2013. Wade had another stout showing in the Florida State League. The 6-foot-1, 180-pound shortstop hit .280/.349/.353 with 11 doubles, five triples, two homeruns, and 31 stolen bases (in 46 attempts) in 98 games with Tampa. The front office bumped him up to Class AA in early August and Wade batted a paltry .204/.224/.265 as he looked – and was – overmatched by the minors' biggest test. For his young career, Wade is sporting a solid .271/.349/.342 with 49 doubles, 11 triples, four homeruns, and 66 stolen bases in 306 games.

**Projection**: First off, CAL thinks fairly highly of the former fourth rounder, linking him to Francisco Lindor and former top prospect Hak-Ju Lee, whose promising career never rebounded after a devastating knee injury. Wade has a lot of things working in his favor: he's willing to take more than the occasional walk, burns up the base paths, and has handled himself well (most of the time) against much older competition. His downfall (for now) is his complete and utter lack of pop – he's never posted an Isolated Power above .077 at any stop along the way. *If* he can start to work the gaps for more power he has a chance to develop into a league-average regular, but right now that looks like a big if.

**Ceiling:** 1.5- to 2.0-win player
**Risk:** High
**MLB ETA:** 2018

## 16. Johnny Barbato, RHP

**MiLB Rank:** N/A
**Position Rank:** N/A

| Born: 07/11/92 | Age: 23 | Bats: R | **Top CALs:** Maikel Cleto, Aaron Blair, |
|---|---|---|---|
| Height: 6-2 | Weight: 230 | Throws: R | Chris Withrow, Wade Davis, Jake Mcgee |

| YEAR | Age | Level | IP | W | L | ERA | FIP | K/9 | BB/9 | K% | BB% | HR/9 | LOB% |
|---|---|---|---|---|---|---|---|---|---|---|---|---|---|
| 2013 | 20 | A+ | 88.0 | 3 | 6 | 5.01 | 4.26 | 9.10 | 3.38 | 23.4% | 8.7% | 0.82 | 63.7% |
| 2014 | 21 | AA | 31.3 | 2 | 2 | 2.87 | 3.31 | 9.48 | 2.87 | 25.6% | 7.8% | 0.86 | 76.2% |
| 2015 | 22 | AA | 42.3 | 2 | 2 | 4.04 | 3.62 | 9.35 | 2.98 | 24.4% | 7.8% | 0.85 | 74.9% |
| 2015 | 22 | AAA | 25.0 | 4 | 0 | 0.36 | 2.92 | 9.36 | 3.96 | 27.4% | 11.6% | 0.36 | 100.0% |

**Background:** Acquired in an overlooked deal that shipped free-agent-to-be Shawn Kelley to San Diego in a one-for-one swap, Barbato successfully avoided undergoing the knife to repair a wonky elbow, an injury that limited him to just 31.1 innings two years ago, to post arguably his finest season to date. A seven-figure Bonus Baby taken in the sixth round in 2010, Barbato opened the year up with a tremendous outing against the Erie SeaWolves in mid-April, fanning four without issuing a walk or surrendering a hit in an inning-and-two-thirds of work – and he never looked back. The 6-foot-2, 230-pound right-hander tossed a total of 42.1 innings with Trenton in the Eastern League, posting a 3.62 FIP to go along with a 44-to-14 strikeout-to-walk ratio. On a bit of a side note: he allowed 19 ER during his time in Class AA, nine of which were allowed in a pair of appearances that covered 1.1 innings; in other words, his ERA outside of those two games was a paltry 2.20. Barbato continued to impress in 25 innings with Scranton/Wilkes-Barre following his promotion, posting a 0.36 ERA with 26 punch outs and 11 walks.

**Projection**: Hard-throwing and knocking loudly on the club's big league door. Barbato has a rather lengthy history of missing bats – he's fanned nearly a quarter of the batters he's faced in his career – with solid average control/command. The long ball is a bit of an issue and likely will be as he moves into the not-so-friendly confines of Yankee Stadium. One final word – or words: he will need to prove that his elbow woes are firmly in the past.

**Ceiling:** 1.0- to 1.5-win player
**Risk:** Moderate
**MLB ETA:** 2016

## 17. Jonathan Holder, RHP

**MiLB Rank: N/A**
**Position Rank: N/A**

| Born: 06/09/93 | Age: 23 | Bats: R | **Top CALs:** Gregory Billo, Paul Phillips, |
|---|---|---|---|
| Height: 6-2 | Weight: 235 | Throws: R | Brian Flynn, Freddy Ballestas, Bryan Price |

| YEAR | Age | Level | IP | W | L | ERA | FIP | K/9 | BB/9 | K% | BB% | HR/9 | LOB% |
|---|---|---|---|---|---|---|---|---|---|---|---|---|---|
| 2014 | 21 | R | 3.7 | 1 | 1 | 12.27 | 3.78 | 9.82 | 7.36 | 21.1% | 15.8% | 0.00 | 50.0% |
| 2014 | 21 | A- | 32.7 | 1 | 2 | 3.03 | 2.92 | 8.27 | 2.76 | 22.2% | 7.4% | 0.28 | 66.5% |
| 2015 | 22 | A+ | 103.3 | 7 | 5 | 2.44 | 2.79 | 6.79 | 1.83 | 18.4% | 4.9% | 0.26 | 74.7% |
| 2015 | 22 | AAA | 5.7 | 0 | 1 | 6.35 | 6.16 | 6.35 | 6.35 | 16.7% | 16.7% | 1.59 | 60.6% |

**Background:** In terms of pure production vary few collegiate hurlers could stack up against the former Mississippi State Bulldog closer. In his three-year run with the school Holder, a 6-foot-2, 235-pound right-hander, tossed 136.0 innings, fanned 191, walked just 31, and accumulated a 1.59 ERA. For those keeping track at home: he averaged 12.64 strikeouts and just 2.05 walks per nine innings during that time. But Holder, who doesn't possess the typical hard-throwing mentality of today's top relievers, fell to the sixth round in 2014 where the Yankees happily snapped him up.

And immediately converted him into a starting pitcher.

After failing to make one start in any in of his three seasons with the Bulldogs, the front office put Holder on a throwing regimen to stretch him out as soon as he debuted in the Gulf Coast League two years ago. Of his 12 appearances that year – 10 of which were in the NYPL – Holder made it through three frames seven times and pitched into a second inning every other instance.

Last year, the burly right-hander made 18 starts (and one relief appearance) for the Tampa Yankees in High Class A, throwing 103.1 innings (nearly his total during his entire time at MSU) with 78.1 strikeouts and just 21 walks. He also made a 5.2-inning appearance with Scranton/Wilkes-Barre in early September as well.

**Projection**: Here's what I wrote prior to the 2014 draft:

*"Personally, I'd love to see an organization think outside the box and stretch Holder out in the rotation (slowly, of course). But given his extensive track record of – wait for it! – saving games it's not likely. After all, who in their right mind would want a Tony Cingrani when you can have a fulltime reliever?!?*

*Cynicism aside, the stocky right-hander is one of the top relievers in college, one that could move every quickly through a team's farm system. He's not quite an elite "relief prospect," but [he] should settle into a late inning (seventh/eighth) role down the line."*

Chalk that up for some pretty darn good prognosticating skills on my behalf. Holder's not going to be a front- of even mid-rotation caliber arm, but he does have some upside. His control/command has been impeccable through his year-plus in the minors, which has to be the case given some low strikeout numbers. But he's proven the ability to take the ball every fifth day and has the (round) frame to chew innings as well. He'll likely get a couple cups as a starter before New York moves onto to another nine-figure contract, but teams could certainly to worse in the sixth round.

**Ceiling:** 1.0- to 1.5-win player
**Risk:** Moderate
**MLB ETA:** 2017

## 18. Mason Williams, CF

**MiLB Rank: N/A**
**Position Rank: N/A**

| Born: 08/21/91 | Age: 24 | Bats: L | **Top CALs:** L.J. Hoes, Rafael Ortega, |
|---|---|---|---|
| Height: 6-1 | Weight: 185 | Throws: R | Brandon Roberts, Jose Martinez, Jonathan Jones |

| Season | Age | LVL | PA | 2B | 3B | HR | AVG | OBP | SLG | ISO | BB% | K% | wRC+ |
|---|---|---|---|---|---|---|---|---|---|---|---|---|---|
| 2013 | 21 | A+ | 461 | 21 | 3 | 3 | 0.261 | 0.327 | 0.350 | 0.089 | 8.5% | 13.2% | 95 |
| 2014 | 22 | AA | 563 | 18 | 4 | 5 | 0.223 | 0.290 | 0.304 | 0.081 | 8.3% | 12.1% | 66 |
| 2015 | 23 | AA | 144 | 7 | 0 | 0 | 0.317 | 0.407 | 0.375 | 0.058 | 13.2% | 11.8% | 131 |
| 2015 | 23 | AAA | 91 | 7 | 1 | 0 | 0.321 | 0.382 | 0.432 | 0.111 | 8.8% | 6.6% | 136 |
| 2015 | 23 | MLB | 22 | 3 | 0 | 1 | 0.286 | 0.318 | 0.571 | 0.286 | 4.5% | 13.6% | 139 |

**Background:** A longtime member of the club's top prospect list, Williams is seemingly the last man standing as part of the system's three-headed prospect monster which included Slade Heathcott and Tyler Austin. Williams, a lefty-swinging center fielder plucked out of West Orange High School in the fourth round way back in 2010, has lost most of his minor league sheen as his offense failed to live up to his low level production lines. As a 19-year-old with Staten Island in the New York-Penn League, he torched the short-season pitchers to the tune of .349/.395/.468 with 11 doubles, six triples, three homeruns, and 28 stolen bases, and then he followed that up with another outstanding performance the next season as he hit .298/.346/.474 between his time with Charleston and Tampa.

And then the wheels started wobbling.

Williams opened up the next year, 2013, back with Tampa in the Florida State League with a decent showing, hitting .261/.327/.350 with 21 doubles, three triples, three homeruns, and 15 stolen bases (in 24 attempts) as his overall production fell to 5% *below* the league average. He also looked lost and overmatched in a 17-game stint with Trenton at the end of the year as well (.153/.164/.264).

Undeterred, the club pushed the once-top prospect back to Trenton where his struggles were only compounded: he hit .223/.290/.304 with just 27 extra-base hits in 128 contests, and his overall production plummeted to a lowly 66 wRC+. So once again Williams found himself back in the Eastern League – for the third time – to open the 2015 season, and the results were much improved: .317/.407/.375. After 34 games at the level the front office bumped him up to Class AAA, where he batted .321/.382/.432 until right shoulder surgery abruptly prematurely ended his season.

**Projection**: I've mentioned numerous times – probably more than I realize – in this year's book about how important and difficult Class AA tends to be on prospects. It is the single biggest test for a minor league player, hitter *or* pitcher. And it's clear (now) that Williams wasn't the prospect many thought he was.

With that being said, there are certainly some useful big league qualities here: solid-average eye at the plate, some speed, and above-average defense. The problems, of course, are two-fold: he can't stay healthy and his power has all but disappeared (even in his reemergence, which also has to do with a BABIP spike, he posted a lowly .080 ISO). He's also had some issues against LHP as well.

Williams is a spot starter/fourth or fifth outfielder.

**Ceiling:** 1.0- to 1.5-win player
**Risk:** Moderate
**MLB ETA:** Debuted in 2015

## 19. Mark Montgomery, RHP

MiLB Rank: N/A
Position Rank: N/A

| Born: 08/30/90 | Age: 21 | Bats: R | Top CALs: Barrett Browning, Brad Mills, |
| Height: 6-0 | Weight: 210 | Throws: R | Kam Mickolio, Ronald Uviedo, Colton Murray |

| YEAR | Age | Level | IP | W | L | ERA | FIP | K/9 | BB/9 | K% | BB% | HR/9 | LOB% |
|------|-----|-------|------|---|---|------|------|------|------|------|------|------|------|
| 2013 | 22 | AAA | 40.0 | 2 | 3 | 3.38 | 4.00 | 11.03 | 5.63 | 28.0% | 14.3% | 0.90 | 79.8% |
| 2014 | 23 | AA | 21.7 | 1 | 0 | 0.83 | 3.63 | 7.06 | 3.32 | 20.7% | 9.8% | 0.42 | 82.5% |
| 2014 | 23 | AAA | 29.7 | 1 | 1 | 3.03 | 3.96 | 10.31 | 5.46 | 26.6% | 14.1% | 0.61 | 75.9% |
| 2015 | 24 | AA | 43.0 | 3 | 3 | 2.93 | 2.90 | 9.42 | 3.35 | 25.7% | 9.1% | 0.42 | 74.7% |
| 2015 | 24 | AAA | 7.7 | 1 | 1 | 1.17 | 1.46 | 9.39 | 1.17 | 30.8% | 3.9% | 0.00 | 66.7% |

**Background:** A minor league dark horse candidate to sit atop Mariano Rivera's heralded throne, Montgomery's once rapid rise through the franchise's system suddenly sputtered as his control began to waver in the Arizona Fall League in 2012. An 11th round pick out of Longwood University in Farmville, Virginia, Montgomery burst onto the scene during his first full taste of minor league action four years ago; in 64.1 innings between the Florida State and Eastern Leagues, he fanned a mind-boggling 99 and walked just 22 en route to posting a 1.54 ERA. But Montgomery promptly followed that up by walking 25 in 40 innings with Scranton/Wilkes-Barre in 2013 and coughed up another 26 free passes in 51.1 innings between Trenton and Class AAA the next year as well. Last year, though, Montgomery seemingly regained his feel for the strike zone as he spent the majority of the year back in Class AA, averaging 3.3 free passes per nine innings.

**Projection**: Though parts of five minor league seasons – and one stint in the Arizona Fall League – there is one thing for certain: strikeouts are going to come in bunches for the diminutive right-hander. But Montgomery's control tends to bounce between average and well below that, depending upon the year. One wonders if he'll ever get an extended shot in the Yankees' pen because the front office may have soured on him as he didn't earn an invite to Spring Training last season. There's potential for a late-inning role, but, again, I doubt it's with this organization.

**Ceiling:** 1.0- to 1.5-win player
**Risk:** Moderate
**MLB ETA:** 2016

## 20. Domingo Acevedo, RHP

MiLB Rank: N/A
Position Rank: N/A

| Born: 03/06/94 | Age: 22 | Bats: R | Top CALs: Marc Rzepczynski, Ronny Morla, |
| Height: 6-7 | Weight: 190 | Throws: R | Scott Gorgen, Bud Norris, Carlos Hernandez |

| YEAR | Age | Level | IP | W | L | ERA | FIP | K/9 | BB/9 | K% | BB% | HR/9 | LOB% |
|---|---|---|---|---|---|---|---|---|---|---|---|---|---|
| 2013 | 19 | R | 41.0 | 1 | 2 | 2.63 | 1.95 | 9.44 | 2.41 | 24.2% | 6.2% | 0.00 | 63.6% |
| 2014 | 20 | R | 15.3 | 0 | 1 | 4.11 | 2.14 | 12.33 | 3.52 | 31.3% | 9.0% | 0.00 | 65.2% |
| 2015 | 21 | A- | 48.0 | 3 | 0 | 1.69 | 2.85 | 9.94 | 2.81 | 27.2% | 7.7% | 0.38 | 75.7% |
| 2015 | 21 | A | 1.7 | 0 | 0 | 5.40 | 4.08 | 5.40 | 5.40 | 12.5% | 12.5% | 0.00 | 66.7% |

**Background:** A lanky 6-foot-7, 190-pounder fire-ballling right-hander out of the Dominican Republic, Acevedo didn't make his debut until the age of 19 and even then it was spent as an older prospect in the DSL. Acevedo moved stateside in 2014, but managed to appear in just five games that year. Last season he got aggressively pushed up to Staten Island where he posted a 53-to-15 strikeout-to-walk ratio and he would make a one game relief appearance in the Sally as well.

**Projection**: Owner of one of the system's top fastballs, the big right-hander has shown brief flashes of dominance throughout his career, particularly during last season: over his last four starts with Staten Island he posted 29 and walked just six in 23.1 innings of work. He's always shown a fantastic ability to miss bats and limit walks, but let's see how he handles (A) full season ball and (B) an age-appropriate level of competition, which won't happen until he makes it up to High Class A in the second half of 2016. Acevedo's a potential sleeper breakout player this year.

**Ceiling:** 1.5-win player
**Risk:** High
**MLB ETA:** 2018

## 21. Bryan Mitchell, RHP

MiLB Rank: N/A
Position Rank: N/A

| Born: 04/19/91 | Age: 25 | Bats: L | Top CALs: Cody Martin, Chris Stratton, |
| Height: 6-2 | Weight: 200 | Throws: R | Sean Stidfole, Patrick Schuster, Casey Coleman |

| YEAR | Age | Level | IP | W | L | ERA | FIP | K/9 | BB/9 | K% | BB% | HR/9 | LOB% |
|---|---|---|---|---|---|---|---|---|---|---|---|---|---|
| 2013 | 22 | A+ | 126.7 | 4 | 11 | 5.12 | 3.51 | 7.39 | 3.77 | 18.3% | 9.3% | 0.36 | 61.2% |
| 2013 | 22 | AA | 18.7 | 0 | 0 | 1.93 | 2.57 | 7.71 | 2.41 | 21.6% | 6.8% | 0.00 | 75.0% |
| 2014 | 23 | AA | 61.3 | 2 | 5 | 4.84 | 4.09 | 8.80 | 4.26 | 22.1% | 10.7% | 0.88 | 67.4% |
| 2014 | 23 | AAA | 41.7 | 4 | 2 | 3.67 | 4.44 | 7.34 | 3.46 | 19.1% | 9.0% | 1.08 | 79.6% |
| 2015 | 24 | AAA | 75.0 | 5 | 5 | 3.12 | 3.18 | 7.32 | 4.44 | 19.3% | 11.7% | 0.12 | 72.0% |

**Background:** The front office and player development engine tried like hell to develop the 2009 16th round pick into a viable starting pitcher, but after parts of six seasons in the organization they finally came to the realization that Mitchell – and his mid-90s fastball – are better suited in quick bursts and not someone who can turn over a lineup multiple times. Mitchell has always shown a knack for missing bats – he fanned one per inning as a 21-year-old in the Sally and averaged more than eight strikeouts per nine innings two years later between the Eastern and International Leagues – but his control, or lack thereof, was ultimately his undoing. Mitchell split last season between Scranton/Wilkes-Barre (as a starting pitcher) and New York (as a reliever), the latter his most likely permanent landing spot. He posted a 29-to-16 strikeout-to-walk ratio in 29.2 big league innings.

**Projection**: Sometimes it takes longer than expected for hurlers to develop solid-average control, but Mitchell's now entering his seventh season and has averaged more than four free passes every nine innings up to this point. As expected, his fastball ticked up from the 93 mph range to an impressive 96.0 mph during his relief stints with the Yankees last season. He'll mix in a hard low-90s cutter as well as a low-80s curveball. Mitchell has the arsenal to pitch in high-leverage situations, but he's better suited in middle relief roles with the team up or down by a couple runs.

**Ceiling:** 1.0-win player
**Risk:** Low to Moderate
**MLB ETA:** 2014

## 22. James Pazos, LHP

**MiLB Rank:** N/A
**Position Rank:** N/A

| Born: 05/05/91 | Age: 25 | Bats: R | **Top CALs:** Dan Jennings, Daniel Webb, |
| Height: 6-3 | Weight: 230 | Throws: L | Ryan Rowland-Smith, Sam Demel, Ian Kennedy |

| YEAR | Age | Level | IP | W | L | ERA | FIP | K/9 | BB/9 | K% | BB% | HR/9 | LOB% |
|------|-----|-------|-----|---|---|------|------|-------|------|-------|-------|------|--------|
| 2013 | 22 | A- | 1.0 | 0 | 0 | 0.00 | 4.10 | 9.00 | 9.00 | 20.0% | 20.0% | 0.00 | 100.0% |
| 2013 | 22 | A | 33.3 | 3 | 1 | 4.05 | 3.72 | 8.64 | 2.16 | 23.4% | 5.8% | 0.81 | 68.1% |
| 2014 | 23 | A+ | 25.0 | 0 | 2 | 3.96 | 1.71 | 11.88 | 2.16 | 31.1% | 5.7% | 0.00 | 58.1% |
| 2014 | 23 | AA | 42.0 | 0 | 1 | 1.50 | 2.78 | 9.00 | 4.07 | 25.0% | 11.3% | 0.00 | 85.4% |
| 2015 | 24 | AA | 9.7 | 0 | 0 | 1.86 | 2.13 | 11.17 | 0.00 | 37.5% | 0.0% | 0.93 | 76.9% |
| 2015 | 24 | AAA | 33.0 | 3 | 1 | 1.09 | 2.46 | 10.09 | 4.09 | 26.8% | 10.9% | 0.00 | 85.7% |

**Background:** The twice-drafted lefty went from being a 13th round pick out of the University of San Diego in 2012 to a legitimate contender for a long, extended look in New York in 2016. Pazos, who was originally selected in the 40th round out of Highland High School in 2009, made stops at three different levels last year, going from six appearances in Class AA to another 21 games with Scranton/Wilkes-Barre, and finally getting called up to The Show in early September for another 11 contests. Pazos would tally an impressive 49-to-15 strikeout-to-walk ratio with an aggregate 1.27 ERA in 42.2 minor league innings, and he fanned three and walked another trio in 5.0 innings with the Yankees. For his MiLB career, Pazos struck out 26.0% and walked 9.0% of the total batters he's faced.

**Projection**: Older lefties with mid-90s heat will certainly get more than a few chances to figure it out at the big league level and Pazos is no different. Along with an above-average fastball, the big lefty also flashed a low-80s slider during his debut. Historically, he's missed a whole bunch of bats with league average control. He could be a useful second lefty out of a big league bullpen.

**Ceiling:** 1. 0-win player
**Risk:** Low to Moderate
**MLB ETA:** Debuted in 2015

## 23. Jordan Montgomery, LHP

**MiLB Rank:** N/A
**Position Rank:** N/A

| Born: 12/27/92 | Age: 23 | Bats: L | **Top CALs:** Paul Phillips, Graham Stoneburner, |
| Height: 6-4 | Weight: 225 | Throws: L | Doug Brandt, Alex Meyer, Aaron Blair |

| YEAR | Age | Level | IP | W | L | ERA | FIP | K/9 | BB/9 | K% | BB% | HR/9 | LOB% |
|------|-----|-------|------|---|---|------|------|-------|------|-------|------|------|-------|
| 2014 | 21 | R | 5.7 | 0 | 1 | 4.76 | 2.80 | 7.94 | 3.18 | 20.8% | 8.3% | 0.00 | 42.9% |
| 2014 | 21 | A- | 13.3 | 1 | 0 | 3.38 | 2.09 | 10.13 | 2.70 | 27.3% | 7.3% | 0.00 | 60.0% |
| 2015 | 22 | A | 43.7 | 4 | 3 | 2.68 | 2.09 | 11.34 | 2.47 | 31.4% | 6.9% | 0.21 | 70.8% |
| 2015 | 22 | A+ | 90.7 | 6 | 5 | 3.08 | 2.87 | 7.64 | 2.38 | 20.7% | 6.5% | 0.40 | 70.0% |

**Background**: A three-year member of South Carolina's rotation, Montgomery was as consistent as they come during his collegiate career. The big lefty posted three consecutive seasons with a walk rate under 2.62 BB/9 while showing a decent ability to miss bats. Montgomery, a fourth round pick two years ago, breezed through the low levels of the minors, making his way up to High Class A in 2015. Between Charleston and Tampa last season, Montgomery tallied 132 punch outs and just 36 free passes in 134.1 innings of work. For his brief professional career, he's averaging nearly a strikeout per inning with a sub-3.0 walk rate.

**Projection**: One of these lefties that won't continue to miss bats in the mid-levels of the minors, but has a chance to succeed because of pitchability. Montgomery isn't overpowering, but knows how to pound the strike zone. He's looked incredibly promising in his year-and-a-half in professional baseball as he's never posted a FIP north of 2.89. Most guys like this don't pan out, but once in a blue moon they do. Montgomery could be one of the guys that do.

**Ceiling:** 1.0- to 1.5-win player
**Risk:** Moderate to High
**MLB ETA:** 2017

## 24. Brady Lail, RHP

MiLB Rank: N/A
Position Rank: N/A

| Born: 08/09/93 | Age: 22 | Bats: R | Top CALs: Amalio Diaz, Deolis Guerra, |
| Height: 6-2 | Weight: 205 | Throws: R | Tim Alderson, Kyle Waldrop, Richard Castillo |

| YEAR | Age | Level | IP | W | L | ERA | FIP | K/9 | BB/9 | K% | BB% | HR/9 | LOB% |
|------|-----|-------|------|---|---|------|-------|-------|------|-------|-------|------|-------|
| 2013 | 19 | R | 54.0 | 4 | 1 | 2.33 | 1.90 | 8.50 | 0.83 | 25.0% | 2.5% | 0.00 | 66.7% |
| 2013 | 19 | A+ | 7.7 | 1 | 0 | 7.04 | 4.81 | 5.87 | 3.52 | 12.5% | 7.5% | 1.17 | 64.1% |
| 2014 | 20 | A | 97.0 | 8 | 4 | 3.71 | 2.99 | 8.81 | 1.58 | 23.4% | 4.2% | 0.56 | 67.5% |
| 2014 | 20 | A+ | 37.3 | 3 | 1 | 3.38 | 3.77 | 5.06 | 2.17 | 14.3% | 6.1% | 0.48 | 69.9% |
| 2015 | 21 | A+ | 5.0 | 1 | 0 | 0.00 | -0.43 | 16.20 | 0.00 | 47.4% | 0.0% | 0.00 | 100.0% |
| 2015 | 21 | AA | 106.3 | 6 | 4 | 2.45 | 3.06 | 5.33 | 2.20 | 14.6% | 6.0% | 0.17 | 74.4% |
| 2015 | 21 | AAA | 37.0 | 3 | 2 | 4.62 | 5.32 | 3.16 | 4.14 | 7.8% | 10.2% | 0.97 | 73.6% |

**Background:** Another late, late round pick to find himself among the system's top prospects list. Lail was originally tabbed as the club's 18th round pick out of Bingham High School in 2012. And since then he's breezed through the Gulf Coast League, dominate the Sally, and looked OK between the Florida State and Eastern Leagues over the past couple of years. Lail made his initial foray into High Class A in 2014, but his strikeout took a noticeable dip as he averaged just 5.1 punch outs per nine innings. Then he followed that up with a similar swing-and-miss rate in Trenton and Scranton/Wilkes-Barre last season as well. Between both 2015 stops he fanned 76 in 143.1 innings of work.

**Projection**: Lail isn't what he appeared to be a couple years ago, namely a pitcher with a strong ability to miss bats. As soon as he crossed the bridge to High Class A he simply hasn't missed a reasonable amount of bats. Granted, he's just entering his age-22 season but he's nearing the 200-inning point of well below-average strikeout rates. He's a candidate to get pushed into a bullpen where his strikeout would likely rebound.

**Ceiling:** 1.0-win player
**Risk:** Moderate
**MLB ETA:** 2016

## 25. Jordan Foley, RHP

MiLB Rank: N/A
Position Rank: N/A

| Born: 07/12/93 | Age: 22 | Bats: R | Top CALs: Luke Jackson, Christian Meza, |
| Height: 6-4 | Weight: 215 | Throws: R | Yeliar Castro, Ryne Slack, Kelvin Vasquez |

| YEAR | Age | Level | IP | W | L | ERA | FIP | K/9 | BB/9 | K% | BB% | HR/9 | LOB% |
|------|-----|-------|------|---|---|------|------|------|------|-------|-------|------|--------|
| 2014 | 20 | R | 3.0 | 0 | 0 | 0.00 | 4.51 | 0.00 | 3.00 | 0.0% | 9.1% | 0.00 | 100.0% |
| 2014 | 20 | A- | 34.3 | 0 | 2 | 4.46 | 3.15 | 9.70 | 3.67 | 24.8% | 9.4% | 0.26 | 66.5% |
| 2015 | 21 | A | 84.3 | 3 | 7 | 2.88 | 3.39 | 9.92 | 3.84 | 26.5% | 10.3% | 0.43 | 74.7% |
| 2015 | 21 | AAA | 6.0 | 0 | 1 | 4.50 | 3.99 | 7.50 | 7.50 | 17.9% | 17.9% | 0.00 | 70.0% |

**Background:** After two up-and-down seasons at Central Michigan University – he walked more than he fanned during his freshman campaign and followed that up with a 90-to-40 strikeout-to-walk ratio in 15 starts the next year – things quietly came together for the 6-foot-4, 215-pound Texas-born hurler. In a career best 97.2 innings, Foley finished with – by the far – the best strikeout-to-walk ratio of his run with the Chippewas during his junior stint: 81-to-to-28. New York took him in the fifth round, 152nd overall, and signed him to a deal worth roughly $300,000. In an abbreviated 2015 – he missed roughly five weeks early in the season – Foley appeared in 19 games with Charleston in the South Atlantic League, throwing 84.1 innings with 93 punch outs, 36 walks, and a 3.39 FIP. He also made two brief appearances with Scranton/Wilkes-Barre midseason.

**Projection**: Here's what I wrote prior to the 2014 draft:

> "Certainly not overpowering, but the strides in his control/command suggest that Foley can at least stay in the rotation for the time being. On the downside, however, is that the right-hander's K-rate [in 2014], 7.46, took a rather large step backward.
>
> Another fringe #4-type arm if everything breaks right. But his work in the Cape [in 2013], which came almost exclusively out of the pen, could be a harbinger of things to come. Foley could be a potential late-inning reliever."

Foley's control/command, while much improved over the past two seasons, remains a...*cough, cough*...work in progress. But he did miss a career best 9.8 bats per nine innings last season, so he's likely bought himself a couple more seasons to show steady progress in the rotation. Thanks to a late birthday – he was born on July 12th, 1993 – Foley's only entering his age-22 season as he heads into High Class A. As I wrote two years ago, he remains a fringy backend starter, but his above-average fastball could tick-up a few notches when – not if – the club moves into a relief role.

**Ceiling:** 1.0-win player
**Risk:** Moderate
**MLB ETA:** 2017/2018

## *Barely Missed:*

- **Abiatal Avelino, SS** – The front office aggressively pushed the then-20-year-old shortstop up to High Class A after a 20-game refresher course in the Sally last season, and the results were…better than expected. After batting a lowly .232/.296/.323 in Low Class A in 2014, Avelino batted a league average-ish .252/.309/.321 as he bumped up to the more advanced league. He's likely a member of next year's Top 25 list.

- **Jose Campos, RHP** – Once touted as the system's next-best-thing, Campos has hardly pitched over the three seasons as he's dealt with elbow injuries and an eventual Tommy John surgery. He made it up to High Class A last season, posing an unsightly 7.05 ERA, but his underlying numbers (6.25 K/0, 2.01 BB/9, 3.97 FIP) were much more promising.

- **Cole Coshow, RHP** – The 6-foot-5, 260-pound right-hander opened the season up in dominant fashion as a member of Charleston's bullpen (16 IP, 20 K, 4 BB) and closed it out as starting pitcher in Class AA. There's some upside here, but his strikeout rate declined when he moved up at each spot. He's likely to be pushed back to the pen.

- **Luis Torrens, C** – The then-18-year-old backstop looked quite promising in the New York-Penn League last season, hitting .270/.327/.405 with 13 doubles, three triples, and two homeruns. He also threw out 42% of would-be base stealers. Another one that's nearly guaranteed a spot in the Top 25 next year.

- **Tyler Webb, LHP** – Former Gamecock made 25 appearances with Scranton/Wilkes-Barre last season, averaging nearly 10 strikeouts and just 2.6 walks per nine innings. He's another that barely missed this year's list. Webb could be a solid second lefty out of a lot of big league pens.

## Bird Doggin' It – Additional Prospects to Keep an Eye in 2016

| Player | Age | POS | Notes |
|---|---|---|---|
| Tyler Austin | 24 | 1B/LF/RF | A once-budding Sabermetric darling fell on hard times when his offensive production stagnated in Class AA in 2013. Last year he batted a paltry – and disappointing – .235/.309/.311 with an 82 wRC+. |
| Nestor Cortes | 21 | LHP | A bit too old for the Appalachian League last season, but the then-20-year-old hurler posted a 66-to-10 strikeout-to-walk ratio in 63.2 innings. He might be ready for full season action. |
| Gabriel Encinas | 24 | RHP | Lanky 6-foot-3 right-hander fanned 116 in 98.1 innings with Tampa in High Class A. The problem: he walked 63 in that span as well. |
| Thairo Estrada | 20 | 2B/SS | The then-19-year-old middle infielder hit .267/.338/.360 with a 108 wRC+ in the New York-Penn League. |
| Drew Finley | 19 | RHP | The club's most recent third round pick, Finley blew away the competition in 32.0 innings with Pulaski; he struck out 41, but battled control issues. |
| Nick Goody | 24 | RHP | Smallish right-hander armed with an average-ish 90 mph fastball posted an aggregate 1.59 ERA between Trenton and Scranton/Wilkes-Barre. He also appeared in seven games with New York as well. |
| Slade Heathcott | 25 | CF | Much hype was heaped on the 2009 first round pick, but he's never topped 81 games in his seven professional seasons. He also hasn't looked like a top prospect since 2012. |
| Chaz Hebert | 23 | LHP | 6-foot-2 southpaw posted an 82-to-26 strikeout-to-walk ratio in 106.2 innings in High Class A. He also made a trio of starts in Class AAA as well. |
| Hoy Jun Park | 20 | SS | Korean-born shortstop looked overmatched in the Appalachian League last season during his pro debut, hitting .239/.351/.383. |
| Gosuke Katoh | 21 | 2B | Looked like an absolute steal coming off of his debut season in 2013 when he slugged .310/.402/.522, but the former second round pick hasn't come close to matching that level of production since. |
| Conner Kendrick | 23 | LHP | Southpaw made stops at four different levels last season, going from the Sally to High Class A to Trenton to the International League, though he wasn't all that effective above Low Class A. |
| Jaron Long | 24 | RHP | Finesse righty out of The Ohio State University, Long posted an aggregate 103-to-30 strikeout-to-walk ratio in 154.2 innings in Class AA and Class AAA. |
| Jose Mesa | 22 | RHP | Son of former big league closer with the same name, the younger Mesa has a knack for the punch out but has trouble hitting the strike zone at certain points. |
| Mark Payton | 24 | OF | Pocket-sized outfielder has a knack for first base – he's sporting a career .404 OBP – but hasn't shown much else. |
| Nick Rumblelow | 24 | RHP | Former LSU hurler unleashed a low- to mid-90s fastball during his 15.2-inning stint with New York. Rumbelow could be a serviceable middle relief arm with a favorable K/BB ratio. |

**State of the Farm System:** Ever the tinkerer, General Manager Billy Beane continued to move prospects in and veterans out as the club quickly

fell out of contention. Here's a run-down of Beane's deals beginning in late July:

- July 23rd, 2015: Dealt lefty Scott Kazmir to the Astros for right-hander Daniel Mengden and backstop Jacob Nottingham, the stereotypical Oakland Atheltic-type prospect.
- July 27th, 2015: Traded veteran setup man Tyler Clippard to the Mets for young arm Casey Meisner.
- July 28th, 2015: Flipped Ben Zobrist to the eventual World Champion Kansas City Royals for big southpaw Sean Manaea and right-hander Aaron Brooks.
- July 31st, 2015: Purchased southpaw Felix Doubront from the Toronto Blue Jays.
- July 31st, 2015: Traded one-time All-Star Ryan Cook to the Red Sox for a player to be named later.
- August 4th, 2015: Sent lefty Eric O'Flaherty to the Mets for Darwin Frias.
- November 20th, 2015: Flipped Jesse Chavez to the Blue Jays for Liam Hendriks.
- November 25th, 2015: Dealt Brendan McCurry to Houston for veteran infielder Jed Lowrie.
- December 2nd, 2015: Traded Jose Torres, Drew Pomeranz, and Jabari Blash to San Diego for Yonder Alonso and Marc Rzepczynski.
- December 8th, 2015: Sent Evan Scribner to Seattle for Trey Cochran-Gill.
- December 9th, 2015: Traded veteran second/third baseman Brett Lawrie to the White Sox for Zack Erwin and Jeffrey "J.B." Wendelken.

For those counting at home that's 11 deals – 10 trades and the Felix Doubront contract purchase – 139 days. After the dust settled Oakland acquired five prospects that rank in their Top 25 and another one, Erwin, who barely missed.

| Rank | Name | POS |
|------|------|-----|
| 1 | Sean Manaea | LHP |
| 2 | Franklin Barreto | SS |
| 3 | Matt Olson | 1B |
| 4 | Jacob Nottingham | C/1B |
| 5 | Dillon Overton | LHP |
| 6 | Renato Nunez | 1B/3B |
| 7 | Daniel Mengden | RHP |
| 8 | Chad Pinder | SS |
| 9 | Casey Meisner | RHP |
| 10 | Sean Nolin | LHP |
| 11 | Matt Chapman | 3B |
| 12 | R.J. Alvarez | RHP |
| 13 | Rangel Ravelo | 1B |
| 14 | Richie Martin | SS |
| 15 | Bobby Wahl | RHP |
| 16 | Yairo Munoz | SS |
| 17 | Raul Alcantara | RHP |
| 18 | J.B. Wendelken | LHP |
| 19 | Chris Kohler | LHP |
| 20 | Dakota Chalmers | RHP |
| 21 | Daniel Gossett | RHP |
| 22 | Mikey White | SS |
| 23 | Sam Bragg | RHP |
| 24 | Brett Graves | RHP |
| 25 | B.J. Boyd | OF |

**Review of the 2015 Draft:** Oakland doubled up with their first two selections last season by taking a pair of collegiate shortstops with the 20th and 63rd picks. University of Florida standout Richie Martin was a solid, average-ish offensive performer during his run with the school, hitting .284/.376/.376 with 27 doubles, seven triples, seven homeruns, and 45 stolen bases in 176 games. White, a three-year starter at the University of Alabama, hit .308/.403/.448 with 39 doubles, nine triples, and 13 dingers in 184 contests.

Prep right-hander Dakota Chalmers battled control issues during his debut in the Arizona Summer League. And fourth rounder Skye Bolt never lived up to the lofty expectations following his dominant freshman season.

## 1. Sean Manaea, LHP

**MiLB Rank: #51**
**Position Rank: N/A**

| Born: 02/01/92 | Age: 24 | Bats: L | Top CALs: Jake Arrieta, CC Lee, |
| Height: 6-5 | Weight: 235 | Throws: L | Jhonny Nunez, Brad Mills, Scott Elbert |

| YEAR | Age | Level | IP | W | L | ERA | FIP | K/9 | BB/9 | K% | BB% | HR/9 | LOB% |
|------|-----|-------|-----|---|---|------|------|-------|------|-------|------|------|--------|
| 2014 | 22 | A+ | 121.7 | 7 | 8 | 3.11 | 3.11 | 10.80 | 3.99 | 28.4% | 10.5% | 0.37 | 69.5% |
| 2015 | 23 | R | 5.0 | 0 | 0 | 1.80 | 5.22 | 10.80 | 1.80 | 31.6% | 5.3% | 1.80 | 100.0% |
| 2015 | 23 | A+ | 19.7 | 1 | 0 | 3.66 | 1.78 | 10.07 | 1.83 | 27.2% | 4.9% | 0.00 | 55.6% |
| 2015 | 23 | AA | 49.7 | 6 | 1 | 2.36 | 3.24 | 11.23 | 3.81 | 29.7% | 10.1% | 0.72 | 82.8% |

**Background:** One of my favorite prospects in the entire 2013 draft class, Manaea, nonetheless, tumbled to the 34th overall pick due to some hip issues. And the Royals, playing the under-slot early-pick-and-spend-big-later-game, grabbed Manaea and signed him to a hefty $3.5 million deal. Two years later KC packaged the former Indiana State hurler along with right-hander Aaron Brooks for the services of Ben Zobrist, a move that's already paid off in a big way for Kansas City, but could also come up huge for Oakland in the coming years. Assuming Manaea can stay healthy. Last year, in another injury-shortened campaign, the 6-foot-5 southpaw made 13 starts between the Carolina and Texas Leagues, totaling just 69.1 innings with 84 punch outs and 25 walks with a 2.73 ERA. For his brief professional career, he's sporting an impressive 236-to-80 strikeout-to-walk ratio in just 196.0 innings of work.

**Projection**: Relax. The injury was an abdominal strain, not of the arm variety. Ignoring his ability – or inability – to put together a healthy campaign, Manaea's numbers have been nothing short of phenomenal since entering pro ball. He's punched out nearly 29% of the batters he's faced while walking 9.7%. He's breezed through two stints in High Class A and made it look quite easy in his seven-game tryout in Class AA. Outside of the Dodgers' Julio Urias, you'd be hard-pressed to find a better southpaw pitching prospect. As long as he stays healthy.

**Ceiling:** 3.3- to 3.5-win player
**Risk:** Moderate
**MLB ETA:** 2017

## 2. Franklin Barreto, SS

**MiLB Rank: #52**
**Position Rank: #8**

| Born: 02/27/96 | Age: 20 | Bats: R | Top CALs: Alen Hanson, Richard Urena, |
| Height: 5-9 | Weight: 175 | Throws: R | Corey Seager, Bryan Cuevas, Claudio Bautista |

| Season | Age | LVL | PA | 2B | 3B | HR | AVG | OBP | SLG | ISO | BB% | K% | wRC+ |
|--------|-----|-----|-----|----|----|----|-------|-------|-------|-------|------|-------|------|
| 2013 | 17 | R | 194 | 16 | 6 | 4 | 0.299 | 0.368 | 0.529 | 0.230 | 6.7% | 21.6% | 161 |
| 2014 | 18 | A- | 328 | 23 | 4 | 6 | 0.311 | 0.384 | 0.481 | 0.170 | 7.9% | 19.5% | 141 |
| 2015 | 19 | A+ | 364 | 22 | 3 | 13 | 0.302 | 0.333 | 0.500 | 0.198 | 4.1% | 18.4% | 122 |

**Background:** Clearly things don't look well for Oakland's chances to come out ahead in the Josh Donaldson-for-Brett-Lawrie offseason deal with Toronto. For those counting at home Donaldson mashed to the tune of .297/.371/.568 while setting career bests in nearly every single offensive category: doubles (41), homeruns (41), RBI (123), wRC+ (154), wins above replacement (8.8 bWAR and 8.7 fWAR), and slugging percentage (.568). Brett Lawrie, on the other hand, performed like...Brett Lawrie. The new Oakland third baseman batted .261/.316/.406 between 2012 and 2014, his last three full seasons in Toronto. He followed that up by hitting .260/.299/.407 in Oakland. It's nearly identical. Two other players acquired by Oakland in the deal – Kendall Graveman and Sean Nolin – are backend starters, at best. So it's up to Barreto, a foot-nothing shortstop, to help firm up Oakland's side of the deal. And he's doing just that.

A tiny-sized shortstop, Barreto packs more offensive punch than his 5-foot-9, 175-pound frame belies. And he's continued to defy anyone that suggests otherwise too.

Barreto opened up his professional career as a 17-year-old in the Gulf Coast League, hitting .299/.368/.529. Toronto bumped him up for a quick – and largely underwhelming – 15-game crash course in the Appalachian League to close out his debut. He spent the next year, his final in the Toronto organization, batting .311/.384/.481 with 33 extra-base hits in Short-Season ball.

Upon acquiring Barreto, Oakland made another bold decision and pushed the promising shortstop straight up to Stockton. And he was nothing short of spectacular. In an injury-shortened campaign, he slugged .302/.333/.500 with 22 doubles, three triples, and 13 homeruns – in just 90 games. Prorating that over a full minor league season: 34 doubles, five triples, and 20 homeruns.

Just one more interesting tidbit: the last time a 19-year-old shortstop posted a wRC+ total of at least 122 was in 2013, former Oakland A's top prospect Addison Russell.

**Projection**: In last year's book I wrote:

> "And now the bad news, sort of: the Venezuelan-born shortstop, who originally signed with Toronto for a shade under $1.5 million in 2012, stands just 5-foot-9. To put that into perspective, only five players – David Eckstein, Jimmy Rollins, Miguel Tejada, Omar Vizquel, and Rafael Furcal – have stood 5-foot-9 or less, posted an OPS+ [of] 100 or better, and appeared in at least 120 games.
>
> And not to throw out something so cliché, but this is such an Oakland move – acquiring a promising offensive-minded prospect despite any perceived physical limitations. You really do have to love that type of mentality. CAL is also a pretty big fan of Barreto's just two seasons into his career, linking him to Dilson Herrera, Alen Hanson, and former A's shortstop of the future Addison Russell."

Well, he didn't add any height to his vertically challenged frame. And CAL is still a fan by tying him to Dodgers current shortstop of the future Corey Seager.

While Stockton's home field tends to inflate power numbers – his overall production, according to StatCorner, drops from .302/.333/.500 to .300/.330/.481 – Barreto has such a strong foundation in place for future success: above-average power, strong contact rates, solid-average or better hit tool, and speed. His lone red flag is a bit nitpick-y: he walked just 4.1% of the time last season, but that number was a lot higher in Short-Season ball two years ago. It remains to be seen if his small stature will allow him to stay at shortstop, but there's plenty of offensive firepower here.

**Ceiling:** 3.0- to 3.5-win player
**Risk:** Moderate
**MLB ETA:** 2017

## 3. Matt Olson, 1B

**MiLB Rank: #84**
**Position Rank: #4**

| Born: 03/29/94 | Age: 22 | Bats: L | Top CALs: Chris Parmelee, Chris Carter, |
| Height: 6-5 | Weight: 230 | Throws: R | Jonathan Rodriguez, Nick Weglarz, Jaff Decker |

| Season | Age | LVL | PA | 2B | 3B | HR | AVG | OBP | SLG | ISO | BB% | K% | wRC+ |
|---|---|---|---|---|---|---|---|---|---|---|---|---|---|
| 2013 | 19 | A | 558 | 32 | 0 | 23 | 0.225 | 0.326 | 0.435 | 0.210 | 12.9% | 26.5% | 114 |
| 2014 | 20 | A+ | 634 | 31 | 1 | 37 | 0.262 | 0.404 | 0.543 | 0.281 | 18.5% | 21.6% | 145 |
| 2015 | 21 | AA | 585 | 37 | 0 | 17 | 0.249 | 0.388 | 0.438 | 0.189 | 17.9% | 23.8% | 132 |
| 2015 | 21 | AA | 585 | 37 | 0 | 17 | 0.249 | 0.388 | 0.438 | 0.189 | 17.9% | 23.8% | 132 |

**Background:** If you were to sculpt the prototypical Oakland's A's slugging prospect it'd probably look something like the former supplemental first rounder: Olson stands a hulking 6-foot-5 and 230 pounds, bats left and throws right, offers up oodles and oodles of power, walks at elite clips, and posts incredibly wRC+ totals despite some poor batting averages. And Olson continued to perform like...well...the typical Oakland A's brooding slugger. In 133 games for Midland, the then-21-year-old first baseman slugged .249/.388/.438 with 37 doubles, 17 homeruns, and a ridiculously favorable 139-to-105 strikeout-to-walk ratio. His walk percentage last season, 17.9%, ranked fifth among all stateside prospects in full season ball.

**Projection**: Left-handers have given Olson some fits throughout the past couple of seasons: he's posted OPSs of .613, .895, and .722 over the past three seasons. And while he's not completely helpless against them, he could be a potential platoon bat if everything doesn't work out. And just as I pointed out in last year's book, CAL seems a little...hesitant at this point, linking him to Chris Parmelee, Chris Carter, Jonathan Rodriguez, Nick Weglarz, and Jaff Decker.

**Ceiling:** 2.5- to 3.0-win player
**Risk:** Moderate
**MLB ETA:** 2016

## 4. Jacob Nottingham, C/1B

MiLB Rank: #88
Position Rank: #2 (C), #5 (1B)

| Born: 04/03/95 | Age: 21 | Bats: R | Top CALs: Gary Sanchez, Tyler Marlette, |
| Height: 6-3 | Weight: 230 | Throws: R | Luis Exposito, Alex Murphy, Juan Apodaca |

| Season | Age | LVL | PA | 2B | 3B | HR | AVG | OBP | SLG | ISO | BB% | K% | wRC+ |
|---|---|---|---|---|---|---|---|---|---|---|---|---|---|
| 2013 | 18 | R | 173 | 10 | 2 | 1 | 0.247 | 0.347 | 0.363 | 0.116 | 12.1% | 22.0% | 114 |
| 2014 | 19 | R | 200 | 10 | 1 | 5 | 0.230 | 0.307 | 0.385 | 0.155 | 9.0% | 27.0% | 98 |
| 2015 | 20 | A | 253 | 18 | 1 | 10 | 0.326 | 0.387 | 0.543 | 0.217 | 7.1% | 20.2% | 169 |
| 2015 | 20 | A+ | 258 | 15 | 1 | 7 | 0.306 | 0.357 | 0.468 | 0.162 | 5.8% | 18.6% | 123 |

**Background:** And this is how the A's do it: Never afraid of taking calculated risks, Oakland signed a resurgent Scott Kazmir during the 2012/2013 offseason to a two-year deal; a year-and-a-half later the organization turned around and dealt the southpaw to the contending Astros for Nottingham and right-hander Daniel Mengden. Nottingham, a sixth round pick in 2013, was in the midst of a breakout season before being dealt; he batted .326/.387/.543 with 29 extra-base hits in 59 games in the Midwest League and continued to torch the California League for his final 17 games in the Houston franchise (.324/.368/.606). After his acquisition, the A's kept him in the Cal League and he continued to mash: .299/.352/.409. His final 2015 triple-slash line: .316/.372/.505 with 33 doubles, one triple, and 17 homeruns.

**Projection**: One of the bigger risers in 2015, Nottingham always had a firm foundation in place prior to his coming out party: over his first two professional seasons he walked in 10.5% of his plate appearances and posted a solid-average .137 Isolated Power, both traits typically sought out by Oakland (and other analytically savvy front offices). Last season the patience took a little bit of a step backward, which isn't too worrisome given his ability to make strong contact, and the power took another step forward. Defensively, he continues to split time from behind the plate and first base, but he's been fairly valuable donning the tools of ignorance, having thrown out about 40% of would-be base stealers of the last two seasons. I like Nottingham, a lot actually. He has the skill set in place to be one of the top minor league backstops come this time next year.

**Ceiling:** 2.5- to 3.0-win player
**Risk:** Moderate
**MLB ETA:**

## 5. Renato Nunez, 1B/3B

MiLB Rank: #146
Position Rank: #10 (1B), #7 (3B)

| Born: 04/04/94 | Age: 22 | Bats: R | Top CALs: Aderlin Rodriguez, Christian Villanueva, |
| Height: 6-1 | Weight: 200 | Throws: R | Brandon Laird, Jeimer Candelario, Matt Davidson |

| Season | Age | LVL | PA | 2B | 3B | HR | AVG | OBP | SLG | ISO | BB% | K% | wRC+ |
|---|---|---|---|---|---|---|---|---|---|---|---|---|---|
| 2013 | 19 | A | 545 | 27 | 0 | 19 | 0.258 | 0.301 | 0.423 | 0.165 | 5.1% | 25.0% | 102 |
| 2014 | 20 | A+ | 562 | 28 | 3 | 29 | 0.279 | 0.336 | 0.517 | 0.238 | 6.0% | 20.1% | 117 |
| 2015 | 21 | AA | 416 | 23 | 0 | 18 | 0.278 | 0.332 | 0.480 | 0.202 | 6.7% | 15.9% | 124 |

**Background:** Another year, another quietly favorable year of production for Nunez. But it also marks the second consecutive year his wRC+ total has crept up. Going back to his debut in full season ball in 2013, Nunez has posted wRC+ marks of 102, 117, and 124 all the while being much younger than his competition. Last season, he slugged .278/.332/.480 with 23 doubles and 18 homeruns. But his overall production spiked tremendously after a slow start. Nunez batted .298/.331/.522 over his final 71 games. For his career, he's sporting a .276/.32/.473 triple-slash line, with 108 doubles, six triples, and 75 homeruns in 440 games.

**Projection**: In last year's book I wrote:

> "Sort of a light Three True Outcomes hitter, Nunez has always flashed impressive power – he owns a career .195 Isolated Power – and a questionable bat. He's always been young for his level of competition. But CAL isn't overly impressed. Defensively, he took a hufe step forward last season."

Nunez more or less matched his previous season's triple-slash line (.279/.336/.517 vs. .278/.332/.480) despite moving up to arguably the most challenging minor league level. The power still grades out as an above-average skill and he shows a surprisingly strong contact rate. Oakland began shifting him from the hot corner to third base last season, so it'll be interesting to see where he fits long term. There's some offensive upside here, but CAL remains utterly unimpressed. If everything breaks the right way, Nunez could be a .260/.320/.415-type big league stick.

**Ceiling:** 2.0- to 2.5-win player
**Risk:** Moderate
**MLB ETA:**

## 6. Dillon Overton, LHP

MiLB Rank: #147

Position Rank: N/A

| Born: 08/17/91 | Age: 24 | Bats: L | Top CALs: Tom Boleska, Chris Schwinden, |
|---|---|---|---|
| Height: 5-11 | Weight: 175 | Throws: L | Chad Jenkins, Zack Segovia, Zachary Neal |

| YEAR | Age | Level | IP | W | L | ERA | FIP | K/9 | BB/9 | K% | BB% | HR/9 | LOB% |
|---|---|---|---|---|---|---|---|---|---|---|---|---|---|
| 2014 | 22 | R | 22.0 | 0 | 2 | 1.64 | 1.90 | 12.68 | 1.23 | 35.2% | 3.4% | 0.00 | 66.7% |
| 2014 | 22 | A- | 15.0 | 0 | 1 | 2.40 | 0.91 | 13.20 | 0.60 | 37.9% | 1.7% | 0.00 | 69.2% |
| 2015 | 23 | A+ | 61.3 | 2 | 4 | 3.82 | 4.07 | 8.66 | 1.76 | 23.9% | 4.9% | 1.03 | 71.4% |
| 2015 | 23 | AA | 64.7 | 5 | 2 | 3.06 | 3.34 | 6.54 | 2.09 | 17.7% | 5.6% | 0.56 | 78.0% |

**Background:** I pegged the former Sooner left-hander as one of my Top 25 Breakout Prospects for 2015 and wrote the following: *"Healthy for the first time since he was fronting Oklahoma's rotation as a sophomore in 2012, Overton, who missed the second half of 2013 and the majority of [2014], sparkled during his brief return last season. He should have everyone talking by midseason."* Well, didn't have everyone talking, but put together an incredibly strong campaign in 2015 – some would say even a breakout. Overton began the year by making 14 appearances, 12 of which were starts, with Stockton in the California League, averaging nearly a punch out per inning while displaying incredible control. Oakland bumped him up to Midland in early July and he made another 13 starts (64.2 innings, 47 strikeouts, and 15 walks). He would finish his first healthy campaign by averaging 7.6 strikeouts and just 1.9 free passes per nine innings.

**Projection:** It's hard to remember that it was Overton, not Jonathan Gray, who was supposed to front the Sooners' rotation heading into his injury-plagued junior campaign. But life happens. And Overton's already gained his previously promising form. He won't miss a whole lot of bats at the big league level, maybe something like 7.2 or 7.3 K/9 during his peak years, but he commands the zone well to help compensate for the lack of punch outs. He's a bit fly ball-prone, so it's fortunate he'll be spending half of his time pitching in the Coliseum. Solid #4-caliber arm with a peak as a decent #3.

**Ceiling:** 2.0- to 2.5-win player
**Risk:** Moderate
**MLB ETA:** 2016

## 7. Daniel Mengden, RHP

MiLB Rank: #168

Position Rank: N/A

| Born: 02/19/93 | Age: 23 | Bats: R | Top CALs: Cy Sneed, Justin Souza, |
|---|---|---|---|
| Height: 6-2 | Weight: 190 | Throws: R | Sammy Solis, Paul Phillips, Eric Gonzalez |

| YEAR | Age | Level | IP | W | L | ERA | FIP | K/9 | BB/9 | K% | BB% | HR/9 | LOB% |
|---|---|---|---|---|---|---|---|---|---|---|---|---|---|
| 2014 | 21 | R | 6.3 | 0 | 0 | 4.26 | 0.51 | 15.63 | 0.00 | 44.0% | 0.0% | 0.00 | 40.0% |
| 2014 | 21 | A- | 4.7 | 0 | 0 | 1.93 | 1.51 | 11.57 | 1.93 | 31.6% | 5.3% | 0.00 | 83.3% |
| 2015 | 22 | A | 38.7 | 4 | 1 | 1.16 | 2.65 | 8.38 | 1.86 | 23.5% | 5.2% | 0.23 | 85.5% |
| 2015 | 22 | A+ | 92.0 | 6 | 3 | 4.79 | 4.30 | 8.71 | 2.74 | 22.2% | 7.0% | 0.98 | 66.4% |

**Background:** Not to be confused with Daniel Gossett, Mengden, a fourth round pick out of Texas A&M two years ago, was acquired from the Astros at the trade deadline for Scott Kazmir. The handlebar-mustachioed right-hander made quick work of the Midwest League in eight games, showed promise in 10 starts with Lancaster, but was ultimately plagued by some bad luck, and was equally solid following his acquisition. Overall, Mengden, a former position-player-turned-pitcher, tossed 130.2 innings across both levels (and in both organizations) while fanning 125 and walking just 36. Again, his aggregate ERA, 3.72, is a bit inflated thanks to his bloated BABIP (.367) with Lancaster and inflated homerun rate (1.28 HR/9) with Stockton.

**Projection:** I've always, always been a big fan of the former fourth round pick. Here's what I wrote before the 2014 draft:

> *"I have a thing for position-players-turned-pitchers. Their arms have less wear-and-tear, they're still learning to hone the craft and, subsequently, there's still quite a bit of projection left, more so than the average collegiate player. My all-time favorite, of course, is Royals' top prospect Kyle Zimmer.*
>
> *And Mengden's no different.*
>
> *He's already shown above-average control/command and an impressive ability to miss bats in the tough SEX, which should only improve as he gains more experience. Mengden's not an elite pitching prospect, but he does have a pretty high ceiling, something along the lines of a steady #3."*

Mengden was able to maintain his strikeout rate while showing a strong feel for the zone in High Class A last season – a definite positive. Add in his ability to generate a ton of action on the ground – his groundball rate was typically been better than average – and Mengden looks like a big league, middle-of-the-rotation caliber arm.

**Ceiling:** 2.0-win player
**Risk:** Moderate
**MLB ETA:** 2017

## 8. Chad Pinder, SS

| Born: 03/29/92 | Age: 24 | Bats: R | Top CALs: Adolfo Gonzalez, Jeff Bianchi, |
|---|---|---|---|
| Height: 6-2 | Weight: 190 | Throws: R | Daniel Mayora, Derek Dietrich, Junior Lake |

| Season | Age | LVL | PA | 2B | 3B | HR | AVG | OBP | SLG | ISO | BB% | K% | wRC+ |
|---|---|---|---|---|---|---|---|---|---|---|---|---|---|
| 2013 | 21 | A- | 161 | 4 | 0 | 3 | 0.200 | 0.286 | 0.293 | 0.093 | 7.5% | 25.5% | 81 |
| 2014 | 22 | A+ | 436 | 32 | 5 | 13 | 0.288 | 0.336 | 0.489 | 0.201 | 5.0% | 22.7% | 112 |
| 2015 | 23 | AA | 522 | 32 | 2 | 15 | 0.317 | 0.361 | 0.486 | 0.170 | 5.4% | 19.7% | 135 |

**Background:** After dabbling with the move from second base to diamond's most important defensive position two years ago, the organization made the full commitment to switch Pinder to shortstop in 2015. And, of course, there were noticeable bumps along the way; he committed 26 errors at the position last season. But Pinder's offensive game didn't seem to mind the change. In fact, he flourished. Spending the entire season in Class AA, the former second round pick out of Virginia batted .317/.361/.486 while setting a career high in homeruns (15) and tying his previous best in doubles (32). His overall production, according to *Weighted Runs Created Plus*, topped the league average mark by 35% -- also a professional best.

**Projection:** I have two thoughts about Pinder. Well, two *main* thoughts:

1. He sort of reminds of former Oakland farmhand Mark Teahen, whom the A's – and GM Billy Beane – shipped off as part of the three-team mega-deal involving Carlos Beltran to Houston and Octavio Dotel coming to Oakland. But it's more of a sense that I don't see Pinder playing in the Athletics' organization for much longer because he's probably going to get shipped off at the peak of his value.

2. With that being said, I've never been a particularly huge fan of Pinder, writing in his pre-draft analysis "that he doesn't look like a future big league regular, unless his plate discipline and power numbers improve noticeably." Well, they have and so do his odds of carving out a quasi-regular role at the game's pinnacle level.

**Ceiling:** 1.5-win player
**Risk:** Moderate
**MLB ETA:** 2018

## 9. Casey Meisner, RHP

| Born: 05/22/95 | Age: 21 | Bats: R | Top CALs: Arquimedes Nieto, Jairo Heredia, |
|---|---|---|---|
| Height: 6-7 | Weight: 190 | Throws: R | Colton Cain, Nick Additon, Jayson Aquino |

| YEAR | Age | Level | IP | W | L | ERA | FIP | K/9 | BB/9 | K% | BB% | HR/9 | LOB% |
|---|---|---|---|---|---|---|---|---|---|---|---|---|---|
| 2013 | 18 | R | 35.3 | 1 | 3 | 3.06 | 2.81 | 7.13 | 2.55 | 19.4% | 6.9% | 0.00 | 59.5% |
| 2014 | 19 | A- | 62.3 | 5 | 3 | 3.75 | 3.18 | 9.67 | 2.60 | 24.2% | 6.5% | 0.58 | 64.8% |
| 2015 | 20 | A | 76.0 | 7 | 2 | 2.13 | 3.64 | 7.82 | 2.25 | 21.9% | 6.3% | 0.71 | 84.0% |
| 2015 | 20 | A+ | 32.3 | 3 | 1 | 2.78 | 3.35 | 6.68 | 1.95 | 18.5% | 5.4% | 0.28 | 67.5% |
| 2015 | 20 | A+ | 35.0 | 3 | 2 | 2.83 | 4.71 | 5.91 | 3.60 | 15.0% | 9.2% | 1.03 | 74.9% |

**Background:** Another fantastic pickup at the trade deadline. The club flipped offseason acquisition Tyler Clippard into promising right-hander Casey Meisner. A third round pick by the Mets in 2013, Meisner, like fellow mid-season pick Jacob Nottingham, was in the midst of a breakout season. The 6-foot-7, 190-pound rail-thin right-hander opened the year with 12 dominant starts in the Sally, posting a 3.64 FIP while averaging 7.82 strikeouts and just 2.25 walks per nine innings. Sandy Alderson & Co. bumped him up to the Florida State League in later June for another six starts before agreeing to part with him. After the acquisition, Meisner made another seven starts in High Class A, this time the Florida State League. He finished the year with a combined 2.45 ERA and a 113-to-40 strikeout-to-walk ratio in 143.1 innings of work.

**Projection:** Here's what I wrote in last year's book:

> "It's almost getting too repetitive at this point, a little broken record-esque for those who remember them, but Meisner's another one of the franchise's under-the-radar-type arms. And despite the massive height, he does really well [in] pounding the zone consistently. CAL likens him to Zach McAllister. [He's a] solid back-end of the rotation arm."

After originally pegging him as a 1.0- to 1.5-win player last year, I'd bump that up a notch. Meisner generates a lot of action on the ground, continues to pound the zone with regularity, and still has some projection left in his lanky frame. He won't blow anyone away with his heater, but it obviously plays up due to his size. There's #3/#4-type upside here.

**Ceiling:** 1.5- to 2.0-win player
**Risk:** Moderate
**MLB ETA:** 2017

## 10. Sean Nolin, LHP

**MiLB Rank:** N/A
**Position Rank:** N/A

| Born: 12/26/89 | Age: 26 | Bats: L | Top CALs: Randy Wells, Anthony Ranaudo, Travis Wood, Justin Thomas, Nick Additon |
| Height: 6-4 | Weight: 230 | Throws: L | |

| YEAR | Age | Level | IP | W | L | ERA | FIP | K/9 | BB/9 | K% | BB% | HR/9 | LOB% |
|------|-----|-------|-----|---|---|------|------|-------|------|-------|-------|------|-------|
| 2013 | 23 | AA | 92.7 | 8 | 3 | 3.01 | 2.82 | 10.00 | 2.43 | 26.8% | 6.5% | 0.58 | 77.1% |
| 2013 | 23 | AAA | 17.7 | 1 | 1 | 1.53 | 4.34 | 6.62 | 5.09 | 18.6% | 14.3% | 0.51 | 92.9% |
| 2014 | 24 | A+ | 7.3 | 0 | 1 | 3.68 | 2.57 | 11.05 | 4.91 | 28.1% | 12.5% | 0.00 | 62.5% |
| 2014 | 24 | AAA | 87.3 | 4 | 6 | 3.50 | 3.86 | 7.63 | 3.61 | 20.0% | 9.5% | 0.62 | 73.4% |
| 2015 | 25 | AAA | 47.3 | 2 | 2 | 2.66 | 4.82 | 7.23 | 3.61 | 18.9% | 9.5% | 0.95 | 85.7% |

**Background:** Another cog in the Josh Donaldson deal with Toronto, Nolin lost several weeks of the 2015 season as he battled a lingering groin injury – an issue that would ultimately limit him to just 76.1 innings. Nolin wouldn't make his debut last season until the first week of May and then later missed all of July as well. The big lefty out of San Jacinto College tallied 14 starts in the PCL, punching out 18.9% and walking 9.5%. Nolin made another six starts with Oakland, his second trip to the big leagues, where he tossed 29.0 innings while posting a laughably poor 15-to-12 strikeout-to-walk ratio. And just for a cherry on top of the crap sundae, he also surrendered four dingers, nearly one for every four punch outs.

**Projection**: Certainly not overpowering in the slightest bit, his fringy fastball betrays his lanky 6-foot-4 frame. Nolin's fastball *averaged* a shade over 86 mph during his extended big league look last season, but during his one-inning stint with Toronto three years ago it was sitting at 92 mph. Nolin's exactly how he portrays himself to be: a fringy backend starter, something evidenced by the lefty being tied to Randy Wells, Anthony Ranaudo, and Travis Wood. Though to be fair, Wells and Wood have had some successful runs in the big leagues.

**Ceiling:** 1.5-win player
**Risk:** Low to Moderate
**MLB ETA:** Debuted in 2013

## 11. Matt Chapman, 3B

**MiLB Rank:** N/A
**Position Rank:** N/A

| Born: 04/28/93 | Age: 23 | Bats: R | Top CALs: Tyler Kolodny, Marc Wik, Jose Brizuela, Joe Sanders, David Vidal |
| Height: 6-2 | Weight: 205 | Throws: R | |

| Season | Age | LVL | PA | 2B | 3B | HR | AVG | OBP | SLG | ISO | BB% | K% | wRC+ |
|--------|-----|-----|-----|----|----|----|-------|-------|-------|-------|-------|-------|------|
| 2014 | 21 | A | 202 | 9 | 3 | 5 | 0.242 | 0.287 | 0.400 | 0.158 | 3.5% | 22.3% | 96 |
| 2015 | 22 | A+ | 352 | 21 | 3 | 23 | 0.250 | 0.341 | 0.566 | 0.316 | 11.1% | 22.4% | 139 |

**Background:** The club's first round pick out of Cal State Fullerton two years ago got off to a bit of an auspicious pro debut, hitting a less-than-stellar .237/.282/.389. A former two-way player for the Titans during his three-year tenure, Chapman, who highlighted as a flame-throwing reliever at times, blossomed in the hitters' haven known as Stockton last season. In an injury-shortened season, something that was pretty common in the Oakland farm system, Chapman batted .250/.341/.566 with 21 doubles, a trio of triples, 23 homeruns, and added four stolen bases for good measure. His overall production topped the Cal League average mark 39%, the ninth best showing in the league last year. And now the bad news: according to StatCorner.com, Chapman's triple-slash line drops from .250/.341/.566 to .240/.330/.524 once adjusting for Stockton's home park.

**Projection**: Here's what I wrote prior to the 2014 draft:

> *"Now the bad news: the Titans' home ballpark is incredibly hitter-friendly, so much so, in fact, that his 2013 park-adjusted wOBA (according to CollegeSplits) is 13 points lower than his raw total. On the positive side, Chapman's power is solid-average with the potential to peak in the 17- to 20-HR range; the plate discipline is decent, as is the hit tool.*
>
> *If everything breaks right, Chapman could develop into a league average regular (depending upon his defense). Nice solid prospect, far from elite."*

Apparently, I enjoy the phrase "now the bad news." All joking aside, the analysis still holds true. Chapman has been the beneficiary of some hitter friendly home environments, but his numbers remain solid after adjustments are made. He's basically the poor man's version of Chad Pinder. Nice power, questionable hit too, solid eye at the plate.

**Ceiling:** 1.5-win player
**Risk:** Moderate
**MLB ETA:** 2017

## 12. R.J. Alvarez, RHP

**MiLB Rank: N/A**
**Position Rank: N/A**

| Born: 06/08/91 | Age: 25 | Bats: R | **Top CALs:** Neil Ramirez, CC Lee, |
|---|---|---|---|
| Height: 6-2 | Weight: 215 | Throws: R | Dan Jennings, Brandon Peterson, Jordan Norberto |

| YEAR | Age | Level | IP | W | L | ERA | FIP | K/9 | BB/9 | K% | BB% | HR/9 | LOB% |
|---|---|---|---|---|---|---|---|---|---|---|---|---|---|
| 2013 | 22 | A+ | 48.7 | 4 | 2 | 2.96 | 2.85 | 14.61 | 4.99 | 38.0% | 13.0% | 0.37 | 78.1% |
| 2014 | 23 | AA | 43.3 | 0 | 1 | 1.25 | 1.48 | 12.67 | 2.70 | 36.1% | 7.7% | 0.00 | 84.8% |
| 2015 | 24 | AAA | 35.0 | 3 | 3 | 4.11 | 3.54 | 10.54 | 4.37 | 26.3% | 10.9% | 0.51 | 68.4% |

**Background:** One could make the argument that since 2012, no other minor league reliever has been more dominant – and consistently dominant – than Alvarez. A third round pick out of Florida Atlantic, Alvarez's minor league track record is pretty impressive – and extensive. In 154.1 innings (spread out over four seasons), the hard-throwing right-hander has fanned 219 of the 655 total batters he's faced, or just about one out of every three batters to dig in against him. He continued that trend last season, his first year in the Oakland organization. Making 31 appearances with Nashville in the PCL, Alvarez posted a 41-to17 strikeout-to-walk ratio in 35.0 innings. And for the second consecutive season he spent some time at the big league level – albeit a disastrous time. In 20.0 innings with Oakland he coughed up seven dingers and 22 earned runs. Ouch.

**Projection**: Mid 90s fastball with some spotty control issues. Alvarez has the talent and ability to develop into a late-inning, shutdown reliever – if his control/command can take a step or two forward. Along with the prodigious strikeout rates he's sporting some big walk totals as well. The work in the big leagues last season should prove to just be one horrific blip on the screen.

**Ceiling:** 1.5-win player
**Risk:** Moderate
**MLB ETA:** Debuted in 2014

## 13. Rangel Ravelo, 1B

**MiLB Rank: N/A**
**Position Rank: N/A**

| Born: 04/24/92 | Age: 24 | Bats: R | **Top CALs:** Chris Parmalee, Yonder Alonso, |
|---|---|---|---|
| Height: 6-2 | Weight: 220 | Throws: R | Jose Osuna, David Cooper, Shane Peterson |

| Season | Age | LVL | PA | 2B | 3B | HR | AVG | OBP | SLG | ISO | BB% | K% | wRC+ |
|---|---|---|---|---|---|---|---|---|---|---|---|---|---|
| 2013 | 21 | A+ | 347 | 27 | 2 | 4 | 0.312 | 0.393 | 0.455 | 0.143 | 11.5% | 13.3% | 138 |
| 2014 | 22 | AA | 551 | 37 | 4 | 11 | 0.309 | 0.386 | 0.473 | 0.164 | 10.2% | 14.0% | 142 |
| 2015 | 23 | AA | 98 | 6 | 1 | 2 | 0.318 | 0.378 | 0.477 | 0.159 | 9.2% | 17.3% | 139 |
| 2015 | 23 | AAA | 112 | 5 | 1 | 1 | 0.277 | 0.324 | 0.376 | 0.099 | 6.3% | 19.6% | 86 |

**Background:** Part of the package Oakland received from the White Sox in exchange for Jeff Samardzija, Ravelo, who was dealt along with Josh Phegley, Chris Bassitt, and Marcus Semien, missed a good portion of the 2015 season as he recovered from wrist surgery. The 2010 sixth round pick didn't make his debut until near the end of June and didn't make it back to full-season action until the second week of July. Ravelo appeared in 22 games for Midland, hitting a robust .318/.378/.477 with six doubles, one triple, and a pair of homeruns. He made another 28 appearances with Nashville, hitting .277/.324/.376. For his career, the 6-foot-2, 220-pound first baseman is sporting a .302/.369/.426 triple-slash line.

**Projection**: Despite a hulking frame and manning a power position, Ravelo's never had the typical homerun-swing; his career high is 11 and he's actually swiped more bags, 24, than slugged homeruns, 21. With that being said, he's hit doubles in bunches, 31 in 101 games in 2013 and 37 in 133 contests two years ago. Solid eye, strong contact skills, but his lack of power will ultimately doom him into a life of bench-dom.

**Ceiling:** 1.5-win player
**Risk:** Moderate
**MLB ETA:** 2016

## 14. Richie Martin, SS

MiLB Rank: N/A
Position Rank: N/A

| Born: 12/22/94 | Age: 21 | Bats: R | Top CALs: Pat Valaika, Jon Del Campo, |
| Height: 6-0 | Weight: 192 | Throws: R | Gift Ngoepe, Tzu-Wei Lin, Anthony Phillips |

| Season | Age | LVL | PA | 2B | 3B | HR | AVG | OBP | SLG | ISO | BB% | K% | wRC+ |
|---|---|---|---|---|---|---|---|---|---|---|---|---|---|
| 2015 | 20 | A- | 226 | 6 | 4 | 2 | 0.237 | 0.353 | 0.342 | 0.105 | 11.1% | 20.8% | 112 |

**Background:** A former 38th round pick of the Mariners coming out of high school, Martin, nonetheless, headed to the west coast three years later as Oakland's first round selection last June, 20th overall. Martin, a three-year starter at the University of Florida, rebounded after a disappointing sophomore campaign, hitting a solid .291/.399/.430 while tying or setting several career highs including doubles (11), triples (4), homeruns (6), stolen bases (20), and a remarkable 20 HBPs. His strikeout-to-walk ratio, a perfect 1-to-1, was also a career best as well. Oakland pushed the polished collegiate shortstop straight to the New York-Penn League and the results were…rather disappointing. In 51 games with Vermont, Martin batted a lowly .237/.351/.342 with just 12 extra-base knocks.

**Projection:** I was a bit tough on Martin during his pre-draft evaluation, writing:

*"Lacking a true standout tool, Martin profiles best as a backup middle infielder option. Outside of his 43-games stretch with Bourne last summer, he's never really dominated at any point over the past three-plus years. Average hit tool, a little bit of quickness, very, very little pop, and a decent idea at the plate."*

I also slapped a second/third round draft grade on the young shortstop – so I'm a bit interested as to what the organization sees in Martin with respect to a long term ceiling. Martin's overall career production leaves a lot to be desired at Florida. His career numbers: 9.5% BB-rate, .092 Isolated Power, and a .376 slugging percentage.

His lone saving grace: his defensive aptitude. But, again, he's likely going to need to grade out as at least an above-average defender to compensate for a swing full of holes. Definite bust material here.

**Ceiling:** 1.0- to 1.5-win player
**Risk:** Moderate
**MLB ETA:** 2018

## 15. Bobby Wahl, RHP

MiLB Rank: N/A
Position Rank: N/A

| Born: 03/21/92 | Age: 24 | Bats: R | Top CALs: Juan Minaya, Tyler Bray, |
| Height: 6-2 | Weight: 210 | Throws: R | Billy Muldowney, Stephen Kohlscheen, Carlos Contreras |

| YEAR | Age | Level | IP | W | L | ERA | FIP | K/9 | BB/9 | K% | BB% | HR/9 | LOB% |
|---|---|---|---|---|---|---|---|---|---|---|---|---|---|
| 2013 | 21 | R | 1.0 | 0 | 0 | 9.00 | 8.01 | 9.00 | 18.00 | 20.0% | 40.0% | 0.00 | 50.0% |
| 2013 | 21 | A- | 20.7 | 0 | 0 | 3.92 | 3.24 | 11.76 | 2.61 | 30.3% | 6.7% | 1.31 | 73.4% |
| 2014 | 22 | A | 42.7 | 0 | 4 | 5.06 | 4.54 | 9.07 | 4.01 | 21.8% | 9.6% | 1.05 | 63.9% |
| 2014 | 22 | A+ | 10.7 | 0 | 0 | 4.22 | 4.31 | 16.03 | 5.06 | 39.6% | 12.5% | 1.69 | 62.5% |
| 2015 | 23 | AA | 32.3 | 2 | 0 | 4.18 | 3.17 | 10.02 | 3.90 | 25.2% | 9.8% | 0.56 | 69.9% |

**Background:** One of the players I listed as a Breakout Prospect in 2015, Wahl had a solid season, though one that was mired by injury and bad luck. A collegiate starter at Ole' Miss, the A's gave Wahl a handful of starts between rookie ball and the Midwest League before realizing his power arsenal was better suited for a relief role. Wahl spent the year finishing games, though not slapped with the closer tag, for Midland. Sandwiched around a lat injury, Wahl tossed 32.1 innings of work while punching out more than a quarter of the batters that stepped into the box against him. His 3.17 FIP was nearly one full run below his actual ERA, the result of a .374 BABIP. For his career, Wahl has averaged 10.6 strikeouts and 4.0 walks per nine innings.

**Projection:** There was little chance Wahl was going to convince the club that he belonged in the rotation – partly because his control took a noticeable step backward during his junior campaign and partly because his power arsenal plays better in a relief role. A lot of Wahl's failure(s) from last season come from a poor game. Have to love the life of a reliever, right? If you ignore his disastrous May 1st outing, his ERA drops from 4.18 to 2.87; he essentially surrendered one-third of his total earned runs on that single day. Oakland tends to operate on the modus operandi of plug-and-chug when it comes to the closer's role, so the former Ole' Miss hurler could get a shot in the next week or two.

**Ceiling:** 1.0- to 1.5-win player
**Risk:** Moderate
**MLB ETA:** Debuted in 2015

## 16. Yairo Munoz, SS

MiLB Rank: N/A

Position Rank: N/A

| Born: 01/23/95 | Age: 21 | Bats: R | Top CALs: Mauricio Dubon, Yamaico Navarro, |
| Height: 6-1 | Weight: 165 | Throws: R | Jorge Polanco, Malquin Canelo, Jonathan Mota |

| Season | Age | LVL | PA | 2B | 3B | HR | AVG | OBP | SLG | ISO | BB% | K% | wRC+ |
|---|---|---|---|---|---|---|---|---|---|---|---|---|---|
| 2014 | 19 | A- | 265 | 17 | 3 | 5 | 0.298 | 0.319 | 0.448 | 0.151 | 2.6% | 15.8% | 122 |
| 2015 | 20 | A | 400 | 14 | 3 | 9 | 0.236 | 0.278 | 0.363 | 0.127 | 5.5% | 15.5% | 84 |
| 2015 | 20 | A+ | 165 | 12 | 0 | 4 | 0.320 | 0.372 | 0.480 | 0.160 | 6.7% | 12.1% | 132 |

**Background:** If you ever wanted to see how BABIP can influence a player's triple-slash line look no further than Munoz's work in 2015. The young shortstop's season is basically a tale of two stories: he batted .236/.278/.363 with an 84 wRC+ and an unlucky .257 BABIP. But his production took a dramatic leap forward upon his promotion to High Class A: .320/.372/.480 with a 132 wRC+ and a lucky .346 BABIP. Munoz's final stat line from the year: .260/.306/.397 with 26 doubles, three triples, 13 homeruns, and 11 stolen bases (in 14 attempts). For his career, he's sporting a .262/.307/.398 triple-slash line with 53 doubles, nine triples, 19 homeruns, and 30 stolen bases (in 42 attempts).

**Projection**: Continuing the brief BABIP lesson, consider the following:

| Level | BB% | K% | ISO | wRC+ | BABIP |
|---|---|---|---|---|---|
| A | 5.50% | 15.50% | 0.127 | 84 | 0.257 |
| A+ | 6.70% | 12.10% | 0.160 | 132 | 0.346 |

Munoz's peripherals are nearly the same, sans his spike in BABIP. The other difference, ISO, is the result of Stockton's home ballpark. And once adjusted for that, his Isolated Power drops to .140. In the end, Munoz is a nice little prospect. Not big league starting potential, but he could be flipped to a team during the organization's next turnaround.

**Ceiling:** 1.0- to 1.5-win player
**Risk:** Moderate
**MLB ETA:** 2017

## 17. Raul Alcantara, RHP

MiLB Rank: N/A

Position Rank: N/A

| Born: 12/04/92 | Age: 23 | Bats: R | Top CALs: Jake Ruckle, Brad Bergesen, |
| Height: 6-3 | Weight: 205 | Throws: R | Orlando Castro, Nathan Culp, Ryan Weber |

| YEAR | Age | Level | IP | W | L | ERA | FIP | K/9 | BB/9 | K% | BB% | HR/9 | LOB% |
|---|---|---|---|---|---|---|---|---|---|---|---|---|---|
| 2013 | 20 | A | 77.3 | 7 | 1 | 2.44 | 2.77 | 6.75 | 0.81 | 18.0% | 2.2% | 0.35 | 72.7% |
| 2013 | 20 | A+ | 79.0 | 5 | 5 | 3.76 | 4.21 | 7.52 | 1.94 | 20.2% | 5.2% | 0.91 | 59.2% |
| 2014 | 21 | AA | 19.7 | 2 | 0 | 2.29 | 3.17 | 4.58 | 2.29 | 13.0% | 6.5% | 0.00 | 79.2% |
| 2015 | 22 | A+ | 48.7 | 0 | 2 | 3.88 | 4.00 | 5.36 | 1.48 | 14.4% | 4.0% | 0.55 | 71.9% |

**Background:** The Dominican-born hurler succumbed to elbow issues – and subsequent Tommy John surgery – just three starts into his 2014 campaign, forcing him to miss the remainder of the year as well as the first several weeks last season as well. Finally healthy, Alcantara was slowly eased back in action; he tossed less than four innings in each of his first three appearances and never lasted longer than four innings in 2015. His overall numbers – he tossed 48.2 innings while fanning 29 and walking eight to go along with a 3.88 ERA – are mired by a couple of poor games. In his first two appearances he surrendered six runs in 4.2 innings and another five runs in a third of an inning against Rancho Cucamonga in early August. Ignoring those games, his season ERA drops to a nice and tidy 2.06. For his career, Alcantara is sporting a sound 304-to-95 strikeout-to-walk ratio in 452.2 innings of work.

**Projection**: Assuming that arsenal bounces back fully from the surgery – and it certainly looks like it did – Alcantara has a decent shot to develop into a backend starting pitcher. His control/command, even in his return, remains an above-average or better skill, which helps to compensate for some lackluster swing-and-miss totals. He tossed fewer than 50 innings last season, so his total will likely be capped around 90- to 110-innings in 2016.

**Ceiling:** 1.0- to 1.5-win player
**Risk:** Moderate
**MLB ETA:** 2017

## 18. J.B. Wendelken, LHP

MiLB Rank: N/A
Position Rank: N/A

| Born: 03/24/93 | Age: 23 | Bats: R | Top CALs: Steve Johnson, Dylan Unsworth, |
| Height: 6-0 | Weight: 235 | Throws: R | Johnny Cueto, Tim Barry, Todd Redmond |

| YEAR | Age | Level | IP | W | L | ERA | FIP | K/9 | BB/9 | K% | BB% | HR/9 | LOB% |
|---|---|---|---|---|---|---|---|---|---|---|---|---|---|
| 2013 | 20 | A | 69.7 | 2 | 1 | 3.23 | 3.48 | 8.01 | 2.71 | 21.0% | 7.1% | 0.52 | 77.3% |
| 2013 | 20 | A+ | 9.3 | 0 | 1 | 4.82 | 3.56 | 15.43 | 6.75 | 33.3% | 14.6% | 0.96 | 73.9% |
| 2014 | 21 | A+ | 145.7 | 7 | 10 | 5.25 | 3.87 | 7.97 | 2.04 | 19.9% | 5.1% | 0.93 | 57.6% |
| 2015 | 22 | AA | 43.0 | 6 | 2 | 2.72 | 2.68 | 11.72 | 2.30 | 31.8% | 6.3% | 0.84 | 79.7% |
| 2015 | 22 | AAA | 16.0 | 0 | 0 | 4.50 | 4.09 | 7.31 | 2.81 | 19.1% | 7.4% | 1.13 | 49.4% |

**Background:** Acquired along with fourth rounder Zack Erwin in exchange for third baseman Brett Lawrie. I listed Wendelken among the Top 25 Breakout Prospects for 2015. And you know what? He did just that, though the Sox pushed him into a fulltime relief role last season. Splitting his season between the Southern and International Leagues, he posted a 69-to-16 strikeout-to-walk ratio and a 2.72 ERA in 59 IP.

**Projection:** Here's what I wrote in last year's book:

> "Wendelken, a former 13th round pick by Boston in 2012, suffered from quite a bit of bad luck last season – a .355 BABIP and a 57.6% strand rate chief among them. He is definitely not a lock to even sniff the big leagues, but there's some potential value here. [He's a] fringy starting pitcher/middle reliever."

While he can be a solid middle relief arm, I do wonder if the A's, a progressively thinking organization (obviously), will push him back into the rotation. At the very worst, he's a J.P. Howell clone.

**Ceiling:** 1.0- to 1.5-win player
**Risk:** Moderate
**MLB ETA:** 2016

## 19. Chris Kohler, LHP

MiLB Rank: N/A
Position Rank: N/A

| Born: 05/04/95 | Age: 21 | Bats: L | Top CALs: Robert Hernandez, Joshua Poytress, |
| Height: 6-3 | Weight: 210 | Throws: L | Daniel Oliver, Kyle Rogers, David Baker |

| YEAR | Age | Level | IP | W | L | ERA | FIP | K/9 | BB/9 | K% | BB% | HR/9 | LOB% |
|---|---|---|---|---|---|---|---|---|---|---|---|---|---|
| 2013 | 18 | R | 22.7 | 1 | 2 | 2.78 | 2.51 | 12.71 | 3.57 | 33.0% | 9.3% | 0.00 | 65.5% |
| 2015 | 20 | A- | 38.7 | 2 | 3 | 4.66 | 3.52 | 8.61 | 2.33 | 22.2% | 6.0% | 0.47 | 65.8% |

**Background:** Making his first meaningful appearance in nearly two years, the once promising southpaw quickly made up for lost time. In his second start of 2015, Kohler dazzled the Lowell Spinners for five innings, allowing a pair of hits while fanning seven and walking just one. Five starts later he made it look easy against the Auburn Doubledays: 5 IP, 3 H, 7 K, and 1 BB. Overall, he finished his comeback season with a 3.52 FIP, 37 punch outs, and 10 walks in 38.2 innings of work. For his career, he's tossed 61.1 innings while fanning 26.1% and walking just 7.2% of the batters he's faced.

**Projection:** He's a very promising, if not risky prospect. Add in the fact that he's thrown barely 60 innings in his professional career – albeit 60 really good innings – and Kohler could spin off in any direction. But here's what we know: When he's healthy Kohler will punch out an above-average number of hitters, especially for a southpaw, and showcase solid average control. He could be a solid backend starter, maybe more.

**Ceiling:** 1.5-win player
**Risk:** High
**MLB ETA:** 2018

## 20. Dakota Chalmers, RHP

MiLB Rank: N/A
Position Rank: N/A

| Born: 10/08/96 | Age: 19 | Bats: R | Top CALs: Christian Flecha, Matthew Swilley, |
| Height: 6-3 | Weight: 170 | Throws: R | Andres Heredia, Luis Gonzalez, Jose Torres |

| YEAR | Age | Level | IP | W | L | ERA | FIP | K/9 | BB/9 | K% | BB% | HR/9 | LOB% |
|---|---|---|---|---|---|---|---|---|---|---|---|---|---|
| 2015 | 18 | R | 20.3 | 0 | 1 | 2.66 | 4.70 | 7.97 | 7.52 | 19.6% | 18.5% | 0.00 | 72.7% |

**Background:** A huge over slot signing out of the third round last June. Chalmers, a 6-foot-3, 170-pound right-hander, signed for a cool $1.2 million deal. Chalmers began his pro career in the Arizona Summer League with mixed results: he posted a 2.66 ERA, but a near 1-to-1 strikeout-to-walk ratio.

**Projection**: It's kind of impressive that Chalmers coughed up 17 free passes in 20.1 innings of work and only surrendered just six earned runs. And in his 11 appearances, he walked at least one in 10 of those. Obviously, the sample size is incredibly limited, but it's safe to say he might have some control issues.

**Ceiling**: Too Soon to Tell
**Risk**: N/A
**MLB ETA**: N/A

## 21. Daniel Gossett, RHP

**MiLB Rank: N/A**
**Position Rank: N/A**

| Born: 11/13/92 | Age: 21 | Bats: R | **Top CALs:** Michael Jefferson, Pedro Encarnacion, Ryan Kelly, Brett Lorin, Cole Mccurry |
| Height: 6-2 | Weight: 185 | Throws: R | |

| YEAR | Age | Level | IP | W | L | ERA | FIP | K/9 | BB/9 | K% | BB% | HR/9 | LOB% |
|---|---|---|---|---|---|---|---|---|---|---|---|---|---|
| 2014 | 21 | A- | 24.0 | 1 | 0 | 2.25 | 2.02 | 9.38 | 0.38 | 28.4% | 1.1% | 0.38 | 70.5% |
| 2015 | 22 | A | 144.7 | 5 | 13 | 4.73 | 4.49 | 6.97 | 3.24 | 17.8% | 8.3% | 1.00 | 62.7% |

**Background:** A second round pick out of Clemson two years ago, Gossett had a stellar debut in the New York-Penn League; he posted an absurd 25-to-1 strikeout-to-walk ratio in 24.0 innings of work. Oakland pushed the right-hander up to Beloit for the entire 2015 season, and his overall numbers leave a lot to be desired. In 144.2 innings Gossett fanned 112, walked 52, and posted a sub-mediocre 4.73 ERA. But let's delve into the numbers a bit more, shall we? Gossett got off to a *terrible* start to open up 2015; in his first 69.1 innings he posted a 5.84 ERA with a 61-to-34 strikeout-to-walk ratio. But his numbers over his final 13 starts are far more impressive: 75.1 IP, 51 punch outs, 18 walks, and a 3.70 ERA.

**Projection**: Gossett was never, ever going to even come close to replicating his fantastic debut, but he's not nearly as bad as the overall numbers from 2015 suggest either. Rather, he's somewhere in between. Prior to the draft I listed Gossett as a "potential big league #4 – an innings eater who will miss some bats, limit some walks, and give up the occasional homerun." And he still profiles as such. Average control, average punch out rates, slightly better than average groundball rates.

**Ceiling**: 1.0- to 1.5-win player
**Risk**: Moderate to High
**MLB ETA**: 2017

## 22. Mikey White, SS

**MiLB Rank: N/A**
**Position Rank: N/A**

| Born: 09/03/93 | Age: 22 | Bats: R | **Top CALs:** Rony Peralta, Pedro Vasquez, Taylor Mundein, David Narodowski, Chan Moon |
| Height: 6-1 | Weight: 185 | Throws: R | |

| Season | Age | LVL | PA | 2B | 3B | HR | AVG | OBP | SLG | ISO | BB% | K% | wRC+ |
|---|---|---|---|---|---|---|---|---|---|---|---|---|---|
| 2015 | 21 | A- | 131 | 10 | 0 | 2 | 0.315 | 0.405 | 0.459 | 0.144 | 10.7% | 22.1% | 153 |
| 2015 | 21 | A | 145 | 5 | 0 | 1 | 0.200 | 0.283 | 0.262 | 0.062 | 6.9% | 20.7% | 65 |

**Background:** Oakland doubled down on collegiate shortstops to open up the 2015 draft. First taking Florida Gator Richie Martin with the 20th overall pick and then grabbing White, the 63rd pick, out of the University of Alabama in the second round. Like Martin, White was a three-year mainstay during his career, sporting a .308/.403/.448 triple-slash line in 184 games. His final campaign at school, .339/.444/.537, was by and away his top offensive showing. And, again, just like Marin, White opened his career up in the New York-Penn League, but fared much better, hitting .315/.405/.459 with 10 doubles and two homeruns in 29 games. Oakland bumped him up to Beloit for another 35 games where he…didn't fare as well. He batted .200/.283/.262.

**Projection**: In terms of offensive upside, it's White who is far more valuable. He flashes gap-to-gap power, a tiny amount of speed, and an average eye at the plate – all of which carried over in his showing in the NYPL. On the defensive side, Martin gets the nod. Another potential backup middle infielder.

**Ceiling**: 1.0- to 1.5-win player
**Risk**: Moderate to High
**MLB ETA**: 2017

## 23. Brett Graves, RHP

| Born: 01/30/93 | Age: 23 | Bats: R | **Top CALs:** Michael Jefferson, Blake Hassebrock, Sugar Ray Marimon, Pedro Encarnacion, Justin Garcia |
| Height: 6-1 | Weight: 170 | Throws: R | |

| YEAR | Age | Level | IP | W | L | ERA | FIP | K/9 | BB/9 | K% | BB% | HR/9 | LOB% |
|---|---|---|---|---|---|---|---|---|---|---|---|---|---|
| 2014 | 21 | R | 1.0 | 0 | 0 | 0.00 | 5.03 | 9.00 | 9.00 | 25.0% | 25.0% | 0.00 | 100.0% |
| 2014 | 21 | A- | 21.0 | 3 | 2 | 6.86 | 3.35 | 7.71 | 2.57 | 19.2% | 6.4% | 0.43 | 43.9% |
| 2015 | 22 | A | 142.7 | 12 | 8 | 5.36 | 4.50 | 5.74 | 2.78 | 14.5% | 7.0% | 0.95 | 64.6% |

**Background:** The University of Mississippi product hasn't lived up to the lofty expectations that come with being a polished collegiate arm taken in the early rounds of draft. Graves, a 2014 third round selection, had a solid, far from spectacular debut two years ago, posting a 19-to-7 strikeout-to-walk ratio. And while his control was a shining part of his work in the Midwest League last season, every other thing about him was rather dull. He tossed 142.2 innings while fanning just 5.7 batters per nine innings and posting equally unsightly 5.36 ERA and 4.50 FIP. For what it's worth, those peripherals last season are nearly identical to his career marks with Mizzou: 5.29 K/9 and 2.94 BB/9.

**Projection**: Basically the anti-Daniel Mengden. Graves has always had a lively arm, but he's never, ever missed a sort of bats to make him a valuable prospect. Here's what I wrote two years ago:

> *"Where are the strikeouts? While his K-rate has bounced back nicely from a career worst 4.06 K/9 last season, he still hasn't missed even an average amount of bats. The control is obviously an above-average to plus skill, but at some point he's going to need to miss bats. Period.*
>
> *Backend starting option, maybe a decent fourth[starter] as things stand right now. And per the usual, he could always get pushed into a late-inning role down the line."*

While he gets a solid amount of action on the ground, it's clearly time to move Graves to the pen a la Bobby Wahl. If/when that happens he could move quick. Graves is a potential solid middle relief option.

**Ceiling:** 1.0-win player
**Risk:** Moderate
**MLB ETA:** 2017

## 24. B.J. Boyd, OF

| Born: 07/16/93 | Age: 22 | Bats: L | **Top CALs:** Corey Adamson, Henry Ramos, Mallex Smith, Estarlin Martinez, Mitch Dening |
| Height: 5-11 | Weight: 230 | Throws: R | |

| Season | Age | LVL | PA | 2B | 3B | HR | AVG | OBP | SLG | ISO | BB% | K% | wRC+ |
|---|---|---|---|---|---|---|---|---|---|---|---|---|---|
| 2013 | 19 | A- | 300 | 13 | 2 | 8 | 0.285 | 0.375 | 0.442 | 0.158 | 11.7% | 22.0% | 149 |
| 2014 | 20 | A | 521 | 15 | 5 | 6 | 0.226 | 0.300 | 0.319 | 0.093 | 9.2% | 18.0% | 80 |
| 2015 | 21 | A+ | 511 | 20 | 8 | 5 | 0.277 | 0.344 | 0.389 | 0.111 | 8.0% | 17.4% | 103 |

**Background:** A short-stocky outfielder out of Palo Alto High School, Boyd entered the 2015 season coming off of his first stumble in professional baseball. The former fourth round pick has a strong showing in the Arizona Summer League in 2012, hitting a robust .301/.401/.434 with plenty of extra-base firepower and sneaky speed on the base paths. He was able to carry that momentum – and then some – into the New York-Penn League a year later: he slugged .285/.375/.442 while tying the Phillies' Zachary Green for best offensive production (149 wRC+) among all teenage bats in the league. And then the stumble happened. The organization pushed Boyd up to full season ball in 2014 and 5-foot-11, 230-pounder never got his feet under him. He batted .226/.300/.319 with 15 doubles, five triples, six homeruns, 15 stolen bases, and a career low 80 wRC+. Undeterred, however, Boyd convinced the club to push him up to Stockton and his overall production rebounded nicely: .2747/.344/.389 with a 103 wRC+.

**Projection**: It was a very typical Boyd-type year – he walked an average amount of time, flashed gap-to-gap pop, swiped some bags, and hit for a decent average. He's a very nice fourth outfield prospect; he does a lot of things, some of them well, but no true standout tool. He has to recapture his 2013 form against southpaws, though.

**Ceiling:** 1.0-win player
**Risk:** Moderate to High
**MLB ETA:** 2017

## 25. Sam Bragg, RHP

MiLB Rank: N/A

Position Rank: N/A

| Born: 03/23/93 | Age: 23 | Bats: R | Top CALs: Josh Taylor, Dan Griffin, |
| Height: 6-2 | Weight: 190 | Throws: R | Yao-Lin Wang, Henry Sosa, Clint Dempster |

| YEAR | Age | Level | IP | W | L | ERA | FIP | K/9 | BB/9 | K% | BB% | HR/9 | LOB% |
|------|-----|-------|-----|---|---|------|------|-------|------|-------|-------|------|--------|
| 2013 | 20 | R | 7.3 | 1 | 0 | 0.00 | 1.01 | 17.18 | 2.45 | 51.9% | 7.4% | 0.00 | 100.0% |
| 2013 | 20 | A- | 19.7 | 0 | 2 | 1.83 | 3.10 | 9.15 | 4.12 | 24.1% | 10.8% | 0.46 | 80.5% |
| 2013 | 20 | A | 2.0 | 0 | 0 | 0.00 | 0.34 | 13.50 | 0.00 | 50.0% | 0.0% | 0.00 | 100.0% |
| 2014 | 21 | A | 75.3 | 4 | 0 | 3.23 | 3.74 | 8.12 | 3.11 | 21.8% | 8.3% | 0.60 | 74.2% |
| 2015 | 22 | A+ | 74.0 | 7 | 2 | 3.65 | 3.75 | 11.19 | 2.80 | 30.1% | 7.5% | 0.97 | 66.0% |

**Background:** Basically, the anti-Brendan McCurry with similar dominating results. Bragg, a hard-throwing right-hander out of Georgia Perimeter College, has been absolutely dominating during his three-year professional career. A former 18th round pick in 2013, Bragg made stops at three different levels during his pro debut, fanning 14 in 7.2 innings in the Arizona Summer League, punching 20 in 19.2 innings with Vermont, and finally a quick two-inning stint in the Midwest League. He spent the entire 2014 season back in the Midwest League working as a long reliever for Beloit while posting some strong peripherals. He did the same thing with Stockton in 2015 – except with even better results: 11.2 K/9 and 2.8 BB/9 in 74.0 innings.

**Projection**: A potential dominating backend reliever, maybe even filling out the set and/or closer's role in Oakland in a couple years. Elite ability to miss bats with a solid feel for the strike zone. Seems like a winning combination to me…

**Ceiling:** 1.0- to 1.5-win player
**Risk:** Moderate to High
**MLB ETA:** 2017

## Barely Missed:

- **Zack Erwin, LHP** – Not overpowering, Erwin never missed an inordinate amount of bats during his time with Clemson. He was also a bit homer-prone over the past two seasons, surrendering 11 in about 180.0 innings of work. His control/command took a tremendous leap forward last season, something that carried over into pro ball. He looks like a fringy #5 who will likely settle in as a middle relief arm.

- **Sandber Pimentel, 1B** – Sturdy-framed 6-foot-3, 220-pound first baseman flashed some power in the Midwest League as a 20-year-old, slugging 17 doubles and 13 homeruns. Questionable hit tool, but Pimenetel's never failed to top 100 wRC+ in any of his four professional seasons.

- **Joel Seddon, RHP** – Former Gamecock closer spent the year splitting time between Stockton's bullpen and rotation as he's slowly making the transition into a full time starter. Before having his innings throttled, Seddon reeled off 13 consecutive starts where he posted a 56-to-12 strikeout-to-walk ratio to go along with a 3.54 ERA.

- **Max Muncy, 1B** – Last season was a bit of a disappointment for the former fifth round pick out of Baylor – despite getting an extended look in the big leagues for the first time in his career. Coming off of two successful stints in Class AA, Muncy's production hovered around the average mark in the PCL, and he looked overmatched in 45 games with Oakland (.206/.268/.392).

## *Bird Doggin' It – Additional Prospects to Keep an Eye in 2016*

| Player | Age | POS | Notes |
|---|---|---|---|
| Iolana Akau | 20 | C | A late, late round pick in 2013 out of a Hawaii high school, the sparsely-used backstop made the most of his career high 168 trips to the plate, hitting .252/.339/.367 as a teenager in the Midwest League. |
| Trevor Bayless | 24 | RHP | Taken in the 22nd round in 2013, Bayless made stops at three different levels last season: Low Class A, High Class, and Class AA. He posted a respectable 58-to-25 strikeout-to-walk ratio. |
| Skye Bolt | 22 | OF | Donned with one of the more badass names in baseball, Bolt was never able to recapture the superstar status he displayed as a true freshman at UNC. Positional versatility and a solid eye. |
| Ben Bracewell | 25 | RHP | Signed out of the Indy Leagues in 2014, Bracewell made the successful jump from the Arizona Summer League to High Class A. Working exclusively in relief he averaged 8.7 K/9 and just 1.9 BB/9. |
| Jaycob Brugman | 24 | OF | There might be enough talent to carve out a big league role as a backup outfielder. No true standout tool, however. |
| Dylan Covey | 24 | RHP | Had his best professional season to date in 2015: 140.1 IP, 100 K, and 43 BB. However, as a 23-year-old former collegiate arm taken relatively early, it was par for the course. |
| Bowdien Derby | 22 | LHP | A three-year stalwart at the University of San Diego, the club took the little lefty with the 188th overall pick in 2015. He doesn't have the size to start, but could develop into a useful relief arm. |
| Ryan Dull | 26 | RHP | Smallish right-hander showed an average-ish 90 mph heater in his 17-game stint with Oakland last season. Solid control and a standard four-pitch mix could keep him as a useful middle relief arm. |
| Mike Fagan | 24 | LHP | Another personal favorite of mine, the former Ivy League arm posed a 52-to-20 strikeout-to-walk ratio between Vermont and Beloit. There's some upside as a decent southpaw out of the pen, but he needs to rein in his propensity for the walk. Sleeper with some solid strikeout ability. |
| James Harris | 22 | OF | Former supplemental first round pick all the way back in 2011, Harris finally topped the 100 wRC+ mark for the first time in his five-year career. |
| Ryon Healy | 24 | 1B/3B | Passed the most important test along the minor league ladder: Class AA. Healy batted a respectable .302/.339/.426. Not enough power for a corner infield position or enough patience to push him past fringe status. |
| Chris Jensen | 25 | RHP | Former Rockies' prospect hasn't been able to regain his breakout form from 2013 when he average 8.0 strikeouts and 2.3 walks per nine innings. |
| Aaron Kurcz | 25 | RHP | Acquired in early July from the Braves in exchange for $167,000 in international bonus money. Kurcz has always missed a ton of bats while displaying some questionable control. He could be a useful late-inning setup man if everything breaks the right way. |
| Carlos Navas | 23 | RHP | Dominated out of the Beloit pen last season. Of course, that's what you would expect out of a 22-year-old relief specialist in Low Class A. |
| John Nogowski | 23 | 1B | He'd be a fringy backup outfielder is everything broke just the right way. It'd be a long shot, sure, but it could happen. The fact that he's doomed to first base while sporting a career .358 SLG only complicates things. |
| J.P. Sportman | 24 | OF | A 27th round pick out of Central Connecticut State University two years ago, Sportman has done nothing but hit in limited action in the minors, batting .309/.365/.409 in rookie ball and then .292/.335/.435 in High Class A. He's yet to top 258 PA in a season though. |
| Jose Torres | 22 | LHP | Blew away the Midwest League competition out of the pen last season, Torres, who averaged 9.8 punch outs and 2.8 free passes per nine innings, could be a big time sleeper pick heading into 2016. |
| Joey Wendle | 26 | 2B | While his two triple-slash lines since 2014 look vastly different (.253/.311/.414 vs. .289/.323/.442), his overall production is nearly identical (98 wRC+ vs. 101 wRC+) A lesson in context. |

**State of the Franchise:** Former Phillies General Manager Ruben Amaro Jr. was widely criticized over his final few years with the organization. And rightly so. Handing out a foolish nine-figure deal to a bad-bodied declining slugger like Ryan Howard will do that to you. But Amaro will likely never be remembered as the pilot of a potentially franchise-altering deal with the Rangers.

Just months before he would be dismissed Amaro engineered a eight-player deal at the deadline, agreeing to send veteran ace Cole Hamels and hard-throwing reliever Jake Diekman to the Rangers for a plethora of top-tier talent: backstop Jorge Alfaro, right-hander Jake Thompson, outfielder Nick Williams, big league ready starter Alec Asher, Jerad Eickhoff, and the shell of former mid-rotation arm Matt Harrison.

Amaro would also pull off another rather large deal the same day as he shipped center fielder Ben Revere to the Blue Jays for Alberto Tirado and Jimmy Cordero.

And with just those two deals – along with another strong draft class – Amaro was able to thrust the Phillies into having one of the better systems in baseball.

There's plenty of top tier talent with the likes of J.P. Crawford, Nick Williams, Cornelius Randolph, the club's most recent first round pick, the enigmatic Mark Appel, who was acquired by new GM Matt Klentak, Jake Thompson, and Jorge Alfaro.

The system also has more than a few players that could carve out nice enough big league careers if everything breaks the right way as well: Carlos Tocci, who finally was able to overcome the club's mishandling, pinpoint control artist Thomas Eshelman (who was also acquired along with Appel, Vincent Velasquez, and Harold Arauz in the Ken Giles deal this offseason), oft-injured shortstop-turned-center-fielder Roman Quinn, backstop Andrew Knapp, and big lefty Matt Imhof.

One name to watch in 2016: first baseman Rhys Hoskins.

| Rank | Name | POS |
|------|------|-----|
| 1 | J.P. Crawford | SS |
| 2 | Nick Williams | LF/CF |
| 3 | Cornelius Randolph | LF |
| 4 | Mark Appel | RHP |
| 5 | Jake Thompson | RHP |
| 6 | Jorge Alfaro | C |
| 7 | Carlos Tocci | CF |
| 8 | Thomas Eshelman | RHP |
| 9 | Roman Quinn | CF |
| 10 | Andrew Knapp | C |
| 11 | Matt Imhof | LHP |
| 12 | Dylan Cozens | LF/RF |
| 13 | Ricardo Pinto | RHP |
| 14 | Scott Kingery | 2B |
| 15 | Rhys Hoskins | 1B |
| 16 | Ben Lively | RHP |
| 17 | Alec Asher | RHP |
| 18 | Darnell Sweeney | IF/OF |
| 19 | Albert Tirado | RHP |
| 20 | Adonis Medina | RHP |
| 21 | Zach Eflin | RHP |
| 22 | Nick Pivetta | RHP |
| 23 | Jesmuel Valentin | IF/OF |
| 24 | Tom Windle | LHP |
| 25 | Franklyn Kilome | RHP |

**Review of the 2015 Draft:** After briefly breaking the team's mantra of taking high ceiling prep players in the first round two years ago, Amaro and Co. got the organization back on track by grabbing toolsy left fielder Cornelius Randolph with the 10th overall pick. Randolph had an impressive debut in the Gulf Coast League, slugging .302/.425/.442 with 15 doubles, three triples, one homeruns, and six stolen bases. He was originally drafted as a shortstop, and if his power doesn't blossom into 15- to 20-homerun territory the club might think about moving him to second or third bases.

Former University of Arizona second baseman Scott Kingery could be a lite version of Jason Kipnis. And third round pick, prep third baseman Lucas Williams, had a solid debut, though he didn't flash a whole lot of power.

## 1. J.P. Crawford, SS

MiLB Rank: #8
Position Rank: #1

| Born: 01/11/95 | Age: 21 | Bats: L | **Top CALs:** Tyler Pastornicky, Jorge Polanco, Daniel Robertson, Gavin Cecchini, Jose Pirela |
|---|---|---|---|
| Height: 6-2 | Weight: 180 | Throws: R | |

| Season | Age | LVL | PA | 2B | 3B | HR | AVG | OBP | SLG | ISO | BB% | K% | wRC+ |
|---|---|---|---|---|---|---|---|---|---|---|---|---|---|
| 2013 | 18 | R | 168 | 8 | 3 | 1 | 0.345 | 0.443 | 0.465 | 0.120 | 14.9% | 14.9% | 171 |
| 2014 | 19 | A | 267 | 16 | 0 | 3 | 0.295 | 0.398 | 0.405 | 0.110 | 13.9% | 13.9% | 132 |
| 2014 | 19 | A+ | 271 | 7 | 0 | 8 | 0.275 | 0.352 | 0.407 | 0.131 | 10.3% | 13.7% | 119 |
| 2015 | 20 | A+ | 95 | 1 | 0 | 1 | 0.392 | 0.489 | 0.443 | 0.051 | 14.7% | 9.5% | 192 |
| 2015 | 20 | AA | 405 | 21 | 7 | 5 | 0.265 | 0.354 | 0.407 | 0.142 | 12.1% | 11.1% | 121 |

**Background:** If you think about the sheer value of high quality prospects to come out of the first round in the 2013 draft – Crawford, Mark Appel, Jon Gray, Kris Bryant, Clint Frazier, Colin Moran, Austin Meadows, Hunter Harvey, Billy McKinney, Rob Kaminsky, Aaron Judge, Sean Manaea, and Aaron Blair among others – one could make the argument, in convincing fashion, that the Phillies' shortstop of the future is the second best selection behind Bryant. Crawford, the 16th overall pick that year, has been one of the class' fast-moving prep players. He made two stops during his pro debut, including a 14-game stint in the South Atlantic League at the ripe age of 18. He would then split the next season between Lakewood and Clearwater, hitting an aggregate .285/.375/.406 with 23 doubles, 11 homeruns, and 24 stolen bases. And Philadelphia had the young shortstop begin last season back in the Florida State League where he torched the under-matched and outgunned pitching to the tune of .392/.489/.443 in 21 games, though he managed just two extra-base hits during that time. He got promoted to the Eastern League at the end of May, and after a bit of an adjustment period Crawford batted .270/.345/.433 over his final 45 contests.

**Projection:** Here's a bit of perspective for you: Crawford was the only qualified 20-year-old hitter in the Eastern and one of just three in any Class AA level. But here's something more impressive, a list of players younger than 21-years-old in Class to post a walk rate above 12% since 2006:

- 2015: J.P. Crawford, 12.1%
- 2012: Jon Singleton, 15.9%
- 2011: Wil Myers, 12.5%
- 2008: Travis Snider, 12.3%
- 2007: Colby Rasmus, 12.6%

That's it; five players in the last eight seasons. Ready to be impressed again? Good. Here's a list ranking the players by their strikeout rate, lowest to highest:

1. J.P. Crawford, 11.1%
2. Colby Rasmus, 19.4%
3. Wil Myers, 20.9%
4. Jon Singleton, 23.6%
5. Travis Snider, 27.4%

Crawford has a well-rounded offensive toolkit: above-average speed, something in the range of 25 to 30 stolen bases, solid average power with 10-to 12-homeruns and 30+ doubles in his future, a walk rate that should settle in between 9.0% and 10.5%, with a hit tool capable of posting perennial .300 averages.

**Ceiling:** 4.0- to 4.5-win player
**Risk:** Moderate
**MLB ETA:** 2016

## 2. Nick Williams, LF/CF

MiLB Rank: #28
Position Rank: #8

| Born: 09/08/93 | Age: 22 | Bats: L | **Top CALs:** Julio Morban, Aaron Cunningham, Steven Moya, Domingo Santana, Jay Bruce |
|---|---|---|---|
| Height: 6-3 | Weight: 195 | Throws: L | |

| Season | Age | LVL | PA | 2B | 3B | HR | AVG | OBP | SLG | ISO | BB% | K% | wRC+ |
|---|---|---|---|---|---|---|---|---|---|---|---|---|---|
| 2013 | 19 | A | 404 | 19 | 12 | 17 | 0.293 | 0.337 | 0.543 | 0.250 | 3.7% | 27.2% | 148 |
| 2014 | 20 | A+ | 408 | 28 | 4 | 13 | 0.292 | 0.343 | 0.491 | 0.199 | 4.7% | 28.7% | 133 |
| 2015 | 21 | AA | 415 | 21 | 4 | 13 | 0.299 | 0.357 | 0.479 | 0.180 | 7.7% | 18.6% | 133 |
| 2015 | 21 | AA | 100 | 5 | 2 | 4 | 0.320 | 0.340 | 0.536 | 0.216 | 3.0% | 20.0% | 151 |

**Background:** Part of the massive haul package received from the Rangers in exchange for lefties Cole Hamels and Jake Diekman, Williams was acquired along with Jorge Alfaro, Jake Thompson, Alec Asher, Jerad Eickhoff, and the corpse of once promising big leaguer Matt Harrison. Taken in the latter part of the second in

2012, tools-laden outfielder put together his finest season to date last year; he slugged .299/.357/.479 in 97 games in the Texas organization and upped the ante – and likely the city's expectations – by raising that mark to a scorching .320/.340/.536 in 22 games with Reading. Overall, he finished the year with a combined .303/.354/.491 triple-slash line, adding 26 doubles, six triples, 17 homeruns, and 13 stolen bases. His overall production topped the league average mark by 37%, tying Cincinnati's Jesse Winker for the second best showing among all Class AA players under the age of 22.

Originally part of Texas' heralded 2012 draft class, the one that saw the additions of Lewis Brinson, Joey Gallo, new Phillies MiLB'er Alec Asher, Keone Kela as well as some prep player out of Alabama by the name of Jameis Winston; Williams has been a steady riser during his four year professional career. After an impressive debut in the Arizona Summer League, Williams handled the Sally with aplomb, hitting .293/.337/.534 as a 19-year-old. He followed that up with another impressive stint in High Class A (.292/.343/.491) while make the rare (and brief) appearance in Class AA before legal drinking age.

For his career, the well-built center fielder out of Ball High School, home to former big league right-hander Brandon Backe, Williams is sporting a solid .296/.346/.489 line with 84 doubles, 30 triples, 49 homeruns, and 42 stolen bases.

**Projection**: Williams can certainly stuff a stat sheet with the best of them. Since entering pro ball in 2013, he's finished a season with at least than 19 doubles, six triples, 13 homeruns, and six stolen bases in any of his campaigns – all the while facing significantly older pitching. But the 2015 season represented such developmental growth in the supremely talented center fielder.

Cursed with a bit of a swing-from-the-heels approach during his first couple seasons, Williams shaved off some significant strikeout numbers from his previous career norms; between 2012 and 2014 his K-rate was a smidgeon under 27%, right on the border of red flag territory. And during the same stretch he walked in just 4.8% of plate appearances. Last season, however, he fanned just 18.8% of the time while posting a career best 6.8% walk rate. He's evolving into a more complete player. I'm not certain that he'll repeat those numbers moving forward, but at the bare minimum he's a solid league-average starter with a much high upside.

**Ceiling**: 3.5-win player
**Risk**: Moderate
**MLB ETA**: 2016

# 3. Cornelius Randolph, LF

**MiLB Rank: #40**
**Position Rank: N/A**

| Born: 06/02/97 | Age: 19 | Bats: L | Top CALs: Aaron Hicks, Ramon Flores, |
| Height: 5-11 | Weight: 205 | Throws: R | Andrew Lambo, Trent Clark, Royce Consigli |

| Season | Age | LVL | PA | 2B | 3B | HR | AVG | OBP | SLG | ISO | BB% | K% | wRC+ |
|--------|-----|-----|----|----|----|----|-----|-----|-----|-----|-----|-----|------|
| 2015 | 18 | R | 212 | 15 | 3 | 1 | 0.302 | 0.425 | 0.442 | 0.140 | 15.1% | 15.1% | 163 |

**Background:** After a slight detour from the club's typical draft strategy two years ago Philadelphia once again drafted a prepster with their first selection last June. (Note; Of their last 16 first rounders – including supplemental picks – they grabbed a high school player 14 times.) Randolph had one helluva showing in the Gulf Coast League during his debut, hitting a robust .302/.425/.442 with 15 2B, 3 3B, one HR, and six SB.

**Projection**: So, so very promising. Perhaps one of the best statistics to note from Randolph's debut season: he posted a 32-to-32 strikeout-to-walk ratio in 212 plate appearances. Randolph flashed some speed, solid-average or better power, topped the GCL average production by 63%, walked a tremendous amount of time, and showed a promising hit tool. The lone red flag: the lefty-swinging outfielder showed some platoon concerns, batting .250/.358/.337 against LHP, not terrible production but something to note.

**Ceiling**: Too Soon to Tell
**Risk**: N/A
**MLB ETA**: N/A

# 4. Mark Appel, RHP

| Born: 07/15/91 | Age: 24 | Bats: R | Top CALs: Rob Rasmussen, Camilo Vazquez, |
|---|---|---|---|
| Height: 6-5 | Weight: 220 | Throws: R | Adam Bright, Robert Rohrbaugh, Sam LeCure |

| YEAR | Age | Level | IP | W | L | ERA | FIP | K/9 | BB/9 | K% | BB% | HR/9 | LOB% |
|---|---|---|---|---|---|---|---|---|---|---|---|---|---|
| 2013 | 21 | A- | 5.0 | 0 | 0 | 3.60 | 0.70 | 10.80 | 0.00 | 30.0% | 0.0% | 0.00 | 66.7% |
| 2013 | 21 | A | 33.0 | 3 | 1 | 3.82 | 3.40 | 7.36 | 2.45 | 19.3% | 6.4% | 0.55 | 64.5% |
| 2014 | 22 | A+ | 44.3 | 2 | 5 | 9.74 | 5.32 | 8.12 | 2.23 | 18.4% | 5.1% | 1.83 | 47.0% |
| 2014 | 22 | AA | 39.0 | 1 | 2 | 3.69 | 2.99 | 8.77 | 3.00 | 23.0% | 7.9% | 0.46 | 69.9% |
| 2015 | 23 | AA | 63.3 | 5 | 1 | 4.26 | 4.37 | 6.96 | 3.27 | 17.8% | 8.4% | 0.99 | 70.9% |
| 2015 | 23 | AAA | 68.3 | 5 | 2 | 4.48 | 4.36 | 8.03 | 3.69 | 20.3% | 9.3% | 0.79 | 66.2% |

**Background:** The twice Top 10 draft pick out of Stanford put a disastrous – or should I say, a widely *perceived* disastrous – 2014 season behind him. In other words, the out-of-whack numbers that plagued him two seasons ago all came roaring back to earth. The .414 BABIP with Lancaster hovered a touch above .300 and his ungodly homerun rate, 1.83 HR/9, also with Lancaster (go figure), plummeted as well. And now for the bad news, or at least some unfavorable news: his production was not bad, not great, just merely...passable. The 6-foot-5, 220-pound right-hander opened the year back with Corpus Christi where he would post nearly identical marks in ERA and FIP (4.26 vs. 4.37) and his peripherals, 6.96 K/9 and 3.27 BB/9, didn't exactly scream dominance either. The Houston front office pushed him up to Fresno in late June where he would make another 12 decent starts. He would toss 68.1 innings while averaging 8.03 strikeouts and 3.69 walks per nine innings while posting (again) nearly identical ERA/FIP totals: 4.48 vs. 4.36.

**Projection:** What the hell is going on here? This production – more specifically, the homerun rate and some wavering control – just seem...batty. So let's delve a little deeper into the numbers, shall we?

First, the homerun rate: over the past two seasons Appel has surrendered 24 homeruns in 215 innings. And, yes, a large amount of that is attributed to the blip in Lancaster, but he still managed to give up about one per nine innings last season. But that total should even come down as he moves forward; his groundball rate, per StatCorner, was about 44% in 2015 and even higher the previous year (about 48%). Meaning: that's a *ton* of worm-burners, so the homerun clip fits about as well as me in a slim-fitting shirt.

Now onto his actual individual starts: Appel really struggled for the first seven- to eight-weeks last season. But he managed to finish out the year on a high note, posting a combined 81-to-33 strikeout-to-walk ratio and a 3.73 ERA over his final 91.2 innings as opponents batted a lowly .236/.307/.385. This seems to be more indicative of his actual talent.

By all accounts he's still armed with the same arsenal as in college. It just might be all mental, maybe even a case of tipping his pitches? I don't know. And while he doesn't look like the "Next Mark Prior or Stephen Strasburg," Appel should have no issues sliding into a solid mid-rotation role. But there's still upside. I'm still holding out hope that he can/will take the next step toward ace-dom.

**Ceiling:** 3.5- to 4.0-win player
**Risk:** Moderate to High
**MLB ETA:** 2016

# 5. Jake Thompson, RHP

| Born: 01/31/94 | Age: 22 | Bats: R | Top CALs: Randall Delgado, Eduardo Rodriguez, |
|---|---|---|---|
| Height: 6-4 | Weight: 235 | Throws: R | Edwin Diaz, Jacob Turner, Jordan Walden |

| YEAR | Age | Level | IP | W | L | ERA | FIP | K/9 | BB/9 | K% | BB% | HR/9 | LOB% |
|---|---|---|---|---|---|---|---|---|---|---|---|---|---|
| 2013 | 19 | A | 83.3 | 3 | 3 | 3.13 | 3.33 | 9.83 | 3.46 | 24.6% | 8.7% | 0.43 | 72.2% |
| 2014 | 20 | A+ | 83.0 | 6 | 4 | 3.14 | 3.11 | 8.57 | 2.71 | 23.1% | 7.3% | 0.33 | 73.9% |
| 2014 | 20 | AA | 11.0 | 1 | 0 | 2.45 | 3.45 | 5.73 | 3.27 | 14.9% | 8.5% | 0.00 | 80.0% |
| 2014 | 20 | AA | 35.7 | 3 | 1 | 3.28 | 3.34 | 11.10 | 4.54 | 29.7% | 12.2% | 0.76 | 79.4% |
| 2015 | 21 | AA | 87.7 | 6 | 6 | 4.72 | 3.82 | 8.01 | 3.08 | 20.2% | 7.8% | 0.72 | 66.0% |
| 2015 | 21 | AA | 45.0 | 5 | 1 | 1.80 | 3.42 | 6.80 | 2.40 | 20.5% | 7.2% | 0.60 | 88.2% |

**Background:** A second round pick out of Rockwall-Heath High School in 2012, Thompson was part of the three-headed prospect monster Texas shipped to the City of Brotherly Love. Thompson, a 6-foot-4, 235-pound right-hander, spent the year between two Class AA levels, tossing 87.2 innings in the Texas League and another 45.0 innings with Reading in the Eastern League. As one of just three qualified hurlers in any Class AA under the age of 22, Thompson more than held his own, posting a 3.69 FIP while fanning 20.3% and walking 7.6% of the total batters he faced in 2015. And just to put that into some perspective: Among all qualified hurlers under the age of 23 in Class AA, Thompson's strikeout percentage ranked sixth. For his career the oft-passed around right-hander, who's now onto his third professional franchise, has punched out nearly a bat per inning (8.8 K/9) while issuing 131 free passes in 374.0 innings of work.

**Projection**: Two years ago in my first book I wrote the following:

*"Detroit is slowly bringing along Thompson, who's tossed just 111.2 innings through his first 24 games. Solid control, above-average ability to miss bats, and plenty of youth on his side, the big right-hander's name could start to jump this season as the training wheels are taken off."*

And I followed that up with this is last year's book:

*"Only 12 other pitchers with 100+ innings under the age of 22 who pitched above Low Class A had a better strikeout rate. The control took a step forward with Lakewood before regressing some in Class AA. Thompson has the ceiling of a solid #3=type pitcher, maybe squeaking in a few fringe #2-type seasons."*

Clearly, I've been a big fan of Thompson's since I started evaluating minor leaguers. The strikeout ability is still an above-average skill, the control/command bounced back to be average or better, and his groundball rate reached an all-time high of 50% last season. Again, he has all the makings of a quality mid-rotation caliber arm. And if Alfaro and Williams develop into anything close to their potential the Cole Hamels deal could go down as one of the better swaps involving prospects in the last decade or so.

**Ceiling:** 2.5-win player
**Risk:** Moderate
**MLB ETA:** 2016

# 6. Jorge Alfaro, C

**MiLB Rank: #112**
**Position Rank: N/A**

| Born: 06/11/93 | Age: 23 | Bats: R | Top CALs: Kellin Deglan, Gary Sanchez, |
|---|---|---|---|
| Height: 6-2 | Weight: 225 | Throws: R | Eric Haase, Luis Exposito, Justin O'Conner |

| Season | Age | LVL | PA | 2B | 3B | HR | AVG | OBP | SLG | ISO | BB% | K% | wRC+ |
|---|---|---|---|---|---|---|---|---|---|---|---|---|---|
| 2013 | 20 | A | 420 | 22 | 1 | 16 | 0.258 | 0.338 | 0.452 | 0.194 | 6.7% | 26.4% | 128 |
| 2014 | 21 | A+ | 437 | 22 | 5 | 13 | 0.261 | 0.318 | 0.440 | 0.178 | 5.3% | 22.9% | 112 |
| 2015 | 22 | AA | 207 | 15 | 2 | 5 | 0.253 | 0.314 | 0.432 | 0.179 | 4.3% | 29.5% | 107 |

**Background:** Highly coveted as a potential return target during the initial Cole Hamels rumors, the Ruben Amaro Jr.-led front office was able to land their man, as well as the rest of the six-man package, as part of the megadeal with the resurgent Rangers. Alfaro, a slowly developing backstop out of Columbia, first appeared in the professional ranks as a 17-year-old in the Dominican Summer League seven years ago. Since then the 6-foot-2, 225-pound prospect has spent a year in the Northwest League, and parts of two seasons each in the South Atlantic, Carolina, and Texas Leagues. In an injury-shortened campaign last year, Alfaro spent 49 games with the Frisco RoughRiders, hitting a Jorge Alfaro-like .253/.314/.432 with 15 doubles, a pair of triples, five homeruns, and two stolen bases while topping the league average production by 7%. Alfaro underwent the knife in the second week of June, a procedure to repair a tendon in his left ankle, and subsequently missed the remainder of his season. For his career, Alfaro has been a .261/.326/.432 hitter, slugging 101 doubles, 16 triples, 52 homeruns, and 35 stolen bases in 453 games.

**Projection**: Here's what I wrote in last year's book:

*"More hype than production right now, outside of his debut season in 2010 Alfaro's always performed well at each stop without truly standing out with the bat. His Weighted Runs Created Plus totals for each stop beginning in 2010 (150+ PA): 72, 129, 105, 128, and 112. CAL links the Columbian-born backstop with a pair of higher profile catching prospects – Gary Sanchez and Andrew Knapp. Otherwise, it's nothing special. League average starting backstop, maybe a tick or two better depending on how the defense grades out."*

So let's update that bit, shall we? First off, CAL still links Alfaro with Gary Sanchez, but now ties him to Kellin Deglan, Eric Haase, Luis Exposito, and Tampa Bay's Justin O'Conner. It's certainly a decent mix with Sanchez and O'Conner leading the way, but one that's lacking a true standout bat. Secondly, here's what we know about Alfaro in a rather lengthy history, one that encompasses nearly 1,900 MiLB plate appearances: the power is an above-average tool, something in the area of 20 or so homeruns across a full season; the hit tool is underwhelming; the patience at the plate is below-average; and he's going to swing-and-miss a whole lot at the big league level. He's like a bad version of the Three True Outcomes Hitter, offering up the power and strikeouts without the patience.

**Ceiling:** 2.5-win player
**Risk:** Moderate
**MLB ETA:** 2016

## 7. Carlos Tocci, CF

**MiLB Rank: #194**
**Position Rank: N/A**

| Born: 08/23/95 | Age: 20 | Bats: R | Top CALs: Yefri Carvajal, Roderick Bernadina, |
| Height: 6-2 | Weight: 160 | Throws: R | Samir Duenez, Elvis Escobar, Dustin Fowler |

| Season | Age | LVL | PA | 2B | 3B | HR | AVG | OBP | SLG | ISO | BB% | K% | wRC+ |
|--------|-----|-----|----|----|----|----|-----|-----|-----|-----|-----|-----|------|
| 2013 | 17 | A | 459 | 17 | 0 | 0 | 0.209 | 0.261 | 0.249 | 0.040 | 4.8% | 16.8% | 50 |
| 2014 | 18 | A | 538 | 18 | 8 | 2 | 0.242 | 0.297 | 0.324 | 0.082 | 4.6% | 17.8% | 76 |
| 2015 | 19 | A | 261 | 14 | 2 | 2 | 0.321 | 0.387 | 0.423 | 0.103 | 7.7% | 11.9% | 133 |
| 2015 | 19 | A+ | 298 | 9 | 0 | 2 | 0.258 | 0.296 | 0.313 | 0.055 | 4.0% | 17.4% | 86 |

**Background:** After spending a good deal of the previous two books ripping into the Phillies for what can only be described as a piss-poor development plan put in place for the Venezuelan-born center fielder, Tocci finally delivered on his offensive promise in his third season in the Sally – despite the organization's best efforts to derail his career. The front office (infamously) pushed the then-17-year-old up to Low Class A three years ago for an entire season – despite the struggling teenager's inability to hit *anything*; he finished the year with a rancid .209/.261/.249 triple-slash line with just 17 extra-base hits. Undeterred by their own mistakes, Philadelphia allowed Tocci to spend the entire 2014 campaign back in the Sally where his numbers saw a modest – at best – improvement: .242/.297/.324. Finally, though, the no longer overmatched 19-year-old Tocci broke loose from the chains of the Sally last year; he slugged .321/.387/.423 with 14 doubles, a pair of triples, two homeruns, and 14 stolen bases (in 16 attempts). His overall production topped the league average mark by 33%, the second best showing by a teenager in the Sally last season.

**Projection:** I would love to know the thought process on not only pushing a 17-year-old prospect that couldn't hit the league average production line in the GCL up to full season ball, but also why not demote him at any point? Tocci took several developmental steps forward last season, showing improvement in his plate discipline, power, and hit tool all the while trimming his punch out rate way down. He was a well-rounded tool kit with the ability to develop into a league average regular – as long as Philadelphia doesn't muck it up.

**Ceiling:** 2.0- to 2.5-win player
**Risk:** Moderate to High
**MLB ETA:** 2018

## 8. Thomas Eshelman, RHP

**MiLB Rank: N/A**
**Position Rank: N/A**

| Born: 06/20/94 | Age: 22 | Bats: R | Top CALs: N/A |
| Height: 6-3 | Weight: 212 | Throws: R | |

| YEAR | Age | Level | IP | W | L | ERA | FIP | K/9 | BB/9 | K% | BB% | HR/9 | LOB% |
|------|-----|-------|----|----|----|-----|-----|-----|------|-----|-----|------|------|
| 2015 | 21 | R | 4.0 | 0 | 1 | 4.50 | 3.31 | 6.75 | 4.50 | 17.7% | 11.8% | 0.00 | 60.0% |
| 2015 | 21 | A | 6.3 | 0 | 0 | 4.26 | 3.24 | 7.11 | 4.26 | 17.2% | 10.3% | 0.00 | 75.0% |

**Background:** The former Cal State Fullerton hurler is sort of like the Nolan Fontana, the New Greek God of Walks, of pitching. Eshelman wasn't the flashiest pitcher in college. Hell, he was basically like a warm glass of milk for an elderly person. But he did manage to post three consecutive seasons of sub-1.90 ERAs for the Titans. Here's where it gets impressive: Eshelman, a 6-foot-3, 212-pound right-hander, walked 18 hitters *for his career* – a career that spanned 376 innings. In other words, he averaged one free pass every 20+ innings. And his work as a true freshman – he walked three hitters in 115.2 innings – will go down as one of the greatest feats in modern college history.

Led by the analytically-savvy front office, Houston grabbed the production-over-potential hurler with the 46th overall pick. Eshelman would toss 10.1 innings without – you guessed it – issuing a free pass. Philly acquired the pinpoint control artist as part of the Ken Giles deal this offseason.

**Projection:** Prior to the 2015 draft I wrote:

> "He's not overpowering so he'll likely get overlooked by some of the bigger arms in the class (Walker Buehler, Dillon Tate, Phil Bickford, Carson Fulmer, Michael Matuella), but Eshelman is a safe, fast-moving back-of-the-rotation caliber arm that could easily be in the big leagues within a season-plus of the draft.
>
> Something to watch when he does make his pro debut: groundball totals. If Eshelman proves to be an above-average worm-burner, watch out. In terms of big league comparison, think Cincinnati's Mike Leake."

**Ceiling:** 1.5-win player
**Risk:** Low to Moderate
**MLB ETA:** 2017

## 9. Roman Quinn, SS

**MiLB Rank:** N/A
**Position Rank:** N/A

| Born: 05/14/93 | Age: 23 | Bats: B | Top CALs: Shane Peterson, Adron Chambers, |
| Height: 5-10 | Weight: 170 | Throws: R | Casey Craig, Peter Bourjos, Dan Brewer |

| Season | Age | LVL | PA | 2B | 3B | HR | AVG | OBP | SLG | ISO | BB% | K% | wRC+ |
|--------|-----|-----|-----|----|----|----|-------|-------|-------|-------|------|-------|------|
| 2013 | 20 | A | 298 | 7 | 3 | 5 | 0.238 | 0.323 | 0.346 | 0.108 | 9.1% | 21.5% | 97 |
| 2014 | 21 | A+ | 382 | 10 | 3 | 7 | 0.257 | 0.343 | 0.370 | 0.113 | 9.4% | 20.9% | 108 |
| 2015 | 22 | AA | 257 | 6 | 6 | 4 | 0.306 | 0.356 | 0.435 | 0.129 | 7.0% | 16.3% | 129 |

**Background:** A former prep shortstop that could play the position about as well as your little Aunt Betty, Quinn made the oh-so-predictable move to the only up-the-middle position left for him a couple years ago: center field. And the speedy little Quinn responded in kind: his offensive production has been trending skyward over the past two years. Quinn, a former second round pick coming off of a .250/.361/.359 showing in High Class A in 2014, was in the midst of an unsuspected breakout season before a fairly serious injury – a torn hip flexor – shut him down in early June. But before the health issue popped up, He was on pace to set career highs in practically every single offensive category en route to hitting .306/.356/.435.

**Projection**: So the question is: Can the surging – and oft-injured – center fielder repeat his 58-game run of dominance moving forward?

Well, let's delve into the numbers. The speed is clearly a game-changer on both sides of the ball, and Quinn has averaged a smidgeon over 71 steals per 162 games. His walk rate last season, 7.0%, was a touch lower than his career norms (8.8%), so there's hope that it can inch back up. His pop, .129 ISO, is also very similar to his previous total (.119 ISO). And his strikeout rates were a touch lower. But the two main differences last season were a career high .360 BABIP, which isn't out of the realm of possibility for a plus-runner with gap power, and his improved performance against RHP.

The switch-hitting Quinn was coming off of back-to-back showing in which he posted OPSs of .651 and .673 against righties, but hung a .769 mark in 112 plate appearances last season. Can me skeptical, but I'm going to need to see him repeat that level of production before I'm entirely convinced. For now, he looks like a fringy everyday player with some noticeable risk – and that's before you factor in that he's never topped more than 88 games in a season yet. One final thought: CALs best case scenario is Peter Bourjos, another speedy center fielder with a career 90 wRC+ and plus-defensive ability, which seems about right.

**Ceiling:** 1.5- to 2.0-win player
**Risk:** Moderate to High
**MLB ETA:** 2016/2017

## 10. Andrew Knapp, C

**MiLB Rank:** N/A
**Position Rank:** N/A

| Born: 11/09/91 | Age: 24 | Bats: B | Top CALs: Dane Phillips, Travis Scott, |
| Height: 6-1 | Weight: 190 | Throws: R | Ryan Lavarnway, Cael Brockmeyer, Zach Wright |

| Season | Age | LVL | PA | 2B | 3B | HR | AVG | OBP | SLG | ISO | BB% | K% | wRC+ |
|--------|-----|-----|-----|----|----|----|-------|-------|-------|-------|-------|-------|------|
| 2013 | 21 | A- | 247 | 20 | 0 | 4 | 0.253 | 0.340 | 0.401 | 0.147 | 8.9% | 23.1% | 128 |
| 2014 | 22 | A | 314 | 19 | 4 | 5 | 0.290 | 0.354 | 0.438 | 0.148 | 8.6% | 22.6% | 121 |
| 2015 | 23 | A+ | 281 | 14 | 3 | 2 | 0.262 | 0.356 | 0.369 | 0.107 | 10.3% | 22.4% | 125 |
| 2015 | 23 | AA | 241 | 21 | 2 | 11 | 0.360 | 0.419 | 0.631 | 0.271 | 9.1% | 17.8% | 200 |

**Background:** Sometimes the stars just align for a player, just like when Davey Johnson bashed 43 of his 136 career homeruns in 1973 or when Brady Anderson went from hitting 16 or so dingers in season to a mind-boggling 50 moonshots in 1996. It happens from time-to-time. And the former backstop out of UC Berkley's 55-game stint with the Fightin' Phils in the Eastern League last season will likely go down as such. Knapp, a switch-hitting catcher taken in the second round in 2013, had a bit of a disappointing season two years ago as he battled his way back from Tommy John surgery, an injury that ultimately limited him to the team's designated hitter role. He batted just .157/.222/.205 in 23 games in the Florida State League before the organization mercifully bounced him down to the Sally. Well, Knapp found himself back in High Class A for the start of last year where he hit a solid .262/.356/.369 to go along with a 125 wRC+ total. But his numbers ballooned to epic proportions once he got promoted to the Eastern League. In those aforementioned 55 games, Knapp mashed to the tune of .360/.419/.631 with a Babe Ruthian-esque 21 doubles, a pair of triples, and 11 homeruns in just 241 trips to the plate. His overall production with the Fightin' Phils, according to *Weighted Runs Created Plus*, topped the league average make by 100%.

**100%!**

**Projection**: A few things to think about here. Prorating his production in Class AA to a full 162-game season looks like this: 62 doubles, six triples, and 32 homeruns. I don't care where you're playing baseball, be it in a video game or little league or, hell, even if the pitches are served up underhand, that's one helluva stat line. But, unfortunately, Knapp's never going to even sniff that type of production ever again. He's never shown that type of power before, at any level and he finished his 55-game stint with a .405 BABIP. Slow-footed catchers with average power just don't post BABIPs of that caliber.

Here's what I wrote prior to his draft selection a couple years ago:

*"Knapp, a switch-hitter, showed some blossoming power during his sophomore campaign, slugging 21 extra-base hits. It's now developed in a solid-average skill with the potential to be 12 to 17 homeruns down the line. He couples that with a decent eye at the plate, though his walk rates will likely be average or slightly below in pro ball. Defensively , he's nabbed 65% of would-be base stealers."*

So, what the hell is Knapp? Well, he's a nice fringy everyday big league contributor. He won't kill a team with his work behind the plate or with a bat in his hands. He'll flash some pop, hit .260-ish, and do everything he should do.

**Ceiling:** 1.5- to 2.0-win player
**Risk:** Moderate to High
**MLB ETA:** 2016

## 11. Matt Imhof, LHP

| | | MiLB Rank: N/A |
| --- | --- | --- |
| | | Position Rank: N/A |

| Born: 10/26/93 | Age: 22 | Bats: L | Top CALs: Oswaldo Martinez, Jason Ray, |
| --- | --- | --- | --- |
| Height: 6-5 | Weight: 220 | Throws: L | Mitch Ray, Tyler Pike, Deunte Heath |

| YEAR | Age | Level | IP | W | L | ERA | FIP | K/9 | BB/9 | K% | BB% | HR/9 | LOB% |
| --- | --- | --- | --- | --- | --- | --- | --- | --- | --- | --- | --- | --- | --- |
| 2014 | 20 | R | 3.0 | 0 | 0 | 0.00 | 4.17 | 6.00 | 3.00 | 18.2% | 9.1% | 0.00 | 100.0% |
| 2014 | 20 | A- | 12.0 | 1 | 0 | 0.75 | 3.11 | 8.25 | 3.00 | 23.9% | 8.7% | 0.00 | 91.7% |
| 2014 | 20 | A | 27.3 | 0 | 2 | 4.28 | 3.81 | 8.89 | 1.98 | 23.3% | 5.2% | 0.99 | 71.8% |
| 2015 | 21 | A+ | 77.7 | 8 | 5 | 3.94 | 4.49 | 6.84 | 4.52 | 17.7% | 11.7% | 0.93 | 66.1% |

**Background:** Placed in the top ten among all Division 1 hurlers two years ago for Cal Poly, Imhof had a strong debut in the Philadelphia organization: he made a quick three-inning appearance in the Gulf Coast, torched the New York-Penn League for three starts, and continued to roll through the Sally for 27+ innings. Last year the front office aggressively pushed the lanky left-hander up to the Florida State League and the results were...OK. In an injury-shortened campaign the 6-foot-5, 220-pound left-hander posted a 59-to-39 strikeout-to-walk ratio in 77.2 innings of work. Imhof missed a handful of weeks courtesy of a biceps injury.

**Projection**: Here's what I wrote prior to the draft two years ago:

*"[He], obviously, has an above-average ability to miss bats, though that's likely to hover near the league average in the professional ranks. His control is decent, not great. But he's also shown an ability to dominate against some of the better international competition. [He's] a solid mid-rotation-type arm."*

Well, the strikeout rate came plummeting back to earth last season as he averaged 6.84 K/9. And just for comparison's sake: the average for the Florida State League was 7.2 K/9. Not too shabby. After a string of two-plus innings starts upon his return from an eight week trip to the DL, Imhof's numbers normalized some after coughing up 11 earned runs in his previous seven innings. Over his final 55.2 innings Imhof posted a 47-to-26 strikeout-to-walk ratio to go along with a 3.23 ERA. As I wrote two years ago, he has the chance to be a mid-rotation caliber arm, something along the lines of having a #3/#4-type future.

**Ceiling:** 1.5-win player
**Risk:** Moderate
**MLB ETA:** 2017

## 12. Dylan Cozens, LF/RF

| | | MiLB Rank: N/A |
| --- | --- | --- |
| | | Position Rank: N/A |

| Born: 05/31/94 | Age: 22 | Bats: L | Top CALs: Angel Morales, Brandon Jacobs, |
| --- | --- | --- | --- |
| Height: 6-6 | Weight: 235 | Throws: L | Jordan Schafer, Quincy Latimore, Teoscar Hernandez |

| Season | Age | LVL | PA | 2B | 3B | HR | AVG | OBP | SLG | ISO | BB% | K% | wRC+ |
| --- | --- | --- | --- | --- | --- | --- | --- | --- | --- | --- | --- | --- | --- |
| 2013 | 19 | A- | 277 | 19 | 2 | 9 | 0.265 | 0.343 | 0.469 | 0.204 | 10.1% | 23.1% | 146 |
| 2014 | 20 | A | 556 | 25 | 6 | 16 | 0.248 | 0.303 | 0.415 | 0.167 | 7.2% | 26.4% | 97 |
| 2015 | 21 | A+ | 397 | 22 | 5 | 5 | 0.282 | 0.335 | 0.411 | 0.129 | 6.5% | 19.9% | 127 |
| 2015 | 21 | AA | 44 | 2 | 0 | 3 | 0.350 | 0.386 | 0.625 | 0.275 | 6.8% | 15.9% | 188 |

**Background**: One of the more memorable moments from my time at Baseball Info Solutions involved former Rangers first baseman/corner outfielder Jason Botts. See, Botts was an absolute physical specimen, built like a line backer at 6-foot-5 and 250-pounds, and blessed with light tower power. But it was the way

Botts made the bat look in his hands; it's was almost twig-esque. Well, Cozens is a lot like Botts with that respect. A former second round pick in 2012 out of Chaparral High School, home to former backstop-turned-borderline-hall-of famer-Paul-Konerko, Cozens stands an impressive 6-foot-6, but remains remarkably lean at 235 pounds. And after pegging him as a potential breakout prospect in 2014, the toolsy corner outfielder finally came through a year later.

Spending the majority of the year with the Clearwater Threshers in the Florida State League, the then-21-year-old slugger had his finest season to date, hitting .282/.335/.411 with 22 doubles, five triples, five homeruns, and 18 stolen bases en route to posting a 127 wRC+. Cozens also missed a month or so due to an undisclosed lower body injury.

**Projection**: As much power as any player in the Phillies' system. The problem for Cozens, however, is that it hasn't shown up on a consistent basis in actual ballgames yet. Blessed with a plethora of tools – speed, decent eye at the plate and a reasonable contact rate to go along with the power – the problem is that he tends to struggle against left-handers. Over the past three years he's posted OPSs of .695, .660, and .723. He looks like a quality bench option/fringy everyday player – a la Jason Botts.

**Ceiling:** 1.5-win player
**Risk:** Moderate
**MLB ETA:** 2016

## 13. Ricardo Pinto, RHP

**MiLB Rank: N/A**
**Position Rank: N/A**

| Born: 01/20/94 | Age: 22 | Bats: R | **Top CALs:** Ivan Pineyro, Chase Dejong, |
| Height: 6-0 | Weight: 165 | Throws: R | Shane Dawson, David Baker, Jack Spradlin |

| YEAR | Age | Level | IP | W | L | ERA | FIP | K/9 | BB/9 | K% | BB% | HR/9 | LOB% |
|------|-----|-------|------|---|---|------|------|------|------|-------|------|------|-------|
| 2013 | 19 | R | 63.0 | 3 | 5 | 2.86 | 3.66 | 7.29 | 1.71 | 19.5% | 4.6% | 0.57 | 66.3% |
| 2014 | 20 | A- | 47.0 | 1 | 5 | 2.11 | 3.59 | 9.19 | 2.87 | 24.5% | 7.7% | 0.77 | 76.0% |
| 2015 | 21 | A | 67.0 | 6 | 2 | 3.09 | 3.36 | 8.06 | 2.42 | 21.4% | 6.4% | 0.54 | 75.6% |
| 2015 | 21 | A+ | 78.3 | 9 | 2 | 2.87 | 3.82 | 5.17 | 2.18 | 14.9% | 6.3% | 0.69 | 71.8% |

**Background:** The once slowly developing right-hander that took two seasons of prepping to get out of the Venezuelan Summer League took some tremendous strides in his fourth professional year. Pinto, a rail-thin 6-foot, 165-pound hurler coming off of a strong showing in the New York-Penn League as a 20-year-old, made 11 starts for the BlueClaws in 2015, posting a dominant 60-to-18 strikeout-to-walk ratio in 67 innings of work to go along with a 3.36 FIP. Philadelphia promoted the surging prospect up to Clearwater in late June for another 13 starts. Overall, he finished the year with a combined 2.97 ERA with 105 punch outs and 37 walks in a career high 145.1 innings.

**Projection**: Something you certainly don't see often anymore: Pinto's year-to-year workload spiked by nearly 100 innings between 2014 and 2015. I'm not sure that it was the wrong move, but it does seem odd that the team wouldn't want to slowly build him – and his petite frame – up. Pinto offered up flashes of dominance in 2015: in his second start of the year he fanned 10, walked one, and surrendered a pair of hits in seven innings against Greensboro; a handful of starts later he would throw another impressive seven-inning, two-hit gem against the Asheville Tourists, strikeout out eight, and walking two; and his first start in the Florida State League he punched out seven and walked none in another two-hit effort in 6+ innings. But not too many rail-thin kids can handle the rigors of grabbing the ball every fifth day for multiple years. And despite throwing fewer than 80 innings in High Class A, Pinto's a candidate for the Class AA rotation when the team breaks camp.

**Ceiling:** 1.5-win player
**Risk:** Moderate
**MLB ETA:** 2017

## 14. Rhys Hoskins, 1B

**MiLB Rank: N/A**
**Position Rank: N/A**

| Born: 03/17/93 | Age: 23 | Bats: R | **Top CALs:** Vinnie Catricala, Matt Clark, |
| Height: 6-4 | Weight: 225 | Throws: R | Ji-Man Choi, Jordy Lara, Carlos Asuaje |

| Season | Age | LVL | PA | 2B | 3B | HR | AVG | OBP | SLG | ISO | BB% | K% | wRC+ |
|--------|-----|-----|-----|----|----|----|-------|-------|-------|-------|------|-------|------|
| 2014 | 21 | A- | 273 | 15 | 0 | 9 | 0.237 | 0.311 | 0.408 | 0.171 | 7.7% | 19.8% | 112 |
| 2015 | 22 | A | 290 | 17 | 4 | 9 | 0.322 | 0.397 | 0.525 | 0.204 | 9.0% | 17.2% | 161 |
| 2015 | 22 | A+ | 277 | 19 | 2 | 8 | 0.317 | 0.394 | 0.510 | 0.193 | 10.5% | 17.7% | 174 |

**Background:** A three-year middle-of-the-lineup thumper for Sacramento State, Hoskins put together a remarkable collegiate run, leaving the school as a .319/.396/.518 career hitter. Hoskins slipped a bit in the draft two years ago, falling to the fifth round where Philadelphia happily snapped the slugger up. And after a bit of a disappointing pro debut, Hoskins rebounded in a big way; he batted .322/.397/.525 in 68 games in the South Atlantic League, and followed that up with a nearly identical .317/.394/.510 triple-slash line with Clearwater. He finished the year with an aggregate .319/.395/.518 to go along with 36 doubles, six triples, and 17 homeruns.

**Projection**: While I didn't get the opportunity to write up an in-depth pre-draft evaluation on the former collegiate slugger, I did, however, rank him as the 44th overall collegiate prospect in the 2014 draft class, right behind former Indiana basher Sam Travis. And despite lasting until the fifth round, Hoskins is proving to be everything and much more. He showed above-average power, a solid eye, and a decent hit tool. While I remain a bit skeptical of his production moving forward given his back-to-back .360s BABIPs in Low Class A and High Class A last season, there's a strong enough foundation to suggest he can develop into at least part-timer.

**Ceiling:** 1.5-win player
**Risk:** Moderate to High
**MLB ETA:** 2017

## 15. Alec Asher, RHP

**MiLB Rank: N/A**
**Position Rank: N/A**

| Born: 10/04/91 | Age: 24 | Bats: R | Top CALs: Paolo Espino, Brett Oberholtzer, |
|---|---|---|---|
| Height: 6-4 | Weight: 230 | Throws: R | Nick Additon, Wes Roemer, James Houser |

| YEAR | Age | Level | IP | W | L | ERA | FIP | K/9 | BB/9 | K% | BB% | HR/9 | LOB% |
|---|---|---|---|---|---|---|---|---|---|---|---|---|---|
| 2013 | 21 | A+ | 133.3 | 9 | 7 | 2.90 | 3.27 | 9.38 | 2.70 | 24.7% | 7.1% | 0.68 | 69.7% |
| 2014 | 22 | AA | 154.0 | 11 | 11 | 3.80 | 3.74 | 7.13 | 1.87 | 19.3% | 5.1% | 1.05 | 67.2% |
| 2015 | 23 | AA | 43.0 | 1 | 4 | 3.98 | 3.60 | 9.00 | 3.77 | 23.5% | 9.8% | 0.63 | 71.2% |
| 2015 | 23 | AAA | 64.7 | 3 | 6 | 4.73 | 6.03 | 7.52 | 2.64 | 19.5% | 6.9% | 2.23 | 79.9% |
| 2015 | 23 | AAA | 26.0 | 2 | 0 | 2.08 | 4.08 | 4.15 | 1.04 | 11.3% | 2.8% | 1.04 | 89.2% |

**Background:** The Big Cat was one of the lesser known players acquired in the midseason swap with Texas. Asher, a former fourth round pick out of Polk Community College in 2012, made four different stops last season: he made eight starts with Frisco in the Texas League, another 12 contests with Round Rock in the PCL, and a quartet of games with Lehigh Valley before making his big league debut in Philadelphia down the stretch. The 6-foot-4, 230-pound right-hander's final minor league line: 133.2 innings, 109 punch outs, 30 walks, and an aggregate 3.97 ERA. His seven starts with the Phillies were mostly disastrous sans a seven-inning, four-strikeout, three-hitter against the Marlins on September 24th. His final MLB line: 29.0 innings, 4.97 K/9, 3.10 BB/9, and a Freddy Krueger-esque 9.31 ERA.

**Projection**: I've always been a fan of the Asher, who has a lengthy history of solid strikeout rates and low walk totals, something that was clearly on display during his run in the minors last season. He showcased a low-90s fastball, a mid-80s slider, upper-70s deuce, and a hard changeup. CAL remains rather unimpressed, linking him to a handful of questionable big league arms like Paolo Espina, Brett Oberholtzer, and Nick Additon. And, well, CAL seems spot on here too.

**Ceiling:** 1.0- to 1.5-win player
**Risk:** Moderate
**MLB ETA:** Debuted in 2015

## 16. Ben Lively, RHP

**MiLB Rank: N/A**
**Position Rank: N/A**

| Born: 03/05/92 | Age: 24 | Bats: R | Top CALs: Justin Thomas, Robert Rohrbaugh, |
|---|---|---|---|
| Height: 6-4 | Weight: 190 | Throws: R | Michael O'Brien, Ryan Searle, Jeff Manship |

| YEAR | Age | Level | IP | W | L | ERA | FIP | K/9 | BB/9 | K% | BB% | HR/9 | LOB% |
|---|---|---|---|---|---|---|---|---|---|---|---|---|---|
| 2013 | 21 | R | 37.0 | 0 | 3 | 0.73 | 2.49 | 11.92 | 2.92 | 33.6% | 8.2% | 0.00 | 79.4% |
| 2013 | 21 | A | 4.0 | 0 | 1 | 2.25 | 0.59 | 15.75 | 2.25 | 43.8% | 6.3% | 0.00 | 33.3% |
| 2014 | 22 | A+ | 79.0 | 10 | 1 | 2.28 | 2.97 | 10.82 | 1.82 | 31.5% | 5.3% | 0.68 | 82.3% |
| 2014 | 22 | AA | 72.0 | 3 | 6 | 3.88 | 4.01 | 9.50 | 4.50 | 24.8% | 11.8% | 0.88 | 75.4% |
| 2015 | 23 | AA | 143.7 | 8 | 7 | 4.13 | 4.08 | 6.95 | 2.82 | 18.1% | 7.4% | 0.88 | 74.3% |

**Background:** It's not too often that a team will recognize a prospect as their Minor League Pitcher of the year and then a handful of weeks later ship him off for an aging veteran, but that's exactly what the Reds did with Lively during last offseason. A former four round pick out of the University of Central Florida, Lively had a hugely successful sophomore campaign in Cincinnati's player development system two years ago: he jumped straight into High Class A with just one inning of experience above the rookie leagues and didn't miss a beat. In fact, he blew away the California League competition – he posted an impeccable 95-to-16 strikeout-to-walk ratio in 79 innings – and handled the Class AA test with ease (72.0 IP, 76 K, and 36 BB). So it made sense for the Phillies, an aging rebuilding team, to swap Marlon Byrd for the up-and-coming right-hander. But, unfortunately, for the Philadelphia faithful the Lively Express didn't look so...lively.

Spending the entire year in the Eastern League Lively made 25 starts with the Reading Fightin' Phils, tallying 143.1 innings with 111 punch outs and 45 free passes to go along with a mediocre 4.08 FIP.

**Projection**: In terms of overall production that wasn't really that much of a difference between Lively first stint in Class AA and last year's longer, more extended look. While the 6-foot-4, 190-pound right-hander traded in strikeouts for improved control, his FIPs were nearly identical: 4.01 vs. 4.08. Lively looks like a classic backend starting pitcher, nothing special but certainly valuable in the right setting. He'll likely see some action in Philly next year.

**Ceiling:** 1.0- to 1.5-win player
**Risk:** Moderate
**MLB ETA:** 2016

## 17. Scott Kingery, 2B

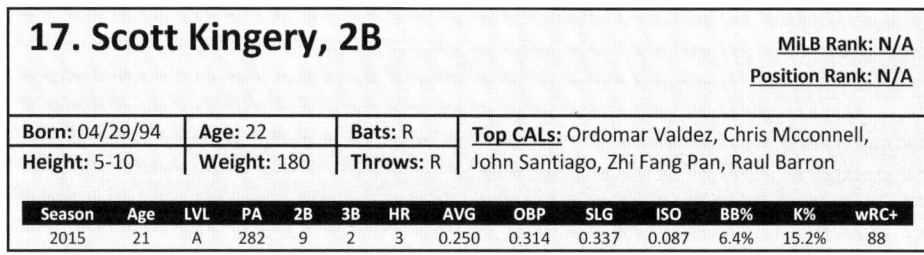

MiLB Rank: N/A
Position Rank: N/A

| Born: 04/29/94 | Age: 22 | Bats: R | Top CALs: Ordomar Valdez, Chris Mcconnell, |
| Height: 5-10 | Weight: 180 | Throws: R | John Santiago, Zhi Fang Pan, Raul Barron |

| Season | Age | LVL | PA | 2B | 3B | HR | AVG | OBP | SLG | ISO | BB% | K% | wRC+ |
|---|---|---|---|---|---|---|---|---|---|---|---|---|---|
| 2015 | 21 | A | 282 | 9 | 2 | 3 | 0.250 | 0.314 | 0.337 | 0.087 | 6.4% | 15.2% | 88 |

**Background:** A sweet-swinging second baseman out of the University of Arizona, Kingery followed up his breakout sophomore campaign (.354/.456/.467) with an even more impressive junior season. In 54 games for the Wildcats, the 5-foot-10, 180-pound infielder slugged a robust .392/.423/.516 with career highs in doubles (15), triples (five), and homeruns (5).

**Projection**: Here's what I wrote during his pre-draft evaluation:

> "Kingery spent his fist two seasons with the Wildcats showcasing a better-than-average eye at the plate, but he's showing far less patience this season, walking in just over 5% of his trips to the plate [at the time of the writing]. That number will likely jump back up to around 7.5% to 8.0% in the professional ranks.
>
> A little bit of speed, not a whole lot of power despite the .515 career slugging percentage, but a strong hit tool.
>
> In terms of absolute upside, think Dustin Pedroia 2014 – .278/.337/.376. Roughly a league-average offensive performer, but that comes with the risk of his production being so inflated by his home park."

**Ceiling:** 1.5- to 2.0-win player
**Risk:** High
**MLB ETA:** 2017/2018

## 18. Darnell Sweeney, IF/OF

MiLB Rank: N/A
Position Rank: N/A

| Born: 02/01/91 | Age: 25 | Bats: B | Top CALs: Tommy Field, Taylor Featherston, |
| Height: 6-1 | Weight: 195 | Throws: R | Tony Thomas, Daniel Mayora, Pedro Florimon |

| Season | Age | LVL | PA | 2B | 3B | HR | AVG | OBP | SLG | ISO | BB% | K% | wRC+ |
|---|---|---|---|---|---|---|---|---|---|---|---|---|---|
| 2013 | 22 | A+ | 613 | 34 | 16 | 11 | 0.275 | 0.329 | 0.455 | 0.179 | 7.0% | 24.6% | 102 |
| 2014 | 23 | AA | 586 | 34 | 5 | 14 | 0.288 | 0.387 | 0.463 | 0.176 | 13.1% | 20.0% | 141 |
| 2015 | 24 | AAA | 522 | 30 | 4 | 9 | 0.271 | 0.332 | 0.409 | 0.138 | 8.0% | 22.2% | 96 |
| 2015 | 24 | MLB | 98 | 4 | 1 | 3 | 0.176 | 0.286 | 0.353 | 0.176 | 13.3% | 27.6% | 77 |

**Background:** Going back to one of Ruben Amaro's favorite trading partners, the Los Angeles Dodgers, the Phillies acquired the switch-hitting utility man and former UNLV rotation stalwart John Richy for 34 games of horrible production from Chase Utley, who batted .202/.291/.363 down the stretch for his new organization. Prior to the trade, Sweeney spent his entire season in Class AAA with the Oklahoma City Dodgers, hitting .271/.332/.409 with 30 doubles, four triples, and nine homeruns while swiping 32 bags in 45 attempts. His overall production was essentially league average; he posted a 96 wRC+. Once he was acquired by the Phils, Sweeney would spend the rest of the year flailing away at big league pitching, hitting a paltry .176/.286/.353 in 98 trips to the plate.

**Projection**: If a team would sculpt the ideal utility man it would likely resemble the former 13th round pick out of the University of Central Florida. Sweeney can bounce around the entire field, having played at least 30 games at second base, shortstop, center field, and left field, and he's also briefly moonlighted as a third baseman as well. He's a switch-hitter with speed, surprising pop, and a solid eye at the plate. As Philadelphia continues to rebuild look for him to get more than a few chances to prove himself as an everyday guy even though he's far better suited in the super-sub role.

**Ceiling:** 1.0-win player
**Risk:** Low
**MLB ETA:** Debuted in 2015

## 19. Alberto Tirado, RHP

**MiLB Rank:** N/A
**Position Rank:** N/A

| Born: 12/10/94 | Age: 21 | Bats: R | Top CALs: Adrian De Horta, Clevelan Santeliz, |
| Height: 6-0 | Weight: 180 | Throws: R | Michael Kirkman, Jack Mcgeary, Hunter Cervenka |

| YEAR | Age | Level | IP | W | L | ERA | FIP | K/9 | BB/9 | K% | BB% | HR/9 | LOB% |
|------|-----|-------|-----|---|---|------|------|------|------|-------|-------|------|-------|
| 2013 | 18 | R | 48.3 | 3 | 0 | 1.68 | 3.62 | 8.19 | 3.72 | 21.3% | 9.7% | 0.19 | 82.8% |
| 2014 | 19 | A- | 35.7 | 1 | 0 | 3.53 | 4.77 | 9.08 | 7.07 | 22.2% | 17.3% | 0.25 | 71.4% |
| 2014 | 19 | A | 40.0 | 1 | 2 | 6.30 | 5.61 | 9.00 | 8.78 | 19.8% | 19.3% | 0.68 | 68.8% |
| 2015 | 20 | A+ | 77.3 | 5 | 3 | 2.68 | 4.25 | 8.96 | 6.17 | 23.6% | 16.2% | 0.47 | 80.1% |

**Background:** A once promising starter in the rookie levels, Tirado – and his control – seemingly lost the way since the calendar flipped to 2014. A 6-foot, 180-pound right-hander out of the Dominican Republic, Tirado began to open some eyes at a 17-year-old making his professional debut in the stateside rookie leagues; he posted a 39-to-17 strikeout-to-walk ratio in 48.0 innings between the Appalachian and Gulf Coast Leagues. He would follow that up with an even better in 2013: 48.1 IP, 1.68 ERA, 44 strikeouts, and 20 walks as he spent the entire year in the advance rookie league. And then he came down with can't-seem-to-find-the-damn-plate-itis, an illness that's plagued him even as he was transitioned into a relief/swing-man. Tirado would cough up 67 walks in 75.2 innings with Lansing and Vancouver in 2014, and he followed that up with only slight improvement in High Class A last season: 53 BB in 77.1 innings of work.

**Projection**: Here's what I wrote in last year's book:

> *"Well, he was clearly on a downswing in 2014, And one wonders if it was the organization's aggressive schedule – he opened the year in the Midwest League – may have clouded his control a bit. He's the very definition of a wild card and even in last year's debacle he showed glimpses of a potential big league starter; his first game of the year, for instance, where he fanned seven and walked one in four innings."*

Clearly the downswing continued into 2015. But, again, Tirado continues to whet the appetite of scouts and analysts alike. He opened the year up as seemingly rejuvenated prospect, posting a 24-to-6 strikeout-to-walk ratio in his first 22.1 innings. He promptly walked seven in his next three appearances spanning a total of six innings, and he coughed up 47 base-on-balls over his final 55 innings. Tirado is an enigma, a puzzle that could lead to developing a promising mid-rotation caliber arm or he could leave the development system telling stories of what may have been.

**Ceiling:** 1.5-win player
**Risk:** High
**MLB ETA:** 2018

## 20. Adonis Medina, RHP

**MiLB Rank:** N/A
**Position Rank:** N/A

| Born: 12/18/96 | Age: 19 | Bats: R | Top CALs: Lino Martinez, Jeurys Familia, |
| Height: 6-1 | Weight: 185 | Throws: R | Jake Woodford, Jacob Johnson, Chad Rodgers |

| YEAR | Age | Level | IP | W | L | ERA | FIP | K/9 | BB/9 | K% | BB% | HR/9 | LOB% |
|------|-----|-------|------|---|---|------|------|------|------|-------|------|------|-------|
| 2014 | 17 | R | 26.3 | 2 | 3 | 1.37 | 2.61 | 7.52 | 1.37 | 20.0% | 3.6% | 0.00 | 66.7% |
| 2015 | 18 | R | 45.3 | 3 | 2 | 2.98 | 3.24 | 6.95 | 2.38 | 18.5% | 6.4% | 0.20 | 66.6% |

**Background:** A wiry right-hander signed out of the Dominican Republic at the age 17, Medina blew away the DSL competition during his debut: in 11 games in the foreign rookie league, the 6-foot-1, 185-pound right-hander posted an impressive 22-to-4 strikeout-to-walk ratio in 26.1 innings. Philadelphia moved Medina stateside to the Gulf Coast last season where he handled the transition with relative ease.

**Projection**: Similar to Franklyn Kilome in a lot of ways, Medina's track record remains quite limited; he's thrown just 71.2 innings since entering pro ball. The control seems like a repeatable skill, even after he moved away from the free-swinging youngsters and into a more polished rookie level. And despite that lack of experience, as well as his relative youth, it wouldn't be surprising to see Medina bypass short-season ball and head straight into the Sally next season.

**Ceiling:** Too Soon to Tell
**Risk:** N/A
**MLB ETA:** N/A

## 21. Zach Eflin, RHP

MiLB Rank: N/A
Position Rank: N/A

| Born: 04/08/94 | Age: 22 | Bats: R | Top CALs: Chris Volstad, Kyle Ryan, |
| Height: 6-4 | Weight: 200 | Throws: R | Wilfredo Boscan, Zeke Spruill, Arquimedes Nieto |

| YEAR | Age | Level | IP | W | L | ERA | FIP | K/9 | BB/9 | K% | BB% | HR/9 | LOB% |
|------|-----|-------|-----|---|---|------|------|------|------|------|------|------|------|
| 2013 | 19 | A | 118.7 | 7 | 6 | 2.73 | 3.54 | 6.52 | 2.35 | 17.1% | 6.2% | 0.53 | 68.1% |
| 2014 | 20 | A+ | 128.0 | 10 | 7 | 3.80 | 4.02 | 6.54 | 2.18 | 17.4% | 5.8% | 0.63 | 72.9% |
| 2015 | 21 | AA | 131.7 | 8 | 6 | 3.69 | 4.04 | 4.65 | 1.57 | 12.6% | 4.3% | 0.82 | 68.4% |

**Background:** After a terribly busy offseason last year, one in which he passed from the Padres to the Dodgers in the Matt Kemp deal and then shipped from Los Angeles to the City of Brotherly Love the following day as part of the Jimmy Rollins package, Eflin was finally able to settle in as the youngest qualified pitcher in the Eastern League in 2015. A former supplemental first rounder back 2012, 33rd overall, Eflin has moved expeditiously through the low levels of the minors: after a quick seven-inning debut in the Arizona Summer League, he spent the next season with Fort Wayne, then followed that up with a full year in High Class A before making his way up to the minors' big test in 2015. And the results were...a bit mixed. In 23 starts with Reading, the 6-foot-4 right-hander tossed a career best 131.2 innings of work and issued a career best 1.6 free passes per nine innings, but alas he managed to barely miss any sticks either (4.6 K/9). For his career, Eflin is sporting a 3.50 ERA to go along with a 251-to-88 strikeout-to-walk ratio.

**Projection**: There's a fairly large difference between competent minor league arm and serviceable big league starter. And, unfortunately, for Eflin; he falls into the former category. While he's been young – sometimes exceptionally young – for his level of competition, he's never really stood out statistically speaking. He's never missed a whole lot of bats and he's posted back-to-back FIPs of 4.02 and 4.04. The lack of strikeouts will ultimately damn him into a relief/spot starter role. And if you need further proof just look at his CALs: Chris Volstad, Kyle Ryan, Wilfredo Boscan, Zeke Spruill, and Arquimedes Nieto.

**Ceiling:** 1.0-win player
**Risk:** Moderate
**MLB ETA:** 2016

## 22. Nick Pivetta, RHP

MiLB Rank: N/A
Position Rank: N/A

| Born: 02/14/93 | Age: 21 | Bats: R | Top CALs: Hector Hernandez, Jake Brigham, |
| Height: 6-5 | Weight: 220 | Throws: R | Robin Leyer, Blake Hassebrock, Deunte Heath |

| YEAR | Age | Level | IP | W | L | ERA | FIP | K/9 | BB/9 | K% | BB% | HR/9 | LOB% |
|------|-----|-------|-----|---|---|------|------|------|------|------|------|------|------|
| 2015 | 22 | A+ | 86.3 | 7 | 4 | 2.29 | 3.27 | 7.51 | 3.02 | 20.7% | 8.3% | 0.42 | 75.5% |
| 2015 | 22 | AA | 43.3 | 2 | 4 | 7.27 | 6.38 | 6.44 | 5.82 | 15.3% | 13.8% | 1.66 | 65.0% |

**Background:** Acquired for what amounted to one infamous choke on NL MVP Bryce Harper, a.k.a. veteran closer Jonathan Papelbon, Pivetta split his season between High Class A and Class AA last year. The big 6-foot-5, 220-pound hard-throwing right-hander opened the year up with 15 starts with Potomac in the Carolina League where he posted a 72-to-29 strikeout-to-walk ratio in 86.1 innings of work. And after a dominant performance in early July against the Wilmington Blue Rocks – he tossed seven innings of two-hit, nine-strikeout, zero-walk ball – the Washington front office promoted the former fourth round pick up to the Eastern League for a couple starts before swapping him for Papelbon at the trade deadline. Pivetta finished the year on a bit of a sour note: of his nine Eastern League starts, he allowed five earned runs or more five different times.

**Projection**: Sort of what you would expect a team would receive for an expensive veteran reliever at the deadline. Pivetta's never missed a whole lot of bats at any point in his career – his work in the Carolina League, 7.5 K/9, was his finest showing to date – and he hasn't shown the type of control to compensate for that yet either. He's one of those guys that will continue to climb through the minor leagues as a starter for a couple more seasons before making the easy transition into a relief role where he'll be a serviceable middle relief/fringy setup arm.

**Ceiling:** 1.0-win player
**Risk:** Moderate
**MLB ETA:** 2017

## 23. Jesmuel Valentin, IF/OF

**MiLB Rank: N/A**
**Position Rank: N/A**

| Born: 05/12/94 | Age: 22 | Bats: B | Top CALs: Luis Mendez, Jordan Cowan, |
| Height: 5-9 | Weight: 180 | Throws: R | Manuel Guzman, Luis Ortiz, Juan Moreno |

| Season | Age | LVL | PA | 2B | 3B | HR | AVG | OBP | SLG | ISO | BB% | K% | wRC+ |
|--------|-----|-----|-----|----|----|----|------|------|------|------|------|------|------|
| 2013 | 19 | R | 293 | 10 | 3 | 4 | 0.284 | 0.379 | 0.396 | 0.112 | 11.3% | 11.6% | 107 |
| 2013 | 19 | A | 122 | 6 | 1 | 0 | 0.212 | 0.325 | 0.293 | 0.081 | 13.1% | 23.0% | 80 |
| 2013 | 19 | A | 122 | 6 | 1 | 0 | 0.212 | 0.325 | 0.293 | 0.081 | 13.1% | 23.0% | 80 |
| 2014 | 20 | A | 462 | 22 | 9 | 7 | 0.280 | 0.349 | 0.430 | 0.150 | 8.2% | 15.6% | 123 |
| 2015 | 21 | A+ | 118 | 10 | 1 | 1 | 0.273 | 0.351 | 0.424 | 0.152 | 10.2% | 12.7% | 136 |

**Background:** Also acquired from Ruben Amaro Jr.'s favorite trade partner, the Los Angeles Dodgers, Valentin was sent eastward as part of the package for Roberto Hernandez two years ago. Valentin, a switch-hitting utility man with experience all over the diamond, missed a good portion of the year for...well...for being a dick. He was arrested in early April and charged with domestic battery in an incident involving his wife. Valentin was subsequently suspended, sought help, and returned to action in late July. He would appear in 31 games with Clearwater in the Florida State League, hitting .273/.351/.424, numbers that more or less far in line with his career norms (.261/.351/.384).

**Projection:** Valentin has all the makings of a quality infielder, not so much towards the makings of a quality human being. The former supplemental first round pick has continued to handle the low level minor league competition. He's shown an above-average eye at the plate, solid gap power, a decent hit tool, the ability to hit from both sides of the plate, and the skill to bounce all around the diamond.

**Ceiling:** 1.0-win player
**Risk:** Moderate
**MLB ETA:** 2017

## 24. Tom Windle, LHP

**MiLB Rank: N/A**
**Position Rank: N/A**

| Born: 03/10/92 | Age: 24 | Bats: L | Top CALs: Michael O'Brien, Kevin Comer, |
| Height: 6-4 | Weight: 215 | Throws: L | Jake Thompson, Ryan Searle, Paul Clemens |

| YEAR | Age | Level | IP | W | L | ERA | FIP | K/9 | BB/9 | K% | BB% | HR/9 | LOB% |
|------|-----|-------|------|---|---|------|------|------|------|------|------|------|------|
| 2013 | 21 | A | 53.7 | 5 | 1 | 2.68 | 3.15 | 8.55 | 3.35 | 22.1% | 8.7% | 0.34 | 76.6% |
| 2014 | 22 | A+ | 139.3 | 12 | 8 | 4.26 | 4.53 | 7.17 | 2.84 | 18.3% | 7.3% | 0.90 | 64.8% |
| 2015 | 23 | AA | 97.3 | 4 | 5 | 4.35 | 4.36 | 5.92 | 4.72 | 15.1% | 12.1% | 0.55 | 66.4% |

**Background:** Trying to disprove the notion that the Big Ten can't churn out a reasonable big league starter, Windle, who hails from the University of Minnesota, was the second piece acquired from – you've guessed it – the Dodgers last season for future Hall of Famer Jimmy Rollins. And, well, let's just say the former second round pick didn't do a whole lot for his former Power Five conference in 2015. In 34 games with the Fightin' Phils, 14 of which were starts, Windle strung together some lackadaisical peripherals: he averaged just 5.9 strikeouts and a worrisome 4.7 walks per nine innings. The club would eventually demote the once-promising lefty to the bullpen in in late June and the results were pretty improved a bit:

| Position | IP | K | BB |
|----------|------|----|----|
| Starter | 70.2 | 43 | 40 |
| Reliever | 27.1 | 21 | 11 |

For his career, the 6-foot-4, 215-pound lefty has fanned 226, walked 115, and posted an even 4.00 ERA in 290.1 innings of work.

**Projection:** It's not like Windle didn't flash some promise as a starting pitcher during his disastrous 2015 campaign. For instance, he twirled a seven-inning, two-hit, nine-strikeout performance against the Harrisburg Senators. But in the end he failed to make the proper adjustments to keep himself in the rotation, like not posting a near one-to-one strikeout-to-walk ratio. And as he enter his age-24 season, it's likely that we've seen the last of him as a starting pitcher, but he does, however, have a chance to develop into a poor man's version of Andrew Miller, the former first round bust turned dominant – and rich! – reliever.

**Ceiling:** 1.0-win player
**Risk:** Moderate
**MLB ETA:** 2016

## 25. Franklyn Kilome, RHP

MiLB Rank: N/A
Position Rank: N/A

| Born: 03/10/92 | Age: 24 | Bats: L | Top CALs: Matt Swynenberg, Manaure Martinez, |
| Height: 6-4 | Weight: 215 | Throws: L | Chris Andujar, Evan Rutckyj, Jose Torres |

| YEAR | Age | Level | IP | W | L | ERA | FIP | K/9 | BB/9 | K% | BB% | HR/9 | LOB% |
|------|-----|-------|-----|---|---|------|------|------|------|-------|-------|------|------|
| 2014 | 19 | R | 40.3 | 3 | 1 | 3.12 | 3.80 | 5.58 | 2.45 | 14.9% | 6.6% | 0.45 | 68.6% |
| 2015 | 20 | A- | 49.3 | 3 | 2 | 3.28 | 4.02 | 6.57 | 3.83 | 17.4% | 10.1% | 0.18 | 71.0% |

**Background:** Philly signed the right-hander out of La Romana, Dominican Republic a couple years back. Kilome made his debut in Philly's GCL affiliate where he posted a mediocre 25-to-11 strikeout-to-walk ratio in 40.1 innings of work. He got bounced up to short-season ball and saw a slight uptick in production in 2015.

**Projection**: Low level wild card arm. Kilome has the size and projectability one would want in a young hurler. But his production has been blasé in his first 89.2 professional innings. On the positive side: he finished the 2015 season with a groundball rate just north of 55%. Kilome is ready for full season action, after which we'll have a better read on his potential

**Ceiling:** 1.0-win player
**Risk:** Moderate
**MLB ETA:** 2016

## Barely Missed:

- **Harold Arauz, RHP** – Acquired from Houston as part of the Ken Giles package, Arauz missed a helluva lot of bats between Gulf Coast League and NYPL, but he was a touch old for those levels.

- **Jonathan Arauz, 2B/SS** –The Panamanian-born middle infielder looked like a promising bat during his debut in the Gulf Coast League, hitting .254/.309/.370 with a 105 wRC+. Of course, that comes with the fact that he was just 16-years-old. Arauz offered up a solid eye, gap-to-gap power, and a reasonable hit tool. He's nearly a lock to be in next year's Top 25.

- **Aaron Brown, OF** – Former two-way star at Pepperdine University took a route that I didn't expect: Philadelphia moved the third round pick to a fulltime bat once he entered pro ball. Brown batted a solid .257/.324/.406 with 17 doubles, four triples, and 11 homeruns en route to topping the league average production by 24%. Here's what I wrote in his pre-draft evaluation: "Brown profiles as a Quad-A type hitter, offering up plenty of power and very little of anything else."

- **Malquin Canelo, SS** – The diminutive shortstop had a BABIP-driven breakout in the Sally last season, hitting .311/.364/.466 while flashing the kind of power he's never shown previously. His numbers tumbled once the club bumped him up to High Class A: he batted .250/.296/.323 as his BABIP dropped to a more reasonable .301.

- **Andrew Pullin, 2B/OF** –Former fifth round pick had a decent showing in with Clearwater last year, hitting .258/.300/.396. He can fill up a stat sheet without truly standing out. Maybe he can carve out a career that sees him bounce up to the big leagues for a couple cups.

- **Lucas Williams, 3B** – Just under 150 plate appearances of data and his lofty draft status to go on, the majority of Williams' production comes from his enormously bloated walk rate, 14.9%. The 6-foot-1, 180-pound third baseman didn't attack pitchers often last season as evidenced by his lack of pop, but it's still too soon to tell if it's just an anomaly.

## *Bird Doggin' It – Additional Prospects to Keep an Eye in 2016*

| Player | Age | POS | Notes |
|---|---|---|---|
| Jimmy Cordero | 24 | RHP | Part of the package acquired from Toronto for the services of Ben Revere. The 6-foot-3 right-hander finished the year with a combined 64-to-24 strikeout-to-walk ratio in 67.0 innings of work between High Class A and Class AA. |
| Joey DeNato | 24 | LHP | Former 19th round pick has been ridiculously dominant since entering pro ball two years ago. DeNato got a late season bump up to Lehigh Valley from the Sally. He could be pitching in Philly as soon as next season. |
| Luis Encarnacion | 18 | 1B | After a disappointing showing as a 16-year-old in the Gulf Coast two years ago, Encarnacion spent 2015 back in the rookie league with a much improved production line: .271/.313/.370. |
| Bailey Falter | 19 | RHP | A fifth round pick out of Chino Hills High School year, Falter posted a remarkable 25-to-3 strikeout-to-walk ratio in 28.2 innings. |
| Elniery Garcia | 21 | LHP | Small-ish left-hander out of the Dominican Republic held his own in the Sally, despite some lackluster peripherals. |
| Edgar Garcoa | 19 | RHP | Garcia made the move to the stateside rookie leagues last season and saw a dramatic rise in his strikeout rate, jumping from 6.7 K/9 to 9.4 K/9. Let's see how he handles a year in which he tosses more than 32.2 innings. |
| Deivi Grullon | 20 | C | The then-19-year-old backstop looked overmatched in his return to the Sally, hitting .221/.273/.335. He's a tough read considering how aggressively the organization is trying to push him through the minors. |
| Ulises Joaquin | 24 | RHP | Spent the year closing out games for Clearwater; he averaged 8.7 punch outs and just 2.0 walks per nine innings. |
| Benton Keys | 21 | LHP | Had a decent showing in the NYPL last season, but the former 11th round prep pick hasn't really stood out in three professional seasons. |
| Brandon Leibrandt | 23 | LHP | Similar to his father – and former big leaguer – Charlie Leibrandt. Brandon is a big finesse lefty who handled High Class A well. He's ready for the Eastern League. |
| Kyle Martin | 23 | 1B | Former South Carolina bopped looked strong in his pro debut as the club bumped him all the way to the Sally, hitting .279/.325/.446. |
| Angelo More | 23 | 2B/SS | The then-22-year-old switch-hitter had a breakout year in 2015 as he hit a combined .312/.356/.447 in limited action between the Florida State and Eastern Leagues. |
| Colton Murray | 26 | RHP | Showed a mid-90s fastball during his brief 7.2-inning stint in Philly last season. Serviceable middle relief arm. Maybe. |
| Edubray Ramos | 23 | RHP | Made quick work of the Florida State League and looked solid in 18 games out of Reading's bullpen. |
| John Richy | 23 | RHP | Ranked the former UNLV starter as the 57th best collegiate prospect in 2014. Richy tallied a 115-to-35 strikeout-to-walk ratio in 137 innings in High Class A between the Dodgers' and Phillies' organization. |
| Yacksel Rios | 23 | RHP | Finished the year with a 3.20 FIP in 88.1 innings in High Class A. |
| Alexis Rivero | 21 | RHP | Fanned 67 in 71.2 innings between the Sally and FSL. |
| Tyler Viza | 21 | RHP | Control artist walked just 5.3% of the batters he faced in the Sally last season to go along with a 3.76 FIP. Not sure if he can overcome the lack of punch outs. |
| Shane Watson | 23 | RHP | Back from missing a year-and-a-half of action due to injury, the former 40th overall pick in 2012 didn't look all that promising in 43.2 innings in the Sally. |

# Pittsburgh Pirates

**State of the Farm System:** Home to three of the top 44 prospects in all of baseball. Pittsburgh has a budding ace in big right-hander Tyler Glasnow, the fifth best prospect in the game, a toolsy center fielder capable of stringing together multiple All-Star caliber seasons in Austin Meadows, the 14th best prospect, and one of the best overall bats in the minor leagues in Josh Bell, the 43rd prospect.

Glasnow, a rail thin 6-foot-8, 225-pound hurler out of Santa Clarita, California, split last season between the Eastern and International Leagues, tallying an impressive 136-to-43 strikeout-to-walk ratio in just over 109 innings of work.

Meadows, the club's first round pick three years ago, spent the majority of the 2015 battering the Florida State League pitching to the tune of .307/.357/.407 with 22 doubles, four triples, and seven homeruns in 121 games.

And Bell, the former big time Bonus Baby, slugged .317/.393/.446 with 24 doubles, nine triples, seven homeruns, and nine stolen bases between his time with Altoona and Indianapolis.

Both Glasnow and Bell figure to be key contributors for the Pirates in 2016 and Meadows shouldn't be too far behind.

Jameson Taillon, the onetime top prospect who was mentioned among the best five in all of baseball, failed to see the diamond for the second straight season as his once promising career was put on hold – again.

Outfielder Willy Garcia and Harold Ramirez give the organization a couple solid middle-tier prospects. Garcia batted .275/.314/.431 between his stints in Class AA and Class AAA. And Ramirez continued his emergence as he slugged .337/.399/.458 with 13 doubles, six triples, four homeruns, and 22 stolen bases in another injury-shortened campaign.

| Rank | Name | POS |
|---|---|---|
| 1 | Tyler Glasnow | RHP |
| 2 | Austin Meadows | CF |
| 3 | Josh Bell | 1B/RF |
| 4 | Jameson Taillon | RHP |
| 5 | Willy Garcia | OF |
| 6 | Harold Ramirez | LF/RF |
| 7 | Kevin Newman | SS |
| 8 | Alen Hanson | 2B/SS |
| 9 | Nick Kingham | RHP |
| 10 | Maxwell Moroff | 2B/SS |
| 11 | Jesse Biddle | LHP |
| 12 | Elias Diaz | C |
| 13 | Trevor Williams | RHP |
| 14 | Cole Tucker | SS |
| 15 | Jose Osuna | 1B/LF/RF |
| 16 | Steven Brault | LHP |
| 17 | Ke'Bryan Hayes | 3B |
| 18 | Yeudy Garcia | RHP |
| 19 | Stephen Tarpley | LHP |
| 20 | Mitch Keller | RHP |
| 21 | Connor Joe | 1B |
| 22 | Kevin Kramer | 2B/SS |
| 23 | Jin-De Jhang | C |
| 24 | Reese Mcguire | C |
| 25 | Clay Holmes | RHP |

One word of caution: infielder Alen Hanson is among the game's most overrated, over-talked-about prospect.

**Review of the 2015 Draft:** Pittsburgh grabbed University of Arizona shortstop Kevin Newman with the 19th overall selection last June. The sweet-swinging infielder ripped the cover off the ball during his final stint with the PAC12 school, hitting a robust .370/.426/.489. But there's a very distinct possibility he fades into a part-time role due to his lack of power and patience.

The club's second pick in the opening round, prep third baseman Ke'Bryan Hayes, hit a respectable .308/.408/.346 during his debut, but he showed very little in terms of power as well.

Pittsburgh also dipped back into the collegiate ranks with their second round pick by taking another highly-touted shortstop with the first name of Kevin. A former UCLA stud, Kevin Kramer, flashed more power and patience during his collegiate career, but lacked the impressive hit tool that his new org-mate showed.

Former Alabama outfielder Casey Hughston looked pitiful during his run in the New York-Penn League.

# 1. Tyler Glasnow, RHP

| Born: 08/23/93 | Age: 22 | Bats: L | Top CALs: Trevor Bauer, Casey Mulligan, |
|---|---|---|---|
| Height: 6-8 | Weight: 225 | Throws: R | Yovani Gallardo, Bruce Rondon, Luis Severino |

| YEAR | Age | Level | IP | W | L | ERA | FIP | K/9 | BB/9 | K% | BB% | HR/9 | LOB% |
|---|---|---|---|---|---|---|---|---|---|---|---|---|---|
| 2013 | 19 | A | 111.3 | 9 | 3 | 2.18 | 3.47 | 13.26 | 4.93 | 36.3% | 13.5% | 0.73 | 79.9% |
| 2014 | 20 | A+ | 124.3 | 12 | 5 | 1.74 | 2.63 | 11.36 | 4.13 | 31.9% | 11.6% | 0.22 | 80.9% |
| 2015 | 21 | A- | 5.3 | 0 | 1 | 3.38 | 2.95 | 10.13 | 3.38 | 26.1% | 8.7% | 0.00 | 33.3% |
| 2015 | 21 | AA | 63.0 | 5 | 3 | 2.43 | 1.98 | 11.71 | 2.71 | 33.1% | 7.7% | 0.29 | 66.4% |
| 2015 | 21 | AAA | 41.0 | 2 | 1 | 2.20 | 2.82 | 10.54 | 4.83 | 27.6% | 12.6% | 0.22 | 73.3% |

**Background:** At one point you just have to stop and ask: How in the *hell* did a prep arm like Glasnow last until the fifth round in 2011? And it's not like he's been a revelation over the past year or two either. He's been a dominant force – and one of the minors' top arms – since making his professional debut in the Gulf Coast League. But that's exactly what happened to the monstrous right-hander out of Santa Clarita, California. A big 6-foot-8, 225-pounder with projectability and a plus-plus-ability to miss bats, Glasnow's dominance was on full display with Altoona in the Eastern League last season. As one of just five hurlers in under the age of 22 with 60+ innings in the EL, Glasnow fanned a mind-boggling 33.1% of the total hitters he faced – the highest mark in the entire league.

And just to take a quick sidestep for a moment, consider this: no one player under the age of 22 has topped that mark in any Class AA level since 2006, the first year of MiLB data is available at FanGraphs.

Pittsburgh promoted the budding ace up to Indianapolis in the International League at the beginning of August for another eight starts, most of which were of the dominant fashion. Glasnow finished his abbreviated campaign with 109.1 innings, 136 punch outs, 43 walks, and a miniscule 2.39. And for his career he's whiffed an inexplicable 32.4% of the hitters he faced to go along with a video game-esque 2.07 ERA.

**Projection**: I've long hitched my analytical wagon on Glasnow's potential as a dominant big leaguer starter. Three years ago in my first book I ranked him as the 13th best prospect in all of baseball, writing at that time:

> *"Dominant. That's it. Just filthy dominance. Although Glasnow stands a towering 6-foot-7, his weight is listed at just 195 pounds, meaning there could still be another gear on his fastball once he begins to fill out. The control/command isn't quite there yet, but there's no reason to suspect that it won't improve. [He has legitimate] ace material."*

Well, I followed that up by moving Glasnow up three spots to the tenth best minor leaguer heading into last season. Here's what I wrote then:

> *"The control is still lagging a bit – he's walked 12.3% of the batters he's faced in his career – but it's definitely trending in the right direction; two years ago his walk percentage was 14.0% and last year he cut that down to 11.6%. Big, big time swing-and-miss ability, he could theoretically see a few upticks in his arsenal as he's lean frame fills out. Glasnow could be – and has the makings of – a special right arm."*

And after another breathtaking performance in 2015 – one that was briefly interrupted by a sprained ankle – there's absolutely nothing else to say that could possibly capture something that I haven't written before. Actually there is: Glasnow's control took the expected step forward last season as he walked a career low 7.7% of batters he faced with Altoona, and if you ignore two disastrous starts in Class AAA, he walked just 10 batters in 36 innings (2.50 BB/9).

**Ceiling:** 5.0- to 5.5-win player
**Risk:** Moderate
**MLB ETA:** 2016

# 2. Austin Meadows, CF

| Born: 05/03/95 | Age: 21 | Bats: L | Top CALs: Brett Phillips, Justin Upton, |
|---|---|---|---|
| Height: 6-3 | Weight: 200 | Throws: L | Harold Ramirez, Estarlin Martinez, Jesse Winker |

| Season | Age | LVL | PA | 2B | 3B | HR | AVG | OBP | SLG | ISO | BB% | K% | wRC+ |
|---|---|---|---|---|---|---|---|---|---|---|---|---|---|
| 2013 | 18 | R | 189 | 11 | 5 | 5 | 0.294 | 0.399 | 0.519 | 0.225 | 12.7% | 22.2% | 169 |
| 2014 | 19 | A | 165 | 13 | 1 | 3 | 0.322 | 0.388 | 0.486 | 0.164 | 8.5% | 18.2% | 144 |
| 2015 | 20 | A+ | 556 | 22 | 4 | 7 | 0.307 | 0.357 | 0.407 | 0.100 | 7.4% | 14.2% | 134 |
| 2015 | 20 | AA | 28 | 2 | 3 | 0 | 0.360 | 0.429 | 0.680 | 0.320 | 7.1% | 17.9% | 213 |

**Background:** It's taken longer than the organization would have liked, but Meadows, the ninth overall pick in 2013, finally put together a full, healthy season. And, boy, it was totally worth the wait. Hailing from Grayson High School, the toolsy outfielder that hadn't topped 48 games in either of two previous professional seasons breezed through the Florida State League last year, hitting an impressive .307/.357/.407 with 22 doubles, four triples, seven homeruns, and swiping 20 bags in 27 attempts. His overall production, per *Weighted Runs Created Plus*, topped the league average mark by 34% – narrowly besting the Mets' Dominic Smith for top showing among all players under the age of 21 in the FSL last season. For his career, Meadows is sporting a .312/.380/.460 triple-slash line with 50 doubles, 14 triples, 17 homeruns, and 26 stolen bases.

**Projection**: A high school rival to the Indians' Clint Frazier, who went a couple picks before Pittsburgh grabbed the toolsy outfielder, Meadows hasn't stalled for any extended length during his 220 minor leagues games – outside of his momentary blip against fellow southpaws two years ago. After struggling against LHP in a limited sample size to the tune of .176/.250/.216, the 6-foot-3 center fielder rebounded in a big way last year, hitting .309/.351/.388. Above-average speed, hit tool, power, and a solid enough eye at the plate. And let's just say CAL is a big fan too, linking him to Brett Phillips, Justin Upton, and Jesse Winker among others. Meadows has the makings of an All-Star caliber big leaguer – perhaps as soon as 2017.

**Ceiling**: 4.0-win player
**Risk**: Moderate
**MLB ETA**: 2017

## 3. Josh Bell, 1B/RF

**MiLB Rank: #44**
**Position Rank: #3 (1B), #12 (OF)**

| Born: 08/14/92 | Age: 23 | Bats: B | Top CALs: Rangel Ravelo, Logan Morrison, |
|---|---|---|---|
| Height: 6-2 | Weight: 235 | Throws: R | Gregory Polanco, Desmond Jennings, Adam Eaton |

| Season | Age | LVL | PA | 2B | 3B | HR | AVG | OBP | SLG | ISO | BB% | K% | wRC+ |
|---|---|---|---|---|---|---|---|---|---|---|---|---|---|
| 2013 | 20 | A | 519 | 37 | 2 | 13 | 0.279 | 0.353 | 0.453 | 0.174 | 10.0% | 17.3% | 131 |
| 2014 | 21 | A+ | 363 | 20 | 4 | 9 | 0.335 | 0.384 | 0.502 | 0.166 | 6.9% | 11.8% | 153 |
| 2014 | 21 | AA | 102 | 2 | 0 | 0 | 0.287 | 0.343 | 0.309 | 0.021 | 7.8% | 11.8% | 86 |
| 2015 | 22 | AA | 426 | 17 | 6 | 5 | 0.307 | 0.376 | 0.427 | 0.120 | 10.3% | 11.7% | 130 |
| 2015 | 22 | AAA | 145 | 7 | 3 | 2 | 0.347 | 0.441 | 0.504 | 0.157 | 14.5% | 10.3% | 174 |

**Background**: One of the most lethal bats in all of baseball down the stretch last season, Bell smoked the International League pitching to the tune of .347/.441/.504 with seven doubles, three triples, and a pair of dingers in his final 31 games of the year. The former second round Bonus Baby who signed a massive $5 million deal, a record for a second round pick, began the year back in the Eastern League following his 24-game stint in the level to cap off his 2014 season. And despite holding his own in the level two years ago – he batted .287/.343/.309 – Bell fared much, much better in his repeat: he slugged .317/.376/.427 with 17 doubles, six triples, and five homeruns. Overall, Bell hit a combined .317/.393/.446 with 24 doubles, nine triples, and seven homeruns between his time with Altoona and Indianapolis.

**Projection**: A plus hit tool with so much power potential, but he quite hasn't figured out how to tap into to it during games. All the doubles – he's averaged nearly 40 every 162 games throughout his career – will eventually start developing into four-baggers at some point. Above-average eye at the plate and a track record of dominant success against older competition, the Pirates have been prepping the former third baseman-turned-corner-outfielder-turned-first-baseman to take over for the recently departed Pedro Alvarez and he's ready to do so – with an even better offensive profile. In terms of his 2016 production, think .280/.350/.420.

**Ceiling**: 3.0- to 3.5-win player
**Risk**: Moderate
**MLB ETA**:

## 4. Jameson Taillon, RHP

**MiLB Rank: #129**
**Position Rank: N/A**

| Born: 11/18/91 | Age: 24 | Bats: R | Top CALs: Eduardo Rodriguez, Jacob Turner, |
|---|---|---|---|
| Height: 6-5 | Weight: 240 | Throws: R | Randall Delgado, Zach Davis, Sean Gallagher |

| YEAR | Age | Level | IP | W | L | ERA | FIP | K/9 | BB/9 | K% | BB% | HR/9 | LOB% |
|---|---|---|---|---|---|---|---|---|---|---|---|---|---|
| 2013 | 21 | AA | 110.3 | 4 | 7 | 3.67 | 3.46 | 8.65 | 2.94 | 22.2% | 7.5% | 0.65 | 69.8% |
| 2013 | 21 | AAA | 37.0 | 1 | 3 | 3.89 | 3.18 | 9.00 | 3.89 | 22.8% | 9.9% | 0.24 | 70.6% |

**Background**: Just to kind of add some perspective – as well as some unwanted, unintended insult to injury – Taillon, the once crown jewel of the Pittsburgh system, was in the same draft class that produced the likes of Bryce Harper, Manny Machado, Matt Harvey, Chris Sale, and Noah Syndergaard, all of whom have established themselves as legitimate impact big leaguers. And at one point it was assumed that Taillon's name would be squarely among his peers, but a Tommy John surgery and a subsequent inguinal hernia, which also required going under the knife, forced him to the miss the entirety of the past two seasons. Before the injuries, Taillon had fanned 22.0% and walked 6.9% of the total hitters he faced between 2011 and 2013.

**Projection**: Star-crossed and snake bitter, what else can you really say? Taillon looked like a potential top-of-the-rotation caliber arm, but his last meaningful game was a 2.0-inning appearance for the Scottsdale Scorpions in the Arizona Fall League on October 8th, 2013. So who the hell knows what he'll resemble when he finally toes the rubber again?

**Ceiling:** 2.5- to 3.0-win player
**Risk:** Moderate to High
**MLB ETA:**        /2017

## 5. Harold Ramirez, LF/RF

**MiLB Rank: #155**
**Position Rank: N/A**

| Born: 09/06/94 | Age: 21 | Bats: R | Top CALs: Dustin Fowler, Manuel Margot, |
|---|---|---|---|
| Height: 5-10 | Weight: 210 | Throws: R | Mason Williams, Danry Vasquez, Joe Dickerson |

| Season | Age | LVL | PA | 2B | 3B | HR | AVG | OBP | SLG | ISO | BB% | K% | wRC+ |
|---|---|---|---|---|---|---|---|---|---|---|---|---|---|
| 2013 | 18 | A- | 310 | 11 | 4 | 5 | 0.285 | 0.354 | 0.409 | 0.124 | 7.4% | 16.8% | 133 |
| 2014 | 19 | A | 226 | 14 | 1 | 1 | 0.309 | 0.364 | 0.402 | 0.093 | 4.9% | 15.5% | 117 |
| 2015 | 20 | A+ | 344 | 13 | 6 | 4 | 0.337 | 0.399 | 0.458 | 0.121 | 7.3% | 14.0% | 163 |

**Background:** The short, stocky corner outfielder out of Columbia had one of biggest breakout last seasons of any prospect in the Pirates' player development engine. Ramirez, who stands a less-than-imposing 5-foot-10 and a round 210 pounds, missed the first seven weeks of the year, but hit a scorching .337/.399/.458 with a 163 wRC+ in 80 games.

**Projection:** Here's what I wrote in last year's book:

*"Ramirez missed a good portion of the year thanks to a stress reaction in his shin. Ouch. Prior to that injury he missed some time with a hamstring issue. When he's healthy he looks like a solid fourth outfielder-type – something that CAL would agree upon. He doesn't walk often; the power's been unnoticeable, but the hit tool and speed could garner some looks."*

OK. Even after his breakout season a lot of the same information could still be said about the plump outfielder: the hit tool and speed are definite, repeatable skills; the power, even though it did take a step forward, is still a below-average skill, and CAL still remains a bit suspicious, linking him to Dustin Fowler, Mason Williams, Danry Vazquez, and Joe Dickerson – though the Manuel Margot comp is incredibly interesting. Curiously enough, Ramirez seems to be able to repeat ridiculously high BABIPs: his last three seasons were .385/.365/.332.

**Ceiling:** 2.5- to 3.0-win player
**Risk:** Moderate to High
**MLB ETA:** 2017/2018

## 6. Willy Garcia, OF

**MiLB Rank: #230**
**Position Rank: N/A**

| Born: 09/04/92 | Age: 23 | Bats: R | Top CALs: Yorman Rodriguez, Fernando Martinez, |
|---|---|---|---|
| Height: 6-2 | Weight: 215 | Throws: R | Quincy Latimore, Joel Guzman, Randal Grichuk |

| Season | Age | LVL | PA | 2B | 3B | HR | AVG | OBP | SLG | ISO | BB% | K% | wRC+ |
|---|---|---|---|---|---|---|---|---|---|---|---|---|---|
| 2013 | 20 | A+ | 480 | 21 | 6 | 16 | 0.256 | 0.294 | 0.437 | 0.180 | 4.8% | 32.1% | 105 |
| 2014 | 21 | AA | 474 | 27 | 5 | 18 | 0.271 | 0.311 | 0.478 | 0.207 | 5.1% | 30.6% | 114 |
| 2015 | 22 | AA | 224 | 7 | 2 | 5 | 0.314 | 0.353 | 0.441 | 0.127 | 4.9% | 21.0% | 127 |
| 2015 | 22 | AAA | 291 | 11 | 4 | 10 | 0.246 | 0.285 | 0.424 | 0.178 | 4.1% | 26.1% | 103 |

**Background:** A toolsy, stat-stuffing free-swinger from the Dominican Republic, Garcia's first half of 2015 just offered up a glimpse of what type of production he's capable of: appearing back in Class AA after a solid showing two years ago, the 6-foot-2, 215-pound outfielder hit .314/.353/.441 with seven doubles, a pair of triples, five homeruns, and three stolen bases to go along with a career best 127 wRC+. The organization's brain-trust bumped Garcia up to the International League in mid-June, and after a bit of an adjustment period – he batted .167/.191/.212 in his first 18 games – he slugged .271/.314/.490 the rest of the way. Overall, Garcia finished the year with an aggregate .275/.314/.431 triple-slash line, hitting 18 doubles, half a dozen triples, 15 homeruns, and four stolen bases in 10 attempts.

**Projection:** There's an awful lot to like about Garcia as a prospect – a package built around speed and power – but his abhorrence to the walk rate will ultimately limit his overall ceiling. He was able to trim off a noticeable amount off of his strikeout rate the second time through the Eastern League, but it spiked back up to just over 26% in Class AAA. The best case scenario, according to CAL, would be St. Louis' Randal Chichuk, another outfielder with questionable strikeout rates, above-average power, and low walk totals.

**Ceiling:** 2.0- to 2.5-win player
**Risk:** Moderate
**MLB ETA:** 2016

## 7. Kevin Newman, SS

**MiLB Rank: #237**
**Position Rank: N/A**

| Born: 08/04/93 | Age: 22 | Bats: R | Top CALs: N/A |
| Height: 6-1 | Weight: 180 | Throws: R | |

| Season | Age | LVL | PA | 2B | 3B | HR | AVG | OBP | SLG | ISO | BB% | K% | wRC+ |
|--------|-----|-----|-----|----|----|----|-------|-------|-------|-------|------|-------|------|
| 2015 | 21 | A- | 173 | 10 | 1 | 2 | 0.226 | 0.281 | 0.340 | 0.113 | 5.8% | 12.7% | 85 |
| 2015 | 21 | A | 110 | 4 | 1 | 0 | 0.306 | 0.376 | 0.367 | 0.061 | 8.2% | 7.3% | 118 |

**Background:** For the second consecutive season the Pirates tabbed a shortstop with their first pick in the draft, this time, though, dipping into the collegiate ranks and selecting University of Arizona's Kevin Newman. The 6-foot-1, 180-pounder hit .337/.396/.421 in his storied three-year career.

**Projection:** Here's what I wrote prior to last year's draft:

> " It's quite simple, really. Will Neman's hit tool, something that's been on display at every point during his collegiate career, be enough to compensate for bupkis power? And even dropping the term "power" is a bit misleading. Through his first 142 collegiate games *and* another 71 Cape Cod contests, the 6-foot-1 shortstop has "slugged" one homerun. That would be fine if he was a doubles machine a la Craig Biggio, but he has just 38 two-baggers to his resume. And not to harp on it – though it's a glaring red flag – but his career ISO at Arizona stands at .072.
>
> Only lessening his potential professional offensive impact is his lack of patience at the plate: he's walk just 48 times in his first 666 plate appearances, or just a little over 7%.
>
> Newman's a fantastic collegiate player, but unless his defense grades out at a Brendan Ryan or Brandon Crawford level there's just not a whole lot of big league impact in his future. Newman's the type that will dominate in the lowest levels and struggle in Class AA/Class AAA.
>
> Solid backup, fringy everyday guy ceiling.

**Ceiling:** 1.5- to 2.0-win player
**Risk:** Moderate
**MLB ETA:** 2017

## 8. Alen Hanson, 2B/SS

**MiLB Rank: #238**
**Position Rank: #10 (2B)**

| Born: 10/22/92 | Age: 23 | Bats: B | Top CALs: Logan Watkins, German Duran, |
| Height: 5-11 | Weight: 180 | Throws: R | Chris Bostick, Trevor Plouffe, Arismendy Alcantara |

| Season | Age | LVL | PA | 2B | 3B | HR | AVG | OBP | SLG | ISO | BB% | K% | wRC+ |
|--------|-----|-----|-----|----|----|----|-------|-------|-------|-------|------|-------|------|
| 2013 | 20 | A+ | 409 | 23 | 8 | 7 | 0.281 | 0.339 | 0.444 | 0.163 | 8.1% | 17.1% | 121 |
| 2013 | 20 | AA | 150 | 4 | 5 | 1 | 0.255 | 0.299 | 0.380 | 0.124 | 5.3% | 17.3% | 86 |
| 2014 | 21 | AA | 527 | 21 | 12 | 11 | 0.280 | 0.326 | 0.442 | 0.162 | 5.9% | 16.7% | 111 |
| 2015 | 22 | AAA | 529 | 17 | 12 | 6 | 0.263 | 0.313 | 0.387 | 0.124 | 7.0% | 17.2% | 101 |

**Background:** It's been four years since Hanson looked like one of the top young minor league shortstops – he batted .309/.381/.528 with 33 doubles, 13 triples, 16 homeruns, and stolen 35 bags with the West Virginia Power at 19-years-old – but since that time, however, his production has slowly dropped from eye-catching to good to slightly better than average to average. Since 2012 through the end of last season, his overall *Weighted Runs Created Plus* totals have dropped from 147 (Low Class A) to 121 (A+) to 111 (AA) to 101 (AAA). A 5-foot-11, 180-pound switch-hitting middle infielder out of the Dominican Republic, Hanson spent the entire 2015 season with Indianapolis in the International League, hitting .263/.313/.383 with 17 doubles, 12 triples, six homeruns, and 35 stolen bases (in 47 attempts). And for his career he's sporting a .284/.343/.444 triple-slash line.

**Projection:** Here's what I wrote in last year's book:

> *"Hanson's CALs leave a lot to be desired – [Arismendy] Alcantara's career got off to an awful start, a level that the overwhelming majority of prospects haven't been able to overcome; [Ronny] Rodriguez's career has sputtered out; [Reid] Brignac was MLB depth at his best, and [German] Duran never made the big leagues. The lone hope is [Nick] Franklin, who hasn't exactly set the world on fire in his first 502 big league plate appearances.*

*As far as Hanson is concerned, the power's average, the speed is a standout tool, but everything else hovers at slightly below-average. He's a fringy everyday game depending upon his defense, which, unfortunately, is pretty porous."*

And after another humdrum offensive showing in 2015 the exact same thing could be said for Hanson again: His CALs remains similarly underwhelming (Logan Watkins, German Duran, Chris Bostick, Trevor Plouffe, and Arismendy Alcantara); the power is strictly gap-to-gap and not the over-the-fence variety, the speed is above-average, and everything is blah.

His defense did improve as he moved across the keystone to second base, and with Neil Walker dealt to New York for Jon Niese, Hanson might be ready to step in for the big league club as decent, cheap option.

**Ceiling:** 1.5- to 2.0-win player
**Risk:** Moderate
**MLB ETA:** 2016

---

## 9. Nick Kingham, RHP

**MiLB Rank: N/A**
**Position Rank: N/A**

| Born: 11/08/91 | Age: 24 | Bats: R | **Top CALs:** Vance Worley, Josh Lindblom, |
|---|---|---|---|
| Height: 6-6 | Weight: 230 | Throws: R | Aaron Blair, Adrian Sampson, Wade Davis |

| YEAR | Age | Level | IP | W | L | ERA | FIP | K/9 | BB/9 | K% | BB% | HR/9 | LOB% |
|---|---|---|---|---|---|---|---|---|---|---|---|---|---|
| 2013 | 21 | A+ | 70.0 | 6 | 3 | 3.09 | 3.20 | 9.64 | 1.80 | 26.5% | 5.0% | 0.77 | 76.2% |
| 2013 | 21 | AA | 73.3 | 3 | 3 | 2.70 | 2.97 | 8.47 | 3.68 | 22.0% | 9.6% | 0.12 | 77.8% |
| 2014 | 22 | AA | 71.0 | 1 | 7 | 3.04 | 3.52 | 6.85 | 3.17 | 17.6% | 8.1% | 0.38 | 67.2% |
| 2014 | 22 | AAA | 88.0 | 5 | 4 | 3.58 | 3.72 | 6.65 | 2.76 | 18.0% | 7.5% | 0.61 | 64.7% |
| 2015 | 23 | AAA | 31.3 | 1 | 2 | 4.31 | 3.22 | 9.19 | 2.01 | 23.5% | 5.2% | 0.86 | 69.6% |

**Background:** Already knocking on the club's big league door before 2014, Kingham was on a mission to force his way into the Pirates' plans through his first six starts last season: he tossed 31.1 innings with Indianapolis, averaging 9.2 punch outs and just 2.0 walks per nine innings. And, unfortunately for Kingham, the young right-hander succumbed to Tommy John surgery.

**Projection:** Prior to the injury – and assuming he can make a full recovery – the former fourth round pick in 2010 looked like a valuable contributor in *any* big league rotation. He showed a strong feel for the strike zone, though he's never going to miss more than a league average amount of bats, and poise beyond his years. Hopefully, he makes a full recovery.

**Ceiling:** 1.5- to 2.0-win player
**Risk:** Moderate to High
**MLB ETA:** 2017

---

## 10. Max Moroff, 2B/SS

**MiLB Rank: N/A**
**Position Rank: N/A**

| Born: 05/13/93 | Age: 23 | Bats: B | **Top CALs:** Logan Watkins, Levi Michael, |
|---|---|---|---|
| Height: 6-0 | Weight: 175 | Throws: R | Karexon Sanchez, Nick Romero, Joey Demichele |

| Season | Age | LVL | PA | 2B | 3B | HR | AVG | OBP | SLG | ISO | BB% | K% | wRC+ |
|---|---|---|---|---|---|---|---|---|---|---|---|---|---|
| 2013 | 20 | A | 506 | 18 | 3 | 8 | 0.233 | 0.335 | 0.345 | 0.112 | 12.8% | 20.2% | 101 |
| 2014 | 21 | A+ | 534 | 30 | 6 | 1 | 0.244 | 0.324 | 0.340 | 0.096 | 10.1% | 24.2% | 93 |
| 2015 | 22 | AA | 612 | 28 | 6 | 7 | 0.293 | 0.374 | 0.409 | 0.117 | 11.4% | 18.1% | 128 |

**Background:** A late-round pick out of Trinity Prep High School in Winter Park, Florida, Moroff quietly had a breakout season in the Eastern League last year, hitting .293/.374/.409 with 28 doubles, six triples, seven homeruns, and 17 stolen bases. His overall production, according to *Weighted Runs Created Plus*, topped the league average mark by 28%.

**Projection:** Here's where it gets interesting – Moroff's breakout campaign, one in which only two other qualified Eastern League players under the age of 23 topped – could be a sustainable level moving forward. His walk rate last season, 11.4%, is nearly identical to his career total (11.8%); his power, .117 ISO, is also close to his previous totals. He did manage to cut down on his punch outs from the previous year, but it was within reason from his 2013 total (18.1% vs. 20.2%). The only red flag was his .356 BABIP, but, again, he's posted something near that in 2014 (.332). And don't forget he's been incredibly young for his levels of competition too. Add it all up and Moroff has the makings of an above-average backup or potential fringy everyday player.

**Ceiling:** 1.5- to 2.0-win player
**Risk:** Moderate to High
**MLB ETA:** 2017

## 11. Jesse Biddle, LHP

**MiLB Rank: N/A**
**Position Rank: N/A**

| Born: 10/22/91 | Age: 24 | Bats: L | **Top CALs:** Dan Cortes, Chris Withrow, |
| Height: 6-5 | Weight: 235 | Throws: L | Alexander Smit, Nick Additon, Travis Chick |

| YEAR | Age | Level | IP | W | L | ERA | FIP | K/9 | BB/9 | K% | BB% | HR/9 | LOB% |
|------|-----|-------|-----|---|---|-----|-----|------|------|-----|-----|------|------|
| 2013 | 21 | AA | 138.3 | 5 | 14 | 3.64 | 3.88 | 10.02 | 5.33 | 26.2% | 14.0% | 0.65 | 74.3% |
| 2014 | 22 | R | 2.0 | 0 | 0 | 4.50 | 8.51 | 13.50 | 4.50 | 37.5% | 12.5% | 4.50 | 100.0% |
| 2014 | 22 | A+ | 10.0 | 2 | 0 | 0.90 | 3.39 | 8.10 | 5.40 | 24.3% | 16.2% | 0.00 | 88.9% |
| 2014 | 22 | AA | 82.3 | 3 | 10 | 5.03 | 4.93 | 8.74 | 4.81 | 21.6% | 11.9% | 1.20 | 60.9% |
| 2015 | 23 | AA | 80.7 | 7 | 2 | 4.24 | 4.29 | 6.36 | 3.79 | 15.9% | 9.5% | 0.78 | 68.6% |
| 2015 | 23 | AAA | 44.7 | 2 | 4 | 6.25 | 4.77 | 6.45 | 5.44 | 14.8% | 12.4% | 0.81 | 65.5% |

**Background:** If you ever need proof of the frailty of prospects take a look at Jesse Biddle, the once crown jewel of the Phillies' development system and budding ace. The Philadelphia-born left-hander absolutely dominated the South Atlantic, Florida State and Eastern Leagues between 2011 and 2013. During that time Biddle tossed 414 innings while tallying 429 punch outs and 202 free passes. For those keeping track at home that's 9.3 strikeouts and 4.39 walks per nine innings *against vastly older competition*. And then...the damn wheels fell of the Biddle Bus to the Big Leagues. The 2014 season was an utter disappointment as his homerun rate spiked to about double his career norm (1.20 HR/9) and he eventually lost time for a mental breather. He finished the year with an unsightly 4.93 FIP.

Biddle followed that up with a third stint in the Eastern League last season, where the numbers – once again – left a lot to be desired: 6.4 K/9 and 3.8 BB/9. The club bumped him up to the International League in early July for nine starts before he succumbed to Tommy John surgery.

Pittsburgh, a place that's become a safe haven for pitchers looking to rebuild their careers, acquired the southpaw after Philly designated him for assignment.

**Projection:** OK. So was Biddle's massive decline in punch outs related to his elbow issues? It's a possibility. But he's been an absolute wreck the past two seasons and as he enters his age-24 season, one in which he'll miss significant time recovering for the elbow surgery, it's highly unlikely he ever regains his once promising sheen. He could be a candidate to be shuffled into the pen in the next 18 months or so. It's a very savvy move for the Burgh.

**Ceiling:** 1.5- to 2.0-win player
**Risk:** Moderate to High
**MLB ETA:** 2017

## 12. Elias Diaz, C

**MiLB Rank: N/A**
**Position Rank: N/A**

| Born: 11/17/90 | Age: 25 | Bats: R | **Top CALs:** Bobby Wilson, Charlie Cutler, |
| Height: 6-0 | Weight: 210 | Throws: R | John Ryan Murphy, Steve Clevenger, Hank Conger |

| Season | Age | LVL | PA | 2B | 3B | HR | AVG | OBP | SLG | ISO | BB% | K% | wRC+ |
|--------|-----|-----|-----|----|----|----|------|------|------|------|------|------|------|
| 2013 | 22 | A+ | 220 | 12 | 2 | 2 | 0.279 | 0.382 | 0.399 | 0.120 | 14.1% | 15.0% | 128 |
| 2014 | 23 | AA | 367 | 20 | 0 | 6 | 0.328 | 0.378 | 0.445 | 0.117 | 8.2% | 13.9% | 129 |
| 2015 | 24 | AAA | 363 | 16 | 4 | 4 | 0.271 | 0.330 | 0.382 | 0.111 | 8.0% | 12.9% | 106 |

**Background:** A member of the organization for parts of seven seasons now, Diaz finally scratched and clawed his way to the game's pinnacle level after 2,122 minor league plate appearances – which precludes include his work in the foreign winter leagues. And much to his credit, the 6-foot-1, 210-pound Venezuelan-born backstop has turned himself into a pretty good stick at the plate. Beginning with his first season in the stateside leagues, Diaz posted OPS totals of .590, .607, and .549 through his second, third, and fourth professional seasons. But something seemed to click in the then-22-year-old MiLB'er because he started showing signs of life: he batted .279/.382/.399 in the Florida State League. He followed that up with a .328/.378/.445 mark in Class AA in 2014 and then held his own in the International League last season as well (.271/.330/.382). Pittsburgh called him up and he appeared in two late, late season games.

**Projection:** Diaz appeared in last year's book as part of the system's *Bird Doggin' It* section where I opined that he had the making of a quality big league backup. Defensively, he remains steady and has thrown out 30% of would-be base stealers over the past two seasons. And he's certainly not going to kill the Pirates when he steps up to the plate: solid eye, gap power, and a decent hit tool.

**Ceiling:** 1.0- to 1.5-win player
**Risk:** Low to Moderate
**MLB ETA:** Debuted in 2015

## 13. Trevor Williams, RHP

**MiLB Rank:** N/A
**Position Rank:** N/A

| Born: 04/25/92 | Age: 24 | Bats: R | Top CALs: Michael Mariot, Keith Couch, |
|---|---|---|---|
| Height: 6-3 | Weight: 230 | Throws: R | Ryan Pope, Robert Rohrbaugh, Joe Gunkel |

| YEAR | Age | Level | IP | W | L | ERA | FIP | K/9 | BB/9 | K% | BB% | HR/9 | LOB% |
|---|---|---|---|---|---|---|---|---|---|---|---|---|---|
| 2013 | 21 | R | 2.0 | 0 | 0 | 4.50 | 2.46 | 4.50 | 0.00 | 10.0% | 0.0% | 0.00 | 33.3% |
| 2013 | 21 | A- | 29.0 | 0 | 2 | 2.48 | 2.65 | 6.21 | 2.48 | 16.1% | 6.5% | 0.00 | 62.9% |
| 2013 | 21 | A | 3.0 | 0 | 0 | 0.00 | 1.48 | 9.00 | 0.00 | 27.3% | 0.0% | 0.00 | 100.0% |
| 2014 | 22 | A+ | 129.0 | 8 | 6 | 2.79 | 3.17 | 6.28 | 2.02 | 16.8% | 5.4% | 0.35 | 73.8% |
| 2014 | 22 | AA | 15.0 | 0 | 1 | 6.00 | 2.52 | 8.40 | 3.60 | 19.7% | 8.5% | 0.00 | 57.1% |
| 2015 | 23 | AA | 117.0 | 7 | 8 | 4.00 | 3.75 | 6.77 | 2.77 | 17.6% | 7.2% | 0.69 | 73.1% |
| 2015 | 23 | AAA | 14.0 | 0 | 2 | 2.57 | 3.46 | 8.36 | 4.50 | 20.0% | 10.8% | 0.00 | 78.3% |

**Background:** It was a move that didn't seem to make a whole lot of sense at the time: the Marlins shipped off Williams, their 2013 second round pick out of Arizona State University, for Richard Mitchell. But as ESPN's Jason Stark reported several weeks after, the deal was done in order to pacify the Pirates' front office after hiring away Marc Delpiano and then Jim Benedict, who, according to Stark, "is also regarded as being among the sport's top pitching gurus." So, see, it's not just the Theo Epsteins of the world that can essentially get dealt to new teams either. As for Williams, well, he spent the majority of 2015 pitching for the Jacksonville Suns in the Southern League, throwing 117.0 innings with an 88-to-36 strikeout-to-walk ratio to go along with a decent 3.75 FIP. Miami bumped the former Sun Devil up to the PCL for an additional three starts as well.

**Projection:** So here's what I wrote three years ago before the 2013 draft:

> "He pounds the zone and knows how to pitch, both of which will help him make it to the big leagues. But Williams is another one of those safe, low ceiling/high floor pitchers in the class. He's very reminiscent of another former ASU hurler, Cincinnati's Mike Leake. The ceiling, however, is lower because the production is rather blah."

Fast forward a couple years and Williams is still making waves as a vanilla arm. He continues to limit base-on-balls, hasn't missed a whole lot of sticks in his career, but he's an innings-eater with some value as a long man of the pen/backend arm. On the plus side: he generates a ton of groundballs as well. Williams should be among the first wave of call-ups for Pittsburgh next season.

**Ceiling:** 1.0- to 1.5-win player
**Risk:** Low to Moderate
**MLB ETA:** 2016

## 14. Cole Tucker, SS

**MiLB Rank:** N/A
**Position Rank:** N/A

| Born: 07/03/96 | Age: 19 | Bats: B | Top CALs: Jose Vinicio, Amed Rosario, |
|---|---|---|---|
| Height: 6-3 | Weight: 185 | Throws: R | Nick Gordon, Cito Culver, Alejandro Salazar |

| Season | Age | LVL | PA | 2B | 3B | HR | AVG | OBP | SLG | ISO | BB% | K% | wRC+ |
|---|---|---|---|---|---|---|---|---|---|---|---|---|---|
| 2014 | 17 | R | 217 | 6 | 2 | 2 | 0.267 | 0.368 | 0.356 | 0.089 | 12.0% | 17.5% | 117 |
| 2015 | 18 | A | 329 | 13 | 3 | 2 | 0.293 | 0.322 | 0.377 | 0.083 | 4.9% | 14.9% | 97 |

**Background:** Proving that arm injuries aren't always reserved for hurlers, the club's 2014 first round pick visited the surgeon's office in late August to repair a torn labrum in his throwing shoulder – something that shouldn't be overlooked given his defensive position. Before the injury, Tucker, a 6-foot-3 switch-hitting shortstop out of Mountain Pointe High School, appeared in 73 games for the West Virginia Power in the South Atlantic League where he held his own by hitting .293/.322/.377 with 13 doubles, a trio of triples, and two homeruns while swiping 25 stolen bases in 31 attempts. His overall production, per *Weighted Runs Created Plus*, fell *below* the league average mark by 3%. It was an OK showing for the then-18-year-old middle infielder as he moved from the Gulf Coast and straight into the Sally, where he batted .267/.368/.356 during his debut.

**Projection:** Viewed as a bit of an over-draft as the 24th overall pick two years ago, Tucker hit better than I would have suspected as an 18-year-old making the transition into full-season ball last season. But that's kind of a backhanded compliment because, well, I thought he'd struggle to hit his weight. With that being said, Tucker's offensive production was empty, one without much power or patience. He's a fringy everyday guy, one which I don't suspect will hack it in the middle- to upper-levels as pitchers realize they can knock the bat out of his hands.

**Ceiling:** 1.5-win player
**Risk:** Moderate to High
**MLB ETA:** 2018

# 15. Jose Osuna, 1B/LF/RF

| | MiLB Rank: N/A |
| | Position Rank: N/A |

| Born: 12/12/92 | Age: 22 | Bats: R | Top CALs: Curt Smith, Christian Marrero, |
| Height: 6-2 | Weight: 213 | Throws: R | Sean Henry, Hunter Cole, Chris Swauger |

| Season | Age | LVL | PA | 2B | 3B | HR | AVG | OBP | SLG | ISO | BB% | K% | wRC+ |
|---|---|---|---|---|---|---|---|---|---|---|---|---|---|
| 2013 | 20 | A+ | 500 | 25 | 1 | 8 | 0.244 | 0.298 | 0.357 | 0.112 | 7.0% | 15.2% | 86 |
| 2014 | 21 | A+ | 408 | 23 | 3 | 10 | 0.296 | 0.347 | 0.458 | 0.162 | 6.9% | 17.6% | 128 |
| 2015 | 22 | A+ | 193 | 12 | 1 | 4 | 0.282 | 0.333 | 0.431 | 0.149 | 7.3% | 17.1% | 131 |
| 2015 | 22 | AA | 349 | 20 | 2 | 8 | 0.288 | 0.327 | 0.437 | 0.149 | 4.9% | 17.5% | 118 |

**Background:** In one of the more curious decisions by the front office, Osuna, who batted a strong .296/.347/.458 with a 128 wRC+ in a repeat of High Class A, found himself back in the Florida State League for the third year in a row. And just like the previous year, Osuna put together a remarkably similar run with the Bradenton Marauders, hitting .282/.333/.431 with 12 doubles, one triple, four homeruns, and a 131 wRC+. Finally convinced after more than 1,100 plate appearances in High Class A – which, by the way, is roughly 45% of his career total – the organization pushed the first baseman/corner outfielder up to Altoona. In 85 games with the Curve, Osuna – once again – was able to hold his own: .288/.327/.437 with 20 doubles, two triples, and eight homeruns to go along with a 118 wRC+.

**Projection**: Despite splitting time between what's typically a team's biggest run producing positions, Osuna's never really shown anything more than solid-average power, and even then it comes in the two-bag variety. Decent eye, solid contact skills, but the problem with him is that he's also never dominated for an extending period of time; he merely tops the league average production by 15% to 30% without eye-catching numbers. He looks like a decent bench stick.

**Ceiling:** 1.0- to 1.5-win player
**Risk:** Moderate
**MLB ETA:** 2017

# 16. Steven Brault, LHP

| | MiLB Rank: N/A |
| | Position Rank: N/A |

| Born: 04/29/92 | Age: 24 | Bats: L | Top CALs: Danny Rosenbaum, Jeff Manship, |
| Height: 6-1 | Weight: 175 | Throws: L | Kea Kometani, Cory Vanallen, Brandon Workman |

| YEAR | Age | Level | IP | W | L | ERA | FIP | K/9 | BB/9 | K% | BB% | HR/9 | LOB% |
|---|---|---|---|---|---|---|---|---|---|---|---|---|---|
| 2013 | 21 | A- | 43.0 | 1 | 2 | 2.09 | 2.61 | 7.95 | 2.51 | 22.5% | 7.1% | 0.21 | 73.5% |
| 2014 | 22 | A | 130.0 | 9 | 8 | 3.05 | 3.09 | 7.96 | 1.94 | 22.2% | 5.4% | 0.28 | 70.3% |
| 2014 | 22 | A+ | 16.3 | 2 | 0 | 0.55 | 2.78 | 4.96 | 1.10 | 15.8% | 3.5% | 0.00 | 88.9% |
| 2015 | 23 | A+ | 65.7 | 4 | 1 | 3.02 | 3.44 | 6.17 | 2.88 | 16.5% | 7.7% | 0.41 | 70.5% |
| 2015 | 23 | AA | 90.0 | 9 | 3 | 2.00 | 2.37 | 8.00 | 1.90 | 22.0% | 5.2% | 0.10 | 77.8% |

**Background:** The Pirates not only doubled up on lefties in their return from Baltimore in the Travis Snider deal, but they also doubled-down on southpaws named Steven (though technically the other one, Tarpley, spells his name S.T.E.P.H.E.N.). Brault, a former 11th round pick out of Regis University where he narrowly missed becoming the school's earliest draft selection, had a wildly successful stint in his new organization in 2015. The 6-foot-1 lefty began the year by posting a 3.44 FIP while averaging 6.17 strikeouts and 2.88 walks per nine innings in 13 starts in High Class A, and then he proceeded to get stronger when the club bumped him up to the Eastern League. In 15 starts with the Altoona Curve, Brault tossed 90 innings, fanned 80, and walked just 19. Overall, he finished the year with an aggregate 2.43 ERA with 125 punch outs and jut 40 walks in 155.2 innings of work.

**Projection**: CAL links him to a pair of quasi-useful big league arms in Brandon Workman and Jeff Manship, who also is coming off of his finest season to date as well. Brault is in the mold of your typical mid-level lefty: he limits walks, won't overpower anyone, but has succeeded up to this point. Expect his strikeout total in Class AA to regress back down to about 6.4 K/9 in 2016. He could be a T.J. House wannabe.

**Ceiling:** 1.0- to 1.5-win player
**Risk:** Moderate
**MLB ETA:** 2016

## 17. Ke'Bryan Hayes, 3B

**MiLB Rank:** N/A
**Position Rank:** N/A

| Born: 01/28/97 | Age: 19 | Bats: R | Top CALs: N/A |
|---|---|---|---|
| Height: 6-1 | Weight: 210 | Throws: R | |

| Season | Age | LVL | PA | 2B | 3B | HR | AVG | OBP | SLG | ISO | BB% | K% | wRC+ |
|---|---|---|---|---|---|---|---|---|---|---|---|---|---|
| 2015 | 18 | R | 175 | 4 | 1 | 0 | 0.333 | 0.434 | 0.375 | 0.042 | 12.6% | 13.7% | 150 |
| 2015 | 18 | A- | 52 | 1 | 0 | 0 | 0.220 | 0.320 | 0.244 | 0.024 | 11.5% | 13.5% | 76 |

**Background:** For the first time in franchise history the Pittsburgh Pirates grabbed a high school third baseman, Ke'Bryan Hayes, in the first round of the June amateur draft. The 32nd overall pick last June, Hayes had a fantastic showing in the Gulf Coast League during his debut, batting .333/.434/.375, though he slugged only five extra-base hits in 175 PA. The organization bumped him up to West Virginia for a quick 12-game crash course, and Hayes' production took a nosedive: in 52 trips to the plate with the Power, the 6-foot-1, 210-pound third baseman hit a lowly .220/.320/.244 with just one extra-base hit, a double. Hayes finished the year with an aggregate .308/.408/.346 triple-slash line, slugging just five doubles and one triple in 56 games.

**Projection**: It's a limited sample size for an incoming prepster – just 227 plate appearances – but Hayes showed next to nothing in terms of the power department. But adding to the concern is the fact over his final 43 games Hays slugged just one double. The eye at the plate looks promising, though.

**Ceiling:** Too Soon to Tell
**Risk:** N/A
**MLB ETA:** N/A

## 18. Yeudy Garcia, RHP

**MiLB Rank:** N/A
**Position Rank:** N/A

| Born: 10/06/92 | Age: 23 | Bats: R | Top CALs: Chris Stratton, Tom Ebert, |
|---|---|---|---|
| Height: 6-3 | Weight: 185 | Throws: R | Russ Savickas, Nelson Gonzalez, Angel Ventura |

| YEAR | Age | Level | IP | W | L | ERA | FIP | K/9 | BB/9 | K% | BB% | HR/9 | LOB% |
|---|---|---|---|---|---|---|---|---|---|---|---|---|---|
| 2014 | 21 | R | 59.7 | 4 | 3 | 2.41 | 3.30 | 7.09 | 3.02 | 18.5% | 7.9% | 0.00 | 71.3% |
| 2015 | 22 | A | 124.3 | 12 | 5 | 2.10 | 3.33 | 8.11 | 2.97 | 22.1% | 8.1% | 0.29 | 77.9% |

**Background:** A definite late bloomer in terms of making waves in the international scene, Garcia didn't make his debut in professional baseball until the age 21 – and even then it was 13 starts in the Dominican Summer League. And just to put that into perspective a bit: the average age in the DSL two years ago was 18. So, clearly, Garcia was expected to pass the rookie league test with ease, which he did – sort of. While he didn't miss a whole lot of bats in 59.2 innings of work, Garcia did post a 2.41 ERA and 3.33 FIP, which subsequently convinced the front office he was ready for full season ball. After beginning his stateside career working multiple innings out of the Power's bullpen, Garcia was moved into the rotation in mid-May and from that point on he tossed 102 innings, fanned 89, walked 36, and posted a miniscule 1.92 ERA.

**Projection**: Even though he bypassed the stateside rookie leagues as well as the New York-Penn League, Garcia was still a touch old for the Sally. With that being said, he offered up more than a few glimpses of promise last season, particularly when he moved back into the rotation. In a late-August game against the Augusta GreenJackets the then-22-year-old hurler fanned 10 and walked one in 5.2 innings. Garcia is a bit tricky to analyze because he's facing off against younger competition, even though he passed the test with flying colors. For now, I'll say he looks like a backend starter with the caveat that there's some added upside as he begins to hone his craft. And I wouldn't be surprised to see him back in the bullpen either.

**Ceiling:** 1.5-win player
**Risk:** High
**MLB ETA:** 2017

## 19. Stephen Tarpley, LHP

**MiLB Rank:** N/A
**Position Rank:** N/A

| Born: 02/17/93 | Age: 23 | Bats: R | Top CALs: Freddy Ballestas, Steven Brault, |
|---|---|---|---|
| Height: 6-1 | Weight: 180 | Throws: L | Mark Cohoon, Po-Hsuan Keng, Bryan Price |

| YEAR | Age | Level | IP | W | L | ERA | FIP | K/9 | BB/9 | K% | BB% | HR/9 | LOB% |
|---|---|---|---|---|---|---|---|---|---|---|---|---|---|
| 2013 | 20 | R | 21.0 | 0 | 1 | 2.14 | 1.79 | 10.71 | 1.29 | 29.8% | 3.6% | 0.00 | 76.0% |
| 2014 | 21 | A- | 66.3 | 3 | 5 | 3.66 | 3.91 | 8.14 | 3.26 | 20.8% | 8.3% | 0.54 | 72.6% |
| 2015 | 22 | A | 116.0 | 11 | 4 | 2.48 | 2.86 | 8.15 | 1.94 | 21.3% | 5.1% | 0.16 | 68.9% |

**Background:** Acquired from the Orioles as part of the package for once-promising power-hitter Travis Snider. Tarpley, who was originally drafted out of high school in the eighth round, bypassed the Indians' offer and headed to Scottsdale Community College where he would hear his name called in the third round by Baltimore two years later. After spending his debut in the Gulf Coast and the following season in the New York-Penn League, the 6-foot-1, 180-pound left-hander finally made it up to full-season ball in 2015. And in 20 starts with West Virginia, Tarpley tossed a season high 116 innings with 105 punch outs and 25 walks. For his career, the young hurler has averaged 8.4 punch outs and just 2.3 walks per nine innings.

**Projection**: Just to add some depth to his production in 2015, consider this: Tarpley walked 24 batters in 66 innings in the NYPL two years ago; last season, in 50 more innings, he walked just one more batter. Tarpley's a bit of back-of-the-rotation sleeper for Pittsburgh – he knows how to limit walks, has missed a bunch of wood in his career, and handled taking the ball every fifth or so day last season. I'm excited to see how he handles High Class A and Class AA in the next year or two.

**Ceiling:** 1.0- to 1.5-win player
**Risk:** Moderate to High
**MLB ETA:** 2018

## 20. Mitch Keller, RHP

**MiLB Rank: N/A**
**Position Rank: N/A**

| Born: 04/04/96 | Age: 20 | Bats: R | Top CALs: Grayson Huffman, Zach Russell, |
|---|---|---|---|
| Height: 6-3 | Weight: 195 | Throws: R | Carlos Salazar, Aaron Wirsch, Robert Fish |

| YEAR | Age | Level | IP | W | L | ERA | FIP | K/9 | BB/9 | K% | BB% | HR/9 | LOB% |
|---|---|---|---|---|---|---|---|---|---|---|---|---|---|
| 2014 | 18 | R | 27.3 | 0 | 0 | 1.98 | 3.14 | 9.55 | 4.28 | 25.7% | 11.5% | 0.00 | 77.1% |
| 2015 | 19 | R | 19.7 | 0 | 3 | 5.49 | 4.54 | 11.44 | 7.32 | 24.8% | 15.8% | 0.46 | 61.0% |

**Background:** Hailing from Xavier High School, home to big league outfielder Ryan Sweeney as well as his older brother Jon Keller, the organization plucked the 6-foot-3, 195-pound right-hander in the second round two years ago. And since then Keller has tallied just 47.0 professional innings.

**Projection**: The hard-throwing right-hander missed the majority of last year as he dealt with a forearm strain, so there's basically no data available on the former second round pick. He's missed a ton of bats in his limited action – 54 in 47.0 innings – but he's struggled locating the ball within a reasonable area code (he's walked 29 during that same time). Just like I did in last year's book, I'm going to reserve any long term prognosticating until he compiles more than 27.1 innings in a season.

**Ceiling:** Too Soon to Tell
**Risk:** N/A
**MLB ETA:** N/A

## 21. Connor Joe, 1B

**MiLB Rank: N/A**
**Position Rank: N/A**

| Born: 08/16/92 | Age: 23 | Bats: R | Top CALs: Bo Thompson, John Nogowski, |
|---|---|---|---|
| Height: 6-0 | Weight: 205 | Throws: R | Shane Brown, Eric Campbell, Mike Paulk |

| Season | Age | LVL | PA | 2B | 3B | HR | AVG | OBP | SLG | ISO | BB% | K% | wRC+ |
|---|---|---|---|---|---|---|---|---|---|---|---|---|---|
| 2015 | 22 | A | 357 | 12 | 1 | 1 | 0.245 | 0.366 | 0.303 | 0.059 | 14.0% | 9.5% | 102 |

**Background:** A supplemental first round pick out of the University of San Diego in 2014, Joe, 39th overall player chosen, spent three years bouncing between catching and patrolling the school's outfield, but all along the way he showed steady offensive progress. After hitting a solid .262/.401/.373 with just eight extra-base knocks during his freshman season, he upped the ante by slugging .319/.397/.470 with 14 doubles and seven triples. And he *exploded* during his junior campaign. In 53 games with the Toreros, the 6-foot, 205-pound part-time backstop mashed to the tune of .367/.462/.606 with 23 doubles, a pair of triples (the first of his career), and nine long balls. A back injury immediately forced the first rounder to miss seeing any low level time in the minors two years ago. Last season, Joe hit .245/.371/.303 in 80 games with West Virginia.

**Projection**: Back injuries, while not quite on the same scale, can warp a player's potential just like arm issues with a pitcher. Remember Michael Aubrey, the Indians former first round pick who never turned the corner thanks to said issues. Anyway, Joe's still showcasing his trademark elite eye at the plate, but his lack of is ill-fitted for a corner position, particularly first base.

**Ceiling:** 1.0-win player
**Risk:** Moderate
**MLB ETA:** 2018

## 22. Kevin Kramer, 2B/SS

**MiLB Rank: N/A**
**Position Rank: N/A**

| Born: 10/03/93 | Age: 22 | Bats: L | **Top CALs:** Tony Kemp, Mitchell Tolman, |
|---|---|---|---|
| Height: 6-1 | Weight: 190 | Throws: R | Darin Mastroianni, Scott Campbell, Seth Spivey |

| Season | Age | LVL | PA | 2B | 3B | HR | AVG | OBP | SLG | ISO | BB% | K% | wRC+ |
|---|---|---|---|---|---|---|---|---|---|---|---|---|---|
| 2015 | 21 | A- | 209 | 7 | 3 | 0 | 0.305 | 0.390 | 0.379 | 0.073 | 12.0% | 13.4% | 132 |
| 2015 | 21 | A | 56 | 2 | 1 | 0 | 0.240 | 0.321 | 0.320 | 0.080 | 8.9% | 14.3% | 88 |
| 2014 | 21 | A- | 160 | 9 | 4 | 7 | 0.276 | 0.363 | 0.560 | 0.284 | 10.0% | 17.5% | 164 |

**Background:** Like a simmering pot of water, Kramer's production had reached a boiling point entering his junior year – and then things got messy for opposing arms. Kramer, who missed the entire 2014 season as he recovered from shoulder surgery, had a breakout season during his

final year with UCLA. The 6-foot-1, 190-pound middle infielder batted .323/.423/.476 while setting career bests in doubles (14) and homeruns (seven). Pittsburgh took Kramer in the second round last June, 62nd overall, signed him to a $900,000 deal, and sent him to the New York-Penn League for his debut. After hitting .305/.390/.379 in 46 games, the front office bumped him up to the Sally for his remaining 12 contests. Overall, Kramer batted .291/.375/.366 with nine doubles, four triples, and 12 stolen bases.

**Projection**: Shortstops galore! The lefty-swinging Kramer offers up doubles power, a strong eye at the plate, and he handled southpaws surprisingly well during his debut (.350/.443/.500). He looks like a potential backup infielder unless he starts showing the type of pop he did during his final run with the Bruins.

**Ceiling:** 1.0-win player
**Risk:** Moderate
**MLB ETA:** 2018

## 23. Jin-De Jhang, C

**MiLB Rank: N/A**
**Position Rank: N/A**

| Born: 05/17/93 | Age: 23 | Bats: L | **Top CALs:** Francisco Hrnandez, John Ryan Murphy, |
|---|---|---|---|
| Height: 5-11 | Weight: 220 | Throws: R | Carlos Paulino, Rob Brantly, Alex Monsalve |

| Season | Age | LVL | PA | 2B | 3B | HR | AVG | OBP | SLG | ISO | BB% | K% | wRC+ |
|---|---|---|---|---|---|---|---|---|---|---|---|---|---|
| 2013 | 20 | A- | 211 | 8 | 1 | 5 | 0.277 | 0.338 | 0.413 | 0.136 | 8.1% | 11.4% | 123 |
| 2014 | 21 | A+ | 293 | 12 | 2 | 2 | 0.219 | 0.263 | 0.301 | 0.082 | 5.1% | 12.3% | 60 |
| 2015 | 22 | A+ | 402 | 16 | 1 | 5 | 0.292 | 0.332 | 0.381 | 0.089 | 5.5% | 10.7% | 117 |

**Background:** The lefty-swinging Taiwanese-born backstop put together back-to-back seasons of solid offensive production to begin his career: he batted .305/.382/.398 in the Gulf Coast in 2013 and .277/.338/.413 a year later in the New York-Penn League. So the Pirates did the (not so) prudent thing and

pushed the then-21-year-old straight up to the Florida State League two years ago, having him completely bypass Low Class A (likely in an effort to give Reese McGuire more playing time). And, of course, Jhang looked overmatched: he batted a lowly .219/.263/.301. The club had the 5-foot-11, 220-pound catcher re-do the FSL last season, and the results, unsurprisingly, were far better: .292/.332/.381.

**Projection**: Jhang still didn't see that much time behind the plate last season as he only donned the tools of ignorance just 46 times – thanks again to Reese McGuire. But make no mistake about it: Jhang has a significantly higher offensive ceiling than his more highly-touted counterpart. Jhang posted a 135 wRC+ in the GCL, a 123 wRC+ in the NYPL, and a solid 117 in the FSL last season. The patience is proving to be below-average and he doesn't pack much of a wallop, but the hit tool is no worse than average. He's another candidate for some backup backstop big league action down the road, though he'll need to be platooned against LHP.

**Ceiling:** 1.0-win player
**Risk:** Moderate
**MLB ETA:** 2018

## 24. Reese McGuire, C

**MiLB Rank: N/A**
**Position Rank: N/A**

| Born: 03/02/95 | Age: 21 | Bats: L | **Top CALs:** Chace Numata, Rossmei Perez, |
|---|---|---|---|
| Height: 6-0 | Weight: 181 | Throws: R | Alex Monsalve, Wilfredo Rodriguez, Rene Garcia |

| Season | Age | LVL | PA | 2B | 3B | HR | AVG | OBP | SLG | ISO | BB% | K% | wRC+ |
|---|---|---|---|---|---|---|---|---|---|---|---|---|---|
| 2013 | 18 | R | 198 | 11 | 0 | 0 | 0.330 | 0.388 | 0.392 | 0.063 | 7.6% | 9.1% | 132 |
| 2014 | 19 | A | 427 | 11 | 4 | 3 | 0.262 | 0.307 | 0.334 | 0.072 | 5.6% | 10.3% | 80 |
| 2015 | 20 | A+ | 411 | 15 | 0 | 0 | 0.254 | 0.301 | 0.294 | 0.040 | 6.3% | 9.5% | 82 |

**Background:** Keeping in mind the two-headed warning that states that (A) outside of prep arms, no other position has a higher attrition rate than high school-aged backstops and (B) catchers typically develop much slower offensively than any other position, but with that being said even McGuire, the

14th overall pick in the 2013, has been a significant disappointment for the organization. The lefty-swinging backstop had a strong showing in the Gulf Coast League three years ago, hitting .323/.388/.392, but promptly followed that up with a disappointing season in the Sally; he batted a lowly .262/.307/.334 with just 11 doubles, four triples, and three homeruns while finishing his sophomore campaign with a production line that fell 20% *below* the league average mark. Undeterred, however, Pittsburgh thought it wise to aggressively push the then-20-year-old catcher up to High Class A last season, and he – once again – looked out of place against the more advanced arms: he slugged .254/.301/.294.

**Projection**: At this point the front office has to be hoping for a Devin Mesoraco turnaround for their young backstop. Mesoraco, who like McGuire was picked in the middle of the first round, struggled mightily through his first three seasons in the minors, posting consecutive OPSs of .580, .710, and .692 between the Gulf Coast, Midwest, and Florida State Leagues. But the now-All-Star backstop had a coming out party during his fourth season: he mashed to the tune of .302/.377/.587 in High Class A and Class AA.

Unlike Mesoraco, though, McGuire has – for those keeping track at home – slugged a total of three homeruns in his first 246 professional games. So it's pretty safe to say that Kentwood High School alum won't be making a whole lot of waves in his fourth season. Decent eye with a high contact rate, the punch-less McGuire has shown a tremendous platoon split against fellow lefties too. Add it all up and it looks like he's a future backup – maybe.

**Ceiling:** 1. 0-win player
**Risk:** Moderate to High
**MLB ETA:** 2018

# 25. Clay Holmes, RHP

**MiLB Rank: N/A**
**Position Rank: N/A**

| Born: 03/27/93 | Age: 23 | Bats: R | Top CALs: Tyler Green, John Younginer, |
| Height: 6-5 | Weight: 230 | Throws: R | Austin Urban, Jason Garcia, Juan Minaya |

| YEAR | Age | Level | IP | W | L | ERA | FIP | K/9 | BB/9 | K% | BB% | HR/9 | LOB% |
|---|---|---|---|---|---|---|---|---|---|---|---|---|---|
| 2013 | 20 | A | 119.0 | 5 | 6 | 4.08 | 4.78 | 6.81 | 5.22 | 17.1% | 13.1% | 0.53 | 72.2% |
| 2015 | 22 | R | 13.3 | 1 | 0 | 2.03 | 2.71 | 6.75 | 0.68 | 17.9% | 1.8% | 0.00 | 70.6% |
| 2015 | 22 | A+ | 23.0 | 0 | 2 | 2.74 | 3.21 | 6.26 | 2.74 | 17.2% | 7.5% | 0.00 | 75.9% |

**Background**: Here's a list of the highest signing bonuses for the players taken in the ninth round in 2011: Clay Holmes ($1.2 million), Garrett Schlecht ($200,000), and Alex Panteliodis ($200,000). And since signing the lofty contract Holmes hasn't really lived up to those lofty standards. The 6-foot-5, 230-pound hurler didn't make his debut until the following season, 2012, and despite a nice 2.28 ERA he posted a troublesome 34-to-29 strikeout-to-walk ratio in 59.1 innings of work. He would spend the next year with West Virginia in the South Atlantic League where he would also finish with a problematic strikeout-to-walk ratio (90-to-69). After that he would miss the entire 2014 season and the majority of last year recovering from Tommy John surgery.

**Projection**: Holmes is now entering his age-23 season and despite getting drafted five years ago he's managed to throw just 214.2 innings in professional ball. He's never missed a lot of bats and last year's control was the first time he posted a walk rate below 4.4 BB/9. In other words, he could be headed down the path of future reliever – and soon.

**Ceiling:** 1.0-win player
**Risk:** Moderate to High
**MLB ETA:** 2018

### *Barely Missed:*

- **Barrett Barnes, LF/CF** –Former first rounder out of Texas Tech University in 2012, 45th overall, Barnes, nonetheless, was left unprotected for the Rule 5 draft after another disappointing campaign in 2015. The short, stocky outfielder hit a combined .256/.352/.403 with 22 doubles, two triples, nine homeruns, and 17 stolen bases. And despite being in the organization for parts of four seasons now, Barnes has never topped 95 games in a season.

- **Adam Frazier, SS** – A sixth round pick out of Mississippi State University three years ago, the lefty-swinging shortstop took to Class AA like fish to water last season. In 103 games with Altoona, Frazier batted .324/.384/.416 with 21 doubles, four triples, two homeruns, and 11 stolen bases. The lack of power limits him to a reserve role.

- **Chad Kuhl, RHP** – A nice little find out of the University of Delaware in 2013, Kuhl, the organization's ninth round pick that year, already made it up to – and succeeded in – Class AA. He spent the year with Altoona, throwing 152.2 innings while averaging just 6.0 punch outs and 2.4 walks per nine innings. Consistency aside, Kuhl has handled some aggressive promotions with aplomb, and he's already knocking on the club's big league door just three seasons after being a late-round pick. His lack of strikeouts will ultimately doom him into a life of middle-relief-dom, but, hey, not bad work for a former ninth round pick.

- **Luis Heredia, RHP** – One of the most enigmatic prospects in recent memory. Heredia first appeared in Low Class A as an 18-year-old and posted a 3.05 ERA as he battled control issues. He repeated the level in 2014 with much less success, and then promptly posted a 54-to-44 strikeout-to-walk ratio in 86.0 innings in the Florida State League last year.

## *Bird Doggin' It – Additional Prospects to Keep an Eye in 2016*

| Player | Age | POS | Notes |
|---|---|---|---|
| Stetson Allie | 25 | 1B/RF | Former second round Bonus Baby couldn't locate his triple-digit fastball, so the team moved him – and his power bat – to a corner position. Big strikeouts, huge power, above-average eye at the plate. |
| Michael De La Cruz | 19 | CF | De La Cruz dominated the Dominican Summer League as a 16-year-old in 2013, hitting .292/.436/.367. He appeared in only 32 games in the GCL the following season, and had a decent showing in a repeat of the level in 2015 (.256/.341/.379). |
| Cody Dickson | 24 | LHP | A 2013 fourth round pick out of Sam Houston State University, the 6-foot-3 southpaw posted a mediocre 98-to-52 strikeout-to-walk ratio in 141.2 innings with Bradenton. |
| Montana Durapau | 24 | RHP | Diminutive right-hander out of Bethune-Cookman via the 32nd round, Durapau made the transition to the bullpen last season and promptly spent time at three different levels (Low Class A, A+, AA). Averaged 8.6 K/9 and just 1.1 BB/9 in 72 innings. |
| Tyler Eppler | 23 | RHP | 6-foot-5, 220-pound right-hander looked solid in 14 games with Bradenton, averaging 6.2 K/9 and just 1.9 BB/9 in 66.1 IP. |
| Elvis Escobar | 21 | OF | Pocket-sized outfielder topped the Sally's average offensive production by 8% last season en route to hitting .296/.326/.407.He could end up in the club's Top 25 next season. |
| Daniel Gamache | 25 | 2B | Second baseman had the best half-season of his entire career in 2015 as he slugged .335/.377/.457 with a 142 wRC+. Unfortunately, it was all BABIP-driven. |
| John Holdzkom | 28 | RHP | Flashed a mid- to upper-90s heater during his brief debut in Pittsburgh two years ago, Holdzkom was limited to just 22.1 innings in 2015 as he battled shoulder issues. |
| Casey Hughston | 22 | CF | Third round pick out of Alabama last year, Hughston batted a paltry .224/.267/.311 in the NYPL during his debut. |
| Jordan Luplow | 22 | 3B/LF | Cal State alum batted .264/.366/.464 with 51 extra-base hits in the Sally as he made the mode from outfielder to third base. Sneaky. |
| Jhondaniel Medina | 23 | RHP | Once-promising strikeout artist whiffed only 44 – and walked 37 – in 62.0 innings with Altoona in the Eastern League in 2015. |
| Tito Polo | 21 | CF | Batted just .236/.313/.328 in the Sally last season, but managed to swipe 46 bags though. |
| Pablo Reyes | 22 | 2B/SS | Held his own with the Power last season, hitting .268/.345/.438 with 12 homeruns. Don't look for a repeat of that production line though. |
| Miguel Rosario | 23 | RHP | Fanned 77 and walked just 23 in 75 innings between the Sally and High Class A. |
| John Sever | 22 | LHP | 6-foot-5 southpaw looked solid in 29 games, nine of which were starts, in the Sally: 86.2 IP, 84 K, and 31 BB. |
| Brandon Waddell | 22 | LHP | Fifth round pick out of Virginia last June, Waddell had a bit of a disappointing junior campaign as he struggled with control/command issues. He never missed a lot of bats at the collegiate level. |

**State of the Farm System:** Well, relatively fresh General Manager A.J. Preller's plan to buy – or trade for – a playoff appearance failed miserably as the club won three fewer games than the season before – despite adding, through mortgaging their future, the likes of Matt Kemp, Derek Norris, Seth Streich, Wil Myers, Brandon Maurer, Craig Kimbrel, and B.J. Upton, who kind of counts as a baseball player still...I think.

Now, to be fair, Preller did well in receiving Manuel Margot, Javier Guerra, Logan Allen, and Carlos Asuaje when he flipped Kimbrel to Boston this offseason. But the once brimming system, even with the latest influx of talent, is still one of the worst in baseball.

It took a bit for Hunter Renfroe to get going in Class AA, but once he got his feet under him he took off like a pistol. But unless the team finally makes the prudent decision to bench Melvin Upton and push the recently acquired Jon Jay to center field, Renfroe will be stuck in Class AAA for at least part of 2016.

Margot and Guerra, the two centerpieces acquired from Boston, are intriguing up-the-middle prospects – both of whom possess above-average potential. Margot batted .276/.324/.419 as a 20-year-old splitting his season between the Carolina and Eastern Leagues. And Guerra hit .279/.329/.449 with 41 extra-base hits as a 19-year-old in the South Atlantic League.

Ruddy Giron, another shortstop prospect, also packed quite a wallop as he mashed nine homeruns in fewer than 100 games in Low Class A – at the age of 18.

Outfielder Travis Jankowski and first baseman/outfielder Alex Dickerson could carve out some roles as useful big leagues as well.

| Rank | Name | POS |
|------|------|-----|
| 1 | Hunter Renfroe | RF |
| 2 | Manuel Margot | CF |
| 3 | Javier Guerra | SS |
| 4 | Ruddy Giron | SS |
| 5 | Travis Jankowski | CF |
| 6 | Alex Dickerson | 1B/LF/RF |
| 7 | Zech Lemond | RHP |
| 8 | Jose Rondon | SS |
| 9 | Franmil Reyes | RF |
| 10 | Enyel De Los Santos | RHP |
| 11 | Jabari Blash | OF |
| 12 | Cory Mazzoni | RHP |
| 13 | Michael Gettys | CF |
| 14 | Colin Rea | RHP |
| 15 | Jose Torres | LHP |
| 16 | Jean Cosme | RHP |
| 17 | Luis Perdomo | RHP |
| 18 | Austin Smith | RHP |
| 19 | Luis Urias | 2B/3B/SS |
| 20 | Carlos Asuaje | 2B |
| 21 | Logan Allen | RHP |
| 22 | Elliot Morris | RHP |
| 23 | Bryan Verbitsky | RHP |
| 24 | Dinelson Lamet | RHP |
| 25 | Tayron Guerrero | RHP |

**Review of the 2015 Draft:** Making matters worse: the organization lost their first round pick due to the James Shields signing last offseason. Oops...

Anyway, the front office went with prep right-hander Austin Smith with their first pick last season, taking him with the 61st pick. Smith was the minor league equivalent of the organization's big league club: he posted a pitiful 11-to-9 strikeout-to-walk ratio in 17.0 innings. Their second pick was Jacob Nix, the former prep right-hander who was caught up in the Brady Aiken scandal with Houston two years ago.

Basically, it has the makings of a piss-poor draft class – which, again, is basically how the big league club is currently viewed.

# 1. Hunter Renfroe, RF

**MiLB Rank: #67**
**Position Rank: #19**

| Born: 01/28/92 | Age: 24 | Bats: R | Top CALs: Matt Spencer, Brandon Jones, |
|---|---|---|---|
| Height: 6-1 | Weight: 215 | Throws: R | Zoilo Almonte, Edgardo Baez, Quincy Latimore |

| Season | Age | LVL | PA | 2B | 3B | HR | AVG | OBP | SLG | ISO | BB% | K% | wRC+ |
|---|---|---|---|---|---|---|---|---|---|---|---|---|---|
| 2013 | 21 | A- | 111 | 9 | 0 | 4 | 0.308 | 0.333 | 0.510 | 0.202 | 4.5% | 23.4% | 142 |
| 2014 | 22 | A+ | 316 | 21 | 3 | 16 | 0.295 | 0.370 | 0.565 | 0.270 | 8.9% | 25.6% | 137 |
| 2014 | 22 | AA | 251 | 12 | 0 | 5 | 0.232 | 0.307 | 0.353 | 0.121 | 10.0% | 21.1% | 90 |
| 2015 | 23 | AA | 463 | 22 | 3 | 14 | 0.259 | 0.313 | 0.425 | 0.166 | 7.1% | 24.2% | 103 |
| 2015 | 23 | AAA | 95 | 5 | 2 | 6 | 0.333 | 0.358 | 0.633 | 0.300 | 4.2% | 21.1% | 158 |

**Background**: Sandwiched between a couple disappointing first rounders, Seattle's D.J. Peterson and Pittsburgh's Reese McGuire, Renfroe – who was taken with the 13th overall pick in the 2013 draft – was thrust into the spotlight after an out-of-nowhere junior campaign for Mississippi State University. Renfroe hit a respectable .271/.308/.459 during stops in the Northwest and Midwest Leagues during his debut. The 6-foot-1, 215-pound corner outfielder followed that up with a dominant 69-game run as the club aggressively pushed him up to High Class A for the start of the 2014 season, hitting .295/.370/.565 with 21 doubles, three triples, 16 homeruns, and nine stolen bases. And that's where the string of dominance promptly ended – at least for a while.

San Diego promoted Renfroe up to the Texas League in mid-June, but he managed to only cobble together a lowly .232/.307/.353 triple-slash line. He would find himself back in Class AA for another extended stint to start last season, though the results were only modestly better: .259/.313/.425 with a 103 wRC+. Renfroe would also make a (dominant) 21-game appearance in Class AAA, which undoubtedly helped buoy his overall yearly production.

**Projection**: Here's the thing about Class AA: it's the single most difficult challenge for a minor league prospect. It's literally *the* make it or break it level – bar none. So, with that being said, it's not overly surprisingly when a player struggles in their first initial run at the level, a la Renfroe, which he certainly did. But here's the thing: something clicked in the former Bulldog after disappointing for more than 100 games in the Texas League and he put together a rather impressive run once the calendar flipped to June last year, hitting .283/.337/.494 in 276 plates.

For those counting at home, he finished the year by slugging .296/.342/.531 with 16 doubles, five triples, and 18 homeruns in his last 88 games. And let's not forget that after leaving college Renfroe spent all of 112 games before making his way up to Class AA. It looks like he just needed a bit of time to get acclimated to the league.

He's not going to be a perennial All-Star caliber bat, but he should settle in as a slightly better-than-average regular.

Finally, here's what I wrote prior to the 2013 draft:

> *"Having spent some time behind the plate as well as on the mound, Renfroe is certainly one of the more athletic prospects in the collegiate class. But with that being said, there's a rather sizeable risk given that his production is relegated to this year. Still, though, he could be an above-average regular, maybe similar to a Hunter Pence or so."*

**Ceiling:** 3.0-win player
**Risk:** Moderate
**MLB ETA:** 2016

# 2. Manuel Margot, CF

**MiLB Rank: #76**
**Position Rank: N/A**

| Born: 09/28/94 | Age: 21 | Bats: R | Top CALs: Jae-Hoon Ha, Albert Almora, |
|---|---|---|---|
| Height: 5-11 | Weight: 170 | Throws: R | Gerardo Parra, Max Kepler, Shannon Wilkerson |

| Season | Age | LVL | PA | 2B | 3B | HR | AVG | OBP | SLG | ISO | BB% | K% | wRC+ |
|---|---|---|---|---|---|---|---|---|---|---|---|---|---|
| 2013 | 18 | A- | 216 | 8 | 2 | 1 | 0.270 | 0.346 | 0.351 | 0.081 | 10.2% | 18.5% | 113 |
| 2014 | 19 | A | 413 | 20 | 5 | 10 | 0.286 | 0.355 | 0.449 | 0.162 | 9.0% | 11.9% | 125 |
| 2015 | 20 | A+ | 198 | 6 | 5 | 3 | 0.282 | 0.321 | 0.420 | 0.138 | 5.6% | 7.6% | 114 |
| 2015 | 20 | AA | 282 | 21 | 4 | 3 | 0.271 | 0.326 | 0.419 | 0.147 | 7.4% | 12.8% | 113 |

**Background:** In a matter of 12 or so months Padres General Manager A.J. Preller has taken the franchise from the brink of despair to the talk of the town as a potential playoff contender and then back down to complete rebuild status – enter Manuel Margot, Javier Guerra, and a couple of minor league wild cards. Preller, who would eventually acquire veteran ace reliever Craig Kimbrel and Melvin Upton's albatross of a contract in early April, turned around and dealt the dominant reliever to Boston for the quartet of prospects in November. Margot, a wiry, quick-twitch center fielder out of the Dominican Republic, has proven to be an offensive force during his four-year tour through the low levels of the minor leagues. He would slug .285/.382/.423 as a 17-year-old in the Dominican Summer League and handled his promotion to short-season ball a year later with aplomb.

He followed that up with a strong showing two years ago between the Sally and Carolina League, hitting .293/.356/.462. Last season, his final as a member in the Red Sox system, Margot – once again – split time between two different levels. He opened up the year by hitting .282/.321/.420 with Salem in High Class A and posted a nearly identical triple-slash line, .271/.326/.419, in the Eastern League.

**Projection**: Ignoring the tons – and *tons* – of lost money the organization agreed to take on with the additional of Melvin Upton's hapless bat, the Padres actually did quite well in the Kimbrel trade. They dealt away Matt Wisler, a backend starter, Carlos Quentin, who eventually retired before appearing in a game for Atlanta, Cameron Maybin, who's more of an overpaid fourth outfielder now, and Jordan Paroubeck, a 2013 second round pick who has yet to make it above the rookie leagues. And in their place – or eventual place – San Diego added a pair of promising young hitters in Margot and Javier Guerra.

Margot has the foundation – though it's not fully developed – in place to become a dynamic big league bat. He's show average power against much older competition with the potential to grow into 15 to 20 homeruns down the line. He combines that with above-average speed, a solid eye, and a hit tool that could develop into .300 down the line.

**Ceiling:** 3.0- to 3.5-win player
**Risk:** Moderate to High
**MLB ETA:** 2016/2017

## 3. Javier Guerra, SS

**MiLB Rank: #99**
**Position Rank: N/A**

**Born:** 09/25/95 **Age:** 20 **Bats:** L
**Height:** 5-11 **Weight:** 155 **Throws:** R

**Top CALs:** Richard Urena, Kenneth People-Walls, Arismendy Alcantara, Yamaico Navarro, Luis Palacios

| Season | Age | LVL | PA | 2B | 3B | HR | AVG | OBP | SLG | ISO | BB% | K% | wRC+ |
|---|---|---|---|---|---|---|---|---|---|---|---|---|---|
| 2013 | 17 | R | 253 | 9 | 0 | 0 | 0.248 | 0.356 | 0.290 | 0.043 | 13.0% | 15.8% | 103 |
| 2014 | 18 | R | 207 | 14 | 4 | 2 | 0.269 | 0.286 | 0.408 | 0.139 | 2.4% | 20.3% | 97 |
| 2015 | 19 | A | 477 | 23 | 3 | 15 | 0.279 | 0.329 | 0.449 | 0.171 | 6.3% | 23.5% | 119 |

**Background:** Another part of the package received from Boston in the Craig Kimbrel deal. Guerra, a 5-foot-11, 155-pound lefty-swinging shortstop out of Panama, originally signed with the Red Sox back in 2012 for a quarter-million dollars – a pittance given his offensive potential. He looked a bit overmatched during his pro debut in the Dominican Summer League three years ago, hitting .248/.356/.290, but he's made steady progress as he's moved stateside into the Gulf Coast and eventually up to the Sally. In 116 games with Greensville last season, Guerra slugged .279/.329/.449 with career highs in doubles (23) and homeruns (15) while adding a trio of triples and seven stolen bases (in 16 attempts). According to *Weighted Runs Created Plus*, his overall production topped the league average mark by 19% last season.

**Projection**: Consider the following: the last time a 19-year-old shortstop slugged at least 15 dingers in a season in the South Atlantic League was four years ago when Colorado's Trevor Story and Pittsburgh's Alen Hanson accomplished the feat (18 and 16, respectively). Overall, San Diego's shiny new prospect finished the year tied for seventh in the league in long balls last season. Guerra showed a tremendous amount of development as his plate discipline jumped from a lowly 2.4% up to an average-ish 6.3%; his power leapt up into above-average territory. It'll be interesting how the organization handles two potential solid shortstop prospects – both of whom are ready for High Class A. The other, of course, being Ruddy Giron.

**Ceiling:** 3.0-win player
**Risk:** Moderate to High
**MLB ETA:** 2018

## 4. Ruddy Giron, SS

**MiLB Rank: #161**
**Position Rank: N/A**

**Born:** 01/04/97 **Age:** 19 **Bats:** R
**Height:** 5-11 **Weight:** 175 **Throws:** R

**Top CALs:** Paul Kelly, Gleyber Torres, Chris Owings, Wilmer Flores, Jake Hager

| Season | Age | LVL | PA | 2B | 3B | HR | AVG | OBP | SLG | ISO | BB% | K% | wRC+ |
|---|---|---|---|---|---|---|---|---|---|---|---|---|---|
| 2014 | 17 | R | 198 | 10 | 0 | 0 | 0.168 | 0.205 | 0.222 | 0.054 | 4.0% | 21.2% | 29 |
| 2015 | 18 | A | 419 | 12 | 4 | 9 | 0.285 | 0.335 | 0.407 | 0.122 | 6.9% | 16.2% | 116 |

**Background:** Signed for a relatively meager amount – at least in terms of baseball dollars – of $600,000 in early July three years, Giron proven to be an incredible bargain for the Friars – especially after his putrid showing in the Arizona Summer League in 2014. Last season, though, San Diego made the incredibly bold move by pushing the then-18-year-old shortstop up to South Atlantic League – despite hitting a lowly .168/.205/.222 with just 10 doubles in 198 plate appearances the year before. And it looks like an absolute stroke of genius for the player development program. In 96 games with the Fort Wayne Tin Caps, the 5-foot-11, 175-pound shortstop slugged an impressive .285/.335/.407 with 12 doubles, four triples, nine homeruns, and 15 stolen base (though, it took 29 attempts to get there). His overall production, according to *Weighted Runs Created Plus*, topped the league average mark by 16%.

**Projection**: A couple things:

- First, prorating his counting stats to a 162-game season: 20 doubles, seven triples, 15 homeruns, and 25 stolen bases.
- Second, here are some interesting facts about Giron:
  - Among all shortstops in the South Atlantic League with 400 plate appearances last season, Giron finished tied for second in homeruns with nine.
  - The last time an 18-year-old shortstop slugged at least nine homeruns in the Midwest League was some guy named Carlos Correa three years ago.
  - Taking it one more step further, Giron and Correa are the only two 18-year-olds to slug nine dingers in a Midwest League season since 2006.

Needless to say, Giron's encroaching on some incredibly interesting territory as a prospect. The power could prove to be an above-average, repeatable skill down the line, with above-average speed, a solid hit tool, and a not-so-terrible eye at the plate. He's very, very, *VERY* underrated as a prospect.

**Ceiling:** 2.5-win player
**Risk:** Moderate to High
**MLB ETA:** 2018

## 5. Travis Jankowski, CF

**MiLB Rank: #195**
**Position Rank: N/A**

| Born: 06/15/91 | Age: 25 | Bats: L | Top CALs: Brian Horwitz, Billy Burns, |
|---|---|---|---|
| Height: 6-2 | Weight: 190 | Throws: R | Javon Moran, Brandon Roberts, Kyle Wren |

| Season | Age | LVL | PA | 2B | 3B | HR | AVG | OBP | SLG | ISO | BB% | K% | wRC+ |
|---|---|---|---|---|---|---|---|---|---|---|---|---|---|
| 2013 | 22 | A+ | 556 | 19 | 6 | 1 | 0.286 | 0.356 | 0.355 | 0.069 | 9.7% | 17.3% | 93 |
| 2014 | 23 | AA | 112 | 4 | 1 | 0 | 0.240 | 0.297 | 0.300 | 0.060 | 7.1% | 12.5% | 72 |
| 2015 | 24 | AA | 321 | 11 | 5 | 1 | 0.316 | 0.395 | 0.401 | 0.085 | 11.2% | 12.5% | 127 |
| 2015 | 24 | AAA | 113 | 6 | 2 | 0 | 0.392 | 0.464 | 0.495 | 0.103 | 11.5% | 8.8% | 164 |
| 2015 | 24 | MLB | 96 | 2 | 2 | 2 | 0.211 | 0.245 | 0.344 | 0.133 | 4.2% | 25.0% | 62 |

**Background:** A supplemental pick in the first round in the famed 2012 draft, Jankowski, the 44th overall pick that year, made up for a lost 2014 season with a strong showing in the Texas League and torching the Pacific Coast League following a late-season promotion. The speedy center, who missed all but 46 games two years ago courtesy of a broken wrist suffered during an unbelievable catch, hit a combined .335/.413/.425 with 17 doubles, a career high seven triples, one dinger (which tied a career high), and 32 stolen bases in 43 attempts. His overall production, according to *Weighted Runs Created Plus*, topped the league average mark by 37%. And for his minor league career Jankowski is sporting a decent .293/.360/.369 triple-slash line. He would also appear in 34 games with the big league club, hitting a paltry .211/.245/.344.

**Projection:** Jankowski's breakout season was buoyed – greatly – by his ridiculous, ungodly 24-game stint in the PCL last season (.392/.464/.495) which, of course, was on the back of an unsustainable .432 BABIP. But that wasn't the only fluky part of his season: in 326 minor league games he's slugged three homeruns; in 34 games with the Padres he slugged two. Jankowski's greatest asset is his speed, an above-average to plus-skill which helps him on the base paths and in the field (obviously). The hit tool is pretty good, but, again, the power is next to nil. He might be able to carve out a couple league-average seasons, but don't expect too much more.

**Ceiling:** 1.5- to 2.0-win player
**Risk:** Low to Moderate
**MLB ETA:** Debuted in 2015

## 6. Alex Dickerson, 1B/LF/RF

**MiLB Rank: N/A**
**Position Rank: N/A**

| Born: 05/26/90 | Age: 26 | Bats: L | Top CALs: Allen Craig, Johan Limonta, |
|---|---|---|---|
| Height: 6-3 | Weight: 230 | Throws: L | Ryan Rua, Rebel Ridling, Mark Canha |

| Season | Age | LVL | PA | 2B | 3B | HR | AVG | OBP | SLG | ISO | BB% | K% | wRC+ |
|---|---|---|---|---|---|---|---|---|---|---|---|---|---|
| 2013 | 23 | AA | 491 | 36 | 3 | 17 | 0.288 | 0.337 | 0.494 | 0.206 | 5.5% | 18.1% | 126 |
| 2014 | 24 | AA | 147 | 11 | 2 | 3 | 0.321 | 0.367 | 0.496 | 0.175 | 6.1% | 19.0% | 146 |
| 2015 | 25 | AAA | 519 | 36 | 9 | 12 | 0.307 | 0.374 | 0.503 | 0.196 | 8.7% | 18.5% | 132 |
| 2015 | 25 | MLB | 8 | 0 | 0 | 0 | 0.250 | 0.250 | 0.250 | 0.000 | 0.0% | 37.5% | 38 |

**Background:** Among the many recent hitters to come out of the University of Indiana, Dickerson was originally taken in the third round of the 2011 draft by the Pirates, but got flipped to San Diego in a late 2013 challenge trade that saw Jaff Decker and Miles Mikolas head back the other way. Dickerson, immediately upon donning a Padres minor league uniform, suffered a pretty severe Spring Training ankle injury and was limited to just 41 games – albeit 41 promising games – in 2014. Last season, the 6-foot-3, 230-pound first baseman/corner outfielder spent the year bashing the Pacific Coast League competition to the tune of .307/.374/.503 while tying a career best 36 doubles with nine triples, 12 homeruns, and a quartet of stolen bases. His overall production, per *Weighted Runs Created Plus*, topped the league average mark by 32%. And for his career, Dickerson is sporting an impressive .300/.360/.485 triple-slash line.

**Projection**: Every once in a while there's a late-blooming minor league veteran that takes everyone by surprise, like Steven Pearce or Brandon Moss or Allen Craig or Stephen Voigt. And Dickerson could be the next in line. He's hit at every stop along the way during his five-year professional career, posting a *Weighted Runs Created Plus* total of at least 126. Solid-average eye with 15- to 18-homer pop and a .270-ish batting average – there's an awful lot of teams that are in need of that type of production. He's likely to get bumped into a DH role in the coming years.

Final note: he handles righties *and* lefties equally well.

**Ceiling:** 1.5-win player
**Risk:** Low to Moderate
**MLB ETA:** Debuted in 2015

## 7. Zech Lemond, RHP

**MiLB Rank:** N/A
**Position Rank:** N/A

| Born: 10/09/92 | Age: 23 | Bats: R | Top CALs: Diogenes Rosario, Kevin Comer, |
|---|---|---|---|
| Height: 6-1 | Weight: 170 | Throws: R | Julian Hilario, Ricky Knapp, Nathan Culp |

| YEAR | Age | Level | IP | W | L | ERA | FIP | K/9 | BB/9 | K% | BB% | HR/9 | LOB% |
|---|---|---|---|---|---|---|---|---|---|---|---|---|---|
| 2014 | 21 | A- | 38.0 | 2 | 3 | 3.79 | 3.08 | 8.05 | 1.18 | 21.4% | 3.1% | 0.24 | 66.5% |
| 2014 | 21 | AA | 4.0 | 0 | 0 | 0.00 | 2.12 | 4.50 | 0.00 | 14.3% | 0.0% | 0.00 | 100.0% |
| 2015 | 22 | A+ | 130.0 | 5 | 10 | 5.54 | 4.58 | 6.99 | 3.05 | 16.9% | 7.4% | 0.83 | 63.9% |

**Background:** One of the few pitchers to make it safely out of Arm Shredder U. – kind of, for now – Lemond spent the majority of his collegiate career as Rice University's late-inning relief specialist. The 6-foot-1, 170-pound hurler was in the midst of transitioning into starting pitcher after the loss of Jordan Stephens before – wait for it – elbow inflammation caused him to be temporarily shutdown. San Diego would grab Lemond in the third round two years, 86th overall, and after a strong showing in Northwest League during his debut he bypassed Low Class A and headed right into the California League last season. In 32 games with Lake Elsinore, 22 of which were starts, Lemond would post an unsightly 5.54 ERA with 101 punch outs and 44 walks in 130.0 innings of work.

**Projection**: Lemond's 4.58 FIP wasn't all that better than his horrible ERA, but he's a candidate for a strong bounce back season in 2016. He got smacked around quite a bit by a .374 BABIP and succumbed to a lower-ish 63.9% strand rate. Plus, he seemed to tire – greatly – over his final 11 starts. Consider the following breakdown:

| Innings | ERA | K | BB |
|---|---|---|---|
| 63.2 | 3.96 | 51 | 19 |
| 46.0 | 9.39 | 33 | 19 |

San Diego would eventually push him back into a relief role in mid-August to help govern his already bloated innings total. There's still an awful lot to like here, especially when you realize that he jumped from being a dominant collegiate reliever straight into a full-time starting pitcher in the California League with just 42.0 innings in between. Best case scenario: he develops into a #4-type arm. Worst case scenario: middle reliever.

**Ceiling:** 1.5-win player
**Risk:** Moderate to High
**MLB ETA:** 2017/2018

## 8. Jose Rondon, SS

**MiLB Rank: N/A**
**Position Rank: N/A**

| Born: 03/03/94 | Age: 22 | Bats: R | **Top CALs:** Reegie Corona, Justin Sellers, |
| Height: 6-1 | Weight: 160 | Throws: R | Jose Pirela, Greg Garcia, Luis Jean |

| Season | Age | LVL | PA | 2B | 3B | HR | AVG | OBP | SLG | ISO | BB% | K% | wRC+ |
|---|---|---|---|---|---|---|---|---|---|---|---|---|---|
| 2013 | 19 | R | 316 | 22 | 2 | 1 | 0.293 | 0.359 | 0.399 | 0.105 | 9.5% | 9.8% | 98 |
| 2014 | 20 | A+ | 478 | 26 | 5 | 1 | 0.319 | 0.365 | 0.409 | 0.090 | 6.3% | 15.3% | 105 |
| 2015 | 21 | A+ | 264 | 12 | 3 | 3 | 0.300 | 0.360 | 0.414 | 0.114 | 8.0% | 14.4% | 113 |
| 2015 | 21 | AA | 107 | 2 | 1 | 0 | 0.190 | 0.219 | 0.230 | 0.040 | 3.7% | 14.0% | 20 |

**Background:** Part of the package the franchised received from the Angels as part of the Huston Street/Trevor Gott deal in July 2014. Rondon, who was acquired along with Taylor Lindsey, Elliot Morris, and R.J. Alvarez, had a bit of breakout season between both organizations two years ago, hitting a combined .315/.363/.404 with 26 doubles, five triples, one homerun, and 13 stolen bases in 111 games, 109 of which were spent in the California League. The 6-foot-1, 160-pound wiry shortstop started last season back in High Class A – a move that seems a bit questionable after his stellar showing the previous year – until he completely flopped in 28 games in the Texas League before a fractured elbow shut him down in late-July. He finished the year with .267/.320/.359 showing, most of which was bogged down by a terrible .190/.219/.230 line with San Antonio.

**Projection**: Despite some strong offensive performances at various points in his five-year minor league career, Rondon profiles as a bit of tweener in terms of his big league ceiling. He runs well, but isn't a burner. He owns a strong hit tool with decent walk rates and handles himself well at shortstop. The problem, though, is his inability to consistently drive the ball – an issue that will likely be further exploited against more advanced pitching.

**Ceiling:** 1.5-win player
**Risk:** Moderate
**MLB ETA:** 2017

## 9. Franmil Reyes, RF

**MiLB Rank: N/A**
**Position Rank: N/A**

| Born: 07/07/97 | Age: 18 | Bats: R | **Top CALs:** Nick Longhi, Henry Ramos, |
| Height: 6-5 | Weight: 240 | Throws: R | Abraham Almonte, Austin Dean, Jorge Bonifacio |

| Season | Age | LVL | PA | 2B | 3B | HR | AVG | OBP | SLG | ISO | BB% | K% | wRC+ |
|---|---|---|---|---|---|---|---|---|---|---|---|---|---|
| 2013 | 17 | R | 186 | 12 | 2 | 3 | 0.315 | 0.387 | 0.467 | 0.152 | 10.8% | 21.0% | 139 |
| 2014 | 18 | A | 552 | 24 | 2 | 11 | 0.248 | 0.301 | 0.368 | 0.120 | 6.9% | 21.4% | 91 |
| 2015 | 19 | A | 509 | 25 | 7 | 8 | 0.255 | 0.320 | 0.393 | 0.138 | 9.0% | 17.9% | 107 |

**Background:** Very few everyday guys – let alone 19-year-olds – can match up with Reyes' imposing stature. Standing 6-foot-5 and a lean 240 pounds, Reyes has the look that would suggest his ability to impose his will on opposing pitchers. And after two mediocre seasons in the Midwest League that's all he has going for him – his look. The young right fielder burst onto the scene as a 16-year-old manhandling the Dominican Summer League four years ago, hitting a solid .267/.360/.416 with 16 doubles, four triples, four homeruns, and a dozen stolen bases. He followed that up with an even better showing in the Arizona Summer League in 2013 (.315/.387/.467) before a late-season promotion to Eugene pulled his overall production down quite a bit. San Diego's aggressiveness reached a simmering point two years ago as they bumped him up to Low Class A, despite his previous struggles in short-season action, and Reyes promptly batted .248/.301/.368. He would repeat the level last year with better – though far from great – results: .255/.320/.393.

**Projection:** I've hitched my analytical wagon to Reyes' tractor trailer-like frame for the past couple of seasons. And he hasn't rewarded my faith – yet. While he's spent the past two seasons developing his approach in the Midwest League it's important to remember that he's only entering his age-20 season. Reyes started to elevate the ball more often last year as his fly ball rate ticked up from 25.3% to 29.2%, taking his ISO with it (it jumped from .120 to .138). He also shows a solid, improving eye at the plate, strong contact skills, and some speed. Don't' give up on the kid yet.

**Ceiling:** 2.0-win player
**Risk:** High
**MLB ETA:** 2019

## 10. Enyel De Los Santos, RHP

MiLB Rank: N/A

Position Rank: N/A

| Born: 12/25/95 | Age: 20 | Bats: R | Top CALs: Kyle Lobstein, Julio Rodriguez, |
| Height: 6-3 | Weight: 170 | Throws: R | Casey Meisner, Jean Cosme, Alex Kisena |

| YEAR | Age | Level | IP | W | L | ERA | FIP | K/9 | BB/9 | K% | BB% | HR/9 | LOB% |
|------|-----|-------|----|----|----|-----|-----|-----|------|-----|-----|------|------|
| 2015 | 19 | R | 24.7 | 3 | 0 | 2.55 | 2.72 | 10.58 | 1.82 | 28.2% | 4.9% | 0.36 | 76.9% |
| 2015 | 19 | A- | 37.7 | 3 | 0 | 4.06 | 3.58 | 10.04 | 3.11 | 26.4% | 8.2% | 0.48 | 69.6% |

**Background:** Acquired along with former Georgia infielder Nelson Ward from the Mariners in November for veteran reliever Joaquin Benoit. De Los Santos looked absolutely brilliant during his professional debut last season. He was merely breathtaking in five starts in the Arizona Summer League and nothing short of amazing upon his promotion to Everett. Overall, he finished with 71 K, and 18 BB in 62.1 IP.

**Projection**: Signed for a measly $15,000 out of the Dominican Republic in July 2014, De Los Santos is proving to be quite the impressive little find. He's tall, lanky, and made quick work out of both low level stops last season. The sample size is only slightly bigger than the typical incoming rookie, but he's certainly one to watch in the coming years.

**Ceiling:** Too Soon to Tell
**Risk:** N/A
**MLB ETA:** N/A

## 11. Jabari Blash, OF

MiLB Rank: N/A

Position Rank: N/A

| Born: 07/04/89 | Age: 26 | Bats: R | Top CALs: Kyle Jensen, Travis Taijeron, |
| Height: 6-5 | Weight: 225 | Throws: R | Andrew Lambo, Joe Gaetti, Richie Shaffer |

| Season | Age | LVL | PA | 2B | 3B | HR | AVG | OBP | SLG | ISO | BB% | K% | wRC+ |
|--------|-----|-----|-----|----|----|----|------|------|------|------|------|------|------|
| 2013 | 23 | A+ | 332 | 16 | 3 | 16 | 0.258 | 0.358 | 0.505 | 0.247 | 12.0% | 25.6% | 124 |
| 2013 | 23 | AA | 120 | 3 | 0 | 9 | 0.309 | 0.442 | 0.619 | 0.309 | 16.7% | 23.3% | 208 |
| 2014 | 24 | AA | 163 | 7 | 1 | 6 | 0.236 | 0.387 | 0.449 | 0.213 | 17.2% | 21.5% | 135 |
| 2014 | 24 | AAA | 189 | 8 | 0 | 12 | 0.210 | 0.312 | 0.481 | 0.272 | 9.0% | 30.2% | 101 |
| 2015 | 25 | AA | 248 | 16 | 2 | 10 | 0.278 | 0.383 | 0.517 | 0.239 | 12.5% | 24.2% | 155 |
| 2015 | 25 | AAA | 228 | 8 | 0 | 22 | 0.264 | 0.355 | 0.640 | 0.376 | 12.3% | 27.6% | 157 |

**Background:** The massive minor league slugger's had a bit of busy offseason as he moved from Seattle to Oakland as part of a waiver claim and then onto San Diego as a piece of the early December Yonder Alonzo deal. Hailing from JuCo powerhouse Miami-Dade, Blash, a 2010 eighth round pick, continued to bash his way through the minor leagues as he cobbled together his finest professional season to date. Splitting his time nearly 50-50 between the Southern and Pacific Coast Leagues, the lean 6-foot-5 corner outfielder slugged a robust .271/.370/.576 with career bests in doubles (24) and homeruns (32) while adding a pair of triples and eight stolen bases to his already-padded stat line. His overall production, according to *Weighted Runs Created Plus*, topped the league average mark by more than 55% last season.

**Projection**: Blash, a career .256/.369/.500, is such an intriguing prospect – one that, at various points in his career, looks like an impact big league option. He's continually shown above-average in-game power (as evidenced by his 32 dingers last season, tied for fourth best among all stateside minor leaguers). But he complements that with an impressive amount of patience and some questionable swing-and-miss tendencies, making his an obvious pick as a Three True Outcomes hitter.

But consider this: Blash has made 10 different stops during his minor league career – only once, his 2014 showing in the PCL, has he failed to top the league by at least 24%. He could be one of those late-blooming, here-for-a-couple-seasons bats. It's another savvy pickup by A.J. Preller.

**Ceiling:** 1.5- to 2.0-win player
**Risk:** High
**MLB ETA:** 2016

## 12. Cory Mazzoni, RHP

**MiLB Rank: N/A**

**Position Rank: N/A**

| Born: 10/19/89 | Age: 26 | Bats: R | **Top CALs:** Ryan Brasier, Andrew Heaney, |
|---|---|---|---|
| Height: 6-1 | Weight: 200 | Throws: R | Jerry Blevins, Dan Jennings, Drew Pomeranz |

| YEAR | Age | Level | IP | W | L | ERA | FIP | K/9 | BB/9 | K% | BB% | HR/9 | LOB% |
|---|---|---|---|---|---|---|---|---|---|---|---|---|---|
| 2013 | 23 | AA | 66.0 | 5 | 3 | 4.36 | 2.82 | 10.09 | 2.59 | 26.2% | 6.7% | 0.55 | 56.2% |
| 2014 | 24 | R | 4.0 | 0 | 1 | 4.50 | 0.76 | 15.75 | 2.25 | 38.9% | 5.6% | 0.00 | 66.7% |
| 2014 | 24 | A+ | 9.0 | 0 | 0 | 5.00 | 2.39 | 9.00 | 3.00 | 22.5% | 7.5% | 0.00 | 64.3% |
| 2014 | 24 | AA | 12.0 | 2 | 0 | 4.50 | 2.69 | 7.50 | 3.00 | 20.0% | 8.0% | 0.00 | 57.1% |
| 2014 | 24 | AAA | 52.0 | 5 | 1 | 4.67 | 4.18 | 8.48 | 2.08 | 22.3% | 5.5% | 1.04 | 66.0% |
| 2015 | 25 | AAA | 34.0 | 1 | 3 | 3.97 | 1.95 | 12.18 | 3.18 | 32.4% | 8.5% | 0.00 | 54.1% |

**Background:** Buried by the Mets' sheer depth of high upside power arms, the Padres acquired Mazzoni, as well as Brad Wieck, in a challenge trade with New York last June in exchange for Alex Torres. And, perhaps driven by the big right-handers inability to stay healthy over the past three seasons, San Diego promptly pushed him into a full-time relief role for the first time in his professional career. The former second round pick spent the year yo-yoing – literally – between El Paso and San Diego. He would make three different trips up to the big leagues in just the first three months of the year before succumbing to shoulder woes. Overall, Mazzoni would tally 34.0 innings in the Pacific Coast League, fanning 46 and walking just 12. And in his three stints with the Padres he would throw another eight innings.

**Projection**: It's hardly surprising that the big right-hander, who previously averaged more than a punch out per inning, saw his already impressive strikeout rate tick up even further in his new – shortened – role. Mazzoni showed a blistering mid-90s fastball, a mid-80s slider, and a hard splitter during his debut. He has the potential to ascend into a closer's role – as long as he can stay healthy.

**Ceiling:** 1.0- to 1.5-win player
**Risk:** Moderate
**MLB ETA:** Debuted in 2015

## 13. Michael Gettys, CF

**MiLB Rank: N/A**

**Position Rank: N/A**

| Born: 10/22/95 | Age: 20 | Bats: R | **Top CALs:** Yorman Rodriguez, Zach Collier, |
|---|---|---|---|
| Height: 6-1 | Weight: 203 | Throws: R | Guillermo Pimentel, Jose Rivero, Willy Garcia |

| Season | Age | LVL | PA | 2B | 3B | HR | AVG | OBP | SLG | ISO | BB% | K% | wRC+ |
|---|---|---|---|---|---|---|---|---|---|---|---|---|---|
| 2014 | 18 | R | 233 | 8 | 5 | 3 | 0.310 | 0.353 | 0.437 | 0.127 | 6.4% | 28.3% | 125 |
| 2015 | 19 | A | 529 | 27 | 6 | 6 | 0.231 | 0.271 | 0.346 | 0.115 | 5.3% | 30.6% | 77 |

**Background:** The club's second round pick out of Gainesville High School two years ago, Gettys got off to a promising start to his professional career, hitting .310/.353/.437 in the Arizona Summer League. San Diego aggressively pushed him up to the Midwest League last year and – predictably (you'll find out below) – he struggled against the full season action, batting .231/.271/.346.

**Projection**: Here's a portion of what I wrote in last year's book: "The long red flag on an otherwise strong debut was his red flag-encroaching K-rate (28.3%)." Well, his punch out rate jumped up a couple more percentage points as he flailed away at the Midwest League pitching. And more importantly, he failed to make any type of adjustments over the course of the season. In fact, he *regressed* as he batted an even worse .218/.260/.322 over his final 105 games. Granted he's still plenty young enough, but it's going to be hard to overcome that K-rate moving forward.

**Ceiling:** 1.0- to 1.5-win player
**Risk:** Moderate
**MLB ETA:** 2019

## 14. Colin Rea, RHP

MiLB Rank: N/A

Position Rank: N/A

| Born: 07/01/90 | Age: 25 | Bats: R | |
|---|---|---|---|
| Height: 6-5 | Weight: 220 | Throws: R | Top CALs: Mike Hauschild, David Goforth, Danny Touchet, Robert Ray, Greg Ross |

| YEAR | Age | Level | IP | W | L | ERA | FIP | K/9 | BB/9 | K% | BB% | HR/9 | LOB% |
|---|---|---|---|---|---|---|---|---|---|---|---|---|---|
| 2013 | 23 | A | 43.0 | 2 | 1 | 2.09 | 3.48 | 7.95 | 4.60 | 20.9% | 12.1% | 0.21 | 82.7% |
| 2013 | 23 | A+ | 43.0 | 0 | 5 | 6.07 | 5.59 | 9.42 | 8.16 | 21.7% | 18.8% | 0.63 | 63.6% |
| 2014 | 24 | A+ | 139.0 | 11 | 9 | 3.88 | 4.02 | 7.64 | 2.40 | 19.8% | 6.2% | 0.71 | 72.4% |
| 2015 | 24 | AA | 75.0 | 3 | 2 | 1.08 | 2.35 | 7.20 | 1.32 | 21.2% | 3.9% | 0.12 | 77.6% |
| 2015 | 24 | AAA | 26.7 | 2 | 2 | 4.39 | 4.65 | 6.75 | 4.05 | 16.7% | 10.0% | 0.68 | 72.1% |

**Background:** A nice little find in the 12th round out of Indiana State University in 2011, Rea made stops at three different levels last season, going from the Texas League to El Paso in the Pacific Coast League and eventually landing in San Diego for a half-dozen starts of decent baseball. The big 6-foot-5, 220-pound right-hander finished his minor league season with 101.2 combined innings with 80 punch outs and 23 walks.

**Projection**: For a brief 12 game span early last year Rea looked like the second coming of Cy Young as he strung together a 1.08 ERA and a 2.35 FIP across 75.0 innings. But he seemed to lose his mojo – that, or his formerly .233 BABIP regressed back to the league average – as he moved up to the PCL. Rea isn't particularly overpowering as his fastball resides in the low-90s. He'll complement it with a mid-80s cutter, a curveball, and a rarely thrown splitter. Don't buy into the hype, he's a backend starter – at best.

**Ceiling:** 1.0-win player
**Risk:** Low
**MLB ETA:** Debuted in 2015

## 15. Jose Torres, LHP

MiLB Rank: N/A

Position Rank: N/A

| Born: 09/24/93 | Age: 22 | Bats: L | |
|---|---|---|---|
| Height: 6-2 | Weight: 175 | Throws: L | Top CALs: David Baker, Yimmi Brasoban, Tyler Vail, Chris Lugo, Travis Ott |

| YEAR | Age | Level | IP | W | L | ERA | FIP | K/9 | BB/9 | K% | BB% | HR/9 | LOB% |
|---|---|---|---|---|---|---|---|---|---|---|---|---|---|
| 2013 | 19 | A- | 30.7 | 3 | 2 | 2.64 | 3.85 | 6.16 | 3.52 | 15.4% | 8.8% | 0.59 | 68.1% |
| 2014 | 20 | A- | 61.7 | 0 | 6 | 4.38 | 3.98 | 6.86 | 3.21 | 17.8% | 8.3% | 0.58 | 61.4% |
| 2015 | 21 | A | 73.7 | 4 | 5 | 2.69 | 3.03 | 9.77 | 2.81 | 26.7% | 7.7% | 0.49 | 75.9% |
| 2015 | 21 | A+ | 3.7 | 0 | 0 | 0.00 | 2.42 | 9.82 | 2.45 | 30.8% | 7.7% | 0.00 | 100.0% |

**Background:** Acquired from Oakland along with Jabari Blash and Drew Pomeranz for the services of Yonder Alonso and and Marc Rzepczynski, the wiry Venezuelan-born southpaw saw a dramatic uptick in his overall production as Oakland pushed him out of the rotation and into a fulltime relief role for the first time. In 47 games last season, all but three coming in the Midwest League, Torres posted an impeccable 84-to-24 strikeout-to-walk ratio to go along with a 2.56 ERA and a FIP hovering around 3.00. For his already lengthy five-year minor league career, the soon-to-be 22-year-old has averaged 7.5 strikeouts and 3.7 walks per nine innings to go along with a decent enough 3.47 ERA.

**Projection**: A very intriguing arm developing in the low levels of the minors – and a fantastic little pickup as well – Torres may have found a home as a quick-moving, multiple-inning relief arm. Or San Diego could see if things finally clicked for the lefty and push him back into the rotation. But there's definite big league potential here. Both the control and swing-and-miss ability took dramatic – and expected – leaps forward last season. He's still a ways off, but I like him.

**Ceiling:** 1.0-win player
**Risk:** Moderate
**MLB ETA:** 2018

## 16. Jean Cosme, RHP

MiLB Rank: N/A

Position Rank: N/A

| Born: 05/24/96 | Age: 20 | Bats: R | |
|---|---|---|---|
| Height: 6-2 | Weight: 155 | Throws: R | Top CALs: Kyle Lobstein, Casey Meisner, Zach Mcallister, Chris Lugo, Parker Bridwell |

| YEAR | Age | Level | IP | W | L | ERA | FIP | K/9 | BB/9 | K% | BB% | HR/9 | LOB% |
|---|---|---|---|---|---|---|---|---|---|---|---|---|---|
| 2014 | 18 | R | 15.3 | 2 | 0 | 4.70 | 4.09 | 9.98 | 4.70 | 25.4% | 11.9% | 0.59 | 69.4% |
| 2015 | 19 | A- | 57.0 | 3 | 5 | 4.74 | 3.17 | 8.37 | 2.84 | 22.8% | 7.7% | 0.32 | 55.4% |

**Background:** Baltimore grabbed the right-hander in the 17th round two years ago. After a short, moderately successful debut in the Gulf Coast League, Cosme seemingly blossomed – or at least is in the opening stage of blossoming – in the NYPL last season, posting a 53-to-18 strikeout K-to-BB ratio in 57 IP. San Diego grabbed the promising young right-hander from the Orioles for replaceable veteran Odrisamer Despaigne.

**Projection:** A complete wild card by the very definition. Cosme, though, looked pretty dominant in his 12 games with Aberdeen – especially over his final four starts when he tallied a 25-to-5 strikeout-to-walk ratio in 22.0 innings. He could be a super sleeper breakout prospect heading into 2016, one in which we could be talking a whole lot about come this time next year.

**Ceiling:** Too Soon to Tell
**Risk:** N/A
**MLB ETA:** N/A

---

## 17. Luis Perdomo, RHP

**MiLB Rank:** N/A
**Position Rank:** N/A

| Born: 05/09/93 | Age: 23 | Bats: R | Top CALs: Kevin Comer, Silfredo Garcia, |
|---|---|---|---|
| Height: 6-2 | Weight: 160 | Throws: R | Brandon Barker, Ryan Searle, Waner Mateo |

| YEAR | Age | Level | IP | W | L | ERA | FIP | K/9 | BB/9 | K% | BB% | HR/9 | LOB% |
|---|---|---|---|---|---|---|---|---|---|---|---|---|---|
| 2013 | 20 | R | 41.7 | 1 | 6 | 5.40 | 4.59 | 6.26 | 3.02 | 14.0% | 6.8% | 0.86 | 46.2% |
| 2014 | 21 | A- | 12.0 | 1 | 0 | 1.50 | 2.61 | 9.75 | 0.75 | 28.3% | 2.2% | 0.75 | 84.9% |
| 2014 | 21 | A | 57.0 | 3 | 6 | 5.05 | 4.27 | 6.47 | 3.32 | 15.7% | 8.1% | 0.63 | 54.0% |
| 2014 | 21 | A+ | 3.0 | 0 | 0 | 0.00 | 1.39 | 9.00 | 0.00 | 30.0% | 0.0% | 0.00 | 100.0% |
| 2015 | 22 | A | 100.3 | 5 | 9 | 3.68 | 3.39 | 8.97 | 2.78 | 23.3% | 7.2% | 0.63 | 67.3% |
| 2015 | 22 | A+ | 26.3 | 1 | 3 | 5.13 | 2.98 | 6.15 | 2.05 | 16.1% | 5.4% | 0.34 | 59.0% |

**Background:** Passed around like a bunch of Christmas leftovers, Perdomo began the offseason as a member of the St. Louis Cardinals but was taken in the Rule 5 Draft by the Rockies and eventually flipped to the Padres for a Player to Be Named Later or cash considerations. Perdomo, a hard-throwing right-hander out of Santo Domingo, had the finest season of his five-year pro career – though most of the damage was done as a 22-year-old making his second trip through the Midwest League. He would post an impressive 118-to-37 strikeout-to-walk ratio in 100.1 innings of work for Peoria. St. Louis would bump him back up to the Florida State League for another six starts beginning in mid-August. Overall, he would finish the year with a career high 126.2 innings while averaging 8.4 punch outs and just 2.6 walks per nine innings.

**Projection:** Perdomo could easily become this year's version of Odubel Herrera, who went from Rule 5 pick to nearly a four-win season for the Phillies this season. Now is Perdomo going to have *that* type of impact? Not at all. But he could be a serviceable, out-of-nowhere middle relief arm for the Padres in 2016. If they can continue to develop him, Perdomo might be able to develop into something better. Very, very savvy pickup.

**Ceiling:** 1.5-win player
**Risk:** High
**MLB ETA:** 2016?

---

## 18. Austin Smith, RHP

**MiLB Rank:** N/A
**Position Rank:** N/A

| Born: 07/09/96 | Age: 19 | Bats: R | Top CALs: Andres Perez-Lobo, Matthew Heidenreich, |
|---|---|---|---|
| Height: 6-4 | Weight: 220 | Throws: R | Austin Willis, Erling Moreno, Santiago Garrido |

| YEAR | Age | Level | IP | W | L | ERA | FIP | K/9 | BB/9 | K% | BB% | HR/9 | LOB% |
|---|---|---|---|---|---|---|---|---|---|---|---|---|---|
| 2015 | 18 | R | 17.0 | 0 | 3 | 7.94 | 4.46 | 5.82 | 4.76 | 13.1% | 10.7% | 0.00 | 57.9% |

**Background:** After the club forfeited their first round pick last June by signing veteran James Shields during the offseason, Smith – by de facto – was the organization's top June pick. Taken with the 51st overall selection, the 6-foot-4, 220-pound right-hander tossed 17.0 innings in his debut, posting a disappointing 11-to-9 strikeout-to-walk ratio en route to surrendering 15 earned runs.

**Projection:** After grabbing a pair of high ceiling collegiate players with their top pick the last two seasons (Trea Turner and Hunter Renfroe), San Diego chose to dip back into the high school ranks and grab the big right-hander. His debut wasn't particularly impressive – then again it was just 17.0 innings. Per the usual, we'll take a wait-and-see approach.

**Ceiling:** Too Soon to Tell
**Risk:** N/A
**MLB ETA:** N/A

## 19. Luis Urias, 2B/3B/SS

**MiLB Rank: N/A**

**Position Rank: N/A**

| Born: 06/03/97 | Age: 19 | Bats: R | Top CALs: Yonathan Mendoza, Isaiah Kiner-Falefa, |
|---|---|---|---|
| Height: 5-9 | Weight: 160 | Throws: R | Josh Morgan, Luis Jean, Luis Carpio |

| Season | Age | LVL | PA | 2B | 3B | HR | AVG | OBP | SLG | ISO | BB% | K% | wRC+ |
|---|---|---|---|---|---|---|---|---|---|---|---|---|---|
| 2014 | 17 | R | 180 | 5 | 1 | 0 | 0.308 | 0.391 | 0.353 | 0.045 | 10.0% | 7.2% | 122 |
| 2015 | 18 | A- | 44 | 1 | 0 | 0 | 0.355 | 0.487 | 0.387 | 0.032 | 11.4% | 2.3% | 166 |
| 2015 | 18 | A | 224 | 5 | 1 | 0 | 0.290 | 0.370 | 0.326 | 0.036 | 7.1% | 8.0% | 110 |

**Background:** A pocket-sized infielder with a knack for finding first base – a *lot*. Urias spent all but two games during his pro debut in the Arizona Summer League, hitting an impressive .310/.393/.355. And after just 10 games with Tri-City last season, Urias earned a promotion to the Midwest League where he made it look relatively easy: .290/.370/.326.

**Projection**: Standing just 5-foot-9 and 160-pounds, Urias has slugged only 13 extra-base hits during his 106 minor leagues games – good enough for a lackluster .337 slugging percentage. But, damn, the kid has proven to be an OBP monster – some of which is driven by higher-ish BABIPs and the other part buoyed by solid walk rates. He's not going to be a particularly strong big leaguer, but he might be able to carve out a semi-useful backup role.

**Ceiling:** 1.0- to 1.5-win player
**Risk:** Moderate to High
**MLB ETA:** 2018

## 20. Carlos Asuaje, 2B

**MiLB Rank: N/A**

**Position Rank: N/A**

| Born: 11/02/91 | Age: 24 | Bats: L | Top CALs: David Adams, Ryan Flaherty, |
|---|---|---|---|
| Height: 5-9 | Weight: 160 | Throws: R | Brad Miller, Nate Spears, Chase d'Arnaud |

| Season | Age | LVL | PA | 2B | 3B | HR | AVG | OBP | SLG | ISO | BB% | K% | wRC+ |
|---|---|---|---|---|---|---|---|---|---|---|---|---|---|
| 2013 | 21 | A- | 204 | 12 | 1 | 1 | 0.269 | 0.366 | 0.368 | 0.099 | 13.2% | 16.2% | 127 |
| 2014 | 22 | A | 383 | 24 | 10 | 11 | 0.305 | 0.391 | 0.542 | 0.237 | 10.7% | 14.6% | 156 |
| 2014 | 22 | A+ | 176 | 14 | 2 | 4 | 0.323 | 0.398 | 0.516 | 0.194 | 10.2% | 19.3% | 157 |
| 2015 | 23 | AA | 570 | 23 | 7 | 8 | 0.251 | 0.334 | 0.374 | 0.123 | 9.8% | 15.4% | 107 |

**Background:** Also part of the package received from the Red Sox in the Craig Kimbrel trade. Asuaje, who is the third highest drafted player out of Nova Southeastern University, looked OK in his first stint in Class AA last season, batting a league average-ish .251/.334/.374 with 23 doubles, seven triples, eight homeruns, and nine stolen bases. His overall production, according to *Weighted Runs Created Plus*, topped the league average mark by 7%. It was marked decline in production as he was coming off of a dominant showing the previous year as he split time between Greenville in the South Atlantic League and Salem in the Carolina League, hitting an impressive .310/.393/.533.

**Projection**: Fun fact: Asuaje's 11th round draft status surpasses both of the school's famous alums: J.D. Martinez, who was taken in the 20th round and Mike Fiers, who was taken two rounds later in the same 2009 draft. Despite some dominance two years ago and a decent showing in the Eastern League last season, Asuaje is fighting an uphill battle for big league playing time. He's been relegated to second base the majority of his career so a bench spot isn't likely as those are typically reserved for players that can handle – effectively – shortstop. He's not overly quick or particularly patient. And his power regressed mightily as he moved up to the minors' toughest challenge.

**Ceiling:** 1.0- to 1.5-win player
**Risk:** Moderate to High
**MLB ETA:** 2016/2017

## 21. Logan Allen, LHP

**MiLB Rank: N/A**

**Position Rank: N/A**

| Born: 05/23/97 | Age: 19 | Bats: R | Top CALs: N/A |
|---|---|---|---|
| Height: 6-3 | Weight: 200 | Throws: L | |

| YEAR | Age | Level | IP | W | L | ERA | FIP | K/9 | BB/9 | K% | BB% | HR/9 | LOB% |
|---|---|---|---|---|---|---|---|---|---|---|---|---|---|
| 2015 | 18 | R | 20.0 | 0 | 0 | 0.90 | 1.06 | 10.80 | 0.45 | 33.8% | 1.4% | 0.00 | 84.6% |
| 2015 | 18 | A- | 4.3 | 0 | 0 | 2.08 | 2.59 | 4.15 | 0.00 | 10.0% | 0.0% | 0.00 | 83.3% |

**Background:** Hailing from the same school as Brady Aiken, Boston coughed up a whole lot of dough to sign Allen. Taken in the eighth round, 231st overall, Allen signed a deal for over $700,000 – money equivalent to third round money. And Allen is starting to pay off in a

# San Diego Padres

*BIG* way. With 24.1 innings between the Gulf Coast and New York-Penn Leagues, Allen tallied a jaw-dropping 26-to-1 – **26-to-1!** – strikeout-to-walk ratio. The 6-foot-3, 200-pound lefty allowed just 18 hits and three earned runs during his first taste of professional baseball.

**Projection**: Well, it's obviously a very, very small sample size. But, *damn*, it's so impressive. Per the usual with incoming prep players, we will take a wait-and-see approach. But he's one to watch in 2016.

**Ceiling:** Too Soon to Tell
**Risk:** N/A
**MLB ETA:** N/A

## 22. Elliot Morris, RHP

MiLB Rank: N/A
Position Rank: N/A

| Born: 04/26/92 | Age: 24 | Bats: R |
|---|---|---|
| Height: 6-4 | Weight: 210 | Throws: R |

**Top CALs:** Ryan Searle, Matthew Hobgood, Michael O'Brien, Paul Clemens, Deunte Heath

| YEAR | Age | Level | IP | W | L | ERA | FIP | K/9 | BB/9 | K% | BB% | HR/9 | LOB% |
|---|---|---|---|---|---|---|---|---|---|---|---|---|---|
| 2013 | 21 | R | 27.3 | 2 | 2 | 3.95 | 4.27 | 8.23 | 3.62 | 21.2% | 9.3% | 0.33 | 74.5% |
| 2014 | 22 | A | 40.0 | 2 | 1 | 2.25 | 3.06 | 9.90 | 2.93 | 27.3% | 8.1% | 0.45 | 72.8% |
| 2014 | 22 | A+ | 93.3 | 6 | 6 | 3.86 | 5.17 | 7.04 | 3.76 | 18.8% | 10.1% | 1.16 | 75.1% |
| 2015 | 23 | R | 1.0 | 0 | 0 | 0.00 | 3.82 | 0.00 | 0.00 | 0.0% | 0.0% | 0.00 | 100.0% |
| 2015 | 23 | AA | 101.7 | 5 | 9 | 4.87 | 4.00 | 6.37 | 3.90 | 15.8% | 9.7% | 0.53 | 64.4% |

**Background:** Acquired from the Angels along with (the disappointing) Taylor Lindsey, Jose Rondon, and R.J. Alvarez in the Huston Street/Trevor Gott deal near the July 2014 trade deadline. Morris spent last season as a member of San Antonio's rotation. In 102.2 innings, the 6-foot-4, 210-pound right-hander posted a mediocre 72-to-44 strikeout-to-walk ratio en route to tallying a lowly 4.82 ERA.

**Projection**: Morris, a former fourth round pick out of Pierce College three years ago, is a poor man's version of Cory Mazzoni – a big, hard-throwing right-hander who's likely headed down the path of relief-dom. Morris' strikeout rate has been in steady decline as he's progressed up the minor league ladder and it now rates as a decent ability, nothing more. He could be a serviceable middle relief arm in the next year or two.

**Ceiling:** 1.0-win player
**Risk:** Moderate
**MLB ETA:** 2016/2017

## 23. Bryan Verbitsky, RHP

MiLB Rank: N/A
Position Rank: N/A

| Born: 06/11/92 | Age: 24 | Bats: R |
|---|---|---|
| Height: 5-11 | Weight: 205 | Throws: R |

**Top CALs:** Tyler Jones, Neil Wagner, Barret Browning, David Carpenter, Mike Hart

| YEAR | Age | Level | IP | W | L | ERA | FIP | K/9 | BB/9 | K% | BB% | HR/9 | LOB% |
|---|---|---|---|---|---|---|---|---|---|---|---|---|---|
| 2013 | 21 | A- | 49.3 | 0 | 6 | 4.01 | 4.37 | 8.57 | 6.93 | 21.4% | 17.3% | 0.36 | 72.0% |
| 2014 | 22 | A- | 27.0 | 2 | 2 | 1.67 | 1.82 | 14.00 | 3.33 | 41.2% | 9.8% | 0.00 | 73.9% |
| 2014 | 22 | A | 8.0 | 0 | 1 | 13.50 | 4.98 | 9.00 | 5.63 | 18.2% | 11.4% | 1.13 | 40.8% |
| 2014 | 22 | A+ | 3.3 | 0 | 1 | 5.40 | 15.74 | 5.40 | 16.20 | 10.5% | 31.6% | 5.40 | 100.0% |
| 2015 | 23 | A | 36.0 | 0 | 0 | 3.00 | 3.23 | 9.50 | 4.25 | 24.5% | 11.0% | 0.25 | 66.5% |
| 2015 | 23 | A+ | 28.0 | 1 | 2 | 4.18 | 3.53 | 10.61 | 3.54 | 26.6% | 8.9% | 0.64 | 62.8% |

**Background:** Hailing from Hofstra University, home to just seven other MLB draft picks, the earliest being 2012 tenth round pick Daniel Poma, Verbitsky easily became the school's most famous baseball alum when the Padres grabbed him in the third round three years ago. A small-ish right-hander, Verbitsky spent the majority of his collegiate career working out of the Pride's bullpen, tallying 87.0 innings while averaging 9.0 strikeouts and 3.10 walks per nine innings. Following his selection, San Diego toyed with the idea of converting the 5-foot-11, 205-pound hurler into a full-time starting pitcher – though the results were mostly disastrous as he walked 38 in 49.1 innings. Verbitsky has spent the past two years making stops for the Northwest League up to High Class A. He's sporting a 170-to-87 strikeout-to-walk ratio in 151.2 innings of work.

**Projection**: Sporting a blistering fastball, Verbitsky was recognized twice as the Diamond Award winner as Nassau's top high school player. He shows a promising ability to miss bats, but his control – even as it ticked forward last season – remains mediocre at best. He has the upside as a potential seventh/eighth-inning arm, but he's still two years away.

**Ceiling:** 1.0-win player
**Risk:** Moderate
**MLB ETA:** 2017/2018

## 24. Dinelson Lamet, RHP

**MiLB Rank: N/A**
**Position Rank: N/A**

| Born: 07/18/92 | Age: 23 | Bats: R | **Top CALs:** Alex Koronis, Anthony Capra, |
| Height: 6-4 | Weight: 187 | Throws: R | Justin Friend, Lee Tabor, Kyle Morrison |

| YEAR | Age | Level | IP | W | L | ERA | FIP | K/9 | BB/9 | K% | BB% | HR/9 | LOB% |
|------|-----|-------|------|---|---|------|------|-------|------|-------|-------|------|-------|
| 2014 | 21 | R | 4.0 | 0 | 0 | 0.00 | 0.63 | 18.00 | 0.00 | 57.1% | 0.0% | 0.00 | 50.0% |
| 2015 | 22 | A | 105.3 | 5 | 8 | 2.99 | 3.74 | 10.25 | 3.76 | 27.2% | 10.0% | 0.77 | 76.0% |

**Background:** Practically an old man when he signed out of the Dominican Republic at the elderly age of 21, Lamet, who inked on the dotted line for $100,000, spent last season working out of Fort Wayne's rotation, throwing 105.1 innings with 120 punch outs, 44 walks, and a decent 3.74 FIP.

**Projection**: Obviously not a whole lot of data to go off of, Lamet was also a bit old – go figure – for the Midwest League, so that further clouds the initial analysis. But the initial returns have been promising nonetheless. It is a bit curious as to why the club didn't bump up the 6-foot-4, 187-pound right-hander up to High Class A. He could be anything at this point, but add his name to the list of players to watch in 2016.

**Ceiling:** Too Soon to Tell
**Risk:** N/A
**MLB ETA:** N/A

## 25. Tayron Guerrero, RHP

**MiLB Rank: N/A**
**Position Rank: N/A**

| Born: 01/09/91 | Age: 25 | Bats: R | **Top CALs:** Jay Buente, Dan Merklinger, |
| Height: 6-7 | Weight: 215 | Throws: R | Barret Browning, Hector Correa, Brad Mills |

| YEAR | Age | Level | IP | W | L | ERA | FIP | K/9 | BB/9 | K% | BB% | HR/9 | LOB% |
|------|-----|-------|------|---|---|------|------|-------|-------|-------|-------|------|-------|
| 2013 | 22 | R | 4.7 | 1 | 0 | 5.79 | 2.51 | 9.64 | 0.00 | 23.8% | 0.0% | 0.00 | 33.3% |
| 2013 | 22 | A- | 32.0 | 1 | 4 | 4.50 | 4.26 | 9.84 | 7.03 | 24.0% | 17.1% | 0.28 | 62.0% |
| 2013 | 22 | A | 3.7 | 0 | 1 | 7.36 | 8.52 | 9.82 | 19.64 | 15.4% | 30.8% | 0.00 | 52.9% |
| 2014 | 23 | A | 36.0 | 6 | 1 | 1.00 | 2.87 | 10.50 | 3.00 | 29.6% | 8.5% | 0.50 | 86.5% |
| 2014 | 23 | A+ | 13.7 | 0 | 0 | 2.63 | 4.62 | 9.22 | 5.27 | 23.7% | 13.6% | 0.66 | 85.2% |
| 2015 | 24 | AA | 42.3 | 1 | 5 | 2.76 | 3.53 | 9.78 | 4.25 | 25.0% | 10.9% | 0.64 | 64.3% |
| 2015 | 24 | AAA | 13.7 | 0 | 0 | 3.95 | 4.04 | 9.88 | 7.24 | 26.3% | 19.3% | 0.00 | 70.0% |

**Background:** The good news: the statue-esque right-hander out of Colombia fanned 61 batters in 56.0 innings of work between the Class AA and Class AAA. The better news: Guerrero finished with the second lowest walk rate of his six-year career. Now, the bad news: that walk rate, which, again, was the tied for the second lowest of his career, was 5.0 BB/9.

**Projection**: A talented, hard-throwing giant wrapped up in an enigma. Guerrero was everything you would want in a pitching prospect – 6-foot-7 frame, an elite ability to miss bats, one of the top fastballs in the system – sans one not-so-tiny thing: his inability to find the strike zone on a consistent basis. And while Guerrero seemed to rein in his control issues two years ago, it, unfortunately, took a big leap backward in 2015. He has a chance to be a dominant backend reliever, just as I have a chance to go down as the greatest baseball writer in history. Sarcasm applied where necessary. But, hey, there's *always* a chance.

**Ceiling:** 1.0- to 1.5-win player
**Risk:** High
**MLB ETA:** 2016/2017

## *Barely Missed:*

- **Michael Dimmock, RHP** – Absolutely dominant between San Antonio and El Paso last season – 60 IP, 70 K, and just six walks – Dimmock "the Dummy" got popped for a drug of abuse for the second time in September, losing a spot in the Arizona Summer League.

- **Sam Holland, RHP** – Side-winding right-hander from Australia got pushed all the way up to California League after spending the previous year in the short-season ball. The club wisely demoted him back to the Northwest League where he picked right up with his level of dominance. He's a strong bounce-back candidate.

- **Jacob Nix, RHP** – The club's most recent third round pick, the big right-hander got caught up in the Brady Aiken drama two years ago. Nix, who was taken in the fifth round, had his $1.5 million offer rescinded as Houston couldn't come to a below-slot deal with Aiken. He would eventually head to IMG Academy – where he would briefly teammate up with Aiken. Somewhere Alanis Morissette is penning a lyric to her song *Ironic* about Nix and Aiken eventually teaming up after the 2014 debacle. Isn't it *Ironic*? Nix would sign for slightly less than a million dollars, so Aiken is on the hook for the other half-mill. Anyway, he would toss 19.2 innings in Arizona Summer League, fanning 19 and walking seven.

## *Bird Doggin' It – Additional Prospects to Keep an Eye in 2016*

| Player | Age | POS | Notes |
|---|---|---|---|
| Carlos Belen | 20 | 3B | He looked overmatched in his promotion up to the Northwest League last season, hitting .218/.299/.383 – a drastic decline from his .256/.348/.541 showing the previous year. |
| Auston Bousfield | 22 | CF | A former fifth rounder out of the University of Mississippi two years ago, Bousfield might be able to carve out a semi-useful role as a backup outfielder in the coming years, but he'll need to flash more power. |
| Jimmy Brasoban | 22 | RHP | The right-hander took to a full-time relief role with relative ease, averaging 10.0 K/9 and 3.1 BB/9 in the Midwest League last season. |
| Franchy Cordero | 21 | SS | Showed surprising power in the Northwest League two years ago, but he struggled to make enough contact as he got exposed in the Low Class A in 2015. |
| Marcus Greene | 21 | C | Acquired from the Rangers for Will Venable, Greene appeared in just 25 games last season, but looked promising in the Northwest League two years ago. |
| Taylor Lindsey | 24 | 2B | Former budding top prospect's production has cratered over the past two seasons. Not sure he if can bounce back. |
| Kyle McGrath | 23 | RHP | Former 36th round pick out of Louisville posted a mind-boggling 79-to-8 strikeout-to-walk ratio in 70.2 innings, all but two coming in the Midwest League. |
| Trevor Megill | 22 | RHP | Former Loyola Marymount flamethrower was plucked out in the seventh round last season and looked overpowering in the Arizona Summer and Northwest Leagues. |
| Gabriel Quintana | 23 | 3B | Failed to make any progress in his second go-round in the California League, hitting a lowly .245/.270/.395. He batted .263/.302/.431 with Lake Elsinore the previous year. |
| Nick Torres | 23 | LF/RF | Hit an aggregate .305/.352/.439 between the Midwest and California Leagues last season. |
| Jose Urena | 21 | LF/RF | Made tremendous, tremendous strides in his plate discipline in a repeat in short-season ball as he posted a 47-to-59 strikeout-to-walk ratio in 277 PA. He could be a sleeper heading into 2016. |
| Brad Wieck | 24 | LHP | Massive, literally, 6-foot-9, 255-pound southpaw acquired from the Mets. He posted a solid 139-to-50 strikeout-to-walk ratio in 123.1 innings, though he was a bit old for the levels of competition. |

**State of the Farm System:** Just like it has in previous years, San Francisco's farm system is brimming with plenty of young, hard-throwing arms.

Phil Bickford, the club's most recent first round pick, looked absolutely brilliant during his debut in the Arizona Summer League. The 6-foot-5, 205-pound right-hander posted an immaculate 32-to-6 strikeout-to-walk ratio in 22.1 innings of work.

The club's first round pick in 2014, former Vanderbilt ace Tyler Beede, had a nice season between San Jose and Richmond as he showed a previously un-displayed knack for finding the strike zone with high regularity. In other words, his walk rate was respectable. Now the bad news, because there's always bad news: Beede didn't miss too many sticks in 2015.

And rounding out the system's version of the Killer B's is savvy control artist Clayton Blackburn, a former 16th round pick who progressed quickly the minors. Last season Blackburn made 23 starts with the Sacramento River Cats, posting 2.85 ERA with 99 strikeouts and just 32 walks in 123.0 innings of work.

In terms of offensive weaponry, the Giants' system has more than a few intriguing names.

Outfielder Mac Williamson is big league ready after returning from Tommy John surgery, but is currently locked in behind San Francisco's starters (Denard Span, Angel Pagan, Hunter Pence, and not to mention backup Gregor Blanco). Williamson could be useable trade bait in the coming months.

Shortstop Christian Arroyo continues to reward the organization's faith in him as the early criticized first round pick slugged a robust .304/.344/.459 as a 20-year-old in an injury-shortened campaign in High Class A.

The club also added collegiate basher Chris Shaw in the first round last June as well as high profile international amateur Lucius Fox.

| Rank | Name | POS |
|------|------|-----|
| 1 | Phil Bickford | RHP |
| 2 | Tyler Beede | RHP |
| 3 | Christian Arroyo | SS |
| 4 | Mac Williamson | LF/RF |
| 5 | Clayton Blackburn | RHP |
| 6 | Chris Shaw | 1B |
| 7 | Lucius Fox | SS |
| 8 | Chase Johnson | RHP |
| 9 | Josh Osich | LHP |
| 10 | Adalberto Mejia | LHP |
| 11 | Aramis Garcia | C |
| 12 | Andrew Suarez | LHP |
| 13 | Jordan Johnson | RHP |
| 14 | Kyle Crick | RHP |
| 15 | Samuel Coonrod | RHP |
| 16 | Hunter Cole | 2B/LF/RF |
| 17 | Derek Law | RHP |
| 18 | Steven Okert | LHP |
| 19 | Chris Stratton | RHP |
| 20 | Austin Slater | 2B/OF |
| 21 | Joan Gregorio | RHP |
| 22 | Ray Black | RHP |
| 23 | Ryder Jones | 3B |
| 24 | Martin Agosta | RHP |
| 25 | Johneshwy Fargas | OF |

**Review of the 2015 Draft:** San Francisco did fantastically well in adding two high profile potentially impact big leaguers in College of Southern Nevada right-hander Phil Bickford and Boston College slugging first baseman Chris Shaw. The organization also picked up polished Miami southpaw Andrew Suarez, who looks like a solid bet to develop into a backend starting pitcher.

Third round prep shortstop Jalen Miller left a lot to be desired as he struggled to the tune of .218/.292/.259 with just six extra-base knocks in 44 games with the organization's Arizona Summer League affiliate.

One name to watch: 11th round pick C.J. Hinosa out of the University of Texas. The former Longhorn batted .296/.328/.481 with 18 doubles, one triple, five dingers, and a pair of stolen bases.

## 1. Phil Bickford, RHP

MiLB Rank: #34

Position Rank: #15

| | | | | |
|---|---|---|---|---|
| **Born:** 07/10/95 | **Age:** 20 | **Bats:** R | **Top CALs:** Cody Kukuk, Kono Kela, | |
| **Height:** 6-5 | **Weight:** 205 | **Throws:** R | Jason Knapp, Felix Sterling, Gavin Dlouhy | |

| YEAR | Age | Level | IP | W | L | ERA | FIP | K/9 | BB/9 | K% | BB% | HR/9 | LOB% |
|---|---|---|---|---|---|---|---|---|---|---|---|---|---|
| 2015 | 19 | R | 22.3 | 0 | 1 | 2.01 | 1.89 | 12.90 | 2.42 | 38.1% | 7.1% | 0.00 | 75.0% |

**Background:** It was a peculiar move at the time, though one that wasn't unprecedented either. But Bickford spurned the Blue Jays' offer as the tenth overall selection in the June amateur draft and opted to take the collegiate route instead. It was reported at that time that the prep right-hander was seeking a deal in excess of $4 million – essentially top five money despite the assigned value for the pick being approximately $2.9 million. Bickford packed his bags and made the trip from Oaks Christian High School to Cal State Fullerton – for a year. After the hard-throwing 6-foot-5, 205-pound hurler dominated the Big West competition as a freshman, throwing 76.0 innings while averaging 8.76 K/9 and a barely-there 1.54 BB/9, he once again packed his bags and headed to another school – the College of Southern Nevada, a JuCo which would allow him to become draft eligible. He, of course, was ridiculously dominant against inferior competition: 86.2 IP, 1.45 ERA, 166 *freakin'* strikeouts, and just 21 walks. He *averaged* more than 17 punch outs every nine innings.

San Francisco would grab Bickford eight picks after his original selection and sign him to a deal that was about $600,000 *less* than what was assigned as the 10th overall pick in 2013.

Anyway, Bickford looked too good for the Arizona Summer League during his pro debut, posting a 32-to-6 strikeout-to-walk ratio in 22.1 innings of work.

**Projection**: Here's what I wrote prior to the draft last season:

"A rare breed, Bickford offers up the perfect trifecta of youth, power, and control. And while his swing-and-miss ability this season puts him in some elite company – he's averaging a smidge over 17 punch outs per nine innings – it's important to add some proper context.

Current Chicago Cubs farmhand – and former third round pick – Donn Roach, owner of a fringy upper 80s fastball, fanned 142 in 111.1 innings during his lone season at Southern Nevada. Roach also fanned 22 in just over 40 innings of work at Arizona during his freshman season.

With that being said, Bickford is one of the better, more promising arms in the class – one that could potentially move quickly through the system despite his relative youth. [He's a] solid #2/#3-type ceiling."

**Ceiling:** 3.5-win player
**Risk:** Moderate
**MLB ETA:** 2017/2018

## 2. Tyler Beede, RHP

MiLB Rank: #92

Position Rank: N/A

| | | | | |
|---|---|---|---|---|
| **Born:** 05/23/93 | **Age:** 23 | **Bats:** R | **Top CALs:** Deunte Heath, Rafael Dolis, | |
| **Height:** 6-4 | **Weight:** 200 | **Throws:** R | Drew Verhagen, Christopher Lee, Chasen Shreve | |

| YEAR | Age | Level | IP | W | L | ERA | FIP | K/9 | BB/9 | K% | BB% | HR/9 | LOB% |
|---|---|---|---|---|---|---|---|---|---|---|---|---|---|
| 2014 | 21 | R | 8.7 | 0 | 1 | 3.12 | 2.88 | 11.42 | 4.15 | 29.0% | 10.5% | 0.00 | 66.7% |
| 2014 | 21 | A- | 6.7 | 0 | 0 | 2.70 | 3.07 | 9.45 | 4.05 | 23.3% | 10.0% | 0.00 | 81.8% |
| 2015 | 22 | A+ | 52.3 | 2 | 2 | 2.24 | 3.43 | 6.36 | 1.55 | 17.2% | 4.2% | 0.34 | 67.0% |
| 2015 | 22 | AA | 72.3 | 3 | 8 | 5.23 | 4.21 | 6.10 | 4.35 | 16.0% | 11.4% | 0.50 | 58.3% |

**Background:** Taking an eerily similar path as his new organization-mate – and future big league rotation-mate – Phil Bickford, Beede was also drafted by the Blue Jays in the opening round of the draft, 21st overall, but spurned the ballclub's best efforts and headed to a big time collegiate program. The 6-foot-4, 200-pound hurler spent three years in Vanderbilt's rotation, throwing 286 innings for Pitcher U. with 287 strikeouts and a whopping 148 walks – or 9.03 K/9 and 4.66 BB/9. He would finish his collegiate career with a 3.56 ERA. Following his junior season, San Francisco grabbed him with the 14th overall selection and sent him to the Arizona Summer League (briefly) before bumping him up to Salem-Keizer. Last season Beede bypassed Low Class A and jumped feet first into the California League without missing a beat; he fanned 37 and walked just nine with some new found above-average control in 52.1 innings. He would spend the second half of the year with the Flying Squirrels in the Eastern League where his previous control problems resurfaced (72.1 IP, 49 K, 35 BB). Overall, Beede finished his first full professional season by averaging 6.2 K/9 and 3.2 BB/9 to go along with a 3.97 ERA.

**Projection**: First off, here's what I wrote prior to the 2014 draft:

> *"One of the best collegiate arms available in this year's class, particularly coming from the rotation, Beede has the makings of a #2-type pitcher, though that depends upon how he [commands] the strike zone at the next level. His control has wavered in the earlier parts of his career, and he'll need to continue to show that this season's strong showing is more than just an aberration. Outside of N.C. State's Carlos Rodon, Beede has [ceiling as] high as any collegiate hurler. That, of course, comes with a little more risk."*

Beede certainly looked the part of a potential upper-rotation caliber arm at points throughout his full-season debut last year: he fanned 11 and walked one in seven innings in his final start in the California League immediately comes to mind as does his seven inning two-hitter in his first start with the Squirrels. But the strides he made in reducing his walk rate quickly dissipated in Class AA; of his 13 starts with Richmond, Beede walked at least three batters nine times.

San Francisco develops arms as well as any organization in baseball, both in terms of pure development but also their uncanny ability to keep hurlers healthy, so Beede still has a shot to reach his #2-type peak. But after last year's run in the Eastern League he looks more like a mid-rotation arm.

**Ceiling:** 2.5- to 3.0-win player
**Risk:** Moderate
**MLB ETA:** 2016/2017

# 3. Christian Arroyo, SS

**MiLB Rank: #140**
**Position Rank: N/A**

| Born: 05/30/95 | Age: 21 | Bats: R | Top CALs: Marco Hernandez, Mauricio Dubon, |
| Height: 6-1 | Weight: 180 | Throws: R | Jorge Polanco, Yamaico Navarro, Starlin Castro |

| Season | Age | LVL | PA | 2B | 3B | HR | AVG | OBP | SLG | ISO | BB% | K% | wRC+ |
|---|---|---|---|---|---|---|---|---|---|---|---|---|---|
| 2013 | 18 | R | 209 | 18 | 5 | 2 | 0.326 | 0.388 | 0.511 | 0.185 | 9.1% | 15.3% | 145 |
| 2014 | 19 | A- | 267 | 14 | 2 | 5 | 0.333 | 0.378 | 0.469 | 0.136 | 6.7% | 11.6% | 135 |
| 2014 | 19 | A | 125 | 3 | 1 | 1 | 0.203 | 0.226 | 0.271 | 0.068 | 3.2% | 17.6% | 35 |
| 2015 | 20 | A+ | 409 | 28 | 2 | 9 | 0.304 | 0.344 | 0.459 | 0.155 | 4.6% | 17.8% | 117 |

**Background:** If anything can be said about longtime San Francisco Giants front office member – and likely future Hall of Famer– Brian Sabean, it's this: never, *ever* offer up snap judgments about any of his latest moves. Take for example the club's selection of Arroyo as the 25th overall pick in the 2013 draft – a move that was widely panned as an overdraft. That is, until the prep shortstop stepped into the Arizona Summer League and torched the rookie level arms to the tune of .326/.388/.511 with 18 doubles, five triples, a pair of homeruns, and three stolen bases in 45 games. After that showing the front office aggressively pushed the then-19-year-old shortstop up to the Sally to begin the 2014 season and after floundering for 31 games – he hit .203/.226/.271 – Arroyo got demoted to the more age-appropriate Northwest League where he would bat .333/.378/.469 the rest of the way.

So he would probably spend at least part of the 2015 season back in the Sally, right?

Wrong.

San Francisco continued to aggressively push the budding shortstop and pushed him right *past* Low Class A and into the California League. This time Arroyo was up for the challenge: in an injury-shortened campaign he slugged .304/.344/.459 with career highs in doubles (28) and homeruns (nine) – despite appearing in just 90 games thanks to a pesky oblique issue.

**Projection**: Granted, the California League tends to inflate offensive numbers a bit – only the Pioneer League and DSL averaged more runs per game in 2015 – but it was an impressive showing for Arroyo. He struggled against southpaws last season, batting .215/.300/.342, but that issue hasn't popped up previously so it should prove to be nothing more than a speed bump. The actual bat is the best of his offensive showings; otherwise; it's mostly an average toolkit. He could be a league average bat, maybe a tick better, maybe a smidge below.

**Ceiling:** 2.0- to 2.5-win player
**Risk:** Moderate
**MLB ETA:** 2017

## 4. Mac Williamson, LF/RF

**MiLB Rank: #141**
**Position Rank: N/A**

| Born: 07/15/90 | Age: 25 | Bats: R | Top CALs: Matt Spencer, Ryan Rua, |
|---|---|---|---|
| Height: 6-5 | Weight: 240 | Throws: R | Johan Limonta, Danny Dorn, Aaron Cunningham |

| Season | Age | LVL | PA | 2B | 3B | HR | AVG | OBP | SLG | ISO | BB% | K% | wRC+ |
|---|---|---|---|---|---|---|---|---|---|---|---|---|---|
| 2013 | 22 | A+ | 597 | 31 | 2 | 25 | 0.292 | 0.375 | 0.504 | 0.212 | 8.5% | 22.1% | 129 |
| 2015 | 24 | AA | 290 | 16 | 2 | 5 | 0.293 | 0.366 | 0.429 | 0.135 | 8.6% | 18.3% | 129 |
| 2015 | 24 | AAA | 227 | 12 | 0 | 8 | 0.249 | 0.370 | 0.439 | 0.190 | 11.5% | 24.2% | 120 |
| 2015 | 24 | MLB | 34 | 0 | 1 | 0 | 0.219 | 0.235 | 0.281 | 0.063 | 0.0% | 23.5% | 42 |

**Background**: Proving that not only pitchers undergo the knife for Tommy John surgery, the former 2012 third round pick out of Wake Forest University got off to a scorching start with San Jose two years ago – he mashed to the tune of .318/.420/.506 – before his season was interrupted by the elbow ligament procedure after 100 plate appearances. Finally healthy, Williamson jumped up to the Eastern League without missing a beat: in 69 games with the Flying Squirrels, the 6-foot-5 corner outfielder slugged .293/.366/.429 with 16 doubles, a pair of triples, five homeruns, and three stolen bases. He got the call up to Sacramento in late June where he batted .249/.370/.439 while topping the league average production by 20%. San Francisco promoted him up to the big league club for help down the stretch.

**Projection**: A very typical San Francisco type prospect, Williamson offers up a well-rounded offensive package without a true standout tool. He'll bat .280 or so with 15- to 18-dingers, a handful a stolen bases, and strong OBPs. He won't be a star by any stretch of the imagination, but Williamson has the potential to carve out a 10-year career as a solid player.

**Ceiling:** 2.0- to 2.5-win player
**Risk:** Moderate
**MLB ETA:** Debuted in 2015

## 5. Clayton Blackburn, RHP

**MiLB Rank: #179**
**Position Rank: N/A**

| Born: 01/06/93 | Age: 23 | Bats: L | Top CALs: Jonathon Niese, Vin Mazzaro, |
|---|---|---|---|
| Height: 6-3 | Weight: 230 | Throws: R | Eduardo Rodriguez, Zach Davies, Liam Hendriks |

| YEAR | Age | Level | IP | W | L | ERA | FIP | K/9 | BB/9 | K% | BB% | HR/9 | LOB% |
|---|---|---|---|---|---|---|---|---|---|---|---|---|---|
| 2013 | 20 | A+ | 133.0 | 7 | 5 | 3.65 | 3.86 | 9.34 | 2.37 | 25.2% | 6.4% | 0.81 | 63.7% |
| 2014 | 21 | AA | 93.0 | 5 | 6 | 3.29 | 2.54 | 8.23 | 1.94 | 22.0% | 5.2% | 0.10 | 67.7% |
| 2015 | 22 | AAA | 123.0 | 10 | 4 | 2.85 | 3.55 | 7.24 | 2.34 | 19.1% | 6.2% | 0.44 | 76.0% |

**Background:** Not in the same mold as the other top arms in the system, Blackburn doesn't rely on a scorching fastball or an ungodly breaking pitch. Instead, he's a steady innings eater with guile and an above-average feel for the strike zone. And that was once again on display as the then-22-year-old right-hander out of Oklahoma made quick work of the Pacific Coast League in 2015. Making 23 appearances with the Sacramento River Cats, 20 of which were starts, Blackburn hurler 123.0 while fanning 19.1% and walking just 6.2% of the total batters he faced. He finished the year with an impressive 2.85 ERA and a 3.55 FIP. For his career, the five-year minor league veteran has averaged 8.7 strikeouts and just 1.9 walks per nine innings to go along with a 2.95 ERA.

**Projection:** I've long been on the 6-foot-3, 230-pound right-hander's bandwagon, originally ranking him as the franchise's #3 prospect two years and their #2 prospect heading into last season. Here's what I wrote in last year's book:

> *"[He's] sort of the anti-Kyle Crick. Blackburn's control is simply on a different planet. The 6-foot-2 right-hander has averaged just 1.7 free passes every nine innings for his entire career. Again, he's solid mid-rotation-type arm. Blackburn should be among the first wave of call ups during the year."*

And while he's not ever remotely close to being overpowering, Blackburn does everything he needs to do to be successful. Limits free passes? Check. Miss an average amount of bats? Check. Generate a ton of action on the ground? Check. Consistently handle older, more advanced competition? Check? Keep the ball in the ballpark? Check.

With Madison Bumgarner, Johnny Cueto, Jeff Samardzija, Jake Peavy, and Matt Cain slated as the club's top five, Blackburn will have trouble cracking the Giants' rotation. So he'll either be (A) called upon when the inevitable injury strikes or (B) a valuable trade commodity for added pieces down the stretch.

**Ceiling:** 1.5- to 2.0-win player
**Risk:** Low to Moderate
**MLB ETA:** 2016

## 6. Chris Shaw, 1B

**MiLB Rank:** #182
**Position Rank:** N/A

| Born: 10/20/93 | Age: 22 | Bats: L | Top CALs: Mark Hamilton, Kevin Cron, |
|---|---|---|---|
| Height: 6-3 | Weight: 229 | Throws: R | Henry Moreno, Steffan Wilson, Chris Vinyard |

| Season | Age | LVL | PA | 2B | 3B | HR | AVG | OBP | SLG | ISO | BB% | K% | wRC+ |
|---|---|---|---|---|---|---|---|---|---|---|---|---|---|
| 2015 | 21 | A- | 200 | 11 | 0 | 12 | 0.287 | 0.360 | 0.551 | 0.264 | 9.5% | 20.5% | 156 |

**Background:** Fun Fact Part I: Prior to Shaw's selection as the 31st overall pick last June, San Francisco has taken just three other first baseman in the first round since 1965, one prep player and two from college. Fun Fact Part II: the last collegiate first baseman taken in the first round by the Giants was none other than borderline Hall of Famer Will Clark, who was the second overall pick in the 1985 draft – a draft, by the way, that featured B.J. Surhoff, Clark, Barry Larkin, and Barry Bonds all going within the top six selections. Anyway, the Giants plucked the 6-foot-3, 229-pound lefty-swinging hulkster after a stout career at Boston College. He would finish his run with the Golden Eagles as not only the third highest drafted player in school history but also a .274/.358/.470 career hitter. San Francisco had Shaw bypass the rookie leagues and pushed him directly into short-season ball; he would bat .287/.360/.551 with 11 doubles and 12 homeruns in 46 games with Salem-Keizer.

**Projection:** Here's what I wrote prior to the 2015 draft:

> "He has a surprisingly strong knack for making contact, especially for a potential middle-of-the-order bat. [He owns] above-average to plus-power potential with the ability to slug 20- to 25-homeruns in a full professional season. It's also important to point out that the Eagles' home park, Eddie Pellagini Diamond at John Shea Field, is incredibly pitcher-friendly. Good, though far from great, eye at the plate.
>
> Shaw looks like a solid, better-than-average first baseman who, once he's further removed from the hamate injury [suffered in 2012], should surprise people with his minor league production.

**Ceiling:** 2.0- to 2.5-win player
**Risk:** Moderate to High
**MLB ETA:** 2017/2018

## 7. Lucius Fox, SS

**MiLB Rank:** #197
**Position Rank:** N/A

| Born: 07/02/97 | Age: 19 | Bats: B | Top CALs: N/A |
|---|---|---|---|
| Height: 6-0 | Weight: 160 | Throws: R | |

**Background:** Signed on the dotted line for a whopping $6 million bonus, money equivalent to the top in the draft.

**Projection:** Typically I avoid writing about newly signed international free agents because the data, even compared to stateside prep prospects, is non-existent. But the pure dollar amount that the young shortstop signed for was eye-catching. Fox's bonus was the highest given out to a non-Cuban player and nearly double that of the next highest, Vladimir Guerrero Jr. It'll be exciting to see Fox in action in 2016.

**Ceiling:** Too Soon to Tell
**Risk:** N/A
**MLB ETA:** N/A

## 8. Chase Johnson, RHP

**MiLB Rank:** #215
**Position Rank:** N/A

| Born: 01/09/92 | Age: 24 | Bats: R | Top CALs: Danny Rosenbaum, Brad Mills, |
|---|---|---|---|
| Height: 6-3 | Weight: 185 | Throws: R | Erik Davis, Scott Alexander, Eric Berger |

| YEAR | Age | Level | IP | W | L | ERA | FIP | K/9 | BB/9 | K% | BB% | HR/9 | LOB% |
|---|---|---|---|---|---|---|---|---|---|---|---|---|---|
| 2013 | 21 | R | 5.3 | 1 | 0 | 1.69 | 1.94 | 11.81 | 1.69 | 33.3% | 4.8% | 0.00 | 83.3% |
| 2013 | 21 | A- | 41.0 | 3 | 2 | 4.17 | 3.64 | 8.12 | 2.63 | 21.8% | 7.1% | 0.66 | 58.6% |
| 2014 | 22 | A | 110.3 | 4 | 7 | 4.57 | 3.83 | 7.67 | 3.26 | 19.5% | 8.3% | 0.41 | 59.7% |
| 2015 | 23 | A+ | 111.0 | 8 | 3 | 2.43 | 3.39 | 9.00 | 2.76 | 24.7% | 7.6% | 0.41 | 77.0% |
| 2015 | 23 | AA | 13.7 | 1 | 1 | 5.93 | 2.39 | 11.85 | 5.27 | 27.3% | 12.1% | 0.00 | 62.5% |

**Background:** A sparsely used hurler during his three years at Cal Poly, Johnson's playing time gradually dropped from 49.0 innings as a part-time starter as a freshman to a full-time reliever the next year to a barely used reliever during his junior campaign at the school. In total, the 6-foot-3, 185-pound right-hander finished his amateur career with 86 punch outs, 43 walks, and a 3.28 ERA in 107 innings of work. Despite the relatively light workload, the Giants grabbed Johnson in the third round in 2013, the 101ˢᵗ overall pick, and immediately converted the hard-throwing hurler into a full-time starting pitcher. Johnson posted a 44-to-13 strikeout-to-walk ratio in 46.1 innings during his debut, and he followed that up with a decent showing in the Sally two years ago. In 110.0 innings with Augusta, Johnson averaged 7.7 strikeouts and 3.3 walks per nine innings. Last year, the club pushed him up to San Jose for 18 dominant starts – he fanned 111 and walked only 34 to go along with a 2.43 ERA – before having him finish with three games in Class AA.

**Projection**: Very, very difficult player to get a handle on. Johnson wasn't good enough to convince the Cal Poly coaches that he was worthy of a spot in the rotation, a staff that did have quite a bit of professional talent, but the Giants, a typically savvy drafting organization, grabbed him in the early rounds.

Then to complicate matters they immediately convert him into a starting pitcher and Johnson – unsurprisingly – struggles during his first full season of action. He, of course, follows that up by posting the fourth highest strikeout percentage of batters in the hitter-friendly Cal League.

I like him, probably more than most. But Johnson has quite a few things working in his favor – namely, his lack of experience. Meaning: he should – theoretically – only get better.

**Ceiling:** 2.0-win player
**Risk:** Moderate to High
**MLB ETA:** 2017

## 9. Josh Osich, LHP

**MiLB Rank: N/A**
**Position Rank: N/A**

**Born:** 09/03/88   **Age:** 28   **Bats:** L   **Top CALs:** Stephen Shackleford, Jay Buente,
**Height:** 6-2   **Weight:** 230   **Throws:** L   Rob Wooten, Ronald Uviedo, Barret Browning

| YEAR | Age | Level | IP | W | L | ERA | FIP | K/9 | BB/9 | K% | BB% | HR/9 | LOB% |
|---|---|---|---|---|---|---|---|---|---|---|---|---|---|
| 2013 | 24 | A+ | 40.3 | 3 | 1 | 2.45 | 2.46 | 10.71 | 2.23 | 29.6% | 6.2% | 0.22 | 71.4% |
| 2013 | 24 | AA | 29.7 | 2 | 3 | 4.85 | 3.53 | 8.49 | 3.64 | 23.0% | 9.8% | 0.61 | 62.5% |
| 2014 | 25 | AA | 33.3 | 1 | 0 | 3.78 | 5.18 | 7.29 | 5.40 | 18.9% | 14.0% | 1.08 | 71.4% |
| 2015 | 26 | AA | 34.0 | 0 | 1 | 1.59 | 2.62 | 9.00 | 2.65 | 24.8% | 7.3% | 0.26 | 85.9% |
| 2015 | 26 | AAA | 7.0 | 0 | 0 | 0.00 | 1.31 | 14.14 | 2.57 | 40.7% | 7.4% | 0.00 | 80.0% |

**Background:** It took longer than expected, but the former 2011 sixth round pick reached the big leagues at the ripe old age of 26 last year. And here's how he did it: after Tommy John surgery – and some other bumps and bruises – San Francisco simultaneously pushed Osich into a fulltime relief role and up to High Class A for his professional debut in 2012. Without missing a beat, the 6-foot-2, 230-pound southpaw posted a promising 34-to-11 strikeout-to-walk ratio in 32.1 innings of work. He followed that up by spending the first half of 2013 back with San Jose in the California League where he would average nearly 10 strikeouts per innings with slightly better control. The club would bump him up to the minors' most challenging test – Class AA – in early June and Osich would see only a slight downturn in production. Then after spending the entire 2014 season back in Richmond – where he posted dominant numbers – the club *once again* pushed the southpaw back into the Eastern League in 2015. He would then spend the remainder of the year yo-yoing between the PCL and San Francisco.

**Projection**: Osich's flashed an above-average, sometime plus heater during his 28.2 innings with the big league club last season, complementing it with a hard low-90s cutter and a mid-80s change. One wonders what took San Francisco so long to promote Osich, but he's here to stay as late-inning southpaw who can handle both lefties *and* righties equally well.

**Ceiling:** 1.5-win player
**Risk:** Low to Moderate
**MLB ETA:** Debuted in 2015

## 10. Adalberto Mejia, LHP

**MiLB Rank: N/A**
**Position Rank: N/A**

**Born:** 06/20/93   **Age:** 23   **Bats:** R   **Top CALs:** James Parr, Brian Flynn,
**Height:** 6-3   **Weight:** 195   **Throws:** L   Richard Castillo, Troy Patton, Jacob Turner

| YEAR | Age | Level | IP | W | L | ERA | FIP | K/9 | BB/9 | K% | BB% | HR/9 | LOB% |
|---|---|---|---|---|---|---|---|---|---|---|---|---|---|
| 2013 | 20 | A+ | 87.0 | 7 | 4 | 3.31 | 4.20 | 9.21 | 2.38 | 25.1% | 6.5% | 1.14 | 77.8% |
| 2013 | 20 | AAA | 5.0 | 0 | 0 | 3.60 | 9.17 | 3.60 | 3.60 | 9.1% | 9.1% | 3.60 | 100.0% |
| 2014 | 21 | AA | 108.0 | 7 | 9 | 4.67 | 3.78 | 6.83 | 2.58 | 17.9% | 6.8% | 0.75 | 64.1% |
| 2015 | 22 | AA | 51.3 | 5 | 2 | 2.45 | 3.41 | 6.66 | 3.16 | 18.1% | 8.6% | 0.35 | 79.3% |

**Background:** The good news: Mejia, 6-foot-3, 195-pound hurler out of the Dominic Republic, continued to look like a burgeoning big league starting pitcher – when he made it to the mound last season. Which brings us to…the bad news: the southpaw got popped for sibutramine, an appetite suppressant, and received a 50-game suspension that began at the start of the season. Now the ugly news: nine starts into his season he hit the DL for a month-plus due to some left shoulder issues. The portly left-hander finished the year with 38 punch outs, 18 walks, and a 2.45 ERA in 51.1 innings of work. And at the time of the writing, Mejia also made another seven starts in the Arizona Fall League as well, posting a less-than-impressive 26-to-14 strikeout-to-walk ratio across 31.0 innings.

**Projection**: Mejia hasn't produced a solid strikeout rate since his dominant showing with San Jose in the California League in 2013. Since then he's totaled 159.1 innings in Class AA while averaging just 6.8 strikeouts per nine innings. He's compensated the subpar swing-and-miss totals with a strong feel for the zone. He looks like a #4/#5-type arm.

**Ceiling**: 1.5-win player
**Risk**: Moderate
**MLB ETA**: 2016

## 11. Aramis Garcia, C

**MiLB Rank: N/A**
**Position Rank: N/A**

| Born: 01/12/93 | Age: 23 | Bats: R | Top CALs: Nick Hundley, Kellin Deglan, |
|---|---|---|---|
| Height: 6-2 | Weight: 220 | Throws: R | Mark Fleury, Adam Moore, Anthony Recker |

| Season | Age | LVL | PA | 2B | 3B | HR | AVG | OBP | SLG | ISO | BB% | K% | wRC+ |
|---|---|---|---|---|---|---|---|---|---|---|---|---|---|
| 2015 | 22 | A | 363 | 15 | 1 | 15 | 0.273 | 0.350 | 0.467 | 0.194 | 9.6% | 21.2% | 131 |
| 2015 | 22 | A+ | 84 | 4 | 0 | 0 | 0.227 | 0.310 | 0.280 | 0.053 | 10.7% | 26.2% | 68 |

**Background**: One of the better offensive backstops in the 2014 draft class, San Francisco grabbed the former Florida International University backstop in the second round, the 52nd overall pick, the fifth catcher taken. Garcia showed steady progress during his three-year run at the school, improving his yearly OPS totals from .761 to .900 to a whopping 1.068 during his junior season. The 6-foot-2, 220-pound Garcia looked overmatched in his professional debut two years ago as he struggled to bat his respective weight during his time in the Arizona Summer and Northwest Leagues. The front office brass opted to take the prudent choice and only pushed him up to Low Class A at the start of last season where he looked more at ease at the plate. He batted .273/.350/.467 with 15 doubles, one three-bagger, and 15 homeruns in 83 games with Augusta. Garcia also earned a late-season promotion to San Jose where he, once again, looked overmatched.

**Projection**: I completely swung-and-missed when it came to projecting Garcia's future projections entering the draft. I even ignored a rather ominous warning as well. Here's what I wrote:

> "Garcia's offensive peak should reside somewhere near .290/.340/.440 with 15 or so homeruns and solid defense behind the plate. The lone knock, though, has been his level of competition and a rather sparse showing in the Cape [Cod Summer League] following his sophomore season."

I was wrong – clearly. But his showing in the Sally wasn't too far off of what I envisioned for the developing backstop (he hit .273/.350/.467). Above-average power potential with a solid eye and the ability to control the running game, Garcia, nonetheless, has a chance to develop into a solid big leaguer, peaking as a fringy everyday backstop.

**Ceiling**: 1.5-win player
**Risk**: Moderate to High
**MLB ETA**: 2016

## 12. Andrew Suarez, LHP

**MiLB Rank: N/A**
**Position Rank: N/A**

| Born: 09/11/92 | Age: 23 | Bats: L | Top CALs: N/A |
|---|---|---|---|
| Height: 6-2 | Weight: 185 | Throws: L | |

| YEAR | Age | Level | IP | W | L | ERA | FIP | K/9 | BB/9 | K% | BB% | HR/9 | LOB% |
|---|---|---|---|---|---|---|---|---|---|---|---|---|---|
| 2015 | 22 | R | 5.0 | 0 | 0 | 1.80 | 2.02 | 10.80 | 1.80 | 33.3% | 5.6% | 0.00 | 66.7% |
| 2015 | 22 | A- | 19.3 | 1 | 0 | 1.40 | 3.71 | 6.98 | 0.93 | 20.3% | 2.7% | 0.93 | 92.6% |
| 2015 | 22 | A+ | 15.0 | 1 | 0 | 1.80 | 3.78 | 9.60 | 1.20 | 28.1% | 3.5% | 1.20 | 98.4% |

**Background**: Let's count the times the 6-foot-2, 185-pound hurler was drafted:

- 2011, Ninth Round, 289th overall, Toronto Blue Jays
- 2014, Second Round, 57th overall, Washington Nationals
- 2015, Second Round, 61st overall, San Francisco Giants

After opting to head back to the University of Miami instead of signing as a second round pick two years ago, Suarez turned in his finest collegiate season in 2015. In 16 games with the Hurricanes, 15 of which were starts, the big southpaw posted a 78-to-22 strikeout-to-walk ratio and a 3.48 ERA in 85.1 innings. He finished his career with 284 innings while averaging 7.07 punch outs and just 1.81 walks per nine innings. Following his selection, San Francisco aggressively pushed the polished southpaw through the Arizona Summer, Northwest, and California Leagues during his debut.

**Projection**: Here's what I wrote prior to the 2014 draft:

> *"Suarez has been one of the biggest risers this spring. He's still not missing a whole lot of bats yet – just 6.82 K/9 this season. The control is a reliable, above-average skill, but he's also been quite hittable too – 11 doubles, four triples, and three homeruns, the most extra-base hits surrendered by any of Miami's top three starters.*
>
> *Solid backend rotation-type arm, peaking as a fringe #3 but should settle in as a solid #4/#5."*

I followed that up prior to last year's draft by writing the following:

> *"Well, nearly 12 months removed and there's virtually no new data to analyze. When he's healthy – which hasn't been the case very often – Suarez does well in limiting walks, will miss a handful of bats, but tends to be a bit too hittable.*
>
> *I'm still sticking to the original ceiling as a solid #4/#5 caliber arm – if injuries aren't a concern. It will be interesting to see where a team grabs him, especially considering that he once again has an option to return to school for his senior season."*

The front office seems content on pushing him as quickly as possible. And given his level of polish and poise, it wouldn't be out of the question to see him start the year in Class AA. Again, he's a backend starter.

**Ceiling:** 1.5-win player
**Risk:** Moderate
**MLB ETA:** 2016/2017

## 13. Jordan Johnson, RHP

**MiLB Rank: N/A**
**Position Rank: N/A**

| | | | |
|---|---|---|---|
| **Born:** 09/15/93 | **Age:** 22 | **Bats:** R | **Top CALs:** Eric Gonzalez, J.J. Pannell, |
| **Height:** 6-3 | **Weight:** 175 | **Throws:** R | Ryan Castellanos, Jose Pena, Sandy Lugo |

| YEAR | Age | Level | IP | W | L | ERA | FIP | K/9 | BB/9 | K% | BB% | HR/9 | LOB% |
|------|-----|-------|-----|---|---|------|------|-------|------|-------|------|------|-------|
| 2014 | 20 | R | 2.7 | 0 | 0 | 0.00 | 4.03 | 10.13 | 6.75 | 30.0% | 20.0% | 0.00 | 100.0% |
| 2015 | 21 | R | 23.3 | 0 | 1 | 1.54 | 1.20 | 12.34 | 0.39 | 36.8% | 1.2% | 0.00 | 70.0% |
| 2015 | 21 | A- | 4.7 | 0 | 1 | 3.86 | 1.03 | 11.57 | 0.00 | 31.6% | 0.0% | 0.00 | 60.0% |
| 2015 | 21 | A+ | 31.3 | 2 | 3 | 4.31 | 3.87 | 9.48 | 2.87 | 24.3% | 7.4% | 0.86 | 67.8% |

**Background:** Fun Fact I: California State University Northridge has produced a pair of big leaguers that topped more than 20 Wins Above Replacement (per Baseball Reference): longtime infielder Adam Kennedy and former first baseman Jason Thompson, who slugged 208 big league homeruns. Fun Fact II: that's more 20-WAR players than The Ohio State University, Clemson University, and Rice University (also known as Arm Shredder U.). Fun Fact III: that's the same number of players to top 20 WAR in their career as Vanderbilt University. Anyway, the Giants unearthed the 6-foot-3, 175-pound right-hander in the 23rd round two years ago. And after a brief three-game debut, he repeated – and dominated – the Arizona Summer League, made a quick four-plus-inning stint in the Northwest League, and posted a 33-to-10 strikeout-to-walk ratio in 31.1 innings with San Jose.

**Projection**: Another difficult player to get a handle on. Johnson looked awfully dominant as the club aggressively challenged him in the second half of 2015. He's shown a promising ability to miss bats *and* limit free passes. Since he's racked up just 62.2 professional innings I'm going to take a wait-and-see approach and hold off further evaluation until following 2016.

Remember this kid's name though.

**Ceiling:** Too Soon to Tell
**Risk:** N/A
**MLB ETA:** N/A

## 14. Kyle Crick, RHP

**MiLB Rank:** N/A
**Position Rank:** N/A

| Born: 11/30/92 | Age: 23 | Bats: L | Top CALs: Jeremy Jeffress, Blake King, |
|---|---|---|---|
| Height: 6-4 | Weight: 220 | Throws: R | Mauricio Robles, Dan Cortes, Shawn Armstrong |

| YEAR | Age | Level | IP | W | L | ERA | FIP | K/9 | BB/9 | K% | BB% | HR/9 | LOB% |
|---|---|---|---|---|---|---|---|---|---|---|---|---|---|
| 2013 | 20 | A+ | 68.7 | 3 | 1 | 1.57 | 2.94 | 12.45 | 5.11 | 33.8% | 13.9% | 0.13 | 78.5% |
| 2014 | 21 | AA | 90.3 | 6 | 7 | 3.79 | 3.96 | 11.06 | 6.08 | 27.9% | 15.3% | 0.70 | 75.3% |
| 2015 | 22 | AA | 63.0 | 3 | 4 | 3.29 | 4.84 | 10.43 | 9.43 | 24.2% | 21.9% | 0.29 | 80.2% |

**Background:** Easily one the most talented arms in the organization and probably on the short list in all of the minor leagues, the problem with the big Texas-born right-hander is, well, obvious: he couldn't throw back-to-back strikes if his life depended on it. And after averaging at least five free passes per nine innings in each of his seasons between 2012 and 2014, Crick's control – or lack thereof – completely bottomed out last year; he walked 66 batted in 63.0 innings of work (yes, he still missed a promising amount of sticks too, 73). But just to give you an idea of how dominant Crick *can* be, the 6-foot-4, 220-pound hurler still managed to post an impressive 3.29 – in spite of seemingly always working with runners on base. Just to add a little perspective on that note, consider the following: Royals minor leaguer Aroni Nina finished with the second worst walk rate in Class AA last season, 8.17 BB/9, but his ERA was north of 5.00.

**Projection**: It was an inevitable move, really, a path that the former first rounder has been traveling down since his debut in the Arizona Summer League in 2011. But the Giants' front office finally bit the bullet and pushed the once-burgeoning ace into a short relief role after 10 disastrous starts last season, though the move didn't help him locate his blistering fastball any better. He posted a 41-to-40 strikeout-to-walk ratio in 42.0 innings as a starter and a 32-to-26 strikeout-to-walk ratio in 21.0 relief innings.

In the end, though, Crick's likely going to go down as another what-if story, but here's hoping he can harness his powerful arsenal and develop into a shutdown, dominant closer. Fingers – and toes, for that matter – firmly crossed.

**Ceiling:** 2.0- to 2.5-win player
**Risk:** High to Extremely High
**MLB ETA:** 2017/2018

## 15. Sam Coonrod, RHP

**MiLB Rank:** N/A
**Position Rank:** N/A

| Born: 09/22/92 | Age: 23 | Bats: R | Top CALs: Austin Kubitza, Armando Rodriguez, |
|---|---|---|---|
| Height: 6-2 | Weight: 225 | Throws: R | Steven Matz, Murillo Gouvea, Garrett Richards |

| YEAR | Age | Level | IP | W | L | ERA | FIP | K/9 | BB/9 | K% | BB% | HR/9 | LOB% |
|---|---|---|---|---|---|---|---|---|---|---|---|---|---|
| 2014 | 21 | R | 27.7 | 1 | 0 | 3.90 | 2.98 | 8.13 | 1.95 | 21.0% | 5.0% | 0.00 | 64.1% |
| 2015 | 22 | A | 111.7 | 7 | 5 | 3.14 | 2.97 | 9.19 | 2.74 | 24.1% | 7.2% | 0.24 | 68.6% |

**Background:** A well-built right-hander out of Southern Illinois University, home to Dave Stieb, Steve Finley, and Jerry Hairston, Coonrod battled a whole lot of control issues during his tenure with the Salukis. After averaging just 2.81 BB/9 during his freshman season, Coonrod posted walk rates north of 5.0 BB/9 over his final two campaigns. The Giants used a fifth round pick on enigmatic hurler two years ago – and the move looks like another savvy one by Brian Sabean & Co. Coonrod rediscovered his long lost control and posted a 25-to-6 strikeout-to-walk ratio in 27.2 innings in the Arizona Summer League during his debut. And he was able to carry that momentum over into the Sally last season as well. Making 22 starts for Augusta, the 6-foot-2, 225-pound hurler posted a phenomenal 114-to-34 strikeout-to-walk ratio in 111.2 innings of work.

**Projection**: Well, I didn't see *that* one coming. After walking 96 batters over his final 164.1 innings Coonrod has somehow cut that rate in half as soon as he buttoned up a pro jersey. His strikeout-to-walk percentage last year, 16.9%, ranked first among all hurlers with at least 100 innings in the Sally last season. With that being said, I'm not entirely convinced by the 180-degree turnaround just yet – especially since he spent the year facing the younger, less experienced South Atlantic League batters. Maybe he develops into a #4/#5-type arm.

**Ceiling:** 1.5-win player
**Risk:** Moderate to High
**MLB ETA:** 2018

## 16. Hunter Cole, 2B/LF/RF

**MiLB Rank: N/A**
**Position Rank: N/A**

| Born: 10/03/92 | Age: 23 | Bats: R | Top CALs: Jose Osuna, Mike Daniel, |
|---|---|---|---|
| Height: 6-1 | Weight: 190 | Throws: R | Brandon Jones, Christian Marreto, Jeremy Baltz |

| Season | Age | LVL | PA | 2B | 3B | HR | AVG | OBP | SLG | ISO | BB% | K% | wRC+ |
|---|---|---|---|---|---|---|---|---|---|---|---|---|---|
| 2014 | 21 | A- | 104 | 5 | 0 | 4 | 0.239 | 0.311 | 0.424 | 0.185 | 7.7% | 19.2% | 104 |
| 2015 | 22 | A | 46 | 6 | 0 | 0 | 0.275 | 0.370 | 0.425 | 0.150 | 10.9% | 26.1% | 129 |
| 2015 | 22 | A+ | 245 | 11 | 5 | 6 | 0.313 | 0.373 | 0.493 | 0.180 | 7.8% | 17.1% | 134 |
| 2015 | 22 | AA | 208 | 16 | 4 | 3 | 0.292 | 0.338 | 0.464 | 0.172 | 6.7% | 22.1% | 130 |

**Background:** Despite a level of above-average consistency throughout his three-year tenure at the University of Georgia, Cole, who posted OPS totals between .814 and .830 in each season with the Bulldogs, didn't hear his name called until the 26th round two years – the 778th overall player chosen. But despite the seemingly long-shot odds already standing in his way, Cole's forcing the outsiders to take notice – even after a largely mediocre showing in the Northwest League two years ago. Cole began last season with the Augusta GreenJackets, a stint that lasted 10 games, and made stops in High Class A and Class AA. In total, the second baseman/outfielder finished the year with an aggregate .301/.358/.425 triple-slash line with 33 doubles, nine triples, nine homeruns, and seven stolen bases (in 12 attempts).

**Projection**: Cole offers up a whole lot of value on both sides of the ball. His ability to man the keystone *and* patrol the corner outfield spots are super-sub worthy. His shows an average eye at the plate, double-digit homerun pop and speed. He also topped the league average production mark by over 30% last season. Think of him as a very poor man's version of Ben Zobrist.

**Ceiling:** 1.0- to s1.5-win player
**Risk:** Moderate
**MLB ETA:** 2017

## 17. Derek Law, RHP

**MiLB Rank: N/A**
**Position Rank: N/A**

| Born: 09/14/90 | Age: 25 | Bats: R | Top CALs: Dan Jennings, Neil Ramirez, |
|---|---|---|---|
| Height: 6-2 | Weight: 210 | Throws: R | Cody Winiarski, Josh Ellis, Drew Pomeranz |

| YEAR | Age | Level | IP | W | L | ERA | FIP | K/9 | BB/9 | K% | BB% | HR/9 | LOB% |
|---|---|---|---|---|---|---|---|---|---|---|---|---|---|
| 2013 | 22 | R | 5.7 | 1 | 0 | 3.18 | 1.36 | 14.29 | 1.59 | 42.9% | 4.8% | 0.00 | 60.0% |
| 2013 | 22 | A | 35.0 | 0 | 3 | 2.31 | 2.05 | 12.34 | 2.57 | 33.3% | 6.9% | 0.26 | 71.0% |
| 2013 | 22 | A+ | 25.7 | 4 | 0 | 2.10 | 1.01 | 15.78 | 0.35 | 45.9% | 1.0% | 0.35 | 72.8% |
| 2014 | 23 | AA | 28.0 | 2 | 0 | 2.57 | 3.35 | 9.32 | 4.50 | 25.7% | 12.4% | 0.32 | 79.8% |
| 2015 | 24 | AA | 25.7 | 0 | 1 | 4.56 | 2.22 | 11.22 | 2.81 | 27.6% | 6.9% | 0.35 | 61.2% |

**Background:** Two years ago Law, a ninth round pick out of Miami-Dade College, Kendall Campus in 2011, was knocking forcefully on the club's big league door. Just 27 games into the 2014 season, the hard-throwing right-hander was averaging slightly more than a punch out per inning while racking up plenty of saves. And then his right elbow gave out as he succumbed to Tommy John surgery. Law made it back to action in late June last season. And he looked as strong as ever. Still unleashing a blistering fastball, the 6-foot-2, 210-pound hurler posted an impressive 32-to-8 strikeout-to-walk ratio in 25.2 innings of work. For his career Law is averaging 11.6 punch outs and just 2.7 free passes per nine innings to go along with a 2.83 ERA.

**Projection**: There's not too much else to say about Law. He was an uncanny ability to miss bats – he's fanned over 31% of the total batters he's faced in his career – while showing an above-average feel for the strike zone. And after a little hiccup in 2012, Law's surrendered just four homeruns in 120 innings of work – or 0.30 homeruns every nine innings. He's not going to be a shutdown dominant closer, but he has the potential to become a Vinnie Pestano-esque setup man.

**Ceiling:** 1.0- to 1.5-win player
**Risk:** Moderate
**MLB ETA:** 2016

## 18. Steven Okert, LHP

MiLB Rank: N/A
Position Rank: N/A

| Born: 07/09/91 | Age: 21 | Bats: L | Top CALs: Heath Hembree, Aaron Blair, |
| Height: 6-3 | Weight: 210 | Throws: L | Daniel Hudson, Garrett Olson, Clay Buchholz |

| YEAR | Age | Level | IP | W | L | ERA | FIP | K/9 | BB/9 | K% | BB% | HR/9 | LOB% |
|---|---|---|---|---|---|---|---|---|---|---|---|---|---|
| 2013 | 21 | A | 60.7 | 2 | 2 | 2.97 | 3.42 | 8.75 | 3.56 | 22.8% | 9.3% | 0.45 | 69.9% |
| 2014 | 22 | A+ | 35.3 | 1 | 2 | 1.53 | 2.53 | 13.75 | 2.80 | 35.5% | 7.2% | 0.51 | 92.6% |
| 2014 | 22 | AA | 33.0 | 1 | 0 | 2.73 | 3.23 | 10.36 | 3.00 | 29.0% | 8.4% | 0.82 | 77.9% |
| 2015 | 23 | AAA | 61.3 | 5 | 3 | 3.82 | 4.35 | 10.13 | 4.26 | 25.6% | 10.7% | 1.03 | 73.3% |

**Background:** Okert's made some quick work of the minor leagues over the past two seasons. The former fourth round pick made stops in the Arizona Summer and Northwest Leagues during his debut, posting a 28-to-12 strikeout-to-walk ratio in 28.2 innings of work. He followed that up with a strong showing in the Sally as he averaged 8.8 punch outs and 3.6 free passes per nine innings. And up to that he seemed to be on a normal development curve. But Okert obliterated the California League competition in the first half of 2014: in 35.1 innings with San Jose, the 6-foot-3, 210-pound southpaw fanned a remarkable 54 and walked just 11. His dominance continued as he got the mid-season promotion to the Eastern League: 33.0 IP, 38 K, 11 BB. Last season the young southpaw spent year biding his time in the Pacific Coast League where he still missed an impressive amount of sticks – 10.1 K/9 – but his control regressed a bit as he walked the highest percentage of batters in his career (10.7%).

**Projection**: Here's what I wrote in last year's book:

> "Big league ready against southpaws (.176/.269/.215), but right-handers have hit Okert pretty well throughout his career (.271/.333/.404). [He's a] solid middle reliever/LOOGY. Definite big league value here, though."

Right-handers continued to still give Okert trouble as they batted .284/.371/.419 against him last season (compared to the .228/.303/.367 line LHs posted against him). San Francisco currently has Javier Lopez as their top lefty, but Okert could be a very serviceable middle relief arm.

**Ceiling:** 1.0-win player
**Risk:** Low to Moderate
**MLB ETA:** 2016

## 19. Chris Stratton, RHP

MiLB Rank: N/A
Position Rank: N/A

| Born: 08/22/90 | Age: 25 | Bats: R | Top CALs: Stephen Fife, Rob Rasmussen, |
| Height: 6-3 | Weight: 190 | Throws: R | Sean Stidfole, Adam Russell, Camilo Vazquez |

| YEAR | Age | Level | IP | W | L | ERA | FIP | K/9 | BB/9 | K% | BB% | HR/9 | LOB% |
|---|---|---|---|---|---|---|---|---|---|---|---|---|---|
| 2013 | 22 | A | 132.0 | 9 | 3 | 3.27 | 3.25 | 8.39 | 3.20 | 22.2% | 8.5% | 0.34 | 76.0% |
| 2014 | 23 | A+ | 99.3 | 7 | 8 | 5.07 | 4.54 | 9.24 | 3.26 | 23.9% | 8.4% | 1.18 | 65.2% |
| 2014 | 23 | AA | 23.0 | 1 | 1 | 3.52 | 4.49 | 7.04 | 4.70 | 16.8% | 11.2% | 0.78 | 81.2% |
| 2015 | 24 | AA | 50.0 | 1 | 5 | 4.14 | 3.87 | 7.02 | 3.96 | 18.4% | 10.4% | 0.54 | 62.9% |
| 2015 | 24 | AAA | 98.0 | 4 | 5 | 3.86 | 4.30 | 6.61 | 3.67 | 17.4% | 9.6% | 0.55 | 69.8% |

**Background:** Taken directly after the selections of Corey Seager and Michael Wacha *and* directly before Lucas Sims and Marcus Stroman in the 2012 draft, Stratton's prospect status doesn't quite line up with those aforementioned players. A three-year stalwart in Mississippi State's rotation, Stratton's strikeout rate has undergone a dramatic decline since he moved into the Eastern League in latter part of the 2014 season. Combined with the work from that year, as well as his 50 innings back in the level in 2015, he's posted a mediocre – and some would say disappointing – 57-to-34 strikeout-to-walk ratio 73 innings. The 6-foot-3, 190-pound right-hander made another 17 blasé starts with Sacramento into the Pacific Coast League last season as well, averaging 6.6 punch outs and 3.7 walks per nine innings.

**Projection**: Slightly below-average control with blah strikeout numbers is certainly not a recipe for future big league success. With San Francisco's bevy of veteran starters in place for the foreseeable future, as well as several better arms ahead of him in the system, it's a high, *high* probability that he winds up as a seventh/eighth-inning relief arm.

**Ceiling:** 1.0-win player
**Risk:** Low to Moderate
**MLB ETA:** 2016

## 20. Austin Slater, 2B/LF/RF

**MiLB Rank:** N/A
**Position Rank:** N/A

| Born: 12/13/92 | Age: 23 | Bats: R | Top CALs: Martin Prado, Walter Ibarra, |
| Height: 6-2 | Weight: 215 | Throws: R | Smelin Perez, Alex Todd, Jorge Flores |

| Season | Age | LVL | PA | 2B | 3B | HR | AVG | OBP | SLG | ISO | BB% | K% | wRC+ |
|---|---|---|---|---|---|---|---|---|---|---|---|---|---|
| 2014 | 21 | A- | 132 | 6 | 0 | 2 | 0.347 | 0.417 | 0.449 | 0.102 | 7.6% | 12.9% | 146 |
| 2015 | 22 | A+ | 265 | 15 | 1 | 3 | 0.292 | 0.321 | 0.396 | 0.104 | 3.8% | 16.6% | 95 |
| 2015 | 22 | AA | 218 | 11 | 1 | 0 | 0.296 | 0.350 | 0.362 | 0.065 | 6.4% | 22.0% | 108 |

**Background:** The 6-foot-2, 215-pound infielder/outfielder shot up the draft charts two years ago, going from a nondescript prospect to one of the better performing collegiate bats by the end of his junior season. Slater, who appeared in only six games during his freshman season, hit a mediocre .269/.361/.411 with little extra-base firepower during his first extended taste of top tier collegiate baseball. And while the production was solid – at best – no one could have foreseen the breakout junior season he had: in 59 games with the Cardinal, Slater slugged a robust .341/.386/.493 with career highs in doubles (17), triples (six), and stolen bases (six). The Giants grabbed the defensive jack-of-all-trades in the eighth round two years ago, 238th overall, and he hasn't stopped hitting since. He batted .347/.417/.449 in 29 games with Salem-Keizer during his debut, and followed that up with an aggregate .294/.334/.381 showing as he spent time between San Jose and Richmond last season.

**Projection:** Another one of these super-sub types. Slater's appeared in 96 games at second base, seven in center field, and 23 in right field. Offensively speaking, he doesn't pack a whole lot of wallop. And while he doesn't walk nearly enough either, the hit tool has a chance to be an above-average offering. He's a lesser version of Hunter Cole.

**Ceiling:** 1.0-win player
**Risk:** Moderate
**MLB ETA:** 2016/2017

## 21. Joan Gregorio, RHP

**MiLB Rank:** N/A
**Position Rank:** N/A

| Born: 01/12/92 | Age: 24 | Bats: R | Top CALs: Cody Hebner, Christian Meza, |
| Height: 6-7 | Weight: 180 | Throws: R | Dennis O'Grady, Dan Merklinger, Hector Santiago |

| YEAR | Age | Level | IP | W | L | ERA | FIP | K/9 | BB/9 | K% | BB% | HR/9 | LOB% |
|---|---|---|---|---|---|---|---|---|---|---|---|---|---|
| 2013 | 21 | A | 69.7 | 6 | 3 | 4.00 | 2.45 | 10.85 | 2.20 | 29.2% | 5.9% | 0.39 | 62.7% |
| 2014 | 22 | A | 68.0 | 2 | 7 | 3.57 | 3.47 | 8.60 | 3.57 | 22.9% | 9.5% | 0.26 | 61.9% |
| 2014 | 22 | A+ | 22.7 | 2 | 2 | 6.75 | 4.23 | 10.72 | 5.16 | 25.5% | 12.3% | 0.79 | 59.1% |
| 2015 | 23 | AA | 78.7 | 3 | 2 | 3.09 | 3.69 | 8.24 | 3.66 | 22.2% | 9.9% | 0.69 | 74.5% |

**Background:** Not nearly the baseball equivalent of former NBA center Shawn Bradley, but the 6-foot-7, 180-pound right-hander isn't too far off either. San Francisco slowly brought the rail-thin Dominican-born hurler back up to speed as he had never topped more than 76.1 innings in a season. Gregorio spent the first portion of the season working out of the Flying Squirrel's bullpen.

**Projection:** Gregorio is as fragile as he is thin – or at least pretty damn close to it. He's been in the Giants' development engine for six seasons now and he's thrown a combined 439.2 innings. A fine number for a reliever, sure, but keep in mind that of Gregorio's 112 games he's made 81 starts. With his age-24 season quickly approaching it might be time to give up on the hope of him developing as a backend starter and just push him into a relief role so as to get something, anything of significant value out of him.

**Ceiling:** 1.0-win player
**Risk:** Moderate
**MLB ETA:** 2016/2017

## 22. Ray Black, RHP

**MiLB Rank:** N/A
**Position Rank:** N/A

| Born: 06/26/90 | Age: 26 | Bats: R | Top CALs: Dario Alvarez, Francisco Rondon, |
| Height: 6-5 | Weight: 225 | Throws: R | Bryce Stowell, Kyle Barraclough, Leonel Campos |

| YEAR | Age | Level | IP | W | L | ERA | FIP | K/9 | BB/9 | K% | BB% | HR/9 | LOB% |
|---|---|---|---|---|---|---|---|---|---|---|---|---|---|
| 2015 | 25 | A+ | 25.0 | 2 | 1 | 2.88 | 3.74 | 18.36 | 9.00 | 45.5% | 22.3% | 0.72 | 79.6% |

**Background:** As I noted in last year's book, Black was a seventh round pick way back in 2011, but didn't make his debut until two years ago thanks to a litany of shoulder/labrum issues. The hard-throwing 6-foot-5, 225-pound right-hander looked promising in the Sally in 2014 as he *averaged* 18.4 K/9 in 35.0 innings. The club bumped Black up to High Class A last season, and he, unfortunately, caught a case of Kyle Crick-itis.

**Projection**: Here's what I wrote in last year's book:

> *"Obviously, the ceiling resides something close to a very good backend reliever, perhaps even as a dominant closer. But, again, we're looking at an old prospect with a checkered injury history dominating in the lowest levels of full season ball. Meaning: there's a lot of swing-and-miss potential for him as a prospect. Pun intended, of course."*

Well, Black continued to miss bats at an epic rate: he fanned 51 guys in 25.0 innings last season. The problem: he walked 25 in that same time span. If Crick is considered a long shot to make it to the big leagues with well below-average control, then Black has to be considered something like 10X that at this point.

**Ceiling**: 2.0-win player
**Risk**: Extremely High
**MLB ETA**: 2018/2019

## 23. Ryder Jones, 3B

**MiLB Rank: N/A**
**Position Rank: N/A**

| Born: 06/07/94 | Age: 22 | Bats: L | Top CALs: Julio Cedeno, Reggie Williams, |
|---|---|---|---|
| Height: 6-3 | Weight: 215 | Throws: R | Mario Martinez, Matt Weaver, David Renfroe |

| Season | Age | LVL | PA | 2B | 3B | HR | AVG | OBP | SLG | ISO | BB% | K% | wRC+ |
|---|---|---|---|---|---|---|---|---|---|---|---|---|---|
| 2013 | 19 | R | 165 | 9 | 0 | 1 | 0.317 | 0.394 | 0.400 | 0.083 | 8.5% | 23.0% | 129 |
| 2014 | 20 | A- | 117 | 5 | 1 | 3 | 0.243 | 0.293 | 0.393 | 0.150 | 6.0% | 17.9% | 90 |
| 2014 | 20 | A | 399 | 21 | 1 | 7 | 0.220 | 0.272 | 0.339 | 0.119 | 4.5% | 23.3% | 71 |
| 2014 | 20 | A | 399 | 21 | 1 | 7 | 0.220 | 0.272 | 0.339 | 0.119 | 4.5% | 23.3% | 71 |
| 2015 | 21 | A+ | 432 | 29 | 2 | 6 | 0.268 | 0.296 | 0.394 | 0.126 | 3.7% | 18.5% | 84 |

**Background:** The club's second round pick three years ago, Jones has hardly looked like the prospect that batted .317/.394/.400 in his debut in the Arizona Summer League. Since then he's cobbled together a .225/.277/.351 triple-slash line in 2014 and then followed that up with another putrid showing in High Class A last year.

**Projection**: It's still tough to get a decent read on Jones thanks to the club's handling of the young third baseman. The front office demoted him to the Northwest League following his first half struggles in the Sally two years. And then pushed him right back up to High Class A – despite the fact that he didn't exactly establish himself in short-season ball. He looks like organizational fodder, nothing more at this point.

**Ceiling**: 1.0-win player
**Risk**: High
**MLB ETA**: 2019

## 24. Martin Agosta, RHP

**MiLB Rank: N/A**
**Position Rank: N/A**

| Born: 04/07/91 | Age: 25 | Bats: R | Top CALs: Alberto Bastardo, Rafael De Paula, |
|---|---|---|---|
| Height: 6-1 | Weight: 180 | Throws: R | Matt Meyer, Pedro Figueroa, Kevin Roberts |

| YEAR | Age | Level | IP | W | L | ERA | FIP | K/9 | BB/9 | K% | BB% | HR/9 | LOB% |
|---|---|---|---|---|---|---|---|---|---|---|---|---|---|
| 2013 | 22 | A | 91.7 | 9 | 3 | 2.06 | 3.31 | 10.70 | 4.22 | 29.3% | 11.6% | 0.39 | 81.9% |
| 2014 | 23 | R | 14.0 | 1 | 0 | 4.50 | 1.75 | 12.21 | 1.29 | 32.2% | 3.4% | 0.00 | 55.6% |
| 2014 | 23 | A+ | 39.0 | 3 | 3 | 9.23 | 6.82 | 5.77 | 7.85 | 12.6% | 17.2% | 1.15 | 55.7% |
| 2015 | 24 | A+ | 106.0 | 5 | 9 | 4.25 | 4.11 | 10.61 | 2.21 | 28.0% | 5.8% | 1.27 | 72.5% |

**Background:** A slowly, *slowly* developing right-hander taken out of St. Mary's College of California in the second round way back in 2012, Agosta rebounded from a disastrous – and I mean a truly *disastrous* – 2014 season to help restore whatever luster is left on his prospect status. After posting a 25-to-34 strikeout-to-walk ratio in 39.0 innings with San Jose in 2014, Agosta started pounding the strike zone with unprecedented frequency last season. The 6-foot-1, 180-pound Agosta fanned a career high 125 while walking a remarkable 26 batters – *nine fewer than he walked the entire 2014 season in roughly three times the innings*. For his career, Agosta is averaging 10.2 punch outs and 3.9 walks per nine innings while sporting a mediocre 4.24 ERA.

**Projection**: Now the bad news: Agosta's entering his age-25 season with *zero* experience above the California League. Now for even worse news: he had a lot of wonky games last season. For example: he allowed five or more runs in five of his 16 starts. He bounced between the rotation and bullpen a bit, so you just have to assume that he's going to be a reliever long term.

**Ceiling:** 1.0-win player
**Risk:** Moderate to High
**MLB ETA:** 2018

## 25. Johneshwy Fargas, OF

**MiLB Rank:** N/A
**Position Rank:** N/A

| Born: 12/15/94 | Age: 21 | Bats: R | Top CALs: Roderick Bernadina, Albert Laboy, Jonathan Jones, Teodoro Martinez, Che Hsuan Lin |
|---|---|---|---|
| Height: 6-1 | Weight: 165 | Throws: R | |

| Season | Age | LVL | PA | 2B | 3B | HR | AVG | OBP | SLG | ISO | BB% | K% | wRC+ |
|---|---|---|---|---|---|---|---|---|---|---|---|---|---|
| 2014 | 19 | A- | 208 | 6 | 0 | 3 | 0.240 | 0.373 | 0.329 | 0.090 | 11.5% | 13.0% | 109 |
| 2015 | 20 | A | 458 | 19 | 2 | 2 | 0.278 | 0.347 | 0.349 | 0.071 | 6.1% | 14.2% | 104 |

**Background:** An 11th round pick out of the Puerto Rico Baseball Academy in 2013, the speedy outfielder had his finest season to date as he moved into the South Atlantic League for the first time. Fargas batted .278/.347/.349 with 19 doubles, a pair of triples, two homeruns, and a whopping 59 stolen bases (in 78 attempts). His overall production, per *Weighted Runs Created Plus*, topped the league average mark by 4%.

**Projection**: Your typical slap-hitting speedster. Fargas has one plus tool – speed, obviously – and very little else. He might be able to carve out a semi-useful role as a pinch runner. Maybe? Probably not.

**Ceiling:** 0.5-win player
**Risk:** Moderate
**MLB ETA:** 2019

### *Barely Missed:*

- **Ty Blach, LHP** – Finesse lefty out of Creighton University spent the year with Sacramento in the PCL. His strikeout rate bottomed out to a career low 5.1 K/9, but he only walked 1.7 BB/9.

- **Dylan Davis, LF/RF** – The 2014 third round pick out of Oregon State University proved that he wasn't ready for High Class A and he didn't exactly establish himself in the Sally either (.250/.322/.406). He was a part-time two-way player in college, so if he fails in the California League again it might be time to start thinking about a switch.

- **Matt Gage, LHP** – 6-foot-4, 240-pounder out of Siena College looked solid in the South Atlantic League last season, posting a 71-to-13 strikeout-to-walk ratio in 77.1 innings. The organization made the unusual move and pushed him right up to Class AA where he looked surprisingly solid. He finished the year with 101 strikeouts and 23 walks in 116.0 innings.

- **Mac Marshall, LHP** – A fourth round pick out of Chipola College last June, Marshall posted fanned 29 in 20.2 innings between the Arizona Summer and Northwest Leagues. The problem: he walked 15 in that same span.

## Bird Doggin' It – Additional Prospects to Keep an Eye in 2016

| Player | Age | POS | Notes |
|--------|-----|-----|-------|
| Carlos Diaz | 22 | RHP | The 6-foot-2 southpaw fanned 75 in 55.1 innings with Augusta in Low Class A last season. It was an age-appropriate level of competition so it'll be interested to see if the strikeout rate carries over in 2016. |
| C.J. Hinojosa | 21 | SS | After a disappointing junior campaign at the University of Texas, Hinojosa rebounded nicely in the Northwest League as he slugged .296/.328/.481. |
| Jalen Miller | 19 | SS | The club's most recent third round pick had a rough go of it during his debut, hitting .218/.292/.259 with a 69 wRC+. |
| Reyes Moronta | 23 | RHP | Dominican-born hurler posted a 64-to-23 strikeout-to-walk ratio in 48.2 relief innings in the Sally. |
| Daniel Slania | 24 | RHP | As round as he is tall, the 6-foot-5, 275-pound right-hander out of Notre Dame posted a 90-to-15 strikeout-to-walk with a 3.53 ERA in 71.1 innings for San Jose. |
| Logan Webb | 19 | RHP | Fourth rounder two years ago tossed 60.1 innings with Salem-Keizer in the Northwest League last season, averaging 6.0 K/9 and 2.4 BB/9. |

**State of the Farm System:** One of the weaker farm systems in the game, Seattle, nonetheless, owns one of the best arms in the all the minor leagues: hard-throwing right-hander Edwin Diaz, a 2012 third round pick out of Caguas Military Academy. The 6-foot-3, 165-pound right-hander, who was named among the Top 25 Breakout Prospects in last year's book, absolutely dominated the California League for seven starts before earning a promotion up to Jackson for the remainder of the year. Diaz finished the season with 145 strikeouts, 46 walks, and a 3.82 ERA in 141.2 combined innings.

And big teenage left-hander Luiz Gohara could be the next line to ascend to the big leagues as Seattle's latest wunderkind, following in the footsteps of Felix Hernandez, Taijuan Walker, and potentially Diaz. Gohara, a 6-foot-3, 210-pounder out of Brazil, tallied a 67-to-38 strikeout-to-walk ratio in 63.1 innings between the Northwest and Midwest Leagues.

Zack Littell, an 11th round pick in 2013, quietly looked solid as a 19-year-old with Clinton in Low Class A.

In terms of bats, the system's sporting one of the more power-packed ones in the minor leagues: former first round pick Alex Jackson, a prep catcher-turned-corner-outfielder. In an injury-shortened campaign the well-built slugger batted .207/.318/.365 with 17 doubles, one triple, and eight homeruns in 318 trips to the plate. As you'll see in the following pages, there's reason to dismiss Jackson's pitiful showing.

Corner outfielder Tyler O'Neill mashed 32 homeruns – more than double that of his career total up to that point. The bad news: he's a poor version of a Three True Outcomes Hitter.

And the recently acquired Boog Powell is nearing big league readiness.

| Rank | Name | POS |
|------|------|-----|
| 1 | Edwin Diaz | RHP |
| 2 | Alex Jackson | LF/RF |
| 3 | Luiz Gohara | LHP |
| 4 | D.J. Peterson | 1B/3B |
| 5 | Tyler O'Neill | LF/RF |
| 6 | Boog Powell | OF |
| 7 | Zack Littell | RHP |
| 8 | Tony Zych | RHP |
| 9 | Andrew Moore | RHP |
| 10 | Joe Wieland | RHP |
| 11 | Dario Pizzano | LF |
| 12 | Nick Neidert | RHP |
| 13 | Tyler Marlette | C |
| 14 | Daniel Altavilla | RHP |
| 15 | Austin Wilson | OF |
| 16 | Ryan Yarbrough | LHP |
| 17 | Jonathan Aro | RHP |
| 18 | Paul Fry | LHP |
| 19 | Dylan Unsworth | RHP |
| 20 | Tyler Smith | SS |
| 21 | Tyler Pike | LHP |
| 22 | Nick Wells | LHP |
| 23 | Gareth Morgan | OF |
| 24 | Dylan Thompson | RHP |
| 25 | Mayckol Guaipe | RHP |

**Review of the 2015 Draft:** The Mariners' first pick didn't come until the 60th selection last June when they took prep right-hander Nick Neidert in the second round. Despite finishing his debut with a tidy 1.53 ERA, the 6-foot-1, 180-pound pitcher managed to fan only 23 batters in over 35 innings of work.

Former Oregon State University right-hander Andrew Moore, another second rounder last June, looked quite promising as he posted a ridiculous 43-to-2 strikeout-to-walk ratio in 39.0 innings with Everett in the Northwest League.

A couple other names to watch moving forward: Dylan Thompson, former Stanford shortstop Drew Jackson, and Bryant College right-hander Kyle Wilcox.

# 1. Edwin Diaz, RHP

| Born: 03/22/94 | Age: 22 | Bats: R | Top CALs: Randall Delgado, Luke Jackson, |
|---|---|---|---|
| Height: 6-3 | Weight: 165 | Throws: R | Eduardo Rodriguez, Jordan Walden, Johnny Barbato |

| YEAR | Age | Level | IP | W | L | ERA | FIP | K/9 | BB/9 | K% | BB% | HR/9 | LOB% |
|---|---|---|---|---|---|---|---|---|---|---|---|---|---|
| 2013 | 19 | R | 69.0 | 5 | 2 | 1.43 | 3.04 | 10.30 | 2.35 | 30.4% | 6.9% | 0.65 | 88.3% |
| 2014 | 20 | A | 116.3 | 6 | 8 | 3.33 | 3.48 | 8.59 | 3.25 | 23.0% | 8.7% | 0.39 | 69.5% |
| 2015 | 21 | A+ | 37.0 | 2 | 0 | 1.70 | 3.62 | 10.22 | 2.19 | 29.8% | 6.4% | 0.73 | 90.6% |
| 2015 | 21 | AA | 104.3 | 5 | 10 | 4.57 | 3.22 | 8.88 | 3.19 | 23.3% | 8.4% | 0.43 | 64.8% |

**Background:** After unleashing Felix Hernandez to wreak havoc on the baseball world more than a decade ago – yes, it's really been that long – Seattle followed that up with the long awaited arrival of Taijuan Walker, another big hard-throwing right-hander a couple years ago. And it appears that Diaz could be the next in line to ascend to the big league throne to complete the triumvirate of dominance. Tall enough to look his future rotation-mates squarely in the eyes, Diaz, who stands a wiry 6-foot-3 and 165 pounds, shook off a horrible debut in the Arizona Summer League five years ago and has been quickly moving through the system's minor league ladder. He torched the Appalachian League, more than held his own – and some might say sparkled – as he moved up to the Midwest League two years ago, dominated – briefly – with Bakersfield, and posted a strikeout-to-walk ratio in the 3-to-1 neighborhood in Class last season.

Diaz, whom I named as one of the Top 25 Breakout Prospects for 2015, was simply breathtaking in his opening seven starts last season – all coming in the California League. He would toss 37.0 innings while fanning 42 and walking just nine to go along with a 1.70 ERA. The Seattle front office would bounce him up to the minors' toughest challenge, Class AA, in mid-May for another 20 starts. Throwing 104.1 innings with the Jackson Generals, Diaz would fan 23.3% and walk 8.4% of the batters he faced. And he was particularly dominant over his final 12 starts with the club: 61.2 IP, 65 K, and 19 BB.

Overall, Diaz would finish the year with an aggregate 3.82 ERA in a career high 141.1 innings, tallying 145 strikeouts and just 46 walks.

**Projection:** There's really nothing poor to say when it comes to Diaz – he's tall and projectable (still), has been missing a ton of bats and continues to do so as he rapidly advances through the system, has succeeded against much older competition, and his control has been trending in the right direction since posting a near one-to-one strikeout-to-walk ratio during his brief pro debut. And CAL seems to be a particularly big fan of the young right-hander as well, comparing him to a lot of hard-throwing, high-strikeout relievers in Luke Jackson, Jordan Walden, and Johnny Barbato. He might not have the ceiling of Walker, but Diaz has the potential to settle in nicely as a rock-solid #3-type arm.

**Ceiling:** 3.0-win player
**Risk:** Low to Moderate
**MLB ETA:** 2016/2017

# 2. Alex Jackson, LF/RF

| Born: 12/25/95 | Age: 20 | Bats: R | Top CALs: Jose Dore, Kyler Burke, |
|---|---|---|---|
| Height: 6-2 | Weight: 215 | Throws: R | Phillips Castillo, Roberto Rodriguez, Guillermo Pimentel |

| Season | Age | LVL | PA | 2B | 3B | HR | AVG | OBP | SLG | ISO | BB% | K% | wRC+ |
|---|---|---|---|---|---|---|---|---|---|---|---|---|---|
| 2015 | 19 | A- | 197 | 11 | 1 | 8 | 0.239 | 0.365 | 0.466 | 0.227 | 10.7% | 31.0% | 140 |
| 2015 | 19 | A | 121 | 6 | 0 | 0 | 0.157 | 0.240 | 0.213 | 0.056 | 5.0% | 28.9% | 37 |

**Background:** Sandwiched between Nick Gordon and Aaron Nola as the sixth selection in the draft two years ago, the Rancho Bernardo product was widely recognized as *the* prep power bat in that year's class. And after signing on the dotted line for more than $4 million dollars, it didn't take long for the backstop-turned-corner-outfielder to display his prodigious pop. Jackson swatted 10 extra-base hits – six doubles, a pair of triples, and two dingers – in just under 100 trips to the plate with the franchise's Arizona Summer League team. His overall production, by the way, topped the league average mark by 28% as he hit a solid .280/.344/.476. Seattle may have gotten a little too greedy – though, that's certainly up for debate – as they pushed the teenage prospect up to the Midwest League to start last season. The 6-foot-2, 215-pound Jackson would bat an utterly disappointing .157/.240/.213 with just six extra-base hits, all doubles, through his first 28 contests with Clinton before an undisclosed left shoulder injury forced him to shut it down for more than a month.

Upon his return Seattle opted to push him down to the Northwest League where he would bat .239/.365/.466 with 11 doubles, one triple, and eight homeruns in 48 games – though he was forced to miss another month with a hand injury. Overall, Jackson would bat an aggregate .207/.318/.365 in just over 300 trips to the plate.

**Projection:** It appears – a key word here – that Jackson's first full season was a quite loss. But let's break it down for a bit. First, I'm willing to ignore the 28-game stint with Clinton last season for a pair of reasons:

1) He was 19 and tallied just 94 plate appearances in professional ball prior to the start of the year. The actual surprise would have been if he *didn't* struggle at the outset of the year.

2) Who knows how long the left shoulder was bothering him before he actually got shutdown. Did it pop up? Was it a lingering issue? I don't know, but in this case it's certainly reasonable enough to look past the poor production line.

Let's breakdown his work with the AquaSox in the Northwest League: after returning from the DL in mid-June Jackson batted a more-than-respectable.259/.355/.444 over the course of his next 23 games. And then the second injury hit, which forced him out for nearly a full month. After he got back from that ailment he would bat .220/.375/.488 – a reasonable facsimile to his pre-injury line. So in a level of competition still a year or two his senior, Jackson would top the league average by 40% on the back of solid OBP skills and that prodigious power.

Not for some bad news: the borderline red flag strikeout rate he displayed during his debut (25.5%) blossomed into a more troublesome mark last season (30.2%). Jackson's never going to his for a high – hell, even a higher-ish – batting average, but he could be a very solid Three True Outcomes hitter in the coming years.

**Ceiling:** 3.0- to 3.5-win player
**Risk:** Moderate to High
**MLB ETA:** 2018

# 3. Luiz Gohara, LHP

**MiLB Rank: #124**
**Position Rank: N/A**

| Born: 07/31/96 | Age: 19 | Bats: L | **Top CALs:** Richard Alvarez, Juan Perez, |
|---|---|---|---|
| Height: 6-3 | Weight: 210 | Throws: L | Jose Martinez, Kelvin De La Cruz, Raynu Guichardo |

| YEAR | Age | Level | IP | W | L | ERA | FIP | K/9 | BB/9 | K% | BB% | HR/9 | LOB% |
|---|---|---|---|---|---|---|---|---|---|---|---|---|---|
| 2013 | 16 | R | 21.7 | 1 | 2 | 4.15 | 3.06 | 11.22 | 3.74 | 27.6% | 9.2% | 0.42 | 60.1% |
| 2014 | 17 | R | 12.7 | 1 | 1 | 2.13 | 1.98 | 11.37 | 1.42 | 31.4% | 3.9% | 0.00 | 69.2% |
| 2014 | 17 | A- | 37.3 | 0 | 6 | 8.20 | 6.26 | 8.92 | 5.79 | 19.8% | 12.8% | 1.45 | 48.1% |
| 2015 | 18 | A- | 53.7 | 3 | 7 | 6.20 | 4.27 | 10.40 | 5.37 | 24.0% | 12.4% | 0.67 | 59.6% |
| 2015 | 18 | A | 9.7 | 0 | 1 | 1.86 | 4.22 | 4.66 | 5.59 | 12.2% | 14.6% | 0.00 | 87.5% |

**Background:** Signed as a 16-year-old out of Brazil in 2013 for a shade under $900,000, Gohara's brief minor league career can be summed up with three different statements: poor luck, problematic control, and a promising ability to miss bats. The 6-foot-3, 210-pounder was aggressively pushed into the Appalachian League immediately after signing with the organization, throwing 21.2 innings while fanning 27 and walking nine. He would make a pair of dominant starts in the Arizona Summer League before spending the rest of his abbreviated sophomore campaign with the Everett AquaSox two years ago, posting a 53-to-26 strikeout-to-walk ratio in 49.2 innings of work. Seattle bounced him between the Midwest League and short-season ball in 2015 where he would total a career high 63.1 innings with 67 punch outs and 38 walks.

**Projection**: Something interesting to note which could be something or just as easily be nothing: opponents have been exceedingly lucky while squaring off against the big lefty as they've posted BABIPs ranging from .333 all the way up to .404 in each of his five (brief) minor league stops. The control remains a work in progress, but teenage southpaws that can fan nearly 10 punch outs per nine innings in the Northwest League are certainly worth watching. There could be some #2/#3-type upside here, but he has a *long* way to go to get there.

**Ceiling:** 3.0- to 3.5-win player
**Risk:** High
**MLB ETA:** 2018/2019

# 4. D.J. Peterson, 1B/3B

**MiLB Rank: #204**
**Position Rank: #10 (3B)**

| Born: 12/31/91 | Age: 24 | Bats: R | **Top CALs:** Luke Hughes, Danny Valencia, |
|---|---|---|---|
| Height: 6-1 | Weight: 210 | Throws: R | Brandon Jones, Kyle Reynolds, Nick Evans |

| Season | Age | LVL | PA | 2B | 3B | HR | AVG | OBP | SLG | ISO | BB% | K% | wRC+ |
|---|---|---|---|---|---|---|---|---|---|---|---|---|---|
| 2013 | 21 | A- | 123 | 6 | 0 | 6 | 0.312 | 0.382 | 0.532 | 0.220 | 10.6% | 14.6% | 162 |
| 2013 | 21 | A | 107 | 5 | 1 | 7 | 0.293 | 0.346 | 0.576 | 0.283 | 6.5% | 22.4% | 155 |
| 2014 | 22 | A+ | 299 | 23 | 1 | 18 | 0.326 | 0.381 | 0.615 | 0.289 | 7.7% | 21.7% | 154 |
| 2014 | 22 | AA | 248 | 8 | 0 | 13 | 0.261 | 0.335 | 0.473 | 0.212 | 8.9% | 20.6% | 126 |
| 2015 | 23 | AA | 393 | 19 | 2 | 7 | 0.223 | 0.290 | 0.346 | 0.123 | 7.9% | 22.9% | 80 |
| 2015 | 23 | AAA | 14 | 1 | 0 | 0 | 0.214 | 0.214 | 0.286 | 0.071 | 0.0% | 21.4% | 24 |

**Background:** Overshadowed by some guy named Kris Bryant in the 2013 draft, though the former New Mexico slugger's offensive output was definitely influenced by the school's home ballpark, Peterson, for the first time since his pre-college days, failed to do the one thing he's *always* done last season: hit. After making quick work of the Northwest and Midwest Leagues during his pro debut three years ago, the 6-foot-1, 210-pound corner infielder slugged .297/.360/.552 during his follow-up campaign with High Desert – another offense-inducing environment – and Jackson in 2014. Last year, however, Peterson looked lost in his return trip to the Southern League, hitting a disappointing .223/.290/.346 in 93 games. Seattle would, nonetheless, bump him up to Tacoma, but an Achilles issue shut him down after only 14 plate appearances. For his career, Peterson's sporting a solid .273/.336/.480 triple-slash line.

**Projection**: Here's what I wrote prior to the draft three years ago:

> *"Peterson is a solid big league prospect, probably being nabbed somewhere in the middle to back half of the first round. He's always shown a strong eye at the plate and his power grades out as a 55 or 60." I also described Peterson as having a ceiling as a .280/.350/.500-type hitter with 25-HR potential."*

And for the first two seasons Peterson looked every bit the part of power-hitting corner infielder. But, for whatever reason, his pop dried up last year as he posted the lowest ISO of his professional – and collegiate – career. Otherwise, all the other numbers fall in line with his career norms: solid eye, BABIP, punch out rate, etc… His power did seem to return in the Arizona Fall League, though he managed to finish that season with another disappointing line: .203/.321/.388. Something inexplicable is up with Peterson, and, unfortunately, it looks like it could warp his career path – if it already hasn't.

**Ceiling:** 2.0-win player
**Risk:** Moderate to High
**MLB ETA:** 2016/2017

# 5. Tyler O'Neill, LF/RF

**MiLB Rank: #212**
**Position Rank: N/A**

| Born: 06/22/95 | Age: 21 | Bats: R | **Top CALs:** Cristian Santana, Trayce Thompson, Cody Johnson, Domingo Santana, Michael Burgess |
|---|---|---|---|
| Height: 5-11 | Weight: 210 | Throws: R | |

| Season | Age | LVL | PA | 2B | 3B | HR | AVG | OBP | SLG | ISO | BB% | K% | wRC+ |
|---|---|---|---|---|---|---|---|---|---|---|---|---|---|
| 2013 | 18 | R | 116 | 5 | 3 | 1 | 0.310 | 0.405 | 0.450 | 0.140 | 10.3% | 23.3% | 143 |
| 2014 | 19 | A | 245 | 9 | 0 | 13 | 0.247 | 0.322 | 0.466 | 0.219 | 8.2% | 32.2% | 124 |
| 2015 | 20 | A+ | 449 | 21 | 2 | 32 | 0.260 | 0.316 | 0.558 | 0.297 | 6.5% | 30.5% | 128 |

**Background:** A short, stocky, built-like-a-brick-shit-house outfielder out of a Canadian prep school three years ago, O'Neill's blossoming power potential falls short to only one other player in the system: 2014 first round pick Alex Jackson. O'Neill, like his budding bash brother, had a phenomenal – albeit short – professional debut in the Arizona Summer League as he slugged .310/.405/.450 with five doubles, three triples, and one homerun while topping the league average mark by 43%. He, like Jackson, suffered through an injury-shortened sophomore campaign in the Midwest League, hitting .247/.322/.466. Last season Seattle continued to aggressively challenge the 5-foot-11, 210-pound corner outfielder by assigning him to the California League. And he looked at ease for the most part as he slugged .260/.316/.558 with 21 doubles, a pair of three-baggers, and 32 long balls, easily one of the best marks in all the minors.

**Projection**: So here's what I wrote in last year's book:

> *"And now the bad news: he punched out in nearly one-third of his plate appearances [in 2014]. Good power, decent eye, O'Neill wasn't really ready for full season ball. He might be this time around though. A poor man's Three True Outcomes hitter. Maybe"*

Well, if 2015 proved anything it was the fact that, yes, O'Neill is on the path of a poor man's Three True Outcomes hitter. Incredible, game altering power? Check. Massive swing-and-miss tendencies? Double-check. Below-average walk rates, the lone skill keeping him from a genuine, real life TTO hitter? Unfortunately, check. And not to complicate matters – or throw salt into the wound – but CAL links him to a bunch of toolsy former top prospects that never panned out due to their high punch out rates.

**Ceiling:** 2.0-win player
**Risk:** High
**MLB ETA:** 2018

## 6. Boog Powell, OF

**MiLB Rank: N/A**
**Position Rank: N/A**

| Born: 01/14/93 | Age: 23 | Bats: L | Top CALs: L.J. Hoes, Mallex Smith, |
|---|---|---|---|
| Height: 5-10 | Weight: 185 | Throws: L | Adam Eaton, Brett Gardner, Dalton Pompey |

| Season | Age | LVL | PA | 2B | 3B | HR | AVG | OBP | SLG | ISO | BB% | K% | wRC+ |
|---|---|---|---|---|---|---|---|---|---|---|---|---|---|
| 2013 | 20 | A- | 245 | 7 | 3 | 0 | 0.283 | 0.364 | 0.344 | 0.061 | 10.6% | 13.9% | 118 |
| 2014 | 21 | A | 311 | 7 | 4 | 3 | 0.335 | 0.452 | 0.429 | 0.094 | 17.0% | 15.8% | 160 |
| 2015 | 22 | AA | 274 | 6 | 6 | 1 | 0.328 | 0.408 | 0.416 | 0.088 | 10.6% | 13.9% | 139 |
| 2015 | 22 | AAA | 246 | 10 | 3 | 2 | 0.257 | 0.360 | 0.364 | 0.107 | 13.0% | 16.7% | 114 |

**Background:** No relation to former MVP slugger Boog Powell, the Rays acquired Powell 2.0 from the A's as part of the Ben Zobrist package in January 2015 and flipped him to Seattle this offseason. The outfielder, unsurprisingly, is the quintessential Oakland-type prospect: an overlooked, late-round draft pick that has had a tremendous amount of success despite some glaring deficiencies, namely power. But despite the obvious lack of pop, Powell continued his climb up through the minor leagues. After getting popped for amphetamines last season, the former 20th round pick out of Orange Coast College opened the year with Montgomery, where he batted .328/.408/.416. Sixty-one games later he got pushed up to Durham, where he would post the second lowest wRC+ mark of his career, a still respectable 114.

**Projection:** Again, there's a clear lack of pop in Powell's bat – his career ISO is a lowly .079 – and he doesn't run a whole lot either. But what he does do is invaluable: get on base. Through his first 294 games, Powell's sporting a .401 OBP with a walk rate approaching 13%. He has the ability to man each of the outfield positions, which only adds value, but I'm not certain he can consistently be a league average regular. He's a less-speedy version of Billy Burns.

**Ceiling:** 1.5-win player
**Risk:** Moderate
**MLB ETA:** 2016

## 7. Zack Littell, RHP

**MiLB Rank: N/A**
**Position Rank: N/A**

| Born: 10/05/95 | Age: 20 | Bats: R | Top CALs: Lucas Lanphere, Casey Shake, |
|---|---|---|---|
| Height: 6-3 | Weight: 190 | Throws: R | Chadwick Kaalekahi, Ronald Herrera, Sam Gibbons |

| YEAR | Age | Level | IP | W | L | ERA | FIP | K/9 | BB/9 | K% | BB% | HR/9 | LOB% |
|---|---|---|---|---|---|---|---|---|---|---|---|---|---|
| 2013 | 17 | R | 33.3 | 0 | 6 | 5.94 | 4.37 | 7.56 | 3.51 | 18.4% | 8.6% | 0.54 | 51.8% |
| 2014 | 18 | R | 69.7 | 5 | 5 | 4.52 | 3.15 | 8.27 | 1.55 | 21.6% | 4.0% | 0.39 | 62.8% |
| 2015 | 19 | A | 112.7 | 3 | 6 | 3.91 | 3.27 | 6.71 | 2.40 | 17.4% | 6.2% | 0.32 | 61.6% |

**Background:** A late-round pick three years ago, Seattle unearthed the promising former prep pitcher in the 11th round, the 327th overall player taken that year. Since then, Littell's been stuffing the stat sheet with impressive strikeout-to-walk ratios: he posted a 28-to-13 mark in the Arizona Summer League; he followed that up with a 64-to-12 showing with Pulaski, and finished with an 84-to-30 strikeout-to-walk ratio in 112.1 innings with Clinton in the Midwest League last season. For his career, Littell is averaging 7.3 strikeouts and just 2.3 walks every nine innings to go along with an unlucky 4.42 ERA.

**Projection:** One of those sneaky good prospects nobody is talking about. Littell hasn't been mentioned a whole lot about likely because of his poor ERA. But he's consistently outperformed them, in particular his 3.15 FIP in 2014 and last year's 3.27 mark. He has some promising swing-and-miss ability, a strong feel for the strike zone, and generates a whole lot of contact on the ground. It's a recipe for success. Hopefully he can avoid the injury nexus and reach his potential as a #4-type arm.

**Ceiling:** 1.5-win player
**Risk:** Moderate
**MLB ETA:** 2019

## 8. Tony Zych, RHP

MiLB Rank: N/A
Position Rank: N/A

| Born: 08/07/90 | Age: 25 | Bats: R | Top CALs: J.R. Graham, Scott Diamond, |
| Height: 6-3 | Weight: 190 | Throws: R | Andrew Heaney, Lucas Luetge, Merrill Kelly |

| YEAR | Age | Level | IP | W | L | ERA | FIP | K/9 | BB/9 | K% | BB% | HR/9 | LOB% |
|---|---|---|---|---|---|---|---|---|---|---|---|---|---|
| 2013 | 22 | AA | 56.0 | 5 | 5 | 3.05 | 3.13 | 6.43 | 3.38 | 16.5% | 8.6% | 0.32 | 61.3% |
| 2014 | 23 | AA | 58.3 | 4 | 5 | 5.09 | 3.74 | 5.40 | 2.78 | 13.8% | 7.1% | 0.46 | 65.4% |
| 2015 | 24 | AA | 16.7 | 0 | 0 | 2.16 | 1.68 | 9.72 | 0.00 | 29.0% | 0.0% | 0.00 | 71.4% |
| 2015 | 24 | AAA | 31.7 | 1 | 2 | 3.41 | 3.13 | 10.52 | 2.56 | 27.4% | 6.7% | 0.57 | 78.2% |

**Background:** A fourth round pick under the Cubs' previous regime in 2011, Seattle just straight up purchased the hard-throwing right-hander from Chicago in early April last season – an incredibly savvy move as the former University of Louisville product easily had his finest season to date. After battling through some lackadaisical strike out rates the previous two seasons, the 6-foot-3, 190-pound hurler exploded in 14 appearances with Jackson – he tossed 16.2 innings with a perfect (literally) 18-to-0 strikeout-to-walk ratio and allowed just four runs, three of which came in one appearance – and tallied another 37-to-9 strikeout-to-walk ratio in 31.2 innings with the PCL Rainiers as he spent the majority of the year yo-yoing between Class AA and Class AAA. Seattle would call him up in early September where he would post another impeccable 24-to-3 strikeout-to-walk in 18.1 innings of work.

**Projection**: It's pretty easy to see how Zich can rack up strikeouts with the best of them: his fastball averaged a smidge over 96 mph during his admittedly brief tenure in the big leagues. He complemented it with a low- to mid-80s slider and a hard, high-80s changeup. And even though the Mariners' bullpen is loaded with a bunch of promising – sometimes dominant – arms, Zych should easily see a fair amount of action, potentially even working his way into some high leverage situations as he continues to earn the trust of new manager Scott Servais. One more thought: CAL seems to be a pretty big fan as well.

**Ceiling:** 1.0- to 1.5-win player
**Risk:** Low to Moderate
**MLB ETA:** Debuted in 2015

## 9. Andrew Moore, RHP

MiLB Rank: N/A
Position Rank: N/A

| Born: 06/02/94 | Age: 22 | Bats: R | Top CALs: Daniel Gossett, Matthew Bowman, |
| Height: 6-0 | Weight: 185 | Throws: R | Justin Masterson, Zachary Neal, Kevin Brady |

| YEAR | Age | Level | IP | W | L | ERA | FIP | K/9 | BB/9 | K% | BB% | HR/9 | LOB% |
|---|---|---|---|---|---|---|---|---|---|---|---|---|---|
| 2015 | 21 | A- | 39.0 | 1 | 1 | 2.08 | 2.29 | 9.92 | 0.46 | 28.5% | 1.3% | 0.46 | 75.3% |

**Background:** The club's second pick in the draft last June – as well as their second pick in the second round – Moore was a three-year mainstay in Oregon State's rotation, leaving the school with 210 strikeouts, just 66 walks, and a 2.00 ERA in 302 innings of work. Seattle sent the 6-foot, 185-pound right-hander to the Northwest League for his debut. And in 39.0 innings with Everett, Moore would post an impressive 43-to-2 strikeout-to-walk ratio with a 2.08 ERA.

**Projection**: Despite a relatively large sample of near-dominance with Oregon State, Moore isn't your prototypical flame-throwing right-hander. He does a fantastic job limiting walks and generally inducing a lot of weak action off the bat. With that being said, he profiles more as a fringy big league starter.

**Ceiling:** 1.0- to 1.5-win player
**Risk:** Low to Moderate
**MLB ETA:** 2018

## 10. Joe Wieland, RHP

MiLB Rank: N/A
Position Rank: N/A

| Born: 01/21/90 | Age: 26 | Bats: R | Top CALs: Tony Pena, Chris Britton, |
| Height: 6-2 | Weight: 205 | Throws: R | Chris Resop, Brad Thompson, Rafael Perez |

| YEAR | Age | Level | IP | W | L | ERA | FIP | K/9 | BB/9 | K% | BB% | HR/9 | LOB% |
|---|---|---|---|---|---|---|---|---|---|---|---|---|---|
| 2014 | 24 | R | 6.0 | 0 | 1 | 3.00 | 1.20 | 15.00 | 1.50 | 45.5% | 4.6% | 0.00 | 50.0% |
| 2014 | 24 | AA | 9.0 | 0 | 1 | 2.00 | 3.56 | 6.00 | 1.00 | 17.7% | 2.9% | 1.00 | 79.0% |
| 2014 | 24 | AAA | 23.7 | 2 | 1 | 3.42 | 3.07 | 7.61 | 1.52 | 20.8% | 4.2% | 0.38 | 69.1% |
| 2015 | 25 | AAA | 113.7 | 10 | 5 | 4.59 | 3.52 | 7.28 | 1.98 | 18.9% | 5.1% | 0.55 | 64.6% |

**Background:** A cog in the massive San Diego overhaul during the 2014-2015 offseason that brought former MVP Matt Kemp to Petco Park. Thanks to a previous round of Tommy John surgery, Wieland topped the 100-inning mark for the first since 2011. Pitching almost exclusively for Oklahoma City in the Pacific

Coast League last season, the former fourth round pick posted peripherals eerily similar to that of his pre-TJ days: 7.28 K/9 and just 1.98 BB/9. He suffered through some bad luck, namely an unsightly .355 BABIP, but his 3.52 FIP is clearly more indicative of his true talent than the 4.59 ERA.

**Projection**: One these guys that often are overlooked because he lacks a traditional out pitch. No blistering fastball (it's hovered around the 90-mph mark during his cups o' coffee at the big league level), no knee-buckling deuce, or Johan Santana-like change up. But Wieland knows how to pitch. And he's been incredibly successful with this approach since entering pro baseball as a fourth round prep arm. Any pitcher that's sporting a *career* MiLB strikeout-to-walk ratio of more than 4.5-to-1 has MLB value. You just get the feeling he's going to be one of these late-blooming quasi-finesse guys that finds a permanent home somewhere.

**Ceiling:** 1.0- to 1.5-win player
**Risk:** Low to Moderate
**MLB ETA:** Debuted in 2012

## 11. Dario Pizzano, LF

**MiLB Rank: N/A**
**Position Rank: N/A**

| Born: 04/09/96 | Age: 20 | Bats: R | Top CALs: Garrett Guzman, Jake Goebbert, |
|---|---|---|---|
| Height: 6-0 | Weight: 170 | Throws: R | Tim Smith, Willie Cabrera, Stephen Piscotty |

| Season | Age | LVL | PA | 2B | 3B | HR | AVG | OBP | SLG | ISO | BB% | K% | wRC+ |
|---|---|---|---|---|---|---|---|---|---|---|---|---|---|
| 2013 | 22 | A | 531 | 40 | 5 | 8 | 0.311 | 0.392 | 0.471 | 0.160 | 11.5% | 9.0% | 142 |
| 2014 | 23 | A+ | 162 | 16 | 2 | 3 | 0.275 | 0.377 | 0.486 | 0.210 | 14.2% | 9.9% | 125 |
| 2014 | 23 | AA | 328 | 14 | 5 | 8 | 0.228 | 0.341 | 0.404 | 0.176 | 13.7% | 11.6% | 111 |
| 2015 | 24 | AA | 243 | 13 | 4 | 4 | 0.308 | 0.366 | 0.457 | 0.149 | 7.8% | 8.2% | 131 |

**Background:** After a brief derailment in his first taste of Class AA two years ago, the former Columbia University masher got back on track as he slugged .308/.366/.457 with 13 doubles, four triples, and four homeruns in 58 games back with Jackson. For his minor league career he's batting an impressive .296/.383/.462.

**Projection**: Pizzano has a shot to be a backup outfielder in the big leagues with a solid eye at the plate and surprising power. And even in his worst professional showing two years ago in Class AA, Pizzano still managed to top the league average production mark by 11%.

**Ceiling:** 1.0- to 1.5-win player
**Risk:** Low to Moderate to High
**MLB ETA:** 2019

## 12. Nick Neidert, RHP

**MiLB Rank: N/A**
**Position Rank: N/A**

| Born: 11/20/96 | Age: 19 | Bats: R | Top CALs: Edwin Linares, Adrian Rosario, |
|---|---|---|---|
| Height: 6-1 | Weight: 180 | Throws: R | Alejandro Barraza, Jeffry Antigua, Samuel Pastrone |

| YEAR | Age | Level | IP | W | L | ERA | FIP | K/9 | BB/9 | K% | BB% | HR/9 | LOB% |
|---|---|---|---|---|---|---|---|---|---|---|---|---|---|
| 2015 | 18 | R | 35.3 | 0 | 2 | 1.53 | 3.65 | 5.86 | 2.29 | 17.0% | 6.7% | 0.25 | 82.8% |

**Background:** Grabbed with the 60th overall pick last June, Seattle signed the prep right-hander to an over-slot $1.2 million bonus. Neidert tossed 35.1 innings in the Arizona Summer League during his debut, fanning 23 and walking nine en route to tallying a 1.63 ERA.

**Projection**: Per the usual, there's not a whole lot of data to go off, but Neidert looked solid during his debut last season. He did a tremendous job of limiting free passes and keeping the ball in the park, though the lone red flag was his inability to miss bats. He's a candidate to get pushed into the Midwest League in 2016.

**Ceiling:** Too Soon to Tell
**Risk:** N/A
**MLB ETA:** N/A

## 13. Tyler Marlette, C

MiLB Rank: N/A
Position Rank: N/A

| Born: 01/23/93 | Age: 23 | Bats: R | Top CALs: Michael Blanke, Luis Sierra, |
|---|---|---|---|
| Height: 5-11 | Weight: 195 | Throws: R | John Ryan Murphy Jair Fernandez, Luis Exposito |

| Season | Age | LVL | PA | 2B | 3B | HR | AVG | OBP | SLG | ISO | BB% | K% | wRC+ |
|---|---|---|---|---|---|---|---|---|---|---|---|---|---|
| 2013 | 20 | A | 297 | 17 | 2 | 6 | 0.304 | 0.367 | 0.448 | 0.144 | 8.1% | 17.8% | 132 |
| 2014 | 21 | A+ | 339 | 23 | 0 | 15 | 0.301 | 0.351 | 0.519 | 0.218 | 7.1% | 18.0% | 123 |
| 2015 | 22 | A+ | 162 | 5 | 1 | 5 | 0.216 | 0.284 | 0.365 | 0.149 | 7.4% | 21.6% | 77 |
| 2015 | 22 | AA | 188 | 13 | 1 | 3 | 0.258 | 0.298 | 0.393 | 0.135 | 5.3% | 16.5% | 94 |

**Background:** Ignoring his abbreviated debut in the Appalachian League in 2011, Marlette, the club's fifth round pick that year, has reeled off four consecutive seasons in which he's failed to top 90 games in a season. After hitting a solid – actually, borderline impressive .301/.351/.519 – in 81 games with High Desert, the system's former bandbox High Class A affiliate, Marlette looked absolutely overwhelmed in a return to the level, hitting a lowly .216/.284/.365 in 39 games with the Bakersfield, the system's *new*, less bandbox-y High Class A affiliate. But the front office opted to push the young catcher up to the Southern League in early June and...viola...his offense improved (thanks to his BABIP regressing back to normal). In 50 contests with the Generals, Marlette batted .258/.298/.393 en route to posting a 94 wRC+.

**Projection**: The conversation begins – and ends – with Marlette's ability to produce the long ball. There aren't too many backstops in the minors that offer up more power potential as a backstop. And just as an example, his career totals pro-rated over a standard 162-season are as follows: 39 doubles, two triples, and 18 homeruns. He shows a fringy average eye at the plate and strong contact numbers – especially for a power-hitter. I'm not particularly sold on the hit tool, but a big league catcher that can slug 15 homeruns and throw out about a third of attempted base stealers will certainly find a home in a lineup more often than not.

**Ceiling:** 1.5-win player
**Risk:** Moderate to High
**MLB ETA:** 2017

## 14. Dan Altavilla, RHP

MiLB Rank: N/A
Position Rank: N/A

| Born: 09/08/92 | Age: 23 | Bats: R | Top CALs: David Palladino, Rick Zagone, |
|---|---|---|---|
| Height: 5-11 | Weight: 200 | Throws: R | Shane Greene, Kevin Comer, Scott Barlow |

| YEAR | Age | Level | IP | W | L | ERA | FIP | K/9 | BB/9 | K% | BB% | HR/9 | LOB% |
|---|---|---|---|---|---|---|---|---|---|---|---|---|---|
| 2014 | 21 | A- | 66.0 | 5 | 3 | 4.36 | 4.84 | 9.00 | 4.36 | 22.5% | 10.9% | 0.95 | 73.9% |
| 2015 | 22 | A+ | 148.3 | 6 | 12 | 4.07 | 4.15 | 8.13 | 3.22 | 21.3% | 8.4% | 0.67 | 63.5% |

**Background:** Fun Fact: since Mercyhurst University's first MLB draft pick in 1983, right-hander John Costello, none of the school's other 13 draft picks have been selected before the 11th round – that is, until the Mariners grabbed Altavilla with the 141st overall pick in the 2014 draft. Fun Fact Part II: both of Mercyhurst University's first two picks in the draft, Costello, a 24th rounder, and David Lee, a 23rd round pick 12 years later, made it to the big leagues – albeit briefly. Anyway, after taking Altavilla in the fifth round two years ago, Seattle pushed the small right-hander straight into the Northwest League for his debut – an aggressive assignment he handled surprisingly well. In 66.0 innings with Everett he fanned 66 and walked 32. Last season Seattle pushed Altavilla straight into High Class A – completely bypassing the Midwest League – and, once again, Altavilla continued to exceed expectations: 148.1 IP, 134 K, 53 BB. He finished the year with a 4.15 FIP.

**Projection**:  Unsurprisingly, the 5-foot-11, 200-pound Altavilla wore down in the season's final weeks last year. He surrendered 27 earned runs over his final 36.0 innings. He was a bit homer-prone during his debut and got bit by the long ball quite often as well during his run with Bakersfield last year as well. So it's not surprising that his groundball rate was only 34.7% last season. He doesn't offer up a tremendous amount of upside in the rotation (especially given his small stature), maybe a fringy #5-type arm, but Altavilla could slide into a late-inning relief role in the coming years.

**Ceiling:** 1.0- to 1.5-win player
**Risk:** Moderate
**MLB ETA:** 2017

## 15. Austin Wilson, OF

**MiLB Rank:** N/A
**Position Rank:** N/A

| Born: 02/07/92 | Age: 24 | Bats: R | Top CALs: Justin Bass, Jeremy Baltz, |
|---|---|---|---|
| Height: 6-4 | Weight: 249 | Throws: R | Joe Holden, Jeremy Synan, Casey Craig |

| Season | Age | LVL | PA | 2B | 3B | HR | AVG | OBP | SLG | ISO | BB% | K% | wRC+ |
|---|---|---|---|---|---|---|---|---|---|---|---|---|---|
| 2013 | 21 | A- | 226 | 11 | 3 | 6 | 0.241 | 0.319 | 0.414 | 0.172 | 7.5% | 18.6% | 114 |
| 2014 | 22 | A | 299 | 17 | 3 | 12 | 0.291 | 0.376 | 0.517 | 0.226 | 8.7% | 21.7% | 153 |
| 2015 | 23 | A+ | 442 | 17 | 2 | 10 | 0.239 | 0.342 | 0.374 | 0.134 | 7.0% | 26.0% | 100 |

**Background:** A three-year starter who garnered plenty of recognition during his solid, though far from dominant, tenure at Stanford, Wilson left the school as a .294/.374/.463 hitter and a second round pick of the Mariners three years ago. Wilson, who was tabbed with the 49th overall selection, rebounded after a rough debut in the Northwest League to slug .291/.376/.517 with 17 doubles, three triples, and 12 homeruns in 72 games in 2014. Last season, though, his production took a noticeable dive as he moved up to the California League, hitting a perfectly league average – and equally uninspiring – .239/.342/.374 with 17 doubles, a pair of triples, 10 homeruns, and eight stolen bases (in 15 attempts). For his professional career, Wilson is sporting a .259/.350/.437 triple-slash line in his first 240 games.

**Projection:** Here's what I wrote in his pre-draft analysis three years ago:

*"He's well-built, but he's never really shown a whole lot of power. And for a player relegated to a corner outfield spot that's a bit concerning. He's more about projectability right now, maybe with 20/20 potential. He might be what Oakland's Michael Taylor was supposed to be, but there's more risk than normal."*

Well, unfortunately for the Mariners and Wilson, the former Cardinal is showing signs of developing into what Michael Taylor actually became: a minor league vagabond with a couple cups of bitter big league coffee. Wilson's power took a tremendous leap backward as he moved up to High Class A all the while taking his strikeout rate up into red flag territory. He looks like a fourth outfielder, nothing more.

**Ceiling:** 1.0- to 1.5-win player
**Risk:** Moderate
**MLB ETA:** 2018

## 16. Ryan Yarbrough, LHP

**MiLB Rank:** N/A
**Position Rank:** N/A

| Born: 12/31/91 | Age: 24 | Bats: R | Top CALs: Jeff Dietz, Nick Waechter, |
|---|---|---|---|
| Height: 6-5 | Weight: 205 | Throws: L | Chad Kerfoot, Casey Fien, Jerad Mccrummen |

| YEAR | Age | Level | IP | W | L | ERA | FIP | K/9 | BB/9 | K% | BB% | HR/9 | LOB% |
|---|---|---|---|---|---|---|---|---|---|---|---|---|---|
| 2014 | 22 | A- | 38.7 | 0 | 1 | 1.40 | 1.88 | 12.34 | 0.93 | 36.6% | 2.8% | 0.23 | 81.1% |
| 2015 | 23 | R | 10.0 | 0 | 0 | 1.80 | 1.52 | 11.70 | 0.90 | 32.5% | 2.5% | 0.00 | 58.3% |
| 2015 | 23 | A | 5.3 | 0 | 1 | 13.50 | 5.83 | 1.69 | 6.75 | 3.2% | 12.9% | 0.00 | 52.9% |
| 2015 | 23 | A+ | 81.3 | 4 | 7 | 3.76 | 3.93 | 8.19 | 1.99 | 21.1% | 5.1% | 0.77 | 65.5% |

**Background:** Originally drafted by the Brewers in the 20th round following his junior season at Old Dominion University, the big lefty, instead, opted to bypass a chance to join the organization and head back to school for his senior year. And the move paid off – kind of. Seattle grabbed the 6-foot-5, 205-pound southpaw in the fourth round two years ago, 111th overall, but signed him to a surprisingly low $40,000 pact. And just to put that into perspective: the Mariners signed their following pick in the 2014 draft, fifth rounder Dan Altavilla, to a deal worth about $300,000. Anyway, Yarbrough quickly exceeded those modest expectations once he entered pro ball. He tallied an aggregate 1.27 ERA in 42.2 innings, most of which was spent in the Northwest League, during his debut. And Yarbrough handled his aggressive promotion to the California League with relative ease last season as well. In an injury-shortened campaign – one that was interrupted with a lengthy stint on the DL courtesy of a groin injury – he tossed 81.1 innings with Bakersfield while fanning 21.1% and walking just 5.1% of the total batters he faced.

**Projection:** One of those fringy big league arms every organization has brewing in the lower levels of the minor leagues. Yarbrough isn't particularly overpowering, but he's performed as you'd expect as a polished collegiate senior. Yarbrough might be able to carve out a useful role as a #5/long man of the big league club's pen in the coming years.

**Ceiling:** Too Soon to Tell
**Risk:** N/A
**MLB ETA:** N/A

## 17. Jonathan Aro, RHP

**MiLB Rank:** N/A
**Position Rank:** N/A

| Born: 10/10/90 | Age: 25 | Bats: R | **Top CALs:** Brad Mills, Scott Maine, |
|---|---|---|---|
| Height: 6-0 | Weight: 175 | Throws: R | A.J. Griffin, Cory Mazzoni, Manny Parra |

| YEAR | Age | Level | IP | W | L | ERA | FIP | K/9 | BB/9 | K% | BB% | HR/9 | LOB% |
|---|---|---|---|---|---|---|---|---|---|---|---|---|---|
| 2013 | 22 | A- | 54.7 | 5 | 3 | 2.14 | 2.55 | 8.07 | 1.98 | 22.4% | 5.5% | 0.33 | 74.3% |
| 2014 | 23 | A | 67.3 | 1 | 3 | 2.27 | 3.04 | 9.89 | 2.94 | 26.7% | 7.9% | 0.40 | 68.3% |
| 2014 | 23 | A+ | 20.0 | 2 | 0 | 1.80 | 2.97 | 10.80 | 3.15 | 30.8% | 9.0% | 0.45 | 75.3% |
| 2015 | 24 | AA | 22.3 | 3 | 2 | 2.82 | 2.78 | 7.66 | 3.22 | 20.2% | 8.5% | 0.00 | 50.0% |
| 2015 | 24 | AAA | 51.7 | 0 | 1 | 3.14 | 2.42 | 9.23 | 1.74 | 25.6% | 4.8% | 0.35 | 72.0% |

**Background:** Despite making his professional debut at the age of 20 in the Dominican Summer League, Aro has quickly ascended through the minor league ranks, making his big league debut just four seasons later. The hard-throwing reliever opened up last season with Portland, which lasted all of eight games before getting the call to report to Pawtucket. He would then yo-yo between the International League and Boston for a couple stints the rest of the year. Aro finished his minor league season with 72 punch outs and just 18 free passes in 74 innings of work, and he would throw another 10.1 innings with the Sox, fanning eight and walking four. For his career he's averaged 8.7 strikeouts and just 2.2 walks per nine innings. Seattle acquired the hard-throwing hurler along with Wade Miley in exchange for Roenis Elias and Carson Smith.

**Projection**: Equipped with a low- to mid-90s fastball, a hard mid-80s slider, and a low 80s changeup; Aro is in the mold of relief pitchers of yesteryear – the ones that could last multiple innings per stint. Of his 41 combined appearances last season, he lasted at least one inning in 33 of those contests. Solid middle relief/long man prospect.

**Ceiling:** 1.0-win player
**Risk:** Low to Moderate
**MLB ETA:** Debuted in 2015

## 18. Paul Fry, LHP

**MiLB Rank:** #4
**Position Rank:** N/A

| Born: 07/26/92 | Age: 23 | Bats: L | **Top CALs:** Casey Mulligan, Dan Jennings, |
|---|---|---|---|
| Height: 6-0 | Weight: 190 | Throws: L | Derek Holland, Greg Mahle, Ian Kennedy |

| YEAR | Age | Level | IP | W | L | ERA | FIP | K/9 | BB/9 | K% | BB% | HR/9 | LOB% |
|---|---|---|---|---|---|---|---|---|---|---|---|---|---|
| 2013 | 20 | R | 34.0 | 2 | 3 | 4.50 | 4.04 | 9.00 | 2.12 | 23.0% | 5.4% | 0.79 | 62.0% |
| 2014 | 21 | A | 66.3 | 4 | 4 | 2.71 | 2.90 | 10.45 | 4.48 | 27.6% | 11.8% | 0.14 | 74.5% |
| 2015 | 22 | A+ | 55.0 | 4 | 3 | 2.13 | 2.16 | 11.45 | 2.29 | 31.5% | 6.3% | 0.00 | 76.2% |
| 2015 | 22 | AA | 25.0 | 0 | 2 | 1.80 | 1.18 | 15.48 | 3.60 | 39.8% | 9.3% | 0.00 | 81.8% |

**Background:** A 17th round pick out of St. Clair County Community College in 2013, Fry has been an absolute gem over the past two seasons. He dominated the Midwest League in 2014, posting a 77-to-33 strikeout-to-walk ratio in 66.0 innings, and he followed that up with an even better showing last season as he split time between the California and Southern Leagues. In 80.0 aggregate innings, the 6-foot, 190-pound southpaw fanned a mind-boggling 113, walked just 24, and tallied a barely-there 2.02 ERA. For his career, he's sporting a 224-to-65 strikeout-to-walk ratio with a 2.75 ERA in just 180.0 innings of work.

**Projection**: Absolute death on both right- and left-handers, Fry's knocking on the big league door just a couple seasons after the Mariners unearthed him late in the draft. He could step into the big league club's bullpen tomorrow and more than hold his own.

**Ceiling:** 1.0-win player
**Risk:** Low to Moderate
**MLB ETA:** 2016

## 19. Dylan Unsworth, RHP

**MiLB Rank:** N/A
**Position Rank:** N/A

| Born: 09/23/92 | Age: 23 | Bats: R | Top CALs: Todd Redmond, Chad Rogers, |
|---|---|---|---|
| Height: 6-1 | Weight: 175 | Throws: R | Ryan Merritt, Luis Cessa, Kendry Flores |

| YEAR | Age | Level | IP | W | L | ERA | FIP | K/9 | BB/9 | K% | BB% | HR/9 | LOB% |
|---|---|---|---|---|---|---|---|---|---|---|---|---|---|
| 2013 | 20 | R | 6.0 | 0 | 0 | 4.50 | 3.34 | 15.00 | 0.00 | 45.5% | 0.0% | 1.50 | 55.6% |
| 2013 | 20 | A | 66.0 | 4 | 1 | 2.32 | 2.43 | 6.27 | 0.27 | 18.4% | 0.8% | 0.27 | 73.4% |
| 2014 | 21 | A+ | 119.3 | 6 | 9 | 5.88 | 4.23 | 8.97 | 1.43 | 22.4% | 3.6% | 1.28 | 59.0% |
| 2015 | 22 | A+ | 40.7 | 1 | 3 | 3.32 | 3.26 | 9.74 | 0.89 | 26.8% | 2.4% | 0.89 | 66.0% |
| 2015 | 22 | AA | 66.3 | 4 | 7 | 4.34 | 3.62 | 6.92 | 1.76 | 18.1% | 4.6% | 0.81 | 63.8% |

**Background:** Signed out of Durban, South Africa, in late June 2010, Unsworth got off to an atrocious start last season in Class AA as he coughed up 11 runs in his first 11.0 innings of work. Seattle would eventually demote him down to Bakersfield after missing two weeks where his numbers rebounded nicely: 40.2 IP, 44 K, 4 BB. He would earn a promotion back to the Generals in mid-July and would finish his season on a high note, posting a 44-to-10 strikeout-to-walk ratio with a 3.42 ERA over his final 55.1 innings. For his career, Unsworth is sporting a 4.35 ERA while averaging 7.8 strikeouts and just 1.2 walks per nine innings.

**Projection**: Another sleeper-type arm the Mariners have brewing, Unsworth has an uncanny ability to pound the strike zone with high regularity – a skill that, undoubtedly, helps buoy his strikeout rates. He's not overpowering, but he generates a lot of groundballs, though he can be a bit homer prone at times. CAL seems to be a fan of sorts, comparing him to Luis Cessa and Kendry Flores. Think of Unsworth as a Josh Tomlin-type arm.

**Ceiling:** 1.0-win player
**Risk:** Low to Moderate
**MLB ETA:** 2017

## 20. Tyler Smith, SS

**MiLB Rank:** N/A
**Position Rank:** N/A

| Born: 07/01/91 | Age: 24 | Bats: R | Top CALs: Ryan Goins, Francisco Soriano, |
|---|---|---|---|
| Height: 6-0 | Weight: 195 | Throws: R | Brock Holt, Daniel Mayora, Andrew Romine |

| Season | Age | LVL | PA | 2B | 3B | HR | AVG | OBP | SLG | ISO | BB% | K% | wRC+ |
|---|---|---|---|---|---|---|---|---|---|---|---|---|---|
| 2013 | 22 | R | 233 | 16 | 3 | 2 | 0.320 | 0.394 | 0.460 | 0.140 | 7.7% | 13.7% | 147 |
| 2014 | 23 | A+ | 492 | 19 | 7 | 9 | 0.286 | 0.378 | 0.428 | 0.142 | 11.6% | 16.5% | 115 |
| 2015 | 24 | AA | 520 | 24 | 2 | 3 | 0.271 | 0.361 | 0.354 | 0.084 | 11.7% | 16.3% | 109 |

**Background:** An eighth round pick out of Oregon State University three years ago, Smith handled his aggressive promotion up to the California League in 2014, hitting a robust – and High Desert inflated – .286/.378/.428. He even earned a late season promotion to Jackson as well. Last season, Smith spent the year back in the Southern League where he hit a respectable .271/.361/.354 with 24 doubles, two triples, three homeruns, and 10 stolen bases. His overall production, according to *Weighted Runs Created Plus*, topped the league average mark by 9%.

**Projection**: Here's what I wrote in the *Bird Doggin' It* section in last year's book:

> *"Jumped from the Appalachian League to High Desert without missing a beat and capped off his season with a 20-game stint with Jackson. Career .294/.387/.433 hitter. Future utility guy."*

After his latest performance in Class AA Smith is one step closer to fulfilling his potential as a decent big league backup. He offers up gap-to-gap power, a tremendous eye at the plate, and a little bit of speed.

**Ceiling:** 1.0-win player
**Risk:** Low to Moderate
**MLB ETA:** 2016/2017

## 21. Tyler Pike, LHP

MiLB Rank: N/A
Position Rank: N/A

| Born: 01/26/94 | | Age: 22 | | Bats: L | | Top CALs: Victor Payano, Clevelan Santeliz, | | | | |
|---|---|---|---|---|---|---|---|---|---|---|
| Height: 6-0 | | Weight: 180 | | Throws: L | | Kyle Smit, Mark Diapoules, Fabian Williamson | | | | |

| YEAR | Age | Level | IP | W | L | ERA | FIP | K/9 | BB/9 | K% | BB% | HR/9 | LOB% |
|---|---|---|---|---|---|---|---|---|---|---|---|---|---|
| 2013 | 19 | A | 110.3 | 7 | 4 | 2.37 | 3.87 | 7.34 | 4.65 | 20.2% | 12.8% | 0.41 | 72.6% |
| 2014 | 20 | A+ | 61.3 | 2 | 4 | 5.72 | 6.60 | 8.36 | 6.75 | 19.9% | 16.1% | 1.47 | 68.4% |
| 2014 | 20 | AA | 49.0 | 3 | 4 | 7.35 | 5.74 | 6.06 | 6.24 | 14.0% | 14.4% | 0.92 | 62.0% |
| 2015 | 21 | A+ | 122.7 | 6 | 6 | 4.26 | 5.52 | 8.36 | 4.62 | 21.0% | 11.6% | 1.32 | 70.0% |
| 2015 | 21 | AA | 11.0 | 0 | 2 | 4.91 | 5.58 | 5.73 | 9.82 | 12.5% | 21.4% | 0.00 | 70.8% |

**Background:** Hailing from bright-and-sunny Winter Haven, Florida, home to 15 big league clubs during Spring Training, Seattle grabbed the 6-foot, 180-pound lefty in the third round four years ago. Pike breezed through his first two professional seasons with (seemingly) little disruption and fanfare – he posted a 57-to-21 strikeout-to-walk ratio in the Arizona Summer League during his debut and followed that up with a 2.37 ERA as a 19-year-old with Clinton in the Midwest League – but his production, and control, hit the skids in 2014. Pike got off to a superficially good start in 2014 as he allowed just four earned runs in his first 18.1 innings, but his control – or lack thereof – was a harbinger of things to come. After walking 12 in his first four starts, Pike would go on to average 6.5 free passes every nine innings that year – including 13 horrific starts in the Southern League. Last season the front office made the prudent decision and sent him back down the California League for the majority of the year where his control rebounded to its previous (subpar) standards.

**Projection**: Going all the way back to his sophomore season in the minor leagues, 2013, Pike's control has been no better than below-average at any point. He walked nearly 13% of the batters he faced in the Midwest League, followed that up with a worrisome 15.3% mark two years ago, and then right back down to 12.5% last season. Pike misses some bats, especially for a young left-hander, but he's now entering his age-22 season with a career walk rate north of 5.0 BB/9. He'll like get a couple more years to figure it out in the rotation, but he's more likely than not going to end up as either (A) career minor league vet or (B) a reliever.

**Ceiling:** 1.0- to 1.5-win player
**Risk:** Moderate to High
**MLB ETA:** 2018

## 22. Nick Wells, LHP

MiLB Rank: N/A
Position Rank: N/A

| Born: 02/21/96 | | Age: 20 | | Bats: L | | Top CALs: Jose Casilla, Christopher Hanna, | | | | |
|---|---|---|---|---|---|---|---|---|---|---|
| Height: 6-5 | | Weight: 185 | | Throws: L | | Robert Wilins, Braden Tullis, Maximo Valerio | | | | |

| YEAR | Age | Level | IP | W | L | ERA | FIP | K/9 | BB/9 | K% | BB% | HR/9 | LOB% |
|---|---|---|---|---|---|---|---|---|---|---|---|---|---|
| 2014 | 18 | R | 34.7 | 1 | 3 | 5.71 | 3.80 | 4.67 | 2.86 | 11.3% | 6.9% | 0.26 | 52.2% |
| 2015 | 19 | R | 32.0 | 1 | 2 | 4.78 | 4.24 | 8.72 | 3.09 | 23.3% | 8.3% | 1.13 | 67.8% |
| 2015 | 19 | A- | 18.0 | 1 | 0 | 1.00 | 2.66 | 8.00 | 2.00 | 24.6% | 6.2% | 0.00 | 81.8% |

**Background:** A third round pick out of Battlefield High School in Haymarket, Virginia, by the Blue Jays two years ago, Wells looks a bit overwhelmed – and ill-prepared – during his foray into professional baseball: in 34.2 innings in the Gulf Coast League he posted a pathetic 18-to-11 strikeout-to-walk ratio. So the club did the smart thing and bumped him up to the advanced rookie leagues where, low and behold, he fared much better. In seven starts with the Bluefield Blue Jays, the 6-foot-5, 185-pound pound southpaw averaged nearly a punch out per inning with solid average control. Toronto would flip the big lefty along with low level arm Jake Brentz and lefty reliever Rob Rasmussen for the services of veteran big leaguer Mark Lowe. Once in his new organization, Seattle would push Wells up to Everett for a quartet of appearances – three of which were starts – to close out his year.

**Projection**: Wells' strong showing last season helped answer some concerns about not missing many bats the previous year. He shows surprising control – especially for a big, young hurler in the low levels of the minors. And if the strikeout rates can remain north of 8.0 K/9, Wells might be able to carve out a big league career as a #4/#5-type starter. Not too shabby for 19.0 innings from Lowe, who signed with the Tigers in early December, by the way.

**Ceiling:** 1.0- to 1.5-win player
**Risk:** High
**MLB ETA:** 2019

## 23. Gareth Morgan, OF

MiLB Rank: N/A

Position Rank: N/A

| Born: 04/12/96 | Age: 20 | Bats: R | Top CALs: David Christensen, Maxwell Walla, |
| Height: 6-4 | Weight: 220 | Throws: R | Chevy Clarke, Jesus Gonzalez, Bladimir Franco |

| Season | Age | LVL | PA | 2B | 3B | HR | AVG | OBP | SLG | ISO | BB% | K% | wRC+ |
|--------|-----|-----|-----|----|----|----|------|------|------|------|------|------|------|
| 2014 | 18 | R | 178 | 8 | 1 | 2 | 0.148 | 0.244 | 0.252 | 0.103 | 9.0% | 41.0% | 52 |
| 2015 | 19 | R | 241 | 12 | 4 | 5 | 0.225 | 0.270 | 0.383 | 0.158 | 5.0% | 36.9% | 88 |

**Background:** Signed for nearly triple the allotted slot bonus as a 74th overall pick in the 2014 draft, Morgan inked his name on the dotted line for an even $2 million, the third highest contract given out to a Canadian-born draft selection. And that's where the good news ends, unfortunately, as his supreme talent has yet to be on full display in either of his first two seasons.

**Projection:** Like it or not, draft picks – in any sport – or more or less a gamble, a lottery. There are very few players that ultimately live up to their pre-draft expectations. And it's quickly looking like the Mariners won't get any return on the sizable investment in Morgan. At 6-foot-4 and 220 pounds, Morgan offers up plenty of power potential (as backed up by his .158 ISO last season), but he makes Russell Branyan's strikeout rates seem like a negligible statistic at this point.

He's fanned 162 times in his first 419 appearances, or about 39% of the time. Philadelphia's Nick Williams was able to eventually move beyond his problematic punch out rates, as did Texas' Lewis Brinson, but Morgan's overall production at this age pales in comparison. He's likely going to be a big draft bust, but he certainly has a lot of desirable tools. Maybe he eventually figures it out?

**Ceiling:** 1.5-win player
**Risk:** High
**MLB ETA:** 2019

## 24. Dylan Thompson, RHP

MiLB Rank: N/A

Position Rank: N/A

| Born: 09/16/96 | Age: 19 | Bats: L | Top CALs: Imani Abdullah, Austin Reed, |
| Height: 6-2 | Weight: 180 | Throws: R | Edgar Arredondo, Carlos Machorro, Dan Tuttle |

| YEAR | Age | Level | IP | W | L | ERA | FIP | K/9 | BB/9 | K% | BB% | HR/9 | LOB% |
|------|-----|-------|------|---|---|------|------|------|------|-------|-------|------|------|
| 2014 | 21 | A- | 26.3 | 3 | 2 | 8.89 | 4.88 | 6.15 | 4.78 | 13.4% | 10.5% | 0.34 | 49.5% |
| 2015 | 18 | R | 26.7 | 2 | 1 | 2.36 | 3.29 | 8.44 | 2.70 | 22.9% | 7.3% | 0.00 | 73.3% |
| 2015 | 22 | A- | 40.7 | 1 | 3 | 4.65 | 4.59 | 6.64 | 5.53 | 15.9% | 13.2% | 0.22 | 61.0% |
| 2015 | 22 | A+ | 2.7 | 0 | 0 | 0.00 | 5.28 | 3.38 | 6.75 | 9.1% | 18.2% | 0.00 | 33.3% |

**Background:** Another recipient of an over-slot bonus last June, the club grabbed the 6-foot-2, 180-pound right-hander in the fourth round. In 26.2 rookie ball innings, Thompson averaged 8.44 K/0 and just 2.70 BB/9 en route to tallying a 3.29 FIP.

**Projection:** Solid, impressive production from the big teenager out of Socastee High School in Myrtle Beach, South Carolina. Thompson originally committed to Coastal Carolina during his junior season. Per the usual, we'll take a wait-and-see approach until next year, but the early returns are quite favorable.

**Ceiling:** 1.0-win player
**Risk:** Moderate
**MLB ETA:** 2016

## 25. Mayckol Guaipe, RHP

MiLB Rank: N/A

Position Rank: N/A

| Born: 08/11/90 | Age: 25 | Bats: R | Top CALs: Robert Ray, Aaron Shafer, |
| Height: 6-4 | Weight: 235 | Throws: R | Brad Meyers, Jeff Manship, Rafael Dolis |

| YEAR | Age | Level | IP | W | L | ERA | FIP | K/9 | BB/9 | K% | BB% | HR/9 | LOB% |
|------|-----|-------|------|---|---|------|------|------|------|-------|-------|------|------|
| 2013 | 22 | A+ | 59.0 | 3 | 4 | 5.64 | 4.82 | 8.69 | 4.42 | 21.8% | 11.1% | 0.76 | 64.0% |
| 2014 | 23 | AA | 56.0 | 1 | 3 | 2.89 | 2.76 | 9.00 | 1.45 | 24.8% | 4.0% | 0.64 | 72.0% |
| 2015 | 24 | AAA | 47.0 | 0 | 4 | 2.87 | 3.60 | 6.89 | 1.91 | 18.6% | 5.2% | 0.57 | 77.1% |

**Background:** After spending parts of nine seasons in the minor leagues – including four stints in the Venezuelan Summer League – the 6-foot-4, 235-pound right-hander finally realized his professional dreams: the Mariners called him up four different times last season, the first coming on June 1st. For his minor league career, Guaipe is averaging 6.9 strikeouts and just 2.9 walk per nine innings, which spans, by the way, more than 200 career games, 35 of which were starts. The hard-throwing Venezuelan-born hurler posted a 22-to-13 strikeout-to-walk ratio in 26.2 innings of work with the big league club.

**Projection:** Grit, determination, and what one would assume a tremendous work ethic. Guaipe's fastball averaged a tick over 93 mph during his time with Seattle, complementing it with a low-80s slider, an upper-70s curveball, and a hard changeup. His control has been otherworldly over the past two seasons in the minors, so there's hope that last year's showing in the big leagues, 4.4 BB/9, will just be a speed bump. He could be a serviceable middle relief arm.

**Ceiling:** 0.5- to 1.0-win player
**Risk:** Low to Moderate
**MLB ETA:** Debuted in 2015

## Barely Missed:

- **Braden Bishop, OF** – Last year's third round pick out of the University of Washington, Bishop has a decent offensive foundation/approach at the plate. The problem, however, is that the little bit of power he flashed in college likely won't translate into the minors.

- **Cody Mobley, RHP** – He's likely a long shot to develop into anything serviceable at the big league club. He had a pretty solid showing in rookie league last June, so he at least should be watched in 2016.

## *Bird Doggin' It – Additional Prospects to Keep an Eye in 2016*

| Player | Age | POS | Notes |
|---|---|---|---|
| Matt Anderson | 24 | RHP | Not to be confused with the former Tigers hurlers, Anderson cobbled together a decent 63-to-23 strikeout-to-walk ratio in 67.0 innings working out of Jackson's bullpen last season. |
| Joe DeCarlo | 22 | 3B | Former 2012 second round pick was a power-first offensive stick, but he posted a career low .333 slugging percentage in his repeat of the Midwest League. |
| Brayan Hernandez | 18 | CF | Signed to a deal just shy of $2 million two years ago, Hernandez looked overmatched in his debut in the Dominican Summer League in 2015, hitting .224/.295/.328. |
| Drew Jackson | 22 | SS | Fifth round pick out of Stanford last year ripped through the Northwest League during his debut, slugging .358/.432/.447. |
| Luis Liberto | 20 | LF/RF | Young corner outfielder batted .260/.341/.453 with 10 doubles, five triples, five homeruns, and 10 stolen bases with Everett last season. |
| Marcus Littlewood | 24 | C | Former shortstop-turned-backstop won't hit much – or at all – but he's thrown out nearly 40% of would-be base stealers in his career. He may be able to carve out a career as a defensive-minded backstop. |
| Tim Lopes | 22 | 2B | The then-21-year-old infielder batted .276/.340/.362 with 27 doubles, four triples, two homeruns, and 35 stolen bases with Bakersfield. |
| Nelson Ward | 23 | 2B/SS | Hit a combined .278/.365/.436 between Clinton and Bakersfield last season. |
| Gianfranco Wawoe | 21 | SS | Shortstop hailing from Curacao batted .263/.325/.381 in the Midwest League last season. His overall production have been trending upward for the past couple of years; he could be a breakout prospect in 2016. |

**State of the Farm System:** The Cardinals' farm system improved quite a bit over the past season-plus, despite graduating the likes of Stephen Piscotty and Randal Grichuk, as well as dealing away promising southpaw Rob Kaminsky. But the majority of the club's most recognizable prospects took some big leaps forward.

Right-hander Alex Reyes, quite frankly, went from being a player with the potential to be one of the best right-handed prospects in baseball to actually becoming one of the best right-handed prospects in baseball. The then 20-year-old right-hander blew away the Florida State League (63.2 IP, 96 K, and 31 BB), continued to shine in Class AA (34.2 IP, 52 K, and 18 BB), and looked strong in the Arizona Fall League (15.0 IP, 14 K, 10 BB). Lucas Giolito and Tyler Glasnow are more promising right-handed MiLB'ers.

The club's 2014 first round pick, fellow right-hander Jack Flaherty, was absolutely brilliant in his first extended look at the minor leagues. In 95.0 innings with Peoria, he fanned 97 and walked just 31 en route to tallying a 2.84 ERA. Their other 2014 first round pick, former Florida State University stud Luke Weaver, made it look ridiculously easy in 19 stars with Palm Beach.

Southpaw Marco Gonzales still has backend starting caliber potential – even after his down season in 2015.

A couple other names to remember in the years moving forward: baby-faced shortstop Edmundo Sosa (.300/.369/.485 in the advanced rookie league), outfielder Magneuris Sierra, Nick Plummer, and right-hander Junior Fernandez.

And, of course, I'd be remiss to forget one of the club's sleeper arms in Andrew Morales.

| Rank | Name | POS |
|------|------|-----|
| 1 | Alex Reyes | RHP |
| 2 | Jack Flaherty | RHP |
| 3 | Luke Weaver | RHP |
| 4 | Marco Gonzales | LHP |
| 5 | Edmundo Sosa | SS |
| 6 | Magneuris Sierra | CF |
| 7 | Nick Plummer | CF |
| 8 | Junior Fernandez | RHP |
| 9 | Andrew Morales | RHP |
| 10 | Sam Tuivailala | RHP |
| 11 | Mariano Llorens | RHP |
| 12 | Jake Woodford | RHP |
| 13 | Tim Cooney | LHP |
| 14 | Anthony Garcia | LF/RF |
| 15 | Harrison Bader | LF/RF |
| 16 | Austin Gomber | LHP |
| 17 | Ronnie Williams | RHP |
| 18 | Corey Littrell | LHP |
| 19 | Zach Petrick | RHP |
| 20 | Charlie Tilson | CF |
| 21 | Trey Nielsen | RHP |
| 22 | Paul Dejong | 3B |
| 23 | Matt Bowman | RHP |
| 24 | Bryce Denton | 3B |
| 25 | Artie Reyes | RHP |

**Review of the 2015 Draft:** St. Louis grabbed prep players with four of their first five selections, taking outfielder Nick Plummer and right-hander Jake Woodford in the first round, third baseman Bryce Denton in the second, and right-hander Jordan Hicks a year later. The lone collegiate player taken was University of Florida overachiever Harrison Bader.

Plummer looked a bit sluggish in his debut, hitting .228/.379/.344 with eight doubles, five triples, one homerun, and eight stolen bases with the organization's Gulf Coast League affiliate. Woodford, on the other hand, handled his transition to the GCL with relative ease: 26.1 IP, 21 strikeouts, and just seven walks. And Denton made Plummer's showing look like Babe Ruth. Hicks did not appear in a professional game.

Bader, a career .312/.391/.466 hitter with the Gators, made quick work of the Midwest League (.301/.364/.505 with 11 doubles, a pair of triples, and nine homeruns).

# 1. Alex Reyes, RHP

| Born: 08/29/94 | Age: 21 | Bats: R | Top CALs: Shelby Miller, Luis Severino, |
|---|---|---|---|
| Height: 6-3 | Weight: 185 | Throws: R | Chance Adams, Lucas Giolito, Ben Hornbeck |

| YEAR | Age | Level | IP | W | L | ERA | FIP | K/9 | BB/9 | K% | BB% | HR/9 | LOB% |
|---|---|---|---|---|---|---|---|---|---|---|---|---|---|
| 2015 | 20 | R | 3.0 | 0 | 0 | 0.00 | 2.31 | 9.00 | 0.00 | 33.3% | 0.0% | 0.00 | 100.0% |
| 2015 | 20 | A+ | 63.7 | 2 | 5 | 2.26 | 1.75 | 13.57 | 4.38 | 36.6% | 11.8% | 0.00 | 75.9% |
| 2015 | 20 | AA | 34.7 | 3 | 2 | 3.12 | 2.32 | 13.50 | 4.67 | 36.4% | 12.6% | 0.26 | 67.4% |

**Background:** Just how good was Reyes last season? Well, he became the third hurler under the age of 21 to lead the entire minor leagues in strikeout percentage since 2006 (minimum 100 innings). The previous two times: Matt Moore (2009) and Tyler Glasnow (2013). The great differentiator between the trio of flame-throwers: Moore and Glasnow accomplished the feat in Low Class A whereas Reyes, the hard-throwing right-hander did so splitting his time between the Florida State and Texas Leagues. Signed out of the Dominican Republic after leaving the States to live with family, Reyes continued his assault on minor league bats last season; in 22 combined starts (101.1 innings of work), the 6-foot-3, 185-pound hurler fanned a mind-boggling 151 while walking 49. For his career, he's averaged nearly 12 punch outs and 4.6 walks per nine innings.

**Projection**: In last year's book I wrote:

> "The control/command still has quite a ways to go, but anytime a teenager fans nearly 30% of the batters he faced in full season ball is definitely noteworthy. The fact that his strikeout percentage ranks third in all of Low Class A is just an added bonus. Reyes is still a minimum of three years from making his big league debut, but there's mid- to front-of-the-rotation potential here."

His dominant showing in 2015 leaves little doubt that there are all kinds of ace potential brewing in his thunderbolt-slinging right arm. The control didn't take a step forward, but it's also important to remember that's he's facing more and more disciplined hitters at an accelerated pace. Meaning: it's not a concern yet.

Simply put, Reyes is just another high ceiling caliber arm in what's seemingly become an endless march up to the big league rotation, ultimately following in the footsteps of Michael Wacha, Carlos Martinez, Lance Lynn, Jaime Garcia, Trevor Rosenthal (he should be in the rotation), etc... True, legitimate #1 starting material – but the control/command needs to take that next step forward.

One final note: Reyes is a candidate for a late-season call up and/or could potentially be placed on the Earl Weaver break-em-in-easy pitching plan (i.e. having him develop in the big leagues as a reliever than transition him into a starting role in 2017).

**Ceiling:** 4.5-win player
**Risk:** Moderate
**MLB ETA:** 2016

# 2. Jack Flaherty, RHP

| Born: 10/15/95 | Age: 20 | Bats: R | Top CALs: Francis Martes, German Marquez, |
|---|---|---|---|
| Height: 6-4 | Weight: 205 | Throws: R | Chris Tillman, Kodi Medeiros, Jake Thompson |

| YEAR | Age | Level | IP | W | L | ERA | FIP | K/9 | BB/9 | K% | BB% | HR/9 | LOB% |
|---|---|---|---|---|---|---|---|---|---|---|---|---|---|
| 2014 | 18 | R | 22.7 | 1 | 1 | 1.59 | 2.54 | 11.12 | 1.59 | 29.8% | 4.3% | 0.40 | 67.8% |
| 2015 | 19 | A | 95.0 | 9 | 3 | 2.84 | 2.83 | 9.19 | 2.94 | 23.7% | 7.6% | 0.19 | 72.3% |

**Background:** "I was born in a cross-fire hurricane; And I howled at my ma in the driving rain; But it's all right now, in fact it's a gas! But it's all right. I'm jumping jack flash; It's a gas, gas, gas." – Jumping Jack Flash, The Rolling Stones. Let's be honest, I kind of shoehorned that reference in, but anytime you can quote the Stones you just go with it. Jumpin' Jack Flaherty's dominant debut momentum from 2014 spilled over into the Midwest League last season. In 19 starts with Peoria (95 innings), Flaherty posted another strong strikeout-to-walk ratio, 97-to-31, while finishing with the lowest FIP among all Midwest League hurlers with at least 90+ innings.

**Projection**: Flaherty's used to walking in some pretty impressive footsteps as he's followed Lucas Giolito and Max Fried as another first round pick hailing from Harvard-Westlake HS. And CAL seems to be a huge fan, linking him to a quintet of very promising arms: Francis Martes, German Marquez, Chris Tillman, Kodi Medeiros, and Jake Thompson.

Here's what I wrote about Flaherty in last year's book:

> *"Another one of the polished pitchers that the club tends to collect. Flaherty overpowered the Gulf Coast during his 22.2-inning stint last season and should follow in the footsteps of both Alex Reyes and Rob Kaminsky and head to Peoria as a 19-year-old."*

Test officially passed – with flying colors. Flaherty was simply too good, too polished for the Low Class A competition. He's likely going to pass the next test, High Class A, with a relative amount of ease as well and could potentially spend a decent amount of the 2016 season in Class AA. Not quite on the same level as Reyes, Flaherty's a nice ##2/3-type arm.

**Ceiling:** 3.0- to 3.5-win player
**Risk:** Moderate
**MLB ETA:** 2017

# 3. Luke Weaver, RHP

<u>MiLB Rank: #91</u>
<u>Position Rank: N/A</u>

| Born: 08/21/93 | Age: 22 | Bats: R | Top CALs: Scott Diamond, Ivan Pneyro, |
| Height: 6-2 | Weight: 170 | Throws: R | Jeff Marquez, Johnny Cueto, Francellis Montas |

| YEAR | Age | Level | IP | W | L | ERA | FIP | K/9 | BB/9 | K% | BB% | HR/9 | LOB% |
|------|-----|-------|-----|---|---|------|------|-------|-------|-------|-------|------|--------|
| 2014 | 20 | R | 6.0 | 0 | 0 | 0.00 | 1.01 | 13.50 | 0.00 | 40.9% | 0.0% | 0.00 | 100.0% |
| 2014 | 20 | A+ | 3.3 | 0 | 1 | 21.60 | 9.09 | 8.10 | 10.80 | 12.5% | 16.7% | 2.70 | 51.5% |
| 2015 | 21 | A+ | 105.3 | 8 | 5 | 1.62 | 2.28 | 7.52 | 1.62 | 20.7% | 4.5% | 0.17 | 72.7% |

**Background:** One of my favorite collegiate arms in the 2014 draft class. Weaver, no relation to either Jeff or Jerad, tumbled to the latter part of the first round following a noticeable downturn in production during his junior campaign at Florida State; his strikeout rate declined from 10.89 K/9 to a career worst 7.19 K/9. But the Cardinals, recognizing value better than any other team in the draft, stopped the rail-thin right-hander's slide and the rest – as they say – is history. Despite throwing just nine innings in his debut, Weaver found himself back in High Class A for the entire 2015 season. He would make 19 starts, throw 105.1 innings, fan 88, walk 19, and post a 2.28 FIP – one of the best marks among all MiLB hurlers with at least 90+ innings.

**Projection**: Just another fantastic draft selection, something that's merely commonplace for one of the best run organizations in baseball. Here's what I wrote about the 6-foot-2, 170-pounder former Seminole prior to the draft two years ago:

> *"Production-wise, Weaver falls into the same category as LSU right-hander Aaron Nola – extreme control pitchers that have historically exhibited some pretty strong strikeout numbers. The difference being, of course, Nola's maintained status quo whereas Weaver's taken a dramatic step backward, which adds some obvious risk associated with his draft selection.*
>
> *Another mid-rotation-type arm poised to move quickly through the minor leagues. His K-rate probably won't be as high as Nola's in the professional ranks, but it should settle in around 7.0 K/9.*
>
> *Plus, considering his slight build – he weighs only 170 pounds – there could be some room for velocity growth [if] he can add the right kind of weight."*

I was spot on with the punch out rate, at least for now, as he averaged a smidgeon over 7.5 strikeouts per nine innings last season. His groundball rates aren't as high as you would like, so his barely-there 0.17 HR-rate last season will likely climb up above the 0.60 HR/9 next year. I originally postulated that he'd ultimately become a #3 caliber arm, which still seams about right.

**Ceiling:** 2.5- to 3.0-win player
**Risk:** Moderate
**MLB ETA:** 2017

## 4. Marco Gonzales, LHP

**MiLB Rank: #109**

**Position Rank: N/A**

| | | | | | | |
|---|---|---|---|---|---|---|
| **Born:** 02/16/92 | | **Age:** 24 | | **Bats:** L | | **Top CALs:** Trevor Bell, Josh Lindblom, |
| **Height:** 6-1 | | **Weight:** 195 | | **Throws:** L | | Pedro Hernandez, Jake Odorizzi, Brett Oberholtzer |

| YEAR | Age | Level | IP | W | L | ERA | FIP | K/9 | BB/9 | K% | BB% | HR/9 | LOB% |
|---|---|---|---|---|---|---|---|---|---|---|---|---|---|
| 2013 | 21 | R | 6.7 | 0 | 0 | 5.40 | 1.81 | 13.50 | 4.05 | 31.3% | 9.4% | 0.00 | 54.6% |
| 2013 | 21 | A+ | 16.7 | 0 | 0 | 1.62 | 3.36 | 7.02 | 2.70 | 21.3% | 8.2% | 0.54 | 88.2% |
| 2014 | 22 | A+ | 37.7 | 2 | 2 | 1.43 | 2.67 | 7.65 | 1.91 | 21.3% | 5.3% | 0.24 | 83.7% |
| 2014 | 22 | AA | 38.7 | 3 | 2 | 2.33 | 2.19 | 10.71 | 2.33 | 28.8% | 6.3% | 0.47 | 72.1% |
| 2014 | 22 | AAA | 45.7 | 4 | 1 | 3.35 | 4.77 | 7.69 | 1.77 | 20.7% | 4.8% | 1.38 | 81.9% |
| 2015 | 23 | A+ | 4.7 | 0 | 0 | 0.00 | 1.45 | 7.71 | 0.00 | 20.0% | 0.0% | 0.00 | 60.0% |
| 2015 | 23 | AA | 6.7 | 0 | 0 | 0.00 | 1.95 | 8.10 | 0.00 | 22.2% | 0.0% | 0.00 | 100.0% |
| 2015 | 23 | AAA | 69.3 | 1 | 5 | 5.45 | 5.08 | 6.62 | 3.12 | 16.4% | 7.7% | 1.30 | 71.6% |

**Background:** The 19th overall pick out of Gonzaga University three years ago, Gonzales yo-yoed his way through practically every stop of the baseball chain. In between dealing with arm/shoulder issues last season, the 6-foot-1 southpaw began the year with six mostly disappointing starts in the PCL, hit the DL for nearly two months, got a pair of tune up games in both the Florida State and Texas League, made another seven starts – with mediocre results – with Springfield, got bumped for a quick one game jaunt with St. Louis, and finally back down to Springfield for one hideous appearance. Overall, Gonzales finished the minor league season with 80.2 innings, 61 punch outs, 24 walks, and an unsightly 4.69 ERA – a rather stark contrast to his wildly successful sophomore campaign two years ago (122.0, 117 K, 27 BB, and a 2.43 between High Class A, Class AA, and the PCL).

**Projection:** Last year was more or less a lost season for Gonzales as injuries – and a subsequent DL vacation – sapped his effectiveness. A silver lining of sorts, though: his average fastball velocity during his MLB debut in 2014 was 89.5 mph; his average heater in his lone start with St. Louis in early September was 89.4 mph.

Even when he's healthy Gonzales will never be mistaken for a dominant frontend starter, but there's some significant MLB value to be extracted from his left arm – as long as it doesn't spontaneously combust. He shows above-average control/command with an average-ish ability to miss the barrel of the bat.

Here's what I wrote prior to the draft:

> "More finesse than anything else, Gonzales grades outs as a mid- to late-first rounder. His work with Team USA [in 2012] adds to his impressive resume (29 Ks in 22 IP). One red flag, however, is the amount of extra-base hits he's surrendered through his 106 innings: 17 doubles and a pair of triples. He's a good #4-type guy."

Again, assuming the arm doesn't fall off, he still remains a safe bet to reach that potential.

**Ceiling:** 2.0- to 2.5-win player
**Risk:** Low to Moderate
**MLB ETA:** Debuted in 2014

## 5. Edmundo Sosa, SS

**MiLB Rank: #183**

**Position Rank: N/A**

| | | | | | | |
|---|---|---|---|---|---|---|
| **Born:** 03/06/96 | | **Age:** 20 | | **Bats:** R | | **Top CALs:** Marco Hernandez, Jorge Polanco, |
| **Height:** 5-11 | | **Weight:** 170 | | **Throws:** R | | Pablo Reyes, Alec Henson, Marcos Almonte |

| Season | Age | LVL | PA | 2B | 3B | HR | AVG | OBP | SLG | ISO | BB% | K% | wRC+ |
|---|---|---|---|---|---|---|---|---|---|---|---|---|---|
| 2013 | 17 | R | 198 | 8 | 3 | 3 | 0.314 | 0.396 | 0.450 | 0.136 | 11.1% | 7.6% | 150 |
| 2014 | 18 | R | 233 | 8 | 5 | 1 | 0.275 | 0.341 | 0.377 | 0.101 | 7.7% | 12.4% | 109 |
| 2015 | 19 | R | 223 | 8 | 4 | 7 | 0.300 | 0.369 | 0.485 | 0.185 | 7.2% | 17.0% | 137 |

**Background:** Originally signed out of Panama for a pretty hefty sum, $425,000, the equivalent of third or fourth round money, Sosa had a strong showing in the Dominical Summer League during his pro debut, slugging .314/.396/.450 with 14 extra-base hits in 47 games. The organization promoted him stateside the following year, 2014, and the 5-foot-11, 170-pound shortstop adapted well; he batted .275/.341/.377 with another 14 extra-base knocks in 52 games. St. Louis strayed a bit from their typical push-em-up, push-em-through development plan with promising young players as they promoted Sosa from the Gulf Coast to the Appalachian League last season. And once again, he continued to hit: .300/.369/.485 with 19 hits going for extra-bases, including a career best seven homeruns.

**Projection:** Sosa failed to crack my Top 20 list for the organization last season, but he earned a honorable mention of sorts by being listed in the *Bird Doggin' It* section. I wrote, "Small teenaged shortstop held his own in the Gulf Coast League [prior to] earning a three-game stint [with]

State College. Decent tools sans power." Well, the power took a pretty important developmental step forward last season as he set a career best with a .185 Isolated Power. He's not overly quick, more sneaky than anything. Decent eye at the plate, strong contact skills, and a potentially above-average hit tool. If he wasn't ready for full season ball last year, he is now.

**Ceiling:** 2.0- to 2.5-win player
**Risk:** Moderate to High
**MLB ETA:** 2018

## 6. Magneuris Sierra, CF

**MiLB Rank: #185**
**Position Rank: N/A**

| Born: 04/07/96 | Age: 20 | Bats: L | **Top CALs:** Elvis Escobar, Jhohan Acevedo, |
| Height: 5-11 | Weight: 160 | Throws: L | Cesar Puello, Mitch Dening, Harold Ramirez |

| Season | Age | LVL | PA | 2B | 3B | HR | AVG | OBP | SLG | ISO | BB% | K% | wRC+ |
|--------|-----|-----|-----|----|----|----|-------|-------|-------|-------|-------|-------|------|
| 2013 | 17 | R | 252 | 6 | 3 | 1 | 0.269 | 0.361 | 0.340 | 0.071 | 11.5% | 13.1% | 115 |
| 2014 | 18 | R | 223 | 12 | 3 | 2 | 0.386 | 0.434 | 0.505 | 0.119 | 7.2% | 13.5% | 170 |
| 2015 | 19 | R | 239 | 8 | 0 | 3 | 0.315 | 0.371 | 0.394 | 0.079 | 7.9% | 17.6% | 117 |
| 2015 | 19 | A | 190 | 1 | 3 | 1 | 0.191 | 0.219 | 0.247 | 0.056 | 3.7% | 27.4% | 33 |

**Background:** After slapping around the Gulf Coast League in epic fashion two years ago (.386/.434/.505), the Midwest League pitchers decided to hit back in 2015 – in a *huge* way. St. Louis aggressively – and rightly so – pushed the Dominican-born center fielder into full season ball, but after 51 putrid games (.191/.219/.247) the club decided to put Sierra's triple-slash line out of its misery and push him back down to the Appalachian League. His numbers saw a noticeable uptick (no surprise) as he slugged .315/.371/.394 with eight doubles, three homeruns, and 15 stolen bases in 239 trips to the plate. For his young career, Sierra is hitting a solid .392/.352/.727. If you subtract his terrible showing with Peoria, his career line jumps to a far, far more impressive .349/.402/.447.

**Projection**: There's a lot to like about the package: the hit tool has a chance to be the best in the system; the power could jump up into 15-HR territory as his lean 160-pound frame fills out, and he's quick enough to swipe 30+ bags in a season. I originally pegged Sierra as a potential fourth outfielder in last year's book, but I'd bump that up to a better-than-average regular – though there's some risk given his youth and failure in Class A.

**Ceiling:** 2.5-win player
**Risk:** Moderate to High
**MLB ETA:** 2018

## 7. Nick Plummer, CF

**MiLB Rank: #190**
**Position Rank: N/A**

| Born: 07/31/96 | Age: 19 | Bats: L | **Top CALs:** Lane Thomas, Michael Crouse, |
| Height: 5-10 | Weight: 200 | Throws: L | Trenton Kemp, Sauris Mejia, Btrett Phillips |

| Season | Age | LVL | PA | 2B | 3B | HR | AVG | OBP | SLG | ISO | BB% | K% | wRC+ |
|--------|-----|-----|-----|----|----|----|-------|-------|-------|-------|-------|-------|------|
| 2015 | 18 | R | 228 | 8 | 5 | 1 | 0.228 | 0.379 | 0.344 | 0.117 | 17.1% | 24.6% | 127 |

**Background:** The club's first pick last June, 23rd overall, Plummer hails from the same alma mater as big league infielder D.J. LeMahieu (Brother Rice High School in Bloomfield, MI). The toolsy center fielder got off to a rocky start in the Gulf Coast League, but managed to pick it up down the stretch as he batted .299/.411/.455 with three doubles, three triples, and one homerun in his final 21 games.

**Projection**: Per the usual, there's not a whole helluva lot to go off of here. As typically of a lot of high round prepsters, Plummer walked at an enormous clip, 17.1%, and he also fanned a whole lot too (24.6%). And despite the overall poor triple-slash line, he's probably shown the organization enough to start the year in Low Class A.

**Ceiling:** Too Soon to Tell
**Risk:** N/A
**MLB ETA:** N/A

## 8. Junior Fernandez, RHP

MiLB Rank: #196
Position Rank: N/A

| Born: 03/02/97 | Age: 19 | Bats: R | Top CALs: Fernando Romero, Jacob Partridge, |
| Height: 6-1 | Weight: 180 | Throws: R | Brad Hand, Jose Perdomo, Angel Reyes |

| YEAR | Age | Level | IP | W | L | ERA | FIP | K/9 | BB/9 | K% | BB% | HR/9 | LOB% |
|------|-----|-------|-----|---|---|------|------|-------|------|-------|------|------|-------|
| 2014 | 17 | R | 28.0 | 0 | 5 | 5.79 | 4.72 | 4.18 | 3.86 | 10.5% | 9.7% | 0.32 | 47.1% |
| 2015 | 18 | R | 51.0 | 3 | 2 | 3.88 | 2.21 | 10.24 | 2.65 | 26.5% | 6.9% | 0.00 | 63.5% |
| 2015 | 18 | A+ | 6.7 | 0 | 0 | 1.35 | 2.57 | 6.75 | 2.70 | 17.9% | 7.1% | 0.00 | 80.0% |

**Background:** File this one under names to remember. Fernandez, a 6-foot-1, 180-pound right-hander, signed out of the Dominican Republic for a cool $400,000 in early July a couple years back. And his initial return on investment two years ago left a lot to be desired: the then-17-year-old hurled 28.0 innings in the Dominican Summer League, punching out 13 and walking 12. But his development took a *gigantic* leap forward in 2015. The organization promoted Fernandez stateside, pushing him into the Gulf Coast, and in 13 games he averaged an impressive 10.2 K/9 and just 2.6 BB/9. The best part: St. Louis had Fernandez bypass the Appalachian, New York-Penn, and Midwest Leagues and sent him directly to Palm Beach for two games to close out a wildly successful year.

**Projection:** Look, Fernandez is 85.2 innings into his pro career, so a lot of things could spiral off into different directions. But the Cards' front office clearly sees something special in the teenaged right-hander, evidenced by having him spend his last two games in the Florida State League. He's a big time power arm with the uncanny ability to hit the zone on a regular basis. Here's one of the bolder predictions I will make in this year's book: Junior Fernandez, a soon-to-be 19-year-old right-hander with 85.2 professional innings under his belt, is the best pitching prospect you've never heard of. Yet.

**Ceiling:** Too Soon to Tell
**Risk:** N/A
**MLB ETA:** N/A

## 9. Andrew Morales, RHP

MiLB Rank: #224
Position Rank: N/A

| Born: 01/16/93 | Age: 23 | Bats: R | Top CALs: Tyler Robertson, Donovan Hand, |
| Height: 6-0 | Weight: 185 | Throws: R | Eddie Mckiernan, Nick Additon, Gary Galvez |

| YEAR | Age | Level | IP | W | L | ERA | FIP | K/9 | BB/9 | K% | BB% | HR/9 | LOB% |
|------|-----|-------|-------|---|---|------|------|-------|------|-------|------|------|-------|
| 2014 | 21 | R | 5.0 | 0 | 1 | 3.60 | 5.51 | 10.80 | 5.40 | 28.6% | 14.3% | 1.80 | 55.6% |
| 2014 | 21 | A+ | 7.3 | 1 | 0 | 1.23 | 2.16 | 7.36 | 0.00 | 24.0% | 0.0% | 0.00 | 66.7% |
| 2015 | 22 | AA | 129.7 | 5 | 8 | 5.00 | 4.85 | 5.90 | 3.19 | 14.4% | 7.8% | 1.18 | 70.7% |

**Background:** In all honesty, Morales was probably – with an almost 100% certainty – my favorite collegiate prospect in the 2014 draft. Just a quick backstory: Morales, 6-foot-nothing, 190-pound-nothing right-hander out of Los Angeles, bypassed the typical four-year school route and headed to tiny Rio Hondo Community College for two years before transferring to – and later dominating for – UC Irvine. He spent two years at the Big West school where he went 21 and 2 with a composite 1.68 ERA in 231 innings. St. Louis grabbed the overlooked right-hander in the second round, had him toss five innings in the Gulf Coast and another 7.1 in the Florida State League during his debut. Then they pushed him directly into the Texas League last season where his overall numbers – 129.2 innings, 5.9 K/9 and 3.19 BB/9 – look far less impressive, until you factor in the his lack of pro experience.

**Projection:** I remain quite smitten with Morales as a pitching prospect. There aren't too many hurlers that could essentially make a successful leap from the amateur level straight into Class AA, the level that typically pushes the prospect pendulum one way or the other. And despite some rather lackluster overall numbers with Springfield, Morales certainly had his moments.

- His production in April, July, and September: 65 innings, 3.05 ERA, 46 K, and 17 BB
- His production in May, June, and August: 64.2 innings, 6.96 ERA, 39 K, and 29 BB

Here's what I wrote before the 2014 draft:

> *"I hate – HATE – throwing around terms like "winner" or "grinder" or "dirt bag". But if they fit any amateur player in the country it is Morales.*
>
> *The strikeout rate is going to hover around 7.5- to 8.0 K/9 in the big leagues; the control is [an] above-average skill, and he's done a solid job keeping the ball in the ballpark. Morales is the type of guy that flies under the radar and then everyone steps back to ask, 'Where'd this guy come from?'" Mid rotation arm.*

*He's going to lose a lot of leverage in signing a deal because he's a senior, so a team could force him into taking a below slot deal – in order to save money for other picks – in exchange for a high selection.*

*Love the potential, though."*

Ditto. I think he's a #4-type arm. Very, very underrated. Watch for a big bounce-back season now that he has his professional feet under him. Final thought: the homerun rate should regress to about 0.80 HR/9; his groundball rate, while not above-average, was still a touch over 40%.

**Ceiling:** 1.5- to 2.0-win player
**Risk:** Moderate
**MLB ETA:** 2016

## 10. Sam Tuivailala, RHP

**MiLB Rank: #226**
**Position Rank: N/A**

| Born: 10/19/92 | Age: 23 | Bats: R | Top CALs: Casey Mulligan, Bruce Rondon, |
|---|---|---|---|
| Height: 6-3 | Weight: 195 | Throws: R | Carlos Rodon, Shawn Armstrong, Blake Snell |

| YEAR | Age | Level | IP | W | L | ERA | FIP | K/9 | BB/9 | K% | BB% | HR/9 | LOB% |
|---|---|---|---|---|---|---|---|---|---|---|---|---|---|
| 2013 | 20 | A | 35.3 | 0 | 3 | 5.35 | 2.55 | 12.74 | 5.09 | 31.5% | 12.6% | 0.00 | 60.0% |
| 2014 | 21 | A+ | 37.7 | 0 | 1 | 3.58 | 1.93 | 15.29 | 4.30 | 39.5% | 11.1% | 0.24 | 69.3% |
| 2014 | 21 | AA | 21.0 | 2 | 1 | 2.57 | 1.69 | 12.86 | 3.86 | 34.1% | 10.2% | 0.00 | 71.4% |
| 2014 | 21 | AAA | 1.3 | 0 | 0 | 0.00 | 1.45 | 20.25 | 0.00 | 50.0% | 0.0% | 0.00 | 100.0% |
| 2015 | 22 | AAA | 45.0 | 3 | 1 | 1.60 | 4.20 | 8.60 | 5.20 | 22.9% | 13.8% | 0.40 | 88.6% |

**Background:** Owner of quite possibly one of the most fun last names to say aloud, Tuivailala – or pronounced too-ee-vai-lull-lah, according to Baseball Reference – spent the majority of 2015 yo-yoing between Memphis and St Louis as he made 43 appearances in the PCL and another 14 at the big league level. Looking specifically at the minor league level, Tuivailala, the name sort of just rolls off the tongue, continued to battle control issues as he failed to average a whiff per inning for the first time in his professional career. In fact, he averaged more than 14 K/9 during the previous three seasons, but only fanned 8.6 K/9 last year. His work with the big league club, though, is more indicative of his actual talent level: he posted a 20-to-8 strikeout-to-walk ratio in 14.2 innings.

**Projection:** Tuivailala first cracked the organization's Top 10 prospects during my mid-season update in 2014, writing at that time: "A converted third baseman, [he] has fanned 67 of the total 168 batters he's faced. A late-inning, high impact reliever waiting to happen. And soon."

Well, Tuivailala is likely as ready as he's ever going to be. Armed with an upper 90s heater, the 6-foot-3 right-hander will never be mistaken for Greg Maddux on the hill, but his ability to rack up tons of strikeouts should help nullify some below-average control. And just for fun: his 30.8% punch out rate nearly missed the top 30 among all big leaguer arms with at least 10 innings pitched last year. Not sure he ever ascends to elite relief status, but he's got more than a puncher's chance.

**Ceiling:** 1.5- to 2.0-win player
**Risk:** Moderate
**MLB ETA:** Debuted in 2014

## 11. Dixon Llorens, RHP

**MiLB Rank: #227**
**Position Rank: N/A**

| Born: 11/18/92 | Age: 23 | Bats: R | Top CALs: Joey Krehbiel, Adrian Rosario, |
|---|---|---|---|
| Height: 5-10 | Weight: 170 | Throws: R | Keith Butler, Clayton Schrader, Blake Snell |

| YEAR | Age | Level | IP | W | L | ERA | FIP | K/9 | BB/9 | K% | BB% | HR/9 | LOB% |
|---|---|---|---|---|---|---|---|---|---|---|---|---|---|
| 2013 | 20 | A | 47.3 | 3 | 3 | 2.85 | 2.35 | 13.50 | 4.37 | 36.0% | 11.7% | 0.38 | 77.5% |
| 2014 | 21 | A+ | 43.7 | 0 | 1 | 2.06 | 2.57 | 15.25 | 5.56 | 40.9% | 14.9% | 0.21 | 80.2% |
| 2014 | 21 | AA | 4.3 | 0 | 0 | 12.46 | 5.89 | 12.46 | 14.54 | 25.0% | 29.2% | 0.00 | 53.9% |
| 2015 | 22 | A | 19.0 | 0 | 1 | 7.11 | 2.55 | 10.89 | 4.26 | 24.7% | 9.7% | 0.00 | 51.4% |

**Background:** Honestly, Lloren's stat line from the Midwest League last season is one of the most bizarre I've ever laid eyes too. It's actually a bit mindboggling as to how *unlucky* the former late-round pick was. In typical Llorens fashion he punched out a *ton* of guys, nearly a quarter of all the hitters he faced, walked more than his fair share, and posted a sub-3.00 FIP, the fifth time he's accomplished that feat. Now the weird part: his ERA was over 7.00 – well, 7.11 to be exact. And this comes without issuing a homerun! Of course, when opponents can hang a .417 BABIP around a pitcher's neck will certainly help do that. Llorens looked to be on the fast-track to the major leagues a couple seasons ago, mowing down whoever was in his way. He posted a 62-to-11 strikeout-to-walk ratio as a 19-year-old splitting his time between Johnson City and Quad Cities. He then dominated the Midwest League for the entire next season. But the wheels on the Llorens Express wobbled quite a bit in 2014 as he battled control issues. A hip injury limited him to just 20 games last season.

**Projection**: I spelled it out in black-and-white in last year's book, writing:

> "Llorens, who came stateside from Cuba via a visa lottery program when he was 10-years-old, has been as dominant as any reliever in the minor leagues since 2012, though he isn't without his flaws. Despite the awe-inspiring strikeout numbersm Llorens control/command has slowly been creeping up as he's jumped from level-to-level, going from 2.8 BB/9 to 4.4 BB/9 a year later and a career high 5.6 BB/9 during his 43.2 innings in Palm Beach. The potential to develop into a future closer is there, where he can reverse the trend and find the plate more often is open for discussion."

I would've loved to have followed that up this year by writing that the small right-hander took a huge developmental step forward last season but it just didn't happen. If anything, he maintained status quo despite bouncing back down to the Midwest League for the third time in his brief career. But, again, any early 20s hurler that's sporting a career strikeout percentage over 37% - yes, 37-freaking-percent – will be given every single opportunity to find his way. Here's hoping he does…

**Ceiling:** 1.5- to 2.0-win player
**Risk:** Moderate
**MLB ETA:** 2017

## 12. Jake Woodford, RHP

**MiLB Rank:** N/A
**Position Rank:** N/A

| Born: 10/28/96 | Age: 19 | Bats: R | Top CALs: Bryan Dobzanski, Adonis Medina, |
| Height: 6-4 | Weight: 210 | Throws: R | Lino Martinez, Marcus Walden, Matt Magil |

| YEAR | Age | Level | IP | W | L | ERA | FIP | K/9 | BB/9 | K% | BB% | HR/9 | LOB% |
|------|-----|-------|------|---|---|------|------|------|------|------|------|------|------|
| 2015 | 18 | R | 26.3 | 1 | 0 | 2.39 | 3.23 | 7.18 | 2.39 | 18.8% | 6.3% | 0.34 | 74.4% |

**Background:** The club's other first round selection last June, Woodford teamed with fellow 2015 first rounder Kyle Tucker, the fifth overall pick, to give H.B. Plant High School one helluva dynamic duo. The 6-foot-4 right-hander tossed 26.1 innings in the Gulf Coast during his debut, punching out 21 and walking seven. He finished the year with a 2.39 ERA and a 3.23 FIP.

**Projection**: Not quite along the same lines as 2014 first rounder pick Jack Flaherty. Woodford was more or less the typical prep arm grabbed early by the Cardinals: he missed some bats, didn't walk a whole lot of hitters, and held his own in the lowest levels. He's proven he's ready for full season ball.

**Ceiling:** Too Soon to Tell
**Risk:** N/A
**MLB ETA:** N/A

## 13. Tim Cooney, LHP

**MiLB Rank:** N/A
**Position Rank:** N/A

| Born: 12/19/90 | Age: 25 | Bats: L | Top CALs: Zach Stewart, Brett Oberholtzer, |
| Height: 6-3 | Weight: 195 | Throws: L | Robert Rohrbaugh, Trevor Bell, Randy Wells |

| YEAR | Age | Level | IP | W | L | ERA | FIP | K/9 | BB/9 | K% | BB% | HR/9 | LOB% |
|------|-----|-------|-------|----|----|------|------|------|------|------|------|------|------|
| 2013 | 22 | A+ | 36.0 | 3 | 3 | 2.75 | 2.74 | 5.75 | 1.00 | 15.8% | 2.7% | 0.25 | 69.7% |
| 2013 | 22 | AA | 118.3 | 7 | 10 | 3.80 | 2.43 | 9.51 | 1.37 | 25.2% | 3.6% | 0.61 | 67.7% |
| 2014 | 23 | AAA | 158.0 | 14 | 6 | 3.47 | 4.93 | 6.78 | 2.68 | 18.0% | 7.1% | 1.20 | 79.9% |
| 2015 | 24 | AAA | 88.7 | 6 | 4 | 2.74 | 4.17 | 6.39 | 1.62 | 18.6% | 4.7% | 0.91 | 71.6% |

**Background:** Statistically speaking, Cooney looked like a budding ace a couple years back after his first – and only – sprint through the Texas League. Cooney, a 6-foot-3 left-hander out of Wake Forest, began the 2013 with six moderately decent starts with Palm Beach in the Florida State League, tossing 35 innings while fanning 23 and walking only four. But, for whatever reason, his K-rate *exploded* once he got Springfield. After averaging just a tick below 6.5 strikeouts per nine innings in his first 91.2 innings, the finesse lefty whiffed 125 in 118.1 in Class A, or 9.5 K/9, or over 25% of the total batters he faced. Since then, however, that total's normalized to his previous career norm as he's spent the majority of the past two seasons fine-tuning his approach in the PCL. Last year Cooney made 14 starts with Memphis, throwing 88.1 innings while fanning 18.6% and walking 4.7% of the batters he faced. He also made another six starts with St. Louis (31.1 IP, 8.33 K/9, 2.87 BB/9, and a 3.58 FIP).

**Projection**: CAL has the right idea, linking Cooney a trio of serviceable big league arms in Zach Stewart, Brett Oberholtzer, and Randy Wells. The former Demon Deacon showed a typical average four-pitch mix during his debut with St. Louis: an upper 80s fastball, low 80s slider, curveball, and changeup. The amount of bats he missed with the Cardinals won't be repeated, though his K- and BB-rates should fall to about 7.2 and 3.0 next year. He's a nice, replaceable #4/#5-type arm.

**Ceiling:** 1.5-win player
**Risk:** Low to Moderate
**MLB ETA:** Debuted in 2015

# 14. Anthony Garcia, LF/RF

<u>MiLB Rank: N/A</u>

<u>Position Rank: N/A</u>

| Born: 01/04/92 | Age: 24 | Bats: R | **Top CALs:** Michael Burgess, John Tolisano, |
|---|---|---|---|
| Height: 6-0 | Weight: 180 | Throws: R | Jose Osuna, Edgardo Baez, Eric Campbell |

| Season | Age | LVL | PA | 2B | 3B | HR | AVG | OBP | SLG | ISO | BB% | K% | wRC+ |
|---|---|---|---|---|---|---|---|---|---|---|---|---|---|
| 2013 | 21 | A+ | 386 | 16 | 1 | 13 | 0.217 | 0.286 | 0.383 | 0.165 | 6.7% | 24.6% | 90 |
| 2014 | 22 | A+ | 391 | 20 | 2 | 10 | 0.227 | 0.320 | 0.385 | 0.157 | 9.7% | 16.4% | 103 |
| 2015 | 23 | AA | 346 | 22 | 0 | 11 | 0.285 | 0.400 | 0.476 | 0.191 | 13.0% | 15.6% | 149 |
| 2015 | 23 | AAA | 64 | 4 | 1 | 2 | 0.276 | 0.344 | 0.483 | 0.207 | 9.4% | 17.2% | 119 |

**Background:** It took a couple seasons – and a whole helluva lot of elbow grease – but Garcia's polished his prospect status enough to give it back some of the sheen he lost. In the beginning Garcia did nothing but hit since entering pro ball, recording wRC+ totals of 137, 149, and 143 as he worked his way through the rookie leagues and Low Class A. And then...his stock plummeted as stopped hitting. After posting back-to-back triple-slash lines of .308/.407/.527 and .280/.354/.525, Garcia's production precipitously dropped to a lowly .217/.286/.383 mark in High Class A; and he faired only slightly better in his follow up in the Florida State League, hitting .227/.320/.385. But he seemingly regained his stroke after the club pushed him up to Class AA for the 2015. In 87 games with Springfield, he slugged an impressive .285/.400/.476 with 22 doubles and 11 homeruns; his 149 wRC+ total ranks fifth among all Class AA hitters under the age of 23 with 300 or more plate appearances.

**Projection**: So where do we go from here? Is Garcia's true production level (A) the hitter that's posted a wRC+ mark above 140 at three different levels or (B) the one that batted .220-ish in two go-rounds in the Florida State League? Let's delve into the numbers...

Garcia's walk rate/patience at the plate has typically ranged from good to very good – even in the down years; the same could be said for his in-game power as well. His strikeout rates has never ballooned over 25% – another positive – and has settled around the 17% more or less. The lone red flag, or so it seems, is the hit tool

Let's continue to dive, shall we?

Here's a list of Garcia's BABIPs since 2011:

| Age | Level | BABIP | wRC+ |
|---|---|---|---|
| 19 | R | 0.352 | 149 |
| 20 | A | 0.338 | 143 |
| 21 | A+ | 0.257 | 90 |
| 22 | A+ | 0.252 | 103 |
| 23 | AA | 0.317 | 149 |

So what caused the two-year crater in BABIP? It's a good question, and one that I'm not sure of either. But here's what I would speculate on: Garcia probably wasn't ready for High Class A as a 21-year-old – despite his (brief) track record of minor league success. Just because a player performs well as a young age in Class A, doesn't guarantee success in High Class A. And he was equally poor against LHP and RHP.

But, for whatever reason, he really struggled against fellow right-handers the following year, posting an OPS of .640 against them. Only complicating matters is the fact that he's never topped 110 games in a season in his career.

In the end, he looks like a solid bat hovering around the league average mark. But the hit tool, I think, will ultimately doom him into fringe everyday status.

**Ceiling:** 1.5- to 2.0-win player
**Risk:** Moderate to High
**MLB ETA:** 2016

## 15. Harrison Bader, LF/RF

**MiLB Rank:** N/A
**Position Rank:** N/A

| Born: 06/03/94 | Age: 22 | Bats: R | **Top CALs:** Christian Stewart, Michael Gerber, |
|---|---|---|---|
| Height: 6-0 | Weight: 195 | Throws: R | Granden Goetzman, Derek Fisher, Jacob Scavuzzo |

| Season | Age | LVL | PA | 2B | 3B | HR | AVG | OBP | SLG | ISO | BB% | K% | wRC+ |
|---|---|---|---|---|---|---|---|---|---|---|---|---|---|
| 2015 | 21 | A- | 30 | 2 | 0 | 2 | 0.379 | 0.400 | 0.655 | 0.276 | 0.0% | 16.7% | 209 |
| 2015 | 21 | A | 228 | 11 | 2 | 9 | 0.301 | 0.364 | 0.505 | 0.204 | 6.6% | 19.3% | 152 |

**Background:** The club's most recent third round pick out of the University of Florida, Bader, the 100th overall player chosen last season, was a three-year starter for the Gators. He opened up his collegiate career by batting .312/.371/.376, followed that up with an even better triple-slash line in 2014 (.335/.411/.431), and exploded with a career best season last year (.297/.393/.556). Overall, Bader hit .312/.391/.466 during his collegiate career. St. Louis had the toolsy outfielder start his professional career in the New York-Penn League, which lasted seven games before getting bumped up to the Midwest League. He hit a combined .311/.370/.523 between both levels.

**Projection:** A lot of the important skills trended in the right direction for Bader throughout his collegiate career – most importantly his power, which improved in each of his three seasons. His walk rate also took an important jump during his final campaign as well. With that being said, Bader's never going to be mistaken for Houston's Nolan Fontana when it comes to walks, but he does have an intriguing combination of power and speed. He could be a 15/15 threat if everything breaks the right way.

**Ceiling:** 1.5-win player
**Risk:** Moderate
**MLB ETA:** 2017

## 16. Austin Gomber, LHP

**MiLB Rank:** N/A
**Position Rank:** N/A

| Born: 11/23/93 | Age: 22 | Bats: L | **Top CALs:** Pedro Encarnacion, Brad Furnish, |
|---|---|---|---|
| Height: 6-5 | Weight: 205 | Throws: L | Clint Dempster, Dan Griffin, Chadwick Bell |

| YEAR | Age | Level | IP | W | L | ERA | FIP | K/9 | BB/9 | K% | BB% | HR/9 | LOB% |
|---|---|---|---|---|---|---|---|---|---|---|---|---|---|
| 2014 | 21 | A- | 47.0 | 2 | 2 | 2.30 | 4.08 | 6.89 | 3.45 | 17.4% | 8.7% | 0.57 | 82.2% |
| 2015 | 22 | A | 135.0 | 15 | 3 | 2.67 | 3.06 | 9.33 | 2.27 | 26.0% | 6.3% | 0.67 | 73.7% |

**Background:** Tell me if you've heard this one before: the Cardinals unearthed another potential big league prospect beyond the first two rounds from a school not known for its baseball prowess. Gomber, a tall, lanky lefty out of Florida Atlantic, home to just nine big leaguers since 1984, was a consistent rotation stalwart for three seasons in college. In 245 career innings with the Owls, Gomber averaged nearly a punch out per inning with a sub-3.0 walk rate. And two seasons after being selected in the fourth round, he's likely the next hurler in the organization to be pushed a long quickly. The southpaw spent last season with Peoria, where he averaged 9.3 K/9 and just 2.3 BB/9. His 3.06 FIP ranked seventh among all Low Class A arms.

**Projection:** Armed with a similar repertoire as fellow southpaw Corey Littrell, Gomber's massive wingspan allows his average-ish fastball to play up a couple ticks. Even going back to his college days he's always had a strong feel for the strike zone, especially for a taller hurler. If I had to venture a guess, I bet Gomber makes a handful of starts with Palm Beach before getting bumped up to Springfield 20 or so starts. He's a nice fourth/fifth starter. For what it's worth I ranked Gomber as the 41st overall collegiate prospect heading into the 2014 draft.

**Ceiling:** 1.5-win player
**Risk:** Moderate to High
**MLB ETA:** 2017

## 17. Ronnie Williams, RHP

**MiLB Rank:** N/A
**Position Rank:** N/A

| Born: 01/06/96 | Age: 20 | Bats: R | **Top CALs:** Benjamin Freeman, Eduardo Aldama, |
|---|---|---|---|
| Height: 6-0 | Weight: 170 | Throws: R | Bobby Hansen, Junior Garcia, Blake Bivens |

| YEAR | Age | Level | IP | W | L | ERA | FIP | K/9 | BB/9 | K% | BB% | HR/9 | LOB% |
|---|---|---|---|---|---|---|---|---|---|---|---|---|---|
| 2014 | 18 | R | 36.3 | 0 | 5 | 4.71 | 3.29 | 7.43 | 2.23 | 19.0% | 5.7% | 0.25 | 59.3% |
| 2015 | 19 | R | 56.0 | 3 | 3 | 3.70 | 4.80 | 6.91 | 4.02 | 18.2% | 10.6% | 0.80 | 65.2% |

**Background:** The 2014 second round pick went winless during his pro debut two years ago – despite some favorable underlying numbers. He fanned 19.0% and walked less than 6.0% the batters he faced and only surrendered one homerun in 36.1 innings. His production took a noticeable dip as the club pushed him up to the more advanced rookie level last year; the result of some problematic control. His walk percentage nearly doubled as it jumped to a below-average 10.6%. For his career, Williams has averaged 7.1 strikeouts and 3.3 walks per nine innings.

**Projection**: He's likely to get pushed up to full season ball to stat 2016, a result of his second half turnaround. After posting a 24-to-17 strikeout-to-walk ratio in his first 28 innings but regained his form previous form over his final 28.0 innings (19-to-8 strikeout-to-walk ratio). He's ready for the Midwest League. Williams could help round out the backend of a rotation.

**Ceiling**: 1.0- to 1.5-win player
**Risk**: Moderate
**MLB ETA**: 2018

## 18. Corey Littrell, LHP

**MiLB Rank: N/A**
**Position Rank: N/A**

| Born: 03/21/92 | Age: 24 | Bats: L | Top CALs: Rick Zagone, Rob Rasmussen, |
|---|---|---|---|
| Height: 6-3 | Weight: 185 | Throws: L | Mike Tarsi, Amaury Rivas, Silfredo Garcia |

| YEAR | Age | Level | IP | W | L | ERA | FIP | K/9 | BB/9 | K% | BB% | HR/9 | LOB% |
|---|---|---|---|---|---|---|---|---|---|---|---|---|---|
| 2013 | 21 | A- | 31.0 | 0 | 3 | 1.74 | 2.23 | 8.71 | 2.90 | 22.9% | 7.6% | 0.00 | 76.9% |
| 2014 | 22 | A+ | 100.0 | 5 | 5 | 3.60 | 4.09 | 8.19 | 3.42 | 21.2% | 8.8% | 0.72 | 76.4% |
| 2014 | 22 | A+ | 31.7 | 0 | 2 | 4.55 | 4.78 | 5.40 | 2.84 | 13.6% | 7.1% | 1.14 | 60.7% |
| 2015 | 23 | A+ | 130.3 | 9 | 9 | 2.69 | 2.77 | 6.42 | 1.45 | 17.7% | 4.0% | 0.35 | 70.9% |

**Background:** The John Lackey (at a discounted price)-for-Joe Kelly-and-Allen-Craig would have been laughably one-sided by itself. But for some odd reason the Red Sox decided to throw in Littrell, a former fifth round pick out of the University of Kentucky. And like Lackey, the 6-foot-3 southpaw also turned in his finest professional season to date, though that comes with a massive caveat: St. Louis, for some reason, decided to have Littrell repeat High Class A despite an overwhelmingly positive showing in 2014. Last season, however, Littrell made 27 appearances, 17 of which were starts, throwing 130.1 innings while fanning 17.7% and walking just 4.0% of the batters he faced. His 2.77 FIP was the second lowest among all Florida State League starters as well as fifth best among all qualified pitchers in any High Class A league.

**Projection**: Here's a bit of an interesting fact: Littrell, a 2013 draft pick, has thrown 293.0 career minor league innings, 262.0 of those coming at the High Class A level. Suffice it to say, we have pretty clear read on his ability relative to the level. Here's what we know at this point: Littrell's more of a finesse lefty, sort of another Tim Cooney-type arm. He'll miss a couple bats every start, and he typically keeps the ball around the plate, on the ground, and in the park. He's ready – again – to take the next leap to Class AA and profiles as a archetypical #5 starter.

**Ceiling**: 1.0- to 1.5-win player
**Risk**: Moderate
**MLB ETA**: 2017

## 19. Zach Petrick, RHP

**MiLB Rank: N/A**
**Position Rank: N/A**

| Born: 07/29/89 | Age: 26 | Bats: R | Top CALs: Tanner Roark, Randy Wells, |
|---|---|---|---|
| Height: 6-3 | Weight: 195 | Throws: R | Elih Villanueva, Daniel Barone, Clayton Mortensen |

| YEAR | Age | Level | IP | W | L | ERA | FIP | K/9 | BB/9 | K% | BB% | HR/9 | LOB% |
|---|---|---|---|---|---|---|---|---|---|---|---|---|---|
| 2013 | 23 | A | 32.7 | 1 | 0 | 0.83 | 1.84 | 12.67 | 2.20 | 34.9% | 6.1% | 0.28 | 89.0% |
| 2013 | 23 | A+ | 33.3 | 3 | 0 | 0.27 | 1.68 | 8.64 | 1.08 | 26.0% | 3.3% | 0.00 | 84.0% |
| 2013 | 23 | AA | 47.3 | 3 | 3 | 3.99 | 3.10 | 8.37 | 2.85 | 22.2% | 7.6% | 0.57 | 68.7% |
| 2014 | 24 | AA | 18.7 | 2 | 0 | 0.48 | 2.32 | 7.23 | 2.41 | 19.7% | 6.6% | 0.00 | 71.4% |
| 2014 | 24 | AAA | 115.0 | 7 | 6 | 4.62 | 5.13 | 6.42 | 2.82 | 16.7% | 7.3% | 1.25 | 71.7% |
| 2015 | 25 | AAA | 157.3 | 7 | 7 | 4.52 | 3.99 | 6.46 | 1.66 | 16.8% | 4.3% | 0.80 | 65.2% |

**Background:** I look forward to writing about Petrick probably more than any other minor league prospect because, well, I love a fantastic underdog story. I've written – at length, on numerous occasions – about Petrick's rise from college free agent to the organization's Minor League Pitcher of the Year just a scant few seasons later. But for those who don't know, let's recap: Petrick played for the University of Northwestern Ohio, a small college located in the Indians' backyard – almost literally. Seriously, it's a little more than 2.5 hours from Progressive Field. Anyway, I digress (though, come on, how do you not scour your own backyard?). Petrick dominated the Appalachian League during his debut in 2012 and then *sprinted* through the Midwest, Florida State, and Texas Leagues in 2013.After three more dominant starts with Springfield to open the 2014 season, Petrick got the call to move up to the PCL, where he continued to limit walks with the best of them. St. Louis kept the promising right-hander with Memphis last season where he outpitched his 4.52 ERA by more than half of a run (according to FIP).

**Projection**: If you ever wonder why St. Louis is one of the best organizations in baseball just reference Petrick. Even if his big league career is as brief as his older brother Billy's, you have to wonder how in the hell did they unearth a quality Class AAA hurler from a school no one's heard of? Petrick is big league ready and should step in as a decent #5 starter with some upside as a good middle relief option. Hop on the bandwagon for one of the better feel-good stories in baseball.

**Ceiling:** 1.0-win player
**Risk:** Low to Moderate
**MLB ETA:** 2016

## 20. Charlie Tilson, CF

**MiLB Rank:** N/A
**Position Rank:** N/A

| Born: 12/02/92 | Age: 23 | Bats: L | Top CALs: Shane Peterson, Jake Cave, |
|---|---|---|---|
| Height: 5-11 | Weight: 175 | Throws: L | Glynn Davis, Teodoro Martinez, Ty Morrison |

| Season | Age | LVL | PA | 2B | 3B | HR | AVG | OBP | SLG | ISO | BB% | K% | wRC+ |
|---|---|---|---|---|---|---|---|---|---|---|---|---|---|
| 2013 | 20 | A | 411 | 8 | 6 | 4 | 0.303 | 0.349 | 0.388 | 0.085 | 6.1% | 14.1% | 109 |
| 2014 | 21 | A+ | 402 | 8 | 8 | 5 | 0.308 | 0.357 | 0.414 | 0.105 | 6.0% | 18.9% | 121 |
| 2014 | 21 | AA | 145 | 4 | 1 | 2 | 0.237 | 0.269 | 0.324 | 0.086 | 4.1% | 19.3% | 68 |
| 2015 | 22 | AA | 594 | 20 | 9 | 4 | 0.295 | 0.351 | 0.388 | 0.093 | 7.7% | 12.1% | 107 |

**Background:** A bit of a late-blooming former high school player, but not in the traditional sense. Tilson appeared in just eight games during his 2011 debut, but would next play in a meaningful contest nearly two years later in 2013 – courtesy of a severe shoulder injury he suffered on an outfield dive. But the slightly-framed center fielder hasn't looked back since, hitting at each stop along the way sans a minor blip as a 21-year-old making his Class AA debut two years ago. Tilson spent the entire 2015 campaign back with Springfield where – unsurprisingly – his numbers were much improved. In 134 games, the 5-foot-11, 175-pounder batted a more-than-respectable .295/.351/.388 with 20 doubles, nine triples, four homeruns, and 46 stolen bases (in 65 attempts). His overall production, per *Weighted Runs Created Plus*, topped the league average by seven percent.

**Projection:** Molded by the baseball gods in the image of the prototypical fourth/fifth outfielder. Tilson excels on the base paths and hits for a solid average thanks to that speed. But every other offensive skill is below-average. His Isolated Power has only topped .100 once in his career; he's never walked more than 7.7% of the time in a season. On a positive note: his work against southpaws improved last season (.287/.333/.367). CAL's not overly optimistic either, linking him to Shane Peterson, Jake Cave, Glynn Davis, Teodoro Martinez, and Ty Morrison.

**Ceiling:** 1.0-win player
**Risk:** Low to Moderate
**MLB ETA:** 2016

## 21. Trey Nielsen, RHP

**MiLB Rank:** N/A
**Position Rank:** N/A

| Born: 09/01/91 | Age: 24 | Bats: R | Top CALs: Manolin De Leon, Jordan Harrison, |
|---|---|---|---|
| Height: 6-1 | Weight: 190 | Throws: R | Williams Perez, Danny Rosenbaum, Chris Jones |

| YEAR | Age | Level | IP | W | L | ERA | FIP | K/9 | BB/9 | K% | BB% | HR/9 | LOB% |
|---|---|---|---|---|---|---|---|---|---|---|---|---|---|
| 2014 | 22 | A- | 50.3 | 3 | 2 | 2.50 | 3.22 | 8.76 | 2.50 | 25.0% | 7.1% | 0.54 | 75.3% |
| 2015 | 23 | A+ | 111.0 | 9 | 6 | 2.59 | 3.11 | 6.32 | 2.76 | 16.9% | 7.4% | 0.24 | 68.0% |

**Background:** Once again, another late, late round pick making his way into the club's Top 25 Prospects List. Nielson's story is like so many others: he spent the first three seasons of his collegiate career at Utah as the club's starting third baseman, with some success too. He also made four appearances on the mound – for a total of six innings – before an elbow injury shortened that little experiment. The Cards took Nielsen in the 30th round, 905th overall, sent him under the knife for Tommy John surgery, and the rest, as they say, is history. Nielsen spent the year with Palm Beach in the Florida State League, throwing 111.0 innings while averaging 6.3 strikeouts and just 2.8 BB/9. Just adding to the intrigue: he made the jump to High Class A from the New York-Penn League.

**Projection:** The most impressive statistic concerning Nielsen – his *career* groundball rate is north of 65% through his first 160+ innings of work. The control is solid, the ability to miss bats is meh. But, damn, those groundball totals sure have statheads foaming at the mouth. He could be a decent backend starter with the right defense behind him.

**Ceiling:** 1.0- to 1.5-win player
**Risk:** Moderate to High
**MLB ETA:** 2017

## 22. Paul DeJong, 3B

MiLB Rank: N/A
Position Rank: N/A

| Born: 08/02/93 | Age: 22 | Bats: R | Top CALs: Ryne Malone, Brent Morel, |
| Height: 6-1 | Weight: 195 | Throws: R | Michael Wing, Jacob May, Tony Granadillo |

| Season | Age | LVL | PA | 2B | 3B | HR | AVG | OBP | SLG | ISO | BB% | K% | wRC+ |
|---|---|---|---|---|---|---|---|---|---|---|---|---|---|
| 2015 | 21 | R | 45 | 6 | 0 | 4 | 0.486 | 0.578 | 0.973 | 0.486 | 13.3% | 20.0% | 309 |
| 2015 | 21 | A | 247 | 12 | 3 | 5 | 0.288 | 0.360 | 0.438 | 0.151 | 9.3% | 17.4% | 133 |

**Background:** Just how good was DeJong over his final two collegiate seasons? The 6-foot-1, 195-pound third baseman posted back-to-back 1.000 OPS seasons; no other stick for the Illinois State Red Bird an .888 OPS in either season. Well, DeJong traded in one Red Bird uniform for another as the Cardinals grabbed him in the fourth round, 131st overall, last June. And DeJong immediately started paying dividends for his new organization: he went 18-for-37 in the Appalachian League and continued to command a presence at the plate upon his promotion to Peoria (.288/.363/.438). Overall, he batted a combined .316/.397/.516 with 18 doubles, three triples, nine homeruns, and 13 stolen bases (in 17 attempts).

**Projection:** It's interesting, isn't it? How the draft, no matter how much you research or study or scout a player, a lot of comes down to a roll of the dice. Take for example DeJong, a fourth round pick out of less-than-impressive baseball university, and 2012 first round pick Patrick Wisdom. DeJong blew the doors off of the NYPL and handled himself adequately in the Midwest League; Wisdom, on the other hand, spent his debut in Short-Season ball and batted a solid .282/.373/.465, but he followed that up with a paltry .231/.312/.411 showing with Peoria the next season. DeJong is another excellent value pick by the organization. He may not have the prototypical pop the average run-producing third baseman shows, but he'll run into 15 or so homeruns once he gets above the A-levels.

**Ceiling:** 1.0- to 1.5-win player
**Risk:** Moderate to High
**MLB ETA:** 2018

## 23. Matt Bowman, RHP

MiLB Rank: N/A
Position Rank: N/A

| Born: 05/31/91 | Age: 25 | Bats: R | Top CALs: Randy Wells, Jeff Locke, |
| Height: 6-0 | Weight: 165 | Throws: R | Luis Cessa, Kyle Lobstein, Jeff Manship |

| YEAR | Age | Level | IP | W | L | ERA | FIP | K/9 | BB/9 | K% | BB% | HR/9 | LOB% |
|---|---|---|---|---|---|---|---|---|---|---|---|---|---|
| 2013 | 22 | A | 30.7 | 4 | 0 | 2.64 | 2.27 | 7.63 | 1.17 | 21.0% | 3.2% | 0.00 | 72.7% |
| 2013 | 22 | A+ | 96.3 | 6 | 4 | 3.18 | 3.54 | 8.41 | 2.90 | 22.6% | 7.8% | 0.75 | 76.8% |
| 2014 | 23 | AA | 98.3 | 7 | 6 | 3.11 | 3.35 | 8.42 | 2.47 | 22.1% | 6.5% | 0.64 | 71.4% |
| 2014 | 23 | AAA | 36.3 | 3 | 2 | 3.47 | 3.04 | 7.93 | 2.23 | 20.9% | 5.9% | 0.25 | 70.2% |
| 2015 | 24 | AAA | 140.0 | 7 | 16 | 5.53 | 5.03 | 4.95 | 3.28 | 12.0% | 7.9% | 0.96 | 64.8% |

**Background:** Another one of my personal favorites. The Ivy League educated right-hander, however, had a rough go of it – or flat out shit time – in his second stint through the PCL last season. In 28 games with Las Vegas, 26 of which were starts, the former Princeton University star posted the lowest strikeout percentage of his career, 12.0%, as well the highest walk percentage of his career, 7.9%, to go along with an equally disappointing 5.53 ERA and 5.03 FIP. It's quite the fall for the former 13th round pick that was coming off of two back-to-back promising campaigns as he made his way up from the South Atlantic League all the way to the PCL. For his career, Bowman has averaged 7.3 punch outs and just 2.6 walks per nine innings. And just to add insult to injury: his 16 losses were tied for the fourth most losses among all minor league hurlers. St. Louis grabbed him from the Mets in the Rule 5 draft this offseason.

**Projection:** I wish I could write something along the lines about how it was all just a whole lot of shit luck. But, unfortunately, that isn't the case. His .339 BABIP is just a hair higher than his showing in 2014; his homerun rate, 0.96, is also slightly up but not by a whole helluva lot; and his strand rate was a touch low, but, again, by not a whole lot. Bowman was simply overmatched in the minors' last stop. His track record is lengthy enough that a rebound to his previous form isn't out of the question. And he does sport a groundball rate hovering around 50%, so there's hope the HR-rate eases back down. But right now he looks like a long relief/swing man.

**Ceiling:** 1.0-win player
**Risk:** Moderate
**MLB ETA:** 2016

## 24. Bryce Denton, 3B

**MiLB Rank: N/A**
**Position Rank: N/A**

| Born: 08/01/97 | Age: 18 | Bats: R | Top CALs: Romulo Ruiz, Andury Acevedo, |
| Height: 6-0 | Weight: 190 | Throws: R | Rory Rhoades, Michael Pasek, Miles Gordon |

| Season | Age | LVL | PA | 2B | 3B | HR | AVG | OBP | SLG | ISO | BB% | K% | wRC+ |
|---|---|---|---|---|---|---|---|---|---|---|---|---|---|
| 2015 | 17 | R | 169 | 1 | 2 | 1 | 0.194 | 0.254 | 0.245 | 0.052 | 6.5% | 18.9% | 56 |

**Background:** Proof that not every incoming draft pick blows through the lowest levels of the minor leagues once they suit up in a St. Louis uniform. The Gulf Coast League pitching mowed down the 2015 second round pick, holding him to a paltry .194/.254/.245 triple-slash line and just four extra-base hits.

**Projection**: Not only isn't there much to write about, there's nothing positive to report on with regards to Denton's debut. His overall production was a staggeringly poor 56 wRC+; his walk rate was below average; and he showed next to nothing in the power department. Suffice to say Denton's a candidate to repeat the GCL in 2016.

**Ceiling:** Too Soon to Tell
**Risk:** N/A
**MLB ETA:** N/A

## 25. Artie Reyes, RHP

**MiLB Rank: N/A**
**Position Rank: N/A**

| Born: 04/06/92 | Age: 24 | Bats: R | Top CALs: Danny Rosenbaum, Brad James, |
| Height: 5-11 | Weight: 185 | Throws: R | Jeff Manship, John Gast, Robert Rohrbaugh |

| YEAR | Age | Level | IP | W | L | ERA | FIP | K/9 | BB/9 | K% | BB% | HR/9 | LOB% |
|---|---|---|---|---|---|---|---|---|---|---|---|---|---|
| 2013 | 21 | A- | 43.3 | 1 | 2 | 2.08 | 4.02 | 5.19 | 3.12 | 14.1% | 8.5% | 0.62 | 82.3% |
| 2014 | 22 | A | 122.7 | 6 | 8 | 3.67 | 3.59 | 7.63 | 2.49 | 19.9% | 6.5% | 0.59 | 71.0% |
| 2015 | 23 | A+ | 14.7 | 1 | 1 | 2.45 | 3.30 | 4.91 | 3.68 | 12.3% | 9.2% | 0.00 | 84.0% |
| 2015 | 23 | AA | 99.0 | 7 | 7 | 2.64 | 2.94 | 7.27 | 2.55 | 19.1% | 6.7% | 0.18 | 72.5% |
| 2015 | 23 | AAA | 25.3 | 1 | 3 | 7.82 | 5.53 | 6.04 | 5.68 | 13.4% | 12.6% | 0.71 | 63.2% |

**Background:** Maybe it's the Howard Stern fan in me, but every time I hear/see the name Artie I think of the shock jock's former sidekick, Artie Lange. Anyway, if Petrick and the countless other late round picks turned legitimate big league prospects weren't enough examples take Reyes, a former 40th round pick out of Gonzaga. Another underrated, undersized, overlooked right-hander, Reyes, who stands a pint-sized 5-foot-11 and 185 pounds, spent his debut in the New York Penn League where he posted an impressive 2.08 ERA despite some lackluster peripherals (5.2 K/9 and 3.1 BB/9). He spent the following season with Peoria, but his stock – and developmental curve – jumped into the fast lane in 2015. Reyes mad three starts with Palm Beach, another 17 with Springfield, and five more with Memphis. For those keeping track at home: within two-and-a-half plus seasons a former 40th round pick jumped all the way up to Class AAA in fewer than 280 professional innings. Overall, Reyes tossed 139.0 innings, punched out 105, and walked 50.

**Projection**: You have to wonder why the organization opted to push Reyes so aggressively last season, but decided to keep another polished collegiate arm, Corey Littrell, mired away in the High Class A. Reyes has a couple things going for him: a pretty ERA, above-average groundball totals, and solid control. But the ability to miss wood – or lack thereof – limits his ceiling rather severely. He's fringy big league starter/swingman.

**Ceiling:** 0.5- to 1.0-win player
**Risk:** Moderate High
**MLB ETA:** 2016

***Barely Missed:***

- **Sandy Alcantara, RHP** – Tall, lanky right-hander out of the Dominican, Alcantara made his stateside debut in 2015. In 12 starts in the Gulf Coast, the 6-foot-4, 170-pound hurler posted a 51-to-20 strikeout-to-walk ratio in 64.1 innings of work. He will likely find his way into the club's Top 25 next season.

- **Ian McKinney, LHP** – A smallish left-hander out of William R. Boone High School, McKinney made stops at three different levels last season, seeing action with State College, Peoria, and Palm Beach. In total, the 5-foot-11 southpaw tossed 87 innings with 74 punch outs and just 20 free passes. Sort of a poor man's version of former Cardinals lefty Rob Kaminsky.

- **Chris Perry, RHP** – A tale of two seasons for the former 17th round pick out of Methodist College. Perry was as dominant as any pitcher in the Florida State League to begin 2015. In 32.0 innings for Palm Beach, the 6-foot-2 right-hander punched out 34, walked 16, and posted a miniscule 1.97 ERA. Then the club bumped him up to Springfield and his year spiraled out of control. In 28.0 innings, Perry fanned 24, but walked a staggering 18. He posted a 6.11 ERA during that span.

- **Darren Seferina, 2B** –Lefty-swinging second baseman out of Miami-Dade had a solid showing in the Midwest League in 2015, hitting a robust .295/.354/.446 with a career best 132 wRC+. Not overly big, just 5-foot-9 and 175 pounds, isn't overly efficient on the base paths, but has solid-average power, a decent eye at the plate, and strong contact skills. He could be a fringy regular down the line.

## *Bird Doggin' It – Additional Prospects to Keep an Eye in 2016*

| Player | Age | POS | Notes |
|---|---|---|---|
| Luis Bandes | 20 | 1B/OF | Had a big breakout in the Gulf Coast League last season, hitting .319/.349/.449 with six doubles and four homeruns in 38 games. He might be ready for at least Short-Season ball. |
| Bruce Caldwell | 24 | 2B/3B | Posted some impressive wRC+ totals in High Class A and Class AA (111 and 125). Not enough stick to compensate for his inability to handle shortstop, so that limits his likelihood of carving out a backup role at the big league level. |
| Kyle Grana | 25 | RHP | Typically, I don't write about 24-year-old in the Midwest League. But Grana finished the year with a 0.78 ERA with Peoria. This, of course, comes on the heels of his 0.89 ERA with State College. And then the 1.88 mark in the rookie leagues. His career ERA: 1.07. |
| Mason Katz | 25 | IF/OF | Former LSU stalwart hasn't taken to wood like I would have guessed. Katz hit .259/.347/.375 as a 24-year-old in the Florida State League last season. |
| Carson Kelly | 21 | C | Former second round pick made the move from the hot corner to behind the plate two years ago. He posted a 100 wRC+ as a 19-year-old in the Midwest League, but his production cratered with Palm Beach (.219/.263/.332). |
| Josh Lucas | 25 | RHP | 6-foot-6 right-hander tallied a 1.29 ERA as a game finisher for Palm Beach and tossed another 5.2 scoreless innings in Springfield. |
| Michael Mayers | 24 | RHP | Former third round pick took a huge step backward in a shortened season. |
| Oscar Mercado | 21 | SS | Former second round pick in 2013, Mercado has the speed and a lofty draft status. That's it. His triple-slash line in the Midwest League last season, .254/.297/.341, was the best of his three-year career. |
| Elehuris Montero | 17 | 3B | 6-foot-3, 195-pound man-child hit .252/.328/.339 as a 16-year-old in the Dominican Summer League. |
| Mike Ohlman | 25 | C | Acquired after being designated by the Orioles, Ohlman was once a budding saber-star. Or at least a minor saber-star. He rebounded – unsurprisingly – in his second go-round in Class AA, posting a 118 wRC+. |
| David Oca | 20 | LHP | Small left-hander out of Venezuela started the season in the Dominican Summer League and ended it in the NYPL. Averaged 8.6 punch outs and just 1.9 walks per nine innings. |
| Rafael Ortega | 24 | OF | The shine has clearly dulled on the former Rockies prospect. Ortega, who got a small taste of the big leagues as a 21-year-old in 2012, spent the year performing at the league average mark in Class AAA. Quintessential fourth/fifth outfielder. |
| Matt Pearce | 22 | RHP | Control artist surrendered just 22 free passes in 144.2 innings with Peoria. The bad news: he averaged just 5.9 K/9. |
| Daniel Poncedeleon | 24 | RHP | Not to be confused with the Spanish explorer, the former ninth round pick made it look easy by totaling a 2.12 ERA between Class A and High Class A. |
| Collin Radack | 24 | LF/RF | Built like a classical run-producing corner outfield bat, but hits like a 5-foot-nothing fifth outfielder. Radack, 6-foot-3 and 205 pounds, owns a career .288/.388/.351 triple-slash line. |
| Jonathan Rodriguez | 26 | 1B/3B/RF | Typical Quad-A bat. |
| Kender Villegas | 23 | RHP | Made three stops last season, showing a promising combination of low walk totals and an above-average ability to miss sticks. |
| David Washington | 25 | 1B/OF | Massive, massive 6-foot-5, 200-pound first base/corner outfielder. Washington had a career year in the Texas League, hitting .274/.338/.471 with 16 dingers in just 97 games. |
| Patrick Wisdom | 24 | 1B/3B | Former first round pick, 52nd overall in 2012 has solid-average or better power and decent contact rates, but routinely fails to square the ball up. He's now batted .225/.285/.386 in over 1,700 plate appearances in the Texas League. |

**tate of the Farm System:** I stood out from the pack as I declared the Rays as having the fourth best minor league system heading into the 2015 season. And that was *before* Blake Snell had his massive breakout season. Now I'm prepared to double down on that and declare Tampa Bay as having the second best farm system in all of baseball – narrowly trailing the Dodgers for the top spot.

Tampa Bay has three potential mid- to upper-rotation caliber arms in Blake Snell, Brent Honeywell, and Taylor Guerrieri.

Snell, as I wrote in last year's book, looks like a Chris Archer-type arm. Honeywell is sporting a dominant 169-to-33 strikeout-to-walk ratio covering his 164.0 career innings, including posting a 129-to-27 mark between Low Class A and High Class A last season. And Guerrieri, fresh off of Tommy John surgery and a drug suspension, was equally dominant between his stints with Charlotte and Montgomery: 78.0 IP, 72 K, and 19 BB.

And behind the three power-packed arms are several promising bats.

Infielder Daniel Robertson batted a solid .274/.363/.415 in an injury-shortened campaign in the Southern League. First baseman Jake Bauers, who I named as one of the Top 25 Breakout Prospects for 2015 in last year's book, hit a combined .272/.342/.418 as a 19-year-old between the Florida State and Southern Leagues. Willy Adames slugged .258/.342/.379 with 24 doubles, six triples, and four homeruns as a 19-year-old in High Class A. And former Wichita State University first baseman looked solid with Bowling Green before his season prematurely ended.

It's a very, very deep, highly underrated farm system with plenty of impact talent sprinkled throughout.

A few names to keep an eye in 2016: corner outfielder Justin Williams and right-hander Hunter Wood.

| Rank | Name | POS |
|------|------|-----|
| 1 | Blake Snell | LHP |
| 2 | Brent Honeywell | RHP |
| 3 | Taylor Guerrieri | RHP |
| 4 | Daniel Robertson | SS |
| 5 | Willy Adames | SS |
| 6 | Jake Bauers | 1B |
| 7 | Jacob Faria | RHP |
| 8 | Garrett Whitley | CF |
| 9 | Casey Gillaspie | 1B |
| 10 | German Marquez | RHP |
| 11 | Enny Romero | LHP |
| 12 | Chris Betts | C |
| 13 | Justin Williams | LF/RF |
| 14 | Andrew Velazquez | IF |
| 15 | Ryan Brett | 2B |
| 16 | Tyler Goeddel | OF |
| 17 | Hunter Wood | RHP |
| 18 | Chih-Wei Hu | RHP |
| 19 | Greg Harris | RHP |
| 20 | Ryne Stanek | RHP |
| 21 | Richie Shaffer | 1B/3B |
| 22 | Kean Wong | 2B |
| 23 | Justin O'Conner | C |
| 24 | Patrick Leonard | 1B/3B/RF |
| 25 | Cameron Varga | RHP |

Expect a big bounce back season from second baseman Ryan Brett. He could very easily supplant Logan Forsythe as the Rays' starting second baseman by the end of the year.

**Review of the 2015 Draft:** The Rays grabbed talented outfielder Garrett Whitley with the 13th overall pick last June, though he looked a bit underwhelming as he batted .174/.293/.312 with four doubles, three triples, and three homeruns between the Gulf Coast and New York-Penn Leagues.

Their second round pick, prep backstop Chris Betts, didn't appear in a game due to elbow woes. And fourth round selection Brandon Koch, out of Dallas Baptist University, looked absolutely dominating in short-season action: 32.1 IP, 47 K, and five walks. Joe McCarthy, a fifth round pick out of the University of Virginia, could be a budding sabermetric darling.

# 1. Blake Snell, LHP

MiLB Rank: #11
Position Rank: #7

| Born: 12/04/92 | Age: 23 | Bats: L | Top CALs: Yordano Ventura, Maikel Cleto, |
| Height: 6-4 | Weight: 180 | Throws: L | Justin De Fratus, Thomas Palica, Matt Harvey |

| YEAR | Age | Level | IP | W | L | ERA | FIP | K/9 | BB/9 | K% | BB% | HR/9 | LOB% |
|---|---|---|---|---|---|---|---|---|---|---|---|---|---|
| 2013 | 20 | A | 99.0 | 4 | 9 | 4.27 | 4.52 | 9.64 | 6.64 | 23.7% | 16.3% | 0.73 | 71.5% |
| 2014 | 21 | A | 40.3 | 3 | 2 | 1.79 | 3.14 | 9.37 | 4.24 | 26.1% | 11.8% | 0.22 | 80.3% |
| 2014 | 21 | A+ | 75.3 | 5 | 6 | 3.94 | 3.19 | 9.20 | 4.42 | 23.3% | 11.2% | 0.12 | 64.8% |
| 2015 | 22 | A+ | 21.0 | 3 | 0 | 0.00 | 2.17 | 11.57 | 4.71 | 32.9% | 13.4% | 0.00 | 100.0% |
| 2015 | 22 | AA | 68.7 | 6 | 2 | 1.57 | 3.26 | 10.35 | 3.80 | 29.5% | 10.8% | 0.66 | 91.2% |
| 2015 | 22 | AAA | 44.3 | 6 | 2 | 1.83 | 2.12 | 11.57 | 2.64 | 33.3% | 7.6% | 0.41 | 79.6% |

**Background:** The Rays' front office has carefully groomed the 6-foot-4 left-hander since drafting him in the supplemental first round in 2011. Snell was eased into the Gulf Coast for his debut (26.1 IP), slowly bumped up to the Appalachian League the following season (47.1 IP), expanded the reins a bit when he debuted in full season ball in 2013 (99.0 IP), and finally allowed to crack the 100-inning mark as he split time between Bowling Green and Charlotte two years ago. Well, apparently the franchise's plan has paid off – *in a HUGE way*. Snell began the year back in the Florida State, where he dominated for 21.0 innings (27-to-11 strikeout-to-walk ratio), would eventually get bumped up to Montgomery for another 12 spectacular starts, and capped off 2015's biggest breakout performance by knocking on the big league club's door by posting a 57-to-13 strikeout-to-walk ratio in 44.1 innings. When the dust settled Snell's final numbers were among the best – if not the best – in all the minors': 134 IP, 163 strikeouts, 53 walks, and a tidy 1.53 ERA.

**Projection:** Prior to his extraordinary run here's what I wrote in last year's book:

> *"A lot like Chris Archer, Snell has battled control/command issues early in his career. The swing-and-miss ability – he's whiffed 24.5% of the batters he's faced in his career – hint at a potential big league career, whether it's as a #2/#3-type arm a la Archer (his #3 CAL) or in the back of a bullpen remains to be seen."*

It certainly looks like he's a lot – *a lot* – closer to capturing his Chris Archer upside after his most recent showing. And CAL even stepped up the ante by linking the southpaw to Yordano Ventura and Mets ace Matt Harvey. The control/command grades out as fringy-average at the moment, but if it approaches his Class AAA levels than he could be one of the top frontline starters in baseball in the coming years. Oh, and just for safe measure, he generates a massive amount of action on the ground as well.

**Ceiling:** 4.0- to 4.5-win player
**Risk:** Moderate
**MLB ETA:** 2016

# 2. Brent Honeywell, RHP

MiLB Rank: #23
Position Rank: #10

| Born: 03/31/95 | Age: 21 | Bats: R | Top CALs: Drew Hutchison, Luis Severino, |
| Height: 6-2 | Weight: 180 | Throws: R | Edgar Osuna, A.J. Cole, Robert Stephenson |

| YEAR | Age | Level | IP | W | L | ERA | FIP | K/9 | BB/9 | K% | BB% | HR/9 | LOB% |
|---|---|---|---|---|---|---|---|---|---|---|---|---|---|
| 2014 | 19 | R | 33.7 | 2 | 1 | 1.07 | 2.20 | 10.69 | 1.60 | 31.3% | 4.7% | 0.27 | 77.2% |
| 2015 | 20 | A | 65.0 | 4 | 4 | 2.91 | 2.40 | 10.52 | 1.66 | 29.0% | 4.6% | 0.42 | 64.8% |
| 2015 | 20 | A+ | 65.3 | 5 | 2 | 3.44 | 2.72 | 7.30 | 2.07 | 20.2% | 5.7% | 0.28 | 67.4% |

**Background:** A second round pick out Walters State Community College two years ago, Honeywell, who was the second highest player selected from the Senators, has jumped up the prospect lists as any player following the 2015 season. The 6-foot-2, 180-pound right-hander tore up the Midwest League. Of his 12 starts with the Bowling Green Hot Rods, Honeywell punched out a least seven in four starts, walked three batters just once, and allowed more than three runs one time. His overall line in Low Class A: 65 innings, 76 strikeouts, 12 walks, and a 2.40 FIP. He got the bump up to Charlotte near the end of June and after two poor starts he finished out the season on a high note: he coughed up 14 earned runs in 57.0 innings while posting a 48-to-13 strikeout-to-walk ratio. His combined line for the year: 130.1 IP, 129 punch outs, and just 27 free passes.

**Projection:** Above-average or better control, Honeywell, who's walked just 5% of the batters he's faced in his career, has as high of a ceiling as any pitcher in the system – including budding ace Blake Snell. Honeywell has missed a ton of bats, shows poise beyond his years, and could be in the big leagues as soon as 2017 – as another front-of-the rotation caliber arm. And Cal remains a *huge* fan as well, linking him to Luis Severino, Robert Stephenson, Drew Hutchison, and A.J. Cole.

**Ceiling:** 4.0- to 4.5-win player
**Risk:** Moderate to High
**MLB ETA:** 2017

## 3. Taylor Guerrieri, RHP

**MiLB Rank: #25**
**Position Rank: #11**

| Born: 12/01/92 | Age: 23 | Bats: R | Top CALs: Brian Flynn, Andrew Gagnon, |
|---|---|---|---|
| Height: 6-3 | Weight: 195 | Throws: R | Chi-Chi Gonzalez, Jesse Beal, Chad Rogers |

| YEAR | Age | Level | IP | W | L | ERA | FIP | K/9 | BB/9 | K% | BB% | HR/9 | LOB% |
|---|---|---|---|---|---|---|---|---|---|---|---|---|---|
| 2013 | 20 | A | 67.0 | 6 | 2 | 2.01 | 3.77 | 6.85 | 1.61 | 19.5% | 4.6% | 0.67 | 85.5% |
| 2014 | 21 | R | 9.3 | 0 | 0 | 0.00 | 2.01 | 9.64 | 1.93 | 26.3% | 5.3% | 0.00 | 66.7% |
| 2015 | 22 | A+ | 42.0 | 2 | 2 | 2.14 | 2.00 | 9.43 | 2.36 | 25.6% | 6.4% | 0.00 | 72.0% |
| 2015 | 22 | AA | 36.0 | 3 | 1 | 1.50 | 3.39 | 7.00 | 2.00 | 18.8% | 5.4% | 0.50 | 82.9% |

**Background:** Incredibly hyped despite barely topping 200 innings in his four-year professional career, Guerrieri's been side-tracked by a midseason 2013 Tommy John surgery and he was popped – for a second time – months later for a drug suspension. Finally healthy – and with the 50-game suspension in his rearview mirror – the former first round pick made it back onto the mound for a little over nine innings in 2014. Last season, with the reins eased a bit, Guerrieri dominated the Florida State League by posting a 44-to-11 strikeout-to-walk ratio in 42.0 innings and he would breeze through eight starts in the Southern League as well; he fanned 28 and walked eight in 36.0 innings.

**Projection**: Obviously ERA is an archaic, misleading statistic but it's fun when pitchers post some Bob Gibson-esque numbers. Take Guerrieri's numbers for example: in 206.1 innings the 6-foot-3 right-hander's *career* ERA is a laughably low 1.61. Despite having an above-average fastball, Guerrieri doesn't miss a whole lot of bats – he's averaged 7.8 K/9 in his career – but he compensates by sporting some of the best control/command in the minors *and* generates a metric-ton of action on the ground as well; he's posted a groundball rate above 60% in each season. He could be a top-of-the-rotation caliber arm and could team with Blake Snell, Chris Archer, Matt Moore, Brent Honeywell, and Jake Odorizzi to form an elite level rotation.

**Ceiling:** 3.0- to 3.5-win player
**Risk:** Low to Moderate
**MLB ETA:** 2017

## 4. Daniel Robertson, SS

**MiLB Rank: #56**
**Position Rank: #9**

| Born: 03/22/94 | Age: 22 | Bats: R | Top CALs: Jorge Polanco, Yamaico Navarro, |
|---|---|---|---|
| Height: 6-1 | Weight: 205 | Throws: R | J.P. Crawford, Marcus Lemon, Cristhian Adames |

| Season | Age | LVL | PA | 2B | 3B | HR | AVG | OBP | SLG | ISO | BB% | K% | wRC+ |
|---|---|---|---|---|---|---|---|---|---|---|---|---|---|
| 2013 | 19 | A | 451 | 21 | 1 | 9 | 0.277 | 0.353 | 0.401 | 0.125 | 9.1% | 17.5% | 116 |
| 2014 | 20 | A+ | 642 | 37 | 3 | 15 | 0.310 | 0.402 | 0.471 | 0.161 | 11.2% | 14.6% | 132 |
| 2015 | 21 | AA | 347 | 20 | 5 | 4 | 0.274 | 0.363 | 0.415 | 0.140 | 9.5% | 16.7% | 123 |

**Background:** Acquired from the A's for Ben Zobrist right after the calendar flipped to 2015, Robertson's long been a personal favorite of mine. A 6-foot-1, 205-pound well-built shortstop out of a California high school, Robertson has consistently performed better-than-expected against older competition. He posted a 116 wRC+ as a 19-year-old in the Midwest League, followed that up with a 132 wRC+ in High Class A the next season, and proved his worth as a 21-year-old in Southern League last season, hitting .274/.363/.415 with 20 doubles, five triples, four homeruns, and a pair of stolen bases in an injury-shortened 2015 campaign. The young shortstop suffered a broken hamate bone, an injury that typically saps a player's power after recovery for a bit.

**Projection**: The injury aside, there's really nothing Robertson can't do at this point: he walks at a favorable clip, has the ability to slug 12- to 15-homeruns, makes solid contact, and handles shortstop well enough. The overall package is far greater than the individual parts, but don't be surprised when Robertson make his debut in mid-2015 and establishes himself as an above-average regular a year later.

**Ceiling:** 2.5- to 3.0-win player
**Risk:** Low to Moderate
**MLB ETA:** 2016

## 5. Willy Adames, SS

**MiLB Rank: #61**

**Position Rank: #10**

| Born: 09/02/95 | Age: 20 | Bats: R | Top CALs: Wendell Rijo, Jonathan Galvez, |
|---|---|---|---|
| Height: 6-1 | Weight: 180 | Throws: R | Ryan Dent, Tim Beckham, Junior Lake |

| Season | Age | LVL | PA | 2B | 3B | HR | AVG | OBP | SLG | ISO | BB% | K% | wRC+ |
|---|---|---|---|---|---|---|---|---|---|---|---|---|---|
| 2013 | 17 | R | 267 | 12 | 5 | 1 | 0.245 | 0.419 | 0.370 | 0.125 | 21.0% | 16.5% | 144 |
| 2014 | 18 | A | 514 | 19 | 14 | 8 | 0.271 | 0.353 | 0.429 | 0.158 | 10.5% | 24.5% | 124 |
| 2015 | 19 | A+ | 456 | 24 | 6 | 4 | 0.258 | 0.342 | 0.379 | 0.121 | 11.8% | 27.0% | 121 |

**Background:** Part of the price the Tigers paid for what would eventual amount to 355 days and 32 starts from David Price. Adames, a 20-year-old shortstop from the Dominican Republic turned in another remarkably consistent campaign, despite spending the entire year as a 19-year-old in the Florida State League. Adames batted .258/.342/.379 with 24 doubles, six triples, four homeruns, and 10 stolen bases (in 11 attempts). His overall production topped the league average mark by 21%. For his career, Adames is sporting a .261/.363/.399 triple-slash line in 291 games.

**Projection:** Similar to Jake Bauers in a sense because Adames is also one of the more underrated prospects in the game, especially considering his position (shortstop). To be fair, though, he remains a work in progress on the defensive side of the ball. With a bat in his hands, though, Adames has a solid eye at the plate – he's walked in more than 13% of his plate appearances – with pop and a decent hit tool.

**Ceiling:** 3.0-win player
**Risk:** Moderate
**MLB ETA:** 2017

## 6. Jake Bauers, 1B

**MiLB Rank: #65**

**Position Rank: #3**

| Born: 10/06/95 | Age: 20 | Bats: L | Top CALs: Freddie Freeman, Francisco Rivera, |
|---|---|---|---|
| Height: 6-1 | Weight: 195 | Throws: L | Anthony Rizzo, Jon Singleton, Billy Mckinney |

| Season | Age | LVL | PA | 2B | 3B | HR | AVG | OBP | SLG | ISO | BB% | K% | wRC+ |
|---|---|---|---|---|---|---|---|---|---|---|---|---|---|
| 2013 | 17 | R | 188 | 8 | 2 | 1 | 0.282 | 0.341 | 0.374 | 0.092 | 7.4% | 16.5% | 102 |
| 2014 | 18 | A | 467 | 18 | 3 | 8 | 0.296 | 0.376 | 0.414 | 0.118 | 10.9% | 17.1% | 128 |
| 2015 | 19 | A+ | 249 | 14 | 2 | 6 | 0.267 | 0.357 | 0.433 | 0.166 | 11.6% | 13.3% | 142 |
| 2015 | 19 | AA | 285 | 18 | 0 | 5 | 0.276 | 0.329 | 0.405 | 0.128 | 7.4% | 14.4% | 105 |

**Background:** Listed among my Top 25 Breakout Prospects for 2015, Bauers lived up to my lofty expectations last year. The 19-year-old, lefty-swinging first baseman opened the season by torching the Florida State League as he topped the average production mark by a whopping 42% en route to hitting .267/.357/.433 with 14 two-baggers, a pair of triples, and six homeruns. After 59 games the front office promoted Bauers up to the Southern League, where he continued to perform exceptionally well especially considering his youth; he slugged .276/.329/.405 while posting a solid 105 wRC+. Overall, the former Padres seventh round pick in 2013 batted a combined .272/.342/.418 with 32 doubles, two triples, 11 homeruns, and eight stolen bases.

**Projection:** Here's an interesting tidbit: Bauers' overall production in High Class A, 142 wRC+, has been topped by only two other 19-year-olds since 2006: Byron Buxton (155 wRC+, 2013) and Giancarlo Stanton (178 wRC+, 2009).

One of the more underrated prospects in baseball, CAL links Bauers to an impressive list of players highlighted by Freddie Freeman and Anthony Rizzo. Here's what I wrote in last year's book:

> *"His power really seemed to be developing at the onset of [2014] when he was sporting a .169 ISO, but [it] really trailed off after that. Either way, though, he's slugged just nine homeruns in his first 159 games. If the power takes a step forward, he has a chance to be a middle-of-the-lineup thumper. If not, maybe like an Eric Hosmer, post hype."*

Well, after noting Bauers' power in the first part of 2014, he posted an eerily similar mark in the Florida State League last year (.166). It's also incredibly promising that the power he showed in Class AA, .128 ISO, is also the second highest mark of his young career. He might be the best prospect you've never heard of – YET.

**Ceiling:** 3.0-win player
**Risk:** Moderate
**MLB ETA:** 2017

## 7. Jacob Faria, RHP

**MiLB Rank:** #85
**Position Rank:** N/A

| Born: 07/30/93 | Age: 22 | Bats: R | **Top CALs:** Randall Delgado, Johnny Cueto, |
|---|---|---|---|
| Height: 6-4 | Weight: 200 | Throws: R | Edwin Diaz, Eduardo Rodriguez, Josh Hader |

| YEAR | Age | Level | IP | W | L | ERA | FIP | K/9 | BB/9 | K% | BB% | HR/9 | LOB% |
|---|---|---|---|---|---|---|---|---|---|---|---|---|---|
| 2013 | 19 | R | 62.3 | 3 | 3 | 2.02 | 2.10 | 10.25 | 1.30 | 28.6% | 3.6% | 0.29 | 70.3% |
| 2014 | 20 | A | 119.7 | 7 | 9 | 3.46 | 3.55 | 8.05 | 2.41 | 21.5% | 6.4% | 0.68 | 65.0% |
| 2015 | 21 | A+ | 74.3 | 10 | 1 | 1.33 | 2.53 | 7.63 | 2.66 | 22.2% | 7.8% | 0.12 | 83.8% |
| 2015 | 21 | AA | 75.3 | 7 | 3 | 2.51 | 2.85 | 11.47 | 3.58 | 31.9% | 10.0% | 0.60 | 76.3% |

**Background:** Just another one of baby-faced Tampa arms blowing through the lower levels of the minor leagues. Faria, a late round pick all the way back in 2011, didn't make his full season debut until two years ago when he made 23 impressive starts with Bowling Green. But the 6-foot-4, 200-pound right-hander sure as hell made up for lost time in 2015 as he breezed through the Florida State League and saw a noticeable uptick in dominance with Montgomery in the Southern League. Faria would finish his breakout 2015 with a combined 1.92 ERA to go along with 159 whiffs and 52 base-on-balls while surrendering just six homeruns.

Among all minor league starters with at least 140+ innings of work in 2015, Faria's 18.3% strikeout-to-walk percentage ranked third, trailing only Minnesota's Jose Berrios and Chicago's Jordan Guerrero – coincidentally all three were 21-year-olds.

**Projection:** In last year's book I wrote:

> *"Only two other qualified 20-year-old hurlers finished with a better strikeout-to-walk percentage in the Midwest League in [2014]. He's ready to be pushed aggressively. Let's see if the franchise recognizes it."*

How's that for spot-on analysis? The only thing I neglected to do was put Faria among the biggest breakout prospects for last season. Faria isn't overpowering, but optimizes his talent incredibly well by limiting walks, pounding the zone, and keeping the ball in park. He's not the same caliber arm as Snell or Honeywell, but he's not far from it. Solid #2/#3-type arm. He's knocking on the big league club's door. Remember the name. CAL's a big fan as well, linking him to Randall Delgado, Johnny Cueto, Edwin Diaz, Eduardo Rodriguez, and Josh Hader.

**Ceiling:** 2.5- to 3.0-win player
**Risk:** Moderate
**MLB ETA:** 2016

## 8. Garrett Whitley, CF

**MiLB Rank:** #96
**Position Rank:** N/A

| Born: 03/13/97 | Age: 19 | Bats: R | **Top CALs:** Dylan Cozens, Jiandido Tromp, |
|---|---|---|---|
| Height: 6-0 | Weight: 200 | Throws: R | Derek Hill, Lane Thomas, Thomas Hickman |

| Season | Age | LVL | PA | 2B | 3B | HR | AVG | OBP | SLG | ISO | BB% | K% | wRC+ |
|---|---|---|---|---|---|---|---|---|---|---|---|---|---|
| 2015 | 18 | R | 116 | 4 | 2 | 3 | 0.188 | 0.310 | 0.365 | 0.177 | 13.8% | 21.6% | 107 |
| 2015 | 18 | A- | 48 | 0 | 1 | 0 | 0.143 | 0.250 | 0.190 | 0.048 | 10.4% | 25.0% | 41 |

**Background:** The second prep outfielder grabbed last June, 13th overall, Whitley didn't take to wood bats and better pitching as well as the organization would have liked during his debut. The 6-foot, 200-pound, well-built center fielder batted a paltry .188/.310/.365 in 30 games in the Gulf Coast League and took a noticeable step backward when he got (inexplicably) pushed up to the NYPL (.143/.250/.190).

**Projection:** Tampa Bay's never been shy about taking high ceiling prep players, particularly in the first round. Since 1996 the franchise has spent 19 first round selections on high school kids, one on a JuCo prospect, and 11 on collegiate players. As far as Whitley's production is concerned: despite struggling to consistently square up GCL pitching he did manage to top the league average production by 7% thanks to a strong walk rate and above-average power. Obviously, there's not enough data to truly evaluate him at this point so it'll be a wait-and-see approach until following the 2016 season.

**Ceiling:** Too Soon to Tell
**Risk:** N/A
**MLB ETA:** N/A

## 9. Casey Gillaspie, 1B

**MiLB Rank:** #154

**Position Rank:** N/A

| Born: 01/25/93 | Age: 23 | Bats: B | **Top CALs:** Chris Mcguiness, Lucas Duda, |
| Height: 6-4 | Weight: 240 | Throws: L | Matt Clark, Ernie Banks Jr, Dennis Guinn |

| Season | Age | LVL | PA | 2B | 3B | HR | AVG | OBP | SLG | ISO | BB% | K% | wRC+ |
|---|---|---|---|---|---|---|---|---|---|---|---|---|---|
| 2014 | 21 | A- | 308 | 16 | 1 | 7 | 0.262 | 0.364 | 0.411 | 0.148 | 13.6% | 21.1% | 129 |
| 2015 | 22 | R | 7 | 0 | 0 | 0 | 0.000 | 0.143 | 0.000 | 0.000 | 0.0% | 28.6% | -31 |
| 2015 | 22 | A | 268 | 11 | 0 | 16 | 0.278 | 0.358 | 0.530 | 0.252 | 10.4% | 16.0% | 155 |
| 2015 | 22 | A+ | 45 | 0 | 1 | 1 | 0.146 | 0.222 | 0.268 | 0.122 | 8.9% | 20.0% | 51 |

**Background:** The club's first round pick, 20th overall, two years ago out of Wichita State, Gillaspie disappointed a bit, at least for a polished collegiate stick, during his debut in short-season ball when he batted .262/.364/.411 in 71 games. Last season, though, Gillaspie had a coming out party in full-season ball, slugging .278/.358/.530. The switch-hitting first baseman finished second in the Midwest League in homeruns with 16 – despite playing in just 64 games. Gillaspie earned a midseason promotion to the Florida State League but succumbed to a left wrist injury just five games later and missed the next seven or so weeks. He did make it back for eight games, but his overall production with Charlotte is skewed for obvious reasons.

**Projection:** As I noted in last year's book, here's what I wrote prior to Gillaspie's selection in 2014 draft:

*"My favorite collegiate bat – bar none. Above-average power and patience, improving hit tool, the ability to hit from both sides of the plate, and a reasonably strong glove at first. And while he's not going to be a game changer in the professional ranks, I do think he's the cream of the draft crop in terms of [collegiate] offensive upside, perhaps peaking around a .280/.360/.490-type hitter."*

The analysis still seems on point. Gillaspie posted a .252 Isolated Power in Low Class A last season, walked in more than 10% of his plate appearances, and topped the average production by more than 55%. The problem, of course, is that he's now entering his age-23 season with just 13 games above the Midwest League. Meaning: he's performed how a collegiate high round pick should perform against inferior competition. And we likely won't get a better feel until he faces off against Class AA.

**Ceiling:** 2.5-win player
**Risk:** Moderate to High
**MLB ETA:** 2017

## 10. Kevin Padlo, 3B

**MiLB Rank:** N/A

**Position Rank:** N/A

| Born: 07/15/96 | Age: 19 | Bats: R | **Top CALs:** Jonathan Galvez, Dilson Herrera, |
| Height: 6-2 | Weight: 200 | Throws: R | Travis Blankenhorn, Rafael Devers, Dylan Cozens |

| Season | Age | LVL | PA | 2B | 3B | HR | AVG | OBP | SLG | ISO | BB% | K% | wRC+ |
|---|---|---|---|---|---|---|---|---|---|---|---|---|---|
| 2014 | 17 | R | 198 | 15 | 4 | 8 | 0.300 | 0.421 | 0.594 | 0.294 | 15.7% | 19.2% | 155 |
| 2015 | 18 | A- | 308 | 22 | 2 | 9 | 0.294 | 0.404 | 0.502 | 0.208 | 14.6% | 20.1% | 159 |
| 2015 | 18 | A | 99 | 5 | 0 | 2 | 0.145 | 0.273 | 0.277 | 0.133 | 14.1% | 26.3% | 64 |

**Background:** After torching the Pioneer League coming out of Murrieta High School two years ago, Colorado aggressively pushed the former fifth round pick up to the South Atlantic League to begin the 2015 season. And Padlo, a 6-foot-2, 200-pound third baseman, looked overmatched for 27 games before regaining his offensive touch following a demotion to the Northwest League. Despite looking overwhelmed in his brief stint with Asheville last season – he batted a lowly .145/.273/.277 with just seven extra-base hits in 99 plate appearances – Padlo looked as dominant as ever with Boise. In 308 trips to the plate he slugged .294/.404/.502 with 22 doubles, a pair of triples, nine homeruns, and 33 stolen bases (in 38 attempts). The Rays acquired Padlo from the Rockies as part of the Chris Dickerson/Jake McGee swap that also sent German Marquez to Coors.

**Projection:** Above average or better eye at the plate – he walked in over 14% of his plate appearances even during his disastrous showing with Asheville – with 25-homerun potential. Padlo is another one of the club's underrated prospects developing in the low levels of the minors. Look for him to fare much better in 2016 – and a move to High Class A in the second half isn't out of the question either.

**Ceiling:** 2.0- to 2.5-win player
**Risk:** High
**MLB ETA:** 2018

## 11. Enny Romero, LHP

**MiLB Rank:** N/A
**Position Rank:** N/A

| Born: 01/24/91 | Age: 25 | Bats: L | **Top CALs:** Cody Martin, Nick Additon, |
| Height: 6-3 | Weight: 215 | Throws: L | Andy Oliver, Brett Oberholtzer, Chris Reed |

| YEAR | Age | Level | IP | W | L | ERA | FIP | K/9 | BB/9 | K% | BB% | HR/9 | LOB% |
|------|-----|-------|-----|---|---|------|------|------|------|------|------|------|-------|
| 2013 | 22 | AA | 140.3 | 11 | 7 | 2.76 | 3.78 | 7.05 | 4.68 | 18.5% | 12.3% | 0.58 | 77.7% |
| 2013 | 22 | AAA | 8.0 | 0 | 0 | 0.00 | 3.45 | 2.25 | 2.25 | 7.1% | 7.1% | 0.00 | 100.0% |
| 2014 | 23 | AAA | 126.0 | 5 | 11 | 4.50 | 4.13 | 8.36 | 3.71 | 21.2% | 9.4% | 0.93 | 69.0% |
| 2015 | 24 | A+ | 6.7 | 0 | 1 | 6.75 | 3.47 | 6.75 | 5.40 | 16.1% | 12.9% | 0.00 | 58.3% |
| 2015 | 24 | AAA | 46.3 | 1 | 1 | 4.86 | 3.78 | 8.74 | 3.30 | 22.4% | 8.5% | 0.97 | 67.8% |

**Background:** After battling control issues for a couple years Romero seemingly turned the corner in 2014: he posted the second lowest walk rate of professional career and the best one since entering full season ball in 2011. But the Rays opted to push the talented, though enigmatic southpaw to the bullpen last season, and the results were – shockingly – quite positive. The lanky 6-foot-3 lefty spent the year bouncing between The Show and the International League as a bit of swing man, compiling strikeout-to-walk ratios of 31-to-13 and 45-to-17, respectively. His production in Tampa Bay was a bit overshadowed by poor luck as evidenced by his 5.10 ERA and 3.62 SIERA, or Skill Independent ERA.

**Projection:** Romero certainly has the talent to succeed as starter at the game's pinnacle level – he flashed a mid- to upper-90s heater with a history of strong strikeout rates from the left-side – but he's simply caught in a numbers game, pitching behind Chris Archer, Jake Odorizzi, Drew Smyly, Matt Moore, etc… So with that respect, it's not surprisingly to see the move to the pen where the Rays can minimalize his control issues. With his ability to handle multiple innings, it wouldn't be surprising to see him approach 1.5 wins above replacement as a reliever.

**Ceiling:** 1.5-win player
**Risk:** Low to Moderate
**MLB ETA:** Debuted in 2013

## 12. Chris Betts, C

**MiLB Rank:** N/A
**Position Rank:** N/A

| Born: 03/10/97 | Age: 19 | Bats: L | **Top CALs:** N/A |
| Height: 6-1 | Weight: 215 | Throws: R | |

**Background:** Tampa Bay's second round pick last season, 52nd overall, failed to make his professional debut after elbow issues forced him to undergo the knife for Tommy John surgery.

**Projection:** Nothing to go off of except his lofty draft status. Betts was viewed as a potential first round pick prior to the injury, so the organization likely found a nice little deal.

**Ceiling:** 1.0-win player
**Risk:** Moderate to High
**MLB ETA:** 2018

## 13. Justin Williams, LF/RF

**MiLB Rank:** N/A
**Position Rank:** N/A

| Born: 08/20/95 | Age: 20 | Bats: L | **Top CALs:** Cesar Puello, Elvis Escobar, |
| Height: 6-2 | Weight: 215 | Throws: R | Nick Longhi, Alfredo Escalera-Maldonado, Ramon Marcelino |

| Season | Age | LVL | PA | 2B | 3B | HR | AVG | OBP | SLG | ISO | BB% | K% | wRC+ |
|--------|-----|-----|-----|----|----|----|------|------|------|------|------|------|------|
| 2013 | 17 | R | 161 | 12 | 0 | 1 | 0.345 | 0.398 | 0.446 | 0.101 | 5.0% | 21.7% | 138 |
| 2014 | 18 | R | 208 | 6 | 2 | 2 | 0.386 | 0.433 | 0.471 | 0.085 | 8.2% | 21.2% | 138 |
| 2014 | 18 | A | 112 | 6 | 3 | 2 | 0.284 | 0.348 | 0.461 | 0.176 | 6.3% | 20.5% | 131 |
| 2015 | 19 | A | 406 | 25 | 2 | 7 | 0.284 | 0.308 | 0.413 | 0.129 | 3.2% | 18.7% | 107 |
| 2015 | 19 | A+ | 84 | 5 | 0 | 0 | 0.241 | 0.250 | 0.301 | 0.060 | 1.2% | 16.7% | 65 |

**Background:** As Indians announcer Tom Hamilton would say, my prediction of Williams being a breakout prospect last season was a-big-swing-and-a-miss – though to be fair, I was probably just a year early. The former second round pick by the D-Backs spent the majority of the year refining his offensive approach as a 19-year-old in the Midwest League before a late season promotion to High Class A. In 99 games with the Hot Rods, Williams batted a respectable .284/.308/.413 with 25 doubles, two triples, and seven homeruns. His 23-game stint with Charlotte – he batted .241/.250/.301 – tends to cloud his overall production line. For his career, Williams has hit .315/.352/.428.

**Projection:** Combined between his 2014 promotion to the Midwest League and last year's work, Williams is sporting a .281/.316/.418 triple-slash line in 130 games – fantastic work for a teenage prospect. The power hasn't quite developed as expected, but he's been a doubles machine in Low Class A, so that adds to the optimism. On the other end of the spectrum is his walk rate, which was average in rookie ball but declined to sub-average levels in full season ball. As I wrote in last year's book, Williams looks like a fringy big league starter.

**Ceiling:** 1.5- to 2.0-win player
**Risk:** Moderate to High
**MLB ETA:** 2018

## 14. Andrew Velazquez, IF

**MiLB Rank: N/A**
**Position Rank: N/A**

| Born: 07/14/94 | Age: 21 | Bats: B | Top CALs: Yamaico Navarro, Heiker Menses, |
|---|---|---|---|
| Height: 5-8 | Weight: 175 | Throws: R | Malquin Canelo, Jonathan Villar, Tim Beckham |

| Season | Age | LVL | PA | 2B | 3B | HR | AVG | OBP | SLG | ISO | BB% | K% | wRC+ |
|---|---|---|---|---|---|---|---|---|---|---|---|---|---|
| 2013 | 18 | A | 257 | 10 | 4 | 0 | 0.260 | 0.319 | 0.336 | 0.077 | 8.2% | 23.0% | 87 |
| 2014 | 19 | A | 622 | 18 | 15 | 9 | 0.290 | 0.367 | 0.428 | 0.138 | 10.0% | 21.9% | 129 |
| 2015 | 20 | A+ | 203 | 9 | 2 | 0 | 0.290 | 0.343 | 0.360 | 0.070 | 7.4% | 26.1% | 116 |

**Background:** Like Daniel Robertson, Velasquez, who was acquired along with promising outfielder Justin Williams for Jeremy Hellickson, suffered a fractured hamate bone, an injury that eventually required surgery in early May. The former seventh round pick made it back to the Stone Crabs in early July after a quick four-game rehab in the Gulf Coast League. Velazquez was able to sandwich 47 games in the Florida State League around the injury, hitting a respectable .290/.343/.360 with nine doubles, a pair of triples, and five stolen bases while manning shortstop, second and third bases. For his career, he owns a .283/.354/.398 triple-slash line.

**Projection:** Velazquez has always shown a solid amount of pop for a 5-foot-8, 175-pound middle infielder, so his lack of offensive punch last season is likely attributed to the hamate injury. Even in a lost year – and let's be honest, that's what it was – he was still able to top the FSL league average production by more than 15%. He's one of those fringy big league regulars – some make it, most don't. He's always going to have to answer questions about his size, or lack thereof, so it wouldn't be surprising to see him move to the keystone permanently in the coming years.

**Ceiling:** 1.5- to 2.0-win player
**Risk:** Moderate to High
**MLB ETA:** 2017

## 15. Ryan Brett, 2B

**MiLB Rank: N/A**
**Position Rank: N/A**

| Born: 10/09/91 | Age: 24 | Bats: B | Top CALs: Tony Abreu, Chris Bostick, |
|---|---|---|---|
| Height: 5-9 | Weight: 180 | Throws: R | Cory Spangebenberg, Starlin Rodriguez, Trevor Plouffe |

| Season | Age | LVL | PA | 2B | 3B | HR | AVG | OBP | SLG | ISO | BB% | K% | wRC+ |
|---|---|---|---|---|---|---|---|---|---|---|---|---|---|
| 2013 | 21 | A+ | 225 | 11 | 4 | 4 | 0.340 | 0.396 | 0.490 | 0.150 | 6.7% | 12.0% | 155 |
| 2013 | 21 | AA | 114 | 6 | 1 | 3 | 0.238 | 0.289 | 0.400 | 0.162 | 7.0% | 12.3% | 98 |
| 2014 | 22 | AA | 459 | 25 | 6 | 8 | 0.303 | 0.346 | 0.448 | 0.145 | 5.2% | 16.1% | 122 |
| 2015 | 23 | AAA | 354 | 18 | 1 | 5 | 0.247 | 0.288 | 0.354 | 0.107 | 4.2% | 18.1% | 83 |
| 2015 | 23 | MLB | 4 | 1 | 0 | 0 | 0.667 | 0.750 | 1.000 | 0.333 | 25.0% | 0.0% | 372 |

**Background:** Originally taken in the third round way, way back in 2010, Brett failed to do the one thing he's *always* done as professional: hit. After posting a promising .303/.346/.448 triple-slash line with the Montgomery Biscuits in the Southern League two years ago, the pocket-sized switch-hitter batted a disappointing .251/.293/.360 with 18 doubles, one triple, five homeruns, and four stolen bases. His overall production, according to *Weighted Runs Created Plus*, was a career worst 17% *below* the league average mark. For his career, Brett is sporting a .289/.343/.421 triple-slash line with 108 doubles, 22 triples, 29 homeruns, and 138 stolen bases in 170 attempts (81.2% success rate).

**Projection:** Here's what I wrote in last year's book:

> *"Just by looking at Brett one would assume he's destined for future utility-dom. But the power's really starting to develop into an average skill; his ISOs the past two seasons: .152 and .145. He runs well, rarely walks, and has a decent to slightly better than average hit tool. Defensively, he has some ways to go. This might be a bit optimistic, but he could carve out a couple fringy-type everyday seasons, especially if he continues to run."*

And I think there's still reason to believe in Brett – despite his disappointing showing in 2015. Why? Well, the 5-foot-9, 180-pound second baseman suffered a partial shoulder separation while sliding back into first base during his brief early season call-up. So it's not surprising to see his numbers drop, even after a length month-long stint on the DL. Plus, he seemed to turn the corner as he slugged .292/.316/.403 over his final 36 games. I'm still sticking with what I wrote in last year's book.

**Ceiling:** 1.5-win player
**Risk:** Moderate
**MLB ETA:** Debuted in 2015

## 16. Tyler Goeddel, OF

**MiLB Rank: N/A**
**Position Rank: N/A**

| Born: 10/20/92 | Age: 23 | Bats: R | Top CALs: Juan Portes, Peter Bourjos, |
|---|---|---|---|
| Height: 6-4 | Weight: 186 | Throws: R | Sean Henry, Tyler Henson, Casey Craig |

| Season | Age | LVL | PA | 2B | 3B | HR | AVG | OBP | SLG | ISO | BB% | K% | wRC+ |
|---|---|---|---|---|---|---|---|---|---|---|---|---|---|
| 2013 | 20 | A | 497 | 18 | 12 | 7 | 0.249 | 0.313 | 0.389 | 0.140 | 8.0% | 19.7% | 97 |
| 2014 | 21 | A+ | 479 | 25 | 8 | 6 | 0.269 | 0.349 | 0.408 | 0.139 | 9.6% | 20.5% | 118 |
| 2015 | 22 | AA | 533 | 17 | 10 | 12 | 0.279 | 0.350 | 0.433 | 0.154 | 9.0% | 18.4% | 122 |

**Background:** It's taken several years for Goeddel to develop from a supplemental first round pick into a legitimate minor league producer. The Rays, who grabbed the third-basemen-turned-corner-outfielder with the 41st overall pick in 2011, pushed the then-19-year-old straight into the Midwest League the following season and he batted .246/.335/.371. The franchise had him repeat the level the following year with similar results: .249/.313/.389. Goeddel finally got bumped up to Charlotte two years ago and responded by posting a 118 wRC+ to go along with his .269/.349/.408 triple-slash line, his finest season to date.

Until last year.

Goeddel slugged .279/.350/.433 with a career best 122 wRC+ in Class AA, hitting 17 doubles, 10 triples, and 12 homeruns while swiping 28 bases, the fourth consecutive time he's grabbed 20 or more bags in a season.

**Projection:** There's really a lot to like wrapped up in his 6-foot-4, 186-pound frame: above-average speed with the ability to use it efficiently on the base paths (his career success rate is a smidge under 80%), blossoming power that could turn into double-digit homerun pop at the big league level, and a decent hit tool. Tampa Bay has had a tremendous amount of luck – or skill – in developing overlooked outfielders in past seasons (Kevin Kiermaier and Brandon Guyer immediately come to mind), and Goeddel is likely to be the next in line.

**Ceiling:** 1.5-win player
**Risk:** Moderate
**MLB ETA:** 2016

## 17. Hunter Wood, RHP

**MiLB Rank: N/A**
**Position Rank: N/A**

| Born: 08/12/93 | Age: 22 | Bats: R | Top CALs: Ivan Pineyro, Jose Guzman, |
|---|---|---|---|
| Height: 6-1 | Weight: 175 | Throws: R | Robbie Ross Jr, Kevin Comer, Luke Eubank |

| YEAR | Age | Level | IP | W | L | ERA | FIP | K/9 | BB/9 | K% | BB% | HR/9 | LOB% |
|---|---|---|---|---|---|---|---|---|---|---|---|---|---|
| 2013 | 19 | R | 45.0 | 3 | 3 | 3.80 | 3.12 | 11.80 | 2.20 | 31.7% | 5.9% | 1.00 | 70.5% |
| 2014 | 20 | A- | 64.3 | 3 | 4 | 3.08 | 3.35 | 7.97 | 2.24 | 21.3% | 6.0% | 0.42 | 72.4% |
| 2014 | 20 | A | 24.3 | 1 | 0 | 4.07 | 5.75 | 7.77 | 4.44 | 19.6% | 11.2% | 1.48 | 76.4% |
| 2015 | 21 | A | 64.3 | 1 | 4 | 1.82 | 2.28 | 11.33 | 2.24 | 33.3% | 6.6% | 0.42 | 82.0% |
| 2015 | 21 | A+ | 42.0 | 1 | 3 | 2.79 | 2.74 | 6.86 | 1.93 | 19.2% | 5.4% | 0.21 | 67.3% |

**Background:** Originally drafted by the Red Sox in the 32nd round coming out of high school in 2012, Wood headed to JuCO Howard College. And after a rather disappointing freshman season – he finished his lone collegiate season with an unsightly 6.33 ERA and an equally unimpressive 33-to-16 strikeout-to-walk ratio in 27 innings – the Rays took a gamble on the 6-foot-1 righty in the 29th round, where he surprisingly signed. Call it magic. Call it fantastic player development. Call it whatever the hell you want. But since Wood entered the Rays' system he's morphed into a completely different pitcher. After his ugly showing with the Hawks, Wood went out and strung together 45.0-ining stretch no one would have expected – especially from an incoming 29th round pick. He whiffed 59, walked just 11, and tallied a 3.12 FIP.

A nice enough start to a professional career, sure, but he was 19 years old and twirling gems in the Appalachian League. So, yeah, skepticism remained. Until he carried that momentum through the New York-Penn League and right into a six-game stint with Bowling Green two years ago, totaling 88.1 innings of work while averaging 7.9 K/9 and 2.9.

Fine. Twenty-year-olds that rip through the NYPL aren't exactly a rare occurrence. And there goes the skepticism trouncing about. Until he looked like the second coming of Bob freakin' Gibson in the Midwest League last season: he fanned 81 and walked only 16 while posting a 1.82 ERA across 64.1 innings. And now I'm convinced. So what he did in 42 innings in the Florida State League only makes me that much more of a believer: 42.0 IP, 32 K, nine BB.

**Projection**: I'm clearly on the Hunter Wood Express at this point. And it's an incredible scouting find for the Rays to unearth this budding gem in the 29th round *after a horrible showing at a JuCo*. Now is Wood going to be, say, a #1 or #2 caliber arm? Nope. But there's definite MLB starter potential in his right arm, maybe peaking as a good #4. The control's been impeccable; he's averaged more than a punch per inning, and he's ready to be pushed quickly.

**Ceiling:** 1.5-win player
**Risk:** Moderate
**MLB ETA:** Debuted in 2014

## 18. Chih-Wei Hu, RHP

**MiLB Rank:** N/A
**Position Rank:** N/A

| Born: 11/04/93 | Age: 22 | Bats: R | Top CALs: Jose Ortegano, Connor Greene, |
|---|---|---|---|
| Height: 6-1 | Weight: 230 | Throws: R | Ivan Pineyro, Joseph Cruz, Reynaldo Lopez |

| YEAR | Age | Level | IP | W | L | ERA | FIP | K/9 | BB/9 | K% | BB% | HR/9 | LOB% |
|---|---|---|---|---|---|---|---|---|---|---|---|---|---|
| 2013 | 19 | R | 36.7 | 2 | 0 | 2.45 | 1.99 | 9.57 | 1.96 | 26.7% | 5.5% | 0.00 | 69.4% |
| 2014 | 20 | R | 16.0 | 1 | 0 | 1.69 | 2.13 | 9.00 | 1.13 | 27.6% | 3.5% | 0.00 | 70.0% |
| 2014 | 20 | A | 55.0 | 7 | 2 | 2.29 | 2.50 | 7.85 | 2.13 | 22.2% | 6.0% | 0.00 | 63.0% |
| 2015 | 21 | A+ | 103.0 | 5 | 6 | 3.32 | 2.99 | 8.13 | 2.36 | 21.8% | 6.3% | 0.52 | 69.6% |
| 2015 | 21 | AAA | 6.0 | 1 | 0 | 1.50 | 3.16 | 9.00 | 6.00 | 25.0% | 16.7% | 0.00 | 83.3% |

**Background:** A fantastic little pickup at the trade deadline for veteran right-handed reliever Kevin Jepsen. The Taiwanese-born right-hander continued his assault on low level minor league bats last season. Combined between the two organizations Hu tossed 109.0 innings while striking out 99 and walking just 31. He finished the year with a nice 3.22 ERA.

**Projection**: Flying under the radar for the majority of his career, Hu has consistently performed at each stop along the way. He posted a 39-to-8 strikeout-to-walk ratio as a 19-year-old in the GCL; 64-to-15 the following year between the Appalachian and Midwest Leagues, and then the 99-to-33 mark last season. Hu's not quite ready to claim a spot in back of the Rays' pen, but he could be within 12 months.

**Ceiling:** 1.5-win player
**Risk:** Moderate
**MLB ETA:** 2017

## 19. Greg Harris, RHP

**MiLB Rank:** N/A
**Position Rank:** N/A

| Born: 08/17/94 | Age: 21 | Bats: R | Top CALs: Arquimedes Nieto, David Baker, |
|---|---|---|---|
| Height: 6-2 | Weight: 170 | Throws: R | Jordan Walden, Yeiper Castillo, Randall Delgado |

| YEAR | Age | Level | IP | W | L | ERA | FIP | K/9 | BB/9 | K% | BB% | HR/9 | LOB% |
|---|---|---|---|---|---|---|---|---|---|---|---|---|---|
| 2013 | 18 | R | 34.0 | 2 | 3 | 5.29 | 5.30 | 5.82 | 2.38 | 15.3% | 6.3% | 1.06 | 58.4% |
| 2014 | 19 | A | 87.0 | 7 | 6 | 4.45 | 3.55 | 9.52 | 2.90 | 24.5% | 7.5% | 0.72 | 63.9% |
| 2015 | 20 | A | 83.0 | 7 | 5 | 2.17 | 2.65 | 9.11 | 3.04 | 24.1% | 8.1% | 0.11 | 69.5% |
| 2015 | 20 | A+ | 39.7 | 1 | 4 | 3.40 | 3.49 | 5.45 | 3.18 | 14.6% | 8.5% | 0.23 | 69.6% |

**Background:** Acquired from the Dodgers for the aging right arm of Joel Peralta, Harris, who came to Tampa Bay with fellow right-hander Jose Dominguez, split his 2015 campaign between the Midwest and Florida State Leagues last season, totaling 122.2 innings of work with 108 punch outs and 42 free passes. For his

career he's averaging 8.2 K/9 and just 2.9 BB/9.

**Projection**: In last year's book I wrote:

> "The 6-foot-2 right-hander offers a promising swing-and-miss ability and above-average control/command. The sample size is just 121.0 innings, so he could go anywhere from here. But this is exactly the type of gamble the Rays should make in dealing Peralta."

Well, not only did Harris basically double his career total in innings pitched, but his prospect arrow is clearly pointing straight up. He did struggle a bit upon his promotion to High Class A, but he had glimpses of domination as well. For example, of the nine appearances he made with Charlotte, Harris tossed at least six innings with one or fewer runs in three of those games. On the other end of the spectrum, there were three other instances of lasting fewer than five innings with at least three runs allowed. He could be a breakout prospect in 2016. Harris is another mid-rotation caliber arm with high upside as a late-inning reliever.

**Ceiling:** 1.5-win player
**Risk:** Moderate
**MLB ETA:** 2018

## 20. Ryne Stanek, RHP

MiLB Rank: N/A
Position Rank: N/A

| Born: 07/26/91 | Age: 24 | Bats: R | Top CALs: Ryan Searle, Lucas Luetge, |
|---|---|---|---|
| Height: 6-4 | Weight: 180 | Throws: R | Pedro Figueroa, Billy Muldowney, Joseph Krebs |

| YEAR | Age | Level | IP | W | L | ERA | FIP | K/9 | BB/9 | K% | BB% | HR/9 | LOB% |
|---|---|---|---|---|---|---|---|---|---|---|---|---|---|
| 2014 | 22 | R | 1.0 | 0 | 0 | 0.00 | 3.51 | 0.00 | 0.00 | 0.0% | 0.0% | 0.00 | 100.0% |
| 2014 | 22 | A | 44.7 | 3 | 4 | 3.63 | 2.95 | 9.27 | 2.62 | 24.7% | 7.0% | 0.40 | 65.3% |
| 2014 | 22 | A+ | 13.0 | 1 | 1 | 5.54 | 3.93 | 2.77 | 3.46 | 7.3% | 9.1% | 0.00 | 55.6% |
| 2015 | 23 | A+ | 50.7 | 4 | 2 | 1.78 | 3.07 | 6.75 | 2.66 | 19.9% | 7.9% | 0.36 | 77.4% |
| 2015 | 23 | AA | 61.7 | 4 | 3 | 4.09 | 5.01 | 5.98 | 4.52 | 15.7% | 11.9% | 1.02 | 72.8% |

**Background:** Once upon a time in the not-so-distant past Stanek was drawing high praise – almost universally – as a pre-season potential #1 pick in the 2013 draft. But a rather disappointing junior campaign for Arkansas pushed the 6-foot-4 hurler down many draft lists. The Rays would eventually stop Stanek's slide with the 29th overall pick two years ago, but had to wait nearly a year later for his debut, courtesy of hip surgery. After a quick one inning get-your-feet-wet appearance in the Gulf Coast, Stanek made his full season debut with the Bowling Green Hot Rods, throwing 44.2 innings of solid ball before getting bumped up to Charlotte for a three-game stint to close out his season. Last year, at the age of 23, Stanek found himself back in the Florida State League, where he made quick work of the competition, before getting bumped up to Class AA. He would finish the year with a combined 3.04 ERA to go along with 79 punch outs and 46 walks in 112.1 innings. The organization pushed him into a relief role late in the season, likely to cap his inning-limit.

**Projection**: I've never been a particularly large fan of the former Razorback; not in the sense that he isn't big league material – because he most definitely is – but rather he's always been a bit overrated. Outside of his punch-out-per-inning nine-game stretch in the Midwest League two years ago, Stanek's never missed a solid amount of bats: he averaged a lowly 7.19 K/9 in three years in college and currently sports a 6.8 K/9 mark in pro ball. Throw in some fringy-average control and one gets the sense that he's a backend option or late-inning relief arm.

**Ceiling:** 1.0- to 1.5-win player
**Risk:** Moderate
**MLB ETA:** 2016

## 21. Richie Shaffer, 1B/3B

MiLB Rank: N/A
Position Rank: N/A

| Born: 03/15/91 | Age: 25 | Bats: R | Top CALs: Luke Hughes, Pedro Alvarez, |
|---|---|---|---|
| Height: 6-3 | Weight: 220 | Throws: R | Matt Joyce, Travis Tijeron, Josh Fields |

| Season | Age | LVL | PA | 2B | 3B | HR | AVG | OBP | SLG | ISO | BB% | K% | wRC+ |
|---|---|---|---|---|---|---|---|---|---|---|---|---|---|
| 2013 | 22 | A+ | 519 | 33 | 1 | 11 | 0.254 | 0.308 | 0.399 | 0.145 | 6.7% | 20.4% | 99 |
| 2014 | 23 | AA | 491 | 28 | 4 | 19 | 0.222 | 0.318 | 0.440 | 0.218 | 11.4% | 24.2% | 112 |
| 2015 | 24 | AA | 175 | 10 | 0 | 7 | 0.262 | 0.362 | 0.470 | 0.208 | 13.1% | 28.0% | 137 |
| 2015 | 24 | AAA | 282 | 17 | 1 | 19 | 0.270 | 0.355 | 0.582 | 0.311 | 11.0% | 26.2% | 166 |
| 2015 | 24 | MLB | 88 | 3 | 0 | 4 | 0.189 | 0.307 | 0.392 | 0.203 | 11.4% | 36.4% | 98 |

**Background:** This one clearly goes under the "it's-about-damn-time" file as he was touted as one of the most polished collegiate bats coming out of Clemson. Shaffer, the 25th overall pick in 2012, owned some impressive career numbers for the Tigers: he slugged .325/.449/.562 with 81 extra-base hits in 162 games. But with several seasons of uninspiring numbers – including a .222/.318/.440 showing in the Southern League two year ago – it looked as though he was quickly encroaching on bust territory. And then 2015 happened – in a BIG way. Shaffer's Class AA refresher course only last 39 games – of course, batting .262/.362/.470 certainly helps – before the club deemed him ready for the final step: the International League. And that's when Shaffer shifted into high gear: he slugged .270/.355/.582 en route to topping the league average mark by 66%. The Rays would eventually call him up for the stretch run, and despite hitting .192 his patience and power pushed his overall production towards league average status.

**Projection**: So here's what we know: through four minor league seasons spanning more than 380 games Shaffer's sporting a solid, run-of-the-mill .252/.334/.458 triple-slash line, and he's only topped an .800 OPS twice at any level. He'll walk at least eight or nine percent of the time, run into enough fastballs to jack 15- to 20-homeruns and struggle to hit above .240. There's value here, something the Rays can take advantage of, but he's like a poor man's Brandon Moss. CAL links him to a bunch of one-dimensional slugger types as well.

**Ceiling:** 1.0-win player
**Risk:** Low to Moderate
**MLB ETA:** Debuted in 2015

## 22. Kean Wong, 2B

MiLB Rank: N/A

Position Rank: N/A

| Born: 04/17/95 | Age: 21 | Bats: L | Top CALs: Carlos Sanchez, Reegie Corona, |
| Height: 5-11 | Weight: 190 | Throws: R | Odubel Herrera, Jose Pirela, Edilio Colina |

| Season | Age | LVL | PA | 2B | 3B | HR | AVG | OBP | SLG | ISO | BB% | K% | wRC+ |
|---|---|---|---|---|---|---|---|---|---|---|---|---|---|
| 2013 | 18 | R | 194 | 7 | 2 | 0 | 0.328 | 0.377 | 0.390 | 0.062 | 5.7% | 11.3% | 130 |
| 2014 | 19 | A | 454 | 15 | 3 | 2 | 0.306 | 0.347 | 0.370 | 0.064 | 5.9% | 16.1% | 108 |
| 2015 | 20 | A+ | 438 | 14 | 3 | 1 | 0.274 | 0.319 | 0.332 | 0.058 | 6.6% | 14.8% | 99 |

**Background:** Coming from a baseball favorable lineage, Wong, who's older brother Kolten owns the second base starting job for St. Louis, also hails from the same high school, Waiakea HS, as Brewers lefty Kodi Medeiros. The younger Wong, a former 2013 fourth round pick, has acquitted himself nicely during his three-year run in professional baseball. After ripping through the Gulf Coast League (.328/.377/.390), he moved into full season ball with ease by hitting .306/.347/.370 as a 19-year-old in the Midwest League. Last he got bumped up to the California League where he continued to hover around the league average production line; he hit .274/.319/.332 with 14 doubles, three triples, one homerun, and 15 stolen bases (in 21 attempts) en route to tallying a 99 wRC+.

**Projection**: Eerily similar skill set to his older brother, Kean, also a lefty-swinging second baseman, has a fairly advanced approach at the plate considering his youth and level of competition. He showcases a line-drive stroke with gap power, a decent eye at the plate, some speed, and a potential above-average hit tool. It the power can take another step or two forward he could develop into a league average or slightly better regular.

**Ceiling:** 1.0- to 1.5-win player
**Risk:** Moderate
**MLB ETA:** 2018

## 23. Justin O'Conner, C

MiLB Rank: N/A

Position Rank: N/A

| Born: 03/31/92 | Age: 24 | Bats: R | Top CALs: Kellin Deglan, Sebastian Valle, |
| Height: 6-0 | Weight: 190 | Throws: R | Jorge Alfaro, Brian Peacock, William Swanner |

| Season | Age | LVL | PA | 2B | 3B | HR | AVG | OBP | SLG | ISO | BB% | K% | wRC+ |
|---|---|---|---|---|---|---|---|---|---|---|---|---|---|
| 2013 | 21 | A | 439 | 17 | 0 | 14 | 0.233 | 0.290 | 0.381 | 0.148 | 7.1% | 25.3% | 88 |
| 2014 | 22 | A+ | 340 | 31 | 2 | 10 | 0.282 | 0.321 | 0.486 | 0.204 | 4.4% | 22.9% | 127 |
| 2015 | 23 | AA | 444 | 27 | 3 | 9 | 0.231 | 0.255 | 0.371 | 0.140 | 2.9% | 29.1% | 72 |

**Background:** One of the bigger pleasant surprises two years ago, O'Conner, a former first round pick in 2010, 31st overall, had a coming out party during his time with Charlotte. After posting sub-.700 OPSs during his first four professional seasons (which doesn't include his .200/.264/.322 showing with Brisbane in the Australian Baseball League), O'Conner slugged .282/.321/.486 with 31 doubles, a pair of triples, and 10 homeruns. The front office would bump him up to Montgomery for the final 21 games of the year, and the numbers, while not as impressive, were a solid showing for a young backstop (.263/.298/.388). This season, however, the wheels on O'Conner's bus fell off. In a big way. A sluggish April (.188/.243/.328) turned into a depressing May (.232/.241/.329) which gave way to a pathetic June (.210/.229/.358). And even his production spike in July (.267/.298/.478) wasn't enough to help right the ship as he batted .217/.234/.337 in August.

**Projection**: Here's what I wrote in last year's book:

*"He's always shown solid-average pop but it took another step forward [in 2014]. The hit tool and walk rate are questionable, but he can control the running game like few others in the minors; he's thrown out 43% of would-be base stealers throughout his career."*

Pretty much the same thing could be said after his poor showing in 2015. O'Conner posted a solid .140 ISO, but struggled to hit for any type of respectable average and walked in just 2.9% of his plate appearances. On the defensive side of the ball, he did manage to throw out a staggering 48% of potential base thieves. He looks like a solid back up backstop, capable of providing some defensive value while packing a little bit of a punch at the plate.

**Ceiling:** 1.0- to 1.5-win player
**Risk:** Moderate to High
**MLB ETA:** 2017

## 24. Patrick Leonard, 1B/3B

| Born: 10/20/92 | Age: 23 | Bats: R | Top CALs: Lance Ray, Tyler Henson, |
| Height: 6-4 | Weight: 225 | Throws: R | Matt Helm, Michael A. Taylor, Michael Burgess |

| Season | Age | LVL | PA | 2B | 3B | HR | AVG | OBP | SLG | ISO | BB% | K% | wRC+ |
|---|---|---|---|---|---|---|---|---|---|---|---|---|---|
| 2013 | 20 | A | 493 | 26 | 0 | 9 | 0.225 | 0.303 | 0.345 | 0.120 | 8.5% | 23.9% | 85 |
| 2014 | 21 | A+ | 515 | 26 | 5 | 13 | 0.284 | 0.359 | 0.448 | 0.165 | 9.5% | 20.8% | 131 |
| 2015 | 22 | AA | 514 | 32 | 3 | 10 | 0.256 | 0.350 | 0.408 | 0.152 | 10.5% | 25.1% | 118 |

**Background:** The lessen known part of the blockbuster deal involving James Shields and the Kansas City Royals, Leonard continued to put his stumble with Bowling Green in 2013 further in his rearview mirror. The corner infielder who has also moonlighted briefly as a right fielder batted a lowly .225/.303/.345 during his full season debut with the Hot Rods, but rebounded the following season in High Class A, hitting .284/.359/.448 with 26 doubles, five triples, and 13 homeruns with Charlotte. Last season his numbers took a modest step backward as he faced off against the more advanced Class AA pitching: he slugged .256/.350/.408 with a career high 32 doubles, three triples, 10 homeruns, and 11 stolen bases.

**Projection:** I've been intrigued by Leonard's offensive potential since prior to the inclusion in the December 2012 mega-deal. A 6-foot-4 and 225 pounds, he built solidly, has always shown solid-average or better power, surprising speed, and slightly better-than-average patience at the plate. And outside of his poor showing in the Midwest League two years ago, he's always performed well against older competition. The lone red flag so far is his rather questionable hit tool. Leonard has the potential to be a fringy big leaguer with added coming from his ability to man multiple positions.

**Ceiling:** 1.0- to 1.5-win player
**Risk:** Moderate to High
**MLB ETA:** 2017

## 25. Cameron Varga, RHP

| Born: 08/19/94 | Age: 21 | Bats: R | Top CALs: Jamaine Cotton, Rudy Owens, |
| Height: 6-2 | Weight: 189 | Throws: R | Cesar Cabral, Jake Buchanan, Jayson Aquino |

| YEAR | Age | Level | IP | W | L | ERA | FIP | K/9 | BB/9 | K% | BB% | HR/9 | LOB% |
|---|---|---|---|---|---|---|---|---|---|---|---|---|---|
| 2014 | 19 | R | 19.0 | 1 | 1 | 4.74 | 4.20 | 5.21 | 3.32 | 12.9% | 8.2% | 0.47 | 66.5% |
| 2014 | 19 | R | 14.3 | 2 | 0 | 2.51 | 1.76 | 8.79 | 0.63 | 25.9% | 1.9% | 0.00 | 69.2% |
| 2015 | 20 | A- | 57.7 | 3 | 6 | 2.97 | 3.19 | 6.09 | 1.72 | 16.1% | 4.5% | 0.31 | 64.7% |

**Background:** The club's second round pick two years ago out of Cincinnati Hills Christian Academy, Varga has been slowly pushed through his first two professional seasons. After splitting his debut between the Appalachian and Gulf Coast Leagues while totaling a 25-to-8 strikeout-to-walk ratio. The organization pushed him up to the New York-Penn League last season and Varga once again limited free passes (1.7 BB/9), missed a couple bats (6.1 K/9), and posted another solid FIP (3.19). For his career Varga has averaged 6.3 strikeouts and just 1.9 base on balls per nine innings.

**Projection:** Similar production as org-mate Taylor Guerrieri in the sense that the duo has above-average control and sub-optimal strikeout rates. And despite the slow climb up the minor league ladder Varga looks primed to start moving quickly. He could be a nice mid- to back-of-the-rotation caliber arm if everything breaks just the right way.

**Ceiling:** 1.0- to 1.5-win player
**Risk:** Moderate to High
**MLB ETA:** 2018

## *Barely Missed:*

- **Riley Unroe, 2B** – The club shifted the 2013 second round pick from shortstop to across the keystone last season, but the move did little to inspire his lagging offense. After a promising, though OBP-driven, debut in the Gulf, Unroe batted a lowly .226/.315/.325 in the Appalachian League the following season and performed modestly better after his promotion to full season ball last season (.255/.333/.321). Little power, but a nose for first.

- **Andrew Bellatti, RHP** – During his 23.1-inning debut with Tampa Bay, Bellatti showcased a low 90s fastball, a slow, low 80s slider, and a changeup. He's been plagued by the long ball at various points in his career, with 2015 being no exception. But solid average control with the ability to miss a handful of bats likely guarantees him some middle relief work.

## *Bird Doggin' It – Additional Prospects to Keep an Eye in 2016*

| Player | Age | POS | Notes |
|--------|-----|-----|-------|
| Kyle Bird | 23 | LHP | 35th round pick out of Flagler College two years ago, Bird spent the year pitching out of relief for Bowling Green, averaging 9.0 K/9 and 2.4 BB/9. |
| Blake Bivens | 20 | RHP | The 6-foot-2 right-hander showed some decent signs of prospect life as a 19-year-old in the Appalachian League last season, fanning 18.3% and walking 7.7% of the total batters he faced. |
| Brock Burke | 19 | LHP | Taken in the third round two years ago, the 6-foot-2 southpaw posted a 35-to-11 strikeout-to-walk ratio. He likely ready for full season ball. |
| Henry Centeno | 21 | RHP | It took the Centeno three years to get out of the Venezuelan Summer League, but since coming stateside in 2014 he hasn't looked back. Centeno posted a nearly identical 3.89 ERA and 4.02 FIP. |
| Yonny Chirinos | 22 | RHP | Dominated the NYPL for three starts, easily handled the Midwest League competition for another 10. Extreme control pitcher who's averaged about seven punch outs per nine innings in his career. |
| Nick Cuiffo | 21 | C | The 21st overall pick in 2013, Cuiffo has yet to top a .625 OPS at any point in his three-year career. Last season's walk rate, 1.9%, and power, .067 ISO, are almost comical if they weren't sad. |
| Johnny Field | 24 | OF | Former University of Arizona outfielder filled the stat sheet in Class AA: .255/.329/.447 with 33 doubles, four triples, 14 homeruns, and 18 stolen bases. |
| Dylan Floro | 25 | RHP | Owner of some of the finest control in the minors, Floro's walked just 3.5% of the batters he's faced *in his career*. Should be a bounce-back candidate based on his 5.02 ERA and 3.39 FIP. There might be a chance for some positive MLB impact here. |
| Mike Franco | 24 | RHP | Ridiculous stat line between the Midwest and Florida State Leagues last season: 67.1 IP, 1.47 ERA, 71 K, and 22 BB. |
| Garrett Fulenchek | 20 | RHP | Acquired the 2014 second rounder from the Braves for draft pool bonus money. Fulenchek couldn't hit the broad side of a barn last season, walking 22 in 17.2 innings. |
| Ryan Garton | 26 | RHP | Former 34th round pick nearly doubled his strikeout rate from the previous season, going from 5.9 K/9 in High Class A to 10.2 K/9 in Class AA. |
| Moises Gomez | 17 | OF | Mashed to the tune of .317/.393/.494 as a 16-year-old in the Venezuelan Summer League. He could be something. Or not. But he looks ready for the next challenge. |
| Jake Hager | 22 | SS | The 32nd pick in 2011 has basically hovered around league average production throughout his career. Last season's showing in Class AA, .271/.316/.376 with a 93 wRC+, is just the latest. |
| Bralin Jackson | 22 | OF | Toolsy outfield can superficially look like a promising prospect – he slugged 19 doubles, three triples, and three homeruns while swiping 14 stolen bases last season – but he's very inefficient. |
| Christopher Kirsch | 24 | LHP | 6-foot-2 southpaw had a decent year as he split time between Charlotte and Montgomery: 137 IP, 103 K, and 49 BB. |
| Brando Koch | 22 | RHP | Ridiculously dominant in Short Season ball during his debut, fanning more than 36% of the hitters he faced. Yeah, that'll play. |
| Matt Lollis | 25 | RHP | Minor league veteran averaged 8.8 K/9 and 4.4 BB/9 in Class AA. Despite spending seven seasons in the minors Lollis has tallied just 11 Class AAA innings. |
| Brandon Lowe | 21 | 2B | Grabbed the University of Maryland second baseman in the third round last year. Lowe owns a .338/.448/.509 and showed promising pop as a middle infielder in the Big 10 during his final season. |
| Mikie Mahtook | 26 | OF | Played way over his head during his run with the Rays last season, but he's a nice fourth outfielder. Average eye, decent hit tool, a little bit of pop and speed. |
| Joe McCarthy | 22 | 1B/OF | Back surgery and his subsequent decline in production caused the collegiate sabermetric superstar to tumble to the fifth round. Batted a solid .277/.362/.337 and could be poised to move quick if the injury is fully behind him. |
| Thomas Milone | 21 | CF | Speedy center field doesn't pack much of an offensive punch might have the potential to be a fourth/fifth outfielder. |

## *Bird Doggin' It – Additional Prospects to Keep an Eye in 2016*

| Player | Age | POS | Notes |
|---|---|---|---|
| Benton Moss | 23 | RHP | Turned in one of the better debuts among the entire draft class last season, Moss looked like a budding ace in the NYPL: 58.1 IP, 66 K, 10 BB, and a 2.93 ERA. He has a rather limited ceiling, but, damn, what a debut. |
| Taylor Motter | 26 | IF/OF | Defensive jack-of-all-trades had his finest professional season to date with Durham: .292/.366/.471 with 43 doubles, one triple, 14 homeruns, and 26 stolen bases. He's entering his age-26 season, but should at least be bench worthy. |
| Jose Mujica | 20 | RHP | Impressive statistic to remember: he's walked 13 in his 100.0 career innings. |
| Travis Ott | 21 | LHP | Part of the Steven Souza package acquired from the Nats, Ott spent the year with Hudson Valley: 60 IP, 56 K, and 20 BB. |
| Austin Pruitt | 26 | RHP | Always a bit old for his level of competition, Pruitt, nonetheless, posted a 122-to-38 strikeout-to-walk ratio with Montgomery in the Southern League. He might be a decent big league relief option. |
| Joey Rickard | 25 | OF | Began the year with Charlotte (.268/.436/.310), but soon caught fire and didn't slow down throughout the rest of the year. He batted .322/.420/.479 with Montgomery and .360/.437/.472 with Durham. |
| Adrian Rondon | 17 | SS | Got knocked around as a 16-year-old in the GCL last season (.166/.256/.234). But any time a kid that young makes his pro debut at that level is at least intriguing. |
| Cameron Seitzer | 26 | 1B/3B/LF | Slugged .308/.383/.475 in his third round at Class AA. He's now entering his age-26 season with just 30 plate appearances above the Southern League. |
| Angel Yepez | 21 | RHP | Young right-hander with pinpoint control and decent punch out rates. He's finally ready for full season ball. |

# Texas Rangers

**State of the Farm System:** The very definition of a boom-or-bust farm system, the Rangers are chock full of some of the best power hitters, lively-armed pitchers, and overall world class athletes found in a single organization.

Joey Gallo can hit 'em to the moon and eventually get there by in a rocket propelled solely on free passes, but the amount of hacks he'll eventually accrue will create a large enough force to propel the world a couple extra rotations. Outfielder Nomar Mazara, the club's top prospect, has plenty of God-given ability oozing from every single pore, but he'll need to continue to take the proper strides against southpaws; otherwise he'll be eaten alive. Center fielder Lewis Brinson, another gifted athlete, took advantage of High Desert's hitter-friendly ballpark by slugging .337/.416/.628, but he managed to shave off some needed strikeouts.

And then there's three of the club's more promising arms: right-handers Dillon Tate, Luis Ortiz, and Michael Matuella – each, of course, bringing their own red flags to the party.

Tate, the club's most recent first round pick, fourth overall, was a revelation during his time with UC Santa Barbara, but will his body be able to withstand the rigors of grabbing the ball every fifth day? The 6-foot-2, 165-pound right-hander was moved into the rotation for the first time last season.

Ortiz, a first round pick in 2014, was absolutely brilliant in his first taste of the South Atlantic League, averaging 8.3 strikeouts and just 1.6 walks per nine innings. The problem: a strained flexor muscle forced him to miss about three months of action.

Matuella, the behemoth right-hander out of Duke University, was widely lauded as a potential #1 overall pick during the preseason, but continued injury issues forced him to tumble all the way down to the third round.

The Rangers have easily one of the most talented systems in baseball, but that comes at a very real cost: it's highly volatile.

Two or three years down the road we all could be talking about the sheer amount of talent the system's churned out. Just as easily we could be lamenting how the system was one of the contributing factors in the Rangers' collapse.

**Review of the 2015 Draft:** Keeping with the organizational theme of Go Big or Go Home, the Rangers grabbed two of the most sought after collegiate arms in the draft, taking Dillon Tate with the fourth overall pick and then grabbing University – oft-injured – stud Michael Matuella two rounds later. If either achieves their big league potential it's an easy win for Texas.

Second round pick Eric Jenkins, a prep outfielder, had a mediocre showing with the bat (.262/.348/.349), but was a speed demon on the base paths. And thrice-drafted lefty Adam Choplick, who was taken in the 14th round out of Oklahoma, could be a nice little find.

But, again, a lot of the draft class' success hinges on the right arms of Tate and Matuella.

| Rank | Name | POS |
|---|---|---|
| 1 | Nomar Mazara | LF/RF |
| 2 | Lewis Brinson | CF |
| 3 | Joey Gallo | 3B/LF |
| 4 | Dillon Tate | RHP |
| 5 | Luis Ortiz | RHP |
| 6 | Ariel Jurado | RHP |
| 7 | Michael Matuella | RHP |
| 8 | Luke Jackson | RHP |
| 9 | Jairo Beras | OF |
| 10 | David Perez | RHP |
| 11 | Andrew Faulkner | LHP |
| 12 | Josh Morgan | 2B/3B/SS |
| 13 | Yohander Mendez | LHP |
| 14 | Evan Van Hoosier | 2B/OF |
| 15 | Frank Lopez | LHP |
| 16 | Ronald Guzman | 1B |
| 17 | Eric Jenkins | CF |
| 18 | Brett Martin | LHP |
| 19 | Joe Jackson | LF |
| 20 | Jose Leclerc | RHP |
| 21 | Drew Robinson | IF/OF |
| 22 | Travis Demeritte | 2B/3B |
| 23 | Juremi Profar | IF |
| 24 | Yeyson Yrizarri | SS |
| 25 | Ti'Quan Forbes | 3B/SS |

# 1. Nomar Mazara, LF/RF

**MiLB Rank: #12**
**Position Rank: #2**

| Born: 04/26/95 | Age: 21 | Bats: L | **Top CALs:** Andrew Lambo, Caleb Gindl, |
| Height: 6-4 | Weight: 195 | Throws: L | Chris Marrero, Josh Bell, Marcell Ozuna |

| Season | Age | LVL | PA | 2B | 3B | HR | AVG | OBP | SLG | ISO | BB% | K% | wRC+ |
|--------|-----|-----|-----|----|----|----|-------|-------|-------|-------|-------|-------|------|
| 2013 | 18 | A | 506 | 23 | 2 | 13 | 0.236 | 0.310 | 0.382 | 0.146 | 8.7% | 25.9% | 101 |
| 2014 | 19 | A | 461 | 21 | 2 | 19 | 0.264 | 0.358 | 0.470 | 0.206 | 12.4% | 21.5% | 130 |
| 2015 | 20 | AA | 470 | 22 | 2 | 13 | 0.284 | 0.357 | 0.443 | 0.159 | 10.0% | 19.6% | 123 |
| 2015 | 20 | AAA | 88 | 4 | 0 | 1 | 0.358 | 0.409 | 0.444 | 0.086 | 5.7% | 11.4% | 132 |

**Background:** Signed to a then-record $4.95 million deal on the international free agent market as a precocious 16-year-old during Texas' wildly busy 2011 spending spree which also added fellow top prospect Ronald Guzman on a pact worth more than $3 million. Mazara, who stands an imposing 6-foot-4 and 195 pounds, has quickly risen through the minors as one of the game's top young bats. The Dominican-born prospect made his professional debut in 2012 at the age of 17, slugging .264/.383/.448 with plenty of extra-base firepower in the Arizona Summer League. He struggled a bit the next season as the organization aggressively pushed him straight up to the South Atlantic League as he batted a lowly .236/.310/.382, but fared much better in his return to the level in 2014. Still one of Low Class A's youngest everyday bats Mazara hit .264/.358/.470 with 21 doubles, a pair of triples, and 19 homeruns in 106 with Hickory. And, once again, the organization continued to forcefully challenge the developing hitter by bouncing him all the way up the Texas League for his remaining 24 games.

Last season, just his fourth in professional baseball, Mazara ripped through the Class AA pitching, hitting .284/.357/.443, and torched the Pacific Coast League for 20 games (.358/.409/.444). He finished the year with an aggregate .296/.366/.443 triple-slash line to go along with 26 doubles, two triples, and 14 homeruns.

**Projection**: First, here's what I wrote in last year's book when I ranked the surging teenager as the system's sixth best prospect:

*"Plus-power potential with a tremendous feel for the strike zone and strong contact skills – against right-handers. Southpaws, on the hand, are a totally different issue.*

*In 317 plate appearances against left-handed pitching, Mazara's hit .194/.290/.276 (compared to .276/.364/.486 vs. RHP). And [2014's] work against lefties – .200/.268/.331 – was hardly better. So with all these potential platoon issues, one was to wonder why the club decided to push the then-19-year-old past High Class A and straight into the Texas League. CAL doesn't seem to be particularly impressed with Mazara either, for what it's worth. But he has plenty of time to [LHP] out."*

OK. Let's update that a bit, shall we? Mazara tallied a .599 OPS against fellow southpaws in 2014, but he improved upon that total by nearly a 100 full points in 2015; he batted .239/.336/.358. But, again, just seven of his 42 extra-base hits came against LHP. Improvements are improvements, and it's especially important given his youth, developmental path, and level of competition.

Mazara's still flashing above-average to potentially plus-power, a solid eye at the plate, and incredibly strong contact skills for a middle-of-the-lineup thumper. And CAL seems to be coming around on Mazara as well, linking him to the Pirates' Josh Bell and Miami's Marcell Ozuna. If he can continue to make strides against lefties the world better watch out because he's an impact bat waiting to happen.

**Ceiling:** 4.0- to 4.5-win player
**Risk:** Moderate
**MLB ETA:** 2016

# 2. Lewis Brinson, CF

**MiLB Rank: #20**
**Position Rank: #5**

| Born: 05/08/94 | Age: 22 | Bats: R | **Top CALs:** Oswaldo Arcia, Brett Phillips, |
| Height: 6-3 | Weight: 170 | Throws: R | Brett Jackson, Zoilo Almonte, Jay Bruce |

| Season | Age | LVL | PA | 2B | 3B | HR | AVG | OBP | SLG | ISO | BB% | K% | wRC+ |
|--------|-----|-----|-----|----|----|----|-------|-------|-------|-------|-------|-------|------|
| 2013 | 19 | A | 503 | 18 | 2 | 21 | 0.237 | 0.322 | 0.427 | 0.190 | 9.5% | 38.0% | 117 |
| 2014 | 20 | A | 186 | 8 | 1 | 10 | 0.335 | 0.405 | 0.579 | 0.244 | 9.7% | 24.7% | 172 |
| 2014 | 20 | A+ | 199 | 8 | 1 | 3 | 0.246 | 0.307 | 0.350 | 0.104 | 7.5% | 25.1% | 87 |
| 2015 | 21 | A+ | 298 | 22 | 7 | 13 | 0.337 | 0.416 | 0.628 | 0.291 | 10.4% | 21.5% | 177 |
| 2015 | 21 | AA | 120 | 8 | 1 | 6 | 0.291 | 0.328 | 0.545 | 0.255 | 5.0% | 23.3% | 138 |
| 2015 | 21 | AAA | 37 | 1 | 0 | 1 | 0.433 | 0.541 | 0.567 | 0.133 | 18.9% | 16.2% | 207 |

**Background:** Overshadowed by his draft mates, Brinson has a chance to develop into the best overall player taken by the Rangers in their vaunted 2012 class (which included Gallo, Nick Williams, and Alex Asher). The 29th overall selection that year, Brinson spent time at three levels last season, making stops at High Class A and Class AA before finishing with a quick eight-game jaunt through the Pacific Coast League. The toolsy center fielder, who sounds like he should be packin' a pocket protector and not an offensive skill set loaded with above-average tools, hit a combined .332/.403/.601 with career bests in doubles (31), triples (8), and homeruns (20) while finishing with his second highest total in stolen bases (18). And just to add a little perspective with regards to his overall production consider the following: Brinson's overall production topped the league average mark by a mind-boggling 69% last season; the next best showing for a player under the age of 22 with at least 400 plate appearances was Cleveland's Bobby Bradley, who posted a 149 wRC+ in Low Class A.

**Projection**: Let's run down the checklist: Above-average power? Yes. Solid or better patience at the plate? Yup. Speed? You got it. Defensive prowess? Right on. Promising hit tool? Check. Most importantly, unlike his more famous organizational mate Joey Gallo, Brinson's strikeout rates have been trending in the right direction the past couple of years, going from 38% in the Sally in 2013 all the way down to a far more reasonable 21.5% last season. CAL seems to be a big believer in Brinson as well, tying him to Oswaldo Arcia, Brett Phillips, and Jay Bruce, who was once widely recognized as the game's top prospect.

**Ceiling**: 3.5- to 4.0-win player
**Risk**: Moderate
**MLB ETA**: 2017

# 3. Joey Gallo, 3B/LF

**MiLB Rank: #46**
**Position Rank: #2 (3B), #14 (OF)**

| Born: 11/19/93 | Age: 22 | Bats: L | Top CALs: Cody Johnson, Miguel Sano, |
| Height: 6-5 | Weight: 230 | Throws: R | Telvin Nash, Mark Reynolds, Pedro Alvarez |

| Season | Age | LVL | PA | 2B | 3B | HR | AVG | OBP | SLG | ISO | BB% | K% | wRC+ |
|---|---|---|---|---|---|---|---|---|---|---|---|---|---|
| 2013 | 19 | A | 446 | 19 | 5 | 38 | 0.245 | 0.334 | 0.610 | 0.365 | 10.8% | 37.0% | 163 |
| 2014 | 20 | A+ | 246 | 9 | 3 | 21 | 0.323 | 0.463 | 0.735 | 0.413 | 20.7% | 26.0% | 221 |
| 2014 | 20 | AA | 291 | 10 | 0 | 21 | 0.232 | 0.334 | 0.524 | 0.292 | 12.4% | 39.5% | 141 |
| 2015 | 21 | AA | 146 | 10 | 1 | 9 | 0.314 | 0.425 | 0.636 | 0.322 | 16.4% | 33.6% | 192 |
| 2015 | 21 | AAA | 228 | 9 | 0 | 14 | 0.195 | 0.289 | 0.450 | 0.255 | 11.8% | 39.5% | 90 |
| 2015 | 21 | MLB | 123 | 3 | 1 | 6 | 0.204 | 0.301 | 0.417 | 0.213 | 12.2% | 46.3% | 85 |

**Background**: Sharing the same personal hitting coach as Chicago's Kris Bryant – who also happens to be Bryant's father – Gallo failed to live up to expectations for first time in his four-year professional career. Part of the Rangers' better draft classes in recent memory – the 2012 class infused the system with the likes of Gallo, Lewis Brinson, Nick Williams, and Alex Asher, the latter two being dealt to Philadelphia in the Cole Hamels trade – Gallo regularly sent the Texas League pitchers ducking for cover as he mashed a robust .314/.425/.636 with 20 extra-base hits in just 34 games. The Rangers called up the former supplemental first rounder in early June. And after a 3-for-5 showing against the White Sox in his Big League game, Gallo batted just .193/.280/.386 over his next 24 games with Texas before getting demoted to the Pacific Coast League.

After that Gallo never seemed to be able to right the ship: he had his worst showing at any minor league level, hitting .195/.289/.450 in 53 games with Round Rock and went 3-for-21 in his second call-up to Texas down the stretch.

**Projection**: Blessed with as much power as *anyone* at any level of baseball, both nationally and internationally. Gallo has posed three questions during his tear through the minor leagues:

1. Where's it going to land?
2. Is he going to make enough contact?
3. And can he do enough damage against left-handed pitching or will he ultimately be forced into a platoon role?

Here are the answers:

1. Probably the moon. Maybe even Mars.
2. I don't think so. Gallo is whiffing at some pretty prodigious rates: since entering Class AA two years ago – and including his work with Texas – the lefty-swinging third baseman has punched out 311 times in 788 trips to the plate, or just a shade less than 40% of the time. It's awfully hard to be a valuable player at any level when you're punching out at that rate.
3. Outside of last year's pitiful showing against southpaws, Gallo has always performed exceptionally well against LHP: he posted OPS totals of 1.393, 1.186, and 1.049 from 2012 through 2014. So last year's .151/.234/.317 was likely just a blimp on the screen.

It's not really surprising that CAL links Gallo to a bunch of all-or-nothing bats in Miguel Sano, Mark Reynolds, and Pedro Alvarez. And just like the later two, I think Gallo will be a solid big league bat capable of mashing 35+ homeruns, but he'll ultimately be a victim of his own hype (which is unfortunate).

**Ceiling**: 3.0- to 3.5-win player

**Risk:** Moderate
**MLB ETA:** Debuted in 2015

## 4. Dillon Tate, RHP

**MiLB Rank: #77**
**Position Rank: N/A**

| Born: 05/01/94 | Age: 22 | Bats: R | Top CALs: N/A |
|---|---|---|---|
| Height: 6-2 | Weight: 165 | Throws: R | |

| YEAR | Age | Level | IP | W | L | ERA | FIP | K/9 | BB/9 | K% | BB% | HR/9 | LOB% |
|---|---|---|---|---|---|---|---|---|---|---|---|---|---|
| 2015 | 21 | A- | 2.0 | 0 | 0 | 0.00 | 5.10 | 13.50 | 13.50 | 37.5% | 37.5% | 0.00 | 100.0% |
| 2015 | 21 | A | 7.0 | 0 | 0 | 1.29 | 3.91 | 6.43 | 0.00 | 21.7% | 0.0% | 1.29 | 100.0% |

**Background:** One of the – if not *the* – biggest draft riser in last year's class, Tate had a successful conversion into UC Santa Barbara's rotation after spending the previous two years pitching out of the school's bullpen. In 14 starts, the bespectacled right-hander posted a strong 111-to-28 strikeout-to-walk ratio in a career best 103.1 innings. The club grabbed Tate with the fourth overall pick last June.

**Projection**: Here's what I wrote prior to the draft last season:

> "An interesting tidbit: Since 1967, there have been just four players out of UC Santa Barbara drafted before the fourth round: Maury Ornest, Barry Zito, Chris Valaika, and Joe Gardner – all of whom were third round picks.
>
> Obviously, Tate, who's in the running for the top overall pick, will easily surpass them as the earliest Gaucho selection.
>
> For his part, Tate offers up plenty of upside in the rotation to go along with an incredibly high floor as potential shutdown reliever. Because of his relative lack of his experience he has far less wear-and-tear than many of the other collegiate arms available, but that does come with a caveat of sorts: how will his arm/body respond to multiple seasons of 160+ innings?
>
> It's certainly encouraging that his strikeout rate during his season as UC Santa Barbara's closer, 9.55, and this season, 9.37 [at that point], are nearly identical. And while he lacks a lengthy track record against premium opponents, he has shined against Kentucky (7.0 IP, 9K, 2BB), Oregon (7.1 IP, 8K, 4BB), Long Beach State (9.0 IP, 10K, 1BB), and Cal State Fullerton (5.2 IP, 8K, 4BB).
>
> Tate looks like a potential upper-half-of-the-rotation caliber starting pitcher, maybe eventually peaking as a true #1."

**Ceiling:** 3.5- to 4.0-win player
**Risk:** High
**MLB ETA:** 2017/2018

## 5. Luis Ortiz, RHP

**MiLB Rank: #95**
**Position Rank: N/A**

| Born: 09/22/95 | Age: 20 | Bats: R | Top CALs: David Holmberg, Casey Kelly, |
|---|---|---|---|
| Height: 6-3 | Weight: 230 | Throws: R | Arodys Vizcaino, Nick Adenhart, Luis Severino |

| YEAR | Age | Level | IP | W | L | ERA | FIP | K/9 | BB/9 | K% | BB% | HR/9 | LOB% |
|---|---|---|---|---|---|---|---|---|---|---|---|---|---|
| 2014 | 18 | R | 13.3 | 1 | 1 | 2.03 | 2.68 | 10.13 | 2.03 | 27.8% | 5.6% | 0.00 | 81.3% |
| 2014 | 18 | A | 7.0 | 0 | 0 | 1.29 | 5.59 | 5.14 | 3.86 | 13.8% | 10.3% | 1.29 | 100.0% |
| 2015 | 19 | A | 50.0 | 4 | 1 | 1.80 | 2.50 | 8.28 | 1.62 | 22.9% | 4.5% | 0.18 | 80.2% |

**Background:** The club's first round pick out of Sanger High School two years ago put on a clinic of dominance during his abbreviated sophomore campaign. Ortiz, who missed nearly three months with a strained flexor muscle, strung together a 46-to-9 strikeout-to-walk ratio in 50.0 innings of work in the Sally. For his career, the 6-foot-3, 230-pound right-hander has fanned 22.9% and walked just 5.2% of the batters he's faced in his brief, 70-inning career.

**Projection**: Not a whole lot of information to go off of here, just 70.1 innings of work spread across the Arizona Summer League and the Sally, Ortiz, nonetheless, has looked as dominant as any pitcher in the organization during that time. He's missing bats, limiting walks, and succeeding against older competition. But after dealing with some arm concerns heading up to the draft last year, one wonders whether this is going to be a reoccurring theme throughout his career. CAL's impressed: Casey Kelly, Arodys Vizcaino, Nick Adenhart, and Luis Severino.

**Ceiling:** 3.5-win player
**Risk:** High
**MLB ETA:** 2018

## 6. Ariel Jurado, RHP

| Born: 01/30/96 | Age: 20 | Bats: R | Top CALs: David Oca, Jayson Aquino, |
| Height: 6-1 | Weight: 180 | Throws: R | Luis Cedeno, Miguel Sulbaran, Alexis Tapia |

| YEAR | Age | Level | IP | W | L | ERA | FIP | K/9 | BB/9 | K% | BB% | HR/9 | LOB% |
|------|-----|-------|------|----|----|------|------|------|------|-------|------|------|-------|
| 2013 | 17 | R | 49.0 | 6 | 0 | 2.39 | 1.93 | 8.63 | 0.55 | 23.7% | 1.5% | 0.18 | 64.1% |
| 2014 | 18 | R | 38.7 | 2 | 1 | 1.63 | 3.26 | 8.15 | 1.86 | 21.7% | 5.0% | 0.23 | 68.1% |
| 2015 | 19 | A | 99.0 | 12 | 1 | 2.45 | 2.62 | 8.64 | 1.09 | 24.4% | 3.1% | 0.45 | 70.4% |

**Background:** How's this for a dominant start to a professional career: through his first 186.2 innings Jurado is sporting a paltry 2.27 ERA while averaging nearly a punch out per inning with a walk rate just over one per every nine innings. The 6-foot-1, 180-pound right-hander handled a big promotion last season as the club bumped him from the Arizona Summer League straight into the Sally – at the ripe age of 19. And Jurado barely missed a beat. In 22 games, 15 of which were starts, the promising hurler posted an impressive 95-to-12 strikeout-to-walk ratio with a barely there 2.65 FIP. He's ready to start moving quickly.

**Projection**: A member of the *Bird Doggin' It* section in last year's book. Let's just put Jurado's performance up against some of his peers: among all Low Class A hurlers with at least 90 innings last season no one topped his strikeout-to-walk percentage, 21.3%. And the last two 19-year-old pitchers to post a strikeout-to-walk percentage above 21% were Lucas Giolito and Tyler Glasnow, two of the minors' best young arms.

Jurado does everything you could ever want a young pitcher to do: he limits walks with the best of them, misses a whole lot of bats, handles aggressive promotions, and has succeeded against much older competition. Throw in one of the minors' top groundball rates, 66%, and there's a strong foundation for at least a mid-rotation arm.

**Ceiling:** 2.0- to 2.5-win player
**Risk:** Moderate
**MLB ETA:** 2018

## 7. Michael Matuella, RHP

| Born: 06/03/94 | Age: 22 | Bats: R | Top CALs: N/A |
| Height: 6-6 | Weight: 220 | Throws: R | |

**Background:** And sometimes the rich only continue to get richer – unless, of course, it's dealing with real money in the real world, because that's how it always seems to come down. Well, that's what's going to happen if the big right-hander out of Duke can finally free himself from the injuries that plagued him throughout his amateur career. Matuella had Tommy John surgery just six starts and 25.0 innings into what was supposed to be a dominant junior season. He has also dealt with some serious back issues as well, specifically when he was diagnosed with spondylosis, a degenerative osteoarthritis of the joints between the center of the spinal vertebrae and/or neural foramina. For his injury-shortened collegiate career, Matuella posted a 119-to-38 strikeout-to-walk ratio in 139 innings.

**Projection**: Here's what I wrote in his pre-draft evaluation:

> *"Front-of-the-rotation potential, especially after posting a 93-to-26 strikeout-to-walk ratio [in] his previous 93.1 innings of work, Matuella offers a tantalizing mix of swing-and-miss ability with strong control, particularly for a bigger pitcher.*
>
> *And in draft class that lacks a true standout #1 pick, Matuella could have easily settled that argument had he not required Tommy John surgery.*
>
> *In terms of ceiling – and the assumption he can fully bounce back from TJ – Matuella has the upside of a #2-type arm, though that comes with some added risk: (A) he really[hasn't] faced, at least on a consistent basis, top tier talent and (B) he's tallied just 139 innings of work over the last three seasons. He could very easily be pushed into a late-inning role as well.*
>
> *Finally, a pair of high-ceiling pitchers – Jeff Hoffman and Erick Fedde – both managed to land in the 18 selections last season despite going down with wonky elbows as well."*

**Ceiling:** 2.5- to 3.0-win player
**Risk:** High to Extremely High
**MLB ETA:** 2017/2018

## 8. Luke Jackson, RHP

| Born: 08/24/91 | Age: 24 | Bats: R | Top CALs: Maikel Cleto, Jake Barrett, |
|---|---|---|---|
| Height: 6-2 | Weight: 205 | Throws: R | Mark Montgomery, Dan Cortes, Zack Wheeler |

| YEAR | Age | Level | IP | W | L | ERA | FIP | K/9 | BB/9 | K% | BB% | HR/9 | LOB% |
|---|---|---|---|---|---|---|---|---|---|---|---|---|---|
| 2013 | 21 | A+ | 101.0 | 9 | 4 | 2.41 | 3.55 | 9.27 | 4.19 | 24.9% | 11.3% | 0.53 | 82.1% |
| 2013 | 21 | AA | 27.0 | 2 | 0 | 0.67 | 2.17 | 10.00 | 4.00 | 29.1% | 11.7% | 0.00 | 92.0% |
| 2014 | 22 | AA | 83.3 | 8 | 2 | 3.02 | 2.92 | 8.96 | 2.59 | 24.8% | 7.2% | 0.54 | 73.4% |
| 2014 | 22 | AAA | 40.0 | 1 | 3 | 10.35 | 6.73 | 9.68 | 6.30 | 21.4% | 13.9% | 2.03 | 50.4% |
| 2015 | 23 | AAA | 66.3 | 2 | 3 | 4.34 | 3.43 | 10.72 | 4.75 | 26.9% | 11.9% | 0.41 | 65.0% |

**Background:** After battling control issues since entering pro ball as the 45th overall pick in 2010, the organization made the prudent decision and pushed the fire-balling right-hander into a late-inning relief role for the first time in his five-year career last season, a move that precipitated his late season call-up to help the club for the stretch run. Jackson, a 6-foot-2, 205-pounder out of Calvary Christian High School, opened the year in Round Rock's rotation, posting an unsightly 5.64 ERA while the opposition batted .318/.396/.482 against him through 22+ innings. After those five starts, four of which were less-than-stellar, Jackson made the move towards short-inning work and finished his Class AAA season by posting a 62-to-22 strikeout-to-walk ratio in 44 innings of work to go along with a 3.68 ERA. Texas promoted the young right-hander in early September for another 6.1 innings.

**Projection**: Jackson unleashed a flurry of mid- to upper-90s fastballs during his run with the Rangers last season, adding a hard curveball and low-80s changeup to his power arsenal. Personally, I would have liked to see the club stick with him as a starting pitcher for the remainder of the season especially since the move was just two starts after he looked dominant against Colorado Springs in late April (6.2 IP, 8K, 0BB), but it was almost an inevitability anyway. Late-inning, high leverage power arm.

**Ceiling:** 1.5-win player
**Risk:** Low to Moderate
**MLB ETA:** Debuted in 2015

## 9. Jairo Beras, OF

| Born: 12/25/94 | Age: 21 | Bats: R | Top CALs: Yorman Rodriguez, Guillermo Pimentel, |
|---|---|---|---|
| Height: 6-5 | Weight: 178 | Throws: R | Greg Burns, Elier Hernandez, Billy Rowell |

| Season | Age | LVL | PA | 2B | 3B | HR | AVG | OBP | SLG | ISO | BB% | K% | wRC+ |
|---|---|---|---|---|---|---|---|---|---|---|---|---|---|
| 2014 | 18 | A | 427 | 18 | 0 | 7 | 0.242 | 0.305 | 0.342 | 0.100 | 7.7% | 31.1% | 83 |
| 2015 | 19 | A | 350 | 18 | 2 | 9 | 0.291 | 0.332 | 0.440 | 0.150 | 5.4% | 25.1% | 119 |

**Background:** Similar to Nomar Mazara is a handful of ways: Beras has plenty of size, 6-foot-5 and 178 pounds, patrols the outfield, and signed to a massive $4.5 million deal. And just like Mazara, Beras looked overmatched during his initial run through the South Atlantic League, but fared much better during his second run. Two years ago, at the age of 19, Beras batted .242/.305/.342 with 18 doubles, seven homeruns, and five stolen bases with an 83 wRC+. Those numbers improved to .291/.332/.440 with a 119 wRC+ last season. For his career, the Dominican-born outfielder is sporting a .263/.317/.391 triple-slash line with 38 doubles, four triples, and 18 homeruns in 215 games.

**Projection**: One gets the feeling that he hasn't even begun to tap into his vast power potential. His eye at the plate is subpar and he's already battling some borderline red flag strikeout totals. His production did improve after a bit of a slow start: he batted .204/.271/.241 through his fist 59 plate appearances, but followed that up with by batting .308/.345/.480 the rest of the way. There's some tremendous sleeper value here – assuming the age issues that clouded his signing are completely out of the way.

**Ceiling:** 1.5- to 2.0-win player
**Risk:** High
**MLB ETA:** 2018

## 10. David Perez, RHP

**MiLB Rank: N/A**
**Position Rank: N/A**

| Born: 12/20/92 | Age: 23 | Bats: R | Top CALs: Scott Mitchinson, Chad Jenkins, |
|---|---|---|---|
| Height: 6-5 | Weight: 200 | Throws: R | Christian Meza, Brett Lorin, Ryan Berry |

| YEAR | Age | Level | IP | W | L | ERA | FIP | K/9 | BB/9 | K% | BB% | HR/9 | LOB% |
|---|---|---|---|---|---|---|---|---|---|---|---|---|---|
| 2013 | 20 | R | 2.7 | 0 | 1 | 6.75 | 5.13 | 10.13 | 6.75 | 25.0% | 16.7% | 0.00 | 66.7% |
| 2014 | 21 | A- | 27.7 | 1 | 0 | 3.90 | 5.85 | 7.81 | 6.83 | 19.1% | 16.7% | 0.65 | 75.8% |
| 2015 | 22 | A | 29.0 | 2 | 1 | 0.93 | 3.38 | 11.48 | 4.34 | 31.4% | 11.9% | 0.62 | 83.9% |
| 2015 | 22 | A+ | 55.0 | 4 | 3 | 4.42 | 4.00 | 9.82 | 2.29 | 26.0% | 6.1% | 0.98 | 66.0% |

**Background:** A big 6-foot-5, 200-pound right-hander out of the Dominican Republic, Perez has quietly, consistently put together one solid season after the next while the organization has experimented with him as a starting pitcher and a relief arm. Last season, his sixth in the Texas, Perez split his time between Hickory and High Desert while posting a 97-to-28 strikeout-to-walk ratio.

**Projection**: It was a strong return for Perez, who missed the majority of 2012 and 2013 due to injury. He continues to offer up a tantalizing combination of high punch out rates with very little walks. Texas started extending the promising hard-thrower towards the end of the season as he made six consecutive starts in High Class A. And here's why you should stop and take notice of Perez: his first two starts in the rotation he tossed 10 total innings with 20 punch outs and zero walks. That type of production – at any level – won't happen very often. He's a candidate for biggest breakout in 2016.

**Ceiling:** 2.5-win player
**Risk:** High to Extremely High
**MLB ETA:** 2017

## 11. Andrew Faulkner, LHP

**MiLB Rank: N/A**
**Position Rank: N/A**

| Born: 09/12/92 | Age: 23 | Bats: R | Top CALs: Ryan Searle, Jeanmar Gomez, |
|---|---|---|---|
| Height: 6-3 | Weight: 200 | Throws: L | Brooks Pounders, Shawn Morimando, Richard Castillo |

| YEAR | Age | Level | IP | W | L | ERA | FIP | K/9 | BB/9 | K% | BB% | HR/9 | LOB% |
|---|---|---|---|---|---|---|---|---|---|---|---|---|---|
| 2013 | 20 | A | 111.3 | 6 | 5 | 3.48 | 4.04 | 6.79 | 2.99 | 17.1% | 7.6% | 0.65 | 72.2% |
| 2014 | 21 | A+ | 104.3 | 10 | 1 | 2.07 | 2.70 | 8.63 | 2.67 | 23.8% | 7.4% | 0.09 | 79.3% |
| 2014 | 21 | AA | 30.7 | 2 | 4 | 4.99 | 3.61 | 9.68 | 4.11 | 24.6% | 10.5% | 0.88 | 52.9% |
| 2015 | 22 | AA | 92.3 | 7 | 4 | 4.19 | 4.34 | 8.77 | 4.58 | 22.2% | 11.6% | 0.88 | 69.9% |
| 2015 | 22 | AAA | 8.0 | 0 | 0 | 0.00 | 0.72 | 14.63 | 1.13 | 50.0% | 3.9% | 0.00 | 100.0% |

**Background:** A late-round find all the way back in 2011, Faulkner continued towards the game's pinnacle level as he made stops with Frisco and Round Rock before earning a late-season call up with the big league club. The 6-foot-3 lefty out of South Aiken High School opened the year with 16 up-and-down starts with the RoughRiders (78.2 IP, 75 strikeouts, and 42 walks) before the organization – for whatever reason – pushed the then-22-year-old hurler into the bullpen, a move that hopefully isn't permanent. Faulkner tossed another 13.1 innings (15 K and 5 BB) with Frisco before getting briefly bumped up to Round Rock for eight innings of zero-run baseball then the Rangers came knocking. He would post a 10-to-1 K/BB ratio in 9.2 innings with the big league club.

**Projection**: Faulkner showed off a mid-90s heater, a low-80s slider, and a hard splitter. I hope that the move to the pen was only in an effort to bolster the club's big league pen, because he's always shown a strong feel for the strike zone with solid-average control. He's shown a slight platoon split against right-handers, but nothing drastic. It's still too early to give up on the soon-to-be 23-year-old as a starting pitcher.

**Ceiling:** 1.5-win player
**Risk:** Moderate
**MLB ETA:** 2016

## 12. Josh Morgan, 2B/3B/SS

**MiLB Rank: N/A**
**Position Rank: N/A**

| Born: 11/16/95 | Age: 20 | Bats: R | Top CALs: Isaiah Kiner-Falefa, Luis Guillorme, |
|---|---|---|---|
| Height: 5-11 | Weight: 185 | Throws: R | Brallan Perez, Yonathan Mendoza, Manuel Guzman |

| Season | Age | LVL | PA | 2B | 3B | HR | AVG | OBP | SLG | ISO | BB% | K% | wRC+ |
|---|---|---|---|---|---|---|---|---|---|---|---|---|---|
| 2014 | 18 | R | 141 | 2 | 1 | 0 | 0.336 | 0.468 | 0.372 | 0.035 | 13.5% | 9.2% | 155 |
| 2014 | 18 | A- | 102 | 1 | 0 | 0 | 0.303 | 0.392 | 0.315 | 0.011 | 9.8% | 9.8% | 110 |
| 2015 | 19 | A | 416 | 15 | 1 | 3 | 0.288 | 0.385 | 0.362 | 0.074 | 10.8% | 12.7% | 121 |

**Background:** Admittedly, that went better than expected. Of course, the development – or at least the quasi-step forward – in the power department played a key role in Morgan's production in the Sally last season. After batting a nice enough .322/.436/.347 in 56 games between the Arizona

Summer League and Spokane during his debut, Morgan proved that the club was right in promoting him up to the Sally as a 19-year-old; he batted .288/.385/.362 with 15 doubles, one triple, three homeruns, and nine stolen bases in 13 attempts. For his career, Morgan is sporting a .300/.404/.356 triple-slash line.

**Projection**: After warning that unless Morgan developed some type of power he would eventually get the bat knocked out of his hands, the former third round pick showed glimpses of solid-average power – despite finishing the year with a lowly .362 slugging percentage. Between April 22nd and July 4th, a span of 61 games and 251 plate appearances, Morgan batted .316/.402/.405 with 14 extra-base hits. His power numbers will likely spike as he moves in the Texas League due to a favorable home ballpark, but Morgan has the potential to develop into solid backup infielder. He shows a decent eye, some speed, and a potential average or better hit tool.

**Ceiling:** 1.5-win player
**Risk:** Moderate
**MLB ETA:** 2017

## 13. Yohander Mendez, LHP

MiLB Rank: N/A
Position Rank: N/A

**Background:** A tall, lanky left-hander out of Venezuela, Mendez has been slowly developing in the lowest levels of the minors since signing as part of Nomar Mazara/Ronald Guzman international class. Mendez debuted in the Dominican Summer League as a 17-year-old in 2012, tossed 33.1 innings with Spokane,

| Born: 01/17/95 | Age: 21 | Bats: L | Top CALs: Kelvin De La Cruz, Jose Guzman, |
| Height: 6-4 | Weight: 178 | Throws: L | Tyler Vail, Jason Mceachern, Felix Doubront |

| YEAR | Age | Level | IP | W | L | ERA | FIP | K/9 | BB/9 | K% | BB% | HR/9 | LOB% |
|---|---|---|---|---|---|---|---|---|---|---|---|---|---|
| 2013 | 18 | A- | 33.3 | 1 | 2 | 3.78 | 5.30 | 6.21 | 4.59 | 15.2% | 11.3% | 1.08 | 72.7% |
| 2014 | 19 | R | 5.7 | 0 | 1 | 4.76 | 2.62 | 11.12 | 3.18 | 25.9% | 7.4% | 0.00 | 60.0% |
| 2014 | 19 | A | 31.0 | 3 | 0 | 2.32 | 3.65 | 8.13 | 0.58 | 24.1% | 1.7% | 1.16 | 84.8% |
| 2015 | 20 | A | 66.3 | 3 | 3 | 2.44 | 2.41 | 10.04 | 2.04 | 27.5% | 5.6% | 0.27 | 75.8% |

twirled another 36.2 between the Arizona Summer League and Hickory two years ago, and settled in nicely in a repeat with the Crawdads last season. In 21 games in the Sally, eight of which were starts, the 6-foot-4, 178-pound left-hander whiffed nearly 28% and walked just 5.6% of the total batters he's faced.

**Projection**: Mendez has now been in the Rangers' organization for parts of four seasons and has tallied just 181.2 innings of work – or just about 45 innings per year. His strikeout percentage spiked to a career high and he seemed to carry those numbers as the team stretched him out in the rotation at the end of the year. In his final nine appearances, which covered 40.0 innings, Mendez posted a 34-to-8 strikeout-to-walk ratio. Let's see what happens when the organization eases the reins a bit.

**Ceiling:** 1.5- to 2.0-win player
**Risk:** High
**MLB ETA:** 2018

## 14. Evan Van Hoosier, 2B/OF

MiLB Rank: N/A
Position Rank: N/A

**Background:** File this one under the young-and-dumb category: Van Hoosier, who had a breakout season before a leg injury shut him down for five-plus weeks, was suspended 50 games for testing positive for amphetamines *and* a drug of abuse while he was in the Arizona Fall League, a level of competition that's typically reserved for top prospects.

| Born: 12/24/93 | Age: 22 | Bats: R | Top CALs: Claudio Bautista, Jonathan Mota, |
| Height: 5-11 | Weight: 185 | Throws: R | David Bote, Frank Martinez, Chris Bostick |

| Season | Age | LVL | PA | 2B | 3B | HR | AVG | OBP | SLG | ISO | BB% | K% | wRC+ |
|---|---|---|---|---|---|---|---|---|---|---|---|---|---|
| 2013 | 19 | A- | 191 | 9 | 2 | 2 | 0.249 | 0.332 | 0.361 | 0.112 | 8.4% | 16.2% | 107 |
| 2014 | 20 | A | 493 | 27 | 8 | 11 | 0.268 | 0.339 | 0.442 | 0.174 | 8.9% | 17.2% | 116 |
| 2015 | 21 | R | 30 | 3 | 0 | 0 | 0.286 | 0.333 | 0.393 | 0.107 | 6.7% | 20.0% | 113 |
| 2015 | 21 | R | 30 | 3 | 0 | 0 | 0.286 | 0.333 | 0.393 | 0.107 | 6.7% | 20.0% | 113 |
| 2015 | 21 | A+ | 281 | 16 | 10 | 2 | 0.331 | 0.374 | 0.494 | 0.163 | 6.4% | 20.3% | 134 |

Stupid, just plain stupid. Van Hoosier, a former eighth round pick out of the College of Southern Nevada, hit .331/.374/.494 while topping the High Class A league average production by 34%. And it was the second consecutive year in which Van Hoosier's proved to a legitimate big league prospect; he batted .268/.339/.442 with 27 doubles, eight triples, 11 homeruns, and 14 stolen bases with a 116 wRC+ in the Sally in 2014.

**Projection**: Stupidity aside, Van Hoosier has some potential as an offensive-minded second baseman. Decent eye, solid-average power, a little bit of speed. With that being said, a lot of his production last season was buoyed by an unsustainable .411 BABIP so look for him to decline next season *after he serves his 50-game suspension.*

**Ceiling:** 1.5-win player
**Risk:** Moderate to High
**MLB ETA:** 2017

## 15. Frank Lopez, LHP

MiLB Rank: N/A
Position Rank: N/A

| Born: 02/18/94 | Age: 22 | Bats: L | Top CALs: Juan Sosa, Nick Additon, |
|---|---|---|---|
| Height: 6-1 | Weight: 175 | Throws: L | Eric Hurley, Alexander Smit, Edwin Diaz |

| YEAR | Age | Level | IP | W | L | ERA | FIP | K/9 | BB/9 | K% | BB% | HR/9 | LOB% |
|---|---|---|---|---|---|---|---|---|---|---|---|---|---|
| 2013 | 19 | A | 73.3 | 3 | 7 | 4.79 | 3.28 | 9.70 | 4.30 | 24.0% | 10.6% | 0.25 | 60.8% |
| 2014 | 20 | R | 6.0 | 0 | 0 | 1.50 | 4.36 | 10.50 | 1.50 | 30.4% | 4.4% | 1.50 | 100.0% |
| 2014 | 20 | A | 73.3 | 4 | 3 | 2.82 | 3.30 | 9.82 | 2.82 | 25.9% | 7.4% | 0.49 | 79.0% |
| 2015 | 21 | A+ | 42.7 | 4 | 1 | 2.95 | 3.83 | 9.07 | 1.69 | 25.4% | 4.7% | 0.84 | 72.5% |
| 2015 | 21 | AA | 75.0 | 3 | 7 | 4.92 | 4.79 | 6.96 | 4.08 | 17.1% | 10.0% | 1.08 | 70.9% |

**Background:** Typically young lefties that have breezed through the rookie levels on up to High Class A will garner quite a bit more attention, but Lopez has continued to fly under the radar a bit. Standing a less-than-imposing 6-foot-1 and 175 pounds, the Venezuelan-born southpaw dominated the Dominican Summer League, posted a 53-to-14 strikeout-to-walk ratio in 52 innings in the Arizona Summer League the next year, averaged a remarkably strong 9.7 punch outs per nine innings in the Sally in 2013, and was even better in his repeat with Hickory two years ago. After rediscovering his control in 2014, Lopez was promoted up to High Class A to begin the 2015 season and despite High Desert's hitter-friendly confines the young lefty more than held his own: 42.2 IP, 43 whiffs, and just eight base-on-balls. The club promoted the then-21-year-old hurler up to the Texas League in last May for his final 16 games.

**Projection:** Here's what I wrote in last year's book about the young lefty:

> "Despite being in pro ball for parts of four seasons now, Lopez has never topped 80 innings in a year. A potential breakout candidate for 2015, Lopez has averaged 9.5 punch outs and 3.3 walks per nine innings for his career. He's a backend arm."

For the first part of 2015, Lopez looked like he was on the cusp of a breakout season – something that continued through his first two Class AA starts. But after that he failed to make the necessary adjustments needed to succeed in the Texas League: his homerun rate spiked, he lost command of the strike zone, and for the first time in his career he stopped missing bats. Still, though, he's only entering his age-22 season with a tremendously strong track record. Lopez isn't a young fire-baller, but he's not your typical soft-tossing lefty either. He's a solid #5-type arm.

**Ceiling:** 1.0- to 1.5-win player
**Risk:** Moderate
**MLB ETA:** 2016

## 16. Ronald Guzman, 1B

MiLB Rank: N/A
Position Rank: N/A

| Born: 10/20/94 | Age: 21 | Bats: L | Top CALs: Daryl Jones, Austin Gallagher, |
|---|---|---|---|
| Height: 6-5 | Weight: 205 | Throws: L | Francisco Rivera, Jaime Ortiz, Jose Osuna |

| Season | Age | LVL | PA | 2B | 3B | HR | AVG | OBP | SLG | ISO | BB% | K% | wRC+ |
|---|---|---|---|---|---|---|---|---|---|---|---|---|---|
| 2013 | 18 | A | 191 | 8 | 0 | 4 | 0.272 | 0.325 | 0.387 | 0.116 | 5.8% | 14.1% | 106 |
| 2014 | 19 | A | 492 | 32 | 0 | 6 | 0.218 | 0.283 | 0.330 | 0.112 | 7.5% | 21.7% | 72 |
| 2015 | 20 | A | 104 | 3 | 0 | 3 | 0.309 | 0.346 | 0.433 | 0.124 | 5.8% | 14.4% | 121 |
| 2015 | 20 | A+ | 452 | 25 | 7 | 9 | 0.277 | 0.319 | 0.434 | 0.156 | 6.0% | 22.3% | 103 |

**Background:** Guzman's huge signing bonus, which was just shy of $3.5 million, was widely overshadowed by Nomar Mazara's deal which was worth nearly $1.5 million and signed around the same time. And like Mazara, Guzman has an impressive frame – 6-foot-5 and 205 pounds – with above-average potential, though he's yet to fully tap into it. The left-handed first baseman had a strong showing in the Sally, his third stop in the league, before spending the majority of the year in High Class A where he batted a league-average-ish .277/.319/.434 with 25 doubles, an eye-catching seven triples, and nine homeruns to go along with a 103 wRC+. For his career, Guzman is sporting a .266/.318/.394 triple-slash line.

**Projection:** And now here's a list of the bad news:

- As I previously mentioned, it took parts of three seasons for the man-child to get out of Low Class A where he batted .243/.301/.358 in nearly 800 plate appearances.
- High Desert, Texas' High Class A affiliate, is a very favorable place for hitters, so much so, in fact, that according to StatCorner Guzman's production dropped from .277/.319/.434 to a more mundane .264/.306/.401

- Finally, beginning with 2015 here are his OPS totals against fellow lefties: .679, .593, .496. Granted, it's definitely trending in the right direction, but remember he was repeating the same level.

Throw in the fact that CAL isn't at all impressed – the system links him to Daryl Jones, Austin Gallagher, Francisco Rivera, Jaime Ortiz, and Jose Osuna – and it doesn't offer up a whole lot of hope for Guzman moving forward.

**Ceiling:** 1.0- to 1.5-win player
**Risk:** Moderate to High
**MLB ETA:** 2018

## 17. Eric Jenkins, CF

**MiLB Rank: N/A**
**Position Rank: N/A**

| Born: 01/30/97 | Age: 19 | Bats: L | Top CALs: Connor Lien, Clay Fuller, |
| Height: 6-1 | Weight: 170 | Throws: R | Derrick Robinson, Michael Crouse, Angel Castillo |

| Season | Age | LVL | PA | 2B | 3B | HR | AVG | OBP | SLG | ISO | BB% | K% | wRC+ |
|--------|-----|-----|-----|----|----|----|------|------|------|------|------|------|------|
| 2015 | 18 | R | 205 | 4 | 6 | 0 | 0.249 | 0.342 | 0.339 | 0.090 | 11.2% | 27.8% | 105 |
| 2015 | 18 | A | 19 | 1 | 0 | 0 | 0.389 | 0.421 | 0.444 | 0.056 | 5.3% | 21.1% | 150 |

**Background:** Texas grabbed the speedy center fielder in the second round out of West Columbus High School, home to former big league outfielder Donell Nixon, last June. Jenkins batted .249/.342/.339 with 27 stolen bases in 30 attempts in the Arizona Summer League before a quick five-game crash course in the Sally.

**Projection:** Jenkins swiped 28 bags and knocked six triples in 56 games last season. Prorating that over a full 162-game schedule is 81 stolen bases and 17 triples. So, clearly, there's an awful lot of speed in play here. Jenkins didn't show a whole lot of pure power last season and the hit tool was a bit underwhelming, but plus-plus speed will catch a lot of eyes.

**Ceiling:** Too Soon to Tell
**Risk:** N/A
**MLB ETA:** N/A

## 18. Brett Martin, LHP

**MiLB Rank: N/A**
**Position Rank: N/A**

| Born: 04/28/95 | Age: 21 | Bats: L | Top CALs: Michael Blazek, Kendry Flores, |
| Height: 6-4 | Weight: 190 | Throws: L | David Baker, Andry Ubiera, Jeffry Antigua |

| YEAR | Age | Level | IP | W | L | ERA | FIP | K/9 | BB/9 | K% | BB% | HR/9 | LOB% |
|------|-----|-------|------|---|---|------|------|------|------|------|------|------|------|
| 2014 | 19 | R | 35.0 | 1 | 4 | 5.40 | 4.12 | 10.03 | 3.09 | 25.2% | 7.7% | 0.77 | 52.4% |
| 2015 | 20 | A | 95.3 | 5 | 6 | 3.49 | 3.67 | 6.80 | 2.45 | 18.6% | 6.7% | 0.57 | 67.2% |

**Background:** A fourth round pick out of Walters State Community College two years ago, Martin handled the move to Hickory with relative ease in 2015. In 20 games, 18 of which were starts, the 6-foot-4, 190-pound lefty fanned 72, walked 26, and posted a 3.67 FIP.

**Projection:** The data is still rather limited on the big lefty – he's thrown just 130.1 innings in his two professional seasons – but Martin's quickly proving to be a solid big league prospect. Promising control with a decent ability to miss bats, everything you would want out of a young lefty. There's still some projection left in his lanky frame. Martin could be a bit of backend sleeper. The 2016 season will go a long way towards determining that, though.

**Ceiling:** 1.0- to 1.5-win player
**Risk:** Moderate to High
**MLB ETA:** 2018

## 19. Joe Jackson, LF

**MiLB Rank: N/A**
**Position Rank: N/A**

| Born: 05/05/92 | Age: 24 | Bats: L | Top CALs: Casey Craig, Jimmy Van Ostrand, |
| Height: 6-1 | Weight: 180 | Throws: R | Wally Crancer, Ryan Khoury, Justin Miller |

| Season | Age | LVL | PA | 2B | 3B | HR | AVG | OBP | SLG | ISO | BB% | K% | wRC+ |
|--------|-----|-----|-----|----|----|----|------|------|------|------|------|------|------|
| 2013 | 21 | A- | 179 | 5 | 1 | 2 | 0.215 | 0.307 | 0.297 | 0.082 | 11.2% | 20.1% | 83 |
| 2014 | 22 | A | 385 | 18 | 4 | 6 | 0.293 | 0.364 | 0.422 | 0.129 | 9.4% | 15.3% | 121 |
| 2015 | 23 | A+ | 486 | 33 | 2 | 10 | 0.298 | 0.366 | 0.455 | 0.157 | 9.5% | 20.0% | 123 |

**Background:** Not to be confused with his deserving Hall of Fame namesake that had a problem with footwear. Jackson, who isn't related to Shoeless Joe, moved out from behind the plate and to a corner outfield spot and put together another solid professional season. Coming off of a .293/.364/.422 showing in the Sally two years ago, Jackson batted .298/.366/.455 with 33 doubles, four triples, 10 homeruns, and five stolen bases in six attempts. The former Citadel star topped the league average production by 23% last season.

**Projection**: And now for some bad news: Jackson's above-average triple-slash line was superficially inflated by High Desert's friendly confines. It drops down to a more modest .288/.355/.429, according to StatCorner. Jackson, a former fifth rounder, doesn't have the prototypical power associated with a corner outfield bat, but shows a decent eye at the plate, doubles pop and solid-average hit tool. CAL links him to a bunch of minor league flameouts, so it doesn't look good for the former backstop now.

**Ceiling:** 1.0-win player
**Risk:** Moderate
**MLB ETA:** 2018

## 20. Jose Leclerc, RHP

**MiLB Rank: N/A**
**Position Rank: N/A**

| Born: 12/19/93 | Age: 22 | Bats: R | Top CALs: Lucas Sims, Jeremy Jeffress, |
| Height: 6-0 | Weight: 165 | Throws: R | Aaron Sanchez, Steve Johnson, Oswaldo Sosa |

| YEAR | Age | Level | IP | W | L | ERA | FIP | K/9 | BB/9 | K% | BB% | HR/9 | LOB% |
|------|-----|-------|-----|---|---|------|------|-------|------|-------|-------|------|-------|
| 2013 | 19 | A | 59.0 | 3 | 4 | 3.36 | 2.68 | 11.75 | 3.20 | 30.3% | 8.3% | 0.31 | 70.0% |
| 2014 | 20 | A+ | 57.3 | 4 | 1 | 3.30 | 4.62 | 12.40 | 5.81 | 32.5% | 15.2% | 1.26 | 82.3% |
| 2015 | 21 | AA | 103.0 | 6 | 8 | 5.77 | 4.70 | 8.56 | 6.38 | 20.8% | 15.5% | 0.70 | 66.8% |

**Background:** Chalk this one up as a bit...surprising. Leclerc's control all but abandoned him during his run as Myrtle Beach's closer last season as he walked a career worst 15.2% of the batters he faced. Undeterred, the Rangers not only bumped the hard-throwing right-hander up to Class AA last season, but they also converted him into a fulltime starting pitcher for the first time in his career. And just for added effect: before last season Leclerc's last professional start was in the Dominican Summer League in 2011, just his third appearance in professional baseball. As expected, the 6-foot, 165-pound hurler had a bit of a rough go of it last season: he tossed a career best 103.0 innings, nearly double his previous career best, while fanning 20.8% and walking a whopping 15.5% of the batters he faced.

**Projection**: After two back-to-back seasons in which he's walked a total of 110 in 160.1 innings, he has to be a candidate to move back into the bullpen, right? Earlier in his career Leclerc looked like a budding dominant relief pitcher, but the last two seasons have really, *really* clouded his potential. He's only entering his age-22 season, so there's plenty of time to rediscover his once solid-average control but I wouldn't count on it.

**Ceiling:** 1.0- to 1.5-win player
**Risk:** High
**MLB ETA:** 2017

## 21. Drew Robinson, IF/OF

**MiLB Rank: N/A**
**Position Rank: N/A**

| Born: 04/20/92 | Age: 24 | Bats: L | Top CALs: John Tolisano, Bruce Caldwell, |
| Height: 6-1 | Weight: 200 | Throws: R | Trayce Thompson, Patrick Wisdom, Kyle Kubitza |

| Season | Age | LVL | PA | 2B | 3B | HR | AVG | OBP | SLG | ISO | BB% | K% | wRC+ |
|--------|-----|-----|-----|----|----|----|-------|-------|-------|-------|-------|-------|------|
| 2013 | 21 | A+ | 523 | 26 | 7 | 8 | 0.257 | 0.369 | 0.404 | 0.147 | 13.8% | 23.7% | 119 |
| 2014 | 22 | AA | 377 | 15 | 5 | 11 | 0.190 | 0.273 | 0.366 | 0.175 | 9.8% | 33.2% | 81 |
| 2015 | 23 | AA | 519 | 23 | 5 | 21 | 0.231 | 0.360 | 0.454 | 0.222 | 16.0% | 26.8% | 127 |
| 2015 | 23 | AAA | 28 | 2 | 0 | 0 | 0.304 | 0.407 | 0.391 | 0.087 | 14.3% | 14.3% | 123 |

**Background:** One of the very first prospects I ever analyzed in what seems like many, many years ago. Robinson's production stagnated the past couple of seasons. A former fourth round pick out of Silverado High School in Las Vegas, Robinson once looked like a budding sabermetric darling: back in 2012, his finest season to date, the infielder/outfielder batted .273/.409/.444 as a 20-year-old in the South Atlantic League. He followed that up with a good, not great, showing with Myrtle Beach (.257/.369/.404), and then the Texas League proved to be too much. In his initial debut in Class AA, Robinson looked overmatched and outclassed by the minors' biggest test as he strung together a putrid .190/.273/.366 line. The 6-foot-1 lefty-swinger had a quasi-bounce back season in a repeat of the Texas League, though it remains another disappointing showing; he batted .231/.360/.454.

**Projection**: Power and patience. Robinson is the type of guy who likely bounces between a couple organizations before settling for a couple cups of big league coffee. He's still walking as much as anyone – his walk rate was 16% last season in Class AA – and the power blossomed into an above-average skill. The hit tool, though, or lack thereof, is going to be too much to overcome. Lefties have eaten him up the past several seasons, so maybe, just maybe, he can develop into a platoon guy.

**Ceiling:** 1.0-win player

**Risk:** Moderate to High
**MLB ETA:** 2016

## 22. Travis Demeritte, 2B/3B

**MiLB Rank: N/A**
**Position Rank: N/A**

| Born: 09/30/94 | Age: 21 | Bats: R | Top CALs: Karexon Sanchez, Michael Chavis, |
|---|---|---|---|
| Height: 6-0 | Weight: 180 | Throws: R | Hector Veloz, Angelo Gumbs, Javier Azcona |

| Season | Age | LVL | PA | 2B | 3B | HR | AVG | OBP | SLG | ISO | BB% | K% | wRC+ |
|---|---|---|---|---|---|---|---|---|---|---|---|---|---|
| 2013 | 18 | R | 175 | 5 | 3 | 4 | 0.285 | 0.411 | 0.444 | 0.160 | 16.6% | 28.0% | 144 |
| 2013 | 18 | R | 175 | 5 | 3 | 4 | 0.285 | 0.411 | 0.444 | 0.160 | 16.6% | 28.0% | 144 |
| 2014 | 19 | A | 466 | 16 | 2 | 25 | 0.211 | 0.310 | 0.450 | 0.239 | 10.7% | 36.7% | 110 |
| 2015 | 20 | A- | 22 | 0 | 0 | 0 | 0.150 | 0.227 | 0.150 | 0.000 | 9.1% | 50.0% | 18 |
| 2015 | 20 | A | 198 | 12 | 1 | 5 | 0.241 | 0.343 | 0.412 | 0.171 | 12.6% | 34.8% | 117 |

**Background:** The former first round pick with promising power potential led the Sally in homeruns in 2014, Demeritte got popped on a drug test and subsequently banned for 80 games. The culprit: Furosemide, a water pill that prevents your body from absorbing too much salt. And even before the suspension Demeritte was only making tiny strides in his overall production as he repeated Low Class A. In 48 games with Hickory, the former 30th overall pick batted a lowly .241/.343/.412, but managed to improve his *Weighted Runs Created Plus* total from 110 to 117. Demeritte came back in early September for a handful of games with the Spokane Indians in the New York-Penn League where he promptly went 3-for-20.

**Projection:** Here's what I wrote in last year's book:

> *"Just as we've seen in the past with Joey Gallo, Lewis Brinson, and to a lesser extent Nick Williams, Demeritte is just the latest baby Ranger to create a windstorm while hacking away in the Sally. And all of the previous three have been able to shed some of the concerns as they moved up the ladder. The difference being, of course, Demeritte's production in Low Class A ranks fourth among the group. The power's legit as is the strong eye at the plate, but if Demeritte doesn't show some tangible step forward in 2015 he's not long for many top prospect lists".*

Well, Demeritte is still flailing away – and missing – at a high rate; he fanned in nearly 35% of his plate appearances last season in the Sally. He's willing to walk a whole lot and the power is still a legit skill. But, damn, that's a tremendously high punch out rate. Still, though, he's entering his age-21 season with already 850+ plate appearances under his belt.

**Ceiling:** 1.0-win player
**Risk:** Moderate to High
**MLB ETA:** 2019

## 23. Juremi Profar, IF

**MiLB Rank: N/A**
**Position Rank: N/A**

| Born: 01/30/96 | Age: 20 | Bats: R | Top CALs: Rangel Ravelo, Juan Mota, |
|---|---|---|---|
| Height: 6-1 | Weight: 185 | Throws: R | Carson Kelly, Janluis Castro, Jose Salazar |

| Season | Age | LVL | PA | 2B | 3B | HR | AVG | OBP | SLG | ISO | BB% | K% | wRC+ |
|---|---|---|---|---|---|---|---|---|---|---|---|---|---|
| 2013 | 17 | R | 251 | 13 | 1 | 0 | 0.281 | 0.361 | 0.350 | 0.069 | 8.8% | 5.2% | 118 |
| 2014 | 18 | A- | 283 | 10 | 0 | 1 | 0.247 | 0.307 | 0.299 | 0.052 | 7.8% | 16.6% | 74 |
| 2015 | 19 | A | 262 | 17 | 1 | 3 | 0.272 | 0.313 | 0.387 | 0.115 | 5.3% | 10.3% | 98 |
| 2015 | 19 | A+ | 58 | 2 | 1 | 1 | 0.240 | 0.304 | 0.380 | 0.140 | 6.9% | 15.5% | 81 |

**Background:** The younger brother of the snake-bitten, star-crossed former top prospect Jurickson Profar, Juremi, nonetheless, is climbing up the Rangers' list. A 6-foot-1, 185-pound infielder that's seen games at shortstop and first, second, and third bases in his brief career, the younger Profar got a late start to 2015 but looked promising in High Class A as a 19-year-old, hitting .240/.304/.380 in 58 plate appearances before getting shoved back down to the Sally for the remainder of the season. In 262 trips to the plate with Hickory, Profar batted a solid .272/.313/.387 with 17 doubles, one triple, and three homeruns en route to posting a 98 wRC+. For his career, he's sporting a .265/.325/.348 triple-slash line.

**Projection:** Certainly not the prospect his brother Jurickson is – or was. But Juremi has a decent offensive skill set of his own: solid hit tool, a slightly subpar walk rate, developing power, and, of course, plenty of positional versatility. He's not going to develop into a big league regular, but he could carve out a career as a nice backup.

**Ceiling:** 1.0-win player
**Risk:** Moderate to High
**MLB ETA:** 2018

## 24. Yeyson Yrizarri, SS

**MiLB Rank: N/A**
**Position Rank: N/A**

| Born: 02/02/97 | Age: 19 | Bats: R | **Top CALs:** Helder Velazquez, Mario Martinez, |
|---|---|---|---|
| Height: 6-0 | Weight: 175 | Throws: R | Humberto Arteaga, Alejandro Paulino, Adrian Valerio |

| Season | Age | LVL | PA | 2B | 3B | HR | AVG | OBP | SLG | ISO | BB% | K% | wRC+ |
|---|---|---|---|---|---|---|---|---|---|---|---|---|---|
| 2014 | 17 | R | 206 | 13 | 1 | 1 | 0.237 | 0.275 | 0.332 | 0.095 | 4.4% | 17.5% | 76 |
| 2014 | 17 | R | 206 | 13 | 1 | 1 | 0.237 | 0.275 | 0.332 | 0.095 | 4.4% | 17.5% | 76 |
| 2015 | 18 | A- | 257 | 10 | 1 | 2 | 0.265 | 0.290 | 0.339 | 0.073 | 2.3% | 17.9% | 81 |
| 2015 | 18 | AAA | 34 | 1 | 1 | 0 | 0.273 | 0.294 | 0.364 | 0.091 | 2.9% | 14.7% | 72 |

**Background:** Another one of the club's big dollar international free agent expenditures, Yrizarri had a bit of a bizarre 2015 season – at least when it comes to his development path. Like Juremi Profar, Yrizarri had a late start to the season; he didn't appear in a game until early June. But the club, in a surprising move, pushed the then-18-year-old shortstop up the PCL – despite never appearing above the Arizona Summer League. And Yrizarri looked competent against the vastly superior pitching. He went 9-for-33 with one double and one triple in nine games. After that the club demoted him back down to the Northwest League where he basically replicated that production for 62 games. He batted .265/.290/.339.

**Projection**: A solid low-level shortstop with a touch of offensive upside. Yrizarri hasn't walked a whole lot during his career or flashed a whole lot of power either. But the hit tool could carry him through the lowest levels.

**Ceiling:** 1.0-win player
**Risk:** Moderate
**MLB ETA:** 2018

## 25. Ti'Quan Forbes, 3B/SS

**MiLB Rank: N/A**
**Position Rank: N/A**

| Born: 08/26/96 | Age: 19 | Bats: R | **Top CALs:** Joantoni Garcia, Jose Rodriguez, |
|---|---|---|---|
| Height: 6-3 | Weight: 180 | Throws: R | Jacob Cordero, Gerald Bautista, Griffin Garabito |

| Season | Age | LVL | PA | 2B | 3B | HR | AVG | OBP | SLG | ISO | BB% | K% | wRC+ |
|---|---|---|---|---|---|---|---|---|---|---|---|---|---|
| 2014 | 17 | R | 204 | 3 | 2 | 0 | 0.241 | 0.338 | 0.282 | 0.040 | 11.3% | 23.0% | 90 |
| 2015 | 18 | A- | 236 | 11 | 1 | 0 | 0.263 | 0.315 | 0.323 | 0.060 | 5.9% | 22.9% | 87 |

**Background:** The club's second round pick two years ago out of Columbia High School, home to just three other draft picks, none of whom are noteworthy, Forbes hasn't quite figured out how to handle either (A) wood bats or (B) minor league arms. The 6-foot-3, 180-pound infielder didn't offer up a whole lot of promise during his debut in 2014, hitting .241/.338/.282 with just five extra-base hits, and he followed that up with an equally blasé showing in the Northwest League last year; he batted .263/.315/.323 with just 12 extra-base hits in 59 games.

**Projection**: Despite a promising frame, one that would belie at least average power, Forbes has batted slugged just 17 extra-base hits – 14 doubles and three triples – in his first 107 games. He's likely headed to the South Atlantic League next year, but it's only going to end in further disappointment.

**Ceiling:** 0.5- to 1.0-win player
**Risk:** Moderate
**MLB ETA:** 2019

### *Barely Missed:*

- **Alex Claudio, LHP** –Claudio's had a couple cups with Texas after some solid minor league seasons working out of the system's various bullpens. But his fastball has barely cracked 84 mph during his big league time – despite that, though, he's tallied a 2.89 ERA in 28 big league innings. He could be a useful LOOGY.

- **Adam Parks, RHP** – Another late round find by the Rangers' scouting department. Park, a 6-foot-3 right-hander taken in the 33rd round out of Liberty University in 2014, made stops at three different levels last season: the Sally, California League, and Class AA. He tallied 86 punch outs and just 19 walks in 73.1 innings of work. He's likely to find his way into the club's Top 25 next season.

## *Bird Doggin' It – Additional Prospects to Keep an Eye in 2016*

| Player | Age | POS | Notes |
|---|---|---|---|
| Ryan Cordell | 24 | IF/OF | Former 11th rounder breezed through the Sally and High Class A, but looked overmatched during his 56-game run in Class AA last season. |
| Michael De Leon | 19 | SS | Another example of the organization's push-'em-till-they-fail mantra. De Leon spent the year with Hickory at the ripe age of 18, though he batted just .222/.277/.281. |
| John Fasola | 24 | RHP | Fantastic buy-low draft pick out of Kent State in 2014. Fasola has averaged 11.5 punch outs and just 2.0 walks per nine innings across his 81.2 innings in professional ball. |
| Christopher Garcia | 23 | OF | Had the best run of his entire professional life in High Class A last season, hitting .327/.378/.531. Of course, it came with High Desert and a .384 BABIP. Bust. |
| Isaiah Kiner-Falefa | 21 | 2B/SS | Fourth round pick in 2013 was a league average performer between the Sally and High Class A last season. The problem: he's never slugged a homerun in three professional seasons. |
| Will Lamb | 25 | LHP | Big lefty out of Clemson continued to battle control issues. |
| Luke Lanphere | 20 | RHP | Promising late round prep pick spent the year in short-season ball and posted a decent 48-to-13 strikeout-to-walk ratio in 68 innings. |
| David Ledbetter | 24 | LHP | Small right-hander struggled mightily in High Class A, posting a 7.46 ERA in 120.2 innings. |
| Ryan Ledbetter | 24 | RHP | Posted a nearly identical ERA as his brother, 7.50, but averaged far more punch outs working out of the pen. |
| Shane McCain | 24 | LHP | Former Troy University lefty has averaged 11.0 punch outs and 2.5 walks per nine innings during his two professional seasons. |
| Sal Mendez | 21 | LHP | Former 40th round pick in 2013 finally made his professional debut last year, fanning 50 in 52.1 innings in the Arizona Summer League. |
| Victor Payano | 23 | LHP | Big lefty has always racked up an enormous amount of punch outs during his six-year career, but he's averaged nearly six free passes per nine innings. |
| Pedro Payano | 21 | RHP | Ridiculous final line during his time between the Arizona Summer and South Atlantic Leagues: 89 IP, 101 K, 22 BB, and a 1.11 ERA. |
| Richelson Pena | 22 | RHP | Posted an 87-to-23 strikeout-to-walk ratio in 111.2 innings with High Desert. |
| Ryne Slack | 23 | LHP | 6-foot-2, 220-pound lefty spent the season missing about a bat per inning between the California and Texas Leagues last season. |

**State of the Farm System:** Stripped like a stolen car at a chop shop, Toronto's system underwent a massive exodus as the front office pushed for a playoff appearance – and potentially even more. Here's a quick rundown:

| Rank | Name | POS |
|---|---|---|
| 1 | Anthony Alford | CF |
| 2 | Sean Reid-Foley | RHP |
| 3 | Max Pentecost | C |
| 4 | Connor Greene | RHP |
| 5 | Rowdy Tellez | 1B |
| 6 | Vladimir Guerrero Jr. | 3B/OF |
| 7 | Richard Urena | SS |
| 8 | Jon Harris | RHP |
| 9 | Clinton Hollon | RHP |
| 10 | Ryan Borucki | LHP |
| 11 | D.J. Davis | CF |
| 12 | Shane Dawson | LHP |
| 13 | Andy Burns | IF/OF |
| 14 | Mitch Nay | 3B |
| 15 | Dwight Smith | OF |
| 16 | Brady Dragmire | RHP |
| 17 | Matt Dean | 1B/3B |
| 18 | Angel Perdomo | LHP |
| 19 | Matt Smoral | LHP |
| 20 | Justin Maese | RHP |
| 21 | Dan Barnes | RHP |
| 22 | Guadalupe Chavez | RHP |
| 23 | Carl Wise | 3B |
| 24 | Jeremy Gabryszwski | RHP |
| 25 | Juan Meza | RHP |

- November 28$^{th}$, 2014: Acquired All-Star – and eventual MVP – third baseman Josh Donaldson for Brett Lawrie, Franklin Barreto, Kendall Graveman, and Sean Nolin.
- July 28$^{th}$, 2015: Traded Jeff Hoffman, Jesus Tinoco, Miguel Castro, and Jose Reyes to the Rockies for Troy Tulowitzki and LaTroy Hawkins.
- July 30$^{th}$, 2015: Flipped Daniel Norris, Jairo Labourt, and Matt Boyd to Detroit for ace southpaw David Price.
- July 31$^{st}$, 2015: Dealt Jake Brentz, Nick Wells, and Rob Rasmussen to the Mariners for veteran reliever Mark Lowe.
- July 31$^{st}$, 2015: Traded Jimmy Cordero and Alberto Tirado to the Phillies for Ben Revere.
- August 8$^{th}$, 2015: Sent Dawel Lugo to the Diamondbacks in exchange for utility man extraordinaire Cliff Pennington.

Granted, each move would be made again because prospects are just that...prospects – not proven commodities. But, damn, thats an awful lot of talent leaving the system, something that new front office czar Mark Shapiro was not happy with according to reports. But, again, as the saying goes: flags fly forever.

What's left are a couple potentially dominant, high risk, high reward prospects.

Center fielder Anthony Alford, a third round pick all the way back in 2012, finally committed to baseball fulltime after spending a couple seasons playing big time college football. And Alford shined: the tools-laden center fielder batted .298/.398/.421 with 25 doubles, seven triples, four homeruns, and 27 stolen bases between his stints with Lansing and Dunedin.

Sean Reid-Foley, the hyphenated assassin, can run it up there with the best of them – resulting in high strikeout totals – but he hits the strike zone as often as Bartolo Colon will leg out an extra-base knock. The big right-hander fanned a remarkable 125 in just 96.0 innings between the Midwest and Florida State Leagues. The downside: he walked 67.

Backstop Max Pentecost, a first round pick two years ago, missed the entire year due to injury.

**Review of the 2015 Draft:** Just like the club had in every opening round beginning in 2009, Toronto grabbed a hurler in the first round. The club grabbed Missouri State University right-hander Jon Harris with the 29$^{th}$ overall pick. The organization followed that up by selecting – and ultimately failing to sign – prep right-hander Brady Singer with the 56$^{th}$ pick.

Their third round selection, prep right-hander Justin Maese, didn't miss hardly any bats, but managed to post a 1.01 ERA in the Gulf Coast League. And fourth round pick Carl Wise batted .235/.273/.310 during his debut.

## 1. Anthony Alford, CF

MiLB Rank: #54
Position Rank: #15

| Born: 07/20/94 | Age: 21 | Bats: R | Top CALs: Cameron Maybin, Angel Morales, |
|---|---|---|---|
| Height: 6-1 | Weight: 205 | Throws: R | Jpe Benson, Dan Brewer, Brandon Nimmo |

| Season | Age | LVL | PA | 2B | 3B | HR | AVG | OBP | SLG | ISO | BB% | K% | wRC+ |
|---|---|---|---|---|---|---|---|---|---|---|---|---|---|
| 2015 | 20 | A | 232 | 14 | 1 | 1 | 0.293 | 0.418 | 0.394 | 0.101 | 16.8% | 25.9% | 143 |
| 2015 | 20 | A+ | 255 | 11 | 6 | 3 | 0.302 | 0.380 | 0.444 | 0.142 | 11.0% | 19.2% | 153 |

**Background:** Easily the system's top athlete – even before the mass exodus left the organization thin on minor league talent – Alford opted to take the two-sport approach and head to Ole Miss after Toronto grabbed the young center fielder in the third round four years ago. The backup safety/backup punt returner decided to ply his athleticism to the diamond fulltime last season, a move that is only cemented as the right decision following by his breakout 2015 campaign. Seeing the ball field for just 25 games between 2012 and 2014, Alford looked at ease as the organization pushed him up to the Lansing Lugnuts in the Midwest League – a promotion that lasted all of 50 games. After topping the Low Class A league average production mark by a whopping 43%, the speedy 6-foot-1, 205-pound outfielder continued his torrid stretch with Dunedin for another 57 contests. Overall, the former football player-turned-top-baseball-prospect slugged a combined .298/.398/.421 with 25 doubles, seven triples, four homeruns, and swiped 27 bags in 34 attempts. His overall production, according to *Weighted Runs Created Plus*, topped the average mark by a mind-boggling 48%.

**Projection**: The most impressive part: remember Alford tallied just 25 games between 2012 through the end of 2014. Meaning: he basically sat out for three years, playing football in the meantime, and came back to establish himself as of the best young outfielders in baseball. Tremendous, tremendous eye at the plate, above-average to plus-speed, and enough wallop in his bat to keep pitchers honest as he moves up the minor league chain. Alford has the potential to a legitimate leadoff stick with the ability to change the game with the bat, on the base paths, and in the field. Simply put, he's the single best prospect you've never heard of – *yet*.

**Ceiling:** 3.0- to 3.5-win player
**Risk:** Moderate
**MLB ETA:** Debuted in 2017/2018

## 2. Sean Reid-Foley, RHP

MiLB Rank: #58
Position Rank: N/A

| Born: 08/30/95 | Age: 20 | Bats: R | Top CALs: Tyler Matzek, Wilmer Font, |
|---|---|---|---|
| Height: 6-3 | Weight: 220 | Throws: R | Jeremy Jeffress, Blake King, Angel Reyes |

| YEAR | Age | Level | IP | W | L | ERA | FIP | K/9 | BB/9 | K% | BB% | HR/9 | LOB% |
|---|---|---|---|---|---|---|---|---|---|---|---|---|---|
| 2014 | 18 | R | 22.7 | 1 | 2 | 4.76 | 2.76 | 9.93 | 3.97 | 25.5% | 10.2% | 0.00 | 62.5% |
| 2015 | 19 | A | 63.3 | 3 | 5 | 3.69 | 3.44 | 12.79 | 6.11 | 30.7% | 14.7% | 0.43 | 71.4% |
| 2015 | 19 | A+ | 32.7 | 1 | 5 | 5.23 | 3.81 | 9.64 | 6.61 | 23.7% | 16.2% | 0.28 | 62.5% |

**Background:** Plucked out of Sandalwood High School in Jacksonville, Florida, in the second round two years ago, Reid-Foley continued to miss a helluva lot of bats during his brief professional career. After fanning more than a quarter of the hitters he faced in his debut in the Gulf Coast League, the hyphened assassin fanned a remarkable 90 batters in just 63.1 innings with Lansing and averaged more than a whiff per inning after his promotion to the Florida State League. Reid-Foley finished the year with 125 punch outs in just 96.0 innings of work – or just under 12 strikeouts every nine innings. And now the bad news: he walked 67 of the 441 hitters he's faced last season. Or in other words: nearly 15.5% or over six per nine innings.

**Projection**: Harkening back to memories of a young Aaron Sanchez, Reid-Foley can fan, and walk, hitters with exceedingly high frequency. Consider the following:

| Player | Age | Level | IP | K% | BB% |
|---|---|---|---|---|---|
| Sean Reid-Foley | 19 | A/A+ | 96.0 | 28.34% | 15.19% |
| Aaron Sanchez | 19 | A | 90.1 | 25.73% | 13.53% |

How's this for impressive: among all hurlers with at least 60 innings in the Midwest League, Reid-Foley finished with the second highest punch out percentage. And how's this for impressive Part II: Reid-Foley was the only teenager hurler to throw at least 30+ innings in the Florida State League. Anyway, he clearly has front of the rotation caliber potential, whether he can eventually harness it or become the next Kyle Crick is an entirely different question.

**Ceiling:** 3.5-win player
**Risk:** Moderate to High
**MLB ETA:** 2018

## 3. Max Pentecost, C

| Born: 03/10/93 | Age: 23 | Bats: R | Top CALs: N/A |
|---|---|---|---|
| Height: 6-2 | Weight: 191 | Throws: R | |

**Background:** Outside of hurlers, arm injuries – particularly of the shoulder variety – are the most damning for backstops. The fact that Pentecost, the 11th overall pick two years ago, underwent two procedures in a matter of four months is incredibly worrisome for his prospects as a catcher. He missed the entire 2015 season.

**Projection**: Here's what I wrote prior to the 2014 draft:

> "I'm a big believer in the bat. He's done nothing but hit since turning down the Rangers' contract offer [out of high school] and heading to college. Through more than two and half seasons of data, Pentecost has slugged .330/.402/.472 while making strides in his contact rate.
>
> Now, Kennesaw's home field tends to inflate offensive numbers a bit, but the power, patience, hit tool, and speed are average across the board. And according to his spray chart, he used the whole field fairly well last summer (warning: sample size of about 150 plate appearances).
>
> Pentecost is a potential solid everyday backstop, [who should peak] around 3.0, maybe 3.5-wins above replacement. The total package is better than the individual pieces, though. Think .280/.335/.430 with 15 homeruns and solid defense."

So now the question is: Will he remain behind the plate after two back-to-back shoulder procedures? Obviously, the bat doesn't play nearly as well at, say, first or third base, or even a corner outfield position. Here's hoping for a full recovery.

**Ceiling:** 3.0-win player
**Risk:** Moderate to High
**MLB ETA:** 2018

## 4. Conner Greene, RHP

| Born: 04/04/95 | Age: 21 | Bats: R | Top CALs: Arquimedes Nieto, Eduardo Rodriguez, Jacob Turner, Randall Delgado, Nick Additon |
|---|---|---|---|
| Height: 6-3 | Weight: 165 | Throws: R | |

| YEAR | Age | Level | IP | W | L | ERA | FIP | K/9 | BB/9 | K% | BB% | HR/9 | LOB% |
|---|---|---|---|---|---|---|---|---|---|---|---|---|---|
| 2013 | 18 | R | 30.7 | 1 | 1 | 5.28 | 4.05 | 5.87 | 4.40 | 14.5% | 10.9% | 0.29 | 65.2% |
| 2014 | 19 | R | 27.7 | 1 | 2 | 4.23 | 3.93 | 6.83 | 3.90 | 17.7% | 10.1% | 0.33 | 61.2% |
| 2014 | 19 | R | 31.7 | 2 | 2 | 1.99 | 3.10 | 8.53 | 1.71 | 24.2% | 4.8% | 0.57 | 71.9% |
| 2015 | 20 | A | 67.3 | 7 | 3 | 3.88 | 3.22 | 8.69 | 2.54 | 22.7% | 6.6% | 0.53 | 71.1% |
| 2015 | 20 | A+ | 40.0 | 2 | 3 | 2.25 | 2.34 | 7.88 | 1.80 | 21.6% | 4.9% | 0.23 | 77.5% |
| 2015 | 20 | AA | 25.0 | 3 | 1 | 4.68 | 4.15 | 5.40 | 4.32 | 13.9% | 11.1% | 0.36 | 65.6% |

**Background:** The former seventh round pick had one of the quieter breakout seasons in 2015 as he opened the year up with Lansing in the Midwest League and capped it off with five starts with New Hampshire in the Eastern League – at the age of 20. Greene, a sturdy 6-foot-3, 165-pound right-hander out of Santa Monica High School, home to Tyler Skaggs and Tony Tarasco, more than doubled his career high in innings, throwing a combined 132.1 frames, fanning 115, walking just 39, and tallying a solid 3.54 FIP. For his three-year career, Greene is sporting a 186-to-72 strikeout-to-walk ratio in 222.1 innings. One interesting tidbit: Greene's final start with Dunedin was an absolute gem: 7.0 IP, two hits, 10 punch outs, and zero walk issued.

**Projection**: Greene's overall numbers are clouded by his five-game stint in Class AA last season. Ignoring those for a moment, his production between Class A and High Class A are as follows: 107.1 innings, 100 strikeouts, just 27 walks, and a 3.51 ERA. He's one of the more interesting players in the entire minors, perhaps with the potential to peak as a solid #3 in the next two year or three years. CAL seems to like him by comparing him to Eduardo Rodriguez, Jacob Turner, and Randall Delgado.

**Ceiling:** 2.5-win player
**Risk:** Moderate
**MLB ETA:** 2018

## 5. Rowdy Tellez, 1B

**MiLB Rank: #121**
**Position Rank: #9**

| Born: 03/16/95 | Age: 21 | Bats: L | Top CALs: Anthony Rizzo, Beau Mills, |
|---|---|---|---|
| Height: 6-4 | Weight: 245 | Throws: L | Jose Jimenez, Chris Marrero, Kyle Blanks |

| Season | Age | LVL | PA | 2B | 3B | HR | AVG | OBP | SLG | ISO | BB% | K% | wRC+ |
|---|---|---|---|---|---|---|---|---|---|---|---|---|---|
| 2013 | 18 | R | 141 | 5 | 3 | 2 | 0.234 | 0.319 | 0.371 | 0.137 | 10.6% | 18.4% | 105 |
| 2014 | 19 | R | 218 | 11 | 1 | 4 | 0.293 | 0.358 | 0.424 | 0.131 | 8.7% | 12.4% | 125 |
| 2015 | 20 | A | 299 | 19 | 0 | 7 | 0.296 | 0.351 | 0.444 | 0.148 | 8.0% | 18.7% | 130 |
| 2015 | 20 | A+ | 148 | 5 | 0 | 7 | 0.275 | 0.338 | 0.473 | 0.198 | 9.5% | 18.9% | 143 |

**Background:** With a name straight out of the movie Road House, Toronto unearthed the budding slugger – aptly named Rowdy Tellez – in the 30th round three years ago, the 895th overall selection, and signed to a deal just south of a cool million dollars. And just 202 games later, the 6-foot-4, 245-pound hulking first baseman is proving to be quite the bargain – particularly after his massive breakout in 2015. In 103 games split between the Midwest and Florida State Leagues, Tellez slugged an impressive .289/.347/.454 with 24 doubles, 14 homeruns, and five stolen bases. His overall production, according to *Weighted Runs Created Plus*, topped the league average mark by 33%. He also earned a trip to the Arizona Fall League as well, hitting .293/.352/.488 with four doubles and four homeruns in 21 games.

**Projection**: As impressive as his season was in 2015, imagine what his overall numbers would have looked like had he not batted a lowly .228/.265/.337 against fellow left-handers. If he can prove that to be nothing more than a speed bump, Tellez has a chance to develop into a middle-of-the-order thumper: above-average power, solid eye at the plate, strong hit tool. Again, there's some risk here, but he has a chance to be a perennial 20- to 25-HR threat down the line.

**Ceiling:** 2.5-win player
**Risk:** Moderate
**MLB ETA:** 2018

## 6. Vladimir Guerrero Jr., 3B/OF

**MiLB Rank: #125**
**Position Rank: #5**

| Born: 03/16/99 | Age: 17 | Bats: R | Top CALs: N/A |
|---|---|---|---|
| Height: 6-2 | Weight: 220 | Throws: R | |

**Background:** The Blue Jays handed out a hefty $3.9 million bonus to Vladimir Guerrero Jr., the son of future Hall of Famer by the same name.

**Projection**: Here's what Ismael Cruz, the Jays' special assistant of Latin American operations said, according to an MLB.com report: "Those kind[s] of guys don't come across very often. So it was either play all your marbles on one guy or it was go out and get a couple players that are fine, but for us, Vladimir is a difference-maker. He has the potential to be a very, very special kid." Guerrero Jr. – perhaps, the new Kid – didn't make an appearance in a game last season. But let's see what the future holds for him.

**Ceiling:** Too Soon to Tell
**Risk:** N/A
**MLB ETA:** N/A

## 7. Richard Urena, SS

**MiLB Rank: #131**
**Position Rank: N/A**

| Born: 02/26/96 | Age: 20 | Bats: B | Top CALs: Yamaico Navarro, Javier Guerra, |
|---|---|---|---|
| Height: 6-1 | Weight: 170 | Throws: R | Arismendy Alcantara, Kenneth Peoples-Walls, Franklin Barreto |

| Season | Age | LVL | PA | 2B | 3B | HR | AVG | OBP | SLG | ISO | BB% | K% | wRC+ |
|---|---|---|---|---|---|---|---|---|---|---|---|---|---|
| 2013 | 17 | R | 280 | 19 | 2 | 1 | 0.296 | 0.381 | 0.403 | 0.107 | 10.7% | 15.4% | 137 |
| 2014 | 18 | R | 236 | 15 | 2 | 2 | 0.318 | 0.363 | 0.433 | 0.115 | 6.8% | 21.6% | 129 |
| 2015 | 19 | A | 408 | 13 | 4 | 15 | 0.266 | 0.289 | 0.438 | 0.172 | 3.2% | 20.6% | 107 |
| 2015 | 19 | A+ | 128 | 3 | 1 | 1 | 0.250 | 0.268 | 0.315 | 0.065 | 2.3% | 20.3% | 76 |

**Background:** Signed out of the Dominican Republic on July 3rd, 2012, the switch-hitting Urena continued to cement himself as one of the more promising shortstops in the low levels of the minors last season. Urena torched the Dominican Summer League competition and earned a brief promotion up to the Gulf Coast during his debut a year after signing his professional pact. He followed that up by slugging .308/.354/.424 with 17 doubles, three triples, a pair of long balls, and six stolen bases between the Appalachian and Northwest Leagues in 2014. Last season, his first taste of full season action, Urena batted a respectable .266/.289/.438 in 91 games with Lansing, and he posted a .250/.268/.315 triple-slash mark in 30 games with Dunedin. Overall, he finished the year with an aggregate .262/.284/.407 line with 16 doubles, and career bests in triples (five) and homeruns (16).

**Projection**: Two interesting things to note here:

1. Urena's power took a tremendous step forward last season, going from below-average to slugging the sixth most homeruns among all minor league shortstops.
2. Urena's patience took an equally large step *backward* last season, going from average to non-existent.

As I noted in last year's book, Urena's power was definitely trending upward so it's likely here to stay. And on the flip-side, he posted two seasons of average-ish walk rates so it's very likely we see a big swing back towards respectability in 2016.

One final note: Urena's production has been swallowed whole by his inability to handle southpaws as he slugged just .205/.227/.279 against them last season. It might be worth scrapping the whole switch-hitting thing in a season or two.

**Ceiling**: 2.5- to 3.0-win player
**Risk**: Moderate to High
**MLB ETA**: 2018

## 8. Jon Harris, RHP

**MiLB Rank: #145**
**Position Rank: N/A**

| Born: 10/16/93 | Age: 22 | Bats: R | Top CALs: Benjamin Wells, Kelvin Lopez, |
| Height: 6-3 | Weight: 160 | Throws: R | William Waltrip, Cory Hamilton, Harold Guerrero |

| YEAR | Age | Level | IP | W | L | ERA | FIP | K/9 | BB/9 | K% | BB% | HR/9 | LOB% |
|------|-----|-------|-----|---|---|------|------|------|------|------|------|------|------|
| 2015 | 21 | A- | 36.0 | 0 | 5 | 6.75 | 4.02 | 8.00 | 5.25 | 18.2% | 11.9% | 0.25 | 56.9% |

**Background**: After taking – and failing to sign – the big right-hander in the 33rd round out of high school in 2012, Toronto finally got their man in the latter part of the first round last season. Harris spent his collegiate career as a three-year starter for Missouri State, but

blossomed during his final season: 103.0 IP, 116 K, and 36 BB.

**Projection**: Here's what I wrote prior to draft last season:

> *"Big and projectable, Harris finally took a large developmental leap forward after two good, not great seasons. His control is merely average, but his ability to miss bats should help him grow into another steady mid-rotation arm. At the very least, he's a potential dominant backend reliever. There is some risk given his relatively short track record of better-than-average production, especially considering his ho-hum work in the Cape [in 2014]."*

**Ceiling**: 2.0- to 2.5-win player
**Risk**: Moderate
**MLB ETA**: 2018

## 9. Clinton Hollon, RHP

**MiLB Rank: N/A**
**Position Rank: N/A**

| Born: 12/24/94 | Age: 21 | Bats: R | Top CALs: Rookie Davis, Francisco Rios, |
| Height: 6-1 | Weight: 195 | Throws: R | Ian Mckinney, Jose Rodriguez, Isaac Gil |

| YEAR | Age | Level | IP | W | L | ERA | FIP | K/9 | BB/9 | K% | BB% | HR/9 | LOB% |
|------|-----|-------|------|---|---|-------|------|------|------|------|------|------|-------|
| 2013 | 18 | R | 5.3 | 0 | 1 | 10.13 | 5.68 | 8.44 | 5.06 | 19.2% | 11.5% | 1.69 | 26.3% |
| 2013 | 18 | R | 12.0 | 1 | 0 | 0.00 | 2.54 | 7.50 | 2.25 | 25.0% | 7.5% | 0.00 | 100.0% |
| 2015 | 20 | A- | 45.3 | 2 | 2 | 3.18 | 3.32 | 7.94 | 2.98 | 21.5% | 8.1% | 0.20 | 69.0% |
| 2015 | 20 | A | 13.3 | 1 | 1 | 4.05 | 4.67 | 3.38 | 4.73 | 8.6% | 12.1% | 0.00 | 65.0% |

**Background**: Toronto grabbed the wiry right-hander in the 2nd round out of Woodford County HS three years ago. And after a promising debut between the both rookie leagues, Hollon missed the entire 2014 season as he recovered from Tommy John surgery. Finally healthy, he posted a 45-to-22 K/BB ratio between short-season

and Low Class A.

**Projection**: Sure, it's still a small sample size – he's thrown just 76.0 total innings in his brief career – but it is still been fairly impressive, particularly his post-op results. Typically, hurlers – especially young hurlers – will battle control issues on the road back from Tommy John, but Hollon basically picked up right where he left off during his debut. He's probably in line for about 100 or so innings in the Midwest League in 2016.

**Ceiling:** 1.0- to 1.5-win player
**Risk:** Moderate
**MLB ETA:** 2018/2019

## 10. Ryan Borucki, LHP

**MiLB Rank: N/A**
**Position Rank: N/A**

| Born: 03/31/94 | Age: 22 | Bats: L | Top CALs: N/A |
|---|---|---|---|
| Height: 6-4 | Weight: 175 | Throws: L | |

| YEAR | Age | Level | IP | W | L | ERA | FIP | K/9 | BB/9 | K% | BB% | HR/9 | LOB% |
|---|---|---|---|---|---|---|---|---|---|---|---|---|---|
| 2014 | 20 | R | 33.3 | 2 | 1 | 2.70 | 3.18 | 8.10 | 1.62 | 22.9% | 4.6% | 0.54 | 72.9% |
| 2014 | 20 | A- | 23.7 | 1 | 1 | 1.90 | 3.02 | 8.37 | 1.14 | 25.0% | 3.4% | 0.38 | 57.7% |
| 2015 | 21 | R | 1.0 | 0 | 0 | 0.00 | 1.31 | 9.00 | 0.00 | 25.0% | 0.0% | 0.00 | 100.0% |
| 2015 | 21 | A- | 4.7 | 0 | 1 | 3.86 | 2.96 | 11.57 | 5.79 | 26.1% | 13.0% | 0.00 | 77.8% |

**Background:** Just another one of the system's promising lefties that have had their brief careers ravaged by injury. Borucki, a 15th round pick four years ago, underwent Tommy John surgery and missed the entire 2013. Two years later tennis elbow and shoulder woes would limit him to just 5.2 innings.

**Projection:** You know, the Mets' budding ace Steven Matz missed a tremendous amount of time during his first couple years after getting drafted – so at least Borucki has some company. And like Matz, when he's healthy the 6-foot-4 Borucki has been dominant, averaging nine strikeouts and just 1.6 walk per nine innings. Hopefully, he can stay on the mound for more than a couple dozen innings in 2016. If he does, he might be one of the most talked about prospects after 2016.

**Ceiling:** 1.0- to 1.5-win player
**Risk:** High to Extremely High
**MLB ETA:** 2019

## 11. D.J. Davis, CF

**MiLB Rank: N/A**
**Position Rank: N/A**

| Born: 07/25/94 | Age: 21 | Bats: L | Top CALs: Rafael Fernandez, Brian Pointer, Keon Broxton, Joe Dunigan, Michael A. Taylor |
|---|---|---|---|
| Height: 6-1 | Weight: 180 | Throws: R | |

| Season | Age | LVL | PA | 2B | 3B | HR | AVG | OBP | SLG | ISO | BB% | K% | wRC+ |
|---|---|---|---|---|---|---|---|---|---|---|---|---|---|
| 2013 | 20 | R | 258 | 8 | 7 | 6 | 0.240 | 0.323 | 0.418 | 0.178 | 10.1% | 29.5% | 111 |
| 2014 | 21 | A | 542 | 13 | 7 | 8 | 0.213 | 0.268 | 0.316 | 0.103 | 6.6% | 30.8% | 67 |
| 2015 | 22 | A | 554 | 19 | 7 | 7 | 0.282 | 0.340 | 0.391 | 0.109 | 7.0% | 21.5% | 113 |

**Background:** How's this for frustrating: the two players taken immediately following Davis, the 17th overall pick in 2012, were shortstop Corey Seager and right-hander Michael Wacha, both of whom would have looked awfully nice in a Toronto uniform during the club's stretch run last season. Anyway, Davis looked like a complete lost cause during his first two stints in the minor leagues, something seemed to click for the toolsy – albeit enigmatic – outfielder in 2015. After hitting a lowly .213/.268/.316 with Lansing in 2014, Davis followed that up with a far improved .282/.340/.391 showing in a repeat of the league, setting career highs in doubles (19) to go along with seven triples, seven homeruns, and 21 stolen bases. His overall production, according to *Weighted Runs Created Plus*, topped the Midwest League average by 13%.

**Projection:** Here's what I wrote in last year's book:

> "Above-average or better speed with no idea how to employ it. Solid average pop, huge strikeout rates, decent eye at the plate. Davis is one of the more athletic prospects in the system, but the red flags are likely going to be too much to overcome."

Well, after fanning in more than 25% of his plate appearances before 2015, Davis went out and posted a 21.5% punch out rate – a development that led to a huge increase in his production. But let's remember something: it occurred in a repeat of Low Class A as a 21-year-old. Meaning: it's incredibly likely that we'll see a big spike in his strikeout rate as he moves up to High Class A. And even if you want to ignore his previous strikeout totals for a minute, Davis' production was far from dominant. At best he's a fourth outfielder.

**Ceiling:** 1.0- to 1.5-win player
**Risk:** Moderate to High
**MLB ETA:** 2018

## 12. Shane Dawson, LHP

MiLB Rank: N/A
Position Rank: N/A

| Born: 09/09/93 | Age: 22 | Bats: R | Top CALs: Myles Jaye, Ryan Searle, |
| Height: 6-1 | Weight: 200 | Throws: L | Ryan Crowley, David Baker, Nick Traviieso |

| YEAR | Age | Level | IP | W | L | ERA | FIP | K/9 | BB/9 | K% | BB% | HR/9 | LOB% |
|------|-----|-------|------|----|---|------|------|-------|------|-------|-------|------|------|
| 2013 | 19 | R | 27.3 | 1 | 3 | 3.29 | 2.12 | 11.52 | 1.98 | 33.7% | 5.8% | 0.33 | 62.0% |
| 2013 | 19 | A- | 18.7 | 1 | 1 | 2.89 | 1.50 | 12.54 | 1.93 | 34.2% | 5.3% | 0.00 | 73.9% |
| 2014 | 20 | A | 56.0 | 3 | 5 | 3.38 | 4.11 | 7.39 | 3.86 | 19.2% | 10.0% | 0.64 | 78.0% |
| 2015 | 21 | A | 101.7 | 12 | 4 | 3.01 | 3.19 | 8.68 | 2.12 | 23.9% | 5.9% | 0.62 | 72.4% |
| 2015 | 21 | A+ | 26.0 | 3 | 2 | 3.12 | 3.74 | 7.62 | 2.77 | 20.0% | 7.3% | 0.69 | 74.5% |

**Background:** Here's a brief anatomy lesson (and, yes, get your heads out of the gutter): the infraspinatus muscle is located just below each shoulder blade. And this triangle-shaped muscle, apparently, can cause shoulder and elbow pain when it atrophies, a rather common occurrence in volleyball players, a sport Dawson participated in during his high school days. Well, Dawson began feeling unbearable pain in his left shoulder and elbow three years ago and was forced to shut it down in the middle of July. After the season concluded the young southpaw was sent to see the team's doctors and they discovered a "huge divot" where the muscle was, according to a NationalPost.com news story. Finally healthy, the 6-foot-1, 200-pound lefty tossed a career high 127.2 innings last season – a miracle given his health issues – with 120 punch outs and 32 walk en route to totaling a 3.03 ERA between his time with Lansing and Dunedin.

**Projection**: Assuming the health issues are firmly in the past, Dawson quickly made up for lost time last season. And it wouldn't be surprising to see him finish the 2016 season in Class AA. He's not overpowering, but he's shown a relatively strong feel for the strike zone with average or better groundball numbers. He might be able to develop into a good #5 down the line.

**Ceiling:** 1.0- to 1.5-win player
**Risk:** Moderate to High
**MLB ETA:** 2018

## 13. Andy Burns, IF/OF

MiLB Rank: N/A
Position Rank: N/A

| Born: 08/07/90 | Age: 25 | Bats: R | Top CALs: Conor Gillaspie, Casey Mcgehee, |
| Height: 6-2 | Weight: 205 | Throws: R | Russ Mitchell, Christian Villanueva, Sean Henry |

| Season | Age | LVL | PA | 2B | 3B | HR | AVG | OBP | SLG | ISO | BB% | K% | wRC+ |
|--------|-----|-----|-----|----|----|----|-------|-------|-------|-------|-------|-------|------|
| 2013 | 22 | A+ | 282 | 15 | 5 | 8 | 0.327 | 0.383 | 0.524 | 0.198 | 8.9% | 13.5% | 156 |
| 2013 | 22 | AA | 291 | 19 | 2 | 7 | 0.253 | 0.309 | 0.419 | 0.166 | 7.9% | 18.9% | 99 |
| 2014 | 23 | AA | 553 | 32 | 5 | 15 | 0.255 | 0.315 | 0.430 | 0.176 | 7.4% | 17.9% | 104 |
| 2015 | 24 | AA | 24 | 0 | 0 | 1 | 0.238 | 0.333 | 0.381 | 0.143 | 12.5% | 12.5% | 111 |
| 2015 | 24 | AAA | 527 | 26 | 0 | 4 | 0.293 | 0.351 | 0.372 | 0.079 | 7.2% | 13.1% | 112 |

**Background:** A late-round pick out of the University of Arizona five years ago, Burns has quietly marched through the minor leagues since then. He spent his debut between rookie ball and the Northwest League, a year in Low Class A, half a season with Dunedin, 203 games with New Hampshire in the Eastern League, and majority of 2015 producing league average offense with the Bisons of Buffalo. In 126 games in the International League, the 6-foot-2, 205-pound infielder batted .293/.351/.376 with 26 doubles, four homeruns, and six stolen bases, though it took 15 attempts to do so. His overall production, according to *Weighted Runs Created Plus*, topped the league average mark by 12%.

**Projection**: I'll just let CAL lead the analysis hear. Burns' top five comparables: Conor Gillaspie, Casey McGehee, Russ Mitchell, Christian Villanueva, and Sean Henry. If it looks like a future utility guy, produces like a future utility guy, and is compared to a bunch of utility guys...well...he's a future utility guy. Burns packs surprising pop – at times. He'll flash an average eye at the plate, some speed, and a decent hit tool. Throw in his ability to man the entire infield – sans pitcher and catcher – as well as both corner outfield positions and it's all pointing to future utility-dom. If I had to pin a future offensive performance down I would go with a .260/.315/.380 triple-slash line.

**Ceiling:** 1.0-win player
**Risk:** Moderate
**MLB ETA:** 2017

## 14. Mitch Nay, 3B

**MiLB Rank: N/A**

**Position Rank: N/A**

| Born: 09/20/93 | Age: 22 | Bats: R | **Top CALs:** Edinson Rincon, Cheslor Cuthbert, |
| Height: 6-3 | Weight: 200 | Throws: R | Jeimer Candelario, Daniel Mateo, Jake Smolinski |

| Season | Age | LVL | PA | 2B | 3B | HR | AVG | OBP | SLG | ISO | BB% | K% | wRC+ |
|---|---|---|---|---|---|---|---|---|---|---|---|---|---|
| 2013 | 19 | R | 258 | 11 | 0 | 6 | 0.300 | 0.364 | 0.426 | 0.126 | 9.7% | 13.6% | 129 |
| 2014 | 20 | A | 518 | 34 | 3 | 3 | 0.285 | 0.342 | 0.389 | 0.104 | 7.5% | 15.3% | 111 |
| 2015 | 21 | A+ | 437 | 18 | 5 | 5 | 0.243 | 0.303 | 0.353 | 0.110 | 7.3% | 17.2% | 100 |

**Background:** Taken with the third to last pick in the first round in 2012 draft, 58th overall, Nay's production has been in slow, steady decline since his strong showing in the Appalachian League three years ago. The well-built third base batted a solid .300/.364/.426 with 11 doubles and six homeruns with Bluefield as a 19-year-old. But he followed that up with a slightly worse season when the organization bumped him up to Lansing two years ago; he batted .285/.342/.389 with the club before earning a quick 11-game stint with Dunedin. Back for a full taste of the Florida State League, Nay batted a disappointingly league average .243/.303/.353 with just 18 doubles, five triples, and five homeruns en route to posting a 100 wRC+. For his career, he's sporting a .271/.330/.378 triple-slash line with 64 doubles, eight triples, and just 14 homeruns in 304 games.

**Projection**: Here's what I wrote in last year's book:

> "Ignoring the .189/.250/.216 triple-slash line he strung together with Dunedin, Nay finished the year on a relatively strong note; he batted .307/.359/.424 over his final 66 games in Low Class A. But for a high round draft pick, at a run-producing position with a good build/frame, Nay hasn't shown a whole lot of pop. He posted a .126 ISO two years ago and followed that up with a .104 mark with Lansing; even during his hot stretch his power was below-average (.117). The culprit, as it seems, is a groundball approaching 50%. It's awfully hard to hit dingers when you're consistently putting the ball on the ground."

Well, it's not surprisingly that Nay's power continued to flounder as his groundball rate is still hovering around the 50% mark last season. But here's something just as troubling: outside of his red hot July – he batted .333/.369/.469 – Nay never topped a monthly OPS above .661. If it's not time to slap the draft bust label on him, it's quickly approaching.

**Ceiling:** 1.0-win player
**Risk:** Moderate
**MLB ETA:** 2018

## 15. Dwight Smith, OF

**MiLB Rank: N/A**

**Position Rank: N/A**

| Born: 10/26/92 | Age: 23 | Bats: L | **Top CALs:** Juan Portes, Sean Henry, |
| Height: 5-11 | Weight: 195 | Throws: R | Christian Marrero, Ramon Flores, Isaias Velasquez |

| Season | Age | LVL | PA | 2B | 3B | HR | AVG | OBP | SLG | ISO | BB% | K% | wRC+ |
|---|---|---|---|---|---|---|---|---|---|---|---|---|---|
| 2013 | 20 | A | 479 | 17 | 3 | 7 | 0.284 | 0.365 | 0.388 | 0.104 | 10.9% | 17.1% | 117 |
| 2014 | 21 | A+ | 533 | 28 | 8 | 12 | 0.284 | 0.363 | 0.453 | 0.169 | 10.9% | 12.9% | 134 |
| 2015 | 22 | AA | 512 | 26 | 2 | 7 | 0.265 | 0.335 | 0.376 | 0.111 | 9.2% | 12.5% | 108 |

**Background:** The son of former big league outfielder by the same name, the younger Smith turned in another solid, yet uninspiring campaign in 2015. The 2011 supplemental first round pick batted a league average-ish .265/.335/.376 with 26 doubles, a pair of triples, seven homeruns, and four stolen bases in 512 trips to the plate.

**Projection**: The power surge Smith showed in High Class A proved to be a mirage as his ISO declined back down to his previous career norms. He has average tools – and minor league production – across the board, nothing really worth noting here. Maybe he can a late bloomer like his old man, but I doubt it.

**Ceiling:** 1.0-win player
**Risk:** Moderate
**MLB ETA:** 2017

## 16. Brady Dragmire, RHP

MiLB Rank: N/A

Position Rank: N/A

| Born: 02/05/93 | Age: 23 | Bats: R | Top CALs: Ryan Weber, Ivan Pineyro, |
| Height: 6-1 | Weight: 180 | Throws: R | Sebastian Vader, Jayson Aquino, Orlando Castro |

| YEAR | Age | Level | IP | W | L | ERA | FIP | K/9 | BB/9 | K% | BB% | HR/9 | LOB% |
|------|-----|-------|------|---|---|------|------|------|------|------|------|------|------|
| 2013 | 20 | R | 50.0 | 3 | 2 | 2.16 | 3.85 | 7.20 | 1.44 | 19.9% | 4.0% | 0.90 | 77.3% |
| 2014 | 21 | A | 77.3 | 3 | 6 | 2.91 | 3.20 | 5.24 | 1.05 | 14.4% | 2.9% | 0.23 | 62.8% |
| 2015 | 22 | A+ | 63.3 | 2 | 2 | 5.26 | 2.52 | 8.10 | 2.84 | 20.1% | 7.1% | 0.14 | 57.8% |

**Background:** Something clicked for the groundball specialist last season as his previous career strikeout rate jumped from 6.63 K/9 to a solid 8.1 K/9 as he moved into the Florida State League for the first time. In 63.1 innings with Dunedin, the 6-foot-1, 180-pound right-hander posted a 57-to-20 K-to-BB ratio.

**Projection:** The victim of some heinously shit luck last season, Dragmire outpitched his bloated 5.26 ERA by nearly three full runs; his FIP registered as a dominant 2.52. The main culprit: a craptastically high .385 BABIP and a criminally low 57.8% strand rate. And one could draw the likely correct assumption that Dunedin's infield defense is pretty shitty because Dragmire's groundball rate was north of 65.1% Meaning: there weren't an awful lot of balls caught. He looks like a solid middle relief option down the line.

**Ceiling:** 1.0-win player
**Risk:** Moderate
**MLB ETA:** 2017

## 17. Matt Dean, 1B/3B

MiLB Rank: N/A

Position Rank: N/A

| Born: 12/22/92 | Age: 23 | Bats: R | Top CALs: Mike Mcdade, Calvin Anderson, |
| Height: 6-3 | Weight: 215 | Throws: R | Ernesto Mejia, Stefan Welch, Lance Ray |

| Season | Age | LVL | PA | 2B | 3B | HR | AVG | OBP | SLG | ISO | BB% | K% | wRC+ |
|--------|-----|-----|-----|----|----|----|------|------|------|------|------|------|------|
| 2013 | 20 | R | 233 | 14 | 3 | 6 | 0.338 | 0.390 | 0.519 | 0.181 | 6.0% | 24.5% | 159 |
| 2014 | 21 | A | 485 | 29 | 5 | 9 | 0.281 | 0.332 | 0.429 | 0.147 | 5.6% | 24.1% | 117 |
| 2015 | 22 | A+ | 521 | 27 | 3 | 14 | 0.253 | 0.313 | 0.410 | 0.157 | 6.9% | 26.7% | 122 |

**Background:** A late-round pick in 2011, Dean didn't make his professional debut until the following season – an admittedly pitiful showing with Bluefield in the Appalachian League when he batted .222/.282/.353 with just 14 extra-base hits in 49 games. Toronto kept the hefty corner infielder at the level the following year – with much improved results – before bumping him up to full-season action in 2014. Last season, Dean, a former 13th round pick out of The Colony High School, hit a respectable .253/.313/.410 in his first taste of the Florida State League, slugging 27 doubles, three triples, and a career best 14 homeruns. For his career, Dean is sporting a .272/.328/.427 triple-slash line in 348 games.

**Projection:** A member of the *Bird Doggin' It* section in last year's book, Dean graduated to the system's Top 25 list in large part – and by that I mean, just because – of the front office's prospect purge to vastly improve the big league club. Dean doesn't possess the type of in-game power that his hulking 6-foot-3, 215-pound frame would suggest. Add in some questionable strikeout rates and a slightly below-average eye at the plate and it's pretty clear to see Dean's limited ceiling.

**Ceiling:** 1.0-win player
**Risk:** Moderate
**MLB ETA:** 2018

## 18. Angel Perdomo, LHP

MiLB Rank: N/A

Position Rank: N/A

| Born: 05/07/94 | Age: 22 | Bats: L | Top CALs: N/A |
| Height: 6-6 | Weight: 200 | Throws: L | |

| YEAR | Age | Level | IP | W | L | ERA | FIP | K/9 | BB/9 | K% | BB% | HR/9 | LOB% |
|------|-----|-------|------|---|---|------|------|-------|------|-------|-------|------|------|
| 2013 | 19 | R | 26.7 | 0 | 1 | 3.04 | 3.05 | 14.51 | 6.08 | 36.1% | 15.1% | 0.34 | 72.5% |
| 2014 | 20 | R | 46.0 | 3 | 2 | 2.54 | 2.81 | 11.15 | 4.11 | 29.1% | 10.7% | 0.20 | 79.9% |
| 2015 | 21 | R | 48.0 | 4 | 1 | 2.63 | 3.83 | 6.75 | 2.63 | 18.0% | 7.0% | 0.56 | 70.6% |
| 2015 | 21 | A- | 21.3 | 2 | 0 | 2.53 | 3.70 | 13.08 | 6.75 | 36.5% | 18.8% | 0.42 | 82.0% |

**Background:** Another big lefty developing in the lowest levels of the minors – though he's still not as large as Matt Smoral – Perdomo, who stands an impressive 6-foot-6 and 200-pounds, made his way up to the Appalachian League for nine starts before getting bumped up to Vancouver for five abbreviated – and often

dominant – games.

**Projection:** Yes, Perdomo battled control issues at various points last season, but he also fanned at least seven and walked fewer than two on four occasions – or just 28% of his starts last season. Granted, he was too old for both levels, but just as I said in Matt Smoral's projection piece, big lefties with promising strikeout potential and a blistering fastball don't exactly grow on trees.

**Ceiling:** 1.0- to 1.5-win player
**Risk:** High
**MLB ETA:** 2019

## 19. Matt Smoral, LHP

**MiLB Rank:** N/A
**Position Rank:** N/A

| Born: 03/18/94 | Age: 22 | Bats: L | Top CALs: Billy Flamion, Wendy Rosa, |
|---|---|---|---|
| Height: 6-8 | Weight: 220 | Throws: L | Aaron Wirsch, Tyler Sample, Omar Duran |

| YEAR | Age | Level | IP | W | L | ERA | FIP | K/9 | BB/9 | K% | BB% | HR/9 | LOB% |
|---|---|---|---|---|---|---|---|---|---|---|---|---|---|
| 2013 | 19 | R | 25.7 | 0 | 2 | 7.01 | 6.07 | 9.47 | 9.12 | 20.5% | 19.7% | 0.35 | 61.8% |
| 2014 | 20 | R | 33.7 | 2 | 3 | 3.48 | 2.41 | 13.63 | 4.81 | 32.5% | 11.5% | 0.00 | 71.2% |
| 2014 | 20 | A- | 20.0 | 2 | 0 | 2.70 | 4.47 | 8.55 | 6.75 | 23.2% | 18.3% | 0.00 | 80.7% |
| 2015 | 21 | R | 10.7 | 0 | 0 | 5.06 | 5.02 | 13.50 | 11.81 | 28.6% | 25.0% | 0.00 | 65.2% |
| 2015 | 21 | A+ | 3.7 | 1 | 0 | 14.73 | 6.98 | 12.27 | 14.73 | 19.2% | 23.1% | 0.00 | 60.0% |

**Background:** Another year in the books, another lost season for the big lefty. Smoral, who stands a Red Wood-esque 6-foot-8 and 220 pounds, has thrown just 93.2 innings over his three professional seasons as he's dealt with a litany of injuries.

**Projection:** At this point, who the hell really knows? Smoral has everything you'd want in a pitching prospect – massive frame, left-handed, above-average or better heater, projectability, etc... – except for the fact that, you know, he sees the mound as often as a blind squirrel finding a nut. Still, though, 6-foot-8, hard-throwing southpaws don't exactly grow on trees...

**Ceiling:** 1.5-win player
**Risk:** High to Extremely High
**MLB ETA:** 2019? 2025? 2040?

## 20. Justin Maese, RHP

**MiLB Rank:** N/A
**Position Rank:** N/A

| Born: 10/24/96 | Age: 19 | Bats: R | Top CALs: Josh Stinson, Alejandro Solarte, |
|---|---|---|---|
| Height: 6-3 | Weight: 190 | Throws: R | Jesse Beal, Richard Bielski, Luca Panerati |

| YEAR | Age | Level | IP | W | L | ERA | FIP | K/9 | BB/9 | K% | BB% | HR/9 | LOB% |
|---|---|---|---|---|---|---|---|---|---|---|---|---|---|
| 2015 | 18 | R | 35.7 | 5 | 0 | 1.01 | 2.75 | 4.79 | 1.51 | 13.3% | 4.2% | 0.00 | 86.8% |

**Background:** Fun fact: there have been two players drafted out of Ysleta High School: Maese, a third round pick last June, and James Greggerson, who was originally drafted in the 30th round way back in 1969. Anyway, Maese slapped a 1.01 ERA together in his debut in the Gulf Coast League.

**Projection:** How's this for interesting: Maese, a 6-foot-3, 190-pound right-hander, allowed just four earned runs in 35.2 innings last season – despite fanning just 19 batters. Of course, walking only six certainly helps. But if he doesn't start missing bats – like, now – don't expect to see his name on the club's Top 25 Prospects list next season.

**Ceiling:** Too Soon to Tell
**Risk:** N/A
**MLB ETA:** N/A

## 21. Danny Barnes, RHP

**MiLB Rank:** N/A
**Position Rank:** N/A

| Born: 10/21/89 | Age: 26 | Bats: L | Top CALs: Ramon Ramirez, Dave Johnson, |
|---|---|---|---|
| Height: 6-1 | Weight: 195 | Throws: R | Henry Centeno, Julio Mateo, Chris Armstrong |

| YEAR | Age | Level | IP | W | L | ERA | FIP | K/9 | BB/9 | K% | BB% | HR/9 | LOB% |
|---|---|---|---|---|---|---|---|---|---|---|---|---|---|
| 2013 | 23 | R | 1.0 | 0 | 0 | 0.00 | 2.54 | 27.00 | 0.00 | 100.0% | 0.0% | 0.00 | 100.0% |
| 2013 | 23 | A+ | 2.0 | 1 | 1 | 22.50 | 2.74 | 9.00 | 4.50 | 16.7% | 8.3% | 0.00 | 16.7% |
| 2014 | 24 | A+ | 38.7 | 0 | 5 | 4.19 | 3.21 | 11.41 | 2.79 | 29.9% | 7.3% | 0.93 | 66.8% |
| 2015 | 25 | AA | 60.7 | 3 | 2 | 2.97 | 2.89 | 10.98 | 2.82 | 28.2% | 7.3% | 0.74 | 77.9% |

**Background:** A late round pick out of Princeton University in 2010, Barnes, once again, turned in a phenomenal campaign last year – his sixth season in the minor leagues. The 6-foot-1, 195-pound right-hander posted a 74-to-19 strikeout-to-walk ratio in 60.2 innings of work.

**Projection**: He's averaging an impeccable 12.0 strikeouts and just 2.9 walks per nine innings. He looks like a potential solid middle relief arm – something that's typically overlooked…until your bullpen goes Ka-Blooey! Teams could do a lot worse than running Barnes out there at an inning at a time.

**Ceiling**: 0.5- to 1.0-win player
**Risk**: Low to Moderate
**MLB ETA**: 2016

## 22. Guadalupe Chavez, RHP

**MiLB Rank: N/A**
**Position Rank: N/A**

| Born: 12/03/97 | Age: 19 | Bats: R |
| Height: 6-2 | Weight: 150 | Throws: R |

**Top CALs**: Juan Robles, Carlos Rodriguez, Cristofer Cabrera, Andy Beltre, Jhondaniel Medina

| YEAR | Age | Level | IP | W | L | ERA | FIP | K/9 | BB/9 | K% | BB% | HR/9 | LOB% |
|---|---|---|---|---|---|---|---|---|---|---|---|---|---|
| 2015 | 17 | R | 42.3 | 4 | 1 | 2.98 | 2.76 | 9.57 | 2.98 | 24.7% | 7.7% | 0.00 | 66.7% |
| 2015 | 17 | R | 19.0 | 3 | 1 | 2.37 | 2.94 | 6.63 | 2.84 | 17.7% | 7.6% | 0.00 | 78.3% |

**Background**: Signed out of Mexico as a 16-year-old in July 2014, Chavez didn't make his professional debut until last season, throwing 42.1 dominant innings in the organization's DSL affiliate and another 19.0 innings in the Gulf Coast. Combined, Chavez posted a 59-to-20 strikeout-to-walk ratio in 61.1 innings of work.

**Projection**: He's a basically a low level wild card at this point. As expected, Chavez blew through Dominican Summer League and looked decent in four games in the Gulf Coast. He's more or less the equivalent of an incoming prep prospect – just a year younger. Let's see what 2016 season holds for the young hurler.

**Ceiling**: Too Soon to Tell
**Risk**: N/A
**MLB ETA**: N/A

## 23. Carl Wise, 3B

**MiLB Rank: N/A**
**Position Rank: N/A**

| Born: 05/25/94 | Age: 22 | Bats: R | Top CALs: N/A |
| Height: 6-2 | Weight: 210 | Throws: R | |

| Season | Age | LVL | PA | 2B | 3B | HR | AVG | OBP | SLG | ISO | BB% | K% | wRC+ |
|---|---|---|---|---|---|---|---|---|---|---|---|---|---|
| 2015 | 21 | R | 33 | 2 | 0 | 0 | 0.258 | 0.303 | 0.323 | 0.065 | 6.1% | 18.2% | 76 |
| 2015 | 21 | A- | 194 | 9 | 1 | 1 | 0.231 | 0.268 | 0.308 | 0.077 | 4.1% | 22.2% | 66 |

**Background**: A three-year starter at the College of Charleston, Wise left the school as a .308/.3403/.516 hitter. Toronto grabbed the 6-foot-2, 210-pound third baseman in the fourth round last June, 122nd overall, and sent him briefly to Bluefield before promoting him up to Vancouver.

**Projection**: He's sort of a lite version of a Moneyball player; he showed a strong ability to control the strike zone during his collegiate career, posting a 100-to-82 strikeout-to-walk ratio in more than 700 plate appearances. That discipline, though, all but evaporated during his tenure in the pros. He's probably nothing more than org. fodder but in an organization as bereft on top talent as Toronto, Wise is definitely worth noting.

**Ceiling**: 0.5- to 1.0-win player
**Risk**: Moderate to High
**MLB ETA**: 2019

## 24. Jeremy Gabryszwski, RHP

**MiLB Rank: N/A**
**Position Rank: N/A**

| Born: 03/16/93 | Age: 23 | Bats: R |
| Height: 6-4 | Weight: 195 | Throws: R |

**Top CALs**: B.J. Hermsen, Joely Rodriguez, Ryan Searle, Keith Couch, Mike Broadway

| YEAR | Age | Level | IP | W | L | ERA | FIP | K/9 | BB/9 | K% | BB% | HR/9 | LOB% |
|---|---|---|---|---|---|---|---|---|---|---|---|---|---|
| 2013 | 20 | A- | 76.7 | 5 | 2 | 2.82 | 2.74 | 4.70 | 1.17 | 12.9% | 3.2% | 0.00 | 57.8% |
| 2014 | 21 | A | 141.3 | 6 | 7 | 4.27 | 3.61 | 5.79 | 1.34 | 14.9% | 3.5% | 0.64 | 64.3% |
| 2014 | 21 | A+ | 10.0 | 1 | 1 | 5.40 | 5.09 | 8.10 | 2.70 | 19.6% | 6.5% | 1.80 | 75.8% |
| 2015 | 22 | A+ | 129.0 | 9 | 8 | 3.77 | 3.30 | 6.35 | 2.16 | 16.6% | 5.6% | 0.49 | 69.1% |

**Background**: A second round pick all the way back in 2011, the slowly developing right-hander turned in an average campaign in the Florida State League last season, posting a 91-to-31 strikeout-to-walk ration in 129.0 innings of work. For his career, he's averaging just 5.7 strikeouts and 1.5

walks per nine innings.

**Projection**: A control pitcher with phenomenal walk rates and average groundball numbers, Gabryszwski found his way onto the list because, well, someone has to help round out the incredibly thin system. He might be a useful reliever. And I might hit the damn lottery.

**Ceiling:** 0.5-win player
**Risk:** Moderate
**MLB ETA:** 2018

## 25. Juan Meza, RHP

**MiLB Rank: N/A**
**Position Rank: N/A**

| Born: 02/04/98 | Age: 18 | Bats: R | **Top CALs:** Hernando Guzman, Henry Centeno, |
| Height: 6-2 | Weight: 172 | Throws: R | Carlos Hiraldo, Dan Urbina, Felix Ramos |

| YEAR | Age | Level | IP | W | L | ERA | FIP | K/9 | BB/9 | K% | BB% | HR/9 | LOB% |
|------|-----|-------|-----|---|---|-------|------|-------|-------|-------|-------|------|-------|
| 2015 | 17 | R | 25.7 | 0 | 0 | 6.66 | 4.21 | 7.36 | 4.91 | 17.5% | 11.7% | 0.35 | 51.6% |
| 2015 | 17 | R | 5.0 | 1 | 0 | 10.80 | 8.71 | 14.40 | 14.40 | 25.8% | 25.8% | 1.80 | 68.5% |

**Background:** Signed to a hefty $1.6 million bonus on July 2nd, 2014, Meza didn't make his anticipated debut until last season when he split time between the Dominican Summer League and Gulf Coast. Overall, he finished the year with 29 strikeouts, 22 walks, and a piss-poor 7.34 ERA in 30.2 innings of work.

**Projection**: Nothing really to go on, but, again, the state of the system mandates a mention – mostly on the back of his big signing bonus.

**Ceiling:** Too Soon to Tell
**Risk:** N/A
**MLB ETA:** N/A

### _Barely Missed:_

- **Yennsy Diaz, RHP** – Wiry right-hander out of the Dominican Republic, Diaz had a fine debut between the Dominican Summer and Gulf Coast Leagues last season: 56.1 IP, 58 K, and 23 BB. He could be a candidate to move into the Midwest League in 2016. Certainly, a name to watch in the coming years.

- **Jose Espada, RHP** – Smallish right-hander taken in the fifth round last June, Espada looked brilliant during his 34.1-inning run in the GCL during his debut, averaging 8.1 strikeouts and just 2.1 walks per nine innings. Another name to watch in the coming years.

## *Bird Doggin' It – Additional Prospects to Keep an Eye in 2016*

| Player | Age | POS | Notes |
|---|---|---|---|
| Deiferson Barreto | 21 | 2B/3B | Hit a solid .302/.347/.402 with eight doubles, one triple, and three homeruns in 51 games in the advanced rookie league. Let's see how he handles short-season, let's alone the Midwest League. |
| Jorge Flores | 24 | IF/OF | Four-year minor league vet spent the season with New Hampshire, batting .276/.360/.347 with 20 doubles, one triple, and a pair of dingers. |
| Chad Girodo | 25 | RHP | Posted a 1.34 ERA mostly between his time with Dunedin and New Hampshire last season, averaging 8.7 strikeouts and 1.3 walks per nine innings. |
| Danny Jansen | 21 | C | Regressed mightily after slugging .282/.390/.484 in the Appalachian League two years ago. Former 16th round pick batted .210/.300/.343, mostly spent in the Midwest League. |
| Reggie Pruitt | 19 | CF | 24th round pick last June signed for $500,000, but batted a lowly .223/.309/.289 in the Gulf Coast League during his debut. |
| Hansel Rodriguez | 19 | RHP | The then-18-year-old looked decent in the GCL last season, his second stint at the level, averaging 7.9 strikeouts and just 2.1 walks per nine innings. |
| Evan Smith | 20 | LHP | Big lefty taken in the fourth round three years ago fanned just 27 in 49.2 innings with Vancouver. |
| Lane Thomas | 29 | 2B | 2014 fifth round pick made the move to second base last season and, not surprisingly, his production at the plate tanked: .206/.244/.353. |

**State of the Farm System:** Whether it's good fortune or tremendous planning, the Nationals' farm system has been home to arguably the top player in baseball, Bryce Harper, and one of the game's better starting pitchers – when healthy – Stephen Strasburg. And now there's a third name on that elite list: Lucas Giolito, the onetime contender to become the first ever high school righty to be taken with the top pick until elbow woes, and subsequent Tommy John surgery, forced him to tumble to the middle of the first round.

So, again, one time is lucky. Twice is a coincidence. But what do you call it when it happens a third time – *in a matter of a few short years*?

Giolito, the third best prospect in baseball, trailing only Minnesota's Byron Buxton and the Dodgers' lefty wunderkind Julio Urias, was as dominant as just about any player in the minor leagues last season: in a career best 117.0 innings he fanned 131 and walked 37 as he split time against much older competition in High Class A and Class AA.

Washington's system is also sporting one of the better middle infield prospects in Trea Turner. The Nats stole the 2014 first round pick as part of the three-team deal involving Tampa Bay and San Diego last season. Turner batted .322/.370/.458 between Class AA and Class AAA. He also appeared in 27 games with the big league club as well.

Dominican-born center fielder Victor Robles continued to assert himself as a player worth watching in the coming years. In 261 plate appearances between the Gulf Coast and New York-Penn Leagues he slugged a whopping .352/.445/.507 with 11 doubles, five triples, and four homeruns.

Right-hander Reynaldo Lopez looked solid in his second season as a full time starting pitcher. And former 2014 first round pick Erick Fedde made a successful return from Tommy John surgery.

In all, Washington has a very top-heavy farm system – one that could potentially burp up five above-average big leaguers. But after that it gets awfully thin, awfully quick.

| Rank | Name | POS |
|------|------|-----|
| 1 | Lucas Giolito | RHP |
| 2 | Trea Turner | 2B/SS |
| 3 | Reynaldo Lopez | RHP |
| 4 | Victor Robles | CF |
| 5 | Erick Fedde | RHP |
| 6 | A.J. Cole | RHP |
| 7 | Austin Voth | RHP |
| 8 | Abel De Los Santos | RHP |
| 9 | Drew Ward | 3B |
| 10 | Andrew Stevenson | CF |
| 11 | Pedro Severino | C |
| 12 | Wilmer Difo | IF |
| 13 | Jakson Reetz | C |
| 14 | Sammy Solis | LHP |
| 15 | Chris Bostick | 2B |
| 16 | Matt Skole | 1B/3B |
| 17 | Osvaldo Abreu | 2B/SS |
| 18 | Blake Perkins | CF |
| 19 | Telmito Agustin | OF |
| 20 | Brian Goodwin | CF |
| 21 | Jake Johansen | RHP |
| 22 | Raudy Read | C |
| 23 | Anderson Franco | 3B |
| 24 | Cody Gunter | RHP |
| 25 | Nick Lee | LHP |

**Review of the 2015 Draft:** Forfeited their first round pick by signing Max Scherzer last season – which seemed to work out pretty well – Washington grabbed LSU slap-hitting center fielder Andrew Stevenson, who left the school as a career .311/.372/.392 hitter, though he slugged just 32 extra-base knocks in 177 games, with the 58th overall pick.

The Nationals grabbed another outfielder, prepster Blake Perkins, with their other second round pick. Perkins batted a lowly .211/.265/.283 during his debut.

Third round pick Rhett Wiseman, from Vanderbilt University, also struggled in his debut: .248/.307/.376 with Auburn in the NYPL.

One name to remember: Mariano Rivera Jr., son of the great Yankees closer.

# Washington Nationals

## 1. Lucas Giolito, RHP

**MiLB Rank: #3**
**Position Rank: #2**

| Born: 07/14/94 | Age: 21 | Bats: R | **Top CALs:** Randall Delgado, Julio Teheran, |
|---|---|---|---|
| Height: 6-6 | Weight: 1255 | Throws: R | Drew Hutchison, Arodys Vizcaino, Noah Syndergaard |

| YEAR | Age | Level | IP | W | L | ERA | FIP | K/9 | BB/9 | K% | BB% | HR/9 | LOB% |
|---|---|---|---|---|---|---|---|---|---|---|---|---|---|
| 2013 | 18 | R | 22.7 | 1 | 1 | 2.78 | 2.58 | 9.93 | 3.97 | 26.6% | 10.6% | 0.00 | 72.4% |
| 2013 | 18 | A- | 14.0 | 1 | 0 | 0.64 | 3.31 | 9.00 | 2.57 | 26.4% | 7.6% | 0.64 | 100.0% |
| 2014 | 19 | A | 98.0 | 10 | 2 | 2.20 | 3.16 | 10.10 | 2.57 | 28.5% | 7.3% | 0.64 | 79.6% |
| 2015 | 20 | A+ | 69.7 | 3 | 5 | 2.71 | 1.96 | 11.11 | 2.58 | 29.5% | 6.9% | 0.13 | 73.9% |
| 2015 | 20 | AA | 47.3 | 4 | 2 | 3.80 | 3.18 | 8.56 | 3.23 | 22.3% | 8.4% | 0.38 | 72.1% |

**Background:** At one point in time – namely before tearing ligaments in his elbow – Giolito looked destined to become the first high school right-hander – and the third prep arm – to go #1 overall in the June draft. Alas, Tommy John is a bitch – or at least impending elbow injuries are a bitch. The Washington Nationals step in and take one very wise, calculated risk. The franchise ended the right-hander's first round skid and grabbed him with the 16th overall pick that year, squarely between the likes of Tyler Naquin and D.J. Davis. Giolito wouldn't see much action over his first two professional seasons – he would throw two innings in the Gulf Coast during his abbreviated debut before finally succumbing to Tommy John surgery and would throw another 36.2 innings when he made it back a year later – but since his return he's simply been one of the most electrifying arms in all of baseball.

Two years ago the hard-throwing hurler twirled gem after gem after gem with Hagerstown in the South Atlantic League. He would finish 2014 with an impeccable 110-to-28 strikeout-to-walk ratio in just 98.0 innings of work, posting a 2.20 ERA and a 3.16 FIP. Washington started to ease the reins a bit last season and pushed Giolito through two levels. He opened the year with 69.2 innings in High Class A and would finish with another 47.1 innings in the Eastern League. Overall, Giolito would throw a career-high 117.0 innings while fanning 26.6% and walking 7.5% of the total batters he faced.

**Projection:** Whatever awe inspiring adjective you could hurl towards a budding ace can – and should – be said about the 6-foot-6, 255-pound hurler. His swing-and-miss potential outranks any minor league hurler, starter *or* reliever. He's shown a tremendous ability to limit free passes – despite being a bigger pitcher. Oh, and then there's his groundball rate, which tends to hover around 50%. Simply put, everything Lucas Giolito does is for his benefit. He's a true, genuine legitimate ace-in-waiting.

**Ceiling:** 6.5-win player
**Risk:** Moderate
**MLB ETA:** 2016/2017

## 2. Trea Turner, 2B/SS

**MiLB Rank: #36**
**Position Rank: #2 (2B), #6 (SS)**

| Born: 06/30/93 | Age: 23 | Bats: R | **Top CALs:** Chris Taylor, Brad Miller, |
|---|---|---|---|
| Height: 6-1 | Weight: 175 | Throws: R | Erik Gonzalez, Jason Donald, Jordany Valdespin |

| Season | Age | LVL | PA | 2B | 3B | HR | AVG | OBP | SLG | ISO | BB% | K% | wRC+ |
|---|---|---|---|---|---|---|---|---|---|---|---|---|---|
| 2014 | 21 | A- | 105 | 2 | 0 | 1 | 0.228 | 0.324 | 0.283 | 0.054 | 10.5% | 18.1% | 80 |
| 2014 | 21 | A | 216 | 14 | 2 | 4 | 0.369 | 0.447 | 0.529 | 0.160 | 11.1% | 22.2% | 180 |
| 2015 | 22 | AA | 254 | 13 | 3 | 5 | 0.322 | 0.385 | 0.471 | 0.150 | 9.4% | 18.9% | 141 |
| 2015 | 22 | AA | 41 | 4 | 1 | 0 | 0.359 | 0.366 | 0.513 | 0.154 | 2.4% | 19.5% | 149 |
| 2015 | 22 | AAA | 205 | 7 | 3 | 3 | 0.314 | 0.353 | 0.431 | 0.117 | 6.3% | 20.0% | 126 |
| 2015 | 22 | MLB | 44 | 1 | 0 | 1 | 0.225 | 0.295 | 0.325 | 0.100 | 9.1% | 27.3% | 72 |

**Background:** While Turner's official time in the San Diego organization lasted a total of 127 games, the reality is that he was gone about half way through. The Nationals agreed to a three-team deal that listed Turner as a player-to-be-named later, though he was decidedly included in the mid-December deal but couldn't officially be named until he spent an entire season in the Padres' organization thanks to some archaic rules. Turner, who was in running as a potential #1 overall pick in the draft two years ago, ripped through the ACC competition during his three-year run with N.C. State, hitting a combined .342/.435/.507 with 38 doubles, nine triples, 20 homeruns, and 113 stolen bases (in just 127 attempts, or a success rate of about 89%). The 6-foot-1, 175-pound middle infielder shined during his abbreviated debut two years ago, hitting a combined .323/.406/.448 with 16 doubles, a pair of triples, five homeruns, and 23 stolen bags during his time in the Northwest and Midwest Leagues.

San Diego, perhaps throwing a bit of caution to the wind, sent the former first rounder up to Class AA to start 2015. And Turner didn't miss a beat. He slugged .322/.385/.471 in 58 games before the trade – finally – became official. Washington would push him to their Class AA affiliate, the Harrisburg Senators, for another 10 games before bumping him up to the International League. He got promoted up to the big leagues in late August.

**Projection**: Here's what I wrote about the quick-rising infielder prior to the 2014 draft:

> "He's going to be an above-average base stealer, showcasing plus-speed and a knack for a high success rate, but the actual hit tool and patience look like average skills at this point. And it's not likely he'll top 10 homeruns in a season either."

I continued:

> "Turner's a nice prospect, one with a league average or slightly better ceiling. And, really, how much separation is there between someone like Turner and some recent failed first round collegiate shortstops like Christian Colon or Deven Marrero?"

Whoops. I definitely got this one wrong. Not only has Turner exceeded my admittedly modest expectations, but he absolutely torched the minor leagues for 185 games before making his big league debut.

Needless to say, Turner's here to stay – I think.

He shows a decent eye at the plate, plus speed, and slightly below-average power. But the hit tool has proven to be much better than I expected. He's likely to make a handful of All-Star contests before he calls it quits.

**Ceiling:** 3.0-win player
**Risk:** Low to Moderate
**MLB ETA:** Debuted in 2015

## 3. Victor Robles, CF

**MiLB Rank:** #72
**Position Rank:** N/A

| Born: 05/19/97 | Age: 19 | Bats: R | **Top CALs:** Jose Osuna, Ivan Gonzalez, |
|---|---|---|---|
| Height: 6-0 | Weight: 185 | Throws: R | Hector Gomez, Juan Herrera, Junnell Ledezma |

| Season | Age | LVL | PA | 2B | 3B | HR | AVG | OBP | SLG | ISO | BB% | K% | wRC+ |
|---|---|---|---|---|---|---|---|---|---|---|---|---|---|
| 2014 | 17 | R | 213 | 14 | 4 | 3 | 0.313 | 0.408 | 0.484 | 0.170 | 8.0% | 12.7% | 157 |
| 2015 | 18 | R | 94 | 6 | 1 | 2 | 0.370 | 0.484 | 0.562 | 0.192 | 10.6% | 12.8% | 209 |
| 2015 | 18 | A- | 167 | 5 | 4 | 2 | 0.343 | 0.424 | 0.479 | 0.136 | 4.8% | 12.6% | 168 |

**Background:** Signed out of the Dominican Republic at the age of 16 for nearly a $250,000, Robles have proven to be quite the bargain during his two seasons. After torching the DSL competition two years ago to the tune of .313/.408/.484, Robles didn't stop bashing as he moved up to the Gulf Coast and the New York-Penn Leagues, hitting a combined .352/.445/.507 with 11 doubles, five triples, four dingers, and 24 stolen bases.

**Projection:** Well, that's one way to announce your arrival as a potential top prospect. Robles topped the DSL average production mark by 57%, the GCL average by 109%, and he was better than the NYPL by 69%. And while his career is limited to just 108 games, it's a damn near perfect 108 games. Speed, power, average, strong contact rates, average eye at the plate – it has the potential to be a very, very dynamic offensive toolkit. Very, very bold prediction: Robles finishes the 2016 season in Class AA.

**Ceiling:** 3.5-win player
**Risk:** High
**MLB ETA:** 2018/2019

## 4. Reynaldo Lopez, RHP

**MiLB Rank:** #94
**Position Rank:** N/A

| Born: 01/04/94 | Age: 22 | Bats: R | **Top CALs:** Keury Mella, Luke Jackson, |
|---|---|---|---|
| Height: 6-0 | Weight: 185 | Throws: R | Dustin Antolin, Jordan Walden, Jose Guzman |

| YEAR | Age | Level | IP | W | L | ERA | FIP | K/9 | BB/9 | K% | BB% | HR/9 | LOB% |
|---|---|---|---|---|---|---|---|---|---|---|---|---|---|
| 2013 | 19 | A- | 1.3 | 0 | 1 | 47.25 | 5.35 | 0.00 | 0.00 | 0.0% | 0.0% | 0.00 | 12.5% |
| 2013 | 19 | A | 4.0 | 0 | 0 | 6.75 | 5.48 | 9.00 | 2.25 | 20.0% | 5.0% | 2.25 | 79.0% |
| 2014 | 20 | A- | 36.0 | 3 | 2 | 0.75 | 3.14 | 7.75 | 3.75 | 22.5% | 10.9% | 0.00 | 84.4% |
| 2014 | 20 | A | 47.3 | 4 | 1 | 1.33 | 2.91 | 7.42 | 2.09 | 22.4% | 6.3% | 0.19 | 84.7% |
| 2015 | 21 | A+ | 99.0 | 6 | 7 | 4.09 | 2.95 | 8.55 | 2.55 | 23.3% | 6.9% | 0.45 | 65.8% |

**Background:** While it's clear that Lucas Giolito possesses the most electric arm in the system, it's worth pointing out that the wiry Lopez isn't as far behind as one would think. The 6-foot, 185-pound right-hander out of the Dominican Republic burst onto the scene two years ago as he was nearly unhittable in the New York-Penn and South Atlantic Leagues. He would finish the 2014 season with an aggregate 1.08 ERA – enter whatever explicative you would like – in 83.1 innings, posting a 70-to-26 strikeout-to-walk ratio. Washington pushed the then-21-year-old hurler up to the Carolina League last season. And he proved that his previous showing was no outlier. In 19 starts with Potomac, Lopez, who hit the DL with a back injury, tossed a career best – believe it or not – 99.0 innings with 94 punch outs and 28 free passes. He finished the year with a neat-and-tidy 2.95 FIP.

**Projection:** Here's what I wrote in last year's book:

> *"With just 99.1 innings under his belt, Lopez could turn out to be anything from a potential front-of-the-rotation arm to a dominant backend reliever to a forgotten minor leaguer. But any time a 20-year-old posts that kind of line in a level – or levels – were the competition is slightly older, it's definitely promising. Oh, yeah, he's sporting a groundball rate north of 56%. Lopez is definitely, definitely, definitely one worth watching – closely."*

Needless to say, I'm convinced at this point. Among all hurlers with at least 90 innings in the Carolina League last season, Lopez's strikeout percentage, 23.3%, finished as the third highest mark; his strikeout-to-walk percentage, 16.3%, finished as the fourth best, and his 2.95 FIP was the sixth lowest. His groundball rate regressed some last season, but it still finished at an above-average 43.7%.

There is some risk involved given his relatively low career innings total, but he might peak as a #2/#3-type arm.

**Ceiling:** 3.0- to 3.5-win player
**Risk:** Moderate to High
**MLB ETA:** 2018

## 5. Erick Fedde, RHP

**MiLB Rank:** #128
**Position Rank:** N/A

| Born: 02/25/93 | Age: 23 | Bats: R | Top CALs: Jasner Severino, Bryan Price, |
| Height: 6-4 | Weight: 180 | Throws: R | Ethan Katz, Paul Phillips, Ethan Carnes |

| YEAR | Age | Level | IP | W | L | ERA | FIP | K/9 | BB/9 | K% | BB% | HR/9 | LOB% |
|------|-----|-------|-----|---|---|------|------|------|------|-------|------|------|-------|
| 2015 | 22 | A- | 35.0 | 4 | 1 | 2.57 | 2.60 | 9.26 | 2.06 | 23.5% | 5.2% | 0.26 | 68.0% |
| 2015 | 22 | A | 29.0 | 1 | 2 | 4.34 | 3.48 | 7.14 | 2.48 | 19.3% | 6.7% | 0.31 | 62.5% |

**Background:** Since it worked out so well the last time, the Nationals once again took a calculated risk by taking a recent Tommy John recipient in the opening round of the draft. After striking gold with Lucas Giolito and his elbow woes in 2012, the front office nabbed

Fedde – and his elbow woes – with the 18th overall selection two years ago. The former UNLV ace finally made it back last season as he split time between the New York-Penn and South Atlantic Leagues. Fedde would finish the year with a combined 3.38 ERA across 64.0 innings while fanning 21.7% and walking just 5.9% of the total batters he faced.

**Projection:** Here's what I wrote prior to the 2014 draft:

> *"One of the more intriguing arms in college baseball, Fedde is another upper-rotation-type arm, perhaps peaking as a lower end #2. He's going to miss a good amount of bats, limit free passes, and if the current trend holds, keep the ball on the ground with some regularity."*

Obviously, the minor league data remains sparse, but Fedde proved that his surgically repaired elbow is back up to his previous form. The organization will likely cap his innings to somewhere around 110 or so in 2016.

**Ceiling:** 2.5- to 3.0-win player
**Risk:** Moderate to High
**MLB ETA:** 2017/2018

## 6. A.J. Cole, RHP

**MiLB Rank:** N/A
**Position Rank:** N/A

| Born: 01/05/92 | Age: 24 | Bats: R | Top CALs: Sean O'Sullivan, Robert Rohrbaugh, |
| Height: 6-5 | Weight: 200 | Throws: R | Brett Oberholtzer, Michael O'Brien, Anthony Swarzak |

| YEAR | Age | Level | IP | W | L | ERA | FIP | K/9 | BB/9 | K% | BB% | HR/9 | LOB% |
|------|-----|-------|-------|---|---|------|------|------|------|-------|------|------|-------|
| 2013 | 21 | A+ | 97.3 | 6 | 3 | 4.25 | 3.69 | 9.43 | 2.13 | 25.1% | 5.7% | 1.11 | 68.7% |
| 2013 | 21 | AA | 45.3 | 4 | 2 | 2.18 | 2.69 | 9.73 | 1.99 | 28.0% | 5.7% | 0.60 | 76.1% |
| 2014 | 22 | AA | 71.0 | 6 | 3 | 2.92 | 2.58 | 7.73 | 1.90 | 19.8% | 4.9% | 0.13 | 70.1% |
| 2014 | 22 | AAA | 63.0 | 7 | 0 | 3.43 | 4.48 | 7.14 | 2.43 | 18.7% | 6.4% | 1.29 | 76.6% |
| 2015 | 23 | AAA | 105.7 | 5 | 6 | 3.15 | 3.90 | 6.47 | 2.90 | 17.2% | 7.7% | 0.77 | 76.5% |

**Background:** It took six years and two different stints within the organization, but Cole finally reached the pinnacle of professional baseball last season as he made his anticipated big league debut. Originally drafted by the Nationals in the fourth round – 116th overall – way back in 2010, Washington dealt the promising right-hander to

Oakland in 2011 as part of the package to receive Gio Gonzalez. A little more than two years later Cole was re-acquired as part of a three-team deal with the Mariners and Athletics. All along the way, however, Cole maintained his typical strong feel for the strike zone – he's averaged just 2.3 walks per nine innings in his career – though his once-promising strikeout numbers have tumbled from above-average to average to mediocre last season. The 6-foot-5, 200-pound right-hander tossed 105.2 innings with Syracuse in 2015, fanning a career low 17.5% and walking 7.7% of the total batters he faced. He also made two brief appearances in Washington as well.

**Projection**: Cole showed the typical four-pitch mix during his short tenure with the Nationals – a 90 mph fastball, a low-80s slider, curveball, and changeup. He's a nice #5 – maybe #4 – caliber starting pitcher. He'll chew a bunch of innings, limit walks, and average about 6.5 strikeouts per nine innings. CAL, for what it's worth, isn't all that impressed either, comparing him to Sean O'Sullivan, Robert Rohrbaugh, Brett Oberholtzer, Michael O'Brien, and Anthony Swarzak.

**Ceiling:** 1.0- to 1.5-win player
**Risk:** Low
**MLB ETA:** Debuted in 2015

## 7. Austin Voth, RHP

**MiLB Rank: N/A**
**Position Rank: N/A**

| Born: 06/26/92 | Age: 24 | Bats: R | Top CALs: Brad Mills, Andrew Heaney, |
|---|---|---|---|
| Height: 6-1 | Weight: 190 | Throws: R | Hector Noesi, Aaron Blair, Jeffrey Johnson |

| YEAR | Age | Level | IP | W | L | ERA | FIP | K/9 | BB/9 | K% | BB% | HR/9 | LOB% |
|---|---|---|---|---|---|---|---|---|---|---|---|---|---|
| 2013 | 21 | R | 5.0 | 0 | 0 | 0.00 | 1.86 | 7.20 | 0.00 | 23.5% | 0.0% | 0.00 | 100.0% |
| 2013 | 21 | A- | 30.7 | 2 | 0 | 1.47 | 0.85 | 12.33 | 1.17 | 36.8% | 3.5% | 0.00 | 76.9% |
| 2013 | 21 | A | 10.7 | 1 | 0 | 3.38 | 2.36 | 7.59 | 1.69 | 20.9% | 4.7% | 0.00 | 60.0% |
| 2014 | 22 | A | 69.7 | 4 | 3 | 2.45 | 2.68 | 9.56 | 2.84 | 26.7% | 7.9% | 0.13 | 67.9% |
| 2014 | 22 | A+ | 37.7 | 2 | 1 | 1.43 | 2.64 | 9.56 | 1.67 | 29.6% | 5.2% | 0.48 | 84.2% |
| 2014 | 22 | AA | 19.3 | 1 | 3 | 6.52 | 5.63 | 8.84 | 4.19 | 21.8% | 10.3% | 1.86 | 68.2% |
| 2015 | 23 | AA | 157.3 | 6 | 7 | 2.92 | 3.07 | 8.47 | 2.29 | 23.2% | 6.3% | 0.57 | 72.1% |

**Background:** A fast-rising right-hander out of the University of Washington, Voth was immediately placed on the quick path to the big leagues following his selection in the fifth round three years ago. After making stops in the Gulf Coast and New York-Penn Leagues during his debut, the 6-foot-1, 190-pound right-hander breezed through three

different levels in 2014 – he made 13 strong starts with Hagerstown in the Sally, another six starts of the dominating variety with Potomac in the Carolina League, and he finished up with five games in Class AA. Last season the organization opted to keep Voth with Harrisburg for the entire year. He would throw a career best 157.1 innings while averaging 8.5 punch outs and just 2.3 walks per nine innings to go along with a 2.92 ERA and a 3.07 FIP.

**Projection**: Voth continues to defy some long-shot odds. But he's been able to maintain his ability to miss bats and limit free passes as he's quickly pushed through the system. Basically, he hasn't shown anything to suggest that he can't carve out a career as a backend starting pitcher.

**Ceiling:** 1.5-win player
**Risk:** Moderate
**MLB ETA:** 2016

## 8. Abel De Los Santos, RHP

**MiLB Rank: N/A**
**Position Rank: N/A**

| Born: 11/21/92 | Age: 23 | Bats: R | Top CALs: Johnny Barbato, Aaron Blair, |
|---|---|---|---|
| Height: 6-2 | Weight: 200 | Throws: R | Eric Hurley, Eduardo Sanchez, Edgmer Escalona |

| YEAR | Age | Level | IP | W | L | ERA | FIP | K/9 | BB/9 | K% | BB% | HR/9 | LOB% |
|---|---|---|---|---|---|---|---|---|---|---|---|---|---|
| 2013 | 21 | R | 15.0 | 0 | 2 | 3.00 | 3.02 | 12.00 | 3.60 | 33.3% | 10.0% | 0.00 | 47.1% |
| 2013 | 20 | A- | 41.3 | 4 | 1 | 3.48 | 3.34 | 10.45 | 2.83 | 28.4% | 7.7% | 0.87 | 75.5% |
| 2013 | 21 | A | 9.3 | 1 | 0 | 14.46 | 9.98 | 5.79 | 11.57 | 11.3% | 22.6% | 1.93 | 35.7% |
| 2014 | 21 | A | 10.7 | 0 | 1 | 1.69 | 2.84 | 10.13 | 0.84 | 29.3% | 2.4% | 0.84 | 75.8% |
| 2014 | 21 | A+ | 45.7 | 5 | 2 | 1.97 | 2.93 | 10.45 | 3.35 | 28.0% | 9.0% | 0.20 | 78.6% |
| 2015 | 22 | AA | 57.7 | 4 | 4 | 3.43 | 3.39 | 8.58 | 1.87 | 23.0% | 5.0% | 0.94 | 72.9% |

**Background:** Acquired along with second base prospect Chris Bostick in deal that sent Ross Detwiler to Texas. The 6-foot-2, 200-pound right-hander spent the majority of the year uncorking mid-90s heat out of the Senators bullpen. De Los Santos finished the season with an impressive 55-to-12 strikeout-to-walk ratio in 57.2 innings of work.

**Projection**: During his brief two-game stint with the Nationals near the end of July De Los Santos showed a four-pitch power arsenal highlighted by a mid-90s fastball. He complemented it with a hard, mid-80s slider, a curveball, and changeup. Unsurprisingly, he has a lengthy history of promising punch out rates; he's averaged a smidge more than a bat per inning in his career. But, surprisingly, he's combined that with a solid feel for the plate; he's walked just 94 of the 1,306 total batters he's faced in his career – or just about 6.7%. De Los Santos seems like a safe bet to develop into a seventh/eighth-inning arm.

**Ceiling:** 1.0- to 1.5-win player
**Risk:** Low to Moderate
**MLB ETA:** Debuted in 2015

## 9. Drew Ward, 3B

MiLB Rank: N/A
Position Rank: N/A

| Born: 11/25/94 | Age: 21 | Bats: L | Top CALs: Billy Rowell, Trey Michalczewski, |
| Height: 6-3 | Weight: 215 | Throws: R | Matt Helm, Tyler Goeddel, Matt West |

| Season | Age | LVL | PA | 2B | 3B | HR | AVG | OBP | SLG | ISO | BB% | K% | wRC+ |
|---|---|---|---|---|---|---|---|---|---|---|---|---|---|
| 2013 | 18 | R | 199 | 13 | 0 | 1 | 0.292 | 0.402 | 0.387 | 0.095 | 12.6% | 22.1% | 141 |
| 2014 | 19 | A | 478 | 26 | 3 | 10 | 0.269 | 0.341 | 0.413 | 0.144 | 8.8% | 25.3% | 112 |
| 2015 | 20 | A+ | 426 | 19 | 2 | 6 | 0.249 | 0.327 | 0.358 | 0.109 | 9.2% | 25.8% | 103 |

**Background:** Ward turned in a bit of a disappointing season in 2015. After hitting a solid .269/.341/.413 as a 19-year-old in the Sally, the lefty-swinging third baseman cobbled together a lowly .249/.327/.358 triple-slash line – though he did manage to top the league average production by 3%. For his career, Ward is sporting a .264/.346/.387 line with 58 doubles, five triples, and 18 homeruns in 279 games.

**Projection:** Ward's pop really took a step backward after a strong showing in the Sally two years ago; his Isolated Power dropped from .144 to a subpar .109 mark last season. But more importantly: Ward didn't seem to make the necessary adjustments as the season wore on. The strikeout rates are borderline red flag territory. He's a candidate to repeat High Class A, but that wouldn't necessarily follow the organization's mantra.

**Ceiling:** 1.5-win player
**Risk:** Moderate to High
**MLB ETA:** 2018

## 10. Andrew Stevenson, CF

MiLB Rank: N/A
Position Rank: N/A

| Born: 06/01/94 | Age: 22 | Bats: L | Top CALs: Cody Podraza, Todd Cunningham, |
| Height: 6-0 | Weight: 185 | Throws: L | Jesus Loya, Narciso Mesa, Danny Mars |

| Season | Age | LVL | PA | 2B | 3B | HR | AVG | OBP | SLG | ISO | BB% | K% | wRC+ |
|---|---|---|---|---|---|---|---|---|---|---|---|---|---|
| 2015 | 21 | R | 6 | 0 | 0 | 0 | 0.200 | 0.333 | 0.200 | 0.000 | 16.7% | 33.3% | 78 |
| 2015 | 21 | A- | 80 | 1 | 2 | 0 | 0.361 | 0.413 | 0.431 | 0.069 | 8.8% | 15.0% | 150 |
| 2015 | 21 | A | 153 | 3 | 2 | 1 | 0.285 | 0.338 | 0.358 | 0.073 | 5.2% | 10.5% | 100 |

**Background:** A 6-foot, 185-pound center fielder out of LSU, Stevenson came a long way since his poor showing as a true freshman when he batted .193/.289/.218 with just one extra-base hit – a homerun – in 143 trips to the plate. But he established himself as one of college's most lethal offensive weapons during his sophomore season with the Tigers, hitting .335/.393/.419 with seven doubles, five triples, and nine stolen bases. He, of course, upped the ante during his final season in Baton Rouge: he set career highs in plate appearances (274), batting average (.348), OBP (.396), slugging percentage (.453), doubles (13), and stolen bases (26) while tying his previous best in triples (five) and homeruns – err...homerun. Washington grabbed Stevenson with the 58th overall pick last June and pushed him through three levels during his debut. He would bat .308/.363/.379 with four doubles, four triples, one homerun, and 23 stolen bases (in 30 attempts) between the Gulf Coast, New York-Penn, and South Atlantic Leagues.

**Projection:** Stevenson falls into that fringy big league regular category. He has a solid hit tool with speed, but his lack of power and average-ish walk rates limit his overall ceiling. One other (very cherry) red flag: lefties ate him alive during his debut last season; he batted a paltry .214/.323/.232 against them.

**Ceiling:** 1.0- to 1.5-win player
**Risk:** Moderate
**MLB ETA:** 2018

## 11. Pedro Severino, C

**MiLB Rank: N/A**
**Position Rank: N/A**

| Born: 07/20/93 | Age: 22 | Bats: R | |
|---|---|---|---|
| Height: 6-2 | Weight: 200 | Throws: R | **Top CALs:** Roberto Pena, Austin Hedges, Wilfredo Gimenez, Miguel Gonzalez, John Ryan Murphy |

| Season | Age | LVL | PA | 2B | 3B | HR | AVG | OBP | SLG | ISO | BB% | K% | wRC+ |
|---|---|---|---|---|---|---|---|---|---|---|---|---|---|
| 2013 | 19 | A | 302 | 19 | 2 | 1 | 0.241 | 0.274 | 0.333 | 0.092 | 4.3% | 17.9% | 74 |
| 2014 | 20 | A+ | 326 | 15 | 1 | 9 | 0.247 | 0.306 | 0.399 | 0.151 | 6.4% | 17.5% | 98 |
| 2015 | 21 | AA | 357 | 13 | 0 | 5 | 0.246 | 0.288 | 0.331 | 0.085 | 5.3% | 14.3% | 77 |
| 2015 | 21 | MLB | 4 | 1 | 0 | 0 | 0.250 | 0.250 | 0.500 | 0.250 | 0.0% | 25.0% | 97 |

**Background:** A lifetime .236/.288/.338 hitter – and that's including his .246/.288/.331 showing with Harrisburg last season – Severino's calling card is his tremendous work behind the dish. The 6-foot-2, 200-pound Dominican-born backstop threw out an impressive 38% of would-be base stealers last season. And before that he tossed out 36% in the Carolina League. And before that he gunned down 40% in the South Atlantic League. See a trend? The man can clearly control the running game. Back to the offense for a moment: Severino slugged 13 doubles and five long balls last season en route to finishing the year 23% below the league average production line.

**Projection**: Defense. Defense. Defense. The conversation will *always* focus on that side of the ball – which is clearly an above-average skill. Offensively, though, he's never going to hit enough to earn more than the occasional spot start. For instance, here are his stop-by-stop *Weighted Runs Created Plus* totals since 2011: 62, 77, 74, 98, and 77. Zero power with matching on-base skills.

**Ceiling:** 1.0-win player
**Risk:** Low to Moderate
**MLB ETA:** Debuted in 2015

## 12. Wilmer Difo, 2B/SS

**MiLB Rank: N/A**
**Position Rank: N/A**

| Born: 04/02/92 | Age: 24 | Bats: B | |
|---|---|---|---|
| Height: 6-0 | Weight: 195 | Throws: R | **Top CALs:** Ramon Torres, Taylor Harbin, Jordany Valdespin, J.T. Riddle, Chase D'Arnaud |

| Season | Age | LVL | PA | 2B | 3B | HR | AVG | OBP | SLG | ISO | BB% | K% | wRC+ |
|---|---|---|---|---|---|---|---|---|---|---|---|---|---|
| 2013 | 21 | A- | 136 | 3 | 4 | 1 | 0.217 | 0.291 | 0.333 | 0.117 | 7.4% | 12.5% | 91 |
| 2014 | 22 | A | 610 | 31 | 7 | 14 | 0.315 | 0.360 | 0.470 | 0.156 | 6.1% | 10.7% | 131 |
| 2015 | 23 | AA | 381 | 21 | 6 | 2 | 0.279 | 0.312 | 0.387 | 0.109 | 3.1% | 20.7% | 99 |
| 2015 | 23 | MLB | 11 | 0 | 0 | 0 | 0.182 | 0.182 | 0.182 | 0.000 | 0.0% | 18.2% | -9 |

**Background:** When it comes to slow moving prospects Difo might just be the winner – or the last one, I guess, depending upon your outlook on life. The switch-hitting middle infielder spent parts of two seasons in the Dominican Summer League, three stints in the Gulf Coast League, two trips to the South Atlantic League, and two more with Potomac. And that's not including his 33-game stint in the New York-Penn League or his 87 games with Harrisburg or even his 15 games with the Nationals too. One has to assume he owns a great set of luggage, right? Anyway, the well traveled infielder hit a combined .286/.325/.412 with 28 doubles, six triples, five homeruns, and 30 stolen bases – though most of that is buoyed by his dominant stint with Potomac.

**Projection**: Your typical run-of-the-mill backup middle infield fodder. Difo flashes decent power, above-average speed, and a decent hit tool. Even with all of that, he's never really stood out.

**Ceiling:** 1.0-win player
**Risk:** Low to Moderate
**MLB ETA:** Debuted in 2015

## 13. Jakson Reetz, C

**MiLB Rank: N/A**
**Position Rank: N/A**

| Born: 01/03/96 | Age: 20 | Bats: R | |
|---|---|---|---|
| Height: 6-1 | Weight: 195 | Throws: R | **Top CALs:** Jesus Sanchez, Nick Ciuffo, David Rodriguez, Rainis Silva, Nelfi Zapata |

| Season | Age | LVL | PA | 2B | 3B | HR | AVG | OBP | SLG | ISO | BB% | K% | wRC+ |
|---|---|---|---|---|---|---|---|---|---|---|---|---|---|
| 2014 | 18 | R | 155 | 6 | 1 | 1 | 0.274 | 0.429 | 0.368 | 0.094 | 16.8% | 19.4% | 142 |
| 2015 | 19 | A- | 132 | 4 | 0 | 0 | 0.212 | 0.326 | 0.248 | 0.035 | 9.8% | 28.0% | 83 |

**Background:** Touted as one of the top prep backstops in the 2014 draft, Reetz, the club's third round pick that season, looked promising during his debut in the Gulf Coast League, hitting .274/.429/.368 with an OBP-inflated 142 wRC+. The organization bumped 6-foot-1, 195-pound catcher up to the New York-Penn League, and – well – let's just says he wasn't as ready they thought he was. He cobbled together a putrid .212/.326/.248 triple-slash line in 132 trips to the plate.

**Projection:** It's not unusual to see an incoming prep player post an absurd walk rate during his debut in the lower rookie levels. And it's also not unusual to see said player with a walk rate far less impressive as he move up the following season. Oh, hell, Jakson Reetz. The young backstop's walk rate dropped from 16.8% to a more typical 9.8%. He's showing so little pop that I'd check to actually see if he's swinging a piece of wood and not some wet noodle.

**Ceiling:** 1.5-win player
**Risk:** High
**MLB ETA:** 2019

## 14. Sammy Solis, LHP

MiLB Rank: N/A
Position Rank: N/A

| Born: 08/10/88 | Age: 27 | Bats: R | Top CALs: N/A |
| Height: 6-5 | Weight: 230 | Throws: L | |

| YEAR | Age | Level | IP | W | L | ERA | FIP | K/9 | BB/9 | K% | BB% | HR/9 | LOB% |
|---|---|---|---|---|---|---|---|---|---|---|---|---|---|
| 2013 | 24 | R | 2.0 | 0 | 0 | 0.00 | 0.46 | 13.50 | 0.00 | 50.0% | 0.0% | 0.00 | 100.0% |
| 2013 | 24 | A+ | 57.7 | 2 | 1 | 3.43 | 3.63 | 6.24 | 2.97 | 16.9% | 8.0% | 0.47 | 74.2% |
| 2014 | 25 | A | 6.0 | 1 | 0 | 0.00 | 1.25 | 10.50 | 0.00 | 33.3% | 0.0% | 0.00 | 100.0% |
| 2014 | 25 | A+ | 5.3 | 1 | 0 | 1.69 | 2.58 | 6.75 | 1.69 | 16.0% | 4.0% | 0.00 | 87.5% |
| 2014 | 25 | AA | 3.3 | 0 | 1 | 21.60 | 3.65 | 2.70 | 2.70 | 5.0% | 5.0% | 0.00 | 10.0% |
| 2015 | 26 | AA | 13.3 | 0 | 3 | 6.75 | 3.19 | 7.43 | 3.38 | 17.2% | 7.8% | 0.00 | 61.5% |
| 2015 | 26 | AAA | 13.3 | 0 | 0 | 2.03 | 2.86 | 7.43 | 3.38 | 20.8% | 9.4% | 0.00 | 78.6% |

**Background:** The oft-injured enigma once again failed to top 50 innings in a season as he yo-yoed between the Harrisburg, Syracuse, and Washington last season. Of his six years in the Nationals' organization the big lefty out of the University of San Diego has thrown 205.0 total innings and no more than 96.2 in any season – which sounds OK until you realize that he's appeared in just 58 games, 38 of which coming as starts.

**Projection:** It's easy to see why the Nationals continue to stand by ~~their man~~...err...Solis. His fastball sizzled in at 94 mph during his debut with the Nationals. And then there's the actual production: he tallied an impressive 13.8% strikeout-to-walk percentage with the big league club. The front office – finally – moved Solis into a relief role, and as long as he stays healthy – which won't happen for too long given his track record – he could be a viable late-inning weapon.

**Ceiling:** 1.0-win player
**Risk:** Moderate
**MLB ETA:** Debuted in 2015

## 15. Chris Bostick, 2B

MiLB Rank: N/A
Position Rank: N/A

| Born: 03/24/93 | Age: 23 | Bats: R | Top CALs: Shelby Ford, Yadiel Rivera, |
| Height: 5-11 | Weight: 185 | Throws: R | Wes Darvill, Nick Romero, Logan Watkins |

| Season | Age | LVL | PA | 2B | 3B | HR | AVG | OBP | SLG | ISO | BB% | K% | wRC+ |
|---|---|---|---|---|---|---|---|---|---|---|---|---|---|
| 2013 | 20 | A | 555 | 25 | 8 | 14 | 0.282 | 0.354 | 0.452 | 0.170 | 9.2% | 22.0% | 127 |
| 2014 | 21 | A+ | 556 | 31 | 8 | 11 | 0.251 | 0.322 | 0.412 | 0.162 | 8.5% | 20.9% | 106 |
| 2015 | 22 | A+ | 264 | 10 | 3 | 4 | 0.274 | 0.344 | 0.393 | 0.120 | 7.2% | 16.7% | 118 |
| 2015 | 22 | AA | 317 | 12 | 5 | 8 | 0.247 | 0.286 | 0.402 | 0.155 | 3.8% | 17.7% | 96 |

**Background:** Here's the thing about Bostick: he's a pest. But I mean that in the best sense possible. A late, *late* round pick in 2011, Bostick, who was chosen with the 1,336th overall pick, continued to successfully navigate his way through the low – and now mid – levels of the minor leagues last season. After appearing in just 14 games during his pro debut, Bostick held his own with the Athletics' short-season affiliate, the Vermont Lake Monsters, hitting a league average-ish – remember that term, it's going to used a lot – .251/.325/.369. Bostick followed that up with another solid showing in the Midwest League in 2013: he batted .282/.354/.452 with 25 doubles, eight triples, 14 homeruns, and 25 stolen bases. Oakland would then ship the young second baseman to the Rangers as part of the Craig Gentry deal. The Rangers would bump Bostick up to the Carolina League where he would put together a .251/.322/.412 line with a career best 31 doubles, eight triples, 11 homeruns, and 24 stolen bases but his overall production remained...league average-ish. And then the Rangers would flip Bostick and right-hander Abel De Los Santos in the Ross Detwiler deal.

Now in his third organization, Bostick repeated High Class A for the first half of the year before getting the call up to the Eastern League. Overall, he would bat a...league average-ish .258/.312/.398.

**Projection:** The individual pieces are far more promising than the actual results: he'll consistently flash a surprising amount of power from the second base position with a decent eye and above-average speed. He's a bit underappreciated in a sense that his worst showing during his five-year career was last season's stint in Class AA when he posted a 96 wRC+. With that being said, he's a fringy big leaguer.

**Ceiling:** 1.0-win player
**Risk:** Moderate
**MLB ETA:** 2017

## 16. Matt Skole, 1B/3B

**MiLB Rank: N/A**
**Position Rank: N/A**

| Born: 07/30/89 | Age: 26 | Bats: L | **Top CALs:** Kevin Keyes, Jacob Butler, |
| Height: 6-4 | Weight: 225 | Throws: R | Jeff Larish, Josh Whitesell, Chris Mcguiness |

| Season | Age | LVL | PA | 2B | 3B | HR | AVG | OBP | SLG | ISO | BB% | K% | wRC+ |
|---|---|---|---|---|---|---|---|---|---|---|---|---|---|
| 2014 | 24 | AA | 544 | 29 | 1 | 14 | 0.241 | 0.352 | 0.399 | 0.158 | 14.3% | 23.3% | 112 |
| 2015 | 25 | AA | 365 | 14 | 1 | 12 | 0.232 | 0.332 | 0.398 | 0.166 | 12.1% | 25.2% | 113 |
| 2015 | 25 | AAA | 182 | 9 | 0 | 8 | 0.238 | 0.357 | 0.457 | 0.219 | 15.4% | 19.2% | 137 |

**Background:** Once upon a time in the not-so-distant past Skole, a former fifth round pick, was one of the most lethal bats in all of college baseball. Starring for the Georgia Tech Yellow Jackets, the lefty-swinging corner infielder scorched the competition to the tune of .335/.446/.682 during his sophomore season and followed that up with another impressive campaign a year later, hitting .348/.445/.545. And for a time it looked as if Skole would be able to carry that momentum into – and all the way through – the minor leagues. He ripped through the New York-Penn League during his debut, hitting .290/.382/.438. Then in 2012 he bashed the Midwest League pitching to the tune of .286/.438/.574 before earning a late-season call-up to Potomac. And then life happened: Skole underwent the knife to repair ligament tears in his elbow – also known as Tommy John surgery – and a small procedure to clean up his wrist.

Skole would make only seven trips to the plate the following season and he struggled through his full-season return in 2014. Finally healthy in 2015, the 6-foot-4, 225-pound infielder struggled through the first two months of the season – he batted .190/.304/.373 over his first 41 games – but things seemed to click once the calendar flipped to June. He would slug .254/.356/.437 the rest of the way.

**Projection:** An above-average eye and matching power might be enough to get him to the big leagues, whether or not he'll be able to overcome his below-average hit tool is an entirely other question. He's a Quad-A guy.

**Ceiling:** 1.0-win player
**Risk:** Moderate
**MLB ETA:** 2016

## 17. Osvaldo Abreu, 2B/SS

**MiLB Rank: N/A**
**Position Rank: N/A**

| Born: 06/13/94 | Age: 22 | Bats: R | **Top CALs:** Jonathan Mota, Everth Cabrera, |
| Height: 6-0 | Weight: 170 | Throws: R | Abiatal Avelino, Yamaico Navarro, Greg Garcia |

| Season | Age | LVL | PA | 2B | 3B | HR | AVG | OBP | SLG | ISO | BB% | K% | wRC+ |
|---|---|---|---|---|---|---|---|---|---|---|---|---|---|
| 2013 | 19 | R | 171 | 12 | 1 | 0 | 0.286 | 0.369 | 0.381 | 0.095 | 11.1% | 14.0% | 126 |
| 2014 | 20 | A- | 231 | 7 | 3 | 1 | 0.229 | 0.279 | 0.305 | 0.076 | 3.9% | 17.7% | 73 |
| 2015 | 21 | A | 513 | 35 | 4 | 6 | 0.274 | 0.357 | 0.412 | 0.138 | 9.7% | 17.3% | 121 |

**Background:** The 6-foot, 170-pound middle infielder out of the Dominican Republic continued his one-level-a-year development plan as he moved up to the South Atlantic League last season. After initially spending a year in the Dominican Summer League in 2012 – one, by the way, that wasn't overly successful – Abreu spent another decent season in the Gulf Coast League before moving into short-season action two years ago. Last year Abreu end-capped three solid months of production with two lousy ones en route to hitting a combined .274/.357/.412 with a whopping 35 doubles, four triples, six homeruns, and 30 stolen bases (in 41 attempts). His overall production, per *Weighted Runs Created Plus*, topped the league average production by 21%.

**Projection:** So the first thing that captures one's imagination when it comes to his 2015 production is the sheer amount of doubles he slugged. But let's compare Abreu's numbers against another (former) infielder in the Nat's system during his stop with Hagerstown a couple years ago:

| Player | Age | PA | AVG | OBP | SLG | 2B | 3B | HR | SB | wRC+ |
|---|---|---|---|---|---|---|---|---|---|---|
| Osvaldo Abreu | 21 | 513 | 0.274 | 0.357 | 0.412 | 35 | 4 | 6 | 30 | 121 |
| Tony Renda | 22 | 606 | 0.294 | 0.380 | 0.405 | 43 | 3 | 3 | 30 | 130 |

Granted, Abreu's a year younger but those numbers are incredibly similar. Abreu shows decent tools across the board – maybe the speed is a tick better than average – without a true standout. If he sticks at shortstop he might be able to get a couple cups of coffee in the big leagues as an end-of-the-bench option.

**Ceiling:** 1.0-win player
**Risk:** Moderate
**MLB ETA:** 2018

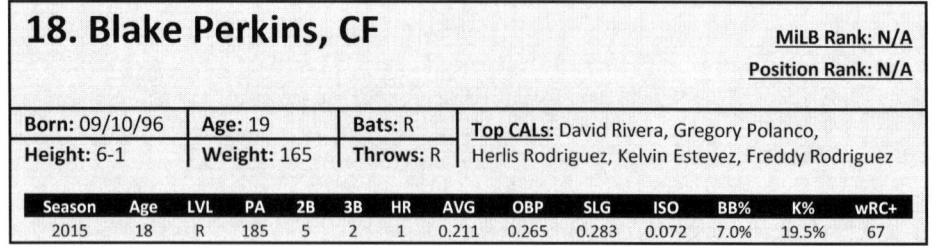

## 18. Blake Perkins, CF

<u>MiLB Rank:</u> N/A

<u>Position Rank:</u> N/A

| Born: 09/10/96 | Age: 19 | Bats: R | Top CALs: David Rivera, Gregory Polanco, |
|---|---|---|---|
| Height: 6-1 | Weight: 165 | Throws: R | Herlis Rodriguez, Kelvin Estevez, Freddy Rodriguez |

| Season | Age | LVL | PA | 2B | 3B | HR | AVG | OBP | SLG | ISO | BB% | K% | wRC+ |
|---|---|---|---|---|---|---|---|---|---|---|---|---|---|
| 2015 | 18 | R | 185 | 5 | 2 | 1 | 0.211 | 0.265 | 0.283 | 0.072 | 7.0% | 19.5% | 67 |

**Background:** Number two among the club's second round picks, 11 selections after Andrew Stevenson was taken; Perkins looked overmatched in the Gulf Coast League during his debut. He hit a lowly .211/.265/.283 en route to posting a disgusting 67 wRC+.

**Projection:** The sample size is way too small to be reliable, but on the flip side he didn't exactly offer up a whole of hope.

**Ceiling:** Too Soon to Tell
**Risk:** N/A
**MLB ETA:** N/A

## 19. Brian Goodwin, CF

<u>MiLB Rank:</u> N/A

<u>Position Rank:</u> N/A

| Born: 11/02/90 | Age: 25 | Bats: L | Top CALs: Xavier Avery, Daryl Jones, |
|---|---|---|---|
| Height: 6-0 | Weight: 195 | Throws: R | Jordan Danks, Kes Carter, Evan Marzilli |

| Season | Age | LVL | PA | 2B | 3B | HR | AVG | OBP | SLG | ISO | BB% | K% | wRC+ |
|---|---|---|---|---|---|---|---|---|---|---|---|---|---|
| 2013 | 22 | AA | 533 | 19 | 11 | 10 | 0.252 | 0.355 | 0.407 | 0.155 | 12.4% | 22.7% | 115 |
| 2014 | 23 | AAA | 329 | 10 | 4 | 4 | 0.219 | 0.342 | 0.328 | 0.109 | 15.2% | 28.9% | 92 |
| 2015 | 24 | AA | 472 | 17 | 4 | 8 | 0.226 | 0.290 | 0.340 | 0.114 | 8.1% | 19.7% | 81 |

**Background:** The last two seasons haven't exactly been a walk in the park for the Miami-Dade center fielder. Goodwin started making waves during his debut in 2012 when he slugged .324/.438/.542 with plenty of extra-base firepower in the Midwest League. Washington would bounce the former first rounder up to Class AA in the second half of the season, completely bypassing High Class A. Since then, well, Goodwin's pretty much stopped hitting. In those final 42 games with Harrisburg, the lefty-swinging center fielder batted .223/.306/.373. He would follow that up with a solid – though far from inspiring – showing when he returned to Harrisburg, hitting .252/.355/.407. Goodwin would spend the next year flailing away at Class AAA and the club bounced him back down to the Easter League in 2015 – where he continued to flail away.

**Projection:** Here's what I wrote in last year's book:

> *"Another Washington outfield prospect loaded with a promising skill set – solid-average power and speed with keen patience at the plate – but is seemingly undone by a lacking hit tool. Goodwin's hit a combined .236 since leaving the Sally midway through the 2012 season. And then you have to consider his work against southpaws since turning pro: .217/.322/.344. CAL's suggesting a typical fourth outfielder/Quad-A guy, which seems spot on."*

Well, after that terrible showing in his third trip through Class AA Washington would be *lucky* if he developed into a toolsy fourth outfielder. And, of course, CAL remains thoroughly pessimistic: Xavier Avery, Daryl Jones, Jordan Danks, Kes Carter, and Evan Marzilli.

**Ceiling:** 1.0-win player
**Risk:** Moderate to High
**MLB ETA:** 2017

## 20. Telmito Agustin, CF

**MiLB Rank: N/A**
**Position Rank: N/A**

| Born: 10/09/96 | Age: 19 | Bats: L | **Top CALs:** Juan Herrera, Yeison Melo, |
|---|---|---|---|
| Height: 5-10 | Weight: 160 | Throws: L | Ramon Beltre, Anthony Garcia, Jose Osuna |

| Season | Age | LVL | PA | 2B | 3B | HR | AVG | OBP | SLG | ISO | BB% | K% | wRC+ |
|---|---|---|---|---|---|---|---|---|---|---|---|---|---|
| 2014 | 17 | R | 274 | 14 | 10 | 3 | 0.301 | 0.415 | 0.498 | 0.196 | 14.6% | 16.8% | 158 |
| 2015 | 18 | R | 141 | 8 | 2 | 1 | 0.331 | 0.371 | 0.446 | 0.115 | 6.4% | 12.1% | 145 |
| 2015 | 18 | A- | 32 | 1 | 2 | 0 | 0.400 | 0.419 | 0.567 | 0.167 | 3.1% | 15.6% | 188 |

**Background:** A quickly little outfielder out of the U.S. Virgin Islands, Agustin tore through the Dominican Summer League two years ago, hitting .300/.413/.495 with 14 doubles, 10 triples, three homeruns, and 25 stolen bases. The franchise moved Agustin stateside for the first time last year with very little change in the results: he hit an aggregate .344/.380/.469

**Projection**: Agustin's previously patient ways all but dried up as he jumped in the Gulf Coast League – which is entirely expected. His walk rate dropped from an elite 14.5% to a more average-ish 6.4%. Agustin's power also dissipated as well. With that being said, he still managed to torch the stateside rookie league by topping the average production line by 45%. He looks like a fourth outfielder as it stands.

**Ceiling:** 1.0- to 1.5-win player
**Risk:** Moderate to High
**MLB ETA:** 2018

## 21. Jake Johansen, RHP

**MiLB Rank: N/A**
**Position Rank: N/A**

| Born: 01/23/91 | Age: 26 | Bats: R | **Top CALs:** Pedro Figueroa, Atahualpa Severino, |
|---|---|---|---|
| Height: 6-6 | Weight: 235 | Throws: R | Mike Mcguire, Dennis O'Grady, Jose Jimenez |

| YEAR | Age | Level | IP | W | L | ERA | FIP | K/9 | BB/9 | K% | BB% | HR/9 | LOB% |
|---|---|---|---|---|---|---|---|---|---|---|---|---|---|
| 2013 | 22 | A- | 42.3 | 1 | 1 | 1.06 | 2.67 | 9.35 | 3.83 | 26.0% | 10.7% | 0.21 | 83.3% |
| 2013 | 22 | A | 9.3 | 0 | 2 | 5.79 | 4.98 | 6.75 | 4.82 | 15.2% | 10.9% | 0.96 | 54.2% |
| 2014 | 23 | A | 100.7 | 5 | 6 | 5.19 | 4.05 | 7.96 | 4.92 | 19.1% | 11.8% | 0.27 | 63.0% |
| 2015 | 24 | R | 5.3 | 0 | 1 | 1.69 | 2.18 | 5.06 | 0.00 | 13.0% | 0.0% | 0.00 | 50.0% |
| 2015 | 24 | A+ | 48.0 | 1 | 7 | 5.44 | 4.69 | 9.00 | 5.06 | 20.5% | 11.5% | 1.13 | 58.3% |

**Background:** Interesting tidbit: there have been only two players taken before the third round in the June amateur draft that have called Dallas Baptist University home – Vic Black, a supplemental first round pick in 2009, and Jake Johansen, a big reach as a second round pick in 2013. Standing an impressive 6-foot-6 and 235 pounds, Johansen failed to rein in his problematic – an understatement of sorts – control issues until his junior campaign at the university. Since getting selected as the 68th overall pick three years ago Johansen continued to average about a strikeout per inning, though that's come with a walk rate hovering near 5.0 BB/9. Last season he tossed 48.0 innings with Potomac, posting a strikeout-to-walk ratio of 48-to-27 en route to tallying a 5.44 ERA.

**Projection**: Well, he's now entering his age-25 season and owns just 48.0 innings above the South Atlantic League. The organization made the prudent decision to push him into a relief role last season, so maybe he can begin to move quickly? Maybe? Maybe?

**Ceiling:** 1.0-win player
**Risk:** Moderate to High
**MLB ETA:** 2017

## 22. Raudy Read, C

**MiLB Rank: N/A**
**Position Rank: N/A**

| Born: 10/29/93 | Age: 22 | Bats: R | **Top CALs:** Mayo Acosta, Jair Fernandez, |
|---|---|---|---|
| Height: 6-0 | Weight: 170 | Throws: R | John Ryan Murphy Ryan Casteel, Sean Rooney |

| Season | Age | LVL | PA | 2B | 3B | HR | AVG | OBP | SLG | ISO | BB% | K% | wRC+ |
|---|---|---|---|---|---|---|---|---|---|---|---|---|---|
| 2013 | 19 | R | 158 | 5 | 0 | 2 | 0.252 | 0.287 | 0.327 | 0.075 | 3.8% | 10.8% | 83 |
| 2014 | 20 | A- | 229 | 20 | 0 | 6 | 0.281 | 0.332 | 0.462 | 0.181 | 6.1% | 16.2% | 131 |
| 2015 | 21 | A | 327 | 20 | 1 | 5 | 0.244 | 0.307 | 0.369 | 0.125 | 7.6% | 15.3% | 93 |
| 2015 | 21 | A+ | 20 | 2 | 0 | 0 | 0.389 | 0.450 | 0.500 | 0.111 | 10.0% | 15.0% | 181 |

**Background:** Another backstop in the mold of Pedro Severino. Read spent the year in the Sally, hitting a slightly below-average .244/.307/.369 with 20 doubles, one triple, and five homeruns. He also appeared in five games with Potomac. For his career, Read is sporting a .245/.301/.390 triple-slash line.

**Projection**: Again, very similar to Severino in a lot of ways, minus his relatively quick path through the minor leagues. Below-average power and hit tool and speed and eye at the plate, the saving grace for Read is his ability to control the running game.

**Ceiling:** 1.0-win player
**Risk:** Moderate to High
**MLB ETA:** 2018

## 23. Anderson Franco, 3B

**MiLB Rank: N/A**
**Position Rank: N/A**

| Born: 08/15/97 | Age: 18 | Bats: R | **Top CALs:** Bill Pujols, Wander Franco, |
| Height: 6-3 | Weight: 190 | Throws: R | Jean Carlos Valdez, Griffin Garabito, Carlos Montero |

| Season | Age | LVL | PA | 2B | 3B | HR | AVG | OBP | SLG | ISO | BB% | K% | wRC+ |
|---|---|---|---|---|---|---|---|---|---|---|---|---|---|
| 2014 | 16 | R | 237 | 8 | 1 | 4 | 0.272 | 0.346 | 0.379 | 0.107 | 11.0% | 19.4% | 111 |
| 2015 | 17 | R | 170 | 6 | 1 | 4 | 0.281 | 0.347 | 0.412 | 0.131 | 8.2% | 15.3% | 130 |
| 2015 | 17 | A- | 47 | 1 | 1 | 0 | 0.225 | 0.340 | 0.300 | 0.075 | 14.9% | 4.3% | 98 |

**Background:** Originally signed for $900,000 in August 2013, Franco didn't make his pro debut until the following year, hitting a league average-ish .272/.346/.379 as a 16-year-old in the Dominican Summer League (thanks to a late birthday). Washington pushed him stateside last season and

Franco handled the GCL surprisingly well before earning a late-season promotion to Auburn.

**Projection**: Again, another prospect with an incredibly limited sample size – even if you want to consider his work in the DSL, which is hard enough to analyze. Average eye, average power, average hit tool, but each has a chance to blossom into a little better.

**Ceiling:** Too Soon to Tell
**Risk:** N/A
**MLB ETA:** N/A

## 24. Cody Gunter, RHP

**MiLB Rank: N/A**
**Position Rank: N/A**

| Born: 04/18/94 | Age: 22 | Bats: L | **Top CALs:** Feliberto Sanchez, Jake Cuffman, |
| Height: 6-3 | Weight: 195 | Throws: R | Jonah Nickerson, Trevor Kelley, Lino Martinez |

| Season | Age | LVL | PA | 2B | 3B | HR | AVG | OBP | SLG | ISO | BB% | K% | wRC+ |
|---|---|---|---|---|---|---|---|---|---|---|---|---|---|
| 2015 | 21 | A- | 21.7 | 1 | 0 | 4.15 | 3.84 | 9.55 | 3.32 | 25.0% | 8.7% | 0.83 | 60.3% |

**Background:** Originally drafted as a third baseman in the sixth round out of Grayson Country College, Gunter made two unsuccessful attempts at figuring out the New York-Penn League before packing up his bat and moving to the mound with a career .228/.302/.337

triple-slash line hung around his neck. Last year he tossed 21.2 innings in the NYPL, fanning 23 and walking eight.

**Projection**: The only thing we do know at this point is that Gunter can't hit for shit. He's one of those low level wild cards – with a relatively fresh arm – that bears watching. In his brief stay in Auburn last season he showed a tremendous ability to miss bats and the control wasn't horrible either.

**Ceiling:** Too Soon to Tell
**Risk:** N/A
**MLB ETA:** N/A

## 25. Nick Lee, LHP

**MiLB Rank: N/A**
**Position Rank: N/A**

| Born: 01/13/91 | Age: 25 | Bats: L | **Top CALs:** Kevin Whelan, Rob Bryson, |
| Height: 5-11 | Weight: 185 | Throws: L | Christopher Perry, Leyson Septimo, Louis Head |

| YEAR | Age | Level | IP | W | L | ERA | FIP | K/9 | BB/9 | K% | BB% | HR/9 | LOB% |
|---|---|---|---|---|---|---|---|---|---|---|---|---|---|
| 2013 | 22 | A | 91.0 | 6 | 4 | 3.96 | 3.82 | 10.09 | 4.25 | 26.3% | 11.1% | 0.69 | 68.5% |
| 2014 | 23 | R | 8.0 | 1 | 0 | 6.75 | 10.38 | 6.75 | 4.50 | 16.7% | 11.1% | 4.50 | 95.2% |
| 2014 | 23 | A | 8.3 | 1 | 0 | 7.56 | 7.31 | 6.48 | 9.72 | 13.3% | 20.0% | 1.08 | 71.4% |
| 2014 | 23 | A+ | 14.3 | 0 | 2 | 10.05 | 2.19 | 14.44 | 5.02 | 33.3% | 11.6% | 0.00 | 30.8% |
| 2015 | 24 | A+ | 28.0 | 1 | 1 | 2.57 | 3.33 | 9.00 | 4.50 | 24.4% | 12.2% | 0.32 | 71.4% |
| 2015 | 24 | AA | 24.0 | 2 | 0 | 3.75 | 3.48 | 10.88 | 7.13 | 26.6% | 17.4% | 0.00 | 73.2% |

**Background:** Given every opportunity to shine as a starting pitcher over the previous four seasons, the organization decided that Lee had run out of chances and pushed the enigmatic southpaw into a relief role in 2015. And he continued to frustrate. In 52.0 innings between Potomac and Harrisburg, Lee posted a 57-to-33 strikeout-to-walk ratio

but he did finish the year with a 3.12 ERA.

**Projection**: Lefties that can average a punch out per inning will *always* get more than their share of looks. But Lee's control has been trending in the wrong direction since 2012. He's now entering his age-25 season with just 24.0 innings above High Class A. And those 24.0 innings were a bit...terrible. He walked 19. At this point, the organization would be lucky to squeeze any type of positive big league value out of once-promising arm.

**Ceiling:** 1.0-win player
**Risk:** High
**MLB ETA:** 2018

## *Barely Missed:*

- **Gilberto Mendez, RHP** – Dominican-born right-hander is sporting an impressive 8.8 K/9 and 2.0 BB/9 during his five-year pro career. He spent last season working out of Harrisburg's bullpen, posting a 52-to-17 strikeout-to-walk ratio.

- **Mariano Rivera, RHP** – Son of the greatest reliever in the history of baseball, Rivera was taken out of Iona College in the fourth round last year. He put together a 26-to-3 strikeout-to-walk ratio in 33.0 innings with Auburn. He could move quickly and profile as a solid middle relief arm.

## *Bird Doggin' It – Additional Prospects to Keep an Eye in 2016*

| Player | Age | POS | Notes |
|---|---|---|---|
| Kelvin Gutierrez | 21 | 3B/SS | Gutierrez batted a respectable .305/.358/.414 with 21 doubles, one triple, and one homerun with Auburn last season. Little homerun pop and huge swing-and-miss tendencies. |
| Bryan Harper | 26 | LHP | Bryce Harper's older brother, a difficult job in itself, Bryan posted a 33-to-15 strikeout-to-walk ratio with Harrisburg. He could be a decent LOOGY in the next year or two. |
| Taylor Hearn | 21 | LHP | 6-foot-5, 215-pound southpaw out of Oklahoma Baptist University was taken in the fifth round last June. He made 10 successful starts with Auburn. |
| Alec Keller | 24 | OF | Former Princeton outfielder hit .294/.341/.374 between Low Class A and High Class A last season. He might be able to get a cup of coffee or two in the big leagues. |
| Tyler Mapes | 24 | RHP | A 30th round pick out of Tulane two years ago, Mapes is sporting a career 2.02 ERA while averaging 6.8 K/9 and just 1.7 BB/9 in his first 120.1 innings. |
| Jose Marmolejos-Diaz | 23 | 1B/LF | Hit .310/.363/.485 with 55 extra-base hits, but was a touch too old for Hagerstown. |
| Bryan Mejia | 22 | IF/OF | Prior to the year Mejia never topped an OPS above .697; then in 62 games with Hagerstown he slugged .345/.369/.555. He's going to come crashing back to earth. |
| Mario Sanchez | 21 | RHP | Made eight starts and 21 relief appearances with Hagerstown last season. Strong control, not much of anything else. |
| Max Schrock | 21 | 2B/SS | A late round pick out of the University of South Carolina, Schrock made quick work of the NYPL during his debut, hitting .308/.355/.448 with 10 doubles, four triples, and a pair of homeruns. |
| Austen Williams | 23 | RHP | 6-foot-3, 220-pound right-hander tossed a career best 139.2 innings while averaging 6.8 strikeouts and just 2.1 walks per nine innings – most of which was spent in the Sally and Carolina Leagues. |
| Rhett Wiseman | 22 | OF | Plucked out of Vanderbilt University in the third round last June, Wiseman hit a disappointing .248/.307/.376 with Auburn during his debut. |

Made in the USA
Middletown, DE
05 March 2016